Annual Report
on
Exchange Arrangements and Exchange Restrictions
2000

International Monetary Fund

Library of Congress Cataloging-in-Publication Data

International Monetary Fund.
  Annual report on exchange arrangements and exchange restrictions.
1979—

Continues: International Monetary Fund. Annual report on exchange
restrictions, 1950–1978
  1. Foreign exchange — Law and legislation — Periodicals. 2. Foreign
exchange — Control — Periodicals. I. Title.
K4440.A13 I57 [date] 341.7′5] 79-644506
ISSN 0250-7366
ISBN 1-55775-898-0

Price: US$95.00
(US$47.50 to full-time university faculty members and students)

Please send orders to:
International Monetary Fund, Publication Services
700 19th Street, N.W., Washington, D.C. 20431, U.S.A.
Tel.: (202) 623-7430   Telefax: (202) 623-7201
E-mail: publications@imf.org
Internet: http://www.imf.org

recycled paper

Letter of Transmittal to Members
and Governors of the Fund

August 28, 2000

Dear Sir or Madam:

I have the honor to transmit to you a copy of the International Monetary Fund's *Annual Report on Exchange Arrangements and Exchange Restrictions, 2000*, which has been prepared in accordance with the provisions of Article XIV, Section 3 of the Articles of Agreement.

On behalf of the Executive Board, I should like to express our appreciation of the cooperation of the countries in the preparation of the Report.

Sincerely yours,

Horst Köhler
*Chairman of the Executive Board
and Managing Director*

CONTENTS

CONTENTS

Note: The term "country," as used in this publication, does not in all cases refer to a territorial entity that is a state as understood by international law and practice; the term also covers some territorial entities that are not states but for which statistical data are maintained and provided internationally on a separate and independent basis.

PREFACE

The Annual Report on Exchange Arrangements and Exchange Restrictions has been published by the IMF since 1950. It draws on information available to the IMF from a number of sources, including that provided in the course of official visits to member countries, and has been prepared in close consultation with national authorities. The information is presented in a tabular format.

This project was coordinated in the Monetary and Exchange Affairs Department by a staff team comprising Virgilio A. Sandoval and Harald Anderson, directed by Akira Ariyoshi, and coordinated by Judit Vadasz. It draws on the specialized contribution of that department (for specific countries), with assistance from staff members of the IMF's six area departments, together with staff of other departments. The report was edited by Gail Berre and Martha Bonilla of the External Relations Department, and was produced by Mr. Anderson and the IMF Graphics Section.

DEFINITION OF ACRONYMS

ACP	Atlantic, Caribbean, and Pacific countries
ACU	Asian Clearing Union (integrated by Bangladesh, India, Islamic Republic of Iran, Myanmar, Nepal, Pakistan, and Sri Lanka)
AFTA	ASEAN free trade area (see ASEAN, below)
AMU	Asian monetary unit
ANZCERTA	Australia-New Zealand Closer Economic Relations and Trade Agreement
ASEAN	Association of Southeast Asian Nations (integrated by Brunei Darussalam, Indonesia, Malaysia, Philippines, Singapore, and Thailand)
ATC	Agreement of Textiles and Clothing
BCEAO	Central Bank of West African States (Banque centrale des états de l'Afrique de l'ouest); the West African states are Benin, Burkina Faso, Côte d'Ivoire, Guinea-Bissau, Mali, Niger, Senegal, and Togo
BEAC	Bank of Central African States (Banque des états de l'Afrique centrale); the Central African states are Cameroon, Central African Republic, Chad, Republic of Congo, Equatorial Guinea, and Gabon
BLEU	Belgium-Luxembourg Economic Union
CACM	Central American Common Market (integrated by Costa Rica, El Salvador, Guatemala, Honduras, and Nicaragua)
CAEMC	Central African Economic and Monetary Community (integrated by the members of the BEAC)
CAP	Common agricultural policy (of the EU)
CARICOM	Caribbean Community and Common Market (integrated by Antigua and Barbuda, The Bahamas, Barbados, Belize, Dominica, Grenada, Guyana, Haiti, Jamaica, Montserrat, St. Kitts and Nevis, St. Lucia, St. Vincent and the Grenadines, Suriname, and Trinidad and Tobago)
CEEAC	Economic Community of Central African States (integrated by Angola, Burundi, Cameroon, Central African Republic, Chad, Democratic Republic of the Congo, Republic of Congo, Equatorial Guinea, Gabon, Rwanda, and São Tomé and Príncipe)
CEFTA	Central European Free Trade Area (integrated by Bulgaria, Czech Republic, Hungary, Poland, Romania, Slovak Republic, and Slovenia)
CEPGL	Economic Community of the Great Lakes Countries (integrated by Burundi, Democratic Republic of the Congo, and Rwanda)
CEPT	Common effective preferential tariff of the ASEAN free trade zone
CET	Common external tariff
CFA	Communauté financière d'Afrique (administered by the BCEAO) and Coopération financière en Afrique centrale (administered by the BEAC)
CIS	Commonwealth of Independent States (integrated by Armenia, Azerbaijan, Belarus, Georgia, Kazakhstan, Kyrgyz Republic, Moldova, Russian Federation, Tajikistan, Turkmenistan, Ukraine, and Uzbekistan)
CMA	Common monetary area (a single exchange control territory comprising Lesotho, Namibia, South Africa, and Swaziland)
CMCF	Caribbean Multilateral Clearing Facility
CMEA	Council for Mutual Economic Assistance (dissolved; formerly integrated by Bulgaria, Cuba, Czechoslovakia, Hungary, Mongolia, Poland, Romania, the U.S.S.R., and Vietnam)
COMESA	Common Market for Eastern and Southern Pacific (integrated by Angola, Burundi, Comoros, Democratic Republic of the Congo, Djibouti, Egypt, Eritrea, Ethiopia, Kenya, Madagascar, Malawi, Mauritius, Namibia, Rwanda, Seychelles, Sudan, Swaziland, Tanzania, Uganda, Zambia, and Zimbabwe)
EAC	East African Community
ECB	European Central Bank
ECCB	Eastern Caribbean Central Bank (Anguilla, Antigua and Barbuda, Dominica, Grenada, Montserrat, St. Kitts and Nevis, St. Lucia, and St. Vincent and the Grenadines)
ECCU	Eastern Caribbean Common Union
ECOWAS	Economic Community of West African States (CEDEAO) (integrated by Benin, Burkina Faso, Cape Verde, Côte d'Ivoire, The Gambia, Ghana, Guinea, Guinea-Bissau, Liberia, Mali, Mauritania, Niger, Nigeria, Senegal, Sierra Leone, and Togo)
ECSC	European Coal and Steel Community
ECU	European currency unit
EEA	European economic area
EFTA	European Free Trade Association (integrated by Iceland, Liechtenstein, Norway, and Switzerland)
EMS	European monetary system
EMU	European Economic and Monetary Union
ERM	Exchange rate mechanism (of the EMS)
EU	European Union (formerly European Community; integrated by Austria, Belgium, Denmark, Finland, France, Germany, Greece, Ireland, Italy, Luxembourg, Netherlands, Portugal, Spain, Sweden, and United Kingdom)

FSU	Former Soviet Union
GCC	Gulf Cooperation Council (Cooperation Council for the Arab States of the Gulf; integrated by Bahrain, Kuwait, Oman, Qatar, Saudi Arabia, and United Arab Emirates)
GSP	Generalized system of preferences
LAIA	Latin American Integration Association (integrated by Argentina, Bolivia, Brazil, Chile, Colombia, Ecuador, Mexico, Paraguay, Peru, Uruguay, and República Bolivariana de Venezuela)
LC	Letter of credit
LIBOR	London interbank offered rate
MERCOSUR	Southern Cone Common Market (integrated by Argentina, Brazil, Paraguay, and Uruguay)
MFA	Multifiber Arrangement
MFN	Most favored nation
MOF	Ministry of Finance
NAFTA	North American Free Trade Agreement
NATO	North Atlantic Treaty Organization
OECD	Organization for Economic Cooperation and Development (integrated by Australia, Austria, Belgium, Canada, Czech Republic, Denmark, Finland, France, Germany, Greece, Hungary, Iceland, Ireland, Italy, Japan, Republic of Korea, Luxembourg, Mexico, Netherlands, New Zealand, Norway, Poland, Portugal, Spain, Sweden, Switzerland, Turkey, United Kingdom, and United States)
OECS	Organization of Eastern Caribbean States (integrated by Antigua and Barbuda, Dominica, Grenada, Montserrat, St. Kitts and Nevis, St. Lucia, and St. Vincent and the Grenadines)
OGL	Open general license
PTA	Preferential trade area for eastern and southern African states
RCPSFM	Regional Council on Public Savings and Financial Markets (an institution of WAEMU countries that is involved in the authorization for issuance and marketing of securities)
SACU	Southern African Customs Union (integrated by Botswana, Lesotho, Namibia, South Africa, and Swaziland)
SADC	Southern Africa Development Community (integrated by Angola, Botswana, Democratic Republic of the Congo, Lesotho, Malawi, Mauritius, Mozambique, Namibia, Seychelles, South Africa, Swaziland, Tanzania, Zambia, and Zimbabwe)
SDR	Special drawing rights
SIBOR	Singapore interbank offered rate
SPARTECA	South Pacific Regional Trade and Economic Cooperation Agreement (signed by Australia, Cook Islands, Fiji, Kiribati, Marshall Islands, Federated States of Micronesia, Nauru, New Zealand, Niue, Palau, Papua New Guinea, Samoa, Solomon Islands, Tonga, Tuvalu, and Vanuatu)
UDEAC	Central African Customs and Economic Union (Union douanière et économique de l'Afrique centrale; integrated by Cameroon, Central African Republic, Chad, Republic of Congo, Equatorial Guinea, and Gabon)
UN	United Nations
UNITA	National Union for the Total Independence of Angola
VAT	Value-added tax
WAEMU	West African Economic and Monetary Union (formerly WAMU; integrated by the members of the BCEAO)
WAMA	West African Monetary Agency (formerly WACH)
WTO	World Trade Organization

Note: This list does not include acronyms of purely national institutions mentioned in the country chapters.

INTRODUCTION

The report provides a detailed description of the exchange arrangements and exchange restrictions of individual member countries, as well as Aruba and the Netherlands Antilles, for which the Kingdom of the Netherlands has accepted the IMF Articles of Agreement, and Hong Kong SAR. In general, the description relates to the exchange and trade systems as of the end of 1999, but, in appropriate cases, reference is made to significant developments that took place in early 2000.

The description of the exchange and trade system is not necessarily confined to those aspects involving exchange restrictions or exchange controls. As in previous reports, questions of definition and jurisdiction have not been raised, and an attempt has been made to describe exchange and trade systems in their entirety, except for the tariff structure and, in most cases, direct taxes on imports and exports.

Following a standardized approach, the description of each system is broken down into similar headings, and the coverage for each country includes a final section that lists chronologically the more significant changes during 1999 and early 2000.

The report is presented in a tabular format that enhances transparency and the uniformity of treatment of the information across countries and includes coverage on the regulatory framework for capital movements. The information is drawn from the exchange arrangements and exchange restrictions database maintained by the IMF. The country tables present an abstract of the relevant information that is available to the IMF. The table on Summary Features of Exchange Arrangements and Regulatory Frameworks for Current and Capital Transactions in Member Countries (Appendix I) provides an overview of the characteristics of the exchange and trade systems of IMF member countries. The Country Table Matrix (Appendix II) provides a full listing of the rubrics used in the database.

When information in a particular category within a section is not available at the time of publication, the category is displayed with a note to that effect (that is, n.a.). When information is available on all but a particular item or items within a category, these items are not included in the table. In cases where members provided the IMF with the information that a category or an item is not regulated, these are marked by "n.r."

1

COMPILATION GUIDE

Status Under IMF Articles of Agreement

Article VIII	The member country has accepted the obligations of Article VIII, Sections 2, 3, and 4 of the IMF's Articles of Agreement.
Article XIV	The member country continues to avail itself of the transitional arrangements of Article XIV, Section 2.

Exchange Arrangement

Currency	The official legal tender of the country.
Other legal tender	The existence of another currency that is allowed to be used officially in the country.
Exchange rate structure	The existence of more than one exchange rate that may be used simultaneously for different purposes and/or by different entities. If there is one exchange rate, the system is called unitary; if there are more than one, the system is called dual or multiple.
Classification	
Exchange arrangement with no separate legal tender	The currency of another country circulates as the sole legal tender, or the member belongs to a monetary or currency union in which the same legal tender is shared by the members of the union.
Currency board arrangement	A monetary regime based on an explicit legislative commitment to exchange domestic currency for a specified foreign currency at a fixed exchange rate, combined with restrictions on the issuing authority to ensure the fulfillment of its legal obligation.
Conventional pegged arrangement	The country pegs its currency (formally or de facto) at a fixed rate to a major currency or a basket of currencies, where the exchange rate fluctuates within a narrow margin of at most ±1% around a central rate.
Pegged exchange rate within horizontal bands	The value of the currency is maintained within certain margins of fluctuation around a formal or de facto fixed peg. The margins are wider than ±1% around the central rate.
Crawling peg	The currency is adjusted periodically in small amounts at a fixed, preannounced rate or in response to changes in selective quantitative indicators.
Crawling band	The currency is maintained within certain fluctuation margins around a central rate adjusted periodically at a fixed preannounced rate, or in response to changes in selective quantitative indicators.
Managed floating with no preannounced path for the exchange rate	The monetary authority influences the movements of the exchange rate through active intervention in the foreign exchange market without specifying, or precommitting to, a preannounced path for the exchange rate.
Independently floating	The exchange rate is market determined, with any foreign exchange intervention aimed at moderating the rate of change and preventing undue fluctuations in the exchange rate, rather than at establishing a level for it.
Exchange tax	The existence of a special tax on foreign exchange transactions.
Exchange subsidy	Foreign exchange transactions are subsidized by using separate, nonmarket exchange rates.
Forward exchange market	The existence of a forward exchange market.
Official cover of forward operations	Official coverage of forward operations refers to the case where an official entity (the central bank or the government) assumes the exchange risk of certain foreign exchange transactions.

Arrangements for Payments and Receipts

Prescription of currency requirements	The official requirements affecting the selection of currency and the method of settlement of transactions with other countries. When a country has concluded payment agreements with other countries, the terms of these agreements often lead to a prescription of currency for specified categories of payments to and from the countries concerned.
Payment arrangements	
Bilateral payment arrangements	Two countries conclude an agreement to prescribe specific rules for payments to each other, including cases when private parties are also obligated to use specific currencies. These agreements can be either operative or inoperative.
Regional arrangements	More than two parties participate in a payment agreement.
Clearing agreements	The official bodies of two or more countries agree to offset with some regularity the balance that arises in the payments to each other as a result of exchange of goods, services, or less often, capital.
Barter agreements and open accounts	The official bodies of two or more countries agree to offset exports of goods and services to one country with imports of goods and services from the same country, without payment.
Administration of control	The authorities' division of responsibility for policy and the administration of exchange controls, and the extent of delegation of powers to outside agencies (often banks authorized to effect foreign exchange transactions).
International security restrictions	Restrictions on payments and transfers for international transactions imposed by member countries for reasons of national or international security.
In accordance with Executive Board Decision No. 144-(52/51)	International security restrictions on the basis of IMF Executive Board Decision No. 144-(52/51) establishing the obligation of members to notify the IMF before imposing such restrictions, or, if circumstances preclude advance notification, as promptly as possible.
In accordance with UN sanctions	Sanctions imposed against a second body on the basis of a UN decision.
Payment arrears	Official or private residents of a member default on their payments or transfers to nonresidents. This category includes only the situation in which the domestic currency is available for the residents to settle their debts, but they are unable to obtain foreign exchange, for example, because of the presence of an officially announced or unofficial queuing system. The category does not cover nonpayment of private parties due to the bankruptcy of the party concerned.
Controls on trade in gold (coins and/or bullion)	The existence of separate rules for trading with gold both domestically and with foreign countries.
Controls on exports and imports of banknotes	The existence of regulations for the physical movement of means of payment between countries. When information is available, the category distinguishes between separate limits for the (1) export and import of banknotes by travelers and (2) export and import of banknotes by banks and other authorized financial institutions.

Resident Accounts

The category describes the manner in which the country treats resident accounts, if allowed, that are maintained in the national currency or in foreign currency, locally or abroad, and the facilities and limitations attached to such accounts. When there is more than one type of resident account, the nature and operation of the various types of accounts are also described: for example, if residents are allowed to open foreign exchange accounts with or without approval from the foreign exchange authority or if these accounts are allowed to be held domestically or abroad; or likewise whether the balances on accounts held by residents in domestic currency are allowed to be converted into foreign currency.

Nonresident Accounts

The category describes the manner in which the country treats local nonresident accounts, if allowed, that are maintained in the national currency or in foreign currency, and the facilities and limitations attached to such accounts. When there is more than one type of nonresident account, the nature and operation of the various types of accounts are also described.

Blocked accounts

Blocked accounts of nonresidents are usually accounts in domestic currency. Regulations do not allow or limit the conversion and/or transfer of the balances of such accounts.

Imports and Import Payments

The category describes the nature and extent of exchange and trade restrictions on imports.

Foreign exchange budget

Information on the existence of a foreign exchange plan, i.e., a prior allocation of a certain amount of foreign exchange, usually on an annual basis, for the importation of specific types of goods and services; in some cases, also differentiating between individual importers.

Financing requirements for imports

Information on specific import financing regulations limiting the rights of residents to conclude private contracts in which the financing options differ from the official regulations.

Documentation requirements for release of foreign exchange for imports

Domiciliation requirements

The obligation to domicile the transactions with a specified (usually domestic) financial institution.

Preshipment inspection

Most often a compulsory government measure aimed at establishing the veracity of the import contract in terms of volume, quality, and price.

Letters of credit

Private parties are obligated to use letters of credit as a form of payment for their imports.

Import licenses used as exchange licenses

The import licenses are not used for trade purposes but to restrict the availability of foreign exchange for legitimate trade.

Other

Import licenses and other nontariff measures

Positive list

A list of goods that may be imported.

Negative list

A list of goods that may not be imported.

Open general licenses

The item indicates arrangements whereby certain imports or other international transactions are exempt from the restrictive application of licensing requirements.

Licenses with quotas

The item refers to cases where a license for the importation of a certain good is granted, but a specific limit is imposed on the amount to be imported.

Other nontariff measures

The item may include the prohibition to import certain goods or all goods from a certain country. Several other nontariff measures are used by members (e.g., phyto-sanitary examinations, setting of standards, etc.), but these are not covered fully by the annual report.

Import taxes and/or tariffs

A brief description of the import tax/tariff system, including taxes levied on the foreign exchange made available for imports.

Taxes collected through the exchange system	Indicates if any taxes apply to the exchange side of an import transaction.
State import monopoly	Private parties are not allowed to engage in the import of certain commodities or they are limited in their activity.

Exports and Export Proceeds

	Identifies restrictions on the use of export proceeds, as well as regulations on exports.
Repatriation requirements	Refers to the obligation of exporters to bring back into the country export proceeds.
Surrender requirements	Refers to regulations requiring the recipient of repatriated export proceeds to sell, sometimes at a specified exchange rate, any foreign exchange proceeds in return for local currency to the central bank, commercial banks, foreign exchange markets, or exchange dealers authorized for this purpose.
Financing requirements	Information on specific export financing regulations limiting the rights of residents to conclude private contracts in which the financing options differ from the official regulations.
Documentation requirements	The same categories are used as in the case of imports.
Export licenses	Restrictions on the right of residents to export goods. These restrictions may take the form of quotas (when a certain quantity of shipment abroad is allowed) or the absence of quotas (when the licenses are issued at the discretion of the foreign trade authority).
Export taxes	A brief description of the export tax system, including the existence of taxes that are levied on the foreign exchange earned by exporters.

Payments for Invisible Transactions and Current Transfers

Controls on these transfers	Describes the procedures for effecting payments abroad for current transactions in invisibles with reference to prior approval requirements, the existence of quantitative and indicative limits, and/or bona fide tests. Detailed information on the most common categories of transactions is provided only when regulations differ for the various categories. Indicative limits establish maximum amounts up to which the purchase of foreign exchange is allowed upon declaration of the purpose of the transaction, mainly for statistical purposes. Amounts above those limits are granted if the bona fide nature of the transaction is established by the presentation of appropriate documentation. Bona fide tests also may be applied for transactions for which quantitative limits have not been established.
Trade-related payments	The comprehensive category includes freight/insurance (including possible regulations on non trade–related insurance payments and transfers); unloading/storage costs; administrative expenses; commissions; and customs duties and fees.
Investment-related payments	The comprehensive category includes profits/dividends; interest payments (including interest on debentures, mortgages, etc.); amortization of loans or depreciation of direct investments; and payment and transfer of rent.
Payments for travel	Includes international travel for pleasure, recreation, business, etc.
Personal payments	The comprehensive category includes medical costs; study abroad costs; pensions (including regulations on the payment and transfer of pensions by both state and private pension providers on behalf of nonresidents, as well as the transfer of pensions due to residents); and family maintenance/alimony (including regulations on the payment and transfer abroad of family maintenance/alimony by residents and the transfer of family maintenance/alimony received by residents from abroad).
Foreign workers' wages	Transfer abroad of earnings by nonresidents working in the country.
Credit card use abroad	Use of credit and debit cards to pay for invisible transactions.

Other payments | The comprehensive category includes subscription/membership fees, authors' royalties, consulting/legal fees, and so forth.

Proceeds from Invisible Transactions and Current Transfers

Encompasses all regulations governing exchange receipts derived from transactions in invisibles, as well as a description of any limitation on their conversion into domestic currency and the use of those receipts.

Repatriation requirements | The concepts of repatriation and surrender requirements are similar to those applied to export proceeds.

Restrictions on use of funds | Refers mainly to the limitations imposed on the use of receipts previously deposited in certain bank accounts.

Capital Transactions

Describes regulations influencing capital movements. The concepts of controls and capital transactions are interpreted broadly. Thus, controls on capital movements include prohibitions; need for prior approval, authorization, and notification; multiple currency practices; discriminatory taxes; and reserve requirements or interest penalties imposed by the authorities that regulate the conclusion or execution of transactions or transfers with respect to both inward and outward capital flows or the holding of assets at home by nonresidents and abroad by residents. The coverage of the regulations would apply to receipts as well as payments and to actions initiated by nonresidents and residents. Moreover, because of their close association with capital movements, information is also provided on local financial operations conducted in foreign currency. Regarding the latter, it indicates specific regulations in force limiting residents and nonresidents to issue a security denominated in foreign currency or, generally, limitations on agreeing upon a contract expressed in terms of foreign exchange.

Controls on capital and money market instruments | Refers to the public offering or private placement on a primary market or listing on a secondary market.

On capital market securities | Refers to shares and other securities of a participating nature, and bonds and other securities with an original maturity of more than one year.

Shares or other securities of a participating nature | Transactions with shares and other securities of a participating nature are included in the category if the investment is not made to acquire a lasting economic interest in the management of the enterprise concerned. Investment to acquire a lasting economic interest is treated under direct investments.

Bonds or other debt securities | Refers to bonds and other securities with an original maturity of more than one year. The term "other securities" includes notes and debentures.

On money market instruments | Refers to securities with an original maturity of one year or less and includes short-term instruments, such as certificates of deposit and bills of exchange. It also includes treasury bills and other short-term government paper, banker's acceptances, commercial paper, interbank deposits, and repurchase agreements.

On collective investment securities | Includes share certificates and registry entries or other evidence of investor interest in an institution for collective investment, such as mutual funds, and unit and investment trusts.

Controls on derivatives and other instruments | Refers to operations in other negotiable instruments and nonsecuritized claims not covered under the above subsections. These may include operations in rights; warrants; financial options and futures; secondary market operations in other financial claims (including sovereign loans, mortgage loans, commercial credits, negotiable instruments originating as loans, receivables, and discounted bills of trade); forward operations (including those in foreign exchange); swaps of bonds and other debt securities; credits and loans; and other swaps (interest rate, debt/equity, equity/debt, foreign currency, as well as swaps of any of the instruments listed above). Controls on operations in foreign exchange without any other underlying transaction (on spot or forward trading on the foreign exchange markets, on forward cover operations, etc.) are also included here.

Controls on credit operations

Commercial credits

Covers operations directly linked with international trade transactions or with the rendering of international services.

Financial credits

The category includes credits other than commercial credits granted by all residents, including by banks to nonresidents or vice versa.

Guarantees, sureties, and financial backup facilities

The category includes sureties, guarantees, and financial backup facilities by residents to nonresidents and vice versa. It also includes guarantees and sureties, including securities pledged for payment or performance of a contract, such as warrants or avals, performance bonds, and standby letters of credit; and financial backup facilities, which are credit facilities used as a guarantee for independent financial operations.

Controls on direct investment

Refers to investment for the purpose of establishing lasting economic relations both abroad by residents and in the country by nonresidents. These investments are essentially for the purpose of producing goods and services, and, in particular, investments that allow investor participation in the management of the enterprise. It includes the creation or extension of a wholly owned enterprise, subsidiary, or branch and the acquisition of full or partial ownership of a new or existing enterprise that results in effective influence over the operations of this enterprise.

Controls on liquidation of direct investment

Refers to the transfer of principal, including the initial capital and capital gains, of a direct investment as defined above.

Controls on real estate transactions

Refers to the acquisition of real estate not associated with direct investment. It would include, for example, investments of a purely financial nature in real estate or the acquisition of real estate for personal use.

Controls on personal capital movements

Covers transfers initiated on behalf of private persons and intended to benefit another private person. It includes transactions involving property to which a promise of a return to the owner with payments of interest is attached (loans, settlements of debt in their country of origin by immigrants), or transfers free of charge to the beneficiary (gifts and endowments, loans, inheritances and legacies, and emigrants' assets).

Provisions specific to commercial banks and other credit institutions

Describes regulations that are specific to these institutions, such as monetary, prudential, and foreign exchange controls. Inclusion of an entry in this part does not necessarily signify that the aim of the measure is to control the flow of capital. Some of these items (borrowing abroad, lending to nonresidents, purchase of locally issued securities denominated in foreign exchange, investment regulations) could merely be repetitions of the entries under respective categories of controls on capital and money market instruments, controls on credit operations, or direct investments when the same regulations apply to commercial banks as to other residents.

Open foreign exchange position limits

The item describes the existence and contents of regulations on certain commercial bank balance sheet items (including capital) or absolute limits covering commercial banks' positions in foreign currencies (including gold).

Provisions specific to institutional investors

Describes controls specific to institutions, such as insurance companies and pension funds.

Other restrictions imposed by securities laws

Refers to additional regulations on capital movements imposed by those laws, such as restrictions on the listing of foreign securities on local security markets.

ISLAMIC STATE OF AFGHANISTAN

(Position as of December 31, 1994)

Status Under IMF Articles of Agreement

Article XIV	Yes.

Exchange Arrangement

Currency	The currency of the Islamic State of Afghanistan is the Afghani.
Exchange rate structure	
Dual	The Da Afghanistan Bank (DAB), the central bank, maintains an official rate defined in terms of the U.S. dollar. The official rate is applied to no more than 10% of convertible currency transactions, including a few transactions of the central government (mainly debt-service payments) and certain foreign currency incomes earned in the Islamic State of Afghanistan. Almost all other official transactions are conducted at a commercial rate set by the government. A free market, in the form of a money bazaar, is also operative. The exchange rate applied to transactions of international organizations is set at 80% of the level of the commercial exchange rate.
Classification	
Independently floating	Most convertible currency transactions are effected at the floating commercial market rate. The DAB posts rates for deutsche marks, French francs, Indian rupees, Pakistan rupees, pounds sterling, and Swiss francs.
Exchange tax	n.a.
Exchange subsidy	n.a.
Forward exchange market	There are no arrangements for forward cover against exchange rate risk operating in the official market or the commercial banking sector.

Arrangements for Payments and Receipts

Prescription of currency requirements	Settlements with countries with which the Islamic State of Afghanistan maintains bilateral payment agreements are made in bilateral accounting dollars in accordance with the procedures set forth in these agreements. Exchange rates for trade under bilateral payment agreements are determined under each agreement. The proceeds from exports of karakul to all countries must be obtained in convertible currencies. There are no other prescription of currency requirements.
Payment arrangements	
Bilateral payment arrangements	The Islamic State of Afghanistan maintains bilateral payment agreements with Bulgaria, China, and Russia. Some of these have been inactive for several years, and others are being phased out.
Operative	Yes.
Inoperative	Yes.
Administration of control	Foreign exchange transactions are controlled by the government through the DAB. No restrictions apply to transactions in the free exchange market.
International security restrictions	n.a.
Payment arrears	n.a.
Controls on trade in gold (coins and/or bullion)	
Controls on external trade	Imports and reexports of gold are permitted, subject to regulations. Exports of gold bullion, silver, and jewelry require permission from the DAB and the Ministry of Finance.

Commercial exports of gold and silver jewelry and other articles containing minor quantities of gold or silver do not require a license. Customs duties are payable on imports and exports of silver in any form, unless the transaction is made by, or on behalf of, the monetary authorities.

Controls on exports and imports of banknotes

On exports

Domestic currency — Travelers may take out up to Af 2,000 in domestic banknotes and Af 50 in coins.

On imports

Domestic currency — Travelers may bring in up to Af 2,000 in domestic banknotes and Af 50 in coins.

Foreign currency — Travelers entering the Islamic State of Afghanistan are required to spend a minimum of the equivalent of $26 a day in foreign exchange. They may bring in any amount of foreign currency but must declare it when entering the country if they intend to take out any unspent amount on departure, subject to the above minimum conversion requirement.

Resident Accounts

Foreign exchange accounts permitted — n.a.

Accounts in domestic currency convertible into foreign currency — n.a.

Nonresident Accounts

Foreign exchange accounts permitted — n.a.

Domestic currency accounts — n.a.

Blocked accounts — n.a.

Imports and Import Payments

Foreign exchange budget — An annual import program drawn up by the Ministry of Commerce covers both public and private sector imports. Adjustments in the public sector import plan are made as circumstances change. The import plan for the private sector, drawn up on the basis of proposals submitted by the Chamber of Commerce, is indicative.

Financing requirements for imports — n.a.

Documentation requirements for release of foreign exchange for imports

Letters of credit — Payments for imports through the banking system to countries with which the Islamic State of Afghanistan has payment agreements may usually be made only under LCs. Payments to other countries may be made under LCs, against bills for collection, or against an undertaking by the importer to import goods of at least an equivalent value to the payment made through the banking system. Except for public sector imports under the government budget, all importers are required to lodge minimum import deposits with banks when they open LCs. The deposit ratios, based on the c.i.f. value of imports, are 20% for essential products and range from 30% to 60% for other products.

Import licenses and other nontariff measures — Imports are not subject to licenses, but import transactions must be registered before orders are placed abroad.

Positive list — Most bilateral agreements, however, specify quantities (and sometimes prices) for commodities to be traded.

Negative list	The importation of certain drugs, liquor, arms, and ammunition is prohibited on grounds of public policy or for security reasons; in some instances, however, special permission to import these goods may be granted. The importation of a few textiles and selected nonessential consumer goods is also prohibited.
Licenses with quotas	There are no quantitative restrictions on most imports, but tariff rates on most consumer items range from 30% to 50%.
Import taxes and/or tariffs	No.
State import monopoly	No.

Exports and Export Proceeds

Repatriation requirements	Export proceeds from bilateral accounts may be retained in bilateral clearing dollar accounts with the DAB. These retained proceeds may either be used directly by the original exporter or sold to other importers. In either case, the retained proceeds are converted at the clearing rate applicable to that particular bilateral arrangement. In the case of exports to countries trading in convertible currencies, export proceeds may be retained abroad for three, six, or twelve months, depending on the country of destination. During the relevant period, the exporter may use these funds to import any goods not included on the list of prohibited goods. Alternatively, at the end of the relevant holding period limit, foreign exchange holdings abroad must be repatriated and held in a foreign currency account with a bank in the Islamic State of Afghanistan or sold at the commercial exchange rate.
Surrender requirements	Proceeds from exports of raisins, fresh fruits, animal casings, skins, licorice roots, medicinal herbs, and wool must be surrendered immediately at the commercial exchange rate.
Financing requirements	n.a.
Documentation requirements	n.a.
Export licenses	Export transactions must be registered. The exportation of opium and museum pieces is prohibited. Otherwise, control is exercised only over exports to bilateral agreement countries.
Without quotas	Yes.
Export taxes	n.a.

Payments for Invisible Transactions and Current Transfers

Controls on these transfers	Foreign exchange for most private purposes may be acquired in the money bazaar.
Investment-related payments	Information is not available on amortization of loans or depreciation of direct investments.
Payments for travel	The DAB levies a charge of Af 0.75 per $1 and 1% of hard currency for permits that approve the exportation of convertible currency by authorized travelers.
Prior approval	Yes.
Quantitative limits	The limit for tourist travel is $1,000, except for private travel to India, for which the limit is the equivalent of $700. The limit for business travel is $15,000.
Personal payments	For medical treatment, the central bank levies a commision of Af 0.75 per $1. No information is available for other types of personal payments other than medical costs.
Quantitative limits	Normally, the DAB grants $2,500 for medical treatment.
Foreign workers' wages	Foreign employees working in the Afghan public and private sectors must convert 60% of their foreign currency salaries into Afghanis at the official rate.
Quantitative limits	Yes.

Proceeds from Invisible Transactions and Current Transfers

Repatriation requirements	n.a.
Restrictions on use of funds	n.a.

Capital Transactions

Controls on capital and money market instruments	n.a.
Controls on derivatives and other instruments	n.a.
Controls on credit operations	n.a.
Controls on direct investment	
Inward direct investment	Investments require prior approval and are administered by the Investment Committee. The law stipulates that foreign investment in the Islamic State of Afghanistan can take place only through joint ventures, with foreign participation not exceeding 49%, and that an investment approved by the Investment Committee requires no further license in order to operate in the Islamic State of Afghanistan. The Foreign and Domestic Private Investment Law includes the following provisions: (1) income tax exemption for four years (six years outside Kabul province), beginning with the date of the first sale of products resulting from the new investment; (2) exemption from import duties on essential imports (mainly for capital goods); (3) exemption from taxes on dividends for four years after the first distribution of dividends, but not more than seven years after the approval of the investment; (4) exemption from personal income and corporate taxes on interest on foreign loans that constitute part of an approved investment; (5) exemption from export duties, provided that the products are not among the prohibited exports; and (6) mandatory procurement by government agencies and departments from enterprises established under the law, as long as the prices are not more than 15% higher than those of foreign suppliers.
Controls on liquidation of direct investment	Capital may be repatriated after five years at an annual rate not exceeding 20% of the total registered capital.
Controls on real estate transactions	n.a.
Controls on personal capital movements	n.a.
Provisions specific to commercial banks and other credit institutions	n.a.
Provisions specific to institutional investors	n.a.
Other controls imposed by securities laws	n.a.

Changes During 1995–99

The IMF has not received from the authorities the information required for a description of the exchange and trade system since 1995.

ALBANIA

(Position as of January 31, 2000)

Status Under IMF Articles of Agreement

Article XIV　　　　　　　　　　Yes.

Exchange Arrangement

Currency　　　　　　　　　The currency of Albania is the Albanian lek.

Other legal tender　　　　　　In special cases, and with prior approval from the Bank of Albania (BOA), foreign exchange may serve as a means of payment.

Exchange rate structure　　Unitary.

Classification

Independently floating　　　　The exchange rate of the lek is determined on the basis of supply and demand for foreign exchange. The BOA calculates and announces the daily average exchange rates for the dollar and 22 other major currencies. No margins are set between buying and selling rates for the official exchange rate. Government transactions are conducted at market rates. However, the commercial banks charge commissions ranging from 0.2% to 2%, depending on the amount, for cashing traveler's checks.

Exchange tax　　　　　　　No.

Exchange subsidy　　　　　No.

Forward exchange market　No.

Arrangements for Payments and Receipts

Prescription of currency requirements　　Payment for all merchandise trade is made in convertible currencies. All transactions under bilateral payment agreements were suspended in 1992, and the settlement of clearing accounts is pending the outcome of negotiations.

Payment arrangements

Bilateral payment arrangements

Inoperative　　　　　Albania maintains bilateral payment agreements in nonconvertible currencies with Algeria, Bulgaria, Cuba, the Czech Republic, Egypt, Hungary, the Democratic People's Republic of Korea, Poland, Romania, the Russian Federation, and Vietnam. Albania also maintains bilateral payment agreements in convertible currencies with Bulgaria, China, Cuba, the Czech Republic, Greece, the Democratic People's Republic of Korea, Romania, Turkey, Vietnam, and the Federal Republic of Yugoslavia (Serbia/Montenegro).

Administration of control　　The BOA is vested with the powers to administer exchange controls. The BOA is the only authority that has the right to (1) license, authorize, regulate, supervise, and revoke the licenses of foreign exchange market operations, as well as second tier banks; (2) define the limits of their activities; and (3) regulate and supervise foreign exchange operations and international payments in order to prevent any participant from dominating the market and undermining the value of the lek through speculation.

There is a reporting requirement on banks and exchange dealers for transactions above $15,000 or its equivalent at the exchange rate prevailing on the date the transaction is effected.

International security restrictions　　No.

Payment arrears

Official　　　　　　　Albania has arrears on debts with China, Greece, Italy, the Russian Federation, Turkey, and with a number of commercial creditors. Official payment arrears to Italy and the Russian

Federation are subject to the July 1998 Paris Club Agreement and their rescheduling awaits the completion of bilateral negotiations.

Private	Yes.
Controls on trade in gold (coins and/or bullion)	n.r.

Controls on exports and imports of banknotes

On exports

Domestic currency — Natural and juridical persons are allowed to take out up to lek 100,000 a person in banknotes and coins. The BOA may authorize larger amounts.

Foreign currency — Foreign natural persons may take abroad in cash or traveler's checks foreign exchange in an amount equal to the amount declared when entering the country. Albanian natural or juridical persons are not allowed to export amounts larger than $10,000 or its equivalent. This limit was increased to $25,000 on May 27, 1999.

On imports

Domestic currency — Natural and juridical persons are allowed to import up to lek 100,000 in domestic banknotes and coins. The BOA may authorize larger amounts.

Foreign currency — Natural and juridical persons are allowed to import foreign currency and traveler's checks up to $10,000 or its equivalent in any other currency.

Resident Accounts

Foreign exchange accounts permitted	Yes.
Held domestically	Yes.
Held abroad	Residents—natural or juridical persons—may open and maintain foreign currency–denominated accounts with banks and financial institutions abroad only with the prior approval of the BOA, which may control and monitor transactions effecting such accounts.
Accounts in domestic currency convertible into foreign currency	Yes.

Nonresident Accounts

Foreign exchange accounts permitted	Yes.
Domestic currency accounts	Yes.
Convertible into foreign currency	Yes.
Blocked accounts	Yes.

Imports and Import Payments

Foreign exchange budget	No.
Financing requirements for imports	No.
Documentation requirements for release of foreign exchange for imports	For imports equal to or larger than $5,000 or its equivalent (increased to $10,000 on May 27, 1999), the following documents must be submitted: (1) an application for carrying out the transaction as well as a declaration specifying in detail the nature of the transaction; (2) a contract and an invoice (or a pro forma invoice) issued by the natural or juridical person supplying the goods; and (3) a declaration issued by the natural or juridical person wishing to carry out the transaction with the bank that the underlying document has not been used to support previous transactions.

Letters of credit	LCs, bank guarantees, or cash against documents should be used for the payment of imports equal to or in excess of $200,000 or its equivalent.
Import licenses used as exchange licenses	Yes.
Import licenses and other nontariff measures	The import of the following products are prohibited: (1) dangerous waste, as toxic corrosives, residual waste from explosives, and radioactive materials; (2) military poisons, chemical weapons, and other strong poisons; (3) narcotics and psychotropic substances; and (4) animal products from infected countries.
Positive list	Yes.
Open general licenses	Yes.
Licenses with quotas	On January 1, 1999, automatic licensing restrictions were introduced on fuel products to support the implementation of domestic technical standards.
Import taxes and/or tariffs	Since January 1, 1999, excise taxes on domestic and imported goods are unified and the tariff on diesel was increased to 20% from 10% to provide temporary protection to the local petroleum industry while undergoing restructuring. There are four tariff rates, which are applied to the c.i.f. value: zero, 5%, 10%, and 20%. Effective January 1, 2000, the maximum tariff rate was reduced to 18% from 20%.
State import monopoly	No.

Exports and Export Proceeds

Repatriation requirements	All private and public companies or individuals operating in the export sector are required to repatriate their foreign exchange receipts.
Financing requirements	No.
Documentation requirements	No.
Export licenses	Until September 1999, there were export bans on raw hides and skins; metal scraps; copper and articles thereof; works of art, arms and ammunitions, as well as parts and accessories therefor; and explosives and pyrotechnic products. Effective September 30, 1999, the export ban on raw skins and hides and on scrap metals was removed.
Without quotas	Yes.
Export taxes	No.

Payments for Invisible Transactions and Current Transfers

Controls on these transfers	Supporting documents for transactions exceeding $5,000 are required. Effective May 27, 1999, this amount was increased to $10,000.

Proceeds from Invisible Transactions and Current Transfers

Repatriation requirements	Yes.
Restrictions on use of funds	No.

Capital Transactions

Controls on capital and money market instruments	Purchases of these instruments abroad by residents require prior approval of the BOA. Trade in these instruments is subject to the control by the Albanian Securities Commission.

On capital market securities

Shares or other securities of a participating nature

Sale or issue locally by nonresidents	Yes.
Purchase abroad by residents	Yes.
Sale or issue abroad by residents	Yes.

Bonds or other debt securities

Sale or issue locally by nonresidents	Yes.
Purchase abroad by residents	Yes.
Sale or issue abroad by residents	Yes.

On money market instruments

Sale or issue locally by nonresidents	Yes.
Purchase abroad by residents	Yes.
Sale or issue abroad by residents	Yes.

On collective investment securities

Sale or issue locally by nonresidents	Yes.
Purchase abroad by residents	Yes.
Sale or issue abroad by residents	Yes.

Controls on derivatives and other instruments	Transactions in these instruments are subject to the control of the Albanian Securities Commission, but these are not yet regulated.
Sale or issue locally by nonresidents	Yes.
Purchase abroad by residents	Yes.
Sale or issue abroad by residents	n.r.

Controls on credit operations

Commercial credits

By residents to nonresidents	Commercial banks may not, without the prior approval of the BOA, extend credit to nonresidents, except to banks and other financial institutions.

Financial credits

By residents to nonresidents	Commercial banks may not, without the prior approval of the BOA, extend credit to nonresidents, except to banks and other financial institutions.

Guarantees, sureties, and financial backup facilities

By residents to nonresidents	Yes.
Controls on direct investment	
Outward direct investment	Outward direct investments are subject to the prior approval of the BOA.
Controls on liquidation of direct investment	No.
Controls on real estate transactions	
Purchase abroad by residents	Purchases are subject to the prior approval of the BOA.
Purchase locally by nonresidents	The controls relate only to the purchase of land.

Controls on personal capital movements

Loans

   By residents to nonresidents   Yes.

Gifts, endowments, inheritances, and legacies

   To residents from nonresidents   n.r.

Provisions specific to commercial banks and other credit institutions

Lending to nonresidents (financial or commercial credits)   Commercial banks may not, without the prior approval of the BOA, extend credit to nonresidents, except to banks and other financial institutions.

Lending locally in foreign exchange   BOA may impose credit ceilings on outstanding stock of credits for each commercial bank.

Differential treatment of deposit accounts held by nonresidents

   Credit controls   Yes.

Investment regulations

   Abroad by banks   Yes.

   In banks by nonresidents   Yes.

Open foreign exchange position limits   The limit is 10% of the bank's capital for a single currency and 20% for all currencies. Effective January 12, 1999, these limits were increased to 20% and 30%, respectively.

   On resident assets and liabilities   Yes.

   On nonresident assets and liabilities   Yes.

Provisions specific to institutional investors   n.r.

Other controls imposed by securities laws   n.r.

Changes During 1999

Arrangements for payments and receipts   *May 27.* The limit of foreign currency exports by Albanian natural and juridical persons was increased to $25,000 from $10,000.

Imports and import payments   *January 1.* Excise taxes on domestic and imported goods were unified at rates at least revenue neutral, and the tariff on diesel was increased to 20% from 10% to provide temporary protection for the local petroleum industry while undergoing restructuring.

January 1. Automatic licensing restrictions were introduced on fuel products to support the implementation of domestic technical standards.

May 27. The amount for imports subject to exchange licenses was increased to $10,000 from $5,000.

Exports and export proceeds   *September 30.* The export ban on raw skins and hides, and on scrap metals was removed.

Payments for invisible transactions and current transfers   *May 27.* The amount for which supporting documents are required was increased to $10,000 from $5,000.

Capital transactions

Provisions specific to commercial banks and other credit institutions   *January 12.* Open foreign exchange position limits of a bank's capital for a single currency were increased to 20% from 10% and, for all currencies, to 30% from 20%.

Changes During 2000

Imports and import payments   *January 1.* The maximum tariff rate was reduced to 18% from 20%.

ALGERIA
(Position as of December 31, 1999)

Status Under IMF Articles of Agreement

Article VIII   Date of Acceptance: September 15, 1997

Exchange Arrangement

Currency

The currency of Algeria is the Algerian dinar.

Exchange rate structure

Unitary.

Classification

Managed floating with no pre-announced path for the exchange rate

The external value of the dinar is set at the interbank foreign exchange market rate. No margin limits are imposed on the buying and selling exchange rates in the interbank foreign exchange market. However, a margin of DA 0.017 has been established between the buying and selling rates of the Bank of Algeria (BOA) for the dinar against the dollar.

Exchange tax

No.

Exchange subsidy

No.

Forward exchange market

Authorized banks may provide forward cover to residents, but this has not taken place.

Arrangements for Payments and Receipts

Prescription of currency requirements

Settlements with countries with which no payment agreements are in force are made in convertible currencies. Payments under foreign supply contracts may be made in either the currency in use at the headquarters of the supplier or that of the country of origin of the merchandise, except that transactions with Morocco may be effected in dollars through special clearing accounts maintained at the central banks of the respective countries.

Payment arrangements

Clearing agreements

Specified noncommercial settlements with Morocco and Tunisia are made through a Moroccan dirham account at the Bank of Morocco and a Tunisian dinar account at the Bank of Tunisia.

Administration of control

The BOA has general jurisdiction over exchange controls. Authority for a number of exchange control procedures has been delegated to seven commercial banks and the Postal Administration.

International security restrictions

No.

Payment arrears

No.

Controls on trade in gold (coins and/or bullion)

Controls on domestic ownership and/or trade

Residents may purchase, hold, and sell gold coins in Algeria for numismatic purposes. Unworked gold for industrial and professional use is distributed by the Agence nationale pour la distribution et la transformation de l'or et des autres métaux précieux (AGENOR); this agency is also authorized to purchase gold in Algeria and to hold, process, and distribute any other precious metals.

Controls on external trade

AGENOR is authorized to import and export any precious metals, including gold. Gold used by dentists and goldsmiths is imported by AGENOR. Gold and other precious metals are included on the list of items importable by concessionaires.

Controls on exports and imports of banknotes

On exports

Domestic currency

Resident travelers may take out up to DA 200 a person.

Foreign currency

Foreign nonresident travelers may reexport any foreign currency they declared upon entry. Resident travelers may export foreign currency withdrawn from their foreign currency accounts up to the equivalent of F 50,000 a trip for an unlimited number of trips a year.

On imports

Domestic currency

Resident travelers may reimport up to DA 200 a person. Nonresidents are not permitted to bring in Algerian dinar banknotes.

Foreign currency

There are no restrictions on the importation of foreign banknotes, but residents and non-residents must declare them when they enter Algeria.

Resident Accounts

Foreign exchange accounts permitted

Yes.

Held domestically

These accounts may be freely credited with book transfers of convertible currencies from abroad using either postal or banking facilities, imported convertible foreign currencies that were declared at the time of the account holder's entry into the country, and domestic bank-to-bank book transfers between accounts held by individuals. These accounts may be debited freely for book transfers abroad but only through the banking system. They may also be debited for purchases of dinars, for book transfers in dinars, and for purchases of convertible foreign currencies to be physically exported by the account holder. The interest rate payable on deposits in these accounts is fixed quarterly by the BOA.

Economic entities are also allowed to open foreign currency accounts for receiving and making foreign currency transfers, including the retained portion of their export proceeds. They may transfer funds in these accounts to other foreign currency accounts or use them to make payments in Algeria or to make foreign currency payments for goods and services pertaining to their business.

Held abroad

No.

Accounts in domestic currency convertible into foreign currency

These accounts are permitted in limited cases, such as for embassies.

Nonresident Accounts

Foreign exchange accounts permitted

These accounts may be credited with foreign currency banknotes and other means of payment denominated in foreign currency, as well as other dinar-denominated funds that meet all requirements for transfers abroad. They may be debited without restrictions to make transfers abroad, to export through withdrawals of foreign banknotes, and to make dinar payments in Algeria. These accounts pay interest and may not show a net debit position.

Domestic currency accounts

Final departure accounts may be opened, without prior authorization, in the name of any natural person residing in Algeria who is not of Algerian nationality, and who intends to leave Algeria to return to his or her country of origin. These accounts may be credited with an amount equivalent to the holdings as of October 20, 1963, of the person concerned; with the proceeds from sales of real estate by the account holder, provided that the funds are paid directly by a ministerial officer; with the proceeds of the sale of securities through a bank; and with any other payments up to DA 2,000. These accounts may be debited without prior approval for certain payments in Algeria on behalf of the account holder.

Convertible into foreign currency

Outward transfers require individual approval from the BOA.

Blocked accounts

Individual suspense accounts may be opened without authorization and may be credited with payments from any country.

Imports and Import Payments

Foreign exchange budget

No.

Financing requirements for imports

Payments for imports of gold, other precious metals, and precious stones must be made from foreign currency accounts. External borrowing by importers for import financing purposes must be arranged through the authorized intermediary banks.

Advance payment requirements

Except when otherwise indicated by the BOA, down payments for imports may not exceed 15% of the total value of imports. When a public agency, public enterprise, or ministry incurs expenditures for imports deemed to be urgent or exceptional, the bank may effect payment before exchange and trade control formalities have been completed.

Advance import deposits

Although not an official regulation, domiciled banks may require from the importer, as part of their normal commercial operations, a deposit in dinars up to the full value of the imports.

Documentation requirements for release of foreign exchange for imports

Domiciliation requirements

All imports are subject to obligatory domiciliation at an authorized intermediary bank, which an importer must establish by submitting a commercial contract or pro forma invoice. Import payments may be made freely but only through the domiciled bank, which effects payments in foreign exchange and debits the importer's account with corresponding amounts in dinars valued at the official exchange rate. Imports must be insured by Algerian insurers.

Preshipment inspection

Yes.

Letters of credit

Yes.

Import licenses and other nontariff measures

Any juridical or natural person registered under the Commercial Register (including concessionaires and wholesalers) may import goods without prior authorization; no license is needed.

Negative list

There are no legal restrictions against Israel, but there are no imports from Israel in practice. A small number of imports are prohibited for religious or security reasons.

Import taxes and/or tariffs

No.

State import monopoly

No.

Exports and Export Proceeds

Repatriation requirements

Proceeds must be repatriated within 120 days. Petroleum companies are subject to the same rule, but proceeds may be deposited in a guaranteed account with a foreign correspondent bank of the BOA.

Surrender requirements

All export proceeds from crude and refined hydrocarbons, byproducts from gas, and mineral products must be surrendered to the BOA. Exporters of other products must surrender 50% of the proceeds to the interbank market; the remaining portion may be retained in a foreign currency account. Exporters may use the funds in these accounts for imports or other payments pertaining to their business, or they may transfer the funds to another foreign currency account. Proceeds from exports of nonhydrocarbons, and nonminerals may be surrendered to commercial banks and other authorized participants in the interbank foreign exchange market.

Financing requirements

No.

Documentation requirements

The requirements are not enforced in practice.

Letters of credit

Yes.

Guarantees

Yes.

Domiciliation

Yes.

Preshipment inspection	Yes.
Export licenses	All exports to Israel are prohibited, and certain exports are prohibited for social or cultural reasons regardless of destination.
Export taxes	No.

Payments for Invisible Transactions and Current Transfers

Controls on these transfers	
Investment-related payments	Information is not available on the payment or transfer of amortization of loans or depreciation of direct investments.
Prior approval	Profit remittances are permitted, provided tax obligations have been met.
Payments for travel	Foreign exchange allocation for tourism by Algerian residents was suspended in October 1986. Pilgrims traveling to Saudi Arabia receive an allowance in Saudi Arabian riyals. The amount is fixed for each pilgrimage and may be provided in the form of checks that may be cashed on arrival for those traveling by air or by sea. Travel tickets purchased by nonresidents for travel abroad must be paid for with imported foreign exchange.
Prior approval	Yes.
Quantitative limits	The quantitative limit is DA 15,000.
Indicative limits/bona fide test	Yes.
Personal payments	
Prior approval	Approval of the BOA is required for transfers of pension income. For family maintenance and alimony payments, the BOA must authorize the granting of foreign exchange. Limits are set on a case-by-case basis.
Quantitative limits	The limits for medical costs are DA 15,900 for adults and DA 7,600 for children under 15 years old. For studies abroad, the limit is DA 7,500.
Indicative limits/bona fide test	Information is not available on family maintenance and alimony transfers.
Foreign workers' wages	Residents of other countries working in Algeria under technical cooperation programs for public enterprises and agencies or for certain mixed companies may transfer abroad up to 100% of their salaries.
Indicative limits/bona fide test	Yes.
Other payments	
Prior approval	Approval of the BOA is required for payments relating to subscriptions and membership fees and consulting and legal fees.
Indicative limits/bona fide test	Yes.

Proceeds from Invisible Transactions and Current Transfers

Repatriation requirements	Yes.
Surrender requirements	Fifty percent of receipts must be surrendered to the banks.
Restrictions on use of funds	No.

Capital Transactions

Controls on capital and money market instruments	Capital transfers to any destination abroad are subject to individual approval by the BOA.

On capital market securities

Shares or other securities of a participating nature

   Purchase abroad by residents   Yes.

On money market instruments

  Purchase abroad by residents   Yes.

On collective investment securities

  Purchase abroad by residents   Yes.

Controls on derivatives and other instruments

Purchase abroad by residents   Yes.

Controls on credit operations   There are controls on all credit transactions, guarantees, sureties, and financial backup facilities by residents to nonresidents.

Controls on direct investment

Outward direct investment   Yes.

Inward direct investment   Foreign direct investment is permitted freely except in certain specified sectors, provided that it conforms to the laws and regulations governing regulated activities and that prior declaration is made to the authorities.

Controls on liquidation of direct investment   No.

Controls on real estate transactions

Purchase abroad by residents   Yes.

Controls on personal capital movements   n.a.

Provisions specific to commercial banks and other credit institutions

Borrowing abroad   Banks and financial institutions may borrow from abroad for their own needs or for those of their clients.

Lending locally in foreign exchange   Banks and financial institutions may on-lend foreign funds borrowed abroad.

Differential treatment of deposit accounts in foreign exchange

  Interest rate controls   The interest rates applicable to foreign currency accounts are determined quarterly by the BOA.

Open foreign exchange position limits   Banks and financial institutions are required to meet the following: (1) a maximum spread of 10% between their position (short or long) in each currency and the amount of their counterpart funds in domestic currency; and (2) a maximum spread of 30% between total exposure (short and long positions, whichever is highest) for all foreign currencies and domestic currency resources.

Provisions specific to institutional investors   No.

Other controls imposed by securities laws   n.a.

Changes During 1999

No significant changes occurred in the exchange and trade system.

ANGOLA

(Position as of December 31, 1999)

Status Under IMF Articles of Agreement

Article XIV	Yes.

Exchange Arrangement

Currency

Until November 30, 1999, the currency of Angola was the Angolan readjusted kwanza. A new currency, the kwanza, was introduced on December 1, 1999.

Exchange rate structure

Unitary.

Classification

Independently floating

On May 21, 1999, a package of foreign exchange liberalization measures was implemented and since then, the kwanza has floated freely, with the central bank setting a reference rate for its transactions based on the previous day's average market rate. Prior to that date, all legal transactions took place at the official exchange rate, and exchange houses were obliged to deal at the official exchange rate set for commercial banks. Thus, the exchange rate arrangement of Angola has been reclassified to the category independently floating from the category crawling peg. Authorized foreign exchange dealers may deal among themselves and with their customers at freely negotiated rates. The National Bank of Angola (BNA) intervenes in the foreign exchange market.

Exchange tax

Foreign exchange operations, except transactions with banknotes and traveler's checks, checks in favor of natural persons, and transactions between banking institutions are subject to a stamp duty of 1.5%.

Exchange subsidy

No.

Forward exchange market

No.

Arrangements for Payments and Receipts

Prescription of currency requirements

The BNA prescribes the currency to be used in import and export transactions, which is either that of the country of origin of imports or the country of destination of exports, or the dollar.

Payment arrangements

Bilateral payment arrangements

  Operative

Yes.

Clearing agreements

Angola is a member of COMESA.

Barter agreements and open accounts

Bilateral arrangements, which do not contain bilateral payment features, are maintained with Brazil, Portugal, and Spain.

Administration of control

The BNA is the exchange authority and may delegate its powers pertaining to specific activities to other entities. All capital transactions and invisible operations exceeding $50,000 require a prior authorization by the BNA. The BNA has authorized commercial banks and exchange bureaus to carry out transactions in the official foreign exchange market. Foreign exchange bureaus are licensed to deal in banknotes and traveler's checks and execute current invisible operations of private nature. Banks are allowed to execute capital movements (after an authorization from the BNA has been issued), permitted invisible operations, and foreign exchange transactions related to foreign trade.

International security restrictions

n.a.

Payment arrears

Official

Yes.

Private	Yes.

Controls on trade in gold (coins and/or bullion)

Controls on domestic ownership and/or trade	Residents are permitted to hold and trade gold only in the form of jewelry.
Controls on external trade	Imports and exports of gold are the monopoly of the BNA.

Controls on exports and imports of banknotes

On exports

Domestic currency	Exports of domestic currency are prohibited.
Foreign currency	Residents are permitted to take out more than $10,000 in foreign exchange only if they present exchange purchase documents, including the reason for the purchase. Nonresidents are allowed to bring into the country any amount of foreign exchange, but when leaving Angola are allowed to take with them more than $5,000 only if the excess was declared upon arrival into the country. The export and reexport of banknotes and traveler's checks by banking institutions requires a prior authorization issued by the BNA.

On imports

Domestic currency	Yes.
Foreign currency	There are no limits on the amount of foreign banknotes or traveler's checks that a resident person may bring into the country; for nonresidents, any amount in excess of $5,000 must be declared upon arrival. Banking institutions are free to import banknotes and traveler's checks, but they must submit a monthly report to the BNA.

Resident Accounts

Foreign exchange accounts permitted	Yes.
Held domestically	Checkbooks may not be issued against these accounts. On May 21, 1999, restrictions on the use of foreign currency accounts were eased to allow deposits without declaring source of funds, and to allow debits for purchases of kwanza and for settlements of international payments on behalf of the depositor.
Held abroad	After prior approval, enterprises are allowed to open foreign exchange accounts to pay for imports of goods and services. For natural persons, no approval is required for opening such accounts.
Accounts in domestic currency convertible into foreign currency	No.

Nonresident Accounts

Foreign exchange accounts permitted	These accounts may be credited with foreign exchange transferred from abroad or the deposit of proceeds from the account holder's activities in Angola. They may be debited with the sale of foreign exchange, payments for foreign currency expenditures, or the repatriation of authorized amounts. On May 21, 1999, restrictions on the use of nonresident accounts (in foreign currency and kwanza) were eased to allow shifting of balances between both types of accounts and the transferring of funds from abroad into those accounts.
Domestic currency accounts	Nonresidents may open two types of domestic currency accounts: type A and type B. The type A account may be credited with the proceeds of the sale of cash from the foreign exchange account and, after prior BNA authorization, with receipts from the nonresident's activities in Angola. These accounts may be debited for payments of local expenses and against purchases of foreign currency to be deposited in a foreign currency account held by the same entity.

The type B account may only be credited with receipts of the nonresident's activity in the country (when allowed by the BNA), and may only be debited for payment of local expenses.

Blocked accounts   No.

Imports and Import Payments

Foreign exchange budget   No.

Financing requirements for imports   No.

Documentation requirements for release of foreign exchange for imports

Preshipment inspection   Yes.

Import licenses and other nontariff measures

Negative list   There are restrictions on the imports of ammunition, money, toxic products, and certain drugs by private persons.

Open general licenses   Imports of goods under $5,000 do not require trade licenses.

Import taxes and/or tariffs   The tariff system comprises eight rates: 1%, 2%, 5%, 10%, 20%, 25%, 30%, and 35%.

Taxes collected through the exchange system   The stamp duty is collected through the exchange system.

State import monopoly   Imports of oil products can only be effected by the public oil company.

Exports and Export Proceeds

Repatriation requirements   Yes.

Surrender requirements   Foreign oil companies are allowed, under an authorization, to retain their export receipts abroad for payment of imports of goods and services, profits transfer, and the amortization of capital. These companies must import funds for payment of royalties, taxes, and local expenses. Domestic oil companies must surrender all their export proceeds to the BNA. In the non-oil sector, foreign exchange earnings must be surrendered to the domestic banks. Diamond companies are allowed to retain in banks in the country a percentage of the receipts of exports for payment of imports of goods and services. They may also retain part of their receipts abroad in escrow accounts.

Financing requirements   n.a.

Documentation requirements

Letters of credit   Yes.

Domiciliation   Yes.

Preshipment inspection   Yes.

Export licenses

Without quotas   All exports of goods and services are subject to licensing. Exports of arms and ammunition, and ethnological collections are prohibited. Special export regimes apply to aircraft, animals and animal products, historical objects, and petroleum. Reexports of goods other than personal belongings are also prohibited.

Export taxes   On September 3, 1999, export taxes were changed to the rates of 1%, 2%, 3%, 4%, 5%, and 10%.

Payments for Invisible Transactions and Current Transfers

Controls on these transfers

As of May 21, 1999, authorization of the BNA is required for nongovernment payments for invisibles in excess of $50,000; below that, banks may sell the foreign exchange but must report to the BNA; lower limits are applied for travel and private transfers, as indicated below.

Trade-related payments

Above $50,000, service contracts with nonresidents are subject to licensing.

Prior approval

Yes.

Investment-related payments

Prior approval

Yes.

Quantitative limits

Foreign investors have to obtain MOF authorization to remit dividends, which are routinely granted, provided the investment in the resident company exceeds $250,000.

Payments for travel

Quantitative limits

Depending on the documented purpose of the travel, the limits are as follows: (1) for individuals, up to $10,000 a person a trip to any country; (2) for business travel, $500 a day for up to 30 days.

Personal payments

Prior approval

Prior approval is required for the payment of pensions above $50,000.

Quantitative limits

For extended education travel, the limit is $2,000 a month. For family maintenance and alimony payments, up to the equivalent of $2,000 a month may be granted to Angolans or foreigners residing abroad who are direct ascendants or descendants of, and financially dependent on, residents in Angola, subject to presentation of documents establishing kinship. For medical expenses, the limit is $5,000.

Foreign workers' wages

Prior approval

Yes.

Other payments

Prior approval

Yes.

Proceeds from Invisible Transactions and Current Transfers

Repatriation requirements

Yes.

Surrender requirements

Service earnings must be surrendered to the banks, unless the provider is authorized by the BNA to retain a certain proportion of the proceeds.

Restrictions on use of funds

No.

Capital Transactions

Controls on capital and money market instruments

Foreign investment activities (i.e., the setting up of new companies or branches, but also acquisition of equity, total or partial takeover of operations, and lending related to profit sharing) are subject to the provisions of the Foreign Investment Law as well as the provisions of foreign exchange legislation and regulations. Implementation is the responsibility of the Foreign Investment Institute. Foreign investments in the areas of petroleum production, diamond mining, and financial institutions are governed by separate legislation. All capital transfers, except supplier credits, are subject to BNA licensing.

Controls on derivatives and other instruments

There are controls on all derivatives transactions.

Controls on credit operations

Commercial credits	Operations are subject to licensing for statistical purposes only.
By residents to nonresidents	Yes.
To residents from nonresidents	Yes.
Financial credits	
By residents to nonresidents	Yes.
To residents from nonresidents	Yes.
Guarantees, sureties, and financial backup facilities	
By residents to nonresidents	Yes.
To residents from nonresidents	Yes.

Controls on direct investment

Outward direct investment	According to the Exchange Control Law, Angolan citizens are permitted to invest abroad.
Inward direct investment	Effective May 21, 1999, a minimum amount of $60,000 was set for authorized foreign investments. Such investments in amounts up to $250,000 need BNA clearance; for those above $250,000, government approval is required. Foreign investment is prohibited in the following areas: (1) defense, internal public order, and state security; (2) central banking and currency issue; and (3) other areas reserved for the state.
Controls on liquidation of direct investment	Foreign investors are guaranteed the right to transfer abroad the proceeds of the sale of investments, including gains and amounts owed to them after payments of taxes due, but prior approval of the MOF is required.
Controls on real estate transactions	There are controls on all real estate transactions.
Controls on personal capital movements	There are controls on all personal capital movements.

Provisions specific to commercial banks and other credit institutions

Borrowing abroad	Yes.
Maintenance of accounts abroad	Yes.
Lending to nonresidents (financial or commercial credits)	Yes.
Lending locally in foreign exchange	Banks may lend locally in foreign exchange to resident exporters.
Differential treatment of deposit accounts in foreign exchange	
Liquid asset requirements	Liquid asset requirements are 50% of the foreign exchange portfolio.
Credit controls	Yes.
Differential treatment of deposit accounts held by nonresidents	
Reserve requirements	Yes.
Investment regulations	
Abroad by banks	Yes.
In banks by nonresidents	Yes.
Open foreign exchange position limits	Banks may hold daily foreign exchange positions of up to $500,000; for foreign exchange bureaus, the amount is up to $150,000.
On resident assets and liabilities	Yes.

On nonresident assets and liabilities	Yes.
Provisions specific to institutional investors	n.a.
Other controls imposed by securities laws	n.a.

Changes During 1999

Exchange arrangement

May 21. Foreign exchange transactions were authorized at market exchange rates. Thus, the exchange rate arrangement of Angola has been reclassified to the category independently floating from the category crawling peg.

May 21. Commercial banks and foreign exchange bureaus were authorized to settle international trade and services transactions up to certain limits, without requesting BNA authorization.

December 1. A new currency, the kwanza, replaced the readjusted kwanza.

Resident accounts

May 21. Restrictions on the use of foreign currency accounts were eased to allow deposits without declaring source of funds, and to allow debits for purchases of kwanza and for settlements of international payments on behalf of the depositor.

Nonresident accounts

May 21. Restrictions on the use of nonresident accounts (in foreign currency and kwanza) were eased to allow shifting of balances between both types of accounts and the transferring of funds from abroad into those accounts.

Imports and import payments

September 3. The import tariff code was simplified through a reduction in tariff levels (with a new maximum rate of 35%) and in the levels of bands (to 8 from 43).

Exports and export proceeds

September 3. The export tariff code was simplified to six levels of bands and tariff levels were reduced (with a new maximum rate of 10%).

Payments for invisible transactions and current transfers

May 21. Banks and foreign exchange bureaus were authorized to settle invisible transactions up to amounts of $50,000 without requesting BNA authorization; travel allowances were raised for all travelers; the limit on transfers to relatives abroad was reduced to the equivalent of $2,000 a month.

Capital transactions

Controls on direct investment

May 21. A minimum amount of $60,000 was set for authorized foreign investments. Such investments in amounts up to $250,000 need BNA clearance; for those above $250,000, government approval is required.

Provisions specific to commercial banks and other credit institutions

May 21. Banks were authorized to provide credit in foreign currency to exporters, up to a limit of 50% of the lending bank's deposits in that specific currency.

ANTIGUA AND BARBUDA

(Position as of January 31, 2000)

Status Under IMF Articles of Agreement

Article VIII   Date of acceptance: November 22, 1983.

Exchange Arrangement

Currency   The currency of Antigua and Barbuda is the Eastern Caribbean dollar issued by the ECCB.

Exchange rate structure   Unitary.

Classification

Exchange arrangement with no sepa-   The Eastern Caribbean dollar is pegged to the U.S. dollar, the intervention currency, at
rate legal tender   EC$2.70 per US$1. The ECCB also quotes daily rates for the Canadian dollar and the
                                     pound sterling.

Exchange tax   A foreign exchange levy of 1% is applied on purchases of foreign currency.

Exchange subsidy   n.a.

Forward exchange market   No.

Arrangements for Payments and Receipts

Prescription of currency   Settlements with residents of member countries of the CARICOM must be made either in
requirements   the currency of the country concerned or in Eastern Caribbean dollars. Exports to Jamaica
                                     are settled in U.S. dollars. Settlements with residents of other countries may be made in any
                                     foreign currency or in Eastern Caribbean dollars.

Payment arrangements

Regional arrangements   Antigua and Barbuda is a member of the CARICOM.

Clearing agreements   No.

Administration of control   The MOF applies exchange control to all foreign currency transactions.

International security restrictions No.

Payment arrears   Yes.

**Controls on trade in gold (coins   No.
and/or bullion)**

Controls on exports and imports of n.a.
banknotes

Resident Accounts

Foreign exchange accounts permitted External accounts may be opened, especially in tourist-oriented industries or export trade
                                         where receipts are primarily in foreign currency and a large number of inputs are imported
                                         or financed in foreign currency.

Held domestically   Yes.

Approval required   Commercial banks are required to report external accounts operations to the MOF on a
                                     monthly basis.

Accounts in domestic currency   n.a.
convertible into foreign currency

Nonresident Accounts

Foreign exchange accounts permitted	External accounts may be maintained in any currency and may be credited with receipts from sales of merchandise (whether from export-oriented or local production) or from remittances.
Approval required	Commercial banks are required to report external accounts operations to the MOF on a monthly basis.
Domestic currency accounts	n.a.
Blocked accounts	n.a.

Imports and Import Payments

Foreign exchange budget	n.a.
Financing requirements for imports	n.a.
Documentation requirements for release of foreign exchange for imports	Payments for authorized imports are permitted upon application and submission of documentary evidence.
Import licenses and other nontariff measures	Certain commodities require individual licenses, unless imported from CARICOM countries. Antigua and Barbuda follows the CARICOM rules of origin adopted.
Open general licenses	Most goods may be freely imported under OGLs granted by the MOF and the Ministries of Industry and Commerce.
Import taxes and/or tariffs	Antigua and Barbuda applies the CARICOM's CET. Tariff rates range from zero to 25% for nearly all items. There are no tariffs on a number of items, including milk and poultry. Exemptions from import duties exist for some goods, including basic foods and agricultural goods. Other exemptions for machinery, equipment, and raw materials are granted on a case-by-case basis. On January 1, 2000, the fourth phase of the CARICOM CET went into effect.
State import monopoly	n.a.

Exports and Export Proceeds

Repatriation requirements	n.a.
Financing requirements	n.a.
Documentation requirements	n.a.
Export licenses	No.
Export taxes	Reexports are not subject to any tax if transactions take place within the bonded area.

Payments for Invisible Transactions and Current Transfers

Controls on these transfers	Payments for invisibles (related to authorized imports) exceeding EC$100,000 require prior approval for certain categories, except for payments for freight, insurance, unloading and storage costs, administrative expenses, commissions, and profits and dividends, which are not subject to controls.
Investment-related payments	Profits may be remitted in full after compliance with corporate income tax payments. Verification is not applied in practice; the authorities, however, can decide to undertake such verification. Information is not available on the amortization of loans or depreciation of direct investments.
Prior approval	Yes.

Quantitative limits	Yes.
Indicative limits/bona fide test	Yes.
Payments for travel	
Prior approval	Approval is required only for amounts exceeding the equivalent of EC$100,000.
Quantitative limits	Yes.
Indicative limits/bona fide test	Yes.
Personal payments	Information is not available on the transfer of pensions.
Prior approval	Payments related to family maintenance and alimony are allowed if provided for in the contract.
Quantitative limits	For payments related to medical and studies abroad, approval on a case-by-case basis is required only for amounts exceeding the equivalent of EC$100,000.
Indicative limits/bona fide test	Yes.
Foreign workers' wages	
Prior approval	These remittances are allowed, if provided for in the contract.
Quantitative limits	Yes.
Indicative limits/bona fide test	Yes.
Other payments	
Prior approval	Payments for consulting and legal fees are allowed, if provided for in the contract.
Quantitative limits	The limit for subscriptions and membership fees is EC$10,000 a year.
Indicative limits/bona fide test	Yes.

Proceeds from Invisible Transactions and Current Transfers

Repatriation requirements	No.
Restrictions on use of funds	No.

Capital Transactions

Controls on capital and money market instruments	No.
Controls on derivatives and other instruments	No.
Controls on credit operations	No.
Controls on direct investment	
Outward direct investment	Large transfers abroad for investment purposes may be phased over time by the Financial Secretary.
Controls on liquidation of direct investment	No.
Controls on real estate transactions	
Purchase locally by nonresidents	An alien landholding license is required, and the purchase must be approved by the Cabinet.
Controls on personal capital movements	No.

Provisions specific to commercial banks and other credit institutions	As a result of laws governing offshore financial institutions, (1) the International Financial Sector Authority was created, with responsibility for licensing offshore financial institutions; (2) there are annual inspections of offshore financial institutions; (3) the minimum capital requirement for offshore banks is US$5 million, of which US$1.5 million is to be deposited in the domestic banking system; (4) all bank directors are to be natural persons, at least one of whom must be Antiguan (thus making bank ownership more transparent); and (5) offshore banks are allowed to extend credit to the Antiguan government.
Lending to nonresidents (financial or commercial credits)	MOF approval is required for these transactions. Loans are subject to a 3% stamp duty.
Provisions specific to institutional investors	n.a.
Other controls imposed by securities laws	n.a.

Changes During 1999

No significant changes occurred in the exchange and trade system.

Changes During 2000

Imports and import payments	*January 1.* The fourth phase of the CARICOM CET went into effect.

ARGENTINA

(Position as of December 31, 1999)

Status Under IMF Articles of Agreement

Article VIII   Date of acceptance: May 14, 1968.

Exchange Arrangement

Currency   The currency of Argentina is the Argentine peso.

Other legal tender   Transactions in convertible currencies are permitted, and contracts in these currencies are legally enforceable, although the currencies are not legal tender.

Exchange rate structure   Unitary.

Classification

Currency board arrangement   The external value of the peso is pegged to the dollar under a currency board type of arrangement. Exchange rates of other currencies are based on the buying and selling rates for the dollar in markets abroad.

Exchange tax   No.

Exchange subsidy   No.

Forward exchange market   Swap transactions and forward exchange operations are permitted in any currency, and the rates may be freely negotiated.

Arrangements for Payments and Receipts

Prescription of currency requirements   Transactions with countries with which there are no payment agreements must be settled in freely convertible currencies.

Payment arrangements

Regional arrangements   Within the framework of the multilateral clearing system of the LAIA, payments between Argentina and other LAIA countries are settled voluntarily through payment agreements and a reciprocal credit mechanism.

                                     Argentina has agreements with Cuba, Malaysia, and Russia. Payments between Argentina and these countries are settled on a voluntary basis through accounts opened with the Central Bank of Argentina (BCRA) and the other central banks concerned, with the exception of Cuba, where settlement through the accounts specified in the agreements is obligatory.

Clearing agreements   Yes.

Administration of control   All exchange transactions are carried out through entities authorized expressly for this purpose, with no restrictions on the purchase or sale of foreign exchange at market prices. These authorized entities include banks, exchange agencies, exchange houses, exchange offices, and financial companies. Each type of institution is subject to separate regulations.

International security restrictions

In accordance with UN sanctions   Restrictions on current payments with respect to Iraq, Libya, and the Federal Republic of Yugoslavia (Serbia/Montenegro) are imposed.

Payment arrears   No.

Controls on trade in gold (coins and/or bullion)

Controls on domestic ownership and/or trade   Residents may hold gold coins and gold in any other form in Argentina or abroad. Financial institutions, exchange houses, and exchange agencies may buy or sell gold in the form of coins or good delivery bars among themselves, and may buy such gold from their clients, as well as other precious metals, the market value of which is based on the daily list prices of major transactions.

Controls on external trade	The importation of gold coins and bars is not restricted. Gold exports must be paid for in convertible currencies. Imports of gold by industrial users are subject to a statistical duty of 0.5%, as well as a sales tax. Institutions may carry out arbitrage operations with their clients in gold coins or bars against foreign banknotes. Authorized institutions may export gold to entities abroad.
Controls on exports and imports of banknotes	No.

Resident Accounts

Foreign exchange accounts permitted	Authorized banks may open accounts in pesos or in foreign exchange, provided that identification requirements aimed, among others, at preventing money laundering have been met. Foreign exchange accounts must be denominated in convertible currencies and may be credited only with cash or with remittances in the following currencies: U.S. dollars for current accounts, savings, and fixed-term deposits; and other currencies that the BCRA explicitly authorizes at the request of financial institutions for savings deposits and fixed-term accounts. Credit balances may be used freely in Argentina or abroad. Transfers between accounts may be made freely. The use of checking accounts denominated in U.S. dollars is allowed for domestic transactions.
Held domestically	Yes.
Held abroad	Yes.
Accounts in domestic currency convertible into foreign currency	Yes.

Nonresident Accounts

Foreign exchange accounts permitted	Authorized banks may open accounts in pesos or in foreign exchange, provided that identification requirements aimed, among others, at preventing money laundering have been met. Checking account requirements include the establishment of a domicile in Argentina.
Domestic currency accounts	Yes.
Convertible into foreign currency	Due to the currency board regime, the convertibility of peso-dollar accounts is allowed.
Blocked accounts	No.

Imports and Import Payments

Foreign exchange budget	No.
Financing requirements for imports	No.
Documentation requirements for release of foreign exchange for imports	
Preshipment inspection	Inspection is required for a reduced list of products.
Import licenses and other nontariff measures	Effective September 9, 1999, import licenses are prescribed for paper products and footwear imported from non-MERCOSUR countries.
Negative list	Restrictions are in force solely for security, hygiene, and public health reasons.
Open general licenses	OGL are required for a reduced list of products.
Licenses with quotas	Quantitative restrictions are applied to the automobile sector and to footwear from MERCOSUR countries.
Other nontariff measures	Nontariff barriers are not applied to intra-MERCOSUR trade. Argentina, however, applies

a special regime to automobile and sugar imports with the authorization of MERCOSUR, pending agreement on a common regime for these sectors. Quantitative restrictions are applied to automobiles. Quantitative restrictions on some textile products imported from Brazil, the People's Republic of China, and Pakistan were introduced on August 1, 1999, and, effective November 1, 1999, on some textile products imported from the Republic of Korea. The imports of secondhand clothing, tires, and some capital goods are prohibited.

Import taxes and/or tariffs

There is no common regime in MERCOSUR for automobiles and sugar.

Argentina and the MERCOSUR countries apply a CET to imports from the rest of the world that encompasses all products. CET rates currently range from zero to 20%. The majority of products are taxed with an additional 3% tariff until December 31, 2000. There are three lists of exceptions to the CET: (1) the national list for 300 products until 2001, with an average rate of 18% in 1999; (2) the capital goods list with 14% CET until 2001; and (3) the computers and telecommunications list with a maximum CET of 16% until 2006. On January 21, 1999, a resolution was adopted, according to which the import tariffs on some capital goods may in some cases be reduced to 6% from 14%.

State import monopoly

No.

Exports and Export Proceeds

Repatriation requirements

No.

Financing requirements

No.

Documentation requirements

No.

Export licenses

Without quotas

Licenses are required for arms, sensitive goods, and war materials.

With quotas

There are quantitative restrictions on exports only on protected animal species.

Export taxes

A 5% export duty is applied to untanned, pickled aplite and wet blue leathers, and a 3.5% duty is applied to cotton, flax, groundnuts, soybeans, sunflower seeds, and turnips.

Payments for Invisible Transactions and Current Transfers

Controls on these transfers

No.

Proceeds from Invisible Transactions and Current Transfers

Repatriation requirements

No.

Restrictions on use of funds

No.

Capital Transactions

Controls on capital and money market instruments

On capital market securities

Shares or other securities of a participating nature

Sale or issue locally by nonresidents

Under the regulations of the National Securities Commission (CNV), foreign investors must meet the same requirements as those applicable to Argentine investors to make a public offering of securities in Argentina. In each case, they must establish a permanent representative office and a domicile in Argentina to receive notices. They must state whether the securities are also being offered to the public in their country of origin, and specify the initial and periodic information requirements to which they are subject. If the CNV believes that the regulations in the country of origin properly protect local investors and guarantee an adequate flow of information, the CNV may lower the requirements for these investors. The CNV may authorize foreign investors on a case-by-case basis to submit only such information as they would periodically submit to the corresponding authority in their jurisdiction of origin.

Bonds or other debt securities

   Sale or issue locally by nonresidents   The same conditions apply as for the sale or issue of shares of a participating nature.

On money market instruments

   Sale or issue locally by nonresidents   Control is applied only for commercial papers.

On collective investment securities

   Sale or issue locally by nonresidents   Yes.

Controls on derivatives and other instruments

Sale or issue locally by nonresidents   Approval of the CNV is required for public offerings.

Controls on credit operations   No.

Controls on direct investment

Inward direct investment   Yes.

Controls on liquidation of direct investment   No.

Controls on real estate transactions

Purchase locally by nonresidents   For purchases of real estate in border areas, a foreign investor must seek prior approval for the project from the Border Superintendency of the Ministry of Defense. This limitation exists for national security reasons.

Controls on personal capital movements   No.

Provisions specific to commercial banks and other credit institutions

Lending to nonresidents (financial or commercial credits)   The credit granted by financial intermediaries must be used in the country and must finance investment, production, commercialization, and consumption of goods and services for internal demand or exports.

Purchase of locally issued securities denominated in foreign exchange   There are limits on the maximum amount of securities a bank may hold from a particular issuer.

Investment regulations

   Abroad by banks   These controls are related only to the constitution of minimum liquidity requirements.

Open foreign exchange position limits   There are regulations on the minimum capital held against market risks.

Provisions specific to institutional investors

Limits (max.) on securities issued by nonresidents and on portfolio invested abroad   Yes.

Limits (max.) on portfolio invested abroad   There is a 25% limit on the investment trust portfolio, but this limit does not apply to MERCOSUR. For diversification and according to law, no more than 10% of pension funds may be invested in securities issued by a foreign sovereign, or in securities of foreign corporations issued abroad.

Limits (min.) on portfolio invested locally	In the event that the trust's assets consist of the securities, a tender offer should be made in Argentina or abroad with a minimum of 75% of the investment being made in assets issued and traded in Argentina.
Currency-matching regulations on assets/liabilities composition	Yes.
Other controls imposed by securities laws	Due to the implicit list associated with positions in different currencies other than the dollar, additional capital is required to cover those lists. Deposits and loans in those currencies are computed to build the position.

Changes During 1999

Imports and import payments

January 21. A resolution was adopted, according to which the import tariffs on some capital goods may in some cases be reduced to 6% from 14%.

August 1. Quantitative restrictions were introduced on the imports of some textile products from Brazil, the People's Republic of China, and Pakistan.

September 9. Import licenses were introduced for paper products and footwear from non-MERCOSUR countries.

November 1. Quantitative restrictions were introduced on the imports of some textile products from the Republic of Korea.

ARMENIA

(Position as of April 30, 2000)

Status Under IMF Articles of Agreement

Article VIII

Date of acceptance: May 29, 1997.

Exchange Arrangement

Currency

The currency of Armenia is the Armenian dram.

Exchange rate structure

Unitary.

Classification

Independently floating

The exchange rate of the dram against the dollar is determined on the basis of exchange rates in the interbank market and at foreign exchange auctions held five times a week in the Yerevan Stock Exchange (YSE) and twice a week in the Gjumry Stock Exchange (GSE). Banks and financial dealers holding licenses from the Central Bank of Armenia (CBA) may participate in the auctions. Anyone may buy and sell at the auctions through banks. However, foreign exchange transactions are taking place predominantly in the interbank market in which the CBA also participates. The CBA intervention in the foreign exchange market is limited to the smoothing of exchange rate fluctuations. The CBA quotes official rates in terms of dollars daily on the basis of the weighted average rate in the interbank market and at the foreign exchange auctions on the previous trading day. This rate is used for accounting valuation of all foreign exchange transactions of all economic agents, including the MOF. Exchange rates for other major currencies are calculated either on the basis of quotations on the YSE, when applicable, or solely on the basis of quotations for the dollar in major international interbank markets against the currencies concerned. Foreign exchange is also freely bought and sold by enterprises and persons, without restrictions, through authorized banks and licensed exchange bureaus that conduct cash transactions.

Exchange tax

No.

Exchange subsidy

No.

Forward exchange market

Residents and nonresidents may freely negotiate forward exchange contracts for both commercial and financial transactions in all leading convertible currencies in the domestic exchange market and at major international foreign exchange markets. However, for the time being, the forward exchange market in Armenia is still undeveloped, although some banks sign forward contracts in small amounts.

Official cover of forward operations

Yes.

Arrangements for Payments and Receipts

Prescription of currency requirements

No.

Payment arrangements

Bilateral payment arrangements

Inoperative

Armenia maintains agreements with Russia and Turkmenistan.

Regional arrangements

Armenia is a signatory of the 1993 Treaty of Economic Union (with Azerbaijan, Belarus, Kazakhstan, Kyrgyz Republic, Moldova, Russia, Tajikistan, and Uzbekistan), which provides for the eventual establishment of a customs union, a payments union, cooperation on investment, industrial development, and customs procedures. Armenia also joined the Agreement on the Establishment of Payments Union of CIS member countries. Armenia is a member of the Black Sea Economic Cooperation (BSEC), together with Albania, Azerbaijan, Bulgaria, Georgia, Greece, Moldova, Romania, Russia, Turkey, and Ukraine. Bilateral free trade agreements have been signed with Georgia, the Kyrgyz Republic,

Moldova, Russia, Tajikistan, and Ukraine, though only the agreement with Russia is in operation.

Clearing agreements	There is an arrangement with Turkmenistan for the importation of natural gas. In addition, bilateral clearing agreements with the Baltic countries and the other countries of the FSU exist, but all have become largely inoperative.
Administration of control	The CBA has overall responsibility for regulating financial relations between Armenia and other countries in close collaboration with the MOF. Resident and nonresident currency dealers, including banks, may undertake foreign exchange transactions without restriction. There are no restrictions on current and capital movements unless otherwise specified by the CBA (in which case, one month's notice is required).
International security restrictions	n.a.
Payment arrears	No.
Controls on trade in gold (coins and/or bullion)	A license is required for trading.
Controls on domestic ownership and/or trade	Yes.
Controls on external trade	Yes.
Controls on exports and imports of banknotes	
On exports	
Foreign currency	Individuals are authorized to transfer, deliver, and export currency denominated in foreign exchange up to $10,000 in cash or its equivalent without any restriction. Exports exceeding that amount are permitted through bank transfers.

Resident Accounts

Foreign exchange accounts permitted	Yes.
Held domestically	Yes.
Held abroad	These accounts are permitted, but approval is required.
Accounts in domestic currency convertible into foreign currency	Yes.

Nonresident Accounts

Foreign exchange accounts permitted	Yes.
Domestic currency accounts	Yes.
Convertible into foreign currency	Yes.
Blocked accounts	No.

Imports and Import Payments

Foreign exchange budget	No.
Financing requirements for imports	No.
Documentation requirements for release of foreign exchange for imports	No.

Import licenses and other nontariff measures

Negative list

Import licenses from the Ministry of Agriculture and the Ministry of Health are required and granted on a case-by-case basis to import medicinal preparations and pesticides. Imports of weapons, military equipment and parts, and explosives require special authorization from the government.

Import taxes and/or tariffs

There are two rates of customs duties: zero and 10%; most imports are zero rated. Products imported from countries in the CIS are exempted. On January 1, 1999, the tariff schedule was revised, with tariffs being reduced to zero from 10% for a few agricultural products, textiles, and vehicles, and increased to 10% from zero for a variety of new materials and manufactured products.

State import monopoly

n.a.

Exports and Export Proceeds

Repatriation requirements

The CBA has the power, as specified by legislation, to impose repatriation requirements on export proceeds.

Financing requirements

No.

Documentation requirements

No.

Export licenses

Export licenses are required for medicines, wild animals and plants, and textile products exported to the EU. In addition, special government permission is required for the export of nuclear technology, nuclear waste, related nonnuclear products, and technology with direct military applications. Minimum threshold prices for the export of ferrous and nonferrous metals and the reexport of foreign-produced goods therefrom remain in force.

Without quotas

Yes.

Export taxes

No.

Payments for Invisible Transactions and Current Transfers

Controls on these transfers

No.

Proceeds from Invisible Transactions and Current Transfers

Repatriation requirements

No.

Restrictions on use of funds

No.

Capital Transactions

Controls on capital and money market instruments

No.

Controls on derivatives and other instruments

No.

Controls on credit operations

No.

Controls on direct investment

No.

Controls on liquidation of direct investment

No.

Controls on real estate transactions

Purchase locally by nonresidents   In accordance with the constitution, nonresidents are not allowed to acquire land in Armenia.

Controls on personal capital movements   No.

Provisions specific to commercial banks and other credit institutions

Differential treatment of deposit accounts held by nonresidents

Reserve requirements   Effective April 9, 1999, the CBA eliminated the option for banks to hold 50% of required reserves against deposits in foreign exchange in either foreign or domestic currency and introduced an 8% reserve requirement in local currency against deposits in either foreign or domestic currency. The reserve requirement is remunerated at an interest rate of 10% a year.

Open foreign exchange position limits   The long foreign exchange position (the positive difference between foreign assets and liabilities) at the end of any business day must not exceed 40% of the bank's total capital, while the open position in nonconvertible currencies must not exceed 10% of the bank's total capital. Effective April 1, 1999, the limit on the overall foreign exchange position was lowered to 30% from 40%. Effective April 1, 2000, it was lowered further to 25%, while the open position limit in nonconvertible currencies was lowered to 5%.

On resident assets and liabilities   Yes.

On nonresident assets and liabilities   Yes.

Provisions specific to institutional investors   No.

Other controls imposed by securities laws   No.

Changes During 1999

Imports and import payments   *January 1.* The tariff schedule was revised, with tariffs being reduced to zero from 10% for a few agricultural products, textiles, and vehicles, and increased to 10% from zero for a variety of new materials and manufactured products.

Capital transactions

Provisions specific to commercial banks and other credit institutions   *April 1.* The limit on the overall foreign exchange position of banks was lowered to 30% of their capital.

April 9. The CBA eliminated the option for banks to hold 50% of required reserves against deposits in foreign exchange in either foreign or domestic currency.

Changes During 2000

Capital transactions

Provisions specific to commercial banks and other credit institutions   *April 1.* The limit on the overall foreign exchange position of banks was lowered to 25% of their capital, while the open position limit in nonconvertible currencies was lowered to 5%.

ARUBA

(Position as of December 31, 1999)

Status Under IMF Articles of Agreement

Article VIII   Date of acceptance: February 15, 1961.

Exchange Arrangement

Currency	The currency of Aruba is the Aruban florin.
Exchange rate structure	Unitary.
Classification	
Conventional pegged arrangement	The florin is pegged to the dollar at Af. 1.79 per $1. The Centrale Bank van Aruba (CBA), the central bank, deals with local commercial banks within margins of 0.002795% on either side of parity.
Exchange tax	A foreign exchange commission of 1.3% is levied on all payments to nonresidents, except when settled in Netherland Antillean guilders. Certain institutions or groups are exempted from this rule.
Exchange subsidy	No.
Forward exchange market	No.

Arrangements for Payments and Receipts

Prescription of currency requirements	No.
Payment arrangements	No.
Administration of control	The CBA administers foreign exchange control.
International security restrictions	
In accordance with UN sanctions	Yes.
Payment arrears	No.
Controls on trade in gold (coins and/or bullion)	No.
Controls on exports and imports of banknotes	
On exports	
Domestic currency	The exportation of domestic banknotes is prohibited.
Foreign currency	The exportation of foreign banknotes requires a license, except for traveling purposes.

Resident Accounts

Foreign exchange accounts permitted	Yes.
Held domestically	Through March 31, 1999, approval to open these accounts was required.
Held abroad	The opening of an account held abroad must be reported to the CBA.
Accounts in domestic currency convertible into foreign currency	These accounts are not allowed.

Nonresident Accounts

Foreign exchange accounts permitted	Yes.
Domestic currency accounts	Yes.
Convertible into foreign currency	Balances up to Af. 200,000 are convertible. Approval of the CBA is required for balances in excess of Af. 200,000.
Blocked accounts	No.

Imports and Import Payments

Foreign exchange budget	No.
Financing requirements for imports	No.
Documentation requirements for release of foreign exchange for imports	No.
Import licenses and other nontariff measures	
Licenses with quotas	The importation of eggs may be subject to quotas, depending on the domestic supply situation.
Import taxes and/or tariffs	Yes.
State import monopoly	No.

Exports and Export Proceeds

Repatriation requirements	Yes.
Surrender requirements	Unless specifically exempted, export proceeds must be converted into local currency within eight working days or credited to a foreign currency account with a local foreign exchange bank or deposited in a foreign bank account approved by the CBA.
Financing requirements	No.
Documentation requirements	No.
Export licenses	No.
Export taxes	No.

Payments for Invisible Transactions and Current Transfers

Controls on these transfers	Most restrictions on these transactions have been eliminated.
Investment-related payments	
Indicative limits/bona fide test	Interest payments on all types of loans may be executed if a license has been obtained from the CBA to conclude the loan. As regards profits and dividends, documents should be submitted to the CBA with respect to the amount involved. Authorization may proceed only if a license was obtained for the loan. In the case of depreciation of direct investments, a special license is required.

Proceeds from Invisible Transactions and Current Transfers

Repatriation requirements	Yes.
Surrender requirements	Unless specifically exempted, proceeds must be converted into local currency within eight

working days or credited to a foreign currency account with a local foreign exchange bank or deposited in a foreign bank account approved by the CBA.

Restrictions on use of funds	No.

Capital Transactions

Controls on capital and money market instruments	Transactions of less than Af. 200,000 a year for natural persons and Af. 500,000 a year for juridical persons (excluding commercial banks and institutional investors) are free. These ceilings are not only applicable to investments but also to all capital transactions with nonresidents. This implies that a CBA license is only required for capital transactions in excess of these ceilings.
On capital market securities	There are controls on all these transactions.
Shares or other securities of a participating nature	
Purchase locally by nonresidents	A CBA license is required.
Controls on derivatives and other instruments	There are controls on all these transactions.
Controls on credit operations	There are controls on all these transactions.
Controls on direct investment	
Outward direct investment	The CBA may require divestment, repatriation, and surrender of proceeds to the CBA.
Inward direct investment	Yes.
Controls on liquidation of direct investment	Yes.
Controls on real estate transactions	There are controls on all these transactions.
Controls on personal capital movements	Personal capital transactions must be settled through the banking system and foreign accounts approved by the CBA.
Loans	
By residents to nonresidents	Yes.
To residents from nonresidents	Yes.
Gifts, endowments, inheritances, and legacies	
By residents to nonresidents	Yes.
To residents from nonresidents	Yes.
Settlement of debts abroad by immigrants	Yes.
Provisions specific to commercial banks and other credit institutions	
Lending to nonresidents (financial or commercial credits)	The CBA's approval is required for lending in domestic currency.
Differential treatment of deposit accounts in foreign exchange	
Reserve requirements	Yes.
Liquid asset requirements	Yes.
Differential treatment of deposit accounts held by nonresidents	
Reserve requirements	Yes.

Liquid asset requirements	Yes.
Provisions specific to institutional investors	
Limits (max.) on portfolio invested abroad	Yes.
Limits (min.) on portfolio invested locally	The limits are 40% of the first Af. 10 million of outstanding liabilities; 50% of the second Af. 10 million; and 60% of the remaining liabilities.
Other controls imposed by securities laws	No.

Changes During 1999

Resident accounts	*April 1.* The CBA's approval is no longer required for residents to open foreign currency accounts.

AUSTRALIA

(Position as of July 31, 2000)

Status Under IMF Articles of Agreement

Article VIII	Date of acceptance: July 1, 1965.

Exchange Arrangement

Currency	The currency of Australia is the Australian dollar. It also circulates in several other countries, including Kiribati, Nauru, and Tuvalu.
Exchange rate structure	Unitary.
Classification	
Independently floating	The exchange rate of the Australian dollar is market-determined. Authorized foreign exchange dealers may deal among themselves, with their customers, and with overseas counterparties at mutually negotiated rates for both spot and forward transactions in any currency with regard to trade- and non-trade-related transactions. However, the Reserve Bank of Australia (RBA) retains discretionary power to intervene in the foreign exchange market. There is no official exchange rate for the Australian dollar. The RBA publishes an indicative rate for the Australian dollar based on market observation at 4 p.m. daily.
Exchange tax	No.
Exchange subsidy	No.
Forward exchange market	Active trading takes place in forward and futures contracts.

Arrangements for Payments and Receipts

Prescription of currency requirements	No.
Payment arrangements	No.
Administration of control	The RBA has responsibility for oversight of the foreign exchange market, including the authorization of foreign exchange dealers. The Australian Transaction Reports and Analysis Center (AUSTRAC), a law enforcement agency, receives information on international transactions including those in cash, which it can pass on to a number of other enforcement and governmental agencies.
International security restrictions	
In accordance with UN sanctions	In accordance with UN Security Council resolutions, restrictions are placed on certain payments and transfers relating to Iraq, Libya, and the Federal Republic of Yugoslavia (Serbia/Montenegro). On December 22, 1999, restrictions were imposed on financial transactions with the Taliban (the Islamic State of Afghanistan) and the UNITA movement in Angola.
Payment arrears	No.
Controls on trade in gold (coins and/or bullion)	No.
Controls on exports and imports of banknotes	Exportation or importation of notes and coins totaling $A 10,000 or more must be reported to AUSTRAC.
On exports	
Foreign currency	Residents must purchase foreign currency from an authorized dealer. Nonresident travelers may take out any foreign currency they brought into Australia.

Resident Accounts

Foreign exchange accounts permitted	Yes.
Held domestically	Local purchases and sales of foreign currency must be through an authorized dealer.
Held abroad	Yes.
Accounts in domestic currency convertible into foreign currency	Conversion must be effected through an authorized foreign exchange dealer.

Nonresident Accounts

Foreign exchange accounts permitted	Local purchases and sales of foreign currency must be through an authorized dealer.
Domestic currency accounts	Yes.
Convertible into foreign currency	Conversion must be effected through an authorized foreign exchange dealer.
Blocked accounts	Only those accounts affected by UN sanctions are blocked.

Imports and Import Payments

Foreign exchange budget	No.
Financing requirements for imports	No.
Documentation requirements for release of foreign exchange for imports	No.
Import licenses and other nontariff measures	There are no import-licensing requirements or quotas on imports other than the tariff quota, which applies to certain cheeses and curd.
Negative list	For some products, imports are allowed only if written authorization is obtained from the relevant authorities or if certain regulations are complied with. Among the goods subject to control are narcotic, psychotropic, and therapeutic substances; firearms and certain weapons; certain chemicals and primary commodities; some glazed ceramic ware; and various dangerous goods. These controls are maintained mainly to meet health and safety requirements; to meet certain requirements for labeling, packaging, or technical specifications; and to satisfy certain obligations arising from Australia's membership in international commodity agreements.
Import taxes and/or tariffs	General tariffs have been reduced to 5%. On January 1, 2000, the tariff on passenger motor vehicles was reduced to 15% and it will remain at that level until January 1, 2005. On July 1, 2000, the tariff on textiles, clothing, and footwear was also reduced to a maximum of 25%. These tariffs will be terminated in 2005.
	The ANZCERTA establishes free trade in goods. The SPARTECA provides nonreciprocal, duty-free access to most markets in Australia and New Zealand for other members. Trade between Papua New Guinea and Australia is covered by the Agreement on Trade and Commercial Relations between Australia and Papua New Guinea.
	Developing countries receive tariff preferences on exports to Australia under the Australian System of Tariff Preferences for Developing Countries, with a uniform preferential margin of 5%. Preferences have been eliminated on imports of certain industries such as textiles, clothing and footwear, chemicals, vegetable and fruit preparations, tuna, and sugar, except from the least-developed countries and South Pacific Island Territories.
State import monopoly	No.

Exports and Export Proceeds

Repatriation requirements	No.

Financing requirements	No.
Documentation requirements	No.
Export licenses	Export prohibitions and restrictions in effect are designed to ensure quality control, administer trade embargoes, and meet obligations under international arrangements. These prohibitions are also set up to restrict the exportation of certain defense materials; regulate the exportation of goods that involve high technology and have dual civilian and military applications; maintain adequate measures of control over designated cultural property, resources, flora, and fauna; secure conservation objectives; and respond to specific market distortions abroad. Remaining controls on primary products apply mainly to food and agricultural products.
	Export controls apply to uranium and related nuclear materials (including uranium-bearing sands) to ensure compliance with Australia's nonproliferation policy obligations. Restrictions also apply to certain other nuclear and related materials. Licenses are required for exports of unprocessed wood, including wood chips. The Australian Dairy Corporation administers export control powers in relation to prescribed dairy products under the provisions of the Dairy Produce Act. All exporters of controlled dairy products must be licensed. This system allows the control of exports to markets where quantitative restrictions apply and ensures that export prices do not fall below minimum prices agreed to under the WTO for these products.
	Exports of cattle, sheep or goat meat, and livestock can be made only by persons or firms licensed by the Commonwealth Department of Agriculture, Fisheries, and Forestry (AFFA). If other countries impose quantitative restrictions on imports of meat or livestock, the AFFA may, in conjunction with industry, introduce measures to control Australian exports to conform with those restrictions.
	Other Commonwealth statutory marketing authorities that have export control powers are the Australian Horticultural Corporation, the Australian Honey Board, the Australian Wheat Board, and the Australian Wine and Brandy Corporation. The Australian Wheat Board's powers make it the sole exporter of Australian wheat.
With quotas	Australia has a complete ban on the export of merino ewes, genetic material, ova, and embryos to any country other than New Zealand. However, merino breeding rams purchased at designated export auctions and semen from rams included in the National Register of Semen Export Donors may be exported, subject to an annual quota (currently limited in total to 900 rams a year), and the AFFA's approval. No ram sold and nominated for the collection of semen for export may be physically exported. There is no restriction on the export of merino rams or reproductive material to New Zealand. The above restrictions do not apply to merino rams intended for slaughter; however, the export of these rams is subject to controls to ensure they do not enter breeding flocks.
Export taxes	No.

Payments for Invisible Transactions and Current Transfers

Controls on these transfers	No.

Proceeds from Invisible Transactions and Current Transfers

Repatriation requirements	No.
Restrictions on use of funds	No.

Capital Transactions

Controls on capital and money market instruments	The purchase of shares and other securities of a participatory nature, which may be affected by laws and policies on inward direct investment, is restricted. Foreign governments, their agencies, and international organizations are not permitted to issue bearer bonds and, when

borrowing in the Australian capital market, must advise the Australian authorities of the details of each borrowing after its completion. Subject to certain disclosure requirements, overseas banks may issue securities in the wholesale capital market in amounts of $A 500,000 or more.

On capital market securities

Shares or other securities of a participating nature

    Purchase locally by nonresidents   Yes.

    Sale or issue abroad by residents   Yes.

Bonds or other debt securities

    Sale or issue locally by nonresidents   Yes.

On money market instruments

Sale or issue locally by nonresidents   Yes.

Controls on derivatives and other instruments

Sale or issue locally by nonresidents   Yes.

Controls on credit operations

Commercial credits

By residents to nonresidents   Yes.

Financial credits

By residents to nonresidents   Yes.

Controls on direct investment

Inward direct investment   Prior authorization is required for (1) proposals by foreign interests that would result in the ownership of a shareholding of 15% or more by a single foreign interest or associates, or 40% or more by two or more unrelated foreign interests in an Australian corporation; however, foreign investment in businesses, other than those in the restricted sectors, with total assets of less than $A 50 million (before September 20, 1999, less than $A 5 million and less than $A 3 million for rural properties) is exempt from examination and notification; (2) all investments in the banking, civil aviation, airports, shipping, media, and telecommunication sectors, which are subject to special restrictions; (3) direct investments by foreign governments or their agencies irrespective of size; and (4) proposals to establish new businesses in other than the restricted sectors of the economy where the total amount of the investment is $A 10 million or more.

Controls on liquidation of direct investment   No.

Controls on real estate transactions

Purchase locally by nonresidents   All acquisitions of vacant and residential real estate must be notified, unless exempt by regulation. Acquisitions of nonresidential commercial real estate for development are normally approved as are acquisitions of developed nonresidential commercial real estate. Acquisition of developed nonresidential commercial real estate is exempt where the total value of the property is less than $A 50 million (less than $A 5 million before September 20, 1999).

Approval is also normally granted for residential land for development or for the acquisitions of dwellings (including condominiums) direct from a developer, either "off the plan," while under construction, or completed but never occupied, provided that no more than 50% of the total number of dwellings are sold to foreign investors.

Foreign acquisitions of established residential real estate are not normally approved except in cases involving temporary residents who acquire accommodation for a period in excess of 12 months, subject to resale of the property upon departure. Foreign persons who are entitled to reside permanently in Australia or, effective September 20, 1999, those who purchase as joint tenants with an Australian spouse, are not required to seek approval to acquire any form of residential real estate. Foreign acquisition of residential real estate (including condominiums) within a designated integrated tourist resort is exempt from authorization.

Controls on personal capital movements

No.

Provisions specific to commercial banks and other credit institutions

Banks are subject to prudential requirements, e.g., liquidity management, credit concentration.

Investment regulations

In banks by nonresidents

Nonresidents may invest in authorized deposit-taking institutions up to a limit of 15%. Any investment larger than this limit must be approved by the Treasurer.

Provisions specific to institutional investors

No.

Other controls imposed by securities laws

The rules of the Australian Stock Exchange require that, to be a participating organization of the Australian Stock Exchange, a majority of the directors of a brokerage must be Australian residents. This rule does not prohibit foreigners from owning a brokerage.

Changes During 1999

Arrangements for payments and receipts

December 22. Restrictions were imposed on financial transactions with Libya, the Taliban (the Islamic State of Afghanistan), and the UNITA movement in Angola.

Capital transactions

Controls on direct investment

September 20. The threshold for notification purposes for foreign investment in existing businesses was raised to $A 50 million.

Controls on real estate transactions

September 20. The notification limit of acquisition of vacant and residential real estate was raised to $A 50 million. Australian citizens and their foreign spouses purchasing as joint tenants are no longer required to seek approval of purchases of residential property.

Changes During 2000

Imports and import payments

January 1. The tariff on passenger motor vehicles was reduced to 15%.

July 1. The tariff on textiles, clothing, and footwear was reduced to a maximum of 25%.

AUSTRIA

(Position as of December 31, 1999)

Status Under IMF Articles of Agreement

Article VIII   Date of acceptance: August 1, 1962.

Exchange Arrangement

Currency

As of January 1, 1999, the currency of Austria is the euro. In cash transactions, however, the legal tender remains the Austrian schilling until 2002, when euro banknotes and coins will be issued.

Exchange rate structure

Unitary.

Classification

Exchange arrangement with no separate legal tender

Austria participates in a currency union (EMU) comprising 11 members of the EU: Austria, Belgium, Finland, France, Germany, Ireland, Italy, Luxembourg, the Netherlands, Portugal, and Spain. Internal conversion rates in respect to the national currencies of EMU participants were fixed to the euro on January 1, 1999, whereas the external exchange rate of the euro is market determined. The conversion rate between the euro and the Austrian schilling was set at S 13.7603 per €1. The ECB has the right to intervene to smooth out fluctuations in external exchange rates.

Exchange tax   No.

Exchange subsidy   No.

Forward exchange market   No.

Arrangements for Payments and Receipts

Prescription of currency requirements

Settlements with all countries may be made either in foreign currencies or through free euro accounts.

Payment arrangements   No.

Bilateral payment arrangements

There are no bilateral payment agreements; however, several bilateral agreements exist for the promotion and protection of investments, which include provisions on transfers between the signatories.

Administration of control

Most exchange transactions are effected through Austrian banks authorized by the central bank.

International security restrictions

In accordance with UN sanctions

Restrictions imposed on certain current payments and transfers to Libya in accordance with a UN Security Council resolution were lifted on May 1, 1999. Certain restrictions on payments and transfers for current international transactions to the government of Iraq are still in force. In compliance with EU regulations, restrictions on payments and transfers are imposed on the Federal Republic of Yugoslavia (Serbia/Montenegro).

Payment arrears   No.

Controls on trade in gold (coins and/or bullion)

No.

Controls on exports and imports of banknotes

No.

Resident Accounts

Foreign exchange accounts permitted	Yes.
Held domestically	Yes.
Held abroad	Yes.
Accounts in domestic currency convertible into foreign currency	Yes.

Nonresident Accounts

Foreign exchange accounts permitted	Yes.
Domestic currency accounts	Yes.
Convertible into foreign currency	Yes.
Blocked accounts	These are accounts affected by UN sanctions against Iraq and, by the virtue of EU regulations, sanctions against the Federal Republic of Yugoslavia (Serbia/Montenegro).

Imports and Import Payments

Foreign exchange budget	No.
Financing requirements for imports	No.
Documentation requirements for release of foreign exchange for imports	No.
Import licenses and other nontariff measures	Export and import licenses must be issued by the Federal Ministry for Economic Affairs for industrial products and by the Federal Ministry of Agriculture and Forestry for agricultural products. As a member of the EU, Austria applies all import regulations based on the common commercial policy, i.e., for industrial products import restrictions in the textile and clothing sectors and statistical surveillance for products falling under the scope of the ECSC Treaty. There are also regulations vis-à-vis China for imports of some consumer products based on current EU law.
Positive list	Yes.
Licenses with quotas	Yes.
Import taxes and/or tariffs	Austria applies the Common Import Regime of the EU.
State import monopoly	No.

Exports and Export Proceeds

Repatriation requirements	No.
Financing requirements	No.
Documentation requirements	No.
Export licenses	Licenses for exports must be obtained from the relevant ministry or at the time of clearance from the customs authorities. For most exports, licenses are not required. Export licenses are issued with due consideration for the provisions of relevant EU trade agreements and the fulfillment of quotas established in accordance with such agreements, and the needs of the Austrian economy.
Without quotas	Yes.
With quotas	Yes.

Export taxes	No.

Payments for Invisible Transactions and Current Transfers

Controls on these transfers	No.

Proceeds from Invisible Transactions and Current Transfers

Repatriation requirements	No.
Restrictions on use of funds	No.

Capital Transactions

Controls on capital and money market instruments	In some cases, reporting requirements to the Austrian National Bank exist.
Controls on derivatives and other instruments	No.
Controls on credit operations	No.
Controls on direct investment	
Inward direct investment	In the auditing and legal professions, the transport sector, and the electric power generation sector certain restrictions apply for investments by nonresidents and Austrian residents who are not nationals of one of the countries of the EEA.
Controls on liquidation of direct investment	No.
Controls on real estate transactions	
Purchase locally by nonresidents	The acquisition of real estate is subject to approval by local authorities.
Controls on personal capital movements	No.
Provisions specific to commercial banks and other credit institutions	
Differential treatment of deposit accounts in foreign exchange	
Reserve requirements	Reserve requirements apply only to deposits held in euro.
Liquid asset requirements	Liquid asset requirements apply only to deposits held in euro.
Open foreign exchange position limits	The net amount of an open foreign exchange position must not exceed 30% of own funds at the end of any business day; the total sum of all open positions must not exceed 50% of own funds. The euro is not considered a foreign currency.
On resident assets and liabilities	Yes.
On nonresident assets and liabilities	Yes.
Provisions specific to institutional investors	
Limits (max.) on securities issued by nonresidents and on portfolio invested abroad	Yes.
Limits (max.) on portfolio invested abroad	Yes.

Limits (min.) on portfolio invested locally	Yes.
Currency-matching regulations on assets/liabilities composition	Yes.
Other controls imposed by securities laws	No.

Changes During 1999

Exchange arrangement	*January 1*. The currency of Austria became the euro. The conversion rate between the euro and the Austrian schilling was set irrevocably at S 13.7603 per €1.
Arrangements for payments and receipts	*May 1*. Restrictions imposed on certain current payments and transfers to Libya in accordance with a UN Security Council resolution were lifted.

AZERBAIJAN

(Position as of December 31, 1999)

Status Under IMF Articles of Agreement

Article XIV	Yes.

Exchange Arrangement

Currency	The currency of Azerbaijan is the Azerbaijan manat.
Exchange rate structure	Unitary.
Classification	
Managed floating with no pre-announced path for the exchange rate	Until July 8, 1999, the external value of the manat was determined on the basis of morning trading sessions. The morning session was limited to Baku Interbank Currency Exchange (BICEX) member banks. The official exchange rate was determined by the Azerbaijan National Bank (ANB) on the basis of BICEX trading. The afternoon trading was operated by the Organized Interbank Foreign Currency Exchange (OICEX), which included all banks with foreign exchange licenses. The OICEX used BICEX facilities for clearing and operated under trading rules and procedures laid out in a collective agreement signed by each participating member. Trading under OICEX was, however, restricted to a band of ±0.5% of the official ANB rate. Trading has also been allowed on the open interbank market, which also included all banks with foreign exchange licenses.
	On July 8, 1999, the telephone market, the auction market, and the interbank market were unified and the administrative regulations were lifted. The official rate is now determined based on a weighted average of these markets; the open interbank exchange market has the dominant weight.
Exchange tax	No.
Exchange subsidy	No.
Forward exchange market	No.

Arrangements for Payments and Receipts

Prescription of currency requirements	Settlements with the Baltic countries, Russia, and the other countries of the FSU are effected through correspondent accounts of the commercial banks in these countries or through correspondent accounts of the respective central banks.
Payment arrangements	
Bilateral payment arrangements	
Inoperative	Yes.
Clearing agreements	Azerbaijan is a member of the Payment Union of the CIS countries, which has become inoperative.
Barter agreements and open accounts	Yes.
Administration of control	The ANB regulates foreign exchange transactions, conducts foreign currency operations, and administers official gold and convertible currency reserve holdings. The ANB also has overall responsibility for issuing licenses to deal in foreign exchange and to open foreign exchange accounts abroad; for regulating foreign exchange operations, including implementing and monitoring compliance with the law; and for establishing prudential rules governing foreign exchange operations. The Ministry of Trade regulates foreign trade, while the Customs Service Law regulates the organization and operation of customs.
International security restrictions	No.

Payment arrears	n.a.
Controls on trade in gold (coins and/or bullion)	Controls are administered by the cabinet of ministries jointly with the ANB.
Controls on external trade	A license is required to conduct international trade in gold.
Controls on exports and imports of banknotes	The exportation and importation of foreign banknotes are regulated by the ANB and the customs agencies.
On exports	
Domestic currency	No more than manat 50,000 in banknotes may be taken out of the country, on the condition that they be returned.
Foreign currency	Yes.
On imports	
Foreign currency	Yes.

Resident Accounts

Foreign exchange accounts permitted	Yes.
Held domestically	No declaration of the origin of foreign exchange is required for individuals, who may transfer freely foreign exchange held in these accounts to their close relatives up to $10,000 and, upon authorization, larger amounts, or may freely convert it into domestic currency.
Held abroad	Resident enterprises may open and use foreign exchange bank accounts in banks abroad, subjopect to authorization by the ANB. Enterprises are obliged to repatriate the foreign exchange held in accounts abroad (except the amount used to pay for imports).
	There is no regulation for individuals who open and use foreign exchange bank accounts in banks abroad.
Accounts in domestic currency convertible into foreign currency	Natural and juridical persons may purchase foreign exchange through authorized banks and authorized banks may also purchase foreign exchange in these markets on their own account, in accordance with the regulations of the ANB. These regulations do not set any limit.

Nonresident Accounts

Foreign exchange accounts permitted	Foreign exchange in these accounts may be transferred abroad or sold to the banks for manat. However, prior approval is required.
Domestic currency accounts	Nonresident enterprises may also open and operate accounts in manat and use them for domestic transactions, in accordance with instructions issued by the ANB.
Convertible into foreign currency	The same regulations apply as for resident accounts.
Blocked accounts	No.

Imports and Import Payments

Foreign exchange budget	No.
Financing requirements for imports	
Advance payment requirements	Advance import payments of more than 180 days prior to the delivery of goods are not allowed. Prepayments by bank transfers for import contracts of goods and services are limited to the equivalent of $10,000. Subject to authorization of the ANB, the amount may exceed the indicative limit.

Documentation requirements for release of foreign exchange for imports

Letters of credit

Prepayments by bank transfers in excess of $10,000 require either an LC or the authorization of the ANB.

Import licenses and other nontariff measures

Negative list

Yes.

Import taxes and/or tariffs

Tariffs are unified at 15% for most goods and for imports from all countries. Capital and input goods are subject to tariff rates of zero or 5%. A customs fee of 0.15% is levied on imports from all sources.

State import monopoly

No.

Exports and Export Proceeds

Repatriation requirements

Residents are required to repatriate all proceeds from exports within 180 days and transfer them to a licensed bank in Azerbaijan within 10 days of receipt, unless specifically exempted by the government. Expenses, commissions, and taxes paid abroad relating to economic activities may be deducted from the proceeds prior to transfer to a licensed bank.

Financing requirements

Yes.

Documentation requirements

Letters of credit

All export operations must be secured by a 100% prepayment or an irrevocable LC.

Guarantees

Yes.

Export licenses

No.

Export taxes

No.

Payments for Invisible Transactions and Current Transfers

Controls on these transfers

Resident individuals are allowed to purchase noncash foreign exchange for transfer abroad for paying of bona fide current international transactions.

Trade-related payments

Indicative limits/bona fide test

Any amount may be paid without limitation, on the basis of documents confirming that trade-related costs have been actually incurred. General limitations apply to advance payments.

Investment-related payments

Indicative limits/bona fide test

Yes.

Payments for travel

Indicative limits/bona fide test

The indicative limit is $10,000. This limit may be exceeded on the basis of an expense estimate.

Personal payments

Indicative limits/bona fide test

The limit is $10,000 for payments related to medical costs, studies abroad, and family maintenance and alimony.

Foreign workers' wages

Prior approval

Yes.

Other payments

Indicative limits/bona fide test

The indicative limit for subscriptions and membership fees varies from $1,000 to $5,000 a year.

Proceeds from Invisible Transactions and Current Transfers

Repatriation requirements	Proceeds must be repatriated within six months and transferred to a licensed bank within 10 days of receipt.
Restrictions on use of funds	No.

Capital Transactions

Controls on capital and money market instruments

On capital market securities

Shares or other securities of a participating nature

Purchase locally by nonresidents	There are no controls, except for banks that sell their shares to nonresidents within the quota specified by the ANB.
Sale or issue locally by nonresidents	This process is regulated by the government in coordination with the ANB by establishing quotas and trading authorization procedures.
Purchase abroad by residents	The transfer of funds is permitted with the approval of the ANB.
Sale or issue abroad by residents	Regulated by the laws on joint-stock companies, securities, and stock exchanges, and by in-house instruction of the ANB. Sale is mainly by prior subscription (an organized market is just emerging).

Bonds or other debt securities

Sale or issue locally by nonresidents	The same regulations apply as for shares or other securities of a participating nature.
Purchase abroad by residents	The same regulations apply as for shares or other securities of a participating nature.
Sale or issue abroad by residents	The same regulations apply as for shares or other securities of a participating nature.

On money market instruments

Purchase abroad by residents	Yes.
Sale or issue abroad by residents	Yes.

On collective investment securities

Sale or issue locally by nonresidents	Yes.
Purchase abroad by residents	Yes.
Sale or issue abroad by residents	Yes.

Controls on derivatives and other instruments	These instruments are currently not available, and the legislation concerning derivatives has not been formulated.

Controls on credit operations

Commercial credits

By residents to nonresidents	Subject to authorization by the ANB.

Financial credits

By residents to nonresidents	Yes.

Controls on direct investment

Outward direct investment	Direct investment abroad requires ANB authorization.
Inward direct investment	Profits may be reinvested in local currency held in Azerbaijan or converted into foreign currency and transferred without controls. Foreign investors are granted certain privileges: enterprises or joint ventures with foreign equity capital ownership of more than 30% are entitled to a two-year holiday on profit taxes, imports and exports of goods and services

may be undertaken without licenses, and exporters of manufactured goods are allowed to retain 100% of their foreign exchange earnings.

Controls on liquidation of direct investment	No.
Controls on real estate transactions	No.
Controls on personal capital movements	
Loans	
By residents to nonresidents	Yes.
Gifts, endowments, inheritances, and legacies	
By residents to nonresidents	These transactions are permitted, but a court ruling is required.
Settlement of debts abroad by immigrants	Subject to presentation of satisfactory documents and based on a court ruling.
Transfer of assets	
Transfer abroad by emigrants	Subject to authorization by the ANB.
Transfer of gambling and prize earnings	Yes.
Provisions specific to commercial banks and other credit institutions	
Borrowing abroad	Yes.
Maintenance of accounts abroad	Yes.
Lending to nonresidents (financial or commercial credits)	Subject to authorization by the ANB.
Lending locally in foreign exchange	Yes.
Purchase of locally issued securities denominated in foreign exchange	Yes.
Differential treatment of deposit accounts in foreign exchange	Yes.
Reserve requirements	There is a 10% reserve requirement on deposit accounts.
Liquid asset requirements	Liquid assets must be equal to at least 30% of total liabilities.
Credit controls	These controls are in the form of different classifications and provisions.
Differential treatment of deposit accounts held by nonresidents	
Reserve requirements	These controls are in the form of different classifications and provisions.
Liquid asset requirements	These controls are in the form of different classifications and provisions.
Credit controls	These controls are in the form of different classifications and provisions.
Investment regulations	The Law on Banks and Banking grants the ANB the right to set quotas for participation in banks' equity capital by foreign investors. This same law establishes regulations governing the investment of funds in shares of other banks, nonbank enterprises, institutions, and organizations.
In banks by nonresidents	Subject to authorization by the ANB.
Open foreign exchange position limits	
On resident assets and liabilities	Yes.
On nonresident assets and liabilities	Yes.

Provisions specific to institutional investors	
Limits (max.) on securities issued by nonresidents and on portfolio invested abroad	The regulations and procedures governing participation by nonresidents in the securities market are determined in accordance with the Azerbaijan Republic Law on Securities and by the Committee on Securities under the president of Azerbaijan.
Limits (max.) on portfolio invested abroad	n.r.
Other controls imposed by securities laws	In accordance with the Azerbaijan Republic Law on Securities, the circulation of securities of foreign issuers in Azerbaijan is regulated by the Committee on Securities. Securities of issuers registered in Azerbaijan may be placed outside Azerbaijan with the authorization of that same body.

Changes During 1999

Exchange arrangement	*July 8.* The three foreign exchange markets were unified and the official exchange rate is now determined on the basis of the weighted average of these markets.

THE BAHAMAS

(Position as of January 31, 2000)

Status Under IMF Articles of Agreement

Article VIII Date of acceptance: December 5, 1973.

Exchange Arrangement

Currency The currency of The Bahamas is the Bahamian dollar.

Other legal tender Commemorative coins in denominations of B$10, B$20, B$50, B$100, B$150, B$200, B$250, B$1,000, and B$2,500 in gold, and B$10 and B$25 in silver are legal tender but do not circulate. The U.S. dollar circulates concurrently with the Bahamian dollar.

Exchange rate structure

Dual In addition to the official exchange market, there is a market in which investment currency may be negotiated between residents through the Central Bank of The Bahamas (CBB); the current premium bid and offer rates are 20% and 25%, respectively. The use of investment currency is prescribed for the purchase of foreign currency securities from nonresidents and direct investments outside The Bahamas. In certain circumstances, the CBB may also permit residents to retain and use foreign currency from other sources to make such outward investments.

Classification

Conventional pegged arrangement The Bahamian dollar is pegged to the U.S. dollar, the intervention currency, at par. Buying and selling rates for the pound sterling are also officially quoted, with the buying rate based on the rate in the New York market; the selling rate is 0.5% above the buying rate. The CBB deals only with commercial banks. For transactions with the public, commercial banks are authorized to charge a commission of 0.50% buying and 0.75% selling per US$1, and 0.50% buying or selling per £1.

Exchange tax A stamp tax of 1.5% is applied to all outward remittances.

Exchange subsidy No.

Forward exchange market Commercial banks may provide forward cover for residents who are due to receive or must pay foreign currency under a contractual commitment. Commercial banks may not, however, sell foreign currency spot to be held on account in cover of future requirements without the CBB's permission. Authorized dealers may deal in foreign currency forward with nonresidents without prior approval from the CBB. Commercial banks may execute forward deals among themselves at market rates and must ensure when carrying out all forward cover arrangements that their open spot or forward position does not exceed the equivalent of B$500,000 long or short.

Arrangements for Payments and Receipts

Prescription of currency requirements The exchange control system of The Bahamas makes no distinction between foreign territories. Settlements with residents of foreign countries may be made in any foreign currency or in Bahamian dollars through an external account. Foreign currencies comprise all currencies other than the Bahamian dollar.

Payment arrangements No.

Regional arrangements The Bahamas is a member of the CARICOM.

Administration of control Exchange control is administered by the CBB, which delegates to authorized dealers the authority to approve allocations of foreign exchange for certain current payments, including payments for imports up to B$100,000; approval authority for cash gifts is not delegated, except in the Family Islands.

International security restrictions	No.
Payment arrears	No.
Controls on trade in gold (coins and/or bullion)	
Controls on domestic ownership and/or trade	Residents, other than authorized dealers, are not permitted to hold or deal in gold bullion. However, residents who are known users of gold for industrial purposes may, with the approval of the CBB, meet their current industrial requirements. There is no restriction on residents' acquisition or retention of gold coins.
Controls on external trade	Authorized dealers are not required to obtain licenses for bullion or coins, and no import duty is imposed on these items. Commercial imports of gold jewelry do not require a license and are duty free, although a 10% stamp tax is required. A 1.5% stamp tax payable to customs is also required on commercial shipments of gold jewelry from any source.
Controls on exports and imports of banknotes	
On exports	
Domestic currency	A traveler may export banknotes up to B$200.
Foreign currency	Bahamian travelers need CBB approval to export foreign banknotes.
On imports	
Domestic currency	Importation is subject to CBB approval.

Resident Accounts

Foreign exchange accounts permitted	Yes.
Held domestically	These accounts are permitted, but approval is required.
Held abroad	These accounts are permitted, but approval is required.
Accounts in domestic currency convertible into foreign currency	No.

Nonresident Accounts

Foreign exchange accounts permitted	Yes.
Domestic currency accounts	With the prior approval of the CBB, authorized banks may also open external accounts in Bahamian dollars for nonresident companies that have local expenses in The Bahamas and for nonresident investors. Authorized banks may freely open external accounts denominated in Bahamian dollars for winter residents and for persons with residency permits who are not gainfully employed in The Bahamas. Persons of a foreign nationality who have been granted temporary resident status are treated in some respects as nonresidents but are not permitted to hold external accounts in Bahamian dollars. External accounts in Bahamian dollars are normally funded entirely from foreign currency originating outside The Bahamas, but income on registered investments may also be credited to these accounts with the approval of the CBB.
Convertible into foreign currency	Yes.
Blocked accounts	The accounts of residents emigrating from The Bahamas who are redesignated upon departure as nonresidents are blocked for amounts in excess of B$25,000 for a period of four years. Balances on blocked accounts are transferable through the official exchange market after that time or through the Investment Currency Market at any time; they may also be invested with the approval of the CBB in certain resident-held assets, or they may be spent locally for any other purpose.

Imports and Import Payments

Foreign exchange budget	No.
Financing requirements for imports	No.
Documentation requirements for release of foreign exchange for imports	Prior approval from the CBB is required to make payments for imports exceeding B$100,000, irrespective of origin, except in the Family Islands, where this authority is delegated to clearing bank branches. This approval is normally given automatically upon submission of pro forma invoices or other relevant documents proving the existence of a purchase contract.

Import licenses and other nontariff measures

Negative list	The importation of certain commodities is prohibited or controlled for social, humanitarian, or health reasons. For all imports of agricultural products, a permit must be obtained from the Ministry of Agriculture. All other goods may be imported without a license. Customs entries are subject to a stamp tax of 7%.
Import taxes and/or tariffs	Import duties vary from zero to 210%. The tariff rate on most goods is 42%, and the average tariff rate is 35%. Stamp duties on imports vary from 2% to 7%. There is no import duty on certain tourist-related goods, but these goods are subject to stamp duties ranging from 8% to 20%. On January 1, 2000, the fourth phase of the CARICOM CET came into effect.
State import monopoly	No.

Exports and Export Proceeds

Repatriation requirements	Yes.
Surrender requirements	The proceeds of exports must be offered for sale to an authorized dealer as soon as the goods have reached their destination or within six months of shipment; alternatively, export proceeds may be used in any manner acceptable to the CBB.
Financing requirements	No.
Documentation requirements	No.
Export licenses	
Without quotas	Export licenses are not required, except for crawfish, conch, and arms and ammunition.
Export taxes	Yes.

Payments for Invisible Transactions and Current Transfers

Controls on these transfers	There are no restrictions on current payments. However, there are limits on the approval authority delegated to commercial banks by the CBB. Authorized dealers may make payments to nonresidents on behalf of residents for certain services and other invisibles, such as commissions, royalties, education, and non–life insurance premiums, within specified limits. CBB approval is required for payments in excess of those limits or for categories of payments not delegated.
Trade-related payments	
Prior approval	For unloading and storage costs and commissions, CBB approval is required for transactions over B$3,000 and B$6,000, respectively.
Indicative limits/bona fide test	Yes.
Investment-related payments	Information is not available for amortization of loans or depreciation of direct investments.
Prior approval	For all investments with approved status, permission is given upon application for the transfer.

Payments for travel

Prior approval   Yes.

Quantitative limits   Under delegated authority, the limits for tourist travel are B$1,000 a person above the age of 18 years and B$500 a person up to the age of 18 years a trip. For business or professional travel, the limit is B$10,000 a person a year. The allowance for tourist travel excludes the cost of fares and travel services, which are normally obtained against payment in Bahamian dollars to a travel agent in The Bahamas. Foreign exchange obtained for travel may not be retained abroad or used abroad for purposes other than travel; any unused balance must be surrendered within a week of issue or, if the traveler is still abroad, within one week of returning to The Bahamas.

Indicative limits/bona fide test   Yes.

Personal payments

Quantitative limits   Under delegated authority, residents are entitled to a foreign exchange allowance of B$3,000 a person a trip for study-related costs.

Indicative limits/bona fide test   Subject to adequate documentary evidence, an education allowance is granted by the CBB without a limit. Apart from a B$1,000 cash allowance, authorized dealers may approve all medical payments to doctors or medical establishments.

Foreign workers' wages

Prior approval   Yes.

Quantitative limits   The limit is 50% of wages and salaries.

Indicative limits/bona fide test   If commitments outside The Bahamas are more than 50% of wages and salaries, additional amounts may be remitted. Temporary residents may also repatriate all of their accumulated savings resulting from their employment in The Bahamas.

Credit card use abroad

Prior approval   Approval is required for residents to hold an international credit card, which may not be used to pay for life insurance premiums and capital items.

Other payments

Prior approval   There is prior approval for consulting and legal fees.

Quantitative limits   Under delegated authority, the limit for subscription and membership fees is B$1,000, and that for consulting and legal fees is B$3,000.

Indicative limits/bona fide test   An indicative limit is applied to consulting and legal fees.

Proceeds from Invisible Transactions and Current Transfers

Repatriation requirements   Residents are obliged to collect all proceeds without delay.

Surrender requirements   All foreign currency proceeds must be offered for sale to an authorized dealer without delay.

Restrictions on use of funds   No.

Capital Transactions

Controls on capital and money market instruments   All outward capital transfers require exchange control approval, and outflows of resident-owned capital are restricted. Inward transfers by nonresidents, which are encouraged, are required to go through the exchange control approval process, although the subsequent use of the funds in The Bahamas may require authorization.

On capital market securities

Shares or other securities of a participating nature

Purchase locally by nonresidents

In principle, inward investment by nonresidents is unrestricted. However, the consent of the CBB is required for the issue or transfer of shares in a Bahamian company to a nonresident and for the transfer of control of a Bahamian company to a nonresident. The extent of such approvals generally reflects the government's economic and investment policy guidelines.

Sale or issue locally by nonresidents

Yes.

Purchase abroad by residents

Residents are not permitted to purchase foreign currency securities with official exchange, export proceeds, or other current earnings; payment must be made with investment currency. All purchases, sales, and swaps of foreign currency securities by Bahamian residents require permission from the CBB and are normally transacted through authorized agents, who are free to act on behalf of nonresidents in relation to such transactions without any further approval from the CBB. All foreign securities purchased by residents of The Bahamas must be held by, or to the order of, an authorized agent.

Sale or issue abroad by residents

Sale proceeds from such resident-held foreign currency securities, if registered at the CBB by December 31, 1972, are eligible for sale in the investment currency market. Unregistered securities may be offered for sale at the official rate of exchange.

Bonds or other debt securities

Purchase locally by nonresidents

Nonresident buyers of Bahamian dollar–denominated securities must fund the acquisition of such securities from foreign currency sources. Interest, dividends, and capital payments on such securities may not be remitted outside The Bahamas, unless the holdings have been properly acquired by nonresidents.

Sale or issue locally by nonresidents

Yes.

Purchase abroad by residents

Yes.

Sale or issue abroad by residents

Yes.

On money market instruments

The same regulations apply as for shares or securities of a participating nature.

On collective investment securities

The same regulations apply as for shares or securities of a participating nature.

Controls on derivatives and other instruments

The same regulations apply as for shares or securities of a participating nature.

Controls on credit operations

Commercial credits

By residents to nonresidents

A resident company wholly owned by nonresidents is not allowed to raise fixed capital in Bahamian dollars, although approval may be granted to obtain working capital in local currency. If the company is partly owned by residents, the amount of local currency borrowing for fixed capital purposes is determined in relation to residents' interest in the equity of the company. Banks and other lenders resident in The Bahamas must have permission to extend loans in domestic currency to any corporate body (other than a bank) that is also resident in The Bahamas but is controlled by any means, whether directly or indirectly, by nonresidents. However, companies set up by nonresidents primarily to import and distribute products manufactured outside The Bahamas are not allowed to borrow Bahamian dollars from residents for either fixed or working capital. Instead, they must provide all their financing in foreign currency, and foreign currency loans are normally permitted on application.

To residents from nonresidents

Residents other than authorized banks must obtain permission to borrow foreign currency from nonresidents, and authorized dealers are subject to exchange control direction of their foreign currency loans to residents. Residents must also obtain permission to pay interest on, and to repay the principal of, foreign currency loans by conversion of Bahamian dollars. When permission is granted for residents to accept foreign currency loans, it is conditional upon the currency being offered for sale without delay to an authorized dealer, unless the funds are required to meet payments to nonresidents for which permission has been specifically given.

Financial credits

> By residents to nonresidents

Yes.

> To residents from nonresidents

Yes.

Guarantees, sureties, and financial
backup facilities

> By residents to nonresidents

Yes.

> To residents from nonresidents

Yes.

Controls on direct investment

Outward direct investment

The use of official exchange for direct investment abroad is limited to B$100,000 or 30%
of the total cost of the investment (whichever is greater) for investments from which the
additional benefits expected to accrue to the balance of payments from export receipts,
profits, or other earnings within 18 months of the investment will at least equal the total
amount of investment and will continue thereafter. Investments abroad that do not meet the
above criteria may be financed by foreign currency borrowed on suitable terms, subject to
individual approval from the CBB, by foreign currency purchased in the investment currency market, or by the retained profits of foreign subsidiary companies. Permission is not
given for investments that are likely to have adverse effects on the balance of payments.

Inward direct investment

CBB approval is required.

**Controls on liquidation of direct
investment**

In the event of a sale or liquidation, nonresident investors are permitted to repatriate the
proceeds, including any capital appreciation, through the official foreign exchange market.

Controls on real estate transactions

Purchase abroad by residents

Residents require the specific approval of the CBB to buy property outside The Bahamas;
such purchases, if for personal use, may be made only with investment currency, and
approval is limited to one property a family. Incidental expenses connected with the
purchase of property for personal use may normally be met with investment currency.
Expenditures necessary for the maintenance of the property or arising directly from its
ownership may, with permission, be met with foreign currency bought at the current
market rate in the official foreign exchange market.

Purchase locally by nonresidents

Foreigners intending to purchase land for commercial purposes or property larger than five
acres in size must obtain a permit from the Investments Board. If such an application is
approved, payment for the purchase may be made either in Bahamian dollars from an external source or in foreign currency. Nonresidents wishing to purchase property for residential purposes may do so without prior approval but are required to obtain a Certificate
of Registration from the Foreign Investment Board on completion of the transaction.

Sale locally by nonresidents

Approval is required.

**Controls on personal capital
movements**

Loans

> By residents to nonresidents

Yes.

> To residents from nonresidents

Yes.

Gifts, endowments, inheritances, and
legacies

> By residents to nonresidents

Yes.

Settlement of debts abroad by
immigrants

Yes.

Transfer of assets

> Transfer abroad by emigrants

Yes.

Transfer of gambling and prize earnings

Residents are not allowed to remit funds for gaming purposes.

Provisions specific to commercial banks and other credit institutions

Borrowing abroad | Yes.

Lending locally in foreign exchange | Exchange control approval is required to make loans to residents.

Open foreign exchange position limits | The limit is B$500,000 for a long or short position.

On resident assets and liabilities | Yes.

On nonresident assets and liabilities | Yes.

Provisions specific to institutional investors | No.

Other controls imposed by securities laws | In the securities market, a Mutual Funds Act and regulation that provides for licensing of Mutual Funds Administrators and Registration of Mutual Funds is enforced. Effective May 1, 1999, the Securities Industry Act provides for the Securities Commission to regulate the stock exchange and stock exchange operations.

Changes During 1999

Capital transactions

Other controls imposed by securities laws | *May 1.* The Securities Industry Act provided for the Securities Commission to regulate the stock exchange and stock exchange operations.

Changes During 2000

Imports and import payments | *January 1.* The fourth phase of the CARICOM CET came into effect.

BAHRAIN

(Position as of December 31, 1999)

Status Under IMF Articles of Agreement

Article VIII   Date of acceptance: March 20, 1973.

Exchange Arrangement

Currency   The currency of Bahrain is the Bahrain dinar.

Exchange rate structure   Unitary.

Classification

Conventional pegged arrangement   The Bahrain dinar has a fixed relationship to the SDR at the rate of BD 0.47619 per SDR 1. The exchange rate of the dinar in terms of the SDR may be set with margins of ±7.25% of this fixed relationship. In practice, however, the dinar has maintained a stable relationship with the dollar, the intervention currency. The middle rate of the dinar for the dollar is quoted by the Bahrain Monetary Agency (BMA) and has remained unchanged since December 1980. The BMA provides daily recommended rates to banks for amounts up to BD 1,000 in dollars, deutsche mark, and pounds sterling based on the latest available dollar rates against those currencies. The BMA does not deal with the public. In their dealings with the public, commercial banks are required to use the BMA's rates for dollars, deutsche mark, and pounds sterling, but they are authorized to charge a commission of 2% (special rates of commission apply for transactions up to BD 1,000). The banks' rates for other currencies are based on the BMA's dollar rates and the New York market rates against the dollar.

Exchange tax   No.

Exchange subsidy   No.

Forward exchange market   The BMA monitors the forward exchange transactions of commercial banks through the open position of banks' monthly returns.

Arrangements for Payments and Receipts

Prescription of currency requirements   All settlements with Israel are prohibited. Otherwise, no requirements are imposed on exchange payments or receipts.

Payment arrangements   No.

Administration of control   There is no exchange control legislation.

International security restrictions

In accordance with Executive Board Decision No. 144-(52/51)   Yes.

In accordance with UN sanctions   Yes.

Payment arrears   No.

Controls on trade in gold (coins and/or bullion)

Controls on external trade   Imports of gold jewelry are subject to a 10% customs duty, but gold ingots are exempt. Brokers doing business in gold and other commodities must obtain BMA approval before they can register with the Ministry of Commerce.

Controls on exports and imports of banknotes   No.

Resident Accounts

Foreign exchange accounts permitted	Yes.
Held domestically	Yes.
Held abroad	Yes.
Accounts in domestic currency convertible into foreign currency	Yes.

Nonresident Accounts

Foreign exchange accounts permitted	Yes.
Domestic currency accounts	Yes.
Convertible into foreign currency	Yes.
Blocked accounts	No.

Imports and Import Payments

Foreign exchange budget	No.
Financing requirements for imports	No.
Documentation requirements for release of foreign exchange for imports	
Letters of credit	Yes.
Import licenses and other nontariff measures	Mandatory government procurements give preference to goods produced in Bahrain and member countries of the GCC, provided that the quality and prices of these goods are within specified margins of the prices of imported substitutes (10% for goods produced in Bahrain and 5% for goods produced in member countries of the GCC).
Negative list	Licenses are required for imports of arms, ammunition, and alcoholic beverages. All imports from Israel are prohibited. Imports of a few commodities are prohibited from all sources for reasons of health, public policy, or security. Imports of cultured pearls are prohibited.
Import taxes and/or tariffs	The rates of customs tariffs range between 5% and 10% on most commodities but the rate is 20% on vehicles, launches, and yachts; 100% on tobacco; and 125% on alcoholic beverages. On January 2, 2000, the Bahrain government eliminated the 5% custom duty on foodstuffs and cut the tariffs on consumer goods to 7.5% from 10%.
State import monopoly	No.

Exports and Export Proceeds

Repatriation requirements	No.
Financing requirements	No.
Documentation requirements	No.
Export licenses	All exports to Israel are prohibited.
Export taxes	No.

Payments for Invisible Transactions and Current Transfers

Controls on these transfers	No.

Proceeds from Invisible Transactions and Current Transfers

Repatriation requirements	No.
Restrictions on use of funds	Proceeds from invisibles from Israel are prohibited.

Capital Transactions

Controls on capital and money market instruments	No exchange control requirements are imposed on capital receipts or payments by residents or nonresidents, but payments may not be made to or received from Israel.
On capital market securities	
Shares or other securities of a participating nature	
Purchase locally by nonresidents	Yes.
Sale or issue locally by nonresidents	Yes.
Purchase abroad by residents	Yes.
Sale or issue abroad by residents	Yes.
Bonds or other debt securities	
Purchase locally by nonresidents	Yes.
Purchase abroad by residents	Yes.
Sale or issue abroad by residents	Yes.
Controls on derivatives and other instruments	No.
Controls on credit operations	No.
Controls on direct investment	
Inward direct investment	As of March 3, 1999, GCC nationals are allowed to own 100% in domestic enterprises, and non-GCC nationals are allowed to own up to 49% with the exception of a few strategic sectors.
Controls on liquidation of direct investment	No.
Controls on real estate transactions	
Purchase locally by nonresidents	Purchase of real estate by nonresidents is prohibited, except for GCC nationals.
Controls on personal capital movements	No.
Provisions specific to commercial banks and other credit institutions	Banks are subject to special rules regarding the payment of dividends and the remittance of profits without exchange control restrictions. Licensed offshore banking units may engage in transactions with nonresidents freely, although transactions with residents are not normally permitted.
Lending to nonresidents (financial or commercial credits)	Yes.
Lending locally in foreign exchange	Lending is limited to 15% of each bank's capital base.

Differential treatment of deposit accounts in foreign exchange	
Credit controls	Yes.
Differential treatment of deposit accounts held by nonresidents	
Liquid asset requirements	Yes.
Credit controls	Yes.
Open foreign exchange position limits	Banks are allowed to set their own individual limits.
Provisions specific to institutional investors	
Limits (max.) on securities issued by nonresidents and on portfolio invested abroad	Yes.
Other controls imposed by securities laws	n.a.

Changes During 1999

Arrangements for payments and receipts	*March 31.* The exchange rate arrangement was reclassified to conventional pegged arrangement from pegged exchange rate within horizontal bands.
Capital transactions	
Controls on direct investment	*March 3.* GCC nationals are allowed to own 100% in domestic enterprises, and non-GCC nationals are allowed to own up to 49%.

Changes During 2000

Imports and import payments	*January 2.* The 5% customs duty on foodstuffs was eliminated, and the tariff on consumer goods was decreased to 7.5% from 10%.

BANGLADESH

(Position as of December 31, 1999)

Status Under IMF Articles of Agreement

Article VIII

Date of acceptance: April 11, 1994.

Exchange Arrangement

Currency

The currency of Bangladesh is the Bangladesh taka.

Exchange rate structure

Unitary.

Classification

Conventional pegged arrangement

The taka is pegged to a weighted currency basket of Bangladesh's major trading partners. The Bangladesh Bank (BB) deals with authorized domestic banks only in dollars, the intervention currency. Authorized banks are free to set their own buying and selling rates for the dollar and the rates for other currencies, based on cross rates in international markets. At the end of 1999, the buy/sell margin was approximately 0.6%.

Exchange tax

No.

Exchange subsidy

No.

Forward exchange market

Forward contracts are available from authorized banks, covering periods of up to six months for export proceeds and import payments, and up to three months of remittances of surplus collection from foreign shipping companies and airlines. Authorized banks are permitted to retain working balances with their foreign correspondents. Currency swaps and forward exchange transactions are permitted when they are effected against underlying approved commercial transactions.

Official cover of forward operations

The BB does not transact in the forward market, nor does it regulate transactions beyond the normal requirements of prudential supervision.

Arrangements for Payments and Receipts

Prescription of currency requirements

Settlements normally take place in convertible currencies and, in some cases, through nonresident taka accounts. Settlements with ACU member countries are required to be effected through the ACU in terms of the AMU (equivalent in value to the dollar). Payments for imports may be made to any country (with the exception of countries from which importation is prohibited). They may be made (1) in taka for credit in Bangladesh to a nonresident bank account of the country concerned; (2) in the currency of the country concerned; or (3) in any freely convertible currency. Export proceeds must be received in freely convertible foreign exchange or in taka from a nonresident taka account.

Payment arrangements

Bilateral payment arrangements

Operative

There are operative bilateral payment arrangements with some countries.

Regional arrangements

Bangladesh is a member of the ACU.

Clearing agreements

Yes.

Administration of control

Exchange control is administered by the BB in accordance with general policy formulated in consultation with the MOF. Banks are issued licenses as authorized dealers (authorized banks) in foreign exchange. The Chief Controller of Imports and Exports of the Ministry of Commerce is responsible for registering exporters and importers and for issuing the Import Policy Order (IPO). Registered importers may make their imports in terms of the IPO against LCs. LC authorization forms (LCAFs) are issued by authorized dealers and do not require a separate import license.

International security restrictions

In accordance with UN sanctions

On the basis of a UN Security Council resolution, all settlements with Iraq, the Taliban (the Islamic State of Afghanistan), and the Federal Republic of Yugoslavia (Serbia/Montenegro) are prohibited.

Payment arrears

No.

Controls on trade in gold (coins and/or bullion)

Controls on domestic ownership and/or trade

There are no restrictions on the internal sale, purchase, or possession of gold or silver ornaments (including coins) and jewelry, but there is a prohibition on the holding of gold and silver in all other forms except by licensed industrialists or dentists.

Controls on external trade

The importation and exportation of gold and silver require special permission. However, adult female travelers are free to bring in or take out any amount of gold jewelry without prior approval from the BB. Exports of gold jewelry and imports of gold and silver for the export/manufacture of jewelry are allowed under the Jewelry Export Scheme.

Controls on exports and imports of banknotes

On exports

  Domestic currency

A resident or a nonresident may take out up to Tk 500 in domestic currency.

  Foreign currency

Nonresidents may take out the foreign currency and traveler's checks they declared on entry or up to $5,000 or the equivalent brought in without declaration. They may also, without obtaining the approval of the BB, reconvert taka notes up to Tk 6,000 into convertible foreign currencies at the time of their departure. Residents may take out foreign currency and traveler's checks up to the amount of any travel allocation they are granted, and also up to $5,000 brought in without declaration when returning from a previous visit abroad.

On imports

  Domestic currency

The importation of Bangladesh currency notes and coins exceeding Tk 500 is prohibited.

  Foreign currency

Foreign currency traveler's checks and foreign currency notes may be brought in freely up to $5,000, but larger amounts should be declared to customs upon arrival in Bangladesh.

Resident Accounts

Foreign exchange accounts permitted

Yes.

Held domestically

Bangladesh nationals and persons of Bangladesh origin who are working abroad are permitted to open foreign currency accounts denominated in dollars, euros, pounds sterling, or Japanese yen. These accounts may be credited with (1) remittances in convertible currencies received from abroad through normal banking and postal channels; (2) proceeds of convertible currencies (banknotes, traveler's checks, drafts, etc.) brought into Bangladesh by the account holders, provided that amounts exceeding $5,000 have been declared to customs upon arrival in Bangladesh; (3) transfers from other foreign currency accounts opened under the former Wage Earners' Scheme; and (4) transfers from nonresident foreign currency deposit accounts. The accounts may be debited without restriction, subject to reporting to the BB.

Residents, when returning from abroad, may bring in any amount of foreign currency and may maintain a resident foreign currency deposit account with the foreign exchange brought in. However, proceeds of exports of goods and services from Bangladesh or commissions arising from business deals in Bangladesh are not allowed to be credited to such accounts. Balances in these accounts are freely transferable abroad and may be used for travel in the usual manner. These accounts may be opened in dollars, euros, pounds sterling, and Japanese yen. Exporters and local joint-venture firms executing projects financed by a foreign donor or international agency may open foreign currency accounts. Foreign currency accounts may also be opened in the names of diplomatic missions in Bangladesh, their expatriates, and diplomatic bonded warehouses (duty-free shops). Approval is required to open these accounts.

Held abroad	Residents who had opened an account abroad when previously residing abroad may maintain such an account after returning to Bangladesh.
Accounts in domestic currency convertible into foreign currency	No.

Nonresident Accounts

Foreign exchange accounts permitted	Bangladesh nationals residing abroad; foreign nationals, companies, and firms registered or incorporated abroad; banks and other financial institutions, including institutional investors; officers and staff of Bangladesh missions and government institutions; autonomous bodies; and commercial banks may open interest-bearing nonresident foreign currency deposit accounts denominated in dollars, euros, pounds sterling, or Japanese yen. These accounts may be credited in initial minimum amounts of $1,000 or $500 ($25,000 for foreigners), with remittances in convertible currencies and transfers from existing foreign currency deposit accounts maintained by Bangladesh nationals abroad. The accounts bear interest if their terms range from one month to one year. Bangladesh nationals may maintain a foreign currency account abroad while residing abroad and may continue to hold the account after returning to Bangladesh. The balance, including interest earned, may be transferred in foreign exchange by the account holder to any country or to any foreign currency deposit account maintained by Bangladesh nationals abroad. The balances in the accounts, which are freely convertible into taka, must be reported monthly by banks to the BB. Nonresident Bangladeshis who do not open or maintain a foreign currency deposit account while abroad may open a nonresident foreign currency deposit account with foreign exchange brought in from abroad within six months of the date of their return to take up permanent residence in Bangladesh. All nonresident accounts are regarded for exchange control purposes as accounts related to the country in which the account holder is a permanent resident (the accounts of the United Nations and its agencies are treated as resident accounts).
Approval required	Nonresident foreign currency accounts may be opened by authorized dealers without prior approval from the BB for Bangladesh nationals and foreign nationals who reside abroad and for foreign firms operating abroad. Specified debits and credits to these accounts may be made in the account holder's absence by authorized dealers without prior approval from the BB. Certain other debits and credits may be made without prior approval from the BB, but are subject to ex post recording.
Domestic currency accounts	Foreign missions and embassies, their expatriate personnel, foreign airline and shipping companies, and international nonprofit organizations in Bangladesh may open interest-bearing accounts, but the interest earned may be disbursed only in local currency.
Convertible into foreign currency	All diplomatic missions operating in Bangladesh, their diplomatic officers, home-based members of the mission staffs, international nonprofit organizations (including charitable organizations functioning in Bangladesh and their respective personnel), foreign oil companies engaged in oil exploration in Bangladesh and their expatriate employees, UN organizations and other international organizations, foreign contractors and consultants engaged in specific projects, and foreign nationals residing in Bangladesh (regardless of their status) are allowed to maintain convertible taka accounts. These accounts may be credited freely with the proceeds of inward remittances in convertible foreign exchange and may be debited freely at any time for local disbursements in taka, as well as for remittances abroad in convertible currencies. Transfers between convertible taka accounts are freely permitted.
Approval required	Yes.
Blocked accounts	Nonresident taka accounts of Bangladesh nationals may be blocked by the BB.

Imports and Import Payments

Foreign exchange budget	No.
Financing requirements for imports	
Advance payment requirements	Advance payments for imports require approval from the BB, which is normally given only for specialized or capital goods.

Documentation requirements for release of foreign exchange for imports

Domiciliation requirements

Yes.

Preshipment inspection

An inspection is required for all imports, with a few exceptions.

Letters of credit

Payment against imports is generally permissible only under cover of irrevocable LCs. However, perishable food items of value not exceeding $7,500 a consignment may be imported overland without LCs; capital machinery and industrial raw materials may also be imported without LCs. Recognized export-oriented units operating under the bonded warehouse system may effect imports of up to four months' requirements of their raw and packing materials by establishing import LCs without reference to any export LC. They may also effect such imports by opening back-to-back LCs (either on a sight basis under the Export Development Fund, or up to 180 days on a usance basis) against export LCs received by them. Authorized dealers may establish LCs on an f.o.b. basis without the approval of the BB, subject to certain conditions. Foreign exchange for authorized imports is provided automatically by authorized dealers when payments are due.

Import licenses and other nontariff measures

All importers (including all government departments, with the exception of the Ministry of Defense) are required to obtain LCAFs for all imports. Under the authority of the IPO issued by the Chief Controller, importers are allowed to effect imports against LCAFs issued by authorized dealer banks without an import license. Single-country LCAFs are issued for imports under bilateral trade or payments agreements and for imports under tied-aid programs. LCAFs are otherwise valid worldwide, except that imports from Israel and imports transported on flag vessels of Israel are prohibited. Goods must be shipped within 17 months of the date of issuance of LCAFs in the case of machinery and spare parts, and 9 months in the case of all other items.

Positive list

Items not specified in the control list of the IPO are freely importable, provided that the importer has a valid import registration certificate.

Negative list

The controlled list contains 110 items in about 1,400 categories at the four-digit level of the Harmonized System Codes. The importation of these items is restricted or prohibited either for public safety, religious, environmental, and social reasons, or because similar items are produced locally. Up to 26 items are restricted purely for trade purposes (7 of which are banned and 19 restricted). Imports from Israel are prohibited.

Open general licenses

All items not on the control list are freely importable by registered importers.

Licenses with quotas

Imports of specified raw materials and packing materials by industrial consumers are governed by an entitlement system, based on the requirements for various industries during each import program period established by the Board of Investment. Firms in the industrial sector are given an entitlement to import specified raw materials and packing materials, and LCAFs are issued on the basis of the entitlement. The entitlement system does not apply to raw materials and packing materials that are freely importable but does apply to items appearing on the controlled list. Separately, industrial consumers may be issued with LCAFs for parts and accessories of machinery. Goods imported against LCAFs issued to industrial consumers must be used in the industry concerned and must not be sold or transferred without prior approval.

Import taxes and/or tariffs

There are five tariff bands: zero, 5%, 15%, 25%, and 37.5%.

State import monopoly

No.

Exports and Export Proceeds

Repatriation requirements

Yes.

Surrender requirements

Proceeds from exports must be received within four months of shipment unless otherwise allowed by the BB. Exporters are permitted to retain 7.5% of the proceeds of exports of ready-made garments and 40% of the proceeds from other exports; they may use retained earnings for bona fide business purposes, such as business travel abroad; participation in trade fairs and seminars; and imports of raw materials, spare parts, and capital goods. They may also be used to set up offices abroad without prior permission from the BB. Joint ventures, other than in the garment industry, located in export processing zones (EPZs) are allowed to retain 80% of their export earnings in a foreign currency deposit account and to place the remaining 20% in a bank account in domestic currency.

Financing requirements	n.a.
Documentation requirements	
Domiciliation	Yes.
Export licenses	Exports to Israel are prohibited. Exports of about 20 product categories are banned. Some of these are restricted for nontrade reasons, while others are restricted to ensure the supply of the domestic market. Export licenses are required for all banned or restricted items.
With quotas	Quotas are imposed on garment exports by the Chief Controller of Imports and Exports on the basis of the previous year's performance. The Export Promotion Bureau monitors quota use in order to reallocate unfilled quotas.
Export taxes	Exports of jute are taxed.

Payments for Invisible Transactions and Current Transfers

Controls on these transfers	Payments for invisibles related to authorized trade transactions are generally not restricted.
Trade-related payments	There are controls on administrative expenses and commissions.
Prior approval	For unloading and storage costs, prior approval is required. Up to 5% of export receipts (up to 33.3% in the case of books) may be remitted abroad for commissions without prior approval from the BB.
Investment-related payments	Authorized dealers are allowed to remit dividends to nonresident shareholders without the prior approval of the BB on receipt of applications from the companies concerned; applications must be supported by an audited balance sheet and profit-and-loss account, a board resolution declaring dividends out of profits derived from the normal business activities of the company, and an auditor's certificate that tax liabilities are covered. Authorized dealers may remit profits of foreign firms, banks, insurance companies, and other financial institutions operating in Bangladesh to their head office on receipt of applications supported by documentation. These remittances are, however, subject to ex post checking by the BB.
Prior approval	No approval is required if loan agreements have been cleared by the Board of Investment (BOI).
Quantitative limits	Information is not available for amortization of loans or depreciation of direct investments.
Indicative limits/bona fide test	Information is not available for amortization of loans or depreciation of direct investments.
Payments for travel	
Quantitative limits	The limit for personal travel by resident Bangladesh nationals to countries other than Bhutan, India, Maldives, Myanmar, Nepal, Pakistan, and Sri Lanka is $3,000 a year; the allowance for air travel to these seven countries is $1,000 a person a year. For new exporters, the indicative limit for business travel is $6,000, while established exporters are permitted to use balances held under the Export Retention Scheme (7.5% of exports of ready-made garments and 40% of other export proceeds). Manufacturers producing for the domestic market and importers are granted business travel allowances equivalent to 1% of turnover as declared in tax returns, and 1% of the value of imports, respectively. There is an annual ceiling of $5,000 in both cases.
Indicative limits/bona fide test	Yes.
Personal payments	Foreign currency for education is made available up to the cost of tuition and living expenses, as estimated by the educational institution concerned. No prior permission is required for the remittance of fees for undergraduate, postgraduate, and some professional courses. Foreign exchange is available for the costs of dependents abroad, after production of a certificate from the Bangladesh embassy in the country concerned, up to a reasonable level based on prevailing prices.
Prior approval	Prior approval is required for the transfer of pensions.

Quantitative limits	Up to $10,000 may be obtained for medical costs without prior approval. Larger amounts are subject to the approval of the BB.
Indicative limits/bona fide test	Applications for foreign exchange for studies abroad and for family maintenance are accepted upon verification of their bona fide nature.

Foreign workers' wages

Quantitative limits	Foreign nationals may freely remit up to 50% of net salary in connection with service contracts approved by the government. The entire amount of their leave salaries and savings may also be freely remitted.
Indicative limits/bona fide test	Yes.

Credit card use abroad

Prior approval	General approval is given for the use by exporters against the foreign exchange retention entitlement and for the use against the travel allowance by other residents.
Quantitative limits	Credit cards may be used up to the amounts authorized for travel allowance and up to balances held in foreign currency deposit accounts.

Other payments

Prior approval	No prior permission is required for the remittance of royalties and technical fees of up to 6% of sales, and of training and consulting fees of up to 1% of sales.
Indicative limits/bona fide test	Industrial enterprises producing for local markets may remit up to 1% of sales receipts declared in the previous year's tax return.

Proceeds from Invisible Transactions and Current Transfers

Repatriation requirements	Yes.
Surrender requirements	Exporters of services are permitted to retain 5% of the proceeds and to use retained earnings for bona fide business purposes. Bangladesh nationals working abroad may retain their earnings in foreign currency accounts or in nonresident foreign currency deposit accounts. Unless specifically exempted by the BB, all Bangladesh nationals who reside in Bangladesh must surrender any foreign exchange coming into their possession, whether held in Bangladesh or abroad, to an authorized dealer within one month of the date of acquisition. However, returning residents may keep, in foreign currency accounts opened in their names, foreign exchange brought in at the time of return from abroad, provided that the amount does not represent proceeds from exports from Bangladesh or commissions earned from business activities in Bangladesh. Residents may retain up to $5,000 brought into the country without declaration. Foreign nationals residing in Bangladesh continuously for more than six months are required to surrender within one month of the date of acquisition any foreign exchange representing their earnings with respect to business conducted in Bangladesh or services rendered while in Bangladesh.
Restrictions on use of funds	Foreign exchange retainable as above may be used for travel abroad or bona fide business purposes.

Capital Transactions

Controls on capital and money market instruments	
On capital market securities	
Shares or other securities of a participating nature	
Purchase locally by nonresidents	Nonresidents may buy Bangladesh securities through stock exchanges against payment in freely convertible currency remitted from abroad through banking channels.

Sale or issue locally by nonresidents	Proceeds from sales, including capital gains and dividends earned on securities purchased in Bangladesh, may be remitted abroad in freely convertible currency. Nonresidents may not issue securities in Bangladesh.
On money market instruments	These transactions are not allowed.
On collective investment securities	
Purchase locally by nonresidents	These transactions are not allowed.
Sale or issue locally by nonresidents	These transactions are not allowed.
Purchase abroad by residents	These transactions are not allowed.
Sale or issue abroad by residents	These transactions are subject to prior approval of the Securities and Exchange Commission. If an instrument is denominated in foreign currency, prior BB approval is required.

Controls on derivatives and other instruments

Purchase locally by nonresidents	These transactions are not allowed.
Sale or issue locally by nonresidents	These transactions are not allowed.
Purchase abroad by residents	Authorized dealer banks may obtain hedging abroad against exchange rate risks on underlying trade transactions.
Sale or issue abroad by residents	Yes.

Controls on credit operations

Commercial credits

By residents to nonresidents	Export payments deferred for more than 120 days require BB authorization.
To residents from nonresidents	Deferred import payments are permitted for up to 360 days for capital machinery and for up to 180 days for industrial raw materials. Private industrial units may borrow funds from abroad with the approval of the BOI.

Financial credits

By residents to nonresidents	Except in specific cases, credits are subject to prior BB approval.
To residents from nonresidents	Authorized dealers (i.e., commercial banks) may obtain short-term loans and overdrafts from overseas branches and correspondents for a period not exceeding seven days at a time.

Guarantees, sureties, and financial backup facilities

By residents to nonresidents	Banks may issue guarantees/sureties in favor of nonresidents in relation to permissible current transactions on behalf of residents.
To residents from nonresidents	Receipt of guarantees/sureties by residents from abroad requires full disclosure of the underlying transaction.

Controls on direct investment

Outward direct investment	All outward transfers of capital require approval, which is sparingly granted for resident-owned capital.
Inward direct investment	Investments, except in the industrial sector, require approval. The Foreign Private Investment (Promotion and Protection) Act provides for the protection and equitable treatment of foreign private investment, indemnification, protection against expropriation and nationalization, and guarantee for repatriation of investment. There is no ceiling on private investment. Tax holidays are granted for periods of up to nine years, depending on the location.
Controls on liquidation of direct investment	Requests for repatriation of the proceeds from liquidation of direct investment (in unlisted companies) are subject to prior scrutiny of the BB.

Controls on real estate transactions

Purchase abroad by residents	Remittances of funds for these purchases are not permitted.

Purchase locally by nonresidents	Purchases of real estate by a nonresident with funds from abroad are allowed.
Sale locally by nonresidents	Repatriation of sales proceeds are subject to prior approval by the BB, which is not normally granted.

Controls on personal capital movements

Loans

  By residents to nonresidents — These transactions are not allowed.

  To residents from nonresidents — These transactions are not allowed, except for industrial enterprises borrowing according to BOI guidelines/approval.

Gifts, endowments, inheritances, and legacies

  By residents to nonresidents — Transfer of title to nonresidents by way of inheritances is not restricted, but income from, and sale proceeds of, such assets are normally not transferable abroad and are required to be used locally with prior authorization from the BB.

  To residents from nonresidents — A resident Bangladesh national requires the prior approval of the government of Bangladesh for receiving any gift/endowment from a foreign donor. Inheritances are to be disclosed to the BB. Net current income from estates inherited abroad are to be repatriated.

Settlement of debts abroad by immigrants	These transactions are normally not allowed, except for repayments on borrowing for industrial investments according to BOI guidelines.
Transfer of assets	These transactions are not allowed, except for movable personal effects.
Transfer abroad by emigrants	These transactions are not allowed, except for normal travel allowance permissible to residents.
Transfer into the country by immigrants	These transactions are permitted, subject to the declaration requirement in respect of foreign exchange in excess of $5,000.
Transfer of gambling and prize earnings	Gambling is prohibited in Bangladesh.

Provisions specific to commercial banks and other credit institutions

Borrowing abroad	The same regulations apply as for financial credits.
Maintenance of accounts abroad	The maintenance of these accounts is subject to notification to the BB.
Lending to nonresidents (financial or commercial credits)	Lending to nonresidents is not allowed, except with prior BB approval and in specific cases.
Lending locally in foreign exchange	Lending is subject to prior approval by the BB.
Purchase of locally issued securities denominated in foreign exchange	Purchases are subject to prior approval by the BB.

Differential treatment of deposit accounts in foreign exchange

  Interest rate controls — Banks are required to maintain interest rates on foreign currency deposits in line with international market rates.

Open foreign exchange position limits	The BB places limits on each authorized dealer's net open position, not to exceed 12.5% of capital.

Provisions specific to institutional investors

Limits (max.) on portfolio invested abroad	Domestic institutional investors may not acquire investment assets abroad.
Other controls imposed by securities laws	n.a.

Changes During 1999

No significant changes occurred in the exchange and trade system.

BARBADOS

(Position as of December 31, 1999)

Status Under IMF Articles of Agreement

Article VIII

Date of acceptance: November 3, 1993.

Exchange Arrangement

Currency

The currency of Barbados is the Barbados dollar.

Other legal tender

Gold coins with face values of BDS$50, BDS$100, BDS$150, BDS$200, and BDS$500 are legal tender and are in limited circulation.

Exchange rate structure

Unitary.

Classification

Conventional pegged arrangement

The Barbados dollar is pegged to the U.S. dollar, the intervention currency, at BDS$2 per US$1. Buying and selling rates for the Canadian dollar, the euro, and the pound sterling are also officially quoted on the basis of their cross-rate relationships to the U.S. dollar. The quoted rates include commission charges of 0.125% buying and 1.75% selling against the U.S. dollar, and 0.1875% buying and 1.8125% selling against the Canadian dollar, euro, and pound sterling. Certain businesses are allowed to change foreign currency.

Exchange tax

No.

Exchange subsidy

No.

Forward exchange market

The Central Bank of Barbados (CBB) periodically obtains forward cover in the international foreign exchange market to cover or hedge its own or the central government's exchange risks associated with foreign exchange loans that are not denominated in U.S. dollars. Commercial banks are allowed to obtain forward cover in the international markets. The CBB and commercial banks enter into swap transactions in U.S. dollars, while commercial banks freely switch between nonregional currencies.

Arrangements for Payments and Receipts

Prescription of currency requirements

Settlements with residents of countries outside the CARICOM area may be made in any foreign currency or through an external account in Barbados dollars. Settlements with residents of CARICOM countries other than Jamaica, Suriname, and Trinidad and Tobago may be made in the currency of the CARICOM country. Settlements with residents of Jamaica, Suriname, and Trinidad and Tobago may be made in U.S. dollars. Retail outlets are permitted to issue change in the same foreign currency in which purchases were made.

Payment arrangements

Yes.

Regional arrangements

Barbados is a member of the CARICOM.

Clearing agreements

Under clearing arrangements with regional monetary authorities, the CBB currently sells only three CARICOM country currencies: the Bahamian dollar, the Eastern Caribbean dollar, and the Belize dollar. The Trinidad and Tobago, Guyana, and Jamaica dollars float against the U.S. dollar, and the CBB sets indicative selling rates based on rates supplied by the monetary authorities of these countries. These rates are applicable only to government transactions.

Administration of control

Exchange control applies to all countries, except those in the OECS, and is administered by the CBB, which delegates to authorized dealers (ADs) the authority to approve normal import payments and foreign exchange for cash gifts. Further authority is delegated to commercial banks in respect of current account transactions ranging from BDS$7,500 to BDS$250,000. Trade controls are administered by the Ministry of Commerce, Consumer Affairs and Business Development (MCCABD). The authority to approve payments to OECS countries is delegated to ADs.

International security restrictions	No.
Payment arrears	No.

Controls on trade in gold (coins and/or bullion)

Controls on domestic ownership and/or trade — Residents, other than the monetary authorities, ADs, and industrial users, are not permitted to hold or acquire gold in any form other than jewelry or coins for numismatic purposes. Any gold acquired in Barbados must be surrendered to an AD, unless exchange control approval is obtained for its retention.

Controls on external trade — The importation of gold by residents is permitted for industrial purposes and is subject to customs duties and charges. Licenses to import gold are issued by the MCCABD. Exchange control permission is required to export gold.

Controls on exports and imports of banknotes

On exports

Domestic currency — Travelers may take out up to BDS$500.

Foreign currency — Travelers may take out up to the equivalent of BDS$1,000. Nonresident visitors may export freely any foreign currency they previously brought in.

Resident Accounts

Foreign exchange accounts permitted — Yes.

Held domestically — Subject to specific conditions under delegated authority, ADs may maintain foreign currency accounts in the names of individuals and companies resident in Barbados. Certain receipts and payments may be credited and debited to foreign currency accounts under conditions established at the time the account is opened. Other credits and debits require individual approval. However, where authority has not been delegated to ADs, the permission of the CBB is required. Approval is given on the basis of the anticipated frequency of receipts and payments in foreign currency.

Held abroad — Permission of the CBB is required.

Accounts in domestic currency convertible into foreign currency — n.a.

Nonresident Accounts

Foreign exchange accounts permitted — The same regulations apply as for resident accounts.

Domestic currency accounts — These accounts may be credited with the proceeds from the sale of foreign currencies, with transfers from other external accounts, with bank interest, and with payments by residents for which the CBB has given general or specific permission. The accounts may be debited for payments to residents of Barbados for the cost of foreign exchange required for travel or business purposes and for any other payment covered by delegated authority to ADs. Other debits and any overdrafts require individual approval.

Convertible into foreign currency — Balances on external accounts are convertible. Nonresident holders of foreign currency accounts are not required to obtain central bank approval to remit funds abroad when the funds were not the result of payment for trade or nontrade transactions.

Blocked accounts — The CBB may require certain payments in favor of nonresidents that are ineligible for transfer to be credited to blocked accounts. Balances in blocked accounts may not be withdrawn without approval, other than for the purchase of approved securities.

Imports and Import Payments

Foreign exchange budget	No.
Financing requirements for imports	
Advance payment requirements	ADs may release foreign exchange up to the equivalent of BDS$250,000 (c.i.f.) for advance payments for imports into Barbados. Other advance payments require the prior approval of the CBB.
Documentation requirements for release of foreign exchange for imports	Payments for authorized imports are permitted upon application and submission of documentary evidence (invoices and customs warrants) to ADs; payments for imports of crude oil and its derivatives are subject to the approval of the CBB.
Import licenses and other nontariff measures	Certain imports require individual licenses. Some items on the import-licensing list may be freely imported throughout the year, while others are subject to temporary restrictions (particularly agricultural products, which tend to be subject to seasonal restrictions). Individual licenses are also required for imports of commodities that are subject to the provisions of the Oils and Fats Agreement between the governments of Barbados, Dominica, Grenada, Guyana, St. Lucia, St. Vincent, and Trinidad and Tobago whether the goods are being imported from CARICOM countries or from elsewhere. Special licensing arrangements have been made for the regulation of trade between Barbados and other CARICOM countries in 22 agricultural commodities.
Licenses with quotas	Not all goods that are subject to licensing are subject to quantitative restrictions or import surcharges.
Import taxes and/or tariffs	Customs duties correspond to the CET of CARICOM, which is in the range of 5%–20%. There is a surtax of 75% on some imports that had been previously subject to quantitative restrictions. A VAT of 15% is levied.
State import monopoly	n.a.

Exports and Export Proceeds

Repatriation requirements	Yes.
Surrender requirements	Yes.
Financing requirements	n.a.
Documentation requirements	n.a.
Export licenses	Specific licenses are required for the exportation of certain goods to any country, including rice, sugarcane, rum, molasses, certain other food products, sewing machines, portland cement, and petroleum products. All other goods may be exported without license.
Without quotas	Yes.
With quotas	Exports of sugar to the United Kingdom and the United States are subject to bilateral export quotas, as are exports of rum to the EU.
Export taxes	n.a.

Payments for Invisible Transactions and Current Transfers

Controls on these transfers	
Trade-related payments	
Prior approval	Approval is required for amounts above the quantitative limits.
Quantitative limits	For freight and insurance, the limit is BDS$250,000 a transaction, including insurance payments and premiums, as long as the amount is approved for payment by the Supervisor

of Insurance. The same limit is applied for unloading and storage costs and administrative expenses; the limit for commissions is BDS$100,000.

Indicative limits/bona fide test	Yes.
Investment-related payments	Information is not available on the payment of amortization loans or depreciation of direct investments.
Prior approval	Yes.
Quantitative limits	The limit for interest payments is BDS$50,000 a year for individuals. For payments of profits and dividends, approval is required for amounts above BDS$250,000, except for listed companies from the CARICOM region on the securities exchange of Barbados, where the limit is BDS$2 million.
Indicative limits/bona fide test	Yes.
Payments for travel	
Quantitative limits	The limits are BDS$7,500 a person a calendar year for private travel, and BDS$750 a day for business travel, up to BDS$50,000 a person a calendar year.
Indicative limits/bona fide test	Yes.
Personal payments	
Prior approval	Approval is required for amounts above the limit.
Quantitative limits	The limits are as follows: for medical costs, BDS$100,000 a year; for studies abroad, BDS$50,000 a person a year; for cash gifts, BDS$5,000; and for alimony and other maintenance expenses, BDS$50,000. Nonresidents may have their pensions remitted to them while residing outside Barbados.
Indicative limits/bona fide test	Yes.
Foreign workers' wages	
Prior approval	Yes.
Quantitative limits	Nonresidents are allowed to remit amounts to cover commitments while employed in Barbados.
Indicative limits/bona fide test	Yes.
Credit card use abroad	
Prior approval	Yes.
Quantitative limits	The limits are the same as for travel.
Indicative limits/bona fide test	Yes.
Other payments	
Prior approval	Approval is required for amounts above the limit.
Quantitative limits	The limit for subscriptions and membership fees is BDS$50,000 a person a year, and, for consulting and legal fees, BDS$100,000 for each nonresident beneficiary.
Indicative limits/bona fide test	Yes.

Proceeds from Invisible Transactions and Current Transfers

Repatriation requirements	Yes.
Surrender requirements	Foreign currency proceeds from invisibles must be sold to ADs.
Restrictions on use of funds	n.a.

Capital Transactions

Controls on capital and money market instruments

On capital market securities

Shares or other securities of a participating nature

  Purchase locally by nonresidents

The issuance and transfer to nonresidents of securities registered in Barbados require exchange control approval, which is freely given provided that an adequate amount of foreign currency is brought in for their purchase.

  Purchase abroad by residents

These purchases require exchange control approval, and certificates of title must be lodged with an authorized depository in Barbados except for regional securities purchased through the Securities Exchange of Barbados. Earnings on these securities must be repatriated and surrendered to an AD.

  Sale or issue abroad by residents

Exchange control approval is required.

Bonds or other debt securities

The same regulations apply as for shares or other securities of a participating nature.

On money market instruments

Purchase locally by nonresidents

The same regulations apply as for shares and other securities of a participating nature.

Purchase abroad by residents

The same regulations apply as for shares and other securities of a participating nature.

On collective investment securities

Purchase locally by nonresidents

The same regulations apply as for shares and other securities of a participating nature.

Purchase abroad by residents

The same regulations apply as for shares and other securities of a participating nature.

Controls on derivatives and other instruments

n.a.

Controls on credit operations

The approval of the CBB is required for all credit operations.

Controls on direct investment

Direct investments require exchange control approval.

Controls on liquidation of direct investment

Liquidation of proceeds is permitted, provided that evidence documenting the validity of the remittance is submitted, all liabilities related to the investment have been discharged, and the original investment was registered with the CBB.

Controls on real estate transactions

Purchase abroad by residents

Purchases require exchange control approval.

Purchase locally by nonresidents

Nonresidents may acquire real estate in Barbados for private purposes with funds from foreign currency sources; local currency financing is not ordinarily permitted.

Sale locally by nonresidents

Proceeds from the realization of such investments equivalent to the amount of foreign currency brought in may be repatriated freely. Capital sums realized in excess of this amount may be repatriated freely on the basis of a calculated annual rate of return on the original foreign investment as follows: for the last five years, at 8%; for the five years immediately preceding the last five years, at 5%; and for any period preceding the last 10 years, at 4%. Amounts in excess of the sum so derived are restricted to remittances of BDS$30,000 a year.

Controls on personal capital movements

Loans

Exchange control permission is required for the granting or receiving of loans.

Gifts, endowments, inheritances, and legacies

By residents to nonresidents

The annual limit is BDS$5,000 for gifts and BDS$30,000 for endowments, inheritances, and legacies.

Settlement of debts abroad by immigrants	Yes.
Transfer of assets	
Transfer abroad by emigrants	The limit is BDS$100,000.
Transfer of gambling and prize earnings	Nonresidents may take out winnings.

Provisions specific to commercial banks and other credit institutions

Borrowing abroad	Any borrowing abroad by ADs to finance their domestic operations requires the approval of the CBB. ADs may assume short-term liability positions in foreign currencies for the financing of approved transfers in respect of both trade and nontrade transactions.
Maintenance of accounts abroad	Accounts must be maintained with overseas correspondent banks.
Lending to nonresidents (financial or commercial credits)	Exchange control permission is required.
Purchase of locally issued securities denominated in foreign exchange	Investment in local securities requires CBB approval.
Differential treatment of deposit accounts in foreign exchange	
Reserve requirements	There is no reserve requirement on deposits in foreign exchange. For domestic currency deposits in commercial banks, there is a liquidity requirement of 26% (12% in treasury bills; 8% in government debentures; and, since May 31, 1999, 6% in cash).
Liquid asset requirements	There is no liquidity requirement on deposits in foreign exchange. For domestic currency deposits in commercial banks, there is a liquidity requirement of 25% (12% in treasury bills, 8% in government debentures, and 5% in cash).
Differential treatment of deposit accounts held by nonresidents	Nonresident deposit accounts are treated the same as resident deposit accounts. Differential treatment is based on whether the amount is in domestic currency.
Open foreign exchange position limits	Limits are set by the CBB.
Provisions specific to institutional investors	Approval is required for investment of pension funds abroad. A 6% tax is levied on portfolio investments of pension funds with foreign companies that are not registered with the Barbados Supervisor of Insurance.
Other controls imposed by securities laws	n.a.

Changes During 1999

Capital transactions

Provisions specific to commercial banks and other credit institutions	*May 31.* The cash portion of the liquidity requirement for domestic currency deposits in commercial banks was raised to 6% from 5%.

BELARUS

(Position as of March 31, 2000)

Status Under IMF Articles of Agreement

Article XIV	Yes.

Exchange Arrangement

Currency

The currency of Belarus is the Belarussian rubel.

Exchange rate structure

Multiple

As of March 31, 1999, there were two official exchange rates—the official noncash exchange rate and the "recommended" cash rate. The official noncash exchange rate has been set by the National Bank of Belarus (NBB) in daily trading in the Belarussian Stock and Currency Exchange (BSCE) since March 1, 1999 (when the two previously existing official noncash exchange rates were unified). As of March 31, 1999, the reported interbank rate was virtually identical to the official noncash exchange rate, in part owing to tax liabilities arising from the difference between the unified noncash exchange rate and the actual transaction rate. As of March 31, 1999, the spread between the "recommended" cash rate and the "street" rate was 13%. On June 30, 1999, there were five exchange rates in existence (two official rates and three parallel rates). As of December 31, 1999, four exchange rates are legally quoted in Belarus: (1) the official exchange rate set by the NBB on the basis of trading sessions on the BSCE, which is applied to surrender requirements and accounting transactions; (2) the exchange rate set on the supplementary trading sessions of the BSCE; (3) the weighted average exchange rate in the interbank market; and (4) the cash exchange rate.

Classification

Managed floating with no pre-announced path for the exchange rate

The official exchange rate of the rubel was managed within an exchange rate band established in January 1996. Most transactions take place through the interbank market exchange rate.

The official exchange rate and rate of supplementary sessions of the BSCE are administratively set by the NBB. The cash exchange rate is informally recommended by the NBB, but it reflects supply and demand conditions. The interbank exchange rate is believed to be underreported due to the taxation of the differential between the official and transaction exchange rates.

All foreign exchange transactions above a stipulated amount involving the rubel and any one of four foreign currencies (the dollar, the euro, the hryvnia, or the Russian ruble) and above the amounts sold according to the existing mandatory 30% surrender requirement are to be undertaken in the supplementary session of the Minsk Interbank Currency Exchange (MICE) rather than on the interbank market, as before.

Effective January 22, 1999, foreign currency above the mandatory surrender amount may be sold on the interbank market. On December 3, 1999, the limits on volumes of transactions on the interbank market were abolished.

Exchange tax

Repatriation of profits in convertible currency is subject to a 15% tax, payable in convertible currency.

Exchange subsidy

n.a.

Forward exchange market

The forward market is regulated by the same provisions as the spot market. On February 10, 1999, foreign currency swap operations by the NBB were discontinued.

Arrangements for Payments and Receipts

Prescription of currency requirements

In accordance with the Agreement on the Establishment of a Payment Union of Member Countries of the CIS and bilateral payment agreements between Belarus and the central banks of those countries, settlements between Belarus and CIS member countries are effected in the national currencies of the parties involved in the settlements, in the currencies of the Payment Union Member Countries of the CIS and in freely convertible currencies, in accordance with legislation in effect within the territory of the country. Settlements between Belarus and CIS member countries and the Baltic countries are effected using noncash procedures via correspondent accounts of authorized banks and central banks.

In accordance with bilateral payment agreements between the NBB and the central banks of Armenia, Azerbaijan, the Kyrgyz Republic, Latvia, Moldova, Tajikistan, and Uzbekistan, only settlements for operations ensuing from the functions of central banks are effected via correspondent accounts of central banks. Settlements for all other accounts are effected via correspondent accounts of authorized banks.

In accordance with bilateral payment agreements between the NBB and the central bank of Estonia, settlements between economic agents may be effected both via correspondent accounts of authorized banks and via correspondent accounts of central banks. Effective December 29, 1999, Belarussian rubel payments for exports are allowed, but import invoicing in rubels is generally prohibited for most goods, but the NBB can grant ad hoc waivers on a case-by-case basis.

Payment arrangements	
Bilateral payment arrangements	Belarus maintains bilateral payment agreements with 14 countries, including the CIS countries.
Operative	Yes.
Regional arrangements	There are arrangements with Moscow and various other regions in Russia.
Clearing agreements	There is an agreement with Uzbekistan calling for the exchange of cotton for strategic goods from Belarus on a balanced basis. There are also agreements with Moldova and Ukraine.
Barter agreements and open accounts	Barter trade of certain goods requires approval from the Ministry of Foreign Affairs (MFA). Barter agreements are effected at the level of economic agents.
Administration of control	The Parliament is responsible for legislating exchange control regulations and the NBB for administering them.
International security restrictions	No.
Payment arrears	
Official	Yes.
Controls on trade in gold (coins and/or bullion)	
Controls on domestic ownership and/or trade	Residents are required to obtain a license from the MOF to deal in precious stones and metals.
Controls on external trade	Licenses for residents to export precious metals and stones are issued by the MFA.
Controls on exports and imports of banknotes	
On exports	
Domestic currency	Residents and nonresidents may export up to the equivalent of 100 times the minimum wage.
Foreign currency	Any person may export Russian rubles up to the equivalent of 500 times the minimum wage set in Russia. Resident and nonresident natural persons may export $500 in cash and any sum in traveler's checks without permission and any sum with the permission of an authorized bank.
On imports	
Domestic currency	Up to the previously exported amount may be imported.

Foreign currency

There are no limitations on the import of foreign currency other than Russian rubles. For Russian rubles, up to the equivalent of 500 times the minimum wage set in Russia may be imported.

Resident Accounts

Foreign exchange accounts permitted

Yes.

Held domestically

Without declaring the sources of their foreign exchange, residents may open foreign currency accounts at commercial banks authorized to transact in foreign exchange.

Held abroad

These accounts may be held abroad, but approval of the NBB is required.

Accounts in domestic currency convertible into foreign currency

Balances may be converted for payments to import goods, labor, and services; payments for business trip expenditures and training abroad; and repayments of loans and interest. Insurance companies may convert balances to establish insurance funds from net profits.

Nonresident Accounts

Foreign exchange accounts permitted

Nonresident juridical persons may maintain foreign exchange accounts with authorized banks in Belarus. The source of the funds may be receipts from abroad; proceeds from the sales of goods and services in the territory of Belarus, including sales to residents; debt-service payment; interest earned on balances in the accounts; funds from other foreign exchange accounts of nonresidents in Belarus; and earnings from investments from the performance of other operations with residents and nonresidents. These accounts may be debited for purchases of goods and services and for investments, as well as for payments to residents and nonresidents. Funds from these accounts may be freely repatriated or exchanged for Belarussian rubels at the market exchange rate through authorized banks. However, approval is required to open accounts for nonresident juridical persons, with countries for which the appropriate agreements have been concluded between the governments or the national banks.

Domestic currency accounts

Nonresident juridical persons may open I (investment), T (current), and C (investment in government securities) accounts at authorized commercial banks. I accounts may be credited with the Belarussian rubel counterpart of foreign exchange sales, dividends, resources from the liquidation of enterprises, and compensation in the event of the nationalization of enterprises. Resources from I accounts may be used to purchase foreign currency, shares of enterprises, privatization checks, etc.

T accounts are used for current operations. Proceeds from the sale of foreign currencies and of goods and services, and resources from the placement of money in deposits and other debt obligations of banks, etc. are transferred into them. Resources from T accounts may be used to purchase goods and services and bonds, and to pay for current expenditures. Funds in C accounts are used for investments in securities issued by the Belarussian government and the NBB. Proceeds from the sale of freely convertible currencies and/or Russian rubles, as well as proceeds from the redemption or sale of government and NBB securities by nonresidents, are deposited in C accounts if the original purchases were made with payments from C accounts.

Convertible into foreign currency

Balances on I and C accounts may be converted into foreign currency. In this process, balances on C accounts may be converted into foreign currency under condition that the nonresident was a holder of securities of the government or the NBB for a period of time established by the NBB. Approval is required to convert these accounts into foreign currency.

Blocked accounts

n.a.

Imports and Import Payments

Foreign exchange budget

n.a.

Financing requirements for imports	Imports for goods and services for Belarussian rubels with payment to correspondent accounts of nonresident banks are permitted only with NBB approval.
Advance payment requirements	For down payments for goods or services exceeding $100,000, a foreign bank guarantee is required. For payments for imported services more than 90 days in advance of the performance of the services and for imported goods more than 60 days in advance of the receipt of the goods, permission of the MFA is required; for advance payment of more than 180 days, NBB approval is required.
Documentation requirements for release of foreign exchange for imports	
Import licenses used as exchange licenses	Yes.
Import licenses and other nontariff measures	Import licenses are required for importing certain herbicides and industrial wastes.
Positive list	All goods may be imported freely, except those subject to prohibitions and restrictions.
Negative list	The importing of radioactive or toxic wastes, as well as publications or videos that are against state morals, health, or security, is prohibited.
Licenses with quotas	Importers are required to obtain a license in order to apply for an import quota for ethyl alcohol and alcoholic beverages.
Import taxes and/or tariffs	The Republic of Belarus has abolished customs controls and customs processing of goods moving between Belarus and Russia. Efforts are under way to establish a uniform trade policy in relation to third countries. The tariff structure consists of higher rates (from 30% to 100%) that apply to goods such as weapons, ammunition, precious metal products, carpets, motor vehicles, alcohol, and certain others. Regular (base) import duty rates apply to countries with MFN status. The preferential treatment given to goods from developing countries (duties that are 75% of the base rates) and from the least developed countries that have this status (goods from which are imported duty-free) is applied to a certain list of goods imported onto the customs territory of Belarus. Duties are applied at twice the MFN rate on imports from countries without MFN status. On January 1, 2000, customs duties on textiles from the EU were temporarily reduced. On July 1, 1999, a temporary surcharge for barter transactions was introduced at the following rates: 5% for barter transactions carried out in accordance with decisions of the Republic of Belarus Council of Ministers or that entail the delivery to Belarus of raw materials, supplies, components, and equipment to support economic agents' own production operations; and 15% for other barter transactions. Economic agents are not subject to the surcharge for barter transactions that entail the delivery to Belarus of goods that appear on a list established by the Republic of Belarus Council of Ministers.
State import monopoly	No.

Exports and Export Proceeds

Repatriation requirements	Foreign exchange proceeds from exports of goods and services must be repatriated within 90 days (60 days within Europe) of shipping, including goods exported under a barter or clearing contract. Special approval of the MFA is needed for longer periods of time; special approval of the NBB is needed for periods in excess of 180 days.
Surrender requirements	A temporary 10% mandatory surrender requirement in the afternoon session of the MICE was introduced on December 11, 1999, and was in effect until January 1, 2000. The exchange rate applicable to this surrender was the rate prevailing in the main session.
	In the first quarter of 2000, 35.2% of the foreign exchange acquired through the surrender requirement was earmarked to pay for fuel and energy resources. The remainder was generally applied to other priority imports.
	The surrender requirement for freely convertible currency and Russian rubles at the official exchange rate is currently 30%. On March 1, 2000, however, an additional 10% surrender requirement was introduced temporarily for subsequent sale of these funds to the

Belarussian State Petroleum and Chemical Concern for the purchase of petroleum, other hydrocarbon raw materials, and petroleum products.

Financing requirements	No.
Documentation requirements	A transaction certificate and a statistical declaration are required.

Export licenses

Without quotas

Export bans exist for some medicinal herbs, art and antique collections, certain wild animals, and goods imported into Belarus on a humanitarian basis. Exports of certain goods, including amber, ores and concentrates, and precious metals and stones, require a license that is subject to the approval of the MOF.

With quotas

Mineral fertilizers and waste, and scrap of ferrous and nonferrous metals are subject to export quotas and licensing requirements.

Export taxes

Effective December 1, 1999, in the context of the common customs area, customs duties were established that are analogous to those of Russia on natural and liquefied gas that are exported from the customs territory of Belarus outside the member states of the Customs Union. VAT and excise taxes are collected on excisable goods that are exported to CIS countries, with the exception of Kazakhstan, the Kyrgyz Republic, Moldova, Tajikistan, and Ukraine.

Other export taxes

A rent payment applies for exported timber and products thereof.

Payments for Invisible Transactions and Current Transfers

Controls on these transfers

Payments for travel

Quantitative limits

Individuals (residents and nonresidents) are permitted to acquire cash foreign currency up to $200 a day at a single exchange office. There are no restrictions on the purchase of foreign exchange for bona fide expenses related to business travel, up to the standard business travel allowances established by the legislation.

Proceeds from Invisible Transactions and Current Transfers

Repatriation requirements

All service export proceeds must be repatriated within 90 days unless special permission for a longer period of repatriation has been granted by the MFA. Special permission from the NBB is required for a period exceeding 180 days.

Surrender requirements

A requirement of 40% applies to receipts in freely convertible currencies and Russian rubles.

Restrictions on use of funds

n.a.

Capital Transactions

Controls on capital and money market instruments

The MOF and the NBB establish quotas and procedures for transactions by residents and nonresidents in securities. The export and import of securities is allowed without limitation. There is a registration procedure for control purposes with the Belarus State Committee on Securities (BSCS).

On capital market securities

Shares or other securities of a participating nature

Purchase locally by nonresidents

BSCS registration is required for shares to be exported.

Sale or issue locally by nonresidents

BSCS registration is required for shares to be imported.

Purchase abroad by residents	A permit from the NBB and registration with the BSCS are required.
Sale or issue abroad by residents	Yes.
Bonds or other debt securities	Registration of securities is required. The NBB regulates the issue of CDs and saving certificates by banks. These may be issued both in domestic currency and in foreign exchange. Banks are not allowed to export bank certificates.
Purchase locally by nonresidents	The same regulations apply as for shares or other securities of a participating nature.
Sale or issue locally by nonresidents	Yes.
Purchase abroad by residents	The same regulations apply as for shares or other securities of a participating nature.
Sale or issue abroad by residents	Yes.
On money market instruments	
Purchase locally by nonresidents	An NBB permit is required to purchase government securities or securities issued by the NBB.
Sale or issue locally by nonresidents	Yes.
Purchase abroad by residents	An NBB permit is required.
Sale or issue abroad by residents	Yes.
On collective investment securities	
Purchase abroad by residents	An NBB permit is required.

Controls on derivatives and other instruments

Purchase abroad by residents	An NBB permit is required.

Controls on credit operations

Commercial credits

To residents from nonresidents	External borrowing by residents must be registered with the NBB.

Financial credits

By residents to nonresidents	An NBB permit is required if the credit is for more than 180 days.
To residents from nonresidents	Yes.

Controls on direct investment

Outward direct investment	Yes.
Inward direct investment	Foreign investment must be registered at the Ministry of Foreign Economic Relations; financial institutions must also register it at the NBB. In the case of insurance institutions, foreign investment must also be registered at the State Insurance Oversight Committee. Certain activities require special approval (license). When establishing an enterprise with foreign investments, the size of a foreign investor's share is not restricted, except for insurance organizations and banks, where it may not exceed 49%.

Controls on liquidation of direct investment	Foreign investors are guaranteed full repatriation of their initial investment capital and profits earned in Belarus.

Controls on real estate transactions

Purchase abroad by residents	An NBB permit is required.

Controls on personal capital movements	n.a.

Provisions specific to commercial banks and other credit institutions

Lending to nonresidents (financial or commercial credits)	Lending in rubels to nonresidents is prohibited.

Lending locally in foreign exchange	These transactions are permitted only for settlements with nonresidents.
Differential treatment of deposit accounts held by nonresidents	
Reserve requirements	Rubel deposits of nonresident banks are subject to a 46% reserve requirement.
Investment regulations	
Abroad by banks	An NBB permit is required.
Open foreign exchange position limits	Open foreign exchange position limits are established depending on the type of foreign currency (freely convertible currency and currency with restricted convertibility). Requirements are also established with regard to limits on the differential between off-balance-sheet assets and liabilities. Limits are computed as a whole by type of foreign currency regardless of whether the asset (liability) belongs to a resident or nonresident.
Provisions specific to institutional investors	n.a.
Other controls imposed by securities laws	n.a.

Changes During 1999

Exchange arrangement	*January 22.* Foreign currency above the mandatory surrender amount may be sold on the interbank market.
	February 10. Foreign currency swap operations by the NBB were discontinued.
	March 31. Two exchange rates remained in operation.
	June 30. Five exchange rates were in existence.
	December 3. The limits on volumes of transactions on the interbank market were abolished.
	December 31. Four exchange rates are legally quoted in Belarus.
Arrangements for payments and receipts	*December 29.* Invoicing of exports in rubels was allowed.
Imports and import payments	*July 1.* A temporary surcharge of 5% or 15% was introduced on barter transactions.
Exports and export proceeds	*December 1.* Customs duties were introduced on natural and liquefied gas exported outside the customs union with Russia.
	December 11. A temporary 10% surrender requirement on the afternoon trading session of the currency exchange was introduced to which the prevailing rate in the main session was applicable.

Changes During 2000

Imports and import payments	*January 1.* Customs duties on textiles from the EU were reduced for a period of six months.
Exports and export proceeds	*January 1.* The temporary 10% surrender requirement was abolished.
	March 1. An additional 10% surrender requirement was introduced temporarily for the subsequent sale of these funds to the Belarussian State Petroleum and Chemical Concern for the purchase of petroleum, petroleum products, and other new hydrocarbon materials.

BELGIUM

(Position as of January 31, 2000)

Status Under IMF Articles of Agreement

Article VIII   Date of acceptance: February 15, 1961.

Exchange Arrangement

Currency

As of January 1, 1999, the currency of Belgium is the euro. In cash transactions, however, the legal tender remains the Belgian franc until 2002, when euro banknotes and coins will be issued.

Exchange rate structure

Unitary.

Classification

Exchange arrangement with no separate legal tender

Belgium participates in a currency union (EMU) comprising 11 members of the EU: Austria, Belgium, Finland, France, Germany, Ireland, Italy, Luxembourg, the Netherlands, Portugal, and Spain. Internal conversion rates in respect to the national currencies of EMU participants were fixed to the euro on January 1, 1999, whereas the external exchange rate of the euro is market determined. The conversion rate between the euro and the Belgian franc was set at BF 40.3399 per €1. The ECB has the right to intervene to smooth out fluctuations in external exchange rates.

Exchange tax

No.

Exchange subsidy

No.

Forward exchange market

Banks are allowed to engage in spot and forward exchange transactions in any currency, and they may deal among themselves and with residents and nonresidents in foreign notes and coins.

Arrangements for Payments and Receipts

Prescription of currency requirements

No.

Payment arrangements

No.

Administration of control

No.

International security restrictions

In accordance with Executive Board Decision No. 144-(52/51)

Belgium applies exchange restrictions against Iraq, and on June 15, 1999, in line with an EU council decision, imposed more sanctions against the Federal Republic of Yugoslavia (Serbia/Montenegro).

In accordance with UN sanctions

Yes.

Payment arrears

No.

Controls on trade in gold (coins and/or bullion)

No.

Controls on exports and imports of banknotes

No.

Resident Accounts

Foreign exchange accounts permitted

Yes.

Held domestically

Yes.

Held abroad	Yes.
Accounts in domestic currency convertible into foreign currency	Yes.

Nonresident Accounts

Foreign exchange accounts permitted	Yes.
Domestic currency accounts	Yes.
Convertible into foreign currency	Yes.
Blocked accounts	These are accounts affected by international security restrictions.

Imports and Import Payments

Foreign exchange budget	No.
Financing requirements for imports	No.
Documentation requirements for release of foreign exchange for imports	No.
Import licenses and other nontariff measures	
Positive list	Individual licenses are required for certain specified imports from all countries (most imports do not require an import license when imported from member countries of the EU), including many textile and steel products, diamonds, weapons, and nontextile products from China. Effective January 1, 2000, licenses are required for imports of shoes from Vietnam. All other commodities are free of license requirements.
Licenses with quotas	Along with other EU countries, the BLEU applies quotas on a number of textile products from non-EU countries in the framework of the MFA, quotas on a number of steel products from Kazakhstan, Russia, and Ukraine, and quotas on a number of products from China (ceramic, porcelain, and shoes).
Import taxes and/or tariffs	Belgium applies the Common Import Regime of the EU to imports of most other agricultural and livestock products from non-EU countries.
State import monopoly	No.

Exports and Export Proceeds

Repatriation requirements	No.
Financing requirements	No.
Documentation requirements	No.
Export licenses	Export licenses are required only for a few products (mostly of a strategic character), for weapons, and for diamonds.
Without quotas	Yes.
Export taxes	No.

Payments for Invisible Transactions and Current Transfers

Controls on these transfers	No.

Proceeds from Invisible Transactions and Current Transfers

Repatriation requirements	No.
Restrictions on use of funds	No.

Capital Transactions

Controls on capital and money market instruments
Most of the controls on transactions with securities of non-EU origin were eliminated on April 5, 1999.

On collective investment securities

  Sale or issue locally by nonresidents
The public issue or sale of collective investment securities that are not of EU origin is controlled.

Controls on derivatives and other instruments
No.

Controls on credit operations
No.

Controls on direct investment

Inward direct investment
No authorization is required for inward direct investment in Belgium, except for the acquisition of Belgian flag vessels by shipping companies not having their principal office in Belgium.

Controls on liquidation of direct investment
No.

Controls on real estate transactions
No.

Controls on personal capital movements
No.

Provisions specific to commercial banks and other credit institutions
No.

Provisions specific to institutional investors

Currency-matching regulations on assets/liabilities composition
These regulations are maintained, but the introduction of the euro has considerably reduced the significance of such regulations. The EU gives the right to its member states to maintain such regulations.

Other controls imposed by securities laws
No.

Changes During 1999

Exchange arrangement
January 1. The currency of Belgium became the euro. The conversion rate between the euro and the Belgian franc was set irrevocably at BF 40.3399 per €1.

Arrangements for payments and receipts
June 15. Sanctions against the Federal Republic of Yugoslavia (Serbia/Montenegro) were strengthened.

Capital transactions
April 5. Most of the controls on transactions with securities of non-EU origin were eliminated.

Changes During 2000

Imports and import payments
January 1. An individual import license is required for the import of shoes from Vietnam.

BELIZE

(Position as of January 31, 2000)

Status Under IMF Articles of Agreement

Article VIII	Date of acceptance: June 14, 1983.

Exchange Arrangement

Currency	The currency of Belize is the Belize dollar.
Exchange rate structure	Unitary.
Classification	
Conventional pegged arrangement	The Belize dollar is pegged to the U.S. dollar, the intervention currency, at the rate of BZ$1 per US$0.5. The Central Bank of Belize (CBB) quotes daily rates for the Canadian dollar, the pound sterling, and a number of currencies of CARICOM member countries.
Exchange tax	A stamp duty of 1.25% is levied on all conversions from the Belize dollar to a foreign currency.
Exchange subsidy	No.
Forward exchange market	No.

Arrangements for Payments and Receipts

Prescription of currency requirements	No.
Payment arrangements	
Regional arrangements	Belize is a member of CARICOM.
Clearing agreements	Belize participates in the CMCF.
Administration of control	The CBB is responsible for administering exchange control, which applies to all countries. Authority covering a wide range of operations is delegated to the commercial banks in their capacity as authorized dealers. Only in exceptional cases or in applications involving substantial amounts is reference made directly to the CBB. However, all applications for foreign exchange processed by authorized dealers are regularly forwarded to the CBB for audit and record keeping.
International security restrictions	No.
Payment arrears	No.
Controls on trade in gold (coins and/or bullion)	
Controls on domestic ownership and/or trade	Residents may not hold gold except with specific authorization from the CBB.
Controls on external trade	Gold may not be imported or exported without the approval of the CBB.
Controls on exports and imports of banknotes	
On exports	
Domestic currency	Each traveler may take abroad up to BZ$100. Amounts beyond this limit require the approval of the CBB, which is liberally granted when justified.
Foreign currency	The amount of foreign currency that each resident traveler may take abroad is left to the discretion of the commercial banks. It is subject to availability and guided by limits. Nonresidents may take out up to the amount imported or the limits specified.

On imports

   Domestic currency   Each traveler may bring in up to BZ$100.

Resident Accounts

Foreign exchange accounts permitted   These accounts may be opened both domestically and abroad, but approval is required.

Accounts in domestic currency convertible into foreign currency   No.

Nonresident Accounts

Foreign exchange accounts permitted   Banks must have permission from the CBB to open external or foreign currency accounts.

Domestic currency accounts   These accounts may be credited with proceeds from the sale of foreign currency.

Convertible into foreign currency   Yes.

Blocked accounts   The CBB may stipulate that sums to be credited or paid to foreign residents be credited to a blocked account.

Imports and Import Payments

Foreign exchange budget   Yes.

Financing requirements for imports   No.

Documentation requirements for release of foreign exchange for imports   Prepayments for imports require authorization from the CBB; in most cases, such authorization is delegated to the commercial banks. The CBB rations its sales of foreign exchange to commercial banks on an ad hoc basis, except for a few essential import items, such as fuel and pharmaceuticals.

Letters of credit   Yes.

Import licenses and other nontariff measures

Negative list   For reasons of health, standardization, and protection of domestic industries, import licenses from the Ministry of Commerce and Industry are required for a number of goods—mostly food and agricultural products, and certain household and construction products; such licenses are liberally granted.

Import taxes and/or tariffs   Import tariff rates range from 5% to 25%, with a number of items (particularly agricultural inputs) entering duty free. Imports by most of the public sector and certain nonprofit entities, imports of an emergency or humanitarian nature, and goods for reexport are exempt from import duties; goods originating from the CARICOM area are also exempt. Some items are subject to revenue replacement duties ranging from 15% to 25%. Specific duties and surcharges apply to certain products. On June 30, 1999, the 15% VAT was replaced with a sales tax of 12% on alcohol, tobacco, and fuel, and 8% for all other goods and services, except exempt goods and services. On January 1, 2000, the fourth phase of the CARICOM CET came into effect.

State import monopoly   No.

Exports and Export Proceeds

Repatriation requirements   Yes.

Surrender requirements   Export proceeds must be surrendered to authorized dealers not later than six months after the date of shipment, unless otherwise directed by the CBB. The CBB makes direct purchases of sugar export proceeds, bypassing the traditional practice of purchasing from commercial banks.

Financing requirements	No.
Documentation requirements	No.
Export licenses	Export licenses are required for live animals, excluding pets; fish, crustaceans, and mollusks, excluding agricultural species; lumber and logs; beans; citrus fruits; and sugar.
Without quotas	Yes.
Export taxes	Effective June 30, 1999, transshipments are subject to a 1.5% customs administration fee.

Payments for Invisible Transactions and Current Transfers

Controls on these transfers	The CBB rations its sale of foreign exchange for invisible payments to commercial banks on an ad hoc basis, except for a few essential items, such as insurance.
Trade-related payments	There are controls on the payment of commissions.
Prior approval	For the payment and transfer of commissions, approval is granted by the CBB, subject to clearance by the Commissioner of Income Tax (CIT).
Investment-related payments	Information is not available on the payment of amortization of loans or depreciation of direct investments.
Prior approval	For interest payments, approval is granted by the CBB, subject to clearance by the CIT. For transfer of profits and dividends, an income statement and a declaration of dividends must be presented along with clearance from the CIT.
Payments for travel	
Quantitative limits	The following limits are in effect: (1) for nonbusiness travel by residents, up to BZ$5,000 a person a trip; (2) for business travel by residents, BZ$500 a person a day, up to a maximum of BZ$20,000 a year; (3) for business or nonbusiness travel by nonresidents, BZ$500 a person a year, unless payment is made from an external account or from proceeds of foreign currency. Resident travelers are required to sell their excess holdings of foreign currencies to an authorized dealer upon returning to Belize.
Indicative limits/bona fide test	Yes.
Personal payments	Payments related to medical costs are made directly to a doctor or hospital with original invoices or bills supporting the application.
Prior approval	For transfer of pension and payments for family maintenance and alimony, approval by the CBB is required.
Quantitative limits	The limit for gifts is BZ$100 a donor.
Indicative limits/bona fide test	Foreign exchange is provided by authorized dealers for payment of correspondence courses when applications are properly documented.
Foreign workers' wages	
Prior approval	Approval is granted by the CBB, subject to clearance by the CIT.
Other payments	
Prior approval	For the transfer of consulting and legal fees, approval is granted by the CBB, subject to clearance by the CIT.
Indicative limits/bona fide test	Similar requirements apply for subscriptions and membership fees as for study abroad.

Proceeds from Invisible Transactions and Current Transfers

Repatriation requirements	Yes.
Surrender requirements	Proceeds must be sold to an authorized dealer.
Restrictions on use of funds	No.

Capital Transactions

Controls on capital and money market instruments	All capital transfers require the approval of the CBB, but controls are liberally administered.
Controls on derivatives and other instruments	There are controls on all these transactions.
Controls on credit operations	There are controls on all these transactions.
Controls on direct investment	
Outward direct investment	Yes.
Inward direct investment	Inward direct investment must be registered with the CBB if the profits are to be repatriated in the future.
Controls on liquidation of direct investment	Repatriation of proceeds requires clearance by the CIT.
Controls on real estate transactions	There are controls on all these transactions.
Controls on personal capital movements	n.a.
Provisions specific to commercial banks and other credit institutions	
Borrowing abroad	Yes.
Maintenance of accounts abroad	Yes.
Lending to nonresidents (financial or commercial credits)	Yes.
Lending locally in foreign exchange	Yes.
Purchase of locally issued securities denominated in foreign exchange	Yes.
Provisions specific to institutional investors	No.
Other controls imposed by securities laws	No.

Changes During 1999

Imports and import payments	*June 30*. The 15% VAT was replaced with a sales tax of 12% on alcohol, tobacco, and fuel, and 8% for all other goods and services, except exempt goods and services.
Exports and export proceeds	*June 30*. Transshipments are subject to a 1.5% customs administration fee.

Changes During 2000

Imports and import payments	*January 1*. The fourth phase of the CARICOM CET came into effect.

BENIN

(Position as of January 31, 2000)

Status Under IMF Articles of Agreement

Article VIII

Date of acceptance: June 1, 1996.

Exchange Arrangement

Currency

The currency of Benin is the CFA franc.

Exchange rate structure

Unitary.

Classification

Exchange arrangement with no separate legal tender

Effective January 1, 1999, the CFA franc peg to the French franc was replaced with a peg to the euro, the intervention currency, at the fixed rate of CFAF 100 per €0.8385, which is the official buying and selling rate. Exchange rates for other currencies are derived from the rate for the currency concerned with the euro and the fixed rate between the euro and the CFA franc. They include a bank commission of 0.25% on transfers to all countries outside the WAEMU, which must be surrendered to the Treasury. Banks are authorized to charge a maximum commission of 2% on manual exchange transactions in French francs.

Exchange tax

No.

Exchange subsidy

No.

Forward exchange market

Effective February 1, 1999, residents were authorized to contract forward exchange cover to settle payments related to imports and exports of goods and services.

Arrangements for Payments and Receipts

Prescription of currency requirements

Because Benin is linked to the French Treasury through an Operations Account, settlements with France, Monaco, and other Operations Account countries (WAEMU and CAEMC members and the Comoros) are made in French francs or the currency of any other Operations Account country.

Payment arrangements

Yes.

Bilateral payment arrangements

Inoperative

Yes.

Regional arrangements

An Operations Account is maintained with the French Treasury that links Operations Account countries. All purchases or sales of foreign currencies or euros against CFA francs are ultimately settled through a debit or credit to the Operations Account.

Clearing agreements

A clearing agreement exists between the WAMA members and Cape Verde, The Gambia, Ghana, Guinea, Liberia, and Sierra Leone.

Administration of control

Exchange control is administered jointly by the MOF and the BCEAO. The only transactions that remain subject to the prior authorization of these institutions relate to inward direct investment and all outward investment, the soliciting of funds in Benin for placement in foreign countries, and domestic and foreign currency accounts of residents. Effective February 1, 1999, regulations governing the external financial relations of WAEMU member states entered into force, delegating to authorized banks the approval process for most foreign exchange transactions. On that same date, the amount of transfers authorized without supporting documentation was raised to CFAF 300,000 from CFAF 100,000. In the context of the regional financial market, the issuance, advertising, or marketing of securities, whether foreign or domestic, requires the prior authorization of the Public Savings and Financial Markets Regional Council (PSFMRC).

International security restrictions

No.

Payment arrears	No.
Controls on trade in gold (coins and/or bullion)	
Controls on domestic ownership and/or trade	Residents are free to hold, acquire, and dispose of gold in any form in Benin.
Controls on external trade	Imports and exports of gold from or to any other country require prior authorization of the MOF.
Controls on exports and imports of banknotes	
On exports	
Domestic currency	The export of CFAF banknotes by travelers is allowed. However, repurchase of exported banknotes by the BCEAO remains suspended. Furthermore, the shipment of BCEAO banknotes between authorized intermediaries and their correspondents located outside the WAEMU zone is strictly forbidden.
Foreign currency	The reexportation of foreign banknotes by nonresident travelers is allowed up to the equivalent of CFAF 500,000; the reexportation of foreign banknotes above these ceilings requires documentation demonstrating either the importation of the foreign banknotes or their purchase against other means of payment registered in the name of the traveler or through the use of nonresident deposits in local banks. Resident travelers outside the BCEAO zone are allowed to export foreign currency equivalent to CFAF 2 million. Amounts in excess of this ceiling may be exported in the form of traveler's checks, bank checks, or other means of payment.
On imports	
Domestic currency	Travelers may import freely CFAF banknotes; however, the amounts must be declared at customs.
Foreign currency	Resident and nonresident travelers may bring in any amount of foreign banknotes and coins (except gold coins) of countries outside the Operations Account area. Nonresidents bringing in foreign banknotes and foreign currency traveler's checks exceeding the equivalent of CFAF 1 million must declare them to customs upon entry. Residents bringing in foreign banknotes exceeding the equivalent of CFAF 300,000 must surrender the excess amount to an authorized intermediary bank within eight days of their return.

Resident Accounts

Foreign exchange accounts permitted	Effective February 1, 1999, residents are allowed to open foreign exchange accounts with local banks or with banks abroad after obtaining authorization from the MOF with the approval of the BCEAO. The approval of the president of the Council of Ministers of the WAEMU is no longer required.
Held domestically	Accounts in foreign currency held by residents with domestic financial institutions are subject to prior authorization by the MOF.
Held abroad	Effective February 1, 1999, residents are allowed to hold foreign exchange accounts abroad. The opening of these accounts requires the prior authorization of the MOF with the approval of the BCEAO.
Accounts in domestic currency convertible into foreign currency	Only nonresidents may hold convertible accounts without restriction.

Nonresident Accounts

Foreign exchange accounts permitted	Effective February 1, 1999, nonresidents were allowed to hold foreign exchange accounts with local banks, but BCEAO authorization is required.

Domestic currency accounts	Because the BCEAO has suspended the repurchase of banknotes circulating outside the territories of the WAEMU zone, nonresident accounts may not be credited or debited with BCEAO banknotes. These accounts may not be overdrawn without prior authorization of the MOF. Transfers of funds between nonresident accounts are not restricted.
Convertible into foreign currency	Nonresidents may freely debit their foreign accounts in francs for the purpose of purchasing foreign currency on the official foreign exchange market.
Blocked accounts	No.

Imports and Import Payments

Foreign exchange budget	No.
Financing requirements for imports	No.
Documentation requirements for release of foreign exchange for imports	
Domiciliation requirements	Effective February 1, 1999, the domiciliation requirement was increased to CFAF 5 million.
Preshipment inspection	All imports exceeding CFAF 3 million are subject to inspection.
Import licenses and other nontariff measures	
Negative list	Certain imports, e.g., narcotics, are prohibited from all sources.
Import taxes and/or tariffs	The WAEMU import classification was implemented on July 1, 1999. On January 1, 2000, the WAEMU introduced a CET with four rates (zero, 5%, 10%, and 20%) for all member countries except Guinea-Bissau. A statistical tax of 1% is levied on the c.i.f. value of imports.
State import monopoly	No.

Exports and Export Proceeds

Repatriation requirements	Receipts must be collected within 120 days of the arrival of the shipment at its destination. Effective February 1, 1999, proceeds from exports to WAEMU countries are no longer required to be repatriated.
Surrender requirements	Proceeds must be surrendered to authorized banks within 30 days of the payment due date. They must then be surrendered to the BCEAO by the authorized intermediaries as transfers via the issuing institution.
Financing requirements	No.
Documentation requirements	
Letters of credit	Yes.
Domiciliation	Proceeds must be domiciled with an authorized intermediary bank when valued at more than CFAF 5 million. Effective February 1, 1999, exports to WAEMU countries need not be domiciled.
Other	Yes.
Export licenses	
Without quotas	Exports are permitted on the basis of a simple authorization from the Directorate of Foreign Trade, which issues a certificate of origin, as needed. Exports of diamonds, gold, and all other precious metals, however, require prior authorization of the MOF, with the exception of articles with a small gold content, travelers' personal effects weighing less than 500 grams, and coins (fewer than 10 pieces, irrespective of their face value and denomination).

With quotas	Exports of teakwood and other varieties of unprocessed wood and charcoal are banned.
Export taxes	No.

Payments for Invisible Transactions and Current Transfers

Controls on these transfers	Payments for invisibles to France, Monaco and Operations Account countries (WAEMU and CAEMC members and the Comoros) are permitted freely; those to other countries are subject to approval. Payments for invisibles related to trade are permitted by a general authorization when the basic trade transaction has been approved or does not require authorization. Bona fide tests are conducted by authorized intermediary banks. Effective February 1, 1999, payments and incomes of foreign ships in the WAEMU zone and WAEMU ships abroad are included under current operations.
Trade-related payments	
Indicative limits/bona fide test	Yes.
Investment-related payments	
Prior approval	The transfer of funds to service loans is no longer subject to restrictions, but must be made through an authorized bank and reported to the MOF for statistical purposes. Payments for the depreciation of direct investment are not expressly provided for in the regulation and, as such, require prior approval from the MOF.
Indicative limits/bona fide test	Yes.
Payments for travel	
Quantitative limits	Effective February 1, 1999, limits on foreign exchange allowances were eliminated. The threshold of foreign exchange to be surrendered by residents after travel was raised to CFAF 300,000 from CFAF 50,000.
Personal payments	
Quantitative limits	There are no limits on transfers related to studies abroad, family maintenance, or alimony. Such payments are made through an authorized bank upon presentation of the appropriate documentation.
Indicative limits/bona fide test	Bona fide tests are conducted by authorized intermediary banks.
Foreign workers' wages	
Prior approval	Yes.
Quantitative limits	Payments abroad related to wages, salaries, and honoraria; contributions and benefits; pensions and work-related activities; and service contracts are generally authorized upon presentation of the appropriate documentation.
Indicative limits/bona fide test	Yes.
Other payments	
Indicative limits/bona fide test	Yes.

Proceeds from Invisible Transactions and Current Transfers

Repatriation requirements	Receipts from transactions with all countries, including France, Monaco, and Operations Account countries, must be repatriated.
Surrender requirements	Effective February 1, 1999, all amounts due from residents of other countries with respect to services, and all income earned in those countries from foreign assets must be collected and surrendered within one month of the due date or the date of receipt.
Restrictions on use of funds	No.

Capital Transactions

Controls on capital and money market instruments	Capital movements between Benin and France, Monaco, and the Operations Account countries are free of controls. Capital transfers to all other countries require authorization from the MOF, and a maximum of 75% of investment abroad may be financed by foreign loans.
	The liquidation of foreign investment is subject to reporting to the MOF, and the reinvestment of proceeds is subject to prior authorization, except the countries mentioned above. If no authorization is given for the reinvestment, the proceeds in foreign exchange must be surrendered to an authorized intermediary bank within one month. Transfers of capital abroad are subject to controls. Capital inflows to WAEMU countries are unrestricted, with the exception of direct investment, which is subject to prior declaration, and certain borrowing operations, which require prior authorization.
	In line with the new direction of economic policy aimed at attracting foreign investment, new exchange laws currently being adopted by the WAEMU member states provide for the elimination of all controls on capital inflows.
	In implementation of the provisions indicated in this document, the term "foreigner" refers to countries that are not members of the franc zone. However, with respect to the local issue and offer for sale of foreign securities, the term "foreigner" means all the countries outside the territory of the member state concerned.
	With the exception of the issue and sale in the country of foreign securities, operations in securities are not covered explicitly by specific laws. However, by their nature, these operations are still subject to the provisions governing foreign investment and lending.
	Effective February 1, 1999, transfers related to the sale of foreign securities by residents and to proceeds of disinvestments by nonresidents were allowed. Foreign investment in WAEMU countries became unrestricted. Such operations are subject to reporting for statistical purposes. The prior authorization of the PSFMRC is required for the issuance and marketing of securities and capital assets of foreign entities, as well as for publicity and advertising of investments abroad. Any investment by residents abroad requires the prior approval of the MOF.
On capital market securities	
Shares or other securities of a participating nature	
Sale or issue locally by nonresidents	The sale or issue of securities in Benin by nonresidents is subject to prior PSFMRC authorization.
Purchase abroad by residents	Yes.
Sale or issue abroad by residents	Yes.
Bonds or other debt securities	The same provisions apply as for shares or other securities of a participating nature.
On money market instruments	
Sale or issue locally by nonresidents	Yes.
Purchase abroad by residents	Yes.
Sale or issue abroad by residents	Yes.
On collective investment securities	
Sale or issue locally by nonresidents	Yes.
Purchase abroad by residents	Yes.
Controls on derivatives and other instruments	These instruments, which are virtually unknown in Benin, are governed by the regulations generally applicable to securities and investments, except options, which, effective February 1, 1999, residents may purchase or sell abroad freely.
Purchase locally by nonresidents	Yes.

Sale or issue locally by nonresidents	Yes.
Purchase abroad by residents	Yes.
Sale or issue abroad by residents	Yes.
Controls on credit operations	The issue of a loan in the form of securities requires prior approval by the MOF. Such approval is not required, however, for loans contracted by authorized intermediaries or for borrowing under specific conditions in terms of the amount and interest rate. Effective February 1, 1999, foreign borrowing by residents became unrestricted and is subject only to reporting for statistical purposes.
Commercial credits	
By residents to nonresidents	Granting of such credits is subject to two provisions. (1) Claims resulting from exports of goods must be collected and the corresponding amounts repatriated through the BCEAO within 30 days of the payment due date stipulated in the commercial contract. In general, the period allowed for payment must not exceed 120 days following the arrival of the merchandise at its destination. (2) Claims resulting from services must also be collected and subsequently surrendered to an authorized dealer or to the BCEAO within a maximum of 30 days from the payment due date.
To residents from nonresidents	These credits may be granted freely. Repayment is usually authorized, subject to presentation of the relevant proof of execution of the commercial operation or provision of the service and of the payment due date.
Financial credits	
By residents to nonresidents	The granting of financial credits is subject to prior authorization by the MOF. The transfer of funds abroad for this purpose requires a foreign exchange authorization, submitted to the MOF for approval, along with the appropriate documentation.
To residents from nonresidents	These credits may be granted freely. Transfers of such funds must be processed through an authorized intermediary. However, if these operations take place between a direct investment company established in Benin and its parent company located abroad, they are considered direct investments and are therefore subject to prior declaration to the MOF.
Guarantees, sureties, and financial backup facilities	
By residents to nonresidents	The granting of guarantees, backing, and security is subject to prior authorization by the MOF.
To residents from nonresidents	These facilities are granted freely, and the funds involved must be transferred from abroad by an authorized intermediary. However, if these operations take place between a direct investment company established in Benin and its parent company located abroad, they are considered direct investments and are therefore subject to prior declaration to the MOF.
Controls on direct investment	
Outward direct investment	Investment abroad by a resident, including the purchase of real property, is subject to prior approval by the MOF. A maximum of 75% of such investments may be financed by foreign loans. The investor must submit a written request indicating the authorized intermediary charged with making the payment. Whether the funds are transferred abroad or deposited to a foreign account in francs, the payment may not be made before the end of the period agreed to by the parties.
Inward direct investment	These investments are subject to reporting to the MOF for statistical purposes. The transfer of a direct investment by one nonresident to another nonresident is also subject to reporting to the MOF for statistical purposes.
Controls on liquidation of direct investment	Proceeds from the sale or liquidation of foreign direct investments or the sale of real property may be transferred freely abroad or credited to a foreign account in francs upon presentation of the required documentation to the authorized intermediary responsible for payment.
	The liquidation of investments abroad by a resident requires a declaration to the MOF for information purposes. The reinvestment of the proceeds of the liquidation is subject to the

prior authorization of the MOF. If the reinvestment has not been authorized, the proceeds of the liquidation must be repatriated within one month through an authorized intermediary.

Controls on real estate transactions

Purchase abroad by residents

Investment abroad by a resident, including the purchase of real property, is subject to prior approval by the MOF. The investor must submit a written request indicating the authorized intermediary charged with making the payment. Whether the funds are transferred abroad or deposited to a foreign account in francs, the payment may not be made before the end of the period agreed to by the parties.

Purchase locally by nonresidents

There are no controls on purchases, except in the case of direct investment in an enterprise, branch, or corporation.

Sale locally by nonresidents

Proceeds from the sale or liquidation of foreign direct investments and the sale of real property may be freely transferred abroad or credited to a foreign account in francs upon presentation of the required documentation to the authorized intermediary responsible for payment.

Controls on personal capital movements

Personal capital movements between residents and nonresidents must be made through the Central Bank, the Postal Service, or an authorized intermediary bank, unless prior authorization is obtained from the MOF.

Loans

By residents to nonresidents

Lending by residents to nonresidents requires the prior authorization of the MOF.

The individuals concerned may not engage in such operations as a regular profession without first being licensed and included in the list of financial institutions.

Loans of any kind granted by authorized intermediaries to nonresidents; overdrafts in francs; and, in general, any advance granted to a nonresident are subject to the prior authorization of the MOF with the approval of the BCEAO.

To residents from nonresidents

The borrower must obtain prior authorization from the MOF if the amount of the loan exceeds CFAF 50 million and if the interest rate exceeds the normal market rate. Loans contracted to finance imports and exports are exempt from authorization. Effective February 1, 1999, loans granted by nonresidents to residents are free of controls. These transactions must, however, be reported to the MOF for statistical purposes when they are made and when they are repaid.

Gifts, endowments, inheritances, and legacies

By residents to nonresidents

Inheritances and legacies are generally authorized. Gifts and endowments to nonresidents are subject to the prior authorization of the MOF.

Settlement of debts abroad by immigrants

Immigrants who have obtained resident status must obtain prior authorization from the MOF for the settlement of debts contracted abroad while they were nonresidents.

Transfer of assets

Transfer abroad by emigrants

Upon presentation of emigration documents, the parties concerned may transfer a maximum of CFAF 300,000 a person without prior authorization. Amounts over and above this ceiling may be transferred with authorization from the MOF.

Transfer of gambling and prize earnings

Yes.

Provisions specific to commercial banks and other credit institutions

Borrowing abroad

Authorized intermediaries may borrow freely abroad. Such borrowing must be reported to the MOF for statistical purposes.

Maintenance of accounts abroad

Banks and financial institutions are not authorized to hold liquid assets outside the WAEMU zone, except to cover current operations.

Lending to nonresidents (financial or commercial credits)

These transactions may be conducted freely in the case of commercial credits. Effective February 1, 1999, for other loans and financial credits or the purchase of securities issued abroad, prior authorization by the MOF is required with the approval of the BCEAO.

Lending locally in foreign exchange	Domestic lending denominated in foreign exchange or purchases of foreign currency–denominated securities issued in Benin require prior authorization by the MOF with approval of the BCEAO.
Purchase of locally issued securities denominated in foreign exchange	These purchases require prior approval by the MOF.
Differential treatment of deposit accounts in foreign exchange	
Credit controls	Any overdraft or advance granted to a nonresident requires the prior authorization of the MOF with the approval of the BCEAO.
Investment regulations	The same regulations apply as for foreign investment.
Abroad by banks	Yes.
In banks by nonresidents	Yes.
Open foreign exchange position limits	There are no prudential ratios; open positions result through special derogations.
Provisions specific to institutional investors	Effective February 1, 1999, controls are imposed by the Insurance Code of the Inter-African Conference on Insurance Markets.
Limits (min.) on portfolio invested locally	The Insurance Code in effect in Benin (the CIMA Code) includes rules applicable specifically to the use of the technical reserves of insurance companies.
Other controls imposed by securities laws	Yes.

Changes During 1999

Exchange arrangement	*January 1.* The CFA franc peg to the French franc was replaced with a peg to the euro.
	January 1. Residents were authorized to contract forward exchange cover to settle payments related to imports and exports of goods and services.
Arrangements for payments and receipts	*February 1.* The amount of transfers authorized without supporting documentation was raised to CFAF 300,000 from CFAF 100,000.
Resident accounts	*February 1.* Residents were allowed to open foreign exchange accounts with local banks or with banks abroad after obtaining authorization from the MOF with the approval of the BCEAO. The approval of the president of the Council of Ministers of the WAEMU is no longer required.
Nonresident accounts	*February 1.* Authorizations to open nonresident accounts are issued by the BCEAO. These operations no longer involve the MOF or the president of the Council of Ministers of the WAEMU.
Imports and import payments	*February 1.* The limit for the domiciliation requirement was raised to CFAF 5 million.
	July 1. The WAEMU import classification was implemented.
Exports and export proceeds	*February 1.* Exports to WAEMU countries need not be domiciled.
	February 1. Proceeds from exports to WAEMU countries are no longer required to be repatriated.
Payments for invisible transactions and current transfers	*February 1.* Indicative limits on foreign exchange allowances for travel were eliminated. The threshold of foreign exchange to be surrendered by residents after travel was raised to CFAF 300,000 from CFAF 50,000.
	February 1. Payments and incomes of foreign ships in the WAEMU zone and WAEMU ships abroad are included under current operations.
Proceeds from invisible transactions and current transfers	*February 1.* All amounts due from residents of other countries with respect to services and all income earned in those countries from foreign assets must be collected and surrendered within one month of the due date or the date of receipt.

Capital transactions	*February 1.* Transfers related to the sale of foreign securities by residents and to proceeds of disinvestments by nonresidents were allowed. Restrictions on foreign investment in WAEMU countries and borrowing from residents abroad were abolished. Such operations are subject to reporting for statistical purposes. The prior authorization of the RCPSFM is required for the issuance and marketing of securities and capital assets of foreign entities and for canvassing, publicizing, and advertising investments abroad. Any investments by residents abroad require the prior approval of the MOF.
Controls on derivatives and other instruments	*February 1.* Transfers relating to option purchases were allowed.
Controls on credit operations	*February 1.* Restrictions on foreign borrowing by residents were abolished; such transactions are subject to reporting only for statistical purposes.
Provisions specific to commercial banks and other credit institutions	*February 1.* Loans granted to nonresidents are subject to the prior authorization of the MOF with the approval of the BCEAO.
Provisions specific to institutional investors	*February 1.* Restrictions are imposed by the Insurance Code of the Inter-African Conference of Insurance Markets.

Changes During 2000

Imports and import payments	*January 1.* The WAEMU introduced a CET with four rates (zero, 5%, 10%, and 20%) for all member countries except Guinea-Bissau.

BHUTAN

(Position as of December 31, 1999)

Status Under IMF Articles of Agreement

Article XIV   Yes.

Exchange Arrangement

Currency   The currency of Bhutan is the Bhutanese ngultrum.

Other legal tender   The Indian rupee is also legal tender.

Exchange rate structure   Unitary.

Classification

Conventional pegged arrangement   The ngultrum is pegged to the Indian rupee at par. The rates for currencies other than the Indian rupee are determined on the basis of the prevailing quotations by the State Bank of India for those currencies.

Exchange tax   No.

Exchange subsidy   No.

Forward exchange market   No.

Arrangements for Payments and Receipts

Prescription of currency requirements   No.

Payment arrangements

Bilateral payment arrangements

  Operative   Yes.

Administration of control   The MOF controls external transactions and provides foreign exchange for most current and capital transactions. The MOF has delegated to the Royal Monetary Authority (RMA) the authority to release foreign exchange (other than Indian rupees) for current transactions. The RMA is charged with implementing the surrender requirements for proceeds from merchandise exports and approving the use of foreign exchange for payments for invisible transactions.

Payments and remittances by residents to nonresidents other than in cash and traveler's checks are required to be channeled through authorized banks in Bhutan.

International security restrictions   No.

Payment arrears   No.

Controls on trade in gold (coins and/or bullion)

Controls on external trade   Imports of gold and silver, up to stipulated quantities, by Bhutanese citizens are permitted. Imports beyond this require special permission from the MOF.

Controls on exports and imports of banknotes   The importation and exportation of cash and securities are subject to declaration of value at the customs point of entry into, and departure from, Bhutan.

On exports

  Domestic currency   Yes.

  Foreign currency   Yes.

On imports

Domestic currency Yes.

Foreign currency Foreign currency notes purchased from authorized banks or declared on entry may be exported freely.

Resident Accounts

Foreign exchange accounts permitted The following categories of persons are permitted to open and maintain U.S. dollar–denominated foreign currency accounts with authorized banks in Bhutan: (1) diplomatic missions in Bhutan and their expatriate employees, (2) representative offices of donor agencies and their expatriate employees, (3) third country contracting firms and their expatriate employees engaged to execute projects financed by donor agencies, and (4) any person who is a national of a third country and resides in Bhutan.

Held domestically The accounts may be opened, but approval of the RMA is required.

Held abroad Residents of Bhutan are not allowed to hold foreign exchange accounts abroad. However, Bhutanese citizens living abroad must close foreign exchange accounts upon return and repatriate any balances to Bhutan.

Accounts in domestic currency convertible into foreign currency No.

Nonresident Accounts

Foreign exchange accounts permitted These accounts are permitted, but approval is required.

Domestic currency accounts Yes.

Convertible into foreign currency These accounts are permitted, but approval is required.

Blocked accounts Yes.

Imports and Import Payments

Foreign exchange budget Yes.

Financing requirements for imports No.

Documentation requirements for release of foreign exchange for imports

Domiciliation requirements Yes.

Letters of credit Yes.

Import licenses and other nontariff measures Import licenses are governed by Rules and Procedures for Imports of Goods from Third Countries issued by the MOF. An import license is required for the importation of capital and intermediate goods from countries other than India. Foreign exchange for all payments related to merchandise imports is automatically made available by authorized banks against import licenses.

Import taxes and/or tariffs Imports from India are free from tariffs and are subject only to the Bhutan sales tax. Tax rates range from zero for essential commodities to 50% on tobacco products and alcoholic beverages.

Imports from countries other than India are subject to tariffs. The maximum tariff rate is 30%, with the exception of the rates for beer (50%), and for tobacco and other alcoholic beverages and spirits (100%).

State import monopoly n.a.

Exports and Export Proceeds

Repatriation requirements	Yes.
Surrender requirements	Proceeds in currencies other than the Indian rupee must be surrendered to the RMA either directly or through the Bank of Bhutan within 90 days.
Financing requirements	No.
Documentation requirements	
Letters of credit	Yes.
Guarantees	Yes.
Domiciliation	Yes.
Preshipment inspection	Yes.
Other	Yes.
Export licenses	
Without quotas	Yes.
With quotas	Yes.
Export taxes	Export taxes are applied only to exports of unprocessed timber, apples, oranges, and cardamom. Exports to countries other than India receive a rebate at rates ranging from 5% to 20% of the c.i.f. value, with the lowest rate applying to unprocessed primary products and the highest rate applying to processed products.

Payments for Invisible Transactions and Current Transfers

Controls on these transfers	All invisible payments, other than those made in Indian rupees, must be approved by the RMA. The RMA is charged with setting limits (indicative in most cases) up to which foreign exchange may be made available for payments for invisible transactions.
Trade-related payments	
Prior approval	Yes.
Investment-related payments	Information is not available on the payment of amortization of loans or depreciation of direct investments.
Prior approval	Yes.
Payments for travel	
Prior approval	Yes.
Quantitative limits	There is a travel allowance of $1,500 per ticketed passenger per calendar year. In case of business travel, the foreign exchange cost of an air ticket and country-specific per diem covering accommodation are provided to travelers. There are no time limits, but two weeks is considered the norm.
Indicative limits/bona fide test	Yes.
Personal payments	Educational fees and tuition are covered fully and without any limits through direct payments to the universities or institutions abroad. Students also receive a monthly stipend of $900 and a one-time settling-in allowance of $1,500; the settling-in allowance and three monthly stipends are paid in advance.
	For medical expenses, subject to referral by a local physician for treatment abroad, foreign exchange is provided to cover the cost of treatment and medicine and for living expenses abroad. Living expenses vary from country to country, but there are no set limits for the other expenses, and all reasonable expenses are covered.
Prior approval	Yes.

Quantitative limits	A citizen of Bhutan who, under the recommendation of a medical specialist, is proceeding to a third country for medical treatment is permitted to purchase foreign exchange from authorized banks, within the limit prescribed by the RMA for the cost of treatment, medicine, and living expenses.
Foreign workers' wages	
Prior approval	Any national of a third country who, with the prior approval of the royal government of Bhutan, is employed directly by a public or private organization in Bhutan is permitted to remit his or her salary and savings in foreign exchange through an authorized bank.
Quantitative limits	The RMA may set limits on any or all such remittances as it deems necessary.
Credit card use abroad	
Prior approval	Yes.
Other payments	
Prior approval	Yes.

Proceeds from Invisible Transactions and Current Transfers

Repatriation requirements	Foreign exchange proceeds of any receipts or holdings by Bhutanese citizens and companies should be repatriated to Bhutan by transferring such claims and funds to authorized banks in Bhutan.
Surrender requirements	All receipts from invisible transactions in currencies other than the Indian rupee must be surrendered to the RMA.
Restrictions on use of funds	No.

Capital Transactions

Controls on capital and money market instruments	All capital transactions must be approved by the RMA.
Controls on derivatives and other instruments	There are controls on all derivative transactions.
Controls on credit operations	There are controls on all credit operations.
Controls on direct investment	There are controls on all direct investment transactions.
Controls on liquidation of direct investment	Yes.
Controls on real estate transactions	There are controls on all real estate transactions.
Controls on personal capital movements	
Gifts, endowments, inheritances, and legacies	
To residents from nonresidents	Yes.
Transfer of assets	
Transfer into the country by immigrants	Yes.
Transfer of gambling and prize earnings	Yes.
Provisions specific to commercial banks and other credit institutions	
Maintenance of accounts abroad	Yes.

Investment regulations

   Abroad by banks   Up to $5 million (gross) investment is allowed.

Open foreign exchange position limits   Yes.

Provisions specific to institutional investors

Limits (max.) on portfolio invested abroad   Yes.

Other controls imposed by securities laws   n.a.

Changes During 1999

No significant changes occurred in the exchange and trade system.

BOLIVIA

(Position as of December 31, 1999)

Status Under IMF Articles of Agreement

Article VIII	Date of acceptance: June 5, 1967.

Exchange Arrangement

Currency	The currency of Bolivia is the Bolivian boliviano.
Exchange rate structure	Unitary.
Classification	
Crawling peg	The official selling rate is determined at auctions held daily by the Central Bank of Bolivia (CBB). The official exchange rate is the average of the bid rates accepted in the latest auction and applies to all foreign exchange operations in Bolivia. The auctions are conducted by the Committee for Exchange and Reserves in the CBB. Before each auction, the Committee decides on the amount of foreign exchange to be auctioned and a floor price below which the CBB will not accept any bids. This floor price is the official exchange rate and is based on the exchange rate of the dollar. The CBB is required to offer in all auctions unitary lots of $5,000 or multiples thereof; the minimum allowable bid is $5,000. Successful bidders are charged the exchange rate specified in their bid. In general, the spreads between the maximum and minimum bids have been less than 2%. Economic agents may buy and sell foreign exchange freely. All public sector institutions, including public enterprises, must purchase foreign exchange for imports of goods and services through the CBB auction market. Until January 13, 1999, sales of foreign exchange by the CBB to the public were subject to a commission of Bs 0.01 per $1 over its buying rate when the commission was raised to Bs 0.02.
Exchange tax	No.
Exchange subsidy	No.
Forward exchange market	No.

Arrangements for Payments and Receipts

Prescription of currency requirements	No.
Payment arrangements	
Regional arrangements	Payments between Bolivia and Argentina, Brazil, Chile, Colombia, Ecuador, Mexico, Paraguay, Peru, Uruguay, and Venezuela must be made through accounts maintained with each other by the CBB and the central bank of the country concerned, within the framework of the multilateral clearing system of the LAIA.
Clearing agreements	Yes.
Administration of control	The CBB is in charge of operating the auction market for foreign exchange. The MOF, together with the CBB, is in charge of approving public sector purchases of foreign exchange for debt-service payments.
International security restrictions	No.
Payment arrears	No.
Controls on trade in gold (coins and/or bullion)	Gold may be traded freely, subject to the following tax scale in accordance with the gross value of the sale of gold bullion: 7% for official quotations larger than $700 a troy ounce; 1% for official quotations between $400 and $700 a troy ounce; and 4% for official quotations of less than $400 a troy ounce.
Controls on exports and imports of banknotes	No.

Resident Accounts

Foreign exchange accounts permitted	Yes.
Held domestically	Yes.
Held abroad	Yes.
Accounts in domestic currency convertible into foreign currency	Yes.

Nonresident Accounts

Foreign exchange accounts permitted	Yes.
Domestic currency accounts	Yes.
Convertible into foreign currency	Yes.
Blocked accounts	No.

Imports and Import Payments

Foreign exchange budget	No.
Financing requirements for imports	No.
Documentation requirements for release of foreign exchange for imports	
Letters of credit	LCs have to be opened at a bank in the Bolivian banking system.
Import licenses and other nontariff measures	
Negative list	Certain imports are controlled for reasons of public health or national security.
Import taxes and/or tariffs	Bolivia has a general uniform import tariff of 10%. A tariff of 5% is applied to capital goods and a rate of 2% is applied to imports of books and printed matter. Donations of food, including wheat, are exempt from the import tariff.
State import monopoly	No.

Exports and Export Proceeds

Repatriation requirements	No.
Financing requirements	No.
Documentation requirements	
Preshipment inspection	Effective April 1, 1999, the process of export verification has been eliminated and replaced by a revision process by public entities. If necessary, however, exporters may contract specialized agencies for verification.
Export licenses	No.
Export taxes	There is a system of tax rebates for indirect taxes and import duty paid on production costs of exported goods and services, including the duty component of depreciation of capital goods used. Exporters of small items whose value in Bolivia's annual exports is less than $3 million receive tax rebates of 2% or 4% of the f.o.b. export value under a simplified procedure. Other exporters receive tax and import duty rebates based on annually determined coefficients that reflect their documented cost structure. Effective April 1, 1999, tax rebates for large exporters are based on the duties paid on total production costs.

Payments for Invisible Transactions and Current Transfers

Controls on these transfers

Investment-related payments	There are no controls on the payment for amortization of loans or depreciation of direct investments.
Prior approval	Public sector purchases of foreign exchange for debt service must be approved by the MOF and the CBB. Profit remittances are subject to a 12.5% tax, which is computed as equivalent to the 25% income tax times the presumed net profit of 50% of the amount remitted.

Proceeds from Invisible Transactions and Current Transfers

Repatriation requirements	No.
Restrictions on use of funds	No.

Capital Transactions

Controls on capital and money market instruments	No.
Controls on derivatives and other instruments	No.
Controls on credit operations	
Commercial credits	
To residents from nonresidents	All foreign credits, including suppliers' credits to government agencies and autonomous entities, and credits to the private sector with official guarantees are subject to prior authorization by the MOF and to control by the CBB. All proceeds of borrowings from foreign public sector agencies must be surrendered to the CBB.
Financial credits	
To residents from nonresidents	Yes.
Controls on direct investment	No.
Controls on liquidation of direct investment	No.
Controls on real estate transactions	No.
Controls on personal capital movements	No.
Provisions specific to commercial banks and other credit institutions	
Borrowing abroad	Financial institutions may make loans in the form of credits denominated in foreign currency for imports of capital goods and inputs for the external sector with resources from international financial institutions, foreign government agencies, or external lines of credit. All overseas credits of less than a two-year term are subject to reserve requirements.
Differential treatment of deposit accounts in foreign exchange	
Reserve requirements	Reserve requirements for domestic and foreign exchange deposits are equal at 2%, except for time deposits for a period of more than six months and less than one year, for which foreign exchange deposits have a reserve requirement of 2%, while domestic currency time deposits are exempt.
Open foreign exchange position limits	The limit is 80% of the value of the banks' net worth minus their fixed assets.

On resident assets and liabilities	Yes.
On nonresident assets and liabilities	Yes.
Provisions specific to institutional investors	
Limits (max.) on portfolio invested abroad	The maximum limit that pension fund administrators may invest abroad varies between 10% and 50% of the total value of the Individual Capitalization Fund. The specific limit is decided by the CBB. Pension fund administrators may invest abroad through authorized primary and secondary markets.
Other controls imposed by securities laws	No.

Changes During 1999

Exchange arrangement	*January 13.* The commission on the sales of foreign exchange by the CBB to the public was increased to BS 0.02 per $1.
Exports and export proceeds	*April 1.* Tax rebates for large exporters are based on the duties paid on their total production costs, while the process of export verification was eliminated and replaced by a pension process managed by public entities.

BOSNIA AND HERZEGOVINA

(Position as of December 31, 1999)

Status Under IMF Articles of Agreement

Article XIV	Yes.

Exchange Arrangement

Currency	The currency of Bosnia and Herzegovina is the convertible marka.
Other legal tender	The deutsche mark circulates widely in the two constituent entities of Bosnia and Herzegovina. In addition, the Croatian kuna circulates widely in the Croat majority area of Bosnia and Herzegovina, and the Yugoslav dinar circulates in the Republika Srpska.
Exchange rate structure	Unitary.
Classification	
Currency board arrangement	The convertible marka is pegged to the deutsche mark at par. The Central Bank of Bosnia and Herzegovina (CBBH) no longer publishes indicative exchange rates for other currencies. The CBBH guarantees unrestricted convertibility of the convertible marka for deutsche mark.
Exchange tax	No.
Exchange subsidy	No.
Forward exchange market	No.

Arrangements for Payments and Receipts

Prescription of currency requirements	No.
Payment arrangements	No.
Administration of control	There are no foreign exchange controls in place for transactions in convertible marka.
International security restrictions	n.a.
Payment arrears	n.a.
Controls on trade in gold (coins and/or bullion)	n.a.
Controls on exports and imports of banknotes	
On exports	
Domestic currency	Yes.
Foreign currency	There are no limits on the amount of foreign currency that may be taken across international borders.

Resident Accounts

Foreign exchange accounts permitted	Yes.
Held domestically	Individuals and exporters may hold foreign exchange in accounts with commercial banks and do not need to supply evidence of the source of these funds.
Held abroad	These accounts may be opened, but approval is required from the MOF in the two entities.

| Accounts in domestic currency convertible into foreign currency | The conversion of convertible marka deposits into deutsche mark is guaranteed, and commercial banks may convert balances on these accounts into any other currency. |

Nonresident Accounts

Foreign exchange accounts permitted	No approval is required if the investment is registered in accordance with the investment law.
Domestic currency accounts	Yes.
Convertible into foreign currency	These accounts may be converted, but approval is required.
Blocked accounts	Yes.

Imports and Import Payments

Foreign exchange budget	No.
Financing requirements for imports	No.
Documentation requirements for release of foreign exchange for imports	No.
Import licenses and other nontariff measures	
Positive list	Yes.
Negative list	Yes.
Open general licenses	Yes.
Licenses with quotas	Yes.
Other nontariff measures	Yes.
Import taxes and/or tariffs	No.
State import monopoly	No.

Exports and Export Proceeds

Repatriation requirements	Yes.
Surrender requirements	Yes.
Financing requirements	No.
Documentation requirements	Exporters have to be authorized to engage in foreign trade. Customs requires that exporters provide documents accompanying the goods.
Export licenses	No.
Export taxes	No.

Payments for Invisible Transactions and Current Transfers

Controls on these transfers	No.

Proceeds from Invisible Transactions and Current Transfers

Repatriation requirements	Yes.

Restrictions on use of funds	Following an agreement with Germany, the CBBH will provide documentation to Germany on pensions from Germany that are being paid by the commercial banks under its jurisdiction to the workers concerned.

Capital Transactions

Controls on capital and money market instruments	No.
Controls on derivatives and other instruments	No.
Controls on credit operations	
Commercial credits	
By residents to nonresidents	Yes.
To residents from nonresidents	Yes.
Financial credits	
By residents to nonresidents	Yes.
Guarantees, sureties, and financial backup facilities	
By residents to nonresidents	Only prudential regulations on banks apply.
Controls on direct investment	No.
Controls on liquidation of direct investment	Full repatriation of capital is permitted after compliance with tax laws.
Controls on real estate transactions	
Purchase abroad by residents	MOF approval is required.
Purchase locally by nonresidents	Yes.
Controls on personal capital movements	
Loans	
By residents to nonresidents	Yes.
To residents from nonresidents	The foreign exchange law prescribes limits.
Gifts, endowments, inheritances, and legacies	
By residents to nonresidents	Yes.
Transfer of assets	
Transfer abroad by emigrants	Yes.
Transfer into the country by immigrants	Yes.
Transfer of gambling and prize earnings	Yes.
Provisions specific to commercial banks and other credit institutions	
Borrowing abroad	Yes.
Maintenance of accounts abroad	Yes.
Lending locally in foreign exchange	Yes.

Purchase of locally issued securities denominated in foreign exchange	Yes.
Differential treatment of deposit accounts in foreign exchange	
Reserve requirements	Yes.
Liquid asset requirements	Yes.
Credit controls	Yes.
Investment regulations	
Abroad by banks	Yes.
In banks by nonresidents	Yes.
Open foreign exchange position limits	Yes.
Provisions specific to institutional investors	No.
Other controls imposed by securities laws	There are legal controls on stocks, shares, and securities.

Changes During 1999

No significant changes occurred in the exchange and trade system.

BOTSWANA

(Position as of December 31, 1999)

Status Under IMF Articles of Agreement

Article VIII

Date of acceptance: November 17, 1995.

Exchange Arrangement

Currency

The currency of Botswana is the Botswana pula.

Exchange rate structure

Dual

Some external loans undertaken by parastatals before October 1, 1990, are protected from exchange rate movements under a Foreign Exchange Risk-Sharing Scheme (FERSS). Under the scheme, risks associated with exchange rate fluctuations up to 4% are fully borne by the borrower, while the next 6% and the following 5% of fluctuations are shared between the borrower and the government in ratios of 50:50 and 25:75, respectively. Risks associated with exchange rate fluctuations in excess of 15% are fully borne by the government. The scheme is symmetrical in that the borrower and the government share any gains from an appreciation in the external value of the pula on the same basis. Under the FERSS, borrowers obtain foreign exchange for servicing their external debt at exchange rates that may differ from the market rate by more than 2%. The scheme is to be phased out once the existing loans are fully repaid. No new loans will be issued under this scheme.

Classification

Conventional pegged arrangement

The exchange rate of the pula is determined with reference to a weighted basket of currencies comprising the SDR and the South African rand. The central bank deals in four currencies: the dollar, the South African rand, the euro, and the pound sterling. Foreign exchange bureaus are licensed to deal in foreign currencies, on a spot basis only.

Exchange tax

No.

Exchange subsidy

No.

Forward exchange market

Forward exchange cover is offered by the commercial banks, and the maturity dates of forward exchange contracts/transactions are not restricted.

Official cover of forward operations

Yes.

Arrangements for Payments and Receipts

Prescription of currency requirements

The requirement that payments from abroad be made in foreign currency was abolished with the removal of exchange controls on February 8, 1999. Transacting parties are now free to determine the currency of the transaction. Residents are permitted to make payments for goods and services sourced from outside Botswana using pula-denominated checks, provided that the traders outside Botswana are willing to accept their collection by banks outside Botswana. Such transactions are subject to supporting documentation for checks in amounts exceeding P 10,000.

Payment arrangements

Bilateral payment arrangements

Botswana is a signatory to various bilateral trade agreements with the following countries: China, the Czech Republic, Republic of Korea, Malawi, Romania, Russia, the Slovak Republic, the Federal Republic of Yugoslavia (Serbia/Montenegro), Zambia, and Zimbabwe.

Operative

Yes.

Inoperative

Yes.

Regional arrangements

Botswana is a member of the SACU, which allows for free import movements and, hence, has no restrictions on trade-related payments to or from SACU countries.

Administration of control	Until the abolition of exchange controls on February 8, 1999, the Bank of Botswana administered exchange controls on behalf of the government of Botswana. For practical/operational purposes, several administrative powers of the Bank of Botswana had been delegated to commercial banks.
International security restrictions	No.
Payment arrears	No.
Controls on trade in gold (coins and/or bullion)	Until the abolition of exchange controls on February 8, 1999, dealing in gold was restricted. Since then, there are no restrictions on trading or owing precious metals in the form of articles of commerce, such as coins, but there are restrictions on possession of unwrought precious metals, such as bullion, as per section 3 of the Unwrought Precious Metal Act, §20.03.
Controls on exports and imports of banknotes	No.
On exports	
Domestic currency	Until February 8, 1999, residents were allowed to export up to P 10,000 a person a day. Since then, travelers may export any amount and are only required to complete a declaration form for amounts equal to or in excess of P 10,000 at the time of travel.
Foreign currency	Until February 8, 1999, residents were allowed to take out up to the equivalent of P 10,000 a trip. Visitors may take out any foreign currency that they legitimately own, subject to completion of a declaration form for any amount equal to or greater than P 10,000.

Resident Accounts

Foreign exchange accounts permitted	Yes.
Held domestically	Commercial banks are authorized to open foreign currency accounts for permanent, temporary residents, and nonresidents. These accounts facilitate foreign receipts and payments for approved transactions, without having to convert foreign currency receipts into pula and vice versa, and to protect against fluctuations in exchange rates. Commercial banks are authorized to open foreign currency accounts for their customers for any amount in any currency at the discretion of banks.
Held abroad	Residents are permitted to open and maintain foreign currency abroad without prior approval from the Bank of Botswana.
Accounts in domestic currency convertible into foreign currency	No.

Nonresident Accounts

Foreign exchange accounts permitted	Yes.
Domestic currency accounts	Yes.
Convertible into foreign currency	Yes.
Blocked accounts	No.

Imports and Import Payments

Foreign exchange budget	No.
Financing requirements for imports	
Advance payment requirements	Until February 8, 1999, when exchange controls were abolished, advance payments were permitted only for a legitimate commercial need.

Documentation requirements for release of foreign exchange for imports	Until February 8, 1999, payments for imports of value exceeding P 10,000 a transaction required supporting documentation before the foreign exchange was released.
Import licenses and other nontariff measures	Import licenses are regulated by customs and excise legislation.
Negative list	Yes.
Open general licenses	n.r.
Licenses with quotas	n.r.
Other nontariff measures	n.r.
Import taxes and/or tariffs	As a member of the SACU, Botswana applies a common external tariff only on imports from outside the SACU.
State import monopoly	No.

Exports and Export Proceeds

Repatriation requirements	Until February 8, 1999, residents were obligated to receive proceeds in a foreign currency or from a nonresident pula account within six months of the date of exportation. Effective February 8, 1999, repatriation requirements were abolished. The maximum limits for exports free of payments for the following goods are: bona fide nonmonetary gifts, P 20,000 for a permanent resident a year; rejected goods, P 100,000 a transaction, subject to providing documentary evidence; and commercial samples (i.e., goods for exhibitions or other promotional purposes), P 150,000 a transaction.
Surrender requirements	Retention of export proceeds for up to one year to finance certain transactions was permitted by the Bank of Botswana on a case-by-case basis. Effective February 8, 1999, surrender requirements were abolished.
Financing requirements	n.r.
Documentation requirements	No.
Export licenses	Certain exports are subject to licensing, mainly for revenue reasons. The exportation of a few items, such as precious and semiprecious stones, requires permits.
Without quotas	Yes.
Export taxes	No.

Payments for Invisible Transactions and Current Transfers

Controls on these transfers	Until February 8, 1999, when exchange controls were abolished, authorized dealers required documentary evidence for payments in excess of P 10,000 a transaction to establish that the payment is for a legitimate purpose and a current account transaction.
Investment-related payments	Authorized dealers may authorize remittances of interim dividends without reference to the Bank of Botswana for companies listed in the Botswana Stock Exchange (BSE) and may approve other remittances of dividends/profits without reference to the Bank of Botswana subject to satisfactory supporting documentation.
Quantitative limits	Authorized dealers were permitted to authorize interest payments at a rate not exceeding 2% a month on import-related payment charges, i.e., interest charged on arrears, but prior Bank of Botswana approval was required if the charge was more than 2% a month. The repayment of loans was not to be more than P 2 million for a company and P 200,000 for individuals. Effective February 8, 1999, these requirements were abolished.
Indicative limits/bona fide test	Until February 8, 1999, there were indicative limits for the payment of interest.
Payments for travel	
Quantitative limits	Permanent and temporary residents were permitted to retain unused foreign exchange travel facilities in foreign currency notes, coins, or traveler's checks up to the equivalent of

P 10,000 instead of P 2,000. Any excess amount was to be surrendered to an authorized dealer within six months of the date of return. Effective February 8, 1999, these requirements were abolished.

Personal payments

Prior approval

Until February 8, 1999, residents required prior approval of the Bank of Botswana to take up pension from nonresidents.

Foreign workers' wages

Quantitative limits

Effective February 8, 1999, no restrictions are imposed on remittances of foreign workers' wages.

Proceeds from Invisible Transactions and Current Transfers

Repatriation requirements

No.

Surrender requirements

The amount of unused foreign currency for travel that a resident was allowed to retain for future travel use was the equivalent of P 10,000 in currency or traveler's checks. Any excess amount was to be surrendered within six months of the date of return. Effective February 8, 1999, foreign currencies received in payment for goods and services in Botswana by traders may be retained and surrendered to authorized dealers or other foreign exchange dealers at the discretion of such traders.

Restrictions on use of funds

No.

Capital Transactions

Controls on capital and money market instruments

On capital market securities

Shares or other securities of a participating nature

Purchase locally by nonresidents

No controls are placed on the participation of nonresidents in debt instruments issued in the domestic market, except that nonresidents are not permitted to purchase central bank bills (Bank of Botswana certificates), or any money market instrument, the purpose of which is to mop up excess liquidity in the system.

Sale or issue locally by nonresidents

Nonresidents are permitted to issue long-term, pula-denominated bonds traded on the BSE, subject to the listing requirements of the BSE.

Purchase abroad by residents

Individuals and business entities could invest abroad up to P 1 million and P 30 million, respectively, in offshore securities. These limits were abolished on February 8, 1999.

On money market instruments

Purchase locally by nonresidents

Nonresidents are not permitted to buy the monetary instruments used by the Bank of Botswana to absorb excess liquidity.

Controls on derivatives and other instruments

These controls are subject to foreign exposure limits of a particular bank.

Controls on credit operations

Commercial credits

By residents to nonresidents

Nonresident-controlled companies (including branches of foreign companies) were allowed to borrow locally from all sources up to P 1 million. Banks and other credit institutions in Botswana were permitted to grant loans and other credit facilities to nonresident-controlled entities up to 10:1 debt-to-equity ratio (after the initial tranche of P 1 million), without prior authorization from the Bank of Botswana. These limits were abolished on February 8, 1999.

| *To residents from nonresidents* | Authorized dealers are permitted to receive loan funds from nonresident sources on behalf of the permanent resident customers up to an equivalent of P 200,000 and P 2 million in respect of individuals and companies, respectively, without any prior reference to the Bank of Botswana. Interest on these loans was restricted to 1% above the relevant LIBOR and 0.5% above the bank prime lending rate for foreign-denominated and pula loans, respectively. These limits were abolished on February 8, 1999. |

Controls on direct investment

| Outward direct investment | Authorized dealers were allowed to make foreign currency available to individuals and companies of amounts of up to P 1 million and P 30 million, respectively, for either acquiring interest in existing business ventures or establishing new business. Companies must have been in operation for two years and registered with the Commissioner of Taxes. These limits and requirements were abolished on February 8, 1999. |

| **Controls on liquidation of direct investment** | Proceeds up to P 100 million could be repatriated immediately, but the excess of that amount was allowed to be repatriated in tranches as agreed upon with the Bank of Botswana. With the abolition of exchange controls on February 8, 1999, these limits were removed. |

Controls on real estate transactions

| Purchase abroad by residents | Purchases limited to P 1 million for individuals and P 30 million for business entities were allowed, provided they used their foreign exchange allowances. These limits were removed on February 8, 1999. |
| Sale locally by nonresidents | n.r. |

| **Controls on personal capital movements** | No. |

Provisions specific to commercial banks and other credit institutions

| Lending to nonresidents (financial or commercial credits) | Loans to nonresident customers are restricted to 25% of unimpaired capital of a commercial bank, and in aggregate, loans to nonresidents should not exceed 800% of a bank's unimpaired capital. |

| Purchase of locally issued securities denominated in foreign exchange | These transactions are subject to the listing requirements of the BSE. |

Open foreign exchange position limits	Prudential limits are set for exposure per currency and for the overall foreign currency risk exposure. For major dealing currencies, the limit is 15% of a bank's unimpaired capital and for others, it is 5%. The limit for the overall foreign exchange exposure is 30% of the unimpaired capital of a bank using the shorthand method.
On resident assets and liabilities	n.r.
On nonresident assets and liabilities	n.r.

Provisions specific to institutional investors

| Limits (max.) on securities issued by nonresidents and on portfolio invested abroad | n.r. |

| Limits (max.) on portfolio invested abroad | Institutional investors, such as pension funds and life insurance companies, may invest not more than 70% of their assets outside Botswana. This control is imposed by the Registrars of Insurance and Pension and Provident Funds. |

| Currency-matching regulations on assets/liabilities composition | n.r. |

| **Other controls imposed by securities laws** | n.r. |

Changes During 1999

Arrangements for payments and receipts	*February 8.* All exchange controls were abolished.
Exports and export proceeds	*February 8.* Repatriation and surrender requirements were abolished.

BRAZIL

(Position as of March 31, 2000)

Status Under IMF Articles of Agreement

Article VIII   Date of acceptance: November 30, 1999.

Exchange Arrangement

Currency   The currency of Brazil is the Brazilian real.

Exchange rate structure   Unitary.

Classification

Independently floating   Before February 1, 1999, there were two official exchange markets. In both exchange markets, the rates were freely negotiated between authorized dealers and their clients. Banks conducted arbitrage operations between both markets; spot transactions had to be settled within two working days. The Central Bank of Brazil (CBB) established an adjustable band for the external value of the national currency. Before January 13, 1999, the spread of the intraband was 140 basis points between R$1.1975 per US$1 (floor) and R$1.2115 per US$1 (ceiling). Rates for other currencies were based on the dollar rates in Brazil and the rates for specific currencies in the international market.

Effective January 13, 1999, the CBB widened the exchange rate band within which the real fluctuated to between R$1.20 and R$1.32. Widening the band allowed for a gradual depreciation of the real. The CBB also announced that it was to adjust the band every three days. The new band allowed for a 10% variation between the floor and ceiling rates. On February 1, 1999, the exchange rate was unified.

CBB interventions in the foreign exchange market will be occasional, limited, and designed to counter disorderly market conditions. On June 21, 1999, a presidential decree was issued adopting an inflation-targeting framework as the guide for monetary policy.

Transactions in the exchange markets are carried out by banks, brokers, and tourist agencies authorized to deal in foreign exchange; the tourist agencies and brokers deal only in banknotes and traveler's checks.

Exchange tax   The maximum tax on credit, foreign exchange operations, insurance operations, and on transactions in financial instruments or securities (IOF) is limited by law to 25%. For foreign exchange transactions, this tax is zero. A 0.5% tax is applied to the following transactions: (1) investments in Brazilian fixed-income funds; (2) inflows related to interbank operations between foreign financial institutions and banks authorized to conduct foreign exchange transactions in Brazil; and (3) holdings of short-term assets in Brazil by nonresidents. Effective March 12, 1999, the tax applied to fixed-income funds was reduced to 2% from 5%. A 2.5% tax is applied to remittances related to obligations of credit card administration companies to pay for purchases by their customers. This tax was reduced to 2% on December 9, 1999. Effective December 29, 1999, inflows related to external loans with a minimum average maturity of 90 days were allowed, but these remittances are taxed at 5%.

Exchange subsidy   No.

Forward exchange market   Banks are permitted to trade foreign exchange on a forward basis within the statutory limits (bought, sold) of the exchange position; such transactions must be settled within 360 days.

Arrangements for Payments and Receipts

Prescription of currency requirements   Prescription of currency is related to the country of origin of imports or the country of final destination of exports, unless otherwise prescribed or authorized. Settlements with Hungary are made under the terms specified in the bilateral agreement.

Payment arrangements

Bilateral payment arrangements

   Operative | Settlements with Hungary are made in dollars every 90 days, and interest rates payable on balances are based on those in the international capital market.

Regional arrangements | Brazil is a member of the LAIA.

Clearing agreements | Payments between Brazil and Argentina, Bolivia, Chile, Colombia, the Dominican Republic, Ecuador, Mexico, Paraguay, Peru, Uruguay, and Republica Bolivariana de Venezuela may be made through special central bank accounts within the framework of the multilateral clearing system of the LAIA.

Administration of control | The National Monetary Council (NMC) is responsible for formulating the overall foreign exchange policy. In accordance with the guidelines established by the Council, exchange control regulations affecting foreign capital and the management of international reserves are under the jurisdiction of the CBB. The Ministry of Planning, Management, and Budget enforces limits on foreign borrowing by the public sector. Foreign trade policy is formulated by the Ministry of Development, Industry, and Trade, implemented by the Secretariat of Foreign Trade (SECEX) and carried out by the Department of Foreign Trade Operations (DECEX). The Department of International Negotiations (DEINT) or the SECEX is responsible for formulating guidelines for tariff policy. The DEINT also decides on changes in customs duties under the provisions of existing legislation. The MOF coordinates public sector import policy.

International security restrictions

In accordance with UN sanctions | There are restrictions imposed on Iraq, Libya, the Taliban (the Islamic State of Afghanistan), and the UNITA movement in Angola.

Payment arrears | No.

Controls on trade in gold (coins and/or bullion) | There are two separate markets for gold transactions: the financial and commercial markets. Transactions that occur in the financial market are regulated by the CBB. The first domestic negotiation of newly mined gold on this market is subject to a 1% financial transactions tax. Rules regarding gold transactions for industrial purposes are defined separately by the federal states, which also establish different rates for the commercial tax levied on them. The CBB and authorized institutions are empowered to buy and sell gold on the domestic and international markets. Purchases of gold are made at current domestic and international prices; the international price is considered a target price.

Controls on domestic ownership and/or trade | Yes.

Controls on external trade | The CBB and authorized institutions may buy and sell gold for monetary use on the international market. Imports and exports of gold for nonmonetary use are subject to the same procedures as those that are applied through the SECEX in respect of other products.

Controls on exports and imports of banknotes | Travelers may take out or bring in domestic or foreign banknotes, checks, or traveler's checks without restriction but must declare to customs any amount over the equivalent of US$10,000.

Resident Accounts

Foreign exchange accounts permitted | These accounts may be held by authorized foreign exchange dealers; Brazilian citizens living abroad; the Brazilian Post Administration; insurance and reinsurance companies and reinsurance brokers; and, effective February 24, 2000, companies responsible for the development and execution of projects in the energy sector.

Held domestically | Yes.

Held abroad | Yes.

Accounts in domestic currency convertible into foreign currency | Only funds deposited in accounts held in Brazil by foreign banks are convertible.

Nonresident Accounts

Foreign exchange accounts permitted

These accounts may be held by embassies, foreign delegations, international organizations, foreign transportation companies, foreign citizens in transit in the country, foreign insurance companies, and Brazilian citizens living abroad. Effective September 10, 1999, the NMC authorized energy companies to open accounts in foreign exchange.

Domestic currency accounts

Yes.

Convertible into foreign currency

Natural and juridical persons (financial and nonfinancial institutions) may hold these accounts. Only the resources deposited in nonresident banks or the resources that have entered Brazil through foreign currency sales and have not been withdrawn may be repatriated to foreign countries. These resources continue to be available to nonresidents once they are withdrawn, but only in the national currency.

Blocked accounts

No.

Imports and Import Payments

Foreign exchange budget

n.a.

Financing requirements for imports

External financing of imports for periods in excess of 360 days must be registered in the Financial Operations Registry, an electronic system. Financing is considered approved by the CBB if the registration is not refused by its Department of Foreign Capital (FIRCE) within five days. The time to finalize anticipatory settlements for critical imports is 30 days.

Documentation requirements for release of foreign exchange for imports

All importers must be registered in the SECEX Importer and Exporter Register. Goods may be imported by firms and persons and must be registered by the CBB, except for imports by the public sector (federal, state, and municipal); imports by PETROBRAS (the Brazilian government oil enterprise) and contracting or subcontracting firms engaged in oil exploration through risk contracts; imports of medicine by individuals up to US$5,000; imports of samples without commercial value, except for pharmaceutical products up to US$1,000; imports of products, except for those prohibited or under special control, by individuals for personal consumption; and imports of goods considered as passengers' baggage for personal use. The import subsystem of the Integrated Foreign Trade System (SISCOMEX/IMPORT) allows importers, carriers, banks, and brokers to register the various stages of an import process directly through the interlinked computers of SECEX, customs, and the CBB. Imports are grouped into the following three broad categories: (1) imports that do not require prior administrative documentation, including samples without commercial value and certain educational materials; (2) imports that require prior import licenses issued by the SISCOMEX/IMPORT; and (3) prohibited imports. Importers were permitted to purchase foreign exchange in the exchange market within 360 days of the settlement date. Effective October 28, 1999, the CBB eliminated the requirement for contracting foreign exchange for transactions related to imports. There is also a limit on the direct importation and purchase on the domestic market of consumer goods by the public sector (the government, autonomous agencies, and public enterprises).

Domiciliation requirements

Required for imports originating or proceeding from countries under restrictions determined by the UN Security Council and imports of bovines in any form originating or proceeding from the United Kingdom.

Letters of credit

The drafts or LCs must be settled on maturity against the presentation of the appropriate documents by the importer. Exchange contracts for imports financed under LCs must be closed on the date of settlement or two working days before the maturity date of the LCs.

Other

Federal ministries and subordinate agencies and public enterprises are required to submit for approval by the Ministry of Planning, Management, and Budget an annual investment program specifying their expected import requirements.

Import licenses and other nontariff measures

Some imports require prior approval (i.e., an import license) from the DECEX. This approval is usually given promptly to registered importers of nonprohibited items. As a rule, licenses are valid for 60 days, except for imports of custom-made capital goods. The Secretariat of Federal Revenue issues clearance certificates for certain groups of commodities to special bonded warehouse importers. Import licenses for a number of specified imports may be obtained after the commodities have been landed and customs clearance obtained. The importation of certain products requires approval of the Ministry of Science and Technology. For some products, eligibility for exemption from import duties may be precluded by the existence of a satisfactory domestic equivalent. Most imports are exempt from prior approval requirements. As of January 1, 1999, all trade between MERCOSUR partners was liberalized, with the exception of trade in automobiles and sugar.

Negative list	Imports of agrochemical products not authorized under Brazilian regulations; weapons; and certain drugs that are not licensed for reasons of security, health, morality, or industrial policy are prohibited.
Open general licenses	OGLs are no longer issued by the SECEX. Issuance is restricted to their annexes, up to the existing remainder of issued OGLs.
Licenses with quotas	In addition to imports under Brazilian concessions covered by the LAIA agreement, goods imported into the Manaus and Tabatinga free zones are subject to an annual quota. Foreign goods up to the equivalent of US$2,000 imported into the Manaus free trade zone may be transferred to other parts of Brazil (as a passenger's baggage) free of import taxes. In accordance with WTO rules, quotas are imposed on imports of textiles from China, Hong Kong SAR, Korea, Panama, and Taiwan Province of China due to their effect on the domestic industry. The tariff rate on imports of toys is 25% plus a possible safeguard extension of 15%. For vehicles carrying more than nine persons, the tariff is 65%. For automobiles, transport vehicles, motorcycles, and bicycles, tariffs are 35%, while assemblers established in Brazil may be favored with a special tariff of 17.5%.
Other nontariff measures	Sanitation and measurement requirements must be observed.
Import taxes and/or tariffs	The MERCOSUR customs union agreement stipulates a CET ranging from zero to 20% on about 85% of traded goods, and the remaining 15% of goods (including a list of national exceptions, capital goods, and computer goods) are subject to a schedule of adjustments designed to bring them into line with the CET within five or six years. The adjustment regime allowed Brazil and Argentina to maintain tariffs on some intra-area trade until January 1, 1999, and Paraguay and Uruguay to maintain some intra-area tariffs until January 1, 2000. The number of goods on Brazil's list of national exceptions to MERCOSUR is 450.
Taxes collected through the exchange system	Foreign exchange transactions related to imports of goods have IOF exemption, and foreign exchange transactions related to imports of services have a tariff of zero.
State import monopoly	Imports of petroleum and derivatives are conducted by the state.

Exports and Export Proceeds

Repatriation requirements	Yes.
Surrender requirements	Proceeds must be surrendered before 180 days from the shipment date or 20 days after receipt of proceeds, whichever comes first.
Financing requirements	Advances on foreign exchange contracts are allowed for operations with terms up to 360 days.
Documentation requirements	Documentation includes invoices, international shipment notification, and export registration. There is a simplified arrangement for foreign exchange transactions related to exports up to the equivalent of US$10,000.
Preshipment inspection	Inspection is required for commodities subject to standardization.
Export licenses	Exports of wild animals and their hides, hair, plumes, or eggs in any form; jacaranda-da-Bahia wood; ipecacuanha plants; red and drab varieties of honey; and antiques of more than 100 years are prohibited. Exports of certain goods require prior approval of the SECEX, including those effected through bilateral accounts, exports without exchange cover, exports on consignment, reexports, commodities for which minimum export prices are fixed by the SECEX, and exports requiring prior authorization from government agencies. SISCOMEX integrates the activities related to the registration, monitoring, and control of

foreign trade operations into a single computerized flow of information. The SISCOMEX comprises two subsystems (exports and imports). The exports subsystem allows exporters, carriers, banks, and brokers to register the various stages of an export process directly through the interlinked computers of the SECEX, customs, and the CBB.

With quotas	Exports of sawed or cleft pine woods, mahogany, Brazilian walnut, and virola are subject to quotas. For exports of ethyl alcohol and sugar in any form, including sugarcane syrup inappropriate for human consumption, the eligibility for exemption from the export tax of 40% is subject to quotas on the basis of an annual quantity exceeding domestic necessity authorized by the Industry, Trade, and Tourism Minister and the MOF. Imports under Brazilian concessions subject to quotas due to agreements in the LAIA member countries and goods imported into the Manaus and Tabatinga free zones are subject to an annual quota. Foreign goods up to the equivalent of US$2,000 imported into the Manaus free trade zone may be transferred to other parts of Brazil (as a passenger's baggage) free of import taxes.
Export taxes	Exports are free from these taxes or are subject to a zero rate duty, with the exception of exports of (1) raw hides, which are subject to an export duty of 9%; and (2) cigarettes to Latin America, which are subject to an export duty of 150%. On January 31, 1999, the interest rate equalization feature of the federal export financing facility was eliminated on exports of consumer goods destined to MERCOSUR countries.

Payments for Invisible Transactions and Current Transfers

Controls on these transfers	Payments for current invisibles not covered by current regulations require approval from the CBB's Exchange Department (DECAM) or the FIRCE. Indicative limits/bona fide tests apply to all payments for invisible transactions and current transfers.
Trade-related payments	For unloading and storage costs there are established rules and surveillance procedures related to the operations freely conducted in the commercial market. Regulations on insurance and reinsurance transactions in foreign currency are set by the National Council on Private Insurance.
Prior approval	Yes.
Indicative limits/bona fide test	Yes.
Investment-related payments	In addition to certain restrictions on remittances stipulated in the Foreign Investment Law, limits on income tax deductions are placed on remittances of royalties and technical assistance fees. It has been possible, however, to make payments of interest on own capital. This kind of payment may be deducted from income tax liability to determine the taxable income of companies, subject to a 15% income withholding tax. Profit remittances related to direct investments are exempt from withholding for income tax purposes. Payments due to depreciation of direct investments are not established by the laws and regulations. As a result, remittances abroad from direct investments are treated as dividends, interest on own capital, capital gains, and return (repatriation) of capital.
Prior approval	Payments for medium- and long-term external debt are subject to prior approval by, and registration with, the CBB's FIRCE, and require a certificate of registration, which is the authorization to remit abroad the related interest, expenses, and fees, provided that due taxes are paid. Profit and dividend remittances are allowed only when the initial foreign capital concerned, including reinvestments, contracts for patents and trademarks, and for technical, scientific, and administrative assistance, has been registered with the CBB's FIRCE. Those contracts must be registered with the Financial Registration, which is an electronic system.
Quantitative limits	Amounts due as royalties for patents or for the use of trademarks, as well as for technical, scientific, and administrative assistance and the like, may be deducted from income tax liability to determine the taxable income, up to the limit of 5% of gross receipts in the first five years of the company's operation. Amounts exceeding this limit are considered profits.
Indicative limits/bona fide test	Yes.

Payments for travel

    Indicative limits/bona fide test   Yes.

Personal payments

    Indicative limits/bona fide test   Yes.

Foreign workers' wages

    Indicative limits/bona fide test   Yes.

Credit card use abroad

    Indicative limits/bona fide test   Yes.

Other payments

    Indicative limits/bona fide test   Yes.

Proceeds from Invisible Transactions and Current Transfers

Repatriation requirements   Yes.

Surrender requirements   Exchange proceeds from current invisibles must be sold to the authorized banks at the prevailing market rate.

Restrictions on use of funds   n.a.

Capital Transactions

Controls on capital and money market instruments   Residents are allowed to purchase bonds or other debt securities, money market securities, and collective investment securities through dedicated offshore investment funds (FIEX).

Foreign investment funds are organized in the form of open-end mutual funds. Participation is limited exclusively to natural and juridical persons, and to funds and other collective investment entities resident, domiciled, or headquartered in Brazil. Foreign investment funds may be managed by a multipurpose bank, commercial bank, investment bank, brokerage firm, or securities distributor under the supervision and direct responsibility of the manager of the institution.

Until February 10, 1999, a minimum of 60% of the fund's investments had to be in securities representative of the federal government's external debt and a maximum of 40% in other securities traded in the international market. Then, the minimum share of Brady bonds in FIEX funds was increased to 80%. These securities must be kept abroad in a custodian account in the fund's name. The fund is authorized to conduct operations in organized derivative markets abroad solely for the purpose of hedging the securities making up the respective portfolio.

Inward and outward transfers of resources through foreign investment funds are subject to registration with the CBB for purposes of monitoring and controlling Brazilian investment, as well as the respective income, investment repatriation, and capital gains. Transfers are processed in foreign currency through the free exchange rate market.

On June 17, 1999, a 0.38% tax was levied on all financial transactions.

Earnings from the redemption of shares of foreign investment funds are subject to an IOF of 0.38%. There is also a 20% income tax to be withheld by the managing institution of the foreign investment funds on the date of the redemption payment or credit and to be paid within three working days of the two-week period following the occurrence of the taxable event. Effective July 1, 1999, a 15% tax was levied on foreign investment profits from Brazilian fixed-income funds.

On capital market securities

*Shares or other securities of a
participating nature*

   Purchase locally by nonresidents

The direct purchase of shares of Brazilian companies by nonresidents basically occurs through direct investments and portfolio investments made by the representatives in the country. Effective March 31, 2000, nonresidents were allowed to purchase shares and other securities listed in the Brazilian stock market. Depositary receipts (DRs) constitute another method of acquiring shares through stock exchanges in the MERCOSUR environment.

The representative of nonresidents in the country is responsible for the registration of foreign investment with the CBB, foreign exchange settlements, the collection of taxes, portfolio bookkeeping, and the safekeeping of documents related to the portfolio.

There is no limit or hold period for financial transfers resulting from inflows, flowbacks, and profits or dividends from capital duly registered with the CBB, provided that the accounting rules and tax laws are complied with. The transfers must be processed through banks authorized to conduct foreign exchange operations, with guaranteed access to the free foreign exchange market to purchase foreign currency.

Natural and juridical persons resident or domiciled in MERCOSUR countries may invest freely in Brazilian stock exchanges without the necessity of trading through investment funds or portfolios. The Brazilian market may be accessed directly by contacting a member institution of the Brazilian securities distribution system, or indirectly through the intermediation of an institution in the securities distribution system of the investor's country.

The Brazilian intermediary institution, through which the foreign investor trades, represents the investor vis-à-vis the Brazilian authorities with respect to the operational, exchange, and tax aspects, and provides information on the operations executed. These investments may be made in dollars, in the currency of the country of origin of the investment, or in reais. Operations involving the repatriation of capital are exempt from income tax withholding.

Earnings from variable-income investments are subject to a 10% income tax withholding (but exempt from income tax on capital gains), and those from fixed-income investments are subject to a 15% income tax withholding, except those from fixed-income funds, which are not taxed.

   Sale or issue locally by nonresidents

The sale of shares of foreign enterprises in Brazil is regulated essentially for the MERCOSUR environment through share custody certificates or directly. The only way to sell other foreign securities in Brazil is through DRs, which allow the placement of certificates representing these shares in the Brazilian market. Inward and outward remittances associated with investments must be processed through banks authorized to conduct foreign exchange operations in the floating exchange rate market for transactions from MERCOSUR countries and in the free exchange rate market for DR transactions. There are no limits or hold periods for the investments, although authorization is required for DR issues.

   Purchase abroad by residents

Brazilian natural and juridical persons may make investments through the purchase of custody certificates on Brazilian stock exchanges representing shares issued by companies headquartered in MERCOSUR countries. These securities may be purchased through foreign investment funds or through direct equity investments in enterprises abroad. Regulations permit employees of firms belonging to foreign economic groups to purchase shares of the main company up to US$20,000. Outside MERCOSUR, residents are allowed to purchase depositary receipts issued abroad based on securities issued in Brazil by resident issuers.

   Sale or issue abroad by residents

In addition to the rules already mentioned governing the purchase of shares on stock exchanges by residents and the specific regulations for MERCOSUR, collective investments may be made through Brazilian investment companies and funds.

Issues of securities abroad by residents are accorded the same treatment as direct external borrowing operations. Thus, exchange contracts involving the entry of foreign currencies must be authorized in advance by the CBB. Fund transfers associated with issues of securities abroad are subject to the conditions of the respective certificates of registration issued by the CBB, the conditions of which are set forth in the contract between the debtor and the creditor.

Bonds or other debt securities

    Purchase locally by nonresidents   Nonresidents are allowed to purchase bonds or other debt securities through dedicated investment funds.

    Sale or issue locally by nonresidents   n.r.

    Purchase abroad by residents   Yes.

    Sale or issue abroad by residents   Bonds and some other debt securities may be issued by residents but are subject to prior approval by, and registration with, the CBB's FIRCE and the issue of a certificate of registration, which is the authorization to remit abroad the related interest, expenses, fees, and amortization of principal, provided that due taxes are paid. There is a minimum average maturity of 90 days. Effective December 29, 1999, the minimum average maturity was eliminated. Foreign loans of less than 90 days are instead subject to an IOF of 5%.

On money market instruments

    Purchase locally by nonresidents   Nonresidents are allowed to purchase money market instruments issued by the central bank through dedicated investment funds.

    Purchase abroad by residents   Yes.

    Sale or issue abroad by residents   Yes.

On collective investment securities   Residents are allowed to issue commercial paper subject to approval by and registration with the CBB's FIRCE and the issue of a certificate of registration, which is the authorization to remit abroad the related principal and other payments, provided that due taxes are paid.

    Purchase locally by nonresidents   Portfolio investments by foreign investors in fixed-income instruments are restricted to two classes of fixed-income funds: those that are subject to a transaction tax of 0.5% from March 17, 1999, through June 30, 1999, and 2% thereafter, and the privatization funds, which are tax free.

Effective March 31, 2000, nonresidents were allowed to purchase collective investments in other securities as well as portfolios of stocks and securities, DRs, conversion funds, privatization funds, real estate investment funds, and emerging enterprises investment funds. The constitution of these funds must be announced in writing to the CBB within a maximum of five days. Funds entering the country are subject to registration with the CBB for purposes of controlling foreign capital and future remittances abroad of cash dividends or bonuses and capital gains realized in the sale of the company's shares.

Inward and outward remittances associated with investments must be processed through banks authorized to conduct foreign exchange operations and having guaranteed access to the free exchange rate market to purchase foreign currency.

    Sale or issue locally by nonresidents   n.r.

    Purchase abroad by residents   Yes.

    Sale or issue abroad by residents   Yes.

Controls on derivatives and other instruments   Effective July 29, 1999, the CBB allowed forward, future, and options transactions in farm products by nonresidents.

Effective March 31, 2000, foreign investors were given access to derivative markets for the first time.

Purchase locally by nonresidents   Any operation by a nonresident investor in derivatives or other future settlements markets may only be performed or registered in stock exchanges, commodities and futures exchanges, or over-the-counter markets organized by an entity authorized by the securities commission or settlement and custody system accredited by the CBB or authorized by the securities commission under their respective jurisdictions. In addition, resident and domiciled natural persons and corporations, including those having their head office abroad; funds; and other entities of foreign collective investment may perform transactions in commodities and futures exchanges involving forwards, futures, and options contracts in farm products. There are no restrictions on investments in derivative operations in Brazil by recipients of direct investments.

Sale or issue locally by nonresidents	Nonresident financial institutions are allowed to issue swaps in the domestic market, subject to constituting the regulatory capital charge against the counterparty credit risk of such operations if they are not guaranteed by a clearinghouse.
Purchase abroad by residents	Private sector entities may engage in hedging operations with financial institutions or stock exchanges abroad to protect themselves against the risk of variations in interest rates, exchange rates, and commodity prices. The costs of such operations must conform to the parameters in force in the international market. The CBB may, at its sole discretion, require foreign exchange compensation sufficient to eliminate the effects of operations not in line with the established objective, or executed outside those parameters, without prejudice to other sanctions that may apply. Payments and receipts in foreign currency scheduled or expected to occur in the future in connection with commercial or financial rights or obligations may also be protected by hedging. Hedging operations, however, are subject to the following limits at any time: (1) in interest rate and currency swaps, the operations are limited to the amount of the underlying commercial or financial rights and obligations remaining in foreign currency; and (2) in commodities swaps, open positions are limited to the physical volume of the commodity to be exported, imported, or traded in the domestic market.
Sale or issue abroad by residents	The same regulations apply as for purchases abroad by residents.

Controls on credit operations

Commercial credits

By residents to nonresidents	Only two forms of credits are permitted: (1) the Exporting Financing Program (PROEX), which is financed with national budget funds—PROEX resources may not be used to establish any facility for foreign public or private entities, insofar as financing is granted on a case-by-case basis and because credit may not be made available to nonresidents for use in several installments spread over a period of time; and (2) the Machinery and Equipment Export Financing Program (FINAMEX), which is operated through agent banks by the Special Agency for Industrial Financing (FINAME). FINAMEX provides funds so that financial institutions (FINAME agents) can grant loans to national exporters at rates and on terms similar to those available to their foreign competitors.
To residents from nonresidents	Commercial credits with terms in excess of 360 days must be authorized by and registered with the FIRCE of the CBB.
	Prepayment of exports must be authorized by the CBB prior to the entry of the foreign exchange into Brazil. Operations governed by these regulations have a 361-day minimum term and are exempt from income tax and from the taxes on credit, exchange, insurance operations, and securities operations. The CBB authorizes and registers external financing for imports of capital goods, intermediate goods, raw materials, and other goods and merchandise, regardless of the type of importer or the destination of the merchandise, if the operations have a term of at least one year.
	In private sector import operations without the direct or indirect surety or guarantee of a public sector entity, the financing terms—interest rate, spread, down payment—are freely contracted by the parties. In the case of a public sector entity and in cases involving the direct or indirect surety or guarantee of a public sector entity, interest rates may not exceed the LIBOR rate for the reference period plus specified maximum spreads.

Financial credits

By residents to nonresidents	Requests for authorization may be approved by the CBB, as there is no legal impediment to doing so.
To residents from nonresidents	The proceeds of financial credits granted to residents must be kept within the country, and the resources must be used for investment in economic activities. Exchange contracts involving the entry of foreign exchange in connection with borrowing are subject to prior approval by the CBB. The minimum average maturity for external loans is 90 days. Effective December 28, 1999, the minimum average maturity was eliminated. Foreign loans of less than 90 days are instead subject to an IOF of 5%.

Guarantees, sureties, and financial
backup facilities

   By residents to nonresidents

Guarantees by nonfinancial juridical persons in credit operations for their foreign subsidiaries are subject to prior authorization by the CBB.

Exchange operations involving financial transfers abroad in the execution of bank sureties and guarantees are carried out exclusively through the floating exchange rate market when such guarantees relate or are linked to (1) imports and other foreign currency operations not covered by certificates issued by the CBB or by a facility; and (2) repatriation of amounts entering the country as advance payment for exports in the event of nonshipment of the goods.

Exchange operations involving financial transfers associated with the execution of payment guarantees for imports, loans, or external financing covered by certificates of authorization or registration issued by the CBB are processed through the free exchange rate market.

   To residents from nonresidents

There are no controls on guarantees provided by nonresidents to residents in connection with foreign capital registered with the CBB, subject to the presentation of a formal statement by the foreign entity furnishing the guarantee. Data concerning the guarantee and the costs incurred in obtaining it are included in the Certificate of Authorization or Registration of the guaranteed operation. If costs are incurred in obtaining the guarantee, the credit operation must be authorized in advance by the CBB.

There are no specific regulations governing other operations. In the event of execution of a guarantee, the beneficiary must arrange for the entry of the corresponding foreign exchange directly through the banking system.

Controls on direct investment

Outward direct investment

Banks authorized to conduct foreign exchange operations may transfer up to US$5 million for each financial group, including all remittances in the last 12 months, and they are basically required to keep on file and make available to the CBB the documents mentioned in said regulations. Transfers exceeding the established limit must first be submitted to the CBB no less than 30 days in advance of the exchange contract, irregardless of the amount. Exchange operations in which the purchaser of the foreign exchange is an entity belonging to the direct or indirect public administration are subject to prior authorization by the CBB. In this case, remittances must be processed through the free exchange rate market.

Brazilian enterprises may invest in financial institutions abroad through the floating exchange rate market. However, such investments by nonfinancial enterprises require prior approval of the CBB and must meet some specified conditions. Investments abroad by institutions authorized to operate by the CBB must obtain the prior opinion of the CBB's Department of Financial System Organization and satisfy several conditions, especially with respect to paid-up capital, net assets, time in operation, fixed-asset ratio, and borrowing ceilings.

Inward direct investment

Applications for the registration of foreign direct investment and technology are not subject to prior authorization. Investments in commercial banks are limited to 30% of the voting capital, if there are controls on the operations of Brazilian banks in the markets where their main offices are located. The establishment in Brazil of new branches of financial institutions domiciled abroad is prohibited. Also, any increase in the percentage of equity participation in financial institutions headquartered in Brazil by natural or juridical persons resident or domiciled abroad is prohibited, except for authorizations resulting from international agreements, from reciprocity arrangements, or in the interest of the Brazilian government as expressed by presidential decree.

In the case of highway freight transportation, there are limitations on equity participation of up to one-fifth of the voting capital stock, except for companies established before July 11, 1980, to which different rules apply. In future capital increases by subscription, however, such entities are required to pay up to four-fifths of said increases in ordinary registered shares through national underwriters.

Foreign participation in journalistic and radio and television broadcasting enterprises is prohibited. Direct or indirect equity participation by foreign enterprises or capital in the health care sector in Brazil is also prohibited, except in special cases.

The registration of foreign investment through the verification of patent or trademark rights as a means of paying in capital is subject to prior recording of the deed of transfer or assignment of the rights to use the patent or trademark with the National Institute of Industrial Property, and is limited to the value stated in the latter. The investment is registered in the currency of the country where the beneficiary is domiciled or headquartered, and must be requested from the CBB by the party receiving the investment.

Foreign investments via the contribution of goods without exchange cover are subject to electronic registration with the CBB and authorization by the SECEX. The goods, machinery, or equipment must be used in the production of goods or the provision of services, must have a useful life of more than five years, and must be part of the enterprise's assets for at least five years.

Investments through currency transfers are not subject to prior authorization. This type of investment may take place through the free exchange rate market to pay up the subscribed capital of enterprises already operating in Brazil, to organize a new enterprise, or to acquire an interest in an existing Brazilian enterprise.

Branches of foreign companies may be opened, subject to the prior issuance of an authorizing decree by the president of the Republic. A branch is considered an office of a foreign enterprise. Enterprises established in Brazil with any degree of foreign equity participation are not covered by this restriction.

The entry of resources associated with the investment must be processed through a banking institution authorized to conduct foreign exchange operations.

Controls on liquidation of direct investment	Remittances of proceeds must be processed through banks authorized to conduct foreign exchange operations.
Controls on real estate transactions	No.
Controls on personal capital movements	
Loans	n.r.
Gifts, endowments, inheritances, and legacies	
By residents to nonresidents	Gifts and endowments require the approval of the CBB.
To residents from nonresidents	There are no controls, but documentary support is required.
Settlement of debts abroad by immigrants	Yes.
Transfer of assets	
Transfer abroad by emigrants	The beneficiary must prove he or she is leaving Brazil, and certificates of the Secretariat of the Federal Revenue are required.
Transfer into the country by immigrants	There are no controls, but documentary support is required.
Transfer of gambling and prize earnings	Remittances for gambling are not permitted.
Provisions specific to commercial banks and other credit institutions	
Borrowing abroad	Foreign borrowing for terms exceeding 360 days is subject to authorization and registration with the CBB. The CBB requires that banks authorized to conduct foreign exchange operations obtain facilities abroad for terms of up to 360 days to extend commercial credit in Brazil.

The National Bank for Economic and Social Development, private investment or development banks, commercial banks authorized to conduct foreign exchange operations, and multipurpose banks with a commercial portfolio (if authorized to conduct foreign exchange operations and holding an investment or development portfolio) are permitted to contract loans abroad to be onlent to enterprises in Brazil by issuing commercial paper. They may also borrow abroad by issuing floating-rate notes, fixed-rate notes, floating-rate certificates of deposit, fixed-rate certificates of deposit, government bonds, and private bonds.

Financial institutions in the National Rural Credit System may borrow abroad to finance costs, investment, or the marketing of agricultural and livestock production.

Banks may raise funds abroad to be onlent to natural or juridical persons to finance the construction or purchase of new real estate. Banks authorized to conduct foreign exchange operations may use facilities contracted for terms exceeding 360 days with banks abroad to finance imports by resident enterprises. The public sector may engage in external credit operations for the settlement of internal debt. The rate of the IOF applied to lending operations in foreign currency is zero.

Effective January 3, 2000, banks may borrow funds abroad to be applied freely in the domestic market.

Lending to nonresidents (financial or commercial credits)	There are no legal provisions authorizing banks or credit institutions headquartered in Brazil to grant financial loans to nonresidents or to purchase securities issued abroad for terms exceeding 360 days. This restriction does not apply to the foreign branches of Brazilian banks with regard to commercial credit.
Lending locally in foreign exchange	All contracts, securities, or other documents, as well as any obligations executable in Brazil that require payment in foreign currency, are null and void. Consequently, banks are prohibited from granting foreign currency loans within Brazil. However, this regulation does not apply to the onlending of external foreign currency loans.
Purchase of locally issued securities denominated in foreign exchange	Domestic operations in foreign currencies are prohibited.
Open foreign exchange position limits	Until February 1, 1999, the limits differed according to the exchange market in which the transactions took place. After February 1, 1999, the following limits were in effect:

(1) Banks authorized to conduct foreign exchange operations could hold long positions of up to US$6 million, including all currencies and all of each bank's branches. Amounts exceeding this ceiling had to be deposited with the CBB in dollars. The ceiling on banks' short exchange position was contingent upon each bank's adjusted net worth. Effective May 27, 1999, open positions in foreign exchange are not to exceed 60% of capital, and banks must increase capital by 50% of the excess of their open positions over 20% of capital.

(2) For licensed dealers (brokerage firms; securities distributors; and credit, financing, and investment enterprises), the ceiling on the long exchange position is US$500,000, and no short exchange position is allowed.

(3) Licensed tourism agencies may not maintain exchange positions, but they are required to observe the daily operational ceiling (cash) of US$200,000; any surpluses have to be sold to licensed banks or dealers.

(4) Providers of tourist accommodations may have cash holdings in foreign currencies of up to US$100,000 to meet their operational needs; any surplus has to be sold to licensed banks or dealers.

Effective October 28, 1999, banks' short foreign exchange position became unlimited.

On resident assets and liabilities	Yes.
On nonresident assets and liabilities	Yes.

Provisions specific to institutional investors

Limits (max.) on portfolio invested abroad	Institutional investors may invest up to 10% of their technical reserves in investment fund shares abroad. Private social security agencies may also invest up to 50% of their reserves, together with other investments up to the same ceiling, in shares of open companies, publicly issued convertible debentures, bonds for subscriptions to shares issued by open companies, and certificates of deposit for shares issued by companies headquartered in MERCOSUR countries.

142

Capital tr ...oney market

Controls to commercial
instrur credit institutions

Provi
ban

March 31. Nonresidents were allowed to purchase shares and other securities listed in the Brazilian stock market.

March 1. Foreign investors were given access to derivative markets for the first time.

January 3. Banks were allowed to borrow funds abroad to be applied freely in the domestic market.

Status Under IMF Articles of Agree...

Article VIII   Date of acceptance: October 10, 1995.

Exchange Arrangement

Currency   The currency of Brunei Darussalam is the Brunei dollar.

Other legal tender   The Singapore dollar is also legal tender.

Exchange rate structure   Unitary.

Classification

Currency board arrangement   The Brunei dollar is issued by the Brunei Currency Board (BCB) only against payments in Singapore dollars and at par. Under the terms of a 1967 Currency Interchangeability Agreement (CIA) between the BCB and the Board of Commissioners of Currency of Singapore (BCCS), the Singapore dollar is customary tender in Brunei Darussalam and the Brunei dollar in Singapore. The BCB and BCCS have accepted each other's currency and have agreed to mutual exchange at par and without charge. They have instructed their banks to do the same with their customers. Any excess currency is repatriated regularly, with the issuing institution bearing the costs, and settlements are made in the other country's currency. The BCB deals only in Singapore dollars and does not quote rates for other currencies. Banks, however, are free to deal in all currencies, with no restrictions on amount, maturity, or type of transaction.

The Brunei Association of Banks fixes daily buying and selling rates for electronic transfers and sight drafts in 17 other currencies on the basis of the interbank quotations for these currencies in relation to the Singapore dollar. Banks in Brunei Darussalam must apply these rates for transactions with the general public for amounts up to B$100,000. Exchange rates for amounts exceeding B$100,000 are set competitively by each bank on the basis of the current interbank quotations for the Singapore dollar on the Singapore market.

Exchange tax   No.

Exchange subsidy   No.

Forward exchange market   There is no forward market for foreign exchange in Brunei Darussalam. However, as a result of the CIA, foreign exchange risk can be hedged in terms of Singapore dollars by resorting to facilities available in that country, including foreign currency futures and options traded on the Singapore International Monetary Exchange, over-the-counter forward transactions arranged by banks in Singapore, and the short-term foreign exchange swap market operated among the banks in the Singapore money market.

Arrangements for Payments and Receipts

**Prescription of currency   No.
requirements**

Payment arrangements

Regional arrangements   Brunei Darussalam is a member of the ASEAN.

Administration of control   There are no formal exchange controls, but the MOF retains responsibility for exchange control matters.

International security restrictions   No.

Payment arrears   No.

Controls on tra~~de~~ and/or and/or bullio~~n~~

Only banks licensed to operate in Brunei Darussalam, and gold dealers and jewelers specifically authorized by the MOF may buy and sell gold bars. Gold bars are not subject to import duty, but a 10% duty is levied on the importation of gold jewelry.

Controls on trade ~~in~~ trade Yes.

Cont~~rols on exports~~ .ports and imports of No.

~~Co~~

Resident Accounts

Foreign exchange accounts permitted	Yes.
Held domestically	Yes.
Held abroad	Yes.
Accounts in domestic currency convertible into foreign currency	Yes.

Nonresident Accounts

Foreign exchange accounts permitted	There is no distinction between accounts of residents and nonresidents of Brunei Darussalam.
Domestic currency accounts	Yes.
Convertible into foreign currency	Yes.
Blocked accounts	No.

Imports and Import Payments

Foreign exchange budget	No.
Financing requirements for imports	No.
Documentation requirements for release of foreign exchange for imports	No.
Import licenses and other nontariff measures	
Negative list	A few imports are banned or restricted for environmental, health, safety, security, or religious reasons.
Import taxes and/or tariffs	Except for cigarettes and alcoholic beverages, most imports are subject to tariff rates of up to 200%. Some 70% of items (including basic foodstuffs, construction materials, and educational materials) are zero rated. Most other goods are subject to tariff rates of 5%, 15%, or 20%. Fireworks are subject to a 30% duty, while automobiles are subject to duties ranging between 40% and 200%, depending on engine size. In accordance with the CEPT scheme for the AFTA, Brunei Darussalam will eliminate its tariffs on imports from other ASEAN members by 2003, with the exception of about 120 tariff lines that are permanently excluded from the plan.
State import monopoly	No.

Exports and Export Proceeds

Repatriation requirements	No.
Financing requirements	n.a.
Documentation requirements	No.
Export licenses	Export licenses are required for alcoholic beverages, cigarettes, diesel, ~~rosene,~~ rice, salt, and sugar.
Without quotas	Yes.
Export taxes	No.

Payments for Invisible Transactions and Current Transfers

Controls on these transfers	There are indicative limits/bona fide tests for all payments for invisible transactions and current transfers.
Investment-related payments	Interest payments are subject to a 20% withholding tax. Information is not available on the payment of amortization of loans and depreciation of direct investments.

Proceeds from Invisible Transactions and Current Transfers

Repatriation requirements	No.
Restrictions on use of funds	No.

Capital Transactions

Controls on capital and money market instruments	No.
Controls on derivatives and other instruments	No.
Controls on credit operations	No.
Controls on direct investment	
Inward direct investment	There are no sectoral controls, but activities relating to national food security and those based on local resources require some degree of local participation. Industries producing for the local market that are not related to national food security and industries that solely export may be fully foreign owned. Joint ventures are particularly encouraged in export-import industries and activities supporting such industries. At least one-half of the directors of a company must be either Brunei citizens or residents of Brunei Darussalam.
Controls on liquidation of direct investment	No.
Controls on real estate transactions	
Purchase locally by nonresidents	Only Brunei citizens are allowed to own land. However, foreign investors may lease land on a long-term basis, including sites destined for industry, agriculture, agroforestry, and aquaculture.
Controls on personal capital movements	
Transfer of gambling and prize earnings	Yes.

...ercial
...titutions

Provisions _deposit_
banks and change

Differen...
accoun... _...nents_   Yes.

Res...atment of deposit
...d by nonresidents
Dif...

a..e requirements   Yes.

...ovisions specific to institutional   No.
investors

Other controls imposed by securities   No.
laws

Changes During 1999

No significant changes occurred in the exchange and trade system.

BULGARIA

(Position as of January 31, 2000)

Status Under IMF Articles of Agreement

Article VIII

Date of acceptance: September 24, 1998.

Exchange Arrangement

Currency

The currency of Bulgaria is the Bulgarian lev.

Exchange rate structure

Unitary.

Classification

Currency board arrangement

An amendment to the Law on the Bulgarian National Bank (BNB) effectively established a currency board arrangement. The deutsche mark was chosen as the peg currency, and the lev was pegged at the rate of lev 1,000 per DM 1, close to the market rate at that time. Effective January 1, 1999, the euro replaced the deutsche mark as a peg at the rate of lev 1,955.83 per €1. The peg was changed to 1.95583 per €1 with the redenomination of the Bulgarian lev on July 5, 1999. The BNB is required to sell and purchase on demand and without restriction currencies of the former EMU member countries for lev on the basis of spot exchange rates that may not differ from the official exchange rate by more than 0.5%.

Exchange tax

No.

Exchange subsidy

No.

Forward exchange market

No.

Arrangements for Payments and Receipts

Prescription of currency requirements

Balances remain on clearing accounts maintained under former bilateral arrangements. These arrangements are now inoperative, and the only transactions that take place on clearing accounts are those that are intended to settle the balances. Valuation and settlement of the balances take place in convertible currencies.

Payment arrangements

Bilateral payment arrangements

Operative

A free trade agreement with Turkey came into effect on January 1, 1999, and one with the former Yugoslav Republic of Macedonia on January 1, 2000.

Inoperative

There are arrangements with Albania, Cambodia, Guinea, the People's Democratic Republic of Korea, the Lao People's Democratic Republic, Romania, and Syria. Bulgaria has outstanding transferable ruble accounts with Cuba, Mongolia, and Romania. The settlement of the debit balance with Romania is under negotiation.

Regional arrangements

Effective January 1, 1999, Bulgaria became a member of the CEFTA.

Barter agreements and open accounts

There are inactive agreements with the Islamic State of Afghanistan, Ethiopia, Ghana, Guyana, Mozambique, Nicaragua, and Tanzania.

Administration of control

Foreign exchange control is exercised by the MOF, the BNB, the customs administration, and the postal authorities.

International security restrictions

In accordance with Executive Board Decision No. 144-(52/51)

Yes.

Payment arrears

Private

Four commercial banks that are in bankruptcy have outstanding debt-service arrears.

147

Controls on trade in gold (coins and/or bullion)

Controls on domestic ownership and/or trade

The MOF controls the acquisition, possession, processing, and disposal of gold, silver, and platinum. The BNB is the only institution entitled to purchase, sell, and hold gold. All domestic transactions for industrial purposes must be conducted at current prices through the BNB. Commercial banks are allowed to make transactions in precious metals. Resident individuals may hold gold but may not trade or deal in it. Effective January 1, 2000, residents carrying out extracting, processing, or other transactions involving precious metals and stones as their business activity are obliged to register with the MOF within 14 days of starting their activity. These activities are included in the banking licenses of commercial banks.

Controls on external trade

Residents carrying out external trade transactions in precious metals and stones are obliged to register with the MOF within 14 days of starting their activity. Natural persons may export and import freely precious metals and stones for personal use after declaring them to the customs authorities. All amounts exceeding personal use are subject to the trade provisions of the Customs Law.

The export and import of precious metals and stones by mail are prohibited. This prohibition does not apply to the BNB and the commercial banks.

Controls on exports and imports of banknotes

On exports

Residents and nonresidents may export domestic or foreign currencies without declaration if the amount is below lev 5,000. Exports of lev 5,001 to lev 20,000 must be declared; nonresidents must also declare the origin of the funds. In the case of exports exceeding lev 20,000, residents must obtain a permit from the BNB, while nonresidents may export the currency after declaration, provided they previously declared it to customs.

   Domestic currency

Yes.

   Foreign currency

Yes.

On imports

Resident and nonresident natural persons may import unlimited amounts of domestic and foreign currency. Amounts exceeding lev 5,000 must be declared to customs.

   Domestic currency

Yes.

Resident Accounts

Foreign exchange accounts permitted

Yes.

Held domestically

Residents may maintain these accounts in Bulgaria. Balances on these accounts earn interest at international market rates. The crediting and debiting of foreign currency accounts are not subject to any regulations. Transfers abroad may be made only by commercial banks after declaring the reason for the transfer or, in the case of amounts exceeding lev 20,000, after documenting the reason for the transfer. If the transfer is related to transactions for which BNB registration is needed, the commercial bank will verify the registration with the BNB.

Held abroad

While opening accounts with foreign banks is not explicitly banned, like all transfers abroad, transfers from Bulgaria to these accounts are subject to regulation. Prior permission from the BNB and MOF is required.

Accounts in domestic currency convertible into foreign currency

No.

Nonresident Accounts

Foreign exchange accounts permitted

The crediting and debiting of these accounts are not subject to any regulations.

Domestic currency accounts

Yes.

Blocked accounts	No.

Imports and Import Payments

Foreign exchange budget	No.
Financing requirements for imports	No.
Documentation requirements for release of foreign exchange for imports	
Other	Yes.
Import licenses and other nontariff measures	Effective January 1, 1999, the registration regime was abolished for tobacco products, livestock and meat, dairy products, and certain grains and sugar. A registration regime was introduced for natural gas and scrap. Effective January 1, 2000, the registration regime applies to goods previously under nonautomatic licensing, such as narcotics, arms, nuclear weapons, etc. Licenses are required for imports of military hardware and related technologies, natural gas, endangered flora and fauna, radioactive and nuclear materials, pharmaceuticals, herbicides, pesticides, unbottled alcohol, jewelry, rare and precious metals, asbestos, asbestos products, narcotic and psychotropic products, gambling machines, etc.
Negative list	Imports of certain goods (dangerous substances with ozone-depleting potential, machinery and equipment for air conditioning using Freon 12, refrigerators, freezers, and other equipment using Freon 11 or 12) are banned for health and security reasons.
Import taxes and/or tariffs	Import tariffs range from zero to 74%, and are calculated on a transaction-value basis in foreign currency and converted to leva. The maximum rate of import tariffs for non-agricultural goods is 30%, and for agricultural goods it is 74%. Certain products are allowed temporarily to be imported without customs duties within specified quantities (active substances for the production of insecticides, fungicides, and herbicides, some agricultural machinery and their spare parts, flour, live breeding animals, etc.). Other products are allowed temporarily to be imported without customs duties (equipment, spare parts, information technology products, and chemicals for control of the environment and emissions control; special installations for recovery of poisoned lands; substances, materials, and equipment for replacement of ozone-destruction technologies; equipment, machines, and spare parts used in mines and geological research activities; installations, equipment, and spare parts for production of energy from nontraditional alternative sources; medical equipment for human and veterinary medicine; etc.). On January 1, 2000, the import surcharge was eliminated and the arithmetic mean tariff for all products was reduced to 16.18% from 17.88%. On January 1, 2000, this mean tariff was reduced to 13.76% from 15.2%. Also on that date, certain temporary import tariff quotas were abolished.
State import monopoly	No.

Exports and Export Proceeds

Repatriation requirements	Proceeds from exports must be repatriated.
Surrender requirements	Proceeds do not have to be surrendered; they may be retained in foreign currencies or sold in the interbank exchange market.
Financing requirements	No.
Documentation requirements	Exports of gold, silver, platinum and articles thereof; solutions; electronic scrap and other products containing precious metals; precious stones; and some varieties of wood must be registered with the Ministry of Trade and Tourism. Effective January 1, 1999, registration (automatic licensing) requirements were abolished for live animals, meat, dairy products, Christmas trees, grapes, wheat, barley, maize, rice, cereal flour, sunflower seeds and oils, sugar, yeast, alcohol, brans, oil cakes, forage, tobacco, skins and hides, and wool. A registration requirement was introduced for scrap metal. Permit requirements (nonautomatic

licensing) were abolished for imports of natural gas and exports of live animals. Effective January 1, 2000, registration requirements were abolished for coal, petroleum, textiles, CDs, and ferrous and nonferrous metals and alloys.

Export licenses	Special licenses are required for the settlement of outstanding balances of multilateral clearing arrangements. Export licenses are required for exports of military hardware and related technologies, endangered flora and fauna, wild plants and animals, livestock, radio-active materials, crafts and antiques, seeds, untreated wood, jewelry, and rare and precious metals. Licenses are normally granted within two working days. On April 27, 1999, the exports to the Federal Republic of Yugoslavia (Serbia/Montenegro) of oil products and some chemical goods (with dangerous substances) were banned for health and ecological reasons.
Without quotas	Yes.
Export taxes	Effective January 1, 1999, the export tax on livestock, scrap, copper products, wool, grain, and raw hides was eliminated. Effective January 1, 2000, the export tax on unprocessed lumber and profiled lumber was eliminated.

Payments for Invisible Transactions and Current Transfers

Controls on these transfers

Trade-related payments

Indicative limits/bona fide test	If the amount exceeds lev 20,000, payments abroad needed for trade are processed by banks against appropriate documents that prove the necessity of the transfer.
Personal payments	These remittances are free if the amount is below lev 20,000. Above that limit, documentary evidence is required.
Indicative limits/bona fide test	Yes.
Foreign workers' wages	Foreign workers' wages may be transferred abroad, provided they have paid their taxes.
Other payments	These payments are free if the amount is below lev 20,000. Above that limit, documentary evidence is required.
Indicative limits/bona fide test	Yes.

Proceeds from Invisible Transactions and Current Transfers

Repatriation requirements	Yes.
Restrictions on use of funds	No.

Capital Transactions

Controls on capital and money market instruments

On capital market securities

Shares or other securities of a participating nature

Purchase abroad by residents	Prior registration with the BNB is required.

Bonds or other debt securities

Purchase abroad by residents	Prior registration with the BNB is required.

On money market instruments

Purchase abroad by residents	Prior registration with the BNB is required.

On collective investment securities

   Purchase abroad by residents   Prior registration with the BNB is required.

Controls on derivatives and other instruments

Purchase abroad by residents   Prior registration with the BNB is required.

Controls on credit operations

Financial credits   Prior registration with the BNB is required.

   By residents to nonresidents   Yes.

   To residents from nonresidents   Yes.

Guarantees, sureties, and financial backup facilities

   By residents to nonresidents   Prior registration with the BNB is required.

Controls on direct investment   No.

Controls on liquidation of direct investment   No.

Controls on real estate transactions

Purchase locally by nonresidents   Prior permission of the MOF is required. Nonresidents may not purchase or own land. If they inherit land, they must dispose of it within a three-year period.

Controls on personal capital movements

Loans   Prior registration with the BNB is required.

   By residents to nonresidents   Yes.

   To residents from nonresidents   Yes.

Provisions specific to commercial banks and other credit institutions

Borrowing abroad   Prior registration with the BNB is required if the bank is only licensed to carry out domestic transactions.

Maintenance of accounts abroad   Prior registration with the BNB is required if the bank is only licensed to carry out domestic transactions.

Open foreign exchange position limits   Each bank is required to observe daily (1) a maximum ratio of up to 25% between its open position in any particular currency and the amount of its own funds, excluding the euro and the currencies of the EMU countries; and (2) a maximum ratio of up to 60% between its net open foreign currency position and the amount of its own funds, excluding the euro and the currencies of the EMU countries.

   On resident assets and liabilities   Yes.

Provisions specific to institutional investors   No.

Other controls imposed by securities laws   No.

Changes During 1999

Exchange arrangement   *January 1.* The euro replaced the deutsche mark as a peg at the rate of lev 1,955.83 per €1.

    July 5. The lev was redenominated by removing three zeros and the key peg was changed to lev 1.95583 per €1.

Arrangements for payments and receipts	*January 1.* Bulgaria became a member of the CEFTA.
	January 1. A free trade agreement with Turkey came into effect.
Imports and import payments	*January 1.* The Export and Import Trade Policy Measures eliminated import licenses for natural gas. The registration regime was abolished for tobacco products, livestock and meat, dairy products, and certain grains and sugar. A registration regime was introduced for natural gas and scrap. The temporary import tariff quotas were abolished. The arithmetic mean tariff for all products was reduced to 16.18% from 17.88%. The maximum rate of import tariffs for nonagricultural goods was set at 35% and for agricultural goods, at 74%.
	January 1. The import surcharge was eliminated.
Exports and export proceeds	*January 1.* The Export and Import Trade Policy Measures abolished the registration requirements for tobacco products, meat, dairy products, wine, and several other products. The license requirements for the export of sunflower oil and livestock were abolished. The export of scrap was required to be registered. The export tax on livestock, scrap, copper products, wool, grain, and raw hides was eliminated.
	April 27. Exports to the Federal Republic of Yugoslavia (Serbia/Montenegro) of oil products and some chemical goods (with dangerous substances) were banned for health and ecological reasons.
Capital transactions	
Controls on direct investment	*January 1.* Tax measures introduced in 1999 carried on the reforms, further broadening the tax base and lowering marginal tax rates. Tax holidays and incentives were removed from the Foreign Investment Act and partially offset by a 10% regional investment tax credit under the Profits Tax Act.
Provisions specific to commercial banks and other credit institutions	*January 1.* Each bank is required to observe daily (1) a maximum ratio of up to 25% between its open position in any particular currency and the amount of its own funds, excluding the euro and the currencies of the EMU countries; and (2) a maximum ratio of 60% between its net open foreign currency position and the amount of own funds, excluding the euro and the currencies of the EMU countries.

Changes During 2000

Arrangements for payments and receipts	*January 1.* Residents carrying out transactions involving precious metals and stones were obliged to register with the MOF within 14 days of starting their activity.
	January 1. A free trade agreement with the former Yugoslav Republic of Macedonia came into effect.
Imports and import payments	*January 1.* The arithmetic mean tariff for all products was reduced to 13.76% from 15.2%.
	January 1. The registration regime was also applied to goods previously under nonautomatic licensing.
Exports and export proceeds	*January 1.* The export tax on unprocessed lumber and profiled lumber was eliminated.
	January 1. The registration of coal, petroleum, textiles, CDs, and ferrous and nonferrous metals and alloys was abolished.

BURKINA FASO

Status Under IMF Articles of Agreement

Article VIII   Date of acceptance: June 1, 1996.

Exchange Arrangement

Currency   The currency of Burkina Faso is the CFA franc.

Exchange rate structure   Unitary.

Classification

Exchange arrangement with no sepa-   The CFA franc is pegged to the euro, the intervention currency, at the fixed rate of
rate legal tender   CFAF 100 per €0.8385. Exchange rates for other currencies are derived from the rate
                                        for the currency concerned in the Paris foreign exchange market and the fixed rate be-
                                        tween the euro and the CFA franc.

Exchange tax   There is a proportional bank commission of 0.25% on transfers to all countries outside
                                    the WAEMU that must be surrendered in its entirety to the treasury. In addition, banks
                                    are allowed to charge an exchange commission of up to 2% on over-the-counter exchange
                                    for French francs.

Exchange subsidy   No.

Forward exchange market   Effective February 1, 1999, residents were authorized to contract forward exchange cover
                                    to cover payments related to imports and exports of goods and services.

Arrangements for Payments and Receipts

Prescription of currency   Because Burkina Faso is linked to the French Treasury through an Operations Account,
requirements   settlements with France, Monaco, and other Operations Account countries (WAEMU
                                    and CAEMC members and the Comoros) are made in CFA francs, euros, or the cur-
                                    rency of any other Operations Account country. Certain settlements are channeled
                                    through special accounts. Settlements with all other countries are usually effected
                                    through correspondent banks in France in the currencies of those countries or in euros
                                    through foreign accounts in euros.

Payment arrangements

Bilateral payment arrangements

  Inoperative   Yes.

Regional arrangements   An Operations Account is maintained with the French Treasury that links Operations
                                    Account countries. All purchases or sales of foreign currencies or euros against CFA
                                    francs are ultimately settled through a debit or credit to the Operations Account.

Clearing agreements   A multilateral clearing agreement exists within the framework of the WAMA between
                                    WAEMU members, Cape Verde, The Gambia, Ghana, Guinea, Liberia, Mauritania,
                                    Nigeria, and Sierra Leone.

Administration of control   Exchange control is administered jointly by the MOF and the BCEAO. Since February 1,
                                    1999, most of the authority to supervise foreign exchange transactions has been delegated
                                    to authorized banks, which are required to report these operations to the MOF. The only
                                    operations that continue to require prior approval from the MOF or the BCEAO involve
                                    residents' investments abroad, domestic accounts in foreign exchange, and resident ac-
                                    counts abroad. The BCEAO is also authorized to collect—either directly or through banks,
                                    financial institutions, the Postal Administration, or judicial agents—any information neces-
                                    sary to compile balance of payments statistics.

Effective February 1, 1999, the amount of transfers authorized without supporting documentation was raised to CFAF 300,000 from CFAF 100,000.

The advertising or offering for sale of foreign or domestic securities in Burkina Faso requires RCPSFM authorization.

International security restrictions   No.

Payment arrears

Official   Restructuring of arrears to Libya and the countries of the FSU is in progress.

Controls on trade in gold (coins and/or bullion)

Controls on external trade   Imports of gold require prior MOF authorization. Exempt from this requirement are (1) imports by or on behalf of the Treasury or the BCEAO; (2) imports of manufactured articles containing minor quantities of gold (such as gold-filled or gold-plated articles); and (3) imports by travelers of gold objects up to a combined weight of 500 grams. Both licensed and exempt imports of gold are subject to customs declaration. Exports of gold are liberalized.

Controls on exports and imports of banknotes

On exports

Domestic currency   The exportation of CFA franc banknotes by nonresident travelers is not prohibited. However, repurchases by the BCEAO of exported banknotes are still suspended. In addition, shipments of BCEAO banknotes among authorized intermediaries and their correspondents situated outside the WAEMU are officially prohibited.

Foreign currency   The reexportation of foreign banknotes by nonresident travelers is allowed up to the equivalent of CFAF 500,000; the reexportation of foreign banknotes above this ceiling requires documentation demonstrating either the importation of the foreign banknotes or their purchase against other means of payment registered in the name of the traveler or through the use of nonresident deposits lodged in local banks.

On imports

Domestic currency   There are no restrictions on the importation by resident or nonresident travelers of banknotes and coins issued by the BCEAO.

Foreign currency   Residents and nonresidents may bring in any amount of foreign banknotes and coins (except gold coins) of countries outside the Operations Account area. Residents bringing in foreign banknotes and foreign currency traveler's checks exceeding the equivalent of CFAF 300,000 must declare them to customs upon entry and sell them to an authorized intermediary bank within eight days.

Resident Accounts

Foreign exchange accounts permitted   Effective February 1, 1999, residents are allowed to open foreign exchange accounts with local banks or with banks abroad after obtaining authorization from the MOF, subsequent to the approval of the BCEAO.

Held domestically   The holding of these accounts is subject to prior approval by the MOF upon the recommendation of the BCEAO and in coordination with the Chairman of the Council of Ministers of the WAEMU.

Held abroad   The opening of accounts abroad by residents is subject to the prior authorization of the MOF, subsequent to the approval of the BCEAO.

Accounts in domestic currency convertible into foreign currency   No.

Nonresident Accounts

Foreign exchange accounts permitted
Effective February 1, 1999, authorization for these accounts is issued by the BCEAO.

Domestic currency accounts
Because the BCEAO has suspended the repurchase of banknotes circulating outside the WAEMU territories, nonresident accounts may not be credited or debited with BCEAO banknotes. These accounts may not be overdrawn without the prior authorization of the MOF, upon recommendation from the BCEAO. Transfers of funds between nonresident accounts are not restricted.

Convertible into foreign currency
Foreign accounts denominated in CFA francs may be freely debited for the purpose of purchases by nonresidents of any foreign currencies on the official exchange market.

Blocked accounts
No.

Imports and Import Payments

Foreign exchange budget
No.

Financing requirements for imports
No.

Documentation requirements for release of foreign exchange for imports

Domiciliation requirements
All import transactions exceeding CFAF 3 million must be domiciled with an authorized bank. The threshold was raised to CFAF 5 million on February 1, 1999.

Preshipment inspection
An inspection is required for quality and price.

Import licenses and other nontariff measures
A technical import visa (certificat de conformité) is required for sugar, insecticides, wheat and cereal flour, tires and inner tubes for motorcycles, vegetable oil, milk, electrical batteries, food preserves, and rice. The Ministry of Industry, Commerce, and Crafts may, on the basis of criteria established by the MOF, waive the prescribed formalities for imports from countries with which Burkina Faso has concluded a customs union or free trade–area agreement.

Positive list
Import licenses were eliminated and replaced with preimport declarations issued for all import operations valued at CFAF 500,000 and over.

Negative list
Imports of ivory and fishing nets with a mesh smaller than three square centimeters are restricted.

Import taxes and/or tariffs
On January 1, 2000, the WAEMU introduced a CET with four rates (zero, 5%, 10%, and 20%) for all member countries except Guinea-Bissau. Imports are further subject to a statistical tax of 1% and a community solidarity tax of 1%. A temporary protection tax of 15% (in other cases 7.5%) may be levied on products upon the authorization of the WAEMU commission, if the effective protection rate has declined by more than 50% (or more than 25%).

All imports from outside the ECOWAS are subject to a solidarity communal levy of 1%, and imports of certain goods that are also locally produced are subject to a protection tax ranging from 10% to 30%. Effective April 1, 1999, the new common tariff categorization for imported products adopted by the WAEMU was introduced.

State import monopoly
No.

Exports and Export Proceeds

Repatriation requirements
Effective February 1, 1999, exports between WAEMU countries are excluded from the repatriation requirement.

Surrender requirements
Export proceeds must be surrendered within one month of the date on which payments fall due. The authorized intermediary banks must then surrender such foreign exchange to the BCEAO via transfer through the bank of issue.

Financing requirements	No.
Documentation requirements	
Domiciliation	All export transactions of more than CFAF 5 million must be domiciled with an authorized intermediary bank, except for exports between WAEMU countries, which, effective February 1, 1999, need not be domiciled.
Export licenses	Export licenses were eliminated and replaced with preexport declarations issued for exports valued at CFAF 500,000 and over. Exports of gold, diamonds, and all other precious metals are subject to MOF authorization. Exports of ivory are subject to special regulations.
Export taxes	Most exports are subject to a customs stamp tax of 6% and a statistical duty of 3%.

Payments for Invisible Transactions and Current Transfers

Controls on these transfers	In the case of transfers not exceeding CFAF 100,000, no supporting document is required. This threshold was increased to CFAF 300,000 on February 1, 1999. Residents are required to pay through a licensed intermediary. Effective February 1, 1999, payments and incomes of foreign ships in the WAEMU zone and WAEMU ships abroad are included under current operations.
Trade-related payments	
Indicative limits/bona fide test	Yes.
Investment-related payments	
Prior approval	Payments for the depreciation of direct investments require the approval of the MOF, since depreciation is not specifically mentioned in the regulations.
Indicative limits/bona fide test	There are no indicative limits or bona fide tests for the transfer of profits and dividends.
Payments for travel	
Quantitative limits	Effective February 1, 1999, limits on foreign exchange allowances were eliminated.
Indicative limits/bona fide test	Allowances in excess of the equivalent of CFAF 2 million in foreign banknotes must be exported in the form of traveler's checks, bank drafts, or other means of payment.
Personal payments	
Indicative limits/bona fide test	Payments for medical costs and studies abroad are granted upon submission of supporting documentation to authorized banks.
Foreign workers' wages	
Indicative limits/bona fide test	Yes.
Other payments	
Indicative limits/bona fide test	Yes.

Proceeds from Invisible Transactions and Current Transfers

Repatriation requirements	Proceeds from invisible transactions with non-WAEMU member countries must be repatriated.
Surrender requirements	Effective February 1, 1999, all proceeds from invisible transactions with non-WAEMU member countries must be surrendered to an authorized dealer within one month of the due date. Resident travelers must declare to customs any foreign means of payment in excess of CFAF 50,000 that they bring in and must surrender these to an authorized bank within eight days of their return. This amount was raised to CFAF 300,000, effective February 1, 1999.
Restrictions on use of funds	No.

Capital Transactions

Controls on capital and money market instruments	Transfers of capital abroad by residents for investment purposes are subject to controls. Capital inflows to WAEMU countries are unrestricted with the exception of direct investment, which is subject to prior declaration, and certain borrowing operations, which require prior authorization of the MOF. If, however, the purchase of the securities has been authorized by the RCPSFM, MOF authorization is not required.
	In line with the new direction of economic policy aimed at attracting foreign investment, new exchange laws currently being adopted by the WAEMU member states provide for the elimination of all controls on capital inflows.
	In the implementation of the provisions indicated in this document, the term "foreigner" refers to countries that are not members of the franc zone. However, with respect to the local issue and offer for sale of foreign securities, the term "foreigner" refers to all the countries outside the territory of the member state concerned.
	With the exception of the issue and sale in the country of foreign securities, operations in securities are not covered explicitly by specific laws. However, by their nature, these operations are still subject to the provisions governing foreign investment and lending.
	Effective February 1, 1999, transfers by nonresidents related to the sale of an investment were allowed. The reinvestment abroad by a resident of proceeds from the sale of an investment is subject to the prior approval of the MOF. Foreign investment in WAEMU countries became unrestricted. Such operations are subject to reporting for statistical purposes. The prior authorization of the RCPSFM is required for the issuance and marketing of securities and capital assets of foreign entities, as well as for the advertising of investments abroad. Any investment by residents abroad requires the prior approval of the MOF.
On capital market securities	
Shares or other securities of a participating nature	
Sale or issue locally by nonresidents	Effective February 1, 1999, prior authorization is required from the RCPSFM. The issuance and sale of securities in Burkina Faso must be declared to the MOF for statistical purposes.
Purchase abroad by residents	The purchase of foreign securities by residents and the transfer abroad of funds for this purpose are subject to the prior authorization of the MOF.
Sale or issue abroad by residents	Yes.
Bonds or other debt securities	
Sale or issue locally by nonresidents	Yes.
Purchase abroad by residents	Yes.
Sale or issue abroad by residents	Yes.
On money market instruments	
Sale or issue locally by nonresidents	Yes.
Purchase abroad by residents	Yes.
Sale or issue abroad by residents	Yes.
On collective investment securities	
Sale or issue locally by nonresidents	Yes.
Purchase abroad by residents	Yes.
Controls on derivatives and other instruments	These instruments, which are virtually nonexistent in Burkina Faso, are governed by the regulations generally applicable to securities and investments, except commodity and security call and put options, which, effective February 1, 1999, residents may purchase freely abroad.
Purchase locally by nonresidents	Yes.

Sale or issue locally by nonresidents	Yes.
Purchase abroad by residents	Yes.
Sale or issue abroad by residents	Yes.

Controls on credit operations

Commercial credits

By residents to nonresidents — There are no controls on credits related to exports of goods, provided that the date on which payment falls due is not more than 120 days after the date of shipment. The transfer of funds abroad for this purpose is subject to prior MOF authorization.

To residents from nonresidents — There are no controls, and repayments of commercial credits are generally approved, subject to the presentation of documents attesting to the validity of the commercial operation or of the services rendered, as well as the payment due date.

Financial credits

By residents to nonresidents — These credits require prior approval from the MOF. Outward transfers necessary to service such facilities require an exchange authorization, subject to the approval of the BCEAO acting on behalf of the MOF and substantiated by documentation.

To residents from nonresidents — There are no controls on these credits, but they must be reported for statistical purposes. The necessary funds must be transferred from abroad through an authorized agent. There are no controls on repayments of loans, provided that the authorized agent handling the settlement is provided with documentation attesting to the validity of the transaction.

Guarantees, sureties, and financial backup facilities — The same regulations apply as for financial credits.

By residents to nonresidents — Yes.

To residents from nonresidents — There are no controls on the granting of these facilities, and the funds involved must be transferred from abroad through an authorized intermediary.

Controls on direct investment

Outward direct investment — All investment abroad by residents is subject to the prior authorization of the MOF. A maximum of 75% of such investments may be financed by foreign loans. Authorization is not required for purchases of foreign securities whose issuance or offering for sale in WAEMU member countries has been authorized by the RCPSFM.

Inward direct investment — Inward investments must be reported for statistical purposes.

Controls on liquidation of direct investment — The liquidation of investments abroad must be reported to the MOF for information purposes. Reinvestment of the proceeds from the liquidation is subject to prior MOF authorization. If reinvestment is not authorized, the proceeds from the liquidation must be repatriated within one month through an authorized intermediary. The sale of foreign investments in Burkina Faso is unrestricted but must be reported to the MOF for statistical purposes.

Controls on real estate transactions

Purchase abroad by residents — Investments abroad by residents require prior authorization from the MOF. The investor must make the request in writing and designate the authorized intermediary that will execute the payment. Whether the payment is made by an outward transfer of funds or by deposit to a foreign account in francs, it cannot be executed until after the period agreed to by the parties.

Controls on personal capital movements

Loans — The same regulations apply as for securities and investments.

By residents to nonresidents — Yes.

To residents from nonresidents — Yes.

Gifts, endowments, inheritances, and legacies

By residents to nonresidents In general, inheritances and dowries are authorized; endowments require prior approval.

To residents from nonresidents Yes.

Settlement of debts abroad by immigrants Immigrants who have acquired resident status must obtain prior approval from the MOF to settle debts incurred abroad when they were nonresidents.

Transfer of assets

Transfer abroad by emigrants These transfers are subject to the prior authorization of the MOF.

Transfer into the country by immigrants This requires authorization of the MOF.

Transfer of gambling and prize earnings Yes.

Provisions specific to commercial banks and other credit institutions The same regulations apply as for lending to nonresidents.

Borrowing abroad Authorized agents are free to borrow from abroad.

Maintenance of accounts abroad Banks and financial institutions are authorized to open accounts with their correspondent banks for settling transactions for their own account or the account of their customers. However, banks are not authorized to hold amounts in these accounts that exceed their current requirements.

Lending to nonresidents (financial or commercial credits) There are no controls if these operations involve commercial credits. Prior authorization from the MOF is required for financial credits.

Lending locally in foreign exchange There are no regulations that apply specifically to these transactions. However, prior MOF approval is required.

Purchase of locally issued securities denominated in foreign exchange These purchases require the prior approval of the RCPSFM.

Differential treatment of deposit accounts in foreign exchange

Credit controls Yes.

Differential treatment of deposit accounts held by nonresidents Monetary regulations make no distinction between resident deposit accounts, nonresident deposit accounts, and foreign deposit accounts.

Investment regulations The same regulations apply as for foreign investments.

Abroad by banks Yes.

In banks by nonresidents Yes.

Open foreign exchange position limits There are no prudential ratios. Open positions result from special dispensations.

Provisions specific to institutional investors Effective February 1, 1999, controls are imposed by the Insurance Code of the Inter-African Conference on Insurance Markets.

Limits (max.) on securities issued by nonresidents and on portfolio invested abroad n.r.

Limits (max.) on portfolio invested abroad n.r.

Limits (min.) on portfolio invested locally n.r.

Currency-matching regulations on assets/liabilities composition n.r.

Other controls imposed by securities laws No.

Changes During 1999

Exchange arrangement	*January 1.* The CFA franc peg to the French franc was replaced with one to the euro.
	February 1. Residents were authorized to contract forward exchange cover to settle payments related to imports and exports of goods and services.
Arrangements for payments and receipts .	*February 1.* The amount that may be transferred without supporting documents was increased to CFAF 300,000.
Resident accounts	*February 1.* Residents were allowed to open foreign exchange accounts with local banks or with banks abroad after obtaining authorization from the MOF, with the approval of the BCEAO.
Nonresident accounts	*February 1.* Authorization to open foreign exchange accounts is now issued by the BCEAO.
Imports and import payments	*February 1.* The domiciliation threshold for import operations was raised to CFAF 5,000,000.
	April 1. The new common tariff categorization for imported products adopted by the WAEMU was introduced.
Exports and export proceeds	*February 1.* Exports between WAEMU countries are no longer subject to domiciliation and repatriation requirements.
Payments for invisible transactions and current transfers	*February 1.* Limits on foreign exchange allowances for travel were abolished.
	February 1. Payments and incomes of foreign ships in the WAEMU zone and WAEMU ships abroad, are included under current operations.
Proceeds from invisible transactions and current transfers	*February 1.* All proceeds must be surrendered to an authorized dealer within one month of the due date. The amount resident travelers must declare to customs and surrender to authorized dealers within eight days of their return was raised to CFAF 300,000.
Capital transactions	*February 1.* Prior authorization of the RCPSFM was required for the issue and offer for sale of securities by foreign entities.
Controls on derivatives and other instruments	*February 1.* Transfers relating to option purchases were allowed.
Provisions specific to institutional investors	*February 1.* Controls were imposed by the Insurance Code of the Inter-African Conference on Insurance Markets.

Changes During 2000

Imports and import payments	*January 1.* The customs duty rates are zero, 5%, 10%, and 20% plus taxes of 2%. A temporary protection tax may also be applied.

BURUNDI

(Position as of December 31, 1999)

Status Under IMF Articles of Agreement

Article XIV	Yes.

Exchange Arrangement

Currency	The currency of Burundi is the Burundi franc.

Exchange rate structure

Dual	Effective November 12, 1999, there are two foreign exchange markets. The first market (the Bank of the Republic of Burundi (BRB) window) comprises export proceeds from coffee, cotton, and tea, which amount to about 95% of the total export proceeds. The second market (the second window) is operated by foreign exchange bureaus.

Classification

Managed floating with no pre-announced path for the exchange rate	The Burundi franc was pegged to a basket of currencies of Burundi's main trading partners through June 30, 1999. Since then, the exchange rate of the Burundi franc has been de facto managed to limit the spread between the official exchange rate and the parallel market rate. Thus, Burundi's exchange rate arrangement has been reclassified to the category managed floating with no preannounced path for the exchange rate from the category conventional pegged arrangement. The BRB quotes the exchange rate for 15 currencies, the euro, and the SDR.
	Effective November 12, 1999, foreign exchange bureaus were allowed to officially operate in the foreign exchange market, creating a second foreign exchange market with a freely determined exchange rate.
Exchange tax	No.
Exchange subsidy	No.
Forward exchange market	n.r.

Arrangements for Payments and Receipts

Prescription of currency requirements	Settlements relating to trade with the Democratic Republic of the Congo and Rwanda in products specified in the commercial agreements with these countries are effected through a clearing process, with balances paid in convertible currencies. Nonresidents staying in a hotel or guesthouse in Burundi must pay their hotel bills by selling convertible currencies or by using a credit card. Payment in Burundi francs is, however, acceptable in the case of guests for whom a resident company or individual has assumed responsibility with prior authorization from the BRB and in the case of nationals of the Democratic Republic of the Congo and Rwanda, who produce declarations of means of payment issued under the auspices of the CEPGL.

Payment arrangements

Bilateral payment arrangements

Operative	There are trade agreements with the Democratic Republic of the Congo and Rwanda. These agreements are not fully operational due to the unfavorable economic situation.
Regional arrangements	Regional agreements exist with Eastern and Southern African countries.
Clearing agreements	Clearing agreements exist with members of COMESA and CEPGL.
Administration of control	Control over foreign exchange transactions and foreign trade is vested in the BRB; authority to carry out some transactions is delegated to seven authorized banks. Effective November 12, 1999, the BRB issued regulations permitting foreign exchange bureaus to operate officially. Transactions above $5,000 are subject to approval based on the production of supporting documentation.

International security restrictions	No.
Payment arrears	
Official	Yes.
Controls on trade in gold (coins and/or bullion)	
Controls on domestic ownership and/or trade	Holders of gold mining permits issued by the ministers responsible for mining and customs may open purchasing houses for gold mined by artisans in Burundi. Gold produced by artisans may be sold only to approved houses.
Controls on external trade	Exports of gold must be declared in Burundi francs at the average daily rates communicated by the BRB. Gold exports are authorized jointly by the mining and customs departments.
Controls on exports and imports of banknotes	
On exports	
Domestic currency	All travelers may take out up to FBu 5,000.
Foreign currency	If the amount exceeds $5,000, a license based on supporting documents is required.
On imports	
Domestic currency	Travelers may bring in up to FBu 5,000.
Foreign currency	Travelers may bring in any amount of foreign currency quoted by the BRB in addition to traveler's checks.

Resident Accounts

Foreign exchange accounts permitted	Effective November 12, 1999, the regulation pertaining to foreign exchange bureaus and foreign exchange accounts authorized resident natural persons or legal entities to open foreign exchange accounts with local banks. Foreign exchange accounts may be credited freely. Withdrawals of Burundi francs are unlimited. Supporting documentation is not required for withdrawals of foreign exchange in the form of banknotes, traveler's checks, or checks up to the equivalent of $5,000 per operation. Supporting documentation is required for transactions involving payments for imports of goods and services, withdrawals of banknotes, traveler's checks, or checks in excess of $5,000. Foreign exchange accounts may bear interest freely.
Held domestically	Authorized banks may freely open foreign exchange accounts, but must forward copies of relevant documents to the BRB.
Held abroad	Prior BRB authorization is required to open these accounts.
Accounts in domestic currency convertible into foreign currency	Yes.

Nonresident Accounts

Foreign exchange accounts permitted	Effective November 12, 1999, any nonresident natural or juridical person may open a foreign exchange account in an authorized bank. Nonresident foreign exchange accounts may be credited freely. Supporting documentation justifying the nature of the transaction is required for all forms of payments or transfers by residents. These accounts may bear interest freely. Amounts of less than or equal to $5,000 may be withdrawn in banknotes on presentation of travel documentation. Withdrawals in excess of this amount require supporting documentation.
Domestic currency accounts	Yes.
Convertible into foreign currency	Yes.
Blocked accounts	n.a.

Imports and Import Payments

Foreign exchange budget	No.
Financing requirements for imports	No.
Advance import deposits	The advance import deposit, which was suspended on March 1, 1999, was 50% of the import value, with the exception of key products, which were subject to a rate of 25%, and oil products and those imported by Brassière et Limonadière du Burundi, which were subject to a rate of 10%.
Documentation requirements for release of foreign exchange for imports	In the base of imports financed at the primary window, the task of verifying import declarations and payments by commercial banks requires prior approval of the BRB. All goods imported into Burundi must be insured by approved Burundi insurers, and premiums must be paid in Burundi francs.
Preshipment inspection	All consignments of imports exceeding $5.000 c.i.f. in value may, in principle, be subject to preshipment inspection with regard to quality, quantity, and price by an international supervising and oversight organization on behalf of the Burundi authorities.
Letters of credit	Yes.
Import licenses used as exchange licenses	Yes.
Import licenses and other nontariff measures	Verification of import declarations at the primary window takes into account the available foreign exchange and the level of market supply.
Positive list	These imports must pass through the primary window.
Negative list	Imports on this list may not be traded at the official exchange rate.
Open general licenses	Yes.
Import taxes and/or tariffs	Burundi is a member of the COMESA. There are five customs duty bands (10%, 12%, 15%, 40%, and 100%) applied to imports from countries not belonging to COMESA. Imports of petroleum products are subject to import duties ranging from 6% to 40%. A 6% service tax, which replaced the statistical tax, is levied on the c.i.f. value of imports, in addition to any applicable customs duties and fiscal duties.
State import monopoly	No.

Exports and Export Proceeds

Repatriation requirements	Export proceeds must be collected within 30 days of the date of export declaration at customs for shipment by air or within 90 days for all other shipments. Deadlines for the collection of proceeds from exports of nontraditional products are set by the commercial bank carrying out the operation.
Surrender requirements	All proceeds from traditional exports must be surrendered to an authorized bank. Exporters of nontraditional products may retain 100% of proceeds. Exporters operating in the free trade area are not required to surrender their export proceeds to an authorized bank. Effective November 12, 1999, only proceeds from exports of coffee, tea, and cotton are required to be surrendered to the BRB.
Financing requirements	No.
Documentation requirements	
Guarantees	Yes.
Export licenses	Yes.
Export taxes	Export taxes are levied on a range of exports. The generally applicable rate is 5%. For green coffee, the rate is set at each crop season. The export tax on coffee is 31%.

Payments for Invisible Transactions and Current Transfers

Controls on these transfers	All payments for invisibles in excess of $5,000 require approval. Effective November 12, 1999, foreign exchange bureaus are authorized to administer payments for invisible transactions.
Trade-related payments	Shipping insurance on coffee exports normally must be taken out in Burundi francs with a Burundi insurer.
Prior approval	Yes.
Indicative limits/bona fide test	Unloading and storage costs are limited to amounts indicated by the invoice.
Investment-related payments	Private joint-stock companies may transfer 100% of the return on foreign capital and of the share allocated to foreign directors after payment of taxes. Airlines are authorized to transfer abroad 100% of their earnings after deduction of local expenses. Transfer of rental income is permitted (after payment of taxes and a deduction of 20% for maintenance expenses). Transfers for income from rents and sale of real estate are suspended.
Prior approval	Yes.
Indicative limits/bona fide test	Information is not available on payments of interest.
Payments for travel	Commercial banks and the BRB grant foreign exchange for private and public travel, respectively.
Prior approval	Yes.
Quantitative limits	Yes.
Indicative limits/bona fide test	Yes.
Personal payments	Commercial banks grant foreign exchange for personal payments within the limits of their available foreign exchange. Pension transfers are effected through the Social Security Institute.
Prior approval	Yes.
Quantitative limits	The limit for medical costs is FBu 700,000, with additional transfers allowed upon presentation of invoices. For studies abroad and for family maintenance and alimony payments, allowances are suspended.
Indicative limits/bona fide test	Yes.
Foreign workers' wages	Transfers are covered on the second market except for those workers who have government contracts.
Prior approval	Yes.
Quantitative limits	Upon presentation of evidence of payment of taxes, foreign nationals residing and working in Burundi are permitted to transfer abroad up to 70% of their net annual income (80% in the case of foreign nationals working for companies that export at least 50% of their production).
Indicative limits/bona fide test	A work contract is required.
Credit card use abroad	The use of credit cards is not permitted.
Other payments	
Prior approval	Yes.
Quantitative limits	Consulting and legal fees are limited to amounts indicated by invoices.
Indicative limits/bona fide test	Yes.

Proceeds from Invisible Transactions and Current Transfers

Repatriation requirements	Yes.
Restrictions on use of funds	Yes.

Capital Transactions

Controls on capital and money market instruments	Capital transfers abroad by residents require individual authorization.
On capital market securities	
Shares or other securities of a participating nature	
Purchase locally by nonresidents	The purchase must be effected in foreign exchange.
Purchase abroad by residents	Yes.
Bonds or other debt securities	
Purchase abroad by residents	Yes.
On money market instruments	
Purchase abroad by residents	BRB authorization is required.
On collective investment securities	
Purchase abroad by residents	BRB authorization is required.
Controls on derivatives and other instruments	n.r.
Controls on credit operations	
Commercial credits	
By residents to nonresidents	Yes.
To residents from nonresidents	Yes.
Financial credits	
By residents to nonresidents	Yes.
Guarantees, sureties, and financial backup facilities	
By residents to nonresidents	Yes.
Controls on direct investment	
Outward direct investment	The provision of foreign exchange for outward direct investments is suspended. Even with the emergence of the free foreign exchange market, banks are not authorized to sell foreign exchange for outward direct investments.
Inward direct investment	Yes.
Controls on liquidation of direct investment	Transfers of foreign capital on which a repatriation guarantee has been granted do not require individual authorization.
Controls on real estate transactions	
Purchase abroad by residents	Yes.
Purchase locally by nonresidents	Purchases must be effected in foreign exchange.
Sale locally by nonresidents	Transfer of the proceeds from the sale of real estate is suspended unless the purchaser is the holder of an adequately funded foreign exchange account.
Controls on personal capital movements	
Loans	
By residents to nonresidents	Yes.
Gifts, endowments, inheritances, and legacies	
By residents to nonresidents	Yes.

Settlement of debts abroad by immigrants	n.r.
Transfer of assets	
Transfer abroad by emigrants	Yes.
Transfer into the country by immigrants	Yes.
Transfer of gambling and prize earnings	n.r.
Provisions specific to commercial banks and other credit institutions	
Lending locally in foreign exchange	Yes.
Purchase of locally issued securities denominated in foreign exchange	n.r.
Differential treatment of deposit accounts in foreign exchange	
Credit controls	Yes.
Differential treatment of deposit accounts held by nonresidents	
Reserve requirements	Yes.
Credit controls	Debit balances are not permitted on foreign exchange accounts.
Investment regulations	
Abroad by banks	Prior approval of the BRB is required.
Provisions specific to institutional investors	No.
Other controls imposed by securities laws	n.a.

Changes During 1999

Exchange arrangement	*July 1.* The exchange rate arrangement has been reclassified to the category managed floating with no preannounced path for the exchange rate from the category conventional pegged arrangement.
	November 12. Foreign exchange bureaus were allowed to officially operate in the foreign exchange market, creating a second foreign exchange market with a freely determined exchange rate. Transactions above $5,000 are subject to approval based on supporting documentation.
Arrangements for payments and receipts	*November 12.* Foreign exchange bureaus were allowed to officially operate with a freely determined exchange rate. Transactions above $5,000 are subject to approval based on supporting documentation.
Resident accounts	*November 12.* The BRB allowed residents to keep foreign exchange deposits in domestic commercial banks.
Nonresident accounts	*November 12.* The BRB allowed residents to keep foreign exchange deposits in domestic commercial banks.
Imports and import payments	*March 1.* The advance import deposit requirement was suspended.
Exports and export proceeds	*November 12.* Only proceeds from exports of coffee, cotton, and tea must be surrendered to the BRB.

CAMBODIA

(Position as of December 31, 1999)

Status Under IMF Articles of Agreement

Article XIV	Yes.

Exchange Arrangement

Currency	The currency of Cambodia is the Cambodian riel.
Other legal tender	The dollar circulates freely and is used for payments.

Exchange rate structure

Dual	The exchange rate system comprises two rates: the official rate and the market rate. Adjustments to the official exchange rate are made daily by the National Bank of Cambodia (NBC) to limit the spread between the official and parallel market rates to less than 1%. The official exchange rate applies mainly to external transactions conducted by the government and state-owned enterprises.

Classification

Managed floating with no pre-announced path for the exchange rate	The NBC quotes daily official rates, at which the Foreign Trade Bank of Cambodia buys and sells foreign exchange. Other commercial banks are free to buy and sell foreign exchange at their own rates. Exchange transactions take place at the market rate. Foreign exchange dealers are permitted to buy and sell banknotes and traveler's checks at the market rate.
Exchange tax	No.
Exchange subsidy	No.
Forward exchange market	No.

Arrangements for Payments and Receipts

Prescription of currency requirements	No.
Payment arrangements	No.
Administration of control	The responsibility for the management of foreign exchange rests with the Ministry of Economy and Finance and the NBC. The NBC is authorized to license commercial banks and other agents to engage in foreign exchange transactions and to regulate current and capital transactions. In practice, no restrictions apply.
International security restrictions	No.
Payment arrears	No.
Controls on trade in gold (coins and/or bullion)	
Controls on external trade	The import or export of raw gold is subject to prior declaration to the NBC if the value of each transaction equals or exceeds $10,000.
Controls on exports and imports of banknotes	
On exports	The export of means of payment equaling or exceeding $10,000 in foreign exchange or its equivalent in domestic currency by a traveler must be declared to customs officers at border crossings of Cambodia.
Domestic currency	Yes.

Foreign currency	Exports are subject to prior notification to the NBC.
On imports	The same regulations apply as for exports.
Domestic currency	Yes.
Foreign currency	There are no limits, but imports exceeding $10,000 or equivalent must be declared on entry.

Resident Accounts

Foreign exchange accounts permitted	Yes.
Held domestically	There are no limits on the balances of these accounts, and the funds may be used to settle domestic obligations, and all transactions may be settled in foreign currency.
Accounts in domestic currency convertible into foreign currency	No.

Nonresident Accounts

Foreign exchange accounts permitted	Regulations applied to residents also apply to nonresidents.
Domestic currency accounts	No.
Blocked accounts	No.

Imports and Import Payments

Foreign exchange budget	No.
Financing requirements for imports	Loans and borrowings, including trade credits, may be freely contracted between residents and nonresidents, provided that the loan disbursements and the repayments thereof are made through authorized intermediaries.
Documentation requirements for release of foreign exchange for imports	
Domiciliation requirements	Authorized intermediaries may be required by the NBC to submit proof of payment of imports by banker's order in support of their applications to purchase foreign exchange, and later also be required to provide various documentary evidence confirming the entry of goods into the country. When the collection is made, the proceeds from exports of goods or services shall be credited to the exporter's account with the domiciled bank in accordance with the existing law.
Preshipment inspection	Preshipment import inspection was temporarily suspended on June 30, 1999.
Import licenses and other nontariff measures	
Negative list	Imports of certain products are subject to control or are prohibited for reasons of national security, health, environmental well-being, or public morality.
Import taxes and/or tariffs	Import duties are levied, and an excise tax of 10% applies to selected imports.
State import monopoly	No.

Exports and Export Proceeds

Repatriation requirements	Exporters or importers of goods and services must make payments for their commercial transactions with the rest of the world through authorized intermediaries.
Surrender requirements	Yes.

Financing requirements	Loans and borrowings, including trade credits, may be freely contracted between residents and nonresidents, provided that the loan disbursements and the repayments thereof are made through authorized intermediaries.
Documentation requirements	
Domiciliation	The proceeds from exports of goods or services must be credited to the exporter's account with a domiciled bank in accordance with the existing law.
Export licenses	
Without quotas	Exports of a limited list of goods by both state-owned and private sector entities must be licensed by the Ministry of Commerce. Export licenses are required for sawed timber, logs, and rice.
With quotas	Effective June 30, 1999, exports of garments, gems, and rice to the United States and sawed timber are subject to a quota. Exports of antiques and several categories of logs are restricted.
Export taxes	An export tax of 10% of the estimated market value applies to exports of timber and other selected exports.

Payments for Invisible Transactions and Current Transfers

Controls on these transfers	Payments for invisibles related to trade are not restricted, but are regulated by the Investment Law.
Payments for travel	
Quantitative limits	An exchange allowance of $10,000 a person is granted at the official rate for all types of travel, irrespective of the length of stay; amounts in excess of this limit must be approved by the NBC. In practice, however, there are no limits.
Indicative limits/bona fide test	Yes.

Proceeds from Invisible Transactions and Current Transfers

Repatriation requirements	The requirement applies only to state-owned enterprises.
Surrender requirements	Only proceeds from invisibles earned by state-owned enterprises must be surrendered.
Restrictions on use of funds	n.a.

Capital Transactions

Controls on capital and money market instruments	There are no specific laws on capital market securities, and there are no securities markets in Cambodia.
Controls on derivatives and other instruments	n.a.
Controls on credit operations	Loans and borrowing, including trade credits, may be freely contracted between residents and nonresidents, provided that the loan disbursements and the repayments thereof are made through authorized intermediaries.
Commercial credits	
By residents to nonresidents	Yes.
Financial credits	
By residents to nonresidents	Yes.

Guarantees, sureties, and financial backup facilities	
By residents to nonresidents	Yes.
To residents from nonresidents	Yes.

Controls on direct investment

Outward direct investment	The requirement of government approval is not enforced.
Inward direct investment	Foreign investors are required to obtain approval from the Council for Development of Cambodia, but there are no foreign exchange restrictions.

Controls on liquidation of direct investment	Proceeds from the liquidation of foreign direct investment taking place in accordance with the provisions of the investment law of the Kingdom of Cambodia may be transferred freely. However, such transfers have to be made through authorized intermediaries, which must report to the NBC all amounts equal to or exceeding $100,000.

Controls on real estate transactions

Purchase locally by nonresidents	Nonresidents may not own land in Cambodia.

Controls on personal capital movements

Loans	Loans and borrowings, including trade credits, may be freely contracted between residents and nonresidents, provided that the loan disbursements and the repayments thereof are made through authorized intermediaries.
Gifts, endowments, inheritances, and legacies	
To residents from nonresidents	Yes.
Transfer of assets	Such operations must take place through authorized intermediaries.
Transfer abroad by emigrants	Yes.

Provisions specific to commercial banks and other credit institutions	Authorized intermediaries must provide the NBC with periodic statements of transfers or settlements and of outflows and inflows of capital carried out between Cambodia and the rest of the world. Any export of foreign currency banknotes by authorized intermediaries is subject to prior declaration to the NBC. Loans and borrowing, including trade credits, may be freely contracted between residents and nonresidents, provided that the loan disbursements and repayments thereof are made through authorized intermediaries. However, in the event of foreign exchange crisis, the NBC may issue regulations to be implemented for a maximum period of three months, imposing certain temporary restrictions on the activity of authorized intermediaries, particularly on certain transactions specified in the law, their foreign exchange position, or any loans in domestic currency extended to nonresidents.
Lending to nonresidents (financial or commercial credits)	Banks may lend to nonresidents doing business within Cambodia.
Differential treatment of deposit accounts in foreign exchange	
Reserve requirements	Yes.
Investment regulations	
Abroad by banks	Yes.
In banks by nonresidents	Yes.
Open foreign exchange position limits	Banks are not allowed to exceed their short or long position in any single foreign currency by more than 5% and in all foreign currencies by more than 15% of the bank's net worth. Residents and nonresidents are not treated differently.
On resident assets and liabilities	Yes.
On nonresident assets and liabilities	Yes.

Provisions specific to institutional investors	There are no institutional investors in Cambodia.
Other controls imposed by securities laws	There are no securities laws.

Changes During 1999

Imports and import payments	*June 30*. Preshipment inspection of goods was temporarily suspended.
Exports and export proceeds	*June 30*. Garment, gem, and rice exports to the United States became the subject of quotas.

CAMEROON
(Position as of December 31, 1999)

Status Under IMF Articles of Agreement

Article VIII   Date of acceptance: June 1, 1996.

Exchange Arrangement

Currency   The currency of Cameroon is the CFA franc.

Exchange rate structure   Unitary.

Classification

Exchange arrangement with no sepa-   The CFA franc is pegged to the euro at the fixed rate of CFAF 100 per €0.1524. Exchange
rate legal tender   transactions in euros between the BEAC and commercial banks take place at the same rate.
Buying and selling rates for certain other foreign currencies are also officially posted, with
quotations based on the fixed rate for the euro and the rates in the Paris exchange market
for the currencies concerned. The commission levied by commercial banks is freely set by
each bank. However, such commission does not apply to government operations, transfers
in settlement of imports covered by an import declaration domiciled with a bank, scheduled
repayments of loans properly obtained, and travel allowance or representation expenses
paid for official missions.

Exchange tax   n.r.

Exchange subsidy   No.

Forward exchange market   Yes.

Arrangements for Payments and Receipts

Prescription of currency   Because Cameroon is an Operations Account country, settlements with France, Monaco,
requirements   and the Operations Account countries are made in CFA francs, euros, or the currency of
any other Operations Account country. Settlements with all other countries are usually
made through correspondent banks in France in any of the currencies of those countries
or in euros through foreign accounts in French francs.

Payment arrangements

Regional arrangements   An Operations Account is maintained with the French Treasury that links Operations Account countries. All purchases or sales of foreign currencies or euros against CFA francs
are ultimately settled through a debit or credit to the Operations Account.

Clearing agreements   There are clearing arrangements in the context of the CEEAC.

Barter agreements and open accounts   n.r.

Administration of control   Exchange control is administered by the Directorate of Economic Controls and External
Finance of the Ministry of Economy and Finance (MEF). Exchange transactions relating to
all countries must be effected through authorized intermediaries (i.e., the Postal Administration and authorized banks). Exchange bureaus are also authorized to effect foreign exchange transactions.

International security restrictions   There are no such restrictions under the legislation in force. However, in practice, decisions are taken in accordance with the resolutions of the international community
(IMF, UN, etc.).

Payment arrears   n.a.

Controls on trade in gold (coins and/or bullion)

Controls on domestic ownership and/or trade

Residents are free to hold, acquire, and dispose of gold jewelry in Cameroon. Approval of the Ministry of Mines, Water, and Energy (MMWE) is required to hold gold in any other form. Such approval is normally given only to industrial users, including jewelers. Newly mined gold must be declared to the MMWE, which authorizes either its exportation or its sale to domestic industrial users. Exports are made only to France.

Controls on external trade

Imports and exports of gold require prior authorization of the MMWE and the MEF, although such authorization is seldom granted for imports. Exempt from this requirement are (1) imports and exports by or on behalf of the monetary authorities, and (2) imports and exports of manufactured articles containing a small quantity of gold (such as gold-filled or gold-plated articles). Both licensed and exempt imports of gold are subject to customs declaration.

Controls on exports and imports of banknotes

On exports

Domestic currency

Exports of all coins and banknotes are subject to a prior declaration.

Foreign currency

All resident travelers, regardless of destination, must declare in writing all means of payment at their disposal at the time of departure. The reexportation of foreign banknotes is allowed up to the equivalent of CFAF 250,000; reexportation above this ceiling requires documentation showing either the importation of foreign banknotes or their purchase against other means of payment registered in the name of the traveler or through the use of deposits lodged in local banks.

On imports

Domestic currency

Resident travelers are authorized to import into Cameroon a maximum of CFAF 300,000 to cover their initial expenses upon their return to Cameroon.

Foreign currency

Yes.

Resident Accounts

Foreign exchange accounts permitted

Residents are permitted to open foreign currency accounts at commercial banks.

Held domestically

The opening of foreign exchange accounts exclusively for use by enterprises in the strategic sector (petroleum), which are also allowed to maintain their accounts in a foreign currency, is subject to the prior authorization of the MEF.

Held abroad

The opening and maintenance of accounts abroad are forbidden.

Accounts in domestic currency convertible into foreign currency

No.

Nonresident Accounts

Foreign exchange accounts permitted

Only accounts of CFA francs convertible into foreign currency are permitted.

Domestic currency accounts

The regulations pertaining to nonresident accounts are based on those applied in France. Since the BEAC has suspended the repurchase of BEAC banknotes circulating outside its zone of issue, BEAC banknotes received by the foreign correspondents of authorized banks and mailed to the BEAC agency in Yaoundé (capital of Cameroon) may not be credited to foreign accounts in CFA francs.

Nonresidents are allowed to maintain bank accounts in euros. These accounts, held mainly by diplomatic missions, international institutions, and their nonresident employees, may be credited only with (1) proceeds of spot or forward sales of foreign currencies transferred from abroad by account owners; (2) transfers from other nonresident euro accounts; and (3) payments by residents in accordance with exchange regulations. These accounts may be debited only for (1) purchases of foreign currencies; (2) transfers to other nonresident euro accounts; and (3) payments to residents in accordance with exchange regulations. Nonresidents may not maintain accounts in CFA francs abroad or accounts in foreign currency in Cameroon.

Convertible into foreign currency	Such accounts may be credited and debited only in foreign currency. Prior authorization of the MEF is required.
Blocked accounts	n.r.

Imports and Import Payments

Foreign exchange budget	No.
Financing requirements for imports	Import payments are made in accordance with the terms of the underlying contracts. However, advance payments (i.e., before the actual delivery of goods) are authorized up to 50% of the value of imports.
Minimum financing requirements	There are no restrictions on import financing. The amounts to be transferred must correspond to those contained in the pertinent import declaration.
Advance payment requirements	Up to 50% of prefinancing is authorized; the balance is authorized only upon presentation of the pertinent trade documents.
Advance import deposits	Advance import deposits are permitted if stipulated by underlying contracts.
Documentation requirements for release of foreign exchange for imports	
Domiciliation requirements	All import transactions for domestic consumption and valued at more than CFAF 2 million must be domiciled with a licensed bank. Transactions involving goods in transit must be domiciled with a bank in the country of final destination.
Preshipment inspection	All imports are subject to inspection by the Société générale de surveillance (SGS).
Letters of credit	LCs are allowed but are optional.
Import licenses and other nontariff measures	Import licenses are almost totally abolished. Importers of more than CFAF 2 million are required to fill out an import declaration with the SGS. The importing of certain products, which are included on a list established each year by the Ministry of Industrial and Commercial Development (MINDIC), remains subject to licensing.
Positive list	A list of products still subject to authorization is published annually by the MINDIC in the Programme générale des echanges.
Negative list	Certain imports are prohibited for ecological, health, or safety reasons.
Open general licenses	Such licenses are available especially for long-term supply contracts.
Licenses with quotas	Quotas are applicable to imports by container.
Import taxes and/or tariffs	Import tariffs range from 5% to 30%. Import surcharges apply only to imports from countries outside the UDEAC.
Taxes collected through the exchange system	Surcharges apply only to imports from countries outside the UDEAC and to imports of maize meal and cement.
State import monopoly	There is a state import monopoly only for imports relating to sovereign expenditure (such as defense and security).

Exports and Export Proceeds

Repatriation requirements	Proceeds from exports to all countries must be repatriated within 30 days of the payment date stipulated in the sales contract. Oil companies are exempt from the repatriation requirement. However, waivers may be granted by the President of the Republic to companies of a strategic nature and representing the national interests.

Surrender requirements	Export proceeds must be surrendered within the eight-day period following repatriation.
Financing requirements	No.
Documentation requirements	For exports of fresh food products (vegetables, fruits), a health certificate is required before shipment.
Letters of credit	n.r.
Guarantees	n.r.
Domiciliation	Exports to all countries are subject to domiciliation requirements for the appropriate documents. Export transactions valued at CFAF 2 million or more must be domiciled with an authorized bank.
Preshipment inspection	Exports to all countries are subject to inspection by the SGS.
Export licenses	Licenses are required for all exports valued at the equivalent of at least CFAF 2 million. Export licenses are issued by the MEF.
Without quotas	Yes.
Export taxes	Export taxes established in the Budget Law are collected by the Directorate of Customs.
Other export taxes	All nonforestry export taxes were eliminated on July 1, 1999. An export tax of 17.5% is applied to timber, and a rate of 12.5% is applied to the log equivalent of processed woods.

Payments for Invisible Transactions and Current Transfers

Controls on these transfers	Payments in excess of CFAF 2 million for invisibles to France, Monaco, and the Operations Account countries require prior declaration and are subject to presentation of relevant invoices. Payments for invisibles related to trade follow the same regime as basic trade transactions, as do transfers of income accruing to nonresidents in the form of profits, dividends, and royalties.
Trade-related payments	With the exception of insurance expenses, agents may obtain authorization for the payment of all other trade-related expenses.
Prior approval	The payment of such expenses is authorized upon presentation of invoices and related documents when the latter are not taken into account in the basic commercial contract.
Quantitative limits	Yes.
Indicative limits/bona fide test	Yes.
Investment-related payments	Distributed profits, dividends, and other interest paid by residents to nonresidents may be transferred.
Prior approval	Yes.
Quantitative limits	Transfers are authorized on the basis of conventions, contracts, minutes of annual meetings (as regards profits and dividends), and loan repayment schedules (as regards interest).
Indicative limits/bona fide test	Yes.
Payments for travel	
Prior approval	Authorization is required for any acquisition of foreign currency by residents traveling to countries other than member countries of the franc zone.
Quantitative limits	The limit on foreign exchange allowances for travelers was increased to $10,000 from $1,000 a person a trip. The number of trips allowed is no longer limited. Returning resident travelers are required to declare all means of payment in their possession upon arrival at customs and to surrender them within eight days.
Indicative limits/bona fide test	Yes.
Personal payments	
Prior approval	Yes.

Quantitative limits	Yes.
Foreign workers' wages	Foreigners working in Cameroon are authorized to transfer up to 50% of their remuneration upon presentation of their pay slip and their most recent statement of income.
Prior approval	Yes.
Quantitative limits	Yes.
Indicative limits/bona fide test	Limits are determined on the basis of the supporting documents provided.
Credit card use abroad	
Prior approval	Yes.
Quantitative limits	Yes.
Indicative limits/bona fide test	Yes.
Other payments	
Prior approval	Yes.
Quantitative limits	Yes.
Indicative limits/bona fide test	Limits are determined on the basis of supporting documents provided.

Proceeds from Invisible Transactions and Current Transfers

Repatriation requirements	All receipts from services and all income earned abroad must be collected within one month of the due date.
Surrender requirements	Foreign currency receipts must be surrendered within one month of collection. Returning resident travelers are required to declare all means of payment in their possession upon arrival at customs and to surrender them within the following eight-day period.
Restrictions on use of funds	No.

Capital Transactions

Controls on capital and money market instruments	Capital transactions between Cameroon and France, Monaco, and the Operations Account countries are free of exchange control. Outward capital transfers to all other countries require exchange control approval and are restricted. Inward capital transfers are free of controls, except for foreign direct investments and borrowing, which are subject to registration and authorization.
On capital market securities	
Shares or other securities of a participating nature	
Purchase locally by nonresidents	Transactions are permitted, provided declaration is made to the MEF.
Sale or issue locally by nonresidents	Yes.
Purchase abroad by residents	The issuing, advertising, or offering for sale of foreign securities in Cameroon requires prior authorization of the MEF and must subsequently be reported to it. Exempt from authorization, however, and subject only to a report after the fact, are operations in connection with shares similar to securities, when their issuing, advertising, or offering for sale in Cameroon has already been authorized. All foreign securities and titles embodying claims on nonresidents must be deposited with an authorized intermediary and are classified as foreign, whether they belong to residents or nonresidents.
Sale or issue abroad by residents	Yes.
Bonds or other debt securities	The same regulations apply as for shares or other securities of a participating nature.

On money market instruments	Transactions in money market instruments require authorization from the MEF.
Purchase locally by nonresidents	Yes.
Sale or issue locally by nonresidents	Yes.
Purchase abroad by residents	Yes.
Sale or issue abroad by residents	Yes.
On collective investment securities	
Purchase locally by nonresidents	Prior authorization of the MEF is required.
Sale or issue locally by nonresidents	Prior declaration to the MEF is required.
Purchase abroad by residents	Prior authorization of the MEF is required.
Sale or issue abroad by residents	Prior declaration to the MEF is required.
Controls on derivatives and other instruments	n.r.
Controls on credit operations	
Commercial credits	
By residents to nonresidents	Lending abroad by natural and juridical persons, whether public or private, whose normal residence or registered office is in Cameroon, or by branches or subsidiaries in Cameroon of juridical persons whose registered office is abroad, requires prior authorization of the MEF and must subsequently be reported to it. The following are, however, exempt from prior authorization and require only a report: (1) loans constituting a direct investment abroad for which prior approval has been obtained, as indicated above; (2) loans directly connected with the rendering of services abroad by the persons or firms mentioned above, or with the financing of commercial transactions either between Cameroon and countries abroad or between foreign countries, in which these persons or firms take part; and (3) loans of up to CFAF 500,000, provided the maturity does not exceed two years and the rate of interest does not exceed 6% a year.
To residents from nonresidents	Borrowing abroad by natural and juridical persons, whether public or private, whose normal residence or registered office is in Cameroon, or by branches or subsidiaries in Cameroon of juridical persons whose registered office is abroad, requires prior authorization of the MEF and must subsequently be reported to it. The following are, however, exempt from this authorization and require only a report: (1) loans directly connected with the rendering of services abroad by the persons or firms mentioned above, or with the financing of commercial transactions either between Cameroon and countries abroad or between foreign countries, in which these persons or firms take part; (2) loans contracted by registered banks and credit institutions; and (3) loans backed by a guarantee from the government.
Financial credits	
By residents to nonresidents	The authorization of the MEF is required.
To residents from nonresidents	Prior declaration is required.
Guarantees, sureties, and financial backup facilities	
By residents to nonresidents	Yes.
To residents from nonresidents	Yes.
Controls on direct investment	
Outward direct investment	Direct investments abroad (including those made through foreign companies that are directly or indirectly controlled by persons in Cameroon and those made by branches or subsidiaries abroad of companies in Cameroon) require prior approval of the MEF, unless they take the form of a capital increase resulting from the reinvestment of undistributed profits or do not exceed 20% of the fair market value of the company being purchased.

Inward direct investment	Foreign direct investments in Cameroon (including those made by companies in Cameroon that are directly or indirectly under foreign control and those made by branches or subsidiaries of foreign companies in Cameroon) require prior declaration to the MEF, unless they take the form of a capital increase resulting from reinvestment of undistributed profits; the MEF has a period of two months from receipt of the declaration during which it may request postponement.
Controls on liquidation of direct investment	The full or partial liquidation of direct investments in Cameroon requires only a report to the MEF, unless the operation involves the relinquishing of a participation that had previously been approved as constituting a direct investment in Cameroon.
Controls on real estate transactions	
Purchase abroad by residents	Prior authorization of the MEF is required.
Purchase locally by nonresidents	Prior declaration to the MEF is required.
Sale locally by nonresidents	Prior declaration to the MEF is required.
Controls on personal capital movements	
Loans	Loans, except for those representing an authorized investment, those relating to the provision of services or to the financing of commercial transactions, and those for amounts not exceeding CFAF 500,000, are subject to the prior authorization of the MEF.
By residents to nonresidents	Yes.
To residents from nonresidents	Yes.
Gifts, endowments, inheritances, and legacies	The authorization of the MEF is required for transfers related to these operations.
Settlement of debts abroad by immigrants	Prior authorization of the MEF is required.
Transfer of assets	n.r.
Transfer of gambling and prize earnings	n.r.
Provisions specific to commercial banks and other credit institutions	
Maintenance of accounts abroad	Correspondent accounts are permitted.
Lending to nonresidents (financial or commercial credits)	Yes.
Purchase of locally issued securities denominated in foreign exchange	Yes.
Differential treatment of deposit accounts held by nonresidents	Only deposits in convertible CFA francs are permitted for nonresidents.
Open foreign exchange position limits	Yes.
Provisions specific to institutional investors	
Limits (max.) on portfolio invested abroad	Yes.
Other controls imposed by securities laws	n.a.

Changes During 1999

Exchange arrangement	*January 1.* The CFA peg to the French franc was replaced with a peg to the euro.
Exports and export proceeds	*July 1.* All nonforestry export taxes were eliminated.

CANADA

(Position as of April 30, 2000)

Status Under IMF Articles of Agreement

Article VIII   Date of acceptance: March 25, 1952.

Exchange Arrangement

Currency	The currency of Canada is the Canadian dollar.
Exchange rate structure	Unitary.
Classification	
Independently floating	The exchange rate of the Canadian dollar is determined on the basis of supply and demand; however, the authorities intervene from time to time to promote orderly conditions in the market.
Exchange tax	No.
Exchange subsidy	No.
Forward exchange market	Forward exchange rates are determined freely in the exchange market.

Arrangements for Payments and Receipts

Prescription of currency requirements	No.
Payment arrangements	
Regional arrangements	Canada is a member of NAFTA.
Administration of control	There are no exchange controls. The licensing of imports and exports, when required, is handled mostly by the Department of Foreign Affairs and International Trade, but other departments also issue licenses in specialized fields.
International security restrictions	
In accordance with Executive Board Decision No. 144-(52/51)	Canada maintains certain restrictions on the making of payments and transfers for current international transactions in respect of the Federal Republic of Yugoslavia (Serbia/ Montenegro).
In accordance with UN sanctions	In accordance with UN Security Council resolutions, Canada imposes restrictions on financial transactions with Bosnia and Herzegovina.
Payment arrears	No.
Controls on trade in gold (coins and/or bullion)	
Controls on external trade	Reexports of gold of U.S. origin to all countries except the United States require a permit. Commercial imports of articles containing minor quantities of gold, such as watches, are unrestricted and free of license.
Controls on exports and imports of banknotes	No.

Resident Accounts

Foreign exchange accounts permitted	Yes.
Held domestically	Yes.

Held abroad	Yes.
Accounts in domestic currency convertible into foreign currency	Yes.

Nonresident Accounts

Foreign exchange accounts permitted	Yes.
Domestic currency accounts	Yes.
Convertible into foreign currency	Yes.
Blocked accounts	Certain assets connected to Iraq, Libya, and the Federal Republic of Yugoslavia (Serbia/Montenegro) are frozen, pursuant to resolutions of the UN Security Council.

Imports and Import Payments

Foreign exchange budget	No.
Financing requirements for imports	No.
Documentation requirements for release of foreign exchange for imports	No.
Import licenses and other nontariff measures	
Negative list	Import permits are required for the importation of certain agricultural products, certain textile products and clothing, certain endangered species of fauna and flora, natural gas, material and equipment for the production or use of atomic energy, certain military armaments, and certain internationally controlled drugs. In addition, Health Canada does not permit the importation of drugs not registered with it. Commercial imports of used motor vehicles (less than 15 years old) have been generally prohibited, except from the United States. The prohibition on imports of used vehicles from Mexico will be phased out by January 1, 2019.
Open general licenses	Yes.
Licenses with quotas	Imports of some clothing and certain textile products, usually in the form of bilateral restraint agreements concluded under the MFA negotiated within the framework of the GATT, are also subject to quantitative restrictions. In accordance with the provisions of the Uruguay Round Agreement on Textiles and Clothing, Canada's system of import controls on textiles and clothing is being liberalized in stages over a 10-year period beginning January 1, 1995. As a result of the commitments made under the Uruguay Round Agreement, Canada replaced all agricultural import restrictions with tariff rate quotas to ensure import access levels as negotiated in the Uruguay Round (or under the NAFTA).
Other nontariff measures	Measures consistent with international trade obligations (e.g., antidumping and countervailing duties) are in place. Following a review of Canada's trade remedy system that was initiated in 1996, changes to the Special Import Measures Act were made to improve efficiency, fairness, and transparency. These changes came into force on April 15, 1999. Under the terms of the 1997 Canada-Chile Free Trade Agreement, the two countries agreed to mutual exemption from antidumping measures for each other's goods when the applicable tariff has been eliminated in both countries or after six years, whichever is earlier.
Import taxes and/or tariffs	No.
State import monopoly	Certain monopolies exist at the federal level.

Exports and Export Proceeds

Repatriation requirements	No.
Financing requirements	No.
Documentation requirements	No.
Export licenses	
Without quotas	The Export Control List identifies all goods that are controlled in order to implement intergovernmental arrangements, maintain supplies, or ensure security. It includes all items identified in the International Munitions List, the International Dual Use List, and the International Atomic Energy List. In addition, controls are maintained for supply reasons to ensure the orderly export marketing of certain products that are subject to import limitations by other countries; to promote further processing in Canada (e.g., of logs and herring roe); and for nonproliferation purposes (i.e., chemical, biological, and nuclear weapons and their delivery systems). The Area Control List includes a limited number of countries to which all exports are controlled. At present, the following countries are on the Area Control List: Angola, Myanmar, and the Federal Republic of Yugoslavia (Serbia/Montenegro). Permits are required for the exportation of listed goods to all countries except, in most cases, the United States, as well as for all goods destined to countries on the Area Control List, unless otherwise exempted.
Export taxes	No.

Payments for Invisible Transactions and Current Transfers

Controls on these transfers	No.

Proceeds from Invisible Transactions and Current Transfers

Repatriation requirements	No.
Restrictions on use of funds	No.

Capital Transactions

Controls on capital and money market instruments	No.
Controls on derivatives and other instruments	No.
Controls on credit operations	No.
Controls on direct investment	
Inward direct investment	Specific restrictions exist on inward direct investments in the broadcasting, telecommunications, transportation, financial, fishery, and energy sectors. In addition, under the provision of the Investment Canada Act, new foreign investments are generally subject to notification requirements but not to review requirements. For WTO investors, only direct acquisitions of businesses with assets exceeding Can$184 million for 1999 (Can$192 million for 2000) are subject to review. Indirect acquisitions are no longer subject to review, except in rare circumstances. These provisions were multilateralized as part of Canada's implementation of the Uruguay Round results. Investments subject to review are required only to pass a test proving that they will yield a net benefit to Canada.

Different thresholds apply in the case of investments made by non-WTO investors and in culturally sensitive sectors. Investments subject to review are required to pass a test proving that they will be of net benefit to Canada. |

The establishment of a new business, the direct acquisition of a business with assets of less than Can$184 million for 1999 (Can$192 million for 2000), and the indirect acquisition of a business by investors from WTO members are not subject to review and need only be notified, except in cases when the Canadian business represents 50% or more of the value of the total assets acquired in the international acquisition. (The acquisition of a Canadian enterprise may be considered "direct" when it involves the acquisition of control of a corporation carrying on a Canadian business and "indirect" when it involves the transfer of control by share acquisition of a non-Canadian corporation that controls a Canadian corporation carrying on a Canadian business.)

The direct acquisition of a business whose assets exceed the above-mentioned limit is reviewed and assessed according to its net benefit to Canada, authorization being generally granted. All acquisitions or investments to establish a new business in cultural sectors such as book publishing, sound recording, and film production are normally subject to review. Reviewable cases must be resolved within 75 days, unless the investor agrees to a longer time period. In practice, most cases are resolved within 45 days.

Controls on liquidation of direct investment	No.
Controls on real estate transactions	
Sale locally by nonresidents	There are no controls; however, withholding taxes apply.
Controls on personal capital movements	No.
Provisions specific to commercial banks and other credit institutions	
Investment regulations	
Abroad by banks	Banks are limited in the type of entities they can invest in domestically or abroad when the investment leads to the ownership of more than 10% of the voting rights of all shares outstanding, to the ownership of more than 25% of shareholders' equity, or to control of the entity.
In banks by nonresidents	No controls are placed on the ownership of banks that specifically preclude nonresident ownership. However, there is a general prohibition on any person, resident or nonresident, directly owning more than 10% of all outstanding shares of any class of shares of a bank. Specific exceptions are made to allow, for example, the ownership of a bank by a foreign bank.
Provisions specific to institutional investors	No.
Other controls imposed by securities laws	No.

Changes During 1999

No significant changes occurred in the exchange and trade system.

Changes During 2000

Imports and import payments	*April 15.* Changes to the Special Import Measures Act were made to improve efficiency, fairness, and transparency.

CAPE VERDE

(Position as of December 31, 1999)

Status Under IMF Articles of Agreement

Article XIV	Yes.

Exchange Arrangement

Currency	The currency of Cape Verde is the Cape Verde escudo.
Exchange rate structure	Unitary.
Classification	
Conventional pegged arrangement	The Cape Verde escudo is pegged to the euro at the rate of CVEsc 110.27 per €1.
Exchange tax	No.
Exchange subsidy	No.
Forward exchange market	No.

Arrangements for Payments and Receipts

Prescription of currency requirements	Most dealings in foreign exchange with the general public are conducted by the two commercial banks, Banca Commercial do Atlantico (BCA) and Caija Economia de Cabo Verde (CECV). Proceeds from invisibles must be repatriated in convertible currencies.
Payment arrangements	
Bilateral payment arrangements	
Operative	There are agreements with São Tomé and Príncipe, under which Cape Verde is a net creditor.
Inoperative	There are agreements with Angola and Cuba, under which Cape Verde is a net creditor.
Administration of control	All foreign exchange transactions are under the control of the Bank of Cape Verde (BCV), the central bank. Current account transactions, investments in securities, and foreign borrowing and lending in connection with current transactions have been liberalized.
International security restrictions	n.a.
Payment arrears	
Official	There are external arrears to Russia and Spain, for which rescheduling negotations are under way.
Controls on trade in gold (coins and/or bullion)	
Controls on external trade	Imports and exports of gold require prior licensing by the BCV.
Controls on exports and imports of banknotes	
On exports	
Domestic currency	The exportation of domestic currency by travelers is permitted up to CVEsc 20,000.
Foreign currency	Residents traveling abroad may take out the equivalent of CVEsc 1 million (approximately $10,000).
On imports	
Domestic currency	The importation of domestic currency is permitted up to specified limits.

| *Foreign currency* | Foreign travelers may import foreign currency up to specified limits. |

Resident Accounts

Foreign exchange accounts permitted	Residents are permitted to open foreign currency accounts at commercial banks authorized to deal in foreign exchange. The operation of these accounts is free, but must follow the BCV regulations.
Held domestically	These accounts are permitted, but prior approval is required.
Held abroad	These accounts are permitted, but prior approval is required.
Accounts in domestic currency convertible into foreign currency	n.a.

Nonresident Accounts

Foreign exchange accounts permitted	These accounts may be opened and operated as demand or term deposit accounts. Term deposit acounts may be maintained for no more than one year. Approval is required to open these accounts.
Domestic currency accounts	Nonresidents may open nonremunerated demand deposit accounts in local currency. The operation of these accounts is free, but must follow the BCV regulations.
Convertible into foreign currency	Yes.
Blocked accounts	n.a.

Imports and Import Payments

Foreign exchange budget	Yes.
Financing requirements for imports	No.
Advance import deposits	For all imports payable in foreign exchange, a 25% deposit in domestic currency was required, which was remunerated at market rates. This advance deposit requirement was eliminated on January 1, 1999.
Documentation requirements for release of foreign exchange for imports	Imports of goods exceeding CVEsc 100,000 and not involving payments from the country's foreign exchange resources are subject to a preregistration requirement.
Letters of credit	Yes.
Import licenses and other nontariff measures	Licenses, which are issued by the General Directorate of Commerce in the Ministry of Economy, Transportation, and Communications, require the endorsement of the BCV and are generally valid for 90 days; they are renewable. The provision of foreign exchange is guaranteed when the license has been previously certified by the BCV. Licenses are, in general, granted liberally for imports of medicines, capital goods, and other development-related equipment. Imports with a value of less than CVEsc 100,000 are exempt from the licensing requirement.
Positive list	Yes.
Import taxes and/or tariffs	Effective January 1, 1999, all quantitative import restrictions were replaced with a tariff protection scheme, providing tariff protection for certain domestically produced sensitive goods in the order of 50%.
State import monopoly	The importation of maize, rice, sugar, and cooking oil is conducted by state monopolies.

Exports and Export Proceeds

Repatriation requirements	Export proceeds must be repatriated within three months, but this period may be extended.
Surrender requirements	Yes.
Financing requirements	No.
Documentation requirements	No.
Export licenses	No.
Export taxes	No.

Payments for Invisible Transactions and Current Transfers

Controls on these transfers	
Trade-related payments	
Indicative limits/bona fide test	Yes.
Investment-related payments	
Indicative limits/bona fide test	Yes.
Payments for travel	Travel allowances were liberalized on May 21, 1999. The purchase of more than CVEsc 1 million in foreign currency a person a trip is subject to the submission of appropriate supportive documents.
Personal payments	
Indicative limits/bona fide test	Yes.
Foreign workers' wages	Transfers by foreign technical assistance personnel working in Cape Verde are authorized within the limits specified in the individual contracts. These contracts, as well as other contracts involving foreign exchange expenditures, are subject to prior screening by the BCV. Requests by other foreigners are examined on a case-by-case basis.
Prior approval	Yes.
Indicative limits/bona fide test	Yes.
Credit card use abroad	
Indicative limits/bona fide test	Yes.
Other payments	
Indicative limits/bona fide test	Yes.

Proceeds from Invisible Transactions and Current Transfers

Repatriation requirements	Proceeds from invisibles must be repatriated in convertible currencies.
Surrender requirements	Yes.
Restrictions on use of funds	n.a.

Capital Transactions

Controls on capital and money market instruments	Capital transactions, except those for investments in securities and foreign borrowing and lending in connection with current account transactions, must be approved in advance by the BCV. Transactions between residents and nonresidents through the CECV are free.

On capital market securities

Shares or other securities of a participating nature

    Purchase locally by nonresidents   Yes.

    Purchase abroad by residents   Yes.

On money market instruments

Purchase abroad by residents   Yes.

Controls on derivatives and other instruments   These instruments do not exist.

Controls on credit operations   Foreign borrowing and lending in connection with current transactions have been liberalized. However, these transactions are subject to verification by institutions authorized to deal in foreign exchange or by the BCV.

Commercial credits

By residents to nonresidents   Yes.

To residents from nonresidents   Yes.

Financial credits   Special authorization from the BCV is required for these transactions.

By residents to nonresidents   Yes.

To residents from nonresidents   Yes.

Guarantees, sureties, and financial backup facilities

By residents to nonresidents   Yes.

Controls on direct investment

Outward direct investment   Yes.

Inward direct investment   For direct investments exceeding $100,000, a permit is required.

Controls on liquidation of direct investment   No.

Controls on real estate transactions   Special authorization from the BCV is required for these transactions.

Controls on personal capital movements   There are controls on all personal capital movements.

Provisions specific to commercial banks and other credit institutions

Borrowing abroad   Special authorization from the BCV is required for these transactions.

Maintenance of accounts abroad   These accounts may be freely opened and operated.

Lending to nonresidents (financial or commercial credits)   Special authorization from the BCV is required for these transactions.

Differential treatment of deposit accounts in foreign exchange

Reserve requirements   Accounts in foreign exchange constitute the assessment base.

Credit controls   Special authorization from the BCV is required for these transactions.

Open foreign exchange position limits   The BCA and the CECV are allowed net foreign exchange positions of up to the equivalent of $1.5 million and $1 million, respectively.

Provisions specific to institutional investors   n.a.

Other controls imposed by securities laws	n.a.

Changes During 1999

Exchange arrangement	*January 1.* The peg to the Portuguese escudo was replaced with a peg to the euro.
Imports and import payments	*January 1.* The advance import deposit requirement was eliminated.
	January 1. All quantitative import restrictions were replaced with a tariff protection scheme.
Payments for invisible transactions and current transfers	*May 21.* Travel allowances were liberalized.

CENTRAL AFRICAN REPUBLIC

(Position as of December 31, 1999)

Status Under IMF Articles of Agreement

Article VIII   Date of acceptance: June 1, 1996.

Exchange Arrangement

Currency   The currency of the Central African Republic is the CFA franc.

Exchange rate structure   Unitary.

Classification

Exchange arrangement with no sepa-   The CFA franc is pegged to the euro, the intervention currency, at the fixed rate of
rate legal tender   CFAF 100 per €0.1524. Exchange transactions in euros between the BEAC and
                                     commercial banks take place at that rate, free of commission. Buying and selling rates
                                     for certain other foreign currencies are also officially posted, with quotations based on
                                     the fixed rate for the euro and the rates in the Paris exchange market for the currencies
                                     concerned. A commission of 0.25% is levied on all capital transfers to countries that are
                                     not members of the BEAC, except those made for the account of the Treasury and for
                                     the expenses of students.

Exchange tax   No.

Exchange subsidy   No.

Forward exchange market   There are no forward exchange markets. However, as allowed by the fixed peg with
                                     the euro, exporters and importers may always cover their position on the Paris foreign
                                     exchange market.

Arrangements for Payments and Receipts

Prescription of currency   Because the Central African Republic is linked to the French Treasury through an Opera-
requirements   tions Account, settlements with France, Monaco, and other Operations Account countries
                                     (WAEMU and CAEMC members and the Comoros) are made in French francs or the cur-
                                     rency of any other Operations Account country. Settlements with all other countries are
                                     usually made in the currencies of those countries or in euros through foreign accounts in
                                     French francs.

Payment arrangements

Regional arrangements   An Operations Account is maintained with the French Treasury that links Operations
                                     Account countries. All purchases or sales of foreign currencies or euros against CFA
                                     francs are ultimately settled through a debit or credit to the Operations Account.

Administration of control   All draft legislation, directives, correspondence, and contracts having a direct or indirect
                                     bearing on the finances of the state require the prior approval of the MOF. The Debt
                                     Directorate of the MOF supervises borrowing abroad. The Office of Foreign Financial
                                     Relations of the same ministry supervises lending abroad; the issuing, advertising, or
                                     offering for sale of foreign securities in the Central African Republic; and inward and
                                     outward direct investment. Exchange control is administered by the MOF, which has
                                     delegated some approval authority to the BEAC (control over the external position of
                                     the banks, granting of exceptional travel allocations in excess of the basic allowances,
                                     and control over the repatriation of net export proceeds), to authorized banks, and to the
                                     Postal Administration. All exchange transactions relating to foreign countries must be
                                     effected through authorized banks. Export declarations are to be made through the Direc-
                                     torate of Foreign Trade of the Ministry of Commerce and Industry, except those for gold,
                                     which are to be made through the BEAC.

International security restrictions   n.a.

Payment arrears	Yes.
Controls on trade in gold (coins and/or bullion)	
Controls on external trade	Imports and exports of gold require a license, which is seldom granted. In practice, imports and exports are made by an authorized purchasing office. Exempt from prior authorization are (1) imports and exports by or on behalf of the Treasury, and (2) imports and exports of manufactured articles containing a small quantity of gold (such as gold-filled or gold-plated articles). Both licensed and exempt imports of gold are subject to customs declaration. Certain companies have been officially appointed as Offices for the Purchase, Import, and Export of Gold and Raw Diamonds.
Controls on exports and imports of banknotes	
On exports	
Domestic currency	There is no limit on the amount of banknotes that residents and nonresidents may export from one CAEMC country to another. Exports of banknotes outside the CAEMC zone are prohibited.
Foreign currency	All resident travelers, regardless of destination, must declare in writing all means of payment at their disposal at the time of departure. The reexportation of foreign banknotes is allowed up to the equivalent of CFAF 250,000; the reexportation of foreign banknotes above this ceiling requires documentation demonstrating either their importation or their purchase against other means of payment registered in the name of the traveler or through the use of nonresident deposits held in local banks.
On imports	
Domestic currency	There is no limit on the amount of banknotes that residents and nonresidents may import from another CAEMC country. Imports of banknotes from outside the CAEMC zone are prohibited.

Resident Accounts

Foreign exchange accounts permitted	Yes.
Held domestically	n.a.
Held abroad	n.a.
Accounts in domestic currency convertible into foreign currency	n.a.

Nonresident Accounts

Foreign exchange accounts permitted	n.a.
Domestic currency accounts	The regulations pertaining to nonresident accounts are based on regulations applied in France. The principal nonresident accounts are foreign accounts in euros. As the BEAC has suspended the repurchase of BEAC banknotes circulating outside the territories of its member countries, BEAC banknotes received by the foreign correspondents of authorized banks and mailed to the BEAC agency in Bangui may not be credited to foreign accounts in euros.
Blocked accounts	n.a.

Imports and Import Payments

Foreign exchange budget	n.a.

Financing requirements for imports

Minimum financing requirements	Yes.
Advance payment requirements	Yes.
Advance import deposits	Yes.

Documentation requirements for release of foreign exchange for imports

Domiciliation requirements — All import transactions relating to foreign countries must be domiciled with an authorized bank.

Preshipment inspection — Preshipment inspection is required for coffee, cotton, and diamonds.

Import licenses used as exchange licenses — Import declarations are required for all imports, and the import license entitles importers to purchase the necessary exchange, provided that the shipping documents are submitted to the authorized bank.

Import licenses and other nontariff measures

Negative list — Imports of firearms of any origin are prohibited.

Import taxes and/or tariffs — The CAEMC CET applies. There are four rates: 5% for essential commodities, 10% for capital goods and inputs, 20% for intermediates, and 30% for consumer goods. The intra-CAEMC tariff is 20% of the CET.

State import monopoly — n.a.

Exports and Export Proceeds

Repatriation requirements — Proceeds must be collected and repatriated within one month of the due date, which must not be later than 90 days after the arrival of the goods at their destination, unless special authorization is obtained.

Surrender requirements — Export proceeds received in currencies other than euros or those of an Operations Account country must be surrendered.

Financing requirements — n.a.

Documentation requirements

Domiciliation — All export transactions must be domiciled with an authorized bank.

Preshipment inspection — Preshipment inspection for coffee is required.

Export licenses — All exports require a declaration.

Without quotas — Yes.

Export taxes — Effective February 11, 1999, the export duties and the export turnover tax were consolidated into a single export tax.

Payments for Invisible Transactions and Current Transfers

Controls on these transfers — Payments for invisibles to France, Monaco, and the Operations Account countries are permitted freely; those to other countries are subject to approval. Approval authority for many types of payment has been delegated to authorized banks. Payments for invisibles related to trade are permitted freely when the basic trade transaction has been approved or does not require authorization.

Trade-related payments

Prior approval — Yes.

Investment-related payments	Transfers of profits and dividends are permitted freely when the basic transaction has been approved.
Prior approval	Yes.
Payments for travel	
Prior approval	Yes.
Quantitative limits	Residents traveling to other countries of the franc zone may obtain an unlimited allocation in French francs. Within the BEAC zone, BEAC banknotes may be exported without limit. The allowances for travel to countries outside the franc zone are subject to the following limits: (1) for tourist travel, CFAF 100,000 a day, maximum CFAF 2 million a trip; (2) for business travel, CFAF 250,000 a day, maximum CFAF 5 million a trip; (3) allowances in excess of these limits are subject to the authorization of the MOF or, by delegation, the BEAC. Returning resident travelers are required to declare all means of payment in their possession upon arrival at customs and surrender within eight days all means of payment exceeding the equivalent of CFAF 25,000. All resident travelers, regardless of destination, must declare in writing all means of payment at their disposal at the time of departure. The reexportation by nonresident travelers of means of payment other than banknotes registered in their name and issued abroad is not restricted. However, documentation is required to prove that such means of payment have been purchased with funds drawn from a foreign account in CFA francs or with other foreign exchange.
Indicative limits/bona fide test	Bona fide requests for allowances in excess of the limits are normally granted.
Personal payments	
Prior approval	Prior approval is not required for costs covering studies abroad.
Quantitative limits	The allowance for sick persons traveling to countries outside the franc zone for medical reasons is CFAF 100,000 a day, maximum CFAF 2.5 million. For studies abroad, the limit is CFAF 1 million.
Indicative limits/bona fide test	Indicative limits or bona fide tests are applied to medical costs and the costs of study abroad.
Foreign workers' wages	
Prior approval	Yes.
Quantitative limits	Foreign nationals working in the CAEMC are allowed to transfer 50% of their net salary upon presentation of their pay vouchers, provided that the transfers take place within three months of the pay period concerned.
Credit card use abroad	
Prior approval	Yes.
Quantitative limits	The use of credit cards, which must be issued by resident financial intermediaries and approved by the MOF, is limited to the ceilings set for tourism and business travel.
Indicative limits/bona fide test	Bona fide requests for allowances in excess of limits are normally granted.
Other payments	
Prior approval	Prior approval is required for consulting and legal fees.

Proceeds from Invisible Transactions and Current Transfers

Repatriation requirements	Proceeds from transactions in invisibles with France, Monaco, and the Operations Account countries may be retained. All amounts due from residents of other countries in respect of services, and all income earned in those countries from foreign assets, must be collected within one month of the due date.
Surrender requirements	If payment is received in foreign currency, it must be surrendered within one month of the date of receipt.
Restrictions on use of funds	n.a.

Capital Transactions

Controls on capital and money market instruments	Capital movements between the Central African Republic, France, and the Operations Account countries are free of exchange control. Capital transfers to all other countries require exchange control approval and are restricted, but capital receipts from such countries are permitted freely.

On capital market securities

Shares or other securities of a participating nature

  Sale or issue locally by nonresidents   The issuing, advertising, or offering for sale of foreign securities in the Central African Republic requires prior authorization from the MOF. Exempt from authorization, however, are operations in connection with (1) loans backed by a guarantee from the government; and (2) shares similar to securities, when the issuing, advertising, or offering for sale in the Central African Republic has previously been authorized.

  Purchase abroad by residents   Yes.

On money market instruments

  Purchase abroad by residents   Yes.

On collective investment securities

  Purchase abroad by residents   Yes.

Controls on derivatives and other instruments

Purchase abroad by residents   Yes.

Controls on credit operations

Commercial credits

  By residents to nonresidents   Lending abroad by residents or by branches or subsidiaries of juridical persons in the Central African Republic whose registered office is abroad requires prior authorization from the MOF. Exempt from this authorization are (1) loans granted by registered banks, and (2) other loans when the total amount of loans outstanding does not exceed CFAF 50 million for any one lender. The contracting of loans that are exempt from authorization and each repayment must be reported to the Office of Foreign Financial Relations within 20 days of the operation, except when the amount of the loan granted abroad by the lender is less than CFAF 500,000.

  To residents from nonresidents   Foreign borrowing by the government or its public and semipublic enterprises, as well as all foreign borrowing with a government guarantee, requires the prior approval of the Director of the Budget. Borrowing abroad by residents or by branches or subsidiaries of juridical persons in the Central African Republic whose registered office is abroad requires prior authorization from the MOF. Exempt from this authorization are (1) loans constituting a direct investment abroad for which prior approval has been obtained, as indicated above; (2) loans directly connected with the rendering of services abroad by the persons or firms mentioned above, or with the financing of commercial transactions either between the Central African Republic and countries abroad, or between foreign countries in which those persons or firms take part; (3) loans contracted by registered banks; and (4) loans other than those mentioned above, when the total amount of loans outstanding does not exceed CFAF 50 million for any one borrower. Loans referred to under (4) and each repayment must be reported to the Office of Foreign Financial Relations within 20 days of the operation, unless the total outstanding amount of all loans contracted abroad by the borrower is less than CFAF 500,000.

Financial credits

  By residents to nonresidents   Yes.

  To residents from nonresidents   Yes.

Guarantees, sureties, and financial backup facilities

By residents to nonresidents　　　Yes.

To residents from nonresidents　　Yes.

Controls on direct investment

Outward direct investment

Direct investments abroad, including those made through foreign companies that are directly or indirectly controlled by persons in the Central African Republic and those made by branches or subsidiaries abroad of companies in the Central African Republic, require the prior approval of the MOF, unless they take the form of a capital increase resulting from the reinvestment of undistributed profits.

Inward direct investment

Investments must be declared to the MOF, unless they take the form of a capital increase resulting from the reinvestment of undistributed profits; the MOF may request a postponement of up to two months from receipt of the declaration.

Controls on liquidation of direct investment

The liquidation of investments requires prior approval from the MOF, unless the operation involves the relinquishing of a participation that had previously been approved.

Controls on real estate transactions　　n.a.

Controls on personal capital movements

Transfer of gambling and prize earnings　　Yes.

Provisions specific to commercial banks and other credit institutions　　n.a.

Provisions specific to institutional investors　　n.a.

Other controls imposed by securities laws　　n.a.

Changes During 1999

Exchange arrangement

January 1. The CFA franc peg to the French franc was replaced with a peg to the euro.

Exports and export proceeds

February 11. The export turnover tax was consolidated into a single export tax.

CHAD

(Position as of December 31, 1999)

Status Under IMF Articles of Agreement

Article VIII   Date of acceptance: June 1, 1996.

Exchange Arrangement

Currency   The currency of Chad is the CFA franc.

Exchange rate structure   Unitary.

Classification

Exchange arrangement with no sepa-   The CFA franc is pegged to the euro at the fixed rate of CFAF 100 per €0.1524. Exchange
rate legal tender   transactions in euros between the BEAC and commercial banks take place at the same rate
                                      and are free of commission. Buying and selling rates for certain other foreign currencies are
                                      also officially posted, with quotations based on the fixed rate for the euro and the rates in
                                      the Paris exchange market for the currencies concerned. All transfers and exchange opera-
                                      tions are subject to a commission levied by the Treasury. The commission rate amounts to
                                      0.25% in the CFA franc zone and 0.5% outside the CFA franc zone.

Exchange tax   No.

Exchange subsidy   No.

Forward exchange market   Forward cover for imports is permitted only for specified commodities and requires the
                                prior approval of the MOF.

Official cover of forward operations   Yes.

Arrangements for Payments and Receipts

Prescription of currency   Because Chad is an Operations Account country, settlements with France, Monaco, and
requirements   other Operations Account countries (WAEMU and CAEMC members and the Comoros)
                                are made in CFA francs, euros, or the currency of any other Operations Account country.
                                Settlements with all other countries are usually made in the currencies of those countries
                                or in euros through foreign accounts in francs.

Payment arrangements

Regional arrangements   An Operations Account is maintained with the French Treasury that links Operations Ac-
                                count countries. All purchases or sales of foreign currencies or euros against CFA francs
                                are ultimately settled through a debit or credit to the Operations Account.

Clearing agreements   Yes.

Administration of control   Exchange control is administered by the MOF, but it has delegated approval authority in
                                part to the External Finance and Exchange Control Subdirectorate, which issues instruc-
                                tions to the authorized banks. All exchange transactions relating to countries outside the
                                Operations Account area must be made through authorized banks. The MOF supervises
                                public and private sector borrowing and lending abroad; the issuing, advertising, or offer-
                                ing for sale of foreign securities in Chad; and inward and outward direct investment. It
                                also issues import and export authorizations for gold.

International security restrictions   No.

Payment arrears

Official   Yes.

Controls on trade in gold (coins and/or bullion)

Controls on external trade

Imports and exports of gold require prior authorization from both the MOF and the Directorate of Geological and Mining Research, as well as a visa from the External Finance Department. Exempt from this requirement are (1) imports and exports by, or on behalf of, the monetary authorities; and (2) imports and exports of manufactured articles containing a small quantity of gold (such as gold-filled or gold-plated articles). Unworked gold may be exported only to France. Both licensed and exempt imports of gold are subject to customs declaration.

Controls on exports and imports of banknotes

On exports

Domestic currency

The exportation of banknotes issued by the BEAC to areas outside that of the BEAC is prohibited. Nonresidents traveling from one BEAC member country to another may take with them an unlimited amount of CFA franc zone banknotes and coins.

Foreign currency

Residents visiting other CFA franc zone countries may obtain an unlimited allocation in French francs. This allocation may be provided in banknotes, traveler's checks, bank drafts, and bank or postal transfers, etc. For travel to countries outside the CFA franc zone, the exchange allocation depends on the type of travel and may be made in banknotes, traveler's checks, bank drafts, or postal transfers. Nonresident travelers may take out foreign exchange or other foreign means of payment up to the amount they declared on entry into the BEAC area. If they have made no declaration on entry into one of the BEAC countries, they may take out only up to the equivalent of CFAF 500,000.

On imports

Domestic currency

Resident and nonresident travelers may bring in any amount of banknotes and coins issued by the BEAC, the Bank of France, or any other bank of Operations Account countries. The importation of banknotes issued by the BEAC from areas outside the BEAC area is prohibited.

Foreign currency

Resident and nonresident travelers may bring in any amount of foreign banknotes and coins (except gold coins) of countries outside the Operations Account area.

Resident Accounts

Foreign exchange accounts permitted

Yes.

Held domestically

These accounts are permitted, but prior approval is required.

Held abroad

These accounts are permitted, but prior approval is required.

Accounts in domestic currency convertible into foreign currency

Yes.

Nonresident Accounts

Foreign exchange accounts permitted

These accounts are permitted, but prior approval is required. Principal nonresident accounts are foreign accounts in francs.

Domestic currency accounts

The regulations pertaining to nonresident accounts are based on regulations applied in France. Because the BEAC has suspended the repurchase of BEAC banknotes circulating outside the territories of the CFA franc zone, BEAC banknotes received by the foreign correspondents of authorized banks and mailed to the BEAC agency in Chad by the Bank of France or the BCEAO may not be credited to foreign accounts in francs.

Convertible into foreign currency

These accounts may be converted, but prior approval is required.

Blocked accounts

Yes.

Imports and Import Payments

Foreign exchange budget — No.

Financing requirements for imports — No.

Documentation requirements for release of foreign exchange for imports

Domiciliation requirements — Imports in excess of CFAF 100,000 and relating to countries outside the BEAC must be domiciled with an authorized bank.

Letters of credit — Yes.

Import licenses and other nontariff measures

Negative list — A special import authorization by the Ministry of Commerce and Industrial Promotion is required for imports of sulphur and other explosives.

Import taxes and/or tariffs — Import tariffs on products from countries that are not members of the UDEAC range from 5% to 30% with four tariff bands.

State import monopoly — No.

Exports and Export Proceeds

Repatriation requirements — Export proceeds normally must be received within 180 days of the arrival of the commodities at their destination.

Surrender requirements — Export proceeds received in currencies other than those of France or of an Operations Account country must be surrendered. The proceeds must be collected and, if received in a foreign currency, surrendered within one month of the due date.

Financing requirements — No.

Documentation requirements

Letters of credit — Yes.

Guarantees — Yes.

Domiciliation — Export transactions to foreign countries exceeding CFAF 50,000 must be domiciled with an authorized bank.

Export licenses

Without quotas — Yes.

Export taxes — No.

Payments for Invisible Transactions and Current Transfers

Controls on these transfers — Payments for invisibles to France, Monaco, and the Operations Account countries are permitted freely. Payments for invisibles related to trade are permitted freely if the basic trade transaction has been approved or does not require authorization.

Some current payments, however, may be subject to delay. On a temporary basis, nonresidents, except diplomatic missions and their staff, international organizations and their staff, agencies with equivalent status and their staff, as well as employees and self-employed members of the professions (professionally active in Operations Account area countries for less than a year), are not permitted to send transfers to countries that are not CFA franc zone members without prior authorization from the proper authorities. They may, however, receive transfers from abroad. A simple declaration is required for transfers to countries outside the BEAC area not exceeding CFAF 500,000 by residents; for transfers of more than CFAF 500,000, prior authorization must be obtained from the competent authorities.

For many types of payment, approval authority has been delegated to authorized banks, which are required to execute promptly all duly documented transfer orders and to dispatch cable transfers within 48 hours of receipt of the relevant request.

Trade-related payments	Insurance on all imports with f.o.b. values exceeding CFAF 500,000 must be arranged with local insurance companies by the importer.
Prior approval	Yes.
Quantitative limits	Yes.
Indicative limits/bona fide test	Yes.
Investment-related payments	Information is not available on the payment of amortization of loans or depreciation of direct investments.
Prior approval	Yes.
Quantitative limits	Yes.
Indicative limits/bona fide test	Yes.
Payments for travel	Travelers—civil servants on missions, students, persons on pilgrimage, etc.—must use the following payment instruments: foreign exchange, traveler's checks, bank drafts, bank and postal transfers, etc. Residents visiting other CFA franc zone countries may obtain an unlimited allocation in French francs. This allocation may be provided in banknotes, traveler's checks, bank drafts, bank or postal transfers, etc.
Prior approval	For travel to countries outside the CFA franc zone, the exchange allocation is subject to prior authorization from the relevant administrative authorities.
Quantitative limits	Residents traveling outside the CFA franc zone for tourism, sporting events, participation in expositions, organization of fairs, participation in seminars or international meetings of a personal capacity, pilgrimages, etc., may obtain an exchange allocation equivalent to CFAF 200,000 a day up to a maximum of CFAF 4 million a person a trip for those over 10 years of age; for children under 10, the allocation is reduced by one-half. Residents traveling to countries outside the CFA franc zone for business may obtain an exchange allocation equivalent to CFAF 500,000 a day, up to a maximum of CFAF 10 million a trip.
	Civil servants and government employees traveling on official business to countries outside the CFA franc zone may obtain the same exchange allocation as tourists, but only if their mission costs are less than a daily allocation of CFAF 200,000, up to a limit of CFAF 4 million. For amounts exceeding these limits, higher exchange allocation is subject to the presentation of supporting documents.
Indicative limits/bona fide test	Yes.
Personal payments	
Prior approval	Yes.
Quantitative limits	For countries outside the CFA franc zone, the exchange allocation for medical costs is equivalent to CFAF 250,000 a day, up to a limit of CFAF 5 million. For studies abroad, the exchange allocation for countries outside the CFA franc zone is equivalent to a three-month scholarship plus expenses for supplies. However, a student, whether or not the holder of a scholarship, may obtain an exchange allocation not exceeding the equivalent of CFAF 2 million. Higher exchange allocations are subject to the presentation of supporting documents.
Indicative limits/bona fide test	Yes.
Foreign workers' wages	
Prior approval	Yes.
Quantitative limits	Yes.
Indicative limits/bona fide test	Yes.

Other payments

Prior approval	Yes.
Quantitative limits	Yes.
Indicative limits/bona fide test	Yes.

Proceeds from Invisible Transactions and Current Transfers

Repatriation requirements   Yes.

Surrender requirements   Proceeds from transactions in invisibles with France, Monaco, and the Operations Account countries may be retained. All amounts due from residents of other countries in respect of services, and all income earned in those countries from foreign assets, must be collected and, if received in foreign currency, surrendered within two months of the due date.

Restrictions on use of funds   No.

Capital Transactions

Controls on capital and money market instruments   Capital movements between Chad and France, Monaco, and the Operations Account countries are free of exchange control; capital transfers to all other countries require exchange control approval and are restricted, but capital receipts from such countries are permitted freely. All foreign securities, foreign currencies, and titles embodying claims on foreign countries or nonresidents held by residents or nonresidents in Chad must be deposited with authorized banks in Chad.

Additional special controls are maintained over borrowing and lending abroad; inward and outward direct investment; and the issuing, advertising, or offering for sale of foreign securities in Chad. These controls relate only to the transactions themselves, not to payments or receipts. With the exception of those controls over the sale or introduction of foreign securities in Chad, the measures do not apply to France, Monaco, and the Operations Account countries.

On capital market securities

Shares or other securities of a participating nature

    Sale or issue locally by nonresidents   The issuing, advertising, or offering for sale of foreign securities in Chad requires prior authorization from the MOF. Exempt from authorization, however, are operations in connection with loans backed by a guarantee from the Chadian government and shares similar to securities, when their issuing, advertising, or offering for sale in Chad has already been authorized.

    Purchase abroad by residents   Yes.

    Sale or issue abroad by residents   Yes.

On money market instruments

Sale or issue locally by nonresidents   Yes.

Purchase abroad by residents   Yes.

Sale or issue abroad by residents   Yes.

On collective investment securities

Sale or issue locally by nonresidents   Yes.

Purchase abroad by residents   Yes.

Sale or issue abroad by residents   Yes.

Controls on derivatives and other instruments

Sale or issue locally by nonresidents | Yes.

Purchase abroad by residents | Yes.

Sale or issue abroad by residents | Yes.

Controls on credit operations

Commercial credits

By residents to nonresidents | Lending requires prior MOF authorization. The following are, however, exempt from this authorization: (1) loans directly connected with the rendering of services abroad by the persons or firms concerned, or with the financing of commercial transactions either between Chad and countries abroad or between foreign countries in which these persons or firms take part; and (2) other loans when the total outstanding amount of these loans does not exceed CFAF 5 million for any one lender. The making of loans referred to under (2) requires no authorization, but each repayment must be declared to the MOF within 30 days of the operation.

To residents from nonresidents | Borrowing requires prior MOF authorization. The following are, however, exempt from this authorization: (1) loans constituting a direct investment abroad for which prior approval has been obtained, as indicated above; (2) loans directly connected with the rendering of services abroad by the persons or firms concerned, or with the financing of commercial transactions either between Chad and countries abroad or between foreign countries in which these persons or firms take part; and (3) loans other than those mentioned above when the total outstanding amount of the loan does not exceed CFAF 10 million for any one borrower, the interest rate is no higher than 7%, and the maturity is two years or less. The contracting of loans referred to under (3) requires no authorization, but each repayment must be declared to the MOF within 30 days of the operation.

Financial credits | The same regulations apply as for commercial credits.

By residents to nonresidents | Yes.

To residents from nonresidents | Yes.

Guarantees, sureties, and financial backup facilities

By residents to nonresidents | Yes.

To residents from nonresidents | Yes.

Controls on direct investment

Outward direct investment | Investments require the prior approval of the MOF.

Inward direct investment | Investments require the prior approval of the MOF, unless they take the form of a mixed-economy enterprise.

Controls on liquidation of direct investment | The full or partial liquidation of direct investments in Chad must be declared to the MOF within 30 days of each operation.

Controls on real estate transactions

Purchase abroad by residents | Yes.

Purchase locally by nonresidents | Yes.

Sale locally by nonresidents | Yes.

Controls on personal capital movements

Transfer of gambling and prize earnings | Yes.

Provisions specific to commercial banks and other credit institutions

Borrowing abroad	Yes.
Maintenance of accounts abroad	Yes.
Lending to nonresidents (financial or commercial credits)	Yes.
Lending locally in foreign exchange	Yes.
Purchase of locally issued securities denominated in foreign exchange	Yes.

Differential treatment of deposit accounts in foreign exchange

Reserve requirements	Yes.
Liquid asset requirements	Commercial banks must maintain a specified minimum amount of their assets in Chad.
Interest rate controls	Yes.
Credit controls	Yes.
Provisions specific to institutional investors	n.a.
Other controls imposed by securities laws	No.

Changes During 1999

Exchange arrangement	*January 1.* The CFA franc peg to the French franc was replaced with a peg to the euro.

CHILE

(Position as of January 31, 2000)

Status Under IMF Articles of Agreement

Article VIII   Date of acceptance: July 27, 1977.

Exchange Arrangement

Currency   The currency of Chile is the Chilean peso.

Exchange rate structure

Unitary   There are two foreign exchange markets, but the exchange rate prevailing in both markets is the same: (1) the official market, through which all current payments and authorized capital transactions, including loan receipts, must be transacted; and (2) the informal market, through which all transactions not required to be channeled through the formal market take place. The official foreign exchange market consists of commercial banks and exchange houses licensed by the Central Bank of Chile (CBC).

Classification

Independently floating   In both exchange markets, economic agents are free to negotiate rates; the CBC conducted transactions in the official exchange market within margins of ±8% around the reference rate and, as of December 1998, both limits of the band were to be widened by a factor of 0.0135% a day. On September 2, 1999, the central bank suspended the crawling band and allowed the peso to float. Thus, the exchange rate arrangement was reclassified to the category independently floating from the category crawling band.

Exchange tax   No.

Exchange subsidy   The CBC provides a subsidy (in the form of notes indexed to inflation with a minimum maturity of six years and an interest rate of 3%) on the following service payments on some debts contracted before August 6, 1982 (the original amount of the debt was about US$8 billion): (1) payments to Chilean banks or financial companies whose debt is indexed to the official exchange rate, and (2) payments abroad on debt obligations registered with the CBC. The subsidized rate is the official reference rate.

Forward exchange market   Free access is given for the purchase of dollars through forward contracts in the forward exchange market. Banks inform the CBC daily about their domestic operations and monthly about their operations abroad.

Arrangements for Payments and Receipts

Prescription of currency requirements   Currencies listed in the Compendium of International Foreign Exchange Regulations are permitted, while operations with other currencies require a special authorization from the CBC.

Payment arrangements

Regional arrangements   Settlements between Chile and the other LAIA countries are made through accounts maintained with each other by the CBC and the central banks of each of the countries concerned within the framework of the multilateral clearing system of the LAIA.

Clearing agreements   Yes.

Administration of control   Exchange market regulations and their administration are the responsibility of the CBC.

International security restrictions   No.

Payment arrears   No.

Controls on trade in gold (coins and/or bullion)

Controls on domestic ownership and/or trade

Monetary gold may be traded only by authorized dealers, but ordinary transactions in gold between private individuals are unrestricted.

Controls on external trade

Trade is unrestricted, subject to normal export and import formalities, including registration with the CBC.

Controls on exports and imports of banknotes

No.

Resident Accounts

Foreign exchange accounts permitted

Yes.

Held domestically

Both natural and juridical persons may hold foreign currency checking accounts. The average balance is subject to legal reserve requirements. Juridical persons must take into account legal restrictions on investments, given their commercial activities (i.e., pension funds administrators). In the case of checking accounts, the commercial banks must certify the domicile reported.

Held abroad

Juridical persons subject to regulations on investment abroad (i.e., banks and pension funds) must abide by such regulations.

Accounts in domestic currency convertible into foreign currency

No.

Nonresident Accounts

Foreign exchange accounts permitted

Checking accounts may not be held by nonresidents because holders must be domiciled in the country.

Domestic currency accounts

No.

Blocked accounts

No.

Imports and Import Payments

Foreign exchange budget

No.

Financing requirements for imports

There is a period during which foreign exchange may be bought in the formal market after the obligation's expiration date has been documented on the import report. On December 9, 1999, this period was extended to 360 days from 90 days.

Documentation requirements for release of foreign exchange for imports

Foreign exchange can be bought on both the official and the informal market. However, if payments are made through the official foreign exchange market, they require an import report issued by the CBC, which must be obtained from, and processed through, the intermediary of a local commercial bank.

Domiciliation requirements

Only resident natural or juridical persons may engage in import activities.

Preshipment inspection

The CBC may reject the import report if prices are not market prices.

Import licenses and other nontariff measures

All imports above $3,000 require an import report issued by the CBC. Imports of wheat, maize, edible oil, and sugar are subject to after-duty price margin limits. Antidumping and countervailing duty laws are applied.

Negative list

Imports of used motor vehicles are restricted.

Import taxes and/or tariffs

Starting from January 1, 1999, the uniform tariff was reduced by 1 percentage point a year so as to reduce it to 6% from 10% by 2003. Imports are subject to a uniform 9% tariff rate with a few exceptions (including on imports from LAIA countries and under a number of bilateral trade agreements).

State import monopoly	No.

Exports and Export Proceeds

Repatriation requirements	Generally, export receipts do not have to be brought back into the country; however, the exporter should inform the CBC on the use of the proceeds. A share of receipts from copper exports of CODELCO (state copper company) must be deposited in the account of the Copper Stabilization Fund at the CBC; withdrawals are permitted only under prescribed circumstances.
Financing requirements	Exports may be financed with advances from foreign buyers or with external or internal credits, as agreed between the trading parties. Until July 12, 1999, when this requirement was eliminated, such advances had to be channeled through the formal exchange market. Credits must be identified with shipments and paid immediately after proceeds are received.
Documentation requirements	The exporter must submit an export report to the CBC through a banking company, establishing the exporter's identity and the terms of the operation.
Letters of credit	The commercial bank that receives the letter prior to payment of the foreign exchange will demand from the exporter the shipping documents of the merchandise and the additional requirements established in the LC.
Domiciliation	Yes.
Preshipment inspection	Inspections are done by customs agents, who perform the role of "customs ministers of faith"; subsequently, a shipment order is issued, which is subject to customs control.
Export licenses	No.
Export taxes	No.

Payments for Invisible Transactions and Current Transfers

Controls on these transfers	
Investment-related payments	There are no controls on the transfer of interest payments.
Prior approval	Transfers of profits require the authorization of the CBC for access to the formal market. In the case of loans, the purchase of currency for amortization must be made in the formal exchange market, subject to prior approval by the CBC, within a period either before the expiration date that appears in the loan repayment program or 10 days after the expiration date.
	In the case of capital repatriation, which may only be done after complying with the minimum one-year holding period, permission must be obtained from the CBC for access to the formal exchange market.
Credit card use abroad	The CBC authorizes the commercial banks to issue credit cards. Card users must pay balances due for purchases abroad with their own resources. However, under the concept of extraordinary expenditures, each person may acquire foreign exchange in the formal market without declaring the purpose.

Proceeds from Invisible Transactions and Current Transfers

Repatriation requirements	Yes.
Surrender requirements	Proceeds from selected transactions (e.g., royalties and copyright fees, commissions, proceeds from insurance, and other benefits related to foreign trade) are subject to a 100% surrender requirement.
Restrictions on use of funds	No.

Capital Transactions

Controls on capital and money market instruments

On capital market securities

Shares or other securities of a participating nature

Purchase locally by nonresidents

Nonresidents may invest in domestic securities in three ways:

(1) Through acquisition by foreign investment funds (FICE). These are formed by foreign capital and administered by an open society established in Chile. Investments may not exceed 5% of social capital in any one company and 10% of the funds' total assets. These funds may not invest more than 40% of their portfolios in equities of the same holding period, and all FICEs as a group may not hold more than 25% of the equities of the same open society. Other requirements for FICEs are a five-year minimum holding period, a profit tax of 10%, and some portfolio restrictions that vary with the duration of the holding period;

(2) Through a financial investment (purchase of fixed-income securities and equities). These are, however, subject to a minimum holding period requirement of one year and to the general income tax law. Equities that have American Depository Receipts (ADRs) may be acquired in the country and converted into ADRs. The issuance of primary ADRs is exempt from the above restrictions, but the issuers are subject to minimum international rating requirements. Holders of ADRs are permitted to participate in preferential share offerings, changing shares thus acquired into ADRs; and

(3) Through loans. These may also be used to finance the purchase of securities in the country. They are subject to a 4% tax on interest payments, and a 1.2% stamp duty.

Sale or issue locally by nonresidents

Proceeds from the sale of domestic securities by nonresidents are subject to the one-year holding period requirement if the capital inflow entered as a financial investment. The sale of equities that are the property of foreigners due to the ADR mechanism is possible, since Chilean ADRs can be converted into domestic stock. However, the resources obtained through the sale must be repatriated. ADRs issued from equities directly acquired in the Chilean stock market (also called secondary ADRs) are tightly restricted, both for the authorized period for acquiring stocks domestically and for the authorized period for acquiring foreign exchange after a local stock sale. Issuance of foreign securities by nonresidents is subject to the same procedures applied to domestic securities. In practice, no foreign securities are traded domestically. Once the respective taxes have been paid, profits may be transferred freely without delay.

Purchase abroad by residents

Except for banks and pension funds, there are no controls on the acquisition of international fixed-income assets and current account deposits. Pension funds are authorized to hold up to 16% of their funds in foreign assets, including up to 10% in variable-income assets.

Sale or issue abroad by residents

Residents may issue equities and bonds abroad, and the associated foreign exchange operations must be effected through the formal exchange market. Equities may be sold according to the rules that regulate capital inflows through the mechanism of ADRs. Primary ADR issues are only subject to a minimum international risk-rating requirement for long-term debt of BBB– for banks and financial institutions.

Bonds or other debt securities

Purchase locally by nonresidents

Such investments must be authorized by, and registered with, the CBC. Currency must be brought in and sold in the formal exchange market. A minimum holding period of one year is required.

Sale or issue locally by nonresidents

These operations are not permitted.

Purchase abroad by residents

Residents may acquire bonds or other investment instruments abroad. However, the foreign exchange must be purchased in the formal exchange market and transferred abroad through the same market after informing the CBC. In the case of pension fund managers (PFMs), insurance companies, mutual funds, and international investment funds, limits are applied with regard to instrument types and amounts.

Sale or issue abroad by residents	Banking firms or juridical persons registered with the Superintendency of Securities and Insurance may issue bonds, subject to prior authorization by the CBC. The long-term foreign debt instruments of the firms issuing them must have a minimum classification of BBB+. Banking firms or financial institutions must have a minimum classification of A/B (BBB+ in the case of subordinate bonds). The weighted average term of the bonds should not be less than two years. In the case of subordinate bonds, the term must not be less than five years. Effective April 15, 1999, for entities other than banks and financial firms, bond issues were permitted with terms of more than two years and less than four years, with a minimum BB classification being required. In the case of bond issues for terms of four years or longer, the minimum classification required is BB– (previously BB).

On money market instruments

Purchase locally by nonresidents	In general, these acquisitions are authorized for nonresidents, but there are regulations governing the mode of inflow. The associated capital inflow liquidation and the subsequent repatriation of proceeds must be effected through the formal exchange market. Acquisitions through external loans are subject to a tax on interest of 4% and a stamp tax of 1.2%. Acquisitions through FICEs are subject to a minimum holding period of five years in addition to a 10% profit tax. In the case of financial investments, there is a minimum holding period of one year, and they are subject to the general income tax law.
Sale or issue locally by nonresidents	These transactions are not authorized and neither is the promotion of these or other financial services from abroad. To operate in the domestic financial market, the company must be registered and established, and must have brought in capital for operational purposes. The legal mechanism used is the creation of a Chilean agency of the foreign corporation.
Purchase abroad by residents	The acquisition of money market instruments by individuals and nonfinancial companies is not restricted.
Sale or issue abroad by residents	Yes.

On collective investment securities

Purchase locally by nonresidents	These purchases are considered financial investments subject to a minimum holding period of one year. Funds that enter Chile through an FICE are subject to a minimum holding period of five years.
Sale or issue locally by nonresidents	These transactions are not permitted. To operate in the domestic financial market, the company must be registered and established, and must have brought in capital for operational purposes. Once this has occurred, the sales of collective investment securities are subject to the same domestic rules as any other investment, with no controls on the repatriation of profits.
Purchase abroad by residents	There are no controls for nonfinancial agents. Pension funds are restricted by the type of fund (mainly to avoid leveraged and hedged funds), country risk, regulation, liquidity, experience of the fund, and participant's concentration.
Sale or issue abroad by residents	In practice, Chilean mutual funds (open funds) and investment funds (closed funds) are not offered directly abroad. To operate abroad, such funds must meet the existing regulations of the foreign country. Domestically issued instruments may be sold to nonresidents, but funds must be repatriated. These inflows are considered a financial investment subject to a one-year holding requirement. FICEs that come into Chile under foreign ownership may be sold and traded in the New York or the London stock exchanges. The capital committed by the FICE must remain invested in Chile for five years.

Controls on derivatives and other instruments	On April 27, 1999, the CBC authorized financial institutions to make foreign interest rate forwards, futures, and swaps in the local markets. Agents must inform the CBC.
Purchase locally by nonresidents	The market is not well developed. Nonresidents may not participate in the formal market for currency derivatives, although they may conduct these transactions with nonbank institutions.
Sale or issue locally by nonresidents	To operate, foreign agents must have resident status.
Purchase abroad by residents	The CBC regulates derivative operations undertaken on external markets in foreign currencies, international interest rate commodities, and variable-return instruments. Speculative positions with derivatives abroad may be taken (banks may not take over-the-counter interest rate options), but the currency must be remitted and returned through the

formal exchange market. Provisions relating to the hedging operations that banks may carry out are maintained, as well as those relating to derivative operations in variable return instruments. The latter may also be undertaken by nonbank financial institutions.

Sale or issue abroad by residents

Derivatives for currency and interest rates exist for operations with foreign agents in over-the-counter operations, with security dealers or brokers that are authorized by the foreign authorities, or with foreign banks. There is access to formal spot exchange markets for hedging purposes. Currency and interest rate options are allowed, except for banks. For residents, including banks, other derivative contracts (interest rates, currencies, and commodity prices) are permitted up to the amount of the underlying external asset or liability position that needs to be covered. However, these contracts cannot be effected on the formal market, except by banks and institutional investors.

Controls on credit operations

Commercial credits

By residents to nonresidents

All types of nonfinancial agents (except pension funds and insurance companies) are allowed to engage in international trade lending, but these operations must be effected through the informal exchange market.

To residents from nonresidents

Commercial credits may be contracted with foreign banks and financial entities under a 4% tax on interest. Associated foreign exchange transactions must be effected through the formal exchange market.

Financial credits

By residents to nonresidents

Operations by insurance companies, pension funds, and institutional investors are restricted. Others must operate through the informal market. Access to the formal market is extended to all credits.

To residents from nonresidents

Financial credits may be contracted with foreign banks and financial entities, subject to a 4% tax on interest and a stamp tax of 1.2%. Under the CEIR, debtors may use the formal market to prepay credits or to maintain the resources in an account abroad as a guarantee to creditors.

Guarantees, sureties, and financial backup facilities

By residents to nonresidents

These transactions are not allowed except for banks, which have to be authorized by the CBC. Only the following operations may be guaranteed or backed up by banks: external credits received by domestic enterprises, financial credits, the issuance of documents abroad, and forward contracts with authorized agents abroad.

To residents from nonresidents

Yes.

Controls on direct investment

Outward direct investment

Foreign exchange for investment may be bought both in the formal or the informal market, but the funds must be transferred through the former. If proceeds of such investments are brought back into the country, they have to be channeled through the formal market, but there is no surrender requirement. Investments by commercial banks are limited to a percentage of their effective capital and are subject to minimum international risk ratings.

The following transactions are permitted in the formal market: investments abroad, including acquisition of real or financial assets; and participation in companies and in contracts for the exploration and exploitation of domestic resources.

Inward direct investment

Capital contributions to new establishments or shares in existing ones are subject to a one-year minimum holding period and a minimum amount of US$1 million. Projects of significant size may be undertaken; there is a minimum holding period of one year, and the investor enjoys favorable taxation treatment with regard to the choice between the general income tax law or the guaranteed payment profit tax of 42%. There is also guaranteed access to the formal exchange market for repatriation.

Controls on liquidation of direct investment

Investments must be held in Chile for at least one year to qualify for repatriation. After that period, it must be demonstrated that the assets were sold and applicable taxes paid.

Controls on real estate transactions

Purchase abroad by residents	Insurance companies may invest only 3% of their capital in noninhabitable urban real estate.
Purchase locally by nonresidents	Purchases are treated as a financial investment and are subject to a minimum investment requirement of US$100,000 and a minimum holding period of one year.
Sale locally by nonresidents	The investment must have been held for one year in Chile, and it must be demonstrated that the asset was sold and applicable taxes paid.

Controls on personal capital movements

Loans

By residents to nonresidents	Chilean regulations establish that both juridical and natural persons may lend abroad. However, the currency from such loans must be remitted through the formal exchange market. The CBC must be informed about such operations.
To residents from nonresidents	The requirement that these loans be authorized by and registered with the CBC was eliminated on April 15, 1999.
Gifts, endowments, inheritances, and legacies	n.r.
Settlement of debts abroad by immigrants	Transfers may be made only through the informal market.

Transfer of assets

Transfer into the country by immigrants	These operations are permitted but are subject to the same restrictions applicable to loans.

Provisions specific to commercial banks and other credit institutions

Maintenance of accounts abroad	Nonbank financial institutions are not allowed to maintain accounts abroad. Banks may hold foreign time deposits within the margin for financial investment abroad. External current accounts are not controlled.
Lending to nonresidents (financial or commercial credits)	Banks may purchase debt instruments and sovereign bonds issued abroad. Time deposits are considered part of the margin for financial investments. Banks satisfying a capital adequacy ratio of at least 10% may acquire stocks of foreign banks or establish branches abroad. Deposits, loans, and other assets of Chilean banks with foreign banks of Chilean ownership may not exceed 40% of the capital and reserves of the foreign bank. Banks are authorized to extend loans to natural or juridical persons resident abroad in order to finance foreign trade operations between third countries.
Lending locally in foreign exchange	Banks may grant loans or acquire securities denominated or expressed in foreign exchange provided they remain within the open position limits.
Purchase of locally issued securities denominated in foreign exchange	These purchases are subject to open position limits.

Differential treatment of deposit accounts in foreign exchange

Liquid asset requirements	Yes.
Interest rate controls	By law, there are ceilings on interest rates for both domestic and foreign currency loans. Those ceilings are defined as one-and-a-half times the average market interest rate.
Investment regulations	Yes.
Abroad by banks	Effective May 27, 1999, foreign financial investments by commercial banks are limited to 70% of each bank's effective capital, and are restricted to bills and bonds issued or guaranteed by foreign governments or central banks and private enterprises. Effective December 9, 1999, the total exposure to any one country may not exceed 50% (previously 40%) of each bank's effective capital. If the investment is made in one foreign financial institution, it may not exceed 30% of the domestic bank's effective capital. The general

minimum long-term international debt risk rating (and its equivalent for short-term debt) for the financial instruments is BBB–, and up to 20% may be invested in BB– instruments. The foreign exchange needed to invest abroad must be obtained in the formal exchange market. Investments require the prior authorization of the CBC.

In banks by nonresidents
Nonresidents may invest in banks, but such investments are subject to a one-year holding period.

Open foreign exchange position limits
The limit is 20% of capital and reserves. This margin includes derivative and spot instruments, foreign investment, and assets and liabilities issued abroad or denominated in foreign exchange. Additionally, there is a foreign financial investment ceiling of 40% of the capital and reserves of each bank, a maximum investment in subsidiaries and branches abroad of 20% of the capital and reserves of domestic banks, and a requirement that the balance of all acquisitions and sales of foreign exchange for a bank be positive.

On resident assets and liabilities
Yes.

On nonresident assets and liabilities
Yes.

Provisions specific to institutional investors
Pension funds and insurance companies may hold only foreign instruments of a minimum international long-term risk rating requirement of BBB. These investors may also acquire foreign instruments guaranteed by the U.S. Treasury, such as Brady Bonds. Acquisition of equities and variable-income assets by pension funds is restricted to instruments in some international markets. Specifically, there are rules on the transparency, regulation, and information of the stock exchange where these instruments can be acquired. However, for insurance companies, the possible stock exchange options are wider; insurance companies may invest in markets where there is a daily average of at least US$10 million of equity transactions. Mutual funds may use the formal exchange market to make investments abroad.

Limits (max.) on portfolio invested abroad
Effective January 28, 1999, pension funds are permitted to invest up to 16% of their resources (previously 12%). Variable income securities from any issuer should not exceed 10% of the fund. Insurance companies may invest 3% of their reserves and risk net worth. Life insurance companies may invest their technical reserves and their risk net worth with global limits of 15% in financial investments and 3% in real estate. The limits for general insurance companies differ from those of the life insurance companies only in the case of financial investment abroad. The limit for the former is 20%.

Currency-matching regulations on assets/liabilities composition
Pension funds and insurance companies are only allowed to cover themselves against currency volatility up to a maximum of their foreign financial investments on a currency-by-currency basis.

Other controls imposed by securities laws
No.

Changes During 1999

Exchange arrangement
September 2. The central bank suspended the crawling band and allowed the peso to float. Thus, the exchange rate arrangement was reclassified to the category independently floating from the category crawling band.

Imports and import payments
January 1. The tariff rate was reduced by 1 percentage point to 10%.

December 9. The period during which foreign exchange may be bought in the formal market was extended to 360 days from 90 days.

Exports and export proceeds
July 12. The CBC allowed advances from foreign buyers or external credits to be channeled through the informal market.

Capital transactions
April 15. For entities other than banks and financial firms, bond issues were permitted with terms of more than two years and less than four years, with a minimum BB classification being required. In the case of bond issues for terms of four years or longer, the minimum classification required is BB–.

Controls on derivatives and other instruments
April 27. The CBC authorized financial institutions (banks must inform the CBC) to make foreign interest rate forwards, futures, and swaps in the local market.

Controls on personal capital movements	*April 15*. The requirement that loans by residents to nonresidents be authorized by the CBC was eliminated.
Provisions specific to commercial banks and other credit institutions	*May 27*. Banks were allowed to have financial investments of up to 70% of their effective capital.
	December 9. Banks were allowed to invest up to 50% of their effective capital in a single country.
Provisions specific to institutional investors	*January 28*. The maximum amount of investment abroad allowed to pension funds was increased to 16% from 12% of the fund. For life insurance companies, the margin authorized for financial investments was widened to 15% from 10%. In the case of general insurance companies, the margin was increased to 20% from 15%.
	April 15. The limit on investment in variable return instruments was increased to 10% from 8% of the fund.

Changes During 2000

Imports and import payments	*January 1*. The tariff rate was reduced by 1 percentage point to 9%.

PEOPLE'S REPUBLIC OF CHINA

(Position as of December 31, 1999)

Status Under IMF Articles of Agreement

Article VIII	Date of acceptance: December 1, 1996.

Exchange Arrangement

Currency

The currency of the People's Republic of China is the Chinese renminbi. The currency unit is the yuan.

Exchange rate structure

Unitary.

Classification

Conventional pegged arrangement

The exchange rate of the renminbi is determined in the interbank foreign exchange market. The People's Bank of China (PBC) announces a reference rate for the renminbi against the U.S. dollar, the Hong Kong dollar, and the yen based on the weighted average price of foreign exchange transactions during the previous day's trading. Daily movement of the exchange rate of the renminbi against the U.S. dollar is—in the interbank foreign exchange market—limited to 0.3% on either side of the reference rate as announced by the PBC. The buying and selling rates of the renminbi against the Hong Kong dollar and the yen may not deviate more than 1% from the reference rate. When the banks designated for foreign exchange business formulate the quoted spot exchange rate of the renminbi against the U.S. dollar, the buying and selling rates may not exceed 0.15% of the reference rate announced by the PBC. The deviation of their quoted buying and selling rates of renminbi against the Hong Kong dollar and the yen must not exceed 1% of the reference rate. The margin between the spot buying rate and the spot selling rate of other quoted currencies may not exceed 0.5%. The selling price for cash transactions is the same as the spot selling rate for all quoted currencies, and the buying price for cash should not exceed 2.5% of the median of its buying and selling spot rates.

The Shanghai-based China Foreign Exchange Trading System (CFETS) is a nationally integrated electronic system for interbank foreign exchange trading. At present, it is electronically linked with 36 foreign exchange trading subcenters located in major cities. All foreign exchange transactions are conducted through the system. Financial institutions involved in foreign exchange transactions must become members of the CFETS.

Exchange tax

No.

Exchange subsidy

No.

Forward exchange market

The PBC operates forward purchase and sale of renminbi against verification of authenticity of transactions on a trial basis. Effective April 1, 1999, the longest maturity was extended to six months from four months.

Arrangements for Payments and Receipts

Prescription of currency requirements

The currencies used in transactions are determined by the respective contracts.

Payment arrangements

No.

Administration of control

The State Administration of Foreign Exchange (SAFE) is responsible for foreign exchange administration, under the administration of the PBC.

International security restrictions

No.

Payment arrears

No.

Controls on trade in gold (coins and/or bullion)

Controls on domestic ownership and/or trade	Private persons may hold gold but not trade it. Nonresidents may buy gold and gold products and silver and silver products but must present the invoice to take them abroad. Effective October 18, 1999, restrictions on domestic ownership and trade of silver and silver products were lifted.
Controls on external trade	Trading of gold and silver is restricted to pharmaceutical, industrial, and other approved users. Unlimited amounts may be imported but must be declared. Exportation requires a permit.

Controls on exports and imports of banknotes

On exports

Domestic currency	The exportation of domestic currency is limited to Y 6,000.
Foreign currency	Residents and nonresidents are allowed to take their personal legitimate foreign currencies abroad as follows: (1) except in special cases, residents may take foreign currencies in cash up to $10,000 or its equivalent abroad; (2) amounts exceeding $10,000 may be taken abroad in the form of traveler's checks or other payment certificates; (3) residents taking foreign currencies up to $2,000 abroad do not need to apply for a License for Carrying Foreign Currencies Abroad (LCFCA). For amounts of more than $2,000 but less than $4,000, an LCFCA from the bank is required; for amounts of more than $4,000, prior authorization from the SAFE is required. Nonresidents taking foreign currencies up to $5,000 abroad do not need an LCFCA; for amounts of more than $5,000 but less than $10,000, an LCFCA from the bank is required; for amounts of more than $10,000, prior authorization from the SAFE is required.

On imports

Foreign currency	Residents and nonresidents importing more than $2,000 and $5,000, respectively, need to declare the amounts to customs.

Resident Accounts

Foreign exchange accounts permitted	Domestic-funded enterprises (DFEs) may maintain foreign exchange settlement accounts with approved balances for current account purposes based on certain criteria on export/import volume and amount of capital set by the SAFE. Domestic establishments involved with receipts and payments as an agent, temporary receipts and payments, and temporary receipts and pending payments in external contract projects, large machinery and electric product exports, donations, and aid may maintain foreign exchange accounts with approval of the SAFE and settle receipts and payments within the scope stipulated by the SAFE. Foreign-funded enterprises (FFEs) may open (1) foreign exchange settlement accounts for receipts and payments under the current account and for verified payments under the capital account with a maximum amount stipulated by the SAFE for each enterprise; and (2) for-eign exchange specified accounts for receipts under the capital account, payments under the current account, and approved payments under the capital account. Natural persons may open foreign currency savings accounts with authorized banks.
Held domestically	These accounts are permitted, but approval is required.
Held abroad	These accounts are permitted, but approval is required.
Accounts in domestic currency convertible into foreign currency	Agencies in need of foreign exchange may convert domestic currency into foreign currency at authorized banks by presenting valid proof and commercial documents when external payments are made.

Nonresident Accounts

Foreign exchange accounts permitted	Nonresidents staying in China for a short time may open foreign currency savings accounts.

Domestic currency accounts	Yes.
Convertible into foreign currency	Yes.
Blocked accounts	No.

Imports and Import Payments

Foreign exchange budget	No.
Financing requirements for imports	The SAFE requires foreign currency bank accounts of companies operating in bonded zones to use their own foreign exchange to buy imported goods, barring them from purchasing foreign exchange with renminbi to finance imports. Additionally, domestic sales of imported goods by bonded zone firms must be in foreign currency, and such proceeds must be deposited in the firms' foreign currency bank accounts.
Advance payment requirements	Importers need prior registration with the SAFE of advance payments exceeding 15% of the contract amount and the equivalent of $100,000; importers need to present a registration form, valid proof, and commercial documents, and carry out reconciliation procedures according to regulations.
Advance import deposits	The same regulations apply as for advance payment requirements.
Documentation requirements for release of foreign exchange for imports	Importers must provide valid proof and commercial bills—mainly import permits, automatic registration permits, proof of import, customs declarations, verification forms for foreign exchange payments, import contracts, and the like—to obtain foreign exchange or to pay directly from their foreign exchange accounts.
Import licenses and other nontariff measures	On December 2, 1999, China began to implement the agreement on agricultural cooperation with the United States, which sets resolutions on the quarantine of wheat, citrus, and meat existing between the two countries.
Positive list	To engage in foreign trade, all enterprises must obtain approval from the foreign trade administration and register with the administrations for industry and commerce, according to the law.
Negative list	Imports of all secondhand garments, poisons, narcotic drugs, diseased animals, and plants are prohibited. In addition, the importation of weapons; ammunition and explosives; manuscripts; printed and recorded materials; and films that are deemed to be detrimental to Chinese political, economic, cultural, and moral interests is prohibited.
Open general licenses	Yes.
Licenses with quotas	Yes.
Import taxes and/or tariffs	Import tariff rates fall into two categories: general and preferential. Preferential rates are granted to imports from countries with which China has a trade treaty or agreement. Other imports are subject to the general rate of duty. Imports of inputs and capital goods of FFEs are exempt from tariffs.
State import monopoly	Products subject to designated trading include wheat, chemical fertilizers, cotton, natural rubber, plant oil, plywood, steel, sugar, timber, tobacco and its products, and wool.

Exports and Export Proceeds

Repatriation requirements	Yes.
Surrender requirements	Qualifying DFEs are allowed to retain 15% of the value of their foreign trade (exports plus imports) of the previous year. Qualifying enterprises are foreign trade companies (FTCs) with a trade volume greater that $30 million and with registered capital greater than Y 10 million, and product-oriented enterprises with foreign trade rights whose volume of trade exceeds $10 million and registered capital exceeds Y 30 million. FFEs may retain their export earnings provided these earnings do not exceed the maximum amount allowed for a foreign exchange account as prescribed by the SAFE; otherwise, the balance, if any,

must be sold to authorized banks. The purchases and sales of foreign exchange by FFEs have been included under the banking surrender system.

Financing requirements	No.
Documentation requirements	No.
Export licenses	
With quotas	Quotas for 33 products in the first half of 1999 and for 29 products in the latter part of 1999 were allocated through a bidding system.
Export taxes	Export duties are levied on 36 products.

Payments for Invisible Transactions and Current Transfers

Controls on these transfers	Nontrade payments by FFEs and DFEs are subject to the same provisions. Resident individuals are subject to different regulations.
Trade-related payments	
Quantitative limits	The payment of export commission proceeds are allowed according to the export contracts and the commission contracts. For a hidden commission exceeding 2% of the contract amount and a stated commission exceeding 5% of the contract amount and the equivalent of $10,000, prior approval of the SAFE is required. A hidden commission not exceeding 2% of the contract amount or a stated commission not exceeding 5% or the equivalent of less than $10,000 may be settled directly through a bank.
Indicative limits/bona fide test	Proof of transaction is required for all trade-related payments. SAFE approval is required for amounts exceeding the prescribed limits for commissions. Traders may pay directly at authorized banks by presenting valid proof and commercial bills.
Investment-related payments	
Indicative limits/bona fide test	Yes.
Payments for travel	The foreign exchange requirements of companies within the budget are provided according to the prescribed limits. There are no restrictions on payments for travel of FFE staff, whereas the amount of foreign exchange that may be bought by other corporations is limited.
	Residents traveling to Hong Kong SAR and Macao SAR for personal reasons may purchase up to $1,000 worth of foreign currencies; individuals traveling to other countries or regions (including the Taiwan Province of China) may purchase up to $2,000 worth of foreign currencies. For amounts exceeding these ceilings, verification of authenticity by the SAFE is required.
	When residents travel abroad as part of touring parties, their registration fees may be purchased and remitted abroad by touring agencies. Effective October 1, 1999, the restriction of providing foreign exchange once a year to residents traveling abroad for private reasons, excluding residents who hold a multiple pass to and from Hong Kong SAR and Macao SAR, was removed.
Prior approval	Verification and approval of the SAFE are required for amounts exceeding the specified limits.
Quantitative limits	Yes.
Indicative limits/bona fide test	Yes.
Personal payments	
Quantitative limits	Residents may purchase foreign exchange up to $1,000 for payments of medicines and medical equipment abroad; for larger amounts, they must submit appropriate documentation for SAFE verification. Persons paying for their own studies abroad may be allowed a onetime purchase of foreign exchange of up to $2,000. Larger amounts require the verification and approval of the SAFE.

Indicative limits/bona fide test	Yes.
Foreign workers' wages	
Indicative limits/bona fide test	Proof of earnings and tax clearance is required.
Other payments	
Indicative limits/bona fide test	For transfers regarding subscriptions and membership fees, proof of transaction is required.

Proceeds from Invisible Transactions and Current Transfers

Repatriation requirements	Yes.
Surrender requirements	Foreign grants and financial aid received by domestic establishments, and foreign exchange earmarked for external payments as prescribed by aid contracts may be maintained with the approval of the SAFE. Foreign embassies and consulates, representative offices of international organizations and affiliates of foreign juridical persons, resident persons, and foreign expatriates may retain their foreign exchange. FFEs may retain foreign exchange earnings from current account transactions, provided the retained amount does not exceed the maximum limit allowed by the SAFE. Balances, if any, must be sold to authorized banks. The purchase and sale of foreign exchange by FFEs have been included under the banking surrender system.
Restrictions on use of funds	n.a.

Capital Transactions

Controls on capital and money market instruments	
On capital market securities	
Shares or other securities of a participating nature	
Purchase locally by nonresidents	Nonresidents may only purchase B shares. The face value of B shares is denominated in U.S. dollars or Hong Kong dollars. These shares are listed on the Chinese Securities Exchange and can only be bought by foreign investors.
Sale or issue locally by nonresidents	These transactions are not permitted.
Purchase abroad by residents	Residents, except financial institutions permitted to engage in foreign borrowing, and authorized industrial and trade enterprises or groups, are not permitted to purchase securities abroad. A qualifications review by the SAFE is required in order for financial institutions to purchase securities abroad.
Sale or issue abroad by residents	Prior approval by the China Securities Regulatory Committee (CSRC) is required.
Bonds or other debt securities	
Purchase locally by nonresidents	These transactions are not permitted.
Sale or issue locally by nonresidents	These transactions are not permitted.
Purchase abroad by residents	Prior approval by the external investment administrative department and the SAFE is required. Residents are allowed to make payments for such securities with privately owned foreign exchange but are not allowed to purchase foreign exchange to make the relevant payments.
Sale or issue abroad by residents	Prior approval by the SAFE is required. The issuing of bonds abroad must be integrated into the state's plan for the use of foreign capital. Bonds may only be issued by financial institutions or authorized enterprises approved by the SAFE.
	Prepayment of external debt is prohibited when there is no prepayment clause in borrowing contracts. If there is such a clause, borrowers may use their own foreign exchange to prepay with the verification of the SAFE. Prepayments with purchased foreign exchange are

prohibited. Borrowers are not allowed to purchase foreign exchange from a bank located outside the local area to repay foreign debt.

On money market instruments

Purchase locally by nonresidents   Nonresidents are not allowed to purchase money market instruments.

Sale or issue locally by nonresidents   Nonresidents are not allowed to sell or issue money market instruments.

Purchase abroad by residents   The same regulations apply as for bonds or other debt securities.

Sale or issue abroad by residents   The sale or issue abroad of securities, other than stocks, requires SAFE approval.

On collective investment securities

Purchase locally by nonresidents   These transactions are not allowed.

Sale or issue locally by nonresidents   n.r.

Purchase abroad by residents   The same regulations apply as for the purchase of money market instruments.

Sale or issue abroad by residents   The same regulations apply as for the sale or issue of money market instruments.

Controls on derivatives and other instruments

Purchase locally by nonresidents   These transactions are not allowed.

Sale or issue locally by nonresidents   These transactions are not allowed.

Purchase abroad by residents   Domestic establishments must entrust authorized financial institutions to make these purchases. If the entrusted institution is abroad, prior approval from the SAFE is required. Operations in such instruments by financial institutions are subject to prior review of qualifications and to limits on open foreign exchange positions. FFEs do not need prior approval; for them, ex post registration is required.

Sale or issue abroad by residents   The same regulations apply as for purchases.

Controls on credit operations

Commercial credits

By residents to nonresidents   n.r.

To residents from nonresidents   Only domestic-funded financial institutions are permitted by the SAFE to engage in external borrowing, and authorized industrial and commercial enterprises or groups may engage in external borrowing of commercial credit. For credit over a one-year maturity, the loan must be part of the state plan for utilizing foreign capital and must be approved by the SAFE. Financial institutions permitted to engage in foreign borrowing are free to conduct short-term foreign borrowing, with a maturity of one year or less, within the target balance without obtaining approval, but they must register the borrowing with the SAFE.

Forward LCs with a maturity exceeding 90 days but less than 365 days are included in the category of short-term credits, while those exceeding one year are included in medium- and long-term international commercial loans.

FFEs may borrow from nonresidents without obtaining approval but must register the borrowing with the SAFE.

If there are no provisions on the advance repayment in the lending contract, no redemption of debt is permitted. If there are provisions on advance repayment, enterprises may redeem debt with their own foreign exchange, provided that approval has been granted by the SAFE, but they may not purchase foreign exchange for that purpose. Renminbi credits extended by banks to domestic institutions should be used only for productive purposes and may not be used to purchase foreign exchange for debt service. At the same time, domestic banks are prohibited from accepting foreign bank guarantees for renminbi loans to domestic-funded enterprises. However, domestic banks may accept guarantees from foreign banks and enterprises to extend renminbi loans. Commercial banks are to ensure that companies do not borrow from bank branches in different locations to evade controls.

Financial credits

By residents to nonresidents   n.r.

To residents from nonresidents   The same regulations apply as for commercial credits.

Guarantees, sureties, and financial
backup facilities

By residents to nonresidents   The provision of guarantees by authorized financial institutions and nonfinancial legal entities that have foreign exchange receipts is allowed. Without the approval of the State Council, government agencies or institutions cannot provide guarantees.

The new definition of guarantees includes collateral, liens, and pledges; and domestic-funded banks need approval from the SAFE for each guarantee for financing transactions. They do not need approval to issue guarantees of nonfinancing transactions but must register them with the SAFE.

Domestic banks are allowed to extend renminbi loans to FFEs with a foreign exchange lien or guarantee provided by foreign banks. Until July 15, 1999, when these controls were eased, it was also required that (1) liens in foreign exchange pledged by FFEs be restricted to their foreign exchange proceeds from external borrowing; (2) institutions providing guarantees be restricted to domestic foreign banks and overseas banks with good credit ratings; (3) guarantees only be granted in the form of stand-by LC or unconditional letter of guarantee for the honoring of a contract; (4) renminbi loans with guarantee in foreign exchange only be used to meet the working capital shortage of enterprises; and (5) FFEs that have obtained renminbi loans from domestic Chinese banks by pledging foreign exchange proceeds from external borrowing in lien or as a guarantee in foreign exchange arranged by foreign banks must register with local SAFE branches within a certain period of time.

Controls on direct investment

Outward direct investment   Foreign exchange is provided for the investment after (1) examination of sources of foreign exchange and an assessment of the foreign exchange risk involved, (2) approval by the Ministry of Foreign Trade and Economic Cooperation (MOFTEC), and (3) approval and registration of outward foreign exchange remittance with the SAFE.

Inward direct investment   Nonresidents are free to invest in China as long as they meet requirements under Sino-foreign joint-venture laws and other relevant regulations, and are approved by the MOFTEC. There is no restriction on the inward remittance of funds as far as exchange control is concerned. For environmental and security reasons, inward direct investment in some industries is prohibited.

**Controls on liquidation of direct
investment**   No.

Controls on real estate transactions The same regulations apply as for direct investment.

**Controls on personal capital
movements**

Loans

By residents to nonresidents   Yes.

To residents from nonresidents   Yes.

Gifts, endowments, inheritances, and
legacies

By residents to nonresidents   In the case that a resident's directly related family member abroad encounters illness, death, or unexpected disaster, the resident is allowed to purchase and remit abroad up to $1,000 or its equivalent, once the resident has valid, notarized proof or proof from the Chinese embassy or consulate; application from the patient's local agency (work unit) or prescription from the hospital; the relevant documents from the resident's work unit (if without a work unit, from the local subdistrict office or the people's government department above the town level); and proof of the documents related to foreign exchange payments. As for other foreign exchange purchases, amounts of up to $500 may be provided by the bank. For a onetime purchase of foreign exchange for private purposes with an amount exceeding the stipulated standard and up to $50,000 or its equivalent, application to the local SAFE offices against specific documented proof is required, and, after verification by the local SAFE office, the foreign exchange needed may be purchased from the bank and remitted or taken abroad. When a onetime purchase exceeds the stipulated standard or $50,000 or its equivalent, the transaction must be reported to the SAFE by the local SAFE office for verification before the bank provides the foreign exchange.

Remittances from a resident's foreign currency account abroad for payments for gifts, donations, inheritances, or legacies, for a onetime amount of less than $10,000 or its equivalent, may be made directly through a bank. For amounts of more than $10,000 but less than $50,000 or their equivalents, application to the local SAFE office is required with stipulated documented proof, and, after verification by the local SAFE office, remittances may be made through a bank. For amounts of more than $50,000 or its equivalent, the transaction must be reported to the SAFE by the local SAFE office for verification before the bank makes the foreign exchange remittances.

Transfers of a resident's foreign currency cash or deposits from a resident's foreign currency cash account abroad for payments of gifts, donations, inheritances, or legacies, for a onetime amount of less than $2,000 or its equivalent, may be made directly by a bank. For amounts of more than $2,000 but less than $10,000 or their equivalents, application to the local SAFE office is required with specific documented proof and corresponding customs declaration documents to remit foreign currency before remittances may be made by a bank. For amounts above $10,000 or its equivalent, the transaction must be reported to the SAFE by the local SAFE office for verification before the bank makes the foreign exchange remittances.

To residents from nonresidents

If the foreign currency income from donations and legacies needs to be paid in foreign currency cash or converted into renminbi and if the onetime amount is less than $10,000 or its equivalent, payments may be made directly by banks. When the amount is above $10,000 but less than $50,000 or their equivalents, relevant documented proof must be provided to the banks or the SAFE. For inherited foreign currency, the required documentation includes proof of identification of authenticity, a notarized statement, and proof of tax clearance abroad. For household use of foreign currency, proof of identification of authenticity and documentation of kinsfolk relationship are required. For foreign currency donations, proof of identification of authenticity and a donation agreement are needed. Banks may make the payments after verifying the documented proof and recording the transaction. When the amount is above $50,000 but less than $200,000 or their equivalents, application to the local SAFE office is required with documented proof, and after the verification of authenticity by the local SAFE office, payments may be made through banks. For amounts above $200,000 or its equivalent, application to the local SAFE office is required with documented proof and the transaction must be reported to the SAFE by the local SAFE office for verification before the bank makes the foreign exchange remittances.

Provisions specific to commercial banks and other credit institutions

Borrowing abroad

The same regulations apply as for commercial credits.

Maintenance of accounts abroad

Registration with the SAFE is required for domestic banks to open foreign exchange accounts abroad. As for domestic nonbank financial institutions and nonfinancial enterprises, prior approval by the SAFE is required.

Lending to nonresidents (financial or commercial credits)

n.r.

Lending locally in foreign exchange

Lending is mainly subject to review of qualifications by the PBC and to asset-liability ratio requirements. Borrowers need to register ex post the transaction with the SAFE and should get a permit from the SAFE to repay the principal.

Purchase of locally issued securities denominated in foreign exchange

China does not issue securities denominated in foreign currency.

Differential treatment of deposit
accounts in foreign exchange

   Reserve requirements | There are different reserve requirements for deposits in renminbi and in foreign currency, and also within the latter for domestic banks and for FFEs (i.e., for FFEs 13% for deposits in renminbi, 5% for any foreign currency deposit for domestic banks, and 3% for deposits of foreign currency of over three months and 5% for less than three months).

   Liquid asset requirements | Banks' foreign exchange liquid assets (one year or less) should not be less than 60% of liquid liabilities (one year or less) and 30% of total foreign exchange assets. Total deposits with three-month maturities, deposits in both domestic and foreign banks, funds used for purchasing transferable foreign currency–denominated securities, deposits with the central bank, and cash holdings should not be less than 15% of banks' total foreign exchange assets. Nonbank foreign exchange liquid assets (one year or less) should not be less than 60% of liquid liabilities (one year or less) and 25% of total assets. Total deposits with three-month maturities, deposits in both domestic and foreign banks, funds used for purchasing transferable foreign currency–denominated securities, deposits with the central bank, and cash holdings should not be less than 10% of nonbank total foreign exchange assets.

   Credit controls | Total loans, investment guarantees (calculated as 50% of the balance guaranteed), and other foreign exchange credits provided to a legal entity by a bank or nonbank financial institution should not exceed 30% of the foreign exchange capital owned by the bank or nonbank financial institution.

Investment regulations | Bank equity investment should not exceed the difference between bank capital and mandatory paid-in capital. Nonbank financial institutions' total equity investment (excluding trust accounts) should not exceed the difference between their capital and mandatory paid-in capital.

   Abroad by banks | Investment in foreign securities other than equities on foreign securities markets by banks is subject to quarterly approval by the PBC.

   In banks by nonresidents | PBC approval is required.

Open foreign exchange position limits | For financial institutions trading foreign exchange on their own behalf, the daily total amount traded (total open foreign exchange position) should not exceed 20% of the foreign exchange working capital. As authorized by the highest level of management, financial institutions trading foreign exchange on their own behalf may retain a small amount of overnight open position, but this should not exceed 1% of the foreign exchange working capital.

   On resident assets and liabilities | Yes.

   On nonresident assets and liabilities | Yes.

Provisions specific to institutional investors | No.

Other controls imposed by securities laws | No.

Changes During 1999

Exchange arrangement | *April 1.* The longest maturity of forward purchase and sale of foreign exchange was extended to six from four months.

Arrangements for payments and receipts | *October 18.* Restrictions on domestic ownership and trade of silver and silver products were lifted.

Imports and import payments | *December 2.* Certain restrictions on imports of wheat, citrus, and meat from the United States were eliminated.

Payments for invisible transactions and current transfers | *October 1.* The restriction of providing foreign exchange once a year to residents traveling abroad for private reasons, excluding residents who hold a multiple pass to and from Hong Kong SAR and Macao SAR, was removed.

Capital transactions

Controls on credit operations

July 15. Some controls on renminbi loans to FFEs under foreign exchange liens or guarantees were eased.

Status Under IMF Articles of Agreement

Article VIII   Date of acceptance: February 15, 1961.

Exchange Arrangement

Currency   The currency of Hong Kong SAR is the Hong Kong dollar.

Other legal tender   Commemorative gold coins of HK$1,000 are legal tender, but are mostly kept by collectors and seldom circulated.

Exchange rate structure

Unitary   The authorities do not maintain margins in exchange transactions.

Classification

Currency board arrangement   The currency board system in Hong Kong SAR, adopted on October 17, 1983, requires the monetary base to be backed by the reserve currency (i.e., the U.S. dollar) at the fixed exchange rate of HK$7.80 to US$1. In Hong Kong SAR, the monetary base includes the amount of banknotes and coins issued, the balance of clearing accounts of the licensed banks held with the Hong Kong Monetary Authority (HKMA) (i.e., aggregate balance), and the outstanding amount of exchange fund bills and notes. Operating under the rule-based currency board system, the HKMA has undertaken to issue additional exchange fund paper only when there is an inflow of funds, but the size of the program is allowed to expand along with the interest payments on such papers.

The issue and redemption of Certificates of Indebtedness, which provide backing for banknotes issued by the note-issuing banks, are required to be made against U.S. dollars at the fixed exchange rate of HK$7.80 to US$1. Starting from April 1, 1999, the issue and withdrawal of coins are settled against the U.S. dollar at the fixed rate of HK$7.80 per US$1.

An explicit convertibility undertaking was made by the HKMA to licensed banks to convert Hong Kong dollar balances in their clearing accounts into U.S. dollars at the fixed exchange rate of HK$7.75 per US$1. This convertibility rate has been moving to HK$7.80 from HK$7.75 by 1 pip (i.e., HK$0.0001) per calendar day starting from April 1, 1999. It would take 500 calendar days to complete the move to the rate of HK$7.80, where it will remain.

Exchange tax   No.

Exchange subsidy   No.

Forward exchange market   The forward exchange markets are operated on private sector initiatives, and the government has no official role.

Arrangements for Payments and Receipts

Prescription of currency requirements   No.

Payment arrangements   No.

Administration of control   No.

International security restrictions

In accordance with UN sanctions   UN sanctions are implemented by the Hong Kong SAR government in accordance with the relevant regulations made under the UN Sanctions Ordinance by the Chief Executive on the instructions of the Ministry of Foreign Affairs of the People's Republic of China.

Payment arrears	No.
Controls on trade in gold (coins and/or bullion)	No.
Controls on exports and imports of banknotes	No.

Resident Accounts

Foreign exchange accounts permitted	Yes.
Held domestically	Yes.
Held abroad	Yes.
Accounts in domestic currency convertible into foreign currency	Yes.

Nonresident Accounts

Foreign exchange accounts permitted	No distinction is made between resident and nonresident accounts.
Domestic currency accounts	Yes.
Convertible into foreign currency	Yes.
Blocked accounts	No.

Imports and Import Payments

Foreign exchange budget	No.
Financing requirements for imports	No.
Documentation requirements for release of foreign exchange for imports	No.
Import licenses and other nontariff measures	
Negative list	Imports of certain articles are subject to licensing control by the Director-General of Trade. Import licenses are required for reasons of public health, safety, environmental protection, security, or for the fulfillment of Hong Kong SAR's international trade obligations.
Licenses with quotas	There is no quota on import quantity covered by a license, whereas the total import quantity of ozone-depleting substances covered by the Montreal Protocol is subject to quotas. The same applies to the import of rice where the quota arrangement is to ensure a stable and sufficient supply of the staple food in Hong Kong SAR. In accordance with Hong Kong SAR's commitment under the Asia Pacific Economic Cooperation, the rice trade will be fully liberalized by 2010.
Import taxes and/or tariffs	All imports are free of duty, although an excise tax for revenue and health purposes is levied on imported and domestically produced cigarettes and other tobacco products, liquors, methyl alcohol, and hydrocarbon oils.
State import monopoly	No.

Exports and Export Proceeds

Repatriation requirements	No.

Financing requirements	No.
Documentation requirements	No.
Export licenses	
Without quotas	Exports of certain articles are subject to licensing control by the Director-General of Trade. Export licenses are required for reasons of public health, safety, environmental protection, security, or for the fulfillment of Hong Kong SAR's international trade obligations.
With quotas	Exports of certain textile articles to some importing countries are subject to quotas as a result of the quantitative restrictions maintained by these countries on textile exports from Hong Kong SAR. According to the WTO Agreement on Textiles and Clothing, textile quotas would be abolished by 2005.
Export taxes	No.

Payments for Invisible Transactions and Current Transfers

Controls on these transfers	No.

Proceeds from Invisible Transactions and Current Transfers

Repatriation requirements	No.
Restrictions on use of funds	There are no limitations on receipts from invisibles. Income from foreign sources, capital gains, distributions from trusts, and dividends is not taxed in Hong Kong SAR; interest income from domestic sources received by licensed banks and corporations carrying on business in Hong Kong SAR is subject to a profits tax. Interest earned on bank deposits by individuals is not subject to the salaries tax.

Capital Transactions

Controls on capital and money market instruments	No exchange control requirements are imposed on capital receipts or payments by residents or nonresidents. A license or an authorization is required for companies, whether incorporated in Hong Kong SAR or elsewhere, to conduct banking, insurance, securities, and futures dealings. Otherwise, all overseas companies are required only to register with the Companies Registry within one month of establishing a business in Hong Kong SAR.
On capital market securities	As part of the government's measures to fortify the financial system against market manipulation, the Stock Exchange of Hong Kong has strictly enforced the T+2 settlement rule, reinstated the tick rule on short selling, and reviewed the list of securities eligible for short selling.
Controls on derivatives and other instruments	The Hong Kong Futures Exchange imposes a special margin rate on open interest exceeding 10,000 contracts.
Controls on credit operations	No.
Controls on direct investment	No.
Controls on liquidation of direct investment	No.
Controls on real estate transactions	No.
Controls on personal capital movements	No.
Provisions specific to commercial banks and other credit institutions	The limits and restrictions stated below are set by the HKMA for prudential reasons only.
Differential treatment of deposit accounts held by nonresidents	No distinction is made between resident and nonresident deposit accounts.

Investment regulations

Abroad by banks

No authorized institution incorporated in Hong Kong SAR or its holding company incorporated in Hong Kong SAR may establish or acquire by whatever means without the approval of the HKMA an overseas banking corporation that becomes the subsidiary of the institution or its holding company. In addition, the Banking Ordinance imposes a requirement on a locally incorporated authorized institution to seek HKMA's prior approval for any acquisition in a company (including establishment) that amounts to 5% or more of the institution's capital base, except if it acquires the shares in the course of satisfaction of debts due to the institution or under an underwriting or subunderwriting contract for a period not exceeding seven days.

Open foreign exchange position limits

All authorized institutions are required to report to the HKMA their foreign currency positions (including options) monthly. Locally incorporated institutions are required to report their consolidated foreign currency positions. The aggregate net open position (calculated as the sum of net long/short positions of individual currencies) should normally not exceed 5% of the capital base of the institution, and the net open position in any individual currency should not exceed 10% of the capital base. For subsidiaries of foreign banks where the parent bank consolidates the foreign exchange risk on a global basis and for which there is adequate home supervision, the HKMA may accept higher limits. For branches of foreign banks, the HKMA reviews and monitors their internal limits, which are usually set by their head offices and home supervisory authorities.

In addition to these limits, locally incorporated institutions are required to provide regulatory capital for foreign exchange risk such that their adjusted capital adequacy ratio (incorporating market risk) should be above the respective statutory minimum ratios.

Provisions specific to institutional investors

No.

Other controls imposed by securities laws

No.

Changes During 1999

Exchange arrangement

April 1. The issue and withdrawal of coins is settled against the U.S. dollar at the fixed rate of HK$7.80 per US$1.

COLOMBIA

(Position as of December 31, 1999)

Status Under IMF Articles of Agreement

Article XIV	Yes.

Exchange Arrangement

Currency	The currency of Colombia is the Colombian peso.
Other legal tender	Various commemorative gold coins are also legal tender.
Exchange rate structure	Unitary.
Classification	
Independently floating	The Banco de la República (BR) conducts foreign exchange transactions with the MOF and authorized financial intermediaries. The BR announces the upper and lower limits of a band 10 days in advance for indicative purposes. Effective June 28, 1999, the central parity of the trading band was depreciated by 9% against the dollar. The upper and lower limits of the band were also widened to allow for a maximum daily fluctuation of 20% in the value of the peso, and the slope of the band was changed to 10% from 13%. On September 25, 1999, the BR abandoned the crawling band and allowed the peso to float. Monetary policy is now guided to pursue an inflation target and uses the monetary base as an intermediate target. The exchange rate arrangement of Colombia has been reclassified to the category independently floating from the category crawling band.

The BR quotes buying and selling rates for certain other currencies daily on the basis of the buying and selling rates for the dollar in markets abroad. All foreign exchange operations take place at a market-determined exchange rate. The Superintendency of Banks calculates a representative market exchange rate based on market rates (i.e., the weighted average of buying and selling effected by foreign exchange market intermediaries, excluding teller transactions and forward transactions). The government purchases foreign exchange for all public debt payments and other expenditures included in the national budget under the same conditions as other authorized intermediaries.

Exchange tax	Surtaxes include a 7% surtax on remittances of earnings on existing oil and non-oil foreign investments, unless earnings are reinvested for five years. Also, a 3% withholding tax on foreign exchange receipts from personal services and other transfers is applied.
Exchange subsidy	No.
Forward exchange market	Residents are permitted to buy forward cover against exchange rate risks with respect to foreign exchange debts in convertible currencies registered at the BR on international markets. Residents may also deal in over-the-counter forward swaps and options in dollars.

Arrangements for Payments and Receipts

Prescription of currency requirements	Payments and receipts are normally effected in dollars, but residents and financial intermediaries are allowed to carry out operations in any currency.
Payment arrangements	
Regional arrangements	Settlements between Colombia and the other LAIA countries may be made through accounts maintained within the framework of the multilateral clearing system of the LAIA.
Clearing agreements	Colombia maintains reciprocal credit agreements with China.
Administration of control	The MOF enforces ex post control and supervision over trade transactions and is responsible for applying penalties for any violation of the trade regulations. The Superintendency of Societies and the Superintendency of Banks are also responsible for the enforcement of exchange regulations. The authorized foreign exchange intermediaries are commercial and mortgage banks, financial corporations, commercial finance companies, the Financiera

Energética Nacional, the Banco de Comercio Exterior de Colombia (BANCOLDEX), and savings and loans corporations. Exchange houses are authorized to carry out a limited range of foreign exchange activities (buying and selling foreign currency and, in some cases, transferring money). The BR keeps an accounting record both of foreign investments in Colombia and of debts abroad and tracks the movement of foreign capital as well as the transfer of profits, dividends, and commissions.

International security restrictions	No.
Payment arrears	No.
Controls on trade in gold (coins and/or bullion)	
Controls on domestic ownership and/or trade	The BR makes domestic sales of gold for industrial use directly at a price equivalent to the average quotation in the London gold market during the previous day; this price is converted into pesos at the representative market exchange rate.
Controls on exports and imports of banknotes	
On exports	
Domestic currency	Except for the BR, all imports and exports of domestic currencies should be effected through authorized financial intermediaries. For travelers, the maximum amount allowed is the equivalent of Col$1 million. This limit is increased annually based on the consumer price index. For amounts exceeding this limit, a customs report must be filed.
Foreign currency	Yes.
On imports	
Domestic currency	Yes.
Foreign currency	Individuals entering the country with foreign exchange or securities denominated in foreign currency in excess of the equivalent of US$7,000 must report it to customs.

Resident Accounts

Foreign exchange accounts permitted	Yes.
Held domestically	Such accounts are restricted to travel agencies, international transport companies in bond stores, and companies in free-trade areas.
Held abroad	Residents may maintain foreign accounts registered at the BR (compensation accounts), funds from which may be used to pay for imports, to invest abroad in financial assets, or to carry out any other foreign exchange operations. Proceeds from services (except interest and profits) and transfers may be used to maintain foreign accounts abroad; these accounts do not have to be registered at the BR. Special foreign accounts (special compensation accounts) are authorized for transactions among residents.
Accounts in domestic currency convertible into foreign currency	n.a.

Nonresident Accounts

Foreign exchange accounts permitted	Credit institutions are authorized to receive current account deposits in foreign currency from nonresident individuals or firms; these deposits are freely available to the holders, but banks must report transactions through these accounts to the BR.
Domestic currency accounts	Deposits in these accounts need not be registered at the BR; they may be used only for trade-related transactions. Banks must report transactions through these accounts to the BR.
Convertible into foreign currency	Yes.
Blocked accounts	No.

Imports and Import Payments

Foreign exchange budget

No.

Financing requirements for imports

Importers may purchase foreign exchange directly from the exchange market. In addition, they may use the proceeds from deposits held abroad. However, foreign enterprises in the oil, coal, and natural gas sectors are not permitted to purchase foreign exchange from financial intermediaries.

Documentation requirements for release of foreign exchange for imports

All imports must be registered at the Colombian Institute of Foreign Trade (INCOMEX).

Preshipment inspection

Yes.

Letters of credit

Yes.

Import licenses and other nontariff measures

Most imports are free and require registration only with INCOMEX if the f.o.b. value exceeds US$1,000. There is a global free list applicable to all countries, a national list applicable only to LAIA member countries, and special lists applicable only to LAIA member countries and the Andean Pact countries. Imports of medicines, chemical products, and weapons and munitions are subject to licensing requirements.

Reimbursable imports involve purchases of official foreign exchange from a financial intermediary, including imports of machinery and equipment financed by international credit institutions. Nonreimbursable imports consist mainly of aid imports under grants and commodities constituting part of a direct investment. Import registrations are granted automatically. However, import registrations by some public sector agencies are screened by INCOMEX to determine whether local substitutes are available. Both import licenses and registrations are valid for six months, except those for agricultural and livestock products and for capital goods, which are valid for three months and for 12 months, respectively. Import licenses may be extended only once.

Import taxes and/or tariffs

With certain exceptions, imports are subject to the CET of the Andean Pact.

State import monopoly

No.

Exports and Export Proceeds

Repatriation requirements

No.

Surrender requirements

All proceeds that are repatriated must be surrendered to authorized financial intermediaries within six months or must be maintained in foreign accounts registered at the BR. Foreign enterprises in the oil, coal, and natural gas sectors and firms in free-trade areas are not required to surrender their foreign exchange. On surrendering export proceeds in the foreign exchange market, exporters of products other than coffee, petroleum and petroleum products, and exports effected through special arrangements (such as barter and compensation) may receive tax credit certificates at any of four rates—2.25%, 3.6%, 4.5%, and 6.5% of domestic value added—depending on the product, the country of destination, and the date of shipment. These certificates, which are freely negotiable and are quoted on the stock exchange, are accepted at par by tax offices for the payment of income tax, customs duties, and certain other taxes.

Exports of coffee are subject to the following regulations: (1) a minimum surrender price is the sales price shown on the export declaration; (2) exporters pay a coffee contribution on the basis of international market prices; (3) the National Coffee Committee (composed of the Ministers of Finance and Agriculture and the Managing Director of the Federation) may establish a physical coffee contingent on the basis of international coffee prices; and (4) the National Coffee Committee establishes a domestic price for export-type coffee expressed in pesos per cargo of 125 kilograms.

Foreign exchange proceeds earned by the public sector may be surrendered to financial intermediaries.

Financing requirements

No.

Documentation requirements

Preshipment inspection	Yes.
Other	Yes.
Export licenses	No.
Export taxes	A 3% withholding tax on foreign exchange receipts for personal services and other transfers is applied.

Payments for Invisible Transactions and Current Transfers

Controls on these transfers

Trade-related payments

Contracts involving royalties, commissions, trademarks, or patents should be registered with INCOMEX for statistical purposes only.

Investment-related payments

Prior approval

Capital must be registered with the BR before profits may be repatriated. Annual transfers of profits abroad and repatriation of capital are not restricted, but they may be temporarily restricted if international reserve holdings of the BR fall below the equivalent of three months of imports.

Quantitative limits

The limit on contractual interest rates for public debt is determined by the BR, which sets the maximum applicable rate.

Proceeds from Invisible Transactions and Current Transfers

Repatriation requirements	No.
Restrictions on use of funds	No.

Capital Transactions

Controls on capital and money market instruments

Purchases of these instruments, whether locally by nonresidents or abroad by residents, must be registered with the BR.

On capital market securities

Shares or other securities of a participating nature

Nonresidents must establish an investment fund to participate in the stock market. Any portfolio investment must be registered with the BR.

Purchase locally by nonresidents

The purchase of 10% or more of the shares of a Colombian financial institution requires the prior approval of the Superintendency of Banks. Foreign investments in the form of placement of shares in a fund established to make investments in the stock exchange and in debt papers issued by the financial sector are permitted.

Purchase abroad by residents

These transactions must be registered with the BR.

Sale or issue abroad by residents

These transactions must be registered with the BR.

Bonds or other debt securities

Purchase locally by nonresidents

Nonresidents must establish an investment fund in order to purchase these securities.

Sale or issue abroad by residents

These transactions must be registered with the BR.

On money market instruments

Purchase locally by nonresidents

Yes.

Sale or issue locally by nonresidents

Yes.

Purchase abroad by residents

Yes.

On collective investment securities

   Purchase locally by nonresidents   Yes.

   Sale or issue locally by nonresidents   Yes.

   Purchase abroad by residents   Yes.

Controls on derivatives and other instruments

Sale or issue locally by nonresidents   Only foreign financial institutions classified as category A and belonging to the Group of Seven (G-7) countries, except for Italy, are authorized to engage in these types of transactions.

Controls on credit operations

Commercial credits

   By residents to nonresidents   Yes.

   To residents from nonresidents   Credits must be registered with the BR. The nonremunerated deposit requirement for external financing is 10% of the disbursement of any loan and the period is six months. Export credits over US$10,000 that are longer than four months are subject to a 10% deposit in dollars for 12 months. Exempted from the deposit requirement are imports financed for less than six months; short-term loans granted by BANCOLDEX to Colombian exporters for up to 12 months for the maximum amount of US$550 million; credit card balances; and loans destined for Colombian investments abroad. Prepayment of the loan is permitted with the authorization of the BR. In case of prepayment of the export credits, exporters must prove that over 85% of the declared value has been in fact exported. All public financing (borrowing and bond issues) in foreign currencies, including by the central and local governments, is also subject to nonremunerated deposit. There is a limit determined by the BR on contractual interest rates for the public sector. Foreign loans for government entities in excess of specified amounts require prior authorization from the MOF. For loans to the government, or guaranteed by the government, the following are also required: prior authorization from the National Council for Economic and Social Policy, prior consultation with the Interparliamentary Committee on Public Credit, and ex post approval from the President of the Republic. Such loans are also subject to the executive decree that authorizes the initiation of negotiations.

Financial credits

   By residents to nonresidents   All residents are allowed to engage in international lending through the formal exchange market. The transactions must be reported to the BR.

   To residents from nonresidents   Yes.

Guarantees, sureties, and financial backup facilities

   By residents to nonresidents   Yes.

   To residents from nonresidents   Yes.

Controls on direct investment

Outward direct investment   Investments should be registered with the BR.

Inward direct investment   Up to 100% ownership in any sector of the economy—except in defense and waste disposal—is allowed. Special regimes remain in effect in the financial, petroleum, and mining sectors.

Controls on liquidation of direct investment   Repatriation of proceeds must be registered with the BR.

Controls on real estate transactions   Purchases should be registered with the BR.

Purchase abroad by residents   Yes.

Purchase locally by nonresidents   Yes.

Sale locally by nonresidents   Yes.

Controls on personal capital movements

Loans

   To residents from nonresidents — Only loans transacted with foreign financial intermediaries are to be reported to the BR, and these must be channeled through the foreign exchange market.

Provisions specific to commercial banks and other credit institutions

Lending to nonresidents (financial or commercial credits) — Banks must inform the BR.

Lending locally in foreign exchange — Yes.

Differential treatment of deposit accounts in foreign exchange

   Reserve requirements — Deposit accounts in foreign exchange are not subject to reserve requirements.

Investment regulations

   Abroad by banks — Credit institutions may invest only in short-term assets abroad or in the capital of foreign financial institutions.

   In banks by nonresidents — Nonresidents may purchase up to 100% of a local financial institution.

Open foreign exchange position limits — Effective February 26, 1999, the limits are 20% and 5% of the net worth. There are no regulations governing the net foreign exchange positions of exchange houses; they may sell their excess foreign holdings to authorized financial intermediaries because they do not have access to the BR.

Provisions specific to institutional investors

Limits (min.) on portfolio invested locally — Yes.

Other controls imposed by securities laws — n.a.

Changes During 1999

Exchange arrangement — *June 28*. The central parity of the trading band was lowered by 9% against the dollar. The upper and lower limits of the band were also widened to allow for a maximum daily fluctuation of 20% in the value of the peso, and the slope of the band was changed to 10% from 13%.

September 25. The central bank abandoned the crawling band and allowed the peso to float. Thus, the exchange rate arrangement of Colombia has been reclassified to the category independently floating from the category crawling band.

Capital transactions

Provisions specific to commercial banks and other credit institutions — *February 26*. The limits for the open foreign exchange position were set at 20% and 5% of the net worth.

COMOROS

(Position as of January 31, 2000)

Status Under IMF Articles of Agreement

Article VIII   Date of acceptance: June 1, 1996.

Exchange Arrangement

Currency   The currency of Comoros is the Comorian franc.

Exchange rate structure   Unitary.

Classification

Conventional pegged arrangement   The Comorian franc is pegged to the euro at CF 491.96775 per €1. Exchange rates for currencies are officially quoted on the basis of the fixed rate of the Comorian franc for the euro and the Paris exchange market rates for other currencies.

Exchange tax   No.

Exchange subsidy   No.

Forward exchange market   Forward cover against exchange rate risk is authorized by the Central Bank of the Comoros (CBC) and is provided to traders by the only authorized commercial bank for up to three months.

Arrangements for Payments and Receipts

Prescription of currency requirements   Because the Comoros is linked to the French Treasury through an Operations Account, settlements with France, Monaco, and other Operations Account countries (WAEMU and CAEMC members) are made in French francs or the currency of any other Operations Account country. Settlements with all other countries are usually made through correspondent banks in France in any of the currencies of those countries or in euros through foreign accounts in euros.

Payment arrangements

Regional arrangements   Comoros is a member of COMESA and the Cross-Border Initiative.

Clearing agreements   Yes.

Administration of control   The Minister of Finance and Budget has sole authority in exchange control matters but has delegated certain exchange control powers to the CBC and to authorized banks. Exchange control is administered by the CBC. The Ministry of Finance and Budget supervises borrowing and lending abroad, inward direct investment, and all outward investment. With the exception of those transactions relating to gold, the country's exchange control measures do not apply to (1) France (and its overseas departments and territories) and Monaco; and (2) all other countries whose bank of issue is linked with the French Treasury by an Operations Account (WAEMU and CAEMC members). A statistical report is required to monitor speculative transactions.

International security restrictions   No.

Payment arrears

Official   Yes.

Controls on trade in gold (coins and/or bullion)

Controls on domestic ownership and/or trade   Yes.

Controls on external trade	Imports and exports of nonmonetary gold require prior authorization. Imports and exports of articles containing gold are subject to declaration, but transfers of personal jewelry within the limit of 500 grams a person are exempt from such declaration.

Controls on exports and imports of banknotes

On exports

Domestic currency	Up to CF 500,000 may be exported.
Foreign currency	Residents traveling to France, Monaco, and the Operations Account countries may take out the equivalent of CF 500,000 in banknotes and any amount in other means of payment. Residents traveling to countries other than France, Monaco, and the other Operations Account countries may take out any means of payment up to the equivalent of CF 500,000 a person a trip. Any amount in excess of these limits is subject to CBC approval, which is granted if supporting documentation is provided. Nonresident travelers may export the equivalent of CF 500,000 in banknotes and any means of payment issued abroad in their name without providing documentary justification. Other cases are authorized pursuant to the exchange regulations when supporting documents can be produced.

Resident Accounts

Foreign exchange accounts permitted	Opening of these accounts is permitted, but no authorization has been granted.
Held domestically	These accounts are permitted, but prior approval is required.
Held abroad	These accounts are permitted, but prior approval is required.
Accounts in domestic currency convertible into foreign currency	No.

Nonresident Accounts

Foreign exchange accounts permitted	These accounts are permitted, but prior approval is required.
Domestic currency accounts	These accounts are permitted if applicants meet the criteria for nonresident eligibility.
Convertible into foreign currency	Yes.
Blocked accounts	Yes.

Imports and Import Payments

Foreign exchange budget	No.
Financing requirements for imports	No.
Documentation requirements for release of foreign exchange for imports	
Domiciliation requirements	All import transactions must be domiciled with the authorized bank if the value is CF 500,000 or more.
Preshipment inspection	Yes.
Letters of credit	Yes.
Import licenses and other nontariff measures	The importation of most goods, except those originating from member countries of the EU, Monaco, and the Operations Account countries, was subject to individual licensing, which was for statistical purposes only. Effective January 31, 2000, this licensing requirement was suspended; however, notification is required for statistical purposes.

Negative list	The importation of certain goods is prohibited from all countries for health or security reasons.
Import taxes and/or tariffs	There are import duty rates of 20%, 30%, and 40% for general merchandise; 150% for tobacco; 180% for spirits; and an administrative fee of 3% for imports exempt from duty.
State import monopoly	No.

Exports and Export Proceeds

Repatriation requirements	Proceeds from exports to foreign countries must be repatriated within 30 days of the expiration of the commercial contract.
Surrender requirements	Proceeds must be sold immediately after repatriation to the authorized bank.
Financing requirements	No.
Documentation requirements	With a few exceptions, exports to any destination are free of licensing requirements.
Letters of credit	Yes.
Domiciliation	All export transactions must be domiciled with an authorized bank if the value is CF 500,000 or more.
Preshipment inspection	Yes.
Export licenses	Licenses were issued mainly for statistical purposes. Effective January 31, 2000, this licensing requirement was suspended; however, notification is required for statistical purposes.
Without quotas	Yes.
Export taxes	There are export taxes, but they do not apply to all exports.
Other export taxes	Certain taxes apply to specific luxury products in favor of professional organizations.

Payments for Invisible Transactions and Current Transfers

Controls on these transfers	Payments for invisibles to France, Monaco, and the Operations Account countries are permitted freely. Payments for invisibles related to authorized imports are not restricted. All other payments, except investment-related transfers, are subject to indicative limits or bona fide tests.
Trade-related payments	
Indicative limits/bona fide test	Yes.
Investment-related payments	Repatriation of dividends and other earnings from nonresidents' direct investments is authorized and guaranteed under the Investment Code.
Payments for travel	
Quantitative limits	Yes.
Indicative limits/bona fide test	Residents traveling to countries other than France, Monaco, and the other Operations Account countries may take out any means of payment up to the equivalent of CF 500,000 a person a trip. Any amount in excess of these limits is subject to the prior approval of the CBC, which is granted if supporting documentation is provided.
Personal payments	These transactions are authorized upon presentation of the pertinent documentation.
Indicative limits/bona fide test	Yes.
Foreign workers' wages	
Indicative limits/bona fide test	Yes.

Credit card use abroad

   Quantitative limits — The same limits apply as for tourist and business travel.

   Indicative limits/bona fide test — Yes.

Other payments

   Prior approval — Yes.

   Indicative limits/bona fide test — Yes.

Proceeds from Invisible Transactions and Current Transfers

Repatriation requirements — Proceeds from transactions with France, Monaco, and the Operations Account countries may be retained. All amounts due from residents of other countries with respect to services and all income earned in those countries from foreign assets must be repatriated within one month of the due date or date of receipt.

Surrender requirements — Export proceeds in foreign currency must be sold to an authorized bank.

Restrictions on use of funds — No.

Capital Transactions

Controls on capital and money market instruments — Capital flows between the Comoros and France, Monaco, and the Operations Account countries are, in principle, free of exchange control. Capital transfers to all other countries require exchange control approval, but capital receipts from such countries are permitted freely.

On capital market securities — CBC authorization is required to effect these transactions.

   Shares or other securities of a participating nature

      Purchase locally by nonresidents — Yes.

      Purchase abroad by residents — Yes.

      Sale or issue abroad by residents — Yes.

   Bonds or other debt securities

      Purchase locally by nonresidents — Yes.

      Sale or issue locally by nonresidents — Yes.

      Purchase abroad by residents — Yes.

      Sale or issue abroad by residents — Yes.

On money market instruments — There is no local market in these instruments.

On collective investment securities — There is no local market in these instruments.

Controls on derivatives and other instruments — There is no local market in these instruments.

Controls on credit operations

Commercial credits

   By residents to nonresidents — Credits must have a maximum maturity of 90 days.

   To residents from nonresidents — Yes.

Financial credits

   By residents to nonresidents — Yes.

To residents from nonresidents	Yes.
Guarantees, sureties, and financial backup facilities	
By residents to nonresidents	Yes.
To residents from nonresidents	Yes.
Controls on direct investment	
Outward direct investment	Controls relate to the approval of the underlying transactions, not to payments or receipts.
Inward direct investment	Yes.
Controls on liquidation of direct investment	n.a.
Controls on real estate transactions	
Purchase abroad by residents	Yes.
Controls on personal capital movements	
Loans	
To residents from nonresidents	Yes.
Gifts, endowments, inheritances, and legacies	
By residents to nonresidents	Yes.
To residents from nonresidents	Yes.
Settlement of debts abroad by immigrants	Settlement of debt is permitted upon presentation of supporting documentation.
Transfer of assets	
Transfer abroad by emigrants	Yes.
Transfer of gambling and prize earnings	Yes.
Provisions specific to commercial banks and other credit institutions	
Borrowing abroad	Yes.
Maintenance of accounts abroad	Yes.
Lending to nonresidents (financial or commercial credits)	Lending is permitted for economic activities in the Comoros.
Lending locally in foreign exchange	Lending does not take place in practice.
Purchase of locally issued securities denominated in foreign exchange	There is no local market in these securities.
Investment regulations	
Abroad by banks	Yes.
In banks by nonresidents	Yes.
Provisions specific to institutional investors	No transactions of this type are carried out.
Other controls imposed by securities laws	n.a.

Changes During 1999

Exchange arrangement	*January 1.* The Comorian franc peg to the French franc was replaced with a peg to the euro.

Changes During 2000

Imports and import payments	*January 31.* The licensing requirements for importing most goods were suspended.
Exports and export proceeds	*January 31.* Export licenses were suspended.

DEMOCRATIC REPUBLIC OF THE CONGO

(Position as of December 31, 1999)

Status Under IMF Articles of Agreement

Article XIV	Yes.

Exchange Arrangement

Currency	The currency of the Democratic Republic of the Congo is the Congo franc.
Exchange rate structure	Unitary.
Classification	
Independently floating	An interbank foreign exchange market is in operation. Charges or commissions are not assessed on interbank market transactions. In their transactions with customers, commercial banks and financial institutions may charge an exchange commission not exceeding 1%. The spread between the buying and selling rates for foreign banknotes set by the commercial banks and financial institutions in the foreign exchange market must not exceed 5%.
Exchange tax	A charge of 0.2% is levied on any exchange operation of authorized banks.
Exchange subsidy	No.
Forward exchange market	Yes.

Arrangements for Payments and Receipts

Prescription of currency requirements	Payments from nonresidents to residents must be made in one of 23 convertible currencies whose rates are published daily by the Central Bank of the Democratic Republic of the Congo (BCC). Residents must make payments to nonresidents in one of the listed convertible currencies or by crediting nonresident accounts in Congo francs or in foreign currency. Settlements with the member countries of the CEPGL and the CEEAC are made in SDRs and through Central African Units of Account (UCAC) accounts established under arrangements concluded by the BCC with the central banks of the countries concerned. Balances on these SDR and UCAC accounts at the end of settlement periods—each quarter for CEPGL countries and each month for CEEAC countries—are transferable into the currency stipulated by the creditor. Virtually all settlements (other than for reexports) with member countries of the CEEAC are effected through accounts with foreign correspondent banks after clearing through the Central African Clearing House through its account with the BCC.
Payment arrangements	
Bilateral payment arrangements	
Inoperative	Yes.
Regional arrangements	Yes.
Clearing agreements	There are arrangements with Burundi and Rwanda. Payments are made through the SDR accounts of the BCC and the central banks of the other two countries.
Administration of control	Effective January 9, 1999, foreign exchange transactions must be conducted through the BCC or authorized foreign exchange dealers. The BCC also supervises authorized banks and dealers, and regulates open foreign exchange positions.
International security restrictions	No.
Payment arrears	
Official	Yes.
Private	Yes.

Controls on trade in gold (coins and/or bullion)

Controls on domestic ownership and/or trade	Only nationals of the Democratic Republic of the Congo are allowed to purchase, transport, sell, or hold gold within the country outside the boundaries of areas covered by exclusive mining concessions. Foreign individuals or corporate persons may do so only on behalf of, and for the account of, authorized marketing agencies.
Controls on external trade	Exports of gold and diamonds by authorized marketing agencies do not require prior authorization from the BCC.

Controls on exports and imports of banknotes

Resident and nonresident travelers must declare their foreign exchange holdings upon entering or exiting the country. Travelers entering the country must deposit their foreign exchange holdings with authorized intermediaries within three days following their entry. They may freely hold means of payment in domestic currency. Travelers exiting the country are authorized to carry an amount of foreign exchange not to exceed $10,000.

On exports	
Domestic currency	Yes.
Foreign currency	Yes.
On imports	
Domestic currency	The importation of banknotes of the Democratic Republic of the Congo is permitted up to the equivalent of $100.
Foreign currency	An unlimited amount of banknotes and other means of payment in foreign currency may be brought into the country.

Resident Accounts

Foreign exchange accounts permitted	These accounts are permitted and may be credited or debited for international transactions without restrictions, may be sight or term accounts, may bear interest, and may be denominated in any currency for which the BCC publishes exchange rates.
Held domestically	Authorized banks are permitted to open accounts in foreign currency for residents and nonresidents without prior approval from the BCC.
Held abroad	Public and/or semipublic enterprises may open foreign bank accounts with prior authorization from the BCC.
Accounts in domestic currency convertible into foreign currency	Yes.

Nonresident Accounts

Foreign exchange accounts permitted	These accounts may be credited or debited for international transactions without restriction. As of June 30, 1999, these accounts may not be in debit position.
Domestic currency accounts	Yes.
Blocked accounts	No.

Imports and Import Payments

Foreign exchange budget	There is a budget for imports by the government and the BCC.
Financing requirements for imports	No.

Documentation requirements for release of foreign exchange for imports

Domiciliation requirements | As of June 30, 1999, importers must obtain a license from an authorized bank.

Preshipment inspection | With a few exceptions, imports are subject to a preshipment inspection. The amount, the invoice price, and the quality of imports must be verified and approved by the foreign agents of the Control Office of the Democratic Republic of the Congo (OCC); however, in special cases verification may be effected upon arrival, subject to a waiver from the BCC. Verification certificates are not required for import values (f.o.b.) of up to the equivalent of SDR 1,000 a tariff item, or up to $2,500 a shipment.

Letters of credit | Yes.

Import licenses and other nontariff measures

Positive list | Yes.

Negative list | Certain imports, including arms, explosives and ammunition, narcotics, materials contrary to public morals, and certain alcoholic beverages, are prohibited or require special authorization from the government.

Other nontariff measures | All goods shipped by sea must be transported on vessels belonging to ship owners who are bonded with the Office congolais du frêt maritime and whose freight charges have been negotiated with that office.

Import taxes and/or tariffs | The customs tariff rates range from 5% to 30%, with a special rate of 5% for some essential industrial imports. The rate of the turnover tax ranges up to 13%.

State import monopoly | No.

Exports and Export Proceeds

Repatriation requirements | Export or reexport proceeds must be repatriated within 30 calendar days from the date of shipment. Proceeds from exports of gold and diamonds must be received at the bank within 10 days after the date of shipment. With exports on consignment, export proceeds must be repatriated as soon as the merchandise has been sold.

Financing requirements | No.

Documentation requirements | As of June 30, 1999, exporters must obtain a license from an authorized bank.

Letters of credit | Yes.

Guarantees | Yes.

Domiciliation | Yes.

Preshipment inspection | All exports require an inspection certificate issued by the OCC; coffee exports also require a quality certificate from the National Coffee Office.

Export licenses

Without quotas | Yes.

Export taxes | The export, turnover, and statistical taxes have been suspended.

Payments for Invisible Transactions and Current Transfers

Controls on these transfers | Payments on account of invisible transactions are regulated.

Trade-related payments | Payment of commissions for representing foreign brand names is regulated.

Indicative limits/bona fide test | Indicative limits or bona fide tests are applied to payment of freight, insurance, and commissions.

Investment-related payments

    Indicative limits/bona fide test   Yes.

Payments for travel

    Indicative limits/bona fide test   Yes.

Personal payments

    Indicative limits/bona fide test   Yes.

Foreign workers' wages

    Quantitative limits   Transfer abroad of foreigners' wages for the preceding year is limited. Transfer abroad of expatriates' wages is limited to 50% of net wages in the case of new employees, provided that the remaining 50% is adequate to cover local needs.

    Indicative limits/bona fide test   Yes.

Other payments

    Indicative limits/bona fide test   Yes.

Proceeds from Invisible Transactions and Current Transfers

Repatriation requirements   Yes.

Surrender requirements   Proceeds must be surrendered to authorized banks. A declaration must be made for each transaction. For some operations, proceeds may be credited to a resident foreign currency account.

Restrictions on use of funds   Receipts credited to a resident's account in foreign exchange are conveyed to the authorized banks as needed by the account holders.

Capital Transactions

Controls on capital and money market instruments   There are controls on treasury bill transactions.

On capital market securities   Yes.

On money market instruments   Yes.

Controls on derivatives and other instruments   No.

Controls on credit operations   Residents may borrow abroad to invest in the Democratic Republic of the Congo.

Commercial credits

    By residents to nonresidents   Yes.

    To residents from nonresidents   Yes.

Financial credits

    By residents to nonresidents   Yes.

    To residents from nonresidents   Yes.

Guarantees, sureties, and financial backup facilities

    To residents from nonresidents   Yes.

Controls on direct investment   Both outward and inward direct investments are permitted, subject to a license from a bank.

Controls on liquidation of direct investment	The repatriation of foreign capital brought in under the provisions of the Investment Code is permitted, subject to prior BCC authorization, only at the time of liquidation, nationalization, or partial or total transfer of shares.
Controls on real estate transactions	
Purchase locally by nonresidents	Yes.
Controls on personal capital movements	Personal capital movements are unrestricted, generally authorized, and do not require licenses. However, they must be carried out through the banking system.
Transfer of gambling and prize earnings	Yes.
Provisions specific to commercial banks and other credit institutions	
Borrowing abroad	Yes.
Maintenance of accounts abroad	Yes.
Lending to nonresidents (financial or commercial credits)	Bridge loans require prior consent of the BCC.
Lending locally in foreign exchange	Yes.
Differential treatment of deposit accounts in foreign exchange	As of June 30, 1999, nonresident accounts in foreign exchange may not be in a debit position.
Credit controls	Yes.
Differential treatment of deposit accounts held by nonresidents	As of June 30, 1999, nonresident accounts in foreign exchange may not be in a debit position.
Credit controls	Yes.
Open foreign exchange position limits	The ceiling on the foreign exchange position of each bank is authorized by the BCC.
Provisions specific to institutional investors	No.
Other controls imposed by securities laws	No.

Changes During 1999

Arrangements for payments and receipts	*January 9.* Foreign exchange transactions must be conducted through the BCC or authorized foreign exchange dealers.
Nonresident accounts	*June 30.* The accounts of nonresidents may not be in a debit position.
Imports and import payments	*June 30.* Importers must obtain a license from an authorized bank.
Exports and export proceeds	*June 30.* Exporters must obtain a license from an authorized bank.
Capital transactions	
Provisions specific to institutional investors	*June 30.* The accounts of nonresidents may not be in a debit position.

REPUBLIC OF CONGO

(Position as of December 31, 1999)

Status Under IMF Articles of Agreement

Article VIII

Date of acceptance: June 1, 1996.

Exchange Arrangement

Currency

The currency of the Republic of Congo is the CFA franc.

Exchange rate structure

Unitary.

Classification

Exchange arrangement with no separate legal tender

The CFA franc is pegged to the euro, the intervention currency, at the fixed rate of CFAF 100 per €0.1524. Exchange transactions in euros between the BEAC and commercial banks take place at the same rate. Buying and selling rates for certain other foreign currencies are also officially posted, with quotations based on the fixed rate for the euro and the rate for the currency concerned in the Paris foreign exchange market. Payments to all countries are subject to a commission of 0.75%, with a minimum charge of CFAF 75; exempt from this commission are payments of the state, the Postal and Telecommunications Administration, the BEAC, salaries of Congolese diplomats abroad, expenditures of official missions abroad, scholarships of persons studying or training abroad, payments made on behalf of individuals for purchases of books and newspapers not intended for sale, and debt-service payments due from companies that have entered into an agreement with the Republic of Congo. An additional commission of 0.25% is levied on all payments to countries that are not members of the BEAC.

Exchange tax

No.

Exchange subsidy

No.

Forward exchange market

There are no spot or forward exchange markets for the CFA franc. However, exporters and importers can always cover their position on the Paris foreign exchange market.

Arrangements for Payments and Receipts

Prescription of currency requirements

Because the Republic of Congo is linked to the French Treasury through an Operations Account, settlements with France, Monaco, and other Operations Account countries (WAEMU and CAEMC members and the Comoros) are made in CFA francs, euros, or the currency of any other Operations Account country. Settlements with all other countries are usually made in any of the currencies of those countries or in French francs through foreign accounts in euros.

Payment arrangements

Regional arrangements

An Operations Account is maintained with the French Treasury. All purchases or sales of foreign currencies or euros against CFA francs are ultimately settled through a debit or credit to the Operations Account.

Clearing agreements

Yes.

Administration of control

Payments to France and the Operations Account countries, although subject to declaration, are unrestricted. Settlements and investment transactions with all foreign countries, however, are subject to control.

The General Directorate of Credit and Financial Relations (DGCRF) in the Ministry of Economy, Planning, and Finance (MEPF) supervises borrowing and lending abroad. Exchange control is administered by the MEPF, which has delegated approval authority to the DGCRF. All exchange transactions relating to foreign countries must be effected through authorized intermediaries—that is, the Postal and Telecommunications Administration and authorized banks.

International security restrictions	No.
Payment arrears	
Official	Yes.

Controls on trade in gold (coins and/or bullion)

Controls on domestic ownership and/or trade — Residents are free to hold gold in the form of coins, art objects, or jewelry; however, to hold gold in any other form, the prior authorization of the MEPF is required.

Controls on external trade — The prior authorization of the MEPF is required to import or export gold in any form. Exempt from the authorization requirement are (1) imports and exports by or on behalf of the Treasury or the BEAC and (2) imports and exports of manufactured articles containing a small quantity of gold (such as gold-filled or gold-plated articles). Both licensed and exempt imports of gold are subject to customs declaration. There are no official exports of gold.

Controls on exports and imports of banknotes

On exports

Domestic currency — There is no limit on the amount of banknotes that residents or nonresidents may export from the Republic of Congo to any member country of the BEAC area of issue, but exports of banknotes outside the CAEMC area are prohibited.

Foreign currency — Residents traveling for tourist or business purposes to France or the Operations Account countries are allowed to take out an unlimited amount in banknotes or other payment instruments in French francs. The reexportation of foreign banknotes is allowed up to the equivalent of CFAF 250,000; the reexportation of foreign banknotes above these ceilings requires documentation demonstrating either the importation of foreign banknotes or their purchase against other means of payment registered in the name of the traveler, or through the use of nonresident deposits lodged in local banks. The reexportation by nonresident travelers of means of payment other than banknotes issued abroad and registered in the name of the nonresident traveler is not restricted, subject to documentation that the banknotes had been purchased with funds drawn from a foreign account in CFA francs or with other foreign exchange.

On imports

Domestic currency — There is no limit on the amount of banknotes that residents and nonresidents may import from a member country of the BEAC area of issue to the Republic of Congo. However, imports of banknotes from outside the area of issue are prohibited.

Foreign currency — Travelers are authorized to enter the Republic of Congo with banknotes and coins other than CFA francs.

Resident Accounts

Foreign exchange accounts permitted	Yes.
Held abroad	These accounts are permitted, but approval is required.
Accounts in domestic currency convertible into foreign currency	n.a.

Nonresident Accounts

Foreign exchange accounts permitted	Foreign exchange accounts are intended primarily for the use of international agencies and embassies. However, prior approval is required.

Domestic currency accounts	The regulations pertaining to nonresident accounts are based on regulations that were applied in France before the abolition of all capital controls in 1989. Because the BEAC has suspended the repurchase of BEAC banknotes exchanged outside the area of issue, these may not be credited to foreign accounts in euros.
Blocked accounts	n.a.

Imports and Import Payments

Foreign exchange budget	No.
Financing requirements for imports	No.
Documentation requirements for release of foreign exchange for imports	
Domiciliation requirements	All import transactions with countries other than France and the Operations Account countries must be domiciled with an authorized bank. Licenses for imports from these countries must be domiciled with an authorized bank and approved by the Foreign Trade Directorate and the DGCRF.
Preshipment inspection	Yes.
Import licenses used as exchange licenses	The approved import license entitles importers to purchase the necessary exchange, provided that the shipping documents are submitted to an authorized bank.
Import licenses and other nontariff measures	An annual import program classifies imports by the following zones: (1) the countries of the CAEMC, (2) France, (3) other Operations Account countries, (4) EU countries other than France, and (5) all remaining countries. Nine product items under this program require licenses, and others are subject to ex post declaration.
Open general licenses	Except for cement, goods from all countries may be imported freely and without licenses. All imports, however, are subject to declaration.
Licenses with quotas	Imports of cement are subject to quotas.
Other nontariff measures	All imports of commercial goods must be insured through authorized insurance companies in the Republic of Congo.
Import taxes and/or tariffs	The common duty rates of the CAEMC member countries are 5% for basic necessities, 10% for raw materials and capital goods, 20% for intermediate and miscellaneous goods, and 30% for consumer goods products requiring special protection. Intra-CAEMC customs duties are 20% of the common external rates.
	Import surcharges of 30% have been introduced on imports of goods previously subject to quantitative restrictions. These surcharges are to be eliminated in three to six years, with the longer period applying to certain agricultural and textile products.
State import monopoly	No.

Exports and Export Proceeds

Repatriation requirements	Proceeds from exports to countries outside the CAEMC zone must be collected and repatriated within 180 days of arrival of the commodities at their destination.
Surrender requirements	Export proceeds must be surrendered within eight days from the payment due date.
Financing requirements	n.a.
Documentation requirements	
Domiciliation	All export transactions relating to countries other than France, Monaco, and the Operations Account countries must be domiciled with an authorized bank.

Export licenses	All exports require an exchange commitment that must be underwritten within eight days from the export date.
Without quotas	Yes.
Export taxes	Export taxes of up to 13% apply to certain goods.

Payments for Invisible Transactions and Current Transfers

Controls on these transfers	Payments for invisibles to France and the Operations Account countries are permitted freely; payments to other countries are subject only to declaration and presentation of appropriate documents to the MEPF for approval. Payments for invisibles related to trade are permitted freely when the basic trade transaction has been approved or does not require authorization.
Investment-related payments	The regulations in force guarantee the repatriation of profits, dividends, and proceeds from disinvestment abroad.
Prior approval	Payments for depreciation of direct investments require DGCRF authorization.
Indicative limits/bona fide test	Yes.
Payments for travel	
Prior approval	Yes.
Quantitative limits	Residents traveling for tourist or business purposes to France or the Operations Account countries are allowed to take out an unlimited amount in banknotes or other payment instruments in CFA francs. The allowances for travel to countries outside the franc zone are subject to the following regulations: (1) for tourist travel, CFAF 100,000 a day, with a maximum of CFAF 2 million a trip; (2) for business travel, CFAF 250,000 a day, with a maximum of CFAF 5 million a trip; (3) for official travel, the equivalent of mission expenses paid to civil servants and other government employees, or for tourists a foreign exchange allowance on the same terms; and (4) for medical expenses, up to CFAF 100,000 a day with a maximum of CFAF 2.5 million a trip. All resident travelers, regardless of destination, must declare in writing all means of payment at their disposal at the time of departure and surrender within eight days all means of payment exceeding the equivalent of CFAF 25,000. Allowances in excess of the limits are subject to the authorization of the MEPF.
Indicative limits/bona fide test	Yes.
Personal payments	
Prior approval	Yes.
Quantitative limits	Payments of pensions, medical expenses, studies abroad, alimony, and family maintenance are authorized upon presentation of supporting documents.
Indicative limits/bona fide test	Yes.
Foreign workers' wages	
Prior approval	Yes.
Quantitative limits	The transfer of the entire net salary of a foreigner working in the Republic of Congo is permitted upon presentation of the appropriate pay voucher, provided that the transfer takes place within three months of the pay period. Transfers by residents of amounts smaller than CFAF 500,000 to nonmember countries of the franc zone are subject to simple declaration, and those exceeding CFAF 500,000 require prior authorization. Transfers to nonmember countries by nonresidents living in the Republic of Congo for less than one year are subject to authorization. Members of diplomatic missions and employees of international organizations are exempt from this requirement.
Indicative limits/bona fide test	Yes.

Credit card use abroad

   Prior approval   Yes.

   Quantitative limits   The use of credit cards, which must be issued by resident financial intermediaries and approved by the MEPF, is limited to the ceilings applied for tourist and business travel.

   Indicative limits/bona fide test   Yes.

Proceeds from Invisible Transactions and Current Transfers

Repatriation requirements   All amounts due from residents of foreign countries with respect to services and all income earned in those countries from foreign assets must be collected when due.

Surrender requirements   Proceeds should be surrendered within one month of the due date.

Restrictions on use of funds   No.

Capital Transactions

Controls on capital and money market instruments   Capital movements between the Republic of Congo, France, Monaco, and the Operations Account countries are free, although ex post declarations are required. Most international capital transactions are subject to prior authorization. Capital transfers abroad require exchange control approval and are restricted, but capital receipts from abroad are generally permitted freely.

All foreign securities, foreign currency, and titles embodying claims on foreign countries or nonresidents that are held in the Republic of Congo by residents or nonresidents must be deposited with authorized banks in the Republic of Congo.

On capital market securities

   Shares or other securities of a participating nature

     Sale or issue locally by nonresidents   The issuing, advertising, or offering for sale of foreign securities in the Republic of Congo requires prior authorization from the MEPF. Exempt from authorization, however, are operations in connection with (1) loans backed by a guarantee from the Congolese government; and (2) shares similar to securities whose issuing, advertising, or offering for sale in the Republic of Congo has previously been authorized.

     Purchase abroad by residents   Yes.

On money market instruments

   Purchase abroad by residents   Yes.

On collective investment securities

   Purchase abroad by residents   Yes.

Controls on derivatives and other instruments

Purchase abroad by residents   Yes.

Controls on credit operations

Commercial credits   Special controls (in addition to any exchange control requirement that may apply) are maintained over borrowing and lending abroad.

   By residents to nonresidents   All lending in CFA francs to nonresidents is prohibited unless special authorization is obtained from the MEPF. The following are, however, exempt from this authorization: (1) loans in foreign currency granted by registered banks, and (2) other loans whose total amounts outstanding do not exceed the equivalent of CFAF 5 million for any one lender. The making of loans that are free of authorization and each repayment must be reported to the General Directorate of Credit and Financial Relations within 20 days.

To residents from nonresidents	Borrowing requires prior authorization from the MEPF. However, loans contracted by registered banks and small loans, where the total amount outstanding does not exceed CFAF 10 million for any one borrower, the interest is no higher than 5%, and the term is at least two years, are exempt from this requirement. The contracting of loans that are free of authorization and each repayment must be reported to the General Directorate of Credit and Financial Relations within 20 days of the operation. Borrowing backed by a guarantee from the government is exempt from authorization.

Financial credits

By residents to nonresidents	Yes.
To residents from nonresidents	Yes.

Guarantees, sureties, and financial backup facilities

By residents to nonresidents	Yes.
To residents from nonresidents	Yes.

Controls on direct investment

Outward direct investment	The prior approval of the MEPF is required.
Inward direct investment	Investments (including those made through foreign companies that are directly or indirectly controlled by persons in the Republic of Congo and those made by overseas branches or subsidiaries of companies in the Republic of Congo) require the prior approval of the MEPF, unless they involve the creation of a mixed-economy enterprise.
Controls on liquidation of direct investment	The full or partial liquidation of direct investments must be declared to the MEPF within 20 days.
Controls on real estate transactions	n.a.
Controls on personal capital movements	n.a.
Provisions specific to commercial banks and other credit institutions	n.a.
Provisions specific to institutional investors	n.a.
Other controls imposed by securities laws	n.a.

Changes During 1999

Exchange arrangement	*January 1.* The CFA franc peg to the French franc was replaced with one to the euro.

COSTA RICA
(Position as of March 31, 2000)

Status Under IMF Articles of Agreement

Article VIII   Date of acceptance: February 1, 1965.

Exchange Arrangement

Currency   The currency of Costa Rica is the Costa Rican colón.

Exchange rate structure   Unitary.

Classification

Crawling peg   The external value of the colón is determined in the interbank market. Foreign exchange trading occurs in the organized electronic foreign exchange market (MONED) among authorized traders, which is where the Central Bank (CB) carries out its intervention operations. Foreign exchange trading also takes place directly between authorized institutions outside the MONED. The government and public sector institutions conduct foreign exchange transactions with the state commercial banks and the CB at the official reference exchange rate, which is calculated at the close of each business day as the weighted average of the exchange rates used in the market during the day. The rate of the crawl is an average of 9 centavos a day (10.5% on an annual basis).

Exchange tax   A tax of 15%, calculated on the average daily spread between buying and selling rates, applied to all foreign exchange transactions in the exchange market. This amount must be transferred to the CB within one day. Effective March 6, 2000, the tax was lowered to 10%.

Exchange subsidy   No.

Forward exchange market   No.

Arrangements for Payments and Receipts

Prescription of currency requirements   Nearly all payments for exchange transactions are made in dollars. Trade payments to Central America may be made in dollars or in local currencies.

Payment arrangements   No.

Regional arrangements   Costa Rica is a member of the CACM.

Administration of control   Regulations are issued by the CB's Superintendency of Banks and Financial Institutions.

International security restrictions   No.

Payment arrears   No.

Controls on trade in gold (coins and/or bullion)

Controls on domestic ownership and/or trade   Natural and juridical persons may buy or sell domestically produced gold (except national archaeological treasures).

Controls on external trade   Licenses from the CB are required for exports of gold.

Controls on exports and imports of banknotes   Imports and exports of foreign currency are free, but are usually carried out through the CB.

Resident Accounts

Foreign exchange accounts permitted   Yes.

247

Held domestically	Yes.
Held abroad	Yes.
Accounts in domestic currency convertible into foreign currency	Yes.

Nonresident Accounts

Foreign exchange accounts permitted	Yes.
Domestic currency accounts	Yes.
Convertible into foreign currency	Yes.
Blocked accounts	n.a.

Imports and Import Payments

Foreign exchange budget	n.a.
Financing requirements for imports	No.
Documentation requirements for release of foreign exchange for imports	No.
Import licenses and other nontariff measures	Imports made on a barter basis require a barter license issued by the Ministry of Economy and Commerce (MEC).
Import taxes and/or tariffs	Customs tariffs on most goods range from 5% to 20%. In addition, the following taxes are levied on imports: (1) a sales tax of 13%, from which certain essential items are exempt; and (2) selective consumption taxes at rates ranging from zero to 75%.
State import monopoly	Imports of fuel are made by Refineria Costa Ricense de Petroleo and imports of grain by the Consejo Nacional de Producción.

Exports and Export Proceeds

Repatriation requirements	Proceeds must be repatriated within 90 days before the end of the fiscal year.
Financing requirements	n.a.
Documentation requirements	An export form must be filed.
Export licenses	
Without quotas	Licenses are required for the following: armaments, munitions, scrap iron, and scrap of nonferrous base metals from the MEC; sugar from the Agricultural Industrial Board for Sugarcane; beans, rice, ipecacuanha root, onions, cotton, meat, and thoroughbred cattle from the National Council of Production; airplanes from the Civil Aviation Board and the MEC; Indian art objects made of gold, stone, or clay from the National Museum; tobacco from the Tobacco Defense Board; textiles, flowers, lumber, certain livestock, and wild animals and plants of the forest from the Ministry of Agriculture and Livestock; bananas from the National Banana Corporation; and coffee from the Coffee Institute. In addition, when there is a lien on coffee in favor of a bank, that bank's approval is required before the CB will grant an export license.
Export taxes	Taxes are levied on traditional exports and, in some cases, are graduated in line with international prices. There are no taxes on nontraditional exports to countries outside Central America, and exporters of these products are entitled to receive freely negotiable tax credit certificates at the following rates based on f.o.b. value: 15% for exports to the United States, Puerto Rico, and Europe; and 20% for exports to Canada. These certificates ceased to be issued to new exporters after 1992, but exporters existing at that time benefit from them, consistent with previous contractual arrangements.

Payments for Invisible Transactions and Current Transfers

Controls on these transfers	No.
Investment-related payments	A 15% withholding tax is levied on all profits and dividends and remittances of interest abroad, except for remittances to foreign banks or their financial entities recognized by the CB as institutions normally engaged in international transactions, and for interest payments on government borrowing abroad.
	Information is not available on the payment of amortization of loans or depreciation of direct investments.

Proceeds from Invisible Transactions and Current Transfers

Repatriation requirements	Repatriation must take place within 90 days of the end of the fiscal year.
Restrictions on use of funds	n.a.

Capital Transactions

Controls on capital and money market instruments	Effective December 22, 1999, the MOF was authorized to issue government bonds denominated in foreign currency aimed at converting domestic debt into foreign currency. Such bonds are to be issued annually, beginning in 2000 and continuing for four years, in amounts equivalent to $250 million, except for the year 2003, when the amount will be increased to the equivalent of $450 million.
Controls on derivatives and other instruments	No.
Controls on credit operations	No.
Commercial credits	The National Budget Authority (composed of the Minister of Finance, the Minister of Planning, and the President of the CB) is in charge of authorizing the negotiation of new external credits contemplated by the central government, decentralized agencies, and state enterprises.
Financial credits	
By residents to nonresidents	Private commercial banks, finance companies, and cooperatives must inform the CB when contracting credits abroad.
Controls on direct investment	No.
Controls on liquidation of direct investment	No.
Controls on real estate transactions	No.
Controls on personal capital movements	n.a.
Provisions specific to commercial banks and other credit institutions	n.a.
Provisions specific to institutional investors	n.a.
Other controls imposed by securities laws	n.a.

Changes During 1999

Capital transactions

December 22. The MOF was authorized to issue government bonds denominated in foreign currency.

Changes During 2000

Exchange arrangement

March 6. The foreign exchange tax was reduced to 10% from 15%.

CÔTE D'IVOIRE

(Position as of January 31, 2000)

Status Under IMF Articles of Agreement

Article VIII   Date of acceptance: June 1, 1996.

Exchange Arrangement

Currency   The currency of Côte d'Ivoire is the CFA franc.

Exchange rate structure   Unitary.

Classification

Exchange arrangement with no sepa- The CFA franc is pegged to the euro, the intervention currency, at the fixed rate of
rate legal tender   CFAF 100 per €0.8385. Exchange rates for other currencies are derived from the rate
                                    for the currency concerned in the Paris exchange market and the fixed rate between the
                                    euro and the CFA franc. The BCEAO levies no commission on transfers to or from all
                                    countries outside the WAEMU.

Exchange tax   Banks levy a proportional commission of 2.5‰ and a freely fixed commission on transfers
                                    to all non-WAEMU countries. The proceeds of the proportional commission are repaid in
                                    full to the Treasury. Transfers between WAEMU member countries are subject to a com-
                                    mission freely fixed by the banks.

Exchange subsidy   No.

Forward exchange market   Effective February 1, 1999, residents were authorized to contract forward exchange
                                    cover to settle payments related to imports and exports of goods and services. Forward
                                    exchange cover for eligible imports must not extend beyond one month for certain spec-
                                    ified goods and three months for goods designated essential commodities, with renewal
                                    of cover only once. Forward cover against exchange rate risk is permitted with prior
                                    authorization from the Directorate of the Treasury of the Ministry of Economy and
                                    Finance (MEF) only for payments for imports of goods and only for the currency stip-
                                    ulated in the commercial contract.

Arrangements for Payments and Receipts

Prescription of currency   Because Côte d'Ivoire is linked to the French Treasury through an Operations Account,
requirements   settlements with France, Monaco, and other Operations Account countries (WAEMU
                                    and CAEMC members and the Comoros) are made in French francs or the currency of
                                    any other Operations Account country. The BCEAO, of which Côte d'Ivoire is a mem-
                                    ber, is authorized to collect, either directly or through the banks, other financial institu-
                                    tions, or the Post Office Administration, any information necessary for compiling the
                                    balance of payments statistics. It also has powers from the MEF to monitor the banks'
                                    external positions.

Payment arrangements

Clearing agreements   Current payments with The Gambia, Ghana, Guinea, Liberia, Mauritania, Nigeria, and
                                    Sierra Leone are usually made through the WAMA.

Administration of control   Exchange control is administered by the Directorate of the Treasury in the MEF. Effective
                                    February 1, 1999, the amount of transfers authorized without supporting documentation
                                    was raised to CFAF 300,000 from CFAF 100,000.

International security restrictions   No.

Payment arrears

Official   Yes.

Controls on trade in gold (coins and/or bullion)

Controls on external trade

Imports and exports of gold from or to any other country require prior authorization from the MEF.

Controls on exports and imports of banknotes

On exports

Domestic currency

The exportation of CFA franc banknotes by travelers is not prohibited. However, repurchasing by the BCEAO of exported banknotes remains suspended. In addition, the sending of BCEAO banknotes between authorized intermediaries and their correspondent banks located outside the WAEMU zone is strictly prohibited.

Foreign currency

The reexportation of foreign banknotes by nonresident travelers is allowed up to the equivalent of CFAF 250,000; the reexportation of foreign banknotes above this ceiling requires documentation demonstrating either the importation of the foreign banknotes or their purchase against other means of payment registered in the name of the traveler or through the use of nonresident deposits at local banks.

On imports

Foreign currency

Residents and nonresidents may bring in any amount of foreign banknotes and coins (except gold coins) of countries outside the Operations Account area. Residents bringing in foreign banknotes and foreign currency traveler's checks must declare them to customs upon entry and sell any amount exceeding the equivalent of CFAF 25,000 to an authorized intermediary bank within eight days.

Resident Accounts

Foreign exchange accounts permitted

Effective February 1, 1999, residents are allowed to open foreign exchange accounts with local banks or with banks abroad after obtaining authorization from the MEF, with the approval of the BCEAO.

Held domestically

Residents may maintain foreign exchange accounts at local financial institutions, subject to prior authorization from the MEF.

Held abroad

The maintenance of bank accounts abroad is not explicitly prohibited by the legislation in force; however, the legislation does prohibit all transfers aimed at the constitution of assets abroad by a resident except where authorized by the MEF.

Accounts in domestic currency convertible into foreign currency

No.

Nonresident Accounts

Foreign exchange accounts permitted

Effective February 1, 1999, authorization is issued by the BCEAO.

Domestic currency accounts

Because the BCEAO has suspended the repurchase of banknotes circulating outside the territories of the WAEMU zone, nonresident accounts may not be credited or debited with BCEAO banknotes. These accounts may not be overdrawn without the prior authorization of the MEF. Transfers of funds between nonresident accounts are not restricted.

Convertible into foreign currency

Yes.

Blocked accounts

No.

Imports and Import Payments

Foreign exchange budget

No.

Financing requirements for imports	No.
Documentation requirements for release of foreign exchange for imports	
Domiciliation requirements	All imports exceeding CFAF 500,000 are subject to this requirement. Effective February 1, 1999, this limit was raised to CFAF 5 million.
Preshipment inspection	Inspection for quality and price is required for imports exceeding CFAF 3 million; imports valued between CFAF 1.5 million and CFAF 3 million may be subject to random inspection.
Letters of credit	LCs are required for goods imported from outside the EU, Operations Account countries, and ACP countries.
Import licenses and other nontariff measures	
Positive list	Imports are classified into three categories: (1) goods requiring prior authorization or the approval of ministries; (2) goods subject to quantitative or other restrictions requiring licenses issued by the Directorate of External Trade Promotions; and (3) freely importable goods.
Open general licenses	Import licenses for a shortlist of controlled products are issued by the Directorate of External Trade Promotions in the Ministry of Commerce.
Other nontariff measures	Yes.
Import taxes and/or tariffs	On January 1, 2000, the WAEMU introduced a CET with four rates (zero, 5%, 10%, and 20%) for all member countries except Guinea-Bissau. A statistical tax of 2.6% is levied on the c.i.f. value of all imports. Imports from members of the WAEMU and the ECOWAS are exempt from these surcharges.
State import monopoly	No.

Exports and Export Proceeds

Repatriation requirements	Proceeds from exports, including those to countries in the Operations Account area, must be received within 120 days of the arrival of the goods at their destination. Effective February 1, 1999, proceeds from exports to WAEMU countries are no longer required to be repatriated.
Surrender requirements	Foreign exchange derived from exports must be surrendered to authorized intermediary banks within 30 days of the payment due date. The authorized intermediary banks shall then surrender the foreign exchange to the BCEAO by transfer through the bank of issue.
Financing requirements	No.
Documentation requirements	Exports require a customs declaration. Exports of cocoa and coffee are subject to a specific unitary export tax and can be effected only by exporters authorized by the Price Stabilization Fund.
Letters of credit	Yes.
Domiciliation	All exports valued at more than CFAF 1 million, regardless of their destination, must be domiciled with an authorized bank. Effective February 1, 1999, exports to WAEMU countries need not be domiciled.
Export licenses	Exports of lumber are subject to quantitative quotas allocated through an auction.
Export taxes	
Other export taxes	Yes.

Payments for Invisible Transactions and Current Transfers

Controls on these transfers	Payments to France, Monaco, and the Operations Account countries are permitted freely; those to other countries must be approved. Payments for invisibles related to trade are permitted freely. Effective February 1, 1999, payments and incomes of foreign ships in the WAEMU zone and WAEMU ships abroad are included under current operations.
Investment-related payments	
Prior approval	The transfer abroad of funds necessary for the repayment of a loan is subject to authorization if the loan itself was subject to prior authorization. For payments of depreciation of direct investments, the prior authorization of the MEF is required, as this is not expressly provided for in the legislation.
Indicative limits/bona fide test	Yes.
Payments for travel	
Quantitative limits	The limits were CFAF 500,000 a trip for tourism and CFAF 75,000 a day up to one month for business travel. Allowances in excess of these limits were subject to authorization from the MEF. Effective February 1, 1999, limits on foreign exchange allowances were eliminated. The threshold of foreign exchange to be surrendered by residents after travel was raised to CFAF 300,000 from CFAF 50,000.
Personal payments	
Indicative limits/bona fide test	For payment of medical costs and studies abroad, indicative limits are used.
Credit card use abroad	Yes.
Other payments	
Indicative limits/bona fide test	Yes.

Proceeds from Invisible Transactions and Current Transfers

Repatriation requirements	All proceeds from transactions with non-Operations Account countries must be collected and repatriated in full. Effective February 1, 1999, the time limit for the repatriation and surrender requirement was set at one month after the due date or the date of receipt.
Surrender requirements	All proceeds from transactions with non-Operations Account countries must be surrendered.
Restrictions on use of funds	No.

Capital Transactions

Controls on capital and money market instruments	Capital movements to foreign countries are controlled. Capital may freely enter the member countries of the WAEMU, except with respect to direct investment that is subject to prior declaration and certain loan operations requiring advance authorization. Exempt from authorization, however, are operations in connection with (1) loans backed by a guarantee from the government of Côte d'Ivoire; and (2) foreign shares similar to securities whose issuing, advertising, or offering for sale in Côte d'Ivoire has already been authorized. With the exception of controls relating to foreign securities, these measures do not apply to relations with France, Monaco, member countries of the WAEMU, and the Operations Account countries. Special controls are also maintained over the soliciting of funds for deposit with foreign natural persons and foreign firms and institutions, and over publicity aimed at placing funds abroad or at subscribing to real estate and building operations abroad; these special controls also apply to France, Monaco, and the Operations Account countries. Effective February 1, 1999, transfers related to the sale of foreign securities by residents and to proceeds of disinvestments by nonresidents were allowed. Foreign investment in WAEMU countries became unrestricted. Such operations are subject to reporting for statistical purposes. The prior authorization of the RCPSFM is required for the issuance and marketing of securities and capital assets of foreign entities, as well as

for publicity and advertising of investments abroad. Any investment by residents abroad requires the prior approval of the MEF. A maximum of 75% of investment abroad may be financed by foreign loans.

On capital market securities

Shares or other securities of a participating nature

Purchase locally by nonresidents

There are no controls, provided that a prior declaration is made in the case of direct investment.

Sale or issue locally by nonresidents

These transactions are subject to the prior authorization of the MEF. Securities that have been authorized in advance may be purchased by a resident only after the latter has obtained prior approval of the MEF. The sale of securities constituting the liquidation of an investment by means of a transfer between a nonresident and a resident may be freely executed, subject to the prescriptions concerning the financial settlement of the operation. Settlement of an operation involving securities by transfer abroad or by crediting a nonresident account requires that an exchange authorization be submitted for the approval of the MEF in conjunction with documents attesting to the validity of the operation.

Purchase abroad by residents

These purchases and the transfer abroad of funds associated with them require the prior authorization of the MEF.

Sale or issue abroad by residents

Residents are free to sell the securities of resident corporations abroad. If these operations result in the foreign control of establishments resident in Côte d'Ivoire, the foreign investors are required to file a declaration in advance with the MEF. The sale of securities constituting the liquidation of an investment abroad is subject to prior declaration to the MEF. The proceeds in foreign exchange from the sale or liquidation must be surrendered to an authorized intermediary bank.

Bonds or other debt securities

n.r.

On money market instruments

Sale or issue locally by nonresidents

These sales are subject to the prior authorization of the MEF (except sales involving the liquidation of an investment, which are restricted).

Purchase abroad by residents

These purchases are subject to the prior authorization of the MEF.

Sale or issue abroad by residents

Residents may freely sell money market instruments abroad. Sales constituting the liquidation of an investment are subject to prior declaration. The proceeds in foreign exchange from the sale or liquidation must be surrendered to an authorized intermediary bank. The issue of money market instruments abroad by residents is governed by the provisions applicable to loans.

On collective investment securities

Sale or issue locally by nonresidents

Yes.

Purchase abroad by residents

Yes.

Sale or issue abroad by residents

Yes.

Controls on derivatives and other instruments

Effective February 1, 1999, transfers relating to option purchases were allowed.

Purchase locally by nonresidents

n.r.

Sale or issue locally by nonresidents

n.r.

Purchase abroad by residents

Yes.

Sale or issue abroad by residents

n.r.

Controls on credit operations

Commercial credits

For the issue of securities constituting a loan, the borrower must request advance authorization from the MEF. However, this authorization is not required for loans contracted by authorized intermediaries or those that comply with specific conditions as to amount and interest rate.

By residents to nonresidents

These credits may be granted, subject to the following provisions: (1) Debts arising from the exporting of goods must be collected and the corresponding amounts repatriated through the BCEAO within 30 days of the payment due date. The payment due date is the date specified in the commercial contract. It must in any case be no more than 120 days after the shipment of the goods. (2) Debts arising from payment for services must also be collected and surrendered on the exchange market no later than two months after the payment due date. No administrative limit is set for this due date.

To residents from nonresidents

These credits may be freely granted. Their repayment is generally authorized, subject to the presentation of documents attesting to the validity of the commercial transaction or the provision of the service, as well as the payment due date.

Financial credits

By residents to nonresidents

The granting of financial credits requires the prior authorization of the MEF. In order to transfer funds abroad to service these facilities, an exchange authorization must be submitted with the required vouchers to the MEF.

To residents from nonresidents

These facilities may be freely granted, and the funds to service them must be transferred from abroad by an authorized intermediary. However, if these operations are carried out between a direct investment company established in Côte d'Ivoire and its parent company abroad, they are considered to be direct investments and are therefore subject to prior declaration to the MEF.

The transfer abroad of the funds necessary to service a loan is subject to authorization if the loan itself required prior authorization. Requests for authorization must be accompanied by all supporting documents necessary to ensure the validity of the operation: authorization to borrow, references from the report prepared in connection with disbursement of the proceeds of the loan, and the like.

Guarantees, sureties, and financial backup facilities

By residents to nonresidents

The granting of these facilities requires the prior authorization of the MEF. In order to transfer funds abroad to service these facilities, an exchange authorization must be submitted with the required vouchers to the MEF.

To residents from nonresidents

These facilities may be freely granted, and the funds to service them must be transferred from abroad by an authorized intermediary. However, if these operations are carried out between a direct investment company established in Côte d'Ivoire and its parent company abroad, they are considered to be direct investments and are therefore subject to prior declaration to the MEF.

Controls on direct investment

Outward direct investment

Investment abroad (including purchases of real estate) by a resident is subject to prior authorization by the MEF, which must be requested by the party concerned in a letter designating the authorized intermediary that will execute payment. This payment, either by the transferring of funds abroad or by the crediting of a foreign account in euros, may not be made before the end of the time period agreed upon by the parties. Effective February 1, 1999, MEF authorization is no longer needed for investments abroad by residents in the form of securities, if the issue or sale by nonresidents was authorized by the RCPSFM.

Inward direct investment

Investments are subject to prior declaration to the MEF, which has a period of two months in which to request the suspension of the operation. The transfer of a direct investment by a nonresident to another nonresident is also subject to prior declaration. Special incentives are provided for foreign and domestic investments in certain priority sectors and priority geographical areas. The incentives include exemption from customs duties and tariffs on all imported capital equipment and spare parts for investment projects, provided that no equivalent item is produced in Côte d'Ivoire. In addition, all such investments are exempt for a specified period, depending on the investment sector or area, from corporate profit taxes, patent contributions, and capital assets taxes. In general, the exemption covers 100% of applicable tax up to the fourth-to-last year of the exemption period and is reduced progressively to 75% of the tax in the third-to-last year, 50% in the second-to-last year, and 25% in the last year. Imports of raw materials for which no equivalents are produced locally are not exempt from import duties and taxes.

Controls on liquidation of direct investment	Proceeds may be freely transferred abroad or credited to a foreign account in euros after presentation of the requisite vouchers to the MEF and the Ministry's approval. Effective February 1, 1999, MEF approval is no longer needed. The liquidation of investments, whether Ivoirien investments abroad or foreign investments in Côte d'Ivoire, must be reported to the Ministry within 20 days of the operation.
Controls on real estate transactions	
Purchase abroad by residents	Purchases are subject to prior authorization by the MEF, which must be requested by the party concerned in a letter designating the authorized intermediary that will execute payment. This payment, either by the transferring of funds abroad or by the crediting of a foreign account in euros, may not be made before the end of the time period agreed upon by the parties.
Purchase locally by nonresidents	Purchases may be freely made if they are not direct investments in a business, branch, or corporation.
Sale locally by nonresidents	Proceeds may be freely transferred abroad or credited to a foreign account in euros after presentation of the requisite vouchers to the MEF and the Ministry's approval.
Controls on personal capital movements	
Loans	
By residents to nonresidents	The granting of a loan by a resident to a nonresident requires the prior authorization of the MEF. Concerned individuals may not carry out such operations as a professional occupation without prior authorization, and they must be registered on the list of financial establishments.
To residents from nonresidents	The borrower must obtain prior authorization from the MEF, unless the amount of the loan does not exceed CFAF 50 million and the interest rate does not exceed the normal market rate. Loans contracted to finance imports and exports are not subject to prior authorization.
Gifts, endowments, inheritances, and legacies	
By residents to nonresidents	Except for inheritances and dowries, for which payments are generally authorized, payments pertaining to other operations require prior authorization of the MEF.
Settlement of debts abroad by immigrants	Immigrants who have obtained resident status must obtain prior authorization from the MEF to settle debts contracted abroad while they were nonresidents.
Transfer of assets	
Transfer abroad by emigrants	On presentation of documentary evidence of emigration, the parties concerned may, without prior authorization, obtain the transfer of a sum equal to a maximum of CFAF 500,000 a person. Amounts in excess may be transferred on authorization of the MEF.
Provisions specific to commercial banks and other credit institutions	
Borrowing abroad	Authorized intermediaries are free to borrow abroad.
Maintenance of accounts abroad	Banks and financial institutions are not permitted to hold liquid assets outside the WAEMU, except to cover the requirements of their current operations.
Lending to nonresidents (financial or commercial credits)	These operations may be freely executed in the case of commercial credits but are subject to the prior authorization of the MEF in the case of loans, financial credits, or the purchase of securities issued abroad. Effective February 1, 1999, the prior approval of the BCEAO is also needed.
Lending locally in foreign exchange	General regulations apply on lending locally in foreign currency or purchasing locally issued securities denominated in foreign exchange.
Differential treatment of deposit accounts in foreign exchange	
Credit controls	Yes.

Investment regulations	The same regulations apply as for foreign investment.
Open foreign exchange position limits	There are no prudential ratios. Open positions result from special dispensations.
Provisions specific to institutional investors	Effective February 1, 1999, controls are imposed by the Insurance Code of the Inter-African Conference on Insurance Markets.
Limits (max.) on portfolio invested abroad	Yes.
Limits (min.) on portfolio invested locally	Yes.
Currency-matching regulations on assets/liabilities composition	Yes.
Other controls imposed by securities laws	No.

Changes During 1999

Exchange arrangement	*January 1.* The CFA franc peg to the French franc was replaced with a peg to the euro.
	February 1. Residents were authorized to contract forward exchange cover to settle payments related to imports and exports of goods and services.
Arrangements for payments and receipts	*February 1.* The amount of transfers authorized without supporting documentation was raised to CFAF 300,000 from CFAF 100,000.
Resident accounts	*February 1.* Residents are allowed to open foreign exchange accounts with local banks or with banks abroad after obtaining authorization from the MEF, with the approval of the BCEAO.
Nonresident accounts	*February 1.* Authorization to open foreign exchange accounts is issued by the BCEAO.
Imports and import payments	*February 1.* The limit for imports requiring domiciliation was raised to CFAF 5 million.
Exports and export proceeds	*February 1.* Proceeds from exports to WAEMU countries are no longer to be repatriated.
	February 1. Exports to WAEMU countries need not be domiciled.
Payments for invisible transactions and current transfers	*February 1.* Payments and incomes of foreign ships in the WAEMU zone and WAEMU ships abroad are included under current operations.
	February 1. Limits on foreign exchange allowances were eliminated. The threshold of foreign exchange to be surrendered by residents after travel was raised to CFAF 300,000 from CFAF 50,000.
Proceeds from invisible transactions and current transfers	*February 1.* The time limit for the repatriation and surrender requirement was set at one month after the due date of receipt.
Capital transactions	
Controls on capital and money market instruments	*February 1.* Transfers related to the sale of foreign securities by residents and to proceeds of disinvestments by nonresidents were allowed. Foreign investment in WAEMU countries became unrestricted. Such operations are subject to reporting for statistical purposes. The prior authorization of the RCPSFM is required for the issuance and marketing of securities and capital assets of foreign entities, as well as for publicity and advertising of investments abroad. Any investment by residents abroad requires the prior approval of the MEF.
Controls on derivatives and other instruments	*February 1.* Transfers relating to option purchases were allowed.
Controls on direct investment	*February 1.* MEF authorization is no longer needed for investments abroad by residents in the form of securities if the issue or sale by nonresidents was authorized by the RCPSFM.
Controls on liquidation of direct investment	*February 1.* MEF approval is no longer needed for nonresidents to transfer the proceeds from the liquidation of direct investments.

Provisions specific to commercial banks and other credit institutions

February 1. The prior approval of the BCEAO is also needed to grant loans and financial credits to nonresidents or to purchase securities abroad.

Provisions specific to institutional investors

February 1. Controls are imposed by the Insurance Code of the Inter-African Conference on Insurance Markets.

Changes During 2000

Imports and import payments

January 1. The WAEMU introduced a CET with four rates (zero, 5%, 10%, and 20%) for all member countries except Guinea-Bissau.

CROATIA

(Position as of December 31, 1999)

Status Under IMF Articles of Agreement

Article VIII	Date of acceptance: May 29, 1995.

Exchange Arrangement

Currency

The currency of Croatia is the Croatian kuna.

Exchange rate structure

Unitary.

Classification

Managed floating with no pre-announced path for the exchange rate

The exchange rate of the kuna is determined in the domestic foreign exchange market. The Croatian National Bank (CNB) may set intervention exchange rates, which it applies in transactions with banks outside the interbank market for leveling undue fluctuations in the exchange rate.

Exchange tax

No.

Exchange subsidy

No.

Forward exchange market

Official cover of forward operations

The CNB has provided, on occasion, swap facilities at par for banks in a limited forward market.

Arrangements for Payments and Receipts

Prescription of currency requirements

No.

Payment arrangements

Bilateral payment arrangements

Operative

There is an arrangement with Italy.

Administration of control

The CNB formulates and administers exchange rate policy and may issue foreign exchange regulations. Companies wishing to engage in foreign trade must register with the commercial courts. Effective May 19, 1999, the CNB subjected imports to exchange controls to prevent fraudulent and fictitious imports and to facilitate enforcement of existing restrictions on certain capital flows.

International security restrictions

In accordance with Executive Board Decision No. 144-(52/51)

Yes.

In accordance with UN sanctions

In compliance with the relevant UN Security Council resolutions, restrictions are imposed on certain financial transactions with Angola, the Federal Republic of Yugoslavia (Serbia/Montenegro), and Iraq.

Payment arrears

Official

Yes.

Controls on trade in gold (coins and/or bullion)

Controls on external trade

The exportation of unprocessed gold and gold coins by producers of gold or by authorized commercial banks is subject to the approval of the CNB. Importation of gold is subject to the approval of the Ministry of Economy (MOE).

260

Controls on exports and imports of banknotes	As a measure against money laundering, kuna or foreign exchange cash transactions above HRK 40,000 should be reported to the Office for the Prevention of Money Laundering.
On exports	The exportation of domestic and foreign currency in cash or checks has to be declared to customs.
Domestic currency	The exportation of Croatian currency by both residents and nonresidents is limited to HRK 2,000 a person; however, larger amounts may be exported with special permission from the CNB.
Foreign currency	Resident natural persons may take abroad up to the equivalent of DM 1,000. An additional amount up to the equivalent of DM 2,000 may be taken out, provided that it is withdrawn from foreign currency accounts or purchased from banks for travel expenses. In both cases, the CNB may allow higher amounts to be taken out on a case-by-case basis.
On imports	
Domestic currency	The importation of Croatian currency by both residents and nonresidents is limited to HRK 2,000 a person; however, larger amounts may be imported with special permission from the CNB.

Resident Accounts

Foreign exchange accounts permitted	Resident natural and juridical persons may, in principle, open and operate foreign exchange accounts only in Croatia. However, the CNB has the authority to allow resident juridical persons to keep foreign exchange in accounts with foreign banks in order to cover the costs of business operations and to meet the requirement of regular foreign trade activities abroad. The law also makes specific provisions for resident juridical persons engaged in capital project construction abroad to maintain accounts with foreign banks, subject to a license issued by the CNB.
Held domestically	Yes.
Held abroad	These accounts are permitted, but approval is required.
Accounts in domestic currency convertible into foreign currency	Resident juridical persons may convert domestic currency into a foreign currency for the purpose of their business operations.

Nonresident Accounts

Foreign exchange accounts permitted	These accounts may be credited freely with foreign exchange and debited for payments abroad for conversion into domestic currency; reconversion of domestic currency into a foreign currency is permitted. As a measure against money laundering, nonresident juridical persons may not credit these accounts with foreign banknotes exceeding the equivalent of $20,000 without special permission from the CNB. Nonresident juridical persons may withdraw up to the equivalent of HRK 15,000 each month from their deposit accounts. Larger amounts may be withdrawn with CNB permission. Nonresidents may open foreign exchange accounts with fully licensed banks in Croatia. On April 20, 1999, a decision was published on the documentation required for opening foreign exchange and domestic currency accounts by nonresidents.
Domestic currency accounts	These accounts may be opened with the proceeds from sales of goods and services or with foreign exchange transferred from abroad and converted into domestic currency.
Convertible into foreign currency	Foreign exchange may be purchased with funds held in these accounts without restriction.
Blocked accounts	Balances in foreign exchange accounts held by residents (natural persons) of the former Socialist Republic of Yugoslavia, blocked since 1992, have been replaced by claims on the Croatian government.

Imports and Import Payments

Foreign exchange budget   No.

Financing requirements for imports

Advance payment requirements   Effective April 20, 1999, advance payments and down payments for imports are permitted under certain circumstances.

Documentation requirements for release of foreign exchange for imports   Effective May 19, 1999, imports are subject to exchange controls. An invoice or agreement is required for transfers.

Import licenses and other nontariff measures   There are no import quotas, although the trade law allows for such quotas in principle, under conditions envisaged by WTO rules. All imports are free from licensing requirements except for a list of products whose importation is controlled by international agreement for noneconomic reasons (such as arms, gold, illegal drugs and narcotics, and artistic and historic work), and a small number of other products (notably iron tubes in bars—except for WTO members—and tractors older than five years). The importation of these items is allowed on a case-by-case basis. Effective May 15, 1999, Croatia reintroduced MFN trade with Bosnia and Herzegovina.

Negative list   Yes.

Import taxes and/or tariffs   Imports are subject to customs tariffs of up to 25% ad valorem. For a number of agricultural and food products, compound duties (ad valorem plus specific customs duty) are applied. The exemption for duty-free imports by travelers is HRK 300. For imports exceeding that value, the regular import tariffs and taxes (VAT 22%) are applied. Goods imported by travelers and postal shipments up to the equivalent of $5,000 are subject to a simplified customs procedure with a unified tariff rate of 10%. For imports exceeding that value, the regular import tariffs and taxes are applied. Returning citizens who have resided abroad for at least five years without interruption may import household effects that were in use for at least twelve months, as well as goods for private business purposes, subject to customs approval, without paying customs tariffs or taxes. Under certain conditions, goods imported by nonresidents for investment purposes are exempt from import duties. Imports under special customs procedures, such as temporary imports and goods to be processed under customs surveillance, are exempt from customs duties.

State import monopoly   No.

Exports and Export Proceeds

Repatriation requirements   Export proceeds must be collected and repatriated in full within 90 days of date of exportation. This period may be extended for 60 days with permission from the CNB. If payment terms in excess of 90 days have been agreed to with foreign importers, the credit arrangement must be registered with the CNB. Export proceeds from the countries of the CIS must be repatriated within 180 days, with the possibility of a further 60-day extension, subject to the approval of the CNB.

Financing requirements   No.

Documentation requirements

Guarantees   Yes.

Export licenses   Exports are free of restrictions except for certain products for which permits must be obtained (e.g., weapons, drugs, and art objects). As of January 1, 1999, quantitative export restrictions were eliminated.

Export taxes   No.

Payments for Invisible Transactions and Current Transfers

Controls on these transfers   No.

Proceeds from Invisible Transactions and Current Transfers

Repatriation requirements Proceeds from services are, in principle, subject to the same regulations as those applying to exports.

Restrictions on use of funds No.

Capital Transactions

Controls on capital and money market instruments Inward portfolio investment is not restricted, except in central bank short-term securities in the primary market. In general, outward investment in capital and money market securities is not allowed for either natural or nonbank juridical persons.

On capital market securities

Shares or other securities of a participating nature

Purchase abroad by residents There are controls in place for all residents, except banks and investment funds.

Bonds or other debt securities

Purchase abroad by residents There are controls in place for all residents, except banks, investment funds, and pension funds.

Sale or issue abroad by residents The same regulations apply as for financial credits.

On money market instruments

Purchase locally by nonresidents Only purchases in the primary market are restricted.

Sale or issue locally by nonresidents Yes.

Purchase abroad by residents The same regulations apply as for bonds and other debt securities.

Sale or issue abroad by residents The same regulations apply as for financial credits.

On collective investment securities

Purchase abroad by residents The same regulations apply as for bonds and other debt securities.

Controls on derivatives and other instruments

Purchase abroad by residents Yes.

Controls on credit operations Effective December 31, 1999, foreign credit operations have to be registered with the CNB.

Commercial credits For statistical purposes only, such transactions have to be registered with the CNB.

By residents to nonresidents Yes.

To residents from nonresidents Yes.

Financial credits

By residents to nonresidents Resident juridical persons may extend financial credits only to nonresident juridical persons in which they have the majority of voting rights.

To residents from nonresidents Resident juridical persons may obtain financial credits from abroad only for performing activities they are registered for.

Guarantees, sureties, and financial backup facilities

By residents to nonresidents Resident juridical persons may issue guarantees, sureties, and financial backup facilities only for performing activities they are registered for.

To residents from nonresidents For statistical purposes only, such transactions have to be registered with the CNB.

Controls on direct investment

Outward direct investment

Natural persons may not make foreign direct investments abroad. Foreign direct investment abroad by juridical persons is free under certain circumstances, but must be registered with the MOE within 30 days from the signature of the contract.

Inward direct investment

Investments must be registered with the commercial courts only.

Controls on liquidation of direct investment

Proceeds may be transferred after settlement of legal obligations, including tax payments.

Controls on real estate transactions

Purchase abroad by residents

A natural person may not transfer capital abroad for the purpose of buying real estate. Juridical persons may buy real estate abroad for the purpose of foreign direct investment.

Purchase locally by nonresidents

Subject to the permission of the Ministry of Foreign Affairs and the Ministry of Justice, foreign natural and juridical persons may, if not otherwise determined by law and if under the assumption of reciprocity, acquire the ownership of real estate in the territory of the Republic of Croatia.

Controls on personal capital movements

For statistical purposes only, such transactions have to be registered with the CNB.

Loans

By residents to nonresidents

Natural persons may not grant credits to nonresidents.

To residents from nonresidents

Resident natural persons are obliged to use foreign financial credits through the authorized domestic banks.

Gifts, endowments, inheritances, and legacies

By residents to nonresidents

Cash gifts and endowments greater than the equivalent of DM 3,000 must be approved by the CNB.

Transfer of assets

Transfer abroad by emigrants

The approval of the CNB is required.

Provisions specific to commercial banks and other credit institutions

Lending locally in foreign exchange

Domestic commercial banks may not give foreign exchange credits to resident natural persons. Commercial banks may, under certain circumstances, give foreign exchange credits to juridical persons for activities they are registered for. Foreign commercial banks may extend credit in foreign exchange to both natural and juridical persons.

Differential treatment of deposit accounts in foreign exchange

Reserve requirements

Commercial banks are required to hold reserve requirements in foreign exchange at 55% of the average balance of household deposits with a remaining maturity of three months. A minimum 50% of these reserves must be held in a special account kept at the CNB, while a maximum 50% may be maintained in accounts earmarked for liquid foreign currency claims and held on accounts with banks not rated lower than AA. In addition, there are reserve requirements on banks' foreign liabilities arising out of foreign credits received for the purposes of conversion into kuna. These reserve requirements, which are payable in kuna and are not remunerated, range from 10% on guarantees and 15% on foreign exchange interbank deposits, to 30% for foreign borrowing of up to one year.

Liquid asset requirements

Short-term foreign exchange liabilities must be covered by 53% short-term foreign exchange assets of a maturity of less than one year.

Open foreign exchange position limits

The limit is 30% of the bank's Tier I capital.

On resident assets and liabilities

Yes.

On nonresident assets and liabilities

Yes.

Provisions specific to institutional investors	On May 13, 1999, a new law on obligatory and voluntary pension funds was enacted.
Limits (max.) on portfolio invested abroad	Investment funds may not invest more than 5% of the value of the fund in the securities of a single issuer. However, this limit may increase to 10% provided that not more than 40% of the assets of the fund are invested in securities of other issuers. In addition, investment funds may acquire bonds of one issuer only if the total face value of these bonds does not exceed 10% of the total face value of all the bonds of the same issuer, if they are in circulation. For purposes of determining this limit, bonds of the Croatian state, member states of the EU, and other member states of the OECD are valued at one-half their face value.
Other controls imposed by securities laws	No.

Changes During 1999

Exchange arrangement	*September 30*. The exchange rate arrangement was reclassified to the category managed floating with no preannounced path for the exchange rate from the category pegged exchange rate within horizontal bands.
Nonresident accounts	*April 20*. A decision was published regarding the documentation requirement for opening nonresident foreign exchange and domestic currency accounts.
Imports and import payments	*April 20*. Advance import payments were allowed under certain circumstances.
	May 15. MFN trade with Bosnia and Herzegovina was reintroduced.
	May 19. Imports are subject to exchange controls.
Exports and export proceeds	*January 1*. Quantitative export restrictions were eliminated.
Capital transactions	
Controls on credit operations	*December 31*. Foreign credit operations have to be registered with the CNB.
Provisions specific to institutional investors	*May 13*. A new law on obligatory and voluntary pension funds was enacted.

CYPRUS

(Position as of February 29, 2000)

Status Under IMF Articles of Agreement

Article VIII   Date of acceptance: January 9, 1991.

Exchange Arrangement

Currency
The currency of Cyprus is the Cyprus pound.

Exchange rate structure
Unitary.

Classification

Pegged exchange rate within
horizontal bands
The Cyprus pound is pegged to the euro at a central rate of €1.7086 per £C 1, with margins of 2.25% around the euro central rate. Subject to certain limitations, including a limit on spreads between buying and selling rates, authorized dealers (banks) are free to determine and quote their own buying and selling rates. The Central Bank of Cyprus (CBC) also quotes daily buying and selling rates for the dollar, the euro, the Greek drachma, and the pound sterling. These rates are subject to change throughout the day. It also quotes indicative rates for other foreign currencies on the basis of market rates in international money market centers.

Exchange tax
No.

Exchange subsidy
No.

Forward exchange market
Authorized dealers may trade in the forward market at rates freely negotiated with their customers. For dollars and pounds sterling, however, forward margins may not be larger than those applied by the CBC for cover for a similar period. Authorized dealers are allowed to purchase forward cover from the CBC at prevailing rates or to conduct forward operations between two foreign currencies for cover in one of the two currencies.

Official cover of forward operations
The CBC offers authorized dealers facilities for forward purchases of dollars and pounds sterling for exports for periods of up to 24 months and for imports normally for up to nine months.

Arrangements for Payments and Receipts

**Prescription of currency
requirements**
No.

Payment arrangements
No.

Administration of control
Exchange controls are administered by the CBC in cooperation with authorized dealers to whom authority has been delegated to approve applications for the allocation of foreign exchange for a large number of bona fide transactions.

International security restrictions

In accordance with Executive Board
Decision No. 144-(52/51)
Although restrictions imposed against the Federal Republic of Yugoslavia (Serbia/Montenegro) were lifted, bank balances belonging to the National Bank of Yugoslavia remain frozen.

In accordance with UN sanctions
Economic sanctions against Iraq, Sierra Leone, and the UNITA movement in Angola pursuant to UN Security Council resolutions are administered by the CBC and relevant government departments. On July 28, 1999, restrictions imposed against Libya were suspended.

Payment arrears
No.

Controls on trade in gold (coins and/or bullion)

Controls on domestic ownership and/or trade

Residents may hold and acquire gold coins in Cyprus for numismatic collection purposes. Residents other than the monetary authorities, authorized dealers in gold, and industrial users are not allowed to hold or acquire gold bullion at home or abroad.

Controls on external trade

The exportation of gold coins or bullion requires the permission of the CBC. Authorized dealers in gold are permitted to import gold bullion only for the purpose of disposing of it to industrial users.

Controls on exports and imports of banknotes

On exports

Domestic currency

Resident travelers may take out up to £C 100. Nonresident travelers may take out any amount of Cypriot banknotes that they imported and declared on arrival. In the case of failure to declare the banknotes imported on arrival, nonresidents may export up to the equivalent of $1,000 in Cypriot or foreign banknotes.

Authorized dealers may dispatch any amount of Cypriot banknotes to foreign banks in exchange for foreign currency.

Foreign currency

Resident travelers may take out any amount of foreign banknotes purchased from authorized dealers as part of their foreign currency allowances. Nonresident travelers may take out any amount of foreign banknotes that they imported and declared on arrival, as well as any amount purchased from banks in Cyprus against external funds. In addition, departing nonresidents may convert, through authorized dealers, Cypriot banknotes up to £C 500 into foreign banknotes, which they can export.

On imports

Foreign currency

Nonresidents entering Cyprus are advised to declare to customs any Cypriot or foreign banknotes in order to facilitate their reexport, deposit with authorized dealers, or use in purchasing immovable property or goods for export.

Resident Accounts

Foreign exchange accounts permitted

Yes.

Held domestically

Residents dealing with transit or triangular trade may deposit up to 97.5% of sale proceeds in these accounts and use balances to pay for the cost of traded goods. Residents engaged in manufacturer-exporter activities may deposit up to 50% of export proceeds in these accounts and use balances to pay for imports of raw materials used in production. Both transit traders and manufacturers-exporters are, however, required to convert into Cyprus pounds at the end of each year any balances in excess of the amount that is necessary for payments of traded goods or raw materials during the following three months. Resident hoteliers may deposit in such accounts part of their receipts in foreign currency that they need to make imminent installment payments on foreign currency loans. Resident lawyers, accountants, and stockbrokers who handle funds of their nonresident clients may also maintain foreign currency accounts or external accounts with authorized dealers. However, approval of the CBC is required for residents other than those referred to above and below.

Held abroad

Cypriot repatriates may keep in foreign currency accounts external accounts with banks in Cyprus, or accounts with banks abroad all of their foreign currency holdings and earnings accruing from properties they own abroad. Resident individuals temporarily working abroad may maintain their foreign currency earnings in foreign currency accounts, external accounts with banks in Cyprus, or accounts with banks abroad. However, approval of the CBC is required for residents other than those referred to in the preceding paragraph. Such approval, however, is granted only in exceptional circumstances.

Accounts in domestic currency convertible into foreign currency

These accounts are designated as external accounts.

Nonresident Accounts

Foreign exchange accounts permitted

Nonresidents may open and maintain accounts with authorized dealers, which may be credited freely with payments from nonresidents (such as transfers from other external accounts or foreign currency accounts), with proceeds from sales of any foreign currency by nonresidents (including declared banknotes), and with authorized payments from residents. Nonresidents who are temporarily employed in Cyprus by residents are allowed to deposit in external or foreign exchange accounts with authorized dealers their entire wages in cases where the terms of employment provides for room and board, or in other cases up to 80% of their monthly wages or £C 400 monthly, whichever is higher, without CBC approval.

The accounts may be debited for payments to residents and nonresidents, for remittances abroad, for transfers to other external accounts or foreign currency accounts, and for payments in cash (Cyprus pounds) in Cyprus. Companies registered or incorporated in Cyprus that are accorded nonresident status (generally designated as international business companies) by the CBC as well as their nonresident employees may maintain foreign currency accounts in Cyprus or abroad, as well as local disbursement accounts for meeting their payments in Cyprus.

Domestic currency accounts

Yes.

Convertible into foreign currency

These accounts are designated as external accounts, and the same regulations as for foreign currency accounts apply.

Blocked accounts

Blocked accounts are maintained in the name of nonresidents for funds that may not immediately be transferred outside of Cyprus. Blocked funds may either be held as deposits or be invested in government securities or government-guaranteed securities. Income earned on blocked funds is freely transferable to the nonresident beneficiary or may be credited to an external account or foreign currency account.

In addition to income, up to one-third of the principal or £C 50,000, whichever is higher, may be released for transfer abroad in each calendar year. Thus, blocked accounts are now in practice transferable abroad within two years after the date of blocking. Also, blocked funds may be released for the following payments in Cyprus: (1) to meet the holder's personal expenses in Cyprus (up to £C 10,000 a year without reference to the CBC); and (2) to purchase any securities quoted on the Cyprus Stock Exchange.

Imports and Import Payments

Foreign exchange budget

No.

Financing requirements for imports

Yes.

Advance payment requirements

Prior approval of the CBC is required for remittances to suppliers exceeding £C 50,000. Authorized dealers are allowed to sell to departing residents foreign exchange up to £C 20,000 for purchases and for the importation of goods into Cyprus; for larger amounts, approval by the CBC is required.

Documentation requirements for release of foreign exchange for imports

Import licenses used as exchange licenses

Import licenses are required for a small number of commodities.

Import licenses and other nontariff measures

Most imports are free of licensing requirements. A license is required for a small number of commodities prescribed by the Minister of Commerce, Industry, and Tourism (MCIT).

Nonresidents may not import commodities into Cyprus unless they are granted a special import license by the MCIT. The importation of goods such as motor vehicles to be used temporarily by visitors or goods to be exhibited in Cyprus and reexported is not subject to this requirement. Imports from Iraq are restricted in accordance with UN Security Council resolutions.

Negative list

Yes.

Import taxes and/or tariffs	Yes.
State import monopoly	No.

Exports and Export Proceeds

Repatriation requirements

All exports whose value exceeds £C 10,000 are subject to exchange control monitoring to ensure the repatriation of the export proceeds.

Surrender requirements

In general, export proceeds must be surrendered to authorized dealers not later than six months after the date of exportation. However, manufacturers are required to convert into domestic currency only 50% of export proceeds; they may deposit the remaining 50% in foreign currency accounts with authorized dealers.

Financing requirements	No.
Documentation requirements	No.
Export licenses	No.
Export taxes	No.

Payments for Invisible Transactions and Current Transfers

Controls on these transfers

Authorized dealers have been delegated the authority to carry out payments for most invisible transactions without reference to the CBC. Invisible transactions that have not been delegated to authorized dealers are still subject to prior approval by the CBC in order to verify the genuineness of each transaction.

Trade-related payments

Authorized dealers may carry out payments for freight, without prior approval of the CBC. However, if the payment exceeds £C 5,000, documentary evidence must be subsequently submitted to the CBC. Until November 28, 1999, the CBC approved applications for the remittance of insurance premiums owed to foreign insurance companies. Effective November 29, 1999, authorized dealers may carry out payments for insurance without reference to the CBC.

Prior approval

Commissions in excess of 5% of the value of exported goods require CBC approval.

Indicative limits/bona fide test

There are indicative limits for the payment of commissions.

Investment-related payments

Profits and dividends and interest from approved foreign investments may be transferred abroad without limitation after payment of due taxes.

Prior approval

Yes.

Payments for travel

Quantitative limits

Authorized dealers are allowed, without reference to the CBC, to sell to resident travelers foreign exchange up to £C 1,000 a person a trip for tourist travel. Moreover, payments for travel may be made through credit cards issued by authorized dealers. The allowance for business travel is £C 150 a day with a maximum of £C 1,500 a trip, or £C 80 a day with a maximum of £C 800 a trip if the traveler holds an international business credit card. Authorized dealers may approve, without reference to the CBC, applications by resident travel agents to pay foreign travel agents and hotels up to £C 10,000 for each organized trip.

Indicative limits/bona fide test

The CBC approves applications for higher amounts to cover bona fide expenses without limitation.

Personal payments

Prior approval

Prior approval is required for the transfer of pensions and for other personal payment exceeding the quantitative or indicative limits.

Quantitative limits	For studies abroad, exchange allowances are based on the cost of living, which is reviewed yearly. The current annual allowance for living expenses for studies in western European countries, except Greece, is £C 7,800; for North America, £C 9,000; for Australia, £C 5,000; and for Greece and all other countries, £C 4,600. There is no limit on the remittance of foreign exchange for payment of tuition fees and greater amounts may be allowed with the approval of the CBC.
Indicative limits/bona fide test	The indicative limit is £C 5,000 for medical expenses abroad. Unlimited additional amounts are provided with the approval of the CBC. For family maintenance and alimony payment, the indicative limit is £C 500 every six months.
Foreign workers' wages	
Quantitative limits	Nonresidents who are temporarily employed in Cyprus by resident firms or individuals and are paid in local currency may deposit with authorized dealers their entire wages in cases where the terms of employment provides for room and board, or in other cases, up to 80% of their monthly remuneration or £C 400 monthly, whichever is higher, in external or foreign currency accounts. The balances in these accounts may be freely transferred abroad without reference to the CBC. For deposits or transfers of amounts in excess of the limits, approval of the CBC is required.
Indicative limits/bona fide test	Yes.
Credit card use abroad	Through December 23, 1999, when the CBC abolished restrictions on the use of credit cards for current payments abroad, authorized dealers were allowed to issue credit cards valid abroad to any resident, except for residents studying abroad or temporarily living abroad. These cards, which were designated as international personal cards, were used abroad for payments to hotels and restaurants; transportation expenses; doctors, clinics, or hospitals; international telephone calls; cash withdrawals up to £C 100 a trip; and any other payments of a total value not exceeding £C 300 a trip. In addition, international personal cards could be used for payments abroad or from Cyprus up to £C 300 for each transaction for the following purposes: examination fees, application fees for admission to foreign educational institutions, subscriptions to professional bodies or societies, fees for enrollment in professional or educational seminars or conferences, and hotel reservation fees. International personal cards were also used for mail orders of books up to £C 300. Authorized dealers now issue credit cards valid abroad to any resident.
Quantitative limits	For cash withdrawals, the limit is £C 300 a trip.
Other payments	Authorized dealers may carry out payments for subscription to professional bodies or societies up to £C 300 a transaction, without reference to the CBC. Prior approval of the CBC is required for amounts exceeding £C 300. Effective March 24, 1999, authorized dealers are empowered to approve payments for royalties and license fees as well as for specialized services in accordance with relevant agreements, without reference to the CBC.
Prior approval	Yes.
Quantitative limits	Yes.
Indicative limits/bona fide test	Yes.

Proceeds from Invisible Transactions and Current Transfers

Repatriation requirements	Yes.
Surrender requirements	Generally, receipts from invisibles must be sold to an authorized dealer. However, a large number of residents have been allowed to maintain part of these proceeds in foreign currency accounts and use these balances for international current payments.
Restrictions on use of funds	Yes.

Capital Transactions

Controls on capital and money market instruments

On capital market securities

Shares or other securities of a participating nature

Purchase locally by nonresidents

Effective July 23, 1999, the acquisition of shares of banks listed in the Cyprus Stock Exchange (CSE) is subject to a ceiling of 50% of each bank's listed capital.

Effective January 7, 2000, the acquisition of shares of other public companies, except banks, by citizens of EU member states is free, while the acquisition of such shares by citizens of non-EU countries continues to be subject to the 49% limit.

Public companies and stockbrokers are authorized to carry out the relevant transactions with nonresidents without reference to the CBC, subject to the limits described above. Applications over these limits may be approved by the CBC.

Sale or issue locally by nonresidents

Securities issued by nonresidents may be admitted to the CSE, but residents are not generally permitted to purchase them.

Purchase abroad by residents

Outside of institutional investors, outward portfolio investment is permitted only for the following residents: Cypriot repatriates and residents temporarily working abroad who may freely use their balances in foreign currency or external accounts to purchase securities abroad, and resident employees of multinational enterprises who participate in the employee stock purchase plan offered by their employers.

Sale or issue abroad by residents

These transactions are subject to the ceilings described above for purchases by nonresidents.

Bonds or other debt securities

Purchase locally by nonresidents

Nonresidents may purchase bonds admitted to the CSE, including bonds issued by public companies and government bonds denominated in Cyprus pounds.

Sale or issue locally by nonresidents

Securities issued by nonresidents may be admitted to the CSE, but residents are not generally permitted to purchase them.

Purchase abroad by residents

Except for banks and institutional investors, only Cypriot repatriates and residents temporarily working abroad may purchase such securities by using their balances in foreign currency or external accounts.

Sale or issue abroad by residents

The same regulations apply as for purchases locally by nonresidents of shares or other securities of a participating nature.

On money market instruments

Purchase locally by nonresidents

Nonresidents may purchase treasury bills denominated in Cyprus pounds.

Sale or issue locally by nonresidents

Prior approval of the CBC is required for residents to purchase such instruments.

Purchase abroad by residents

Except for banks and institutional investors, only Cypriot repatriates and residents temporarily working abroad may purchase money market instruments abroad by using their balances in foreign currency or external accounts.

Sale or issue abroad by residents

Prior approval of the CBC is required.

On collective investment securities

Purchase locally by nonresidents

The purchase of securities issued by public investment companies in Cyprus is permitted within the limits applied to capital market securities. However, effective January 7, 2000, acquisition of such securities is free for citizens of EU states.

Sale or issue locally by nonresidents

Securities issued by nonresidents may be admitted to the Cyprus Stock Exchange, but residents are not generally permitted to purchase them.

Purchase abroad by residents	Except for institutional investors, only Cypriot repatriates and residents temporarily working abroad may purchase such securities abroad by using their balances in foreign currency, or external accounts.
Sale or issue abroad by residents	Prior approval of the CBC is required.

Controls on derivatives and other instruments

There are controls on all transactions in derivatives and other instruments.

Controls on credit operations

Commercial credits

By residents to nonresidents

Credits with a maturity of up to 180 days for the export of goods from Cyprus may be freely granted. Other credits require approval of the CBC.

To residents from nonresidents

Commercial credits with a maturity of up to 200 days for imports of goods to Cyprus may be negotiated freely. Other credits are subject to approval of the CBC.

Financial credits

By residents to nonresidents

Residents other than authorized dealers are not allowed to grant these credits without the approval of the CBC.

To residents from nonresidents

These credits are subject to approval by the CBC, which is usually granted for productive projects.

Guarantees, sureties, and financial backup facilities

By residents to nonresidents

Authorized dealers may issue these guarantees without reference to the CBC in several cases including tender guarantees up to 5% of the tender price, performance bonds up to 10% of the contract price, guarantees for the refund of advance payments, and guarantees in respect of any other transactions where an immediate payment to the nonresident beneficiary could be made under the existing exchange control rules. In other cases, prior approval of the CBC is required.

Controls on direct investment

Outward direct investment

Until January 6, 2000, approval of the CBC was required. The amount of capital that may have been directly transferred abroad was limited to £C 0.5 million. If the issue of a guarantee alone was required, the amount of the guarantee should not have exceeded £C 1 million. In cases where direct transfer of capital as well as a guarantee were required, the total amount should not have exceeded £C 1 million, provided the amount of capital to be directly transferred did not exceed £C 0.5 million. In exceptional cases where it appeared certain that a large part of the investment was to be repatriated in a short time, the governor of the CBC may have approved larger amounts. Effective January 7, 2000, residents of Cyprus are allowed to undertake direct investment abroad without restriction as to the sector of the investment or the amount of foreign exchange involved. The transfer of capital abroad is effected as soon as the CBC is satisfied that the direct investment is genuine. Where the foreign exchange cost is substantial, the CBC reserves the right to take measures in order to mitigate the impact on the balance of payments.

Inward direct investment

In the agricultural sector, foreign participation of up to 49% is allowed. Applications are examined by the CBC in consultation with the Ministry of Agriculture, Natural Resources, and Environment. The indicative minimum amount of investment is £C 100,000.

There is no limit on the percentage of foreign participation in the manufacturing sector, or in wholesale and retail trade. The CBC handles the applications if the foreign participation does not exceed 49% and the amount to be invested is lower than £C 750,000. Otherwise, applications are considered jointly by the CBC and the MCIT.

For most other activities, foreign participation of up to 100% is permitted. Over 70 types of services have been classified into two categories for which the indicative minimum limits of investment are £C 50,000 and £C 100,000.

Investors in the tourism sector are subject to the government tourism policy applicable at the time. The current policy provides for up to 49% of foreign participation in hotels and other tourism establishments. However, up to 100% of foreign participation may be allowed for supplementary tourism projects such as golf courses, marinas, etc. In tourist and travel agencies, up to 49% foreign participation is allowed, provided the foreign investor's contribution is at least £C 150,000. A 49% limit also applies to restaurants and recreational centers as well as agencies representing imported good services.

Applications for direct investment in banking, insurance and other financial companies, public companies, newspaper and magazine publishing houses, and new airlines are considered on a case-by-case basis, and the extent of allowable foreign participation is decided on the merits of each individual case.

Effective January 7, 2000, direct investment in Cyprus by citizens of EU states is free, except in certain sectors that are governed by specific restrictive legislation, i.e., tertiary education and public utilities (no foreign participation is allowed); radio and television stations (foreign shareholding is limited to 2.5% a person); and publication of newspapers and magazines (subject to authorization by the Minister of the Interior). In addition, direct investments in Cyprus by non-EU citizens are subject to the three sector-specific restrictions listed for citizens of EU states. Applications are approved by the CBC for the percentage of foreign participation indicated above, provided national security matters are not compromised, natural and environmental conditions are not threatened, the Cypriot economy is not harmed, and the level (amount) of investment is adequate.

Controls on liquidation of direct investment	Permission of the CBC for the repatriation of the proceeds of sale or liquidation of approved investments (including capital gains) is readily granted at any time after payment of taxes.
Controls on real estate transactions	
Purchase abroad by residents	Residents are generally not allowed to purchase real estate abroad, except when the real estate is part of an authorized direct investment project.
Purchase locally by nonresidents	In accordance with the Immovable Property Acquisition (Aliens) Law, aliens cannot acquire immovable property in Cyprus other than by inheritance, except with the approval of the District Officer, and they are required to pay the purchase price with foreign exchange. When the real estate concerned exceeds two donums (one donum = 1,338 m²), approval may be granted only for the following purposes: (1) a primary or secondary residence not exceeding three donums; (2) professional or commercial premises; or (3) premises for industry sectors deemed beneficial to the Cypriot economy. Nonresidents of Cypriot origin do not need the approval of the District Officer.
Sale locally by nonresidents	Proceeds are transferable abroad after payment of taxes, provided the seller acquired the property by paying with foreign exchange; otherwise, proceeds are transferable abroad through a blocked account.
Controls on personal capital movements	
Loans	Prior approval of the CBC is required.
By residents to nonresidents	Yes.
To residents from nonresidents	Yes.
Gifts, endowments, inheritances, and legacies	
By residents to nonresidents	For gifts or endowments exceeding £C 500 every six months, and for the transfer of funds inherited from residents by nonresidents, prior approval of the CBC is required. Funds inherited are transferable abroad through a blocked account.
Settlement of debts abroad by immigrants	In case the immigrant debtor does not maintain sufficient balances in foreign currency or external accounts to repay a debt abroad, approval of the CBC is granted for repayment through local funds.
Transfer of assets	
Transfer abroad by emigrants	At the time of emigration, emigrants may transfer abroad up to £C 100,000 of their local funds. Any remaining local funds are transferable abroad through blocked accounts. In addition, emigrants who are Cypriot repatriates (i.e., residents of Cyprus who were previously residents in other countries and decide to emigrate again from Cyprus) may

transfer abroad in a lump sum all their funds that they previously imported in Cyprus and converted into local funds.

Transfer of gambling and prize earnings	Prior approval from the CBC is required.

Provisions specific to commercial banks and other credit institutions

Borrowing abroad	Prior approval of the CBC is required.
Maintenance of accounts abroad	Authorized dealers are allowed to maintain working balances with foreign banks within limits prescribed by the CBC, as well as deposits abroad held as cover for their deposit liabilities in foreign currencies.
Lending to nonresidents (financial or commercial credits)	Authorized dealers are allowed to grant medium- and long-term loans in foreign currencies to nonresidents of up to 20% of their deposit liabilities in foreign currencies. They are also allowed to grant loans and credits to international businesses registered in Cyprus of up to 10% of their deposit liabilities in foreign currencies.
	In addition, authorized dealers are allowed to lend Cyprus pounds up to a maximum of £C 5,000 to nonresident individuals temporarily living in Cyprus, without reference to the CBC. For greater amounts, prior approval of the CBC is required.
Lending locally in foreign exchange	Authorized dealers may grant certain short-term credit facilities in foreign currency (e.g., discounting bills of exchange) to residents without reference to the CBC. For other lending to residents in foreign currency, prior approval of the CBC is required. Such approval is usually granted for the following purposes: to finance transit trade, to provide working capital for resident oil companies or for industries operating in the industrial free zone, to meet the financial needs of Cyprus Airways, and to finance other desirable productive projects.
Purchase of locally issued securities denominated in foreign exchange	Yes.
Differential treatment of deposit accounts in foreign exchange	The monetary regulations applied to accounts in foreign currencies, held either by non-residents or by residents, are different from those applied to accounts in Cyprus pounds.
Reserve requirements	A minimum reserve requirement of 7% applies only to deposits in Cyprus pounds.
Liquid asset requirements	Liquid assets in foreign currencies equal to at least 60% of deposit liabilities in foreign currencies must be maintained. For deposits in Cyprus pounds, there is no prescribed liquidity ratio. However, the liquidity positions of banks are monitored by the CBC for prudential purposes.
Interest rate controls	Accounts in Cyprus pounds are subject to an interest rate ceiling of 9%, whereas accounts in foreign currencies are not subject to interest rate ceilings.
Credit controls	Yes.
Differential treatment of deposit accounts held by nonresidents	Nonresidents' deposit accounts in foreign exchange or in domestic currency are not treated differently from deposit accounts of residents.
Investment regulations	There are prescribed assets that may be held with respect to accounts in foreign currencies. Authorized dealers may purchase securities issued abroad, such as securities issued by solvent foreign governments and traded in recognized stock exchanges abroad, within certain limits prescribed by the CBC.
Abroad by banks	Yes.
In banks by nonresidents	Nonresidents may acquire up to 50% of the share capital of resident banks listed on the CSE. The acquisition of 10% or more of a bank's share capital by any resident or nonresident person, either alone or with any associates, is subject to prior approval of the CBC.
Open foreign exchange position limits	The net open/uncovered position in any one foreign currency and the overall aggregate net position in all foreign currencies may not exceed 10% and 15%, respectively, of the authorized dealer's capital base, except with the prior approval of the CBC.

Provisions specific to institutional investors

Limits (max.) on securities issued by nonresidents and on portfolio invested abroad	Yes.

Limits (max.) on portfolio invested abroad

Insurance companies may invest abroad up to 25% (up from 20%) of their trust fund, in securities quoted in a number of foreign stock exchanges. Public investment companies may also invest abroad a maximum of 25% of their portfolio. Other institutional investors are not allowed to invest abroad.

Limits (min.) on portfolio invested locally

Yes.

Other controls imposed by securities laws

The Cyprus Stock Exchange and Securities Laws and the regulations issued under these laws apply to transactions by nonresidents and residents in a nondiscriminating manner.

Effective February 2, 2000, the CBC imposed a ceiling of £C 5 million on investments abroad by public companies. Thus, these companies may invest in securities quoted on foreign stock exchanges up to 25% of their portfolio or £C 5 million, whichever is smaller.

Changes During 1999

Exchange arrangement

January 1. The peg to the ECU was replaced with a peg to the euro.

Arrangements for payments and receipts

July 28. Restrictions imposed against Libya pursuant to UN Security Council resolutions were suspended.

Payments for invisible transactions and current transfers

March 24. Authorized dealers are empowered to approve payments for royalties and license fees as well as for specialized services in accordance with relevant agreements, without reference to the CBC.

November 29. Authorized dealers may carry out payments for insurance without reference to the CBC.

December 23. The CBC abolished restrictions on the use of credit cards abroad.

Capital transactions

Controls on capital and money market instruments

July 23. The limit on total nonresident participation in the share capital of each domestic bank listed on the CSE was raised to 50% from 15%.

Changes During 2000

Capital transactions

Controls on capital and money market instruments

January 7. Except for banks, the CBC abolished exchange controls concerning the percentage of the share capital of Cypriot companies listed on the CSE that may be acquired by citizens of EU member states.

Controls on direct investment

January 7. Direct investments by citizens of EU states were liberalized, except for tertiary education, public utilities, radio and television, and the publication of newspapers and magazines. Non-EU citizens were subject to these restrictions as well.

Provisions specific to institutional investors

February 2. The CBC imposed a ceiling of £C 5 million on investments abroad by public companies. Thus, these companies may invest in securities quoted on foreign stock exchanges up to 25% of their portfolio or £C 5 million, whichever is smaller.

CZECH REPUBLIC

(Position as of April 30, 2000)

Status Under IMF Articles of Agreement

Article VIII   Date of acceptance: October 1, 1995.

Exchange Arrangement

Currency	The currency of the Czech Republic is the Czech koruna.
Exchange rate structure	Unitary.
Classification	
Managed floating with no pre-announced path for the exchange rate	The external value of the koruna is determined by supply and demand conditions in the foreign exchange market. The Czech National Bank (CNB) may intervene in the foreign exchange market in order to smooth large intraday volatility swings of the euro/koruna rate. The CNB publishes daily rates of some selected currencies against the koruna for customs and accounting purposes. Commercial banks set their own exchange rate with no limitation.
Exchange tax	No.
Exchange subsidy	No.
Forward exchange market	Yes.

Arrangements for Payments and Receipts

Prescription of currency requirements	No.
Payment arrangements	
Regional arrangements	The Czech Republic is a member of the CEFTA.
Administration of control	The MOF and the CNB are responsible for the administration of exchange controls and regulations, in accordance with the Foreign Exchange Act. In general, the MOF exercises authority over ministries and other administrative authorities, municipal authorities, budgetary organizations, state funds, and all types of credits being extended to or accepted by the Czech Republic. The CNB exercises authority over the activities of all other agents.
International security restrictions	
In accordance with UN sanctions	Yes.
Payment arrears	No.
Controls on trade in gold (coins and/or bullion)	
Controls on domestic ownership and/or trade	Gold bullion may, with some exceptions, be traded only with authorized agents (generally banks). Trade in gold coins is free.
Controls on external trade	The export and import of gold bullion and/or more than 10 gold coins must be reported.
Controls on exports and imports of banknotes	There are reporting obligations on exports and imports exceeding CZK 200,000.
On exports	
Domestic currency	Yes.
Foreign currency	Yes.

On imports

Domestic currency	Yes.
Foreign currency	Yes.

Resident Accounts

Foreign exchange accounts permitted   Yes.

Held domestically   Yes.

Held abroad   Approval is required with some exceptions.

Accounts in domestic currency convertible into foreign currency   Yes.

Nonresident Accounts

Foreign exchange accounts permitted   Foreign exchange may be deposited freely, and payments may be made from these accounts in the Czech Republic or abroad without restriction.

Domestic currency accounts   Domestic currency accounts may be opened with commercial banks in koruny. Balances on these accounts may be used freely to make payments in the Czech Republic. All transfers abroad from these accounts may be made freely.

Convertible into foreign currency   Yes.

Blocked accounts   There are blocked accounts on the basis of an embargo against the Islamic State of Afghanistan and the Federal Republic of Yugoslavia (Serbia/Montenegro).

Imports and Import Payments

Foreign exchange budget   No.

Financing requirements for imports   No.

Documentation requirements for release of foreign exchange for imports   Foreign invoices may be settled only through bank transfers.

Import licenses and other nontariff measures

Negative list   Yes.

Open general licenses   Import licenses are required for a few strategic items, such as uranium ore and its concentrates, coal, natural gas, poisons, military materials, firearms and ammunition, dual-use goods and technologies, narcotics, and clothing (excluding imports from the EU and the EFTA). In addition, an automatic licensing system accompanied by levies applies to some agricultural products, mineral fuel and oils, iron and steel and their products, and some chemical products.

Licenses with quotas   Imports of hard coal (from Poland and Ukraine), uranium ore and its derivatives, and technological components containing uranium are subject to licenses with quotas.

Imports of cane sugar or beet sugar and chemically pure saccharase from the Slovak Republic were subject to tariff quotas of 3,500 tons for 1999.

Imports of isoglucose from the Slovak Republic were subject to tariff quotas of 5,000 tons for 1999.

Import taxes and/or tariffs   All imports are subject to an ad valorem customs duty of up to 31.5% for industrial goods and up to 146.5% for agricultural goods. Imports are also subject to a value-added tax of 5% or 22%. Imports from the Slovak Republic are exempt from customs duties under a customs union agreement. Imports from developing countries are granted preferences.

State import monopoly	No.

Exports and Export Proceeds

Repatriation requirements	Yes.
Financing requirements	No.
Documentation requirements	No.
Export licenses	
Without quotas	The Ministry of Industry and Trade, after approval by the Ministry of Foreign Affairs, the Ministry of Defense, and the Ministry of the Interior, grants export licenses for armaments. A limited number of products require export licenses for purposes of health control (including livestock and plants); facilitating voluntary restraints on products on which partner countries have imposed import quotas (such as textiles and steel products); or preserving for the internal market natural resources or imported raw materials (such as energy, metallurgical materials, wood, foodstuffs, pharmaceutical products, and construction materials). For the two latter groups of products, neither quantitative nor value limits are in force.
Export taxes	No.

Payments for Invisible Transactions and Current Transfers

Controls on these transfers	
Trade-related payments	n.r.
Investment-related payments	Remittance of investment-related payments is permitted, once tax obligations have been met.
Payments for travel	n.r.
Personal payments	n.r.
Foreign workers' wages	n.r.
Credit card use abroad	n.r.
Other payments	n.r.

Proceeds from Invisible Transactions and Current Transfers

Repatriation requirements	Yes.
Restrictions on use of funds	No.

Capital Transactions

Controls on capital and money market instruments	Effective January 1, 1999, controls were eliminated on most of the operations in foreign securities.
On capital market securities	CNB bonds may be purchased only by resident institutional investors.
Shares or other securities of a participating nature	
Purchase locally by nonresidents	The purchase of shares and other securities of a participating nature may be affected by regulations on inward direct investments.

Bonds or other debt securities

    Sale or issue locally by nonresidents — Prior authorization is required for nonresidents to issue debt securities.

    Sale or issue abroad by residents — Prior authorization is required for issuing debt securities abroad.

On money market instruments

  Sale or issue locally by nonresidents — Prior authorization is required for nonresidents to issue money market securities.

  Sale or issue abroad by residents — Prior authorization is required for issuing debt securities abroad.

On collective investment securities

  Sale or issue locally by nonresidents — Share certificates may be issued in the Czech Republic only by resident investors.

  Sale or issue abroad by residents — Share certificates may be issued by residents having a general license to issue collective investment securities.

Controls on derivatives and other instruments — Effective January 1, 1999, controls were eliminated on transactions in derivatives.

Controls on credit operations — Effective January 1, 1999, controls were eliminated on extending financial credits and operations with guarantees, sureties, and financial backup facilities.

Controls on direct investment

Inward direct investment — There are restrictions on nonresidents investing in local telephone networks and services, air transport, gaming, and setting up branches of mortgage banks.

Controls on liquidation of direct investment — No.

Controls on real estate transactions

Purchase locally by nonresidents — A nonresident who is not a citizen of the Czech Republic may acquire real estate only in the following cases: (1) by heritage; (2) for the diplomatic representation of a foreign country under the terms of reciprocity; (3) if it is real estate acquired in an unapportioned coownership of a married couple of which only one is a nonresident, or where a nonresident acquires property from a husband, wife, parents, or grandparents; (4) through the exchange of domestic real estate that the nonresident owns for other domestic real estate, the usual price of which does not exceed the usual price of the former real estate; (5) if the nonresident has a preemption by reason of a proportioned coownership of real estate; (6) if it is a construction built by a nonresident on his own land; and (7) under the terms explicitly stipulated by the Act on Mitigating the Consequences of Property Injustice. Branches of nonresident corporations may not purchase real estate.

Controls on personal capital movements — No.

Provisions specific to commercial banks and other credit institutions

Lending locally in foreign exchange — The range is determined by the banking license granted.

Purchase of locally issued securities denominated in foreign exchange — The range is determined by the banking license granted.

Investment regulations

  Abroad by banks — n.r.

  In banks by nonresidents — Resident and nonresident investors are treated equally.

Open foreign exchange position limits — Open foreign exchange limits are applied on both on- and off-balance sheet exposures and are 20% of the capital for all currencies and 15% for open koruna positions.

  On resident assets and liabilities — Yes.

  On nonresident assets and liabilities — Yes.

Provisions specific to institutional investors	A portfolio of securities held in a trust or in an investment fund's assets may not be formed by more than 11% of the total nominal value of securities of one kind issued by the same issuer. Effective April 1, 2000, insurance companies and pension funds may place their assets abroad, subject to specific prudential regulations.
Limits (min.) on portfolio invested locally	Yes.
Other controls imposed by securities laws	The Securities Commissions Act of 1998 removed most controls.

Changes During 1999

Capital transactions	*January 1.* A new government decree entered into force, eliminating most controls on capital transactions.
Controls on capital and money market instruments	*January 1.* Controls on operations with foreign securities were eliminated.
Controls on derivatives and other instruments	*January 1.* Controls on operations in derivatives were eliminated.
Controls on credit operations	*January 1.* Controls on extending financial credits and operations with guarantees, sureties, and financial backup facilities were eliminated.

Changes During 2000

Capital transactions	
Provisions specific to commercial banks and other credit institutions	*April 1.* Insurance companies and pension funds may place their assets abroad, subject to specific prudential regulations.

DENMARK

(Position as of December 31, 1999)

Status Under IMF Articles of Agreement

Article VIII

Date of acceptance: May 1, 1967.

Exchange Arrangement

Currency

The currency of Denmark is the Danish krone.

Exchange rate structure

Unitary

Classification

Pegged exchange rate within horizontal bands

As of January 1, 1999, Denmark became a participant in the ERM II and maintains the spot exchange rate between the Danish krone and the euro within margins of 2.25% above or below the central rate.

Exchange tax

No.

Exchange subsidy

No.

Forward exchange market

Yes.

Arrangements for Payments and Receipts

Prescription of currency requirements

No.

Payment arrangements

No.

Administration of control

No.

International security restrictions

In accordance with Executive Board Decision No. 144-(52/51)

Yes.

In accordance with UN sanctions

Denmark maintains exchange restrictions against Iraq and against Libya.

Payment arrears

No.

Controls on trade in gold (coins and/or bullion)

No.

Controls on exports and imports of banknotes

No.

Resident Accounts

Foreign exchange accounts permitted

Yes.

Held domestically

Yes.

Held abroad

Yes.

Accounts in domestic currency convertible into foreign currency

Yes.

Nonresident Accounts

Foreign exchange accounts permitted	Yes.
Domestic currency accounts	Yes.
Convertible into foreign currency	Yes.
Blocked accounts	No.

Imports and Import Payments

Foreign exchange budget	No.
Financing requirements for imports	No.
Documentation requirements for release of foreign exchange for imports	No.
Import licenses and other nontariff measures	
Open general licenses	A few items require a license when originating in Japan and the Republic of Korea. A larger number of items require a license when originating in or purchased from Albania, Bulgaria, China, the Czech Republic, Hungary, the Democratic People's Republic of Korea, Mongolia, Poland, Romania, the Slovak Republic, the Baltic countries, Russia, the other countries of the former Soviet Union, and Vietnam.
Licenses with quotas	Licenses are required for imports of textiles, toys, and footwear.
Import taxes and/or tariffs	No.
State import monopoly	No.

Exports and Export Proceeds

Repatriation requirements	No.
Financing requirements	No.
Documentation requirements	No.
Export licenses	
Without quotas	Except for certain items subject to strategic controls, licenses are required only for exports of waste and scrap of certain metals.
Export taxes	No.

Payments for Invisible Transactions and Current Transfers

Controls on these transfers	No.

Proceeds from Invisible Transactions and Current Transfers

Repatriation requirements	No.
Restrictions on use of funds	No.

Capital Transactions

Controls on capital and money market instruments	No.
Controls on derivatives and other instruments	No.
Controls on credit operations	No.
Controls on direct investment	No.
Controls on liquidation of direct investment	No.
Controls on real estate transactions	
Purchase abroad by residents	Yes.
Purchase locally by nonresidents	Purchases are prohibited, except in the case of acquisitions by: (1) persons who have formerly been residents of Denmark for at least five years; (2) EU nationals working in Denmark and EU-based companies operating in Denmark for residential or business purposes; and (3) non-EU nationals who either are in possession of a valid residence permit or are entitled to stay in Denmark without such a permit for residential or active business purposes.
Controls on personal capital movements	No.
Provisions specific to commercial banks and other credit institutions	The Consolidated Act contains prudential regulations covering capital adequacy, liquidity, and large exposures. These regulations follow the relevant EU directives.
Provisions specific to institutional investors	
Limits (max.) on securities issued by nonresidents and on portfolio invested abroad	A 40% limitation on holdings of foreign equity securities by private insurance companies and pension funds is in effect.
Currency-matching regulations on assets/liabilities composition	Insurance companies are regulated by the "balance principle," which determines that consistency must be ensured between assets and liabilities denominated in the same currency.
Other controls imposed by securities laws	No.

Changes During 1999

Exchange arrangement	*January 1.* Denmark became a participant in the ERM II.

DJIBOUTI

(Position as of January 31, 2000)

Status Under IMF Articles of Agreement

Article VIII   Date of acceptance: September 19, 1980.

Exchange Arrangement

Currency   The currency of Djibouti is the Djibouti franc.

Exchange rate structure   Unitary.

Classification

Currency board arrangement   The Djibouti franc is pegged to the dollar, the intervention currency, at DF 177.721 per $1. The official buying and selling rates for currencies other than the dollar are set by local banks on the basis of the cross rates for the dollar in international markets. There is coverage of the full issue of Djibouti francs in foreign exchange.

Exchange tax   No.

Exchange subsidy   No.

Forward exchange market   No.

Arrangements for Payments and Receipts

Prescription of currency requirements   No.

Payment arrangements   No.

Administration of control   No.

International security restrictions

In accordance with UN sanctions   Yes.

Payment arrears   No.

Controls on trade in gold (coins and/or bullion)   No.

Controls on exports and imports of banknotes   No.

Resident Accounts

Foreign exchange accounts permitted   Yes.

Held domestically   Yes.

Held abroad   Yes.

Accounts in domestic currency convertible into foreign currency   Yes.

Nonresident Accounts

Foreign exchange accounts permitted   Yes.

Domestic currency accounts	Yes.
Convertible into foreign currency	Yes.
Blocked accounts	Yes.

Imports and Import Payments

Foreign exchange budget	No.
Financing requirements for imports	
Advance import deposits	Advance import deposits are permitted up to a certain percentage of the value of imports.
Documentation requirements for release of foreign exchange for imports	Yes.
Preshipment inspection	Yes.
Letters of credit	Yes.
Import licenses and other nontariff measures	
Negative list	Yes.
Import taxes and/or tariffs	Formally, customs duties are not charged on imports, but, in practice, fiscal duties are levied by means of the general consumption tax on imports at three rates (8%, 20%, and 33%). Certain commodities, including alcoholic beverages, noncarbonated mineral water, petroleum products, khat, and tobacco, are subject to a surtax of various rates.
State import monopoly	No.

Exports and Export Proceeds

Repatriation requirements	No.
Financing requirements	Yes.
Documentation requirements	
Letters of credit	Yes.
Guarantees	Yes.
Domiciliation	Yes.
Preshipment inspection	Yes.
Export licenses	No.
Export taxes	No.

Payments for Invisible Transactions and Current Transfers

Controls on these transfers	No.

Proceeds from Invisible Transactions and Current Transfers

Repatriation requirements	No.
Restrictions on use of funds	No.

Capital Transactions

Controls on capital and money market instruments	No.
Controls on derivatives and other instruments	No.
Controls on credit operations	There are controls on all credit transactions by residents to nonresidents, including transactions as regards guarantees, sureties, and financial backup facilities within the limits established by the banking regulations to comply with the prudential standard on customer risk.
Commercial credits	
By residents to nonresidents	Yes.
Financial credits	
By residents to nonresidents	Yes.
Guarantees, sureties, and financial backup facilities	
By residents to nonresidents	Yes.
Controls on direct investment	
Outward direct investment	Yes.
Inward direct investment	Yes.
Controls on liquidation of direct investment	No.
Controls on real estate transactions	No.
Controls on personal capital movements	No.
Provisions specific to commercial banks and other credit institutions	
Lending to nonresidents (financial or commercial credits)	Yes.
Lending locally in foreign exchange	Yes.
Purchase of locally issued securities denominated in foreign exchange	Yes.
Differential treatment of deposit accounts in foreign exchange	
Liquid asset requirements	Yes.
Differential treatment of deposit accounts held by nonresidents	
Liquid asset requirements	Yes.
Provisions specific to institutional investors	
Currency-matching regulations on assets/liabilities composition	There is a matching requirement with respect to both the amount of the transaction and the intervention currency, and also with respect to maturity and interest rate.
Other controls imposed by securities laws	No.

Changes During 1999

No significant changes occurred in the exchange and trade system.

Changes During 2000

Imports and import payments

January 1. The consumption tax on imports was reduced to three rates (8%, 20%, and 33%) from seven rates.

DOMINICA

(Position as of January 31, 2000)

Status Under IMF Articles of Agreement

Article VIII   Date of acceptance: December 13, 1979.

Exchange Arrangement

Currency   The currency of Dominica is the Eastern Caribbean dollar, issued by the ECCB.

Exchange rate structure   Unitary.

Classification

Exchange arrangement with no sepa-   The Eastern Caribbean dollar is pegged to the U.S. dollar, the intervention currency, at
rate legal tender   EC$2.70 per US$1.

Exchange tax   No.

Exchange subsidy   No.

Forward exchange market   No.

Arrangements for Payments and Receipts

Prescription of currency   Settlements with residents of the territories participating in the ECCB Agreement must be
requirements   made in Eastern Caribbean dollars; those with member countries of the CARICOM must be
                                 made in the currency of the CARICOM country concerned. Settlements with residents of
                                 other countries may be made in any foreign currency that is acceptable to the country where
                                 the settlement is being made.

Payment arrangements

Regional arrangements   Dominica is a member of the CARICOM.

Clearing agreements   As a member of CARICOM, Dominica participates in the CMCF.

Administration of control   Exchange control is administered by the MOF and applies to all countries outside the
                                 ECCB area. The MOF has delegated to commercial banks certain powers to approve sales
                                 of foreign currencies but requires that any individual foreign currency transaction in excess
                                 of EC$250,000 must be approved by the MOF. The Ministry of Trade administers import
                                 and export arrangements and controls.

International security restrictions   Trade with Iraq is prohibited.

In accordance with UN sanctions   Yes.

Payment arrears

Official   Yes.

Controls on trade in gold (coins
and/or bullion)

Controls on domestic ownership and/or   Residents are permitted to acquire and hold gold coins for numismatic purposes only.
trade

Controls on external trade   Small quantities of gold may be imported for industrial purposes only with the approval of
                                          the MOF.

Controls on exports and imports of banknotes

On exports

Domestic currency   The exportation of Eastern Caribbean dollar notes and coins outside the ECCB area is limited to amounts prescribed by the ECCB.

Resident Accounts

Foreign exchange accounts permitted   Yes.

Held domestically   These accounts are normally confined to major exporters and may only be credited with foreign currencies obtained abroad. Payments from these accounts do not require approval.

Held abroad   No.

Accounts in domestic currency convertible into foreign currency   Yes.

Nonresident Accounts

Foreign exchange accounts permitted   These accounts are permitted, but approval is required.

Domestic currency accounts   Yes.

Convertible into foreign currency   For any single transaction in excess of EC$250,000, approval from the MOF is required.

Blocked accounts   No.

Imports and Import Payments

Foreign exchange budget   No.

Financing requirements for imports   No.

Documentation requirements for release of foreign exchange for imports   Payments for authorized imports are permitted upon presentation of documentary evidence of purchase to a commercial bank.

Letters of credit   Yes.

Import licenses and other nontariff measures   All imports from Iraq are prohibited.

Negative list   Imports of specified goods originating elsewhere than OECS countries, Belize, and CARICOM countries require a license. Imports of a subset of these goods from the more developed countries of CARICOM (Barbados, Guyana, Jamaica, and Trinidad and Tobago) also require a license.

Open general licenses   Applicable to public health and safety goods.

Licenses with quotas   There are certain quantitative restrictions on imports of beverages, flour, and margarine; quotas are allocated to traditional importers based on their historical market shares.

Import taxes and/or tariffs   Dominica applies the CET of CARICOM. Effective January 1, 1999, most rates are ad valorem, with the maximum rates having been reduced to 25% from 30%. Lower rates apply to machinery (zero to 15%) and some essential foodstuffs (10% to 15%), while higher rates apply to domestic appliances (25% to 40%) and motor vehicles (25% to 45%). Specific duties are applied to some goods. Imports are also subject to a 1% customs service charge. On January 1, 2000, the fourth phase of the CARICOM CET went into effect.

State import monopoly   Bulk imports of sugar and rice are effected by a state agency.

Exports and Export Proceeds

Repatriation requirements	Yes.
Surrender requirements	The conversion of export proceeds to an ECCB currency account is mandatory, unless the exporter has a foreign currency account into which the proceeds may be paid.
Financing requirements	n.a.
Documentation requirements	No.
Export licenses	Exports to Iraq are prohibited, and specific licenses are required for the exportation of protected plant and animal species to any destination.
Without quotas	Yes.
Export taxes	Bananas exported by the Dominica Banana Marketing Corporation are subject to a levy of 1% if the export price is between EC$0.55 and EC$0.60 a pound; if the export price exceeds EC$0.60 a pound, an additional levy equivalent to 25% of the excess is imposed.

Payments for Invisible Transactions and Current Transfers

Controls on these transfers	Commercial banks are authorized to sell foreign currency in amounts up to EC$250,000. Amounts over this limit require approval by the MOF, which is generally granted. Remittances of pensions, family maintenance funds, and subscriptions and membership fees are not subject to controls.
Trade-related payments	
Prior approval	Yes.
Quantitative limits	Yes.
Indicative limits/bona fide test	Yes.
Investment-related payments	
Prior approval	Yes.
Quantitative limits	Yes.
Indicative limits/bona fide test	Yes.
Payments for travel	
Prior approval	Yes.
Quantitative limits	Yes.
Indicative limits/bona fide test	Yes.
Personal payments	There are controls on the payment of medical costs and studies abroad.
Prior approval	Yes.
Indicative limits/bona fide test	Bona fide tests apply to the payment of medical costs.
Foreign workers' wages	
Prior approval	Earnings of foreign workers may be remitted after settlement of all taxes or other public liabilities.
Credit card use abroad	
Prior approval	Yes.
Quantitative limits	Yes.
Indicative limits/bona fide test	Yes.
Other payments	There are no controls on subscriptions and membership fees.

Prior approval	Yes.
Quantitative limits	Yes.
Indicative limits/bona fide test	Yes.

Proceeds from Invisible Transactions and Current Transfers

Repatriation requirements	Yes.
Surrender requirements	Foreign currency proceeds from these transactions must be sold to a bank or deposited into a foreign currency account.
Restrictions on use of funds	No.

Capital Transactions

Controls on capital and money market instruments	All outward transfers of capital in excess of EC$250,000 require MOF approval.
On capital market securities	
Shares or other securities of a participating nature	
Purchase abroad by residents	Yes.
Bonds or other debt securities	
Purchase abroad by residents	Yes.
On money market instruments	
Purchase abroad by residents	Yes.
On collective investment securities	
Purchase abroad by residents	Yes.
Controls on derivatives and other instruments	n.a.
Controls on credit operations	All credit operations by residents to nonresidents require MOF approval.
Commercial credits	
By residents to nonresidents	Yes.
Financial credits	
By residents to nonresidents	Yes.
Guarantees, sureties, and financial backup facilities	
By residents to nonresidents	Yes.
Controls on direct investment	
Outward direct investment	Yes.
Inward direct investment	Nonresidents are generally required to have an alien landholding license to hold shares in private and public companies and to hold property.
Controls on liquidation of direct investment	Proceeds may be remitted after the discharge of any related liabilities.
Controls on real estate transactions	
Purchase abroad by residents	Yes.

Purchase locally by nonresidents	An alien landholding license is required.
Controls on personal capital movements	
Loans	
By residents to nonresidents	Yes.
Gifts, endowments, inheritances, and legacies	
By residents to nonresidents	Yes.
Settlement of debts abroad by immigrants	Yes.
Transfer of assets	
Transfer abroad by emigrants	Yes.
Transfer of gambling and prize earnings	Yes.
Provisions specific to commercial banks and other credit institutions	
Lending to nonresidents (financial or commercial credits)	MOF approval is required.
Lending locally in foreign exchange	These transactions are generally not permitted.
Provisions specific to institutional investors	No.
Other controls imposed by securities laws	No.

Changes During 1999

Imports and import payments	*January 1.* The maximum import tariff under the CARICOM CET was reduced to 25% from 30%.

Changes During 2000

Imports and import payments	*January 1.* The fourth phase of the CARICOM CET went into effect.

DOMINICAN REPUBLIC

(Position as of March 31, 2000)

Status Under IMF Articles of Agreement

Article VIII   Date of acceptance: August 1, 1953.

Exchange Arrangement

Currency   The currency of the Dominican Republic is the Dominican peso.

Exchange rate structure

Dual   In addition to the official exchange rate set by the Central Bank of the Dominican Republic (CBDR), the market exchange rate reflects commercial banks' foreign exchange transactions with the public. There is also an extrabank market rate determined by foreign exchange transactions with exchange houses.

Classification

Managed floating with no pre-   The CBDR occasionally intervenes in the market via the commercial banks and foreign
announced path for the exchange rate exchange dealers.

                                     The official exchange rate is adjusted on a weekly basis in line with a weighted average of the buy rate of commercial banks.

Exchange tax   A commission of 1.75% is charged on all bank sales of foreign currency, which, on October 8, 1999, was increased temporarily to 5%.

Exchange subsidy   No.

Forward exchange market   No.

Arrangements for Payments and Receipts

Prescription of currency   Settlements with Bolivia, Brazil, Chile, Colombia, Ecuador, Mexico, Peru, and Uruguay
requirements   may be made through special accounts established under reciprocal credit agreements within the framework of the LAIA. All payments must be invoiced in dollars; otherwise, no obligations are imposed on importers, exporters, or other residents regarding the currency to be used for payments to nonresidents or with respect to payments in the currency in which the loan is denominated.

Payment arrangements

Bilateral payment arrangements

  Operative   Yes.

Regional arrangements   The Dominican Republic is a member of the LAIA.

Clearing agreements   Yes.

Barter agreements and open accounts Settlements take place under reciprocal credit agreements with Argentina, Brazil, Chile, Colombia, and Venezuela.

Administration of control   Exchange control policy is determined by the Monetary Board and administered by the CBDR.

International security restrictions No.

Payment arrears

Official   Nearly all public sector debt-service payments that were in arrears have been regularized, though some arrears arising mainly from contract disputes remain.

Controls on trade in gold (coins and/or bullion)	Whole bars of gold are to be sold to local industrial and handicraft enterprises through the central bank. Such sales must equal 1% of the physical volume of refined gold and silver produced each year, or no more than 2,000 troy ounces annually.
Controls on domestic ownership and/or trade	Individuals may purchase, hold, and sell gold coins not only for numismatic purposes, but also may buy gold as needed for industrial or handicraft purposes from the central bank, indicating in their request the purpose for which it is to be used.
Controls on external trade	Imports and exports of gold in any form other than jewelry constituting the personal effects of a traveler require licenses issued by the CBDR.

Controls on exports and imports of banknotes

On exports

   Domestic currency   Travelers are allowed to export up to RD$20,000 in domestic banknotes and RD$100 in coins.

   Foreign currency   Travelers are allowed to export up to US$10,000.

On imports

   Domestic currency   Travelers are allowed to import up to RD$20,000 in domestic banknotes and up to RD$100 in coins.

Resident Accounts

Foreign exchange accounts permitted	Yes.
Held domestically	Natural or juridical persons may, with the prior approval of the Monetary Board, locally maintain savings or time deposit accounts in dollars or in any other freely convertible foreign currency at banks authorized to offer full services.
Held abroad	No.
Accounts in domestic currency convertible into foreign currency	Domestic currency may be converted to foreign currency.

Nonresident Accounts

Foreign exchange accounts permitted	Natural or juridical persons may, with the prior approval of the Monetary Board, locally maintain savings or time deposit accounts in dollars or in any other freely convertible foreign currency at banks authorized to offer full services.
Domestic currency accounts	Yes.
Convertible into foreign currency	Approval is required for opening these accounts.
Blocked accounts	No.

Imports and Import Payments

Foreign exchange budget	No.
Financing requirements for imports	No.
Documentation requirements for release of foreign exchange for imports	Payments for oil are transacted through the CBDR at the official exchange rate, and these imports require certification of the use of foreign currency for customs clearance. According to regulations, all other purchases of foreign exchange for imports should be transacted through the commercial banks and are only subject to verification of appropriate documentation, except for the industrial free-trade zones.

Import licenses and other nontariff measures	
Positive list	This list includes beans, corn, garlic, milk, onions, poultry, rice, and sugar.
Negative list	Imports of live animals; seeds; plants; fruits; plant and animal products that are unhealthy, decomposing, or infected with germs or parasites; and substances harmful or injurious to human, plant, or animal health are prohibited.
Licenses with quotas	Imports of beans, corn, garlic, milk, onions, poultry, rice, and refined sugar require licenses.
Other nontariff measures	Sugar may be imported only by domestic producers. The Association of Canned Food Manufacturers has exclusive rights to import tomato paste.
Import taxes and/or tariffs	Tariff rates range from zero to 35%. There is also a temporary import system for the entry into the customs area, free of import duties and taxes, of certain goods that are to be reexported in 12 months or less, after being processed, worked, or repaired. In addition, there is a zero rate for imports of inputs, machinery, and equipment to be used in the textile and agricultural sectors.
Taxes collected through the exchange system	Yes.
State import monopoly	The state refinery has exclusive rights to import certain petroleum products for resale.

Exports and Export Proceeds

Repatriation requirements	Yes.
Surrender requirements	A 100% requirement applies to all traditional exports (i.e., cocoa, sugar, coffee, tobacco, and mineral products).
Financing requirements	Exporters may not extend credit to foreign buyers with a maturity of more than 30 days from the date of shipment without authorization from the CBDR.
Documentation requirements	Yes.
Export licenses	Certain exports are prohibited for environmental protection purposes.
With quotas	Licenses are required for sugar and textile imports and exports to and from the United States. Bananas are subject to quantitative restrictions in the EU, as is coffee in the markets of signatories to the International Coffee Agreement.
Export taxes	No.

Payments for Invisible Transactions and Current Transfers

Controls on these transfers	All invisible payments may be made freely through commercial banks, subject to documentation requirements.
Trade-related payments	
Prior approval	Yes.
Investment-related payments	No controls are exercised on the transfer of profits.
Payments for travel	
Quantitative limits	Yes.
Personal payments	No controls are exercised on the transfer of pensions and family maintenance payments.
Quantitative limits	Yes.
Foreign workers' wages	
Prior approval	Prior approval of the president of the Republic is required for the hiring of Haitian workers to harvest sugarcane.

Other payments

Prior approval Technical assistance fees must be registered with the CBDR.

Indicative limits/bona fide test Yes.

Proceeds from Invisible Transactions and Current Transfers

Repatriation requirements Yes.

Surrender requirements While most exchange proceeds from invisibles may be sold in the interbank market, certain receipts (e.g., for international phone calls, international credit card transactions, jet fuel, foreign embassies' operations, and receipts from insurance claims) must be surrendered to the CBDR.

Restrictions on use of funds No.

Capital Transactions

Controls on capital and money market instruments There are no restrictions on capital inflows to the private sector, but such investments must be registered with the CBDR. External debt contracted by the public sector is subject to controls.

On capital market securities The local capital market is still emerging; shares and bonds are not yet traded. Only the primary market's own operations are effected, with commercial paper denominated in domestic currency.

Bonds or other debt securities

Sale or issue abroad by residents Yes.

Controls on derivatives and other instruments No.

Controls on credit operations

Commercial credits

To residents from nonresidents Prior CBDR approval is required.

Financial credits

By residents to nonresidents Banks may grant unsecured loans to a single individual or legal entity for up to 15% of their capital and reserves, and up to a maximum of 30% when secured with real guarantees, both to residents and nonresidents.

To residents from nonresidents External debt may be contracted directly by the central government, subject to congressional authorization. New loans by other public entities require authorization from the president of the Republic for their subsequent registration by the Monetary Board. Private external debt must be registered with the CBDR, except for foreign exchange advances on future traditional exports, which require approval from the CBDR.

Guarantees, sureties, and financial backup facilities Effective October 7, 1999, banks authorized to offer full services may obtain financing abroad of up to one year, limited to 30% of their paid-up capital and reserves.

By residents to nonresidents Banks authorized to offer full services are allowed, with the prior approval of the CBDR, to offer guarantees in foreign exchange in addition to those offered to cover trade operations as well as to renew guarantees that have been granted through March 2, 2000.

Controls on direct investment

Inward direct investment Investments must be registered with the CBDR. Investment in the following sectors is prohibited: (1) disposal of toxic waste and of dangerous or radioactive substances not produced in the country; (2) activities that affect public health and the environment; and (3) production of materials and equipment that affect defense and national security.

Controls on liquidation of direct investment	No.
Controls on real estate transactions	No.
Controls on personal capital movements	
Transfer of assets	
Transfer abroad by emigrants	Yes.
Transfer into the country by immigrants	Yes.

Provisions specific to commercial banks and other credit institutions

Borrowing abroad — Effective October 7, 1999, banks authorized to offer full services may obtain financing abroad of up to one year, limited to 30% of their paid-up capital and reserves.

Lending locally in foreign exchange — Banks authorized to offer full services may grant loans in dollars to the sectors exporting goods and services to finance activities specific to their functions and to the importing sectors to cover payments abroad for the acquisition of goods and services.

Differential treatment of deposit accounts in foreign exchange

Reserve requirements — Foreign currency deposits taken by commercial and full service banks are subject to a 10% reserve requirement valued at the official exchange rate.

Credit controls — Banks may grant unsecured loans to a single individual or legal entity for up to 15% of their capital and reserves, and up to a maximum of 30% when secured with real guarantees, both to residents and nonresidents.

Differential treatment of deposit accounts held by nonresidents

Reserve requirements — Yes.

Open foreign exchange position limits — Regulations are currently being drafted to prohibit open positions.

Provisions specific to institutional investors — No.

Other controls imposed by securities laws — No.

Changes During 1999

Exchange arrangement — *October 8.* The commission on all bank sales of foreign currency was temporarily increased to 5% from 1.75%.

Capital transactions

Provisions specific to commercial banks and other credit institutions — *October 7.* Banks authorized to offer full services may obtain financing abroad of up to one year, limited to 30% of their paid-up capital and reserves.

October 8. The reserve requirement on foreign currency deposits taken by commercial and full service banks up to an amount in dollars equivalent to three times the bank's capital and reserve was increased to 10% from zero.

Changes During 2000

Capital transactions

Controls on credit operations — *March 9.* Banks authorized to offer full services were allowed to offer guarantees in foreign exchange in addition to those offered to cover trade operations.

ECUADOR

(Position as of March 31, 2000)

Status Under IMF Articles of Agreement

Article VIII   Date of acceptance: August 31, 1970.

Exchange Arrangement

Currency

Effective March 13, 2000, a full dollarization scheme was established. Although the currency of Ecuador is the Ecuadorian sucre, the dollarization legislation makes the dollar the legal tender and provides for a limited issue of domestic coins with small value to remain in circulation to facilitate small transactions and requires that they be fully backed at all times by dollars.

Exchange rate structure

Unitary

Until February 12, 1999, there were two exchange rates: the free market rate and the Central Bank of Ecuador (CBE) official exchange rate. All legally permitted foreign exchange transactions, other than those conducted through the CBE, were conducted in the free market. The dual exchange rate system was unified on February 12, 1999, when the sucre was floated.

Classification

Exchange arrangement with no separate legal tender

Until February 11, 1999, the market rate of the sucre against the dollar moved within a preannounced band. The band was ±7.5% around the midpoint, and the pace of depreciation of the band was 20% a year. On that date, the sucre's lower limit was S/. 7.261 per $1 and the upper limit was S/. 6.284 per $1.

On February 12, 1999, the CBE allowed the sucre to float freely in the foreign exchange market and the exchange rate arrangement of Ecuador was reclassified to the category independently floating from the category crawling band.

Effective March 13, 2000, a full dollarization scheme was established. The dollarization legislation provides for the central bank to exchange on demand sucres at a rate of S/. 25,000 per $1. The central bank has ceased the creation of sucre-denominated liabilities, and it stands ready to redeem sucre coins and banknotes for dollars on demand. It is envisaged that dollarization will be largely completed within 12 months. Thus, the exchange arrangement of Ecuador has been reclassified to the category exchange rate, no separate legal tender from the category independently floating.

Exchange tax   No.

Exchange subsidy   No.

Forward exchange market

Banks and other financial institutions authorized to conduct foreign exchange transactions are permitted to conduct forward swaps and options, and transactions in other financial derivative instruments, subject to the supervision and control of the Superintendency of Banks.

Arrangements for Payments and Receipts

Prescription of currency requirements

Exchange proceeds from all countries, except for LAIA members, must be received in convertible currencies. Whenever possible, import payments must be made in the currency stipulated in the import license. Some settlements with Hungary take place through bilateral accounts.

Payment arrangements

Bilateral payment arrangements

Operative

There are arrangements with Cuba and Hungary; balances are settled every four months.

Regional arrangements	Payments between Ecuador and the other LAIA countries may be made within the framework of the multilateral clearing system of the LAIA.
Clearing agreements	Yes.
Administration of control	Public sector foreign exchange transactions are carried out exclusively through the CBE. Exports must be registered with the CBE to guarantee repatriation of any foreign exchange proceeds from the transaction. Private sector foreign exchange transactions related to the exportation, production, transportation, and commercialization of oil and its derivatives may be carried out through the free market or through the CBE. Private sector foreign exchange transactions may be effected through banks and exchange houses authorized by the Central Bank Board.
International security restrictions	No.
Payment arrears	
Official	Arrears are maintained with respect to public and publicly guaranteed debt-service payments to official and private creditors.
Private	Commercial banks under the control of the Deposit Insurance Agency (AGD) maintain external payment arrears on trade and interbank credit lines.
Controls on trade in gold (coins and/or bullion)	No.
Controls on exports and imports of banknotes	No.

Resident Accounts

Foreign exchange accounts permitted	Yes.
Held domestically	Yes.
Held abroad	Yes.
Accounts in domestic currency convertible into foreign currency	Yes.

Nonresident Accounts

Foreign exchange accounts permitted	Yes.
Domestic currency accounts	Yes.
Convertible into foreign currency	Yes.
Blocked accounts	No.

Imports and Import Payments

Foreign exchange budget	No.
Financing requirements for imports	
Advance payment requirements	Prepayments for imports by the private sector are permitted.
Documentation requirements for release of foreign exchange for imports	No.
Import licenses and other nontariff measures	Prior import licenses are required for agricultural, medical, and psychotropical imports. In addition, Petroecuador (the state oil company) may, without a license, import supplies, materials, and equipment during emergencies.

Negative list	Imports of psychotropics, used vehicles, vehicle parts and pieces, and used clothes are prohibited primarily to protect the environment and health. Imports of antiques and certain items related to health and national security are also prohibited. Certain imports require prior authorization from government ministries or agencies for ecological, health, and national security reasons.
Import taxes and/or tariffs	Tariff rates for most goods are zero, 5%, 10%, 15%, 20%, and 40%. Automobiles are subject to a 40% rate calculated on the basis of a set of reference prices. For certain agricultural goods, tariffs are imposed on those with prices below a certain lower benchmark, and rebates are granted on goods with prices above an upper benchmark. Before concluding the negotiations for accession to the WTO, Ecuador replaced its system of price bans for 130 agricultural products with the one used by the Community of Andean Nations. No timetable for the elimination of this syetem has been agreed to by the WTO. All private sector imports are subject to the 10% VAT. Effective January 1, 2000, the VAT rate was increased to 12%. Effective February 9, 1999, goods imported into Ecuador are subject to additional tariffs ranging from 2% to 10%.
State import monopoly	No.

Exports and Export Proceeds

Repatriation requirements	No.
Surrender requirements	All export proceeds must be surrendered to authorized financial entities. However, exporters may deduct up to 15% from their surrender requirement to cover the actual cost of consular fees and commissions paid abroad. The surrender requirement does not apply to exports effected under authorized barter transactions or to exports to countries with which Ecuador has bilateral payment agreements. In such cases, exporters are required to provide official documentation from the recipient country establishing the applicable forms of payment. Exporters of marine products are permitted to retain up to 30% of the f.o.b. value of their shipments to cover the actual cost of leasing foreign ships. Minimum reference prices are established for exports of bananas, coffee, fish products, cocoa, and semifinished products of cocoa to help ensure that exchange proceeds are fully surrendered. Payment of foreign exchange for petroleum exports is made on the basis of the sale prices stated in the sales contracts and must be surrendered within 30 days of the date of shipment. In addition, exporters may deduct from their surrender requirements the cost of Kraft paper and starch or inputs and raw materials imported under the "Industrial Deposits Temporary Admission" regime when exporters require cardboard boxes for packing that are built with Kraft paper and starch.
Financing requirements	No.
Documentation requirements	Barter transactions require the prior approval of the Ministry of Foreign Trade, Industrialization, and Fisheries, and must be registered with the CBE.
Export licenses	Exports do not require licenses, but must be registered for statistical purposes.
Without quotas	The export prices of bananas, cocoa, coffee, fish, and semifinished cocoa products are subject to minimum reference prices.
Export taxes	All crude oil exports are subject to a tax of $0.5 a barrel. A fee of $1.02 a barrel is applied to crude oil exported through the pipeline. Effective March 10, 2000, this fee was increased to $1.60 a barrel. This fee increases in accordance with the viscosity of the crude oil and the distance it is transported (in kilometers).

Payments for Invisible Transactions and Current Transfers

Controls on these transfers	Residents and nonresidents traveling abroad by air must pay a tax of $25 a person. Airline tickets for foreign travel are taxed at 12%, and tickets for travel by ship are taxed at 8% for departures and 4% for the return trip.

Proceeds from Invisible Transactions and Current Transfers

Repatriation requirements	Yes.
Surrender requirements	All receipts from invisibles must be sold in the free market, except for interest income on exchange reserves of the CBE and all invisible receipts of the public sector, which are transacted at the central bank rate.
Restrictions on use of funds	No.

Capital Transactions

Controls on capital and money market instruments	
On money market instruments	
Sale or issue locally by nonresidents	There are controls on the issue of these instruments.
On collective investment securities	
Sale or issue locally by nonresidents	There are controls on the issue of these instruments.
Controls on derivatives and other instruments	No.
Controls on credit operations	All foreign loans granted to or guaranteed by the government or official entities, whether or not they involve the disbursement of foreign exchange, are subject to prior approval from the Central Bank Board. A request for such approval must be submitted by the Minister of Finance and Public Credit to the Central Bank Board, accompanied by detailed information on the loan contract and the investment projects it is intended to finance. In examining the request, the Central Bank Board considers the effects that the loan and the related investment may have on the balance of payments and on monetary aggregates. For public sector entities, the projects to be financed must be included in the General Development Plan.
	New external credits with a maturity of over one year that are contracted by the private sector, either directly or through the domestic financial system, must be registered with the CBE within 45 days of disbursement. Nonregistered credits are subject to a service charge equivalent to 0.25% of the credit amount.
Commercial credits	
By residents to nonresidents	Yes.
To residents from nonresidents	Yes.
Financial credits	
By residents to nonresidents	Yes.
To residents from nonresidents	Yes.
Guarantees, sureties, and financial backup facilities	
By residents to nonresidents	Yes.
To residents from nonresidents	Yes.
Controls on direct investment	No.
Controls on liquidation of direct investment	No.
Controls on real estate transactions	No.
Controls on personal capital movements	No.

**Provisions specific to commercial
banks and other credit institutions**

Differential treatment of deposit
accounts in foreign exchange

   Reserve requirements   The reserve requirement for dollar-denominated accounts was 4%, while that for sucre-
denominated accounts was 19%. Effective January 27, 2000, the reserve requirements were
unified at 9%.

Open foreign exchange position limits   Until February 11, 1999, there was a limit equivalent to 20% of technical capital of banks.

**Provisions specific to institutional
investors**   No.

**Other controls imposed by securities
laws**   No.

Changes During 1999

Exchange arrangement   *February 11.* The dual exchange rate system was eliminated and the sucre was allowed to
float freely. The exchange rate arrangement of Ecuador was reclassified to the category
independently floating from the category crawling band.

Imports and import payments   *February 9.* Goods imported into Ecuador are subject to additional tariffs ranging from
2% to 10%.

Capital transactions

Provisions specific to commercial   *February 11.* The open foreign exchange position limit equivalent to 20% of technical
banks and other credit institutions   capital was eliminated.

Changes During 2000

Exchange arrangement   *March 13.* A full dollarization scheme was implemented, making the dollar legal tender.

                                    March 31. The exchange arrangement was reclassified to the category exchange arrange-
ment, no separate legal tender from the category independently floating.

Imports and import payments   *January 1.* The VAT on imports was increased to 12% from 10%.

Exports and export proceeds   *March 10.* The fee on crude oil exports was increased to $1.60 a barrel from $1.02 a barrel.

Capital transactions

Provisions specific to commercial   *January 27.* The reserve requirements for dollar-denominated and sucre-denominated ac-
banks and other credit institutions   counts were unified at 9%.

EGYPT

(Position as of December 31, 1999)

Status Under IMF Articles of Agreement

Article XIV	Yes.

Exchange Arrangement

Currency

The currency of Egypt is the Egyptian pound.

Exchange rate structure

Multiple

In addition to the market exchange rate, there is a special rate of LE 1.30 per $1 that is applied to transactions effected under the bilateral payment agreement with Sudan, and a rate of LE 0.3913 per $1 that is used for the liquidation of minimal balances related to terminated bilateral payment agreements.

Classification

Conventional pegged arrangement

The Egyptian pound is pegged to the dollar, which is used as the intervention currency by the Central Bank of Egypt (CBE). Nonbank foreign exchange dealers are permitted to operate in a free (kerb) market. They may buy and sell domestic and foreign means of payment (banknotes, coins, and traveler's checks) on their own account. These transactions may be conducted either in cash or through their accounts maintained with authorized banks in Egypt. In addition, authorized nonbank dealers may broker any foreign exchange operation and transaction, except transfers to and from the country, on the accounts of their bank or nonbank customers. The spread between the CBE buying and selling rates for foreign exchange is about 0.50%.

Exchange tax

No.

Exchange subsidy

No.

Forward exchange market

Authorized commercial banks are permitted to conduct forward foreign exchange transactions for their own account. No prior approval by the CBE is required, and the banks are free to determine the rates applied for forward transactions.

Arrangements for Payments and Receipts

Prescription of currency requirements

For countries with which indemnity agreements concerning compensation for nationalized property are in force, certain settlements are made through special accounts in Egyptian pounds with the CBE. The balances of these accounts are minimal. Suez Canal dues are expressed in SDRs and are paid by debiting free accounts in foreign currency. Settlements with Sudan are made in accordance with the terms of the bilateral agreement.

Payment arrangements

Bilateral payment arrangements

Operative

There is an agreement with Sudan.

Inoperative

There is an agreement with Russia to settle debts between Egypt and the Baltic countries and the other countries of the FSU.

Regional arrangements

Egypt is a member of the COMESA.

Barter agreements and open accounts

Yes.

Administration of control

Banks are authorized to execute foreign exchange transactions within the framework of a general authorization without obtaining specific exchange control approval.

International security restrictions

In accordance with UN sanctions

Restrictions exist against Libya.

Payment arrears	There are limited technical payment arrears with certain non–Paris Club creditors.
Official	Yes.
Private	Yes.
Controls on trade in gold (coins and/or bullion)	
Controls on domestic ownership and/or trade	Banks are not authorized to deal or speculate, on their own or customers' accounts, in precious metals.
Controls on exports and imports of banknotes	
On exports	
Domestic currency	Travelers may take out up to LE 1,000.
On imports	
Domestic currency	Persons arriving in Egypt may import up to LE 1,000.

Resident Accounts

Foreign exchange accounts permitted	Yes.
Held domestically	Yes.
Held abroad	Yes.
Accounts in domestic currency convertible into foreign currency	Balances may be converted through the foreign exchange market.

Nonresident Accounts

Foreign exchange accounts permitted	"Free accounts" may be opened in the name of any entity. These accounts may be credited with transfers of convertible currencies from abroad and transfers from other similar accounts, foreign banknotes (convertible currencies), and interest earned on these accounts. These accounts may be debited for transfers abroad, transfers to other similar accounts, withdrawals in foreign banknotes by the owner or others, and for payments in Egypt.
Domestic currency accounts	Yes.
Convertible into foreign currency	Yes.
Blocked accounts	No.

Imports and Import Payments

Foreign exchange budget	No.
Financing requirements for imports	No.
Documentation requirements for release of foreign exchange for imports	
Letters of credit	On March 2, 1999, margins for LCs were increased to 100% from 10%.
Import licenses and other nontariff measures	
Negative list	Most items may be imported freely.
Import taxes and/or tariffs	Products are classified into seven groups for customs purposes, with tariff rates ranging from 5% to 50% (with several exceptions). Surcharges at rates of 2% and 3% apply to most imports.
State import monopoly	No.

Exports and Export Proceeds

Repatriation requirements	No.
Financing requirements	No.
Documentation requirements	No.
Export licenses	
Without quotas	Exports of raw hides are restricted.
Export taxes	No.

Payments for Invisible Transactions and Current Transfers

Controls on these transfers	No.

Proceeds from Invisible Transactions and Current Transfers

Repatriation requirements	Foreign exchange earned abroad may be held indefinitely abroad or in local free accounts.
Restrictions on use of funds	No.

Capital Transactions

Controls on capital and money market instruments

On capital market securities

Shares or other securities of a participating nature

Sale or issue locally by nonresidents

There are no controls under the Foreign Exchange Law and Regulations on the issue of securities in the country by nonresidents. Trading in securities denominated in foreign currencies must be settled in foreign currencies. The foreign exchange market may be used for transferring proceeds associated with the sale of both Egyptian securities and foreign securities.

Bonds or other debt securities

Sale or issue locally by nonresidents

Prior approval of the Capital Market Authority is required for issuing bonds.

Controls on derivatives and other instruments

Derivatives do not exist in the Egyptian market.

Controls on credit operations

Commercial credits

To residents from nonresidents

No controls are applied if the maturity of the commercial credits is one year or less and if these credits are received by the private sector. Ministries, governmental administrations, public authorities, and public sector companies are all required to refer to the CBE when borrowing from abroad in convertible currencies, in order to register loans of more than one year. If external loans are used to finance capital goods or projects, such a transaction falls under the state investment plan.

Controls on direct investment

Inward direct investment

There are no general controls, but nonbank companies of foreign exchange dealers should be owned entirely by Egyptians.

Controls on liquidation of direct investment

No.

Controls on real estate transactions

Purchase locally by nonresidents   Yes.

Sale locally by nonresidents   Yes.

Controls on personal capital   No.
movements

Provisions specific to commercial
banks and other credit institutions

Differential treatment of deposit   Yes.
accounts in foreign exchange

   Reserve requirements   Deposits in foreign currencies held by either nationals or foreign nationals are subject to a 10% requirement (the interest-free reserve ratio requirement of deposits in Egyptian pounds is 15%), which must be deposited with the CBE at LIBOR.

   Liquid asset requirements   The requirement for assets in foreign currencies is 25%, and 20% for assets in Egyptian pounds.

Investment regulations

   Abroad by banks   All banks operating in Egypt (except branches of foreign banks) are prohibited from depositing or having investment securities worth more than 40% of their capital base or 10% of their total investment abroad, whichever is lower, with a foreign correspondent bank. According to the Banking Law, all banks operating in Egypt are prohibited from owning shares exceeding 40% of issued capital in joint-stock companies, locally or abroad. In addition, the face value of the shares owned by the bank in these companies may not exceed the value of the bank's issued capital and reserves.

   In banks by nonresidents   Shareholdings by residents or nonresidents in any bank in Egypt that exceed 10% of the bank's capital require prior approval from the CBE Board of Directors.

Open foreign exchange position limits   The limits are (1) for each currency (local or foreign): 10% of Tier I and Tier II capital; (2) for total long or short positions: 20% of Tier I and Tier II capital; and (3) total foreign assets to total foreign liabilities, or vice versa, not to exceed 105%.

   On resident assets and liabilities   Yes.

   On nonresident assets and liabilities   Yes.

Provisions specific to institutional
investors

Limits (max.) on securities issued by   Yes.
nonresidents and on portfolio invested
abroad

Limits (max.) on portfolio invested   Yes.
abroad

Limits (min.) on portfolio invested   Yes.
locally

Other controls imposed by securities   Yes.
laws

Changes During 1999

Imports and import payments   *March 2.* Margins for LCs were increased to 100% from 10%.

EL SALVADOR

(Position as of December 31, 1999)

Status Under IMF Articles of Agreement

Article VIII	Date of acceptance: November 6, 1946.

Exchange Arrangement

Currency	The currency of El Salvador is the Salvadoran colón.
Other legal tender	Gold coins in denominations of C 25, C 50, C 100, C 200, and C 2,500 are legal tender, but do not circulate.
Exchange rate structure	Unitary.
Classification	
Conventional pegged arrangement	The Central Reserve Bank (CRB) publishes the daily exchange rates, which are applied to its transactions with the public sector, and the calculation of tax obligations. These exchange rates are the simple average of the exchange rates set by commercial banks and exchange houses on the previous working day. Since January 1, 1994, the CRB has intervened in the foreign exchange market to maintain the exchange rate at C 8.75 per $1.
Exchange tax	No.
Exchange subsidy	No.
Forward exchange market	No.

Arrangements for Payments and Receipts

Prescription of currency requirements	No.
Payment arrangements	
Regional arrangements	El Salvador is a member of the CACM.
Administration of control	The CRB administers exchange regulations. All private sector foreign exchange transactions are delegated to the commercial banks and exchange houses. The Centro de Trámites de Exportación issues certificates of origin and health when foreign importers require them. The Salvadoran Coffee Council issues permits freely to private sector traders to conduct external or domestic trade in coffee.
International security restrictions	No.
Payment arrears	No.
Controls on trade in gold (coins and/or bullion)	
Controls on domestic ownership and/or trade	Yes.
Controls on external trade	Yes.
Controls on exports and imports of banknotes	No.

Resident Accounts

Foreign exchange accounts permitted	Yes.

Held domestically	Balances on these accounts may be sold to the commercial banks and exchange houses or used to make payments abroad without restriction. Transfers of funds between these accounts are not restricted, but the commercial banks are required to submit periodic reports to the CRB on the use of such accounts.
Held abroad	Yes.
Accounts in domestic currency convertible into foreign currency	Yes.

Nonresident Accounts

Foreign exchange accounts permitted	Yes.
Domestic currency accounts	Yes.
Convertible into foreign currency	Yes.
Blocked accounts	No.

Imports and Import Payments

Foreign exchange budget	No.
Financing requirements for imports	No.
Documentation requirements for release of foreign exchange for imports	No.
Import licenses and other nontariff measures	
Positive list	Import permits issued by the Ministry of Economy are required for gasoline, kerosene, fuel oil, asphalt, propane and butane gas, cloth and jute sacks, sugar, and molasses.
Import taxes and/or tariffs	Most import tariffs range up to 10%, although some products are subject to higher tariffs, such as automobiles, 25–30%; alcoholic beverages, 30%; and textiles and luxury goods, 20%. There are no tariffs on capital goods and selected inputs. Exporters of nontraditional products to markets outside Central America receive duty drawbacks on imported raw materials equivalent to 6% of f.o.b. value of exports. In line with commitments under the CACM, on July 31, 1999, tariffs on imports of intermediate goods from outside the Central American region were lowered to 5–10%, and those on consumption goods were lowered to 15%.
State import monopoly	No.

Exports and Export Proceeds

Repatriation requirements	No.
Financing requirements	No.
Documentation requirements	No.
Export licenses	All exports must be registered, with the exception of exports amounting to less than $5,000, unless the product specifications call for such certification. Export permits, issued by the MOF, are required for diesel fuel, liquefied petroleum gas, and gray cement.
Without quotas	Yes.
Export taxes	No.

Payments for Invisible Transactions and Current Transfers

Controls on these transfers	No.

Proceeds from Invisible Transactions and Current Transfers

Repatriation requirements	No.
Restrictions on use of funds	No.

Capital Transactions

Controls on capital and money market instruments	No.
Controls on derivatives and other instruments	No.
Controls on credit operations	No.
Controls on direct investment	
Inward direct investment	Foreign direct investments and inflows of capital with a maturity of more than one year must be registered with the Ministry of the Economy for statistical purposes. Certain minimum capital requirements exist for businesses owned by foreign residents and those having foreign resident shareholders.
Controls on liquidation of direct investment	No.
Controls on real estate transactions	No.
Controls on personal capital movements	No.
Provisions specific to commercial banks and other credit institutions	The new Banking Law was approved on September 2, 1999.
Borrowing abroad	External borrowing by financial institutions is subject to a reserve requirement of 10%. The CRB remunerates reserves on short-term financial system external borrowing at the average LIBOR in the last eight weeks.
Open foreign exchange position limits	The limit on the net foreign asset position of commercial banks is 10% of capital and reserves.
On resident assets and liabilities	Yes.
On nonresident assets and liabilities	Yes.
Provisions specific to institutional investors	No.
Other controls imposed by securities laws	No.

Changes During 1999

Imports and import payments	*July 31.* Tariffs of imports of intermediate goods from outside the Central American region were lowered to 5–10%, and those on consumption goods were lowered to 15%.
Capital transactions	
Provisions specific to commercial banks and other credit institutions	*September 2.* The new Banking Law was approved.

EQUATORIAL GUINEA

(Position as of December 31, 1999)

Status Under IMF Articles of Agreement

Article VIII   Date of acceptance: June 1, 1996.

Exchange Arrangement

Currency   The currency of Equatorial Guinea is the CFA franc.

Exchange rate structure   Unitary.

Classification

Exchange arrangement with no sepa-   The CFA franc is pegged to the euro, the intervention currency, at the fixed rate of
rate legal tender   CFAF 100 per €0.1524. Exchange transactions in euros between the BEAC and
                                       commercial banks take place at the same rate. Buying and selling rates for certain
                                       other foreign currencies are also officially posted, with quotations based on the fixed
                                       rate for the euro and the rates in the Paris exchange market for the currencies concerned.
                                       A commission of 0.5% is levied on transfers to countries that are not members of the
                                       BEAC, except for transfers in respect of central and local government operations,
                                       payments for imports covered by a duly issued license and domiciled with a bank,
                                       scheduled repayments on loans properly obtained abroad, travel allowances paid by the
                                       government and its agencies for official missions, and payments of insurance premiums.

Exchange tax   No.

Exchange subsidy   No.

Forward exchange market   No.

Arrangements for Payments and Receipts

Prescription of currency   Because Equatorial Guinea is linked to the French Treasury through an Operations
requirements   Account, settlements with France, Monaco, and other Operations Account countries
                                 (WAEMU and CAEMC members and the Comoros) are made in French francs or
                                 the currency of any other Operations Account country. Settlements with all other
                                 countries are usually made through correspondent banks in France in the currencies
                                 of those countries or in francs through foreign accounts.

Payment arrangements   Yes.

Regional arrangements   An Operations Account is maintained with the French Treasury that links Operations
                                 Account countries. All purchases or sales of foreign currencies or euros against CFA
                                 francs are ultimately settled through a debit or credit to the Operations Account.

Administration of control   Exchange control is administered by the Directorate General of Exchange Control
                                 (DNCC) of the MOF. Exchange transactions relating to all countries must be effected
                                 through authorized banks.

International security restrictions

In accordance with UN sanctions Yes.

Payment arrears

Official   Yes.

**Controls on trade in gold (coins
and/or bullion)**

Controls on domestic ownership and/or   Residents are free to hold, acquire, and dispose of gold jewelry. They must have the
trade   approval of the Directorate of Mines to hold gold in any other form. Approval is not
                                         normally given because there are no industrial users in Equatorial Guinea. Newly

mined gold must be declared to the Directorate of Mines, which authorizes either its exportation or its sale in the domestic market.

Controls on external trade
Exports are allowed only to France. Imports and exports of gold require prior authorization from the Directorate of Mines and the MOF; authorization is seldom granted for imports. Exempt from this requirement are (1) imports and exports by or on behalf of the monetary authorities, and (2) imports and exports of manufactured articles containing a small quantity of gold (such as gold-filled or gold-plated articles). Both licensed and exempt imports of gold are subject to customs declaration.

Controls on exports and imports of banknotes

On exports

Domestic currency
Residents traveling for tourism or business purposes to countries in the CFA franc zone are allowed to take out BEAC banknotes up to CFAF 2 million; amounts in excess of this limit may be taken out in other means of payment.

Foreign currency
All resident travelers, regardless of destination, must declare in writing all means of payment at their disposal at the time of departure. The reexportation of foreign banknotes is allowed up to the equivalent of CFAF 250,000; the reexportation of foreign banknotes above this ceiling requires documentation demonstrating either the importation of foreign banknotes or their purchase against other means of payment registered in the name of the traveler or through the use of nonresident deposits lodged in local banks.

On imports

Foreign currency
Resident and nonresident travelers may bring in any amount of banknotes and coins issued by the BEAC, the Bank of France, or a bank of issue maintaining an Operations Account with the French Treasury, as well as any amount of foreign banknotes and coins (except gold coins) of countries outside the Operations Account area.

Resident Accounts

Foreign exchange accounts permitted
Yes.

Held domestically
No.

Held abroad
These accounts may opened, but approval is required.

Accounts in domestic currency convertible into foreign currency
Yes.

Nonresident Accounts

Foreign exchange accounts permitted
Accounts in foreign currency include accounts in dollars. Accounts in euros are treated identically to accounts in domestic currency. The regulations pertaining to nonresident accounts are based on regulations applied in France. These accounts are permitted; however, approval is required, except for accounts in euros.

Domestic currency accounts
Because the BEAC suspended in 1993 the repurchase of its banknotes circulating outside the territories of the CFA franc zone, BEAC banknotes received by the foreign correspondents of authorized banks and mailed to the BEAC agency in Equatorial Guinea by the Bank of France or the BCEAO may not be credited to foreign accounts in francs.

Convertible into foreign currency
These accounts may be converted, but prior approval is required.

Blocked accounts
n.a.

Imports and Import Payments

Foreign exchange budget
No.

Financing requirements for imports	Certified bank documents are required.
Minimum financing requirements	Yes.
Documentation requirements for release of foreign exchange for imports	
Domiciliation requirements	All import transactions of which the value exceeds CFAF 500,000 must be domiciled with an authorized bank. Import transactions by residents involving goods for use outside Equatorial Guinea must be domiciled with a bank in the country of final destination.
Letters of credit	Yes.
Import licenses and other nontariff measures	No import licenses are required, except for imports of gold.
Negative list	Certain goods are prohibited for security, health, or safety reasons.
Import taxes and/or tariffs	Equatorial Guinea applies the common duty rates of the UDEAC on imports from non-members (5% for basic necessities, 10% for raw materials and capital goods, 20% for intermediate and miscellaneous goods, and 30% for consumer goods), except for higher rates imposed on a limited number of luxury goods (15% to 40%). Duties on imports from UDEAC members are set at 20% of those for imports from nonmembers. Fiscal duties and turnover taxes are also applied to imports.
State import monopoly	n.a.

Exports and Export Proceeds

Repatriation requirements	Proceeds from exports to all countries must be repatriated within 30 days of the payment date stipulated in the sales contract. Payments for exports must be made within 30 days of the arrival date of the merchandise at its destination.
Financing requirements	No.
Documentation requirements	
Letters of credit	Yes.
Guarantees	Yes.
Domiciliation	Export transactions valued at CFAF 50,000 or more must be domiciled with an authorized bank. Exports to all countries are subject to domiciliation requirements for the appropriate documents.
Export licenses	No.
Export taxes	No.

Payments for Invisible Transactions and Current Transfers

Controls on these transfers	Payments in excess of CFAF 500,000 for invisibles to France, Monaco, and the Operations Account countries require prior declaration but are permitted freely; those to other countries are subject to the approval of the MOF. Payments for invisibles related to trade are permitted freely when the basic trade transaction has been approved or does not require authorization. Transfers of income accruing to nonresidents in the form of profits, dividends, and royalties are also permitted freely when the basic transaction has been approved.
Trade-related payments	
Quantitative limits	Except in the case of expatriates working in Equatorial Guinea on a temporary basis, payments of insurance premiums of up to CFAF 50,000 to foreign countries are permitted; larger amounts may be authorized by the DNCC.
Indicative limits/bona fide test	Applied to the payment of freight and insurance costs.

| Investment-related payments | Information is not available on the payment of amortization of loans or depreciation of direct investments. |

Quantitative limits

The transfer of rental income from real property owned in Equatorial Guinea by foreign nationals is permitted up to 50% of the income declared for taxation purposes, net of tax. Remittances for current repair and management of real property abroad are limited to the equivalent of CFAF 200,000 every two years.

Indicative limits/bona fide test

Applied to the payment of profit and dividends.

Payments for travel

Prior approval

Yes.

Quantitative limits

Residents traveling for tourism or business purposes to countries in the CFA franc zone are allowed to take out BEAC banknotes up to CFAF 2 million; amounts in excess of this limit may be taken out in other means of payment. The allowances for travel to countries outside the CFA franc zone are subject to the following regulations: (1) for tourist travel, CFAF 100,000 a day, up to CFAF 2 million a trip; (2) for business travel, CFAF 250,000 a day, up to CFAF 5 million a trip; (3) allowances in excess of these limits are subject to the authorization of the MOF or, by delegation, the BEAC; and (4) the use of credit cards, which must be issued by resident financial intermediaries and approved by the MOF, is limited to the ceilings indicated above for tourist and business travel. Returning resident travelers are required to declare all means of payment in their possession upon arrival at customs and to surrender within eight days all means of payment exceeding the equivalent of CFAF 25,000. All resident travelers, regardless of destination, must declare in writing all means of payment at their disposal at the time of departure. The reexportation by non-resident travelers of means of payment other than banknotes issued abroad and registered in the name of the nonresident traveler is not restricted, subject to documentation that they had been purchased with funds drawn from a foreign account in CFA francs or with other foreign exchange.

Indicative limits/bona fide test

Yes.

Personal payments

Prior approval

Yes.

Quantitative limits

Yes.

Indicative limits/bona fide test

Yes.

Foreign workers' wages

Prior approval

Yes.

Quantitative limits

The limit is determined as a function of the salary.

Indicative limits/bona fide test

Yes.

Credit card use abroad

The use of credit cards, which must be issued by resident financial intermediaries and approved by the MOF, is limited to the ceilings for tourist and business travel.

Prior approval

Yes.

Quantitative limits

Yes.

Indicative limits/bona fide test

Yes.

Other payments

Prior approval

Yes.

Quantitative limits

Yes.

Indicative limits/bona fide test

Yes.

Proceeds from Invisible Transactions and Current Transfers

Repatriation requirements   Proceeds from transactions in invisibles with France, Monaco, and the Operations Account countries may be retained. All amounts due from residents of other countries in respect of services and all income earned in those countries from foreign assets must be collected within a month of the due date.

Surrender requirements   Proceeds earned in countries outside the franc zone must be surrendered within a month of collection if received in foreign currency.

Restrictions on use of funds   n.a.

Capital Transactions

Controls on capital and money market instruments   Capital movements between Equatorial Guinea and France, Monaco, and the Operations Account countries are free of exchange control. Capital transfers to all other countries require exchange control approval and are restricted, but capital receipts from such countries are permitted freely.

On capital market securities

  Shares or other securities of a participating nature

    Purchase abroad by residents   Yes.

    Sale or issue abroad by residents   Yes.

On money market instruments

  Purchase abroad by residents   Yes.

  Sale or issue abroad by residents   Yes.

On collective investment securities

  Purchase abroad by residents   Yes.

  Sale or issue abroad by residents   Yes.

Controls on derivatives and other instruments

Purchase locally by nonresidents   Yes.

Sale or issue locally by nonresidents   Yes.

Purchase abroad by residents   Yes.

Sale or issue abroad by residents   Yes.

Controls on credit operations

Commercial credits

  To residents from nonresidents   Yes.

Financial credits

  To residents from nonresidents   Yes.

Guarantees, sureties, and financial backup facilities

  To residents from nonresidents   Yes.

Controls on direct investment

Outward direct investment   Yes.

Inward direct investment   Yes.

Controls on liquidation of direct investment	A bona fide test is applied.
Controls on real estate transactions	
Purchase abroad by residents	Yes.
Purchase locally by nonresidents	Yes.
Sale locally by nonresidents	Yes.
Controls on personal capital movements	
Transfer of gambling and prize earnings	Yes.
Provisions specific to commercial banks and other credit institutions	
Borrowing abroad	Yes.
Maintenance of accounts abroad	Yes.
Lending to nonresidents (financial or commercial credits)	Yes.
Lending locally in foreign exchange	Yes.
Differential treatment of deposit accounts in foreign exchange	
Reserve requirements	Yes.
Liquid asset requirements	Yes.
Investment regulations	
Open foreign exchange position limits	Yes.
Provisions specific to institutional investors	
Limits (max.) on portfolio invested abroad	Yes.
Limits (min.) on portfolio invested locally	Yes.
Other controls imposed by securities laws	n.a.

Changes During 1999

Exchange arrangement	*January 1.* The CFA franc peg to the French franc was replaced with a peg to the euro.

ERITREA

(Position as of January 31, 2000)

Status Under IMF Articles of Agreement

Article XIV	Yes.

Exchange Arrangement

Currency
The currency of Eritrea is the Eritrean nakfa.

Exchange rate structure
Unitary.

Classification

Independently floating
The exchange rate for the Eritrea nakfa is determined freely in the foreign exchange market. However, the dealers are required to report their prevailing exchange rates to the Bank of Eritrea (BE) daily, and the midpoint of the reported rates is used to set a daily reference rate.

Exchange tax
The BE prescribes a commission of 0.25% for purchases of foreign exchange and 0.75% for sales of foreign exchange, except for banknote transactions. Authorized dealers are permitted, but not required, to levy a service charge of up to 0.25% for buying and 0.75% for selling for their own account.

Exchange subsidy
No.

Forward exchange market
No.

Arrangements for Payments and Receipts

Prescription of currency requirements
All transactions with Ethiopia are settled in convertible currencies.

Payment arrangements

Regional arrangements
Eritrea is a member of the COMESA.

Clearing agreements
A clearing arrangement exists between the members of the COMESA.

Administration of control
The BE oversees all foreign exchange transactions of the authorized dealers and issues dealers' licenses. It may from time to time issue regulations, directives, and instructions on foreign exchange matters. The National Licensing Office issues licenses for importers, exporters, and commercial agents, and the Ministry of Trade and Industry regulates foreign investments. The Asmara Chamber of Commerce issues certificates of origin for exports.

International security restrictions
No.

Payment arrears
No.

Controls on trade in gold (coins and/or bullion)

Controls on domestic ownership and/or trade
Authorization from the Ministry of Energy and Mines is required for ownership or possession of gold or other precious metals or ores. Residents may own gold jewelry without restrictions.

Controls on exports and imports of banknotes
Travelers are not required to declare their foreign currency holdings upon entry or departure.

Resident Accounts

Foreign exchange accounts permitted
Yes.

Held domestically	Yes.
Held abroad	The opening of these accounts is restricted to resident banks. Nonbank residents may not open accounts abroad, unless specifically authorized by the BE.
Accounts in domestic currency convertible into foreign currency	Yes.

Nonresident Accounts

Foreign exchange accounts permitted	Resident Eritreans working temporarily abroad may maintain nonresident dollar accounts in Eritrea.
Domestic currency accounts	Available only to members of the diplomatic community; welfare organizations; nongovernmental organizations and their personnel; as well as joint ventures and other business firms that invest their capital, wholly or partially, in foreign exchange.
Convertible into foreign currency	Yes.
Blocked accounts	No.

Imports and Import Payments

Foreign exchange budget	No.
Financing requirements for imports	Most imports financed with official foreign exchange are effected under LCs or on a cash-against-documents basis. Suppliers' credits must be registered with the BE.
Advance import deposits	Only for LC type of imports.
Documentation requirements for release of foreign exchange for imports	
Letters of credit	Yes.
Import licenses and other nontariff measures	
Positive list	All commodities may be freely imported with some exceptions.
Negative list	Yes.
Open general licenses	All importers must have a valid trade license issued by the National Licensing Office.
Import taxes and/or tariffs	
Taxes collected through the exchange system	A commission of 2% is collected on imports that do not require official foreign exchange and are not aid-funded (franco valuta imports).
State import monopoly	The imports of military materials, weapons, armaments, and the like are to be conducted by the state.

Exports and Export Proceeds

Repatriation requirements	All export proceeds must be repatriated within 90 days of shipment; where justified, this deadline may be extended by another 90 days.
Surrender requirements	No.
Financing requirements	Exports may be made under LCs on an advance-payment basis or on a consignment basis.
Documentation requirements	All exports require documentation. Certain commodities require clearance from specific government bodies (e.g., the Eritrean Institute of Standards). In particular, livestock and cereals require permission from the Ministry of Agriculture, and marine products require permission from the Ministry of Marine Resources.

Letters of credit	Yes.
Guarantees	Yes.
Preshipment inspection	Yes.
Export licenses	Exporters must be licensed by the National Licensing Office.
Without quotas	Yes.
Export taxes	No.

Payments for Invisible Transactions and Current Transfers

| **Controls on these transfers** | Effective January 1, 2000, all restrictions on payments for invisible transactions and current transfers were abolished. |
| Investment-related payments | Petroleum contractors and subcontractors may freely transfer abroad funds accruing from petroleum operations and may pay subcontractors and expatriate staff abroad. |

Proceeds from Invisible Transactions and Current Transfers

| **Repatriation requirements** | No. |
| **Restrictions on use of funds** | No. |

Capital Transactions

Controls on capital and money market instruments	
On capital market securities	
Shares or other securities of a participating nature	
Purchase locally by nonresidents	Yes.
Purchase abroad by residents	Authorized banks may acquire securities with the approval of the BE.
On money market instruments	
Purchase abroad by residents	Yes.
Controls on derivatives and other instruments	n.a.
Controls on credit operations	
Commercial credits	
To residents from nonresidents	Yes.
Financial credits	
To residents from nonresidents	Authorized banks may borrow abroad or overdraw their correspondent accounts abroad with the approval of the BE.
Controls on direct investment	
Inward direct investment	Foreign direct investment is permitted in all sectors. However, domestic retail and whole-sale trade, and import and commission agencies are open to foreign investors only when Eritrea has a bilateral agreement of reciprocity with the country of the investor; this latter condition may be waived by the government. Approved investments and their subsequent expansion are exempted from customs duties and sales tax for capital goods and spare parts associated with the investment. There are no exemptions from income tax.

Controls on liquidation of direct investment	For investments certified under the Investment Proclamation, foreign investors may freely remit proceeds received from the liquidation of investment and/or expansion, and payments received from the sale or transfer of shares.
Controls on real estate transactions	No.
Controls on personal capital movements	
Loans	
By residents to nonresidents	Yes.
To residents from nonresidents	Yes.
Provisions specific to commercial banks and other credit institutions	
Borrowing abroad	Yes.
Lending to nonresidents (financial or commercial credits)	Yes.
Lending locally in foreign exchange	Yes.
Investment regulations	Yes.
Provisions specific to institutional investors	n.a.
Other controls imposed by securities laws	n.a.

Changes During 1999

No significant changes occurred in the exchange and trade system.

Changes During 2000

Payments for invisible transactions and current transfers	*January 1.* All restrictions were abolished.

ESTONIA

(Position as of January 31, 2000)

Status Under IMF Articles of Agreement

Article VIII	Date of acceptance: August 15, 1994.

Exchange Arrangement

Currency	The currency of Estonia is the Estonian kroon.
Exchange rate structure	Unitary.
Classification	
Currency board arrangement	The exchange rate of the kroon is pegged to the deutsche mark at the rate of EEK 8 per DM 1. This implies an implicit peg to the euro at the rate of EEK 15.6466 per €1. The Bank of Estonia (BOE) provides commercial banks with the possibility of buying or selling foreign exchange to adjust their kroon liquidity. All transactions are initiated by commercial banks. For licensed credit institutions, the BOE is obliged to exchange euros and the other EU currencies, Japanese yen, and U.S. dollars for Estonian krooni and vice versa without limits. There is no spread between the buying and selling rates of the Estonian kroon against the euro or the other EU currencies. Transactions in convertible currencies are freely effected by commercial banks who may freely quote their own exchange rates.
Exchange tax	No.
Exchange subsidy	No.
Forward exchange market	Yes.

Arrangements for Payments and Receipts

Prescription of currency requirements	Settlements with the Baltic countries, Russia, and the other countries of the FSU may be effected through a system of correspondent accounts maintained by the BOE with the respective central banks. Balances accrued in these accounts may in most cases be used freely by their holders to purchase either goods or services in the country concerned. In operating these accounts, the BOE acts as an intermediary only and does not convert any balances to krooni. Kroon balances held by the central banks of the Baltic countries, Russia, and the other countries of the FSU in their correspondent accounts are fully convertible without delay. No swing credits or overdraft facilities are provided by these arrangements.
Payment arrangements	
Bilateral payment arrangements	
Inoperative	Estonia has bilateral agreements with Armenia, Azerbaijan, Belarus, Kazakhstan, the Kyrgyz Republic, Latvia, Lithuania, Moldova, Russia, Tajikistan, Turkmenistan, Ukraine, and Uzbekistan. These agreements provide commercial banks with a facility to effect their payments with the country concerned through correspondent accounts maintained by the BOE with the respective central banks. Commercial banks in Estonia are free to open their own correspondent accounts with commercial banks in the Baltic countries, Russia, and the other countries of the FSU.
Administration of control	The BOE issues and enforces foreign exchange regulations. The MOF controls and monitors imports and exports, and licenses gold trading.
International security restrictions	No.
Payment arrears	Some external debt issues with Russia and certain other countries of the FSU are not yet settled.
Official	All external debt with Russia is official.

Controls on trade in gold (coins and/or bullion)

Controls on domestic ownership and/or trade	Yes.
Controls on external trade	International trade in gold is subject to licensing requirements administered by the MOF.
Controls on exports and imports of banknotes	No.

Resident Accounts

Foreign exchange accounts permitted	Yes.
Held domestically	Yes.
Held abroad	Yes.
Accounts in domestic currency convertible into foreign currency	Yes.

Nonresident Accounts

Foreign exchange accounts permitted	Yes.
Domestic currency accounts	Yes.
Convertible into foreign currency	Yes.
Blocked accounts	No.

Imports and Import Payments

Foreign exchange budget	No.
Financing requirements for imports	No.
Documentation requirements for release of foreign exchange for imports	No.
Import licenses and other nontariff measures	
Negative list	Yes.
Open general licenses	Open general licenses are required for the following goods: alcohol, medicinal products, precious metals and stones, and tobacco.
Licenses with quotas	Licenses or special permits are required for the import of the following goods: explosives; weapons; radio broadcast equipment; rare species of plants and animals and hunting trophies; goods subject to veterinary, food, and phytosanitary control; plant preservatives and fertilizers; narcotic drugs and psychotropic substances; equipment and means for recording of audiovisual production; lottery tickets; strategic goods; radioactive materials; motor vehicles; and dangerous and other waste products.
Import taxes and/or tariffs	Excise duties are levied on tobacco, alcohol, motor vehicles, fuel, and packaging materials. Imports are also subject to a state duty and a VAT of 18%, which is also levied on domestically produced goods.
	Effective January 1, 2000, the law on preferential customs duties came into force. According to the law, foodstuffs originating from third countries, such as those countries with which Estonia has not concluded a free trade agreement, are subject to customs duties. Free trade agreements have been concluded with the EFTA, the EU, the Czech Republic, the

Faroe Islands, Hungary, Latvia, Lithuania, Poland, the Slovak Republic, Slovenia, Turkey, and Ukraine.

State import monopoly	No.

Exports and Export Proceeds

Repatriation requirements	No.
Financing requirements	No.
Documentation requirements	No.
Export licenses	
Without quotas	Licenses or special permits are required for alcohol; tobacco and tobacco goods; items of cultural value; precious metals, precious stones, and articles containing these products; medicinal products; weapons; explosives; rare species of plants and animals and hunting trophies; goods subject to veterinary, food, and phytosanitary control; narcotic drugs and psychotropic substances; strategic goods; radioactive radiation sources; motor vehicles; and dangerous and other waste products.
Export taxes	No.

Payments for Invisible Transactions and Current Transfers

Controls on these transfers	No.

Proceeds from Invisible Transactions and Current Transfers

Repatriation requirements	No.
Restrictions on use of funds	No.

Capital Transactions

Controls on capital and money market instruments	No.
Controls on derivatives and other instruments	No.
Controls on credit operations	No.
Controls on direct investment	
Inward direct investment	According to the Foreign Investment Act, the government can decide in which fields to prohibit the establishment of an enterprise with foreign ownership or the participation of foreign investors. This is a latent restriction that is maintained only to be applied against third countries when needed.
	At present, foreign capital in the aviation sector may not exceed 49%. This control will be abolished upon accession to the EU.
Controls on liquidation of direct investment	No.
Controls on real estate transactions	
Purchase locally by nonresidents	This is subject to approval by the county governor concerned. Acquisition of real estate is prohibited in the following areas: the islands, except for the largest islands; and certain local municipalities bordering Russia.

Controls on personal capital movements

Gifts, endowments, inheritances, and legacies

   By residents to nonresidents   There is a control on the giving of real estate as a gift.

Provisions specific to commercial banks and other credit institutions

Borrowing abroad   Yes.

Differential treatment of deposit accounts held by nonresidents

   Reserve requirements   Net liabilities to foreign credit institutions are subject to a reserve requirement, but liabilities to domestic credit institutions are not. Financial guarantees provided by commercial banks to other financial institutions and nonresident credit institutions are subject to the mandatory reserve requirement.

Open foreign exchange position limits

   On resident assets and liabilities   Yes.

   On nonresident assets and liabilities   Yes.

Provisions specific to institutional investors

Limits (max.) on portfolio invested abroad   Investment funds are restricted from investing their assets in nongovernmental securities of certain countries. No controls are applied to the EU or the EEA countries. In respect to other countries, investment is permitted only in accordance with the respective list made by the MOF.

Investments in foreign real estate may not exceed 25% of total assets.

Other controls imposed by securities laws   No.

Changes During 1999

No significant changes occurred in the exchange and trade system.

Changes During 2000

Imports and import payments   *January 1.* The law on preferential customs duties came into force. It stipulates that food-stuffs originating from third countries, that is, those countries with which Estonia has not concluded a free trade agreement, are subject to customs duties.

ETHIOPIA

(Position as of December 31, 1999)

Status Under IMF Articles of Agreement

Article XIV	Yes.

Exchange Arrangement

Currency
The currency of Ethiopia is the Ethiopian birr.

Exchange rate structure
Unitary.

Classification

Managed floating with no pre-announced path for the exchange rate
The official exchange rate of the birr against the dollar is the marginal rate (i.e., the lowest successful bid) determined in weekly auctions for announced quantities of foreign exchange, as determined by the National Bank of Ethiopia (NBE). An interbank market for trading domestic and foreign exchange funds is operational. A wholesale foreign exchange market replaced the retail auction. Foreign exchange bureaus are allowed to engage in all approved spot/cash external current account transactions.

Exchange tax
Authorized dealers must observe a prescribed commission of 1.5% on selling, which accrues to the NBE, and they may levy service charges of up to 0.25% on buying and 1% on selling for their own accounts.

Exchange subsidy
No.

Forward exchange market
No.

Arrangements for Payments and Receipts

Prescription of currency requirements
Yes.

Payment arrangements

Regional arrangements
Ethiopia is a member of the COMESA.

Clearing agreements
Payments may be made within the framework of COMESA.

Administration of control
The NBE transferred the responsibility for determining compliance of buyers and sellers of foreign exchange with import and export licensing requirements and foreign exchange regulations to commercial banks.

International security restrictions
n.a.

Payment arrears
n.a.

Controls on trade in gold (coins and/or bullion)
Import and export exchange licenses are required by the NBE.

Controls on domestic ownership and/or trade
The ownership of personal jewelry is permitted. However, unless authorized by the Ministry of Mines and Energy, the possession or custody of 50 ounces or more of raw or refined gold or platinum, or gold or platinum in the form of nuggets, ore, or bullion, is not permitted. Effective December 30, 1999, private companies may directly export newly minted gold, silver, and jewelry.

Controls on external trade
Licenses to import or export gold in any form are issued by the NBE.

Controls on exports and imports of banknotes

On exports

  Domestic currency
Travelers may take out Br 100 in Ethiopian banknotes.

Foreign currency	Except for short-term visitors, travelers must have an authorization to reexport foreign exchange. Reconversion of birr to foreign exchange up to $150 may be made without the presentation of any documentary evidence; for amounts exceeding $150, the presentation of authenticated documentary evidence indicating that the equivalent amount of foreign exchange was lawfully converted into local currency is required.
On imports	
Domestic currency	Travelers may bring in Br 100 in Ethiopian currency.

Resident Accounts

Foreign exchange accounts permitted	Commercial banks may open foreign exchange retention accounts for eligible exporters of goods and recipients of inward remittances without prior approval from the NBE.
Held domestically	Exporters of services may open foreign exchange retention accounts with the NBE's approval.
Held abroad	No.
Accounts in domestic currency convertible into foreign currency	No.

Nonresident Accounts

Foreign exchange accounts permitted	Deposits to these accounts must be made in foreign exchange. Balances may be transferred freely abroad, and transfers between nonresident accounts do not require prior approval. Members of the diplomatic community must use transferable or nontransferable birr accounts for payment of local expenses. Joint ventures and individual foreign investors are permitted to open foreign currency accounts or transferable or nontransferable birr accounts to purchase raw materials, equipment, and spare parts not available in Ethiopia. All clients deal directly with commercial banks without the NBE's involvement. Ethiopian nonresidents may maintain interest-bearing accounts. Non-Ethiopians may not hold foreign exchange accounts, except diplomatic bodies and foreign investors. These accounts may only be current accounts. Approval from the NBE is required.
Domestic currency accounts	Yes.
Convertible into foreign currency	Approval is required for the conversion of the balances on nonresident, nontransferable birr accounts into foreign currency accounts.
Blocked accounts	No.

Imports and Import Payments

Foreign exchange budget	No.
Financing requirements for imports	Imports of goods on the negative list (i.e., used clothing) are ineligible for the foreign exchange auctions. Importation under suppliers' credits requires prior approval of the terms and conditions of the credit, and such imports are allowed only for individuals or enterprises engaged in export activities and/or who generate foreign exchange.
Documentation requirements for release of foreign exchange for imports	Final invoices that separately show f.o.b. cost and freight charges and nonnegotiable bills of lading are required. Exchange licenses may be obtained when a valid importer's license is presented. Applications for exchange licenses must be accompanied by information on costs and payment terms and evidence that adequate insurance has been arranged with the Ethiopian Insurance Corporation. Insurance may be arranged with any legally registered insurance company (private insurance companies included), not necessarily with the Ethiopian Insurance Corporation alone.
Domiciliation requirements	Importers are required to insure their goods with local insurance companies.

Preshipment inspection	Effective June 15, 1999, the system of preshipment inspection was introduced.
Letters of credit	n.r.
Import licenses used as exchange licenses	Yes.
Import licenses and other nontariff measures	Imports by federal and regional offices are exempted from the import licensing requirement.
Negative list	The list includes used clothing and items restricted for reasons of health and security. Imports of cars and other vehicles require prior authorization from the Ministry of Transport and Communications.
Open general licenses	n.r.
Import taxes and/or tariffs	The item-weighted average tariff rate is 19% and the trade-weighted average 14.9%.
State import monopoly	No.

Exports and Export Proceeds

Repatriation requirements	Yes.
Surrender requirements	Exporters may retain 10% of their export proceeds in foreign exchange for an indefinite period. The remaining balance may be retained for a period of 28 days after which it must be converted into local currency by the customer's bank using the NBE's marginal rate of the week in the wholesale auction.
Financing requirements	No.
Documentation requirements	All exporters must prove to the NBE that they have repatriated 100% of previous exports before being allowed to export again.
Guarantees	Effective January 18, 1999, an Export Credit Guarantee Scheme was established.
Export licenses	
Without quotas	All exports are processed by commercial banks, with the exception of coffee exports.
With quotas	Exports of raw hides and skins are regulated or prohibited until the needs of local factories are met.
Export taxes	The exportation of coffee is subject to a customs tax of 6.5% of the exported value.

Payments for Invisible Transactions and Current Transfers

Controls on these transfers	
Trade-related payments	
Prior approval	Approval is given by the commercial banks.
Quantitative limits	n.r.
Indicative limits/bona fide test	Verification of documentary evidence is required for unloading, storage, and administrative expenses. For commissions, verification by the NBE of contractual agreement between parties is required.
Investment-related payments	
Prior approval	After paying local taxes, foreign companies may remit dividends on their invested and reinvested capital in any currency. Prior approval for amortization of loans or depreciation of direct investments is required mainly for government transactions made through the MOF.
Indicative limits/bona fide test	These are subject to an assessment based on the NBE's determined criteria. Verification of contractual agreement between parties by the NBE is required.

Payments for travel

Quantitative limits There are no limits for persons traveling abroad for business purposes related to imports or exports. Persons traveling for holiday purposes may purchase up to $1,200 directly from foreign exchange bureaus operated by commercial banks. For government travel, the allowance amounts vary by country and foreign currency, based on the cost of living.

Indicative limits/bona fide test Yes.

Personal payments

Prior approval Yes.

Quantitative limits There are no limits for medical and studies abroad costs. Foreign nationals may remit up to 100% of their net earnings for the education of their children. Government students are granted foreign exchange up to the requirement of the employer.

Indicative limits/bona fide test For transfers of pensions, proof of financial emolument and domicile are required. Verification by a medical board and the Ministry of Health is required for medical payments.

Foreign workers' wages

Prior approval Yes.

Quantitative limits Foreign contractual employees of the government may take out foreign exchange during the terms of their service and upon final departure, not to exceed their earnings. However, the value of fees, accommodations, gratuities, accumulated leave pay, and similar benefits may not be included for remittance purposes. Other expatriate employees may take out foreign exchange on final departure not to exceed their net earnings.

Foreign employees of foreign embassies, legations, consulates, and international organizations whose salaries are fully paid in foreign currency from sources outside Ethiopia may take out and/or transfer their net earnings not to exceed the balance in their nonresident foreign currency account, nonresident transferable birr account, and/or nontransferable birr accounts.

Other payments

Prior approval Yes.

Indicative limits/bona fide test For subscription and membership fees, documentation is required from the overseas institute and approval is given by the commercial banks. The NBE's verification of contractual agreements between the parties is required for the transfer of consulting and legal fees, and applications are considered on a case-by-case basis.

Proceeds from Invisible Transactions and Current Transfers

Repatriation requirements Yes.

Surrender requirements Ten percent of proceeds may be retained indefinitely. The remaining balance may be retained for a period of 28 days only.

Restrictions on use of funds These funds may be used for payments such as imports of goods and services, export promotion, training and education, credit repayment, and other payments approved by the NBE.

Capital Transactions

Controls on capital and money market instruments

On capital market securities

Shares or other securities of a participating nature

Purchase abroad by residents Yes.

On collective investment securities	There is no market in these instruments.
Controls on derivatives and other instruments	There is no market in these instruments.

Controls on credit operations

Commercial credits

To residents from nonresidents	Yes.

Financial credits

To residents from nonresidents	Banks need prior approval from the NBE to borrow funds abroad, but do not need prior approval for overdrawing their accounts with foreign correspondents or accepting deposits. Other residents need to obtain the NBE's prior approval, and the credits should be used for export-generating investments. The equity component of the debt/equity ratio of the loan should not be less than 40%, except when the NBE issues a waiver.

Guarantees, sureties, and financial backup facilities

By residents to nonresidents	Yes.
To residents from nonresidents	Commercial banks may issue guarantees on behalf of foreign banks to resident companies.

Controls on direct investment

Inward direct investment	Foreign investors may hold up to 100% of the shares in any venture, except the banking, insurance, and transport sectors, including trading above a certain limit.
	All investments must be approved and certified by the Ethiopian Investment Authority (EIA). Investments are allowed in areas such as agriculture, livestock and crop production, manufacturing, mining, construction, real estate, machinery leasing, social services, education, health, engineering services, technology-intensive industries, pharmaceutical and fertilizer production, and hotel and tourism. Investment in telecommunications and defense industries is allowed in partnership with the government. Investments in rail transport service, postal service (except courier service), the generation and supply of electricity above an installed capacity of 25 megawatts, as well as transmission and supply of electric energy through the Integrated National Grid System are reserved for the government.
	Exemptions from income taxes are granted for up to five years for new projects and for up to three years for major extensions to existing projects. Imports of investment goods and spare parts for such ventures are also eligible for exemption from customs duties and other specified import levies. The EIA may decide on additional or new incentives when it deems this necessary.

Controls on liquidation of direct investment	Authorization by the EIA is required for repatriation of capital, and registration of capital inflows with the EIA establishes the evidence of inflows that is required for authorization. All recognized and registered foreign investments may be terminated on presentation of documents regarding liquidation and on payment of all taxes and other liabilities. Subject to appropriate documentation, foreign investors, upon final departure from Ethiopia, may transfer their capital without limitations. All foreign investors may also transfer abroad in convertible currency payments for debts, fees, or royalties in respect of technology transfer agreements.

Controls on real estate transactions

Purchase locally by nonresidents	All Ethiopian passport holders may purchase real estate in Ethiopia.
Sale locally by nonresidents	Yes.

Controls on personal capital movements

Loans

To residents from nonresidents	Regulations on financial credits apply.

Gifts, endowments, inheritances, and
legacies

By residents to nonresidents	Yes.
To residents from nonresidents	Yes.

Transfer of assets

Transfer into the country by immigrants	Yes.

Transfer of gambling and prize earnings	These transactions are not allowed.

Provisions specific to commercial banks and other credit institutions

Borrowing abroad	Banks may not borrow from, or enter into a guarantee agreement with, banks abroad unless authorized by the NBE.
Maintenance of accounts abroad	Banks may maintain nostro accounts with their correspondents.
Lending locally in foreign exchange	Domestic banks may grant personal loans to staff members of international institutions.
Purchase of locally issued securities denominated in foreign exchange	Banks may not acquire securities denominated in foreign currencies without the permission of the NBE.

Differential treatment of deposit
accounts in foreign exchange

Liquid asset requirements	Yes.

Differential treatment of deposit
accounts held by nonresidents

Interest rate controls	All nonresident accounts take the form of demand deposits on which no interest is paid.
Open foreign exchange position limits	The overall foreign currency position of each bank should not exceed 15% of its capital at the close of business on each Friday.
On resident assets and liabilities	n.r.
On nonresident assets and liabilities	n.r.

Provisions specific to institutional investors	Residents are not allowed to invest in foreign securities.
Limits (max.) on securities issued by nonresidents and on portfolio invested abroad	Yes.
Limits (max.) on portfolio invested abroad	Yes.
Limits (min.) on portfolio invested locally	n.r.
Currency-matching regulations on assets/liabilities composition	n.r.
Other controls imposed by securities laws	n.a.

Changes During 1999

Arrangements for payments and receipts	*December 30.* The export of newly minted gold, jewelry, and ornaments made of gold and silver was liberalized.
Imports and import payments	*June 15.* The system of preshipment inspections was introduced.
Exports and export proceeds	*January 18.* An Export Credit Guarantee Scheme was introduced.

FIJI

Status Under IMF Articles of Agreement

Article VIII   Date of acceptance: August 4, 1972.

Exchange Arrangement

Currency

The currency of Fiji is the Fiji dollar.

Exchange rate structure

Unitary.

Classification

Conventional pegged arrangement

The external value of the Fiji dollar is determined on the basis of a weighted basket of currencies comprising the Australian dollar, the Japanese yen, the New Zealand dollar, the euro, and the U.S. dollar. The exchange rate of the Fiji dollar in terms of the U.S. dollar, the intervention currency, is fixed daily by the Reserve Bank of Fiji (RBF) on the basis of quotations for the U.S. dollar and other currencies included in the basket.

Exchange tax

No.

Exchange subsidy

No.

Forward exchange market

Forward exchange facilites are provided by authorized dealers for trade transactions for periods of up to six months for exports and nine months for imports, up to a ratio of their capital.

Arrangements for Payments and Receipts

Prescription of currency requirements

Although no specific requirements exist, settlements must be made in convertible currencies acceptable to both countries.

Payment arrangements

n.a.

Administration of control

Exchange control is administered by the RBF acting as an agent of the government; the RBF delegates to authorized dealers the authority to approve current payments and transfers up to the full amount, except for advance payments for imports. Effective January 1, 2000, no documentary evidence is needed for any current or capital transfer, except insurance, for amounts up to F$10,000.

International security restrictions

n.a.

Payment arrears

n.a.

Controls on trade in gold (coins and/or bullion)

Controls on domestic ownership and/or trade

Residents may freely purchase, hold, and sell gold coins but not gold bullion.

Controls on external trade

The exportation of gold coins, except coins and collectors' pieces for numismatic purposes, requires specific permission from the RBF. The importation of gold, other than gold coins, from all sources requires a specific import license from the MOF; these are restricted to authorized gold dealers. Gold coins and gold bullion are exempt from fiscal duty but are subject to a 10% VAT. Gold jewelry is also exempt from fiscal duty but subject to a 10% VAT and is not under licensing control. Samples of gold and gold jewelry sent by foreign manufacturers require import licenses if their value exceeds F$200. Exports of gold jewelry are free of export duty but require licenses if their value exceeds F$1,000. Exports of gold bullion are subject to an export duty of 3%.

Controls on exports and imports of banknotes

On exports

Domestic currency — Exports are allowed up to F$500 a trip for travel-related purposes only.

Foreign currency — Exports are allowed up to the amount declared at the time of arrival. Local travelers are allowed up to a F$5,000 cash equivalent in foreign currency (inclusive of a maximum of F$500 in local currency) for each overseas trip.

On imports

Domestic currency — Travelers may freely bring in Fiji banknotes, but must declare them to customs or immigration officials on arrival.

Foreign currency — Travelers may freely bring in foreign currency banknotes, but must declare them to customs or immigration officials on arrival in order to export the unused balance on departure.

Resident Accounts

Foreign exchange accounts permitted — Applicable to resident individuals and any business entity registered and operating in Fiji.

Held domestically — These accounts are permitted, but prior approval is required. Effective January 1, 2000, commercial banks are authorized to approve local deposits up to the amount of F$1,000 per transaction.

Held abroad — These accounts are permitted, but prior approval is required.

Accounts in domestic currency convertible into foreign currency — Yes.

Nonresident Accounts

Foreign exchange accounts permitted — These accounts may be credited freely with the account holders' salaries (net of tax), with interest payable on the account, or with payments from other external accounts.

Domestic currency accounts — These accounts may be credited freely with the account holders' salaries (net of tax); with interest payable on the account; with payments from other external accounts; with the proceeds of sales of foreign currency or foreign coins by the account holder; and with Fiji banknotes that the account holder brought into Fiji, or acquired by debit to an external account, or acquired through the sale of foreign currency in the country during a temporary visit. External accounts may also be credited with payments by residents for which either general or specific authority has been given. External accounts may be debited for payments to residents of Fiji, transfers to other external accounts, payments in cash in Fiji, and purchases of foreign exchange.

Convertible into foreign currency — These accounts may be converted, but approval is required. Effective January 1, 2000, approval may be granted by the commercial banks.

Blocked accounts — n.a.

Imports and Import Payments

Foreign exchange budget — No.

Financing requirements for imports

Advance payment requirements — Authorized banks may approve advance payments for imports of up to F$500,000 an application without specific approval from the RBF, if such payments are required by the supplier. Documentary evidence is needed for remittances above F$10,000.

Documentation requirements for release of foreign exchange for imports	Payments for authorized imports are permitted upon application and submission of documentary evidence to authorized dealers, who may allow payments for goods that have been imported under either a specific import license or an OGL.
Domiciliation requirements	Yes.
Letters of credit	Yes.
Import licenses and other nontariff measures	Imports of poultry and poultry products and lubrication oils from any source require a specific import license. The Ministry of Commerce and Industry (MCI) is responsible for issuing import licenses, with the exception of those for gold and timber. Import licenses and other nontariff measures for gold are issued by the MOF; for timber, they are issued by the Ministry of Forestry. A wide range of consumer goods are imported by national cooperative societies under a joint arrangement with six other Pacific Island countries. The import license for cyclonic building materials is jointly issued by the Department of Fair Trading and Consumer Affairs and the MOF.
Negative list	The importation of a few commodities is prohibited for security, health, or public policy reasons.
Licenses with quotas	Import licenses for frozen chicken from the United States are issued on a quota basis.
Other nontariff measures	All imports must meet required technical standards on labeling, packaging, and expiration date requirements. All agricultural and forestry products are subject to quarantine clearance.
Import taxes and/or tariffs	Import tariffs range from 5% to 22.5%. A 10% VAT is also levied.
State import monopoly	No.

Exports and Export Proceeds

Repatriation requirements	Exporters are required to collect the proceeds from exports within six months of the date of shipment of the goods from Fiji and may not, without specific permission, grant more than six months' credit to a nonresident buyer. Customs is delegated to process and approve all export of goods with no monetary return.
Surrender requirements	On January 1, 1999, the export retention limit was raised to 40%.
Financing requirements	n.a.
Documentation requirements	n.a.
Export licenses	Export licenses are issued by the customs department and monitored by the Comptroller of Customs. Specific licenses are required only for exports of sugar, wheat bran, copra meal, certain types of lumber, certain animals, and a few other items. The MCI is responsible for issuing export licenses for trochus shells. Irrespective of export-licensing requirements, however, exporters are required to produce an export permit for the commercial consignment of all goods with an f.o.b. value of more than F$1,000; this permit is required for exchange control purposes.
Export taxes	A 3% export duty is levied on exports of sugar, gold, and silver.

Payments for Invisible Transactions and Current Transfers

Controls on these transfers	Most payments have been fully delegated to authorized banks without any restrictions or limits. Effective January 1, 2000, documentation requirements were also eliminated for amounts up to F$10,000, except for insurance transfers.
Trade-related payments	
Indicative limits/bona fide test	Yes.
Investment-related payments	Payment of interest is allowed, provided prior approval for the loan was granted by the RBF, if the loan is in excess of F$500,000.

Quantitative limits	Effective January 1, 1999, limits on remittances of profits and earnings were removed. Authorized banks may make payments of up to F$100,000 an application for profit remittances without prior approval of the RBF.
Indicative limits/bona fide test	Yes.
Payments for travel	
Indicative limits/bona fide test	Yes.
Personal payments	
Prior approval	For payment of medical costs, no approval is required, provided that payment is made directly to the institution.
Quantitative limits	Foreign exchange provided is restricted to amounts due.
Indicative limits/bona fide test	Yes.
Foreign workers' wages	
Indicative limits/bona fide test	Yes.
Credit card use abroad	
Quantitative limits	The use of credit cards for travel-related expenses is not restricted.
Indicative limits/bona fide test	Yes.
Other payments	
Indicative limits/bona fide test	Yes.

Proceeds from Invisible Transactions and Current Transfers

Repatriation requirements	Yes.
Surrender requirements	Residents are required to sell all their foreign currency receipts to an authorized dealer within one month of their return.
Restrictions on use of funds	No.

Capital Transactions

Controls on capital and money market instruments	Effective January 1, 2000, the authority to authorize investments of nonresidents for amounts up to F$100,000 was delegated to the following institutions: (1) the Suva Stock Exchange for investments in listed companies; and (2) commercial banks for investments in Fiji dollar–denominated deposits. Some of the funding for these investments should be from abroad or from earnings in Fiji. The allocation for portfolio investment by private persons is F$10,000, to be utilized as a retail account.
On capital market securities	
Shares or other securities of a participating nature	
Purchase locally by nonresidents	Yes.
Sale or issue locally by nonresidents	Yes.
Purchase abroad by residents	Effective January 1, 1999, locally incorporated companies are allowed to invest up to F$500,000 a company up to an overall national ceiling of F$10 million to buy shares in companies offshore. Effective January 1, 2000, companies are allowed to invest up to F$1 million a company and the overall ceiling was raised to F$30 million. These investments are restricted to the establishment of subsidiary offices and equity purchases in businesses that would assist the growth potential of the Fiji operation.
Sale or issue abroad by residents	Yes.

Bonds or other debt securities	There are controls on all transactions in bonds or other debt securities.
On money market instruments	There are controls on all transactions in money market instruments.
On collective investment securities	There are controls on all transactions in collective investment securities.
Controls on derivatives and other instruments	There are controls on all derivatives transactions.
Controls on credit operations	Residents must obtain prior permission from the RBF to borrow amounts over F$100,000 in foreign currency abroad. Effective January 1, 2000, this limit was increased to F$500,000. Prior RBF permission is required for any up-front fees.
Commercial credits	
By residents to nonresidents	Yes.
To residents from nonresidents	Yes.
Financial credits	
By residents to nonresidents	Yes.
To residents from nonresidents	Yes.
Guarantees, sureties, and financial backup facilities	
By residents to nonresidents	Effective January 1, 1999, the limit on bank guarantees was removed and fully delegated to commercial banks.
To residents from nonresidents	Yes.
Controls on direct investment	
Outward direct investment	Effective January 1, 1999, (1) nonbank financial institutions may invest up to F$65 million in 1999; (2) the limit on overseas investment for individuals and families was increased to F$20,000 a taxpayer, up to an overall ceiling of F$10 million; and (3) the limit on expenditure to set up sales offices or subsidies abroad by local companies was increased to F$500,000 a subsidiary. On January 1, 2000, the limit on establishing sales offices/subsidiaries abroad by local companies was increased to F$1 million. Nonbank financial companies were allowed to invest up to F$70 million.
Inward direct investment	Foreign investment in Fiji is normally expected to be financed from a nonresident source. Such foreign investment may be given "approved status," which guarantees the right to repatriate dividends and capital.
Controls on liquidation of direct investment	Such transactions require specific permission from the RBF, which is readily granted upon evidence that the investment funds originated offshore. Nonresident-owned companies are permitted to repatriate in full the proceeds from sales of assets and capital gains on investments.
Controls on real estate transactions	
Purchase abroad by residents	The purchase of personal property abroad is not permitted.
Purchase locally by nonresidents	Approval by the Ministry of Land is required for purchases of state-owned property. Settlements require RBF approval to ensure proceeds are received in Fiji and that funds originate from abroad.
Sale locally by nonresidents	Controls on settlements are effected to safeguard local interest before proceeds from sales are remitted abroad.
Controls on personal capital movements	
Loans	
By residents to nonresidents	Yes.
To residents from nonresidents	Yes.

Settlement of debts abroad by immigrants	Yes.
Transfer of assets	
Transfer abroad by emigrants	Effective January 1, 1999, the ceiling on emigration allowance was removed. Authorized banks may make payments up to F$100,000 an applicant without the prior approval of the RBF.
Transfer of gambling and prize earnings	Yes.

Provisions specific to commercial banks and other credit institutions

Borrowing abroad	Authorized dealers must obtain permission from the RBF to borrow abroad.
Maintenance of accounts abroad	Yes.
Lending to nonresidents (financial or commercial credits)	Effective January 1, 1999, the limits for lending to a newly established company or a branch of a company in Fiji (other than a bank) that is controlled directly or indirectly by persons who reside outside Fiji was raised to F$1 million. Effective January 1, 2000, this limit was raised to F$5 million. Lenders may also authorize temporary overdrafts without reference to the RBF. Borrowing by nonresident individuals is fully delegated to lending institutions and commercial banks.
Lending locally in foreign exchange	The banks and nonbank financial institutions may not lend foreign currency to any resident of Fiji without the specific permission of the RBF.
Purchase of locally issued securities denominated in foreign exchange	Yes.
Investment regulations	
Abroad by banks	Yes.
In banks by nonresidents	An individual may (together with his or her relatives) own up to 15% of the voting shares of a bank or credit institution. Ownership through a company may be up to 30%. This does not preclude the establishment of branches or subsidiaries incorporated in Fiji of 100% nonresident-controlled financial institutions.
Open foreign exchange position limits	Net open position limits in terms of each bank's actual capital are set at the greater of 12.5% or F$0.4 million, and 25% or F$0.8 million up to a maximum of F$7.5 million, for a single currency and overall foreign currency, respectively.
	The limit on gross outstanding forward foreign exchange sales contracts is set at 50% of each bank's capital in Fiji, provided net outstanding forward exchange sales contracts does not exceed F$15 million.

Provisions specific to institutional investors

Limits (max.) on securities issued by nonresidents and on portfolio invested abroad	Yes.
Limits (max.) on portfolio invested abroad	The limit for 1999 was F$65 million, of which nonbank financial institutions are permitted to place F$15 million offshore, and the Fiji National Provident Fund may place F$50 million.
Other controls imposed by securities laws	n.a.

Changes During 1999

Exports and export proceeds	*January 1.* The export retention limit was raised to 40% from 25% of an exporter's total export earnings for the previous year.
Capital transactions	*January 1.* Locally incorporated companies were allowed to invest up to F$500,000 a company, up to an overall national ceiling of F$10 million to buy shares in companies offshore.

Controls on credit operations	*January 1.* The limit on bank guarantees was removed and fully delegated to commercial banks.
Controls on direct investment	*January 1.* The limit on expenditure to set up sales offices or subsidiaries abroad by local companies was increased to F$500,000 a subsidiary.
	January 1. The limit on overseas investments for individuals and their relatives was increased to F$20,000 a taxpayer, up to an overall ceiling of F$10 million.
	January 1. Nonbank financial institutions may invest up to F$65 million in 1999.
Controls on personal capital movements	*January 1.* The ceilings on the emigration allowance and operating profits for nonresident investors were removed.
Provisions specific to commercial banks and other credit institutions	*January 1.* The limits for lending to a newly established company or a branch of a company in Fiji (other than a bank) that is controlled directly or indirectly by persons who reside outside Fiji was raised to F$1 million.

Changes During 2000

Arrangements for payments and receipts	*January 1.* No documentary evidence is needed for any current or capital transfer below F$10,000.
Resident accounts	*January 1.* Commercial banks may authorize local deposits up to F$1,000 per transaction.
Nonresident accounts	*January 1.* Approval to convert domestic currency balances into foreign exchange is to be granted by commercial banks.
Payments for invisible transactions and current transfers	*January 1.* Documentation requirements were eliminated for amounts up to F$10,000.
	January 1. Only insurance transfers in excess of F$10,000 require documentary evidence.
Capital transactions	
Controls on capital and money market instruments	*January 1.* The authority to authorize investments in a publicly listed company and Fiji dollar–denominated deposits of nonresidents for amounts up to F$100,000 was delegated to the Suva Stock Exchange and the commercial banks.
	January 1. The ceiling of investment abroad by a locally incorporated company was raised to F$5 million a company, and the overall ceiling was raised to F$30 million.
Controls on credit operations	*January 1.* The limit above which RBF authorization is required for residents to borrow from abroad was raised to F$500,000 from F$100,000.
Controls on direct investment	*January 1.* The limit on establishing sales offices/subsidiaries abroad by local companies was increased to F$1 million a company. Nonbank financial institutions may invest up to F$70 million.
Provisions specific to commercial banks and other credit institutions	*January 1.* The limit to establish a new company by nonresidents was raised to F$5 million.
	January 1. The limit for commercial bank lending to a nonresident-owned company was raised to F$5 million from F$1 million.

FINLAND

(Position as of January 31, 2000)

Status Under IMF Articles of Agreement

Article VIII	Date of acceptance: September 25, 1979.

Exchange Arrangement

Currency	As of January 1, 1999, the currency of Finland is the euro. In cash transactions, however, the legal tender remains the Finnish markka until 2002, when euro banknotes and coins will be issued.
Exchange rate structure	Unitary.

Classification

Exchange arrangement with no separate legal tender	Finland participates in a currency union (EMU) comprising 11 members of the EU: Austria, Belgium, Finland, France, Germany, Ireland, Italy, Luxembourg, the Netherlands, Portugal, and Spain. Internal conversion rates in respect to the national currencies of EMU participants were fixed to the euro on January 1, 1999, whereas the external exchange rate of the euro is market-determined. The conversion rate between the euro and the Finnish markka was set at Fmk 5.94573 per €1. The ECB has the right to intervene to smooth out fluctuations in external exchange rates.
Exchange tax	No.
Exchange subsidy	No.
Forward exchange market	Yes.

Arrangements for Payments and Receipts

Prescription of currency requirements	No.
Payment arrangements	No.
Administration of control	There are no exchange controls. Import licensing is administered by the National Board of Customs. Export licensing relating to international export control regimes is administered by the trade department/foreign trade division of the Ministry of Trade and Industry.

International security restrictions

In accordance with Executive Board Decision No. 144-(52/51)	Yes.
In accordance with UN sanctions	Finland maintains exchange restrictions pursuant to UN Security Council resolutions against Iraq and Libya. Exchange restrictions against the Federal Republic of Yugoslavia (Serbia/Montenegro) and certain areas of the Republic of Bosnia and Herzegovina have been terminated, with the exception of certain claims. Finland maintains exchange restrictions against the Federal Republic of Yugoslavia (Serbia/Montenegro) pursuant to EU regulations. A UN Security Council resolution on food for oil (Iraq) is implemented.
Payment arrears	No.
Controls on trade in gold (coins and/or bullion)	No.
Controls on exports and imports of banknotes	No.

337

Resident Accounts

Foreign exchange accounts permitted	Yes.
Held domestically	Yes.
Held abroad	Yes.
Accounts in domestic currency convertible into foreign currency	Yes.

Nonresident Accounts

Foreign exchange accounts permitted	Yes.
Domestic currency accounts	Yes.
Convertible into foreign currency	Yes.
Blocked accounts	No.

Imports and Import Payments

Foreign exchange budget	No.
Financing requirements for imports	No.
Documentation requirements for release of foreign exchange for imports	No.
Import licenses and other nontariff measures	
Negative list	Yes.
Licenses with quotas	The following products are subject to quantitative import restrictions and require an import license when imported into the EU: agricultural products; certain steel products subject to bilateral agreements with Russia and Ukraine; certain steel products subject to autonomous community quota for Kazakhstan; specific textile products subject to bilateral agreements with third countries, particular third-country textile products subject to autonomous community quotas; and certain Chinese industrial products subject to autonomous community quotas.
Import taxes and/or tariffs	No.
State import monopoly	No.

Exports and Export Proceeds

Repatriation requirements	No.
Financing requirements	No.
Documentation requirements	No.
Export licenses	Export licenses are required only for exports of goods related to international export control regimes and are administered by the Ministry of Trade and Industry. The sale of arms is strictly controlled by the Ministry of Defense.
Without quotas	Yes.
Export taxes	No.

Payments for Invisible Transactions and Current Transf[...]

Controls on these transfers	No.

Proceeds from Invisible Transactions and Current Transf[...]

Repatriation requirements	No.
Restrictions on use of funds	No.

Capital Transactions

Controls on capital and money market instruments

On capital market securities

Shares or other securities of a participating nature

Purchase locally by nonresidents — The control applies only to the purchase of shares and other securities of a participatory nature that may be affected by laws on inward direct investment and establishment.

Controls on derivatives and other instruments — No.

Controls on credit operations — No.

Controls on direct investment

Inward direct investment — Acquisition of shares giving at least one-third of the voting rights in a Finnish defense enterprise to a single foreign owner requires prior confirmation by the Ministry of Defense; approval can be denied only if the safeguarding of the public defense is jeopardized.

Controls on liquidation of direct investment — No.

Controls on real estate transactions

Purchase locally by nonresidents — Effective January 1, 2000, acquisition of real estate by nonresidents for recreational purposes or secondary residences for those who have not previously been residents of Finland for at least five years was allowed.

Controls on personal capital movements — No.

Provisions specific to commercial banks and other credit institutions

Open foreign exchange position limits — Prudential regulation harmonized with EU directives is applied.

Provisions specific to institutional investors

Limits (max.) on portfolio invested abroad — Yes.

Limits (min.) on portfolio invested locally — Yes.

Currency-matching regulations on assets/liabilities composition — Yes.

Other controls imposed by securities laws — Yes.

Changes During 1999

Exchange arrangement

January 1. The currency of Finland became the euro. The conversion rate between the euro and the Finnish markka was set irrevocably at Fmk 5.94573 per €1.

Changes During 2000

Capital transactions

Controls on real estate transactions

January 1. The purchase of real estate for recreational purposes or secondary residences by those who have not previously been residents of Finland for at least five years was allowed.

FRANCE

(Position as of December 31, 1999)

Status Under IMF Articles of Agreement

Article VIII   Date of acceptance: February 15, 1961.

Exchange Arrangement

Currency

As of January 1, 1999, the currency of France is the euro. In cash transactions, however, the legal tender remains the French franc until 2002, when euro banknotes and coins will be issued.

Exchange rate structure   Unitary.

Classification

Exchange arrangement with no separate legal tender

France participates in a currency union (EMU) comprising 11 members of the EU: Austria, Belgium, Finland, France, Germany, Ireland, Italy, Luxembourg, the Netherlands, Portugal, and Spain. Internal conversion rates in respect to the national currencies of EMU participants were fixed to the euro on January 1, 1999, whereas the external exchange rate of the euro is market determined. The conversion rate between the euro and the French franc was set at FF 6.55957 per €1. The ECB has the right to intervene to smooth out fluctuations in external exchange rates. Fixed conversion rates in terms of the euro apply to the CFP franc, which is the currency of the overseas territories of French Polynesia, New Caledonia, and Wallis and Futuna Islands. Two groups of African countries are linked to the French Treasury through an Operations Account: Benin, Burkina Faso, Côte d'Ivoire, Guinea-Bissau, Mali, Niger, Senegal, and Togo (franc de la Communauté financière africaine, issued by the BCEAO); and Cameroon, Central African Republic, Chad, Republic of Congo, Equatorial Guinea, and Gabon (franc de la Coopération financière en Afrique centrale, issued by the BEAC). These fixed parities are €1 per CFAF 119.261 and €1 per CFAF 656.168, respectively.

The Comorian franc, issued by the Central Bank of the Comoros, which holds an Operations Account with the French Treasury, is linked to the French franc by a fixed parity of €1 per CF 504.795.

Exchange tax   No.

Exchange subsidy   No.

Forward exchange market

Registered banks in France and Monaco, which may also act on behalf of banks established abroad or in Operations Account countries, are permitted to deal spot or forward in the exchange market in France. Registered banks may also deal spot and forward with their correspondents in foreign markets in all currencies. Nonbank residents may purchase foreign exchange forward in respect of specified transactions. All residents, including private persons, may purchase or sell foreign exchange forward without restriction. Forward sales of foreign currency are not restricted, whether or not they are for hedging purposes.

Arrangements for Payments and Receipts

Prescription of currency requirements   No.

Payment arrangements   No.

Administration of control

The Ministry of Economy is the coordinating agency for financial relations with foreign countries. It is responsible for all matters relating to inward and outward direct investment and has certain powers over matters relating to insurance, reinsurance, annuities, and the like. The execution of all transfers has been delegated to registered banks and stockbrokers and to the Postal Administration.

International security restrictions

In accordance with UN sanctions　　Restrictions on payments have been imposed on Iraq and the UNITA movement in Angola in accordance with a UN Security Council resolution. On October 15, 1999, restrictions on payments were imposed on the Taliban (the Islamic State of Afghanistan).

Payment arrears　　No.

Controls on trade in gold (coins and/or bullion)　　No.

Controls on exports and imports of banknotes　　Amounts exceeding the equivalent of F 50,000 must be declared to customs upon arrival or departure.

On imports

  Foreign currency　　At the request of Algeria, Morocco, and Tunisia, banknotes issued by these countries may not be exchanged in France.

Resident Accounts

Foreign exchange accounts permitted　　Yes.

Held domestically　　Yes.

Held abroad　　Yes.

Accounts in domestic currency convertible into foreign currency　　Yes.

Nonresident Accounts

Foreign exchange accounts permitted　　Yes.

Domestic currency accounts　　Yes.

Convertible into foreign currency　　Yes.

Blocked accounts　　No.

Imports and Import Payments

Foreign exchange budget　　No.

Financing requirements for imports　　No.

Documentation requirements for release of foreign exchange for imports　　A customs declaration is required.

Import licenses and other nontariff measures　　Some imports from non-EU countries are subject to minimum prices; these require an administrative visa issued by the Central Customs Administration or the appropriate ministry and sometimes, exceptionally, an import license. Imports of products of the ECSC require such administrative visas when originating in non-ECSC countries. Imports from non-EU countries of most products covered by the CAP of the EU are subject to variable import levies that have replaced previous barriers. Common EU regulations are also applied to imports from non-EU countries of most other agricultural and livestock products. Quantitative restrictions consist of EU-wide and national restrictions. The former include textile and apparel limits under the MFA and voluntary export restraints.

For some commodities, such as petroleum and petroleum products, global quotas are allocated annually. In other cases, quotas are allocated semiannually and apply to all countries (other than those that have bilaterally negotiated quotas or receive privileged treatment).

Licenses with quotas	Licenses are required for some countries and some products. Imports of goods that originate outside of the EU and are subject to quantitative restrictions require individual licenses. Common EU regulations are also applied to imports from non-EU countries.
Import taxes and/or tariffs	Duties are collected at the time of entry into the EU in relation to the origin of the products and a tariff nomenclature. An agricultural levy (within the CAP) and, if necessary, an anti-dumping levy may be added.
State import monopoly	No.

Exports and Export Proceeds

Repatriation requirements	No.
Financing requirements	No.
Documentation requirements	A customs declaration is required.
Export licenses	
Without quotas	Certain prohibited goods may be exported only under a special license.
Export taxes	Exports are not taxed, except for works of art, which are subject to the value-added tax.

Payments for Invisible Transactions and Current Transfers

Controls on these transfers	No.

Proceeds from Invisible Transactions and Current Transfers

Repatriation requirements	No.
Restrictions on use of funds	No.

Capital Transactions

Controls on capital and money market instruments	
On money market instruments	
Sale or issue locally by nonresidents	Nonresidents may only issue commercial papers.
Sale or issue abroad by residents	Yes.
On collective investment securities	
Sale or issue locally by nonresidents	The restriction does not apply to collective investment securities that are of EU origin and comply with the EU Directive.
Controls on derivatives and other instruments	No.
Controls on credit operations	No.
Controls on direct investment	Direct investments are defined as those in which foreign investors hold more than one-third of the capital. In the case of firms whose shares are quoted on the stock exchange, the threshold is reduced to 20% of the capital and applies to each individual foreign participation but not to the total of foreign participation. To determine whether a company is under foreign control, the Ministry of Economy and Finance (MEF) may also take into account any special relationships resulting from stock options, loans, patents and licenses, and commercial contracts.

Inward direct investment	An authorization is needed for investments in areas pertaining to public order and defense.
Controls on liquidation of direct investment	The liquidation proceeds of foreign direct investment in France may be freely transferred abroad; the liquidation must be reported to the MEF within 20 days of its occurrence. The liquidation of direct investments abroad is free from any prior application, provided that the corresponding funds had been reported to the Bank of France.
Controls on real estate transactions	No.
Controls on personal capital movements	No.
Provisions specific to commercial banks and other credit institutions	No.
Provisions specific to institutional investors	
Currency-matching regulations on assets/liabilities composition	Insurance companies in the EU are required to cover their technical reserves with assets expressed in the same currency.
Other controls imposed by securities laws	No.

Changes During 1999

Exchange arrangement	*January 1*. The currency of France became the euro. The conversion rate between the euro and the French franc was set irrevocably at FF 6.55957 per €1. The fixed parities for Operations Account countries are €1 per CFAF 119.261 and €1 per CFAF 656.168. The Comorian franc is fixed to the euro at €1 per CF 504.795.
Arrangements for payments and receipts	*October 15*. Restrictions were imposed on the Taliban (the Islamic State of Afghanistan).

GABON

(Position as of December 31, 1999)

Status Under IMF Articles of Agreement

Article VIII   Date of acceptance: June 1, 1996.

Exchange Arrangement

Currency   The currency of Gabon is the CFA franc.

Exchange rate structure   Unitary.

Classification

Exchange arrangement with no separate legal tender
The CFA franc is pegged to the euro, the intervention currency, at the fixed rate of CFAF 100 per €0.1524. Exchange transactions in euros between the BEAC and commercial banks take place at the same rate. Buying and selling rates for certain foreign currencies are also officially posted, with quotations based on the fixed rate for the euro and the rate for the currency concerned in the Paris exchange market, and include a commission. Commissions are levied at the rate of 0.25% on transfers made by the banks for their own accounts and on all private capital transfers to countries that are not members of the BEAC, except those made for the account of the Treasury, national accounting offices, national and international public agencies, and private entities granted exemption by the Ministry of Finance, Budget, and Participations (MOFBP) because of the nature of their activities.

Exchange tax   No.

Exchange subsidy   No.

Forward exchange market   There are no forward exchange markets for the CFA franc. However, exporters and importers can always cover their position on the Paris foreign exchange market.

Arrangements for Payments and Receipts

Prescription of currency requirements
Because Gabon is an Operations Account country, settlements with France, Monaco, and the other Operations Account countries (WAEMU and CAEMC members and the Comoros) are made in CFA francs, euros, or the currency of any other Operations Account country. Settlements with all other countries are usually made through correspondent banks in France in the currencies of those countries or in euros through foreign accounts in francs.

Payment arrangements

Regional arrangements
An Operations Account is maintained with the French Treasury that links Operations Account countries. All purchases or sales of foreign currencies or euros against CFA francs are ultimately settled through a debit or credit to the Operations Account.

Clearing agreements   Yes.

Administration of control
The Directorate of Financial Institutions (DFI) of the MOFBP supervises borrowing and lending abroad. Exchange control is administered by the MOFBP, which has partly delegated approval authority to the authorized banks for current payments and to the BEAC for issues related to the external position of the banks. All exchange transactions relating to foreign countries must be effected through authorized intermediaries, that is, the Postal Administration and authorized banks. Import and export authorizations, where necessary, are issued by the Directorate of External Trade of the Ministry of Commerce and Industry.

International security restrictions   n.a.

Payment arrears   No.

Controls on trade in gold (coins and/or bullion)

Controls on domestic ownership and/or trade	Residents are free to hold, acquire, and dispose of gold in any form in Gabon.
Controls on external trade	Imports and exports of gold require the authorization of the MOFBP. Exempt from this requirement are (1) imports and exports by or on behalf of the monetary authorities, and (2) imports and exports of manufactured articles containing a small quantity of gold (such as gold-filled or gold-plated articles). The exportation of gold is the monopoly of the Société gabonaise de recherches et d'exploitation minières. Imports of gold exempted from licensing and authorization requirements are subject to customs declaration.

Controls on exports and imports of banknotes

On exports

Domestic currency	There is no limit on the amount of banknotes that residents and nonresidents may export from one CAEMC country to another, but exports of banknotes outside the CAEMC area are prohibited.
Foreign currency	Residents traveling outside the CAEMC area are subject to the various limits imposed on foreign exchange allowances allocated per trip, depending on the nature of the travel. Nonresident travelers may take with them foreign currency or other foreign means of payment equivalent to the maximum amount declared upon entry into the CAEMC area. Above this ceiling or in the absence of declaration, nonresidents must provide supporting documents explaining the origin of such amounts.

On imports

Domestic currency	There is no limit on the amount of banknotes that residents and nonresidents can import into one CAEMC country from another, but imports of banknotes from outside the CAEMC area, by both residents and nonresidents, are prohibited.
Foreign currency	Resident and nonresident travelers may bring in any amount of banknotes and coins issued by the Bank of France or any other bank of issue maintaining an Operations Account with the French Treasury, as well as any amount of foreign banknotes and coins (except gold coins) of countries outside the Operations Account area.

Resident Accounts

Foreign exchange accounts permitted	Yes.
Held domestically	No.
Held abroad	These accounts are permitted, but prior approval is required.
Accounts in domestic currency convertible into foreign currency	n.a.

Nonresident Accounts

Foreign exchange accounts permitted	These accounts are permitted, but prior approval is required.
Domestic currency accounts	The regulations pertaining to nonresident accounts are based on regulations that were applied in France before the abolition of all capital controls in 1989. Because the BEAC has suspended the repurchase of BEAC banknotes circulating outside the territories of its member countries, BEAC banknotes received by foreign correspondents' authorized banks and mailed to the BEAC agency in Libreville may not be credited to foreign accounts in francs.
Convertible into foreign currency	Yes.
Blocked accounts	n.a.

Imports and Import Payments

Foreign exchange budget
No.

Financing requirements for imports
No.

Documentation requirements for release of foreign exchange for imports

Domiciliation requirements
All import transactions relating to foreign countries must be domiciled with an authorized bank.

Import licenses used as exchange licenses
Import declarations to or licenses approved by the Ministry of Foreign Trade and the DFI of the MOFBP entitle importers to purchase the necessary foreign exchange, provided that the shipping documents are submitted to the authorized bank.

Import licenses and other nontariff measures

Negative list
Some imports are prohibited for security and health reasons.

Open general licenses
Except for sugar, imports from all countries are permitted freely and do not require licenses. All imports, however, are subject to declaration.

Licenses with quotas
Importation of sugar is subject to a surcharge.

Other nontariff measures
All imports of commercial goods must be insured through authorized insurance companies in Gabon.

Import taxes and/or tariffs
The common duty rates of the CAEMC member countries are 5% for basic necessities, 10% for raw materials and capital goods, 20% for intermediate goods, and 30% for consumer goods.

State import monopoly
No.

Exports and Export Proceeds

Repatriation requirements
Proceeds from exports to countries outside the CAEMC area must be collected and repatriated within 30 days of the payment date stipulated in the contract, unless a special waiver is granted by the MOFBP.

Surrender requirements
Export proceeds received in currencies other than those of France or an Operations Account country must be surrendered within one month of collection.

Financing requirements
n.a.

Documentation requirements

Domiciliation
Export transactions relating to foreign countries must be domiciled with an authorized bank.

Export licenses
Exports are subject to declaration to the Ministry of Foreign Trade.

Export taxes
Export taxes are levied on mining products (0.5%) and forest products (5% to 11%).

Payments for Invisible Transactions and Current Transfers

Controls on these transfers
Payments for invisibles to France and the Operations Account countries are permitted freely; payments to other countries are subject to bona fide tests in the form of declaration and presentation of appropriate documents to the MOFBP. For many types of payments, the monitoring function of the MOFBP has been delegated to authorized banks and the Postal Administration. Payments for invisibles related to trade are permitted freely when the basic trade transaction has been approved or does not require authorization.

Payments for travel

Quantitative limits

Residents traveling to other countries of the franc zone may obtain an unlimited allocation of French francs. Within the CAEMC area, BEAC banknotes may be exported without limits. Residents traveling outside the CAEMC area are allowed to take out foreign banknotes and other means of payment up to a limit of CFAF 2 million and CFAF 5 million for tourism and business purposes, respectively.

Indicative limits/bona fide test

Yes.

Personal payments

Information is not available on the payment of pensions and family maintenance.

Quantitative limits

Persons traveling to countries outside the franc zone for medical reasons may obtain an exchange allocation of up to CFAF 2.5 million. Students or trainees leaving Gabon for the first time or returning to their normal place of study to countries outside the CAEMC area may obtain an exchange allowance equivalent to CFAF 1 million.

Indicative limits/bona fide test

Yes.

Foreign workers' wages

Quantitative limits

Foreign workers are allowed to transfer 50% of their net salary upon presentation of their pay vouchers, provided that the transfers take place within three months of the pay period concerned.

Credit card use abroad

Prior approval

Yes.

Quantitative limits

The use of credit cards, which must be issued by resident financial intermediaries and approved by the MOFBP, is limited to the ceilings indicated above for tourism and business travel.

Indicative limits/bona fide test

Yes.

Proceeds from Invisible Transactions and Current Transfers

Repatriation requirements

Proceeds from transactions in invisibles with France, Monaco, and the Operations Account countries may be retained.

Surrender requirements

All amounts due from residents of other countries in respect of services and all income earned in those countries from foreign assets must be collected and, if received in foreign currency, surrendered within a month of the due date. Returning resident travelers are required to declare all means of payment in their possession upon arrival at customs and surrender within eight days all means of payment exceeding the equivalent of CFAF 25,000.

Restrictions on use of funds

No.

Capital Transactions

Controls on capital and money market instruments

Capital movements between Gabon and France, and the Operations Account countries are permitted freely, except for the sale or introduction of foreign securities. Capital transfers to all other countries are restricted and require the approval of the DFI, but capital receipts from these countries are permitted freely. All foreign securities, foreign currency, and titles embodying claims on foreign countries or nonresidents that are held in Gabon by residents or nonresidents must be deposited with authorized banks in Gabon.

On capital market securities

Shares or other securities of a participating nature

Sale or issue locally by nonresidents

The issuing, advertising, or offering for sale of foreign securities in Gabon requires prior authorization from the MOFBP. Exempt from authorization, however, are operations in connection with (1) loans backed by a guarantee from the Gabonese government, and

(2) shares similar to securities whose issuing, advertising, or offering for sale in Gabon has previously been authorized.

Purchase abroad by residents	Yes.
On money market instruments	Yes.
On collective investment securities	Yes.
Controls on derivatives and other instruments	Yes.

Controls on credit operations

Commercial credits

By residents to nonresidents

Lending by residents or by branches or subsidiaries in Gabon of juridical persons whose registered office is abroad requires prior authorization from the MOFBP. The following are, however, exempt from this authorization: (1) loans granted by registered banks; and (2) other loans, of which the total amount outstanding does not exceed CFAF 50 million for any one lender. However, for loans that are free of authorization, each repayment must be declared to the Directorate of Financial Institutions within 20 days of the operation except when the total outstanding amount of all loans granted abroad by the lender does not exceed CFAF 5 million.

To residents from nonresidents

Borrowing by residents or by branches or subsidiaries in Gabon of juridical persons whose registered office is abroad requires prior authorization from the MOFBP. The following transactions are exempt from this requirement: (1) loans constituting a direct investment abroad for which prior approval has been obtained; (2) loans directly connected with the rendering of services abroad by the persons or firms mentioned above, or with the financing of commercial transactions either between Gabon and countries abroad or between foreign countries in which these persons or firms take part; (3) loans contracted by registered banks; and (4) loans other than those mentioned above, of which the total amount outstanding does not exceed CFAF 50 million for any one borrower. However, for the contracting of loans referred to under (4) that are free of authorization, each repayment must be declared to the DFI within 20 days of the operation unless the total outstanding amount of all loans contracted abroad by the borrower is CFAF 5 million or less.

Financial credits

By residents to nonresidents	Yes.
To residents from nonresidents	Yes.
Guarantees, sureties, and financial backup facilities	Yes.

Controls on direct investment

Outward direct investment

Investments, including those made by companies in Gabon that are directly or indirectly under foreign control and those made by branches or subsidiaries of foreign companies in Gabon, must be declared to the MOFBP unless they take the form of a capital increase resulting from reinvestment of undistributed profits.

Inward direct investment

Investments must be declared to the MOFBP within 20 days of the operation unless they take the form of a capital increase resulting from the reinvestment of undistributed profits; within two months of receipt of the declaration, the MOFBP may request the postponement of the project. Foreign companies investing in Gabon must offer shares for purchase by Gabonese nationals for an amount equivalent to at least 10% of the company's capital.

Controls on liquidation of direct investment

The full or partial liquidation of direct investments in Gabon must be declared to the MOFBP within 20 days of the operation unless the operation involves the relinquishing of a shareholding that had previously been approved as constituting a direct investment in Gabon.

Controls on real estate transactions

Purchase locally by nonresidents

Purchases by nonresidents are not permitted.

Controls on personal capital movements	n.a.
Provisions specific to commercial banks and other credit institutions	n.a.
Provisions specific to institutional investors	n.a.
Other controls imposed by securities laws	n.a.

Changes During 1999

Exchange arrangement	*January 1.* The CFA franc peg to the French franc was replaced with a peg to the euro.

THE GAMBIA

Status Under IMF Articles of Agreement

Article VIII
Date of acceptance: January 21, 1993.

Exchange Arrangement

Currency
The currency of The Gambia is the Gambian dalasi.

Exchange rate structure
Unitary.

Classification

Independently floating
The exchange rate of the dalasi is determined in the foreign exchange market. Commercial banks and foreign exchange bureaus are free to transact among themselves, with the Central Bank of The Gambia (CBG), or with customers at exchange rates agreed on by the parties to these transactions. The CBG conducts a foreign exchange market review session on the last working day of each week with the participation of the commercial banks and foreign exchange bureaus. During this session, the average market rate during the week is announced as the rate for customs valuation purposes for the following week.

Exchange tax
No.

Exchange subsidy
No.

Forward exchange market
No.

Arrangements for Payments and Receipts

Prescription of currency requirements
No.

Payment arrangements

Regional arrangements
The Gambia participates in the WAMA.

Clearing agreements
Yes.

Administration of control
No.

International security restrictions
n.a.

Payment arrears
No.

Controls on trade in gold (coins and/or bullion)
No.

Controls on exports and imports of banknotes
No.

Resident Accounts

Foreign exchange accounts permitted
No.

Accounts in domestic currency convertible into foreign currency
n.a.

Nonresident Accounts

Foreign exchange accounts permitted
No.

Domestic currency accounts	Yes.
Convertible into foreign currency	Accounts denominated in dalasis are designated external accounts and may be opened without reference to the CBG when commercial banks are satisfied that the account holder's source of funds is from abroad in convertible foreign currency. Designated external accounts may be credited with payments from residents of other countries, with transfers from other external accounts, and with the proceeds of sales through the banking system of other convertible currencies. They may be debited for payments to residents of other countries, for transfers to other external accounts, and for purchase of other convertible currencies.
Blocked accounts	No.

Imports and Import Payments

Foreign exchange budget	No.
Financing requirements for imports	No.
Documentation requirements for release of foreign exchange for imports	
Preshipment inspection	Yes.
Import licenses and other nontariff measures	
Negative list	Imports of certain goods are subject to prior authorization for health and security reasons.
Open general licenses	Yes.
Import taxes and/or tariffs	Customs duty rates range from zero to 20%. All merchandise imports are subject to a national sales tax of 10% calculated on the c.i.f. value. Imports by the government, diplomatic missions, and charitable organizations are exempt from this tax.
State import monopoly	No.

Exports and Export Proceeds

Repatriation requirements	No.
Financing requirements	No.
Documentation requirements	No.
Export licenses	
Without quotas	The exportation of forestry products is subject to prior authorization from the Forestry Department.
Export taxes	No.

Payments for Invisible Transactions and Current Transfers

Controls on these transfers	No.

Proceeds from Invisible Transactions and Current Transfers

Repatriation requirements	No.
Restrictions on use of funds	No.

Capital Transactions

Controls on capital and money market instruments	There are no capital markets, money markets, or stock exchanges in The Gambia.
Controls on derivatives and other instruments	These instruments do not exist in The Gambia.
Controls on credit operations	
Financial credits	
To residents from nonresidents	Yes.
Controls on direct investment	No.
Controls on liquidation of direct investment	No.
Controls on real estate transactions	There are controls on all real estate transactions.
Controls on personal capital movements	n.a.
Provisions specific to commercial banks and other credit institutions	
Differential treatment of deposit accounts in foreign exchange	There are no deposit accounts in foreign exchange.
Open foreign exchange position limits	The limit in the interbank foreign exchange market set by the CBG must be observed on a weekly basis, and transactions must be reported daily to the CBG. On September 30, 1999, the ceiling on foreign exchange holdings by commercial banks was replaced by foreign exchange exposure limits.
Provisions specific to institutional investors	No.
Other controls imposed by securities laws	No.

Changes During 1999

Capital transactions	
Provisions specific to commercial banks and other credit institutions	*September 30.* The limit on foreign exchange holdings by commercial banks was replaced by foreign exchange exposure limits.

GEORGIA

(Position as of January 31, 2000)

Status Under IMF Articles of Agreement

Article VIII   Date of acceptance: December 20, 1996.

Exchange Arrangement

Currency   The currency of Georgia is the Georgian lari.

Exchange rate structure   Unitary.

Classification

Independently floating   While the National Bank of Georgia (NBG) does not intervene in the market to defend the exchange rate, it purchases foreign exchange when this is consistent with its inflation objectives. The official exchange rate for the dollar is determined daily. The official rates for other currencies are determined on the basis of the cross rates for the dollar and the currencies concerned in the international market. The official exchange rates are used for budget and tax accounting purposes, as well as for all payments between the government and enterprises and other legal entities. The NBG and the major commercial banks participate in the fixing sessions at the Tbilisi Interbank Currency Exchange (TICEX) for all commercial transactions; the exchange rate of the lari is negotiated freely between the banks and foreign exchange bureaus that are licensed by the NBG and their customers. Foreign exchange bureaus are permitted to buy and sell foreign currency notes.

Exchange tax   No.

Exchange subsidy   No.

Forward exchange market   This market is largely inoperative.

Arrangements for Payments and Receipts

Prescription of currency requirements   No.

Payment arrangements   No.

Administration of control   The NBG is responsible for administering exchange control regulations, which are formulated in collaboration with the MOF.

International security restrictions   No.

Payment arrears   Georgia has accumulated official arrears to the People's Republic of China, Russia, Turkmenistan, and Ukraine. The Georgian authorities have initiated negotiations on the second stage of rescheduling agreements for the full amount of the arrears accumulated.

Official   Yes.

Controls on trade in gold (coins and/or bullion)   A license is required to trade in gold.

Controls on domestic ownership and/or trade   Yes.

Controls on external trade   Yes.

Controls on exports and imports of banknotes

On exports   Yes.

Domestic currency	Up to four units of each currency denomination may be taken out without permission. For exports exceeding this limit, NBG authorization is required.
On imports	A declaration is required.
Domestic currency	Yes.

Resident Accounts

Foreign exchange accounts permitted	Yes.
Held domestically	There are no restrictions on the opening and use of these accounts, and the balances may be used for all authorized transactions.
Held abroad	No.
Accounts in domestic currency convertible into foreign currency	No.

Nonresident Accounts

Foreign exchange accounts permitted	No.
Domestic currency accounts	No.
Blocked accounts	No.

Imports and Import Payments

Foreign exchange budget	No.
Financing requirements for imports	No.
Documentation requirements for release of foreign exchange for imports	No.
Import licenses and other nontariff measures	
Negative list	Licenses are required for imports of weapons, narcotics, industrial equipment, pharmaceuticals, and agricultural pesticides; licenses are issued by the State Committee on Foreign Economic Relations (SCFER).
Import taxes and/or tariffs	A customs duty of 12% is levied on most non-CIS imports, as well as imports of fuels from CIS countries; certain goods are subject to a 5% customs duty, including specific capital goods, medical goods and equipment, and certain raw materials. Items exempted from customs duties include mazut, baby food, goods for embassies, imported goods in customs warehouses, reexports, some pharmaceutical products, and raw materials and semifinished goods destined for production of exports within certain limits. All imports are subject to a 0.3% customs processing fee. Effective January 1, 2000, this fee was changed to 0.15% of the value of the product, but not less than lari 50 and not to exceed lari 2,000.
State import monopoly	n.a.

Exports and Export Proceeds

Repatriation requirements	No.
Financing requirements	No.
Documentation requirements	Yes.

Export licenses	Licensing is administered by the SCFER. Licenses are required for logs; scrap metal; pine seeds; numismatic collections considered national treasures; certain biological, paleon-tological, archeological, and ethnographic goods; and raw materials for the production of medicine. Exports of scrap metal are subject to a specific tax equivalent to 20% ad valorem rate. This tax was eliminated on July 20, 1999. Exports of arms and narcotics are subject, in practice, to prohibitions.
Without quotas	Yes.
Export taxes	All exports are subject to a general customs processing fee of 0.3%. Effective January 1, 2000, this fee was changed to 0.15% of the value of the product, but not less than lari 50 and not to exceed lari 2,000.

Payments for Invisible Transactions and Current Transfers

Controls on these transfers	There are indicative limits/bona fide tests in the case of all payments for invisible transactions and current transfers.
Trade-related payments	
Indicative limits/bona fide test	Yes.
Investment-related payments	Information is not available on the payment of amortization of loans or depreciation of direct investments.
Indicative limits/bona fide test	Yes.
Payments for travel	
Indicative limits/bona fide test	Yes.
Personal payments	
Indicative limits/bona fide test	Yes.
Foreign workers' wages	
Indicative limits/bona fide test	Yes.
Credit card use abroad	
Prior approval	Yes.
Indicative limits/bona fide test	Yes.
Other payments	
Indicative limits/bona fide test	Yes.

Proceeds from Invisible Transactions and Current Transfers

Repatriation requirements	No.
Restrictions on use of funds	No.

Capital Transactions

Controls on capital and money market instruments	Inward and outward capital operations are not restricted but are subject to registration re-quirements for monitoring purposes. The issuance, trading, recording, and redemption of government securities are to be regulated by the Law on Securities and Stock Exchanges that is currently being developed.
Controls on derivatives and other instruments	
Purchase locally by nonresidents	Yes.

Sale or issue locally by nonresidents	Yes.
Sale or issue abroad by residents	Yes.
Controls on credit operations	No.
Controls on direct investment	Under the Foreign Investment Law, the taxation and promotion of investment activities by joint ventures and foreign enterprises are regulated by the current tax legislation. Foreign investment enterprises that received licenses before this law came into effect enjoy all the rights and benefits granted under the previous law for a period of five years from the date of issuance of those licenses.
Controls on liquidation of direct investment	No.
Controls on real estate transactions	No.
Controls on personal capital movements	No.
Provisions specific to commercial banks and other credit institutions	
Open foreign exchange position limits	
On resident assets and liabilities	Yes.
On nonresident assets and liabilities	Yes.
Provisions specific to institutional investors	n.a.
Other controls imposed by securities laws	n.a.

Changes During 1999

Exports and export proceeds	*July 20.* The export tax on scrap metal was eliminated.

Changes During 2000

Imports and import payments	*January 1.* The charge for customs processing of both imported and exported goods was changed to 0.15% (previously 0.3%) of the value of the product, but not less than lari 50 and not to exceed lari 2,000.

GERMANY

(Position as of December 31, 1999)

Status Under IMF Articles of Agreement

Article VIII   Date of acceptance: February 15, 1961.

Exchange Arrangement

Currency
As of January 1, 1999, the currency of Germany is the euro. In cash transactions, however, the legal tender is the deutsche mark until 2002, when euro banknotes and coins will be issued.

Exchange rate structure
Unitary.

Classification

Exchange arrangement with no separate legal tender
Germany participates in a currency union (EMU) comprising 11 members of the EU: Austria, Belgium, Finland, France, Germany, Ireland, Italy, Luxembourg, the Netherlands, Portugal, and Spain. Internal conversion rates in respect to the national currencies of EMU participants were fixed to the euro on January 1, 1999, whereas the external exchange rate of the euro is market determined. The conversion rate between the euro and the deutsche mark was set at DM 1.95583 per €1. The ECB has the right to intervene to smooth out fluctuations in external exchange rates.

Exchange tax
No.

Exchange subsidy
No.

Forward exchange market
Residents and nonresidents may freely negotiate forward exchange contracts for both commercial and financial transactions in all leading convertible currencies in the domestic exchange market and at international foreign exchange markets. Germany has no officially fixed rates in the forward exchange market. All transactions are negotiated at free market rates.

Arrangements for Payments and Receipts

Prescription of currency requirements
No.

Payment arrangements
No.

Administration of control
All banks in Germany are permitted to carry out foreign exchange transactions.

International security restrictions

In accordance with UN sanctions
In compliance with UN Security Council resolutions and EU regulations, restrictions have been imposed on the making of payments and transfers for current international transactions regarding Iraq and the Federal Republic of Yugoslavia (Serbia/Montenegro) and against the Taliban (the Islamic State of Afghanistan). Restrictions against Libya were suspended on April 5, 1999.

Payment arrears
No.

Controls on trade in gold (coins and/or bullion)
No.

Controls on exports and imports of banknotes
No.

Resident Accounts

Foreign exchange accounts permitted	Yes.
Held domestically	Yes.
Held abroad	Yes.
Accounts in domestic currency convertible into foreign currency	Yes.

Nonresident Accounts

Foreign exchange accounts permitted	Yes.
Domestic currency accounts	Yes.
Convertible into foreign currency	Yes.
Blocked accounts	Yes.

Imports and Import Payments

Foreign exchange budget	No.
Financing requirements for imports	No.
Documentation requirements for release of foreign exchange for imports	No.
Import licenses and other nontariff measures	
Negative list	Yes.
Licenses with quotas	The importation of certain nontextile goods from China is subject to the EU's annual global quota.
Other nontariff measures	Imports of numerous textile products are subject to the agreement on textiles and clothing and to bilateral agreements and regulations of the EU with various supplier countries. Most goods covered by the CAP are subject to variable import levies. Imports of rolled steel products from Russia and Ukraine are subject to an annual quota under a voluntary restrictions agreement. Imports of rolled steel products from Kazakhstan are subject to an autonomous EU quota.
Import taxes and/or tariffs	No.
State import monopoly	No.

Exports and Export Proceeds

Repatriation requirements	No.
Financing requirements	No.
Documentation requirements	For statistical purposes, an export notification is required for all goods.
Export licenses	
Without quotas	Certain exports (mostly military and dual-use goods) are subject to individual, global, or general licensing. The customs authorities exercise control over export declarations.
Export taxes	No.

Payments for Invisible Transactions and Current Transfers

Controls on these transfers	No.

Proceeds from Invisible Transactions and Current Transfers

Repatriation requirements	No.
Restrictions on use of funds	No.

Capital Transactions

Controls on capital and money market instruments	Effective January 1, 1999, the restriction on purchases of federal savings bonds by nonresident entities and the prohibition on the sale or issue of bonds and/or money market securities and debt instruments denominated in deutsche mark issued by nonresident banks with a maturity of less than two years were abolished, as was the requirement that securities denominated in deutsche mark should only be issued under the lead management of credit institutions domiciled in Germany.
Controls on derivatives and other instruments	No.
Controls on credit operations	No.
Controls on direct investment	No.
Controls on liquidation of direct investment	No.
Controls on real estate transactions	No.
Controls on personal capital movements	No.
Provisions specific to commercial banks and other credit institutions	On January 1, 1999, the provisions on minimum reserve requirements were replaced by corresponding ECB regulations.
Provisions specific to institutional investors	
Limits (max.) on securities issued by nonresidents and on portfolio invested abroad	There are certain provisions for the portfolio of life insurance and pension funds for prudential regulations.
Limits (max.) on portfolio invested abroad	The same regulations apply as for securities.
Currency-matching regulations on assets/liabilities composition	Currency-matching regulation for life insurance, pension funds, and old-age provision investment funds exist.
Other controls imposed by securities laws	No.

Changes During 1999

Exchange arrangement	*January 1*. The currency of Germany became the euro. The conversion rate between the euro and the deutsche mark was set irrevocably at DM 1.95583 per €1.
Arrangements for payments and receipts	*April 5*. Restrictions against Libya were suspended.

Capital transactions

Controls on capital and money market instruments

January 1. The restriction of purchases of federal savings bonds by nonresident entities and the prohibition on the sale or issue of bonds and/or money market securities and debt instruments denominated in deutsche mark issued by nonresident banks with a maturity of less than two years were abolished, as was the requirement that securities denominated in deutsche mark should only be issued under the lead management of credit institutions domiciled in Germany.

Provisions specific to commercial banks and other credit institutions

January 1. The provisions on minimum reserve requirements were replaced by corresponding ECB regulations.

GHANA
(Position as of December 31, 1999)

Status Under IMF Articles of Agreement

Article VIII   Date of acceptance: February 2, 1994.

Exchange Arrangement

Currency	The currency of Ghana is the Ghanaian cedi.
Exchange rate structure	Unitary.
Classification	
Independently floating	The exchange rate of the cedi is determined in the interbank foreign exchange market. Since October 6, 1999, the average exchange rate is based on the average rates reported by authorized banks in their transactions with each other or with their customers. Before that, the exchange rate in the interbank market was not always applied by authorized banks to their customers. Rates are quoted by authorized dealers for certain other currencies, with daily quotations based on the buying and selling rates for the dollar in markets abroad.
Exchange tax	No.
Exchange subsidy	No.
Forward exchange market	No.

Arrangements for Payments and Receipts

Prescription of currency requirements	Settlements related to transactions covered by bilateral payment agreements are made through clearing accounts maintained by the Bank of Ghana (BOG) and the central banks of the countries concerned. Proceeds from exports to countries with which Ghana does not have bilateral payment agreements must be received in the currency of the importing country (if that currency is quoted by the BOG) or debited for authorized inward payments to residents of Ghana for transfers to other official accounts related to the same country and for transfers to the related clearing account at the BOG.
Payment arrangements	
Bilateral payment arrangements	
Inoperative	Ghana has agreements with Bulgaria, China, Cuba, the Czech Republic, Poland, Romania, and the Slovak Republic. The clearing balances on these agreements are being settled.
Administration of control	The BOG records and confirms foreign capital inflows and administers foreign exchange for official payments and travel. All foreign exchange transactions by the private sector are approved and effected by authorized banks without reference to the BOG.
International security restrictions	No.
Payment arrears	No.
Controls on trade in gold (coins and/or bullion)	
Controls on domestic ownership and/or trade	Domestic transactions in gold must be authorized by the Precious Minerals Marketing Company, and certain domestic sales may be carried out only by permit under the Gold Mining Products Protection Ordinance.
Controls on external trade	Ghanaian residents may not buy or borrow any gold from, or sell or lend any gold to, any person other than an authorized dealer. Imports of gold other than those by or on behalf of the monetary authorities are not normally licensed. The import duty on gold, including bullion and partly worked gold, is levied at a uniform rate of 25%. The gold mines export their output in semirefined form.

Controls on exports and imports of banknotes

On exports

Domestic currency — The exportation of Ghanaian banknotes is permitted up to the equivalent of ₵5,000.

Foreign currency — Residents traveling abroad are permitted to carry up to the equivalent of $3,000. In addition, resident travelers are permitted to carry up to $5,000 or its equivalent in traveler's checks or bank drafts for direct purchases.

On imports

Domestic currency — Travelers may reimport up to the equivalent of the ₵5,000 that they were allowed to export.

Resident Accounts

Foreign exchange accounts permitted — Yes.

Held domestically — Yes.

Held abroad — These accounts are permitted, but approval is required.

Accounts in domestic currency convertible into foreign currency — Conversion is not allowed, except for approved purposes.

Nonresident Accounts

Foreign exchange accounts permitted — The accounts may be credited with authorized outward payments, with transfers from other foreign accounts, and with the proceeds from sales of convertible currency. They may be debited for inward payments, for transfers to other foreign accounts, and for purchases of external currencies upon approval by the BOG. Nonresident account status is granted to embassies, delegations, consulates, and offices of high commissioners in Ghana and to the non-Ghanaian members of their staff. It is also available to international institutions and foreign-registered companies operating in Ghana, and to nonresident Ghanaians.

Approval required — Yes.

Domestic currency accounts — Yes.

Convertible into foreign currency — These accounts are permitted, but approval is required.

Blocked accounts — Funds not placed at the free disposal of nonresidents (for example, certain types of capital proceeds) may be deposited in blocked accounts, which may be debited for authorized payments, including for purchases of approved securities.

Imports and Import Payments

Foreign exchange budget — No.

Financing requirements for imports — No.

Documentation requirements for release of foreign exchange for imports

Preshipment inspection — Required for imports above ₵5,000.

Letters of credit — Most imports are effected with confirmed LCs established through authorized banks on a sight basis.

Import licenses and other nontariff measures

Negative list — Yes.

Import taxes and/or tariffs	Tariffs range from zero to 25% of the c.i.f. value of imports. A significant portion of imports, mostly for investment, is exempted. On May 1, 1999, importers without a tax-payer identification number became subject to a 5% income withholding tax on the value of their imports. At the same time, the special tax of 17.5% on certain imported goods was abolished.
State import monopoly	No.

Exports and Export Proceeds

Repatriation requirements	Exporters are required to collect and repatriate in full the proceeds from their exports within 60 days of shipment; proceeds from exports of nontraditional products may be sold at market rates upon receipt in the banks.
Surrender requirements	Nontraditional exports are not subject to surrender requirements, while 20% to 40% of gold and 98% of cocoa export proceeds are surrendered to the BOG.
Financing requirements	No.
Documentation requirements	
Letters of credit	LCs are required, except for nontraditional exports.
Guarantees	Yes.
Domiciliation	Yes.
Preshipment inspection	An inspection is required, except for nontraditional exports.
Other	Yes.
Export licenses	
Export taxes	Only cocoa exports are subject to an export tax that is calculated as the difference between export proceeds and payments to farmers, together with the Cocoa Board's costs if proceeds exceed payments.

Payments for Invisible Transactions and Current Transfers

Controls on these transfers	
Trade-related payments	Freight charges may be paid to the local shipping agents; the transfer of funds to cover such charges is normally permitted, provided that the application is properly documented.
Quantitative limits	Quantitative limits are applied for commissions.
Investment-related payments	
Prior approval	Prior approval is required for the payment of amortization of loans or depreciation of direct investments.
Payments for travel	
Quantitative limits	Residents traveling abroad are permitted to carry up to the equivalent of $3,000. In addition, resident travelers are permitted to carry up to the equivalent of $5,000 in traveler's checks or bank drafts for direct purchases abroad.
Indicative limits/bona fide test	Yes.

Proceeds from Invisible Transactions and Current Transfers

Repatriation requirements	Yes.
Surrender requirements	All receipts from invisibles must be sold to authorized dealers or held in foreign exchange–denominated bank accounts in resident banks.

Restrictions on use of funds	No.

Capital Transactions

Controls on capital and money market instruments

On capital market securities

Shares or other securities of a participating nature

Purchase locally by nonresidents

Nonresidents may purchase securities listed on the Ghana Stock Exchange (GSE); individual holdings and total holdings of all nonresidents in one security listed on the GSE may not exceed 10% and 74%, respectively. For companies not listed on the GSE, nonresident participation requires the following minimum equity injections to acquire shares: (1) $10,000 or its equivalent in capital goods when the enterprise is a joint venture; (2) $50,000 or its equivalent in capital goods when the enterprise is wholly owned by a non-Ghanaian; and (3) $300,000 or its equivalent in capital goods in the case of a trading enterprise involved only in the purchasing and selling of goods that is either wholly or partly owned by a non-Ghanaian and that employs at least 10 Ghanaians.

Sale or issue locally by nonresidents

These transactions require prior approval from the BOG and the MOF. The transfer or repatriation of proceeds from sales must be reported to the BOG.

Purchase abroad by residents

There are no controls on these purchases, but the purchase of foreign exchange to buy securities requires the prior approval of the BOG.

Sale or issue abroad by residents

These transactions require the prior approval of the BOG.

Bonds or other debt securities

Sale or issue locally by nonresidents

These transactions require the prior approval of the BOG.

Purchase abroad by residents

These transactions require the prior approval of the BOG.

Sale or issue abroad by residents

These transactions require the prior approval of the BOG.

On money market instruments

Purchase locally by nonresidents

Current regulations do not allow nonresidents to bring in foreign exchange for the purpose of investing in local money market instruments (BOG and government securities). However, nonresidents holding local currencies may invest in these instruments.

Sale or issue locally by nonresidents

These transactions are not allowed.

Purchase abroad by residents

No controls apply to these purchases, but the purchase of foreign exchange to buy these instruments requires the prior approval of the BOG.

Sale or issue abroad by residents

These transactions are not allowed.

On collective investment securities

Purchase locally by nonresidents

These purchases require prior approval of the BOG.

Sale or issue locally by nonresidents

These transactions, as well as the transfer abroad of proceeds associated with these sales, including those derived from the liquidation of such securities, require BOG approval.

Purchase abroad by residents

The purchase of foreign exchange to buy such securities requires prior approval from the BOG.

Sale or issue abroad by residents

These transactions require the consent of the MOF.

Controls on derivatives and other instruments

Currently, a local market in derivatives and other instruments does not exist.

Purchase locally by nonresidents

Yes.

Sale or issue locally by nonresidents

Yes.

Purchase abroad by residents	The purchase of foreign exchange to effect such transactions requires BOG approval.
Sale or issue abroad by residents	Yes.

Controls on credit operations

Commercial credits

   To residents from nonresidents — BOG approval is required for these credits, which must be channeled through the banking system. Transactions must be supported by relevant documents.

Financial credits

   To residents from nonresidents — These credits require BOG approval.

Controls on direct investment

Outward direct investment — All capital outflows must be approved by the BOG; applications for such transfers must be supported by documentary evidence and are considered on their merits.

Inward direct investment — Certain areas of economic activity are not open to foreigners. Foreign investments in Ghana require the prior approval of the Ghana Investment Promotion Center (GIPC) if they are to benefit from the facilities available under the GIPC Act, under which approved investments are guaranteed, in principle, the right to transfer profits and, in the event of sale or liquidation, capital proceeds. Tax holidays and initial capital allowances are also available for such investments.

The minimum qualifying amounts of investment by a non-Ghanaian are as follows: (1) $10,000 or its equivalent in capital goods by way of equity participation in a joint-venture enterprise with a Ghanaian partner; (2) $50,000 or its equivalent in capital goods by way of equity when the enterprise is wholly owned by a non-Ghanaian; and (3) $300,000 or its equivalent in goods by way of equity capital when the enterprise is either wholly or partly owned by a non-Ghanaian, employs at least 10 Ghanaians, and is involved in the purchasing and selling of goods.

Controls on liquidation of direct investment — The GIPC Act stipulates that the assets of foreign investors may not be expropriated. Disputes over the amount of compensation are settled in accordance with the established procedure for conciliation (for example, through arbitration by the International Center for Settlements of Investment Disputes or the United Nations Commission on International Trade and Law).

Controls on real estate transactions

Purchase abroad by residents	Individuals are allowed up to $500.
Sale locally by nonresidents	Yes.

Controls on personal capital movements — There are controls on all personal capital movements, except for the transfer of assets into the country by immigrants.

Provisions specific to commercial banks and other credit institutions

Borrowing abroad	BOG notification is required.
Maintenance of accounts abroad	BOG notification is required.
Lending to nonresidents (financial or commercial credits)	Yes.
Lending locally in foreign exchange	Yes.
Purchase of locally issued securities denominated in foreign exchange	These purchases are allowed within reasonable or acceptable limits.

Investment regulations

   In banks by nonresidents — Yes.

Open foreign exchange position limits — Based on the volume of foreign exchange transactions of banks. This is subject to periodic review.

On resident assets and liabilities	Yes.
On nonresident assets and liabilities	Yes.
Provisions specific to institutional investors	No.
Other controls imposed by securities laws	No.

Changes During 1999

Exchange arrangement	*October 6.* The average exchange rate is now based on the average rates reported by authorized banks in their transactions with each other or with their customers.
Imports and import payments	*May 1.* Importers without a taxpayer identification number became subject to a 5% income withholding tax on the value of their imports. At the same time, the special tax of 17.5% on certain imported goods was abolished.

GREECE

(Position as of March 31, 2000)

Status Under IMF Articles of Agreement

Article VIII	Date of acceptance: July 22, 1992.

Exchange Arrangement

Currency	The currency of Greece is the Greek drachma.
Exchange rate structure	Unitary.

Classification

Pegged exchange rate within horizontal bands	The exchange rate for the drachma is determined in the domestic and foreign interbank markets, as well as in daily fixing sessions in which the Bank of Greece (BOG) and authorized commercial banks participate. Greece is a member of the ERM of the EMS, and was admitted to the ERM II on January 1, 1999.
Exchange tax	No.
Exchange subsidy	No.
Forward exchange market	No.

Arrangements for Payments and Receipts

Prescription of currency requirements	Settlements with all countries may be made in any convertible foreign currency or through nonresident deposit accounts in drachmas.
Payment arrangements	No.
Administration of control	There are no exchange controls. Resident credit institutions are authorized to carry out all the necessary formalities for the settlement of all transactions with nonresidents and are obliged to provide to the BOG all the information necessary to compile the balance of payments. Until August 5, 1999, natural and juridical persons were required to inform the BOG, for statistical purposes, of transactions with nonresidents of sums greater than €2,000 if a domestic banking institution was not involved.

International security restrictions

In accordance with UN sanctions	Yes.
Payment arrears	No.

Controls on trade in gold (coins and/or bullion)

Controls on domestic ownership and/or trade	Residents may freely purchase new gold sovereigns from the BOG through licensed stock-brokers at a price set by the BOG. These gold coins may be resold only to the BOG or to the Athens Stock Exchange (ASE). Holders of gold coins acquired in the free market that existed before December 22, 1965, may sell them without any formality to the BOG or to an authorized bank at the official price.
	Effective March 2, 2000, natural and juridical persons, residents, and nonresidents may freely purchase and sell gold coins and/or bars that are not used for commercial and industrial purposes. This gold may be purchased by and sold to the BOG and/or any other credit institution operating in Greece authorized to carry out transactions in foreign exchange.
Controls on external trade	Until March 1, 2000, gold bars or coins brought in by travelers and declared upon entry were allowed to be reexported after approval by the BOG. Effective March 2, 2000, residents and nonresidents are required to declare upon entering and/or leaving Greece amounts of gold exceeding the equivalent of €2,000 and €10,000, respectively, or submit

a copy of the document certifying that the relevant latter transaction was carried out by a domestic credit institution.

Controls on exports and imports of banknotes	
On exports	Residents and nonresidents leaving Greece should declare amounts of banknotes and personal checks in domestic and/or foreign currency exceeding the equivalent of €2,000. For amounts up to the equivalent of €10,000, they must also provide in the declaration the purpose of the export of banknotes and additionally: (1) if they are residents of Greece, their fiscal number; (2) if they are residents of other EU member countries, the number of their identification and/or passport number; and (3) if they are residents of other non-EU member countries, their passport number. If the amount exceeds the equivalent of €10,000, residents must also provide a copy of their tax certificate.
Domestic currency	Yes.
Foreign currency	Yes.
On imports	Residents and nonresidents entering Greece should declare imported banknotes and personal checks in domestic and foreign currency if the total amount exceeds the equivalent of €10,000.
Domestic currency	Yes.
Foreign currency	Yes.

Resident Accounts

Foreign exchange accounts permitted	Yes.
Held domestically	Yes.
Held abroad	Yes.
Accounts in domestic currency convertible into foreign currency	Residents are permitted to convert drachma deposits held with resident credit institutions into foreign currency deposits.

Nonresident Accounts

Foreign exchange accounts permitted	Yes.
Domestic currency accounts	Yes.
Convertible into foreign currency	Yes.
Blocked accounts	No.

Imports and Import Payments

Foreign exchange budget	No.
Financing requirements for imports	No.
Documentation requirements for release of foreign exchange for imports	No.
Import licenses and other nontariff measures	Import licenses are required for some specific products from certain low-cost countries under EU surveillance. Special regulations govern imports of certain items such as medicines, narcotics, and motion picture films.
Licenses with quotas	Yes.
Other nontariff measures	Yes.

Import taxes and/or tariffs	No.
State import monopoly	No.

Exports and Export Proceeds

Repatriation requirements	No.
Financing requirements	No.
Documentation requirements	No.
Export licenses	No.
Export taxes	No.

Payments for Invisible Transactions and Current Transfers

Controls on these transfers

Payments for travel

   Quantitative limits — Yes.

   Indicative limits/bona fide test — Effective August 5, 1999, the limit was raised to the equivalent of €10,000 (previously €2,000) a trip a person in domestic or foreign currency without presenting any supporting documentation.

Personal payments

   Quantitative limits — Yes.

   Indicative limits/bona fide test — Effective August 5, 1999, the limit was raised to the equivalent of €10,000 (previously €2,000) for studies abroad in foreign or domestic currency; additional amounts are permitted upon presentation of the relevant documentation.

Foreign workers' wages

   Prior approval — Remittances of earnings by foreign workers are permitted, with the provision of the relevant documentation.

Credit card use abroad

   Indicative limits/bona fide test — The limit on withdrawal in foreign banknotes is the equivalent of €1,000 a month.

Proceeds from Invisible Transactions and Current Transfers

Repatriation requirements	No.
Restrictions on use of funds	No.

Capital Transactions

Controls on capital and money market instruments

On capital market securities

Shares or other securities of a participating nature

   Purchase locally by nonresidents — Existing legislation on inward direct investment and establishment imposes certain control on the purchase of shares and other securities of a participatory nature in the broadcasting and maritime sectors.

Controls on derivatives and other instruments	No.
Controls on credit operations	No.
Controls on direct investment	
Inward direct investment	Investments in border regions by non-EU residents require approval for reasons of national security. There are also controls on the acquisition of mining rights and participation in new or existing enterprises if these are engaged in radio and television broadcasting or maritime and air transport.
Controls on liquidation of direct investment	No.
Controls on real estate transactions	No.
Controls on personal capital movements	
Transfer of gambling and prize earnings	Transfers are permitted with the provision of the relevant documentation.
Provisions specific to commercial banks and other credit institutions	No.
Provisions specific to institutional investors	No.
Other controls imposed by securities laws	Over-the-counter transactions of equities listed on the ASE are not allowed.

Changes During 1999

Exchange arrangement	*January 1*. Greece was admitted to the ERM II.
Arrangements for payments and receipts	*August 5*. The requirement of informing the BOG of transactions above €2,000 carried out between residents and nonresidents was eliminated.
Payments for invisible transactions and current transfers	*August 5*. The limits for personal travel and payments abroad were raised to the equivalent of €10,000 from €2,000.

Changes During 2000

Arrangements for payments and receipts	*March 2*. Natural and juridical persons, residents, and nonresidents were allowed to freely purchase and sell gold coins and/or bars that are not used for commercial and industrial purposes. This gold may be purchased by and sold to the BOG and/or any other credit institution operating in Greece authorized to carry out transactions in foreign exchange. Residents and nonresidents were required to declare upon entering and/or leaving Greece amounts of gold exceeding the equivalent of €2,000 and €10,000, respectively.

GRENADA

(Position as of January 31, 2000)

Status Under IMF Articles of Agreement

Article VIII   Date of acceptance: January 24, 1994.

Exchange Arrangement

Currency   The currency of Grenada is the Eastern Caribbean dollar, which is issued by the ECCB.

Exchange rate structure   Unitary.

Classification

Exchange arrangement with no sepa-   The Eastern Caribbean dollar is pegged to the U.S. dollar, the intervention currency, at
rate legal tender   EC$2.70 per US$1.

Exchange tax   No.

Exchange subsidy   No.

Forward exchange market   No.

Arrangements for Payments and Receipts

**Prescription of currency   Settlements with residents of member countries of the CARICOM must be made either
requirements**   through external accounts in Eastern Caribbean dollars, in the currency of the CARICOM
                                     country concerned, or in U.S. dollars. Settlements with residents of the former Sterling
                                     Area, other than CARICOM countries, may be made in pounds sterling, in any other former
                                     Sterling Area currency, or in Eastern Caribbean dollars to and from external accounts.
                                     Settlements with residents of other countries are made in any foreign currency or through
                                     an external account in Eastern Caribbean dollars.

Payment arrangements

Regional arrangements   Grenada is a member of the CARICOM.

Clearing agreements   Grenada participates in the CMCF.

Administration of control   Exchange control is administered by the MOF and applies to all countries. The MOF dele-
                                     gates to authorized dealers (ADs) the authority to approve some import payments and cer-
                                     tain other outward payments. The Trade Division of the MOF administers trade control.

International security restrictions

In accordance with UN sanctions   There are restrictions on trade relations with Libya.

Payment arrears   No.

**Controls on trade in gold (coins
and/or bullion)**

Controls on domestic ownership and/or   Residents other than the monetary authorities, ADs, and industrial users are not permitted
trade   to hold or acquire gold in any form other than jewelry or coins for numismatic purposes.

Controls on external trade   Imports of gold are permitted for industrial purposes only and are subject to customs duties
                                     and charges. The MOF issues licenses to import gold. The exportation of gold is not
                                     normally permitted.

**Controls on exports and imports of
banknotes**

On exports

  Foreign currency   Nonresident travelers may export, with the approval of the MOF, any foreign currency
                                     they previously brought into Grenada, and both residents and nonresidents must receive

---

permission from the MOF to take out, in any one transaction, sums in excess of EC$250,000.

Resident Accounts

Foreign exchange accounts permitted These accounts may be freely debited but may be credited only with foreign exchange earned or received from outside the ECCB area. Holders of these accounts must submit regular statements of debits and credits to the MOF.

Held domestically Yes.

Held abroad n.a.

Accounts in domestic currency convertible into foreign currency n.a.

Nonresident Accounts

Foreign exchange accounts permitted The same regulations apply as for resident accounts.

Domestic currency accounts These accounts must be credited with funds from an external source.

Convertible into foreign currency Yes.

Blocked accounts No.

Imports and Import Payments

Foreign exchange budget No.

Financing requirements for imports No.

Documentation requirements for release of foreign exchange for imports Payments for documented imports are free of restrictions. Payments for restricted imports and any goods and services in excess of the limits of ADs require permission from the MOF.

Letters of credit Yes.

Import licenses and other nontariff measures

Negative list Prohibited goods include whole chickens, chicken eggs, live breeding poultry, war toys, animal skins, and various drugs deemed to be dangerous.

Open general licenses There are quantitative restrictions on certain items from non-CARICOM sources, including arms and ammunition; carbonated beverages; flour; industrial gas; paints; and miscellaneous items associated with furniture and the construction industry. Items from the CARICOM area that require licenses include curry products, industrial gas, furniture, and solar water heaters.

Licenses with quotas Yes.

Import taxes and/or tariffs All imports from non-CARICOM countries are subject to the following CET rates: zero for agricultural imports; 40% for agricultural products; and 15% to 25% for most other items. All imports are subject to a 5% customs service charge. Imports not granted exemptions from customs duties are subject to a general consumption tax (GCT) regime with three broad rates of 10%, 15%, and 25%. There are three additional GCT rates of 50%, 55%, and 75% that are applied to specific items such as new cars, foreign used cars, and cigarettes, respectively. An environmental levy is charged that consists of an EC$0.25 duty on each imported bottle of liquor, carbonated and noncarbonated beverages, and syrups. The levy also consists of a 1% charge on the c.i.f. of white goods (durable consumer items) and a 2% charge on the c.i.f. of imported cars. Imports of capital equipment are subject to a minimum charge of 5% under the CET and 25% under the consumption tax. However, most capital imports are granted exemptions from import duties, and all capital imports by domestic associations involved in the growing or packaging of bananas, maize, or nutmeg are exempt from import duties, provided that the imports are used for improvements in the industries. On January 1, 2000, the fourth phase of the CARICOM CET came into effect.

State import monopoly
The Marketing and National Importing Board is the sole authorized importer of bulk purchases of milk, flour, and sugar.

Exports and Export Proceeds

Repatriation requirements
Yes.

Surrender requirements
Proceeds must be surrendered to ADs (commercial banks) in foreign exchange.

Financing requirements
n.a.

Documentation requirements
n.a.

Export licenses
Specific licenses are required for the exportation of exotic birds, coral, mineral products, and live sheep and goats to any destination.

Without quotas
Yes.

Export taxes
No.

Payments for Invisible Transactions and Current Transfers

Controls on these transfers
Payments for invisibles related to authorized imports are not restricted but require the approval of the MOF whenever a single transaction exceeds EC$250,000.

Trade-related payments

Prior approval
Yes.

Quantitative limits
Yes.

Indicative limits/bona fide test
Yes.

Investment-related payments

Prior approval
Approval is granted if all related liabilities have been discharged and the investment was registered with the MOF.

Quantitative limits
Yes.

Indicative limits/bona fide test
Yes.

Payments for travel

Prior approval
Yes.

Quantitative limits
Yes.

Indicative limits/bona fide test
Yes.

Personal payments

Prior approval
For studies abroad, MOF approval is required, and permission is usually granted on presentation of documentation of registration and the costs of tuition and other expenses. For transfer of pensions, approval is granted upon proof of immigrant status. For family maintenance and alimony payments, approval is granted upon proof of established liabilities.

Indicative limits/bona fide test
Yes.

Foreign workers' wages

Prior approval
Approval is granted upon proof of immigrant status.

Indicative limits/bona fide test
Yes.

Other payments
There are no restrictions on the payment of subscriptions and membership fees.

Prior approval	MOF approval, which is granted on the basis of agreements incorporating payment for consulting and legal fees services, is required. Payments may be made up to the amount approved, subject, where applicable, to withholding on income tax.
Quantitative limits	Yes.
Indicative limits/bona fide test	Yes.

Proceeds from Invisible Transactions and Current Transfers

Repatriation requirements	Yes.
Surrender requirements	The surrender of foreign currency proceeds from invisibles is mandatory.
Restrictions on use of funds	No.

Capital Transactions

Controls on capital and money market instruments	Any single outward capital transaction in excess of EC$250,000 requires exchange control approval.
On capital market securities	
Shares or other securities of a participating nature	
Purchase locally by nonresidents	MOF approval is required.
Sale or issue locally by nonresidents	Yes.
Purchase abroad by residents	Certificates of title to foreign currency securities held by residents must be lodged with an authorized depository in Grenada, and earnings on these securities must be repatriated.
Bonds or other debt securities	
Purchase locally by nonresidents	MOF approval is required.
Sale or issue locally by nonresidents	Yes.
Purchase abroad by residents	Yes.
On money market instruments	
Sale or issue locally by nonresidents	Yes.
Purchase abroad by residents	Yes.
On collective investment securities	
Sale or issue locally by nonresidents	Yes.
Purchase abroad by residents	Yes.
Controls on derivatives and other instruments	
Sale or issue locally by nonresidents	Yes.
Purchase abroad by residents	Yes.
Controls on credit operations	
Commercial credits	
By residents to nonresidents	Local currency financing is not ordinarily permitted and requires the approval of the MOF.
Financial credits	
By residents to nonresidents	Yes.

Controls on direct investment

Outward direct investment   Yes.

Inward direct investment   Cabinet approval via the Industrial Development Corporation is normally required for non-residents operating manufacturing enterprises and hotels, and an alien landholding license is required for nonresidents to hold both financial and physical property. Nonresident labor services are generally permitted with work permits, which are issued by the Ministry of Labor.

Controls on liquidation of direct investment   Remittances of proceeds are permitted, provided that all related liabilities have been discharged and that the original investment was registered with the MOF.

Controls on real estate transactions

Purchase abroad by residents   An alien landholding license must be issued by the Office of the Prime Minister.

Controls on personal capital movements

Loans

   By residents to nonresidents   Yes.

   To residents from nonresidents   Any borrowing abroad by nationals to finance their domestic operations generally requires the approval of the MOF.

Gifts, endowments, inheritances, and legacies

   By residents to nonresidents   Yes.

Settlement of debts abroad by immigrants   Yes.

Transfer of assets

   Transfer abroad by emigrants   Yes.

Provisions specific to commercial banks and other credit institutions

Borrowing abroad   ADs may freely assume short-term liability positions in foreign currencies to finance approved transfers for both trade and nontrade transactions. Any borrowing abroad by ADs to finance their domestic operations requires the approval of the MOF.

Lending to nonresidents (financial or commercial credits)   Local currency financing requires the approval of the MOF but is not ordinarily permitted.

Provisions specific to institutional investors   No.

Other controls imposed by securities laws   n.a.

Changes During 1999

No significant changes occurred in the exchange and trade system.

Changes During 2000

Imports and import payments   *January 1.* The fourth phase of the CARICOM CET came into effect.

GUATEMALA

Status Under IMF Articles of Agreement

Article VIII	Date of acceptance: January 27, 1947.

Exchange Arrangement

Currency

The currency of Guatemala is the Guatemalan quetzal.

Exchange rate structure

Unitary.

Classification

Managed floating with no pre-announced path for the exchange rate

As of June 30, 1999, on the basis of additional available information, the exchange rate system of Guatemala was reclassified to the category managed floating, no preannounced path from the category independently floating. The exchange rate is determined in the interbank market where the Bank of Guatemala (BOG) intervenes to moderate undue fluctuations, to purchase foreign exchange on behalf of the public sector, and to service its own external debt. All foreign exchange transactions of the public sector must take place through the BOG at a reference rate that is equivalent to the weighted average of the buying and selling rates in the interbank market during the day before the previous business day.

Exchange tax

No.

Exchange subsidy

No.

Forward exchange market

No.

Arrangements for Payments and Receipts

Prescription of currency requirements

In practice, most transactions in foreign exchange are denominated in dollars, domestic currency, or other means of payment, in accordance with special payments agreements.

Payment arrangements

Bilateral payment arrangements

Operative

There are payment arrangements under the Mexico-Guatemala Clearing and Credit Reciprocal Agreement and the Panama-Guatemala Clearing and Credit Reciprocal Agreement.

Inoperative

The Clearing and Credit Reciprocal Agreement between Guatemala and El Salvador, Honduras, and Costa Rica functioned until 1995.

Regional arrangements

Guatemala is a member of the CACM.

Clearing agreements

Yes.

Administration of control

The BOG administers the exchange regime. Foreign exchange transactions in the public sector are carried out exclusively through the BOG; those in the private sector are made through banks and foreign exchange houses authorized by the Monetary Board.

International security restrictions

No.

Payment arrears

Official

Arrears are maintained with respect to certain external payments related to official debt, mostly with Paris Club creditors.

Controls on trade in gold (coins and/or bullion)

Controls on domestic ownership and/or trade

The BOG may buy and sell gold coins and bullion either directly or through authorized banks and is entitled to buy gold holdings surrendered by any resident. The BOG sells gold to domestic artistic or industrial users in accordance with guidelines from the Monetary Board with the government's approval.

Controls on external trade	The exportation of gold is prohibited except when the BOG issues a special export license. Gold is imported only by the BOG.
Controls on exports and imports of banknotes	No.

Resident Accounts

Foreign exchange accounts permitted	Juridical and natural persons are eligible. Banks, however, have not yet offered these accounts because the rules for foreign exchange deposits are still under discussion.
Held domestically	Yes.
Held abroad	No.
Accounts in domestic currency convertible into foreign currency	No.

Nonresident Accounts

Foreign exchange accounts permitted	Juridical and natural persons are eligible. Banks, however, have not yet offered these accounts because the rules for foreign exchange deposits are still under discussion.
Domestic currency accounts	Yes.
Convertible into foreign currency	No.
Blocked accounts	No.

Imports and Import Payments

Foreign exchange budget	No.
Financing requirements for imports	No.
Documentation requirements for release of foreign exchange for imports	No.
Import licenses and other nontariff measures	Imports of most goods are unrestricted and require neither registration nor a license. However, Guatemalan imports of agricultural commodities and animal products have been subject to tariffs. At present, those products are incorporated in and regulated within the WTO charter as very sensitive for the Guatemalan economy.
Open general licenses	Yes.
Import taxes and/or tariffs	Guatemala applies the CET for processed goods of the CACM, which ranges from zero to 15%, with virtually all intra-CACM trade exempt from tariffs. The maximum tariffs on raw materials, and intermediate and capital goods produced in Central America are 5% and 10%, respectively, while there are no tariffs on raw materials and intermediate and capital goods not produced in Central America.
	Some processed products, such as coffee, sugar, oil, wheat, and alcohol, which are traded with the CACM, are subject to tariffs ranging from 1% to 15%. Guatemala's tariff structure continues to exempt certain processed products from the maximum CET rate of 15%. The tariff rates for most textiles and footwear are 20% and 27%, respectively. In addition, certain agricultural products enjoy safeguard provisions and are subject to tariff rate quotas under WTO rules, which also allow tariffs well above the maximum rate for imports in excess of quota. Poultry and poultry parts are subject to a quota of 7,000 metric tons a year, with tariffs of 15% within quota and 45% in excess of quota. Other examples are apples and pears (12% and 25%); corn (5% and 35%); and wheat flour (8.28%). Rice is subject to a quota of 33,435 metric tons a year, with a tariff of zero and a range of tariffs between 18% and 36% in excess of the quota. These quotas are adjusted yearly, following discussions between the private sector and government.

State import monopoly	No.

Exports and Export Proceeds

Repatriation requirements	Yes.
Surrender requirements	Foreign exchange proceeds must be sold to an authorized participant in the interbank market other than the BOG. The granting of export licenses is contingent upon the agreement to sell export proceeds to any authorized participant in the interbank market other than the BOG within 90 days of the date of issue (this period may be extended to 180 days).
Financing requirements	No.
Documentation requirements	No.
Export licenses	Exporters must obtain an export license issued by the BOG before the Guatemalan customs can authorize shipment of the merchandise. A few other items, including gold (unless the BOG issues a special export license) and silver, may not be exported in any form. In the case of exports to Central America, export licenses are required only for statistical purposes.
With quotas	Exports of apparel and textiles to the U.S. market are subject to quotas.
Export taxes	No.

Payments for Invisible Transactions and Current Transfers

Controls on these transfers	No.

Proceeds from Invisible Transactions and Current Transfers

Repatriation requirements	Yes.
Surrender requirements	Proceeds for invisibles must be sold to an authorized financial institution at the market rate.
Restrictions on use of funds	No.

Capital Transactions

Controls on capital and money market instruments	No.
Controls on derivatives and other instruments	No.
Controls on credit operations	
Guarantees, sureties, and financial backup facilities	
To residents from nonresidents	Yes.
Controls on direct investment	
Inward direct investment	Foreign direct investment in the petroleum sector is regulated by special legislation.
Controls on liquidation of direct investment	No.
Controls on real estate transactions	No.
Controls on personal capital movements	No.

Provisions specific to commercial banks and other credit institutions

Borrowing abroad   Yes.

Maintenance of accounts abroad   Yes.

Lending to nonresidents (financial or   Yes.
commercial credits)

Differential treatment of deposit
accounts in foreign exchange

   Reserve requirements   Yes.

   Liquid asset requirements   Yes.

   Credit controls   Yes.

Open foreign exchange position limits   The limit for banks and finance companies is 25% of the value of their paid-up capital and
                                                   reserves; for exchange houses, it is 100%. Foreign exchange exceeding these limits at the
                                                   end of each day must be negotiated in the interbank market or sold to the BOG.

Provisions specific to institutional   No.
investors

Other controls imposed by securities   No.
laws

Changes During 1999

Exchange arrangement   *June 30*. On the basis of additional available information, the exchange rate arrangement of
                                                   Guatemala was reclassified to the category managed floating, no preannounced path from
                                                   the category independently floating.

GUINEA

(Position as of February 29, 2000)

Status Under IMF Articles of Agreement

Article VIII   Date of acceptance: November 17, 1995.

Exchange Arrangement

Currency   The currency of Guinea is the Guinean franc.

Other legal tender   Silver commemorative coins are also legal tender.

Exchange rate structure   Unitary.

Classification

Independently floating   The official exchange rate of the Guinean franc is determined weekly in the auction market for foreign exchange. Commercial banks and foreign exchange bureaus are free to buy and sell foreign exchange at any rate.

Exchange tax   No.

Exchange subsidy   No.

Forward exchange market   No.

Arrangements for Payments and Receipts

Prescription of currency requirements   All current transactions effected in Guinea must be settled in Guinean francs. Settlements on account of transactions covered by bilateral payment agreements are made in currencies prescribed by, and through accounts established under, the provisions of the agreements. Settlements with countries other than members of the WAMA are made in designated convertible currencies quoted by the Central Bank of the Republic of Guinea (CBRG).

Payment arrangements

Bilateral payment arrangements

  Inoperative   Guinea maintains bilateral payment agreements with Bulgaria, China, Egypt, Romania, and Russia.

Clearing agreements   Settlements with the BCEAO and with The Gambia, Ghana, Liberia, Mauritania, Nigeria, and Sierra Leone are generally carried out through the WAMA.

Administration of control   Exchange control authority is vested in the CBRG, which has delegated to the commercial banks authority to (1) sign import descriptions and descriptive import applications; (2) allocate foreign exchange to travelers holding foreign airline tickets; and (3) manage foreign currency accounts. All settlements with foreign countries, including payments for imports, may be effected by the commercial banks.

On February 18, 2000, the national assembly passed the Exchange Control Law, liberalizing current account transactions.

International security restrictions

In accordance with UN sanctions   Yes.

Payment arrears

Official   Yes.

Private   Yes.

Controls on trade in gold (coins and/or bullion)   The CBRG purchases gold only in Guinean francs at international prices.

381

Controls on domestic ownership and/or trade	Transactions in nonmonetary gold are not subject to restrictions.
Controls on external trade	The exportation of gold is subject to prior authorization by the CBRG.
Controls on exports and imports of banknotes	
On exports	
Domestic currency	Exportation is limited to GF 5,000 a person a trip.
Foreign currency	Exportation of foreign currency is made through the CBRG.
On imports	
Domestic currency	Importation is limited to GF 5,000 a person a trip.
Foreign currency	The importation of foreign banknotes and traveler's checks is permitted, subject to declaration on entry. Residents, however, must surrender both to commercial banks within 15 days of their return or exchange them for Guinean francs.

Resident Accounts

Foreign exchange accounts permitted	Yes.
Held domestically	Residents are free to open foreign exchange accounts with local banks. Exporters may hold all of their earnings in foreign currency in local bank accounts.
Held abroad	These accounts are permitted, but prior approval of the CBRG is required.
Accounts in domestic currency convertible into foreign currency	Accounts in convertible Guinean francs may be credited with deposits in foreign exchange, irrespective of their origin. The accounts may be debited freely and converted by commercial banks into foreign currencies without prior authorization from the CBRG. Interest rates on these accounts are negotiated between the account holder and the bank.

Nonresident Accounts

Foreign exchange accounts permitted	Yes.
Domestic currency accounts	The same regulations apply as for resident accounts.
Convertible into foreign currency	Yes.
Blocked accounts	No.

Imports and Import Payments

Foreign exchange budget	Yes.
Financing requirements for imports	
Minimum financing requirements	The minimum financing requirement is $2,000.
Advance payment requirements	Advance payments may be established by the commercial agreement.
Documentation requirements for release of foreign exchange for imports	There are no restrictions on imports financed from own resources or through the foreign exchange market.
Domiciliation requirements	Yes.
Preshipment inspection	Yes.
Letters of credit	Yes.

Import licenses and other nontariff measures

Negative list

Imports of armaments, ammunitions, and narcotics are prohibited.

Import taxes and/or tariffs

All imports are subject to an 18% VAT, a fiscal import duty (DFE) of 8%, and a customs duty (DDE) of 7%, with the following exceptions: animals, flour, sugar, pharmaceutical products, and fertilizers are subject to a DFE of 6% and a DDE of 2%; and food industry imports, cement, and agricultural machinery are subject to a DFE of 8% and a DDE of 2%. In addition, a surtax of 20% to 70% is imposed on all luxury goods, nonalcoholic beverages, certain wines, and spirits. Imports by the three semipublic enterprises in the mining sector are regulated by special agreements and are subject to a 5.6% levy.

State import monopoly

No.

Exports and Export Proceeds

Repatriation requirements

Yes.

Surrender requirements

Private traders may retain all of their proceeds to finance authorized imports. Gold exporters and vendors may retain all of their proceeds. Semipublic enterprises may retain abroad all of their proceeds and may use them for import payments, operating costs, and external debt service.

Financing requirements

No.

Documentation requirements

Letters of credit

Yes.

Guarantees

Yes.

Domiciliation

All private sector exports require domiciliation with a commercial bank and submission of an export description to help prevent shortages of goods needed for domestic consumption and to identify capital outflows. Exports of the mining sector are exempt from this requirement.

Preshipment inspection

Yes.

Export licenses

The exportation of wild animals (dead or alive), meats, articles of historic or ethnographic interest, jewelry, articles made of precious metals, and plants and seeds require special authorization from designated agencies.

Without quotas

These are applicable to agricultural exports.

With quotas

There are quotas on the export of wild animals and articles of historic or ethnographic interest.

Export taxes

Exports of diamonds are subject to a tax of 3%, and exports of gold and other precious metals to a 5% tax.

Other export taxes

Mining and petroleum products are subject to other export taxes.

Payments for Invisible Transactions and Current Transfers

Controls on these transfers

Trade-related payments

There are no controls on the payment of unloading and storage costs.

Indicative limits/bona fide test

Yes.

Investment-related payments

Prior approval

Prior approval is required for government operations.

Indicative limits/bona fide test

Yes.

Payments for travel

  Quantitative limits — Yes.

  Indicative limits/bona fide test — Yes.

Personal payments

  Prior approval — Prior approval is required for the payment of pensions.

  Indicative limits/bona fide test — There are no indicative limits or bona fide rates for the payment of pensions.

Foreign workers' wages

  Prior approval — Approval is granted only for contracts approved by the Ministry of Labor.

  Quantitative limits — Foreign workers may transfer up to 50% of their taxable income.

  Indicative limits/bona fide test — Yes.

Other payments

  Indicative limits/bona fide test — Yes.

Proceeds from Invisible Transactions and Current Transfers

Repatriation requirements — Yes.

Restrictions on use of funds — No.

Capital Transactions

Controls on capital and money market instruments — All capital transfers through the official exchange market require authorization from the CBRG. Outward capital transfers by Guinean nationals through the official market are prohibited.

On capital market securities

  Shares or other securities of a participating nature

    Purchase locally by nonresidents — Yes.

    Sale or issue locally by nonresidents — Yes.

  Bonds or other debt securities — There are currently no transactions involving bonds.

On money market instruments

  Purchase locally by nonresidents — Yes.

  Sale or issue locally by nonresidents — Yes.

Controls on derivatives and other instruments — No.

Controls on credit operations — There are controls on all credit operations.

Controls on direct investment

Outward direct investment — The authorization of the CBRG is required.

Inward direct investment — There are no limits on amounts that nonresidents may invest in Guinea, and all Guinean and foreign nationals may hold controlling interests in Guinean enterprises.

Controls on liquidation of direct investment — No.

Controls on real estate transactions — The authorization of the CBRG is required.

Purchase abroad by residents	Yes.
Purchase locally by nonresidents	Yes.
Sale locally by nonresidents	Yes.
Controls on personal capital movements	There are controls on all these operations.
Provisions specific to commercial banks and other credit institutions	
Borrowing abroad	Yes.
Maintenance of accounts abroad	Yes.
Lending to nonresidents (financial or commercial credits)	The only form of lending to nonresidents that is allowed is overdraft protection on domestic currency checking accounts.
Lending locally in foreign exchange	Yes.
Differential treatment of deposit accounts in foreign exchange	
Reserve requirements	Yes.
Liquid asset requirements	Yes.
Interest rate controls	Yes.
Credit controls	Yes.
Differential treatment of deposit accounts held by nonresidents	
Liquid asset requirements	Yes.
Interest rate controls	Yes.
Credit controls	Yes.
Investment regulations	
Abroad by banks	Yes.
In banks by nonresidents	Yes.
Provisions specific to institutional investors	No.
Other controls imposed by securities laws	No.

Changes During 1999

No significant changes occurred in the exchange and trade system.

Changes During 2000

Arrangements for payments and receipts	*February 18.* The national assembly passed the Exchange Control Law, liberalizing current account transactions.

GUINEA-BISSAU

(Position as of December 31, 1999)

Status Under IMF Articles of Agreement

Article VIII   Date of acceptance: January 1, 1997.

Exchange Arrangement

Currency

The currency of Guinea-Bissau is the CFA franc.

Exchange rate structure

Unitary.

Classification

Exchange arrangement with no separate legal tender

The CFA franc is pegged to the euro, the intervention currency, at the fixed rate of CFAF 100 per €0.8385. Exchange rates for other currencies are derived from the rate for the currency concerned in the Paris foreign exchange market and the fixed rate between the euro and the CFA franc.

Exchange tax

There is a bank commission of 0.25% on transfers to all countries outside the WAEMU, which must be surrendered in its entirety to the Treasury.

Exchange subsidy

No.

Forward exchange market

Effective February 1, 1999, residents were authorized to contract forward exchange cover to settle payments related to imports and exports of goods and services.

Official cover of forward operations

Yes.

Arrangements for Payments and Receipts

Prescription of currency requirements

Because Guinea-Bissau is linked to the French Treasury through an Operations Account, settlements with France, Monaco, and other Operations Account countries (WAEMU and CAEMC members and the Comoros) are made in CFA francs, euros, or the currency of any other Operations Account country. Certain settlements are channeled through special accounts. Settlements with all other countries are usually effected either through correspondent banks in France in the currencies of those countries or in euros through foreign accounts in euros.

Payment arrangements

Bilateral payment arrangements

Inoperative

Yes.

Regional arrangements

An Operations Account is maintained with the French Treasury that links Operations Account countries. All purchases or sales of foreign currencies or euros against CFA francs are ultimately settled through a debit or credit to the Operations Account.

Administration of control

Exchange control is administered by the Directorate of the Treasury in the MOF. The approval authority for exchange control (except for imports and exports of gold, forward exchange cover, and the opening of external accounts in foreign currency) has been delegated to the BCEAO, which is also authorized to collect—either directly or through banks, financial institutions, the Postal Administration, or judicial agents—any information necessary to compile the balance of payments statistics.

All exchange transactions relating to foreign countries must be effected through authorized banks, the Postal Administration, or the BCEAO. Settlements with a country outside the Operations Account area must be formally approved by the customs administration. Effective February 1, 1999, the amount of transfers authorized without supporting documentation was raised to CFAF 300,000 from CFAF 100,000.

International security restrictions

No.

Payment arrears

Official   Yes.

Controls on trade in gold (coins and/or bullion)

Controls on external trade   Exports and imports of gold are prohibited unless expressly authorized.

Controls on exports and imports of banknotes

On exports

  Domestic currency   The exportation of CFA franc banknotes by nonresident travelers is not prohibited. However, repurchases by the BCEAO of exported banknotes are suspended. In addition, shipments of BCEAO banknotes among authorized intermediaries and their correspondents situated outside the WAEMU are officially prohibited.

  Foreign currency   The reexportation of foreign banknotes by nonresident travelers is allowed up to the equivalent of CFAF 500,000; the reexportation of foreign banknotes above these ceilings requires documentation demonstrating either the importation of the foreign banknotes or their purchase against other means of payment registered in the name of the traveler or through the use of nonresident deposits lodged in local banks.

On imports

  Domestic currency   There are no restrictions on the importation by resident or nonresident travelers of banknotes and coins issued by the BCEAO.

  Foreign currency   Residents and nonresidents may bring in any amount of foreign banknotes and coins (except gold coins) of countries outside the Operations Account area. Residents bringing in foreign banknotes and foreign currency traveler's checks exceeding the equivalent of CFAF 50,000 must declare them to customs upon entry and sell them to an authorized intermediary bank within eight days.

Resident Accounts

Foreign exchange accounts permitted   Effective February 1, 1999, residents are allowed to open foreign exchange accounts with local banks or with banks abroad after obtaining authorization from the MOF, and with the approval of the BCEAO.

Held domestically   These accounts are permitted, but approval is required.

Held abroad   The holding of these accounts is not explicitly prohibited, but regulations prohibit any transfer with the aim of increasing a resident's foreign holdings, unless approved by the MOF.

Accounts in domestic currency convertible into foreign currency   No.

Nonresident Accounts

Foreign exchange accounts permitted   Effective February 1, 1999, authorization for these accounts is issued by the BCEAO.

Domestic currency accounts   Because the BCEAO has suspended the repurchase of banknotes circulating outside the WAEMU territories, nonresident acounts may not be credited or debited with BCEAO banknotes. These accounts may not be overdrawn without the prior authorization of the MOF. Transfers of funds between nonresident accounts are not restricted.

Convertible into foreign currency   Foreign accounts denominated in CFA francs may be freely debited for the purpose of purchases by nonresidents of any foreign currency on the official exchange market.

Blocked accounts   No.

Imports and Import Payments

Foreign exchange budget	No.
Financing requirements for imports	No.
Documentation requirements for release of foreign exchange for imports	
Preshipment inspection	Yes.
Import licenses and other nontariff measures	All imports, regardless of whether they involve the use of official or free market foreign exchange, require a prior import license issued by the Ministry of Commerce and Tourism, primarily for statistical purposes. Except for a short negative list, licenses are issued automatically after verification of invoice prices for goods to be taxed.
Negative list	Yes.
Import taxes and/or tariffs	The tariff rates are zero, 5%, 10%, 20%, and 30%.
State import monopoly	No.

Exports and Export Proceeds

Repatriation requirements	Effective February 1, 1999, proceeds from exports to WAEMU countries are no longer required to be repatriated.
Surrender requirements	Export proceeds must be surrendered within one month of the date on which payments fall due. The authorized intermediary bank must then surrender such foreign exchange to the BCEAO via transfer through the bank of issue.
Financing requirements	No.
Documentation requirements	Yes.
Export licenses	All exports require a prior export license. Only exporters registered with the Ministry of Commerce and Tourism may obtain these licenses, which are granted automatically in most cases. Prior licenses are intended primarily for statistical purposes, although they are also used to check the prices of exports. There are no products of which the exportation is reserved solely for the public sector.
Without quotas	Yes.
Export taxes	Cashew nut exports are subject to a special tax of 10%, except those to ECOWAS countries. Other agricultural exports are subject to a rural property tax of 2%.

Payments for Invisible Transactions and Current Transfers

Controls on these transfers	Effective February 1, 1999, payments and incomes of foreign ships in the WAEMU zone and WAEMU ships abroad are included under current operations.
Investment-related payments	Information is not available for payment of amortization of loans or depreciation of direct investments.
Payments for travel	
Indicative limits/bona fide test	Effective February 1, 1999, limits on foreign exchange allowances were eliminated. The threshold of foreign exchange to be surrendered by residents after travel was raised to CFAF 300,000 from CFAF 50,000.
Personal payments	Information is not available for payment of pensions, family maintenance, or alimony.
Foreign workers' wages	
Indicative limits/bona fide test	Yes.

Proceeds from Invisible Transactions and Current Transfers

Repatriation requirements	Yes.
Surrender requirements	Effective February 1, 1999, all amounts due from residents of other countries in respect of services and all incomes earned in those countries from foreign assets must be collected and surrendered within one month of the due date or the date of receipt.
Restrictions on use of funds	No.

Capital Transactions

Controls on capital and money market instruments	Outward capital transfers are subject to authorization from the MOF, and a maximum of 75% of investment abroad may be financed by foreign loans. The liquidation of foreign investment is subject to reporting to the MOF, and the reinvestment of proceeds is subject to prior authorization. If no authorization is given for the reinvestment, the proceeds in foreign exchange must be surrendered to an authorized intermediary bank within one month.
	Capital transfers to the WAEMU member countries are unrestricted, except for direct investments, which are subject to prior declaration, as are certain borrowing operations. Prior authorization is waived, however, in the following cases: (1) borrowing guaranteed by the government of Guinea-Bissau; and (2) foreign shares that are similar to securities, the issuance, public announcement, or sale of which has already been approved in Guinea-Bissau. There is also special surveillance of calls for subscribed funds for purposes of deposit with foreign nationals, corporations, or institutions, as well as of any public announcement for the purpose of investing funds abroad or subscribing to foreign construction or real estate operations. These special provisions also apply to France, Monaco, and Operations Account countries.
On capital market securities	
Shares or other securities of a participating nature	
Sale or issue locally by nonresidents	Yes.
Purchase abroad by residents	Yes.
Sale or issue abroad by residents	Residents are free to sell the shares of resident companies abroad. If the effect of such operations is to place resident Guinea-Bissau companies under foreign control, the foreign investors must make a prior declaration to the MOF.
Bonds or other debt securities	
Purchase abroad by residents	Yes.
Sale or issue abroad by residents	Yes.
On money market instruments	
Sale or issue locally by nonresidents	Yes.
Purchase abroad by residents	Yes.
Sale or issue abroad by residents	Yes.
On collective investment securities	
Purchase abroad by residents	Yes.
Sale or issue abroad by residents	Yes.
Controls on derivatives and other instruments	These investments are governed by the regulations generally applicable to securities and investments, except for commodity and security call and put options, which residents may freely purchase abroad.
Purchase abroad by residents	Yes.

Controls on credit operations

Commercial credits

 By residents to nonresidents   There are no controls on credits related to exports of goods, provided that the date on which payment falls due is not more than 180 days after the goods arrive at their destination. There are no controls on credits in connection with services rendered. In these cases, no deadline is set for the date on which payment falls due.

 To residents from nonresidents There are no controls, and repayments of commercial credits are generally approved, subject to the presentation of documents attesting to the validity of the commercial operation or of the services rendered.

Financial credits

 By residents to nonresidents   Yes.

 To residents from nonresidents If such transactions take place between a direct investment company established in Guinea-Bissau and its parent company situated abroad, the transactions are regarded as direct investments and are therefore subject to prior declaration to the MOF.

Guarantees, sureties, and financial backup facilities

 By residents to nonresidents   Yes.

Controls on direct investment

Outward direct investment   Yes.

Inward direct investment   The Investment Code provides for incentives to investments and protection against the nationalization and expropriation of assets.

Controls on liquidation of direct investment   No.

Controls on real estate transactions   Yes.

Controls on personal capital movements

Loans

 By residents to nonresidents   These transactions are subject to authorization of the MOF.

 To residents from nonresidents Loans from nonresidents require notification to the MOF.

Gifts, endowments, inheritances, and legacies

 By residents to nonresidents   These transactions are subject to authorization of the MOF.

Settlement of debts abroad by immigrants   These transactions are subject to authorization of the MOF.

Transfer of assets

 Transfer abroad by emigrants These transactions are subject to authorization of the MOF.

 Transfer into the country by immigrants These transactions require notification to the MOF.

Provisions specific to commercial banks and other credit institutions

Lending to nonresidents (financial or commercial credits)   There are no controls if these operations involve commercial credits. Effective February 1, 1999, other loans granted to nonresidents are subject to the prior authorization of the MOF, after the approval of the BCEAO.

Lending locally in foreign exchange   The same regulations apply as for lending to residents.

Purchase of locally issued securities denominated in foreign exchange   The same regulations apply as for lending to residents.

Differential treatment of deposit accounts in foreign exchange	
Credit controls	Yes.
Differential treatment of deposit accounts held by nonresidents	Monetary regulations make no distinction between resident deposit accounts, nonresident deposit accounts, and foreign deposit accounts.
Investment regulations	Yes.
Open foreign exchange position limits	Yes.
Provisions specific to institutional investors	Effective February 1, 1999, controls are imposed by the insurance code of the Inter-African Conference on Insurance Markets.
Other controls imposed by securities laws	n.a.

Changes During 1999

Exchange arrangement	*January 1.* The CFA franc peg to the French franc was replaced by a peg to the euro.
	February 1. Residents were authorized to contract forward exchange cover to settle payments related to imports and exports of goods and services.
Arrangements for payments and receipts	*February 1.* The amount of transfers authorized without supporting documentation was raised to CFAF 300,000 from CFAF 100,000.
Resident accounts	*February 1.* Residents were allowed to open foreign exchange accounts with local banks or with banks abroad after obtaining authorization from the MOF and with the approval of the BCEAO.
Nonresident accounts	*February 1.* The authorization to open nonresident accounts must be issued by the BCEAO.
Exports and export proceeds	*February 1.* Proceeds from exports to WAEMU countries are no longer required to be repatriated.
Payments for invisible transactions and current transfers	*February 1.* Payments and incomes of foreign ships in the WAEMU zone and WAEMU ships abroad are included under current operations.
	February 1. Limits on foreign exchange allowances were eliminated. The threshold of foreign exchange to be surrendered by residents after travel was raised to CFAF 300,000 from CFAF 50,000.
Proceeds from invisible transactions and current transfers	*February 1.* All amounts due from residents of other countries in respect of services and all incomes earned in those countries from foreign assets must be collected and surrendered within one month of the due date or the date of receipt.
Capital transactions	
Provisions specific to commercial banks and other credit institutions	*February 1.* Except for commercial credits, loans granted to nonresidents are subject to the prior authorization of the MOF, after the approval of the BCEAO.
Provisions specific to institutional investors	*February 1.* Restrictions are imposed by the Insurance Code of the Inter-African Conference on Insurance Markets.

GUYANA

(Position as of January 31, 2000)

Status Under IMF Articles of Agreement

Article VIII   Date of acceptance: December 27, 1966.

Exchange Arrangement

Currency	The currency of Guyana is the Guyana dollar.
Exchange rate structure	Unitary.
Classification	
Independently floating	The exchange rate of the Guyana dollar is determined freely in the cambio market. The Bank of Guyana (BOG) conducts certain transactions on the basis of the cambio exchange rate by averaging quotations of the three largest dealers on the date the transaction takes place. In accordance with the bilateral agreements with the central banks of the CARICOM, the BOG quotes weekly rates for certain CARICOM currencies.
Exchange tax	No.
Exchange subsidy	No.
Forward exchange market	The only arrangement for forward cover against exchange rate risk operates in the official sector in respect of exchange rate guarantees that are provided to certain deposits in dormant accounts. However, no exchange rate guarantee has been given for deposits made after end-March 1989.
Official cover of forward operations	Yes.

Arrangements for Payments and Receipts

Prescription of currency requirements	No.
Payment arrangements	
Bilateral payment arrangements	
Operative	There are arrangements with all CARICOM central banks.
Regional arrangements	Guyana is a member of the CARICOM.
Administration of control	No.
International security restrictions	No.
Payment arrears	
Official	Arrears exist with Argentina, China, India, Kuwait, Libya, Russia, and the Federal Republic of Yugoslavia (Serbia/Montenegro).
Private	Arrears exist on certain dormant accounts holding domestic currency deposits equivalent in value to pending applications for foreign exchange. A program was initiated to settle debts outstanding under the external payment deposits schemes.
Controls on trade in gold (coins and/or bullion)	
Controls on domestic ownership and/or trade	Residents other than the monetary authorities, authorized dealers, producers of gold, and authorized industrial users are not allowed to hold or acquire gold in any form except for numismatic purposes and jewelry, at home or abroad, without special permission.

| Controls on external trade | Imports and exports of gold in any form by, or on behalf of, the monetary authorities, authorized dealers, producers of gold, and industrial users require permits endorsed by the Guyana Gold Board. |

Controls on exports and imports of banknotes

On imports

   Foreign currency

Travelers entering Guyana with foreign currency in excess of the equivalent of US$10,000 must declare the amount.

Resident Accounts

Foreign exchange accounts permitted	Yes.
Held domestically	Exporters are allowed to maintain and operate foreign exchange accounts. These accounts are approved on merit but are generally granted to bona fide exporters who require imported inputs for production and/or have external loan obligations. These accounts may be credited with all or a portion of retained export proceeds and proceeds of foreign currency loans. They may be debited freely for any payments at the discretion of the account holder.
Held abroad	Yes.
Accounts in domestic currency convertible into foreign currency	The balances of these accounts may be converted at the prevailing cambio exchange rate.

Nonresident Accounts

Foreign exchange accounts permitted	External accounts may be opened by commercial banks without the prior approval of the central bank for citizens of Guyana residing permanently abroad, citizens of other countries temporarily residing in Guyana, nonresidents attached to diplomatic missions or international organizations, branches of companies incorporated outside of Guyana, and companies incorporated in Guyana but controlled by nonresidents abroad. These accounts may be maintained in U.S. dollars, pounds sterling, or Canadian dollars and may be credited with noncash instruments of convertible foreign currencies transferred through the banking system. These accounts may also be credited freely with all authorized payments by residents of Guyana to nonresidents; other credits require approval. They may be debited freely for payments for any purpose to residents of any country, for transfers to other external accounts, for withdrawals by the account holder in Guyana, and for transfers to nonresident accounts.
Domestic currency accounts	Yes.
Convertible into foreign currency	No.
Blocked accounts	No.

Imports and Import Payments

Foreign exchange budget	The BOG prepares a hard currency receipts and payments statement to monitor projected flows.
Financing requirements for imports	Import transactions effected through the cambio exchange market are permitted without restriction. Most imports of consumer goods take place on this basis. Certain payments for official imports effected by commercial banks on behalf of the BOG require the Bank's prior approval.
Documentation requirements for release of foreign exchange for imports	Requirements are related mainly to petroleum products. Documents required include invoices, bills of lading, and certificates of origin.
Import licenses and other nontariff measures	There are no licensing requirements for permissible imports, except for petroleum products and some 20 items affecting national security, public health and safety, and the environment.

Negative list	Imports of unprocessed meat, poultry, fruit, and processed fruit items are restricted, subject to import-licensing controls, from all non-CARICOM sources.
Import taxes and/or tariffs	The CET of CARICOM is applied to all imports from outside the market. Effective March 26, 1999, tariffs range from 5% to 20%. Intra-CARICOM trade is free of import duties. On January 1, 2000, the fourth phase of the CARICOM CET came into effect.
State import monopoly	No.

Exports and Export Proceeds

Repatriation requirements	No.
Financing requirements	No.
Documentation requirements	No.
Export licenses	Licenses are required for exports of gold and wildlife.
Without quotas	Gold exports are not subject to quotas.
With quotas	There are quotas for the supply of some commodities to preferential markets and for wildlife exports.
Export taxes	There are levies on exports of rice and sugar. For exports of timber, bauxite, sugar, live birds, and aquarium fish, an export duty is applied.

Payments for Invisible Transactions and Current Transfers

Controls on these transfers	No.

Proceeds from Invisible Transactions and Current Transfers

Repatriation requirements	No.
Restrictions on use of funds	No.

Capital Transactions

Controls on capital and money market instruments	No.
Controls on derivatives and other instruments	No.
Controls on credit operations	All types of credit operations are controlled.
Controls on direct investment	No.
Controls on liquidation of direct investment	No.
Controls on real estate transactions	No.
Controls on personal capital movements	No.
Provisions specific to commercial banks and other credit institutions	
Lending to nonresidents (financial or commercial credits)	Yes.
Lending locally in foreign exchange	Yes.

Open foreign exchange position limits	Open positions are being monitored.
Provisions specific to institutional investors	No.
Other controls imposed by securities laws	On January 22, 1999, the BOG removed the limit on bid prices in weekly treasury bill auctions.

Changes During 1999

Imports and import payments	*March 26.* The maximum CET of CARICOM was reduced to 20% from 25%.
Capital transactions	
Other controls imposed by securities laws	*January 22.* The BOG removed the limit on bid prices in weekly treasury bill auctions.

Changes During 2000

| **Imports and import payments** | *January 1.* The fourth phase of the CARICOM CET came into effect. |

HAITI

(Position as of December 31, 1999)

Status Under IMF Articles of Agreement

Article VIII	Date of acceptance: December 22, 1953.

Exchange Arrangement

Currency	The currency of Haiti is the Haitian gourde.
Other legal tender	The dollar circulates freely and is generally accepted in Haiti. Several gold coins have been issued that are legal tender but do not circulate.
Exchange rate structure	Unitary.
Classification	
Independently floating	The exchange rate is determined in the exchange market. The Bank of the Republic of Haiti (BRH)—the central bank—operates a dollar clearinghouse. Commercial banks quote buying and selling rates for certain other currencies based on the buying and selling rates of the dollar in exchange markets abroad. The market is dominated by banks, with money changers following this market.
Exchange tax	No.
Exchange subsidy	No.
Forward exchange market	No.

Arrangements for Payments and Receipts

Prescription of currency requirements	No.
Payment arrangements	
Bilateral payment arrangements	
Operative	Haiti's debt toward Argentina was rescheduled until 2001 and that toward Italy until 2028.
Regional arrangements	On July 7, 1999, Haiti became a member of the CARICOM, pending parliament's approval.
Administration of control	The BRH administers the foreign exchange system together with the Ministry of Finance and Economic Affairs (MFEA) and the Ministry of Commerce and Industry (MCI).
International security restrictions	n.a.
Payment arrears	No.
Controls on trade in gold (coins and/or bullion)	
Controls on domestic ownership and/or trade	Residents may hold and acquire gold coins in Haiti for numismatic purposes.
Controls on external trade	The BRH has the exclusive right to purchase gold domestically and to export gold in the form of coins, mineral dust, or bars. Exports of gold require, in addition, prior authorization from the MCI and the MFEA, as well as an endorsement from the MCI, before customs clearance. However, commercial imports of articles containing a small amount of gold, such as gold watches, are freely permitted and do not require an import license or other authorization.
Controls on exports and imports of banknotes	No.

Resident Accounts

Foreign exchange accounts permitted   These accounts may be credited with export proceeds, with transfers from abroad received by exchange houses, or with receipts from maritime agencies and nongovernmental organizations.

Held domestically   Yes.

Held abroad   Yes.

Accounts in domestic currency convertible into foreign currency   Yes.

Nonresident Accounts

Foreign exchange accounts permitted   Yes.

Domestic currency accounts   Yes.

Convertible into foreign currency   Yes.

Blocked accounts   n.a.

Imports and Import Payments

Foreign exchange budget   No.

Financing requirements for imports   No.

Documentation requirements for release of foreign exchange for imports   No.

Import licenses and other nontariff measures   No.

Import taxes and/or tariffs   There are three standard tariff rates, 5%, 10%, and 15%. Several goods have special tariff rates—gasoline, 25%; and cement, rice, and sugar, 3%. A domestic turnover tax is charged on the c.i.f. value plus import duties. All imports, except for inputs used by certain export industries, are subject to a 4% verification fee. As Haiti became a member of the CARICOM, numerous exemptions and suspensions have been negotiated to avoid tariff increases under the CET. These suspensions and extensions are valid until 2005. The suspension mechanism can also be used in case of supply shortages and local price increases for certain goods within the common market.

State import monopoly   No.

Exports and Export Proceeds

Repatriation requirements   No.

Financing requirements   No.

Documentation requirements   n.a.

Export licenses   No.

Export taxes   No.

Payments for Invisible Transactions and Current Transfers

Controls on these transfers   No.

Investment-related payments	Information is not available on the payment of amortization of loans and depreciation of direct investments.
Personal payments	Information is not available on the transfer of pensions, family maintenance, and alimony.

Proceeds from Invisible Transactions and Current Transfers

Repatriation requirements	No.
Restrictions on use of funds	No.

Capital Transactions

Controls on capital and money market instruments	n.a.
Controls on derivatives and other instruments	n.a.
Controls on credit operations	n.a.
Controls on direct investment	
Inward direct investment	Investments require prior government approval. Investments in handicraft industries are not normally approved.
Controls on liquidation of direct investment	n.a.
Controls on real estate transactions	n.a.
Controls on personal capital movements	n.a.
Provisions specific to commercial banks and other credit institutions	Private banks are required to maintain at least 85% of their liabilities in domestic assets for local customers. This requirement, however, is not enforced.
Differential treatment of deposit accounts in foreign exchange	
Reserve requirements	The reserve requirement for local currency deposits was 26.5%, while that on foreign currency deposits was 12.5%. Effective October 22, 1999, these were changed to 28.5% and 15%, respectively.
Provisions specific to institutional investors	n.a.
Other controls imposed by securities laws	n.a.

Changes During 1999

Arrangements for payments and receipts	*July 7*. Haiti became a member of the CARICOM.
Capital transactions	
Provisions specific to commercial banks and other credit institutions	*October 22*. The reserve requirements for local and foreign currencies were increased to 28.5% and 15%, respectively.

HONDURAS

Status Under IMF Articles of Agreement

Article VIII	Date of acceptance: July 1, 1950.

Exchange Arrangement

Currency	The currency of Honduras is the Honduran lempira.
Exchange rate structure	Unitary.
Classification	

Crawling band

The exchange rate for the lempira is determined in foreign exchange auctions. Banks and exchange houses are required to sell all their daily foreign exchange purchases to the Central Bank of Honduras (CBH). Buyers (banks, exchange houses, or private individuals) bid at a price that may not differ from the base price set by the authorities by more than 7% in either direction. The base exchange rate is adjusted every five auctions according to changes in the differential between domestic and international inflation and in the exchange rates of currencies of trading partners of Honduras with respect to the dollar. The amount of foreign exchange offered at each auction must be at least 60% of the CBH's purchase of foreign exchange from its agents. The minimum amount of foreign exchange to be offered and the base price are announced before the auction. Individuals willing to purchase foreign exchange must make offers in lempiras for amounts ranging between $5,000 and $300,000. Foreign exchange agents may purchase for their own account to satisfy private demands lower than $5,000. The maximum amount of foreign exchange that may be purchased for this purpose is $30,000 for commercial banks and $10,000 for foreign exchange houses. Foreign exchange agents may charge up to 1.5% commission on sales to the public lower than $5,000 and up to 1.2% for larger sales. Auction rates may deviate from the base rate by ±7%. Auctions are held once each working day, and each bidder may make up to three offers in each auction.

Exchange tax	No.
Exchange subsidy	No.
Forward exchange market	No.

Arrangements for Payments and Receipts

Prescription of currency requirements	No.
Payment arrangements	
Regional arrangements	Honduras is a member of the CACM.
	Trade transactions with the rest of Central America may be carried out in local currencies or in dollars.
Administration of control	The CBH exercises control.
International security restrictions	No.
Payment arrears	
Official	Most of these arrears were with the Paris Club creditors and were rescheduled through the Agreed Minutes signed on April 30, 1999.
Controls on trade in gold (coins and/or bullion)	No.

Controls on exports and imports of banknotes	No.

Resident Accounts

Foreign exchange accounts permitted	Banks are required to hold these deposits in (1) foreign currency notes in their vaults, (2) deposits in the CBH, (3) special accounts at correspondent banks abroad, (4) investments in high-liquidity foreign instruments, or (5) export or import financing instruments.
Held domestically	Yes.
Held abroad	Yes.
Accounts in domestic currency convertible into foreign currency	No.

Nonresident Accounts

Foreign exchange accounts permitted	Yes.
Domestic currency accounts	Yes.
Convertible into foreign currency	Yes.
Blocked accounts	No.

Imports and Import Payments

Foreign exchange budget	No.
Financing requirements for imports	No.
Documentation requirements for release of foreign exchange for imports	No.
Import licenses and other nontariff measures	Imports of arms and similar items require a license issued by the Ministry of Security.
Import taxes and/or tariffs	Import duties range up to 19%. Over 1,600 items from other Central American countries are exempt from import duties, except for a 0.5% import surcharge. The surcharge will be eliminated in 2000. There are duty-free and industrial-processing zones that benefit from tariff exemptions. The tariff for imports of certain consumer goods was reduced to 17% on December 31, 1999.
State import monopoly	No.

Exports and Export Proceeds

Repatriation requirements	Yes.
Surrender requirements	All export earnings, except those from trade with other Central American countries, must be surrendered to banks or exchange houses within a period of 20 to 85 days. Proceeds from coffee exports must be surrendered within 20 days. Exporters are allowed to retain up to 30% of their foreign exchange proceeds to finance their own imports, as well as to pay for their authorized external obligations. Commercial banks and exchange houses are required to sell all the purchased foreign exchange to the CBH.
Financing requirements	No.
Documentation requirements	
Domiciliation	Yes.

Preshipment inspection	Yes.
Export licenses	No licenses are required, but exports must be registered for statistical purposes.
Export taxes	Bananas were subject to an export tax of $0.50 for a 40-pound box. On June 1, 1999, the export tax was decreased to $0.10, and is to be abolished by June 2000.

Payments for Invisible Transactions and Current Transfers

Controls on these transfers	There are no controls on these payments, but all buyers of foreign exchange are required to fill out a form stating the purpose for which the funds will be used. There are no limits on the amount purchased.

Proceeds from Invisible Transactions and Current Transfers

Repatriation requirements	No.
Restrictions on use of funds	No.

Capital Transactions

Controls on capital and money market instruments	
On capital market securities	
Shares or other securities of a participating nature	
Purchase locally by nonresidents	Purchases of capital shares in existing domestic firms are permitted, with the exception of defense-related industries, hazardous industries, and small-scale industry and commerce.
On collective investment securities	
Purchase locally by nonresidents	There are no controls on activities involving the receipt of foreign exchange and its transfer abroad for investment in mutual funds.
Sale or issue locally by nonresidents	Foreign mutual funds and similar financial institutions must have permission to collect funds in Honduras for deposit or investment abroad.
Controls on derivatives and other instruments	No.
Controls on credit operations	The approval of congress is required for all public sector foreign borrowing. Private sector external debt contracts must be registered with the CBH for statistical purposes only.
Commercial credits	
To residents from nonresidents	Yes.
Financial credits	
To residents from nonresidents	Yes.
Guarantees, sureties, and financial backup facilities	
To residents from nonresidents	Yes.
Controls on direct investment	
Inward direct investment	Investments are permitted in all sectors without control, with the exception of defense-related industries, hazardous industries, and small-scale industry and commerce. Investments in hazardous industries require prior approval. All foreign investments must be registered with the Secretary of Economy and Trade.

Controls on liquidation of direct investment	No.
Controls on real estate transactions	
Purchase locally by nonresidents	There are location and size limitations.
Controls on personal capital movements	No.
Provisions specific to commercial banks and other credit institutions	
Borrowing abroad	The limit of indebtedness is three times their capital and reserves.
Maintenance of accounts abroad	Commercial banks must deposit abroad 38% of foreign exchange deposits held by the private sector.
Lending to nonresidents (financial or commercial credits)	CBH authorization is required.
Lending locally in foreign exchange	Financial institutions may lend 50% of their foreign exchange deposits locally in foreign exchange.
Differential treatment of deposit accounts in foreign exchange	
Reserve requirements	All types of deposits are subject to a 12% requirement.
Liquid asset requirements	Foreign exchange deposits are subject to a 38% requirement.
Credit controls	Credit with 40% of funds from foreign exchange deposits must be granted to export-related activities. The remaining 10% may be lent for any purpose.
Differential treatment of deposit accounts held by nonresidents	
Reserve requirements	Currently, banks, nonbank financial institutions, and savings and loan associations are subject to a nonremunerated reserve requirement of 12% on all deposits both in domestic and foreign currency. In addition, for deposits in domestic currency, financial institutions were required to hold obligatory deposits at the central bank at a market-based interest rate equivalent to 13% of deposits for banks, 3% for nonbank financial institutions, and 5% for savings and loans associations. For deposits in foreign currency, financial institutions are required to deposit 38% in foreign banks, and may lend 50% mainly to export activities. The central bank aims to harmonize all reserve requirements with levels prevailing in other Central American countries by 2000.
Provisions specific to institutional investors	No.
Other controls imposed by securities laws	There is no securities law.

Changes During 1999

Arrangements for payments and receipts	*April 30.* Most of the official payment arrears were rescheduled with Paris Club creditors.
Imports and import payments	*December 31.* The tariff for imports of certain consumer goods was reduced to 17%.
Exports and export proceeds	*June 1.* The export tax on bananas was decreased to $0.10 for a 40-pound box.

HUNGARY

(Position as of July 31, 2000)

Status Under IMF Articles of Agreement

Article VIII   Date of acceptance: January 1, 1996.

Exchange Arrangement

Currency   The currency of Hungary is the Hungarian forint.

Exchange rate structure   Unitary.

Classification

Crawling band   The National Bank of Hungary (NBH) adjusts the official exchange rate of the forint in accordance with a preannounced rate of crawl effected against a currency basket comprising the euro (70%) and the dollar (30%). On January 1, 1999, the monthly rate of depreciation against the basket of currencies was adjusted to 0.6% and on October 1, 1999, to 0.4%. Effective January 1, 2000, the central parity of the forint is determined by a preannounced rate of crawl against the euro. The official exchange rate is fixed at 11:00 a.m. every day and is calculated for 24 convertible currencies, including the euro, within margins of 2.25%, but licensed banks are free to determine their own margins within the band.

Exchange tax   No.

Exchange subsidy   No.

Forward exchange market   Commercial banks may engage in forward transactions at exchange rates negotiated freely between the banks and their customers.

Arrangements for Payments and Receipts

Prescription of currency   No.
requirements

Payment arrangements

Bilateral payment arrangements

  Operative   There are agreements with Brazil and Ecuador, under which outstanding balances are settled every 90 days.

  Inoperative   There are agreements with Albania, Bulgaria, Cambodia, the Lao People's Democratic Republic, Russia, and Vietnam for the settlement of outstanding transferable or clearing ruble balances with shipments of goods.

Regional arrangements   Hungary is a member of the CEFTA.

Administration of control   Authority for enforcing foreign exchange regulations is vested in the NBH.

International security restrictions

In accordance with UN sanctions   Hungary maintains payment restrictions against Iraq and Libya.

Payment arrears   No.

**Controls on trade in gold (coins   No.
and/or bullion)**

Controls on exports and imports of banknotes

On exports

   Domestic currency   Residents and nonresidents may take out of the country up to Ft 350,000 a trip without authorization.

   Foreign currency   Exports are limited to the equivalent of Ft 100,000 a person a trip without authorization.

On imports

   Domestic currency   Imports are limited to Ft 350,000 a person a trip.

   Foreign currency   No.

Resident Accounts

Foreign exchange accounts permitted   Yes.

Held domestically   Resident natural persons may freely maintain convertible currency accounts at authorized commercial banks. Resident juridical persons may open convertible currency accounts with funds originating from specific sources, such as export proceeds, foreign borrowing, capital paid in convertible currency by the foreign owners of joint-venture companies, and proceeds from direct and portfolio investments abroad, inheritance, or donations paid in convertible currency for foundations, churches and social organizations, and budgetary institutions. Approval is required for titles not mentioned above.

Held abroad   Residents may hold, without permission, foreign exchange accounts abroad if they are working or staying abroad, maintain a resident office or are main contractors, for the purpose of an initial capital deposit account in connection with making outward foreign direct investment, or for credit accounts and margin accounts in connection with commodity stock. As of July 1, 2000, resident fund managers were authorized to hold accounts abroad in which to keep the securities and their earnings abroad in order to technically facilitate investment operations. In all other cases, permission to hold foreign exchange accounts abroad is required.

Accounts in domestic currency convertible into foreign currency   Conversion is free for all liberalized items and in all authorized cases.

Nonresident Accounts

Foreign exchange accounts permitted   Yes.

Domestic currency accounts   Yes.

Convertible into foreign currency   Convertible forint accounts may be credited with legally acquired forint; proceeds from the conversion of convertible currency or forint acquired from nonliberalized or unauthorized transactions must be placed in a nonconvertible forint account, which does not bear interest.

Blocked accounts   No.

Imports and Import Payments

Foreign exchange budget   No.

Financing requirements for imports   No.

Documentation requirements for release of foreign exchange for imports   No.

Import licenses and other nontariff measures   Licenses are required for a number of products, including imports destined for the settlement of outstanding balances in transferable or clearing rubles. About 95% of Hungarian imports are fully liberalized.

Negative list	Yes.
Licenses with quotas	Licenses are needed for products falling under the global quota on consumer goods.
Import taxes and/or tariffs	Goods for personal use brought in by returning Hungarian travelers are subject to a general import duty of 15%, based on the actual invoice price with a duty-free allowance of Ft 30,000. Residents, if they are employees of a domestic agency and if they are stationed abroad for more than one year, may import, free of customs duty, goods for personal use up to a value equivalent to 40% of their earnings. Goods imported into Hungary are subject to customs duties in accordance with the established and published tariffs.
State import monopoly	No.

Exports and Export Proceeds

Repatriation requirements	Export proceeds in convertible currencies must be repatriated to Hungary upon receipt of the foreign exchange. Certain exemptions are granted, stipulated in the law, or subject to specific approval by the NBH. In the case of nonconvertible currencies, the exporters are required to make a best effort to exchange them into convertible currency and repatriate the convertible currency.
Surrender requirements	No.
Financing requirements	
Documentation requirements	
Export licenses	Exports of items included in the negative list require a license.
Export taxes	No.

Payments for Invisible Transactions and Current Transfers

Controls on these transfers	No.

Proceeds from Invisible Transactions and Current Transfers

Repatriation requirements	Proceeds are subject to the same requirement as export proceeds.
Surrender requirements	No.
Restrictions on use of funds	No.

Capital Transactions

Controls on capital and money market instruments	
On capital market securities	
Shares or other securities of a participating nature	
Sale or issue locally by nonresidents	Transactions in OECD central government bonds, bonds and shares of OECD-based enterprises (in the case of both bonds, those with an original maturity of one year or longer), and the sale of shares of parent companies to the employees of its subsidiary companies are free. For transactions in other instruments, a foreign exchange authorization is required. The authorization is liberally granted, on a case-by-case basis, after submitting a request and its accompanying documents. All proceeds associated with authorized transactions may be freely converted and transferred abroad by nonresidents.
Purchase abroad by residents	The same regulations apply as for sale or issue locally by nonresidents. Funds required for

transactions may be freely converted and transferred abroad by residents. The transaction must take place through a resident brokerage company.

Bonds or other debt securities

Purchase locally by nonresidents

Permission of the NBH is required if the original maturity of bonds or other debt securities is less than 365 days.

Sale or issue locally by nonresidents

The same regulations apply as for shares or other securities of a participating nature.

Purchase abroad by residents

The same regulations apply as for sale or issue locally by nonresidents. Funds required for transactions may be freely converted and transferred abroad by residents. The transactions must take place through a resident brokerage company.

Sale or issue abroad by residents

The permission of the NBH is required for public or private offering of bonds and other debt securities issued by residents to foreigners or for listing such securities at a recognized securities market in a foreign country if the original maturity of such securities is less than 365 days. Pursuant to the Securities Act, such transactions are subject to the approval of the Hungarian Banking and Capital Markets Supervision.

On money market instruments

These transactions require a foreign exchange authorization, which is granted in exceptional cases on a case-by-case basis, after submitting a request and its accompanying documents. Proceeds associated with the transaction may be freely converted and transferred abroad.

Purchase locally by nonresidents

Yes.

Sale or issue locally by nonresidents

Yes.

Purchase abroad by residents

Yes.

Sale or issue abroad by residents

Yes.

On collective investment securities

Purchase locally by nonresidents

Transactions for closed-end funds are free, but those for open-end funds require authorization, which is granted in exceptional cases.

Sale or issue locally by nonresidents

The same regulations apply as for transactions in money market instruments, except that, effective July 1, 2000, foreign collective investment securities are admitted to the domestic market if (1) the fund manager is registered in an OECD member state; (2) the fund's investment policy focuses on instruments that are already liberalized and freely available for residents of Hungary; and (3) the initial offering of the securities took place in an OECD member country.

Purchase abroad by residents

The same regulations apply as for transactions in money market instruments, except that residents may freely purchase abroad collective investment securities for closed-end funds or ones for which approval was granted through resident investment companies.

Sale or issue abroad by residents

Transactions for closed-end funds are free, but those for open-end funds require authorization, which is granted in exceptional cases.

Controls on derivatives and other instruments

These transactions require authorization, which is granted in exceptional cases on a case-by-case basis.

Purchase locally by nonresidents

As an exception, nonresidents are permitted to trade in futures contracts for individual stocks or the Budapest stock index (BUX) on the Budapest Stock Exchange.

Sale or issue locally by nonresidents

As an exception, nonresidents are permitted to trade in futures contracts for individual stocks or the BUX on the Budapest Stock Exchange.

Purchase abroad by residents

Yes.

Sale or issue abroad by residents

Yes.

Controls on credit operations

Financial credits

By residents to nonresidents

A resident may, without the permission of the foreign exchange authority, grant credit to a direct enterprise abroad acquired in accordance with the Hungarian foreign exchange rules. The maturity of such a credit should exceed five years; otherwise, a foreign exchange authorization is required. On January 1, 2000, residents were allowed to grant foreign exchange credits with a maturity of more than one year to nonresidents of OECD member countries. Credits between close relatives are free; in all other cases, a foreign exchange authority authorization is needed, which is granted liberally in the case of long- and medium-term credits and granted exceptionally in the case of short-term credits.

To residents from nonresidents

For residents, medium- and long-term financial credits in foreign exchange are allowed. For short-term borrowing, an authorization from the foreign exchange authority (NBH) is required. The borrowing may be effected in the form of a bank transfer to an authorized credit institution in Hungary. The repayment should be made proportionally, i.e., the first year's installments may not be higher than the average installment over the entire period.

Borrowing in domestic currency is free for resident enterprises; for organizations and private individuals, it is subject to a foreign exchange authority permit. Borrowing in domestic currency may be effected only from a convertible forint account held by a nonresident.

Guarantees, sureties, and financial backup facilities

These transactions are allowed if they are related to liberalized transactions. In all other cases, authorization is needed, which is granted liberally on a case-by-case basis.

By residents to nonresidents

Yes.

To residents from nonresidents

Yes.

Controls on direct investment

Outward direct investment

Equity participation in a nonresident enterprise is considered as foreign direct investment and is free if the participation in the share or equity capital or the value of assets of the foreign enterprise is more than 10%. The following preconditions should also be met: (1) the laws of the country of incorporation should allow the transfer to Hungary of profits and capital in convertible foreign exchange; (2) the resident's liability should not exceed (except in the case of a branch) its share in the enterprise; (3) the resident should have no custom duty, tax, pension, health insurance, or social security contribution liability outstanding; (4) the resident should not be in bankruptcy or under liquidation, and no such action should have been initiated against him or her in the year of application or the previous two calendar years; (5) during the period stipulated above, there should be no negative decision against the investor made by the foreign exchange authority; and (6) during the same period, no senior employee of the applicant should have been a senior member of the supervisory committee of an enterprise against which the foreign exchange authority had made a negative decision. If the planned investment does not meet any of the listed criteria, the application will automatically fall under the authorization procedure.

Controls on liquidation of direct investment

No.

Controls on real estate transactions

Purchase abroad by residents

Real estate acquisition must be reported within eight days.

Purchase locally by nonresidents

Approval of local municipal authorities is required.

Controls on personal capital movements

Loans

By residents to nonresidents

Credits between close relatives are free. Otherwise, the same regulations apply as for financial credits.

To residents from nonresidents

Yes.

Gifts, endowments, inheritances, and legacies

By residents to nonresidents

A resident may donate convertible foreign exchange or currency to a nonresident, provided an authorization of the NBH is granted. A resident may give a gift of pecuniary value to a nonresident, except for (1) the resident's share or participation in foreign direct investment; (2) the right of ownership in respect of real estate abroad or in Hungary; and (3) securities, money market instruments, and transferable instruments, which may be acquired by nonresidents with a foreign exchange license. (The above-mentioned operations are liberalized only in the case of close relatives.) A resident may establish an endowment abroad or may join a foreign endowment only with authorization. This provision also applies to an assumption of obligation serving public interest.

Transfer of assets

Transfer abroad by emigrants

On first leaving Hungary for any foreign country, a private individual who is entitled to emigrate may take the following out of the country without the permission of the foreign exchange authority: (1) his or her pecuniary value; (2) the currency or foreign exchange originating from the conversion of the domestic payment instruments received for the sale of his or her domestic real estate; and (3) the foreign exchange or currency originating from the conversion of domestic payment instrument(s) deposited with a domestic credit institution in a registered deposit.

Provisions specific to commercial banks and other credit institutions

Borrowing abroad

Financial institutions must report all foreign borrowing to the NBH.

Lending to nonresidents (financial or commercial credits)

Short-term lending is allowed within the following rules: (1) total outstanding lending to nonresidents should not exceed 50% of the total amount of liabilities in foreign exchange less the own capital of the bank in foreign exchange or the amount stipulated in a foreign exchange authority license; and (2) a bank may not have an aggregate lending with an individual borrower of more than 25% of its adjusted capital. Effective January 1, 2000, medium- and long-term lending for nonresidents from OECD member countries is free; lending to other nonresidents is subject to a case-by-case authorization, which is granted liberally. In the case of purchase of short-term securities with an original maturity of less than one year, their aggregate amount should not exceed 50% of the total amount of liabilities in foreign exchange less the own capital of the bank in foreign exchange. In that figure, short-term lending should also be included. In the case of purchase of medium- and long-term securities, the same rules apply as for residents. Short-term lending locally to nonresidents is allowed within the framework stipulated above.

Country risk rules prescribe the placement of specific reserves against possible losses on credits extended to problem countries, the list of which is based on the assessment of the NBH and published by the MOF.

Purchase of locally issued securities denominated in foreign exchange

The purchase and issue of locally issued foreign exchange–denominated securities require a permit from the NBH. This license is granted on a case-by-case basis.

Differential treatment of deposit accounts in foreign exchange

Reserve requirements

The interest paid on all obligatory reserves placed at the NBH is 10%.

Differential treatment of deposit accounts held by nonresidents

As of January 1, 1999, commercial bank liabilities to nonresidents with a maturity of less than one year are subject to the system of reserve requirements, currently with a reserve ratio of zero. Obligatory reserves held against liabilities to nonresidents are remunerated at the same rate as reserves held against liabilities to residents.

Open foreign exchange position limits

The gross aggregate position is limited to 30% of the bank's adjusted capital. Banks should adhere to the limit on a daily basis.

Provisions specific to institutional investors

In the case of insurance companies, these provisions are included in the Law on Insurance Companies and Insurance Activities, which bans foreign investment by insurance companies. In the case of pension funds, a government decree limits the share of foreign investment by pension funds in the compulsory second pillar to 10% of total assets, rising to 30% by 2002, and limits that of other pension funds to 20% of total assets. In the case of mutual funds, these provisions are included in the Central Banking Law.

Limits (max.) on portfolio invested abroad

Yes.

Limits (min.) on portfolio invested locally

Yes.

Other controls imposed by securities laws

No.

Changes During 1999

Exchange arrangement

January 1. The euro replaced the deutsche mark in the currency basket to which the forint is pegged, and the monthly rate of depreciation was adjusted to 0.6%.

October 1. The monthly rate of depreciation was adjusted to 0.4% from 0.6%.

Capital transactions

Provisions specific to commercial banks and other credit institutions

January 1. Commercial bank liabilities to nonresidents with a maturity of less than one year are subject to the system of reserve requirements, currently with a reserve ratio of zero. Obligatory reserves held against liabilities to nonresidents will be remunerated at the same rate as reserves held against liabilities to residents.

Changes During 2000

Exchange arrangement

January 1. The preannounced rate of crawl was effected against the euro.

Resident accounts

July 1. Resident fund managers were allowed to keep foreign exchange accounts abroad.

Capital transactions

July 1. The sale or issue by nonresidents or the purchase by residents of collective investment securities was liberalized once a few preconditions are satisfied.

Controls on credit operations

January 1. Residents were allowed to extend credits with a maturity of more than one year to nonresidents of OECD member countries.

Provisions specific to commercial banks and other credit institutions

January 1. Long- and medium-term lending in foreign exchange to nonresidents from OECD member countries became free.

ICELAND

(Position as of February 29, 2000)

Status Under IMF Articles of Agreement

Article VIII
Date of acceptance: September 19, 1983.

Exchange Arrangement

Currency
The currency of Iceland is the Icelandic króna.

Other legal tender
A commemorative gold coin with face value of ISK 100 is legal tender, but it does not circulate.

Exchange rate structure
Unitary.

Classification

Pegged exchange rate within horizontal bands
The external value of the króna is pegged to a basket of nine currencies: the Canadian dollar, the Danish krone, the euro, the Japanese yen, the Norwegian krone, the pound sterling, the Swedish krona, the Swiss franc, and the U.S. dollar. The Central Bank of Iceland (CBI) intervenes in the exchange market to keep the exchange rate within a margin of ±6% around the central rate. As of February 14, 2000, this margin was raised to ±9%.

Exchange tax
No.

Exchange subsidy
No.

Forward exchange market
Iceland has no organized forward market and the króna has no quoted forward exchange rate. However, forward contracts can be freely negotiated in all currencies.

Arrangements for Payments and Receipts

Prescription of currency requirements
No.

Payment arrangements
No.

Administration of control
The Ministry of Industry and Commerce (MIC) has ultimate responsibilities for imports and, in consultation with the CBI, for capital movements and foreign exchange regulation. The MIC implements the control on inward foreign direct investment. The CBI licenses the foreign exchange dealers on a commercial basis and sets the reporting requirements for statistical purposes and for implementation of control on inward foreign direct investment.

International security restrictions

In accordance with Executive Board Decision No. 144-(52/51)
Yes.

In accordance with UN sanctions
In compliance with UN Security Council resolutions, certain restrictions had been imposed on payments and transfers for current international transactions with respect to the Federal Republic of Yugoslavia (Serbia/Montenegro). Iceland imposes exchange restrictions against Libya in accordance with UN Security Council resolutions.

Payment arrears
No.

Controls on trade in gold (coins and/or bullion)
No.

Controls on exports and imports of banknotes
No.

Resident Accounts

Foreign exchange accounts permitted	Yes.
Held domestically	All accounts in domestic banks must be identified by name and identification number.
Held abroad	Residents must inform the CBI on opening of bank accounts abroad.
Accounts in domestic currency convertible into foreign currency	n.r.

Nonresident Accounts

Foreign exchange accounts permitted	Banks must report to the CBI the monthly positions of nonresident accounts. All accounts in domestic banks must be identified by name and identification number.
Domestic currency accounts	Yes.
Convertible into foreign currency	All accounts in domestic banks must be identified by name and identification number.
Blocked accounts	No.

Imports and Import Payments

Foreign exchange budget	No.
Financing requirements for imports	No.
Documentation requirements for release of foreign exchange for imports	No.
Import licenses and other nontariff measures	Imports of goods and services are free, except when international agreements or provisions in the special legislation provide otherwise.
Negative list	Live animals and certain other agricultural products require health certificates.
Open general licenses	Imports by tourists and foreign visitors are duty-free within general limits on the total, as well as on individual merchandise value, and quantitative limits are set on alcohol and tobacco by the customs authorities.
Import taxes and/or tariffs	Yes.
State import monopoly	Tobacco may be imported only under state trading arrangements.

Exports and Export Proceeds

Repatriation requirements	No.
Financing requirements	No.
Documentation requirements	No.
Export licenses	
Without quotas	Exports of military, fisheries, and agricultural products require licenses from the Ministry of Foreign Affairs and Foreign Trade.
Export taxes	No.

Payments for Invisible Transactions and Current Transfers

Controls on these transfers	No.

Proceeds from Invisible Transactions and Current Transfers

Repatriation requirements	No.
Restrictions on use of funds	No.

Capital Transactions

Controls on capital and money market instruments

The purchase of shares or other equity capital may be affected by laws on foreign investment in Iceland.

On capital market securities

Shares or other securities of a participating nature

Purchase locally by nonresidents

Yes.

Sale or issue locally by nonresidents

Foreign governments and other authorities are prohibited from issuing debt instruments in Iceland unless permitted by the CBI.

Bonds or other debt securities

Sale or issue locally by nonresidents

Foreign governments and other authorities are prohibited from issuing debt instruments in Iceland unless permitted by the CBI.

On money market instruments

Sale or issue locally by nonresidents

Yes.

Controls on derivatives and other instruments

Sale or issue locally by nonresidents

Foreign governments and other authorities are prohibited from issuing debt instruments in Iceland unless permitted by the CBI.

Controls on credit operations

No.

Controls on direct investment

Inward direct investment

Foreign direct investments in Iceland are regulated by a special law on foreign investment: (1) foreign investment is prohibited in the fisheries and primary fish processing industry, as only resident Icelandic citizens or domestically registered entities, where foreign ownership does not exceed 25%, may fish within the Icelandic fishing limit or operate primary fish processing facilities; this limit can be extended to 33% if the foreign investment in domestic entities does not exceed 5% of the total equity; (2) investments by foreign governments and public authorities are prohibited in Iceland; the MIC may grant exemptions from this restriction and restrictions that follow, which do not apply to residents of the EEA; (3) there are controls on the ownership or right to harness waterfalls and geothermal energy, where restrictions apply to investment in power production and distribution companies; (4) investments in domestic airlines may not exceed 49%; and (5) the above and other special laws also stipulate restricted conditions for residency of managers and majority of voting power in holding companies.

Controls on liquidation of direct investment

No.

Controls on real estate transactions

Purchase locally by nonresidents

The conditions to own real estate in Iceland are the following: (1) individual owners must be Icelandic citizens; (2) in the case of unlimited companies, all owners must be Icelandic citizens; and (3) joint-stock companies must be registered in Iceland, with at least 80% owned by Icelandic citizens, and all of the members of the board of directors being Icelandic citizens. Icelandic citizens must control the majority of the voting power at annual meetings. The same conditions apply if the real estate is to be leased for more than three years or if the lease agreement cannot be terminated with less than one year's notice. However, a company that is granted an operating license in Iceland may acquire real estate for its own use as long as the license does not carry with it the right to exploit natural resources. Citizens of the EEA and other foreign citizens who have been domiciled in Iceland for at least five years are exempted from these restrictions. The Minister of Justice may grant others exemption from these requirements.

Controls on personal capital movements

No.

Provisions specific to commercial banks and other credit institutions

Open foreign exchange position limits

The CBI regulates the net foreign exchange position of the banks, particularly in the foreign exchange market.

Provisions specific to institutional investors

Limits (max.) on securities issued by nonresidents and on portfolio invested abroad

Portfolio investments of pension funds are restricted to listed securities of organized markets within the OECD countries or elsewhere and with the approval of the Financial Supervision Authority.

Currency-matching regulations on assets/liabilities composition

Foreign exchange exposure of pension funds is limited to 40% of their total assets.

Other controls imposed by securities laws

No.

Changes During 1999

Exchange arrangement

January 1. The composition of the basket of currencies to which the króna is pegged was changed to reflect the introduction of the euro.

Changes During 2000

Exchange arrangement

February 14. The margin within which the CBI intervenes was raised to ±9% from ±6%.

INDIA

(Position as of December 31, 1999)

Status Under IMF Articles of Agreement

Article VIII   Date of acceptance: August 20, 1994.

Exchange Arrangement

Currency   The currency of India is the Indian rupee.

Exchange rate structure   Unitary.

Classification

Independently floating   The exchange rate of the rupee is determined in the interbank market. The Reserve Bank of India (RBI) purchases and sells spot and forward dollars from and to authorized dealers (ADs) in the interbank market at the market exchange rate.

Exchange tax   No.

Exchange subsidy   No.

Forward exchange market   ADs are allowed to deal forward in any permitted currency. Forward purchases or sales of foreign currencies against rupees with banks abroad are prohibited. The RBI may enter into swap transactions with ADs, under which it buys or sells spot dollars and sells or buys forward dollars for maturities available in the market.

ADs are allowed to offer a forward cover facility to foreign institutional investors (FII) to the extent of the value of their investment in respect of their fresh equity investments in India, and to cover the appreciation in the market value of their existing investment in India. This facility has also been extended to nonresident Indians (NRIs) and overseas corporate bodies (OCBs) to cover their portfolio equity investments. ADs are allowed to extend forward cover to holders of foreign currency nonresident (FCNR) accounts or nonresident external (NRE) accounts to enable them to hedge balances in such accounts.

ADs are also permitted to provide forward exchange cover to FIIs up to 15% of their out-standing equity investment as of the close of business on March 31, 1999, converted into U.S. dollar terms at the rate of Rs 42.43 per $1, as well as for the entire amount of any additional investment made after March 31, 1999. Existing forward contracts booked in accordance with earlier instructions were allowed to continue even if the amount thereof exceeded 15% of the value of the investment on March 31, 1999.

Official cover of forward operations   The Export Credit Guarantee Corporation of India, Ltd. (ECGCI) provides protection against exchange fluctuation with respect to deferred receivables from the date of a bid up to 15 years after the award of a contract. Exchange cover is offered in Australian dollars, euros, Japanese yen, pounds sterling, Swiss francs, U.A.E. dirhams, and U.S. dollars. For payments specified in other convertible currencies, cover is provided at the discretion of the ECGCI.

Arrangements for Payments and Receipts

Prescription of currency requirements   For prescription of currency purposes, countries are divided into two groups: (1) member countries of the ACU (except Nepal) and (2) the external group (all other countries). In the first group, all payments on account of eligible current international transactions, except payments relating to travel, must be settled through the ACU arrangement. In other cases, payments may be settled in any permitted currency. Export-import transactions financed out of loans from international financial institutions are settled outside the ACU mecha-nism. ADs and commercial banks in ACU countries are allowed to transfer ACU dollars among themselves instead of routing the transactions through their respective central banks. Payments to countries in the second group may be made in Indian rupees to the account of a resident of any of these countries or in any permitted currency, and receipts from these countries may be obtained in Indian rupees from accounts of a bank situated in any of these countries or in any permitted currency. However, special rules may apply with respect to exports under lines of credit extended by the government of India to the governments of certain foreign countries.

Payment arrangements

Regional arrangements

India is a member of the ACU.

Clearing agreements

Although Nepal is a member of the ACU, trade between India and Nepal is settled outside the ACU mechanism. Nepal is permitted to import from India against payment in freely convertible currency, in addition to the existing system of payment in Indian rupees. Transactions between all other ACU member countries are settled through ACU dollar accounts.

Administration of control

Exchange control is administered by the RBI in accordance with the general policy laid down by the government, in consultation with the RBI. Much of the routine work of exchange control is delegated to ADs. Import and export licenses, where necessary, are issued by the Director General of Foreign Trade. The RBI is responsible for approving applications for foreign currency loans under a $5 million scheme and for approving applications for short-term loans and credits with maturities of less than three years.

International security restrictions

In accordance with Executive Board Decision No. 144-(52/51)

Yes.

In accordance with UN sanctions

Yes.

Payment arrears

No.

Controls on trade in gold (coins and/or bullion)

Controls on domestic ownership and/or trade

There are no restrictions on internal trade in gold. However, gold mines continue to sell gold to industrial users through the distribution network of the State Bank of India (SBI), as well as through market sales. Forward trading in gold or silver is prohibited. Apart from a few agencies authorized by the government, 14 banks are authorized by the RBI to import gold for sale in the domestic market.

Controls on external trade

Exports of gold in any form other than jewelry produced in India for exportation with a gold value not exceeding 10% of the total value and jewelry constituting the personal effects of a traveler are prohibited, subject to certain monetary limits, unless effected by or on behalf of the monetary authorities. The net exportation of gold from India is not permitted. Exporters of jewelry may import their essential inputs, such as gold, with import licenses granted by the licensing authority. Under this scheme, the foreign buyer may supply gold or silver in advance and free of charge for the manufacture and ultimate export of gold or silver jewelry and articles thereof.

Exporters of gold jewelry and articles are entitled to replenishment of gold through the designated branches of the SBI, or any other agency nominated by the Ministry of Commerce, at a price indicated in the certificate issued by the SBI after the purchase of the gold. This scheme is limited to exports that are supported by an irrevocable LC, payment of cash on a delivery basis, or advance payment in foreign exchange. Exports of gold jewelry may also be allowed on a collection basis (documents against acceptance). The exporter has the option to obtain gold from the SBI in advance. On presentation of the required documents, the appropriate release order and gem replenishment license may be issued by the licensing authority, provided that the exporters satisfy value added and other requirements under the scheme.

Special permission for imports of gold and silver is granted only in exceptional cases where either no foreign exchange transaction is involved or the metals are needed for a particular purpose. Special permission is also granted when the gold or silver is imported for processing and reexportation provided that payments for the importation will not be required, the entire quantity of metal imported will be reexported in the form of jewelry, and the value added will be repatriated to India in foreign exchange through an AD. The government has permitted the import into India of gold and silver up to certain stipulated quantities by persons of Indian nationality or origin coming into India, subject to certain conditions and payment of the prescribed duty in foreign exchange. Gold and silver brought into the country are permitted to be sold to residents against payment in rupees.

Controls on exports and imports of banknotes

On exports

Domestic currency

In general, the exportation of Indian currency notes and coins, except to Bhutan and Nepal, is prohibited. The exportation to Nepal of Indian currency notes in denominations higher than Rs 100 is also prohibited. However, resident Indians may take with them Indian currency notes not exceeding Rs 1,000 a person at any one time to countries other than Nepal when going abroad on a temporary visit.

Foreign currency

ADs, exchange bureaus, and authorized money changers are permitted to sell foreign currency notes and coins up to the equivalent of Rs 100 to travelers going to Bangladesh and up to $50 or its equivalent to those going to other countries except Bhutan, Bangladesh, and Nepal. Nonresidents may take out the foreign currency notes that they brought in (and declared on entry if the amount exceeded $2,500), less the amounts sold to ADs and authorized money changers in India.

On imports

Domestic currency

The importation of Indian currency notes and coins is prohibited. However, any person may bring in Indian currency notes (other than notes of denominations larger than Rs 100) from Nepal. Indian travelers may bring in up to Rs 1,000 a person if they previously took out this amount when traveling abroad on a temporary visit.

Foreign currency

Foreign currency notes may be brought in without limit, provided that the total amount is declared to the customs authorities upon arrival if the value of foreign notes, coins, and traveler's checks exceeds $10,000 or its equivalent and/or if the aggregate value of foreign currency notes brought in at any one time exceeds $2,500 or its equivalent.

Resident Accounts

Foreign exchange accounts permitted

The accounts of Indians and of Bhutanese and Nepalese nationals residing in Bhutan and Nepal, as well as the accounts of offices and branches of Indian, Bhutanese, and Nepalese firms, companies, or other organizations in Bhutan and Nepal, are treated as resident accounts. However, residents of Nepal must obtain their foreign exchange requirements from the Nepal Rastra Bank. Approval of the RBI is required for the opening of foreign currency accounts, both held domestically or abroad, except for those covered by general permission granted by the RBI. Exporters may open Export Earners' Foreign Currency (EEFC) accounts. These accounts may be used to (1) open offices abroad and to meet the expenses of these offices; and (2) make investments from the account balance in overseas joint ventures up to the limit of $15 million without reference to the RBI. Effective April 15, 1999, a new type of account, the Nonresident Special Rupee (NRSR) account for NRIs and persons of Indian origin (PIOs) who would voluntarily undertake not to seek repatriation of funds held in such accounts and interest/income accrued thereon was introduced. These accounts have the same restrictions and facilities as those applicable to domestic resident accounts.

Held domestically

These accounts are permitted, but prior approval is required.

Held abroad

These accounts are permitted, but prior approval is required.

Accounts in domestic currency convertible into foreign currency

NRIs, PIOs, OCBs, and other corporate bodies that are owned directly or indirectly to the extent of at least 60% by NRIs, and overseas trusts in which at least 60% of the interest is irrevocably held by such persons, are permitted to maintain nonresident (external) accounts. Balances in such accounts are freely convertible into foreign currency. The opening of such accounts in the name of Pakistan or Bangladesh nationals, though of Indian origin, requires RBI approval.

Nonresident Accounts

Foreign exchange accounts permitted

1. Ordinary nonresident rupee accounts of individuals or firms may be credited with (i) the proceeds of remittances received in any permitted currency from abroad through normal banking channels, balances sold by the account holder in any permitted currency during his or her visit to India, or balances transferred from rupee accounts of nonresident banks; and (ii) legitimate dues paid in rupees by the account holder in India. For credits and debits exceeding Rs 100,000, ADs are required to submit a report on Form A-4 if the debit transactions relate to investment in shares, securities, or commercial paper of Indian companies or to the purchase of immovable property in India. ADs may debit the ordinary nonresident rupee accounts for all local disbursements, including investments in India that are covered by the general or special permission of the RBI.

2. Nonresident external rupee (NRER) accounts may be opened for NRIs and nonresident PIOs, or for overseas companies and partnership firms of which at least 60% is owned by nonresident PIOs. In addition to ADs holding licenses under the Foreign Exchange Regulation Act, some state cooperative banks, certain urban cooperative banks, and scheduled commercial banks not holding such licenses have also been permitted by the RBI to open and maintain nonresident rupee accounts, subject to certain conditions. Such accounts may also be opened for eligible persons during temporary visits to India against the tender of foreign currency traveler's checks, notes, or coins. They may be credited with (i) new funds remitted through banking channels from the country of residence of the account holder or from any country; (ii) the proceeds of foreign currency traveler's checks, personal checks, and drafts in the name of the account holder; (iii) foreign currency notes and coins tendered by the account holder while in India; (iv) income from authorized investments; and (v) the transfer of funds from other NRER or FCNR accounts. ADs are allowed to transfer funds between NRER accounts of different persons held with the same AD or different ADs for any purpose. The accounts may be debited (i) for disbursement in India and for transfers abroad; (ii) for any other transaction if covered under general or special permission granted by the RBI; and (iii) to purchase foreign currency and rupee traveler's checks or traveler's LC for the use of the account holder and his or her family and dependents. Investments in the shares of Indian companies, in partnership firms and the like, or in immovable property may be made with the approval of the RBI. Interest on deposits in nonresident external accounts in any bank in India is exempt from the personal income tax, although juridical persons are not entitled to this exemption. Interest earnings are transferable. The balances held in such accounts by natural persons are exempt from the wealth tax; gifts to close relatives in India from the balances in these accounts are exempt from the gift tax.

3. FCNR accounts denominated in dollars, euros, Japanese yen, and pounds sterling may be held in the form of term deposits by persons of Indian nationality or origin and by overseas companies as specified above. On June 30, 1999, the minimum maturity on these accounts was raised to one year from six months. These accounts may be credited with amounts received through normal banking channels, including interest earnings. Balances may be repatriated at any time without reference to the RBI. Balances may also be used for the same purposes that debits to NRER accounts are allowed. ADs are allowed to effect transfers of funds between FCNR accounts of different persons maintained with the same AD or other ADs for any purpose, subject to certain conditions. The current FCNR accounts operate in the same manner as the old FCNR accounts, except that the issuing bank (not the RBI) bears the exchange risk.

4. Nonresident, nonrepatriable rupee deposit accounts may be opened by NRIs and owned predominantly by NRIs and PIOs (except Pakistan and Bangladesh nationals). These accounts may be opened with funds in freely convertible foreign exchange remitted from abroad or funds transferred from existing NRER or FCNR accounts. The funds in these accounts may not be repatriated abroad at any time. The transfer abroad of accruing interest is permitted.

Effective May 19, 1999, foreign embassies, missions, and diplomats were permitted to open foreign currency accounts with ADs without the approval of the RBI, subject to certain conditions (previously, such accounts were allowed to be opened only at selected branches of the SBI). Accounts related to all foreign countries other than Bhutan and Nepal are treated as nonresident accounts.

Domestic currency accounts	Yes.
Convertible into foreign currency	Yes.
Blocked accounts	No.

Imports and Import Payments

Foreign exchange budget	No.
Financing requirements for imports	n.a.
Documentation requirements for release of foreign exchange for imports	n.a.
Import licenses and other nontariff measures	
Positive list	The importation of the following is restricted: (1) certain specified precious, semiprecious, and other stones; (2) safety, security, and related items; (3) seeds, plants, and animals; (4) insecticides and pesticides; (5) drugs and pharmaceuticals; (6) chemicals and allied items relating to the small-scale sector; and (7) most consumer goods and certain other items.
Negative list	Importation of tallow, fat and/or oils rendered or unrendered of any animal origin, animal rennet, wild animals (including their parts and products), and ivory is prohibited. Imports from Iraq are also prohibited.
Import taxes and/or tariffs	Yes.
State import monopoly	The importation of certain specified types of petroleum products, fertilizers, edible and nonedible oils, seeds, and cereals is channeled through the state trading enterprises, i.e., Indian Oil Corporation Ltd., Minerals and Metals Trading Corporation of India Ltd., State Trading Corporation of India Ltd., and the Food Corporation of India.

Exports and Export Proceeds

Repatriation requirements	Proceeds must be repatriated by the due date of receipt or within six months of shipment, whichever is earlier. Regarding exports made to Indian-owned warehouses abroad established with the permission of the RBI, a period of up to 15 months is allowed for the realization of export proceeds. Exporters are required to obtain permission from the RBI through ADs in the event that the export value is not realized within the prescribed period. The RBI also administers a scheme under which engineering goods (capital goods and consumer durables) may be exported under deferred credit arrangements, so that the full export value is paid in installments over more than six months.
Surrender requirements	Exporters are permitted to retain up to 50% of foreign exchange receipts in foreign currency accounts with banks in India. In the case of 100% export-oriented units, units in export processing zones, and units in hardware/software technology parts, up to 70% of foreign exchange receipts may be retained. Corporate exporters are permitted to extend trade-related advances to their importer clients out of their EEFC accounts up to $3 million for each EEFC account without obtaining RBI approval. ADs are permitted to allow utilization of funds held in EEFC accounts for making bona fide payments on behalf of the account holders in foreign exchange that are connected with their trade-related current account transactions without any restrictions, except in the case of remittances of agency commissions on exports, which are restricted to 12%.
Financing requirements	n.a.
Documentation requirements	n.a.
Export licenses	Licenses are required for exports of mineral ores and concentrates and chemicals, including those specified in the UN Convention on Chemical Weapons.

Export taxes

Other export taxes   Yes.

Payments for Invisible Transactions and Current Transfers

Controls on these transfers

All bona fide current account transactions qualify for the release of foreign exchange either under the authority delegated to ADs or after obtaining the necessary approval from the RBI.

Trade-related payments

Information is not available on payments of administrative expenses.

Quantitative limits

ADs are permitted to allow cash remittances of commissions on exports up to 12.5% of invoice value.

Investment-related payments

Remittances are allowed, subject to certain conditions, provided that all current taxes and other liabilities have been cleared.

The RBI allows branches of foreign companies operating in India to remit profits to their head offices without the prior approval of the RBI. Foreign banks do not need RBI approval for remittances of profits (net of taxes) earned in the normal course of business with their head offices. The remittance is subject to compliance with the Banking Act and RBI directives.

Prior approval

Yes.

Quantitative limits

Quantitative limits exist for interest payments.

Indicative limits/bona fide test

Yes.

Payments for travel

Prior approval

Yes.

Quantitative limits

Up to $3,000 a person a year may be released by ADs and full-fledged money changers for one or more trips abroad, except for visits to Bhutan and Nepal. The limits for various categories of business travel are as follows: (1) the per diem for senior executives is $500 and for others $350; and (2) Indian firms participating in trade fairs/exhibitions and private printers and publishers wishing to participate in overseas book fairs and exhibitions may obtain unlimited exchange from ADs, subject to rendering accounts.

Indicative limits/bona fide test

ADs may release foreign exchange in certain cases beyond indicative limits.

Personal payments

Quantitative limits

ADs have been delegated the power to release foreign exchange in line with the estimate of overseas doctor and hospital costs. ADs have been delegated the power to release foreign exchange for higher studies abroad on the basis of the cost estimate of the university or institution abroad. ADs may allow remittances of up to $5,000 a year for maintenance of a resident's dependents abroad.

Foreign workers' wages

Quantitative limits

Foreign workers, except those from Pakistan, are permitted to make reasonable remittances to their own countries to pay insurance premiums, to support their families, and for other expenses. ADs may allow such remittances of up to 75% of the net income of a foreign worker, provided that the worker holds a valid employment visa. ADs may also allow such remittances in excess of 75% of net income, provided the remittance meets prerequisites and the worker's family is staying abroad.

Indicative limits/bona fide test

Credit card use abroad

Persons going abroad for any purpose (except for employment or emigration) may use international credit cards (ICCs) for all purposes, including for the purchase of articles for personal use within their entitlement of foreign exchange. The basic travel quota may also be obtained through the use of credit cards. The use of ICCs is allowed for (1) imports of software through the Internet ($18,000 a transaction), (2) payment of services obtained through the Internet, and (3) use by software engineers going abroad on assignment.

Resident Indians are also allowed to hold ICCs to use locally and abroad. Effective April 7, 1999, ADs and/or their subsidiaries were permitted to issue rupee credit cards valid in India, Nepal, and Bhutan to NRIs/PIOs and to allow settlement of bills in rupees arising from use of such cards by debits to their NRSR/NRE accounts or to their ordinary nonresident rupee accounts.

Other payments

Quantitative limits

The limit for subscriptions and membership fees is $25,000 or its equivalent. There are no limits on remittances for legal expenses in connection with trade-related transactions. Remittances by Indian shipping companies for fees for solicitors and adjusters may be allowed by ADs without limit. There is no limit for remittances to foreign data service vendors for the use of international databases.

Indicative limits/bona fide test

Yes.

Proceeds from Invisible Transactions and Current Transfers

Repatriation requirements

Proceeds must be repatriated.

Surrender requirements

Up to 50% of receipts may be retained in foreign currency accounts with banks in India. In the case of export-oriented units, units created in Export Processing Zones, Software Technology Parks, or Electronic Maintenance Technology Parks, 70% of remittances may be obtained from these accounts.

Restrictions on use of funds

n.a.

Capital Transactions

Controls on capital and money market instruments

On capital market securities

Shares or other securities of a participating nature

Purchase locally by nonresidents

FIIs are permitted to make investments in all securities traded on the primary and secondary markets, including equity and other securities, and in instruments of companies listed or to be listed on the stock exchanges in India. FIIs are also allowed to invest in dated government securities, either on behalf of clients or by using proprietary funds. FIIs are required to register initially with the Securities and Exchange Board of India (SEBI) and with the RBI. For FIIs registered for investments in equities, there is no control on the value of their investments in the primary and secondary markets, but investments in debt instruments may not exceed 30% of the total investment. However, FIIs may set up separately 100% debt funds, which may invest their portfolio in debt instruments within the overall approved debt ceiling.

Portfolio investments in the primary or secondary markets are subject to a ceiling of 10% of the issued share capital for individual FII holdings and 24% of issued share capital for the total holdings of all registered FIIs in any one company, with the exception of (1) foreign investments under financial collaboration; and (2) investments through offshore single and regional funds, global depositary receipts (GDRs), and convertibles in the euromarket.

The individual ceiling for NRIs, OCBs, and PIOs is 5% of the paid-up capital, and their aggregate investment ceilings are 10% of the paid-up share capital of a company. In the case of companies listed on the stock exchange, the ceiling may be raised to 24% of paid-up capital by passing a resolution in the general board meeting.

Sale or issue locally by nonresidents

Nonresidents are not permitted to issue securities in the local market. In the case of securities of Indian companies held by nonresidents, transfers to a resident must be confirmed by the RBI. Transfers of sale proceeds are permitted, subject to tax, provided no controls were imposed on the repatriation of sale proceeds while approving the original investment. Transfers between two nonresidents do not require such confirmation, but a nonresident transferee requires permission for the purchase of shares of an Indian company.

The RBI has introduced a scheme for investment by NRIs and OCBs of up to 51% of the new issues by certain Indian companies that are not listed on stock exchanges. The companies providing investments are required to inform all partners of the details of the remittances.

Purchase abroad by residents	RBI permission is required for acquiring, holding, or disposing of any foreign security. If the acquisition is permitted, transfer of the needed funds from India is also permitted. In the case of a sale of foreign securities, the repatriation of sale proceeds to India is required, unless otherwise specified. Indians who have returned to India after a minimum continuous stay of one year abroad have been exempted from the requirement of obtaining RBI permission for continuing to hold securities already purchased prior to their return to India out of incomes earned by them while abroad. They are also free to use sales proceeds of such securities for acquisition of further securities without RBI permission. The RBI considers applications from resident employees of foreign companies and their joint ventures or wholly owned subsidiaries, in which the foreign company holds not less than 51% equity, for remittance up to $10,000 per employee in a block of five years for acquisition of shares of the foreign company. Similarly, applications are considered from employees of Indian software companies for remittance of $10,000 in a block of five years for acquiring shares in overseas joint ventures or wholly owned subsidiaries of Indian companies, subject to certain conditions.
Sale or issue abroad by residents	The same regulations apply as for purchases abroad by residents.

On money market instruments

Purchase locally by nonresidents	NRIs and OCBs (predominantly those owned to the extent of at least 60% by NRIs and nonresident PIOs) are allowed to invest in money market mutual funds floated by commercial banks and public or private sector financial institutions with authorization from the RBI or the SEBI on a nonrepatriation basis.
Sale or issue locally by nonresidents	These transactions require RBI approval.
Purchase abroad by residents	Residents are not permitted to purchase such instruments abroad without the authorization of the RBI.
Sale or issue abroad by residents	These transactions are not permitted.

On collective investment securities

Resident companies are not permitted to issue securities to nonresidents without the approval of the RBI.

Purchase locally by nonresidents	These transactions require the prior approval of the RBI.
Sale or issue locally by nonresidents	The issue of collective investment securities by nonresidents on local markets in India is not permitted.
Purchase abroad by residents	These transactions require the prior approval of the RBI.
Sale or issue abroad by residents	These transactions require permission from the RBI; the Unit Trust of India has been granted permission for issuing certain securities abroad.

Controls on derivatives and other instruments

Purchase locally by nonresidents	Resident companies are not permitted to issue rupee-based derivatives and other instruments in India.
Sale or issue locally by nonresidents	These transactions are not allowed.
Purchase abroad by residents	ADs are allowed to purchase hedge instruments for corporate clients and for their own asset/liability management. Contract length is restricted to six months, after which point RBI clearance is required. Crude oil and petroleum products are excluded.
Sale or issue abroad by residents	These transactions require the permission of the RBI.

Controls on credit operations

Effective June 2, 1999, ADs were permitted to grant credit facilities according to their commercial value against the security of balances held in EEFC accounts.

Commercial credits

By residents to nonresidents

A commercial credit of up to six months is allowed regarding exports on documents-against-acceptance terms. Contracts for exports involving payments to be realized beyond the normal period of six months are treated as deferred payment exports. Such exports are permitted, keeping in mind the credit terms offered, the commodity to be exported, and other related considerations. This applies to turnkey, construction, and service contracts undertaken by Indian exporters on credit terms. Under the Buyer's Credit Scheme, the Export- Import Bank (EXIM Bank) offers credits to foreign buyers in connection with the export of capital goods and turnkey projects in India in participation with commercial banks in India. These are considered by the EXIM Bank depending upon the creditworthiness, standing, and financial position of the overseas borrower; the economic viability of the project; the standing of the Indian exporter; and so forth.

To residents from nonresidents

Proposals for raising foreign currency loans and credits—buyer's credits and supplier's credits or lines of credit by firms, companies, or lending institutions—for financing imports of goods and services for a period of less than three years are considered by the RBI on their terms and conditions in connection with the terms offered in overseas markets. Exporters are allowed to raise external commercial borrowing up to twice the average amount of annual exports during the previous years, subject to a maximum of $100 million without end-use restrictions (i.e., general corporate objectives, excluding investment in stock or in real estate). The maximum level of entitlement in any one year is a cumulative limit and debit outstanding under the existing $15 million exporters scheme netted out to determine annual eligibility. External commercial borrowing guidelines for exporters and shipping companies were eased, facilitating overseas borrowing by eligible corporations.

Financial credits

These transactions require prior permission from the RBI.

By residents to nonresidents

Yes.

To residents from nonresidents

Prepayment of such loans and credits, and payments of interest and other charges on such loans may be made by ADs under general permission of the RBI. Borrowing proposals for loans less than three years and those falling under the $5 million and $10 million scheme must be cleared by the RBI. External borrowing falling outside these schemes requires government approval. External borrowing is permitted for expenditures related to roads, bridges, ports, industrial parks, and urban infrastructure (water supply, sanitation, and sewerage projects). In addition to the previously designated sectors, power, railways, telecommunications, and license fee payments are also approved uses of external borrowing. Holding companies and promoters may raise external borrowing to the equivalent of $50 million to finance equity investment in a subsidiary company implementing infrastructure projects. Corporate borrowers may raise long-term resources with average maturities of 8 and 16 years up to $100 million and $500 million, respectively, and use the funds without any end-use restrictions (i.e., general corporate objectives), excluding investments in the stock market and real estate. However, borrowings of an average maturity of 10 years and above would be outside the ceiling.

Corporate borrowers are permitted to raise external borrowing to acquire ships and vessels from Indian shipyards. Corporate borrowers who had raised funds for the import of capital goods and services through bonds, floating rate notes, or syndicated loans are permitted to remit funds into India and deploy the same, excluding investments in the stock market or in real estate, until their actual import of capital goods and services takes place or up to one year, whichever is less. In case borrowers decide to deploy the funds abroad until the approved end-use requirement arises, they are eligible to do so in line with RBI guidelines. Borrowing limits for telecommunications projects are flexible, and an increase from the present 25% to 50% of the project cost is allowed.

Guarantees, sureties, and financial backup facilities

By residents to nonresidents

The ADs are allowed to give performance bonds or guarantees in favor of overseas buyers in connection with bona fide exports from India, as well as guarantees in the ordinary course of business in respect of missing documents, authenticity of signatures, and other similar purposes. The RBI has granted general permission to shipping agents to give guarantees in respect of any debt or other obligation as liability of their principals. Guarantees in favor of income tax, customs, post, and other central or state government authorities in India subject to such instructions require authorization from the RBI.

To residents from nonresidents

The RBI has permitted ADs to grant loans to residents against guarantees from nonresidents, subject, among other things, to the condition that no direct or indirect payment is made abroad by way of guarantee, commission, or otherwise.

Controls on direct investment

Outward direct investment

Investments are subject to approval of the RBI. Proposals for participation in overseas joint ventures, the setting up of wholly owned subsidiaries abroad that involve remittance of cash, and the export of goods from India, are considered in light of the financial position and track record of the applicant Indian company; the past export performance; and the benefits likely to accrue in terms of foreign exchange earnings by way of exports, technology transfer, profits, dividends, and so forth. ADs are permitted to allow investments up to $15 million (inclusive of investment approved under the fast-track route by the RBI) in a block of three years out of funds held by the Indian investors in their EEFC accounts. Proposals of investment in joint ventures or wholly owned subsidiaries abroad up to a maximum of 50% of GDRs to be raised would be cleared by the MOF under its normal GDR approval process for overseas investment as a permitted end use. The RBI also allows investment in joint ventures or wholly owned subsidiaries abroad uniformly up to $15 million in respect of all countries and Indian rupee investments up to Rs 600 million in Nepal and Bhutan.

For the use of investment by computer software companies with cumulative export or foreign exchange realization of $25 million or more in the preceding three years, blanket investment approval is given by the RBI up to 50% of such foreign exchange earnings, subject to a maximum of $25 million in a block of three consecutive financial years.

Inward direct investment

Foreign equity up to 50%, 51%, and 74% is permitted by the RBI in specified high-priority industries on an automatic basis. The RBI also allows foreign equity holdings up to 51% in trading companies primarily engaged in export activities. Other applications require clearance from the government. A liberal policy is followed for investments in India by NRIs or predominantly owned by OCBs. Foreign companies are also permitted to set up offices in India for the purpose of carrying on liaison activities, provided their entire expenses are remitted from abroad. Applications for investment in areas that do not fall within the authority of the RBI but that are covered by the foreign investment policy are approved by the Foreign Investment Promotion Board (FIPB). Such investments may be approved up to 100% of capital on a case-by-case basis. The Ministry of Industry is the relevant agency for all issues related to foreign direct investment, including approvals. In the case of coal, hydro, and nonconventional energy-based power projects, the Power Ministry may grant automatic approvals of up to 100% foreign equity under certain conditions. Nonresidents, noncitizens, and nonbank companies not incorporated under Indian law must have permission from the RBI to initiate, expand, or continue any business activity in India and to hold or acquire shares of any company carrying on a trading, commercial, or industrial activity in India.

NRIs or PIOs may invest freely in any public or private limited company or in any partnership or proprietary concern engaged in any activity except agricultural or plantation activities and real estate (excluding real estate development, such as construction of houses, etc.), provided (1) funds for investment are either remitted from abroad through normal banking channels or drawn from their nonresident accounts; (2) repatriation of the capital invested will not be requested; and (3) overall limits on holdings of shares and convertible debentures bought through the stock exchange by NRIs (see below) are adhered to.

OCBs, societies, and partnership firms of which at least 60% is owned by NRIs or PIOs and overseas trusts in which at least 60% of the beneficial interest is irrevocably held by NRIs are also allowed to invest in any public or private limited company, in accordance with the above provisions.

NRIs and OCBs, as defined above, may use funds derived from fresh remittances or held in their nonresident (external) or foreign currency (nonresident) accounts to (1) make portfolio investments with repatriation benefits up to 1% of the capital, provided that their total holdings of shares and convertible debentures held on either a repatriable or nonrepatriable basis by all nonresident investors do not exceed 10%, 24%, or 30% of the paid-up capital of the company or of the total paid-up value of each series of convertible debentures issued by the company; (2) invest freely in national savings certificates with full repatriation benefits; (3) invest up to 40% of the new equity capital issued by a company setting up industrial manufacturing projects; hospitals (including diagnostic centers); hotels of at least three-star category; and shipping, software, and oil exploration services with repatriation rights for capital and income, subject to deduction of applicable Indian taxes; (4) place up to 100% in new investments, including expansion of existing industrial undertakings in specified priority industries, with free repatriation of such investments. Foreign direct investment is permitted in trading companies. Trading companies must be registered with the Ministry of Commerce and must obtain a certificate of their status as either export, trading, star trading, or super star trading house before applying to the RBI for remittances or dividends. The RBI has the authority to permit foreign investment of up to 51% of the paid-up capital of such Indian companies. A higher percentage, up to 100%, is considered for approval by the FIPB, provided that the funding company is primarily engaged in exports. Existing joint-venture companies may raise the ratio of foreign equity shares to 51% of their capital through expansion of their capital base or through preferential allocation of shares to the foreign investor. Companies in certain manufacturing and tourist industries may obtain RBI automatic approval for the expansion; (5) invest on a nonrepatriable basis in money market mutual funds (only NRIs and OCBs), subject to RBI approval; (6) invest up to 51% of equity on a repatriable basis in unlisted companies in all industries, except those mentioned in Annex III of the Statement of Industrial Policy; and (7) issue shares to foreign investors of up to 50%, 51%, 74%, or 100% if those Indian companies issuing the shares were engaged in specified high-priority industries, subject to fulfilling certain conditions. The RBI has granted permission for such transactions and has also granted general permission to Indian companies to issue shares to foreign investors up to the level approved by the government (Ministry of Industry).

Controls on liquidation of direct investment	Sale of shares, securities, and immovable property requires approval of the RBI. Repatriation of after-tax sales proceeds is generally permitted, provided no condition of nonrepatriation was imposed when approving the original investment.
Controls on real estate transactions	These transactions require the permission of the RBI.
Purchase abroad by residents	Indians who have returned to India after a minimum continuous stay of one year abroad are, however, permitted to hold immovable property acquired with funds earned while they were abroad. They are also free to dispose of such property or acquire new property from the sale proceeds of such property.
Purchase locally by nonresidents	NRIs and OCBs (predominantly those owned by NRIs) may invest in companies engaged in real estate development (e.g., construction of houses, etc.); up to 100% of new investments may be required to be locked in for a period of three years for disinvestment. After three years, remittances of disinvestment will be allowed up to the original investment in foreign exchange. In the cases of OCBs, profits may be repatriated up to 16%.
Sale locally by nonresidents	Repatriation of after-tax sales proceeds is generally permitted, provided no condition of nonrepatriation was imposed while approving the original investment.
Controls on personal capital movements	
Loans	
By residents to nonresidents	These transactions require the approval of the RBI.
To residents from nonresidents	These transactions require the approval of the RBI. NRIs are permitted to grant non-interest–bearing loans on a nonrepatriation basis to their close relatives in India.
Gifts, endowments, inheritances, and legacies	
By residents to nonresidents	ADs are allowed to permit remittances of gifts up to $1,000 a year by residents.
Transfer of assets	
Transfer abroad by emigrants	These transactions require the approval of the RBI.

Transfer of gambling and prize earnings	Remittances of earnings from sweepstakes and lotteries are not permitted.
Provisions specific to commercial banks and other credit institutions	The interest rate surcharge of 30% on import financing was withdrawn on October 31, 1999.
Borrowing abroad	Borrowing is subject to approval by the government, the MOF, and the Department of Economic Affairs. ADs may avail themselves of loans, overdrafts, and other types of fund-based credit facilities from their overseas branches and correspondents up to 15% of their unimpaired Tier I capital. Loans or overdrafts in excess of this limit may be obtained solely for the purpose of replenishing the dealers' rupee resources in India without prior approval from the RBI. Repayment of such borrowing requires prior approval from the RBI, which may be accorded only when the debtor bank has no outstanding borrowings in India from the RBI or any other bank or financial institution and is clear of all money market borrowings for a period of at least four weeks before the repayment.
Maintenance of accounts abroad	There are no controls on ADs maintaining accounts abroad. In all other cases (e.g., airlines and shipping companies), specific permission by the RBI is required. The RBI has granted general permission to certain categories of persons to maintain foreign currency accounts abroad for specific purposes, subject to certain conditions.
Lending to nonresidents (financial or commercial credits)	Lending is subject to RBI approval on a case-by-case basis and at a limit of $10 million. However, ADs have been permitted to invest their temporary surplus funds in foreign treasury bills and make deposits with banks abroad, subject to a limit of 15% of their Tier I capital.
Lending locally in foreign exchange	Banks may lend to residents to meet bona fide foreign exchange requirements toward preshipment credit in foreign currency for financing domestic inputs. Banks may also use their FCNR deposit resources to grant loans to residents for their bona fide foreign currency requirements.
Purchase of locally issued securities denominated in foreign exchange	No scheme is in place allowing for these transactions.
Differential treatment of deposit accounts in foreign exchange	
Interest rate controls	While interest rates on resident deposits for maturities of over two years have been completely deregulated, interest rates on FCNR (banks), which must be aligned with the international rates, are decided by the RBI. Interest rates on nonresident (nonrepatriable) rupee deposit schemes are deregulated for all maturities. External commercial borrowings for project financing are allowed spreads of up to 350 basis points above LIBOR and U.S. treasury bills. Corporate entities are also allowed to raise 50% of the permissible debt in the form of subordinated debt at a higher interest rate.
Differential treatment of deposit accounts held by nonresidents	
Reserve requirements	Reserve requirements on domestic and foreign currency deposits by nonresidents were reduced to 9% effective November 20, 1999. The requirement for banks to maintain an incremental cash reserve ratio of 10% on the increase in liabilities under the FCNR scheme over the level prevailing on April 11, 1997, was also withdrawn on November 20, 1999. The requirement that banks must charge a minimum 20% interest rate on overdue export bills was withdrawn on October 31, 1999.
Liquid asset requirements	An incremental cash reserve requirement of 10% on foreign currency nonresident deposits is in effect. All other foreign currency accounts remain exempted from the cash reserve requirement.
Open foreign exchange position limits	Banks are required to maintain on an ongoing basis Tier I capital at 5% of the open position limit approved by the RBI, and the overall open position limit should have a reasonable relation to the capital of the bank.
Provisions specific to institutional investors	
Limits (max.) on portfolio invested abroad	Yes.

Other controls imposed by   n.a.
securities laws

Changes During 1999

Exchange arrangement   *March 31.* ADs were permitted to provide forward exchange cover to FIIs to the extent of 15% of their outstanding equity investment.

Resident accounts   *April 15.* A new type of account, the NRSR account for NRIs and PIOs, was introduced.

Nonresident accounts   *May 19.* Foreign embassies, missions, and diplomats were permitted to open foreign currency accounts with ADs without the approval of the RBI, subject to certain conditions.

                                       June 30. The minimum maturity on FCNR accounts was raised to one year from six months.

Payments for invisible transactions *April 7.* ADs and/or their subsidiaries were permitted to issue rupee credit cards valid in
and current transfers   India, Nepal, and Bhutan to NRIs and PIOs and to allow settlement of bills in rupees arising from use of such cards by debit to their NRSR/NRE accounts or to their ordinary nonresident rupee accounts.

Capital transactions

Controls on credit operations   *June 2.* ADs were permitted to grant credit facilities according to their commercial value against the security of balances held in an EEFC account.

Provisions specific to commercial   *October 31.* The stipulation that banks must charge a minimum 20% interest rate on
banks and other credit institutions   overdue export bills was withdrawn.

                                       October 31. The interest rate surcharge on import financing was withdrawn.

                                       November 20. Reserve requirements on domestic and foreign currency deposits by nonresidents were reduced to 9%.

INDONESIA

(Position as of February 29, 2000)

Status Under IMF Articles of Agreement

Article VIII	Date of acceptance: May 7, 1988.

Exchange Arrangement

Currency	The currency of Indonesia is the Indonesian rupiah.
Other legal tender	Two commemorative gold coins are also legal tender.
Exchange rate structure	Unitary.
Classification	
Independently floating	The exchange rate is determined freely in the foreign exchange market.
Exchange tax	No.
Exchange subsidy	No.
Forward exchange market	Forward foreign currency contracts offered by domestic banks to nonresidents are limited to $5 million for each bank and for each customer. These restrictions do not apply to trade- and investment-related transactions.
Official cover of forward operations	Yes.

Arrangements for Payments and Receipts

Prescription of currency requirements	No.
Payment arrangements	
Regional arrangements	Indonesia is a member of the ASEAN.
Barter agreements and open accounts	There are countertrade arrangements as part of bids for government-sponsored construction or procurement projects, whose import component is valued at more than Rp 500 million.
Administration of control	In general, there are no restrictions on foreign exchange transactions. However, the Commercial Offshore Loan Team (COLT) has the authority to institute regulations regarding commercial offshore borrowing. Effective May 1, 1999, the Foreign Exchange Flows and Exchange Rate System Act was approved by parliament. On October 28, 1999, the Foreign Exchange Transactions Law was approved by parliament; the law gives Bank Indonesia (BI) the authority to obtain information on foreign exchange transactions.
International security restrictions	
In accordance with UN sanctions	Restrictions against countries on which the UN has imposed a trade embargo are in effect.
Payment arrears	No.
Controls on trade in gold (coins and/or bullion)	
Controls on external trade	Travelers may freely take out up to Rp 65,000 a person in Indonesian commemorative gold and silver coins issued in August 1970 and up to Rp 130,000 a person in gold and silver coins issued in October 1974; amounts in excess of these limits require the prior approval of the BI. Gold may be imported freely. Imports are subject to a levy of Rp 25 per $1.

Controls on exports and imports of banknotes

On exports

  Domestic currency

Travelers may freely take out Indonesian notes and coins up to Rp 5 million a person. For amounts in excess of this limit and up to Rp 10 million, a declaration must be made to customs officials, while for amounts exceeding Rp 10 million, the prior approval of the BI is required in addition to the customs declaration.

On imports

  Domestic currency

Travelers may bring in Indonesian notes and coins up to Rp 5 million a person. For the repatriation of amounts in excess of this amount limit, the same conditions apply as for exports.

Resident Accounts

Foreign exchange accounts permitted Yes.

Held domestically Only checking and time deposit accounts are permitted.

Held abroad Yes.

Accounts in domestic currency convertible into foreign currency No checks may be drawn on foreign currency accounts.

Nonresident Accounts

Foreign exchange accounts permitted Yes.

Approval required Only checking and time deposit accounts are permitted. No checks may be drawn on foreign currency accounts.

Domestic currency accounts Yes.

Convertible into foreign currency Yes.

Blocked accounts No.

Imports and Import Payments

Foreign exchange budget No.

Financing requirements for imports Requirements in general are set by commercial banks on the basis of their assessment. Exporters, however, require banks to guarantee a 100% face value of red-clause LCs and advance payments.

Documentation requirements for release of foreign exchange for imports Cement/asbestos sheets, dry batteries, steel slabs, low-voltage electric cord, and electric light bulbs are subject to quality control.

Domiciliation requirements Yes.

Letters of credit LCs may be issued by foreign exchange banks in the form of sight or usance LCs. Payment settlement under usance LCs should not be more than 360 days.

Import licenses and other nontariff measures

Negative list Imports from countries against which the United Nations has imposed a trade embargo are prohibited, as are imports from all sources of most secondhand goods and of certain products. Secondhand engines, however, and their parts and other capital goods may be imported by industrial firms for their own use or for the reconditioning of their industry, in accordance with the guidelines of the Ministry of Trade (MOT) and of Industry. Certain categories of agricultural imports, including foodstuffs, beverages, and fruits, may be imported only by registered importers designated by the MOT. The procurement policies of companies approved for the importation of fruit, alcoholic beverages, and chicken are evaluated annually by the government, although explicit quantitative restrictions are not placed on these products.

Open general licenses

There is a registry of authorized importers that includes only Indonesian nationals, although foreign investors are permitted to import the items required for their own projects. Although all imports into Indonesia are subject to licensing requirements, most are classified under the General Importer License.

Import taxes and/or tariffs

Certain products are granted preferential duties within the framework of the AFTA and the WTO.

Taxes collected through the exchange system

Import taxes are collected through foreign exchange banks authorized by the MOF.

State import monopoly

Imports of certain goods remain restricted to approved importers, most of which are state enterprises. Pertamina has a monopoly on the importation of lubricating oil and lubricating fats, and Dahana on the importation of ammunition and explosive gelatin. The monopoly rights of approved importers (sole agents) also remain in effect for the importation of certain heavy equipment and motor vehicles, although this right may be transferred to general importers. The importation of trucks is subject to restriction.

Exports and Export Proceeds

Repatriation requirements

No.

Financing requirements

Exporters (producers or suppliers) may sell their export proceeds to the BI through a rediscount facility. Drafts may be rediscounted in rupiah or foreign currency. Such drafts denominated in currencies other than the dollar, euro, pound sterling, and yen must first be converted into dollars. The maximum remaining period to maturity of drafts that can be rediscounted by foreign exchange banks to the BI is 720 days. The BI sets the discount rate for daily rediscount transactions based on the SIBOR rate for various maturities plus a margin. The BI also provides rediscount facilities for suppliers of related products to exporters. In this case, on the basis of a local LC, a supplier may seek a bank draft and sell to the BI through a foreign exchange bank, provided the remaining days to maturity are between 30 and 180 days. The discount rate for the draft is the BI's six-month money market securities' cut-off rate.

Documentation requirements

Letters of credit

Exports with sight LC conditions must be settled not later than 30 days from the date the exports are registered with the foreign exchange bank.

Domiciliation

Yes.

Preshipment inspection

Exports of goods that contain imported material that received import tax abolishment from the government must be examined before shipment.

Other

Yes.

Export licenses

Exports to countries against which the UN has imposed a trade embargo are prohibited, as are exports to all countries of certain categories of unprocessed or low-quality rubber, brass and copper scrap (except from the island of Irian Jaya), iron scrap, steel scrap, and antiques of cultural value. Exporters are required to obtain trade permits issued by the MOT.

Without quotas

Exports of certain domestically produced commodities must have prior authorization from the MOT in order to meet domestic demand and to encourage domestic processing of certain raw materials. Items affected by such controls include clove seeds, logs, fertilizer, cement, iron for construction reinforcement, automobile tires, paper, asphalt, stearin, cattle, salt, wheat flour, maize, soybeans, rice, copra, olein, raw rattan, meat, and all goods produced from subsidized raw materials. Concern about domestic price stability sometimes leads to the suspension of exports of various items in this category.

With quotas	Manioc may be exported only by approved exporters. Textiles and textile products subject to import quotas in the consumer countries may be exported only by approved textile exporters, who may transfer their allocated quotas to other approved exporters through the Commodity Exchange Board.
Export taxes	Export taxes ranging from $250 to $4,800 per cubic meter are applied to sawed and processed timber. Exports of logs are subject to taxes ranging from $500 to $4,800 per cubic meter. Certain processed wood products are not taxed. Certain other products are subject to export taxes ranging from 5% to 30%.
	On February 1, 1999, taxes on exports of logs and sawn timber were reduced to 20%.
	On June 4, 1999, export taxes on palm oil were reduced to 30% from 40%; on crude palm kernel, to 20% from 30%; and on crude coconut oil, to zero from 15%.
Taxes collected through the exchange system	Taxes are collected through foreign exchange banks authorized by the MOF.

Payments for Invisible Transactions and Current Transfers

Controls on these transfers	No.

Proceeds from Invisible Transactions and Current Transfers

Repatriation requirements	No.
Restrictions on use of funds	No.

Capital Transactions

Controls on capital and money market instruments	
On capital market securities	
Shares or other securities of a participating nature	
Purchase locally by nonresidents	Foreign investors are allowed to purchase without limit shares issued by Indonesian companies in the Indonesian capital market. There is a control on the ownership of a joint securities company, which is a finance company. Effective March 31, 1999, the ceiling on the amount of stock foreigners may require in nonstrategic corporations without the approval of the company's board of directors was raised.
Sale or issue locally by nonresidents	Foreign companies are permitted to issue Indonesian Depository Receipts (IDRs) through custodian banks in Indonesia. IDRs are instruments that facilitate the trading of shares of foreign companies in the Indonesian capital market. Custodian banks in turn issue IDRs based on the shares that the foreign companies have put in the custodian bank.
Sale or issue abroad by residents	No control applies as long as the shares are not listed on the Indonesian Stock Exchange (ISM). If those securities are listed on the ISM, they initially should comply with the Capital Market Act and with the requirement on the maximum percentage of foreign ownership of shares. However, Indonesian companies do not issue shares but rather American Depository Receipts (ADRs) in the U.S. capital market and Global Depository Receipts (GDRs) on the London Stock Exchange.
Bonds or other debt securities	n.r.
On money market instruments	
Sale or issue locally by nonresidents	These transactions are prohibited.

Sale or issue abroad by residents	Banks require approval from the COLT for issuance of instruments with maturities of over two years or for amounts exceeding $20 million a year a creditor; total issuances, however, should not exceed 30% of the bank's capital.

On collective investment securities

Purchase locally by nonresidents — No person may purchase more than 1% of any fund.

Controls on derivatives and other instruments

Derivative transactions, other than those associated with foreign exchange and interest rates, are prohibited. Exception may be made by the BI for derivative transactions related to stock margins. Banks are obliged to enter into a written agreement with their clients and explain the risks of these transactions and also to submit a weekly report to the BI. Losses from derivative transactions exceeding 10% of each bank's capital must immediately be reported to the BI. Forward sales contracts of foreign currency by domestic banks to nonresidents are limited to $5 million a bank a customer. These controls do not apply to trade- and investment-related transactions. Banks are prohibited from maintaining derivative exposure transacted by the bank's owners, director, employees, commissioners, or any other party linked to the bank, as well as from extending credit facilities and overdrafts for the purpose of derivative transactions to the bank's debtors.

Purchase locally by nonresidents — Yes.

Sale or issue locally by nonresidents — Yes.

Purchase abroad by residents — Yes.

Sale or issue abroad by residents — Yes.

Controls on credit operations

Commercial credits

By residents to nonresidents — In general, resident entities are prohibited from granting credit to nonresident entities.

To residents from nonresidents — Resident entities, especially the nonbank private sector, may borrow from nonresidents; however, they have to submit periodic reports to the BI on their borrowing. The following are subject to authorization by the BI: (1) borrowings related to development projects using nonrecourse, limited recourse, advance payment, trustee borrowing, leasing, and similar financing; (2) borrowings related to development projects with financing based on BOT, B&T, and similar schemes; and (3) borrowings related to the government or a state company (including the State Bank or Pertamina), including in the form of government equity participation, guarantee for provision of feedstock supply, or guarantee for products offtaker.

Financial credits

By residents to nonresidents — In general, there are no controls on the granting of credit by residents (excluding banks) to nonresident entities.

To residents from nonresidents — Yes.

Guarantees, sureties, and financial backup facilities

By residents to nonresidents — Banks are allowed to provide sureties and guarantees to nonresident entities only under the following conditions: (1) when there is sufficient contraguarantee from bona fide overseas banks (excluding overseas branches from the relevant bank); and (2) when there is a cash deposit valued at 100% of the guarantee granted.

Controls on direct investment

Inward direct investment — Several sectors are controlled: (1) foreign investment companies in infrastructure projects such as seaports, electricity generation, transmission and distribution for public use, telecommunications, shipping, airlines, potable water supply, public railways, and nuclear electric power generation should be established by way of joint venture between foreign and Indonesian partners, and the share of Indonesian partners should be at least 5% of the total capital issued at the outset of the company; and (2) a foreign investment company may be established as a straight investment, which means that 100% of the shares may be owned by a foreign citizen and/or entities. However, some of the company's shares must be sold to an Indonesian citizen and/or entities through direct placement and/or indirectly through the domestic capital market no later than 15 years after the commencement of commercial operations.

Foreign ownership of direct investments must begin to be divested by the eleventh year of production. For investments above $50 million, divestment of 50% must be completed within 20 years. For smaller investments, the divestment requirement is less stringent.

All foreign enterprises are eligible to receive preferential customs duty treatment for imports of required raw materials for the first two years of production activity. Raw materials may be imported with no time limit. In addition, an enterprise exporting more than 65% of its production is free to hire foreign experts as needed to maintain its export commitments.

On January 31, 1999, a presidential decree was issued granting income tax holdings for up to eight years to newly established corporations in 22 industrial sectors.

On March 31, 1999, takeovers of nonstrategic operations by foreign investors without government approval was permitted.

Controls on liquidation of direct investment

Investors are granted the right to repatriate capital, to transfer profits (after settlement of taxes and financial obligations in Indonesia), and to make transfers relating to expenses connected with the employment of foreign nationals in Indonesia and relating to depreciation allowances. No transfer permit is issued for capital repatriation as long as investment benefits from tax relief are being received; at present, however, foreign payments do not require a transfer permit.

Controls on real estate transactions

Purchase locally by nonresidents

According to the Agrarian Law, nonresidents are only allowed to buy land with the land title status "the right to use of land," but since the land title of real estate in Indonesia is "the right to build on land," they are not allowed to buy real estate. Nonresidents, however, are permitted to engage in inward direct investment in local real estate.

Sale locally by nonresidents

Yes.

Controls on personal capital movements

No.

Provisions specific to commercial banks and other credit institutions

Borrowing abroad

The COLT supervises all foreign commercial loan transactions. COLT's prior approval is required before any public enterprise, commercial bank, or public sector body may accept a loan from abroad. Resident banks or credit institutions, specifically the ones that deal with international trade and finance activities, are allowed to borrow abroad within limits. An annual borrowing ceiling is imposed by the BI for foreign commercial borrowing of more than two years' maturity. In addition, the prospective borrowers must obtain COLT decisions for queuing on the international capital market before soliciting for such borrowings. Besides, banks may receive foreign commercial borrowing with maturities of no more than two years with an amount not exceeding $20 million a creditor on a bilateral basis without prior approval from the BI, but the banks should maintain the total amount of such borrowings at or below a maximum of 30% of their capital. Trade financing, such as the issuance of LCs, red-clause LCs, supplier's and buyer's credits with maturities not exceeding one year and amounts of less than $20 million, are not considered borrowings that require approval from the COLT. A bank that has received a medium- to long-term foreign commercial lending facility (PKLN) ceiling must provide export credit of at least 80% of the PKLN received for the year concerned. Foreign commercial borrowings received by financial institutions, such as leasing companies, factoring companies, and consumer financing companies, may not exceed five times the company's net worth less its equity share.

Lending to nonresidents (financial or commercial credits)

Banks are not allowed to grant loans or financial and commercial credits in either rupiah or foreign exchange to nonresidents, including those with authorization from residents to obtain credit.

Lending locally in foreign exchange

Banks are permitted to lend locally in foreign exchange. Banks may also purchase locally issued securities denominated in foreign exchange, subject to the requirement that the securities must be investment grade and should not be issued by their groups. To do this, banks should take into account other exchange regulations, namely the regulation on net open position aimed at prudential control.

Purchase of locally issued securities denominated in foreign exchange	This is allowed; however, transactions are limited by open position limits.
Differential treatment of deposit accounts in foreign exchange	
Interest rate controls	Banks are free to set their interest rates on both deposits and loans in foreign exchange. In the case of taxes, revenues gained from interest on nonresident deposit accounts are taxed at 20% or at a percentage stipulated on the tax agreement between the government of Indonesia and the government of a nonresident entity, while the revenues gained from interest of resident deposit accounts are taxed at 15%.
Investment regulations	
Abroad by banks	Banks are only permitted to place their investments in financial institutions, and this should not exceed 25% of a bank's capital as well as 15% of the financial institution's capital.
In banks by nonresidents	Until March 30, 1999, equity participation of foreign banks in a joint bank could not exceed 85% of paid-up capital. Effective March 31, 1999, this limit was raised to 99%. A requirement that foreign legal entities obtain a recommendation from the monetary authorities of its country of origin also went into effect. Such a recommendation should at least include information that the foreign legal entity has a good reputation and has never conducted any disgraceful act in the banking business.
Open foreign exchange position limits	At the end of each business day, the total daily consolidated net open position (NOP), which covers both on- and off-balance-sheet items as well as both on- and offshore branches, must not exceed 20% of bank's capital after a transitional period. Banks must submit a weekly report of their daily consolidated net open position to the BI. The transitional period for the NOP regulation is in three phases: (1) the excess amount of NOP in June 1999 had to be up to 70% of that of December 1998; (2) the excess amount of NOP in December 1999 had to be up to 40% of that of December 1998; and (3) the 20% NOP limitation will be effective by June 2000.
On resident assets and liabilities	Yes.
On nonresident assets and liabilities	Yes.
Provisions specific to institutional investors	Insurance and reinsurance companies licensed in Indonesia are not allowed to invest abroad except for private placement in companies conducting insurance business overseas, such as insurance companies, reinsurance companies, insurance brokers, loss adjusters, etc. Indonesian mutual funds are prohibited from investing abroad.
Limits (max.) on portfolio invested abroad	Liabilities denominated in foreign currency of insurance and reinsurance companies exceeding assets denominated in foreign currency shall not be more than 10% of shareholders' equity.
Other controls imposed by securities laws	Yes.

Changes During 1999

Arrangements for payments and receipts	*May 1.* The Foreign Exchange Flows and Exchange Rate System Act was approved by parliament.
	October 28. The Foreign Exchange Transactions Law was approved by parliament.
Exports and export proceeds	*February 1.* The export tax on logs and sawn timber was reduced to 20%.
	June 4. Export taxes on palm oil were reduced to 30% from 40%; on crude palm kernel, to 20% from 30%; and on crude coconut oil, to zero from 15%.
Capital transactions	
Controls on capital and money market instruments	*March 31.* The ceiling on the amount of stock foreigners may acquire in nonstrategic corporations without the approval of the company's board of directors was raised.

Controls on direct investment

January 31. A presidential decree was issued granting income tax holdings for up to eight years to newly established corporations in 22 industrial sectors.

March 31. The takeover of nonstrategic operations by foreign investors without government approval was permitted.

Provisions specific to commercial banks and other credit institutions

March 31. Equity participation of foreign banks in a joint bank was raised to 99% from 85%.

Changes During 2000

Arrangements for payments and receipts

February 1. Restrictions against Israel were removed.

ISLAMIC REPUBLIC OF IRAN

(Position as of March 31, 2000)

Status Under IMF Articles of Agreement

Article XIV	Yes.

Exchange Arrangement

Currency	The currency of the Islamic Republic of Iran is the Iranian rial.
Exchange rate structure	
Dual	Until March 19, 2000, the exchange rate system consisted of three officially approved rates: (1) the official "floating" rate of Rls 1,750 per $1 applied mainly to the imports of essential goods and services of public and publicly guaranteed debt; (2) the official "export" rate of Rls 3,000 per $1 applied to all other transactions; (3) and an effective Tehran Stock Exchange (TSE) rate applied to imports from a positive list of 30 categories of goods (mostly essential industrial raw materials). As of March 20, 2000, the official "export" rate was abolished, and since then the effective TSE rate is applied to all transactions except for the imports of essential goods and for services of public and publicly guaranteed debt.
Classification	
Conventional pegged arrangement	The exchange rates are set by the Bank Markazi (BM).
Exchange tax	No.
Exchange subsidy	Government oil export proceeds, surrendered to the BM at Rls 1,750 per $1, are mostly earmarked for government imports and external debt service, which gives rise to an implicit exchange subsidy.
Forward exchange market	No.

Arrangements for Payments and Receipts

Prescription of currency requirements	No.
Payment arrangements	
Bilateral payment arrangements	All bilateral payment arrangements have been terminated, and the outstanding credit balances are in the process of being settled.
Regional arrangements	Iran is a member of the ACU. Settlements of current transactions with the member countries of the ACU are required to be settled in AMUs.
Clearing agreements	Yes.
Administration of control	Foreign exchange operations are centralized at the BM. The list of allowed imports and exports is regulated and issued periodically by the Ministry of Commerce.
International security restrictions	n.a.
Payment arrears	No.
Controls on trade in gold (coins and/or bullion)	
Controls on external trade	Authority to trade in gold for monetary purposes is reserved for the BM. Exports of gold ingots, coins, or semifinished products are prohibited. Exports of finished articles may be effected in accordance with relevant regulations. Natural and juridical persons, including authorized banks, may import gold, platinum, and silver bullion for commercial purposes, in accordance with the relevant regulations. Travelers may bring in jewelry up to a value equivalent to Rls 5 million and may take out the entire value, provided that it is recorded on

their passport. The importation of personal jewelry with a value exceeding this amount requires approval from the BM. The exportation of Iranian gold coins for numismatic purposes requires prior approval from the BM.

Controls on exports and imports of banknotes

On exports

Foreign currency

Nationals leaving Iran are allowed to purchase up to $1,000 a person a year at the TSE rate. For traveling to neighboring countries and Southeast Asia, the allowance is $300 and $500, respectively. Foreign exchange from foreign currency–denominated (FCD) accounts originating abroad and/or credit cards may be transferred by natural persons without any limitation.

On imports

Domestic currency

Yes.

Foreign currency

There is no limit on the amount of foreign exchange that foreign travelers may bring into the country, but a declaration is required to be able to repatriate the excess amount not used in the Islamic Republic of Iran.

Resident Accounts

Foreign exchange accounts permitted

Yes.

Held domestically

Iranian nationals may open FCD accounts both domestically and abroad, and foreign nationals may maintain accounts in both foreign currency that originated abroad and local currency.

Held abroad

Yes.

Accounts in domestic currency convertible into foreign currency

The balance of accounts is not convertible.

Nonresident Accounts

Foreign exchange accounts permitted

Foreign exchange originating abroad and deposited in these accounts may be transferred abroad without limitations.

Domestic currency accounts

The balance of rial accounts may be used only in the Islamic Republic of Iran.

Blocked accounts

n.a.

Imports and Import Payments

Foreign exchange budget

No.

Financing requirements for imports

Minimum financing requirements

Yes.

Advance payment requirements

Requirements range from 15% to 100%, depending on the type of imports. Import deposits are unremunerated but refundable.

Advance import deposits

Yes.

Documentation requirements for release of foreign exchange for imports

There is a positive import list for 37 broad categories of goods for imports at the effective TSE rate.

Domiciliation requirements

Yes.

Preshipment inspection

Yes.

Letters of credit	Imports through LCs and bills of exchange are permitted.
Import licenses used as exchange licenses	Yes.
Import licenses and other nontariff measures	All importers must obtain import licenses from relevant ministries together with the approval of the central bank for foreign exchange allocation at a particular exchange rate or the opening of LCs with the respective commercial banks. Clearance through customs is authorized upon presentation of shipping documents endorsed by an authorized bank and of a permit issued by the Ministry of Commerce. Certain goods, such as pharmaceuticals, must be accompanied by a special permit issued by the Ministry of Health, Treatment, and Medical Education, and telecommunication devices require a permit issued by the Ministry of the Post, Telegraph, and Telephone.
Positive list	Import regulations distinguish between authorized, conditional, and prohibited goods. Authorized goods cover a broad category of items, which is announced periodically by the Ministry of Commerce.
Negative list	Conditional goods may be imported under certain conditions. Imports from Israel are prohibited.
Open general licenses	At the beginning of each year, the Ministry of Commerce issues the list of goods that may be imported without prior approval.
Licenses with quotas	Yes.
Import taxes and/or tariffs	Most imports are subject to an ad valorem commercial benefit tax in addition to any applicable customs duties.
State import monopoly	No.

Exports and Export Proceeds

Repatriation requirements	Until March 19, 2000, all non-oil export proceeds were fully repatriated and surrendered to commercial banks (except for a "bonus" exemption) against a fixed rate of Rls 3,000 per $1. The banks then surrendered the funds to the central bank after a maximum of 15 days. Upon surrendering, exporters were given the right, in the form of "import certificates," to repurchase the full amount of foreign exchange from the central bank and could either use this right themselves for importing or sell the right on the TSE to other authorized import-ers. The period between the date goods were exported and the date foreign exchange earnings were repatriated to the banking sector was extended to eight months from six months. An exporter could receive a 1% bonus in the form of a retention allowance for each month of early repatriation and surrender. Effective March 20, 2000, exporters receive certificates of deposit (CDs) against the repatriation of their foreign exchange earnings, which they may use for their imports, sell on the TSE to other licensed importers, or sell to the bank at the preceeding day's TSE rate. Also from this date, exporters who export their goods and services with LCs may receive a 1.5% bonus in the form of a retention allowance for each month of early repatriation and surrender.
Surrender requirements	The ratios are the same as those for the repatriation requirement.
Financing requirements	Yes.
Documentation requirements	
Letters of credit	The export of goods and services through LCs and/or trustee transactions and bills of exchange is permitted.
Guarantees	Shorter-term trade financing is currently undertaken through bank-to-bank credit lines, where exporters are certain of receiving their sales proceeds on a sight basis through a postimportation financing facility already established between the BM and the respective foreign banks. Under this umbrella facility, the BM provides an implicit foreign exchange guarantee against rial/dollar devaluation (but not against fluctuations in cross rates, which would have to be met by the importers).
Preshipment inspection	Inspection by the customs authorities generally applies to all exports.

Export licenses	The Ministry of Commerce issues an overall export license for goods on the authorized list.
Without quotas	Yes.
With quotas	Yes.
Export taxes	No.

Payments for Invisible Transactions and Current Transfers

Controls on these transfers

Trade-related payments	Freight charges may only be transferred through LCs or bills of exchange up to a maximum of 30% of the f.o.b. value of goods; to transfer more than 30% requires the approval of the BM. Only Iranian insurance companies may issue insurance policies for the import of goods. Approval is on a case-by-case basis for unloading and storage costs, and payment of administrative charges. There is no control on the payment of commissions.
Prior approval	Yes.
Investment-related payments	
Prior approval	Approval is on a case-by-case basis for profits and dividends.
Indicative limits/bona fide test	There are indicative limits and bona fide tests for the payment of amortization of loans or depreciation of direct investments.
Payments for travel	
Quantitative limits	The limits are $1,000 a year for a person with an individual passport and $500 a person for those traveling with a group passport. In the case of travel to neighboring countries, the limits are $500 a year a person in the case of individual passports, and $150 a year a person in the case of group passports.
Indicative limits/bona fide test	Yes.
Personal payments	Iranian nationals are allowed to pay pensions and family maintenance to nonresidents by obtaining foreign exchange from exchange bureaus and are allowed to transfer pensions and family maintenance through the banking system.
Prior approval	Yes.
Quantitative limits	Budget allowances are provided on a monthly basis to students on scholarships abroad, approved by the Ministry of Higher Education, and may be converted into foreign exchange at the "floating" rate of Rls 1,750 per $1. All other students abroad are allowed to purchase foreign exchange for tuition and boarding at the TSE rate (with limits), and beyond that from externally sourced FCD accounts. For other invisible payments, additional amounts beyond BM limits may also be legally paid for from externally sourced FCD accounts. Individuals who seek medical treatment abroad may obtain a foreign exchange allowance, if it is approved by the High Medical Council of the Ministry of Health, at Rls 1,750 per $1.
Indicative limits/bona fide test	Yes.
Foreign workers' wages	
Prior approval	Yes.
Quantitative limits	Foreign nationals working in the public sector in the Islamic Republic of Iran whose services are considered essential are allowed to remit abroad up to 50% of their net salaries per month at the TSE rate with prior approval of the central bank, up to a monthly limit of $500. Foreign workers in the private sector do not qualify for outward remittances.
Indicative limits/bona fide test	Yes.
Other payments	Payment of consulting/legal fees with the confirmation of the Bureau of Legal Services of Iran is permitted.
Prior approval	Yes.

Quantitative limits	There are quantitative limits for payment of subscriptions and membership fees.

Proceeds from Invisible Transactions and Current Transfers

Repatriation requirements	Yes.
Surrender requirements	Yes.
Restrictions on use of funds	Yes.

Capital Transactions

Controls on capital and money market instruments	
On capital market securities	
Shares or other securities of a participating nature	
Purchase locally by nonresidents	Nonresidents may invest in instruments traded on the TSE, but such investments are not protected under the investment law.
Controls on derivatives and other instruments	n.a.
Controls on credit operations	There are controls on all credit operations and all transactions in sureties, guarantees, and financial backup facilities.
Controls on direct investment	
Outward direct investment	Permitted with the confirmation of the High Council for Investment.
Inward direct investment	Controls are administered by the Organization for Investment and Economic and Technical Assistance of the Ministry of Economic Affairs and Finance, if the investment took place in accordance with the Law Concerning Attraction and Protection of Foreign Capital Investment.
Controls on liquidation of direct investment	The repatriation of capital is guaranteed with the approval of the Organization for Investment and Economic and Technical Assistance of the Ministry of Economic Affairs and Finance and the BM.
Controls on real estate transactions	n.a.
Controls on personal capital movements	
Loans	
By residents to nonresidents	Yes.
To residents from nonresidents	Yes.
Gifts, endowments, inheritances, and legacies	
By residents to nonresidents	Yes.
Settlement of debts abroad by immigrants	Yes.
Transfer of assets	
Transfer abroad by emigrants	Yes.

Provisions specific to commercial banks and other credit institutions	
Borrowing abroad	Yes.
Maintenance of accounts abroad	Yes.
Differential treatment of deposit accounts in foreign exchange	
Interest rate controls	Yes.
Credit controls	Yes.
Differential treatment of deposit accounts held by nonresidents	
Interest rate controls	Yes.
Credit controls	Yes.
Investment regulations	Yes.
Open foreign exchange position limits	Yes.
Provisions specific to institutional investors	n.a.
Other controls imposed by securities laws	n.a.

Changes During 1999

No significant changes occurred in the exchange and trade system.

Changes During 2000

Exchange arrangement	*March 20*. The official "export" exchange rate was abolished, reducing the number of exchange rates to two from three.
Exports and export proceeds	*March 20*. Exporters receive a CD that they may use for imports, sell on the TSE, or sell to their bank.

IRAQ

Status Under IMF Articles of Agreement

Article XIV	Yes.

Exchange Arrangement

Currency	The currency of Iraq is the Iraqi dinar.
Exchange rate structure	Unitary.
Classification	
Conventional pegged arrangement	The Iraqi dinar is pegged to the dollar, the intervention currency. The exchange rates are set by the Central Bank of Iraq (CBI). The CBI undertakes transactions in the listed currencies only with authorized dealers.
Exchange tax	No.
Exchange subsidy	No.
Forward exchange market	No.

Arrangements for Payments and Receipts

Prescription of currency requirements	Settlements with foreign countries normally must be made in any of the listed currencies or in Iraqi dinars from a nonresident account, provided that the funds in the account were obtained originally through credits in any one of the listed currencies. Payments to and receipts from Israel are prohibited.
Payment arrangements	n.a.
Administration of control	Exchange control authority is vested in the Board of Administration of the CBI. Certain approval authority has been delegated to the Department of Foreign Exchange and Banking Supervision of the CBI and to licensed dealers. Foreign exchange transactions must take place through a licensed dealer unless otherwise authorized by the governor of the CBI. Branches of the Rafidain Bank and the Rasheed Bank are licensed dealers. The Ministry of Trade (MOT) formulates import policy and the annual import program.
International security restrictions	
In accordance with UN sanctions	Yes.
Payment arrears	n.a.
Controls on trade in gold (coins and/or bullion)	
Controls on external trade	Residents and nonresidents may bring into Iraq, free of customs duty, worked and unworked gold, regardless of its weight, provided that they declare it upon importation. Residents may take out with them worked gold not exceeding five grams a person, subject to declaration; such gold may be brought back on their return to the country. Nonresident Iraqis are allowed to take out worked gold that they brought with them for personal use.
Controls on exports and imports of banknotes	
On exports	
Domestic currency	The maximum amount allowed is ID 5.
On imports	
Domestic currency	Amounts up to ID 1,000 are allowed.

Foreign currency

Travelers may bring in foreign exchange, including currency notes (other than Israeli currency), in unlimited amounts, provided that they declare the funds on an exchange control form; amounts not intended to be taken out of the country are exempt from declaration.

Resident Accounts

Foreign exchange accounts permitted

Yes.

Held domestically

Resident Iraqis and resident nationals of other Arab countries are allowed to open foreign currency accounts at the commercial banks and to use the balances in these accounts without restriction, provided the accounts have been credited with foreign banknotes.

Held abroad

No.

Accounts in domestic currency convertible into foreign currency

No.

Nonresident Accounts

Foreign exchange accounts permitted

Nonresident Iraqis and nonresident nationals of other Arab countries are allowed to open foreign currency accounts at the commercial banks and to use the balances in these accounts without restriction, provided the accounts have been credited with foreign banknotes. Nonresident accounts are divided into ordinary nonresident accounts, which involve current payment transactions, and special nonresident accounts, which involve capital transfer transactions. Balances on these accounts and any applicable interest are freely transferable abroad in foreign currencies, provided that the funds have been deposited with licensed dealers within three months of transfer. Iraqi nationals residing abroad (or their legal representatives) may withdraw from their nonresident accounts up to ID 100,000 a year in three installments to cover personal expenses in their country of residence. For all other cases, approval is required.

Approval required

Yes.

Domestic currency accounts

No.

Blocked accounts

No.

Imports and Import Payments

Foreign exchange budget

Yes.

Financing requirements for imports

No.

Documentation requirements for release of foreign exchange for imports

Import licenses used as exchange licenses

The Rafidain Bank or the Rasheed Bank provides foreign exchange upon presentation of the exchange control copy of the import license, except in some instances when reference must be made to the CBI.

Import licenses and other nontariff measures

Imports are restricted by UN sanctions. Licenses are issued in accordance with an annual import program. Imports of all goods from Israel are prohibited. All private imports are subject to licenses, except imports of materials constituting basic elements for development projects.

Negative list

Imports of some commodities on a protected list are, in principle, prohibited from all sources.

Import taxes and/or tariffs

To finance the Export Subsidy Fund, a tax of 0.5% is levied on imports of capital goods, and a tax of 0.75% is levied on imports of consumer goods. All imports subject to import duty are also subject to a customs surcharge. Foreign companies implementing development projects in Iraq are exempt from all import duties and domestic taxes accruing from the implementation of these projects, including income taxes due on the earnings of their non-Iraqi workers.

State import monopoly	Imports of commodities are normally handled by the public sector.

Exports and Export Proceeds

Repatriation requirements	Yes.
Surrender requirements	Exporters of 13 goods manufactured by firms in the public sector must repatriate 60% of their foreign exchange proceeds through the Rafidain Bank or the Rasheed Bank and surrender them within two months of shipment. Other exporters may retain their export proceeds in a foreign exchange account with the commercial banks for three years and use them to pay for licensed imports.
Financing requirements	No.
Documentation requirements	n.a.
Export licenses	Exports are restricted by UN sanctions. All exports to Israel and exports of certain goods to all other countries are prohibited. The MOT may prohibit the exportation of any commodity when supply falls short of domestic demand. All exports are licensed freely through the General Company for Exhibitions and Trading Services.
Export taxes	n.a.

Payments for Invisible Transactions and Current Transfers

Controls on these transfers	All payments for invisibles require permission.
Trade-related payments	Information is available only for the payment of freight and insurance. Foreign exchange is not granted to merchants to purchase insurance abroad for their exports.
Prior approval	Yes.
Payments for travel	
Quantitative limits	The basic allowance for travel to Arab countries, Cyprus, Greece, and Turkey is ID 300 a person a trip for travelers 18 years of age or over (ID 50 for persons under 18 years); the basic allowance for other countries is ID 500 a person a trip for travelers 18 years of age or over (ID 250 for persons under 18 years).
Personal payments	Information is available only for payment of medical and study abroad costs.
Prior approval	Yes.
Quantitative limits	Students abroad are allocated a fixed amount in Iraqi dinars to be transferred to the country of their residence, except for certain countries, such as India; the Baltic countries, Russia, and other countries of the FSU; and countries in North Africa, where students are paid a fixed amount in dollars.
Foreign workers' wages	The Rafidain Bank and the Rasheed Bank are permitted to transfer salaries of teachers who are nationals of Arab countries employed by the Ministry of Higher Education, and of scientific researchers and medical doctors, in accordance with the terms of their contracts.
Prior approval	Yes.
Quantitative limits	Certain nonresident private sector workers who have contracts with public institutions in Iraq are permitted to transfer the amounts provided for in those contracts. Those not employed under contracts may transfer abroad a monthly amount of ID 10 a person if not insured and ID 20 a person if insured and working in the private sector. Skilled noncontractual workers employed in the nationalized sector by the government are entitled to ID 40 a person a month. Persons under 16 years or over 55 years of age, however, are not allowed to transfer their earnings abroad.

Proceeds from Invisible Transactions and Current Transfers

Repatriation requirements	Yes.
Surrender requirements	Foreign exchange receipts in excess of ID 100 must be surrendered to a licensed dealer within three months.
Restrictions on use of funds	n.a.

Capital Transactions

Controls on capital and money market instruments	Most capital transactions effected abroad by residents, whether Iraqis or foreign nationals, require prior approval.
On capital market securities	
Shares or other securities of a participating nature	
Sale or issue abroad by residents	Yes.
Bonds or other debt securities	
Purchase abroad by residents	Yes.
On money market instruments	
Purchase locally by nonresidents	Yes.
Sale or issue locally by nonresidents	Yes.
Purchase abroad by residents	Yes.
Sale or issue abroad by residents	Yes.
On collective investment securities	
Purchase abroad by residents	Yes.
Sale or issue abroad by residents	Yes.
Controls on derivatives and other instruments	Yes.
Controls on credit operations	
Commercial credits	Yes.
Financial credits	Yes.
Guarantees, sureties, and financial backup facilities	Yes.
Controls on direct investment	
Outward direct investment	All investments effected abroad by residents, whether Iraqis or foreign nationals, require prior approval.
Inward direct investment	No foreign (defined as non-Arab) participation is allowed in the capital of private sector companies, but citizens of other Arab countries may participate with Iraqis in projects in the industrial, agricultural, and tourism sectors; participation is encouraged by the Arab Investment Law. The law permits (1) Iraqi investors to hold up to 49% of an enterprise, provided that their contribution and profits be paid in Iraqi dinars and that the minimum capital of the enterprise is ID 0.5 million; (2) Arab investors to transfer annually up to 100% of the profits distributed to them, but not exceeding 20% of their paid-in capital; and (3) nationals of Arab countries to bring capital into Iraq in Iraqi currency for industrial and agricultural investments. Arab investors are allowed to transfer capital in a convertible currency through a licensed bank or physical assets that will be used in the enterprises they are planning to establish, provided that used machinery and equipment have at least one-half of their productive life left.

Controls on liquidation of direct investment	Yes.
Controls on real estate transactions	
Purchase locally by nonresidents	Yes.
Controls on personal capital movements	
Gifts, endowments, inheritances, and legacies	
By residents to nonresidents	Yes.
To residents from nonresidents	Yes.
Transfer of assets	
Transfer into the country by immigrants	Yes.
Provisions specific to commercial banks and other credit institutions	Yes.
Investment regulations	Yes.
Open foreign exchange position limits	Yes.
Provisions specific to institutional investors	No.
Other controls imposed by securities laws	n.a.

Changes During 1999

No significant changes occurred in the exchange and trade system.

IRELAND

(Position as of December 31, 1999)

Status Under IMF Articles of Agreement

Article VIII   Date of acceptance: February 15, 1961.

Exchange Arrangement

Currency

As of January 1, 1999, the currency of Ireland is the euro. In cash transactions, however, the legal tender remains the Irish pound until 2002, when euro banknotes and coins will be issued.

Exchange rate structure

Unitary.

Classification

Exchange arrangement with no separate legal tender

Ireland participates in a currency union (EMU) comprising 11 members of the EU: Austria, Belgium, Finland, France, Germany, Ireland, Italy, Luxembourg, the Netherlands, Portugal, and Spain. Internal conversion rates in respect to the national currencies of EMU participants were fixed to the euro on January 1, 1999, whereas the external exchange rate of the euro is market determined. The conversion rate between the euro and the Irish pound was set at IR£0.787564 per €1. The ECB has the right to intervene to smooth out fluctuations in external exchange rates.

Exchange tax   No.

Exchange subsidy   No.

Forward exchange market   Banks are free to provide forward exchange facilities.

Arrangements for Payments and Receipts

Prescription of currency requirements   No.

Payment arrangements   No.

Administration of control   No.

International security restrictions

In accordance with Executive Board Decision No. 144-(52/51)   Yes.

In accordance with UN sanctions   Restrictions on financial transfers with Angola, Iraq, and the Federal Republic of Yugoslavia (Serbia/Montenegro) are applied in accordance with relevant UN Security Council resolutions and EU regulations.

Payment arrears   No.

Controls on trade in gold (coins and/or bullion)   No.

Controls on exports and imports of banknotes   No.

Resident Accounts

Foreign exchange accounts permitted   Yes.

Held domestically   Yes.

Held abroad	Yes.
Accounts in domestic currency convertible into foreign currency	Yes.

Nonresident Accounts

Foreign exchange accounts permitted	Yes.
Domestic currency accounts	Yes.
Convertible into foreign currency	Yes.
Blocked accounts	These are accounts blocked in accordance with UN sanctions.

Imports and Import Payments

Foreign exchange budget	No.
Financing requirements for imports	No.
Documentation requirements for release of foreign exchange for imports	No.
Import licenses and other nontariff measures	
Negative list	For reasons of national policy, imports of certain goods (e.g., specified drugs, explosives, and firearms and ammunition) are prohibited without special licenses.
Licenses with quotas	Imports of certain goods (including textiles, steel, footwear, and ceramic products) originating in certain non-EU countries are subject to either quantitative restrictions or surveillance measures. Imports from non-EU countries of products covered by the CAP are subject to a system of access quotas.
Import taxes and/or tariffs	The EU system of customs duties applies to imports.
State import monopoly	No.

Exports and Export Proceeds

Repatriation requirements	No.
Financing requirements	No.
Documentation requirements	No.
Export licenses	Exports of controlled military and dual-use goods to both EU and non-EU countries may require export licenses.
Export taxes	No.

Payments for Invisible Transactions and Current Transfers

Controls on these transfers	No.

Proceeds from Invisible Transactions and Current Transfers

Repatriation requirements	No.
Restrictions on use of funds	No.

Capital Transactions

Controls on capital and money market instruments	No.
Controls on derivatives and other instruments	No.
Controls on credit operations	No.
Controls on direct investment	
Inward direct investment	Investment by foreign-controlled enterprises does not require authorization, except for a very limited number of sectors that are subject to special conditions.
Controls on liquidation of direct investment	No.
Controls on real estate transactions	
Purchase locally by nonresidents	Persons, individuals, and companies whose principal place of residence/registered office is outside the territory of the EU/EEA must apply to the Land Commission for permission to purchase land. Such permission is rarely withheld.
Controls on personal capital movements	No.
Provisions specific to commercial banks and other credit institutions	No.
Provisions specific to institutional investors	No.
Other controls imposed by securities laws	No.

Changes During 1999

Exchange arrangement	*January 1.* The currency of Ireland became the euro. The conversion rate between the euro and the Irish pound was set irrevocably at IR£0.787564 per €1.

ISRAEL

(Position as of February 29, 2000)

Status Under IMF Articles of Agreement

Article VIII	Date of acceptance: September 21, 1993.

Exchange Arrangement

Currency	The currency of Israel is the Israeli new sheqel.
Exchange rate structure	Unitary.
Classification	
Crawling band	The exchange rate of the new sheqel is managed with regard to a basket of currencies comprising the dollar, the euro, the pound sterling, and the yen. The market exchange rate fluctuates within a crawling band in response to market forces. The upper and lower limits of the band have been adjusted daily, reflecting the annual difference between the domestic inflation target and the projected inflation of the main trading partners. The adjustment of the upper (depreciated) band has been 6% on an annual basis since July 26, 1993; the adjustment of the lower (appreciated) band has been 2% on an annual basis since August 6, 1998. On December 31, 1999, the width of the band was 44.5% (upper limit over lower limit) and the margin from a virtual midpoint was ±18.23%.
Exchange tax	No.
Exchange subsidy	No.
Forward exchange market	Yes.

Arrangements for Payments and Receipts

Prescription of currency requirements	No.
Payment arrangements	No.
Administration of control	Exchange control is the responsibility of the Controller of Foreign Exchange; it is administered by the Bank of Israel (BOI) in cooperation with other government agencies.
International security restrictions	No.
Payment arrears	No.
Controls on trade in gold (coins and/or bullion)	No.
Controls on exports and imports of banknotes	No.

Resident Accounts

Foreign exchange accounts permitted	Effective January 1, 1999, banks are required to classify the accounts of residents of areas under autonomous Palestinian administration as a separate group and to report on the basis of the same principles as applied to nonresident accounts.
Held domestically	Yes.
Held abroad	Yes.
Accounts in domestic currency convertible into foreign currency	Yes.

Nonresident Accounts

Foreign exchange accounts permitted
Account holders may freely effect transfers from their foreign currency account and may also convert funds held in the account into local currency at the market exchange rate. There are no restrictions on the opening of convertible local currency accounts by nonresidents and on transfers made thereof.

Domestic currency accounts
Yes.

Convertible into foreign currency
Yes.

Blocked accounts
No.

Imports and Import Payments

Foreign exchange budget
No.

Financing requirements for imports
No.

Documentation requirements for release of foreign exchange for imports
No.

Import licenses and other nontariff measures
With the exception of agricultural products, imports are free of quantitative restrictions. A special regime applies to imports from countries that restrict or prohibit imports from Israel.

Import taxes and/or tariffs
No.

State import monopoly
No.

Exports and Export Proceeds

Repatriation requirements
No.

Financing requirements
No.

Documentation requirements
No.

Export licenses
Most exports do not require licenses. Exports of oil and certain defense equipment require licensing.

Without quotas
Yes.

Export taxes
No.

Payments for Invisible Transactions and Current Transfers

Controls on these transfers
No.

Proceeds from Invisible Transactions and Current Transfers

Repatriation requirements
No.

Restrictions on use of funds
No.

Capital Transactions

Controls on capital and money market instruments
The Foreign Exchange Control Regulations prescribed direct reporting to the Controller of Foreign Exchange of outward portfolio investments and for offerings abroad by Israeli corporations for amounts above $0.5 million. Effective April 15, 1999, this threshold was

raised to $5 million. On the same date, individuals and nonprofit organizations were required to report to the Controller of Foreign Exchange all outward portfolio investments above $0.5 million. On February 3, 2000, this threshold was raised to $5 million.

On capital market securities

Shares or other securities of a participating nature

Sale or issue locally by nonresidents — Proceeds may be freely transferred.

Purchase abroad by residents — Households may freely purchase securities abroad. Provident funds may make direct portfolio investments abroad of up to 5% of their assets. Pension funds and insurance companies may only purchase abroad securities issued by the Israeli government and Israeli corporations.

Bonds or other debt securities

Purchase abroad by residents — The same regulations apply as for shares or other securities of a participating nature.

On money market instruments

Purchase abroad by residents — The same regulations apply as for shares or other securities of a participating nature.

On collective investment securities

Purchase abroad by residents — The same regulations apply as for shares or other securities of a participating nature.

Controls on derivatives and other instruments — A resident may not undertake with a nonresident derivatives transactions of any kind in which one of the underlying assets is local currency and that involve payment or receipt in foreign currency, unless the transaction is at a predetermined price and for a maximum period of 30 days.

Purchase locally by nonresidents — Yes.

Sale or issue locally by nonresidents — All activities and transactions in foreign currency between Israeli residents and nonresidents are permitted, except for a short list of controls on institutional investors and on several transactions in derivatives made with nonresidents.

Purchase abroad by residents — The same regulations apply as for shares or other securities of a participating nature.

Controls on credit operations — No.

Controls on direct investment

Outward direct investment — Provident funds may make direct and portfolio investments abroad of up to 5% of their assets. Pension funds are not allowed to make any direct investments abroad. The Foreign Exchange Regulations required direct reporting to the Controller of Foreign Exchange of outward direct investments made by corporations above $0.5 million. Effective April 15, 1999, this threshold was raised to $5 million. On the same date, individuals and nonprofit organizations were required to report outward direct investments above $0.5 million. Effective February 3, 2000, this threshold was raised to $5 million. On the same date, new immigrants and Israeli citizens returning to Israel after having resided abroad for seven years or more were exempt from direct reporting for a three-year period.

Controls on liquidation of direct investment — No.

Controls on real estate transactions

Purchase abroad by residents — Individuals are permitted to invest abroad freely in land and in real estate. Provident funds may invest in real estate abroad up to 5% of their assets, while pension funds are not allowed to invest abroad.

Controls on personal capital movements — No.

Provisions specific to commercial banks and other credit institutions

Differential treatment of deposit accounts in foreign exchange

   Reserve requirements   All foreign currency accounts are subject to additional secondary reserve ratios, half of which must be deposited with the BOI in an interest-generating account.

Differential treatment of deposit accounts held by nonresidents

   Reserve requirements   The same reserve ratios apply to bank accounts held by both residents and nonresidents. Reserve requirements against resident foreign currency accounts are denominated in local currency, whereas reserve requirements against nonresident foreign currency accounts are denominated in foreign currency.

Provisions specific to institutional investors

Limits (max.) on securities issued by   Yes.
nonresidents and on portfolio invested
abroad

Limits (max.) on portfolio invested   The limit on direct and portfolio investment abroad by provident funds is 5% of their
abroad   assets. Pension funds and insurance companies are not allowed to invest abroad, except in securities issued by the Israeli government and Israeli corporations.

Other controls imposed by securities   No.
laws

Changes During 1999

Resident accounts   *January 1.* Banks are required to classify and report the accounts of residents of areas under autonomous Palestinian administration as a separate group.

Capital transactions   *April 15.* The threshold for direct reporting to the Controller of Foreign Exchange of outward direct and portfolio investments made by corporations, as well as for offerings abroad by Israeli corporations, was raised to $5 million. Individuals and nonprofit organizations were required to report directly to the Controller of Foreign Exchange all outward direct and portfolio investments above a threshold of $0.5 million.

Controls on direct investment   *April 15.* The threshold for direct reporting to the Controller of Foreign Exchange of outward direct investments made by corporations was raised to $5 million from $0.5 million. Individuals and nonprofit organizations were required to report directly to the Controller of Foreign Exchange all outward direct investments above a threshold of $0.5 million.

Changes During 2000

Capital transactions

Controls on direct investment   *February 3.* The threshold for direct reporting on investments abroad by individuals and nonprofit organizations was raised from $0.5 million to $5 million. New immigrants and Israeli citizens returning to Israel after having resided abroad for seven years or more were exempt from direct reporting for a three-year period.

ITALY

(Position as of January 31, 2000)

Status Under IMF Articles of Agreement

Article VIII   Date of acceptance: February 15, 1961.

Exchange Arrangement

Currency

As of January 1, 1999, the currency of Italy is the euro. In cash transactions, however, the legal tender remains the Italian lira until 2002, when euro banknotes and coins will be issued.

Exchange rate structure

Unitary.

Classification

Exchange arrangement with no separate legal tender

Italy participates in a currency union (EMU) comprising 11 members of the EU: Austria, Belgium, Finland, France, Germany, Ireland, Italy, Luxembourg, the Netherlands, Portugal, and Spain. Internal conversion rates in respect to the national currencies of EMU participants were fixed to the euro on January 1, 1999, whereas the external exchange rate of the euro is market determined. The conversion rate between the euro and the Italian lira was set at Lit 1936.27 per €1. The ECB has the right to intervene to smooth out fluctuations in external exchange rates.

Exchange tax

No.

Exchange subsidy

No.

Forward exchange market

Premiums and discounts in the forward exchange market are normally left to the interplay of market forces.

Arrangements for Payments and Receipts

Prescription of currency requirements

Settlements with foreign countries are normally made in quoted currencies or in euro on foreign accounts.

Payment arrangements

Clearing agreements

Italy maintains clearing accounts with Croatia and Slovenia. The accounts are used for trade in cross-border areas. The balances in these accounts may be used only to finance trade between certain districts of Croatia and Slovenia and the Italian provinces of Trieste and Gorizia. The balances are not transferable. There is no automatic mechanism through which outstanding balances are settled within 90 days. Only Italy is allowed to maintain a debit balance on these accounts.

Administration of control

Effective August 4, 1999, when the requirement for banks to obtain an authorization to carry out foreign exchange transactions was eliminated, residents were allowed to conduct foreign exchange transactions freely, with settlements to be effected either indirectly, through the Bank of Italy (BOI), other financial intermediaries, and the Poste Italiane S.p.a., or directly, by drawing on external accounts or by offsetting debts and credits vis-à-vis other residents or nonresidents. Operators and intermediaries must, for statistical purposes, transmit data to the Italian Foreign Exchange Office on their foreign transactions that exceed the equivalent of Lit 20 million by filling out a foreign exchange statistical return.

International security restrictions

In accordance with Executive Board Decision No. 144-(52/51)

Yes.

In accordance with UN sanctions

Certain restrictions are imposed on the making of payments and transfers for current international transactions with respect to the Federal Republic of Yugoslavia (Serbia/

Montenegro), Iraq, and the UNITA movement in Angola. Sanctions against Libya were suspended on April 5, 1999.

Payment arrears	No.
Controls on trade in gold (coins and/or bullion)	
Controls on domestic ownership and/or trade	Domestic purchases and sales of gold with a total amount exceeding the equivalent of Lit 20 million must be declared to the Foreign Exchange Office.
Controls on external trade	Effective January 17, 2000, purchases and sales of gold with a total amount exceeding the equivalent of Lit 20 million must be declared to the Foreign Exchange Office. Before that date, purchases and sales of gold were reserved for the monetary authorities. Residents were allowed to purchase and import unrefined gold under ministerial license for industrial purposes. The exportation of unrefined gold was subject to licensing by the Ministry of Foreign Trade. The importation and exportation of gold coins, including coins that are legal tender in a foreign country, were unrestricted. Imports of unrefined gold were not subject to a VAT, whereas imports of gold coins were subject to a VAT of 20%.
Controls on exports and imports of banknotes	Residents and nonresidents are allowed to take with them into or out of the country without limits cash and securities in Italian lire and/or foreign currency. For fiscal and antimoney-laundering purposes, the transfer of cash and/or securities with a total amount exceeding the equivalent of Lit 20 million must be declared by filling out a form when crossing the border into or out of non-EU countries and submitting the form to border customs offices; for EU-country entry or exit, this declaration must be submitted at banks, customs offices, post offices, or a customs guard station within 48 hours after entry into Italian territory or 48 hours prior to exit from Italian territory. For transfers by letter, the declaration must be submitted within 48 hours after receipt or at the time of mailing. The declaration has to be sent by banks, customs offices, post offices, or customs guard stations to the Italian Foreign Exchange Office.
On exports	
Domestic currency	Yes.
Foreign currency	Yes.
On imports	
Domestic currency	Yes.
Foreign currency	Yes.

Resident Accounts

Foreign exchange accounts permitted	Yes.
Held domestically	Yes.
Held abroad	Yes.
Accounts in domestic currency convertible into foreign currency	Yes.

Nonresident Accounts

Foreign exchange accounts permitted	Yes.
Domestic currency accounts	Yes.
Convertible into foreign currency	Yes.
Blocked accounts	These are accounts that have been blocked in compliance with UN Security Council resolutions.

Imports and Import Payments

Foreign exchange budget	No.
Financing requirements for imports	No.
Documentation requirements for release of foreign exchange for imports	No.
Import licenses and other nontariff measures	Imports are governed by EU regulations according to which imports of most products, except for textiles and some products originating from China, are free of licensing and quantitative restrictions. Imports from non-EU countries of most products covered by the CAP are subject to variable import levies, which have replaced all previous barriers to imports. Common EU regulations are also applied to imports of most other agricultural and livestock products from non-EU countries. Payments for imports are not regulated, without prejudice to the general rules cited in the section on Administration of Control.
Negative list	Yes.
Licenses with quotas	Yes.
Import taxes and/or tariffs	Yes.
State import monopoly	No.

Exports and Export Proceeds

Repatriation requirements	No.
Financing requirements	No.
Documentation requirements	No.
Export licenses	
Without quotas	Exports to non-EU countries are free, with the exception of high-technology products included in an EU Regulation and of oil extracted from the seabed, which are subject to ministerial authorization.
Export taxes	No.

Payments for Invisible Transactions and Current Transfers

Controls on these transfers	No.

Proceeds from Invisible Transactions and Current Transfers

Repatriation requirements	No.
Restrictions on use of funds	No.

Capital Transactions

Controls on capital and money market instruments	
On collective investment securities	
Sale or issue locally by nonresidents	The public offering in Italy of securities issued by mutual funds that are not covered by EU directives is subject to authorization.

Controls on derivatives and other instruments	No.
Controls on credit operations	No.
Controls on direct investment	No.
Controls on liquidation of direct investment	No.
Controls on real estate transactions	No.
Controls on personal capital movements	No.

Provisions specific to commercial banks and other credit institutions

Open foreign exchange position limits

On resident assets and liabilities	Yes.
On nonresident assets and liabilities	Yes.

Provisions specific to institutional investors

Currency-matching regulations on assets/liabilities composition	Yes.
Other controls imposed by securities laws	The public offering in Italy of financial products is subject to prior communication to the supervisory authority to which the prospectus to be published should be attached.

Changes During 1999

Exchange arrangement	*January 1*. The currency of Italy became the euro. The conversion rate between the euro and the Italian lira was set irrevocably at Lit 1936.27 per €1.
Arrangements for payments and receipts	*April 5*. Sanctions against Libya were suspended.
	June 15. Sanctions were imposed on the Federal Republic of Yugoslavia (Serbia/Montenegro).
	August 4. Banks were no longer required to obtain authorization to carry out foreign exchange transactions.

Changes During 2000

Arrangements for payments and receipts	*January 17*. Transactions involving domestic ownership and trade of gold were liberalized.

JAMAICA

(Position as of June 30, 2000)

Status Under IMF Articles of Agreement

Article VIII   Date of acceptance: February 22, 1963.

Exchange Arrangement

Currency

The currency of Jamaica is the Jamaica dollar.

Other legal tender

Commemorative gold coins in denominations of J$20, J$100, and J$250 are legal tender but do not circulate.

Exchange rate structure

Unitary.

Classification

Managed floating with no pre-announced path for the exchange rate

The exchange rate of the Jamaica dollar is determined in the interbank market. The foreign exchange market is operated by the commercial banks, other authorized dealers (ADs), cambios, and the Bank of Jamaica (BJ). The commercial banks buy and sell for their own account. ADs and cambios are required to sell to the BJ a prescribed minimum amount of foreign exchange that they have purchased. Excess foreign exchange may be sold without restrictions to the commercial banks, other ADs, and the general public. Proceeds from official loans, divestment of government assets, and taxes on the bauxite sector payable in foreign currency are sold directly to the BJ. While there is no restriction on transactions in any currency, the principal foreign currencies accepted in the exchange market are the Canadian dollar, the pound sterling, and the U.S. dollar.

Exchange tax

No.

Exchange subsidy

No.

Forward exchange market

The market is currently inactive.

Arrangements for Payments and Receipts

Prescription of currency requirements

Payments to all countries may be made by crediting Jamaica dollars to an external account or a foreign currency account. Receipts from all countries must be received by debit of an external account or in any foreign currency.

Payment arrangements

Regional arrangements

Jamaica is a member of the CARICOM.

Clearing agreements

The clearing arrangements within the framework of the CARICOM have been suspended since November 1, 1990. The BJ no longer intervenes in CARICOM private sector commercial transactions; settlements for such transactions are effected by the commercial banking sector in convertible currencies.

Administration of control

Trading in foreign exchange, except by and through an AD, is prohibited. The MOF has the authority to issue directions to specified classes of persons regarding the acquisition of foreign assets.

International security restrictions

In accordance with UN sanctions

Repayment of the loan from Iraq has been suspended in line with UN sanctions.

Payment arrears

n.a.

Controls on trade in gold (coins and/or bullion)

There are no restrictions on the purchase, sale, or holding of gold for numismatic or industrial purposes.

Controls on exports and imports of banknotes

No.

Resident Accounts

Foreign exchange accounts permitted   Funds on these accounts ("A" accounts) may be transferred freely between residents and nonresidents. In cases when the transferee is a bank, licensed deposit-taking institution, credit union, building society, cambio operator, unit trust, or pension fund, the acquisition of the foreign currency must be in accordance with directions issued by the MOF. External accounts may be credited with payments by residents of Jamaica, with transfers from other external accounts, and with the proceeds from the sale of gold or foreign currencies to an AD. They may be debited for payments to residents of Jamaica, for transfers to other external accounts, and for the purchase of foreign currencies.

Held domestically   Yes.

Held abroad   Yes.

Accounts in domestic currency convertible into foreign currency   These accounts ("B" accounts) are exempt from tax on interest earned, provided that deposits are held as certificates of deposit with at least one-year maturity. After September 22, 1991, new B accounts may not be opened.

Nonresident Accounts

Foreign exchange accounts permitted   A accounts held by nonresidents are subject to the same regulations applied to those accounts held by residents, but nonresidents may open tax-free foreign currency A accounts. All credits to these accounts must originate directly from foreign remittances and not from the local purchase of foreign exchange.

Domestic currency accounts   The same regulations apply as for accounts held by residents.

Convertible into foreign currency   Yes.

Blocked accounts   No.

Imports and Import Payments

Foreign exchange budget   Yes.

Financing requirements for imports   No.

Documentation requirements for release of foreign exchange for imports   No.

Import licenses and other nontariff measures   Import licenses are required for pharmaceutical products and items that endanger public health or security; otherwise, goods may be imported freely without a license. Import licenses, when required, are issued by the Trade Board, which is responsible to the Minister of Industry and Commerce. Imports of motor vehicles require a permit for government statistical purposes. Payments for imports may be made by commercial banks without reference to the BJ.

Import taxes and/or tariffs   Imports are subject to customs tariffs of up to 20% for nonagricultural products and 40% for agricultural products, in compliance with the CET arrangement of the CARICOM. Some agricultural imports are subject to additional stamp duties of up to 95%. Taxes are collected by customs at the port of entry. On January 1, 2000, the fourth phase of the CARICOM CET came into effect.

State import monopoly   No.

Exports and Export Proceeds

Repatriation requirements   No.

Financing requirements   No.

Documentation requirements	No.
Export licenses	Most goods may be exported without restriction. However, specific licenses are required for exports of certain agricultural products, ammunition, explosives, firearms, antique furniture, motor vehicles, mineral and metal ores, paintings, jewelry, and petroleum products.
Without quotas	n.r.
With quotas	n.r.
Export taxes	No.

Payments for Invisible Transactions and Current Transfers

Controls on these transfers	No.

Proceeds from Invisible Transactions and Current Transfers

Repatriation requirements	No.
Restrictions on use of funds	No.

Capital Transactions

Controls on capital and money market instruments	
On capital market securities	
Bonds or other debt securities	n.r.
On money market instruments	
Sale or issue locally by nonresidents	These transactions are subject to ministerial approval; a prospectus is required under the Companies Act.
Purchase abroad by residents	For banks, licensed deposit-taking institutions, credit unions, building societies, cambio operators, unit trusts, and pension funds, the purchase must be in accordance with directions issued by the MOF.
Sale or issue abroad by residents	The same regulations apply as for purchases.
On collective investment securities	Ministerial approval is required for banks, licensed deposit-taking institutions, credit unions, building societies, cambio operators, unit trusts, and pension funds.
Purchase locally by nonresidents	Yes.
Sale or issue locally by nonresidents	Yes.
Purchase abroad by residents	Yes.
Sale or issue abroad by residents	Yes.
Controls on derivatives and other instruments	n.r.
Controls on credit operations	No.
Controls on direct investment	No.
Controls on liquidation of direct investment	No.
Controls on real estate transactions	No.
Controls on personal capital movements	n.r.

Provisions specific to commercial banks and other credit institutions

Differential treatment of deposit accounts in foreign exchange

Reserve requirements

On February 1, 1999, the cash reserve requirement of commercial banks' domestic currency deposits was lowered to 19% from 21% and on foreign currency deposits to 19% from 20%. Effective May 1, 1999, the cash reserve requirement was equalized at 17%. Effective October 1, 1999, the cash reserve requirement was lowered to 16% from 17%. On March 1, 2000, and on June 1, 2000, this requirement was reduced to 15% and 14%, respectively.

Liquid asset requirements

Effective February 1, 1999, the domestic liquid asset requirement for commercial banks was lowered to 41% from 43% and to 39% on May 1, 1999. For nonbank financial institutions, there is a requirement of 35% for assets in foreign currency and domestic currency. Effective June 1, 2000, the commercial banks' liquid asset requirement was lowered further to 35%, effectively unifying these requirements. Effective October 1, 1999, the liquid asset requirement was reduced to 34%. On March 1, 2000 and June 1, 2000, this requirement was lowered to 33% and 32%, respectively.

Provisions specific to institutional investors

Mutual fund schemes must be approved by the Securities Commission.

Limits (min.) on portfolio invested locally

The minimum to be specified by the Superintendent of Insurance does not exceed 70% of the domestic liabilities of the company.

Currency-matching regulations on assets/liabilities composition

Commercial banks and licensed deposit-taking institutions may be required to match their Jamaica dollar liabilities to their clients with Jamaica dollar assets.

Other controls imposed by securities laws

Nonresident companies must be incorporated or registered in Jamaica or other CARICOM member states in order to obtain a license to deal in securities or give investment advice. The nonresident company must be owned, controlled, or supervised by persons who are citizens of, and are actually residents in, Jamaica or other CARICOM states as may be prescribed.

Changes During 1999

Capital transactions

Provisions specific to commercial banks and other credit institutions

February 1. The cash reserve requirement of commercial banks' domestic currency deposits was lowered to 19% from 21% and on foreign currency deposits to 19% from 20%. The domestic liquid assets requirement for commercial banks was lowered to 41% from 43%.

May 1. The cash reserve requirement on domestic and foreign currency deposits was equalized at 17%

May 1. The liquid asset requirement for foreign currency was lowered to 39% from 40%.

June 1. Commercial banks' liquid asset requirement was reduced to 35%, effectively unifying this requirement with that applied to nonbank financial institutions.

October 1. The cash reserve requirement and the liquid assets requirement were lowered to 15% and 34%, respectively.

Changes During 2000

Imports and import payments

January 1. The fourth phase of the CARICOM CET came into effect.

Capital transactions

Provisions specific to commercial banks and other credit institutions

March 1. The cash reserve requirement and the liquid assets requirement were reduced to 15% and 33%, respectively.

June 1. The cash reserve requirement and the liquid assets requirement were reduced to 14% and 32%, respectively.

JAPAN

(Position as of December 31, 1999)

Status Under IMF Articles of Agreement

Article VIII	Date of acceptance: April 1, 1964.

Exchange Arrangement

Currency	The currency of Japan is the Japanese yen.
Exchange rate structure	Unitary.
Classification	
Independently floating	The exchange rate of the Japanese yen is determined on the basis of supply and demand. However, the authorities intervene when necessary in order to counter disorderly conditions in the markets. The principal intervention currency is the dollar.
Exchange tax	No.
Exchange subsidy	No.
Forward exchange market	There are no officially set rates in the forward market, and forward exchange transactions are based on free market rates.

Arrangements for Payments and Receipts

Prescription of currency requirements	No.
Payment arrangements	No.
Administration of control	The exchange and trade control system is operated mainly by the MOF, the Ministry of International Trade and Industry (MITI), and the Bank of Japan (BOJ) acting as the government's agent. Import- and export-reporting requirements are handled by the MITI.
International security restrictions	
In accordance with UN sanctions	Payments related to imports from, and exports to, Iraq and Libya require permission from the MITI. Intermediary trade of petroleum and its products destined for Angola requires permission from the MITI. For other payments, such as those arising from capital transactions and services from Japan to residents of Iraq, Libya, and Angola or by residents of these countries to foreign countries through Japan, permission from the MOF is required.
Payment arrears	No.
Controls on trade in gold (coins and/or bullion)	No.
Controls on exports and imports of banknotes	No.

Resident Accounts

Foreign exchange accounts permitted	Yes.
Held domestically	Yes.
Held abroad	Yes.
Accounts in domestic currency convertible into foreign currency	Yes.

461

Nonresident Accounts

Foreign exchange accounts permitted	Yes.
Domestic currency accounts	Yes.
Convertible into foreign currency	Yes.
Blocked accounts	No.

Imports and Import Payments

Foreign exchange budget	No.
Financing requirements for imports	No.
Documentation requirements for release of foreign exchange for imports	No.
Import licenses and other nontariff measures	The Import Restriction System covers 77 items (four-digit Harmonized Commodity Description and Coding System, HS base), which are subject to import restrictions falling under the state trading, national security, public health, and moral protection provisions of the WTO. For the restricted items, once importers obtain authorization from the MITI, they receive an import quota certificate that entitles them to receive an import license from a bank automatically upon application. For the importation of certain other goods from certain countries or shipping areas, individual authorization must be obtained from the MITI. Import settlements effected under the special methods require authorization from the MITI.
Negative list	Yes.
Open general licenses	Yes.
Licenses with quotas	Yes.
Import taxes and/or tariffs	No.
State import monopoly	No.

Exports and Export Proceeds

Repatriation requirements	No.
Financing requirements	No.
Documentation requirements	No.
Export licenses	Export restraint may be applied either globally or to certain destinations, and it may cover export volume, export prices, or other conditions. Twenty-seven export cartels are operating under the provisions of the Export and Import Transactions Law. In addition, 228 items are subject to a license to control their exportation to specified destinations either because of short supply in the domestic market (e.g., nickel) or to forestall the imposition of import restrictions by other countries (e.g., certain textiles). Exports under processing contracts and exports for which settlements are effected under the special methods described above require authorization from the MITI. Exports of specified raw materials for foreign processing and reimportation require individual licenses.
Without quotas	Yes.
With quotas	Yes.
Export taxes	No.

Payments for Invisible Transactions and Current Transfers

Controls on these transfers   No.

Proceeds from Invisible Transactions and Current Transfers

Repatriation requirements   No.

Restrictions on use of funds   No.

Capital Transactions

Controls on capital and money   No.
market instruments

Controls on derivatives and other   No.
instruments

Controls on credit operations   No.

Controls on direct investment

Outward direct investment   Outward direct investments by residents in a limited number of industries, such as the manufacture of arms, require a prior notice.

Inward direct investment   Inward direct investments by foreign investors in a limited number of industries, such as the manufacture of arms, require prior notice.

Controls on liquidation of direct   No.
investment

Controls on real estate transactions   No.

Controls on personal capital   No.
movements

Provisions specific to commercial
banks and other credit institutions

Maintenance of accounts abroad   There is (1) a ceiling on the investment by credit cooperatives in foreign currency–denominated bonds, excluding corporate bonds issued by nonresidents, equivalent to 30% of their net worth; and (2) a ceiling of 5% of assets for investment in foreign currency–denominated securities by the loan trust accounts of trust banks.

Provisions specific to institutional
investors

Limits (max.) on portfolio invested   The limits are (1) 30% of total assets for insurance companies holding securities issued by
abroad   nonresidents; (2) the same ratio that applies to purchases of foreign currency–denominated assets; (3) 20% of the reserve funds issued by nonresidents for holding by the Post Office Insurance Fund of bonds; and (4) 30% of pension trust assets for foreign currency–denominated assets purchased by pension funds (for the new money deposited from April 1, 1990, effective December 27, 1991, the ceiling was raised to 50% on the basis of each institutional account, and the ceiling for foreign-affiliated companies was raised to 70%).

Other controls imposed by securities   Yes.
laws

Changes During 1999

No significant changes occurred in the exchange and trade system.

JORDAN

(Position as of April 30, 2000)

Status Under IMF Articles of Agreement

Article VIII   Date of acceptance: February 20, 1995.

Exchange Arrangement

Currency

The currency of Jordan is the Jordan dinar.

Other legal tender

The Central Bank of Jordan (CBJ) issues commemorative gold coins, which, although legal tender and available to residents and nonresidents, do not circulate.

Exchange rate structure

Unitary.

Classification

Conventional pegged arrangement

The dinar is officially pegged to the SDR, but in practice, it has been pegged to the dollar since late 1995. A fee of 0.1% may be levied by the CBJ on foreign currency transfers. Amounts transferred from nonresidents' accounts in foreign currency, as well as transfers made by governmental entities, diplomatic missions, and nonprofit and humanitarian organizations, are exempt from this fee.

Exchange tax

No.

Exchange subsidy

No.

Forward exchange market

Licensed banks may buy foreign currencies without limits against dinars from their customers on a forward deal basis, and they may sell foreign currencies against dinars to their customers on a forward deal basis to pay for imports into Jordan.

Official cover of forward operations

For corporations or projects considered to be of vital national interest, the CBJ may offer a forward exchange facility in respect of forward exchange cover provided by Jordan banks.

Arrangements for Payments and Receipts

Prescription of currency requirements

No.

Payment arrangements

Bilateral payment arrangements

Operative

There is an arrangement with the Syrian Arab Republic.

Inoperative

There is an arrangement with the Republic of Yemen.

Administration of control

No.

International security restrictions

No.

Payment arrears

Official

Yes.

Controls on trade in gold (coins and/or bullion)

No.

Controls on exports and imports of banknotes

No.

Resident Accounts

Foreign exchange accounts permitted	Yes.
Held domestically	Yes.
Held abroad	Yes.
Accounts in domestic currency convertible into foreign currency	Yes.

Nonresident Accounts

Foreign exchange accounts permitted	Yes.
Approval required	For statistical purposes, nonresident accounts are opened upon proof of domicile.
Domestic currency accounts	Yes.
Convertible into foreign currency	Yes.
Blocked accounts	No.

Imports and Import Payments

Foreign exchange budget	No.
Financing requirements for imports	No.
Documentation requirements for release of foreign exchange for imports	No.
Import licenses and other nontariff measures	
Negative list	The list includes imports from countries that have bilateral agreements with Jordan and imports by certain institutions.
Import taxes and/or tariffs	Customs duties are levied at one single rate. On July 21, 1999, the maximum import tariff was reduced to 35% from 40%, and tariffs on industrial imports were reduced to 10%. As a result of these measures, the average tariff rate was reduced to 19.8% from 23.7%. On April 3, 2000, the maximum tariff rate was reduced to 30% from 35%.
State import monopoly	Oil imports are conducted by a state agency.

Exports and Export Proceeds

Repatriation requirements	No.
Financing requirements	No.
Documentation requirements	No.
Export licenses	
Without quotas	Licenses for exports are not required except for exports to countries that have bilateral agreements with Jordan.
Export taxes	No.

Payments for Invisible Transactions and Current Transfers

Controls on these transfers	No.

Proceeds from Invisible Transactions and Current Transfers

Repatriation requirements	No.
Restrictions on use of funds	No.

Capital Transactions

Controls on capital and money market instruments

No.

Controls on derivatives and other instruments

No.

Controls on credit operations

Commercial credits

By residents to nonresidents

Licensed banks and financial companies may extend credit facilities in Jordan dinars to residents and nonresidents against their foreign currency deposits. Credit facilities extended to nonresidents against their foreign currency deposits should not exceed 5% of total credit granted by a bank or a financial company. Furthermore, the balance of the foreign currency deposit used as collateral against the extended credit facilities should not, at any time, be less than the outstanding balance of credit facilities, provided that banks continue to comply with CBJ prudential requirements.

Controls on direct investment

Inward direct investment

Nonresident investments are restricted to a maximum of 50% ownership or subscription in shares of mining, trading and trade services, and construction and contracting sectors. The amount of investment in the project should not be less than JD 50,000.

Controls on liquidation of direct investment

No.

Controls on real estate transactions

Purchase locally by nonresidents

These transactions are allowed only if reciprocal treatment exists. Cabinet approval must be obtained.

Controls on personal capital movements

Transfer of gambling and prize earnings

Gambling is illegal in Jordan, but prize earnings transfers are not restricted.

Provisions specific to commercial banks and other credit institutions

Lending to nonresidents (financial or commercial credits)

Licensed banks are permitted to lend up to 50% of their foreign exchange deposits.

Lending locally in foreign exchange

Licensed banks are permitted to lend up to 50% of their foreign exchange deposits.

Investment regulations

Abroad by banks

There are no restrictions except for foreign exchange exposure limits.

Open foreign exchange position limits

On nonresident assets and liabilities

Yes.

Provisions specific to institutional investors

Licensed banks are permitted to invest up to 50% of their client deposits in foreign currency.

Limits (max.) on securities issued by nonresidents and on portfolio invested abroad

There are no regulations for issuance of these securities, but portfolio investments are not restricted.

Currency-matching regulations on assets/liabilities composition	There are no restrictions except for foreign exposure limits.
Other controls imposed by securities laws	Non-Jordanian investments are restricted to a maximum of 50% ownership or subscription in shares of the three sectors of mining, trade and trade services, and construction and contracting sectors.

Changes During 1999

Imports and import payments	*July 21.* The maximum tariff was reduced to 35% from 40% and that of industrial imports was reduced to 10%.

Changes During 2000

Imports and import payments	*April 3.* The maximum tariff rate was reduced to 30% from 35%.

KAZAKHSTAN

(Position as of January 31, 2000)

Status Under IMF Articles of Agreement

Article VIII   Date of acceptance: July 16, 1996.

Exchange Arrangement

Currency   The currency of Kazakhstan is the Kazakh tenge.

Exchange rate structure   Unitary.

Classification

Independently floating

On April 5, 1999, Kazakhstan shifted to a freely floating exchange regime. Since then, monetary policy is guided by ceilings on monetary aggregates with a view to maintaining a low rate of inflation. Thus, the exchange rate system of Kazakhstan has been reclassified to the independently floating category from managed floating with no preannounced path for the exchange rate.

The official exchange rates of the tenge against the dollar, the euro, and the Russian ruble are determined once a week on the basis of rates in the foreign exchange, interbank, and exchange bureau markets, and are announced each Monday by the National Bank of Kazakhstan (NBK). Official rates for more than 30 other currencies are set on the basis of cross rates in international markets. The currency market includes the Kazakhstan Stock Exchange (KASE), which conducts daily trading in online mode using an electronic trading system, an over-the-counter interbank market, and a network of exchange bureaus handling foreign exchange cash transactions. Banks may participate in auctions on their own account or on behalf of their clients. Banks may also trade in an over-the-counter interbank market at freely negotiated rates. There are more than 2,000 exchange bureaus that conduct foreign exchange cash transactions. Before the floating of the tenge, the NBK had been regulating the nominal exchange rate of the tenge in accordance with the inflation trend forecast via active interventions on the KASE.

Exchange tax

Effective April 2, 1999, a 1% tax was introduced for purchases of foreign exchange by natural persons; this tax was eliminated on January 1, 2000.

Exchange subsidy   No.

Forward exchange market

Foreign exchange futures are quoted on the KASE. Forward exchange operations are also performed in the interbank market.

Arrangements for Payments and Receipts

Prescription of currency requirements

All transactions between residents must be effected in tenge, unless otherwise stipulated by law. Transactions between residents and nonresidents may be made in any currency as long as they comply with the relevant foreign exchange regulations of the NBK. The NBK has the right to impose restrictions on the payment currency for a resident's export operations.

Payment arrangements

Bilateral payment arrangements

Operative

Settlements with foreign partners are made through a system of correspondent accounts of the NBK and commercial banks.

Clearing agreements   Yes.

Barter agreements and open accounts   Yes.

Administration of control

The NBK controls exchange transactions, supervises authorized banks, regulates open foreign exchange positions, and has the authority to reintroduce surrender requirements.

The MOF monitors government and government-guaranteed external debt. The Ministry of

Energy, Industry, and Trade supervises the licensing of a limited number of imports and exports and monitors transactions with precious metals and stones. The Ministry of Government Revenue supervises the payment of export and import duties. Authorized banks and nonbank financial institutions serve as agents for foreign exchange control.

International security restrictions	No.
Payment arrears	No.
Controls on trade in gold (coins and/or bullion)	The refined precious metals market has been liberalized. The principal participants in the market are commercial banks that are engaged in the purchasing of refined precious metals on a competitive basis and in their export on the basis of NBK licenses.
Controls on exports and imports of banknotes	There are simplified customs procedures under which a declaration may be made at the initiative of natural persons, although the customs office has the power to impose full customs control.

On exports

Domestic currency

Domestic currency may be exported without restriction.

Foreign currency

Effective May 1, 1999, resident natural persons may export foreign currency up to the equivalent of $3,000 without documents certifying the legal origin of the funds. When amounts exceed the equivalent of $3,000, documents for the entire amount being exported must be presented to customs authorities. The export of foreign currency by nonresident natural persons is carried out in accordance with the declaration prepared by them at the time of entry. In the event that the amount indicated in the declaration is less, the nonresident is required to present documents certifying the legal origin of the funds.

On imports

Foreign currency

Effective September 19, 1999, a customs duty equivalent to 1% was introduced on imports of foreign currency by juridical persons.

Resident Accounts

Foreign exchange accounts permitted	Yes.
Held domestically	Yes.
Held abroad	These accounts may be held abroad. However, a license from the NBK is required, with the exception of resident natural persons temporarily located abroad (e.g., for purposes of work, study, or medical treatment, or for humanitarian reasons).
Accounts in domestic currency convertible into foreign currency	Resident juridical persons may acquire foreign currency on the domestic market only to effect settlements with nonresidents and to meet obligations with regard to credits in foreign currency received from authorized banks and in other instances stipulated by legislative acts. With a view to protecting depositors' interests from devaluation during the shift to an independently floating exchange rate, effective April 5, 1999, resident natural and juridical persons were given the opportunity to exchange their tenge deposits, if held until October 5, 1999 (for juridical persons) or until January 5, 2000 (for natural persons), into dollar-denominated deposits at the predevaluation exchange rate. This was a onetime opportunity.

Nonresident Accounts

Foreign exchange accounts permitted	Yes.
Domestic currency accounts	Yes.
Convertible into foreign currency	Nonresident juridical persons may acquire foreign currency on the domestic foreign exchange market of Kazakhstan only for resources in tenge received as a result of the performance of current foreign exchange transactions or in other cases as provided by the law.
Blocked accounts	No.

Imports and Import Payments

Foreign exchange budget	No.
Financing requirements for imports	
Advance payment requirements	Prepayment in foreign exchange prior to 180 days requires a license from the NBK.
Documentation requirements for release of foreign exchange for imports	Presentation to an authorized bank of the relevant contract, agreement, or accord is required. A transaction passport must be compiled for each import transaction in excess of $5,000, and the import transaction must be monitored by the Customs Committee and an authorized bank until full completion.
Import licenses and other nontariff measures	Import licenses are required for 12 categories of goods. A certificate of the country of origin must be presented only in instances stipulated by the customs law. A ban on imports of certain categories of goods from Russia was in effect from January 11, 1999, through June 23, 1999.
Negative list	Imports of two categories of goods are subject to approval by the government for public health and security reasons.
Import taxes and/or tariffs	Customs duties and excises are levied on imported goods.
State import monopoly	No.

Exports and Export Proceeds

Repatriation requirements	All proceeds must be repatriated unless a license is granted by the NBK.
Surrender requirements	On April 5, 1999, a 50% surrender requirement was introduced; it was eliminated on November 16, 1999. The NBK reserves the right to introduce surrender requirements at any time.
Financing requirements	No.
Documentation requirements	A transaction passport must be compiled for each export transaction above $5,000, and the transaction must be monitored by the Customs Committee and an authorized bank until full completion.
Export licenses	Export licenses are required for 16 categories of goods. For security and environmental protection reasons, government approval is required for the exports of three groups of goods.
Without quotas	Yes.
Export taxes	No.

Payments for Invisible Transactions and Current Transfers

Controls on these transfers	There are indicative limits or bona fide tests for all transactions.
Trade-related payments	
Quantitative limits	When reinsuring with a foreign insurer (reinsurer), the proportion of the reinsured party's own liability (retention of liability) should represent at least 5% of the total volume of liability.
Indicative limits/bona fide test	Yes.
Investment-related payments	All investments by nonresidents exceeding 180 days and $100,000 must be registered with the NBK.
Indicative limits/bona fide test	When payments are made by residents to nonresidents, presentation to an authorized bank of the relevant documents (contract, agreement, accord, etc.) is required. For payments involving foreign exchange transactions that require a license or registration certification

from the NBK, resident juridical persons are also required to furnish an authorized bank with a copy of the relevant documents.

Payments for travel

Quantitative limits — There are expenditure standards for business travel to various countries in accordance with Ministry of Finance instructions.

Indicative limits/bona fide test — For amounts exceeding $3,000, a document certifying the legal origin of the funds is required.

Personal payments

Indicative limits/bona fide test — Current foreign exchange transactions in the form of onetime transfers by resident and non-resident natural persons in an amount up to the equivalent of $3,000 may be effected through authorized banks without opening an account.

Foreign workers' wages

Indicative limits/bona fide test — Yes.

Credit card use abroad

Indicative limits/bona fide test — Yes.

Other payments

Indicative limits/bona fide test — Yes.

Proceeds from Invisible Transactions and Current Transfers

Repatriation requirements — All proceeds should be repatriated unless the NBK grants a license.

Surrender requirements — On April 5, 1999, a 50% surrender requirement was introduced; it was eliminated on November 16, 1999. The NBK reserves the right to introduce surrender requirements at any time.

Restrictions on use of funds — Resources in foreign currency may be used only for settlements with nonresidents and for repayment of credit in foreign currency and in other cases as stipulated by the law. There are no restrictions on conversion into domestic currency.

Capital Transactions

Controls on capital and money market instruments

On capital market securities

Shares or other securities of a participating nature

Purchase locally by nonresidents — Purchases in excess of the equivalent of $100,000 must be registered with the NBK.

Sale or issue locally by nonresidents — The circulation, issue, or sale requires the approval of the National Securities Commission (NSC).

Purchase abroad by residents — Prior approval of the NBK is required.

Sale or issue abroad by residents — Prior approval of the NSC together with registration with the NBK is required if the amount of issue exceeds the equivalent of $100,000.

Bonds or other debt securities

Purchase locally by nonresidents — Purchases in excess of the equivalent of $100,000 must be registered with the NBK.

Sale or issue locally by nonresidents — Prior approval of the NSC is required for nonresidents.

Purchase abroad by residents — A license from the NBK is required.

Sale or issue abroad by residents	Prior approval of the NSC and registration with the NBK are required if the amount of issue exceeds the equivalent of $10,000.
On money market instruments	Prior approval of the NBK is required for all money market transactions.
Purchase locally by nonresidents	Purchases in excess of the equivalent of $100,000 must be registered with the NBK.
Sale or issue locally by nonresidents	Prior approval of the NSC is required.
Purchase abroad by residents	A license from the NBK is required.
Sale or issue abroad by residents	Prior approval of the NSC and registration with the NBK are required if the amount of issue exceeds the equivalent of $100,000.
On collective investment securities	The same regulations as for money market instruments apply to all collective investment securities.
Controls on derivatives and other instruments	The same regulations as for money market instruments apply to all collective investment securities, except for sale or issue by nonresidents, which is not controlled.
Controls on credit operations	
Commercial credits	
By residents to nonresidents	A license from the NBK is required for operations with a maturity of more than 180 days.
To residents from nonresidents	A registration certificate from the NBK is required for operations with a maturity of more than 180 days and a value exceeding the equivalent of $100,000.
Financial credits	
By residents to nonresidents	A license from the NBK is required for operations with a maturity of more than 180 days.
To residents from nonresidents	A certificate of registration with the NBK is required for credits with a maturity of more than 180 days and in an amount exceeding the equivalent of $100,000.
Controls on direct investment	The law on State Support of Direct Investment clarifies the rules and regulations governing direct investments (both foreign and domestic), and provides government guarantees to protect the interest of investors. The law also strengthens the coordinating roles of the State Committee on Investment with the aim of facilitating the investment process in the country. This law also authorizes the Committee to provide tax privileges on a case-by-case basis for new investors in priority sectors of the economy.
Outward direct investment	Residents must obtain a license from the NBK to invest abroad in foreign exchange.
Inward direct investment	A certificate of registration from the NBK is required for residents to attract foreign investments in excess of the equivalent of $100,000.
Controls on liquidation of direct investment	Yes.
Controls on real estate transactions	
Purchase abroad by residents	A license from the NBK is required.
Purchase locally by nonresidents	Transfers from nonresidents to residents in payment for property rights and other rights to real estate in an amount above the equivalent of $100,000 are subject to registration with the NBK.
Controls on personal capital movements	
Loans	
By residents to nonresidents	Credits by residents to nonresidents in foreign currency for a term of more than 180 days are subject to licensing with the NBK.
To residents from nonresidents	Credits by nonresidents to residents for a term of more than 180 days and in an amount equivalent to more than $100,000 are subject to registration with the NBK.
Transfer of gambling and prize earnings	The legal origin of the funds must be documented.

Provisions specific to commercial banks and other credit institutions

Borrowing abroad

Registration with the NBK is required to receive credits for a term of more than 180 days and in an amount exceeding $100,000.

Maintenance of accounts abroad

A license from the NBK is required.

Lending to nonresidents (financial or commercial credits)

A license from the NBK is required when extending credit for a term of more than 180 days.

Lending locally in foreign exchange

Authorized banks are entitled to provide credits in foreign currency to resident and nonresident juridical persons only in accordance with noncash procedures.

Purchase of locally issued securities denominated in foreign exchange

Payments by residents are effected only in tenge, regardless of the currency in which the securities are denominated.

Investment regulations

Abroad by banks

Investments abroad by resident banks are limited by the ratio set for the placement of equity capital in domestic assets. Bank investments are subject to licensing by the NBK.

In banks by nonresidents

Effective July 16, 1999, a nonresident bank having a minimum rating from one of the main rating agencies may hold 5% or more of a bank's stocks.

A natural or juridical person that is registered in an offshore zone may not be a founder or shareholder of a resident bank of Kazakhstan.

A nonresident bank is entitled to file an application with the NBK for permission to open a subsidiary bank after a representative office of the given bank has been in operation in Kazakhstan for one year.

A nonresident bank that is a founder or a partner of a bank is required to present the relevant documents to the NBK.

The total combined registered capital of banks with foreign participation must not exceed 25% of the total capital of all banks in Kazakhstan. On July 16, 1999, this limit was increased to 50%.

Open foreign exchange position limits

The open position limit was 15% of a bank's capital, and the total open position was 25% of a bank's capital. Effective July 16, 1999, the (long or short) foreign exchange limit is no more than 30% of a bank's equity capital; the net foreign exchange position limit is 50% of a bank's equity capital; and the long foreign exchange position limit for currencies of countries that are not members of the OECD is 5% of a bank's equity capital.

On resident assets and liabilities

Yes.

Provisions specific to institutional investors

On April 9, 1999, pension funds were provided with a onetime opportunity to exchange tenge-denominated securities for foreign exchange–denominated securities.

Limits (max.) on securities issued by nonresidents and on portfolio invested abroad

Yes.

Limits (max.) on portfolio invested abroad

Yes.

Limits (min.) on portfolio invested locally

Yes.

Other controls imposed by securities laws

A license is required for professional activities on the securities market and stock exchanges.

Changes During 1999

Exchange arrangement

January 1. The official exchange rate of the tenge was determined against the euro instead of the deutsche mark.

April 2. A 1% tax was introduced on purchases of foreign exchange.

April 5. Kazakhstan switched to a floating exchange rate regime. Thus, the exchange rate arrangement of Kazakhstan has been reclassified to the independently floating category from managed floating with no preannounced path for the exchange rate.

Arrangements for payments and receipts

May 1. Resident natural persons may export foreign currency up to the equivalent of $3,000 without documenting the legal origin of the funds.

September 19. A 1% customs duty on imports of foreign currency by juridical persons was introduced.

Resident accounts

April 5. Resident natural and juridical persons were given a onetime opportunity to exchange tenge holdings into dollar-denominated deposits at predevaluation exchange rates.

Imports and import payments

January 11. Certain categories of imports from Russia have been banned.

June 23. The ban on certain categories of imports from Russia was lifted.

Exports and export proceeds

April 5. A 50% surrender requirement was introduced.

November 16. The 50% surrender requirement was lifted.

Proceeds from invisible transactions and current transfers

April 5. A 50% surrender requirement was introduced.

November 16. The 50% surrender requirement was lifted.

Capital transactions

Provisions specific to commercial banks and other credit institutions

July 16. The limit on foreign ownership of the aggregate capital of the commercial banking sector was raised to 50%.

July 16. The (long or short) foreign exchange limit was changed to no more than 30% of a bank's equity capital, the net foreign exchange position limit to 50% of a bank's equity capital, and the long foreign exchange position limit for currencies of countries that are not members of the OECD to 5% of a bank's equity capital.

July 16. A nonresident bank having a minimum rating from one of the main rating agencies may hold 5% or more of a bank's stocks.

Provisions specific to institutional investors

April 5. Pension funds were provided with a onetime opportunity to exchange tenge-denominated securities for foreign exchange–denominated securities.

Changes During 2000

Exchange arrangement

January 1. The 1% tax on purchases of foreign exchange was eliminated.

KENYA

(Position as of December 31, 1999)

Status Under IMF Articles of Agreement

Article VIII	Date of acceptance: June 30, 1994.

Exchange Arrangement

Currency	The currency of Kenya is the Kenya shilling.
Exchange rate structure	Unitary.
Classification	
Managed floating with no pre-announced path for the exchange rate	The exchange rate is determined in the interbank market. Foreign exchange bureaus are authorized to deal in cash and foreign traveler's checks. The official exchange rate is set at the previous day's average market rate. The dollar is the principal intervention currency. The official exchange rate applies only to government and government-guaranteed external debt-service payments and to government imports for which there is a specific budget allocation.
Exchange tax	No.
Exchange subsidy	No.
Forward exchange market	Commercial banks are authorized to enter into forward exchange contracts with their customers at market-determined exchange rates in currencies of their choice. There are no limits on the amount or period of cover.

Arrangements for Payments and Receipts

Prescription of currency requirements	No.
Payment arrangements	
Regional arrangements	Kenya is a member of COMESA. On November 30, 1999, a treaty was signed to establish the EAC, of which Kenya is also a member.
Administration of control	The Central Bank Act gives the Central Bank of Kenya (CBK) powers to license and regulate foreign exchange transactions.
International security restrictions	No.
Payment arrears	
Official	Yes.
Controls on trade in gold (coins and/or bullion)	No.
Controls on exports and imports of banknotes	No.

Resident Accounts

Foreign exchange accounts permitted	Yes.
Held domestically	Yes.
Held abroad	Yes.
Accounts in domestic currency convertible into foreign currency	Yes.

Nonresident Accounts

Foreign exchange accounts permitted	Yes.
Domestic currency accounts	Yes.
Convertible into foreign currency	Yes.
Blocked accounts	No.

Imports and Import Payments

Foreign exchange budget	No.
Financing requirements for imports	No.
Documentation requirements for release of foreign exchange for imports	A copy of the import declaration, a final invoice, and a copy of the customs entry must be submitted.
Preshipment inspection	An inspection is required for all imports with an f.o.b. value of more than $5,000. These are subject to inspection for quality, quantity, and price, and require a clean report of findings. Banks are allowed to effect clean payments (for imports) provided they obtain a pledge from the importer to submit the documents at a later date.
Import licenses and other nontariff measures	
Negative list	The list includes a few items for health, security, and environmental reasons.
Import taxes and/or tariffs	Yes.
State import monopoly	No.

Exports and Export Proceeds

Repatriation requirements	No.
Financing requirements	No.
Documentation requirements	No.
Export licenses	
Without quotas	Coffee, tea, and horticultural produce may be exported only if a sales contract is registered with the Coffee Board, Tea Board, and Horticultural Crops Development Authority, respectively. Exports of certain foods and agricultural products require special licenses to ensure adequate supplies in the domestic market. Exports of minerals, precious stones, and other essential strategic materials are also subject to special licensing.
Export taxes	No.

Payments for Invisible Transactions and Current Transfers

Controls on these transfers	No.

Proceeds from Invisible Transactions and Current Transfers

Repatriation requirements	No.
Restrictions on use of funds	No.

Capital Transactions

Controls on capital and money market instruments

On capital market securities

Shares or other securities of a participating nature

Purchase locally by nonresidents	Nonresidents are allowed to purchase a maximum of 40% of shares of primary or secondary issues. A nonresident may not purchase more than 5% of the total of secondary or primary issues.
Sale or issue locally by nonresidents	There is no control on the sale of securities by nonresidents. However, issuance of securities by nonresidents requires prior approval from the Capital Markets Authority (CMA).
Sale or issue abroad by residents	The sale or issue of securities abroad by residents requires prior approval from the CMA.

Bonds or other debt securities

Purchase locally by nonresidents	Yes.
Sale or issue locally by nonresidents	The same regulations apply as for securities of a participating nature.
Sale or issue abroad by residents	The same regulations apply as for securities of a participating nature.

On money market instruments

Sale or issue locally by nonresidents	There are no controls on sales, but the issuing requires prior approval from the CBK.
Sale or issue abroad by residents	The sale or issuance of money market instruments abroad by residents requires prior approval by the CBK.

On collective investment securities

Purchase locally by nonresidents	Yes.
Sale or issue locally by nonresidents	Yes.

Controls on derivatives and other instruments

Sale or issue locally by nonresidents	CBK approval is required for these transactions.
Sale or issue abroad by residents	CBK approval is required for these transactions.
Controls on credit operations	No.
Controls on direct investment	No.
Controls on liquidation of direct investment	No.

Controls on real estate transactions

Purchase locally by nonresidents	Purchases of real estate are subject to government approval.
Controls on personal capital movements	No.

Provisions specific to commercial banks and other credit institutions

Differential treatment of deposit accounts in foreign exchange

Reserve requirements	Yes.

Differential treatment of deposit accounts held by nonresidents

Reserve requirements	Yes.

Open foreign exchange position limits	Foreign exchange exposure is defined as net foreign assets reported on the balance sheet and is limited to a maximum of 20% of paid-up capital (assigned).
On resident assets and liabilities	Yes.
On nonresident assets and liabilities	Yes.
Provisions specific to institutional investors	No.
Other controls imposed by securities laws	No.

Changes During 1999

Arrangements for payments and receipts	*November 30.* A treaty to establish the EAC was signed.

KIRIBATI

(Position as of December 31, 1999)

Status Under IMF Articles of Agreement

Article VIII   Date of acceptance: August 22, 1986.

Exchange Arrangement

Currency

The currency of Kiribati is the Australian dollar.

Other legal tender

A small number of Kiribati coins is also in circulation.

Exchange rate structure

Unitary.

Classification

Exchange arrangement with no separate legal tender

There is no central monetary institution, and the authorities do not buy or sell foreign exchange. The Bank of Kiribati (BOK), the only commercial bank, quotes daily rates for 15 currencies on the basis of their respective values against the Australian dollar.

Exchange tax

No.

Exchange subsidy

No.

Forward exchange market

The BOK provides forward contracts of up to three months of maturity.

Arrangements for Payments and Receipts

Prescription of currency requirements

Outward and inward payments may be settled in Australian currency or in any other currency. Purchases and sales of foreign currencies in exchange for Australian dollars must be undertaken with the BOK, the only authorized foreign exchange dealer.

Payment arrangements

No.

Administration of control

No.

International security restrictions

No.

Payment arrears

No.

Controls on trade in gold (coins and/or bullion)

n.a.

Controls on exports and imports of banknotes

No.

Resident Accounts

Foreign exchange accounts permitted   Yes.

Held domestically   Yes.

Held abroad   Yes.

Accounts in domestic currency convertible into foreign currency   n.a.

Nonresident Accounts

Foreign exchange accounts permitted   Yes.

Domestic currency accounts	n.a.
Blocked accounts	No.

Imports and Import Payments

Foreign exchange budget	No.
Financing requirements for imports	No.
Documentation requirements for release of foreign exchange for imports	n.a.
Import licenses and other nontariff measures	
Negative list	Imports of certain goods are prohibited for health, safety, or environmental reasons.
Import taxes and/or tariffs	Tariffs ranging from zero to 80% apply to most private imports. Specific duties apply to imports of rice, flour, petroleum products, alcoholic beverages, and tobacco products.
State import monopoly	No.

Exports and Export Proceeds

Repatriation requirements	No.
Financing requirements	No.
Documentation requirements	n.a.
Export licenses	Copra may be exported only through the Kiribati Copra Cooperative Society.
Export taxes	No.

Payments for Invisible Transactions and Current Transfers

Controls on these transfers	Information is not available on the payment of amortization of loans or depreciation of direct investments.

Proceeds from Invisible Transactions and Current Transfers

Repatriation requirements	n.a.
Restrictions on use of funds	n.a.

Capital Transactions

Controls on capital and money market instruments	n.a.
Controls on derivatives and other instruments	n.a.
Controls on credit operations	n.a.
Controls on direct investment	
Inward direct investment	The authorities encourage investments in the export-promoting or import-substituting sectors. All applications for foreign investment up to $A 250,000 must be made to the Foreign Investment Commission for approval. Applications with a larger capital contribution are approved by the Cabinet.

Controls on liquidation of direct investment	n.a.
Controls on real estate transactions	n.a.
Controls on personal capital movements	n.a.
Provisions specific to commercial banks and other credit institutions	n.a.
Provisions specific to institutional investors	n.a.
Other controls imposed by securities laws	n.a.

Changes During 1999

No significant changes occurred in the exchange and trade system.

REPUBLIC OF KOREA

(Position as of December 31, 1999)

Status Under IMF Articles of Agreement

Article VIII	Date of acceptance: November 1, 1988.

Exchange Arrangement

Currency	The currency of Korea is the Korean won.
Exchange rate structure	Unitary.
Classification	
Independently floating	The exchange rate of the won is determined on the basis of supply and demand.
Exchange tax	No.
Exchange subsidy	No.
Forward exchange market	Foreign exchange banks may conduct forward transactions, futures transactions, swaps, and options between foreign currencies, as well as between the won and foreign currencies. There are no specific restrictions on the terms of forward contracts.

Arrangements for Payments and Receipts

Prescription of currency requirements	All settlements with other countries may be made in any convertible currency except the won. Nonresidents are permitted to carry out current transactions denominated in won, provided that remittances are made in foreign currencies. For this purpose, nonresidents are allowed to open settlement accounts in won (free won accounts) for current transactions as well as for reinsurance contracts and investments in domestic securities.
Payment arrangements	No.
Administration of control	The Ministry of Finance and Economy (MOFE) initiates policy with respect to prescription of currency, method of settlement, foreign exchange operations, payments for current transactions, and capital transactions and transfers. The Bank of Korea (BOK) executes most of the above functions; it also regulates the operations of the exchange market and may intervene in it. A revised foreign exchange law came into effect on April 1, 1999.
International security restrictions	No.
Payment arrears	No.
Controls on trade in gold (coins and/or bullion)	
Controls on external trade	Residents are allowed to import and export gold other than gold coins in circulation, subject to the same regulations as those applied to merchandise trade.
Controls on exports and imports of banknotes	
On exports	
Domestic currency	Banknotes in excess of the equivalent of $10,000 may not be exported without permission from the BOK.
Foreign currency	Banknotes in excess of the equivalent of $10,000 may not be exported without specific permission. Upon leaving Korea, nonresidents may purchase foreign currency up to the amount they have sold during their stay in Korea.

On imports

   Domestic currency   Residents and nonresidents must notify the customs office of domestic currency they bring into Korea if the amount exceeds the equivalent of $10,000.

   Foreign currency   Residents and nonresidents must notify the customs office of foreign currency they bring into Korea if the amount exceeds the equivalent of $10,000.

Resident Accounts

Foreign exchange accounts permitted   Yes.

Held domestically   The foreign currency composition of these accounts may be changed without restriction.

Held abroad   Institutional investors are permitted to hold deposits abroad for asset diversification purposes without a quantitative ceiling. General corporations and individuals are permitted to hold deposits abroad of up to $5 million and $50,000 a year, respectively.

Accounts in domestic currency convertible into foreign currency   No.

Nonresident Accounts

Foreign exchange accounts permitted   Remittances from these accounts and withdrawals in foreign currency may be made freely. The approval of the bank where the account is held is not required for remittances abroad or transfers to other foreign currency accounts for purchases and withdrawals of foreign means of payment or for payments relating to approved transactions.

Domestic currency accounts   The establishment of such deposits and trust accounts of less than a one-year maturity requires the permission of the BOK.

Convertible into foreign currency   Yes.

Blocked accounts   n.a.

Imports and Import Payments

Foreign exchange budget   No.

Financing requirements for imports   No.

Documentation requirements for release of foreign exchange for imports   No.

Import licenses and other nontariff measures   Under the Imports Diversification Program, there were 113 items for which imports were restricted. The Program was phased out in two stages. In the first, 25 items were liberalized, and on June 1, 1999, the remaining items were liberalized.

Negative list   Yes.

Open general licenses   About 3,000 products are subject to special import approval procedures, mostly due to health and other reasons, under the regulation on import notices. Eight of the 10,859 basic items in the Harmonized System are subject to license.

Licenses with quotas   A trade commission may recommend quotas and quality standards if it has determined that certain imports have harmed domestic industries. There are four quotas on milk products.

Import taxes and/or tariffs   There are adjustment tariffs on 38 products. There are antidumping duties on 14 products.

Taxes collected through the exchange system   Yes.

State import monopoly   There is a state monopoly on the import of 18 agricultural products.

Exports and Export Proceeds

Repatriation requirements	Export earnings exceeding $50,000 must be repatriated to Korea within six months, except in specific cases. However, general trading companies licensed under the Foreign Trade Act and enterprises whose trade value in the previous year exceeded $5 million are allowed to retain overseas deposits up to 50% of this value within the limit of $500 million.
Financing requirements	No.
Documentation requirements	No.
Export licenses	
Without quotas	There are export bans on 14 items for environmental reasons.
With quotas	There are quotas under the ATC and voluntary restraint on nine products under bilateral agreements.
Export taxes	No.

Payments for Invisible Transactions and Current Transfers

Controls on these transfers

Investment-related payments

Prior approval	The transfer of income from securities acquired through inheritance is subject to prior approval.

Payments for travel

Quantitative limits	The monthly allowance for residents staying abroad for over 30 days is $10,000. For those staying abroad over one year, a remittance of $50,000 (including basic travel allowances) is allowed within two months after the time of departure.
Indicative limits/bona fide test	Residents traveling abroad may, in general, purchase foreign exchange up to the equivalent of $10,000 a trip as their basic travel allowance; additional foreign exchange may also be purchased for specified expenses, including transportation costs.

Personal payments

Quantitative limits	The basic monthly allowance for students under 20 years old is $3,000; for students with a dependent family, an additional allowance of $500 for a spouse and each child is allowed. Residents are allowed to remit up to $5,000 a transaction to their parents and children living abroad for living expenses and to their relatives abroad for wedding gifts or funeral donations, with no restrictions on the number of remittances.

Credit card use abroad

Quantitative limits	Residents may make payments abroad by credit card for expenditures relating to travel and tourism; for amounts exceeding $5,000 a month, the foreign exchange authorities must verify the authenticity of the payments.
Indicative limits/bona fide test	Yes.

Proceeds from Invisible Transactions and Current Transfers

Repatriation requirements	Yes.
Surrender requirements	Residents are permitted to hold foreign currency earned from invisible transactions, but once converted into won, a limit applies to reconversion. Residents and nonresidents must notify the customs office of domestic and foreign exchange they bring into Korea if the amount exceeds the equivalent of $10,000. Domestic firms engaged in international construction and service businesses may deposit abroad up to 30% of the amount of foreign currency acquired in the previous year or $3 million, whichever is greater.
Restrictions on use of funds	No.

Capital Transactions

Controls on capital and money market instruments	On April 1, 1999, the new foreign exchange law switched the positive list system to a negative list system.

On capital market securities

Shares or other securities of a participating nature

Sale or issue locally by nonresidents	Foreign institutions are eligible to list their shares on the Korean Stock Exchange (KSE) in the form of depository receipts. These institutions include international financial organizations, central or municipal governments, public organizations, and general companies.

Bonds or other debt securities

Sale or issue locally by nonresidents	Foreign institutions may issue won-denominated bonds in the domestic capital market. However, the issuer must submit a prior report to the MOFE and the Financial Supervisory Council (FSC). Nonresidents are required to obtain a permit before issuing won-denominated bonds with maturities of less than one year.
Sale or issue abroad by residents	The sale or issuance abroad by residents must be reported to the MOFE before the transaction is carried out.

On money market instruments

Sale or issue locally by nonresidents	These transactions require MOFE approval.
Purchase abroad by residents	Purchase of short-term securities abroad denominated in won requires MOFE approval.
Sale or issue abroad by residents	There are no controls for foreign exchange banks to issue money market instruments denominated in foreign currency in foreign money markets. Only issues by enterprises with unsound financial structures require MOFE approval.
	Residents may issue money market instruments denominated in won in the foreign money markets with the approval of the MOFE.

On collective investment securities

Sale or issue locally by nonresidents	Foreign institutions may issue collective investment securities in the domestic market provided that the foreign institutions establish themselves in Korea. However, this is not required for the issue of collective investment securities by foreign investment trust companies that invest their funds exclusively in foreign securities. In the case of the issue of collective investment securities, the issuer must submit a prior report to the FSC.
Sale or issue abroad by residents	According to the Foreign Exchange Transaction Regulation, residents may issue collective investment securities denominated in foreign currency in foreign markets. However, the issuer must submit a prior report to the designated exchange bank. Residents may issue collective investment securities denominated in domestic currency in foreign markets with the approval of the MOFE.
	According to the Securities Investment Trust Company Act, the deed should be approved by the FSC; however, the standard deed has only to be reported to the FSC.
Controls on derivatives and other instruments	There are no controls on the trading of over the counter–related derivatives if the transactions are made through domestic foreign exchange banks.
Sale or issue locally by nonresidents	There are controls on all derivative transactions by nonresidents involving the use of won-denominated financing.
Sale or issue abroad by residents	Yes.

Controls on credit operations

Commercial credits

By residents to nonresidents	Commercial credits in domestic currency of more than W 100 million a borrower that are granted by institutional investors require MOFE approval.
	Commercial credits in foreign currency granted by general trading companies of more than $10 million, and by other enterprises of more than $300,000, require MOFE approval.

| *To residents from nonresidents* | There are no controls for enterprises to borrow commercial credits. Only commercial credits with maturities of one year or less granted to enterprises with unsound financial structures require MOFE approval. |

Financial credits

By residents to nonresidents	Credits and loans denominated in domestic currency of more than W 100 million a borrower require MOFE approval.
To residents from nonresidents	There are no controls for foreign exchange banks and enterprises to borrow financial credits in foreign currency abroad.
	Only financial credits with a maturity of one year or less granted to enterprises with unsound financial structures require MOFE approval.

Guarantees, sureties, and financial backup facilities

| *By residents to nonresidents* | Residents, other than banks, must obtain approval from the BOK, except for the following cases: (1) when a foreign importer is granted an offshore loan by a foreign exchange bank to finance imports from a resident, and said resident pledges a guarantee in foreign currency; (2) when a resident concludes a contract guaranteeing performance or bearing responsibility for the liabilities assumed by the nonresident, who in turn is providing a guarantee, such as bid bonds or other sureties, related to international bids or contracts entered into by a resident; and (3) when residents provide guarantees to serve as collateral for spot financing. There are no controls on the provision of underwritten backup facilities by domestic institutional investors when they participate in an international underwriting syndicate. |

Controls on direct investment

Outward direct investment	Under current regulations, notification to a foreign exchange bank is required. However, investments in excess of US$50 million require prior assessment by the Outward Direct Investment Advisory Committee in the following instances: (1) when the total investment amount of a parent company exceeds its issued capital or half of its total capital and reserves; or (2) the liabilities of the parent company exceed its total assets, i.e., it has negative net worth; or (3) the subsidiary had a negative net worth greater than US$100 million or half of its capital or shows a continuous five-year deficit, excluding the accounting year when the business started to operate.
	Under the new foreign exchange law, investments in excess of $10 million and for which either condition (2) or (3) does not apply, will no longer be assessed by the Outward Direct Investment Advisory Committee, but instead notification to the MOFE must be given.
Inward direct investment	Equity participation is possible by increasing the amount invested in newly established or existing enterprises. Direct investment by means of mergers and acquisitions is also allowed. For the establishment and extension of a domestic branch of a foreign enterprise, approval from the FSC is required for financial institutions; notification to foreign exchange banks is required for nonfinancial institutions and for the establishment of an office. Investments in public utilities, radio, and television are restricted.
	Direct investments are allowed in all industries, except those specified on a "negative" list, including about 0.4% of all industries listed in the Korean standard industrial classification. Direct investment is allowed in all of the industries in the manufacturing sector.
	In general, foreign-financed companies are no longer required to set up partnerships with local firms. There are no controls on the maximum value of foreign investment. Tax privileges may be granted to foreign-financed projects that involve advanced technology. Postinvestment controls have also been relaxed to treat foreign and local companies equally.
	All foreign direct investments, except those in industries on the negative list, are subject to a notification requirement. A notification is deemed accepted by a foreign exchange bank unless it advises to the contrary.

Controls on liquidation of direct investment

No.

Controls on real estate transactions

Purchase abroad by residents

Overseas direct investments in the leasing and sale of real estate, construction, and the operation of golf courses are prohibited. No approvals or notifications are required for acquisition of overseas real estate by foreign exchange banks, government authorities, and residents if given as gifts or through inheritance from nonresidents. However, a notification to the BOK is required for the acquisition of real estate necessary for approved business activities costing up to $10 million. For real estate necessary for approved business activities exceeding $10 million, permission from the BOK is required.

Purchase locally by nonresidents

The following are not restricted: acquisition of domestic land or mortgages, leasing of domestic real estate by nonresidents, and acquisition of real estate or associated rights other than land by nonresidents from nonresidents. Notification to the BOK is required for the acquisition of real estate and its associated rights, including real estate acquired through inheritance or as a gift from nonresidents, and the establishment of fixed collateral not assuming the transfer of ownership. Approval of the MOFE is required for real estate acquisitions other than those specified above.

Sale locally by nonresidents

Approval of the BOK is required.

Controls on personal capital movements

Loans

By residents to nonresidents

Loans by residents to nonresidents have to be approved by the MOFE.

To residents from nonresidents

Yes.

Gifts, endowments, inheritances, and legacies

By residents to nonresidents

Payments that exceed $5,000 have to be approved by the Governor of the BOK. Gifts, endowments, inheritances, and legacies require prior aproval from the BOK.

Transfer of assets

Transfer abroad by emigrants

The ceiling for emigration settlement expenses is $400,000 for a head of household and $200,000 a person for members of a household. After obtaining nationality, the emigrant may withdraw the remaining domestic properties.

Transfer of gambling and prize earnings

Transfer of gambling earnings requires approval from the BOK.

Provisions specific to commercial banks and other credit institutions

There are prudential regulations on the assets/liabilities compositions of foreign exchange banks.

Foreign exchange banks should maintain short-term assets (less than three months) of at least 70% of short-term liabilities and long-term borrowing (more than three months) in excess of 50% of long-term assets.

Foreign exchange banks should maintain positive maturity mismatches from sight to seven days. Any negative mismatch should not exceed 10% of total foreign currency assets from sight to one month.

Borrowing abroad

For reference, the foreign exchange banks are required to report to the MOFE the funding of maturities of one year or more and for amounts exceeding $50 million.

Lending to nonresidents (financial or commercial credits)

Foreign exchange banks and other credit institutions may extend credits without restriction to nonresidents in foreign currency. Credits and loans of more than W 100 million a borrower denominated in domestic currency and granted by institutional investors require MOFE approval.

Lending locally in foreign exchange

There are no controls on loan ceilings, but there are some restrictions on the use of loans.

Differential treatment of deposit accounts in foreign exchange

Reserve requirements

Yes.

Differential treatment of deposit accounts held by nonresidents	
Reserve requirements	Reserve requirements on foreign currency deposit accounts are 7% for resident accounts and 1% for nonresident accounts.
Open foreign exchange position limits	The overall net open position (short-hand position) of foreign exchange banks measured by the sum of the net short positions or the sum of the net long positions, whichever is greater, is limited to 20% of the total equity capital at the end of the previous month.
Provisions specific to institutional investors	
Limits (max.) on portfolio invested abroad	Institutional investors are permitted to hold deposits abroad for asset diversification purposes without a quantitative ceiling. General corporations and individuals are permitted to hold deposits abroad of up to $5 million and $50,000 a year, respectively.
Currency-matching regulations on assets/liabilities composition	Yes.
Other controls imposed by securities laws	Controls imposed by the Securities Laws established by the FSC are as follows: (1) domestic securities investments by nonresident foreign nationals are regulated by "Rules on Sales and Purchases of Securities by Foreigners." The main contents of the Rules include investment ceilings, investment procedures, and the management of foreign investors, etc.; (2) overseas securities investments by residents are regulated by "Rules on Sales and Purchases of Overseas Securities." The main contents of the Rules include securities' eligibility for investment and transaction procedures, etc.; and (3) issuance of overseas securities by residents is regulated by "Rules on Financial Management of Listed Companies." The main contents of the Rules include the eligibility of issuers, the use of funds raised by issuance, and the obligations of issuers on reporting, etc.

Changes During 1999

Arrangements for payments and receipts	*April 1.* A revised foreign exchange law came into effect.
Imports and import payments	*June 1.* The Import Diversification Program was phased out.
Capital transactions	*April 1.* The issuing of securities denominated in foreign currency by nonresidents was allowed, as well as investment in deposits and trusts with maturities of one year or more by nonresidents.
	April 1. The revised foreign exchange law switched the capital control system to a negative list from a positive list.
Controls on derivatives and other instruments	*April 1.* The real demand principle imposed on financial derivatives was abolished.
Controls on credit operations	*April 1.* Borrowing abroad in maturities of one year or less by corporations whose financial structures are sound was allowed.
Controls on direct investment	*April 1.* Outward direct investments in excess of $10 million are no longer assessed by the Outward Direct Investment Advisory Committee but require notification to the MOFE in cases where (1) the liabilities of the parent company do not exceed its total assets, and (2) the subsidiary does not have a negative net worth exceeding $100 million or half its capital and does not show a continuous five-year deficit.
Provisions specific to commercial banks and other credit institutions	*January 1.* The foreign exchange position system was changed from the net aggregate position system to the short-hand position system. The limits of the position were raised to 20% from 15% of the total equity capital at the end of the previous month.
	April 1. Foreign exposure–limit regulations were expanded to include all financial institutions participating in the foreign exchange business.

KUWAIT

(Position as of December 31, 1999)

Status Under IMF Articles of Agreement

Article VIII   Date of acceptance: April 5, 1963.

Exchange Arrangement

Currency   The currency of Kuwait is the Kuwaiti dinar.

Exchange rate structure   Unitary.

Classification

Conventional pegged arrangement   The external value of the Kuwaiti dinar is determined on the basis of a special weighted basket of currencies of Kuwait's trade and financial partners. The Central Bank of Kuwait (CBK) sets the exchange rate vis-à-vis the dollar on the basis of the latest market quotations in relation to the other currencies included in the basket.

Exchange tax   No.

Exchange subsidy   No.

Forward exchange market   Yes.

Official cover of forward operations   Official coverage is extended to forward contracts related to commercial transactions.

Arrangements for Payments and Receipts

Prescription of currency   No.
requirements

Payment arrangements

Regional arrangements   GCC central banks maintain a regional arrangement to exchange GCC banknotes.

Barter agreements and open accounts   Yes.

Administration of control   There is no exchange control, and both residents and nonresidents may freely purchase and sell foreign exchange. All trade with Israel is prohibited. Payments may not be made to or received from Israel for any type of transaction.

International security restrictions   No.

Payment arrears   No.

Controls on trade in gold (coins and/or bullion)

Controls on external trade   Monetary authorities and merchants registered with the Ministry of Commerce and Industry (MCI) may import and export gold in any form if such gold is at least 18-karat fine; gold jewelry may not be imported or sold unless it is properly hallmarked. Jewelry and precious metals in any form, manufactured or unmanufactured, are subject to an import duty of 4%.

Controls on exports and imports of   No.
banknotes

Resident Accounts

Foreign exchange accounts permitted   Yes.

Held domestically   Yes.

Held abroad   Yes.

Accounts in domestic currency convertible into foreign currency	Yes.

Nonresident Accounts

Foreign exchange accounts permitted	Yes.
Domestic currency accounts	Yes.
Convertible into foreign currency	Yes.
Blocked accounts	No.

Imports and Import Payments

Foreign exchange budget	No.
Financing requirements for imports	No.
Documentation requirements for release of foreign exchange for imports	No.
Import licenses and other nontariff measures	Import licenses are required for all commercial imports other than fresh fruits and vegetables. Licenses, except for wheat and flour, are issued freely to registered Kuwaiti merchants and companies. To be registered, the importer must be either a Kuwaiti citizen, a firm in which all partners are Kuwaiti nationals, or a shareholding or limited liability company in which Kuwaiti nationals own at least 51% of the stock.
Negative list	The importation of oxygen, certain steel and asbestos pipes, pork and foodstuffs containing pork, alcoholic beverages, used vehicles over five years old, portable telephones, chewing tobacco, and gas cylinders is prohibited.
Open general licenses	Imports of industrial equipment, machinery, and their spare parts require industrial licenses valid for onetime use only. Licenses are issued to registered and licensed industrial establishments with the approval of the Industrial Development Commission at the MCI. Private imports of personal objects may be permitted under individual or specific licenses. Registered importers handling a variety of commodities may obtain a general license valid for one year. Other importers must obtain specific licenses for individual commodities, which are also valid for one year.
Other nontariff measures	Government procurement policies grant preferences to Kuwaiti-produced goods up to a price margin of 5% over goods produced in other GCC countries, and 10% over goods produced in non-GCC countries.
Import taxes and/or tariffs	Kuwait applies the uniform tariff structure of the GCC. A minimum tariff of 4% applies to non-GCC imports, while no tariffs apply to imports with at least 40% local value added from other GCC members. Imports of foodstuffs, as well as some machinery and equipment, spare parts, and raw materials are exempt from import duties. Kuwait applies higher tariffs in industries where domestic producers cater to at least 40% of the local market. Tariff rates differ depending on the domestic value-added content of the products in question. If the domestically produced goods contain at least 20%, 30%, or 40% of domestic value added, protective duties of 15%, 20%, and 25%, respectively, may be applied to competing imports. The degree of protection given by the formula is reduced by 5% in the case of consumer goods. The maximum duty imposed on products that compete with locally manufactured goods is 100%.
State import monopoly	No.

Exports and Export Proceeds

Repatriation requirements	No.
Financing requirements	No.

Documentation requirements	No.
Export licenses	Exports of live sheep and poultry, sugar, fats, rice, meat, eggs, milk, cheese, butter, olive oil, fresh fruits, vegetables in any form, beans, lentils, chickpeas, jams, and cement may be prohibited in time of emergency or shortage in Kuwait. These items may be exported in limited quantities only under a special license issued by the MCI. Exports of arms and ammunition also require licenses.
With quotas	Yes.
Export taxes	No.

Payments for Invisible Transactions and Current Transfers

Controls on these transfers	No.

Proceeds from Invisible Transactions and Current Transfers

Repatriation requirements	No.
Restrictions on use of funds	No.

Capital Transactions

Controls on capital and money market instruments	The listing of foreign stocks and bonds on the Kuwait Stock Exchange is subject to the approval of the Exchange Committee.
On capital market securities	
Shares or other securities of a participating nature	
Purchase locally by nonresidents	GCC nationals are allowed to purchase local stocks up to a certain limit. Other nonresidents are not allowed to purchase capital market securities, namely, stocks. However, nonresidents may purchase local treasury bills and bonds through local banks and investment companies.
Sale or issue locally by nonresidents	Yes.
Bonds or other debt securities	
Sale or issue locally by nonresidents	Yes.
Sale or issue abroad by residents	Controls apply to banks and financial institutions subject to CBK supervision.
On money market instruments	
Sale or issue locally by nonresidents	Yes.
On collective investment securities	
Purchase locally by nonresidents	Yes.
Sale or issue locally by nonresidents	Yes.
Controls on derivatives and other instruments	
Purchase locally by nonresidents	Yes.
Sale or issue locally by nonresidents	Yes.
Controls on credit operations	No.

Controls on direct investment

Inward direct investment

Government agreement is necessary for the participation of nonresident capital in resident corporations in Kuwait; foreign participation in new Kuwaiti companies must be less than 49%. The participation of GCC nationals in companies established in Kuwait may reach up to 75% of the capital, and there are no restrictions on participation in retail trade enterprises by non-Kuwaiti GCC nationals.

Controls on liquidation of direct investment

No.

Controls on real estate transactions

Purchase locally by nonresidents

Only GCC nationals may purchase real estate for private residence purposes of up to 3,000 square meters.

Sale locally by nonresidents

Yes.

Controls on personal capital movements

No.

Provisions specific to commercial banks and other credit institutions

Borrowing abroad

Controls apply to the sale or issue of bonds or other debt securities abroad.

Lending to nonresidents (financial or commercial credits)

Yes.

Differential treatment of deposit accounts in foreign exchange

Liquid asset requirements

Yes.

Interest rate controls

Yes.

Differential treatment of deposit accounts held by nonresidents

Liquid asset requirements

Yes.

Open foreign exchange position limits

On resident assets and liabilities

Open foreign exchange position limits may not exceed 10% of a bank's capital, and in some cases, lower limits are set.

Provisions specific to institutional investors

No.

Other controls imposed by securities laws

No.

Changes During 1999

No significant changes occurred in the exchange and trade system.

KYRGYZ REPUBLIC

(Position as of January 31, 2000)

Status Under IMF Articles of Agreement

Article VIII	Date of acceptance: March 29, 1995.

Exchange Arrangement

Currency	The currency of the Kyrgyz Republic is the Kyrgyz som.
Exchange rate structure	Unitary.
Classification	
Managed floating with no pre-announced path for the exchange rate	The official exchange rate of the som against the dollar is defined as the average-weighted exchange rate of interbank foreign exchange transactions for the week. The National Bank of the Kyrgyz Republic (NBKR) participates and intervenes in the interbank market as necessary.
Exchange tax	No.
Exchange subsidy	No.
Forward exchange market	No.

Arrangements for Payments and Receipts

Prescription of currency requirements	There are no prescription of currency requirements, and settlements may be made in any currency.
Payment arrangements	
Bilateral payment arrangements	
Operative	There are agreements or settlement procedures with countries of the FSU.
Regional arrangements	There are agreements with the Interstate Bank and the Central Asian Bank for Cooperation and Development.
Administration of control	The NBKR has responsibility for managing its gold and foreign exchange reserves. The som is fully convertible for current payments and transfers with no restrictions on buying, selling, or holding foreign currencies. The NBKR is also responsible for issuing foreign exchange licenses to commercial banks and to foreign exchange bureaus.
International security restrictions	No.
Payment arrears	In 2000, arrears emerged in relation to India, Pakistan, Russia, and Turkey.
Official	Yes.
Controls on trade in gold (coins and/or bullion)	All gold produced is sold at market prices. The government and the NBKR have priority in purchasing and also a right to participate as sellers. If the government and the NBKR do not exercise that right, the gold is sold either in the domestic market or abroad.
Controls on exports and imports of banknotes	No.

Resident Accounts

Foreign exchange accounts permitted	Yes.
Held domestically	Yes.

| Held abroad | These accounts are permitted, but, according to the Law on Operations in Foreign Exchange, the NBKR should be informed about such accounts. |
| **Accounts in domestic currency convertible into foreign currency** | Yes. |

Nonresident Accounts

Foreign exchange accounts permitted	Yes.
Domestic currency accounts	Yes.
Convertible into foreign currency	Yes.
Blocked accounts	No.

Imports and Import Payments

Foreign exchange budget	No.
Financing requirements for imports	No.
Documentation requirements for release of foreign exchange for imports	No.
Import licenses and other nontariff measures	Excise taxes apply to alcoholic goods, tobacco products, jewelry made of precious stones and metals, crystal products, clothing made from fur and skins, gas-operated arms and firearms, petroleum products, coffee, cocoa, and rugs.
Positive list	The list applies to all products.
Negative list	Imports of encryption equipment, armaments, military equipment and uniforms, explosive materials, nuclear materials, precious stones and metals, narcotics and poisons, pesticides, medicines and medicinal equipment, and official and civilian firearms may take place only with the authorization of the government.
Open general licenses	OGLs are issued for the period of time required for the export and import operations, but for a maximum of one calendar year.
Licenses with quotas	Quotas are applied on imports of ethyl alcohol.
Import taxes and/or tariffs	The tariff regime was changed on July 19, 1999, replacing the 10% duty on all imports with tariff bands ranging from zero to 50%. On January 1, 2000, the Customs Tariff for 2000 entered into force, whereby imports are subject to customs duties at the rates of zero, 10%, 17.5%, and 20%.
State import monopoly	No.

Exports and Export Proceeds

Repatriation requirements	No.
Financing requirements	No.
Documentation requirements	No.
Export licenses	Exports of wild and rare animals and plants, fish, raw medicinal materials, encryption equipment, armaments and military equipment, explosives, nuclear materials, precious stones and metals, narcotics and poisons, and antiques may take place only with the authorization of the government.
Without quotas	Yes.
Export taxes	On August 31, 1999, the authorities introduced temporary export duties of 100% on wheat, grain, and milk, and a customs duty ranging from $0.20–$0.30 per kilogram on a range of

other agricultural commodities, including cotton, tobacco, wool, and other products. Most were subsequently eliminated, except for those on grain and flour.

Payments for Invisible Transactions and Current Transfers

Controls on these transfers   No.

Proceeds from Invisible Transactions and Current Transfers

Repatriation requirements   No.

Restrictions on use of funds   No.

Capital Transactions

Controls on capital and money market instruments

On capital market securities   Control is exercised by the National Securities Market Commission (NKRTsB) under the president of the Kyrgyz Republic, except for the following: debt securities of domestic state and local governments; other securities issued or guaranteed by the government of the Kyrgyz Republic, by the NBKR, or by local state authorities (excluding certain certificates); bills of exchange; any documented payment liabilities arising in the course of usual business activities and valid for a period not exceeding one year; and checks.

Shares or other securities of a participating nature

  Purchase locally by nonresidents   The issuer is obliged to provide the NKRTsB with information on the acquisition by any person of a share in its statutory capital exceeding 5% and/or 5% of its stock shares.

  Sale or issue locally by nonresidents   The same regulations apply as for purchases in the country by nonresidents.

  Sale or issue abroad by residents   Securities must be registered with the NKRTsB.

Bonds or other debt securities   The issuance and circulation of corporate bonds is regulated by the NKRTsB.

  Purchase locally by nonresidents   The same regulations apply as for shares or other securities of a participating nature.

  Sale or issue locally by nonresidents   The same regulations apply as for shares or other securities of a participating nature.

  Sale or issue abroad by residents   Securities must be registered with the NKRTsB.

On money market instruments   The main money market instrument consists of government treasury bills.

  Purchase locally by nonresidents   These transactions must be reported to the NBKR.

  Sale or issue locally by nonresidents   Securities must be registered with the NKRTsB.

  Sale or issue abroad by residents   Securities must be registered with the NKRTsB.

On collective investment securities   Securities invested in joint-stock investment funds and mutual funds are regulated; the operations of other funds are not presently regulated.

  Sale or issue locally by nonresidents   The same regulations apply as for shares or other securities of a participating nature.

  Sale or issue abroad by residents   Securities must be registered with the NKRTsB.

Controls on derivatives and other instruments   There is currently no market in these instruments; therefore, they are not regulated.

Controls on credit operations   There are no controls on these transactions; however, all economic entities must report to statistical agencies concerning commercial (trade) credits received and issued.

Financial credits	
To residents from nonresidents	The MOF keeps track of state external debt. In the event that a guarantee of the government of the Kyrgyz Republic is provided, credits must be registered with the MOF. The government does not keep information on private borrowings abroad.
Controls on direct investment	No.
Controls on liquidation of direct investment	No.
Controls on real estate transactions	
Purchase locally by nonresidents	Purchases are subject to approval by the Ministry of Justice.
Controls on personal capital movements	No.
Provisions specific to commercial banks and other credit institutions	
Borrowing abroad	These transactions must be reported to the NBKR.
Maintenance of accounts abroad	These transactions must be reported to the NBKR.
Lending to nonresidents (financial or commercial credits)	These transactions must be reported to the NBKR.
Lending locally in foreign exchange	These transactions must be reported to the NBKR.
Purchase of locally issued securities denominated in foreign exchange	Locally issued securities must be denominated in local currency. However, the use of foreign currency, or of payment documents in foreign currency, is permitted in certain instances and according to procedures established by legislation.
Investment regulations	
Abroad by banks	These transactions must be reported to the NBKR.
In banks by nonresidents	These transactions must be reported to the NBKR.
Open foreign exchange position limits	Limits are established by the NBKR.
On resident assets and liabilities	Yes.
On nonresident assets and liabilities	Yes.
Provisions specific to institutional investors	
Limits (max.) on portfolio invested abroad	Investment funds are not permitted to invest, locally or abroad, more than 10% of their total assets in the securities of a single issuer, or to hold more than 25% of the common stock of an issuer.
Other controls imposed by securities laws	No.

Changes During 1999

Imports and import payments	*July 19.* The 10% uniform duty was replaced with tariff bands ranging from zero to 50%.
Exports and export proceeds	*August 31.* The authorities introduced temporary export duties of 100% on a range of agricultural commodities, including cotton, grain, and flour. Most were subsequently eliminated, except for those on grain and flour.

Changes During 2000

Imports and import payments	*January 1.* The Customs Tariff for 2000 entered into force, whereby imports are subject to customs duties at the rates of zero, 10%, 17.5%, and 20%.

LAO PEOPLE'S DEMOCRATIC REPUBLIC

(Position as of December 31, 1999)

Status Under IMF Articles of Agreement

Article XIV	Yes.

Exchange Arrangement

Currency	The currency of the Lao People's Democratic Republic is the Lao kip.
Other legal tender	The Thai baht and the dollar are widely held and used for payments.
Exchange rate structure	
Dual	The exchange rate system comprises two rates: a rate set by the commercial banks and a parallel market rate.
Classification	
Managed floating with no pre-announced path for the exchange rate	Commercial banks and licensed foreign exchange bureaus are permitted to buy and sell foreign exchange at freely determined rates, provided the spread between buying and selling rates remains less than 2%. In practice, however, la Banque pour le commerce extérieur du Laos (BCEL), the major state-owned commercial bank and the dominant transactor in the official exchange market, sets the commercial bank exchange rate taking into account movements in the parallel market.
Exchange tax	No.
Exchange subsidy	No.
Forward exchange market	No.

Arrangements for Payments and Receipts

Prescription of currency requirements	No prescription of currency requirements are imposed on receipts or payments but, in principle, the Bank of the Lao P.D.R. (BOL), the central bank, provides and accepts only dollars, euros, Japanese yen, pounds sterling, Swiss francs, and Thai baht.
Payment arrangements	
Bilateral payment arrangements	
Operative	A bilateral payment agreement is in effect with Vietnam.
Inoperative	An inoperative bilateral payment agreement exists with Malaysia.
Barter agreements and open accounts	Bilateral trading arrangements are maintained with China and Vietnam.
Administration of control	Official transactions are handled by the BOL. The Ministry of Commerce (MOC) grants import and export authorization to state trading companies, joint ventures between domestic enterprises and foreign investors, cooperatives, and other public and private enterprises.
International security restrictions	n.a.
Payment arrears	n.a.
Controls on trade in gold (coins and/or bullion)	
Controls on external trade	Imports and exports of gold and silver require BOL authorization.

Controls on exports and imports of banknotes

On exports

Domestic currency	Exports of domestic currency require BOL authorization.
Foreign currency	Residents traveling abroad may take out foreign currency within the limit set from time to time by the BOL.
	Nonresidents are authorized to take out foreign currency to the limit of the amount that was brought in and declared upon arrival.

On imports

Domestic currency	Imports of domestic currency require BOL authorization.
Foreign currency	Persons entering the country may bring unlimited amounts of foreign currency and may declare the amount thereof to the immigration officer at the port of entry in case they want to take out the same amount in foreign exchange.

Resident Accounts

Foreign exchange accounts permitted	Foreign exchange accounts may be credited with (1) proceeds from exports of goods and services; (2) other transfers from abroad; (3) transfers or payments from foreign currency accounts opened with commercial banks within Lao P.D.R.; and (4) foreign banknotes and coins. These accounts, which are interest bearing, may be debited for conversion into kip for domestic expenditure, or foreign exchange balances may be used for authorized external payments and transfers.
Held domestically	Yes.
Held abroad	Residents may open accounts abroad in exceptional cases with the approval of the BOL.
Accounts in domestic currency convertible into foreign currency	Kip accounts of nonresidents, namely embassies and international organizations, the credit balance of which is from conversion of foreign currency, are considered as convertible accounts.

Nonresident Accounts

Foreign exchange accounts permitted	These accounts may be credited with (1) remittances from abroad; (2) transfers from other nonresident and resident foreign currency accounts in Lao P.D.R.; and (3) foreign currency brought into the country by the account holder and duly declared upon arrival. Nonresidents are not allowed to accept or deposit to their accounts foreign currency proceeds from exports of goods and services of residents without the approval of the BOL. These accounts, which bear interest, may be debited for (1) conversion into kip; (2) transfers into residents' and nonresidents' foreign currency accounts maintained with an authorized commercial bank; (3) payments in kip to accounts of residents or nonresidents; and (4) payments and transfers abroad.
Domestic currency accounts	These accounts may be credited with (1) sales of foreign currencies and (2) transfers from other convertible kip accounts of holders of the same category. Nonresidents are not permitted to deposit kip belonging to residents into their convertible kip accounts. These accounts may be debited for (1) payments in kip and (2) conversion into foreign currency at the prevailing buying rate of the commercial bank concerned.
Convertible into foreign currency	Yes.
Blocked accounts	n.a.

Imports and Import Payments

Foreign exchange budget	No.

Financing requirements for imports

Advance import deposits

Margin deposits are required against LCs, and the rates are set by the BCEL and other commercial banks.

Documentation requirements for release of foreign exchange for imports

Preshipment inspection

A joint-venture company inspects goods before shipment.

Letters of credit

Yes.

Import licenses and other nontariff measures

Import licenses issued by the trade department under the Vientiene prefecture and provincial government authorities are required for all goods. Imports may be made by any registered export-import business.

Negative list

Yes.

Licenses with quotas

The quota for the imports of vehicles has been abolished.

Other nontariff measures

Yes.

Import taxes and/or tariffs

The tariff structure is composed of six rates (5%, 10%, 15%, 20%, 30%, and 40%). The lowest rates apply to imports of raw materials, certain inputs, and certain essential consumer goods. The highest rates of 30% and 40% apply to luxury consumer goods, certain beverages, and tobacco.

State import monopoly

No.

Exports and Export Proceeds

Repatriation requirements

Yes.

Financing requirements

n.a.

Documentation requirements

n.a.

Export licenses

Export licenses, which are issued by the trade department under the Vientiene prefecture and provincial government authorities, are required for all products.

With quotas

Quotas apply only to timber.

Export taxes

No.

Payments for Invisible Transactions and Current Transfers

Controls on these transfers

Investment-related payments

Information is not available on the payment of amortization of loans or depreciation of direct investments.

Proceeds from Invisible Transactions and Current Transfers

Repatriation requirements

Proceeds from invisibles are, in practice, treated in the same way as proceeds from merchandise exports.

Restrictions on use of funds

No.

Capital Transactions

Controls on capital and money market instruments

All capital transactions require BOL authorization.

Controls on derivatives and other instruments	All derivatives transactions require BOL authorization.
Controls on credit operations	n.a.
Controls on direct investment	Direct investments are subject to the Direct Investment Promotion and Management Law.
Outward direct investment	Yes.
Inward direct investment	Yes.
Controls on liquidation of direct investment	These transactions are permitted after BOL scrutiny. Transfers of large sums may be made in installments according to a plan approved by the BOL.
Controls on real estate transactions	
Purchase abroad by residents	Yes.
Purchase locally by nonresidents	Yes.
Sale locally by nonresidents	Yes.
Controls on personal capital movements	n.a.
Provisions specific to commercial banks and other credit institutions	
Maintenance of accounts abroad	Authorized commercial banks may open accounts abroad.
Differential treatment of deposit accounts in foreign exchange	
Interest rate controls	Yes.
Open foreign exchange position limits	Yes.
Provisions specific to institutional investors	n.a.
Other controls imposed by securities laws	n.a.

Changes During 1999

No significant changes occurred in the exchange and trade system.

LATVIA

(Position as of April 30, 2000)

Status Under IMF Articles of Agreement

Article VIII   Date of acceptance: June 10, 1994.

Exchange Arrangement

Currency   The currency of Latvia is the Latvian lats.

Exchange rate structure   Unitary.

Classification

Conventional pegged arrangement   The lats is pegged to the SDR and, since February 1994, has maintained a constant exchange rate against the SDR of LVL 0.7997 per SDR 1. The Bank of Latvia (BOL) quotes fixing rates of the lats against 46 convertible currencies daily. These rates are used for accounting purposes and are valid through the next day. The BOL also quotes real-time buying and selling rates for the currencies in the SDR basket (i.e., dollars, euros, pounds sterling, and yen). The spread between the buying and selling rate is 2%.

Exchange tax   No.

Exchange subsidy   No.

Forward exchange market   Yes.

Arrangements for Payments and Receipts

Prescription of currency requirements   No.

Payment arrangements

Bilateral payment arrangements

  Inoperative   Inoperative bilateral payment agreements are maintained with Azerbaijan and Kazakhstan.

Administration of control   Government decisions adopted by the cabinet of ministers and approved by parliament prevail in foreign exchange and trade matters, but the authority to issue regulations governing foreign exchange transactions has been delegated to the BOL. All foreign exchange transactions must be effected through authorized banks and enterprises licensed by the BOL.

International security restrictions   No.

Payment arrears   No.

Controls on trade in gold (coins and/or bullion)

Controls on domestic ownership and/or trade   A license is required.

Controls on exports and imports of banknotes   No.

Resident Accounts

Foreign exchange accounts permitted   Resident natural persons and enterprises are allowed to hold foreign currencies in domestic or foreign bank accounts and to use these funds for domestic payments.

Held domestically	Yes.
Held abroad	Yes.
Accounts in domestic currency convertible into foreign currency	Yes.

Nonresident Accounts

Foreign exchange accounts permitted	Nonresident natural persons and enterprises are permitted to hold bank accounts in Latvia denominated in either foreign or domestic currency.
Domestic currency accounts	Yes.
Convertible into foreign currency	Yes.
Blocked accounts	n.a.

Imports and Import Payments

Foreign exchange budget	No.
Financing requirements for imports	No.
Documentation requirements for release of foreign exchange for imports	No.
Import licenses and other nontariff measures	
Negative list	There are virtually no licensing requirements for imports except for reasons of health and safety. Licensing is almost automatic except for pyrotechnic products, arms and ammunition, combat vehicles, and prepared explosives. The processing time for license applications is no more than 10 business days, and license fees reflect processing costs only.
Import taxes and/or tariffs	According to the Law on Customs Duty (Tariffs), there are three specific tariffs on sugar and cigarettes. The average of the basic ad valorem tariffs on nonagricultural goods is 2.46%, with 1% being the most common tariff rate. Some final goods are exempt from customs duties. The average basic rate on agricultural goods is 12.71%, and the average MFN rate is 9.20%.
	On April 1, 2000, parliament abolished fixed tariff rates on alcoholic beverages and abolished tariff rates on cyclic and acyclic hydrocarbons; paper, paperboard, paper pulp, and articles made of paper; iron and steel and articles made thereof; and electrical machinery.
	Latvia maintains trade and economic cooperation agreements providing for MFN status with the following countries: Armenia, Azerbaijan, Belarus, China, Kazakhstan, the Kyrgyz Republic, Moldova, Russia, Tajikistan, Turkmenistan, Ukraine (for agricultural goods), and Uzbekistan. Latvia has free-trade agreements with a total of 27 WTO countries. These are the other Baltic countries, the European Union, the EFTA, the Czech Republic, Hungary, Poland, the Slovak Republic, Slovenia, and Ukraine (for industrial goods).
State import monopoly	No.

Exports and Export Proceeds

Repatriation requirements	No.
Financing requirements	No.
Documentation requirements	No.
Export licenses	No.

Export taxes	All remaining export duties, except on books more than 50 years old and antiques, were removed on January 1, 1999.

Payments for Invisible Transactions and Current Transfers

Controls on these transfers	No.

Proceeds from Invisible Transactions and Current Transfers

Repatriation requirements	No.
Restrictions on use of funds	No.

Capital Transactions

Controls on capital and money market instruments	No.
Controls on derivatives and other instruments	No.
Controls on credit operations	No.
Controls on direct investment	
Inward direct investment	Nonresidents are not allowed to hold more than 49% of shares in companies operating in securities.
Controls on liquidation of direct investment	No.
Controls on real estate transactions	
Purchase locally by nonresidents	The purchase of buildings is permitted. The purchase of land is not restricted, except for areas of land near borders and environmentally protected areas. Land to be used for agricultural and forestry purposes may be bought only if one-half of the paid share capital of the company belongs (1) to citizens of Latvia or to citizens of countries with which Latvia has an agreement on promotion of foreign investment; (2) to a group of the previous categories; or (3) it is a public joint-stock company, shares of which are quoted on the stock exchange.
Controls on personal capital movements	n.a.
Provisions specific to commercial banks and other credit institutions	
Lending to nonresidents (financial or commercial credits)	Exposure (including lending) to any Zone B country must not exceed 25% of a bank's capital. Total exposure to Zone B countries must not exceed 200% of a bank's capital.
Open foreign exchange position limits	The open foreign currency position is limited to 10% of capital for any single foreign currency and 20% of capital for all foreign currencies.
On resident assets and liabilities	Yes.
On nonresident assets and liabilities	Yes.
Provisions specific to institutional investors	Private pension funds are not allowed to invest abroad more than 15% of their pension capital. The law on insurance companies and their supervision restricts investments abroad by the insurance companies to 10% of their technical resources, except when authorization is granted.
Limits (max.) on securities issued by nonresidents and on portfolio invested abroad	Yes.

| Limits (max.) on portfolio invested abroad | Yes. |
| Other controls imposed by securities laws | No. |

Changes During 1999

Exports and export proceeds

January 1. All remaining export duties, except those on books more than 50 years old and antiques, were removed.

Capital transactions

Controls on direct investment

October 4. The foreign investment law was amended to allow foreign ownership in excess of 49% in radio and television.

November 11. Nonresidents were allowed to invest more than 49% in companies operating in gambling and lotteries.

Changes During 2000

Imports and import payments

April 1. Fixed tariff rates on alcoholic beverages and tariff rates on a range of products were abolished.

Capital transactions

Controls on direct investment

February 24. Foreign ownership in companies engaged in logging was allowed.

LEBANON

(Position as of December 31, 1999)

Status Under IMF Articles of Agreement

Article VIII	Date of acceptance: July 1, 1993.

Exchange Arrangement

Currency	The currency of Lebanon is the Lebanese pound.
Exchange rate structure	Unitary.

Classification

Conventional pegged arrangement	Exchange rates are market determined, but the authorities may announce buying or selling rates for certain currencies and intervene when necessary in order to maintain orderly conditions in the exchange market. Banks are allowed to engage in spot transactions in any currency except in Israeli new sheqalim.
Exchange tax	No.
Exchange subsidy	No.
Forward exchange market	Forward operations are allowed, provided that a minimum margin deposit of 20% is constituted for each operation.

Arrangements for Payments and Receipts

Prescription of currency requirements	No.
Payment arrangements	No.
Bilateral payment arrangements	
Operative	Bilateral trade agreements are maintained with Egypt, Iraq, Jordan, Kuwait, the Palestinian Authority, Saudi Arabia, Sudan, and the Syrian Arab Republic.
Administration of control	No.
International security restrictions	No.
Payment arrears	No.
Controls on trade in gold (coins and/or bullion)	The importation, exportation, and domestic sale of foreign gold coins require a certificate issued by the Office for the Protection of the Consumer that indicates the gold content and weight.
Controls on exports and imports of banknotes	No.

Resident Accounts

Foreign exchange accounts permitted	Yes.
Held domestically	Yes.
Held abroad	Yes.
Accounts in domestic currency convertible into foreign currency	Yes.

Nonresident Accounts

Foreign exchange accounts permitted

Yes.

Domestic currency accounts

Nonresident nonfinancial entities may hold accounts in Lebanese pounds freely. However, effective February 2, 1999, banks and financial institutions are prohibited from opening debit or credit accounts (including fiduciary accounts) in Lebanese pounds for nonresident banks, financial institutions, and money dealers.

Convertible into foreign currency

Yes.

Blocked accounts

No.

Imports and Import Payments

Foreign exchange budget

No.

Financing requirements for imports

Advance import deposits

Importers must place with banks a prior deposit of 15% of the value of the LC in the same currency as the LC.

Documentation requirements for re-lease of foreign exchange for imports

No.

Import licenses and other nontariff measures

All imports from Israel are prohibited. Additionally, certain commercial entities listed under the Arab Boycott List are banned from trading with Lebanon.

Negative list

Imports prohibited year-round include live chickens, all chicken meat, except for chicken nuggets, fresh liquid milk, yogurt, spring onions, cauliflowers, cabbages, carrots, parsnips, broad beans, green peppers, spinach, olives, zucchinis, parsley, coriander, watercress, lamb's lettuce, spearmint, potatoes, green almonds, pine nuts, citrus fruits, bananas, figs, grapes, apples, peaches, plums, green plums, sharon fruits, jujubes, strawberries, quinces, apricots, cherries, pears, thyme, olive oil, and pickles.

Imports prohibited during a specified period of the year include tomatoes, cucumbers, egg-plant, green beans, peas, watermelons, muskmelons, onions, garlic, and corncobs. Imports of various seeds (citrus, apple, olive, and nut) and various juices (apple, orange, and lemon) and of certain finished goods, wires, cables, cement, veterinary vaccines, and fertilizers require a license.

Import taxes and/or tariffs

Lebanon uses the Harmonized System Tariff version 96. Customs valuation is on the basis of c.i.f. value; customs duties are generally ad valorem. The rates vary between 2% and 105%. There are preferential duty rates for goods imported for industrial, agricultural, or public use. In addition to ad valorem duties, the following other methods are used: (1) the bracket-based calculation in the case of cars, when the value of a car is divided into three brackets and the total duty is the sum of the duties applied at cash rate; (2) duties calculated on the basis of units of measure, such as weight or volume (e.g., gasoline); (3) combined duty is calculated on an ad valorem and specific basis, so that the higher amount is collected (e.g., tropical fruits and chickens). In addition, excise duties are collected on tobacco, cement, fuels, and cars.

Effective January 1, 1999, Lebanon applied the Arab Free Trade Area Convention.

State import monopoly

Imports of some goods are reserved for the government.

Exports and Export Proceeds

Repatriation requirements

No.

Financing requirements

No.

Documentation requirements	No.
Export licenses	Exports of arms and ammunition, narcotics, and similar products are prohibited.
Without quotas	Yes.
Export taxes	No.

Payments for Invisible Transactions and Current Transfers

Controls on these transfers	No.

Proceeds from Invisible Transactions and Current Transfers

Repatriation requirements	No.
Restrictions on use of funds	No.

Capital Transactions

Controls on capital and money market instruments	
On capital market securities	
Shares or other securities of a participating nature	
Purchase locally by nonresidents	Different ceilings are imposed on nonresidents' shares in companies ranging from 51% to 100%, depending on the nature of the company. Any investor acquiring more than 5% of a bank's category C shares needs the prior approval of the Banque du Liban (BL).
Bonds or other debt securities	
Purchase locally by nonresidents	Foreign financial institutions need the BL's approval when purchasing treasury securities denominated in Lebanese pounds or CDs from the BL, and also when transferring the foreign exchange. The same regulations apply for private persons purchasing treasury securities.
Purchase abroad by residents	Residents may purchase debt securities from abroad freely. Banks and financial institutions, however, are only allowed to purchase bonds issued by G-10 countries.
On money market instruments	
Purchase locally by nonresidents	The same regulations apply as for bonds and other debt securities.
Purchase abroad by residents	The same regulations apply as for bonds and other debt securities.
On collective investment securities	The transfer of shares in excess of 10% per person of a collective investment company is subject to prior BL approval.
Purchase locally by nonresidents	Yes.
Sale or issue locally by nonresidents	Yes.
Controls on derivatives and other instruments	Effective December 28, 1999, the issuance and trading of derivative products require prior BL approval.
Sale or issue locally by nonresidents	Yes.
Purchase abroad by residents	There is no control on purchasing derivatives or any financial instruments from abroad. Banks, however, unlike financial institutions and brokerage firms, need the prior approval of the central bank to engage in derivative transactions for their own account.
Sale or issue abroad by residents	The same regulations apply as for purchases abroad by residents.

Controls on credit operations

Commercial credits

By residents to nonresidents   Yes.

Financial credits

By residents to nonresidents   Yes.

Controls on direct investment

Inward direct investment   All participation in the financial sector and in the holding companies related to banks needs prior approval from the BL. Any investor acquiring more than 5% of a bank's category C shares that are traded in the market needs prior approval of the BL.

Controls on liquidation of direct investment   No.

Controls on real estate transactions

Purchase locally by nonresidents   The right to acquire real estate by non-Arab foreigners requires a license from the Council of Ministers. Arab nationals do not need a license; nevertheless, a ceiling on the total area that can be acquired is imposed.

Controls on personal capital movements   No.

Provisions specific to commercial banks and other credit institutions   Effective December 28, 1999, banks have to inform the Banking Control Commission about any guarantee on derivative transactions. These guarantees should not exceed 7% of the bank's equity.

Borrowing abroad   Effective October 29, 1999, for commercial banks, the volume of debt instruments in foreign exchange should not exceed 4% of total deposits in foreign currencies as of the end of the previous financial year; for investment banks, the limit is 6%.

Lending to nonresidents (financial or commercial credits)   Banks are prohibited from extending credits in Lebanese pounds for nonresident banks and financial institutions. This control does not apply to guarantees issued by nonresident banks and financial institutions as collateral to loans in Lebanese pounds, provided that such loans are for commercial or investment activities in Lebanon. In addition, the net debtor interbank position between a Lebanese bank and its affiliate or sister company abroad should not exceed 25% of core capital.

Differential treatment of deposit accounts in foreign exchange

Reserve requirements   Deposit accounts in foreign exchange are exempted from reserve requirements.

Liquid asset requirements   Effective March 18, 1999, liquid assets in foreign exchange should not be less than 30% of the total clients' deposits of all maturities, net interbank credit accounts, CDs, bonds, and subordinated loans with a maturity of less than one year.

Investment regulations

Abroad by banks   Banks need the prior approval of the central bank to acquire shares in foreign financial institutions.

In banks by nonresidents   Foreigners' participation in Lebanese banks is limited up to two-thirds of capital. Foreign banks may establish fully owned branches subject to central bank approval.

Open foreign exchange position limits   Regardless of resident/nonresident assets or liabilities, banks may maintain a trading position (total open position less total structural position) in foreign currency of up to 5% of the core capital of banks, and a global position (total trading position, short or long) of up to 40% of core capital. Structural positions are long-term positions representing foreign assets in foreign currencies.

On resident assets and liabilities   Yes.

On nonresident assets and liabilities   Yes.

Provisions specific to institutional investors   No.

Other controls imposed by securities laws

Yes.

Changes During 1999

Nonresident accounts

February 2. Banks and financial institutions are prohibited from accepting fiduciary deposits in Lebanese pounds for nonresident banks, financial institutions, and money dealers.

Imports and import payments

January 1. Lebanon applied the Arab Free Trade Area Convention.

Capital transactions

Controls on derivatives and other instruments

December 28. The issuance and trading of derivatives requires prior BL approval.

Provisions specific to commercial banks and other credit institutions

March 18. Liquid assets in foreign exchange should not be less than 30% of the total clients' deposits of all maturities, net interbank credit accounts, CDs, bonds, and subordinated loans maturing in less than one year.

October 29. For commercial banks, the volume of debt instruments in foreign currencies should not exceed 4% of total deposits in foreign currencies as of the end of the previous financial year; for investment banks, the limit is 6%.

December 28. Guarantees issued on derivative transactions should not exceed 7% of the bank's equity.

LESOTHO

(Position as of December 31, 1999)

Status Under IMF Articles of Agreement

Article VIII   Date of acceptance: March 5, 1997.

Exchange Arrangement

Currency   The currency of Lesotho is the Lesotho loti.

Other legal tender   The South African rand is also legal tender.

Exchange rate structure   Unitary.

Classification

Conventional pegged arrangement   The loti is pegged to the South African rand at M 1 per R 1.

Exchange tax   No.

Exchange subsidy   No.

Forward exchange market   Authorized dealers are permitted to conduct forward exchange operations through their correspondent banks abroad at rates quoted by the latter. Forward exchange cover, however, is not common in Lesotho.

Arrangements for Payments and Receipts

Prescription of currency requirements   Settlements by or to residents of the CMA with all countries outside the CMA may be made in rand to and from a nonresident account and in any foreign currency.

Payment arrangements

Regional arrangements   As Lesotho is part of the CMA, payments within the CMA are unrestricted and unrecorded except for statistical and customs purposes. In its relations with countries outside the CMA, Lesotho applies exchange controls that are largely similar to those applied by South Africa and Swaziland.

Administration of control   The Central Bank of Lesotho (CBL) controls foreign exchange transactions and delegates to commercial banks the authority to approve certain types of current payments up to established limits. Permits are issued by the Department of Customs and Excise based on the recommendation of the Department of Trade and Industry. Licenses for financial institutions accepting deposits, insurance companies, brokers, and agents are issued by the CBL.

International security restrictions   No.

Payment arrears   No.

Controls on trade in gold (coins and/or bullion)

Controls on domestic ownership and/or trade   Only authorized dealers may trade in gold, but anyone may hold gold.

Controls on external trade   Exports of gold from the CMA are prohibited.

Controls on exports and imports of banknotes

On exports

  Domestic currency   Exports of currency from the CMA are prohibited.

  Foreign currency   Exports of foreign currency from the CMA by residents are prohibited; visitors may reexport the unspent portion of foreign currency brought into the country.

Resident Accounts

Foreign exchange accounts permitted	Yes.
Held domestically	These accounts may be opened, but prior approval is required.
Held abroad	Only banks may hold these accounts, and prior approval is required.
Accounts in domestic currency convertible into foreign currency	Approval is required.

Nonresident Accounts

Foreign exchange accounts permitted	Loti accounts of nonresidents are divided into nonresident accounts and emigrant blocked accounts.
Domestic currency accounts	Yes.
Convertible into foreign currency	These accounts may be opened, but prior approval is required.
Blocked accounts	Funds in emigrant blocked loti accounts may be invested in quoted securities and other such investments approved by the CBL. The free transfer of income from an emigrant's blocked assets is limited to M 300,000 a family unit a year.

Imports and Import Payments

Foreign exchange budget	No.
Financing requirements for imports	Yes.
Advance payment requirements	Payments are not normally allowed before the date of shipment or dispatch, except with the prior approval or special authorization from the CBL. Authorized dealers may permit, without the CBL's approval, advance payment of up to 33.3% of the ex-factory cost of capital goods if suppliers require it or if it is normal practice in the trade concerned.
Documentation requirements for release of foreign exchange for imports	No.
Import licenses and other nontariff measures	Lesotho is a member of the SACU, and all imports, except certain food imports, originating in any country of the SACU are unrestricted. Imports from countries outside the SACU are usually licensed in conformity with the import regulations of the SACU. Lesotho reserves the right to restrict certain imports. Import permits are valid for all countries and entitle the holder to buy the foreign exchange required to make payments for imports from outside the SACU.
Negative list	With certain exceptions, imports from outside the SACU must conform to a negative list and be licensed.
Licenses with quotas	Certain food imports from within the SACU are subject to import licensing.
Import taxes and/or tariffs	Lesotho applies the external customs tariffs of the SACU.
State import monopoly	No.

Exports and Export Proceeds

Repatriation requirements	All export proceeds must be repatriated.
Surrender requirements	Unless otherwise permitted, all export proceeds must be surrendered within six months of the date of the export transaction.
Financing requirements	A state-supported export credit scheme is in effect, involving credit guarantees, and pre- and postshipment credits.

Documentation requirements n.a.

Export licenses

Without quotas Certain exports are subject to licensing for revenue purposes; this requirement, in practice, is limited to the exportation of diamonds. Most exports are shipped without license to or through South Africa.

Export taxes No.

Payments for Invisible Transactions and Current Transfers

Controls on these transfers No.

Investment-related payments Profit and dividend transfers are not restricted, provided the funds were not obtained through excessive use of local borrowing facilities. Information is not available on payment of amortization of loans or depreciation of direct investments.

Quantitative limits Yes.

Indicative limits/bona fide test There is no indicative limit or bona fide test for the payment of commissions.

Payments for travel

Quantitative limits There is a limit of M 60,000 a year for adults and M 20,000 for children under 12 years of age, at an average daily rate of up to M 2,000 for the duration of the visit. The basic annual exchange allowance for travel to neighboring countries—Angola, Botswana, the Democratic Republic of Congo, Malawi, Mozambique, Zambia, and Zimbabwe—is M 20,000 an adult and M 5,000 a child under 12 years of age, at an average daily rate of up to M 1,000 for the duration of the visit.

Indicative limits/bona fide test Larger allowances may be obtained for business travel.

Personal payments

Prior approval Prior approval is required for payment of study abroad costs.

Quantitative limits For study abroad, the limits are M 4,000 a month for a single student or M 8,000 a month for a student accompanied by a spouse who is not studying.

Other payments

Quantitative limits The limit for professional fees is M 10,000, and the limit for technical services is M 50,000.

Proceeds from Invisible Transactions and Current Transfers

Repatriation requirements Yes.

Surrender requirements Proceeds must be surrendered within seven days of the date of accrual, unless an exemption is obtained.

Restrictions on use of funds No.

Capital Transactions

Controls on capital and money market instruments

On capital market securities

Shares or other securities of a participating nature

Purchase locally by nonresidents Prior approval is required.

Sale or issue locally by nonresidents Quantitative limits exist.

Purchase abroad by residents	Yes.
On money market instruments	
Purchase abroad by residents	Yes.
On collective investment securities	
Purchase abroad by residents	Yes.
Controls on derivatives and other instruments	n.a.
Controls on credit operations	
Commercial credits	
By residents to nonresidents	Export credits are available for up to six months; in certain circumstances, the maturity can be extended by six months. Longer-term credits require exchange control approval.
To residents from nonresidents	These credits require exchange control approval.
Financial credits	
By residents to nonresidents	These credits require prior approval. However, wholly nonresident-owned subsidiaries may borrow locally up to 100% of the total shareholder's investment.
To residents from nonresidents	Prior approval is required to ensure that repayments and servicing of the loans do not disrupt the balance of payments and to ensure that the level of interest rates paid is reasonable in terms of prevailing international rates.
Guarantees, sureties, and financial backup facilities	
By residents to nonresidents	Guarantees of up to M 25,000 in respect of overdraft facilities for residents of Botswana, Malawi, Zambia, and Zimbabwe for domestic, farming, and business purposes may be approved.
Controls on direct investment	The rulings on applications for inward and outward capital transfers may depend on whether the applicant is a temporary resident foreign national, a nonresident, or a resident.
Outward direct investment	Outward direct investment is prohibited.
Inward direct investment	Inward capital transfers should be properly documented to facilitate the subsequent repatriation of interest, dividends, profits, and other income.
Controls on liquidation of direct investment	No.
Controls on real estate transactions	
Purchase abroad by residents	Prior approval is required.
Controls on personal capital movements	
Transfer of assets	Emigrants are allowed to transfer, through normal banking channels, up to M 300,000 of earnings on blocked assets.
Transfer abroad by emigrants	Yes.
Transfer of gambling and prize earnings	Prior approval is required.
Provisions specific to commercial banks and other credit institutions	
Borrowing abroad	Prior approval is required.
Maintenance of accounts abroad	Prior approval is required.
Lending to nonresidents (financial or commercial credits)	Authorized dealers may lend up to M 20,000, provided that the total available to the borrower from any source does not exceed this amount. Facilities in excess of such an amount require prior approval.

Provisions specific to institutional investors	n.a.
Other controls imposed by securities laws	n.a.

Changes During 1999

No significant changes occurred in the exchange and trade system.

LIBERIA

(Position as of March 31, 2000)

Status Under IMF Articles of Agreement

Article XIV	Yes.

Exchange Arrangement

Currency	The currency of Liberia is the Liberian dollar. There were two Liberian dollar notes, Liberty notes and J.J. Roberts notes. Between February and August 1999, in order to prepare for the introduction of a new Liberian currency, the authorities exchanged some J.J. Roberts dollar notes for Liberty dollar notes at the prevailing market exchange rate of two Liberty notes for one J.J. Roberts note. Effective March 29, 2000, a new multi-denominational Liberian dollar was introduced to replace the J.J. Roberts and the Liberty dollar notes.
Other legal tender	The U.S. dollar is also legal tender.
Exchange rate structure	Unitary.
Classification	
Independently floating	The Liberian dollar is market determined, and all foreign exchange dealers including banks are permitted to buy and sell currencies, including the U.S. dollar, at market-determined exchange rates.
Exchange tax	No.
Exchange subsidy	No.
Forward exchange market	No.

Arrangements for Payments and Receipts

Prescription of currency requirements	Import duties and customs fees are payable in U.S. dollars, and exporters must pay export taxes in U.S. dollars. Hotels are required to receive payments from foreign guests in foreign exchange.
Payment arrangements	No.
Administration of control	Export- and import-licensing regulations are administered by the Ministry of Commerce and Industry (MCI).
International security restrictions	No.
Payment arrears	
Official	Yes.
Private	Yes.
Controls on trade in gold (coins and/or bullion)	
Controls on external trade	Imports and exports of gold in any form are subject to licenses issued by the Ministry of Land, Mines, and Energy; import licenses are issued freely, but export licenses are granted restrictively.
Controls on exports and imports of banknotes	No.

Resident Accounts

Foreign exchange accounts permitted	Yes.
Held domestically	Yes.
Held abroad	Yes.
Accounts in domestic currency convertible into foreign currency	Yes.

Nonresident Accounts

Foreign exchange accounts permitted	Yes.
Domestic currency accounts	Yes.
Convertible into foreign currency	Yes.
Blocked accounts	No.

Imports and Import Payments

Foreign exchange budget	No.
Financing requirements for imports	No.
Documentation requirements for release of foreign exchange for imports	
Preshipment inspection	Preshipment inspection is required to ascertain the country of origin, the quality, the quantity, and the value of all goods to be shipped. Both final and intermediate goods are subject to inspection, except for imports with an f.o.b. value of less than US$3,000.
Import licenses and other nontariff measures	
Negative list	There is no general system of import control, but the importation of some items, including safety matches, electrode welding rods, and liquefied petroleum gas, is subject to licensing and quantitative restrictions. Licensing requirements are liberally enforced. Imports of arms, ammunition, and explosives require prior licenses. In addition, imports of certain goods (for example, narcotics, other than for medicinal purposes) are prohibited. Licenses to import inexpensive, widely consumed varieties of rice are issued to private distributors by the MCI. The importation of more expensive rice is not subject to official controls.
Import taxes and/or tariffs	The nominal average tariff rate is 11.7%.
State import monopoly	No.

Exports and Export Proceeds

Repatriation requirements	No.
Financing requirements	No.
Documentation requirements	n.r.
Export licenses	Licenses are generally issued freely, including those for agricultural products, to ensure certification of quality and origin.
Export taxes	An export tax of 5% is imposed on the f.o.b. value of rubber and other agricultural produce, payable in U.S. dollars.
Other export taxes	An export tax of 15% is levied on diamonds.

Payments for Invisible Transactions and Current Transfers

Controls on these transfers	There are no controls on these transfers; however, information on the payment of amortization of loans or depreciation of direct investment is not available.

Proceeds from Invisible Transactions and Current Transfers

Repatriation requirements	No.
Restrictions on use of funds	No.

Capital Transactions

Controls on capital and money market instruments	No exchange control requirements are imposed on capital receipts or payments by residents.
Controls on derivatives and other instruments	No.
Controls on credit operations	No.
Controls on direct investment	No.
Controls on liquidation of direct investment	No.
Controls on real estate transactions	No.
Controls on personal capital movements	No.
Provisions specific to commercial banks and other credit institutions	
Investment regulations	n.r.
Open foreign exchange position limits	n.r.
Provisions specific to institutional investors	No.
Other controls imposed by securities laws	No.

Changes During 1999

No significant changes occurred in the exchange and trade system.

Changes During 2000

Exchange arrangement	*March 29.* A new Liberian dollar was introduced to replace the J.J. Roberts and the Liberty dollars.

SOCIALIST PEOPLE'S LIBYAN ARAB JAMAHIRIYA

(Position as of December 31, 1999)

Status Under IMF Articles of Agreement

Article XIV	Yes.

Exchange Arrangement

Currency

The currency of Libya is the Libyan dinar.

Exchange rate structure

Dual

Effective February 14, 1999, the Central Bank of Libya (CBL) legalized the parallel exchange market and allowed commercial banks to sell foreign exchange for transactions related to personal imports, travel, medical treatment abroad, and hajj and omra at the parallel exchange rate. On February 13, 1999, this rate stood at LD 3.20 per $1.

Classification

Pegged exchange rate within horizontal bands

The Libyan dinar is pegged to the SDR at the rate of LD 1 per SDR 2.80. Margins of up to 77.5% are allowed around this fixed relationship. The dinar has been depreciated to the maximum extent permitted within those margins to LD 1 per SDR 1.577.

Exchange tax

Fees are levied on outward foreign exchange transfers for the purpose of financing the Great Man-Made River Project.

Exchange subsidy

No.

Forward exchange market

No.

Arrangements for Payments and Receipts

Prescription of currency requirements

All settlements with Israel are prohibited. Settlements with other countries are made in convertible currencies.

Payment arrangements

Bilateral payment arrangements

Operative

An agreement is maintained with Malta; outstanding balances are settled in convertible currencies every 90 days.

Administration of control

The CBL administers exchange control and has delegated some powers to authorized banks. The General People's Congress regulates policy on imports and exports, which is executed by the Secretariat of Planning, the Economy, and Trade (SOPET).

International security restrictions

No.

Payment arrears

No.

Controls on trade in gold (coins and/or bullion)

Controls on domestic ownership and/or trade

Residents may freely purchase, hold, and sell gold in any form other than bars.

Controls on external trade

The CBL imports processed and unprocessed gold and precious metals; it also sells gold bars to domestic goldsmiths for manufacture at prices announced from time to time. The gold must be processed before it may be sold to the public. Unworked gold is subject to an import duty of 15%.

Controls on exports and imports of banknotes

On exports

Domestic currency — Travelers may not take out Libyan currency.

Foreign currency — Notes up to the equivalent of LD 300 may be taken out in a calendar year as a basic travel allowance. Additional amounts may be granted in special circumstances. Pilgrims to Saudi Arabia are entitled to a special quota. Temporary residents may take out any foreign currency notes that they had previously brought in and declared to customs. Foreign exchange converted into Libyan dinars by visiting tourists may be reconverted upon departure, with the exception of a minimum local expenditure of $50 for each day spent in the country.

Effective February 14, 1999, residents and nonresidents are allowed to export foreign currency bought from commercial banks.

On imports

Domestic currency — Residents and nonresidents are not allowed to import Libyan currency.

Resident Accounts

Foreign exchange accounts permitted — Yes.

Held domestically — Individual residents are allowed to keep foreign currencies in domestic bank accounts and to transfer balances abroad without restriction. Exporters are allowed to retain foreign exchange earnings in a special account that may be used to finance imports of raw materials, spare parts, and machinery needed for export production. Effective August 25, 1999, no approval is required to open these accounts.

Held abroad — n.a.

Accounts in domestic currency convertible into foreign currency — n.a.

Nonresident Accounts

Foreign exchange accounts permitted — n.a.

Domestic currency accounts — Nonresidents who are gainfully employed in the country are permitted to open these accounts, which may be credited with their legitimate earnings. All other credits to nonresident accounts require the prior approval of the CBL.

Funds brought in by nonresident contractors undertaking contracts in their own names must be kept with an authorized bank. Payments received by contractors in respect of their contracts may also be credited to these accounts. Remittances from these accounts are subject to the prior approval of the CBL after submission of the prescribed evidence, but, in general, remittances are permitted up to the net-of-tax amount specified in the contract.

Convertible into foreign currency — These accounts may be converted, but approval is required.

Blocked accounts — Nonresident-owned capital that is not permitted to be transferred abroad is credited to blocked accounts. With the approval of the CBL, funds in blocked accounts (with certain exceptions) may be used for expenditures in Libya, up to LD 500 a year, to cover the cost of visits by the owner of the funds or a close relative; for payment of legal fees and taxes; for remittances to the owner of the funds in his or her country of permanent residence (up to LD 1,000 in a calendar year); and for remittances in cases of hardship. When the funds have been in a blocked account for five years, they qualify, upon payment of due taxes, for remittance in full to the owner in his or her country of permanent residence. The blocked accounts of persons (with certain exceptions) who have left the country permanently are being released in installments.

Imports and Import Payments

Foreign exchange budget	Yes.
Financing requirements for imports	
Advance import deposits	Authorized banks may not open an LC without an advance import deposit equal to at least 20% of the value of the import.
Documentation requirements for release of foreign exchange for imports	
Letters of credit	Before an LC is established, a marine insurance policy from a local insurance company must be submitted.
Import licenses used as exchange licenses	Exchange permits required for imports are readily granted by the authorized banks following central bank approval, provided that a firm contract exists and an import license has been obtained from the SOPET.
Import licenses and other nontariff measures	Imports undertaken by state-owned enterprises do not require licenses if they are authorized within the annual commodity budget; other imports are subject to licensing. Resident firms undertaking development projects may import needed items not included in the annual commodity budget if the items are not available locally. Imports by nonresidents, however, must be financed with foreign exchange resources from abroad. With the exception of strategic goods (i.e., nine essential food items, medicines, insecticides, petroleum products, tobacco, and gold) retained by public corporations, all other goods may be imported by either public or private entities within the provisions of the annual commodity budget.
Negative list	Imports of mineral water, fruit juices, instant tea, certain types of coffee, green vegetables, poultry, preserved meats and vegetables, alcoholic beverages, peanuts, oriental rugs, soaps, envelopes, crystal chandeliers, toy guns, luxury cars, and furs are prohibited.
Other nontariff measures	All imports from Israel are prohibited. Importers are required to deal directly with producers abroad and not through intermediaries.
Import taxes and/or tariffs	Imports are subject to customs duties and surcharges, the latter being 10% of the applicable customs duties. All products from Arab countries are exempt from customs duties, provided domestic value added is at least 40%.
State import monopoly	A state-owned company controlled by the CBL has a monopoly over the importation of gold and precious metals.

Exports and Export Proceeds

Repatriation requirements	All proceeds must be repatriated within six months of shipment.
Surrender requirements	Exporters are allowed to retain up to 40% of nonhydrocarbon earnings.
Financing requirements	n.a.
Documentation requirements	
Letters of credit	All exports require the opening of LCs.
Export licenses	In general, exporters do not need export licenses but must register with the Export Promotion Council and supply on a regular basis the relevant documentation on their exports. Exports of nonmonetary gold (other than for processing abroad), scrap metals, eggs, chicken, fish, olive oil, paint, tires, steel, and tractors are prohibited. Exports or reexports of wheat, wheat flour, crushed wheat, barley, rice, tea, sugar, tomato paste, and macaroni, which are subsidized commodities, are prohibited. All exports to Israel are prohibited.
Without quotas	Export licenses are required for raw wool, hides and skins, and agricultural products.
Export taxes	n.a.

Payments for Invisible Transactions and Current Transfers

Controls on these transfers	Payments for invisibles related to authorized imports are not restricted. All other payments for invisibles, as well as payments in excess of the approval authority delegated to the banks, require the prior approval of the CBL.
Investment-related payments	Profits generated by foreign capital invested in projects deemed to contribute to the economic development of the country may be transferred freely to the country of origin, provided that the paid-up capital is not less than the equivalent of LD 200,000 and that at least 51% of the shares are held by foreign nationals. Information is not available on the payment of amortization of loans or depreciation of direct investments.
Payments for travel	Foreign exchange allocations for travel were suspended in 1992. Effective February 14, 1999, residents are allowed to purchase foreign exchange for tourism from authorized banks without limits.
Prior approval	Yes.
Foreign workers' wages	
Prior approval	Nonresidents employed by the state, by state-owned enterprises, and by foreign companies may remit (1) up to 50% of their net salaries each month if their contracts do not specify that lodging, board, or both will be made available free of charge by the employer; or (2) up to 75% of their net salaries if their contracts specify that the employer will provide both lodging and board free of charge at work sites in remote areas. Staff of UN agencies, embassies, consulates, and medical institutions are exempt from these regulations.
Quantitative limits	Yes.
Other payments	
Prior approval	Yes.

Proceeds from Invisible Transactions and Current Transfers

Repatriation requirements	Yes.
Surrender requirements	All foreign exchange receipts must be surrendered.
Restrictions on use of funds	n.a.

Capital Transactions

Controls on capital and money market instruments	Purchase abroad of these instruments by residents requires approval.
On capital market securities	
Shares or other securities of a participating nature	
Purchase abroad by residents	Yes.
On money market instruments	
Purchase abroad by residents	Yes.
On collective investment securities	
Purchase abroad by residents	Yes.
Controls on derivatives and other instruments	n.a.
Controls on credit operations	
Commercial credits	Residents must obtain prior CBL approval to borrow funds abroad.

By residents to nonresidents	Yes.
To residents from nonresidents	Yes.
Financial credits	
To residents from nonresidents	Yes.
Guarantees, sureties, and financial backup facilities	
To residents from nonresidents	Yes.
Controls on direct investment	
Outward direct investment	Yes.
Inward direct investment	Foreign participation in industrial ventures set up after March 20, 1970, is permitted on a minority basis, but only if it leads to increased production in excess of local requirements, introduction of the latest technology, and cooperation with foreign firms in exporting the surplus production.
Controls on liquidation of direct investment	Foreign capital invested in projects deemed to contribute to the economic development of the country may be transferred freely to the country of origin, provided that the paid-up capital is not less than the equivalent of LD 200,000 and that at least 51% of the shares are held by foreign nationals.
Controls on real estate transactions	
Purchase abroad by residents	Residents must have prior permission from the Committee of the People's Bureau for Foreign Affairs and International Economic Cooperation to purchase real estate abroad.
Purchase locally by nonresidents	Yes.
Controls on personal capital movements	n.a.
Provisions specific to commercial banks and other credit institutions	n.a.
Provisions specific to institutional investors	n.a.
Other controls imposed by securities laws	n.a.

Changes During 1999

Exchange arrangement	*February 14.* A dual exchange rate market was introduced by legalizing the parallel market and allowing commercial banks to sell foreign exchange at that rate for authorized transactions.
Arrangements for payments and receipts	*February 14.* Residents and nonresidents were allowed to export foreign currency bought from commercial banks.
Resident accounts	*August 25.* No approval is required to open foreign exchange accounts.
Payments for invisible transactions and current transfers	*February 14.* Residents were allowed to purchase foreign exchange for tourism from banks without limit.

LITHUANIA

(Position as of December 31, 1999)

Status Under IMF Articles of Agreement

Article VIII	Date of acceptance: May 3, 1994.

Exchange Arrangement

Currency	The currency of Lithuania is the Lithuanian litas.
Exchange rate structure	Unitary.
Classification	
Currency board arrangement	The litas is pegged to the dollar at LTL 4 per $1 since April 1994 when the currency board arrangement was established.
Exchange tax	No.
Exchange subsidy	No.
Forward exchange market	Yes.

Arrangements for Payments and Receipts

Prescription of currency requirements	No.
Payment arrangements	
Bilateral payment arrangements	
Operative	Correspondent accounts exist between the Bank of Lithuania (BOL) and the central banks of the Baltic countries, Russia, and the other countries of the FSU. These accounts need not be used for payments originating after October 1992.
Inoperative	Ruble-denominated correspondent accounts maintained with the central banks of the Baltic countries, Russia, and the other countries of the FSU have been closed and are in the process of being settled.
Administration of control	Parliament has the legislative authority in foreign exchange and trade matters; it has adopted a banking law delegating to the BOL the authority to issue regulations governing foreign exchange transactions. All foreign exchange transactions must be effected through authorized banks licensed by the BOL. Authorized banks are allowed to transact among themselves, as well as with residents and nonresidents of Lithuania; the BOL may limit the types of transactions that may be conducted on a case-by-case basis.
International security restrictions	No.
Payment arrears	No.
Controls on trade in gold (coins and/or bullion)	No.
Controls on exports and imports of banknotes	
On exports	Natural or juridical persons, excluding the BOL or commercial banks, are not allowed to export more than LTL 500,000 in cash in domestic or foreign currency, except in cases where it is allowed by law or an international agreement.
Domestic currency	Yes.
Foreign currency	Yes.

Resident Accounts

Foreign exchange accounts permitted	Yes.
Held domestically	Yes.
Held abroad	Juridical persons need the permission of the BOL to hold accounts abroad.
Accounts in domestic currency convertible into foreign currency	Yes.

Nonresident Accounts

Foreign exchange accounts permitted	Yes.
Approval required	Approval is required if the legislation of the other country requires approval.
Domestic currency accounts	Yes.
Convertible into foreign currency	Yes.
Blocked accounts	n.a.

Imports and Import Payments

Foreign exchange budget	No.
Financing requirements for imports	No.
Documentation requirements for release of foreign exchange for imports	No.
Import licenses and other nontariff measures	There are no quantitative restrictions or licensing requirements on imports, except for health and national security reasons and as noted below. Certain food products, such as meat semiproducts, poultry, and fish, are subject to licensing.
	Certain agricultural goods and alcoholic beverages are subject to duties, and certain quantitative restrictions are used to control trade in strategic goods and technology to protect Lithuania's cultural heritage. Alcoholic beverages and tobacco may be imported only by traders registered with the government, but import quantities are unrestricted.
Import taxes and/or tariffs	A three-tier tariff structure exists consisting of (1) a "conventional" rate applied to countries granted MFN status; (2) a "preferential" rate applied to countries with which Lithuania has a foreign trade agreement; and (3) an "autonomous" rate that is usually 5% higher than the MFN rate and is applied to all other countries. Imports entering under a majority of tariff lines are duty free; and most other tariff lines carry duty rates of 20% or less; however, rates on agricultural products range as high as 87%. Some non–ad valorem duty rates remain in effect. On June 30, 1999, import tariffs on refined oil products from CIS countries were increased to 15% from 5%.
	A tax at the uniform rate of 0.01% is imposed on imports (and exports) for the sole purpose of collecting statistical information on trade.
State import monopoly	No.

Exports and Export Proceeds

Repatriation requirements	No.
Financing requirements	No.
Documentation requirements	No.
Export licenses	There are license requirements governing trade in strategic goods and technology.

Without quotas	Yes.
With quotas	Yes.
Export taxes	A tax at the uniform rate 0.01% is imposed on exports. Taxes are applied to exports of raw hides, certain types of logs, glands and other organs for therapeutic purposes or for use in the preparation of pharmaceutical products, and feathers.
Other export taxes	Yes.

Payments for Invisible Transactions and Current Transfers

Controls on these transfers	No.

Proceeds from Invisible Transactions and Current Transfers

Repatriation requirements	No.
Restrictions on use of funds	No.

Capital Transactions

Controls on capital and money market instruments	No.
Controls on derivatives and other instruments	No.
Controls on credit operations	No.
Controls on direct investment	
Inward direct investment	There are no controls, except in fields that are subject to prohibition under the Law on Foreign Capital Investments: state defense, production and sale of narcotic substances, and lottery transactions. The law permits the state to sell shares to nonresidents, guarantees nondiscriminatory national treatment to foreign investors, and protects investments against nationalization and expropriation. The purchase of state-owned enterprises is subject to authorization from the Central Privatization Committee. One of the main conditions in this process is that the company must remain engaged in the same type of business for at least one year under the new ownership. While firms with 100% foreign capital ownership are allowed to operate in Lithuania, the government reserves the right to establish limits on foreign investment in Lithuanian enterprises. In joint ventures in the transportation and communication sectors, the domestic partner is required to hold the majority of shares. Wholly owned ventures in the alcoholic beverage or tobacco industries are prohibited. Enterprises with foreign investment must be insured by Lithuanian insurance companies, even if the company retains other insurance services outside Lithuania.
Controls on liquidation of direct investment	No.
Controls on real estate transactions	
Purchase locally by nonresidents	The ownership of land by nonresidents in Lithuania is prohibited, but lease contracts with limits up to two hectares of land in Vilnius and ten hectares outside the capital are permitted for up to 99 years and may be renewed thereafter.
Sale locally by nonresidents	Yes.
Controls on personal capital movements	n.a.

Provisions specific to commercial banks and other credit institutions

Maintenance of accounts abroad

Resident banks or other credit institutions must inform the BOL about their accounts with foreign banks.

Purchase of locally issued securities denominated in foreign exchange

Locally issued securities must be denominated in the national currency.

Differential treatment of deposit accounts held by nonresidents

Reserve requirements

There are reserve requirements on nonresidents' deposits and on commercial banks' borrowing from foreign financial institutions.

Open foreign exchange position limits

Banks' overall open positions may not exceed 30% of their capital, and the open position in individual currencies may not exceed 20% of the banks' capital.

Provisions specific to institutional investors

No.

Other controls imposed by securities laws

No.

Changes During 1999

No significant changes occurred in the exchange and trade system.

LUXEMBOURG

(Position as of December 31, 1999)

Status Under IMF Articles of Agreement

Article VIII   Date of acceptance: February 15, 1961.

Exchange Arrangement

Currency

As of January 1, 1999, the currency of Luxembourg is the euro. In cash transactions, however, the legal tender remains the Luxembourg franc and the Belgian franc until 2002, when euro banknotes and coins will be issued.

Other legal tender

The Belgian franc also circulates as legal tender.

Exchange rate structure

Unitary.

Classification

Exchange arrangement with no separate legal tender

Luxembourg participates in a currency union (EMU) comprising 11 members of the EU: Austria, Belgium, Finland, France, Germany, Ireland, Italy, Luxembourg, the Netherlands, Portugal, and Spain. Internal conversion rates in respect to the national currencies of EMU participants were fixed to the euro on January 1, 1999, whereas the external exchange rate of the euro is market determined. The conversion rate between the euro and the Luxembourg franc was set at Lux F 40.3399 per €1. The ECB has the right to intervene to smooth out fluctuations in external exchange rates.

Exchange tax   No.

Exchange subsidy   No.

Forward exchange market   Yes.

Arrangements for Payments and Receipts

Prescription of currency requirements   No.

Payment arrangements   No.

Administration of control   No.

International security restrictions

Certain restrictions are imposed on the making of payments and transfers for current international transactions in respect of the Federal Republic of Yugoslavia (Serbia/Montenegro), Iraq, Libya, and the UNITA movement in Angola.

In accordance with Executive Board Decision No. 144-(52/51)   Yes.

In accordance with UN sanctions   Yes.

Payment arrears   No.

Controls on trade in gold (coins and/or bullion)   No.

Controls on exports and imports of banknotes   No.

Resident Accounts

Foreign exchange accounts permitted   Yes.

Held domestically	Yes.
Held abroad	Yes.
Accounts in domestic currency convertible into foreign currency	Yes.

Nonresident Accounts

Foreign exchange accounts permitted	Yes.
Domestic currency accounts	Yes.
Convertible into foreign currency	Yes.
Blocked accounts	These are accounts affected by international security restrictions.

Imports and Import Payments

Foreign exchange budget	No.
Financing requirements for imports	No.
Documentation requirements for release of foreign exchange for imports	No.
Import licenses and other nontariff measures	
Positive list	Payments for imports may be made freely. Individual licenses are required for certain specified imports from all countries (most imports do not require an import license when imported from another EU member country), including many textile and steel products, diamonds, weapons, and nontextile products from China. All other commodities are free of license requirements.
Licenses with quotas	Along with EU countries, Luxembourg applies quotas on a number of textile products from non-EU countries in the framework of the MFA. It also applies a system of quotas on some steel products originating in Kazakhstan, Russia, and Ukraine. A double-checking system (without quotas) is applied to imports of some steel products from Bulgaria, the Czech Republic, the former Yugoslav Republic of Macedonia, Poland, Romania, and the Slovak Republic. Quotas are applied on a number of products from China, such as ceramics, porcelain, and shoes.
Import taxes and/or tariffs	Luxembourg applies the Common Import Regime of the EU to imports of most other agricultural and livestock products from non-EU countries.
State import monopoly	No.

Exports and Export Proceeds

Repatriation requirements	No.
Financing requirements	No.
Documentation requirements	No.
Export licenses	Export licenses are required for a few products, mostly of a strategic character, such as arms and dual-use goods, and diamonds. Export licenses are also required for exports to countries under UN embargo.
Without quotas	Yes.
Export taxes	No.

Payments for Invisible Transactions and Current Transfers

Controls on these transfers	No.

Proceeds from Invisible Transactions and Current Transfers

Repatriation requirements	No.
Restrictions on use of funds	No.

Capital Transactions

Controls on capital and money market instruments	No.
Controls on derivatives and other instruments	No.
Controls on credit operations	No.
Controls on direct investment	No.
Controls on liquidation of direct investment	No.
Controls on real estate transactions	No.
Controls on personal capital movements	No.
Provisions specific to commercial banks and other credit institutions	No.
Provisions specific to institutional investors	
Currency-matching regulations on assets/liabilities composition	These are applicable only to insurance undertakings.
Other controls imposed by securities laws	No.

Changes During 1999

Exchange arrangement	*January 1.* The currency of Luxembourg became the euro. The conversion rate between the euro and the Luxembourg franc was set irrevocably at Lux F 40.3399 per €1.

FORMER YUGOSLAV REPUBLIC OF MACEDONIA

(Position as of December 31, 1999)

Status Under IMF Articles of Agreement

Article VIII   Date of acceptance: June 19, 1998.

Exchange Arrangement

Currency

The currency of the former Yugoslav Republic of Macedonia is the Macedonian denar.

Exchange rate structure

Unitary.

Classification

Conventional pegged arrangement

The exchange market operates at two levels: wholesale (enterprises, commercial banks, and the National Bank of the Republic of Macedonia (NBRM)) and retail (households). The NBRM participates in the wholesale market to maintain the value of the denar against the deutsche mark at a level that would meet balance of payments objectives. Buying and selling rates for transactions between authorized banks and enterprises have to be reported to the NBRM, which calculates an average daily rate. Based on this rate and cross rates on the international market, the NBRM publishes rates for 22 currencies. The NBRM deals at the published midpoint rates plus or minus a margin of 0.3%.

The retail level of the foreign exchange market consists of foreign exchange bureaus, which are owned and operated by banks, enterprises, and natural persons. Foreign exchange bureaus may hold foreign exchange positions equivalent to 100% of the net foreign exchange purchases in the preceding 10 days.

Exchange tax

No.

Exchange subsidy

No.

Forward exchange market

Forward foreign exchange contracts for trade transactions are permitted.

Official cover of forward operations

The NBRM may conclude forward foreign exchange contracts.

Arrangements for Payments and Receipts

Prescription of currency requirements

No.

Payment arrangements

No.

Administration of control

The parliament has the authority to legislate laws governing foreign exchange and trade transactions. Certain changes in the trade regime may be made through government regulations. The NBRM is authorized to control foreign exchange operations of banks and other financial institutions. The MOF is authorized to control foreign exchange and trade operations and the credit relations of enterprises abroad, as well as other forms of business activities abroad, encompassing all enterprises that operate internationally. Certain foreign exchange control activities have been delegated to the participants in the foreign exchange market and the customs office. The Ministry of Foreign Relations administers the Commercial Companies Act.

International security restrictions

No.

Payment arrears

Private

Yes.

Controls on trade in gold (coins and/or bullion)

Controls on domestic ownership and/or trade

Gold producers must report all production, including quality and quantity sold. Processors are also required to report all quantities bought and processed.

Controls on external trade

The importation and exportation of gold require NBRM approval.

Controls on exports and imports of banknotes

On exports

Domestic currency

A maximum of MDen 5,000 in denomimations of 100-, 50-, 20-, and 10-denar banknotes may be exported.

Foreign currency

Up to DM 1,000 for private domestic travelers; and for business travelers, up to the amount stated on the bank order form. Nonresidents may export foreign currency up to the amount declared upon arrival in the country.

On imports

Domestic currency

The same limits apply as for exports.

Foreign currency

Foreign travelers must declare foreign currency over DM 300.

Resident Accounts

Foreign exchange accounts permitted

Foreign exchange deposits made after April 26, 1991, are freely disposable, i.e., they can be withdrawn in foreign currency or converted into denars.

Held domestically

Yes.

Held abroad

Enterprises with foreign operations may hold these accounts, but approval is required.

Accounts in domestic currency convertible into foreign currency

No.

Nonresident Accounts

Foreign exchange accounts permitted

These accounts may be credited freely with foreign exchange and debited for payments abroad or for conversion into denars.

Domestic currency accounts

Yes.

Convertible into foreign currency

Yes.

Blocked accounts

No.

Imports and Import Payments

Foreign exchange budget

No.

Financing requirements for imports

No.

Documentation requirements for release of foreign exchange for imports

A contract, invoice, or customs declaration should be submitted to the commercial bank effecting the payment. Generally, payments for imports are permitted after the importation of goods. Only imports of equipment and spare parts, some essential consumer goods, goods financed by foreign loans, and raw materials may be paid in advance.

Import licenses and other nontariff measures

Imports of certain goods, such as weapons and medicines, are subject to licensing requirements for security or public health reasons.

Import taxes and/or tariffs

Customs duties on most items range up to 35%; rates on raw materials range from zero to 8%; machinery and equipment from 5% to 20%; consumer goods from 15% to 35%; and agricultural goods from 20% to 60%. The number of bands was reduced to sixteen and the average rate to about 15%. There is also a 1% documentation fee.

State import monopoly

No.

Exports and Export Proceeds

Repatriation requirements

All export proceeds from transactions that are not based on commodity credits have to be transferred by the exporters into the country within 90 days from the day the exportation was made.

Surrender requirements

Exporters must inform their bank about the origin of their proceeds and how to dispose of them within four business days of transferring the proceeds into the country. Within 90 days of the transfer, exporters may retain the foreign exchange and use it for payments abroad or sell them on the foreign exchange market. After this period, selling the foreign exchange on the market is obligatory.

Financing requirements

No.

Documentation requirements

No.

Export licenses

Generally, exports are liberal. However, in some exceptional cases, the export of certain goods requires a license from the appropriate authorities.

Without quotas

Yes.

Export taxes

Other export taxes

A 0.1% fee is levied for export promotion by the Ministry of Trade.

Payments for Invisible Transactions and Current Transfers

Controls on these transfers

Personal payments

The transfer of pensions is permitted only on the basis of ratified international agreement.

Prior approval

Yes.

Proceeds from Invisible Transactions and Current Transfers

Repatriation requirements

Proceeds from invisibles are subject to the same regulations as those applicable to merchandise exports.

Surrender requirements

Yes.

Restrictions on use of funds

No.

Capital Transactions

Controls on capital and money market instruments

Outward portfolio investment by resident natural and juridical persons is not permitted.

On capital market securities

Shares or other securities of a participating nature

Purchase locally by nonresidents

According to the Commercial Companies Act, nonresidents may acquire shares in domestic companies on the same terms as residents, provided that they obtain approval from the Ministry of Foreign Affairs, if the majority of shares are in question; otherwise, they should only register the investment.

Sale or issue locally by nonresidents

According to the Securities Act, nonresidents may issue securities in the former Yugoslav Republic of Macedonia on the basis of reciprocity and approval of the Commission on Securities.

Purchase abroad by residents	According to the Foreign Trade Act, only foreign direct investments are permitted by the Ministry of Trade. The transfer of foreign exchange requires the approval of the NBRM.
Sale or issue abroad by residents	Yes.
Bonds or other debt securities	
Purchase locally by nonresidents	Yes.
Sale or issue locally by nonresidents	The same conditions apply as for shares or other securities of a participatory nature.
Purchase abroad by residents	The same conditions apply as for shares or other securities of a participatory nature.
Sale or issue abroad by residents	Yes.
On money market instruments	
Purchase locally by nonresidents	Yes.
Sale or issue locally by nonresidents	The same conditions apply as for shares or other securities of a participatory nature.
Purchase abroad by residents	The same conditions apply as for shares or other securities of a participatory nature.
Sale or issue abroad by residents	Yes.
On collective investment securities	n.r.
Controls on derivatives and other instruments	n.r.
Controls on credit operations	
Commercial credits	Short-term commercial banks' credit lines with a maturity exceeding 90 days should be registered.
By residents to nonresidents	Credits for the export of goods and services exceeding 90 days should be registered.
To residents from nonresidents	Credits for the import of goods for consumption are not permitted. Other credits exceeding 180 days should be registered.
Financial credits	
By residents to nonresidents	Financial credits are permitted only if export of goods and services is promoted.
To residents from nonresidents	Private financial credits are permitted only for export-oriented projects.
Guarantees, sureties, and financial backup facilities	
By residents to nonresidents	Only commercial banks may effect these transactions, which should be registered with the NBRM.
Controls on direct investment	
Outward direct investment	Investments require approval from, and registration with, the Ministry of Trade.
Inward direct investment	Nonresidents are allowed to invest in existing firms, establish their own firms, or establish joint ventures except in a few sectors (such as arms production). Imports of raw materials, spare parts, and equipment not produced domestically by joint-venture firms are exempt from customs duties if the foreign share in the investment is at least 20%. All foreign investment registered with the Ministry of Trade is protected from nationalization.
Controls on liquidation of direct investment	No.
Controls on real estate transactions	There are controls on all these transactions.
Controls on personal capital movements	
Loans	According to the Foreign Credit Relation Act, natural persons are not permitted to engage in credit relations.
By residents to nonresidents	Yes.

To residents from nonresidents	Yes.
Gifts, endowments, inheritances, and legacies	Inheritances may be transferred on the basis of an agreement of reciprocity with the respective country.
By residents to nonresidents	Yes.
To residents from nonresidents	Yes.
Transfer of gambling and prize earnings	The transfer of proceeds from gambling is not permitted.

Provisions specific to commercial banks and other credit institutions

Borrowing abroad	Yes.
Maintenance of accounts abroad	Yes.
Lending to nonresidents (financial or commercial credits)	Yes.
Lending locally in foreign exchange	This lending is not permitted.
Differential treatment of deposit accounts in foreign exchange	
Reserve requirements	Nonresident deposits in denars are subject to requirements, but foreign exchange deposits are not. The effective reserve requirements on foreign currency deposits by individuals are 70% on sight deposits, 60% on one-month deposits, 50% on three-month deposits, 40% on six-month deposits, 30% on one-year deposits, and 20% on longer-term deposits.
Liquid asset requirements	Yes.
Credit controls	Credit controls apply only to domestic currency credits.
Differential treatment of deposit accounts held by nonresidents	
Liquid asset requirements	Yes.
Open foreign exchange position limits	Yes.
Provisions specific to institutional investors	n.r.
Other controls imposed by securities laws	No.

Changes During 1999

No significant changes occurred in the exchange and trade system.

MADAGASCAR

(Position as of December 31, 1999)

Status Under IMF Articles of Agreement

Article VIII	Date of acceptance: September 18, 1996.

Exchange Arrangement

Currency	The currency of Madagascar is the Malagasy franc.
Exchange rate structure	Unitary.
Classification	
Independently floating	The exchange rate is determined freely in the official interbank market. The euro, introduced on January 1, 1999, is the only currency quoted on this market, and the exchange rates of other currencies are determined on the basis of the cross-rate relationships of the currencies concerned in the Paris exchange market.
Exchange tax	No.
Exchange subsidy	No.
Forward exchange market	There are limited arrangements for forward cover against exchange rate risk. Importers may buy foreign currency 120 days prior to settlement from their bank.

Arrangements for Payments and Receipts

Prescription of currency requirements	No.
Payment arrangements	
Bilateral payment arrangements	
Inoperative	There is an arrangement with Mauritius that has been inoperative for some time.
Barter agreements and open accounts	Regulations prohibit barter trade.
Administration of control	Exchange control is administered by the Exchange Operations Monitoring Unit of the General Directorate of the Treasury, which also supervises borrowing and lending abroad by residents, and the issue, sale, or introduction of foreign securities in Madagascar. Approval authority for exchange control has been delegated to authorized intermediaries, except for capital operations, and all exchange transactions relating to foreign countries must be effected through such intermediaries.
International security restrictions	n.a.
Payment arrears	
Official	Yes.
Private	Yes.
Controls on trade in gold (coins and/or bullion)	
Controls on domestic ownership and/or trade	Approved collectors acting in their own name and on their own account may purchase gold within the country from holders of valid gold mining titles, from authorized holders of gold washing rights from the Gold Board, and from agencies for approved collectors.
Controls on external trade	Imports and exports of gold require prior authorization from the Ministry of Commerce after review by the Directorate of Energy and Mines. Exempt from this requirement are (1) imports and exports by or on behalf of the Central Bank of Madagascar (CBM), and (2) imports and exports of manufactured articles containing a minor quantity of gold (such

as gold-filled or gold-plated articles). Travelers are authorized to export 50 grams or 250 carats of gold jewelry or gold articles a person, and 50 grams or 250 carats of numismatic items a person. Imports of gold, whether licensed or exempt from license, are subject to customs declaration. Holders of a valid gold mining title or a gold washing permit or rights thereto are free to sell the gold recovered to any approved collector. However, Malagasy authorities, represented by the CBM or its agents, have first rights to purchase gold produced in the country. The Gold Board and agencies authorized by the Ministry of Mining may export gold in all its forms. Jewelers, goldsmiths, and private sector professionals who use gold may export it only in worked form, subject to the decision of the Minister of Mining.

Controls on exports and imports of banknotes

On exports

Domestic currency

Resident and nonresident travelers may take abroad up to FMG 25,000 in Malagasy banknotes.

Foreign currency

Residents and nonresident travelers may take abroad any amount of foreign currency, but a declaration is required if the amount is more than the equivalent of F 50,000.

On imports

Domestic currency

Residents and nonresidents may bring in up to FMG 25,000.

Foreign currency

Resident and nonresident travelers may bring in any amount of foreign currency, but a declaration is required if the amount is equal to F 50,000 or more.

Resident Accounts

Foreign exchange accounts permitted

Yes.

Held domestically

Residents may freely open foreign currency accounts with local commercial banks. Only transfers from abroad or from another foreign currency account, as well as foreign banknotes or traveler's and bank checks may be deposited in these accounts without justification. These accounts may be freely debited either for conversion into Malagasy francs through a sale on the interbank market or by transfer to a foreign account in Madagascar or abroad. Conversion into foreign banknotes is allowed only within the limits stipulated under the applicable foreign exchange control regulation.

Held abroad

MOF authorization is required for opening foreign exchange accounts abroad in foreign banks.

Accounts in domestic currency convertible into foreign currency

No.

Nonresident Accounts

Foreign exchange accounts permitted

Nonresidents are treated the same as residents for the purpose of opening these accounts.

Domestic currency accounts

Transactions between residents and enterprises in the free trade zone are conducted either through the enterprises' special accounts in Malagasy francs or through their foreign exchange accounts.

Blocked accounts

No.

Imports and Import Payments

Foreign exchange budget

No.

Financing requirements for imports

No.

Documentation requirements for release of foreign exchange for imports

Domiciliation requirements	The requirement applies to all imports.
Preshipment inspection	Yes.
Letters of credit	Yes.

Import licenses and other nontariff measures — There is a shortlist of imports subject to administrative control primarily for health and security reasons.

Import taxes and/or tariffs — Effective February 27, 1999, the government introduced import duty rates of 5% and 25%, in addition to the four-rate system of 10%, 15%, 20%, and 30%, and shifted many goods into lower-rate categories, which was in line with the objective of moving toward the three-rate structure (5%, 15%, and 25%) envisaged under the Cross-Border Initiative for Eastern and Southern Africa. Some imports, mostly luxury goods, are subject to excise import taxes of 10% to 120%. A pretax of 3% to 5%, deductible from the corporate tax, is paid on all imports. At end-May 1999, the government introduced a new system of controls on tax privileges for free zone enterprises.

State import monopoly — Petroleum products are imported by a state monopoly.

Exports and Export Proceeds

Repatriation requirements — All export proceeds should be repatriated within 90 days of the shipment date.

Financing requirements — No.

Documentation requirements

Letters of credit	All exports require either a COD or settlement against delivery of documents, excluding free deliveries.
Domiciliation	The requirement applies for exports exceeding FMG 1 million.
Preshipment inspection	Yes.

Export licenses — No.

Export taxes — No.

Payments for Invisible Transactions and Current Transfers

Controls on these transfers — No.

Proceeds from Invisible Transactions and Current Transfers

Repatriation requirements — Proceeds must be repatriated within 30 days of the due date.

Restrictions on use of funds — n.a.

Capital Transactions

Controls on capital and money market instruments — Capital movements between Madagascar and foreign countries, and between residents and nonresidents are subject to prior authorization from the MOF. There are no capital market regulations, due to the absence of a capital market.

On capital market securities

*Shares or other securities of a
participating nature*

    Purchase locally by nonresidents | Yes.

    Sale or issue locally by nonresidents | Exempt from authorization are operations in connection with shares similar to securities whose issuing or offering for sale in Madagascar has previously been authorized.

    Purchase abroad by residents | Yes.

    Sale or issue abroad by residents | Yes.

Bonds or other debt securities | n.r.

On money market instruments | n.r.

On collective investment securities | n.r.

**Controls on derivatives and other
instruments** | n.r.

Controls on credit operations

Commercial credits

    By residents to nonresidents | These operations currently do not take place.

    To residents from nonresidents | Credits for export prefinancing operations are permitted.

Financial credits

    To residents from nonresidents | Borrowing abroad by natural or juridical persons, whether public or private, requires prior authorization from the MOF, although loans contracted by authorized banks or credit institutions with special legal status are exempt. Enterprises in the free trade zone are permitted to contract and service foreign loans freely, and interest and amortization payments on foreign loans contracted directly by these companies are not restricted.

Controls on direct investment

Outward direct investment | Investments abroad by Malagasy nationals, including those made through foreign companies directly or indirectly controlled by persons resident in Madagascar and those made by overseas branches or subsidiaries of companies located in Madagascar, are subject to prior authorization from the MOF.

Inward direct investment | Investments, including those made by companies in Madagascar that are directly or indirectly under foreign control and those made by branches or subsidiaries of foreign companies in Madagascar, as well as corresponding transfers, may be freely conducted within Madagascar without authorization or investment approval.

**Controls on liquidation of direct
investment** | The total or partial liquidation of these investments, whether Malagasy investments abroad or foreign investments in Madagascar, must be reported to the MOF. Proceeds from the liquidation of foreign investment may be repatriated with the prior authorization of the MOF.

Controls on real estate transactions

Purchase abroad by residents | Prohibited, unless otherwise approved by the MOF.

Sale locally by nonresidents | The transfer of proceeds of sales is subject to prior authorization by the MOF.

**Controls on personal capital
movements** | n.a.

**Provisions specific to commercial
banks and other credit institutions** | Controls are implemented through bank supervision.

**Provisions specific to institutional
investors** | n.a.

**Other controls imposed by securities
laws** | n.a.

Changes During 1999

Exchange arrangement	*January 1.* The euro became the only currency to be traded in the official interbank market.
Imports and import payments	*February 27.* Additional import duty rates of 5% and 25% were introduced.
	May 31. A new system of controls on tax privileges for free zone enterprises was introduced.

MALAWI

(Position as of December 31, 1999)

Status Under IMF Articles of Agreement

Article VIII   Date of acceptance: December 7, 1995.

Exchange Arrangement

Currency

The currency of Malawi is the Malawi kwacha.

Exchange rate structure

Unitary.

Classification

Managed floating with no pre-announced path for the exchange rate

The exchange rate of the Malawi kwacha is managed in a flexible manner, with an intervention policy limited to smoothing out fluctuations of the rate and with consideration for international reserve targets. Exchange market participants are free to quote their own central rate, with the condition that the margin between the buying and selling rates should not exceed 2%. The Reserve Bank of Malawi (RBM) quotes reference rates, which are distributed to authorized dealer banks (ADBs). Foreign exchange bureaus are authorized to conduct spot transactions with the general public on the basis of exchange rates negotiated with their clients.

Exchange tax   No.

Exchange subsidy   No.

Forward exchange market   No.

Arrangements for Payments and Receipts

Prescription of currency requirements

Payments to and receipts from nonresidents may be made in any convertible currency traded in Malawi or in Malawi kwacha through nonresident accounts.

Payment arrangements

Clearing agreements

Malawi participates in the COMESA Clearing House Arrangement.

Administration of control

Exchange control is administered by the RBM under the authority of the MOF.

International security restrictions   No.

Payment arrears   No.

Controls on trade in gold (coins and/or bullion)

Controls on domestic ownership and/or trade

Residents may purchase, hold, and sell gold coins for numismatic purposes. Only the monetary authorities may hold or acquire gold at home or abroad in any form other than jewelry.

Controls on external trade

Only the monetary authorities may conduct external trade in gold. Imports of gold in any form other than jewelry require licenses issued by the Ministry of Commerce and Industry (MCI) in consultation with the MOF; such licenses are not normally granted except for imports by or on behalf of the monetary authorities and industrial users.

Controls on exports and imports of banknotes

Malawi and Mozambican monetary authorities are working toward the formalization of a repatriation agreement.

On exports

Domestic currency

Up to MK 3,000 may be exported.

Foreign currency

Approval for exports is granted, subject to verification of need.

On imports

Domestic currency Up to MK 3,000 may be imported.

Resident Accounts

Foreign exchange accounts permitted Yes.

Held domestically Residents receiving foreign exchange regularly from abroad may maintain foreign currency accounts (FCDAs). Balances in FCDAs may be used to make foreign payments and transfers, provided exchange control regulations are satisfied.

Held abroad No.

Accounts in domestic currency convertible into foreign currency No.

Nonresident Accounts

Foreign exchange accounts permitted These accounts are permitted, but approval is required.

Domestic currency accounts These accounts may be credited with the proceeds from sales of any convertible currency, with authorized payments in Malawi kwacha from abroad, and with transfers from other nonresident accounts. These accounts may also be debited to make payments to residents of Malawi for any purpose, transfer freely to other nonresident accounts, and make payments to account holders temporarily residing in Malawi.

Convertible into foreign currency These accounts may be converted, but prior approval is required.

Blocked accounts Credits to and debits from these accounts require prior authorization, and authorization is normally given for balances to be invested in an approved manner. Interest earned on balances may be transferred to the account holder's country of residence.

Imports and Import Payments

Foreign exchange budget No.

Financing requirements for imports Importers are free to choose any method of payment, and imports may be paid for in Malawi kwacha to an appropriate local nonresident account or in any convertible currency. When imports arrive in the country and payment is due, the importer must submit to an ADB application for foreign exchange. Such applications must be accompanied by relevant importation, customs, and preshipment inspection documents.

Advance payment requirements Prepayment for imports is not allowed. Importers are encouraged to use other modes of payment (e.g., LCs).

Advance import deposits Advance import deposits are not required by law; however, commercial banks do require them as a banking practice and depending on the mode of payment (e.g., LCs).

Documentation requirements for release of foreign exchange for imports

Preshipment inspection A clean-report-of-findings certificate is required. All imports into Malawi in the amount of $2,000 (f.o.b.) or its equivalent and above are subject to preshipment inspection.

Import licenses and other nontariff measures

Negative list Imports of clothing and uniforms designed for military or police use, radioactive substances, mist nets for the capture of wild birds, wild animals, live fish, compound products suitable only for use as animal foodstuffs, eggs of domestic or wild birds, live poultry (including day-old chicks), meat dieldrin, aidrin, and kitchen and table salt require specific licenses from the MCI. Specific import licenses are usually issued within one week of application and are normally valid for six months.

Open general licenses	Most imports are subject to the OGL, including imports from Commonwealth countries and from countries that are members of the WTO.
Other nontariff measures	Yes.
Import taxes and/or tariffs	Customs tariffs are ad valorem and range from up to 35% of c.i.f. value, with a weighted average of about 15%. Custom tariffs on all items with MFN status range from zero to 30%. Tariffs on items from the COMESA region range from zero to 13%. Selected government imports are exempt from customs tariffs. Imports are also subject to a surtax ranging up to 20%.
State import monopoly	No.

Exports and Export Proceeds

Repatriation requirements	Yes.
Surrender requirements	ADBs are required to convert 60% of foreign exchange received from exports immediately upon receipt at the prevailing buying exchange rate, and credit the Malawi kwacha proceeds to the customer's account. The remaining 40% may be credited to the exporter's foreign currency account. There are no restrictions on the time period over which such balances may be held. This 60% conversion is also applied to dollar proceeds from the tobacco and tea auctions. In the case of tobacco proceeds, the conversion is 100% until the seller has fully repaid his overdraft with his bankers.
Financing requirements	Yes.
Documentation requirements	Exporters are required to complete form CD1s (exports from Malawi).
Export licenses	
Without quotas	Yes.
Export taxes	No.

Payments for Invisible Transactions and Current Transfers

Controls on these transfers	Commercial banks are authorized to provide foreign exchange, without reference to the exchange control authorities, for all current invisible payments, but certain invisible payments, such as private and business travel, and medical treatment are subject to indicative limits.
Investment-related payments	These payments are allowed, provided the investment and the foreign loan are approved and registered by the RBM.
Payments for travel	
Quantitative limits	Yes.
Indicative limits/bona fide test	The limits are $3,000 a trip for tourist travel and $5,000 a trip for business travel. Foreign exchange in excess of these limits is granted upon proof of need. Subsequent issues of foreign exchange to the same individual with respect to private or business travel is granted upon proof of previous travel.
Personal payments	
Quantitative limits	ADBs may approve up to $1,000 for family maintenance and alimony payments. Limits are also applied for payments of medical costs, family maintenance, and alimony.
Indicative limits/bona fide test	Yes.
Foreign workers' wages	
Quantitative limits	The limit is two-thirds of current net earnings.

Credit card use abroad

Prior approval — Yes.

Proceeds from Invisible Transactions and Current Transfers

Repatriation requirements — Yes.

Surrender requirements — Sixty percent of total proceeds may be converted into local currency upon receipt, and the balance may be held in FCDAs.

Restrictions on use of funds — Funds can only be used in accordance with exchange control regulations.

Capital Transactions

Controls on capital and money market instruments — Inward transfers of non–debt creating capital are not restricted. Outward transfers of capital are controlled mainly for residents.

On capital market securities

Shares or other securities of a participating nature

   Purchase abroad by residents — Specific exchange control approval is required.

Bonds or other debt securities

   Purchase abroad by residents — Specific exchange control approval is required.

On money market instruments

Purchase abroad by residents — Yes.

On collective investment securities

Purchase abroad by residents — Yes.

Controls on derivatives and other instruments

Purchase abroad by residents — Yes.

Controls on credit operations — Borrowing abroad by residents requires prior exchange control approval, which is normally granted provided that the terms of repayment, including the servicing costs, are acceptable.

Commercial credits

To residents from nonresidents — Yes.

Financial credits

To residents from nonresidents — Yes.

Guarantees, sureties, and financial backup facilities

To residents from nonresidents — Yes.

Controls on direct investment

Outward direct investment — Yes.

Controls on liquidation of direct investment — Repatriation of investments is permitted when the original investment was made with funds brought into the country.

Controls on real estate transactions

Purchase abroad by residents — Yes.

Controls on personal capital movements

Loans

   To residents from nonresidents   Borrowing abroad by residents requires prior exchange control approval, which is normally granted provided that the terms of repayment, including the servicing costs, are acceptable.

Gifts, endowments, inheritances, and legacies

   By residents to nonresidents   Yes.

Settlement of debts abroad by immigrants   Yes.

Transfer of assets

   Transfer abroad by emigrants   Yes.

Provisions specific to commercial banks and other credit institutions

Borrowing abroad   Yes.

Lending locally in foreign exchange   Yes.

Purchase of locally issued securities denominated in foreign exchange   Yes.

Differential treatment of deposit accounts in foreign exchange

   Reserve requirements   Yes.

Differential treatment of deposit accounts held by nonresidents

   Reserve requirements   Yes.

Investment regulations

   In banks by nonresidents   Yes.

Provisions specific to institutional investors   n.a.

Other controls imposed by securities laws   No.

Changes During 1999

No significant changes occurred in the exchange and trade system.

MALAYSIA

(Position as of February 29, 2000)

Status Under IMF Articles of Agreement

Article VIII   Date of acceptance: November 11, 1968.

Exchange Arrangement

Currency   The currency of Malaysia is the Malaysian ringgit.

Exchange rate structure   Unitary.

Classification

Conventional pegged arrangement   The exchange rate of the ringgit is pegged against the dollar at RM 3.80 per $1.

Exchange tax   n.a.

Exchange subsidy   n.a.

Forward exchange market   Forward exchange contracts may be effected for both commercial and financial transactions. For financial transactions, prior approval is required. For commercial transactions, forward cover for imports is provided for up to 12 months from the intended date of import, while for export purposes, the forward cover would be up to six months from the export date. Forward exchange contracts against the ringgit with nonresidents require the prior approval of the Controller of Foreign Exchange (COFE).

Arrangements for Payments and Receipts

**Prescription of currency
requirements**   Special rules apply to settlements with Israel and the Federal Republic of Yugoslavia (Serbia/Montenegro).

Payment arrangements

Bilateral payment arrangements

   Operative   There are 15 arrangements.

   Inoperative   There are 11 arrangements.

Regional arrangements   Malaysia is a member of ASEAN.

Clearing agreements   Yes.

Administration of control   The COFE, who is also the Governor of the Bank Negara Malaysia (BNM), administers exchange control.

International security restrictions

In accordance with Executive Board
Decision No. 144-(52/51)   Malaysia imposes certain restrictions on payments and transfers for current international transactions with respect to the Federal Republic of Yugoslavia (Serbia/Montenegro).

In accordance with UN sanctions   Yes.

Payment arrears   No.

**Controls on trade in gold (coins
and/or bullion)**   No.

**Controls on exports and imports of
banknotes**   Effective February 5, 1999, the ceiling allowed for the import and export of ringgit for border trade with Thailand was raised.

On exports

   Domestic currency   The limit on exports of ringgit by resident and nonresident travelers is RM 1,000 a person. The export of domestic currency by other means, irrespective of the amount, requires prior approval.

Foreign currency	The export of foreign currency by nontravelers requires prior approval. A limit of RM 10,000 or its equivalent for exports of foreign currency by resident travelers and up to the amount brought into Malaysia by nonresident travelers is in effect.
On imports	
Domestic currency	The import of currency notes by a traveler is limited to RM 1,000. The importation of ringgit banknotes by institutions other than commercial banks, or by any other means, requires prior approval from the COFE.

Resident Accounts

Foreign exchange accounts permitted	Yes.
Held domestically	Exporters are allowed to retain a portion of their export proceeds in foreign currency accounts with designated banks in Malaysia with an overnight limit between $1 million and $10 million or any other approved amount. Limits imposed on exporters are based on their average export receipts over the last 12 months.
	Corporate residents and domestic borrowers are allowed to open one or more foreign currency or multicurrency accounts to retain foreign currency receivables rather than export the proceeds, subject to an aggregate overnight limit of $0.5 million.
Approval required	Prior approval is required to retain amounts exceeding the permitted limit.
Held abroad	Residents with no domestic borrowing are allowed to open foreign currency accounts with an overseas branch of Malaysian-owned banks for crediting foreign currency receivables other than export proceeds. Resident individuals are allowed to open foreign currency accounts with overseas banks for education and employment purposes with an overnight limit of up to $50,000. Residents with domestic borrowing require prior approval.
Accounts in domestic currency convertible into foreign currency	Yes.

Nonresident Accounts

Foreign exchange accounts permitted	All commercial and merchant banks are allowed to open these accounts.
Domestic currency accounts	Nonresident ringgit accounts in Malaysia are known as external accounts. Credits to this account are limited to sale of foreign currency, ringgit instruments, securities, or other assets in Malaysia; salaries, wages, rentals, commissions, interest, profits, or dividends. Debits to this account are also restricted to settlement for purchase of ringgit assets and placements of deposits; payment of administrative and statutory expenses in Malaysia; payment of goods and services for use in Malaysia; and granting of loans and advances to staff in Malaysia, according to the terms and conditions of services. Prior approval is required for transfer of funds between external accounts and for uses of funds other than permitted purposes. Nevertheless, there are no restrictions on the operation of the external accounts of nonresidents working in Malaysia, embassies, consulates, high commissions, central banks, or supranational or international organizations in Malaysia.
Convertible into foreign currency	There is no restriction on conversion and repatriation of ringgit funds in external or special external accounts, subject to payment of the appropriate levy on profits made from portfolio investments. There continues to be no restriction on conversion and repatriation of sale proceeds of investment by foreign direct investors.
Blocked accounts	All debits and credits to accounts of residents of Israel and the Federal Republic of Yugoslavia (Serbia/Montenegro) require prior approval.

Imports and Import Payments

Foreign exchange budget	No.

Financing requirements for imports	There is a requirement to settle all imports in foreign currency.
Minimum financing requirements	n.r.
Advance payment requirements	n.r.
Advance import deposits	n.r.
Documentation requirements for release of foreign exchange for imports	n.r.
Import licenses and other nontariff measures	The authority for import control rests with the Royal Customs and Excise Department of the MOF. Import licensing throughout Malaysia is administered daily by the Ministry of International Trade and Industry (MITI) together with other specified authorities, such as the Ministry of Primary Industries, the Malaysian Timber Board, the Department of Agriculture, and the Veterinary Department, on behalf of the Royal Customs and Excise Department.
Negative list	Imports from Israel and the Federal Republic of Yugoslavia (Serbia/Montenegro) require licenses. Finished motor vehicle imports are subject to nonautomatic import licensing, which is administered by the MITI. The movement of live animals between peninsular Malaysia, Sabah, and Sarawak is subject to a permit issued by the Veterinary Department. Imports of the meat, bones, hides, hooves, horns, and offal of any animal or any portion of an animal from all countries require an import license. Imports of primates, whether dead or alive, require an import license, subject to approval from the Department of Wildlife and National Parks and all other goods as specified in the Customs Order. Importation of unprocessed food and planting materials from tropical America and Central Africa to Malaysia are prohibited under the Plant Quarantine Act. Effective February 10, 2000, approval is required from the Ministry of Health to import 19 chemicals covered under the 1988 Convention Against Illicit Traffic in Narcotics, Drugs, and Psychotropic Substances.
Licenses with quotas	Certain imports are subject to quantitative restrictions, which are reviewed periodically, to protect local industries temporarily when required.
Other nontariff measures	Yes.
Import taxes and/or tariffs	Antidumping duties have been imposed on PVC floor covering, self-copy paper, and corrugating medium paper from specified companies to their related companies. Effective January 1, 1999, import duty exemptions were provided to intermediate manufacturing goods. Effective February 15, 2000, temporary antidumping duties were imposed on imports of gypsum boards.
State import monopoly	n.a.

Exports and Export Proceeds

Repatriation requirements	Proceeds from exports must be received and repatriated according to the payment schedule specified in the commercial contract, but no longer than six months after the date of exportation. Export proceeds must be received only in foreign currency.
Surrender requirements	Exporters are allowed to retain their export proceeds in foreign currency accounts with designated banks with an overnight limit of between $1 million and $10 million, or any higher approved amount.
Financing requirements	Yes.
Documentation requirements	Exports of rubber from peninsular Malaysia require a certificate issued by the Malaysian Rubber Exchange and Licensing Board.
Letters of credit	n.r.
Guarantees	n.r.
Domiciliation	n.r.
Export licenses	Exports to Israel and the Federal Republic of Yugoslavia (Serbia/Montenegro) require export licenses from the MITI. Exports of logs are restricted and require licenses from the Malaysian Timber Industries Board. Exports of roofing tiles, bricks, minerals, rice and

paddy in any form, milk and specified milk products, textiles, some types of newspapers, as well as a few other goods, are subject to permits issued by the MITI and other specified authorities.

Export taxes   Export incentives are provided to companies that export Malaysian products. The primary incentives include a double deduction of expenses incurred in overseas promotion, export credit refinancing, and duty drawbacks.

Payments for Invisible Transactions and Current Transfers

Controls on these transfers   Payments for invisibles to all countries other than Israel and the Federal Republic of Yugoslavia (Serbia/Montenego) may be made without restriction. Remittances to nonresidents of profits on all bona fide investments are permitted, upon the completion of statistical forms for amounts exceeding the equivalent of RM 10,000. Remittances of interest payments do not require prior approval as long as such payments are in accordance with the terms of the loan obtained.

Proceeds from Invisible Transactions and Current Transfers

Repatriation requirements   Proceeds from invisibles must be repatriated according to the proceeds schedule specified in the agreement.

Surrender requirements   If received in foreign currency, proceeds may be retained in permitted foreign currency accounts.

Restrictions on use of funds   n.a.

Capital Transactions

Controls on capital and money market instruments

On capital market securities

Shares or other securities of a participating nature

　Sale or issue locally by nonresidents   Nonresidents must undertake all purchases and sales of ringgit securities through authorized depository institutions. Nonresident sellers of Malaysian securities were previously required to hold on to their ringgit proceeds for at least 12 months before the investment is repatriated. On February 15, 1999, this requirement was eliminated, and a graduated system of exit taxes was introduced: for investments made prior to February 15, 1999, capital is taxed at 30% if repatriated less than seven months after entry; at 20% if repatriated after seven months; and at 10% if repatriated 9 to 12 months after entry. Capital repatriated more than one year after entry is not taxed. For investments made on or after February 15, 1999, the original capital is not taxed, but the repatriated capital gains are as follows: capital gains repatriated within 12 months after the gain is realized are taxable at 30%, and for those repatriated after more than 12 months are taxable at 10%. Effective September 21, 1999, nonresident sellers of Malaysian securities may repatriate the proceeds at any time. A 10% exit levy on profits is required. Profits made from investments in MESDAQ (Malaysian stock exchange) are exempted from the exit levy regulations.

　Purchase abroad by residents   No controls apply for transactions valued at less than RM 10,000; but for those amounting to RM 10,000 or more, prior approval is required.

　Sale or issue abroad by residents   No exchange controls apply to a resident on the sale of securities abroad. However, a resident must obtain approval to issue securities abroad. Approval is given if the proceeds associated with these issues are used to finance productive activities in Malaysia, particularly for projects that generate foreign exchange earnings or save on the future outflow of foreign exchange through the production of import substitution goods. The proceeds from the sale or permitted issuance of securities are required to be transferred to Malaysia.

Bonds or other debt securities

  Sale or issue locally by nonresidents   Issuance by nonresidents requires approval.

  Purchase abroad by residents   The same conditions apply as for shares or other securities of a participating nature.

  Sale or issue abroad by residents   Issuance by residents requires an approval.

On money market instruments

  Purchase abroad by residents   The same regulations apply as for shares or other securities of a participating nature.

  Sale or issue abroad by residents   When residents issue money market instruments abroad, it is considered to be obtaining credit facilities. Residents are freely permitted to obtain credit facilities in foreign currency only up to RM 5 million or its equivalent. For amounts exceeding this figure, prior approval is required. Approval is given for foreign currency credit facilities raised on reasonable terms to finance productive activities in Malaysia, particularly for projects that generate sufficient foreign exchange to service the external debt so created.

On collective investment securities

  Sale or issue locally by nonresidents   There is no exchange control on the sale of Malaysian securities in the country by nonresidents. However, repatriation of capital or profit is subjected to a 10% exit levy on profits from investments made after February 15, 1999.

  Purchase abroad by residents   The same regulations apply as for shares or other securities of a participating nature.

  Sale or issue abroad by residents   The same regulations apply as for shares or other securities of a participating nature.

Controls on derivatives and other instruments   Effective January 13, 1999, capital flows for the purpose of trading in derivatives in the Commodity and Monetary Exchange of Malaysia and the Kuala Lumpur Options and Financial Futures Exchanges by nonresidents do not require approval when the transactions are conducted through a Designated External Account.

Purchase locally by nonresidents   Prior approval is required for nonresidents to buy or sell forward ringgit vis-à-vis foreign currency. However, nonresidents are allowed to buy outright forward ringgit to settle trades done on the MESDAQ for tenure of not more than five working days. This is only applicable to firm, committed trades and not to anticipated market purchases.

Purchase abroad by residents   A resident must obtain permission to make payments to a nonresident for any spot or forward contract or interest rate futures not transacted at a futures exchange in Malaysia.

Sale or issue abroad by residents   Residents must obtain permission to issue and to sell financial instruments abroad.

Controls on credit operations

Commercial credits

  By residents to nonresidents   No controls apply to residents in the extension of trade credit to nonresidents for export of goods from Malaysia up to a maximum period of six months from the date of export. There is a prohibition of domestic credit facilities to nonresident correspondent banks and nonresident stockbrokerage companies (subject to RM 5 million limit previously), and of residents obtaining ringgit credit facilities from any nonresident individuals (subject to RM 100,000 limit previously).

  To residents from nonresidents   Residents are permitted to obtain credit facilities in foreign currency up to the equivalent of RM 5 million in the aggregate from licensed banks, licensed merchant banks, and nonresidents. Any larger amount would require prior approval. Residents are not allowed to obtain loans in ringgit from nonresidents. There is no control for residents to obtain commercial credits from nonresidents for the importation of capital goods for a period not exceeding 12 months. Extensions of domestic credit facilities by authorized dealers to nonresident stockbroking companies are allowed in amounts up to RM 200 million intraday and RM 5 million overnight in the case of technical or other inadvertent delays.

Financial credits

  By residents to nonresidents   No controls apply to credits granted by residents in foreign currency to nonresidents of less than RM 10,000. Ringgit loans could be extended by banking institutions up to an aggregate amount of RM 200,000 for purposes other than financing immovable properties in Malaysia. For financing a residential property, financing is allowed for up to 60% of the purchase price for construction of property. Approval is required for credit facilities exceeding the limit.

To residents from nonresidents	Residents are permitted to obtain total credit in foreign currency of up to RM 5 million from licensed banks, licensed merchant banks, and nonresidents. Any larger amount would require prior approval. Residents are not allowed to obtain loans in ringgit from nonresidents.

Guarantees, sureties, and financial backup facilities

By residents to nonresidents	These transactions are permitted subject to informing the COFE. However, any payment to a nonresident in relation to or consequential to the guarantee must be made in foreign currency.
To residents from nonresidents	Residents are permitted to obtain financial guarantees, provided the aggregate amount of credit facility, including the financial guarantee, does not exceed RM 5 million. There is, however, no control on the amount of financial guarantee to be obtained from offshore banks in Labuan. In all cases, all payments related to the guarantees are made in foreign currency; otherwise, approval is required.

Controls on direct investment

Outward direct investment

Investments abroad exceeding RM 10,000 in any form require approval.

Inward direct investment

Controls are imposed on equity shares in line with the National Economic Policy. The following inward investments require prior approval from the Foreign Investment Committee (FIC): (1) acquisition of any substantial fixed assets by foreign interests; (2) acquisition of assets or interests, mergers, and takeovers of companies and businesses in Malaysia by any means that will cause ownership or control to pass to foreign interests; (3) acquisition of 15% or more of the voting power (equity interests) by any foreign interest or associated group or by a foreign interest in the aggregate of 30% or more of the voting power of a Malaysian company or business; (4) control of Malaysian companies and businesses through any form of joint-venture agreement, management agreement, or technical assistance arrangement; (5) merger or takeover of any company or business in Malaysia; and (6) any other proposed acquisition of assets or interests exceeding RM 5 million in value.

Incorporation of a Malaysian company by a foreign entity does not require the approval of the FIC. However, increases in the paid-up capital of a Malaysian company that involve any foreign entity require the approval of the FIC under the following circumstances: (1) the total value of the foreign entity's new subscription exceeds RM 5 million; (2) the total of the foreign entity's new subscription exceeds 15% of the voting power in the relevant company; (3) as a result of the increase in paid-up capital, any foreign entity increases its voting power to more than 15% in the relevant company; (4) the total of the new subscription by several foreign entities increases their joint voting power to 30% or more of the voting power in the relevant company; (5) as a result of the increase in paid-up capital, the aggregate holding of several foreign entities increases to 30% or more of the voting power in the relevant company; and (6) an increase in the paid-up capital of any Malaysian company to more than RM 5 million on incorporation, the holdings of foreign entities constitutes more than 15% of the voting power, or the joint holdings of several foreign entities constitutes 30% or more of the voting power of the company concerned.

In addition, the permitted percentage of equity held by foreigners also depends on the percentage of production exported, whether high-technology products are purchased or whether priority products are produced for the domestic market. For projects involving extracting, mining, and processing mineral ores, a majority foreign equity participation of up to 100% is permitted. Multimedia Super Corridor status companies are allowed to have 100% foreign equity.

Controls on liquidation of direct investment

The proceeds of investments may be repatriated freely after resale, upon the completion of a statistical form, for amounts of RM 10,000 or more.

Controls on real estate transactions

Purchase abroad by residents

The same regulations apply as for purchases of shares or other securities of a participating nature abroad by residents.

Purchase locally by nonresidents	Under Special Guidelines, no limitation or condition is imposed on the purchase of residential, shop lot, and office space by foreigners subject to the following criteria: (1) the purchase under consideration must be more than RM 250,000; (2) the project must be newly completed or at least 50% in progress; and (3) financing for the above acquisition must be obtained from overseas financial institutions outside Malaysia.

Controls on personal capital movements

Loans

By residents to nonresidents	The same regulations apply as for financial credits.
To residents from nonresidents	Yes.
Gifts, endowments, inheritances, and legacies	n.r.
Transfer of assets	n.r.

Provisions specific to commercial banks and other credit institutions

Borrowing abroad	Only authorized dealers and permitted merchant banks are allowed to borrow freely in foreign currency from nonresidents. Other financial institutions are subject to prior approval if the aggregate amount exceeds RM 5 million.
Maintenance of accounts abroad	Only authorized dealers in foreign currencies and merchant banks are permitted to maintain accounts abroad. Other credit institutions require approval to maintain these accounts.
Lending to nonresidents (financial or commercial credits)	Authorized dealers are allowed to extend loans in foreign currency to nonresidents. A banking institution is, however, allowed to extend credit in ringgit to: (1) nonresidents, other than banks or stockbroking companies up to an aggregate of RM 200,000 for any purpose except to finance the acquisition or development of immovable property in Malaysia; and (2) nonresidents who are working in Malaysia up to 60% of the purchase price or construction cost for residential property.
	The extension of loans in ringgit to nonresidents exceeding the amounts or for purposes other than those stipulated above requires prior approval.
	Banking institutions are not allowed to extend loans in ringgit to any foreign bank or foreign stockbroking company.
	Stockbroking companies are allowed to extend margin financing facilities to nonresident clients for the purchase of shares listed on the Kuala Lumpur Stock Exchange (KLSE), subject to compliance with rules imposed by the KLSE.
Lending locally in foreign exchange	Authorized dealers and merchant banks are allowed to lend in foreign currency to residents. A resident borrower, however, requires prior approval if total aggregate borrowing exceeds RM 5 million.
Purchase of locally issued securities denominated in foreign exchange	Purchases are allowed, provided that the issuance of the securities has been approved.

Investment regulations

Abroad by banks	Investment in equity and property and purchases of debt securities in excess of RM 10,000 require prior approval.
In banks by nonresidents	Foreigners are generally limited to an aggregate participation of not more than 30% equity interest in a bank.
Open foreign exchange position limits	The criteria in determining banks' net overnight foreign currency open position limits are based on a matrix that takes into account their shareholders' funds and dealing capacity.

Provisions specific to institutional investors

Limits (max.) on portfolio invested abroad	Insurers are required to support the aggregate of their liabilities and margin of solvency (referred to as "the Amount") with admitted assets as specified by the BNM. For the

financial year ending in 1999, insurers are required to maintain a minimum of 70% and 80%, respectively, of "the Amount" in the form of admitted assets.

The rules allow a licensed insurer in respect of its Malaysian insurance fund to hold for investment purposes up to a maximum of 5% of "the Amount" in assets of a foreign jurisdiction with a sovereign rating that is not lower than the sovereign rating of Malaysia. However, investment in any one foreign jurisdiction is restricted to 2% of "the Amount." A licensed insurer is also allowed to hold assets of a foreign jurisdiction where it is carrying on business to enable it to meet its foreign liabilities in that jurisdiction.

Limits (min.) on portfolio invested locally

Employee Provident Fund (EPF) investment in foreign securities is subject to approval of amounts exceeding RM 10,000. The EPF is required to invest a minimum of 50% of its annual investible funds in securities issued or guaranteed by the federal government, provided that the total amount of funds invested in such securities is not less than 70% of its total investment.

Unit trust funds may invest up to 10% of the fund's net asset value in securities listed on foreign stock exchanges. Prior approval from the Securities Commission is required for such investment.

Other controls imposed by securities laws

There are no controls on foreign firms trading in the corporate debt, equity, and derivative market. However, the following guidelines as set out by the FIC should be observed: (1) any proposed acquisition of 15% or more of the voting power by any one foreign interest or associated group, or foreign interests in the aggregate of 30% or more of the voting power of a Malaysian company or business; (2) acquisition of assets or interests, merges, and takeovers of companies and businesses in Malaysia, whether by Malaysian or foreign interests; and (3) any other proposed acquisition of assets or interests exceeding in value RM 5 million, whether by Malaysians or foreign interests require approval. Foreign companies with no substantial business operations in Malaysia are not normally granted listing on the local stock exchange.

Changes During 1999

Arrangements for payments and receipts

February 5. The ceiling allowed for the import and export of ringgit for border trade with Thailand was raised.

Imports and import payments

January 1. Import duty exemptions were provided to intermediate manufacturing goods.

Capital transactions

February 15. Investors were allowed to repatriate the proceeds from portfolio investments, subject to paying a levy.

April 15. Repatriation of investments in MESDAQ are exempt from paying the levy.

September 21. Nonresidents were allowed to repatriate proceeds from sales of securities after paying a 10% exit levy.

Controls on capital and money market instruments

February 15. The requirement that nonresident holdings of Malaysian securities be kept in Malaysia for at least one year was replaced by a graduated system of exit taxes on capital and capital gains.

Controls on derivatives and other instruments

January 13. Capital flows for the purpose of trading in derivatives in the Commodity and Monetary Exchange of Malaysia and the Kuala Lumpur Options and Financial Futures Exchanges by nonresidents do not require approval when the transactions are conducted through a Designated External Account.

Changes During 2000

Imports and import payments

February 10. Approval from the Ministry of Health is required to import 19 chemical substances.

February 15. Temporary antidumping duties were imposed on imports of gypsum boards.

MALDIVES

(Position as of December 31, 1999)

Status Under IMF Articles of Agreement

Article XIV	Yes.

Exchange Arrangement

Currency	The currency of Maldives is the Maldivian rufiyaa.
Exchange rate structure	Unitary.

Classification

Conventional pegged arrangement	The exchange rate is determined on the basis of a trade-weighted basket of currencies. Once the exchange rate is set, the Maldives Monetary Authority (MMA) buys and sells currency at a spread of 10 laari within which commercial banks and foreign exchange dealers must also operate. To promote stability and maintain confidence, the authorities have de facto kept the exchange rate stable vis-à-vis the dollar since October 1994.
Exchange tax	No.
Exchange subsidy	No.
Forward exchange market	No.

Arrangements for Payments and Receipts

Prescription of currency requirements	The MMA sells foreign exchange to trading firms and individuals through the Post Office Exchange Counter (POEC). The POEC imposes daily limits for cash and noncash transactions of $300 and $2,000, respectively.
Payment arrangements	No.
Administration of control	No.

International security restrictions

In accordance with UN sanctions	Imports from Iraq and the Federal Republic of Yugoslavia (Serbia/Montenegro) are prohibited.
Payment arrears	No.
Controls on trade in gold (coins and/or bullion)	Transactions in gold are not subject to regulation.
Controls on exports and imports of banknotes	No.

Resident Accounts

Foreign exchange accounts permitted	Yes.
Held domestically	Yes.
Held abroad	Yes.
Accounts in domestic currency convertible into foreign currency	Yes.

Nonresident Accounts

Foreign exchange accounts permitted	No distinction is made between accounts held by residents and those held by nonresidents.

| Domestic currency accounts | No. |
| Blocked accounts | No. |

Imports and Import Payments

Foreign exchange budget	No.
Financing requirements for imports	No.
Documentation requirements for release of foreign exchange for imports	No.
Import licenses and other nontariff measures	Import operations may only be conducted after being registered and licensed at the Ministry of Trade and Industries (MTI). Imports from Iraq and the Federal Republic of Yugoslavia (Serbia/Montenegro) are prohibited.
Open general licenses	All goods may be imported under an OGL system. Licenses are issued on application.
Licenses with quotas	All private sector imports of rice, wheat flour, and sugar are subject to a quota.
Import taxes and/or tariffs	Duties are levied on all merchandise items other than rice, flour, and sugar.
State import monopoly	No.

Exports and Export Proceeds

Repatriation requirements	No.
Financing requirements	No.
Documentation requirements	No.
Export licenses	Export licenses are issued by the MTI. The private sector may export most items, with the exception of fresh and frozen tuna.
With quotas	Quotas for exports of aquarium fish are in effect.
Export taxes	Exports of fish and fish products and reexports are exempt from duties. However, a 50% tax is levied on the export of ambergris.

Payments for Invisible Transactions and Current Transfers

| Controls on these transfers | No. |

Proceeds from Invisible Transactions and Current Transfers

| Repatriation requirements | No. |
| Restrictions on use of funds | No. |

Capital Transactions

Controls on capital and money market instruments	
On capital market securities	
Shares or other securities of a participating nature	
Purchase locally by nonresidents	Although no law prohibits these purchases, there is a control on the foreign purchase of shares placed by some companies that have floated their securities.

Sale or issue locally by nonresidents	The law permits raising of capital through public offering.
Controls on derivatives and other instruments	n.a.
Controls on credit operations	
Financial credits	
By residents to nonresidents	Except commercial banks, natural and juridical persons may not extend credit and charge interest without the approval of the MMA. However, locally incorporated offshore banks are allowed to extend financial credits to nonresidents.
Guarantees, sureties, and financial backup facilities	
By residents to nonresidents	Yes.
Controls on direct investment	
Inward direct investment	Investments require prior approval from the government. Investors are required to provide at least 75% of their capital investment in cash or goods financed from outside Maldives.
Controls on liquidation of direct investment	No.
Controls on real estate transactions	
Purchase locally by nonresidents	Yes.
Sale locally by nonresidents	Yes.
Controls on personal capital movements	
Loans	
By residents to nonresidents	Yes.
To residents from nonresidents	Yes.
Transfer of gambling and prize earnings	Gambling is not allowed in Maldives.
Provisions specific to commercial banks and other credit institutions	
Lending to nonresidents (financial or commercial credits)	Banks may lend 25% of the initial capital investment made by them.
Differential treatment of deposit accounts in foreign exchange	
Interest rate controls	Interest rate control exists in the case of local currency only, as the annual rate of interest chargeable on loans and advances may not exceed 20%.
Credit controls	Yes.
Differential treatment of deposit accounts held by nonresidents	
Credit controls	Yes.
Provisions specific to institutional investors	
Limits (max.) on securities issued by nonresidents and on portfolio invested abroad	n.r.
Other controls imposed by securities laws	No.

Changes During 1999

No significant changes occurred in the exchange and trade system.

MALI

(Position as of January 31, 2000)

Status Under IMF Articles of Agreement

Article VIII	Date of acceptance: June 1, 1996.

Exchange Arrangement

Currency	The currency of Mali is the CFA franc.
Exchange rate structure	Unitary.
Classification	
Exchange arrangement with no separate legal tender	The CFA franc is pegged to the euro at the rate of CFAF 100 per €0.8385. Exchange rates for other currencies are derived from the rate for the currency concerned in the Paris foreign exchange market and the fixed rate between the euro and the CFA franc.
Exchange tax	There is no exchange tax, but foreign exchange transfers are subject to a stamp duty. In addition, banks charge a commission of 0.25% on transfers to all countries outside the WAEMU, which must be surrendered in its entirety to the Treasury.
Exchange subsidy	No.
Forward exchange market	Effective February 1, 1999, residents were authorized to contract forward exchange cover to settle payments related to imports and exports of goods and services. Forward exchange contracts may be arranged with the prior authorization of the MOF. For certain products, the duration of forward exchange rate cover may be extended to three months but cannot be renewed. For exports, the duration of forward exchange contracts may not exceed 120 days after the arrival of the goods at their destination.

Arrangements for Payments and Receipts

Prescription of currency requirements	Because Mali is linked to the French Treasury through an Operations Account, settlements with France, Monaco, and other Operations Account countries (WAEMU and CAEMC members and the Comoros) are made in French francs or the currency of any other Operations Account country. There are no prescription of currency requirements for transfers to non-WAEMU franc zone countries.
Payment arrangements	
Regional arrangements	An Operations Account is maintained with the French Treasury that links Operations Account countries. All purchases or sales of foreign currencies or euros against CFA francs are ultimately settled through a debit or credit to the Operations Account.
Administration of control	Exchange control is administered jointly by the MOF and the BCEAO. Since February 1, 1999, most of the authority to supervise foreign exchange transactions has been delegated to authorized banks, which are required to report those operations to the MOF. The only operations that continue to require prior authorization of the MOF or the BCEAO involve residents' investments abroad, domestic accounts in foreign exchange, and residents' accounts abroad. Effective February 1, 1999, the amount of transfers authorized without supporting documentation was raised to CFAF 300,000 from CFAF 100,000.
International security restrictions	No.
Payment arrears	No.
Controls on trade in gold (coins and/or bullion)	Authorization from the Directorate of External Commerce, issued after a favorable ruling by the MOF, is required to hold, sell, import, export, or deal in raw diamonds and precious and semiprecious materials.
Controls on external trade	Commercial imports and exports of gold do not require authorization from the MOF but are subject to all foreign trade regulations, including bank domiciliation, customs declaration,

and the obligation to repatriate export proceeds. Travelers may export gold jewelry and personal belongings, other than gold coins and ingots, up to a maximum weight of 500 grams.

Controls on exports and imports of banknotes

On exports

  Domestic currency   Residents traveling to non-BCEAO countries are not allowed to take out BCEAO banknotes.

  Foreign currency   The reexportation of foreign banknotes for amounts exceeding the equivalent of CFAF 500,000 requires documentation demonstrating the importation of the foreign banknotes, or their purchase through a means of payment registered in the name of the traveler or through the use of nonresident deposits in local banks.

On imports

  Foreign currency   Nonresidents may bring in any amount of foreign banknotes and coins (except gold coins) of countries outside the Operations Account area. Residents bringing in foreign banknotes or other means of payment exceeding the equivalent of CFAF 300,000 must declare them to customs upon entry and sell them to an authorized intermediary bank within eight days.

Resident Accounts

Foreign exchange accounts permitted   Effective February 1, 1999, residents are allowed to open foreign exchange accounts with local banks or banks abroad after obtaining authorization from the MOF, subsequent to the approval of the BCEAO.

Held domestically   Holding accounts at local financial institutions requires prior authorization of the MOF.

Held abroad   Yes.

Accounts in domestic currency convertible into foreign currency   Yes.

Nonresident Accounts

Foreign exchange accounts permitted   Effective February 1, 1999, authorization is issued by the BCEAO.

Domestic currency accounts   Because the BCEAO has suspended the repurchase of banknotes circulating outside WAEMU countries, nonresident accounts may not be credited or debited with BCEAO banknotes. These accounts may not be overdrawn without the authorization of the MOF with BCEAO concurrence.

Blocked accounts   Yes.

Imports and Import Payments

Foreign exchange budget   No.

Financing requirements for imports   No.

Documentation requirements for release of foreign exchange for imports

Domiciliation requirements   A domiciliation requirement exists for all imports exceeding CFAF 500,000. Effective February 1, 1999, this limit was raised to CFAF 5 million.

Preshipment inspection   An inspection for quality and price is required.

Letters of credit   LCs are required for imports of goods outside EU, Operations Account, and ACP countries.

Import licenses and other nontariff measures	There are no import licensing requirements, but imports are required to be registered and permits are issued automatically.
Import taxes and/or tariffs	On January 1, 2000, the WAEMU introduced a CET with four rates (zero, 5%, 10%, and 20%) for all member countries except Guinea-Bissau. Imports are also subject to a customs duty of up to 5% and a customs service fee of 5%. Some goods are exempt from these charges. Tariff rates are ad valorem (except for those on petroleum products) and are based on c.i.f. values. Petroleum is subject to a variable levy. Imports are subject to additional taxes ranging from 7.5% to 55%, which have been temporarily suspended since 1994.
State import monopoly	No.

Exports and Export Proceeds

Repatriation requirements	Exports to foreign countries must be recorded with an authorized bank, and all export proceeds, including those originating in France and other countries linked to the French Treasury by an Operations Account, must be repatriated through the BCEAO. Effective February 1, 1999, proceeds from exports to WAEMU countries are no longer required to be repatriated.
Surrender requirements	Proceeds must be surrendered within 30 days of the payment due date or within 120 days of shipment if no payment date is specified in the sales contract.
Financing requirements	No.
Documentation requirements	
Domiciliation	Effective February 1, 1999, exports to WAEMU countries need not be domiciled.
Export licenses	All exports require only a certificate of registration.
Export taxes	No.

Payments for Invisible Transactions and Current Transfers

Controls on these transfers	Payments to France, Monaco, and the countries linked to the French Treasury by an Operations Account are permitted freely. For payments for invisibles to other countries not exceeding CFAF 300,000, no supporting documents are required. Payments related to trade above this amount are permitted freely when the basic trade transaction has been approved or does not require authorization.
	Effective February 1, 1999, payments and incomes from foreign ships in the WAEMU zone and WAEMU ships abroad are included under current operations.
Investment-related payments	Authorized banks may transfer, on their own responsibility, profit payments based on supporting documentation.
Payments for travel	
Quantitative limits	There was a limit of CFA 500,000 a trip for tourist travel and CFAF 2,750,000 for business travel (including tourist trip allocation). Effective February 1, 1999, limits on foreign exchange allowances were eliminated. The threshold of foreign exchange to be surrendered by residents after travel was raised to CFAF 300,000 from CFAF 50,000.
Personal payments	Payment of study abroad costs and medical expenses are allowed freely on the basis of supporting documents.
Indicative limits/bona fide test	Yes.
Foreign workers' wages	The transfer of salaries is permitted upon presentation of the appropriate pay voucher, provided that the transfer takes place within three months of the pay period or that there is a reciprocity agreement with the foreigner's country of nationality.
Prior approval	Yes.
Indicative limits/bona fide test	Yes.

Credit card use abroad	Credit cards issued by specialized resident financial intermediaries and authorized banks may be used abroad.
Prior approval	Yes.
Indicative limits/bona fide test	Yes.
Other payments	
Prior approval	Yes.
Indicative limits/bona fide test	Yes.

Proceeds from Invisible Transactions and Current Transfers

Repatriation requirements	Proceeds from invisible transactions with countries that are not WAEMU members must be repatriated.
Surrender requirements	Proceeds, except those from WAEMU member countries, must be surrendered. Effective February 1, 1999, the time limit for the repatriation and surrender requirement was set at one month after the due date of the receipt.
Restrictions on use of funds	No.

Capital Transactions

Controls on capital and money market instruments	Capital movements between Mali and France, Monaco, and the countries linked to the French Treasury by an Operations Account are free of restrictions. Capital transfers to all other countries require authorization from the MOF, and a maximum of 75% of investment abroad may be financed by foreign loans. Capital receipts from these countries are permitted freely.
	The liquidation of foreign investment is subject to reporting to the MOF, and the reinvestment of proceeds is subject to prior authorization. If no authorization is given for the reinvestment, the proceeds in foreign exchange must be surrendered to an authorized intermediary bank within one month. Effective February 1, 1999, transfers related to the sale of foreign securities by residents and to proceeds of disinvestments by nonresidents were allowed. Foreign investment in WAEMU countries became unrestricted. Such operations are subject to reporting for statistical purposes. The prior authorization of the RCPSFM is required for the issuance and marketing of securities and capital assets of foreign entities, as well as for publicity and advertising of investments abroad.
On capital market securities	
Shares or other securities of a participating nature	
Purchase locally by nonresidents	Yes.
Sale or issue locally by nonresidents	For nonresidents, prior authorization by the MOF is required. Residents may acquire these securities by obtaining a permit from the MOF. There are no restrictions on the sale of securities constituting disinvestment. Payments for sales by transfer abroad or by credit to a nonresident account, however, require an exchange permit approved by the MOF.
Purchase abroad by residents	Prior authorization from the MOF is required.
Sale or issue abroad by residents	Residents are free to transfer these securities abroad. If the effect of these transactions is to place Malian resident institutions under foreign control, the foreign investors concerned are required to report in advance to the MOF. The same rule applies to disinvestments. Foreign currency proceeds from these transactions must be surrendered to a domestic authorized bank.
Bonds or other debt securities	The same regulations apply as for shares and other securities of a participating nature.

On money market instruments

Purchase locally by nonresidents | The purchase may be effected through a domestic bank.

Sale or issue locally by nonresidents | These sales require prior authorization of the MOF, except for disinvestments. Transfers of the proceeds require an exchange permit approved by the MOF.

Purchase abroad by residents | Prior authorization from the MOF is required.

Sale or issue abroad by residents | Residents are free to sell money market instruments abroad. Sales constituting disinvestment are subject to prior disclosure. The foreign currency proceeds of such sale or disinvestment must be surrendered to a licensed banking intermediary. The issue abroad of money market instruments by residents is governed by the provisions applicable to loans.

On collective investment securities

Sale or issue locally by nonresidents | Prior authorization is required.

Purchase abroad by residents | Prior authorization is required.

Controls on derivatives and other instruments | These instruments, which are virtually nonexistent, are governed by the regulations generally applicable to securities and investments. Effective February 1, 1999, residents are allowed to purchase abroad, call, and put options in commodities and securities.

Controls on credit operations

Commercial credits | Special controls apply for borrowing outside the region.

By residents to nonresidents | The granting of these credits is subject to the following provisions:

(1) Any claims generated by the export of goods must be collected, and the corresponding amounts must be repatriated through the BCEAO within 30 days of the due date of the payment stipulated in the commercial contract. In principle, the grace period should not exceed 120 days following the arrival of the merchandise at its destination.

(2) Any claims generated by the provision of services must also be collected and then surrendered on the exchange market within one month, at most, of the due date of the payment, for which no limit is set.

To residents from nonresidents | There are no controls on the granting of these credits; their repayment is generally authorized, subject to the licensed intermediary being presented with documentation attesting to the reality of the commercial transaction or to the provision of services.

Financial credits

By residents to nonresidents | The granting of financial credits is subject to the prior authorization of the MOF. The transfer of funds abroad for this purpose requires prior MOF approval.

To residents from nonresidents | There are no controls on these credits. However, if these transactions are carried out between a direct investment enterprise established in Mali and its parent company abroad, they are considered to be direct investment and, as a result, are subject to prior disclosure to the MOF.

Guarantees, sureties, and financial backup facilities

By residents to nonresidents | The granting of guarantees, sureties, and financial backup facilities is subject to the prior authorization of the MOF. The transfer of funds abroad requires an exchange permit approved by the MOF.

To residents from nonresidents | There are no controls on the granting of these facilities.

Controls on direct investment

Outward direct investment | All outward investments by residents require the prior authorization of the MOF. These investments may be financed up to 75% by external borrowing. Effective February 1, 1999, MOF authorization is no longer needed for purchases of foreign securities issued or sold in WAEMU member states if the issue or sale by nonresidents was authorized by the RCPSFM.

Inward direct investment	Inward investments must be reported in advance to the MOF, which has two months to request deferment of plans. Any transfer of direct investment by a nonresident to another nonresident is also subject to prior disclosure.
Controls on liquidation of direct investment	Liquidation of a resident's foreign investments must be reported for information purposes to the MOF. Reinvestment of the proceeds of the liquidation requires the Ministry's prior authorization. If the reinvestment was not authorized, the proceeds of the liquidation must be repatriated within one month through an authorized intermediary. Foreign investments may be transferred freely from Mali and must be reported for statistical purposes.

Controls on real estate transactions

Purchase abroad by residents	Prior authorization of the MOF is required.
Purchase locally by nonresidents	There are no controls on purchases, provided that they do not represent direct investment in an enterprise, branch office, or company.
Sale locally by nonresidents	The proceeds of the sale or liquidation of foreign direct investment or the sale of real estate may be freely transferred abroad or credited to a foreign account in francs, upon presentation of supporting documentation to the MOF and receipt of the latter's response.

Controls on personal capital movements

Loans

By residents to nonresidents	Prior authorization of the MOF is required.
To residents from nonresidents	The borrower must obtain prior authorization from the MOF if the amount of the loan exceeds CFAF 30 million and if the interest rate is above the normal market rate. No authorization is required for loans contracted to finance imports or exports.

Gifts, endowments, inheritances, and legacies

By residents to nonresidents	Payments relating to inheritances and legacies are generally authorized. Payments in connection with gifts or donations, however, require the prior authorization of the MOF.
Settlement of debts abroad by immigrants	Immigrants acquiring resident status must obtain the prior authorization of the MOF for the payment of debts contracted abroad while they were nonresidents.

Transfer of assets

Transfer abroad by emigrants	These transfers are allowed upon presentation of proof of emigration to the MOF.
Transfer into the country by immigrants	Yes.
Transfer of gambling and prize earnings	Yes.

Provisions specific to commercial banks and other credit institutions

Borrowing abroad	Licensed intermediaries are free to borrow abroad. Other credit institutions are governed by general provisions applicable to other residents.
Maintenance of accounts abroad	Banks and financial institutions are not authorized to hold liquid assets outside the WAEMU zone, except to meet the needs of their current operations.
Lending to nonresidents (financial or commercial credits)	There are no controls on commercial credit operations of this type; the prior authorization of the MOF is required for loans and financial credits. Effective February 1, 1999, the prior approval of the BCEAO is also needed.
Lending locally in foreign exchange	Prior authorization of the MOF is required.
Purchase of locally issued securities denominated in foreign exchange	Prior authorization of the RCPSFM is required.

Differential treatment of deposit accounts in foreign exchange

Reserve requirements	Yes.

Credit controls	Yes.
Differential treatment of deposit accounts held by nonresidents	
Credit controls	Yes.
Investment regulations	The same regulations apply as for other residents.
Open foreign exchange position limits	Yes.
Provisions specific to institutional investors	On February 1, 1999, controls were imposed by the Insurance Code of the Inter-African Insurance Market Conference.
Limits (max.) on portfolio invested abroad	Yes.
Limits (min.) on portfolio invested locally	Yes.
Other controls imposed by securities laws	No.

Changes During 1999

Exchange arrangement	*February 1.* The CFA franc peg to the French franc was replaced with a peg to the euro.
	February 1. Residents were authorized to contract forward exchange cover in connection with payments related to imports and exports of goods and services.
Arrangements for payments and receipts	*February 1.* The list of generally authorized transactions was expanded to include transfers of the proceeds of disinvestment and of the sale of foreign securities to nonresidents relating to option purchases.
	February 1. The amount of transfers authorized without supporting documentation was raised to CFAF 300,000 from CFAF 100,000.
Resident accounts	*February 1.* Residents could be authorized to open foreign exchange accounts with local banks or banks abroad. Such authorization was granted by the MOF after BCEAO approval has been obtained. The opinion of the president of the WAEMU Council of Ministers was no longer required.
Nonresident accounts	*February 1.* Authorization to open nonresident accounts was granted by the BCEAO. The MOF and the president of the WAEMU Council of Ministers no longer have a role in this process.
Imports and import payments	*February 1.* The level of import transactions requiring domiciliation was increased to CFAF 5,000,000 from CFAF 3,000,000.
Exports and export proceeds	*February 1.* Exports between WAEMU countries were no longer subject to domiciliation and repatriation of proceeds.
Payments for invisible transactions and current transfers	*February 1.* Indicative ceilings on foreign currency allocations to resident travelers were eliminated. The amount of foreign currency to be surrendered by residents after travel was increased to CFAF 300,000 from CFAF 50,000.
	February 1. The payments and incomes of foreign ships in the WAEMU zone and WAEMU ships abroad were generally treated as authorized current transactions.
Proceeds from invisible transactions and current transfers	*February 1.* Income or proceeds collected abroad or paid by a nonresident had to be surrendered to a licensed intermediary within one month of the payment due date.
Capital transactions	*February 1.* The prior authorization of the RCPSFM was required for the following operations: issuing and marketing of securities and real assets of foreign entities, canvassing, or advertising for investment abroad.
	February 1. There were no controls on foreign investment in WAEMU countries or on foreign borrowing by residents. These operations became subject only to reporting for statistical purposes.

Controls on derivatives and other instruments	*February 1.* Residents were allowed to purchase abroad, call, and put options in commodities and securities.
Controls on direct investment	*February 1.* Authorization was no longer required for investment abroad consisting of the acquisition by residents of securities for which the issue or marketing by nonresidents had been authorized in advance by the RCPSFM.
Provisions specific to commercial banks and other credit institutions	*February 1.* Loans and other assistance granted to nonresidents became subject to the prior authorization of the MOF after the approval of the BCEAO has been obtained.
Provisions specific to institutional investors	*February 1.* Controls were imposed by the Insurance Code of the Inter-African Insurance Market Conference.

Changes During 2000

Imports and import payments	*January 1.* The WAEMU introduced a CET with four rates (zero, 5%, 10%, and 20%) for all member countries except Guinea-Bissau.

MALTA
(Position as of January 31, 2000)

Status Under IMF Articles of Agreement

Article VIII

Date of acceptance: November 30, 1994.

Exchange Arrangement

Currency

The currency of Malta is the Maltese lira.

Other legal tender

Malta has 23 denominations of gold coins, which are legal tender.

Exchange rate structure

Unitary.

Classification

Conventional pegged arrangement

The exchange rate of the Maltese lira is determined on the basis of a weighted basket of currencies comprising the dollar, the euro, and pound sterling. Unless market conditions indicate otherwise, a variable spread of approximately 0.125% is applied effective January 1, 1999, to the middle rate to compute the buying and selling rates for transactions between the Central Bank of Malta (CBM) and the credit institutions (authorized banks). These transactions may be conducted in dollars, euros, or pounds sterling, normally in amounts not less than Lm 150,000. Transactions in smaller amounts are handled through the interbank market. There is no limit on the spread between the buying and selling rates the credit institutions may quote. Authorized banks may also establish rates for currencies not quoted by the CBM based on the latest international market rates.

Exchange tax

No.

Exchange subsidy

No.

Forward exchange market

Official cover of forward operations

The CBM provides forward cover directly to government departments and public sector bodies in respect of such transactions. Forward rates are based on interest rate differentials between market rates and international money market rates.

Arrangements for Payments and Receipts

Prescription of currency requirements

Authorized payments to and proceeds from exports to all countries may be transacted in any foreign currency.

Payment arrangements

Bilateral payment arrangements

Operative

There is a banking agreement with Libya operated by the respective central banks to clear payments in connection with commercial transactions, outstanding balances being settled in convertible currencies within 90 days.

Administration of control

The CBM, as agent for the MOF, administers exchange controls. Authority to approve and effect particular current and capital account transactions is delegated to authorized credit institutions (mainly foreign exchange bureaus).

Effective January 1, 2000, the MOF delegated responsibility for the approval of inward direct investment by nonresidents to the Malta Financial Services Centre (MFSC), which is the institution that is responsible for the registration of companies and, together with the CBM, for supervising and regulating financial services in Malta.

International security restrictions

In accordance with Executive Board Decision No. 144-(52/51)

Yes.

| In accordance with UN sanctions | Certain restrictions on payments and transfers to Angola, Georgia, the Federal Republic of Yugoslavia (Serbia/Montenegro), Iraq, Liberia, Libya, Rwanda, Sierra Leone, and Somalia remain in force in compliance with UN Security Council Resolutions. Effective April 30, 1999, restrictions on transactions with Libya were suspended following the suspension of such sanctions by the United Nations. Effective December 21, 1999, similar restrictions apply to payments and transfers to the Taliban (the Islamic State of Afghanistan). |

Payment arrears No.

Controls on trade in gold (coins and/or bullion)

| Controls on domestic ownership and/or trade | Residents are allowed to hold gold coins that are legal tender in Malta, but must obtain permission from the CBM to purchase and sell any other gold coins. |
| Controls on external trade | Authorized businesses may import gold bullion solely for the manufacture of gold articles. The importation of gold coins for numismatic purposes and the exportation of unworked gold by residents other than the monetary authorities are subject to CBM approval. Licenses are required for the importation of gold filigree. |

Controls on exports and imports of banknotes

On exports

| *Domestic currency* | Residents and nonresidents may export up to Lm 25 a person. |
| *Foreign currency* | Nonresident travelers may export foreign currency up to the amount they bring into the country. Effective January 1, 2000, the limit for residents was increased to Lm 5,000 a trip (from Lm 2,500). |

On imports

| *Domestic currency* | Only Lm 50 in notes and coins that are or have been legal tender in Malta may be imported. |
| *Foreign currency* | Subject to the provisions of the Money Laundering Act, any amount of foreign currency may be imported. |

Resident Accounts

| **Foreign exchange accounts permitted** | Yes. |
| Held domestically | Effective January 1, 1999, resident individuals may invest up to Lm 8,000 (previously, Lm 5,000) a year in savings and time deposit accounts denominated in foreign currency. Effective January 1, 2000, this limit was increased to Lm 15,000 a year. Export companies in the manufacturing sector may deposit export proceeds in such accounts for a maximum period of six months. Effective January 1, 2000, this facility was extended to firms in all other export-oriented activities.

Effective January 1, 2000, resident businesses in the retailing sector may hold up to Lm 2,500 in foreign currency time and savings deposits on the condition that the funds be used in relation to their business activities and payments to nonresidents in connection with current account transactions.

Effective January 1, 2000, residents may also hold up to Lm 2,500 in demand deposit accounts. Credit balances in these accounts may be used for payments to nonresidents in connection with current account transactions.

CBM approval is required for any transactions involving foreign exchange accounts held by residents with local banking institutions above the limits and conditions stated above. |
| Held abroad | Residents are permitted to open savings and time deposit accounts with nonresident banking institutions and may deposit in such accounts a maximum amount of Lm 15,000 a year.

CBM approval is required for any transactions involving foreign exchange accounts held by residents with nonresident banking institutions outside the limits and conditions stated above. CBM approval is also required if residents wish to open and maintain demand deposit accounts with nonresident banking institutions. |

Accounts in domestic currency convertible into foreign currency	Conversion is allowed freely with regard to all authorized transactions (mainly current payments).

Nonresident Accounts

Foreign exchange accounts permitted	These accounts may be credited with funds from overseas sources or with income earned from permitted activities carried out in Malta.
Domestic currency accounts	The same criteria apply as for foreign exchange accounts.
Convertible into foreign currency	Yes.
Blocked accounts	Balances retained in blocked accounts are usually limited to those arising from the liquidation of investments in real estate in Malta. Such balances are temporarily retained until proof of the validity of any agreements entered into in terms of the underlying transaction is provided, and until it is shown that the relevant legal and financial conditions have been met.

Imports and Import Payments

Foreign exchange budget	No.
Financing requirements for imports	No.
Documentation requirements for release of foreign exchange for imports	Payments for imports may be made freely, provided that currency regulations are complied with and that supporting documents, including the customs entry form for imports with a minimum value of Lm 20,000 and related import license, where applicable, are submitted to the intermediary bank.
Domiciliation requirements	Import payments must be transacted through authorized credit or financial institutions.
Import licenses used as exchange licenses	Where import licenses are required, such licenses must be presented to the authorized credit and financial institutions to obtain foreign exchange.
Import licenses and other nontariff measures	The Director of Imports and Internal Trade in the Ministry for Economic Services administers certain import controls in line with the Importation Control Regulations.
Negative list	Licenses are required only for the importation of items that need clearance for health, safety, security, and environmental reasons, as well as for particularly sensitive items, such as fresh and frozen fish, handmade lace, and gold and silver filigree.
Open general licenses	All other products may be imported without an import license.
Import taxes and/or tariffs	Imports originating from non-EU countries are subject to import duties. Additionally, a number of imports are subject to protective levies.
State import monopoly	The importation of barley, maize, hard and soft wheat, and certain petroleum products is undertaken only by state-owned enterprises.

Exports and Export Proceeds

Repatriation requirements	Proceeds must be received within six months of shipment.
Surrender requirements	Export proceeds must be surrendered to the authorized credit and financial institutions. However, effective January 1, 1999, exporters in the manufacturing sector may retain export proceeds in foreign currency deposit accounts with authorized banks for up to six months to make import payments connected with their exporting business. Effective January 1, 2000, the retention of proceeds in foreign currency deposit accounts was extended to firms in all other export-oriented activities.
Financing requirements	No.
Documentation requirements	Exporters must submit a CBM form for exports over Lm 20,000.

Export licenses	With the exception of works of art and certain essential goods, all products may be exported freely.
Without quotas	Certain items of clothing for export to countries in the EU are subject to indicative ceilings and EU statistical surveillance.
Export taxes	No.

Payments for Invisible Transactions and Current Transfers

Controls on these transfers	Payments for invisibles may be made freely, but supporting documents must be presented to authorized credit and financial institutions before payment is effected. In some cases, such as travel-related payments and gift remittances, these payments are subject to limits on the amounts remitted, to prevent capital transfers.
Payments for travel	There are no quantitative restrictions on payments for accommodation and transportation expenses, as long as they are paid for in Malta or abroad with credit cards.
Quantitative limits	Residents are entitled to a travel allowance equivalent to Lm 2,500 a trip. Effective January 1, 2000, the travel allowance was increased to the equivalent of Lm 5,000 a trip.
Indicative limits/bona fide test	Amounts in excess of the above limit may be granted upon submission of documentary proof of need.
Personal payments	There are no restrictions on the transfer of pensions. Payments that are directly related to medical treatment, education, family maintenance, and alimony are permitted, within reasonable limits.
Quantitative limits	The annual limit each resident may transfer abroad to other family members or as a cash gift was Lm 2,500. Effective January 1, 2000, this limit was increased to Lm 5,000. Remittances above this limit require exchange control approval.
Indicative limits/bona fide test	Supporting documents must be presented to the intermediary bank.

Proceeds from Invisible Transactions and Current Transfers

Repatriation requirements	Proceeds must be received within six months of payments.
Surrender requirements	Receipts must be offered for sale to an authorized credit or financial institution or, if permitted by the CBM, deposited in a foreign currency account with a local institution.
Restrictions on use of funds	Funds deposited in foreign currency accounts may not be utilized for capital transactions without CBM authorization.

Capital Transactions

Controls on capital and money market instruments	Effective January 1, 2000, individuals and nonfinancial companies are permitted to invest up to Lm 15,000 a year. Any investment above this amount requires CMB approval.
On capital market securities	
Shares or other securities of a participating nature	
Purchase locally by nonresidents	Approval from the CBM must be obtained to purchase or acquire securities that are not listed on the Malta Stock Exchange (MSE). Effective January 1, 2000, approval must be obtained from the MFSC.
Sale or issue locally by nonresidents	Securities may not be issued without the approval of the MFSC.
Purchase abroad by residents	Effective January 1, 2000, individuals and companies are permitted to invest up to Lm 15,000 a year (previously Lm 8,000). Any investment above that amount requires exchange control approval from the CBM. Credit institutions and insurance companies are permitted to invest in such securities as long as the holding of such investment is in line

with prudential supervision regulations and currency exposure limits stipulated by the CBM and the MFSC.

Sale or issue abroad by residents	Residents are permitted to sell their approved holdings of foreign portfolio investments and acquire other such investments. Effective January 1, 2000, locally registered companies may list their securities on recognized stock exchanges overseas without CBM approval.
Bonds or other debt securities	The same regulations apply as for shares or other securities of a participating nature.
On money market instruments	The same regulations apply as for shares or other securities of a participating nature.
On collective investment securities	
Sale or issue locally by nonresidents	Sales are permitted, but the issue of these securities requires the approval of the MFSC.
Purchase abroad by residents	The same regulations apply as for shares or other securities of a participating nature.
Sale or issue abroad by residents	The same regulations apply as for shares or other securities of a participating nature.
Controls on derivatives and other instruments	Presently, such transactions take the form of forward currency deals. Such transactions are generally only allowed as a hedging instrument to cover an underlying current account transaction.
Purchase locally by nonresidents	Yes.
Sale or issue locally by nonresidents	Yes.
Purchase abroad by residents	Yes.
Sale or issue abroad by residents	Yes.
Controls on credit operations	
Commercial credits	
By residents to nonresidents	Exchange control approval is not required for commercial credits, but export proceeds must be received within six months of shipment, unless otherwise authorized.
Financial credits	
By residents to nonresidents	Resident credit and financial institutions are permitted to lend to nonresidents in foreign currency. Such lending is subject to prudential directives issued by the CBM. The directives cover large credit exposures and other regulations on currency exposure limits. Resident credit and financial institutions may also lend to nonresidents in local currency any amount, subject to prudential directives issued by the CBM, as long as the funds borrowed by the nonresident are used for financing operations in the local economy.
To residents from nonresidents	Resident credit and financial institutions are permitted to borrow from nonresident financial institutions as long as the maturity period of the borrowing exceeds three years. Borrowings for periods of three years or less require CBM approval. All such borrowings must be reported to the CBM.
Guarantees, sureties, and financial backup facilities	
By residents to nonresidents	These transactions are allowed if related to trade transactions.
Controls on direct investment	
Outward direct investment	Effective January 1, 1999, residents, individuals and companies, were allowed to remit up to Lm 300,000 a year (from Lm 150,000 a year) for direct investment purposes. Investments in excess of that amount required CBM approval. Effective January 1, 2000, all limits on the amount that resident individuals may transfer abroad for direct investment purposes were removed. Approval for such investment, however, remains subject to the condition that the resident acquire a controlling interest in the overseas company. Details of the state of the investment must be reported to the CBM annually.
Inward direct investment	Prior CBM approval is required. Except in a few areas, direct investment by nonresidents is usually permitted. Direct investment is usually prohibited in the real estate, wholesale, and retail trade sectors (particularly the importation of consumer goods for resale). Applications for direct investment in other activities may also be refused if the sectors involved are considered sensitive from a national perspective.

Controls on liquidation of direct investment	Approval is usually granted once financial statements and documentary evidence of the original investment are submitted to the MFSC.

Controls on real estate transactions

Purchase abroad by residents	Effective January 1, 2000, residents may invest up to Lm 50,000 a year in real estate abroad, subject to presentation of documentation to the CBM. Residents are also allowed to purchase real estate overseas using funds already held in portfolio investments abroad.
Purchase locally by nonresidents	Effective January 1, 1999, nonresidents may acquire immovable property in Malta as their own residence, with the permission of the MOF, on the condition that the cost of property to be acquired exceeds Lm 30,000 in the case of an apartment and Lm 50,000 in the case of any other residence (previously Lm 15,000), and that funds originate from overseas; additionally, the ad valorem stamp duty on the value of property sold to nonresidents was reduced to 10% from 17%. The MOF may allow nonresidents to acquire more than one property in specially designated areas.
Sale locally by nonresidents	Nonresidents are not allowed to engage in real estate property transactions in Malta, except to sell any property acquired with the approval of the MOF.

Controls on personal capital movements

Loans

By residents to nonresidents	Effective January 1, 2000, loans extended by residents to nonresidents are permitted up to a limit of Lm 20,000, provided that the loan is for a period of more than three years and related documentation is submitted regularly to the CBM for statistical purposes. Borrowing in excess of Lm 20,000 and/or for a period of three years or less is subject to specific CBM approval.
To residents from nonresidents	Loans in excess of Lm 5,000 may be obtained from foreign sources, provided that the loan is for a period of over three years and related documentation is submitted for statistical purposes. Borrowing in excess of Lm 5,000 with less than three years' maturity is subject to specific CBM approval. Effective January 1, 2000, this limit was increased to Lm 20,000.

Gifts, endowments, inheritances, and legacies

By residents to nonresidents	Effective January 1, 2000, the limit on gifts was increased to Lm 5,000 from Lm 2,500, but there are no limits for endowments, inheritances, and legacies, although documentary evidence must be submitted to an authorized credit or financial institution.
Settlement of debts abroad by immigrants	Yes.

Provisions specific to commercial banks and other credit institutions	Effective January 10, 1999, credit institutions, other than those that are authorized to transact only in currencies other than the Maltese lira, as well as other financial institutions, may hold foreign assets in unlimited amounts, but subject to prudential regulations issued by the CBM.
Borrowing abroad	Resident banks and financial institutions are permitted to borrow from nonresident financial institutions as long as the maturity period of the borrowings exceeds three years. Borrowings for periods of three years or less require CBM approval. All borrowings must be reported to the CBM.
Maintenance of accounts abroad	Credit institutions may hold accounts for both liquidity and investment purposes, subject to prudential regulations.
Lending to nonresidents (financial or commercial credits)	Lending and purchases of securities abroad are permitted, subject to banking directives on large exposures and regulations on currency exposure limits. Resident banks and financial institutions may lend to nonresidents in local currency any amount, subject to prudential directives governing large exposures, as long as the funds borrowed are used for carrying out operations in the local economy.
Lending locally in foreign exchange	Lending is permitted, subject to prudential regulations issued by the CBM with regard to exposure limits.

Purchase of locally issued securities denominated in foreign exchange	This is permitted, subject to prudential regulations issued by the CBM with regard to exposure limits.
Open foreign exchange position limits	Open foreign exchange position limits are subject to prudential regulations issued by the CBM with regard to exposure limits.
Provisions specific to institutional investors	Effective January 1, 2000, overseas portfolio investments by insurance companies were completely liberalized, but remain subject to prudential regulations introduced by the MFSC. These regulations, issued in the form of directives, are in line with those in force in the EU. The regulations also refer to asset quality and currency matching.
	Investment management companies are permitted to invest, without limit, eligible funds that originate from overseas from both resident and nonresident sources. In addition, they are permitted to invest overseas funds that originate from local sources belonging to residents, on the condition that the funds invested by the resident with the investment company do not exceed the yearly portfolio investment allowance (currently Lm 15,000 a person).
Limits (max.) on securities issued by nonresidents and on portfolio invested abroad	Yes.
Limits (max.) on portfolio invested abroad	Yes.
Currency-matching regulations on assets/liabilities composition	Yes.
Other controls imposed by securities laws	No.

Changes During 1999

Exchange arrangement	*January 1.* The composition of the Maltese lira basket was revised to take into account the introduction of the euro. The euro was allocated the previous weight of the ECU component, excluding the sterling weight within the ECU. The latter was allocated to the weight of the sterling in the Maltese lira basket.
	January 1. The variable spread used for the computation of the buying and selling rates for transactions in foreign exchange between the CBM and the credit institutions was reduced to approximately 0.125%.
Arrangements for payments and receipts	*April 30.* Restrictions on transactions with Libya were suspended following the suspension of sanctions by the United Nations.
	December 21. Restrictions were placed on payments and transfers to the Taliban (the Islamic Republic of Afghanistan).
Resident accounts	*January 1.* The allowance for investments in foreign currency by resident individuals and nonfinancial corporate bodies, without specific exchange control approval, was increased to Lm 8,000 from Lm 5,000 a year.
Exports and export proceeds	*January 1.* The period during which exporters in the manufacturing sector are allowed to retain export proceeds in foreign currency deposit accounts was extended to six months from four months.
Capital transactions	*January 1.* The allowance for investments in foreign currency by resident individuals and non-financial corporate bodies, without specific exchange control approval, was increased to Lm 8,000 from Lm 5,000 a year.
Controls on direct investment	*January 1.* The allowance for direct investment abroad by resident individuals and corporate bodies, without specific exchange control approval, was increased to Lm 300,000 from Lm 150,000 a year.
Controls on real estate transactions	*January 1.* The "ad valorem" stamp duty on the value of property sold to nonresidents was reduced to 10% from 17%. The minimum value of property to be acquired by nonresidents was increased to Lm 30,000 from Lm 15,000 in the case of apartments and to Lm 50,000 from Lm 15,000 in the case of other residences.

Provisions specific to commercial banks and other credit institutions	*January 10.* Credit institutions, other than those that are authorized to transact only in currencies other than the Maltese lira, as well as other financial institutions, were allowed to hold foreign assets in unlimited amounts, subject to prudential regulations issued by the CBM.

Changes During 2000

Arrangements for payments and receipts	*January 1.* The MOF delegated responsibility for the approval of inward direct investment by nonresidents to the MFSC.
	January 1. Residents were allowed to export up to Lm 5,000 in foreign currency a trip (previously Lm 2,500).
Resident accounts	*January 1.* The allowance for investment in foreign currency by resident individuals and nonfinancial corporate bodies, without specific exchange control approval, was increased to Lm 15,000 a year from Lm 8,000 a year.
	January 1. Firms in all other export-oriented activities, not just export companies, were allowed to deposit export proceeds in savings and time deposit accounts denominated in foreign currency for a maximum period of six months.
	January 1. Resident businesses in the retailing sector were allowed to hold up to Lm 2,500 in foreign currency time and savings deposits on the condition that the funds be used only for receipts related to their business activities and payments to nonresidents in connection with current account transactions.
Exports and export proceeds	*January 1.* The retention of proceeds in foreign currency deposit accounts was extended to firms in all export-oriented activities.
Payments for invisible transactions and current transfers	*January 1.* The annual limit each resident may transfer abroad to family members or as a cash gift was increased to Lm 5,000 from Lm 2,500.
	January 1. The travel allowance was increased to the equivalent of Lm 5,000 a trip from Lm 2,500 a trip.
	January 1. The allowance for investment in foreign currency by resident individuals and nonfinancial corporate bodies, without specific exchange control approval, was increased to Lm 15,000 a year from Lm 8,000 a year.
Capital transactions	
Controls on capital and money market instruments	*January 1.* Locally registered companies may list their securities on recognized stock exchanges overseas without CBM approval.
	January 1. Approval to purchase or acquire securities that are not listed in the MSE must be obtained from the MFSC, not the CBM.
Controls on direct investment	*January 1.* Limits on the amount that resident individuals may transfer abroad for direct investment purposes were removed.
Controls on real estate transactions	*January 1.* Residents were allowed to invest in real estate abroad up to Lm 50,000 a year.
Controls on personal capital movements	*January 1.* The limit on transfers of gifts was raised to Lm 5,000 from Lm 2,000.
	January 1. Loans extended by residents to nonresidents and by nonresidents to residents for a period of more than three years were increased to Lm 20,000 from Lm 5,000.
Provisions specific to institutional investors	*January 1.* Overseas portfolio investments by insurance companies were completely liberalized, but remain subject to the prudential regulations introduced by the MFSC.

MARSHALL ISLANDS

(Position as of December 31, 1999)

Status Under IMF Articles of Agreement

Article VIII	Date of acceptance: May 21, 1992.

Exchange Arrangement

Currency	The currency of the Marshall Islands is the dollar.
Exchange rate structure	Unitary.
Classification	
Exchange arrangement with no separate legal tender	The authorities do not buy or sell foreign exchange. Foreign exchange transactions are handled by three commercial banks, which are authorized foreign exchange dealers and are regulated by a statutory banking board. The banks buy and sell foreign exchange at the rates quoted in the international markets.
Exchange tax	No.
Exchange subsidy	No.
Forward exchange market	Forward transactions may be conducted through commercial banks without restrictions.

Arrangements for Payments and Receipts

Prescription of currency requirements	Outward and inward payments may be settled in dollars or in any other convertible currency.
Payment arrangements	No.
Administration of control	There are no exchange control regulations.
International security restrictions	No.
Payment arrears	No.
Controls on trade in gold (coins and/or bullion)	n.a.
Controls on exports and imports of banknotes	n.a.

Resident Accounts

Foreign exchange accounts permitted	Yes.
Held domestically	Yes.
Held abroad	Commercial banks are not permitted to transfer abroad more than 25% of deposits received from residents. In practice, this regulation is not strictly enforced and does not prevent a depositor from transferring deposits abroad.
Accounts in domestic currency convertible into foreign currency	Yes.

Nonresident Accounts

Foreign exchange accounts permitted	Yes.

Domestic currency accounts	Yes.
Convertible into foreign currency	Yes.
Blocked accounts	No.

Imports and Import Payments

Foreign exchange budget	No.
Financing requirements for imports	No.
Documentation requirements for release of foreign exchange for imports	No.
Import licenses and other nontariff measures	Imports are not subject to import licensing requirements, but importers must obtain a business license.
Negative list	Imports of certain products are prohibited for environmental, health, safety, or social reasons.
Import taxes and/or tariffs	Specific and ad valorem duties are levied on imports. Ad valorem duties range from 5% to 75%. Most items are charged a 10% tariff rate, while a 5% rate is applied to food items, medicines, building materials, and heavy machinery. Specific duties are applied on cigarettes, certain beverages, and fuels.
State import monopoly	No.

Exports and Export Proceeds

Repatriation requirements	No.
Financing requirements	No.
Documentation requirements	No.
Export licenses	Exports are not subject to licensing requirements, taxes, or quantitative restrictions. The exportation of copra and its by-products is conducted solely by the government-owned Tobolar Copra Processing Plant, Inc.
Export taxes	No.

Payments for Invisible Transactions and Current Transfers

Controls on these transfers	No.

Proceeds from Invisible Transactions and Current Transfers

Repatriation requirements	No.
Restrictions on use of funds	No.

Capital Transactions

Controls on capital and money market instruments	n.a.
Controls on derivatives and other instruments	n.a.
Controls on credit operations	n.a.

Controls on direct investment

Outward direct investment

Foreign investors are required to submit applications to the Cabinet and obtain a license in order to engage in business or to acquire an interest in a business in the Marshall Islands.

Inward direct investment

Yes.

Controls on liquidation of direct investment

n.a.

Controls on real estate transactions

Purchase locally by nonresidents

Foreigners are prohibited from owning land, but investors may obtain long-term leases for up to 50 years with an option to renew on land needed for their business.

Controls on personal capital movements

n.a.

Provisions specific to commercial banks and other credit institutions

n.a.

Provisions specific to institutional investors

n.a.

Other controls imposed by securities laws

n.a.

Changes During 1999

No significant changes occurred in the exchange and trade system.

MAURITANIA

(Position as of December 31, 1999)

Status Under IMF Articles of Agreement

Article VIII   Date of acceptance: July 19, 1999.

Exchange Arrangement

Currency   The currency of Mauritania is the Mauritanian ouguiya.

Exchange rate structure   Unitary.

Classification

Managed floating with no pre-   The Central Bank of Mauritania (CBM) sets each week a central intervention rate based on
announced path for the exchange rate observed and foreseeable market pressures; the reserve accumulation target; and the actual
                                    rate observed in transactions recorded in the preceding days by banks and exchange bu-
                                    reaus. Based on this central intervention rate, the CBM uses a fixed margin of 0.75% in
                                    each direction to obtain bid and offer rates, which are used in all CBM foreign exchange
                                    ouguiya transactions with the treasury. Based on the interbank market overnight rates, the
                                    CBM buys and sells foreign exchange in the full amounts offered or demanded by banks
                                    and exchange bureaus, without limitations. Banks and exchange bureaus continue to freely
                                    determine the bid and offer rates and commissions they use in transactions with their cus-
                                    tomers and among themselves. The average exchange rate is applied to foreign clearing
                                    transactions of the Postal Administration. This exchange rate is also applied to remittances
                                    through the Postal Administration by Mauritanian workers residing abroad.

Exchange tax   No.

Exchange subsidy   No.

Forward exchange market   No.

Arrangements for Payments and Receipts

**Prescription of currency   No.
requirements**

Payment arrangements

Bilateral payment arrangements

  Inoperative   Yes.

Regional arrangements   An inoperative arrangement exists within the framework of the Arab Maghreb Union.

Administration of control   Administration of control is vested in the CBM, the Ministry of Economy and Finance,
                                    and the Ministry of Commerce (MOC). Exchange control authority to approve current
                                    international transactions is delegated to authorized banks and foreign exchange bureaus.
                                    All imports must be registered at the CBM for statistical purposes.

International security restrictions No.

Payment arrears

Private   Yes.

**Controls on trade in gold (coins
and/or bullion)**

Controls on external trade   All imports and exports of gold, except manufactured articles containing a minor quantity
                                    of gold, require prior authorization from the CBM.

Controls on exports and imports of banknotes

On exports

Domestic currency

Travelers are not allowed to take out domestic banknotes and coins.

Foreign currency

Residents are authorized to export foreign exchange obtained legally and must provide documentation to prove the source. Nonresidents of foreign nationality may freely export payment instruments denominated in foreign currencies. Nonresidents are free to export foreign exchange; however, if they wish to repurchase amounts previously surrendered in exchange for ouguiyas, they must present a receipt of sale of foreign exchange to a bank or an exchange bureau. They are exempt from this formality for any sum not exceeding $200. Nonresident holders of foreign accounts denominated in a foreign currency or in convertible ouguiyas and maintained in a licensed banking intermediary may export any amount of traveler's checks denominated in foreign currencies that have been purchased by debit to the aforementioned accounts.

On imports

Domestic currency

Imports are not allowed.

Foreign currency

Residents and nonresidents of Mauritania may freely import foreign banknotes but residents must exchange them at an authorized bank.

Resident Accounts

Foreign exchange accounts permitted

Yes.

Held domestically

Exporters may open these accounts in Mauritanian banks to deposit the portion of their export proceeds that they are authorized to retain. These accounts may be debited for payment for current operations or for surrender of foreign exchange to the market.

Held abroad

Licensed banks and foreign exchange bureaus may freely open accounts with banks abroad to accommodate foreign exchange market transactions. Other residents are not allowed to maintain accounts abroad.

Accounts in domestic currency convertible into foreign currency

These accounts may not be opened, except by exporters, as specified above.

Nonresident Accounts

Foreign exchange accounts permitted

Licensed intermediary banks may open freely the following nonresident accounts: (1) nonresident convertible accounts, which may be denominated in foreign currencies or in convertible ouguiyas, and transit accounts. Nonresident convertible accounts may be credited with transfers from abroad or from another foreign account; proceeds from the encashment of checks drawn on a foreign bank or on another foreign account opened in a Mauritanian bank to the order of the account holder; transfers issued by a licensed intermediary bank by order of a resident in payment of transactions authorized by the exchange control regulations; and proceeds from the surrender of foreign exchange on account on the foreign exchange market (however, banknotes, whether foreign or issued by the CBM, may not be deposited). These accounts may be debited for foreign exchange surrendered on the foreign exchange market, funds made available abroad, withdrawals of traveler's checks denominated in a foreign currency by the holder, transfers in favor of another foreign account or a resident, checks issued by the holder of the account in favor of another nonresident or a resident, and withdrawals of banknotes issued by the CBM; and (2) transit accounts, which may be opened freely by resident consignees on their books in the names of shipping companies.

Domestic currency accounts

Convertible ouguiya accounts may be credited in the same manner as foreign exchange accounts.

Convertible into foreign currency

Yes.

Blocked accounts   No.

Imports and Import Payments

Foreign exchange budget   No.

Financing requirements for imports

Advance payment requirements   Advance payments for imports require the prior approval of the CBM.

Advance import deposits   n.r.

Documentation requirements for release of foreign exchange for imports

Import licenses used as exchange   Upon presentation of the advance import notification, the importer may purchase the
licenses   foreign exchange from an authorized bank or an exchange bureau.

Import licenses and other nontariff The holders of import-export permits had to obtain a certificate that was endorsed by the
measures   CBM. Nonholders of import-export permits were subject to the authorization of the MOC.
                                     Effective December 31, 1999, this requirement was eliminated.

Negative list   Imports of a few goods are prohibited for reasons of health or public policy.

Open general licenses   Yes.

Import taxes and/or tariffs   Four duty rates apply: zero, 5%, 10%, and 20%. In addition, a statistical tax of 3% is levied.
                                     Goods that are imported by some public enterprises or with external financing are exempt
                                     from all import duties.

State import monopoly   No.

Exports and Export Proceeds

Repatriation requirements   On January 1, 1999, the requirement that 15% of the export receipts of the state-owned
                                     Ore Company (SNIM) is to be repatriated via correspondents of the banks and exchange
                                     bureaus was increased to 20%.

Surrender requirements   On December 31, 1999, the surrender requirement of the SNIM export proceeds was
                                     reduced to 40%, the percentage of non-iron export earnings that exporters may keep
                                     was increased to 70%, and the retention period for export earnings was increased to
                                     nine months.

Financing requirements   n.r.

Documentation requirements   Export certificates submitted to the CBM for statistical purposes must specify the quantity,
                                     value, and destination of all goods.

Letters of credit   n.r.

Guarantees   n.r.

Domiciliation   Exports exceeding UM 20,000 must be domiciled.

Preshipment inspection   n.r.

Export licenses   Exports of goods require only a certificate endorsed by the CBM.

Without quotas   Yes.

Export taxes   A tax is levied on exports of fish and crustaceans at rates ranging from 8% to 20% for
                                     specialized catches, and at a rate of 5% for shrimp and crayfish.

Other export taxes   n.r.

Payments for Invisible Transactions and Current Transfers

Controls on these transfers	The signing of a contract for services rendered by nonresidents to residents is subject to the CBM's endorsement; foreign exchange necessary to pay for their services may be acquired upon presentation of the endorsed contract and a bill of costs.
Trade-related payments	
Prior approval	Yes.
Indicative limits/bona fide test	Yes.
Investment-related payments	Information is not available on the payment of amortization of loans or depreciation of direct investments.
Prior approval	Yes.
Indicative limits/bona fide test	Yes.
Payments for travel	On June 7, 1999, restrictions on foreign exchange sales for travel abroad were eliminated.
Personal payments	There are controls on the payment of family maintenance and alimony, but information is not available on other personal payments.
Prior approval	Yes.
Indicative limits/bona fide test	Yes.

Proceeds from Invisible Transactions and Current Transfers

Repatriation requirements	Proceeds must be repatriated within four months.
Surrender requirements	Earnings from services routinely rendered abroad by residents must be domiciled at a licensed intermediary bank. Proceeds must be surrendered in exchange for ouguiyas under the same conditions as proceeds from exports of goods.
Restrictions on use of funds	n.a.

Capital Transactions

Controls on capital and money market instruments	Capital movements are subject to exchange control. Outward capital transfers require CBM approval and are restricted, but capital receipts are normally permitted freely, although the subsequent investment of the funds in Mauritania may require approval.
On capital market securities	
Shares or other securities of a participating nature	
Purchase abroad by residents	Yes.
On money market instruments	
Purchase abroad by residents	Yes.
On collective investment securities	
Purchase abroad by residents	Yes.
Controls on derivatives and other instruments	
Purchase abroad by residents	Yes.
Controls on credit operations	All credit transactions, guarantees, sureties, and financial backup facilities by residents to nonresidents are controlled.

Commercial credits	
By residents to nonresidents	Yes.
Financial credits	
By residents to nonresidents	Yes.
Guarantees, sureties, and financial backup facilities	
By residents to nonresidents	Yes.
Controls on direct investment	Investments must be declared to the CBM before they are made.
Outward direct investment	Yes.
Inward direct investment	Yes.
Controls on liquidation of direct investment	n.a.
Controls on real estate transactions	
Purchase abroad by residents	Yes.
Controls on personal capital movements	n.a.
Provisions specific to commercial banks and other credit institutions	
Open foreign exchange position limits	
On resident assets and liabilities	On July 1, 1999, the limits on commercial banks' net open foreign positions in foreign exchange were adjusted to a maximum of 10% of net capital per currency and to a maximum of 20% of net capital for all currencies.
Provisions specific to institutional investors	n.a.
Other controls imposed by securities laws	n.a.

Changes During 1999

Fund status	*July 19.* Mauritania accepted the obligations of Article VIII, sections 2, 3, and 4.
Imports and import payments	*December 31.* The requirement to obtain a certificate endorsed by the CBM was eliminated.
Exports and export proceeds	*January 1.* The amount of export receipts of the SNIM required to be repatriated was increased to 20% from 15%.
	December 31. The surrender requirement of the SNIM export proceeds was reduced to 40%; the percentage of non-iron export earnings that exporters may keep was increased to 70%; and the retention period for export earnings was increased to nine months.
Payments for invisible transactions and current transfers	*June 7.* Restrictions on foreign exchange sales for travel abroad were eliminated.
Capital transactions	
Provisions specific to commercial banks and other credit institutions	*July 1.* The limits on commercial banks' net open foreign positions in foreign exchange were adjusted to a maximum of 10% of net capital per currency and to a maximum of 20% of net capital for all currencies.

MAURITIUS

(Position as of December 31, 1999)

Status Under IMF Articles of Agreement

Article VIII	Date of acceptance: September 29, 1993.

Exchange Arrangement

Currency	The currency of Mauritius is the Mauritian rupee.
Other legal tender	Gold coins issued in Mauritius are legal tender.
Exchange rate structure	Unitary.
Classification	
Independently floating	The exchange rate of the Mauritian rupee is market determined.
Exchange tax	No.
Exchange subsidy	No.
Forward exchange market	Commercial banks are free to provide forward exchange cover to their clients.

Arrangements for Payments and Receipts

Prescription of currency requirements	No.
Payment arrangements	
Regional arrangements	Mauritius is a member of the COMESA clearinghouse.
Clearing agreements	Yes.
Administration of control	No.
International security restrictions	
In accordance with UN sanctions	Restrictions are imposed in compliance with UN Security Council resolutions.
Payment arrears	No.
Controls on trade in gold (coins and/or bullion)	
Controls on domestic ownership and/or trade	Residents are permitted to hold gold for numismatic purposes or as personal jewelry and ornaments.
Controls on exports and imports of banknotes	No.

Resident Accounts

Foreign exchange accounts permitted	There is no distinction between accounts of residents and nonresidents in Mauritius.
Held domestically	Companies and individuals may maintain accounts denominated in foreign currencies with commercial banks.
Held abroad	Yes.
Accounts in domestic currency convertible into foreign currency	Yes.

Nonresident Accounts

Foreign exchange accounts permitted	Companies and individuals may maintain accounts denominated in foreign currencies with commercial banks. Companies need a specific approval from the bank of Mauritius (BOM).
Domestic currency accounts	Companies and individuals may maintain accounts denominated in Mauritian rupees with commercial banks.
Convertible into foreign currency	Yes.
Blocked accounts	No.

Imports and Import Payments

Foreign exchange budget	No.
Financing requirements for imports	No.
Documentation requirements for release of foreign exchange for imports	
Import licenses used as exchange licenses	Release of foreign exchange for imports of goods that are controlled for the purpose of consumer protection requires the presentation of the original import permit issued by the Ministry of Trade and Shipping.
Import licenses and other nontariff measures	Imports of agricultural, horticultural, and livestock products require phytosanitary inspection. Imports of sugarcane are prohibited.
Open general licenses	Most imports are admitted to Mauritius under the system of OGL.
Licenses with quotas	Imports of potatoes and salt are subject, when necessary, to quotas.
Import taxes and/or tariffs	In certain cases, duty rates range up to 100%, with most items subject to rates up to 20%. Certain items are subject to import excise duties ranging from 15% to 400%.
State import monopoly	No.

Exports and Export Proceeds

Repatriation requirements	No.
Financing requirements	No.
Documentation requirements	No.
Export licenses	A permit is required for exports of textile products to the United States and Canada.
With quotas	Mauritius abides by quotas on exports of textiles and clothing to the United States and Canada under bilateral export restraint agreements. The volume of sugar exports to the EU is restricted under the Sugar Protocol of the Lomé Convention; that to the United States is also subject to quotas.
Export taxes	n.a.

Payments for Invisible Transactions and Current Transfers

Controls on these transfers	No.

Proceeds from Invisible Transactions and Current Transfers

Repatriation requirements	No.
Restrictions on use of funds	No.

Capital Transactions

Controls on capital and money market instruments	There are no controls on the purchase by nonresidents of shares listed on the stock exchange. However, the authorization of the Prime Minister and the Minister of Internal Affairs is required under the Noncitizens Propriety Restriction Act (NPRA) for nonresidents to purchase shares not listed on the stock exchange.
On capital market securities	
Shares or other securities of a participating nature	
Purchase locally by nonresidents	Yes.
Controls on derivatives and other instruments	No.
Controls on credit operations	No.
Controls on direct investment	
Inward direct investment	Yes.
Controls on liquidation of direct investment	No.
Controls on real estate transactions	
Purchase locally by nonresidents	Noncitizens acquiring property in Mauritius must obtain the prior permission of the Prime Minister and Minister of Internal Affairs. The purchase must be financed by funds transferred from abroad through the banking system.
Controls on personal capital movements	No.
Provisions specific to commercial banks and other credit institutions	
Investment regulations	
Abroad by banks	The BOM must approve investments in shares.
In banks by nonresidents	Nonresidents may invest in shares of commercial banks listed on the Stock Exchange of Mauritius (SEM). In the case of banks whose shares are not listed on the SEM, the authorization of the Prime Minister and the Minister of Internal Affairs must be sought. In both cases, bank shareholdings of 15% or more require approval of the BOM.
Open foreign exchange position limits	A daily overall foreign exchange exposure limit of 15% in relation to Tier I capital is applicable to domestic commercial banks.
On resident assets and liabilities	Yes.
On nonresident assets and liabilities	Yes.
Provisions specific to institutional investors	No.
Other controls imposed by securities laws	Noncitizens are not allowed to hold more than 15% of shares in the listed sugar companies.

Changes During 1999

No significant changes occurred in the exchange and trade system.

MEXICO

(Position as of January 31, 2000)

Status Under IMF Articles of Agreement

Article VIII

Date of acceptance: November 12, 1946.

Exchange Arrangement

Currency

The currency of Mexico is the Mexican peso.

Exchange rate structure

Unitary.

Classification

Independently floating

A floating exchange rate policy is maintained by the government, with Banco de Mexico (BOM) intervening in the foreign exchange market on the basis of rules-based mechanisms to minimize volatility and ensure an orderly market. The BOM, on instructions from the Foreign Exchange Commission (made up of officials from the MOF and the BOM), implements a mechanism intended to encourage purchases of foreign exchange by the BOM when there is an excess supply in the foreign exchange market, and discourage such purchases when there is an excess demand. This mechanism was contrived to conserve the nature of the floating foreign exchange regime. Under this mechanism, each month the BOM auctions among banks the rights to sell to the BOM a fixed amount of dollars in exchange for Mexican pesos. These rights may be partially or completely exercised within the month following the respective auction. Holders of these rights may sell dollars to the BOM at the interbank exchange rate published for the previous business day, if the exchange rate is not higher than the average exchange rate for the 20 business days prior to the date on which said rights are exercised. The maximum amount of rights to be auctioned per month is currently fixed at US$250 million.

The BOM also announced that it would be prepared to auction (sell) up to US$200 million a day, but would accept only those bids that are at least 2% more depreciated (in terms of Mexican pesos per U.S. dollar) than the fix of the previous day.

Exchange tax

No.

Exchange subsidy

No.

Forward exchange market

Commercial banks are allowed to enter into forward transactions that involve currencies in over-the-counter markets and formal markets recognized by the BOM (currently, the Chicago Mercantile Exchange, the Chicago Board Options Exchange, the Mid America Commodity Exchange, the Mexican Derivatives Exchange, and the Commodity Exchange Inc.).

Arrangements for Payments and Receipts

Prescription of currency requirements

No.

Payment arrangements

Bilateral payment arrangements

Operative

There is a payment arrangement with the Central Bank of Malaysia.

Regional arrangements

In accordance with the Reciprocal Credits and Payment Agreements entered into by the BOM with the central banks of Argentina, Bolivia, Brazil, Chile, Colombia, the Dominican Republic, Ecuador, Paraguay, Peru, Uruguay, and Venezuela, payments to these countries may be made through the BOM and the central bank of the country concerned within the framework of the multilateral clearing system of the LAIA. A similar payment arrangement exists with the central banks of Costa Rica, El Salvador, Guatemala, Honduras, and Nicaragua. Mexico is also a member of NAFTA.

Clearing agreements	There are clearing agreements in accordance with the regional payment agreements referred to above.
Administration of control	No.
International security restrictions	No.
Payment arrears	No.
Controls on trade in gold (coins and/or bullion)	No.
Controls on exports and imports of banknotes	
On imports	
Domestic currency	The customs law requires that persons bringing into the country an amount of cash, checks, or a combination of both higher than the equivalent of US$20,000 must declare it to the customs authorities.
Foreign currency	The same regulations apply as for imports of domestic currency.

Resident Accounts

Foreign exchange accounts permitted	Yes.
Held domestically	Commercial banks are permitted to hold dollar deposits in checking accounts payable in Mexico provided holders of such accounts are (1) residents of the 20 kilometer–long strip along the northern border area of Mexico or living in Baja California or Baja California Sur, and (2) firms domiciled in Mexico. Commercial banks are also permitted to hold dollar deposits for firms established in Mexico provided such deposits are payable abroad.
Held abroad	Yes.
Accounts in domestic currency convertible into foreign currency	No.

Nonresident Accounts

Foreign exchange accounts permitted	Commercial banks arc only permitted to hold dollar deposits through checking accounts payable in Mexico with respect to official representations of foreign governments and international organizations, including foreign individuals employed in such entities and foreign correspondents. In such cases, they should be registered in Mexico with the appropriate authority.
Domestic currency accounts	Yes.
Convertible into foreign currency	No.
Blocked accounts	No.

Imports and Import Payments

Foreign exchange budget	No.
Financing requirements for imports	No.
Documentation requirements for release of foreign exchange for imports	No.
Import licenses and other nontariff measures	Import licenses from the Secretariat of Commerce and Industrial Promotion (SECOFI) are required for only 69 of the 11,398 items on which Mexico's general import tariff is levied, except for temporary imports of raw materials and intermediate goods for export industries. On average, import licenses cover the applicant's import needs for nine months and may be

extended for three months. Import needs are estimated at 20% above the amount of previous actual imports but may be increased when justified. New licenses are issued only if the applicant can demonstrate that at least 70% of earlier licenses have been effectively used. For some commodities, "open-ended" import licenses may be granted, allowing imports to be effected during a period of six months to one year, subject to an overall limit. Depending on the importer's performance, the license may be renewed repeatedly. Imports of new cars of a given manufacturer are limited to 143% of export levels of the same manufacturer. Imports of used cars are subject to the prior approval of the SECOFI.

Negative list	Yes.
Open general licenses	Yes.
Licenses with quotas	Yes.

Import taxes and/or tariffs   Import tariffs range from zero to 30%, with higher rates for a few products such as clothing, footwear, and leather goods subject to a 35% tariff. Imports from members of LAIA are granted preferential duty treatment. Free trade agreements exist with Bolivia, Chile, Colombia, Costa Rica, Nicaragua, and Venezuela. Trade with the United States and Canada takes place under NAFTA. As part of the 1999 budget, the authorities have increased customs duties on imports from countries that do not have free trade agreements with Mexico. Mexico has applied antidumping duties on a variety of products: corrugated rod, synthetic rubber, and steel products from Brazil; doorknobs, footwear, tools, walkers and carioles, chinaware, dental floss, textiles and articles of apparel, electronic products, toys, lighters, and chemical products from China; bicycle tires from India; beef, sodium hydroxide, polyvinyl chloride, fructose, bond paper, metal plates, seamless tubes and pipes, gasoline additives, hydrogen peroxide, and polyestyrene from the United States; sulfuric acid from Japan; urea from Ukraine; polyester from Korea; steel products from Russia, Venezuela, Canada, and the Netherlands; kitchenware from Taiwan; and polyestyrene from Germany.

State import monopoly   No.

Exports and Export Proceeds

Repatriation requirements   No.

Financing requirements   No.

Documentation requirements   No.

Export licenses   Most exports do not require licenses. Exports of a few specified items related to drugs, narcotic substances, endangered species, and archaeological pieces are prohibited.

Export taxes   Export taxes are limited to endangered species' skins, turtle oil, and electricity, among others.

Payments for Invisible Transactions and Current Transfers

Controls on these transfers   Under the insurance law, it is prohibited for foreign insurance companies to enter into the following types of contracts: (1) insurance of persons when the person is located in Mexico at the time the contract is closed; (2) insurance of hulls of ships or airships and of any class of vehicle against risk proper to the maritime and transport class of insurance when the ships, airships, or vehicles are registered in Mexico or are property of residents of Mexico; (3) credit insurance when the insured is subject to Mexican laws; (4) insurance against civil liability derived from events that may occur in Mexico; and (5) other classes of insurance against risks that may occur in Mexican territory. Reinsurance may be contracted with foreign reinsurance companies.

Proceeds from Invisible Transactions and Current Transfers

Repatriation requirements   No.

Restrictions on use of funds   No.

Capital Transactions

Controls on capital and money market instruments

On capital market securities

Shares or other securities of a participating nature

Purchase locally by nonresidents | Purchase of shares and other securities of a participating nature may be affected by the laws on inward direct investment and establishment. Such laws specify activities where investment is reserved to the government or Mexican investors. Notwithstanding these restrictions, if certain requirements are met, the Foreign Investment Law allows foreign investors to purchase equity securities traded on the Mexican stock exchange (MSE). Thus, with the authorization of the SECOFI, investment trusts may be established by Mexican banks acting as trustees. These trusts issue ordinary participation certificates that may be acquired by foreign investors; the certificates grant only economic rights to their holders and do not confer voting rights in the companies whose stock is held by the trusts (such voting rights being exercisable only by the trustee).

Sale or issue locally by nonresidents | Foreign commercial entities must be authorized by the SECOFI before engaging in habitual commercial activities in the Mexican territory. Foreign securities publicly offered in the domestic market must be approved by the National Banking and Securities Commission (CNBV).

Purchase abroad by residents | Controls apply to the purchases of foreign securities by Mexican securities firms and banks for their own account.

Sale or issue abroad by residents | Domestic securities offered in foreign markets must be registered with the National Registry of Securities and Intermediaries (NRSI).

Bonds or other debt securities

Sale or issue locally by nonresidents | The same regulations apply as for shares or other securities of a participating nature.

Purchase abroad by residents | Controls apply to the purchases of foreign securities by Mexican securities firms and banks for their own account and on the account of their clients.

Sale or issue abroad by residents | The same regulations apply as for shares or other securities of a participating nature.

On money market instruments

Sale or issue locally by nonresidents | The same regulations apply as for shares or other securities of a participating nature.

Purchase abroad by residents | The same regulations apply as for bonds or other debt securities.

Sale or issue abroad by residents | The same regulations apply as for shares or other securities of a participating nature.

On collective investment securities

Purchase locally by nonresidents | Irrespective of the holder's nationality, limits are imposed on individual holdings of shares issued by mutual funds organized pursuant to the Investments Societies Law.

Sale or issue locally by nonresidents | The same regulations apply as for shares or other securities of a participating nature.

Purchase abroad by residents | The same regulations apply as for bonds or other debt securities.

Sale or issue abroad by residents | The same regulations apply as for shares or other securities of a participating nature.

Controls on derivatives and other instruments	Effective March 1, 1999, the Commodity Exchange Incorporated was included as a recognized market in which commercial banks may enter into futures or options transactions. The BOM and the CNBV issued provisions applicable to securities firms regarding derivative operations.
Purchase locally by nonresidents	Foreigners are restricted to invest in options publicly traded when investments in the underlying shares or other securities of a participating nature of such options are reserved exclusively to Mexican residents.
Sale or issue locally by nonresidents	Foreign commercial entities must be authorized by the SECOFI before engaging in habitual commercial activities in the Mexican territory. The underlying asset of equity options publicly traded must be registered with the NRSI and the MSE where the option is traded. Options on foreign stock exchange indices need the approval on the respective index by the MSE where the option is traded. Furthermore, foreign derivatives publicly offered in the domestic market must be approved by the CNBV.
Purchase abroad by residents	Controls apply to Mexican financial institutions with respect to the type of transactions they can enter into and amounts related thereto.
Sale or issue abroad by residents	The same controls apply as for purchases abroad by residents.
Controls on credit operations	
Commercial credits	
By residents to nonresidents	There are limits on the amount that banks may lend to individual borrowers and on the open foreign exchange position of banks.
To residents from nonresidents	There are limits on credits granted to Mexican banks denominated in foreign currency and open foreign exchange position limits.
Financial credits	
By residents to nonresidents	There are limits on the amount that banks are allowed to lend to individual borrowers and on the open foreign exchange position of banks.
Controls on direct investment	
Inward direct investment	If certain conditions are satisfied, the ownership by foreign investors of 100% of the capital stock of a Mexican company is permitted. The law sets forth which activities of the economy are reserved to the government or to Mexican investors and lists the different activities in which foreign investment may not exceed 10%, 25%, and 49% of the total investment.
	Direct or indirect investment by a foreign government or state enterprise in financial institutions is prohibited except for commercial banks, limited-scope financial institutions, financial holding companies, securities specialists, securities firms, general deposit warehouses, financial leasing companies, savings and loan companies, factoring com-panies, and foreign exchange firms where the restriction applies to investment by entities that exercise governmental authority.
	Investments in the following sectors are reserved for the government: petroleum and other hydrocarbons; basic petrochemicals; electricity; nuclear energy generation; radio-active minerals; telegraph; radiotelegraphy; postal service; issuance of paper money; minting of coins; and the control and supervision of ports, airports, and heliports.
	Investments in the following sectors are reserved exclusively for Mexican individuals or Mexican corporations with a foreign exclusion clause: retail trade of gasoline and liquified petroleum gas; radio and television broadcasting services other than cable television; ground transport of passengers, tourism, and loading (excluding courier and packaged goods transport services); credit unions, development banks; and certain professional and technical services. Notwithstanding these restrictions, foreign investors may invest in these activities through the acquisition of ordinary participation certificates—issued by investment trusts established by Mexican banks acting as trustee, which grant only economic rights to their holders.
	Investments exceeding 49% in the following sectors and companies require prior authorization from the National Foreign Investment Commission: acquisition in a Mexican corporation if the total value of assets exceeds the equivalent of approximately

US$75 million; port services for interior navigation; shipping companies dedicated only to the export of high-traffic ships; administration of air terminals; cellular telephones; construction of pipelines for oil and other derivatives; oil and gas drilling; legal services; private education; credit information companies; securities rating institutions; insurance agents; and building, operation, and exploitation of railway lines, if they are for general lines of communication, and the public service of railway transportation. Limits on maximum foreign investments are applied to the following sectors: cooperative production entities (10%); air transportation (25%); certain financial institutions (49%); manufacturing of explosives and firearms (49%); newspapers for national distribution (49%); acquisition of "T" shares that represent the value of land used for agriculture, livestock, and forestry purposes (49%); fishing, other than aquaculture, in coastal and fresh waters or in the Exclusive Economic Zone (49%); interior navigation and coastal sailing, except tourist cruises and the exploitation of dredges and other naval devices for ports (49%); integral harbor administration (49%); port pilot services for interior navigation (49%); supply of fuels and lubricants for ships, aircraft, and railroad equipment (49%); using, utilizing, or exploiting a frequency band in national territory, except for the free use spectrum and the official use spectrum (49%); installing, operating, or exploiting public telecommunications networks (49%); occupying geostationary orbital positions and satellite orbits assigned to the country or exploiting the corresponding frequency bands (49%); and exploiting signal transmission and reception rights of frequency bands associated with foreign satellite systems that may cover or render services in the national territory (49%).

No shareholder, regardless of nationality, is authorized to own directly or indirectly: (1) more than 5% of the shares representing the capital stock of a banking institution, securities firm, or financial holding company. This percentage may be increased to 20% if the financial authorities so authorize. The per-shareholder limits do not apply to any foreign financial institution that, in accordance with an international trade treaty, establishes a subsidiary of any of such institutions; and (2) more than 20% of the shares representing the capital stock of an insurance company, except for any foreign financial institution that, in accordance with a program approved by the Secretariat of Finance and Public Credit (SHCP) to acquire a Mexican-owned insurance company, acquires ultimate control of that insurance company.

Controls on liquidation of direct investment	No.
Controls on real estate transactions	
Purchase locally by nonresidents	These controls apply to the direct acquisition by foreign nonresidents of real estate inside a 100-kilometer strip alongside the Mexican land border and a 50-kilometer strip inland from the Mexican coast. In addition, foreign nonresident investors may acquire real estate through Mexican companies, according to whose bylaws, these residents will con-sider themselves Mexican, and refrain from invoking the protection of their government regarding the property acquired and their rights to the real estate within the zone defined above. Such acquisitions may take place (1) through the acquisition of shares of Mexican companies dedicated to nonresidential activities with prior notification to the Ministry of Foreign Affairs or (2) through a real estate trust for residential activities.
Controls on personal capital movements	No.
Provisions specific to commercial banks and other credit institutions	Effective September 23, 1999, portfolio rating rules issued by the MOF were amended. The MOF issued new capitalization rules, which entered into force on January 1, 2000.
Borrowing abroad	Borrowing abroad is permitted subject to the limits on the liabilities of commercial banks denominated in foreign currency and on open foreign exchange positions.
Maintenance of accounts abroad	Mexican banks may maintain accounts abroad but must maintain an equilibrium between their open positions in foreign exchange and domestic currency.
Lending to nonresidents (financial or commercial credits)	There are limits on the amount that banks may lend to individual borrowers, regardless of their nationality, and on the open foreign exchange position of banks.
Lending locally in foreign exchange	There are limits on the amount that banks may lend to individual borrowers and on the open foreign exchange position of banks.

Purchase of locally issued securities denominated in foreign exchange	Irrespective of the currency denomination, banks may only enter into transactions on their own account with respect to securities registered with the NRSI, through securities firms, except for securities issued by banks.
Differential treatment of deposit accounts in foreign exchange	
Liquid asset requirements	Banks must invest in liquid assets, as determined by the central bank and denominated in foreign currency, an amount calculated through the maturity structure of their liabilities payable in foreign currency. Effective March 1, 1999, the number of instruments in which commercial banks may invest in order to cover the liquid assets requirement was increased to include securities issued abroad by the Mexican government.
Investment regulations	
Abroad by banks	Controls apply on types of transactions into which banks may enter and amounts related thereto.
In banks by nonresidents	No shareholder, regardless of its nationality, is authorized to own, directly or indirectly, more than 5% of the shares representing the capital stock of a banking institution. However, this percentage may be increased to 20% if the SHCP so authorizes. The per-shareholder limits do not apply to any foreign financial institution that, in accordance with a trade treaty, establishes a bank subsidiary.
Open foreign exchange position limits	
On resident assets and liabilities	Irrespective of the counterparty's residence, total liabilities of commercial banks denominated in or referred to foreign currency (excluding cash and highly liquid assets, as determined by the central bank) must not exceed an amount equal to 183% of the basic capital stock of the respective bank (calculation of the basic capital stock reflects the capitalization procedure set under the Basle accord).
	Aggregate short positions subject to foreign exchange risk of each commercial bank must equal the aggregate long positions of that bank each day. Notwithstanding this requirement, the central bank allows short or long aggregate positions, or positions referred to the dollar, at the end of each day provided they do not exceed 15% of the bank's net capital (net capital being calculated pursuant to rules issued by the SHCP). Banks may record short or long positions referred to individual currencies other than the dollar in amounts equal to or less than 2% of the net capital of the respective bank. Such positions are valued pursuant to the guidelines set by the central bank.
	Offshore banking institutions may be authorized by the BOM, such that the positions referred to above may be determined from a long position in dollars.
On nonresident assets and liabilities	The same regulations apply as for nonresident assets and liabilities.
Provisions specific to institutional investors	
Limits (max.) on securities issued by nonresidents and on portfolio invested abroad	Insurance companies may only invest in instruments pursuant to rules issued by the SHCP. Such rules specify the types of instruments and amounts in which insurance companies may invest.
	Common mutual funds and debt instrument mutual funds must invest their portfolios in securities registered with the NRSI, except for those specified by the CNBV.
Limits (max.) on portfolio invested abroad	Insurance companies may only invest in instruments pursuant to rules issued by the SHCP. Such rules specify the types of instruments and amounts in which insurance companies may invest.
	Common mutual funds and debt instrument mutual funds must invest their portfolios in securities registered with the NRSI, except for those specified by the CNBV.
Limits (min.) on portfolio invested locally	Common mutual funds and debt instrument mutual funds must invest their portfolios in securities registered with the NRSI, except for those specified by the CNBV. The investment guidelines determined by such authority establish the types of instruments and the minimum percentage of total assets in which such mutual funds may invest.

Other controls imposed by securities laws	No.

Changes During 1999

Capital transactions

Controls on derivatives and other instruments	*March 1.* The Commodity Exchange Incorporated was included as a recognized market in which commercial banks may enter into futures or options transactions. The CNBV and the BOM issued provisions applicable to securities firms regarding derivative operations.
Controls on direct investment	*January 20.* Existing legislation was amended to permit greater foreign investment in banks, securities firms, and financial holding companies. Under the amendments, the capital stock of banking institutions—other than development banks—securities firms and financial holding companies, was transformed into one class of common stock: Series "O" (an additional capital stock, up to 40% of the common capital stock may be represented by Series "L" shares, which confer to their holders limited voting rights). Thus, the limitation on aggregate foreign shareholdings of Mexican banks, securities firms, and financial holding companies has effectively been lifted.
Provisions specific to commercial banks and other credit institutions	*March 1.* The number of instruments in which commercial banks may invest in order to cover the liquid assets requirement was increased to include securities issued abroad by the Mexican government.
	September 23. Portfolio rating rules issued by the MOF were amended.

Changes During 2000

Capital transactions

Provisions specific to commercial banks and other credit institutions	*January 1.* New capitalization rules issued by the MOF entered into force.

FEDERATED STATES OF MICRONESIA

(Position as of December 31, 1999)

Status Under IMF Articles of Agreement

Article VIII	Date of acceptance: June 24, 1993.

Exchange Arrangement

Currency	The currency of the Federated States of Micronesia is the dollar.
Exchange rate structure	Unitary.
Classification	
Exchange arrangement with no separate legal tender	The authorities do not buy or sell foreign exchange. Foreign exchange transactions are handled by three commercial banks, which are authorized foreign exchange dealers and are regulated by a statutory banking board. The banks buy and sell foreign exchange at the rates quoted in international markets.
Exchange tax	No.
Exchange subsidy	No.
Forward exchange market	Forward transactions may be conducted through commercial banks without restriction.

Arrangements for Payments and Receipts

Prescription of currency requirements	No.
Payment arrangements	No.
Administration of control	No.
International security restrictions	No.
Payment arrears	No.
Controls on trade in gold (coins and/or bullion)	No.
Controls on exports and imports of banknotes	No.

Resident Accounts

Foreign exchange accounts permitted	Yes.
Held domestically	Yes.
Held abroad	Yes.
Accounts in domestic currency convertible into foreign currency	No.

Nonresident Accounts

Foreign exchange accounts permitted	Yes.
Domestic currency accounts	Yes.

Convertible into foreign currency	Yes.
Blocked accounts	No.

Imports and Import Payments

Foreign exchange budget	No.
Financing requirements for imports	No.
Documentation requirements for release of foreign exchange for imports	n.a.
Import licenses and other nontariff measures	Importers must obtain a business license.
Negative list	Imports of certain products are prohibited for environmental, health, safety, or social reasons.
Import taxes and/or tariffs	Import duties are levied on an ad valorem or specific basis as follows: 25% on cigarettes, carbonated nonalcoholic beverages, drink mixes and preparations, coffee, tea, beer, malt beverages, and wines; $10 per U.S. gallon on spirits and distilled alcoholic beverages; and $0.05 per U.S. gallon on gasoline and diesel fuel. Ad valorem duties are 3% on foodstuffs, 100% on laundry bar soap, and 4% on all other products. The ad valorem duties are based on the c.i.f. value of the goods.
State import monopoly	No.

Exports and Export Proceeds

Repatriation requirements	No.
Financing requirements	No.
Documentation requirements	n.a.
Export licenses	Exports are not subject to licensing requirements, taxes, or quantitative restrictions. The purchasing and exportation of copra and dried coconut meat yielding coconut oil are conducted solely by the Coconut Development Authority.
Export taxes	No.

Payments for Invisible Transactions and Current Transfers

Controls on these transfers	No.

Proceeds from Invisible Transactions and Current Transfers

Repatriation requirements	No.
Restrictions on use of funds	No.

Capital Transactions

Controls on capital and money market instruments	n.a.
Controls on derivatives and other instruments	n.a.

Controls on credit operations	n.r.
Controls on direct investment	
Inward direct investment	Foreign investors must obtain an application from the federal government and submit it for review and action to the Foreign Investment Board of the state in which the business will be located. Also, they must obtain a license from the federal government to engage in business or to aquire an interest in a business in the Federated States of Micronesia. If a foreign investor wishes to conduct business in more than one state, an application for each state must be obtained from the federal government and submitted to the Federal Investment Board of each of the states in which the business will be located and operated. Priorities for foreign investment are reviewed by the federal and state authorities from time to time.
Controls on liquidation of direct investment	No.
Controls on real estate transactions	
Purchase locally by nonresidents	Foreign investment in the real estate and construction sectors is prohibited in accordance with the laws prohibiting land ownership by foreigners. Foreign investors normally obtain long-term leases (usually up to 25 years with an option to renew for another 25 years) for land needed for their business.
Sale locally by nonresidents	Yes.
Controls on personal capital movements	n.r.
Provisions specific to commercial banks and other credit institutions	
Investment regulations	
Abroad by banks	Yes.
Provisions specific to institutional investors	n.a.
Other controls imposed by securities laws	n.a.

Changes During 1999

No significant changes occurred in the exchange and trade system.

MOLDOVA

(Position as of April 30, 2000)

Status Under IMF Articles of Agreement

Article VIII	Date of acceptance: June 30, 1995.

Exchange Arrangement

Currency	The currency of Moldova is the Moldovan leu.
Exchange rate structure	Unitary.
Classification	
Independently floating	The official exchange rate of the leu against the dollar is determined daily as the weighted average of all market transactions as announced by the National Bank of Moldova (NBM). The NBM quotes exchange rates of the leu for other currencies on the basis of the leu-dollar rate and the cross-rate relationships between the dollar and the currencies concerned in the international market.
	The official exchange rate is used in accounting and statistical calculations. Institutions eligible to deal in foreign exchange are authorized banks and foreign exchange bureaus. The latter are authorized to purchase from and sell to residents and nonresidents foreign banknotes and traveler's checks in any currency. Authorized banks and foreign exchange bureaus may set their own buying and selling rates in their foreign exchange transactions.
Exchange tax	No.
Exchange subsidy	No.
Forward exchange market	n.a.

Arrangements for Payments and Receipts

Prescription of currency requirements	No.
Payment arrangements	
Bilateral payment arrangements	
Operative	Moldova has concluded agreements on settlements with the CIS countries providing for settlements and payments in accordance with international banking practices.
Regional arrangements	Moldova is a member of the Payments Union within the CIS; however, the arrangement is inoperative.
Administration of control	The NBM has the ultimate authority in the area of foreign exchange arrangements and is responsible for managing the country's foreign exchange reserves, regulating the currency market, and granting licenses to engage in foreign currency transactions. In accordance with the Law on Controls on the Repatriation of Funds, Goods, and Services, the NBM provides the accounting. The MOF is responsible for controls on repatriation.
International security restrictions	No.
Payment arrears	
Official	On April 7, 2000, the government concluded an agreement with the Russian Federation on the restructuring of official debt.
Private	The government is holding negotiations on the restructuring of private debt.

Controls on trade in gold (coins and/or bullion)

Controls on domestic ownership and/or trade

The MOF establishes regulations governing domestic trade.

Controls on external trade

A license from the MOF is required to conduct international trade in gold.

Controls on exports and imports of banknotes

Nonresident banks that have loro correspondent accounts at resident banks may export or import cash in local or foreign currency only with the approval of the NBM. Resident banks with a "B" or "C" type license may freely export or import foreign currency.

On exports

Domestic currency

The export limit is MDL 2,500 for both residents and nonresidents; exports of domestic currency have to be declared.

Foreign currency

For freely convertible currencies, the limit is $50,000 for both residents and nonresidents upon presentation of a customs declaration for the importation of the currency or approval of an authorized bank or the NBM. Without these documents, the limit is $5,000. For non-convertible currencies, there are no limits.

On imports

Domestic currency

The limit is MDL 2,500 for both residents and nonresidents; imports of domestic currency must be declared.

Foreign currency

Imported currency must be declared, but there are no quantitative restrictions.

Resident Accounts

Foreign exchange accounts permitted

Yes.

Held domestically

Residents are entitled to open an unlimited number of type "A" and "B" accounts in freely convertible currencies. All foreign currency earnings of residents must be deposited in their accounts at authorized banks. Account holders may use foreign exchange balances in their accounts to settle current international as well as domestic transactions only after conversion into the national currency, whereas, for capital transactions, NBM approval is required. Other than that, there are no restrictions on the use of funds from type "A" accounts. There are, however, restrictions on the use of funds from type "B" accounts. MOF approval is required only for organizations financed from the budget.

Held abroad

These accounts may be held abroad. However, NBM approval is required, except for banks holding a "B" or "C" license. MOF approval is required only for organizations financed from the budget.

Accounts in domestic currency convertible into foreign currency

Funds from accounts in Moldovan lei may be converted into foreign exchange and may be used for current international transactions and for capital transactions. Approval from the NBM is required for capital transactions.

Nonresident Accounts

Foreign exchange accounts permitted

Nonresidents with foreign currency deposits at authorized banks in Moldova may freely transfer the balances abroad or sell them on the foreign exchange market through authorized banks.

Domestic currency accounts

Accounts in Moldovan lei may be opened by nonresidents from CIS countries with approval from the central bank of the relevant country. Other nonresidents may open accounts in Moldovan lei at authorized banks in Moldova if the funds were received from selling foreign exchange in the foreign exchange market in Moldova or as a result of selling goods, providing services, or other labor.

Convertible into foreign currency

Nonresidents may convert Moldovan lei into foreign exchange provided the Moldovan lei were received as a result of a current international transaction, with the exception of Moldovan lei received from selling restricted currencies (for CIS countries and Romania).

For nonresident natural persons, conversion into a freely convertible currency is allowed if the foreign currency was previously imported or transferred into Moldova and sold to a bank, and documents showing that the foreign currency had been imported into Moldova are submitted to the purchasing bank.

Blocked accounts   No.

Imports and Import Payments

Foreign exchange budget   No.

Financing requirements for imports   No.

Advance payment requirements   If a contract is not executed, the amount of the advance payment must be repatriated into Moldova no later than 90 days after such advance payment was effected.

Documentation requirements for release of foreign exchange for imports   A contract with a nonresident for importation from abroad is required. Foreign exchange purchased on the domestic currency market must be transferred for imports within seven days of the date of purchase. In the event that payment is not made, the foreign exchange must be sold.

Preshipment inspection   On March 21, 2000, a preshipment inspection agreement was signed with a foreign company.

Import licenses and other nontariff measures   Imports of medicine; medical equipment; chemicals; industrial waste; narcotics; psychotropic, high-potency, toxic, poisonous, radioactive, and explosive substances; and hazardous waste are subject to licensing for the purpose of protecting the consumer and ensuring compliance with domestic standards. Imports of ammunition, military hardware, and special compounds for the manufacture thereof (with the exception of hunting rifles and cartridges), as well as work and services in the sphere of military-technical cooperation, are allowed only with permission of a special government commission.

Negative list   Imports of unprocessed ivory into Moldovan territories are prohibited.

Import taxes and/or tariffs   There are four tariff bands for imports (zero, 5%, 10%, and 15%), with the maximum tariff applied to tobacco products, alcoholic beverages, and jewelry. A zero customs tariff is applied to cotton, fertilizers, pharmaceutical products, textbooks, and base metals and products thereof. No import customs duty is imposed on goods and objects produced in and imported from Romania and CIS countries that have ratified the Agreement on the Creation of a Free Trade Zone or with which the Republic of Moldova has conducted bilateral interstate agreements on free trade. Imported goods for which a zero customs duty is applied are subject to a special duty of 5% of the customs value, regardless of the country of origin. Imported goods and services are subject to VAT in the amount of 20%, with the exception of the following types of goods: those intended as assistance in the event of a natural disaster and other emergencies; those identified as humanitarian assistance; transit goods; and goods intended for sale through duty-free shops and shops that exclusively serve diplomatic missions of foreign states in Moldova and their personnel.

State import monopoly   No.

Exports and Export Proceeds

Repatriation requirements   Proceeds from exports must be repatriated no later than 180 days from the issuance of the customs declaration. Proceeds from exports of strategic goods must be repatriated within 90 days, and proceeds from goods sold on consignment within 365 days. The list of these goods is established by the government.

Financing requirements   No.

Documentation requirements   Presentation of an export contract and a declaration on the repatriation of foreign exchange proceeds is required.

Export licenses   Export licenses and normative prices are abolished, except for a limited list of goods considered important, and for health and security reasons.

Export taxes	No.

Payments for Invisible Transactions and Current Transfers

Controls on these transfers	Resident and nonresident natural persons may transfer abroad without restriction freely convertible currencies received from abroad or imported into Moldova, provided they have a customs declaration. Otherwise, for payments in freely convertible currencies of up to $1,000, a resident natural person must show a supporting document confirming the need to effect the transfer. For payments over $1,000, approval by the NBM is required.
	There is no limit on the transfer of nonconvertible currencies by natural persons. Juridical persons may effect transfers for current international payments on the basis of documents confirming the need to effect these payments.
Investment-related payments	Repayment of loans from nonresidents that have been registered with the NBM is permitted. Payments for depreciation of direct investments that are registered with the NBM and that exist on the basis of certificates of registration of direct investments may be made.
Payments for travel	
Prior approval	For amounts in freely convertible currencies in excess of $5,000 a trip, a resident unable to produce evidence of the currency's importation or receipt from abroad must obtain prior approval for exports.
Quantitative limits	Residents may export up to $5,000 of freely convertible currencies.
Personal payments	
Prior approval	The transfer of pensions from abroad as well as expenditures/alimony for the support of families payable to residents of Moldova is not regulated. In the case of payment for medical services, study abroad costs, and the transfer abroad of alimony for the support of families, approval from the NBM is required for freely convertible currencies in excess of $1,000.
Quantitative limits	Yes.
Indicative limits/bona fide test	Yes.
Foreign workers' wages	A labor contract and documents confirming the payment of taxes are required.
Credit card use abroad	Issuance of credit and debit cards against accounts of juridical persons is allowed, and for natural persons, issuance of debit cards against types "A" and "B" accounts and accounts in lei is allowed. Funds from type "B" accounts and those in Moldovan lei may be used for personal current expenses and business travel.
Prior approval	The issuing bank must obtain NBM approval to issue cards from type "B" accounts and from those in Moldovan lei.
Quantitative limits	The limit for the use of cards abroad is $200 a day or $5,000 a month, and not more than $20,000 for settlement of current transactions.
Indicative limits/bona fide test	Yes.
Other payments	
Prior approval	Yes.
Quantitative limits	Resident natural persons may transfer up to $1,000 in freely convertible currencies.
Indicative limits/bona fide test	Amounts in excess of $1,000 are freely approved subject to documentation.

Proceeds from Invisible Transactions and Current Transfers

Repatriation requirements	All proceeds from invisibles, except the earnings of workers residing abroad, must be repatriated unless the NBM approves the opening of an account abroad.

Restrictions on use of funds	Payments and transfers from abroad to natural persons in nonconvertible currencies are made in Moldovan lei.

Capital Transactions

Controls on capital and money market instruments	Approval from the NBM is required for the transfer of capital to nonresidents. Investment income earned abroad by residents must be repatriated. Proceeds from loans and other capital flows from nonresidents are to be registered with the NBM.
On capital market securities	
Shares or other securities of a participating nature	
Purchase locally by nonresidents	Approval by the NBM is required. Effective March 23, 1999, an offer to acquire at least 25% of the total number of shares of a company, or such quantity that would allow control over the company, must be registered with the National Securities Commission.
Sale or issue locally by nonresidents	Foreign securities may be sold in Moldova only in the form of Moldovan Depository Receipts (MDRs) issued by residents who are professional participants in the securities market. NBM approval for the exportation of capital from Moldova is required for registration to issue MDRs.
Purchase abroad by residents	NBM approval is required.
Sale or issue abroad by residents	NBM registration is required.
Bonds or other debt securities	
Purchase locally by nonresidents	Yes.
Sale or issue locally by nonresidents	The same regulations apply as for shares or other securities of a participating nature.
Purchase abroad by residents	Yes.
Sale or issue abroad by residents	NBM registration is required.
On money market instruments	
Purchase locally by nonresidents	MOF approval is required for foreign investors to purchase state securities. A single investor (resident or nonresident) may account for no more than 50% of the issuance of a given government security purchased in an auction or on the secondary market.
Sale or issue locally by nonresidents	NBM approval is required.
Purchase abroad by residents	NBM approval is required.
Sale or issue abroad by residents	NBM registration is required.
On collective investment securities	
Purchase locally by nonresidents	NBM registration is required.
Sale or issue locally by nonresidents	NBM approval is required.
Purchase abroad by residents	NBM approval is required.
Sale or issue abroad by residents	NBM registration is required.
Controls on derivatives and other instruments	
Purchase locally by nonresidents	NBM registration is required.
Sale or issue locally by nonresidents	NBM approval is required.
Purchase abroad by residents	NBM approval is required.
Sale or issue abroad by residents	NBM registration is required.

Controls on credit operations

Commercial credits

  By residents to nonresidents   NBM approval is required.

  To residents from nonresidents   Effective April 16, 1999, the NBM registers those credits with a deferred payment of more than one year.

Financial credits

  By residents to nonresidents   NBM approval is required.

  To residents from nonresidents   NBM registration is required.

Guarantees, sureties, and financial backup facilities

  By residents to nonresidents   NBM approval is required.

  To residents from nonresidents   NBM registration is required.

Controls on direct investment

Outward direct investment   NBM approval is required.

Inward direct investment   NBM registration is required.

Controls on liquidation of direct investment   Yes.

Controls on real estate transactions

Purchase abroad by residents   NBM approval is required.

Sale locally by nonresidents   NBM approval is required to transfer proceeds.

Controls on personal capital movements

Loans

  By residents to nonresidents   NBM approval is required.

  To residents from nonresidents   NBM registration is required mainly for statistical purposes.

Gifts, endowments, inheritances, and legacies

  By residents to nonresidents   Gifts and endowments are permitted with NBM approval only upon presentation of relevant documentation and only by a first-order relative. Inheritances in monetary form are transferred with NBM approval upon the presentation of relevant documentation.

Settlement of debts abroad by immigrants   Limited to income earned and past transfers by immigrants into Moldova.

Transfer of assets

  Transfer abroad by emigrants   NBM approval is required upon presentation of confirming documents.

Transfer of gambling and prize earnings   Residents may export up to $5,000. Nonresidents are not permitted to transfer gambling earnings abroad.

Provisions specific to commercial banks and other credit institutions

Borrowing abroad   NBM registration is required.

Maintenance of accounts abroad   For types "B" and "C" banking licenses, there are no controls on the opening and maintenance of accounts abroad.

Lending to nonresidents (financial or commercial credits)   NBM approval is required.

Lending locally in foreign exchange	Authorized banks are permitted to lend in freely convertible currencies only to importers that are resident juridical persons. Banks holding "B" and "C" licenses are permitted to lend to one another and to other economic agents using funds obtained from foreign and international financial institutions for the financing of certain programs.
Purchase of locally issued securities denominated in foreign exchange	Securities denominated in foreign exchange are not issued in the country.
Differential treatment of deposit accounts in foreign exchange	The charter of accounts does not provide for separate accounts in foreign exchange; banks, however, perform separate accounting for each currency.
Differential treatment of deposit accounts held by nonresidents	The charter of accounts does not provide for separate accounts for nonresidents; banks, however, perform separate accounting for nonresidents.
Investment regulations	
Abroad by banks	NBM approval is required.
In banks by nonresidents	NBM approval is required when a share representing more than 10% of aggregate capital is acquired.
Open foreign exchange position limits	The limit for both long and short exchange positions is 10% of the aggregate normative capital for each currency and 20% for long and short positions individually.
Provisions specific to institutional investors	
Limits (max.) on securities issued by nonresidents and on portfolio invested abroad	Nonresidents may not issue securities without the approval of the National Securities Council.
Limits (max.) on portfolio invested abroad	NBM approval is required.
Limits (min.) on portfolio invested locally	NBM registration is required.
Other controls imposed by securities laws	No.

Changes During 1999

Arrangements for payments and receipts	*January 1.* A new procedure for the import and export of foreign currency was introduced. Nonresident banks that have loro correspondent accounts at resident banks may import/export foreign currency and cash Moldovan lei only with the approval of the NBM. Resident banks with types "B" and "C" licenses may freely import and export foreign currency.
Imports and import payments	*January 1.* Moldova switched to VAT destination principles for all imports, including imports from Russia.
Capital transactions	*March 23.* An offer to acquire at least 25% of the total number of shares of a company, or such quantity that would allow control over the company, must be registered with the National Securities Commission.
Controls on credit operations	*April 16.* The NBM registers commercial credits from nonresidents with a deferred payment of more than one year.

Changes During 2000

Arrangements for payments and receipts	*April 7.* The government concluded an agreement with the Russian Federation on the restructuring of official debt.
Imports and import payments	*March 21.* A preshipment inspection agreement was signed with a foreign company.

MONGOLIA

(Position as of December 31, 1999)

Status Under IMF Articles of Agreement

Article VIII   Date of acceptance: February 1, 1996.

Exchange Arrangement

Currency   The currency of Mongolia is the Mongolian togrog.

Exchange rate structure   Unitary.

Classification

Independently floating   In principle, the official exchange rate of the togrog is set daily by the Bank of Mongolia (BOM) as the midpoint of the previous day's average buying and selling rates established by transactions among participants in the interbank foreign exchange market. However, the volume of trading is very low, and the BOM currently adjusts the official rate only once a week rather than once a day. The official exchange rate is applied to public sector imports and service payments, including debt service, and to trade and service transactions conducted under bilateral payment arrangements. All other transactions, including sales of retained foreign exchange by public sector enterprises, take place through the interbank market. Exchange rates for other convertible currencies are calculated on the basis of the cross rates against the dollar in international markets. The spread between commercial banks' buying and selling rates is limited to 1%.

Exchange tax   No.

Exchange subsidy   No.

Forward exchange market   No.

Arrangements for Payments and Receipts

Prescription of currency requirements   No.

Payment arrangements

Bilateral payment arrangements

Inoperative   Some of the outstanding balances under the clearing arrangements of the former International Bank for Economic Cooperation are still under negotiation. Under inoperative bilateral trade arrangements, there are also outstanding balances with the People's Republic of China, the Islamic State of Afghanistan, and the Federal Republic of Yugoslavia (Serbia/Montenegro).

Clearing agreements   Mongolia maintains a bilateral clearing agreement with the Democratic People's Republic of Korea.

Administration of control   International transactions are governed by the Foreign Exchange Law.

International security restrictions

In accordance with Executive Board Decision No. 144-(52/51)   Restrictions are imposed on certain transactions with the Federal Republic of Yugoslavia (Serbia/Montenegro).

Payment arrears   No.

Controls on trade in gold (coins and/or bullion)

Controls on external trade   Exporters of gold must register their exports with the BOM or a commercial bank.

Controls on exports and imports of banknotes

On exports

Domestic currency　　　　　　Exportation of domestic banknotes is prohibited.

On imports

Domestic currency　　　　　　Importation of domestic banknotes is prohibited.

Resident Accounts

Foreign exchange accounts permitted	Accounts may be held at authorized banks; they may be credited with retained export earnings and foreign exchange transferred from abroad, and the balances may be used for any purpose without restriction.
Held domestically	Yes.
Held abroad	Yes.
Accounts in domestic currency convertible into foreign currency	Yes.

Nonresident Accounts

Foreign exchange accounts permitted	Registration with the State Registry is required.
Domestic currency accounts	Yes.
Convertible into foreign currency	Yes.
Blocked accounts	No.

Imports and Import Payments

Foreign exchange budget	No.
Financing requirements for imports	No.
Documentation requirements for release of foreign exchange for imports	No.
Import licenses and other nontariff measures	
Negative list	Imports of drugs, materials that encourage or depict violence or pornography, and items that could cause environmental damage are banned.
Open general licenses	Imports of historical artifacts, precious metals, weapons, radioactive materials, ferrous and nonferrous metals, and goods and services requiring licenses under international contracts and agreements require a special permit.
Other nontariff measures	Specific excise taxes are levied on imports of alcohol and cigarettes.
Import taxes and/or tariffs	There are no customs duties except on alcoholic spirits, which is assessed at 15%. Effective July 1, 1999, a uniform 5% import duty went into effect.
State import monopoly	No.

Exports and Export Proceeds

Repatriation requirements	No.

Financing requirements	No.
Documentation requirements	No.
Export licenses	
Without quotas	Exports of historical artifacts, precious metals, weapons, radioactive materials, ferrous and nonferrous metals, and goods and services requiring licenses under international contracts and agreements require a special permit.
With quotas	Yes.
Export taxes	Export taxes apply to the export of nonferrous and scrap metals, raw cashmere, and raw camel wool.
Other export taxes	Yes.

Payments for Invisible Transactions and Current Transfers

Controls on these transfers	No.
Investment-related payments	Information is not available on the payment of amortization of loans or depreciation of direct investments.

Proceeds from Invisible Transactions and Current Transfers

Repatriation requirements	No.
Restrictions on use of funds	No.

Capital Transactions

Controls on capital and money market instruments	
On capital market securities	
Shares or other securities of a participating nature	
Sale or issue locally by nonresidents	The issue of capital market securities is prohibited.
On money market instruments	
Sale or issue locally by nonresidents	The issue of money market instruments is prohibited.
On collective investment securities	
Sale or issue locally by nonresidents	The issue of collective investment securities is prohibited.
Controls on derivatives and other instruments	
Sale or issue locally by nonresidents	The issue of derivatives and other instruments is prohibited.
Controls on credit operations	
Commercial credits	
By residents to nonresidents	Registration with the MOF is required.
To residents from nonresidents	Registration with the BOM is required.
Financial credits	
By residents to nonresidents	Registration with the MOF is required.

To residents from nonresidents	Registration with the BOM is required.

Controls on direct investment

Inward direct investment	Investment by private corporations is encouraged particularly in projects involving export promotion, the use of advanced technology, and the exploitation of natural resources. The Law on Foreign Investment guarantees that foreign firms will not be nationalized and that foreign investors will have the right to dispose of their assets. The maximum rate of profit tax is 40%, and foreign investors are exempt from the tax for three to ten years, depending on the sector and export performance. In addition, the law stipulates that entities with foreign participation may export at world prices or other agreed prices, and they may import or export directly or in cooperation with foreign trade enterprises.

Controls on liquidation of direct investment	No.

Controls on real estate transactions

Purchase abroad by residents	Registration with the State Real Estate Registry is required.
Purchase locally by nonresidents	Registration with the State Real Estate Registry is required.

Controls on personal capital movements

Loans	Registration with the BOM and the MOF is required.
By residents to nonresidents	Yes.
To residents from nonresidents	Yes.

Provisions specific to commercial banks and other credit institutions

Borrowing abroad	Registration with the BOM is required.
Maintenance of accounts abroad	BOM permission is required.

Differential treatment of deposit accounts in foreign exchange

Reserve requirements	On January 31, 1999, the BOM introduced a 50% cap on the share of the reserve requirement that may be met by cash in vault, and on the symmetrical treatment of domestic and foreign currency deposits in meeting reserve requirements.
Open foreign exchange position limits	The limit is 20% of capital, including a subceiling of 10% for any individual currency.
Provisions specific to institutional investors	No.
Other controls imposed by securities laws	Securities may be issued only by government institutions upon the approval of the Great Hural or by companies registered in Mongolia.
	It is prohibited to lend securities. Any person owing 5% or more of total shares of any company must report it to the Securities Committee of the Great Hural within five days after acquisition. Any person who intends to own directly or indirectly 20% or more of total shares of any company must make a tender in accordance with the Securities Law of Mongolia.

Changes During 1999

Imports and import payments	*July 1.* A uniform 5% import duty went into effect.

Capital transactions

Provisions specific to commercial banks and other credit institutions	*January 31.* The BOM introduced a 50% cap on the share of the reserve requirement that may be met by cash in vault, and on the symmetrical treatment of domestic and foreign currency deposits in meeting reserve requirements.

MOROCCO

(Position as of December 31, 1999)

Status Under IMF Articles of Agreement

Article VIII	Date of acceptance: January 21, 1993.

Exchange Arrangement

Currency	The currency of Morocco is the Moroccan dirham.
Other legal tender	Commemorative gold coins with a face value of DH 250 and DH 500, and commemorative silver coins with a face value of DH 50, DH 100, DH 150, and DH 200 are also legal tender.
Exchange rate structure	Unitary.
Classification	
Conventional pegged arrangement	The exchange rate is determined freely in an interbank foreign exchange market. Bank Al-Maghrib (BAM)—the central bank—intervenes in the market by setting the buying and selling rates applicable to its operations with banks based on a basket of currencies comprising the dollar, the euro, and the pound sterling, weighted in accordance with the geographic distribution of Morocco's foreign trade and the pattern of currencies of settlement. This quotation system is also based on the observance of the cross exchange rates in the international market. For exchange operations with customers, banks may not exceed the rate limits set by the BAM.
	Morocco imposes a levy of 0.2% on foreign exchange transactions, which is paid to the Foreign Exchange Office (FEO) for its services.
Exchange tax	No.
Exchange subsidy	No.
Forward exchange market	
Official cover of forward operations	The official forward foreign exchange cover facility has been suspended since the creation of the foreign exchange market.

Arrangements for Payments and Receipts

Prescription of currency requirements	No.
Payment arrangements	
Bilateral payment arrangements	
Inoperative	Arrangements with Mali and Guinea have been inoperative since the 1960s. These arrangements were abolished in 1999.
Regional arrangements	There is a regional payment arrangement operated by the central banks of Algeria, Libya, Mauritania, Morocco, and Tunisia.
Administration of control	Exchange control is administered by the FEO, an agency under the MOF. This office has delegated the execution of the main exchange control measures to authorized banks. Import and export licenses, when required, are issued by the Department of Foreign Trade.
International security restrictions	
In accordance with Executive Board Decision No. 144-(52/51)	Yes.
In accordance with UN sanctions	Morocco maintains restrictions for security reasons against Iraq and the Federal Republic of Yugoslavia (Serbia/Montenegro) pursuant to UN Security Council resolutions.

Payment arrears	No.
Controls on trade in gold (coins and/or bullion)	
Controls on domestic ownership and/or trade	Residents may purchase, hold, and sell gold coins in Morocco for numismatic or investment purposes. Ten different types of foreign gold coins are traded on the Casablanca Stock Exchange, which does not, however, deal in gold bars.
Controls on external trade	Imports of gold are subject to authorization from the Customs and Indirect Taxes Administration. Each year, the MOF fixes a quota for the importation of gold ingots. The quota is then allocated among jewelers and industrial users of precious metals. Exports of gold are prohibited.
Controls on exports and imports of banknotes	
On exports	
Domestic currency	The exportation of domestic banknotes is prohibited.
Foreign currency	Visitors to Morocco are permitted to repurchase foreign exchange against the presentation of exchange certificates up to the amount of the original conversion of foreign exchange into dirhams. Residents may also export foreign banknotes following general or special approval by the Exchange Office.
On imports	
Domestic currency	The importation of domestic banknotes is prohibited.
Foreign currency	Nonresident travelers may bring in freely foreign banknotes, traveler's checks, and other means of payment denominated in foreign currency. Resident travelers may also bring in foreign banknotes in any amount, as well as any other means of payment in foreign exchange but must surrender them within 30 days of their return to Morocco.

Resident Accounts

Foreign exchange accounts permitted	Yes.
Held domestically	Any Moroccan exporter of goods or services already holding a convertible export promotion account (CCPEX) is allowed to open a foreign exchange account. Those without a CCPEX must receive prior approval from the Exchange Office. Up to 20% of foreign exchange receipts may be credited to these accounts simultaneously, with the sale of the remaining 80% to domestic banks. There is no restriction on crediting foreign exchange accounts either with the proceeds from financial investments held in the accounts or with transfers from another of the holder's foreign exchange accounts. These accounts may be freely debited for payment of business expenses, as provided for in the exchange regulations, for investing in authorized intermediary banks, for subscribing to bonds issued by the Moroccan Treasury, for crediting another foreign exchange account or a CCPEX held in the exporter's name, or for surrender of foreign currency to banks.
Held abroad	These accounts are permitted; only foreign nationals do not require authorization.
Accounts in domestic currency convertible into foreign currency	Exporters of goods and services may open accounts in convertible dirhams at Moroccan banks, which may be credited with the dirham equivalent of 20% of repatriated foreign currency sold to domestic banks. Funds in these accounts may be used to finance expenses incurred abroad and related to the holder's business activity. Fishing companies may place up to 100% of the dirham equivalent of their repatriated exchange receipts in these accounts. Exporters may choose either a foreign exchange account or a convertible export promotion account, or may hold both kinds, provided the overall percentage of repatriated foreign exchange receipts placed in the accounts does not exceed the 20% limit.

Nonresident Accounts

Foreign exchange accounts permitted

Two types of accounts may be opened. (1) Foreign currency accounts in the names of foreign nationals may be maintained by natural or juridical persons of foreign nationality who are either residents or nonresidents. These accounts may be credited freely with transfers from abroad with foreign banknotes, checks, traveler's checks, or any other means of payment denominated in foreign currency and with foreign currency withdrawn from domestic banks, following general or special authorization from the FEO. They may be debited freely for transfer abroad in favor of the account holder or to a foreign third party, for the surrender of foreign currency to domestic banks, and for the payment of checks denominated in foreign currency. (2) Foreign currency accounts may be opened by individuals of Moroccan nationality residing abroad in their name. These accounts may be credited freely with transfers from abroad, checks or any other means of payment denominated in foreign currency, foreign currency withdrawn from domestic banks following general or special authorization from the FEO, the return on investments effected on the basis of these accounts, and transfers from another foreign currency account or from an account in convertible dirhams. They may be debited freely for transfers abroad, transfers to another account in foreign currency or in convertible dirhams, foreign currency subscriptions for notes issued by the Moroccan Treasury, and for the surrender of foreign currency to domestic banks.

Domestic currency accounts

Yes.

Convertible into foreign currency

These are restricted to resident or nonresident natural and juridical persons of foreign nationality and may be credited freely with generally or specifically authorized transfers, and with dirhams obtained from the sale to banks of foreign exchange, including banknotes. They may be debited freely for payments made in Morocco and for purchases of foreign exchange at banks. There are no restrictions on transfers between foreign accounts in convertible dirhams or on transfers of interest. Holders of these accounts may obtain international credit cards for settlement of all expenses in Morocco and abroad. Convertible dirham accounts may be opened freely in the name of nonresident Moroccans residing abroad. Overdrafts are not allowed, and there are no restrictions on the interest rate payable. These accounts may be credited freely with (1) dirhams from the sale of convertible currencies, including banknotes, to domestic banks; (2) transfers authorized by the FEO; (3) payments of interest accrued on these accounts; (4) transfers from foreign accounts in convertible dirhams; and (5) transfers from term deposits in convertible dirham accounts. They may be debited freely for (1) the purchase of foreign exchange from domestic banks, (2) dirham payments in Morocco, (3) transfers to foreign accounts in convertible dirhams, and (4) transfers to term deposits in convertible dirham accounts.

These accounts may also be debited freely, either for the benefit of the account holder or for other nonresidents, for the purchase of foreign banknotes, traveler's checks, or other foreign currency–denominated means of payment. Convertible dirham accounts for exporters may be opened by exporters of goods or services with Moroccan banks. These accounts may be credited with the equivalent of 20% of the foreign currency repatriated and surrendered to domestic banks.

Balances on these accounts may be used to finance expenditures contracted abroad and linked to the professional activity of those concerned. Fishing companies may credit to these accounts up to 100% of the foreign currency repatriated. Exporters have the choice of maintaining either foreign currency accounts or convertible dirham accounts. They may also hold both accounts simultaneously, provided that the overall percentage of export earnings to be credited to both accounts does not exceed 20% of foreign exchange earnings. Convertible term accounts are designed to attract funds from nonresident foreigners who are not entitled to guaranteed transfers.

These funds may be transferred within a maximum period of five years. The holders of such accounts may use the available funds, without prior authorization from the FEO, to fund investments in Morocco; buy treasury bonds; purchase Moroccan marketable securities; settle expenses incurred in Morocco; and, in the case of foreign corporations, provide their Moroccan subsidiaries with current account advances. They may also transfer freely the balances to resident or nonresident foreigners or to Moroccan nationals residing abroad. The beneficiaries of the proceeds of these accounts may use them to cover expenses incurred by foreign companies shooting films in Morocco; to purchase secondary residences under certain conditions; and to finance up to 50% of an investor's participation in investments in Morocco (the remainder must be financed with funds transferred from abroad). Funds invested with the proceeds of convertible term accounts may be transferred abroad without restriction in the event of liquidation or transfer, except for certain categories that are subject to a three-year waiting period.

Blocked accounts No.

Imports and Import Payments

Foreign exchange budget No.

Financing requirements for imports

Minimum financing requirements For all imports, an import certificate lodged with an authorized bank is required to make payments related to goods and incidental costs. Imports used for the production of export goods may be financed directly from the proceeds of foreign exchange claims of the same exporter within the framework of special lines of credit that commercial banks are authorized to contract with their foreign correspondents. Moroccan commercial banks may make advance payments abroad for imports of capital goods up to 40% of their f.o.b. value.

Advance payment requirements The maximum rate for advance payments on imports of capital goods is 40% of the f.o.b. value of the imports. Advance payment is limited to the foreign exchange equivalent of DH 20,000 for imported spare parts, consumer goods, and samples with payment effected by resident individuals or legal entities.

Documentation requirements for release of foreign exchange for imports Except for goods imported by air, insurance policies for imports must be taken out with insurance companies in Morocco. For a limited group of goods, however, insurance policies may be underwritten abroad. This group includes externally funded imports if the financing terms include foreign insurance; capital goods and equipment under turnkey contracts; or duly authorized investment programs in crude oil, gas, cattle, and wood. Imports are subject to a disembarkation inspection.

Domiciliation requirements Yes.

Import licenses and other nontariff measures On March 16, 1999, Morocco and Tunisia signed a free trade agreement providing for the immediate liberalization of 2,000 products and for the complete phasing out of tariff barriers between the two countries by December 2007.

Certain items are subject to minimum import prices (reference prices) for antidumping or safeguarding purposes.

Positive list Imports of arms and explosives, secondhand clothing, used tires, and chemical products that deplete the ozone layer require licenses.

Negative list Imports of products that affect public security, morale, and health may be prohibited.

Import taxes and/or tariffs Customs duties are levied on an ad valorem basis, with rates ranging from 2.5% to 35% for industrial goods; these tariffs can range up to 300% on certain agricultural products (tariff equivalents). In addition, a 15% levy is applied to imports. However, certain consumer goods not produced in Morocco are exempt from this levy and are subject to a customs duty of 10% only. Imports used for the production of exports are exempt from customs duties and other restrictions.

State import monopoly No.

Exports and Export Proceeds

Repatriation requirements All exporters must sign a guarantee to repatriate and surrender foreign exchange proceeds. Export proceeds collected abroad may be used directly abroad to finance imports of goods and raw materials of goods for export.

Surrender requirements Foreign exchange must be surrendered within one month of the date of payment by foreign buyers specified in the commercial contract; in principle, this date must not be more than 150 days from the date of arrival of the merchandise. This deadline may be extended if warranted by business conditions and approved by the FEO. Residents of Moroccan nationality, including individuals and corporations, must repatriate foreign exchange receipts accruing from all their noncommercial claims and surrender them to an authorized bank. Other residents must surrender noncommercial receipts only if the receipts result from their activities in Morocco. Exporters are authorized to obtain up to 20% of export earnings in convertible dirham or foreign exchange accounts.

Financing requirements	No.
Documentation requirements	
Preshipment inspection	Yes.
Export licenses	
Without quotas	On March 16, 1999, Morocco and Tunisia signed a free trade agreement, providing for the immediate liberalization of 2,000 products, and for the complete phasing out of tariff barriers between the two countries by December 2007. Exports of flour, charcoal, certain animals, plants, archaeological items, and chemical products that deplete the ozone layer are subject to authorization.
Export taxes	A 1% quality control tax is levied on exports of foodstuffs.

Payments for Invisible Transactions and Current Transfers

Controls on these transfers	Authorized banks are permitted to make payments and settle expenses incidental to commercial transactions covered by the relevant import or export documents and for travel and study abroad without authorization from the FEO. Moroccan enterprises are permitted to settle in dirhams the expenses incurred by their foreign managers and nonresident foreigners working for or on behalf of these enterprises. Foreign airlines operating in Morocco may transfer, without prior authorization from the FEO, any surplus revenue from the proceeds of ticket sales, excess baggage, and air freight. Transfers with respect to sea and road transportation may be made directly to authorized banks.
Trade-related payments	Transfers by deep-sea fishing companies for technical insurance and boat management costs are liberalized. There are no restrictions on the payment of unloading and storage costs and administrative expenses.
Indicative limits/bona fide test	Yes.
Investment-related payments	There are no restrictions on the payment of profits and dividends. Information is not available on the payment of amortization of loans or depreciation of direct investments.
Indicative limits/bona fide test	There are indicative limits and bona fide tests on the transfer of interest.
Payments for travel	
Quantitative limits	The maximum allowance for tourist travel is DH 10,000 a person a year. This allowance may be increased by DH 3,000 for a minor child on the passport of the beneficiary parent accompanying said parent at the time of travel abroad. The same allocation may also be granted to Moroccan residents living abroad upon their return to their home country, provided they have not benefited from the 15% allocation on remittances within the previous 12 months up to a limit of DH 20,000. Residents of foreign nationality who wish to travel abroad may be granted the foreign exchange equivalent of all their savings from income. Business travel by exporters of goods and services may be financed without restriction by debiting convertible export promotion accounts or foreign currency accounts maintained with Moroccan banks. In the case of business travel allowances for others, annual foreign exchange allowances are approved by the FEO on the basis of need, with a daily limit of DH 2,000. Banks have been empowered to provide advance allowances of up to DH 40,000 to small and medium-size enterprises and of up to DH 20,000 a year for business travel by individuals not belonging to either of these categories. In all cases, business travel allowances cannot be added to allowances for tourist travel. The FEO grants exemptions as needed.
Indicative limits/bona fide test	Yes.

Personal payments	Transfers for family maintenance and alimony payments are approved upon presentation of documentary evidence. Commercial banks are authorized to transfer retirement pensions provided by public and private agencies in favor of retirees residing abroad permanently.
Prior approval	For medical costs, approval by the Ministry of Health is required.
Quantitative limits	Commercial banks are authorized to sell foreign exchange to Moroccan nationals who must travel abroad for medical treatment up to a maximum allowance of the equivalent of DH 20,000, and to make transfers on patients' behalf for treatment abroad in favor of hospitals and medical institutions concerned. This limit was raised to DH 30,000 on October 5, 1999. School fees to foreign academic institutions, upon submission of documentary evidence, may be transferred without limit; however, the following limits apply: (1) an annual installation allowance equivalent to DH 20,000 and the same amount for a person accom-panying a minor student leaving Morocco for the first time; and (2) an allowance for living expenses amounting to the equivalent of DH 6,000 a month for non-scholarship holders and DH 4,000 a month for scholarship holders. In addition to these funds, banks are authorized to effect the transfer of rent and corresponding charges in favor of the foreign landlord once the student or his or her legal guardian has submitted a lease and a certificate of residence or any other equivalent document. The limit is DH 2,000 a month for foreign nationals residing in Morocco to cover the cost of higher education for a child studying abroad. Foreign retired persons and foreign spouses of Moroccans may transfer all of their income. They may also contribute freely to their retirement or social security fund in their country of origin.
Indicative limits/bona fide test	Applications for additional amounts must be referred to the FEO for approval, which is granted on proof of need.
Foreign workers' wages	
Quantitative limits	Foreigners residing in Morocco and employed in either the private or public sectors or engaged in professions in industry, commerce, and agriculture may transfer all their savings from income.
Credit card use abroad	
Quantitative limits	Yes.
Indicative limits/bona fide test	Yes.
Other payments	There are no restrictions on the payments for subscriptions and membership fees.

Proceeds from Invisible Transactions and Current Transfers

Repatriation requirements	Residents of Moroccan nationality, including individuals and corporations, must repatriate foreign exchange receipts accruing from all their noncommercial claims and surrender them to an authorized bank. Other residents must surrender noncommercial receipts only if the receipts result from their activities in Morocco. Moroccans working abroad must surrender within one month all foreign exchange in their possession, but on departure from Morocco, they may export without restriction foreign banknotes obtained by debiting their accounts in convertible dirhams. If they do not have such an account, they may take out 15% of foreign exchange repatriated and surrendered 12 months before to Moroccan banks up to a limit of DH 20,000. If these facilities are not available, Moroccan residents living abroad may take advantage of the same DH 10,000 tourist allocation that applies to residents. Resident travelers may bring in foreign banknotes in any amount, as well as any other means of payment in foreign exchange but must surrender them within 30 days of their return to Morocco.
Surrender requirements	Exporters of services are required to obtain up to 20% of their export earnings in amounts denominated in foreign currency or convertible dirhams.
Restrictions on use of funds	No.

Capital Transactions

Controls on capital and money market instruments

On capital market securities

Shares or other securities of a participating nature

    Sale or issue locally by nonresidents

The issuance of capital market securities by nonresidents is prohibited. There are, however, no controls on the sale of Moroccan securities by nonresidents. Proceeds from such sales may also be transferred freely, provided that the relevant purchases are financed by foreign exchange inflows or any comparable means.

    Purchase abroad by residents

Purchases of foreign securities by residents of Moroccan nationality and transfers of the funds required for such purchases are subject to the prior approval of the FEO. Residents of foreign nationality are free to purchase securities abroad or, generally speaking, to constitute assets abroad, provided that these purchases are financed from their foreign exchange holdings or holdings of convertible dirhams.

    Sale or issue abroad by residents

Yes.

Bonds or other debt securities

    Sale or issue locally by nonresidents

Yes.

    Purchase abroad by residents

Yes.

    Sale or issue abroad by residents

Yes.

On money market instruments

Purchase locally by nonresidents

When the purchase of such instruments or securities is financed by a foreign exchange inflow or by the proceeds of the sale of other securities previously purchased through the surrender of foreign exchange, the transfer of disinvestment proceeds, including capital gains, and of income generated by such investment is free.

Sale or issue locally by nonresidents

The issuance of these instruments by nonresidents is prohibited.

Purchase abroad by residents

Purchases require the prior authorization of the FEO, which is granted under certain conditions. On the other hand, residents of foreign nationality are free to engage in operations abroad financed with their foreign exchange holdings.

Sale or issue abroad by residents

Yes.

On collective investment securities

Purchase abroad by residents

The same regulations apply as for money market instruments.

Sale or issue abroad by residents

Yes.

Controls on derivatives and other instruments

Purchase locally by nonresidents

These instruments have not been developed in Morocco.

Purchase abroad by residents

Residents of Moroccan nationality may subscribe to such instruments abroad only with the prior approval of the FEO. Authorized intermediaries are allowed to engage in foreign exchange buying and selling operations with foreign banks using foreign currency cash.

Sale or issue abroad by residents

The issue abroad of these instruments by Moroccan residents is subject to prior authorization by the FEO.

Controls on credit operations

Commercial credits

By residents to nonresidents

Merchandise exporters are free to grant commercial credits to nonresidents for up to 150 days; longer terms may be granted with the approval of the FEO, as required for business purposes.

Financial credits

By residents to nonresidents

The granting of financial loans by residents to nonresidents is subject to the approval of the FEO.

To residents from nonresidents

Financial credits are limited to foreign loans for financing investment operations or foreign trade.

Guarantees, sureties, and financial backup facilities

By residents to nonresidents

Moroccan banks may issue or accept in favor of residents sureties issued on behalf of nonresidents in support of the participation of said nonresidents in public or private contracting, the supplying of goods or services, the refund of down payments, and the substitution of guarantee withholdings. Similarly, they may issue sureties on behalf of nonresidents in support of tax liabilities or financial obligations. A counterguarantee from a foreign bank is required for sureties issued by Moroccan banks on behalf of nonresidents. When claims are entered under sureties issued or accepted in favor of residents on behalf of nonresidents, the relevant amounts must be repatriated to Morocco.

To residents from nonresidents

Provisions of guarantees are allowed on the condition that they are contracted through resident Moroccan banks.

Controls on direct investment

Outward direct investment

Outward direct investments are subject to prior approval of the FEO, but residents of foreign nationality are free to invest abroad.

Controls on liquidation of direct investment

There are no controls on transfers made directly with the banking system of the proceeds of the liquidation or sale of foreign investment, including capital gains. For the liquidation of any investment not falling under the convertibility arrangements, the relevant proceeds must be deposited in a convertible time deposit account denominated in dirhams. Funds placed therein may be transferred over a five-year period in equal annuities.

Controls on real estate transactions

These operations are subject to the investment regime.

Purchase abroad by residents

Yes.

Purchase locally by nonresidents

Foreign nationals may not purchase properties outside of urban limits.

Controls on personal capital movements

Loans

These operations are subject to FEO authorization.

Gifts, endowments, inheritances, and legacies

By residents to nonresidents

Gifts and endowments are subject to prior FEO authorization. However, inheritance transfers may be effected freely if the acquisition of the inherited property is financed with foreign exchange.

Settlement of debts abroad by immigrants

These operations are subject to FEO authorization.

Transfer of assets

Transfer abroad by emigrants

Yes.

Transfer of gambling and prize earnings

Yes.

Provisions specific to commercial banks and other credit institutions

Borrowing abroad

Commercial banks may only borrow abroad to finance foreign trade or investment operations.

Lending to nonresidents (financial or commercial credits)	The granting of loans abroad by Moroccan banks is subject to approval by the Exchange Office. However, banks may use cash held in foreign exchange accounts (by foreign nationals, Moroccan citizens residing abroad, and exporters) for granting buyers' credits to foreign, nonresident customers of Moroccan exporters.
Lending locally in foreign exchange	Moroccan banks may grant foreign exchange loans to residents for the financing of foreign trade operations and investment, within the limits of their respective foreign exchange positions, as authorized by the rules of the foreign exchange market.
Purchase of locally issued securities denominated in foreign exchange	Purchases are subject to the prior approval of the FEO.
Differential treatment of deposit accounts in foreign exchange	
Reserve requirements	Convertible dirham and foreign exchange accounts are excluded from reserve requirements.
Liquid asset requirements	All deposits are taken into account for the calculation of liquid asset requirements.
Differential treatment of deposit accounts held by nonresidents	
Credit controls	Debit balances are not permitted in foreign exchange accounts.
Investment regulations	
Abroad by banks	These operations are subject to authorization by the FEO and the monetary authorities.
In banks by nonresidents	These operations are subject to authorization by the monetary authorities.
Open foreign exchange position limits	On January 1, 1999, the open foreign exchange position limit for each currency was increased to 10% from 7% of net capital and reserves.
On resident assets and liabilities	The assets and liabilities of these accounts are included in the calculation of bank foreign exchange positions.
On nonresident assets and liabilities	The same regulations apply as for nonresident assets and liabilities.
Provisions specific to institutional investors	
Limits (max.) on portfolio invested abroad	Prior approval by the FEO is required for portfolio investment abroad.
Other controls imposed by securities laws	n.a.

Changes During 1999

Exchange arrangement	*January 1.* The euro replaced six of the eight currencies to which the dirham is pegged.
Imports and import payments	*March 16.* Morocco and Tunisia signed a free trade agreement providing for the immediate liberalization of 2,000 products.
Capital transactions	
Provisions specific to commercial banks and other credit institutions	*January 1.* The open foreign exchange position limit for each currency was increased to 10% from 7% of net capital and reserves.

MOZAMBIQUE

(Position as of January 31, 2000)

Status Under IMF Articles of Agreement

Article XIV	Yes.

Exchange Arrangement

Currency	The currency of Mozambique is the Mozambican metical.
Exchange rate structure	Unitary.
Classification	
Independently floating	The external value of the metical is determined by supply and demand in the exchange market, where the Bank of Mozambique (BM), the commercial banks, and foreign exchange bureaus participate.
	There is an interbank money market and an interdealer market in foreign exchange outside the fixing sessions. The foreign exchange market is cleared twice daily through telex and telephone transactions.
Exchange tax	No.
Exchange subsidy	No.
Forward exchange market	No.

Arrangements for Payments and Receipts

Prescription of currency requirements	No.
Payment arrangements	Yes.
Administration of control	The BM is responsible for foreign exchange policy and administers its control.
International security restrictions	n.a.
Payment arrears	n.a.
Controls on trade in gold (coins and/or bullion)	
Controls on domestic ownership and/or trade	Residents other than monetary authorities are permitted to hold gold for numismatic purposes or as jewelry or ornaments.
Controls on external trade	The exportation of gold is governed by special regulations, while the same regulations that apply to other import items are applicable to the importation of nonmonetary gold.
Controls on exports and imports of banknotes	
On exports	
Domestic currency	Exports of domestic currency are subject to a limit of Mt 500,000.
Foreign currency	Nonresidents may export foreign banknotes up to the equivalent of $5,000 and above, up to the amount they declared on entry.
On imports	
Domestic currency	Imports of domestic currency are subject to a limit of Mt 500,000, provided they have been previously exported.
Foreign currency	Imports of foreign currencies in excess of the equivalent of $5,000 must be declared.

Resident Accounts

Foreign exchange accounts permitted	Yes.
Held domestically	Yes.
Held abroad	Juridical persons must report to the BM the opening of such accounts.
Accounts in domestic currency convertible into foreign currency	No.

Nonresident Accounts

Foreign exchange accounts permitted	Yes.
Domestic currency accounts	These accounts may be opened with funds from the conversion of foreign currency or from employment and technical assistance contracts approved by the appropriate institutions; transfers of such funds abroad are permitted once the origin of the funds is proven.
Convertible into foreign currency	This is permitted for funds whose origin has been proven.
Blocked accounts	n.a.

Imports and Import Payments

Foreign exchange budget	No.
Financing requirements for imports	
Advance payment requirements	Documentary proof of the arrival of goods has to be presented.
Documentation requirements for release of foreign exchange for imports	
Domiciliation requirements	Yes.
Preshipment inspection	Inspections are performed randomly, depending on the type of merchandise import.
Import licenses and other nontariff measures	A single-document import procedure is required.
Negative list	A negative product list exists for imports financed by donors' or creditors' funds. In order to ensure that donors' requirements are met, the Office for the Coordination of Import Programs and other agencies review import requests. Some import support funds are allocated by the BM to the commercial banks.
Open general licenses	A single-document import procedure is in effect.
Import taxes and/or tariffs	Yes.
State import monopoly	No.

Exports and Export Proceeds

Repatriation requirements	All export proceeds, except in cases authorized by the BM, must be collected through the commercial banks.
Financing requirements	No.
Documentation requirements	
Domiciliation	Yes.
Export licenses	A single-document export procedure is required.

Export taxes	There is a duty of 14% on exports, which, on January 1, 2000, was raised to 18%.
Other export taxes	Yes.

Payments for Invisible Transactions and Current Transfers

Controls on these transfers	Exchange bureaus are authorized to sell foreign exchange up to the equivalent of $5,000 to individuals to pay expenses associated with travel, study, or medical treatment abroad, as well as for film rental, expenses for fairs and exhibitions, contributions to international organizations, and subscriptions to publications. Commercial banks are authorized to sell foreign exchange up to the equivalent of $5,000 for the payment of all types of invisible transactions and current transfers, except for profits and dividends from investment. Operations exceeding the limits and those relating to profits and dividends are subject to prior approval of the BM.
Trade-related payments	
Prior approval	Yes.
Investment-related payments	Remittances of profits and dividends from foreign direct investment may be made in accordance with the specific project authorization.
Prior approval	Yes.
Payments for travel	
Prior approval	Yes.
Personal payments	
Prior approval	Yes.
Foreign workers' wages	Foreign experts working in Mozambique may remit abroad all or part of their salaries, depending on the terms of their employment contracts.
Prior approval	Yes.
Other payments	
Prior approval	Yes.

Proceeds from Invisible Transactions and Current Transfers

Repatriation requirements	Yes.
Surrender requirements	Certain Mozambican nationals working abroad under officially arranged contracts (specifically, miners in the Republic of South Africa) are obligated to remit 60% of their earnings through the BM and to convert them into meticais.
Restrictions on use of funds	No.

Capital Transactions

Controls on capital and money market instruments	There are controls on all capital and money market transactions.
Controls on derivatives and other instruments	There are controls on all derivative transactions.
Controls on credit operations	
Commercial credits	
By residents to nonresidents	Yes.
To residents from nonresidents	Public and private enterprises need BM approval to borrow abroad. All foreign borrowing

	must be registered with the BM. Borrowing by the government must be obtained on concessional terms.
Financial credits	
By residents to nonresidents	Yes.
To residents from nonresidents	Public and private enterprises need BM approval to borrow abroad. All foreign borrowing must be registered with the BM. Borrowing by the government must be obtained on concessionary terms.
Guarantees, sureties, and financial backup facilities	
By residents to nonresidents	Yes.
To residents from nonresidents	Yes.
Controls on direct investment	
Outward direct investment	Yes.
Inward direct investment	Foreign investors are guaranteed the right to repatriate their initial capital. The incentives for foreign investments include tax and customs exemptions for specified periods and for access to domestic credit. Foreign investment proposals are processed by the Investment Promotion Center.
Controls on liquidation of direct investment	Yes.
Controls on real estate transactions	
Purchase abroad by residents	Yes.
Purchase locally by nonresidents	Nonresidents are prohibited from purchasing real estate and may only contract leasing and concessions.
Controls on personal capital movements	These are controls on all personal capital movements.
Transfer of gambling and prize earnings	Earnings from gambling are fully transferable, provided they are confirmed by the casinos, in accordance with a special permanent authorization granted to the casinos by the BM.
Provisions specific to commercial banks and other credit institutions	
Borrowing abroad	No prior approval is required, but the borrowing must be registered at the BM.
Lending to nonresidents (financial or commercial credits)	Yes.
Differential treatment of deposit accounts in foreign exchange	
Reserve requirements	Yes.
Liquid asset requirements	Yes.
Credit controls	Yes.
Investment regulations	
Abroad by banks	Yes.
In banks by nonresidents	Yes.
Open foreign exchange position limits	Limits are set in percent of core capital.
On resident assets and liabilities	Yes.
On nonresident assets and liabilities	Yes.

Provisions specific to institutional investors

Limits (max.) on securities issued by nonresidents and on portfolio invested abroad	Prior BM approval is required.
Limits (max.) on portfolio invested abroad	Prior BM approval is required.
Limits (min.) on portfolio invested locally	Prior BM approval is required.
Currency-matching regulations on assets/liabilities composition	Yes.
Other controls imposed by securities laws	n.r.

Changes During 1999

No significant changes occurred in the exchange and trade system.

Changes During 2000

Exports and export proceeds	*January 1.* The export duty was raised to 18% from 14%.

MYANMAR

(Position as of December 31, 1999)

Status Under IMF Articles of Agreement

Article XIV	Yes.

Exchange Arrangement

Currency	The currency of Myanmar is the Myanmar kyat.

Exchange rate structure

Dual	In addition to the official exchange rate, foreign exchange certificates (FECs) are issued by the Central Bank of Myanmar (CBM) in denominations of 1, 5, 10, and 20 units and are exchangeable with six hard currencies or with acceptable traveler's checks. FECs are widely used and serve the needs of visitors and investors in Myanmar. FECs are available for kyats at the market-determined rate at the exchange centers in Yangon. Seven exchange centers operate in Yangon and 19 in other cities. Holders of FECs may deposit them into their foreign exchange accounts. An unofficial parallel market for foreign exchange also exists.

Classification

Conventional pegged arrangement	The Myanmar kyat is officially pegged to the SDR at K 8.50847 per SDR 1. Myanmar applies margins of 2% to spot exchange transactions, based on the fixed kyat-SDR rate. The buying and selling rates of the kyat for the euro, Japanese yen, Swiss franc, pound sterling, and the U.S. dollar, quoted by the Myanmar Foreign Trade Bank (MFTB), are determined on the basis of the daily calculations of the value of these currencies against the SDR, as are rates for the currencies of some member countries of the ACU (i.e., the Bangladesh taka, Indian rupee, Iranian rial, Nepalese rupee, Pakistan rupee, and Sri Lanka rupee). The buying and selling rates for the Hong Kong dollar, Malaysian ringgit, and Singapore dollar are determined daily on the basis of the appropriate cross rates in the Singapore market, and the buying and selling rates for other currencies are based on the appropriate cross rates published in *The Asian Wall Street Journal* or the *London Financial Times*.
Exchange tax	No.
Exchange subsidy	No.
Forward exchange market	No.

Arrangements for Payments and Receipts

Prescription of currency requirements	Settlements with member countries of the ACU are made in ACU dollars through the ACU mechanism.

Payment arrangements

Regional arrangements	Myanmar is a member of the ACU.
Clearing agreements	Yes.
Barter agreements and open accounts	Bilateral trade arrangements with neighboring countries exist. These arrangements do not provide for the extension of credit.
Administration of control	Exchange control is administered by the CBM in accordance with instructions from the Ministry of Finance and Revenue (MFR). A Foreign Exchange Control Board headed by the Deputy Prime Minister allocates foreign exchange for the public sector. The central bank limits foreign currency operations to two state-owned banks, the MFTB and the Myanmar Investment and Commercial Bank (MICB).

International security restrictions

In accordance with UN sanctions — Yes.

Payment arrears

Official — Arrears are maintained with respect to debt-service payments of the central government.

Controls on trade in gold (coins and/or bullion)

Controls on external trade — Imports and exports of gold are not allowed for the private sector. Jewelry for personal use may be brought into Myanmar, subject to customs declaration at the port of arrival. Personal jewelry of a prescribed value may be taken out, subject to the condition that the jewelry will be brought back into the country. No conditions are attached, however, to the taking out of personal jewelry that was declared to customs when it was brought into Myanmar. Gold bullion may not be imported from any source.

Controls on exports and imports of banknotes

On exports

Domestic currency — The exportation of Myanmar currency is prohibited.

Foreign currency — Residents who have been granted an official permit to travel abroad are allowed to buy $500 from the MFTB and the MICB on presentation of $500 of FECs or the equivalent from their own foreign currency accounts. Nonresidents leaving Myanmar within six months of arriving may take out any balance of foreign currency they brought in with them and may also reconvert the remaining balance of the FECs purchased in excess of the minimum required purchase of $300.

On imports

Domestic currency — The importation of Myanmar currency is prohibited.

Foreign currency — Travelers may bring in up to $2,000 or its equivalent without any declaration. Tourists arriving in Myanmar are required to purchase FECs equivalent to a minimum value of $300, but amounts in excess of this minimum may be reconverted into foreign exchange on departure.

Resident Accounts

Foreign exchange accounts permitted — Yes.

Held domestically — Foreign currency accounts of national firms may be kept with private domestic banks permitted to conduct foreign exchange transactions. Accounts may be opened in U.S. dollars only by Myanmar nationals who earn foreign exchange. Account holders are allowed to import under import licenses issued by the Ministry of Commerce (MOC) on the basis of LCs or on a collection basis.

Approval required — With prior approval, account holders may use funds from their accounts to purchase air tickets for family visits abroad and to make payments for personal imports, for examination fees for their children, and for medical treatment abroad. Transfers of funds between accounts are permitted.

Held abroad — These accounts may be opened, but approval is required.

Accounts in domestic currency convertible into foreign currency — Conversion is permitted only for payment of official expenses.

Nonresident Accounts

Foreign exchange accounts permitted — Foreign currency accounts of diplomatic missions and international organizations and their home-based personnel may be kept with the MFTB only. For other nonresidents, prior approval is required.

Domestic currency accounts	These accounts are permitted, but all debits and credits require prior authorization.
Convertible into foreign currency	These accounts may be converted, but approval is required.
Blocked accounts	No.

Imports and Import Payments

Foreign exchange budget	An import program for the public sector is prepared annually as part of the foreign exchange budget drawn up jointly by the Ministry of National Planning and Economic Development and the MFR.
Financing requirements for imports	All payments for imports not originating from border trade are made through private domestic banks permitted to conduct foreign exchange business. State economic enterprises obtain foreign exchange directly from the MFTB, within the approved foreign exchange budget, after receiving endorsement from the respective ministries. Payments for border imports may be effected directly from the proceeds of border exports. Myanmar nationals who have opened foreign currency accounts are allowed to make unlimited payments for personal imports with the funds from their accounts. Myanmar nationals working abroad under official permits who have not yet opened foreign currency accounts may make payments on their personal imports out of their accumulated savings of legitimate funds.
Advance payment requirements	The state banks require a 100% advance payment, while private bank requirements vary according to the credit standing of their customers.
Advance import deposits	Yes.
Documentation requirements for release of foreign exchange for imports	
Preshipment inspection	Yes.
Letters of credit	Yes.
Import licenses used as exchange licenses	Yes.
Import licenses and other nontariff measures	Imports are free from tariffs, except for those imported from countries under UN embargo or with which Myanmar has severed diplomatic relations. With a few exceptions, private sector imports require import licenses for each transaction and are largely financed from the importer's foreign currency account. Since November 1997, only one type of import license has been issued, under which 60% is allocated to essential goods and the remainder to nonessential goods. An importer wishing to import nonpriority or neutral items is generally required to import priority goods at a value equivalent to 50% and 25% of the values of nonpriority goods and of neutral items, respectively. Private importers must register at the MOC and renew their licenses annually. Border imports require permits. Exporters of agricultural, forestry, and fisheries products are encouraged to import up to the equivalent of 25% of the export value of selected items that will contribute to the production in these sectors. A 2% service charge payable in foreign exchange is charged for issuance of an import license on garments.
Negative list	Certain items, such as opium and other narcotics, playing cards, and gold and silver bullion, may not be imported from any source.
Open general licenses	Joint ventures with private interests may be granted OGLs on a case-by-case basis. State economic enterprises may import goods for their own use and for resale with OGLs, whereas government departments may import only for their own use.
Import taxes and/or tariffs	Tariff rates range from zero to 40%. Agricultural implements, raw materials, and other essential imports are taxed at low rates, while the highest rates are applied to imports of luxury goods.
State import monopoly	No.

Exports and Export Proceeds

Repatriation requirements	Proceeds from exports must be fully repatriated.
Financing requirements	No.
Documentation requirements	
Letters of credit	Yes.
Preshipment inspection	Yes.
Export licenses	Export trade may be conducted with any country without restriction, except those under UN embargo or with which Myanmar has severed diplomatic relations.
Without quotas	In practice, state agencies responsible for production may export any product in excess of what is needed for domestic consumption. Special permits are required for exports of antiques. State enterprises have a monopoly on the exportation of rice, teak, petroleum, natural gas, pearls, jade, and precious stones and metals. Rice is exported by the Myanmar Agricultural Produce Trading through the Myanmar Export-Import Services; private traders and cooperatives are also permitted to export some beans and pulses, rattan, flour, and cut flowers under valid export permits issued by the MOC. Border trade of certain products, including rice, teak, rubber, petroleum, hides, leather, some beans and pulses, maize, cotton, and groundnuts, is not permitted.
Export taxes	Excluding goods under the exemption list, duties were levied on all exports at 5%, provided the proceeds are received in foreign currency. A specific duty of K 10 per metric ton is levied on all varieties of rice. Effective January 1, 1999, export duties were abolished.
Other export taxes	Customs duties are levied on rice, bamboo, cereal, raw hides, and cakes.

Payments for Invisible Transactions and Current Transfers

Controls on these transfers	All payments for invisibles outside the public sector are subject to approval and are considered on a case-by-case basis. Remittances against FECs are permitted up to US$30,000 a month.
Trade-related payments	Remittances of insurance premium payments other than for Myanmar Insurance are not permitted.
Prior approval	Yes.
Investment-related payments	Information is not available on the amortization of loans or the depreciation of direct investments.
Prior approval	Yes.
Payments for travel	
Prior approval	Yes.
Quantitative limits	Yes.
Personal payments	
Prior approval	Yes.
Quantitative limits	Remittances to retired government employees are permitted only if the persons concerned were nonnationals throughout their term of service and are now residing in their native countries. Family remittances are permitted only for foreign technicians employed under contract by the government; the limit is one-half of the net salary if the spouse is living abroad, and one-third of the net salary if the spouse is living in Myanmar.
Foreign workers' wages	Balances of salary and lawful income earned that remain after payment of taxes and deduction of living expenses of the worker and his or her family may be transferred abroad through a bank with the approval of the CBM.
Prior approval	Yes.

Other payments

Prior approval   Yes.

Proceeds from Invisible Transactions and Current Transfers

Repatriation requirements   Yes.

Surrender requirements   Unless exchange control authorities grant a special waiver, 10% of proceeds must be paid
                                         as income tax. Myanmar nationals working abroad with permission from the government
                                         are required to pay an income tax at the rate of 10% of their gross earnings in foreign ex-
                                         change. Myanmar seamen serving abroad and Myanmar nationals working abroad in pri-
                                         vate organizations are required to transfer to Myanmar as tax 10% of their gross earnings
                                         in foreign exchange through embassies in their country of residence. Myanmar nationals
                                         working abroad in UN organizations are not required to pay income tax.

Restrictions on use of funds   Use of funds is subject to exchange control approval.

Capital Transactions

Controls on capital and money   n.a.
market instruments

Controls on derivatives and other   n.a.
instruments

Controls on credit operations

Commercial credits

  To residents from nonresidents   Yes.

Financial credits

  To residents from nonresidents   Yes.

Guarantees, sureties, and financial
backup facilities

  To residents from nonresidents   Yes.

Controls on direct investment

Inward direct investment   The Myanmar Investment Commission may accept proposals for investment from
                                         foreigners for full ownership and under joint venture, with the share of foreign capital
                                         representing at least 35% of the total capital. To facilitate and promote foreign invest-
                                         ment, the commission may grant exemption from customs duties and other internal
                                         taxes on machinery and equipment imported during construction of the project, spare
                                         parts used in business, and raw materials imported for the first three years of commer-
                                         cial production, as well as exemption from the income tax for a period of up to three
                                         consecutive years, including the year when production of goods and services began,
                                         or for longer than three years, depending upon the profitability of the enterprise.
                                         Furthermore, accelerated depreciation allowances may be granted. Types of economic
                                         activity and the sectors open to foreign investment are specified in a detailed positive list.

Controls on liquidation of direct   The government guarantees that an economic enterprise formed under a permit will not be
investment   nationalized during the term of the contract or during an extended term. Repatriation of
                                         capital and profits is allowed through banks after payment of taxes and prescribed funds.

Controls on real estate transa 'ions

Purchase abroad by residents   Yes.

Purchase locally by nonresidents   Land may not be owned by foreign investors but may be leased from the state.

Sale locally by nonresidents   Yes.

Controls on personal capital movements	
Transfer of gambling and prize earnings	Yes.

Provisions specific to commercial banks and other credit institutions	
Borrowing abroad	State approval is required.
Maintenance of accounts abroad	Yes.
Provisions specific to institutional investors	n.a.
Other controls imposed by securities laws	n.a.

Changes During 1999

Exports and export proceeds	*January 1.* All export duties on commodities were abolished.

NAMIBIA

(Position as of December 31, 1999)

Status Under IMF Articles of Agreement

Article VIII   Date of acceptance: September 20, 1996.

Exchange Arrangement

Currency   The currency of Namibia is the Namibia dollar.

Other legal tender   The South African rand is also legal tender.

Exchange rate structure   Unitary.

Classification

Conventional pegged arrangement   The Namibia dollar is pegged to the South African rand at par. The exchange rate of the Namibia dollar against other currencies is determined on the basis of cross rates of the South African rand against the currencies concerned in international markets. The exchange market in Namibia has developed as an extension of the exchange market in South Africa.

Exchange tax   No.

Exchange subsidy   No.

Forward exchange market   Authorized dealers are permitted to conduct forward exchange operations, including forward cover, with residents in any foreign currency in respect of authorized trade and nontrade transactions. Forward exchange contracts may cover the entire period of the outstanding commitments and accruals. Forward cover is also provided to nonresidents, subject to certain limitations. Gold mining companies and houses may sell forward anticipated receipts of their future gold sales. Forward cover is provided in U.S. dollars only and is available to authorized dealers for maturities not exceeding 12 months at a time in the form of swap transactions involving Namibia dollars (South African rand) and U.S. dollars with a margin based on the interest rate differential between the two currencies.

Official cover of forward operations   Special forward cover at preferential rates is provided in respect of import financing.

Arrangements for Payments and Receipts

Prescription of currency requirements   If a particular type of payment is not covered in the Exchange Control Rulings, an application is lodged with the Bank of Namibia (BON). Each application is considered on its own merit.

Payment arrangements

Regional arrangements   Namibia is part of the CMA, and no restrictions are applied to payments within the CMA.

Administration of control   The BON has delegated some powers to authorized dealers who assist the BON in administering exchange control. Where an authorized dealer cannot approve a transaction in terms of the Exchange Control Rulings, an application is lodged with the BON. The norms applied by the BON in scrutinizing applications are subject to policy guidelines established within the CMA.

International security restrictions   No.

Payment arrears   No.

Controls on trade in gold (coins and/or bullion)   The exchange control regulations prohibit the purchase and sale, both domestically and abroad, of unwrought gold by Namibia residents without the specific authority of the BON. All such requests are considered on merit.

Controls on domestic ownership and/or trade   Residents are permitted to purchase, hold, and sell gold coins within the CMA for numismatic and investment purposes only.

Controls on external trade	All export and import of gold require the prior approval of the monetary authority.

Controls on exports and imports of banknotes

On exports

Domestic currency — An individual may export up to N$5,000.

Foreign currency — Export of foreign currency not authorized in terms of exchange control rulings requires prior BON approval.

On imports

Domestic currency — Upon entry from countries outside the CMA, residents and nonresidents may bring in a total of N$5,000 in Namibia banknotes or R 5,000 in South African banknotes. There are no limitations on the importation of domestic currency from Lesotho and Swaziland.

Foreign currency — Importation of foreign currency by nonresidents of the CMA is unrestricted. However, Namibia residents are only allowed to import into Namibia the residual balance of foreign currency initially exported.

Resident Accounts

Foreign exchange accounts permitted	Yes.
Held domestically	Resident private individuals are allowed to operate foreign currency accounts with local authorized dealers; however, prior approval is required.
Held abroad	These accounts are permitted, particularly for import and export enterprises, but approval is required.
Accounts in domestic currency convertible into foreign currency	Payments in foreign currency may be effected from resident accounts, provided the transaction is covered under the Exchange Control Rulings or where prior approval has been obtained in respect thereof.

Nonresident Accounts

Foreign exchange accounts permitted	Only export-processing zones (EPZ) customer foreign currency accounts are allowed. These accounts are kept offshore via a local authorized dealer and are set up to facilitate the foreign currency disbursements of EPZ enterprises. Transactions through these accounts must conform to normal banking practices and must be carried out with the full cognizance and approval of the authorized dealer concerned. For other residents, prior approval is required.
Domestic currency accounts	The regulations that apply to these accounts in South Africa also apply in Namibia. EPZ nonresident accounts are allowed. These are Namibia dollar accounts, funded with foreign currency, and are used for the normal operational requirements and expenditures of EPZ enterprises and to facilitate local investments. Balances remaining in these accounts are freely convertible and transferable abroad.
Convertible into foreign currency	These accounts may be converted, but approval is required.
Blocked accounts	These accounts continue to be subjected to normal emigration procedures.

Imports and Import Payments

Foreign exchange budget	No.
Financing requirements for imports	
Advance payment requirements	Advance payment for the importation of capital goods is allowed upon filing an application with the BON. Authorized dealers may authorize "cash with order" advance payments and approve up to 33.3% of the ex-factory cost of capital goods.

| **Documentation requirements for release of foreign exchange for imports** | Documentation confirming receipt of the imported articles into Namibia (e.g., bill of entry, local post receipts) is required. |

Letters of credit — LCs may be established by authorized dealers locally.

Import licenses and other nontariff measures — There are no restrictions on imports originating in any country of the SACU. Imports from countries outside the SACU are usually licensed in conformity with South Africa's import regulations. Permits are valid for one year, are expressed in value terms, and are valid for imports from any country outside the SACU. At present, about 90% of imports require a permit.

Negative list — Namibia has the right to restrict certain imports (through customs duties or quantitative restrictions) from countries outside the SACU and, under certain conditions, from countries within the SACU.

Import taxes and/or tariffs

Taxes collected through the exchange system — A general sales tax of 10% is levied on all imports in addition to a sales duty between zero and 15%, depending on the type of commodity.

State import monopoly — No.

Exports and Export Proceeds

Repatriation requirements — All export proceeds are normally required to be repatriated.

Surrender requirements — All export proceeds are normally required to be surrendered within six months of shipment or within 30 days of the date of accrual. Corporate entities that operate in the export field and also import goods from abroad are allowed to offset the cost of imports against the proceeds of exports, provided the set-off takes place within 30 days.

Financing requirements — No.

Documentation requirements — All exports from Namibia should be accompanied by an export declaration, and, upon receipt of export proceeds locally, the inflow of foreign currency must be declared.

Letters of credit — Yes.

Guarantees — Yes.

Export licenses — All exports, except to SACU member countries, require a license.

Without quotas — Permits are required for exports of goods in short supply to non-SACU countries.

Export taxes — No.

Payments for Invisible Transactions and Current Transfers

Controls on these transfers — Authorized dealers may approve trade-related invisible payments without limitation and other invisible payments up to established limits. Larger amounts may be granted on presentation of documentary proof of need. Virtually all remaining controls on current account transactions are liberalized, except in cases where the limits were retained to make the remaining controls on capital outflows effective.

Investment-related payments

Prior approval — No prior approval is required, but if a local company is contracting any loans via a local source, an application should be filed with the BON. The repayment of foreign loans requires BON approval.

Payments for travel

Quantitative limits — Residents may obtain up to N$120,000 for a person 12 years or older and N$35,000 for a child under the age of 12 years each calendar year. Residents traveling to destinations outside the CMA are allowed to take the foreign exchange made available in any form.

Indicative limits/bona fide test	Amounts in excess of the indicative limits are approved when the applicant provides documents in support of a bona fide request.
Personal payments	There are no restrictions on payment of medical costs.
Prior approval	As regards transfer of pensions, applications are considered on the merits of the particular case.
Quantitative limits	The annual allowance for study abroad is N$120,000 for a student or N$240,000 for a student accompanied by a nonstudent spouse. Family maintenance transfers are limited to N$4,000 a month for a receiving family unit. Alimony payments are not limited.
Indicative limits/bona fide test	Amounts in excess of the indicative limits for payment of study abroad are approved when applicants provide documents in support of a bona fide request.
Foreign workers' wages	
Prior approval	Yes.
Quantitative limits	Contract workers may transfer two-thirds of their monthly salary.
Credit card use abroad	
Prior approval	Departing residents are required to complete a form prior to departure.
Quantitative limits	Limits must be in accordance with prescribed travel allowances.
Indicative limits/bona fide test	Yes.
Other payments	
Prior approval	Applications are considered on the merits of the particular case.

Proceeds from Invisible Transactions and Current Transfers

Repatriation requirements	Yes.
Surrender requirements	Proceeds from invisibles must be surrendered within 30 days of the date of accrual, unless exemption is obtained.
Restrictions on use of funds	Prior BON approval should be obtained to use such funds outside the CMA.

Capital Transactions

Controls on capital and money market instruments	Inward transfers of capital from non-CMA countries for equity investment are freely permitted, whereas applications by residents to retain funds in, or transfer them to, countries outside the CMA for bona fide long-term investments in specific development projects or for the expansion of existing projects owned or controlled by residents are considered on their own merits. Namibia corporations are allowed to invest substantial amounts in the SADC member countries, and dual listing of companies on both the Namibia Stock Exchange and other SADC stock exchanges is permitted.
On capital market securities	
Shares or other securities of a participating nature	
Sale or issue locally by nonresidents	Proceeds from the sale of quoted or unquoted CMA securities, real estate, and other equity investments by nonresidents are freely transferable.
Purchase abroad by residents	Yes.
Sale or issue abroad by residents	Yes.
Bonds or other debt securities	
Purchase abroad by residents	Yes.
Sale or issue abroad by residents	Yes.

On money market instruments

   Purchase abroad by residents   Prior BON approval is required for the acquisition of money market instruments outside the CMA.

   Sale or issue abroad by residents   Yes.

On collective investment securities

   Purchase abroad by residents   Prior BON approval is required for the acquisition of collective investment securities outside the CMA.

   Sale or issue abroad by residents   Yes.

Controls on derivatives and other instruments

Purchase abroad by residents   Prior BON approval is required.

Sale or issue abroad by residents   Yes.

Controls on credit operations   Interest rates applicable on foreign-currency-denominated loans should not exceed LIBOR plus 2%, while those on local-currency-denominated loans should not exceed the prime overdraft rate plus 3%.

Commercial credits   Credit operations outside the CMA are subject to specific approval from the BON, which is generally given for borrowing abroad with a maturity of at least six months by domestic entrepreneurs, except for speculative borrowings or consumer credit. Authorized dealers are generally permitted to raise funds abroad in their own names for the financing of Namibia's foreign trade and other approved purposes.

   By residents to nonresidents   Yes.

   To residents from nonresidents   Yes.

Financial credits

   By residents to nonresidents   A wholly nonresident-owned company may borrow 100% of shareholder equity locally. Only companies that are 75% or more foreign owned are subject to exchange controls.

   To residents from nonresidents   Yes.

Guarantees, sureties, and financial backup facilities

   By residents to nonresidents   Yes.

   To residents from nonresidents   Yes.

Controls on direct investment

Outward direct investment   Applications by residents to retain funds in, or transfer them to, countries outside the CMA for bona fide long-term investments in specific development projects or for the expansion of existing projects owned or controlled by residents are considered on their own merits.

The limit on foreign investment is N$50 million for countries other than SADC members, and a facility of N$250 million in respect of investment into SADC member countries is established. Consideration is to be given to foreign borrowings to finance these investments being raised with recourse to, or guarantee from, Namibia, implying that the local corporations' balance sheet may be used in negotiating such a facility. Approved foreign subsidiaries may expand activities abroad without prior approval, provided such expansion is financed by foreign borrowings or by the employment of profits earned by the foreign subsidiary.

The BON is now considering applications by private individuals to invest in fixed property, e.g., holiday homes and farms, in the SADC member countries.

Inward direct investment   Inward transfers of capital from non-CMA countries for equity investment are free.

Controls on liquidation of direct investment   Yes.

Controls on real estate transactions

Purchase abroad by residents | Yes.

Controls on personal capital movements

Loans

By residents to nonresidents Residents require prior approval.

To residents from nonresidents Residents require prior approval.

Gifts, endowments, inheritances, and legacies

By residents to nonresidents Cash bequests and the cash proceeds of legacies and distributions from such estates due to nonresidents may be remitted up to N$500,000. Amounts due in excess of this amount require prior BON approval.

To residents from nonresidents Residents must declare funds obtained and repatriate them to Namibia. Alternatively, exemption may be obtained from the BON for retention of such funds abroad. Each application is considered on its own merits.

Settlement of debts abroad by immigrants If the immigrants have formally declared their assets and liabilities and have no cash resources available with which to pay the debt, the BON may consider requests for exemption based on merit.

Transfer of assets

Transfer abroad by emigrants Families emigrating outside the CMA are granted the normal tourist allowance and are permitted to remit up to N$400,000 (N$200,000 for single persons). Any balance exceeding this limit must be credited to an emigrant blocked account. The balance, including earned income, may be transferred under prescribed conditions.

Transfer into the country by immigrants Immigrants are required to furnish the exchange control authorities with a complete account of their foreign assets and liabilities at the time of their arrival. Any foreign assets they transfer to Namibia may, through the same channel, be retransferred abroad.

Transfer of gambling and prize earnings Normally, Namibians are discouraged from participating in international lotteries. Most requests in this regard are declined.

Provisions specific to commercial banks and other credit institutions

Borrowing abroad Authorized dealers are generally permitted to raise funds abroad in their own names for the financing of Namibia's foreign trade and for other approved purposes.

Lending to nonresidents (financial or commercial credits) Prior approval is needed for lending not related to trade transactions. Only companies that are 75% or more foreign owned are subject to exchange controls, and permission is given for local financial assistance to be granted to nonresident-owned companies against a nonresident guarantee, provided the amount made available does not exceed the limit calculated in terms of the formula requirements.

Lending locally in foreign exchange Authorized dealers may lend money locally in Namibia dollars.

Differential treatment of deposit accounts in foreign exchange As long as these deposits are liabilities to the public, arising from operations in Namibia, they will be included in the basis for calculating the minimum liquid assets and reserve requirements.

Credit controls The limit for credit facilities to any person or group of related persons is 30% of a banking institution's capital funds. In addition to the above limit, granted credit facilities that exceed 10% of capital funds may not exceed, in aggregate, 800% of the total capital funds of the banking institution in Namibia. These limits apply to all customers irrespective of their citizenship.

Differential treatment of deposit accounts held by nonresidents As long as these deposits are liabilities to the public, arising from operations in Namibia, they will be included in the basis for calculating the minimum liquid assets and reserve requirements.

Credit controls The same regulations apply as for deposit accounts in foreign exchange.

Investment regulations

   Abroad by banks | Banking institutions are at all times required to maintain minimum local assets situated in Namibia of an aggregate value of not less than 100% of the amount of their liabilities payable in Namibia dollars (excluding capital funds), less any debit balances denominated in South African rand in the clearing account held with their associate banks in South Africa.

Open foreign exchange position limits | There is no distinction between residents and nonresidents. The net open position limit is 15% of a bank's share capital and unimpaired reserves.

   On resident assets and liabilities | Yes.

   On nonresident assets and liabilities | Yes.

Provisions specific to institutional investors | Namibian pension funds and insurance companies are obliged by law to invest 35% of their total assets locally.

Limits (max.) on securities issued by nonresidents and on portfolio invested abroad | The maximum is 65% of the total assets of pension funds and insurance companies.

Limits (max.) on portfolio invested abroad | Investments are allowed only by way of swaps. The foreign currency transfers allowed are 10% of the total value of the local fund. Transfers abroad of up to 3% of the net inflow of funds during the preceding year may be allowed. In addition, 2% of the net inflow of funds during a preceding year could be used for investment into stock exchanges of SADC member countries, subject to the overall limit of 10% of the total assets applicable to asset swaps.

The definition of institutional investor includes the unit trust management company itself. In the past, it included only the fund itself.

Limits (min.) on portfolio invested locally | The minimum is 35% of the total assets of pension funds and insurance companies.

Other controls imposed by securities laws | No.

Changes During 1999

No significant changes occurred in the exchange and trade system.

NEPAL

(Position as of February 29, 2000)

Status Under IMF Articles of Agreement

Article VIII   Date of acceptance: May 30, 1994.

Exchange Arrangement

Currency   The currency of Nepal is the Nepalese rupee.

Exchange rate structure   Unitary.

Classification

Conventional pegged arrangement   The Nepalese rupee has been pegged to the Indian rupee at the rate of NRe 1.6 per Re 1 since February 1993.The reference rate of the dollar quoted by the Nepal Rastra Bank (NRB) is based on the average of the quoted rate of commercial banks. Exchange rates of other major currencies are quoted on the basis of overseas markets. Buying and selling rates are quoted daily for certain other currencies, with quotations based on the buying and selling rates for the dollar in markets abroad.

Exchange tax   No.

Exchange subsidy   No.

Forward exchange market   Banks provide forward exchange cover for trade transactions.

Arrangements for Payments and Receipts

Prescription of currency requirements   Convertibility between the Indian rupee and the Nepalese rupee is unrestricted in Nepal. All current transactions with member countries of the ACU other than India must be effected through the ACU. Payments for selected imports from India may be settled in dollars. Other imports and proceeds from exports to India must be settled in Indian rupees. Proceeds from exports to other countries must be received in convertible currencies.

Payment arrangements

Regional arrangements   Nepal is a member of the ACU.

Clearing agreements   Yes.

Administration of control   Payments in convertible currencies may be made without permission, subject to the procedures prescribed by the NRB. All exchange transactions must be settled through authorized dealers. Nonbank authorized dealers are licensed to accept foreign currencies only for their services to foreign nationals.

International security restrictions   n.a.

Payment arrears   No.

Controls on trade in gold (coins and/or bullion)

Controls on external trade   Persons who have stayed abroad for more than one month and have an official source of foreign earnings may import up to 10 kilograms of gold.

Controls on exports and imports of banknotes

On exports

Foreign currency   Foreign banknotes, other than Indian banknotes, may not be taken out by residents without permission. Nonresidents may take out the unchanged amount of any foreign banknotes they bring in.

On imports

 Domestic currency   Yes.

 Foreign currency   Residents and nonresidents may bring in foreign banknotes freely, but must declare amounts exceeding the equivalent of $2,000. No limit applies to Indian rupees.

Resident Accounts

Foreign exchange accounts permitted Exporters are allowed to deposit up to 100% of export earnings in a foreign exchange account to cover trade-related expenses. Nepalese citizens earning foreign exchange from working abroad (except in Bhutan and India) for more than three months may open these accounts. Commercial banks may accept deposits denominated in most of the freely usable currencies, and are free to determine the rate of interest paid on deposits. Current accounts may be opened with a minimum equivalent to $500, and time deposits with a minimum equivalent to $3,000.

Held domestically   These accounts are allowed, but approval is required.

Held abroad   With prior approval, commercial banks may open these accounts.

Accounts in domestic currency convertible into foreign currency No.

Nonresident Accounts

Foreign exchange accounts permitted Accounts may be maintained in all specified convertible currencies, and balances in these accounts may be freely transferred abroad. Diplomats and foreign nationals, except Indian nationals, may open foreign currency accounts freely with Nepalese banks.

Domestic currency accounts No.

Blocked accounts   No.

Imports and Import Payments

Foreign exchange budget   No.

Financing requirements for imports No.

Documentation requirements for release of foreign exchange for imports On May 24, 1999, three items were added to the list of items imported from India that have to be settled in foreign exchange, and on February 29, 2000, another item was added, bringing the total number to 33.

Letters of credit   Yes.

Import licenses and other nontariff measures Most imports are covered under OGLs. Quantitative restrictions are in effect for the importation of poppy seeds.

Negative list   Imports of arms, ammunition, wireless transmitters, precious metals, and jewelry require special permission from the government.

Open general licenses   Yes.

Import taxes and/or tariffs There are seven tariff rates (5%, 10%, 15%, 25%, and 40% as well as two special rates of 80% and 130%), with most goods subject to either the 15% or the 25% rate. Nepalese citizens returning from abroad who have spent at least 15 nights out of the country are permitted to bring in goods worth NRe 1,000 free of customs duties and sales taxes. Citizens with official sources of foreign exchange earnings and who have stayed abroad for one month or more are allowed additional imports without official documentation.

State import monopoly   No.

Exports and Export Proceeds

Repatriation requirements	Proceeds from exports must be repatriated within 180 days of receipt. Exporters are allowed to accept short payments in export proceeds, if they do not exceed $500 or 1%, whichever is higher. Approval of the NRB is required for amounts above the specified limit.
Surrender requirements	Exporters may retain the export earnings on their foreign currency account with local banks.
Financing requirements	Commercial banks may grant preexport credit of up to 70% of the f.o.b. value of products to all individuals and institutions holding irrevocable LCs opened or endorsed by foreign banks and acceptable to the Nepalese banks. Such credit may be provided for a maximum of three months; this period may be extended without penalty under special circumstances beyond the control of the exporter.
Documentation requirements	
Letters of credit	Exports to countries other than India are allowed only against irrevocable LCs or advance payments by foreign banks.
Guarantees	Effective September 16, 1999, export consignments not exceeding $50,000 may be undertaken on the basis of a bank guarantee also.
Domiciliation	Reexportation to India of non-Nepalese goods and reexportation to any destination of goods imported from India are prohibited.
Export licenses	Exports of items having archaeological and religious value, old coins, narcotics, and explosive materials are prohibited.
With quotas	The export volume of selected ready-made garments to the United States is restricted by a quota system.
Export taxes	No.
Other export taxes	There are nominal export service charges, but no taxes are charged.

Payments for Invisible Transactions and Current Transfers

Controls on these transfers	
Trade-related payments	Yes.
Investment-related payments	
Prior approval	Prior approval is required in the case of private sector loan amortization.
Payments for travel	
Quantitative limits	The limit ranges from $700 to $1,500, depending on destination.
Personal payments	
Prior approval	Prior approval of the government is required for transfers related to medical and study abroad costs.
Foreign workers' wages	
Prior approval	Yes.
Credit card use abroad	The use of credit cards abroad is allowed under specific guidelines.
Other payments	
Prior approval	Yes.

Proceeds from Invisible Transactions and Current Transfers

Repatriation requirements	Yes.
Surrender requirements	Yes.
Restrictions on use of funds	Yes.

Capital Transactions

Controls on capital and money market instruments

On capital market securities

Shares or other securities of a participating nature

Purchase locally by nonresidents	Nonresidents may invest in equity shares up to 25% of the capital of Nepalese companies.
Sale or issue locally by nonresidents	Yes.
Purchase abroad by residents	Yes.
Sale or issue abroad by residents	Yes.

Bonds or other debt securities

Purchase locally by nonresidents	Purchases may only be made for bonds denominated in Nepalese currency.
Sale or issue locally by nonresidents	Sales may only be made for bonds denominated in Nepalese currency.
Purchase abroad by residents	Yes.
Sale or issue abroad by residents	Yes.

On money market instruments	In principle, participation by nonresidents is allowed, but so far no effective participation has been recorded.
Purchase abroad by residents	Yes.
Sale or issue abroad by residents	Yes.
Controls on derivatives and other instruments	No transactions have occurred as yet.
Controls on credit operations	Specified borrowers may borrow from abroad on the basis of guidelines.

Commercial credits

By residents to nonresidents	Yes.
To residents from nonresidents	Yes.

Financial credits

By residents to nonresidents	Yes.
To residents from nonresidents	Yes.

Guarantees, sureties, and financial backup facilities

By residents to nonresidents	Yes.
To residents from nonresidents	Yes.

Controls on direct investment

Outward direct investment	Nepalese citizens, whether or not residing in Nepal, are not allowed to make any type of investment in foreign countries, except as specifically permitted by government notice. The exemptions include the purchase and sale of insurance policies abroad, and investments abroad by any banking or financial institution incorporated in Nepal.

Inward direct investment	Investments require prior approval in the form of a guarantee from the Department of Industry. Foreign investment is not permitted in cottage, small-scale, or defense-related industries. Foreign investors may hold 100% equity in large- and medium-scale industries. Foreign securities firms are permitted to form joint ventures with local state exchange members, but their ownership is limited to 40%.
Controls on liquidation of direct investment	Based on the provisions of the Company Act.
Controls on real estate transactions	There are controls on all real estate transactions.
Controls on personal capital movements	
Loans	
By residents to nonresidents	Yes.
To residents from nonresidents	Yes.
Gifts, endowments, inheritances, and legacies	
By residents to nonresidents	Yes.
To residents from nonresidents	Yes.
Provisions specific to commercial banks and other credit institutions	
Borrowing abroad	Based on specific guidelines.
Lending to nonresidents (financial or commercial credits)	Yes.
Lending locally in foreign exchange	Exporters, tourism-related businesses, and specific industries are entitled to such credits.
Purchase of locally issued securities denominated in foreign exchange	No such transactions have occurred.
Differential treatment of deposit accounts in foreign exchange	Differential treatment is based on the type of currency.
Reserve requirements	Yes.
Liquid asset requirements	Yes.
Interest rate controls	Yes.
Credit controls	Yes.
Provisions specific to institutional investors	n.r.
Other controls imposed by securities laws	n.r.

Changes During 1999

Imports and import payments	*April 24.* Three items were added to the list of items imported from India that have to be settled in foreign exchange.
Exports and export proceeds	*September 16.* Export consignments not exceeding $50,000 may be undertaken on the basis of bank guarantee also.

Changes During 2000

Imports and import payments	*February 29.* One item was added to the list of items imported from India that have to be paid in foreign exchange.

NETHERLANDS

(Position as of December 31, 1999)

Status Under IMF Articles of Agreement

Article VIII	Date of acceptance: February 15, 1961.

Exchange Arrangement

Currency	As of January 1, 1999, the currency of the Netherlands is the euro. In cash transactions, however, the legal tender remains the Netherlands guilder until 2002, when euro banknotes and coins will be issued.
Exchange rate structure	Unitary.

Classification

Exchange arrangement with no separate legal tender	The Netherlands participates in a currency union (EMU) comprising 11 members of the EU: Austria, Belgium, Finland, France, Germany, Ireland, Italy, Luxembourg, the Netherlands, Portugal, and Spain. Internal conversion rates in respect to the national currencies of EMU participants were fixed to the euro on January 1, 1999, whereas the external exchange rate of the euro is market determined. The conversion rate between the euro and the Netherlands guilder was set at f. 2.20371 per €1. The ECB has the right to intervene to smooth out fluctuations in external exchange rates.
Exchange tax	No.
Exchange subsidy	No.
Forward exchange market	Forward exchange contracts are not limited as to delivery period, nor is an underlying trade transaction required.

Arrangements for Payments and Receipts

Prescription of currency requirements	No.
Payment arrangements	No.
Administration of control	No.
International security restrictions	
In accordance with Executive Board Decision No. 144-(52/51)	Yes.
In accordance with UN sanctions	In compliance with the relevant UN Security Council resolutions and/or EU regulations, certain restrictions are imposed on financial transactions with Iraq, Libya, the Federal Republic of Yugoslavia (Serbia/Montenegro), and the UNITA movement in Angola. Effective April 6, 1999, restrictions on financial transactions with Libya were suspended.
Payment arrears	No.
Controls on trade in gold (coins and/or bullion)	No.
Controls on exports and imports of banknotes	No.

Resident Accounts

Foreign exchange accounts permitted	Yes.

Held domestically	Yes.
Held abroad	Yes.
Accounts in domestic currency convertible into foreign currency	Yes.

Nonresident Accounts

Foreign exchange accounts permitted	Yes.
Domestic currency accounts	Yes.
Convertible into foreign currency	Yes.
Blocked accounts	In compliance with relevant UN Security Council resolutions and/or EU regulations, funds belonging to Iraq, Libya, the Federal Republic of Yugoslavia (Serbia/Montenegro), and the UNITA movement in Angola are blocked. Effective April 6, 1999, restrictions on financial transactions with Libya were suspended.

Imports and Import Payments

Foreign exchange budget	No.
Financing requirements for imports	No.
Documentation requirements for release of foreign exchange for imports	No.
Import licenses and other nontariff measures	Imports from Angola and Iraq are prohibited. Imports of most products covered by the CAP from non-EU countries are subject to import levies. Common EU regulations are applied to most agricultural and livestock products.
Negative list	Import licenses are required for imports originating in Hong Kong SAR, Japan, and state trading countries (i.e., the People's Republic of China, the Democratic People's Republic of Korea, and Vietnam), as well as for the importation of goods of unknown origin. In addition, import licenses are required for a limited number of products, mainly those of the agricultural, steel, and textile sectors.
Licenses with quotas	These apply to imports of textiles originating in the Far East and in state trading countries.
Import taxes and/or tariffs	Yes.
State import monopoly	No.

Exports and Export Proceeds

Repatriation requirements	No.
Financing requirements	No.
Documentation requirements	No.
Export licenses	
Without quotas	Export licenses are required for only a few commodities, mostly of a strategic character, for some agricultural products, and for iron and steel scrap and related products.
Export taxes	No.

Payments for Invisible Transactions and Current Transfers

Controls on these transfers	No.

Proceeds from Invisible Transactions and Current Transfers

Repatriation requirements	No.
Restrictions on use of funds	No.

Capital Transactions

Controls on capital and money market instruments	Inward and outward capital transfers by residents and nonresidents are not restricted, but they are subject to reporting requirements based on the External Financial Relations Act.
Controls on derivatives and other instruments	No.
Controls on credit operations	No.
Controls on direct investment	No.
Controls on liquidation of direct investment	No.
Controls on real estate transactions	No.
Controls on personal capital movements	No.
Provisions specific to commercial banks and other credit institutions	
Open foreign exchange position limits	Limits are imposed on banks' total position in foreign currency and precious metals. Banks are required to report to the Nederlandsche Bank their position in each foreign currency and precious metal (spot, forward, and option positions) at the end of each month.
Provisions specific to institutional investors	No.
Other controls imposed by securities laws	No.

Changes During 1999

Exchange arrangement	*January 1.* The currency of the Netherlands became the euro. The conversion rate between the euro and the Netherlands guilder was set irrevocably at f. 2.20371 per €1.
Arrangements for payments and receipts	*April 6.* Restrictions on financial transactions with Libya were suspended.

NETHERLANDS ANTILLES

(Position as of December 31, 1999)

Status Under IMF Articles of Agreement

Article VIII   Date of acceptance: February 15, 1961.

Exchange Arrangement

Currency   The currency of the Netherlands Antilles is the Netherlands Antillean guilder.

Exchange rate structure   Unitary.

Classification

Conventional pegged arrangement   The Netherlands Antillean guilder is pegged to the dollar, the intervention currency, at NA f. 1.7900 per $1. The official selling rate is NA f. 1.82 per $1. Official buying and selling rates for certain other currencies are set daily on the basis of rates of the dollar abroad.

Exchange tax   No.

Exchange subsidy   No.

Forward exchange market   No.

Arrangements for Payments and Receipts

Prescription of currency requirements   No.

Payment arrangements   No.

Administration of control   The Central Bank (CB) issues exchange licenses where required. The Department of Finance (DOF) issues import licenses where required, and authorized banks may provide foreign exchange for all current transactions without prior approval of the CB.

International security restrictions

In accordance with UN sanctions   Sanctions under UN resolutions against Iraq and the Federal Republic of Yugoslavia (Serbia/Montenegro) are in effect.

Payment arrears   No.

Controls on trade in gold (coins and/or bullion)   No.

Controls on exports and imports of banknotes

On exports

   Domestic currency   Exportation is prohibited except for traveling purposes.

   Foreign currency   Nonresidents may take with them on departure any foreign currency that they brought in.

Resident Accounts

Foreign exchange accounts permitted   Resident individuals may hold these accounts without a special license.

Held domestically   Yes.

Held abroad   Transfers from a local bank account to foreign accounts are allowed up to NA f. 10,000 a quarter.

Accounts in domestic currency convertible into foreign currency	Yes.

Nonresident Accounts

Foreign exchange accounts permitted	Yes.
Domestic currency accounts	These accounts are permitted, but approval is required for accounts exceeding NA f. 200,000.
Convertible into foreign currency	Yes.
Blocked accounts	No.

Imports and Import Payments

Foreign exchange budget	No.
Financing requirements for imports	Imports with delivery dates exceeding payment dates by more than 12 months must be reported to the CB.
Documentation requirements for release of foreign exchange for imports	No.
Import licenses and other nontariff measures	No.
Import taxes and/or tariffs	Imported goods for which there are locally produced substitutes are subject to tariffs ranging from 25% to 90%. Certain commodities are subject to import surcharges in Bonaire and Curaçao.
State import monopoly	No.

Exports and Export Proceeds

Repatriation requirements	If export proceeds are not received within 12 months of shipment, the delay must be reported to the CB.
Financing requirements	No.
Documentation requirements	No.
Export licenses	No.
Export taxes	No.

Payments for Invisible Transactions and Current Transfers

Controls on these transfers	Most types of current invisible payments and remittances may be made freely. A license is required if the delivery and payment dates are more than one year apart.
Investment-related payments	There are restrictions on the transfer of profits.
Prior approval	Companies must submit their annual report to the CB for verification of the actual amount of profits and dividends recorded before they may remit them.
Indicative limits/bona fide test	Yes.

Proceeds from Invisible Transactions and Current Transfers

Repatriation requirements	No.

Restrictions on use of funds	No.

Capital Transactions

Controls on capital and money market instruments	Investments by residents in officially listed foreign securities (and in mutual funds whose shares are listed) are permitted free of license up to NA f. 100,000 a year, provided that these payments occur through a local exchange bank. Reinvestment of proceeds from the sales of securities is also allowed.
On capital market securities	There are controls on all capital market transactions.
Controls on derivatives and other instruments	Yes.
Controls on credit operations	Credit operations require licenses, which are normally granted.
Controls on direct investment	
Outward direct investment	Yes.
Inward direct investment	Investments require licenses, which are normally granted.
Controls on liquidation of direct investment	No.
Controls on real estate transactions	
Purchase abroad by residents	A license is required for these purchases.
Controls on personal capital movements	
Loans	
By residents to nonresidents	Only short-term loans are permitted.
To residents from nonresidents	Only short-term loans are permitted.
Transfer of assets	
Transfer abroad by emigrants	Yes.
Transfer into the country by immigrants	Yes.
Provisions specific to commercial banks and other credit institutions	
Differential treatment of deposit accounts in foreign exchange	
Credit controls	Effective January 1, 1999, the ceiling on net domestic credit to the private sector, which stood at 2.5%, was eliminated.
Investment regulations	CB approval is required for the acquisition of more than 5% of shares in other companies.
Abroad by banks	Yes.
In banks by nonresidents	Yes.
Open foreign exchange position limits	Banks are not allowed to have negative net foreign asset positions. Any negative position is subject to penalty.
Provisions specific to institutional investors	Yes.
Limits (min.) on portfolio invested locally	The limits are 40% for the first NA f. 10 million, 50% for the next NA f. 10 million, and 60% for additional amounts of the total provisions and liabilities.
Currency-matching regulations on assets/liabilities composition	There must be sufficient assets in a particular currency to cover the liabilities in that currency (currency exposure is not allowed).

Other controls imposed by securities laws

There is no securities law.

Changes During 1999

Capital transactions

Provisions specific to commercial banks and other credit institutions

January 1. The ceiling on net domestic credit to the private sector was lifted.

NEW ZEALAND

(Position as of December 31, 1999)

Status Under IMF Articles of Agreement

Article VIII	Date of acceptance: August 5, 1982.

Exchange Arrangement

Currency	The currency of New Zealand is the New Zealand dollar.
Exchange rate structure	Unitary.
Classification	
Independently floating	The exchange rate of the New Zealand dollar is determined on the basis of supply and demand in the foreign exchange market.
Exchange tax	No.
Exchange subsidy	No.
Forward exchange market	Yes.

Arrangements for Payments and Receipts

Prescription of currency requirements	No.
Payment arrangements	No.
Administration of control	No.
International security restrictions	
In accordance with Executive Board Decision No. 144-(52/51)	Yes.
In accordance with UN sanctions	Certain restrictions had been imposed on the making of payments and transfers for current international transactions with respect to Iraq, and similarly with respect to the Federal Republic of Yugoslavia (Serbia/Montenegro) in compliance with UN Security Council resolutions. Restrictions with respect to the Federal Republic of Yugoslavia (Serbia/Montenegro) resolution have been suspended since December 1995 in cases where it is clear that the assets, money, and securities are not subject to any claim or interest on the part of the successor states of the Former Socialist Federal Republic of Yugoslavia other than Serbia/Montenegro. Certain restrictions on the making of payments and transfers for current international transactions pursuant to the UN Security Council resolutions have been imposed with respect to the UNITA movement in Angola and Libya. Effective November 25, 1999, certain restrictions were imposed on the making of payments and transfers with respect to the Taliban (the Islamic State of Afghanistan).
Payment arrears	No.
Controls on trade in gold (coins and/or bullion)	No.
Controls on exports and imports of banknotes	The Financial Transactions Reporting Act requires that imports and exports of banknotes be reported. A customs documentation form, required when entering or leaving the country, includes a requirement to declare amounts greater than $NZ 10,000 or its equivalent.

Resident Accounts

Foreign exchange accounts permitted	Yes.

Held domestically	Yes.
Held abroad	Yes.
Accounts in domestic currency convertible into foreign currency	Yes.

Nonresident Accounts

Foreign exchange accounts permitted	Yes.
Domestic currency accounts	Yes.
Convertible into foreign currency	Yes.
Blocked accounts	No.

Imports and Import Payments

Foreign exchange budget	No.
Financing requirements for imports	No.
Documentation requirements for release of foreign exchange for imports	No.

Import licenses and other nontariff measures

Negative list

Import prohibitions and restrictions affect some 70 products or classes of products—primarily plants, animals, and products considered dangerous to human health or not in the public interest.

Import taxes and/or tariffs

Tariffs only apply to goods also produced in New Zealand. Over 90% of imports (by value) are imported free of duty, either because there is no New Zealand–made equivalent or because the imports are from preferential sources.

Most tariffs are ad valorem, except for many clothing products, where "alternative specific" tariffs apply. Tariffs on affected goods are either ad valorem (generally 19%) or a corresponding alternative specific tariff, which is expressed in dollars per unit, whichever is higher. Tariffs for most imports from nonpreferential sources are 6–8%. The only tariffs over 15% apply to some motor vehicle parts (17.5%), clothing (19%), and carpets and footwear (both 17.5%). Tariffs were last decreased on July 1, 1999.

Under the terms of the ANZCERTA and the SPARTECA agreements, imports from the participating countries enter New Zealand duty free. Eligible imports from developing countries are allocated tariff preferences, while the 48 least-developed countries are granted duty-free access for all products, except clothing and footwear.

State import monopoly	No.

Exports and Export Proceeds

Repatriation requirements	No.
Financing requirements	No.
Documentation requirements	No.

Export licenses

Without quotas

Certain items classified as strategic goods may be exported only when specific requirements have been met and an export permit has been issued.

With quotas	Yes.
Export taxes	No.

Payments for Invisible Transactions and Current Transfers

Controls on these transfers	No.

Proceeds from Invisible Transactions and Current Transfers

Repatriation requirements	No.
Restrictions on use of funds	No.

Capital Transactions

Controls on capital and money market instruments	No.
Controls on derivatives and other instruments	No.
Controls on credit operations	No.
Controls on direct investment	
Inward direct investment	Under the Overseas Investment Regulations, there are separate authorization procedures for "nonland," "land," and fishing quota investments, which apply both to new investors and to existing foreign-controlled firms. Nonland investments involving the acquisition of over 25% of the shares of a New Zealand company, and where, effective December 9, 1999, the consideration exceeds $NZ 50 million or which involve the purchase of property in excess of $NZ 50 million used in carrying on a business, are subject to a bona fide investor test. Established foreign-controlled enterprises also need approval for investments exceeding $NZ 50 million in areas unrelated to that consented to originally. However, since these investors were screened when they first invested, the procedure is straightforward. Under the Fisheries Act, a nonresident must obtain either an exemption or a permission to acquire or to continue holding a fishing quota, an interest in quota, annual catch entitlement, or provisional catch history.
Controls on liquidation of direct investment	No.
Controls on real estate transactions	
Purchase locally by nonresidents	Foreign investment in certain types of land is subject to both a bona fide investor test and a "national interest" test. Land acquisitions that require authorization relate to any land exceeding five hectares in area or where the consideration exceeds $NZ 10 million, and islands or land containing or adjoining reserves, historic or heritage areas, and the foreshore or lakes in excess of 0.4 hectares.
Controls on personal capital movements	No.
Provisions specific to commercial banks and other credit institutions	No.
Provisions specific to institutional investors	No.
Other controls imposed by securities laws	No.

Changes During 1999

Arrangements for payments and receipts

November 26. Certain restrictions were imposed on the making of payments and transfers with respect to the Taliban (the Islamic State of Afghanistan).

Imports and import payments

July 1. Tariff rates were decreased.

Capital transactions

Controls on direct investment

December 9. The limits above which authorization is needed for investments was raised to $NZ 50 million from $NZ 10 million.

NICARAGUA

(Position as of December 31, 1999)

Status Under IMF Articles of Agreement

Article VIII	Date of acceptance: July 30, 1964.

Exchange Arrangement

Currency	The currency of Nicaragua is the Nicaraguan córdoba.
Exchange rate structure	Unitary.
Classification	
Crawling peg	As of July 11, 1999, the devaluation of the córdoba against the dollar was slowed to an annual rate of 9% from 12% and as of November 1, 1999, to an annual rate of 6%. The central government and financial institutions are free to undertake purchases or sales of foreign exchange with the Central Bank of Nicaragua (CBN).
Exchange tax	There is no tax, but the CBN charges a commission of 1% on sales of foreign exchange.
Exchange subsidy	No.
Forward exchange market	No.

Arrangements for Payments and Receipts

Prescription of currency requirements	No.
Payment arrangements	
Regional arrangements	Nicaragua is a member of the CACM.
Administration of control	Exchange operations between private agents are not restricted. The CBN allows authorized commercial banks and exchange houses to make foreign exchange transactions.
International security restrictions	No.
Payment arrears	
Official	Payment arrears are maintained with members of the Paris Club and non–Paris Club countries.
Controls on trade in gold (coins and/or bullion)	
Controls on domestic ownership and/or trade	The Nicaraguan Mining Institute manages the country's gold production. An authorization from the CBN is required to operate as a gold exporter. Natural and juridical persons may trade gold coins (commemorative gold coins were issued in 1967, 1975, and 1980) for numismatic purposes only.
Controls on exports and imports of banknotes	No.

Resident Accounts

Foreign exchange accounts permitted	Yes.
Held domestically	Yes.
Held abroad	Yes.

Accounts in domestic currency convertible into foreign currency	Yes.

Nonresident Accounts

Foreign exchange accounts permitted	Yes.
Domestic currency accounts	Córdoba accounts with exchange guarantee (maintenance of value) contracts may be opened with commercial banks.
Convertible into foreign currency	Yes.
Blocked accounts	No.

Imports and Import Payments

Foreign exchange budget	No.
Financing requirements for imports	No.
Documentation requirements for release of foreign exchange for imports	All importers must submit an import declaration form either to commercial banks or to customs when they are using their own resources.
Letters of credit	Some import payments are made with sight drafts, but almost all are made through LCs.
Import licenses and other nontariff measures	
Open general licenses	Yes.
Import taxes and/or tariffs	As of January 1, 1999, imports of 746 items are subject to a temporary import tariff of 15% independent of their origin, and all imports are subject to a sales tax and the Central American Common Tariff. On July 1, 1999, the maximum tariff was reduced to 10%. The maximum import tariff for certain tobacco and alcoholic beverage items is 20%. Effective November 30, 1999, an additional 35% import duty was imposed, a "sovereignty tax," on imports from Honduras and Colombia.
State import monopoly	No.

Exports and Export Proceeds

Repatriation requirements	No.
Financing requirements	No.
Documentation requirements	No.
Export licenses	Export licenses are not required, but all exports must be registered with the Ministry of Economy.
Export taxes	No.

Payments for Invisible Transactions and Current Transfers

Controls on these transfers	No.

Proceeds from Invisible Transactions and Current Transfers

Repatriation requirements	No.
Restrictions on use of funds	No.

Capital Transactions

Controls on capital and money market instruments	No.
Controls on derivatives and other instruments	No.
Controls on credit operations	
Commercial credits	
To residents from nonresidents	For statistical purposes, these credits must be reported to the CBN within 30 days after the credits have been granted.
Financial credits	
To residents from nonresidents	The same requirement applies as for commercial credits.
Controls on direct investment	
Inward direct investment	Foreign exchange originating from new investments or additions to capital must be surrendered to the CBN through commercial banks. However, in practice this regulation has become obsolete as a result of the elimination of exchange controls.
Controls on liquidation of direct investment	No.
Controls on real estate transactions	No.
Controls on personal capital movements	No.
Provisions specific to commercial banks and other credit institutions	
Purchase of locally issued securities denominated in foreign exchange	These instruments may only be issued by the CBN or the government.
Investment regulations	
Abroad by banks	There are prudential limits.
Provisions specific to institutional investors	
Currency-matching regulations on assets/liabilities composition	There are prudential limits established by the Superintendency of Financial Institutions.
Other controls imposed by securities laws	No.

Changes During 1999

Exchange arrangement	*July 11.* The rate of devaluation of the córdoba against the dollar was reduced to an annual 9% from 12%.
	November 1. The rate of devaluation of the córdoba against the dollar was reduced to an annual 6% from 9%.
Imports and import payments	*January 1.* The maximum import tariff was reduced to 15%.
	July 1. The maximum import tariff was reduced to 10%.
	November 30. An additional 35% import duty was imposed on imports from Honduras and Colombia.

NIGER

(Position as of January 31, 2000)

Status Under IMF Articles of Agreement

Article VIII   Date of acceptance: June 1, 1996.

Exchange Arrangement

Currency   The currency of Niger is the CFA franc.

Exchange rate structure   Unitary.

Classification

Exchange arrangement with no sepa- The CFA franc is pegged to the euro, the intervention currency, at a fixed rate of
rate legal tender   CFAF 100 per €0.8385, which is the official buying and selling rate. Exchange rates
                                    for other currencies are derived from the rate for the currency concerned in the Paris
                                    foreign exchange market and the fixed rate between the euro and the CFA franc.

Exchange tax   Authorized banks charge an exchange commission of 2% on exchanges involving French
                                    francs and a commission on purchases and sales of other currencies, the rate of which is
                                    freely determined. In addition, they levy a bank commission of 0.25% on transfers to all
                                    countries outside the WAEMU, which must be surrendered in its entirety to the Treasury.

Exchange subsidy   No.

Forward exchange market   Forward cover is available to residents only for imports of specified categories of goods.
                                    This cover has to be authorized by the MOF and provided in the currency of settlement
                                    stipulated in the commercial contract. Maturities must correspond to the due date of foreign
                                    exchange settlement as per the contract and must not exceed one month, except in the case
                                    of specified products, where it may be extended for up to three months. Effective Feb-
                                    ruary 1, 1999, residents are authorized to contract forward exchange cover to settle pay-
                                    ments related to imports and exports of goods and services, and maturities may not take
                                    place after the payment due date for the imports or exports in question.

Arrangements for Payments and Receipts

**Prescription of currency   Because Niger is linked to the French Treasury through an Operations Account, settlements
requirements**   with France, Monaco, and other Operations Account countries (WAEMU and CAEMC
                                    members and the Comoros) are made in French francs or the currency of any other Opera-
                                    tions Account country or any other currency stipulated in commercial contracts.

Payment arrangements

Regional arrangements   An Operations Account is maintained with the French Treasury that links Operations
                                    Account countries. All purchases or sales of foreign currencies or euros against CFA
                                    francs are ultimately settled through a debit or credit to the Operations Account.

Clearing agreements   A multilateral clearing agreement exists within the WAMA between the member states of
                                    the WAEMU and Cape Verde, The Gambia, Ghana, Guinea, Liberia, Mauritania, Nigeria,
                                    and Sierra Leone.

Administration of control   Exchange control is administered jointly by the MOF and the BCEAO. Since February 1,
                                    1999, most of the authority to supervise foreign exchange transactions has been delegated
                                    to authorized banks, which are required to report those operations to the MOF. The only
                                    operations that continue to require prior authorization of the MOF or the BCEAO involve
                                    residents' investments abroad, domestic accounts in foreign exchange, and residents'
                                    accounts abroad. Effective February 1, 1999, the amount of transfers authorized without
                                    supporting documentation was raised to CFAF 300,000 from CFAF 100,000.

International security restrictions No.

Payment arrears

Official   Yes.

Private   Yes.

Controls on trade in gold (coins and/or bullion)

Controls on external trade

Imports and exports of gold require prior authorization from the MOF. Exempt from this requirement are (1) imports and exports by or on behalf of the Treasury or the BCEAO; (2) imports and exports of manufactured articles containing a minor quantity of gold (such as gold-filled or gold-plated articles); and (3) articles of gold up to a combined weight of 500 grams when carried by a traveler.

Controls on exports and imports of banknotes

On exports

Domestic currency

Travelers are allowed to export CFA franc banknotes within the WAEMU. However, repurchases by the BCEAO of exported banknotes continue to be suspended. In addition, the shipment of BCEAO banknotes between authorized intermediaries and their correspondent banks located outside of the WAEMU zone is strictly prohibited.

Foreign currency

The reexportation of foreign banknotes is allowed up to the equivalent of CFAF 500,000; for larger amounts, documentation demonstrating either the importation of the foreign banknotes or their purchase against other means of payment registered in the name of the traveler or through the use of nonresident deposits in local banks is required.

On imports

Domestic currency

Residents and nonresidents are free to import banknotes and coins issued by the BCEAO.

Foreign currency

Nonresidents may bring in any amount of foreign banknotes and coins (except gold coins) of countries outside the Operations Account area. Residents bringing in foreign banknotes and foreign currency traveler's checks exceeding the equivalent of CFAF 300,000 must declare them to customs upon entry and must surrender them within eight days.

Resident Accounts

Foreign exchange accounts permitted

Effective February 1, 1999, residents are allowed to open foreign exchange accounts with local banks or banks abroad after obtaining authorization from the MOF, subsequent to the approval of the BCEAO.

Held domestically

These accounts are permitted, but prior approval is required.

Held abroad

The opening of accounts abroad by residents is subject to prior MOF authorization, subsequent to the approval of the BCEAO.

Accounts in domestic currency convertible into foreign currency

No.

Nonresident Accounts

Foreign exchange accounts permitted   Effective February 1, 1999, authorization is issued by the BCEAO.

Domestic currency accounts

These accounts may not be credited with banknotes of the BCEAO, French franc notes, or any other banknote issued by a central bank maintaining an Operations Account with the French Treasury.

Convertible into foreign currency

These accounts may be freely debited for the purchase of foreign currencies on the official market.

Blocked accounts   No.

Imports and Import Payments

Foreign exchange budget	No.
Financing requirements for imports	
Advance payment requirements	Advance payments for imports require authorization, and importers may not acquire foreign exchange until the scheduled date of the payment.
Documentation requirements for release of foreign exchange for imports	Exchange authorization and invoices are required.
Domiciliation requirements	All imports exceeding CFAF 3 million must be domiciled with an authorized bank. Effective February 1, 1999, this limit was raised to CFAF 5 million.
Preshipment inspection	An inspection is required for the quality and price of goods exceeding CFAF 3 million f.o.b.
Import licenses and other nontariff measures	Quantitative restrictions may be applied on products for public health and security reasons.
Negative list	Narcotics and firearms are prohibited.
Import taxes and/or tariffs	On January 1, 2000, the WAEMU introduced a CET with four rates (zero, 5%, 10%, and 20%) for all member countries except Guinea-Bissau.
Taxes collected through the exchange system	Yes.
State import monopoly	No.

Exports and Export Proceeds

Repatriation requirements	The due date of payment for exports must fall within 120 days after the goods have been shipped. Proceeds from exports, regardless of the purchasing country, must be repatriated in their entirety through the BCEAO no later than 30 days from the date of receipt. Effective February 1, 1999, proceeds from exports to WAEMU countries are no longer required to be repatriated.
Surrender requirements	Yes.
Financing requirements	No.
Documentation requirements	A customs declaration is required.
Domiciliation	All exports of more than CFAF 5 million must be domiciled with an authorized intermediary bank. Effective February 1, 1999, exports to WAEMU countries need not be domiciled.
Export licenses	Licenses are required for gold and groundnuts.
Export taxes	No.

Payments for Invisible Transactions and Current Transfers

Controls on these transfers	Payments for invisible transactions with France, Monaco, and the countries linked to the French Treasury by an Operations Account are permitted freely. Effective February 1, 1999, (1) payments and incomes of foreign ships in the WAEMU zone and WAEMU ships abroad are included under current operations; (2) indicative ceilings for foreign currency allocations were eliminated; and (3) the amount of foreign currency to be surrendered by residents after travel was raised to CFAF 300,000 from CFAF 50,000.
Trade-related payments	
Indicative limits/bona fide test	Yes.

Investment-related payments

    Prior approval   Yes.

    Indicative limits/bona fide test   Yes.

Payments for travel

    Quantitative limits   Residents traveling as tourists or on business to franc zone countries that are not members of the WAEMU are allowed to take out up to the equivalent of CFAF 2 million in cash in foreign currency. Any sum above this amount may be taken out in the form of traveler's checks, certified checks, or other payment instruments. Foreign currency is issued upon presentation to an authorized bank of a ticket and a valid passport or identity card.

Personal payments

    Prior approval   Required for payment of family maintenance.

    Indicative limits/bona fide test   Yes.

Foreign workers' wages

    Indicative limits/bona fide test   Total net wages may be transferred upon the presentation of pay slips.

Credit card use abroad   Credit cards issued by resident financial intermediaries or foreign financial institutions may be used abroad.

    Quantitative limits   Credit cards issued by resident financial intermediaries and specifically authorized by the MOF may be used up to the ceiling for tourist and business travel.

Other payments

    Indicative limits/bona fide test   Yes.

Proceeds from Invisible Transactions and Current Transfers

Repatriation requirements   Proceeds from invisible transactions with countries that are not WAEMU members must be repatriated.

Surrender requirements   All amounts due, except for transactions with WAEMU members, must be surrendered within one month of the due date or date of receipt.

Restrictions on use of funds   n.a.

Capital Transactions

Controls on capital and money market instruments   Capital inflows to WAEMU countries are unrestricted. Capital transfers to all other countries require MOF approval, but receipts are freely permitted. All investments abroad by residents require MOF authorization; a maximum of 75% of such investments may be financed by foreign loans.

Effective February 1, 1999, there are no controls on foreign investments in WAEMU countries or on capital outflows for repayment of loans, disinvestment abroad, and option contract purchases. These operations must be reported to the MOF for statistical purposes.

Prior authorization of the RCPSFM is required for the issuing and marketing of securities and real assets of foreign entities, canvassing, or advertising investments abroad.

On capital market securities

    Shares or other securities of a participating nature

      Purchase locally by nonresidents   These are subject to declaration to the MOF for statistical purposes.

      Sale or issue locally by nonresidents   Residents may purchase securities sold or issued by nonresidents only after obtaining the authorization of the RCPSFM.

Purchase abroad by residents	The prior authorization of the MOF is required for these operations.
Sale or issue abroad by residents	Residents may sell securities freely to nonresidents for disinvestment purposes, but the settlement by transfer abroad or by a credit to a nonresident's account requires an exchange license issued by the MOF.
Bonds or other debt securities	The same regulations apply as for shares or other securities of a participating nature.

On money market instruments

Sale or issue locally by nonresidents	Yes.
Purchase abroad by residents	Yes.
Sale or issue abroad by residents	Yes.

On collective investment securities

Purchase locally by nonresidents	Yes.
Sale or issue locally by nonresidents	Yes.
Purchase abroad by residents	Yes.
Sale or issue abroad by residents	Yes.

Controls on derivatives and other instruments	These instruments are virtually unknown in Niger. However, instruments of this type are governed by the rules and regulations normally applicable to securities and direct investments. Effective February 1, 1999, residents are authorized to purchase abroad call and put options in commodities and securities.
Purchase locally by nonresidents	Yes.
Sale or issue locally by nonresidents	Yes.
Purchase abroad by residents	Yes.
Sale or issue abroad by residents	Yes.

Controls on credit operations

Commercial credits

By residents to nonresidents	Credits to nonresidents may be granted freely for merchandise exports if the due date of payment is within 120 days following shipment of the goods; commercial credits for services may be granted freely; no time limit has been officially fixed for such payment.
To residents from nonresidents	There are no controls on the granting of loans of this type. Their repayment is, in general, authorized, subject to the submission of documents.

Financial credits

By residents to nonresidents	The granting of financial credit is subject to prior authorization of the MOF. For the transfer abroad of funds in this context, a foreign exchange authorization must be submitted for clearance from the MOF, together with the necessary supporting documents.
To residents from nonresidents	The funds required for servicing these facilities must be transferred by an authorized intermediary. Effective February 1, 1999, foreign borrowing by residents became unrestricted.

Guarantees, sureties, and financial backup facilities

By residents to nonresidents	The same regulations apply as for financial credits.
To residents from nonresidents	There are no controls, but the necessary funds must be transferred from abroad through an authorized intermediary. If, however, these transactions take place between a direct investment company resident in Niger and its parent company located abroad, the transactions are considered direct investments and require a prior declaration to the MOF.

Controls on direct investment

Outward direct investment	Participation in a company is considered direct investment if it exceeds 20%. Until February 1, 1999, all investments made abroad by residents were subject to the prior authorization of the MOF. Effective February 1, 1999, such authorization is no longer required for

investments consisting of the acquisition by residents of securities, for which the issue or marketing by nonresidents has been authorized in advance by the RCPSFM. A maximum of 75% of such investments may be financed with borrowing from abroad.

Inward direct investment	Inward investment is subject to prior reporting to the MOF for statistical purposes.
Controls on liquidation of direct investment	The liquidation of a resident's investments abroad must be reported to the MOF. Reinvestment of the proceeds of such liquidations is subject to prior MOF authorization. If the reinvestment is not authorized, the proceeds must be repatriated within one month through an authorized bank. There are no controls on the sale of foreign investment in Niger, but such operations must be reported to the MOF for statistical purposes.
Controls on real estate transactions	
Purchase abroad by residents	Prior authorization of the MOF is required.
Purchase locally by nonresidents	Purchases for purposes other than direct investment in a business, branch, or company are allowed with prior declaration to the MOF.
Sale locally by nonresidents	Operations may be settled only after the approval of the MOF. Following settlement, the liquidation or sale must be reported to the MOF and to the BCEAO within 20 days.
Controls on personal capital movements	
Loans	
By residents to nonresidents	Prior authorization of the MOF is required.
To residents from nonresidents	A declaration for statistical purposes and submission of a report to the MOF is required.
Gifts, endowments, inheritances, and legacies	
By residents to nonresidents	Gifts and endowments are subject to prior authorization of the MOF. Inheritances and legacies are generally authorized.
To residents from nonresidents	These transactions are subject to declaration to the MOF.
Settlement of debts abroad by immigrants	Immigrants who have acquired resident status must first obtain authorization from the MOF to settle debts contracted abroad while they were nonresidents.
Transfer of assets	
Transfer abroad by emigrants	These transactions are subject to prior authorization to the MOF.
Transfer of gambling and prize earnings	Yes.
Provisions specific to commercial banks and other credit institutions	
Borrowing abroad	The same regulations apply as for financial loans contracted by residents.
Maintenance of accounts abroad	Banks and financial institutions may open accounts with correspondent banks but are not authorized to hold liquid assets, except to meet the needs of their current operations.
Lending to nonresidents (financial or commercial credits)	The prior authorization of the MOF is required.
Purchase of locally issued securities denominated in foreign exchange	Yes.
Differential treatment of deposit accounts in foreign exchange	
Credit controls	Effective February 1, 1999, loans and other assistance granted to nonresidents are subject to prior MOF authorization, after the consent of the BCEAO has been obtained.
Differential treatment of deposit accounts held by nonresidents	
Credit controls	Yes.

Investment regulations	The same regulations apply as for direct investment.
Abroad by banks	Yes.
In banks by nonresidents	Yes.
Provisions specific to institutional investors	Controls were imposed by the Insurance Code of the Inter-African Conference of Insurance Markets.
Limits (min.) on portfolio invested locally	The Insurance Code includes specific rules for the use of insurance companies' technical reserves.
Other controls imposed by securities laws	No.

Changes During 1999

Exchange arrangement	*January 1.* The CFA franc peg to the French franc was replaced with a peg to the euro.
	February 1. Residents were authorized to contact forward exchange cover in connection with payments related to imports and exports of goods and services.
Arrangements for payments and receipts	*February 1.* The amount of transfers authorized without supporting documentation was raised to CFAF 300,000 from CFAF 100,000.
Resident accounts	*February 1.* Residents were allowed to open foreign exchange accounts with local banks or with banks abroad after obtaining authorization from the MOF, with the approval of the BCEAO.
Nonresident accounts	*February 1.* Authorizations to open nonresident accounts are to be issued by the BCEAO.
Imports and import payments	*February 1.* The limit for the domiciliation requirement was raised to CFAF 5 million.
Exports and export proceeds	*February 1.* Proceeds from exports to WAEMU countries were no longer required to be repatriated.
Payments for invisible transactions and current transfers	*February 1.* Limits on foreign exchange allowances were eliminated. The threshold of foreign exchange to be surrendered by residents after travel was raised to CFAF 300,000 from CFAF 50,000.
	February 1. Payments and incomes of foreign ships in the WAEMU zone and WAEMU ships abroad were included under current operations.
Capital transactions	*February 1.* Transfers related to the sale of foreign securities by residents and to proceeds of disinvestments by nonresidents were allowed. Foreign investment in WAEMU countries became unrestricted. Such operations are to be subject to reporting for statistical purposes. The prior authorization of the RCPSFM is required for the issuance and marketing of securities and capital assets of foreign entities, as well as for the advertising of investments abroad. Any investment by residents abroad requires the prior approval of the MOF.
Controls on derivatives and other instruments	*February 1.* Transfers relating to option purchases were allowed.
Controls on credit operations	*February 1.* Foreign borrowing by residents became unrestricted.
Provisions specific to commercial banks and other credit institutions	*February 1.* Loans and other assistance granted to nonresidents require MOF authorization, after the consent of the BCEAO has been obtained.

Changes During 2000

| **Imports and import payments** | *January 1.* The WAEMU introduced a CET with four rates (zero, 5%, 10%, and 20%) for all member countries except Guinea-Bissau. |

NIGERIA

(Position as of December 31, 1999)

Status Under IMF Articles of Agreement

Article XIV   Yes.

Exchange Arrangement

Currency   The currency of Nigeria is the Nigerian naira.

Exchange rate structure

Unitary   Before the inauguration of the interbank market on October 25, 1999, the official foreign exchange rate (mainly from oil receipts) was provided by the Central Bank of Nigeria (CBN) to end users through their banks in weekly allocations in the autonomous foreign exchange market (AFEM). Other CBN transactions (with government agencies, oil companies, etc.) were also made at this rate. Transactions at the official exchange rate were limited to a specific list of official purposes, subject to approval or exception of the head of state. Since the interbank market was created, sales of government receipts of foreign exchange are made by the CBN in the interbank market. Petroleum companies may sell their proceeds from oil exports to the CBN or to approved dealer banks. Payments of Petroleum Profits Tax are required to be in foreign exchange direct to the CBN. Approved dealer banks may buy foreign exchange from the CBN on their own account (subject to prudential requirements on open forward positions), or on behalf of their customers, who are required to justify their purchases of foreign exchange with reference to trade, remittance, travel, or other requirements. In addition, there is a bureau de change and parallel market in foreign exchange. Since the inauguration of the interbank market, the exchange rates in these markets have not diverged significantly from the interbank rate.

Classification

Managed floating with no pre-   The AFEM exchange rate was set weekly in reference to the interbank, bureau de change,
announced path for the exchange rate and parallel market rates. Effective June 23, 1999, all foreign exchange bids at the AFEM were subject to a 200% treasury bill–backing requirement. This requirement was reduced to 100% on September 1, 1999, to 50% on September 20, 1999, and was eliminated on October 28, 1999. Effective October 25, 1999, the interbank rate is set as the outcome of telephone dealing among approved dealer banks and the CBN.

Exchange tax   No.

Exchange subsidy   Yes.

Forward exchange market   Forward exchange transactions in the interbank market are permitted among the authorized foreign exchange dealers and between the dealers and their customers, subject to prudential limits.

Arrangements for Payments and Receipts

Prescription of currency   No.
requirements

Payment arrangements

Regional arrangements   Yes.

Barter agreements and open accounts   Yes.

Administration of control   The CBN formulates basic foreign exchange policy and issues directives as appropriate for the operation of the interbank market. The CBN approves and revokes the appointments of authorized dealers or authorized buyers of foreign currency, and supervises and monitors the operation of the interbank market.

International security restrictions	No.
Payment arrears	External debt-service payments have been limited to approximately 30% of official foreign exchange receipts net of foreign exchange outlays for petroleum investment and operations, resulting in payments being substantially smaller than maturing obligations.
Official	Most of the arrears are to Paris Club bilateral creditors, but there are also small amounts of arrears to multilateral and non-Paris Club bilateral creditors.
Controls on trade in gold (coins and/or bullion)	
Controls on domestic ownership and/or trade	Residents other than the monetary authorities, producers of gold, and authorized industrial users are not allowed, without special permission, to hold or acquire gold in any form other than jewelry or coins, at home or abroad.
Controls on external trade	The importation and exportation of gold in any form other than jewelry require specific licenses issued by the Federal Ministry of Finance (FMF).
Controls on exports and imports of banknotes	
On exports	
Domestic currency	Exportation is prohibited, except for up to ₦1,000 by residents for settlement of local expenses immediately upon return.
Foreign currency	The exportation of amounts in excess of $5,000 or its equivalent must be declared.
On imports	
Domestic currency	The importation is prohibited, except for up to ₦1,000 by residents for settlement expenses immediately upon return.
Foreign currency	The importation of amounts in excess of $5,000 or its equivalent must be declared.

Resident Accounts

Foreign exchange accounts permitted	Yes.
Held domestically	Any person may open, maintain, and operate a domiciliary account designated in foreign currency with an authorized dealer.
Held abroad	No.
Accounts in domestic currency convertible into foreign currency	Yes.

Nonresident Accounts

Foreign exchange accounts permitted	External accounts are maintained for diplomatic representatives of all countries and international organizations. They may be credited with authorized payments by residents of Nigeria to residents of foreign countries, with payments from other external accounts, and with proceeds from sales of foreign currencies. They may be debited for payments to residents of Nigeria, for payments to other external accounts, and for purchases of foreign currencies.
Domestic currency accounts	Funds derived from local sources may be deposited in nonresident accounts.
Convertible into foreign currency	Yes.
Approval required	Nonresident accounts may be credited with proceeds from services rendered locally, and remittance may be effected subject to adequate documentation.
Blocked accounts	No.

Imports and Import Payments

Foreign exchange budget   No.

Financing requirements for imports   No.

Documentation requirements for release of foreign exchange for imports   Unless a "clean report of findings" on the goods to be imported has been issued, foreign exchange settlements for imports may not be effected. Transactions involving the use of bills for collection and open accounts are allowed. However, the transactions executed on private sector initiative do not carry any government guarantee or obligation. The remittances are to be made through the AFEM, or with autonomous funds, while the relevant shipping documents for the transactions are to be channeled through authorized dealers.

Preshipment inspection   All containerized imports, irrespective of their value, are subject to preshipment inspection. The government is responsible for the payment of a service charge for the Comprehensive Import Supervision Scheme.

Letters of credit   Import payments covered by confirmed LCs are made, on presentation of the specified documents to the overseas correspondents, on the understanding that the goods paid for will arrive in Nigeria and that all shipping documents are lodged by importers with the authorized dealers within 21 days of negotiation of the specified documents.

Import licenses and other nontariff measures

Negative list   The importation of mosquito repellant coils, maize, sorghum, millet, wheat flour, barites and bentonites, retreaded or used tires, gypsum, kaolin, and gaming machines is prohibited. Effective January 1, 1999, the import prohibitions on vegetable oils and plastic housewares were removed.

Import taxes and/or tariffs   Import duties range from zero to 100%, with most goods subject to rates between 10% and 40%. The unweighted average duty is about 25%. In addition, five import surcharges apply: a 7% port development surcharge; a 5% levy on imported sugar; a 2% surcharge on automobiles; a 1% Raw Materials and Development Council surcharge; and a 0.02% freight rate stabilization surcharge earmarked for the Nigerian Shippers Council. Certain categories of imports are exempt from import taxes. Effective January 1, 1999, the import duty rebate of 25% was eliminated.

State import monopoly   No.

Exports and Export Proceeds

Repatriation requirements   Export proceeds must be repatriated within 90 days from the date of shipment of the goods.

Surrender requirements   Non-oil exporters are permitted to sell their export proceeds to authorized dealer banks at interbank rates, or use the funds to finance eligible transactions.

Financing requirements   n.a.

Documentation requirements

Letters of credit   Payment for exports should be made with LCs or any other international mode of payment.

Domiciliation   Repatriated non-oil export proceeds and other inflows should be held in domiciliary accounts maintained with authorized dealers in Nigeria. Holders of the domiciliary accounts have easy access to their funds maintained therein, subject to the existing guidelines, and may sell their export proceeds to banks other than those where they maintain their domiciliary accounts.

Preshipment inspection   All exports, both oil and non-oil, from Nigeria are subject to preshipment inspection by government-appointed inspection agents. All exporters are responsible for the payment of a service charge for the Nigerian Export Supervision Scheme at rates determined and advised by the FMF.

Export licenses   Production of unrefined gold and petroleum products is subject to licensing. The exportation of African antiques, works of art, and objects used in African ceremonies is prohibited, except under certain conditions. Exports of timber (rough and sawn), raw hides and skins, scrap metal, and unprocessed rubber latex and rubber lumps are prohibited. Exports of petroleum are handled by the Nigerian National Petroleum Corporation and are subject to special arrangements. Effective January 1, 1999, the export prohibition on beans, rice, and yams was eliminated.

Export taxes   No.

Payments for Invisible Transactions and Current Transfers

Controls on these transfers   Applications for foreign exchange must be submitted to banks; verification is on an ex post basis, and such payments are allowed, subject to documentation requirements.

Trade-related payments

  Quantitative limits   The limit for commissions is 2% on bills for collection.

  Indicative limits/bona fide test   Yes.

Investment-related payments   Transfers of profits are permitted freely when the basic transaction has been approved.

  Prior approval   Applications for the remittance of profits and dividends from capital investment are made through authorized dealers and do not require prior approval but are subject to documentation requirements. Until October 22, 1999, when this limitation was abolished, interest income, profits/dividends, patent license fees, and other invisibles connected with approved projects under the Debt Conversion Program (DCP), subject to documentation requirements, could not have been repatriated for a minimum period of five years from the date of release of redemption proceeds for actual investment or five years after such profits and dividends were made or paid, whichever was later.

  Indicative limits/bona fide test   Interest on bills for collection transactions is subject to a maximum of 2% above the prime rate prevailing in the country of the beneficiary.

Foreign workers' wages

  Quantitative limits   Up to 100% of net salary after tax may be transferred abroad, subject to a documentation requirement.

  Indicative limits/bona fide test   Evidence of income earned must be provided.

Other payments   Up to 5% of consulting and legal fees for projects of a high technological content, for which local expertise is not available, may be remitted.

  Quantitative limits   Yes.

Proceeds from Invisible Transactions and Current Transfers

Repatriation requirements   All proceeds must be received through banks.

Surrender requirements   All proceeds from oil companies are bought by the CBN.

Restrictions on use of funds   Yes.

Capital Transactions

Controls on capital and money market instruments   Applications for private capital transfers abroad are processed by banks, subject to satisfactory documentation. No prior approval is required, except in the case of the DCP.

On capital market securities

  Shares or other securities of a participating nature

    Sale or issue locally by nonresidents   These transactions may be conducted through authorized dealers.

Purchase abroad by residents	Residents of Nigeria may deal in foreign currency securities and may buy from, or sell to, nonresidents of Nigeria any security payable in naira without any prior approval.
Bonds or other debt securities	The DCP regulates the purchase of selected Nigerian foreign debt instruments (mainly CBN promissory notes arising from past consolidation of unsecured trade credit arrears) at a discount and the disposition of the naira proceeds on the conversion of such debt.

On money market instruments

Purchase abroad by residents	While documented investments are permitted, the transfer to external accounts is not.

Controls on derivatives and other instruments — No.

Controls on credit operations

Commercial credits

By residents to nonresidents	Permission of the FMF is not required for nonresident individuals or companies (other than banks) registered in Nigeria that are controlled directly or indirectly from outside Nigeria. However, to enable companies to meet temporary shortages of funds, licensed banks in Nigeria may grant loans or overdrafts for periods of up to 14 days, or may increase the amount of any advance or overdraft by the amount of loan interest or bank charges payable thereon. General permission is also given for any loan, bank overdraft, or other credit facility to be arranged to finance Nigerian imports or exports of goods.
To residents from nonresidents	Approval is not required from the FMF for any individual, firm, company, or branch resident in Nigeria to borrow abroad. However, official agencies and state-controlled corporations need the prior approval of the FMF for any foreign borrowing. The contracting of suppliers' credits abroad by state-controlled corporations or agencies is also subject to approval from the FMF.

Controls on direct investment

Inward direct investment	There are no ceilings for foreign capital participation in the equity capital of enterprises in various sectors of the economy. The Nigerian Investment Promotion Commission deals with all matters relating to registration and the prescription of applicable incentives for direct capital investment in priority areas.
Controls on liquidation of direct investment	Approval of the FMF is not needed. Capital proceeds arising from the subsequent disposal of investments made under the DCP may only be repatriated 10 years after the effective investment of the proceeds, and is limited to 20% a year.

Controls on real estate transactions — No.

Controls on personal capital movements

Gifts, endowments, inheritances, and legacies

By residents to nonresidents	These transactions should not exceed $500 at a time.
Transfer of gambling and prize earnings	Gambling is prohibited.

Provisions specific to commercial banks and other credit institutions

Purchase of locally issued securities denominated in foreign exchange	Yes.

Differential treatment of deposit accounts in foreign exchange

Reserve requirements	Yes.
Liquid asset requirements	Yes.

Open foreign exchange position limits

On nonresident assets and liabilities	Yes.

Provisions specific to institutional investors   No.

Other controls imposed by securities laws   No.

Changes During 1999

Exchange arrangement   *January 1.* The official exchange rate was abolished, and the dual market was unified.

June 23. All foreign exchange bids at the AFEM were subject to a 200% treasury bill–backing requirement. This requirement was reduced to 100% on September 1, 1999, to 50% on September 20, 1999, and was eliminated on October 28, 1999.

October 25. The interbank market was expanded.

October 28. The AFEM was abolished.

Imports and import payments   *January 1.* The import prohibitions on vegetable oils and plastic housewares were removed. The import duty rebate of 25% was eliminated.

Exports and export proceeds   *January 1.* The export prohibition on beans, yams, and rice was eliminated.

Payments for invisible transactions and current transfers   *October 22.* Limitations on profit remittances in respect of investments made while under the debt-equity conversion scheme were abolished.

NORWAY

(Position as of December 31, 1999)

Status Under IMF Articles of Agreement

Article VIII   Date of acceptance: May 11, 1967.

Exchange Arrangement

Currency	The currency of Norway is the Norwegian krone.
Exchange rate structure	Unitary.
Classification	
Managed floating with no pre-announced path for the exchange rate	The monetary policy objective of the Bank of Norway (BN) is to maintain the stability of the Norwegian krone against other European currencies. No fluctuation margins are established.
Exchange tax	No.
Exchange subsidy	No.
Forward exchange market	Yes.

Arrangements for Payments and Receipts

Prescription of currency requirements	No.
Payment arrangements	No.
Administration of control	The BN, in cooperation with the MOF, exercises control.
International security restrictions	
In accordance with UN sanctions	Restrictions are imposed on financial transactions with Iraq. There are blocked accounts and restrictions on financial transactions with respect to the Federal Republic of Yugoslavia (Serbia/Montenegro). Restrictions on financial transactions with Libya have been suspended.
Payment arrears	No.
Controls on trade in gold (coins and/or bullion)	No.
Controls on exports and imports of banknotes	A resident or nonresident who on entry into or departure from Norway is carrying Norwegian and/or foreign banknotes and coins equivalent to an amount in excess of NKr 25,000 a person a journey is obliged to notify the Customs Administration on the prescribed form.
	A resident or nonresident staying in Norway who receives a dispatch by post, courier, or other form of transport containing Norwegian and/or foreign banknotes and coins from abroad, or who sends such a dispatch abroad, equivalent to an amount in excess of NKr 25,000, is obliged to notify the BN in writing.

Resident Accounts

Foreign exchange accounts permitted	Yes.
Held domestically	Yes.
Held abroad	There is a notification and reporting requirement if transactions and/or average balances at the end of the previous 12 months exceed NKr 100 million.

Accounts in domestic currency convertible into foreign currency	Yes.

Nonresident Accounts

Foreign exchange accounts permitted	Yes.
Domestic currency accounts	Yes.
Convertible into foreign currency	Yes.
Blocked accounts	It is prohibited to alter, transfer, or remove from Norway any deposit made in the country by Yugoslav authorities (blocked in accordance with UN resolutions).

Imports and Import Payments

Foreign exchange budget	No.
Financing requirements for imports	No.
Documentation requirements for release of foreign exchange for imports	No.
Import licenses and other nontariff measures	
Negative list	All imports from Iraq are prohibited. There are restrictions on trade with, and payments to and from, the Federal Republic of Yugoslavia (Serbia/Montenegro), while the restrictions on trade with Libya have been suspended. Knotted netting, madeup fishing nets, and other nets are subject to licensing.
Open general licenses	Yes.
Licenses with quotas	These licenses are required for textiles.
Other nontariff measures	There are certain measures imposed for sanitary reasons.
Import taxes and/or tariffs	No.
State import monopoly	No.

Exports and Export Proceeds

Repatriation requirements	No.
Financing requirements	No.
Documentation requirements	No.
Export licenses	
Without quotas	Exports subject to regulation are listed and require licenses.
Export taxes	
Other export taxes	Yes.

Payments for Invisible Transactions and Current Transfers

Controls on these transfers	No.

Proceeds from Invisible Transactions and Current Transfers

Repatriation requirements	No.
Restrictions on use of funds	No.

Capital Transactions

Controls on capital and money market instruments

On capital market securities

Shares or other securities of a participating nature

Purchase locally by nonresidents — The control applies only to the purchase of shares and other securities of a participating nature that may be affected by laws on inward direct investment and establishment.

Controls on derivatives and other instruments — No.

Controls on credit operations — No.

Controls on direct investment

Inward direct investment — The control applies only to the purchase of shares and other securities of a participating nature that may be affected by laws on inward investment and establishment.

Controls on liquidation of direct investment — No.

Controls on real estate transactions — No.

Controls on personal capital movements — No.

Provisions specific to commercial banks and other credit institutions

Open foreign exchange position limits — Credit institutions and investment firms are subject to exposure regulations. Net positions of up to 15% of the institutions' equity and subordinated loan capital may be taken out in individual currencies, and the aggregate position must be kept within 30% of the financial institutions' equity and subordinated loan capital.

Provisions specific to institutional investors

Limits (max.) on securities issued by nonresidents and on portfolio invested abroad — Insurance companies and pension funds are subject to controls regarding classes of investments held against technical provisions to ensure a sufficiently diversified portfolio, e.g., there is a combined cap of 35% on domestic and foreign shares.

Currency-matching regulations on assets/liabilities composition — There are no currency-matching regulations on assets/liabilities composition for investment funds. However, such regulations exist for insurance and pension funds for which net financial assets in a currency have to be equivalent to at least 80% of technical provisions in the same currency at any time. An insurance company cannot have negative financial assets in a currency.

Other controls imposed by securities laws — Other restrictions are included in the Act on Securities Funds and Rules for Asset Management.

Changes During 1999

No significant changes occurred in the exchange and trade system.

OMAN

(Position as of January 31, 2000)

Status Under IMF Articles of Agreement

Article VIII	Date of acceptance: June 19, 1974.

Exchange Arrangement

Currency	The currency of Oman is the rial Omani.
Exchange rate structure	Unitary.
Classification	
Conventional pegged arrangement	The exchange rate of the rial Omani is pegged to the dollar at RO 1 per $2.6008. The commercial banks' rates for other currencies are based on market rates in London.
Exchange tax	No.
Exchange subsidy	No.
Forward exchange market	Yes.
Official cover of forward operations	Yes.

Arrangements for Payments and Receipts

Prescription of currency requirements	All settlements with Israel and the use of its currency are prohibited.
Payment arrangements	No.
Administration of control	The Central Bank of Oman (CBO) has exclusive exchange control authority; there is no exchange control legislation.
International security restrictions	Restrictions are imposed with respect to Israel.
Payment arrears	No.
Controls on trade in gold (coins and/or bullion)	
Controls on external trade	Gold transactions with Israel are prohibited.
Controls on exports and imports of banknotes	No.

Resident Accounts

Foreign exchange accounts permitted	No distinction is made between accounts held by residents and those held by nonresidents.
Held domestically	Yes.
Held abroad	Yes.
Accounts in domestic currency convertible into foreign currency	Yes.

Nonresident Accounts

Foreign exchange accounts permitted	Yes.

Domestic currency accounts	Yes.
Convertible into foreign currency	Yes.
Blocked accounts	No.

Imports and Import Payments

Foreign exchange budget	No.
Financing requirements for imports	No.
Documentation requirements for release of foreign exchange for imports	No.
Import licenses and other nontariff measures	Licenses are required for imports. All imports from Israel are prohibited.
Negative list	Companies operating in Oman and trading in manufactured oil products are prohibited from importing specified products as long as domestic production is deemed adequate to satisfy local demand.
Import taxes and/or tariffs	Customs duties range from 5% for most goods to 100% for imports of alcoholic beverages. Customs duties are not levied on government imports. In January 1999, the custom duty rate for imports of luxury goods was raised to 15% from 5%; this measure was reversed on January 1, 2000.
Taxes collected through the exchange system	Yes.
State import monopoly	No.

Exports and Export Proceeds

Repatriation requirements	No.
Financing requirements	No.
Documentation requirements	No.
Export licenses	All exports to Israel are prohibited.
Export taxes	No.

Payments for Invisible Transactions and Current Transfers

Controls on these transfers	Payments for invisibles are generally not restricted, except for payments to Israel.
Investment-related payments	
Prior approval	Remittances of profit and dividends by commercial banks require prior approval from the CBO.

Proceeds from Invisible Transactions and Current Transfers

Repatriation requirements	No.
Restrictions on use of funds	No.

Capital Transactions

Controls on capital and money market instruments

On capital market securities

Shares or other securities of a participating nature

    Purchase locally by nonresidents | Foreign share ownership in Omani companies is limited to 49%, but it could be raised to 100%.

Controls on derivatives and other instruments | No.

Controls on credit operations

Commercial credits | The Oman Development Bank may provide medium- and long-term loans at preferential interest rates for project financing in the petroleum, agricultural, fishery, and mineral sectors; it may also give assistance in preinvestment research. In addition, the government provides loans at subsidized interest rates for those projects with a majority Omani shareholding that are used for industrial production for exportation, industrial production using indigenous raw materials or labor, or the development of tourism.

Controls on direct investment

Inward direct investment | Investment in business firms in Oman by nonresidents requires prior approval.

Controls on liquidation of direct investment | No.

Controls on real estate transactions

Purchase locally by nonresidents | Yes.

Sale locally by nonresidents | Yes.

Controls on personal capital movements | No.

Provisions specific to commercial banks and other credit institutions

Borrowing abroad | Effective January 9, 1999, overall foreign borrowing by individual commercial banks is restricted to 300% of their net worth. Subceilings of 200% and 100% are applicable for foreign loans with maturity periods of up to five years and up to two years, respectively.

Lending to nonresidents (financial or commercial credits) | Lending to nonresidents is limited to 10% of the loan portfolio of banks.

Open foreign exchange position limits | The limit is 40% of banks' capital and reserves.

Provisions specific to institutional investors | n.a.

Other controls imposed by securities laws | n.a.

Changes During 1999

Imports and import payments | *January 31.* The customs duty rate for imports of luxury goods was raised to 15% from 5%.

Capital transactions

Provisions specific to commercial banks and other credit institutions | *January 9.* The overall foreign borrowing by individual commercial banks was restricted.

Changes During 2000

Imports and import payments   *January 1*. The increase of the customs duty rates on luxury goods was reversed.

PAKISTAN

(Position as of April 30, 2000)

Status Under IMF Articles of Agreement

Article VIII   Date of acceptance: July 1, 1994.

Exchange Arrangement

Currency   The currency of Pakistan is the Pakistan rupee.

Exchange rate structure

Unitary   A multiple exchange rate system comprising an official, a floating interbank (FIBR), and a composite exchange rate, based on a prespecified ratio of the official exchange rate and the FIBR, which was initially prescribed at the ratio of 50:50, respectively, and subsequently amended to a ratio of 20:80 and then to 5:95, was in effect through May 18, 1999.

Effective May 19, 1999, the official exchange rate of PRs 46 per $1 was abolished and the exchange rate system was unified at the composite rate level, and all current international transactions are now conducted at the interbank exchange rate.

Classification

Conventional pegged arrangement   Prior to the unification of the multiple exchange rate system on May 19, 1999, the State Bank of Pakistan (SBP) was setting the exchange rate of the rupee while commercial banks were allowed to quote their own exchange rates for the dollar within the SBP buying and selling bands.

Since June 1999, the exchange rate of the rupee has been de facto pegged to the dollar. Thus, Pakistan's exchange rate arrangement has been reclassified to the category conventional pegged arrangement from the category managed floating with no preannounced path for the exchange rate.

Exchange tax   No.

Exchange subsidy   No.

Forward exchange market   There is a forward market. The maximum tenure of forward cover provided by banks for trade transactions is 12 months, and these facilities are also provided for funds transferred from abroad for portfolio investment.

Official cover of forward operations   Forward exchange cover for private foreign currency deposits, except for deposits brought under FE Circular 45 of 1985, is provided by the SBP, which, from August 9, 1999, charges an annual fee of 8% (increased to 10% on March 4, 1999) on onshore foreign currency deposits to bring them in line with the rates in the interbank forward foreign exchange market. Effective May 19, 1999, the SBP no longer provides forward cover to authorized dealers (ADs).

Arrangements for Payments and Receipts

Prescription of currency requirements   No.

Payment arrangements

Regional arrangements   Pakistan is a member of the ACU.

Clearing agreements   Payments to, and receipts from, member countries of the ACU with respect to current transactions are effected in AMUs, which equal $1.

Administration of control   The SBP has delegated authority to a number of banks and financial institutions to deal in all foreign currencies, and to sell foreign exchange within limits prescribed by the SBP.

672

International security restrictions	No.
Payment arrears	No.
Controls on trade in gold (coins and/or bullion)	
Controls on domestic ownership and/or trade	There is no control on local trade in gold bullion.
Controls on external trade	The exportation of gold is prohibited unless authorized by the SBP; such permission is not usually granted. Imports are allowed through dealers authorized by the government.
Controls on exports and imports of banknotes	
On exports	
Domestic currency	An individual may take out up to PRs 500 to India and PRs 3,000 to other countries.
Foreign currency	No one may take out of Pakistan foreign currency in excess of $10,000 or equivalent without permission.
On imports	
Domestic currency	An individual may bring in up to PRs 500 from India and PRs 3,000 from other countries.

Resident Accounts

Foreign exchange accounts permitted	ADs and nonbank financial institutions are allowed to offer a new foreign currency accounts (FCAs) scheme.
	Holders of frozen (old) FCAs are permitted to purchase special dollar bonds of the government of Pakistan against outstanding balances in their FCAs or to convert the foreign currency into Pakistan rupees.
Held domestically	These accounts may be credited with remittances from abroad, traveler's checks, and foreign currency notes. However, receipts from exports of goods and services, earnings from services of residents, earnings and profits of overseas offices or branches of Pakistan firms or companies and banks, and foreign exchange released from Pakistan for any specified purpose may not be credited to these accounts. Amounts of incremental deposits made on or after July 1, 1998, in these accounts are freely transferable abroad, and there are no limits on amounts of withdrawal. These accounts may be permanently retained, and an upper ceiling on the rate of interest on term deposits (of three months and up to five years) is fixed by the SBP with the approval of the government. The rates are based on the Eurodollar deposit bid rate of Barclays Bank, London. The margins over the Eurodollar deposit bid rates range from 0.75% for three-month deposits to 2% for five-year deposits. Under the new FCAs scheme, institutions are free to keep/invest their deposits abroad or in Pakistan. However, deposits mobilized with effect from June 3, 1999, may be employed only in Pakistan. Lending such funds to borrowers in Pakistan, ADs would be required to observe prudential regulations of the SBP. However, ADs are free to decide the rate of return that they offer to depositors.
Held abroad	Balances of up to $1,000 may be held abroad by residents in any country (except Afghanistan, Bangladesh, India, and Israel) in FCAs, which may not be operated without the approval of the SBP.
Accounts in domestic currency convertible into foreign currency	Yes.

Nonresident Accounts

Foreign exchange accounts permitted	Pakistan nationals residing abroad; foreign nationals, whether residing abroad or in Pakistan; and firms, companies, and charitable bodies owned by persons who are otherwise eligible may open FCAs with banks in Pakistan without the prior approval of the exchange

control authorities. The accounts may be denominated in deutsche mark, dollars, euros, pounds sterling, and yen; credit balances may be transferred abroad, and interest on such accounts is exempt from income tax. Deposit holders wishing to make payments in Pakistan must first convert the foreign exchange drawn from their accounts into Pakistan rupees. If Pakistan nationals holding such accounts return to Pakistan, they may retain the accounts permanently. Authorized dealers under the FCA facility may accept term deposits in foreign currency from their overseas branches and foreign banks operating abroad, including financial institutions owned by them; such term deposits must be at least $0.5 million (or the equivalent in other currencies) for a maturity period of at least six months. The rates of interest paid on these deposits may not exceed 1% above LIBOR. Effective May 26, 1999, the sale of foreign currencies to nonresident bank branches and correspondents against credit balance(s) available in their nonresident rupee account requires prior approval of the State Bank.

On July 5, 1999, the facility to open FCAs was withdrawn from diplomatic missions and the staff of international organizations and they were not allowed to sell or purchase foreign exchange on the interbank market. On April 3, 2000, these restrictions were eliminated.

Holders of frozen (old) FCAs are permitted to purchase dollar bonds of the government of Pakistan against outstanding balances in their FCAs. Funds mobilized under the new FCA scheme are not required to be surrendered to SBP nor would the SBP provide a forward cover in respect of such accounts. ADs are free to decide the rate of return that they offer to depositors.

Domestic currency accounts	The accounts of individuals, firms, or companies residing outside Pakistan are designated nonresident accounts. (Different rules apply to the nonresident rupee accounts of individuals, firms, or companies, on the one hand, and to the nonresident rupee accounts of banks, on the other hand.) Authorized banks are permitted to open nonresident accounts for non-bank nonresidents without prior SBP approval when the accounts are opened with funds received from abroad through banking channels or with rupee funds accepted for remittance abroad. Debits and credits to nonresident accounts for specified purposes may be made by authorized banks without prior approval.
Convertible into foreign currency	Domestic currency accounts are convertible into foreign currency when opened as convertible rupee accounts with funds received from abroad.
Blocked accounts	Accounts of residents of India, other than the accounts of the Indian Embassy and its personnel, are blocked.

Imports and Import Payments

Foreign exchange budget	Yes.
Financing requirements for imports	
Advance payment requirements	Advance payments of up to 33.33% are allowed by the SBP where goods are of specialized or capital nature. The cash margin requirement was eliminated on February 24, 1999, and was reintroduced on October 15, 1999.
Advance import deposits	There is a 35% nonremunerated import deposit requirement for import transactions other than those for industrial new materials, machinery and spare parts, petroleum, edible oil, wheat, and eight other products.
Documentation requirements for release of foreign exchange for imports	Clean-on-board shipped bills of lading and other documentation as per contract or LCs are required. Imports valued at and above $10,000 are required to be subsequently documented with surrender of a Customs Bill of Entry.
Domiciliation requirements	Yes.
Letters of credit	Yes.
Import licenses and other nontariff measures	Import licenses are not required. Imports from Israel are prohibited. Imports of 45 items on the health and safety list are restricted. Imports of 21 items on the procedural list require certain technical expertise (e.g., petroleum) or certain conditions (e.g., unassembled cars).

Negative list	Many of the products on the negative list consist of products banned for religious and health reasons, or to discourage consumption of luxury items, or goods banned under international agreements. The list includes several textile items.
Import taxes and/or tariffs	The maximum customs tariff, except for motor vehicles, liquor, and tobacco, has been reduced to 35% from 45% as of March 31, 1999.
State import monopoly	Imports of wheat are permitted for the public sector only.

Exports and Export Proceeds

Repatriation requirements	Proceeds must be repatriated by the due dates of bills of exchange or within four months of shipment. Effective May 25, 1999, export proceeds may be held in "Special Exporter's Account" for up to three working days only for the purpose of sale to an authorized dealer.
Surrender requirements	Until March 11, 1999, 5% of export proceeds were required to be surrendered to the SBP at the official exchange rate. Effective May 19, 1999, the surrender requirement was eliminated. Exporters are permitted to sell their entire proceeds in the intrabank market within seven days. On May 25, 1999, this was reduced to three days.
Financing requirements	No.
Documentation requirements	The documents required are a firm order, the exporter's registration with the Export Promotion Bureau, and Form "E."
Domiciliation	Yes.
Preshipment inspection	Preshipment inspection is required in only a few cases.
Export licenses	Exporters are required to be registered with the Export Promotion Bureau (EPB). Exports to Israel are not allowed.
With quotas	Export licenses have ceased to be required for maize, cement, gram, split gram, and camels, but export contracts must be registered with the EPB for monitoring purposes.
Export taxes	There are no export duties; however, a nominal fee (export development surcharge) of 0.25% is charged on all exports, except for a few specified items. Regulatory duties are levied on exports of crushed and steamed bones at rates of 10% and 5%, respectively, and on exports of wet blue tanned hides and skins (except for those imported and reexported), at a rate of 20%.
Other export taxes	The standard rate of income tax on export/import proceeds is 1%. It is reduced to 0.75% on exports of goods manufactured in Pakistan, and to 0.5% on exports of jewelry, ceramics, surgical equipment, and sporting goods.

Payments for Invisible Transactions and Current Transfers

Controls on these transfers	
Trade-related payments	There is no restriction on the payment of freight against invoices.
Prior approval	Yes.
Quantitative limits	Commission, brokerage fees, and other charges are generally limited to 5% of invoice values. The rate is 1% for cement and more for a few other goods.
Indicative limits/bona fide test	There are indicative limits/bona fide tests for the payment of commissions.
Investment-related payments	The remittance of dividends declared on current profits is allowed freely to foreign shareholders if the investment was made on a repatriable basis. The remittance of profits by branches of foreign companies other than banks and those engaged in insurance, shipping, and the airline business, and of dividends to foreign portfolio investors credited to their convertible rupee accounts is permitted without restriction provided that the required documents are submitted to the SBP. The same regulation applies to head office expenses charged to a branch's profit-and-loss account and accepted for tax purposes by the Pakistan

income tax authorities. Effective January 18, 2000, ADs are authorized to execute these remittances without prior SBP approval.

Prior approval	Prior approval is required for the transfer of profits.
Quantitative limits	Interest payments are allowed up to 1.5% over LIBOR. However, there is no limit on interest with respect to project loans. The payment of interest is permitted under imports only on usance basis.
Indicative limits/bona fide test	There are no indicative limits or bona fide tests for the payment of profits and dividends.

Payments for travel

Quantitative limits	The allowance for private travel to countries other than the Islamic State of Afghanistan, Bangladesh, and India is $50 a day for up to 42 days during a calendar year on submission of travel documents to the authorized dealers. Requests for foreign exchange in excess of these amounts are to be referred by the authorized dealers to the SBP, giving justification for the additional amount. Unspent foreign exchange, however, must be surrendered to an authorized dealer. The entitlement may be used in installments. There are also specific allowances for pilgrims' travel to Saudi Arabia. Exporters of goods with annual export earnings of more than PRs 2.5 million and exporters of services with annual earnings of more than PRs 0.25 million are granted a renewable business travel allowance of $200 a day, up to $6,000 a business trip. In addition, business travelers may settle credit card charges of up to $100 a day, subject to a maximum of $3,000 for a 30-day visit, with foreign exchange procured from the kerb market.

Effective March 31, 1999, foreign exchange for travel purposes may be bought freely from ADs. |
| *Indicative limits/bona fide test* | Yes. |

Personal payments

	Foreign exchange allowances for students' tuition fees and expenses as required by institutions may be obtained from ADs without approval from the SBP.
Prior approval	For medical costs, approval is required on a case-by-case basis.
Quantitative limits	Allowances for professional training abroad are granted at $1,200 a month. For family maintenance and alimony payments, allowances are determined on a case-by-case basis.

Credit card use abroad

Quantitative limits	In the case of business travelers, they may settle credit card charges of up to $100 a day, subject to a maximum of $3,000 for a 30-day visit. There are no limits if the amount is charged to a foreign currency account of the cardholder, opened under the new FCA scheme.
Indicative limits/bona fide test	Yes.

Other payments

	There is no limit for individuals with regard to subscriptions and membership fees. For professional and specialized organizations, the limit is PRs 20,000 a calendar year.
Prior approval	Prior approval is required for the payment of consulting and legal fees.
Quantitative limits	Yes.

Proceeds from Invisible Transactions and Current Transfers

Repatriation requirements	Yes.
Surrender requirements	Through May 18, 1999, proceeds had to be surrendered to the SBP within three months, and travel agents and tour agents were permitted to retain up to 5% of their foreign exchange earnings for marketing and related export promotion expenses. Effective May 19, 1999, the surrender requirement for foreign exchange earnings was eliminated, but the proceeds must be sold to an AD.
Restrictions on use of funds	Yes.

Capital Transactions

Controls on capital and money market instruments

On capital market securities

Shares or other securities of a participating nature

Sale or issue locally by nonresidents	There are no controls on the sale of securities purchased in Pakistan. Nonresidents, however, are not permitted to issue securities in Pakistan.
Purchase abroad by residents	Prior SBP approval is required.
Sale or issue abroad by residents	Residents may sell or issue securities after obtaining approval from the Securities and Exchange Commission of Pakistan (SECP). The proceeds associated with these issues are required to be transferred to Pakistan or used for purchase of plants and machinery abroad. Transfer of funds required to service these security issues is permitted.

Bonds or other debt securities

Purchase locally by nonresidents	Nonresidents are allowed to trade freely in the registered corporate debt instruments and bonds listed on the stock exchange and in federal investment bonds (FIBs) and in treasury bills (TBs). Foreign bank branches in Pakistan and foreign-controlled investment banks are permitted to make investments in registered listed corporate debt instruments in the primary and secondary markets.
Sale or issue locally by nonresidents	The same regulations apply as for shares or other securities of a participating nature.
Purchase abroad by residents	These transactions are not permitted.
Sale or issue abroad by residents	Specific permission is required, which is granted if the proceeds of the bonds are to be used for the import of plants and machinery.

On money market instruments

Purchase locally by nonresidents	There are no controls on the purchase of TBs and certificates of investment (COIs) by nonresidents.
Sale or issue locally by nonresidents	There are no controls on the sale of TBs and COIs purchased in Pakistan. Nonresidents are, however, not permitted to issue such investments in Pakistan.
Purchase abroad by residents	These transactions are not permitted.
Sale or issue abroad by residents	Residents may sell or issue money market instruments after obtaining approval from the SECP. The proceeds associated with these issues are required to be transferred to Pakistan or used for purchase of plants and machinery abroad. The transfer of funds required to service these security issues is permitted.

On collective investment securities

Purchase locally by nonresidents	Nonresidents are permitted to purchase units of the National Investment Trust, the State Enterprise Mutual Fund of the Investment Corporation of Pakistan, and other mutual funds listed on the Pakistan stock exchanges.
Sale or issue locally by nonresidents	The same regulations apply as for shares and other securities of a participating nature.
Purchase abroad by residents	These transactions are not permitted.
Sale or issue abroad by residents	Residents may sell or issue securities after obtaining approval from the SECP. The proceeds associated with these issues are required to be transferred to Pakistan or used for purchase of plants and machinery abroad. The transfer of funds required to service these security issues is permitted.

Controls on derivatives and other instruments

Purchase locally by nonresidents	Only rights shares exist. There are no other derivatives.
Sale or issue locally by nonresidents	These transactions are not permitted, except for rights issues.

Purchase abroad by residents	These transactions are not permitted.
Sale or issue abroad by residents	These transactions are not permitted.
Controls on credit operations	Credits of up to four months with respect to exported goods, and up to 12½ years with respect to the export of plants and machinery, are permitted.
Commercial credits	
By residents to nonresidents	Credits of up to four months with respect to exported goods, and up to 12½ years with respect to the export of plants and machinery, are permitted.
To residents from nonresidents	Residents have been granted general permission with certain conditions.
Financial credits	
By residents to nonresidents	These credits are not allowed.
To residents from nonresidents	There are no controls on these payments; however, parent companies of the multinationals are also permitted to provide loans for financing the foreign currency cost of the projects, as well as working capital requirements.
Guarantees, sureties, and financial backup facilities	
By residents to nonresidents	There are no controls if the transaction is business related.
To residents from nonresidents	This is subject to compliance with other credit restrictions.
Controls on direct investment	
Outward direct investment	Direct investment abroad requires prior approval under foreign exchange laws. Resident Pakistan nationals require prior approval from the SBP to sell movable or immovable assets held abroad, and liquidation proceeds must be repatriated to Pakistan through normal banking channels.
Inward direct investment	No prior approval is required for investment in the manufacturing sector. Investment in new industrial units for the manufacture of alcohol (except industrial alcohol) is banned. Investment in the specified industries of arms and ammunitions, security printing, currency and minting, high explosives, and radioactive substances requires prior approval. Foreigners are permitted to make investments in services, infrastructure, social, and agriculture sectors subject to the condition that the foreign equity investment must be at least $0.5 million. Foreign investors may hold 100% foreign equity in social and infrastructure sectors. In the case of the services sector, they may hold 100% foreign equity for two years, subject to the following conditions: (1) remittance of profit and dividends will be restricted to 60% of total equity during the two-year period; and (2) a minimum of 40% of the equity is transferred to Pakistan investors within two years' time, including disinvestment through the stock exchange. In the case of the agricultural sector, 40% of the equity must be held by a Pakistan company or investor.
Controls on liquidation of direct investment	No.
Controls on real estate transactions	
Purchase abroad by residents	Residents are not permitted to purchase real estate abroad.
Purchase locally by nonresidents	Purchases for business purposes are not restricted.
Controls on personal capital movements	
Loans	
By residents to nonresidents	Yes.
Gifts, endowments, inheritances, and legacies	
By residents to nonresidents	Up to PRs 500 is permitted.

Transfer of assets

   Transfer abroad by emigrants   Yes.

   Transfer into the country by   There are no quantitative restrictions on transfers through the secondary market.
   immigrants

Transfer of gambling and prize earnings   Remittance is not allowed.

Provisions specific to commercial   Foreign-controlled investment banks are permitted to resort to local borrowing for their
banks and other credit institutions   working capital requirements of up to 100% of their paid capital, reserves, etc., subject to
observance of all other nonbank financial institutions rules.

Borrowing abroad   Transactions are allowed for temporary periods, and only if they become necessary for the
normal course of business.

Maintenance of accounts abroad   Commercial banks and other credit institutions are allowed to maintain foreign accounts;
limits for balances are fixed by the SBP.

Purchase of locally issued securities   Foreign banks and foreign-controlled investment banks are permitted to purchase foreign
denominated in foreign exchange   currency bearer certificates issued locally.

Differential treatment of deposit   Effective June 3, 1999, every bank/nonbank financial institution accepting foreign currency
accounts in foreign exchange   deposits must use, invest, or place them only within Pakistan.

   Interest rate controls   This is linked to the respective London Interbank Bidding Rate (LIBID).

   Credit controls   Yes.

Differential treatment of deposit
accounts held by nonresidents

   Interest rate controls   This is linked to the respective LIBID.

Investment regulations

   Abroad by banks   Banks may not invest abroad except in the case of foreign currency deposits mobilized
up to June 2, 1999.

   In banks by nonresidents   Prior approval is required.

Open foreign exchange position limits   Open position balances in nostro accounts are regulated by the Foreign Exchange Department. There are limits on banks' nostro accounts. The existing system of net open positions
was replaced at end-May 1999 by an aggregate foreign exchange exposure limit for each
bank, equivalent to 10% of its paid-up capital with maximum and minimum limits of PRs
500 million and PRs 50 million (in foreign currency), respectively.

   On resident assets and liabilities   Yes.

   On nonresident assets and liabilities   Yes.

Provisions specific to institutional
investors

Limits (max.) on securities issued by   Nonresidents are not allowed to issue securities in Pakistan, and residents require specific
nonresidents and on portfolio invested   permission to make portfolio investments abroad.
abroad

Limits (max.) on portfolio invested   Yes.
abroad

Other controls imposed by securities   No.
laws

Changes During 1999

Exchange arrangement   *March 4.* The fee charged by the SBP for forward exchange cover was increased to 10%
from 8%.

March 18. The weight of the FIBR and the official exchange rate in the composite exchange rate was changed to 95% and 5%, respectively.

May 19. The multiple exchange system was unified. Also, the SBP no longer provides forward cover to ADs.

June 30. The exchange rate of the rupee has been de facto pegged to the dollar. Thus, the exchange rate arrangement has been reclassified to the category conventional fixed pegged arrangement from the category managed floating with no preannounced path for the exchange rate.

August 9. The fee charged by the SPB for forward exchange cover was reduced to 8% from 10%.

Nonresident accounts

May 26. The sale of foreign currencies to nonresident bank branches and correspondents against credit balance(s) available in their nonresident rupee account required prior approval of the State Bank.

July 5. The facility to open FCAs was withdrawn from diplomatic missions and the staff of international oganizations and they were not allowed to sell or purchase foreign exchange on the interbank market.

Imports and import payments

February 24. The cash margin requirement was eliminated.

March 31. The maximum import tariff was reduced to 35%.

October 15. Cash margin requirements of 10%–35% were reintroduced.

Exports and export proceeds

March 11. The surrender requirement was reduced to 5%.

May 19. The surrender requirement for exports and export proceeds was eliminated.

May 25. The number of days within which exporters must sell their proceeds to the interbank market was reduced to three from seven.

Payments for invisible transactions and current transfers

March 31. Foreign exchange for travel may be bought freely from the ADs.

Proceeds from invisible transactions and current transfers

May 19. The surrender requirement for invisible transactions was eliminated.

Capital transactions

Provisions specific to commercial banks and other credit institutions

June 3. Every bank/nonbank financial institution accepting foreign currency deposits must use, invest, or place them only within Pakistan.

Changes During 2000

Nonresident accounts

April 3. The restriction on opening FCAs and buying and selling foreign exchange on the interbank market by diplomatic missions and the staff of international organizations was eliminated.

Payments for invisible transactions and current transfers

January 18. ADs were authorized to execute investment-related payments without prior SBP approval.

PALAU

(Position as of December 31, 1999)

Status Under IMF Articles of Agreement

Article VIII   Date of acceptance: December 16, 1997.

Exchange Arrangement

Currency   The currency of Palau is the dollar.

Exchange rate structure   Unitary.

Classification

Exchange arrangement with no sepa-   Yes.
rate legal tender

Exchange tax   No.

Exchange subsidy   No.

Forward exchange market   No.

Arrangements for Payments and Receipts

Prescription of currency   No.
requirements

Payment arrangements   No.

Administration of control   No.

International security restrictions   No.

Payment arrears   No.

Controls on trade in gold (coins   No.
and/or bullion)

Controls on exports and imports of   No.
banknotes

Resident Accounts

Foreign exchange accounts permitted   n.r.

Accounts in domestic currency   n.r.
convertible into foreign currency

Nonresident Accounts

Foreign exchange accounts permitted   No.

Domestic currency accounts   No.

Blocked accounts   No.

Imports and Import Payments

Foreign exchange budget   No.

Financing requirements for imports	No.
Documentation requirements for release of foreign exchange for imports	No.
Import licenses and other nontariff measures	
Negative list	The importation of controlled substances, guns, ammunition, nonquarantined fruits, live plants, and animals is restricted.
Import taxes and/or tariffs	The tariff for general imports is 3%; government, personal, medical, and food imports are exempted. The tariff for cigarettes is $0.50 per 20, and for tobacco, it is 150% ad valorem. Cosmetics and toiletries have a tariff of 25%; carbonated soft drinks, $0.10 per 12 ounces; beer, $0.03 per ounce; liquor, $0.30 per ounce; wine, $0.20 per ounce; wine coolers, $0.05 per ounce; liquid fuel, $0.05 per gallon; and vehicles, 5% ad valorem, plus $250.
State import monopoly	No.

Exports and Export Proceeds

Repatriation requirements	No.
Financing requirements	No.
Documentation requirements	No.
Export licenses	
Without quotas	Yes.
Export taxes	Export taxes are levied on fish exports ($0.25 per kilo).

Payments for Invisible Transactions and Current Transfers

Controls on these transfers	No.

Proceeds from Invisible Transactions and Current Transfers

Repatriation requirements	No.
Restrictions on use of funds	No.

Capital Transactions

Controls on capital and money market instruments	No.
Controls on derivatives and other instruments	No.
Controls on credit operations	No.
Controls on direct investment	
Inward direct investment	The Palau National Code restricts foreign direct investment without local ownership.
Controls on liquidation of direct investment	No.
Controls on real estate transactions	
Purchase locally by nonresidents	According to the constitution, only citizens of Palau and corporations wholly owned by citizens of Palau may acquire title to land or waters in Palau.

Controls on personal capital movements	No.
Provisions specific to commercial banks and other credit institutions	Specific provisions are applied only to the Palau National Development Bank, which is not involved in commercial banking.
Provisions specific to institutional investors	No.
Other controls imposed by securities laws	No.

Changes During 1999

No significant changes occurred in the exchange and trade system.

PANAMA

(Position as of December 31, 1999)

Status Under IMF Articles of Agreement

Article VIII	Date of acceptance: November 26, 1946.

Exchange Arrangement

Currency	The currency of Panama is the Panamanian balboa. It is the unit of account and is limited to coins.
Other legal tender	The dollar is legal tender and circulates freely in Panama.
Exchange rate structure	Unitary.
Classification	
Exchange arrangement with no separate legal tender	The currency of Panama is pegged to the dollar at the rate of B 1 per $1.
Exchange tax	No.
Exchange subsidy	No.
Forward exchange market	No.

Arrangements for Payments and Receipts

Prescription of currency requirements	No.
Payment arrangements	No.
Administration of control	No.
International security restrictions	No.
Payment arrears	
Official	Official payment arrears are maintained toward holders of nonrestructured bonds who could not be identified.
Controls on trade in gold (coins and/or bullion)	
Controls on external trade	Imports and exports of gold in any form other than jewelry carried as personal effects by travelers require a license if effected by residents other than the monetary authorities. Exports of unworked gold produced in Panama are subject to an export duty of 1% ad valorem, and exports of gold coins (other than U.S. coins, which are exempt) are subject to a duty of 0.5%.
Controls on exports and imports of banknotes	No.

Resident Accounts

Foreign exchange accounts permitted	Yes.
Held domestically	Yes.
Held abroad	Yes.
Accounts in domestic currency convertible into foreign currency	Yes.

Nonresident Accounts

Foreign exchange accounts permitted	Yes.
Domestic currency accounts	Yes.
Convertible into foreign currency	Yes.
Blocked accounts	No.

Imports and Import Payments

Foreign exchange budget	No.
Financing requirements for imports	No.
Documentation requirements for release of foreign exchange for imports	No.
Import licenses and other nontariff measures	For rice products, pork meat, poultry meat, and tomato paste and puree, a contingent mechanism exists that was negotiated under the WTO agreement facilitating the exchange of permits allowing the imports of these products at preferential tariff rates.
Import taxes and/or tariffs	All tariff rates are on an ad valorem basis and are assessed on the c.i.f. value of imports. Trade reform has resulted in simplified tariff bands of zero, 3%, 5%, 10%, and 15%. The exceptions to the maximum tariff of 15% are automobiles (17%), sugar (50% on imports exceeding a historical average price range), and about 18 products (mainly agricultural products) whose tariffs are the maximum (and declining) levels negotiated with WTO including dairy products (90–173%), rice (130%), onions (90%), beef meat (40%), pork meat (70–90%), some poultry meat (300%), ketchup (70%), and tomato paste and puree (87%). All imports into the area designated as the Colón Free Zone and the newly established export processing zones are exempt from duties.
State import monopoly	No.

Exports and Export Proceeds

Repatriation requirements	No.
Financing requirements	No.
Documentation requirements	No.
Export licenses	Exports of certain drugs, firearms, and ammunition are prohibited or restricted. Any product (including raw materials and machinery) may be imported into the Colón Free Zone and stored, modified, processed, assembled, repacked, and reexported without being subject to customs procedures.
Export taxes	On January 1, 1999, taxes on banana exports were eliminated.
Other export taxes	Export taxes are levied on gold, silver, platinum, manganese, other minerals, unrefined sugar, coconuts, scrap metal, pearls, animal wax, nispero gum, ipecac root, and rubber. Certain nontraditional exports (with a minimum local cost-of-production content of 20%) are eligible for tax credit certificates equivalent to 20% of value added. Export processing zones are exempt from all taxes.

Payments for Invisible Transactions and Current Transfers

Controls on these transfers	No.

Proceeds from Invisible Transactions and Current Transfers

Repatriation requirements	No.
Restrictions on use of funds	No.

Capital Transactions

Controls on capital and money market instruments	No.
Controls on derivatives and other instruments	No.
Controls on credit operations	No.
Controls on direct investment	No.
Controls on liquidation of direct investment	No.
Controls on real estate transactions	No.
Controls on personal capital movements	No.
Provisions specific to commercial banks and other credit institutions	No.
Provisions specific to institutional investors	No.
Other controls imposed by securities laws	No.

Changes During 1999

Exports and export proceeds	*January 1*. Banana export taxes were eliminated.

PAPUA NEW GUINEA

(Position as of December 31, 1999)

Status Under IMF Articles of Agreement

Article VIII   Date of acceptance: December 4, 1975.

Exchange Arrangement

Currency   The currency of Papua New Guinea is the Papua New Guinea kina.

Exchange rate structure   Unitary.

Classification

Independently floating   The exchange rate of the kina is determined freely in the interbank market in which authorized banks participate with the Bank of Papua New Guinea (BPNG) acting as broker. The commercial banks, the only authorized foreign exchange dealers, publish rates for all current transactions with their customers within a maximum spread between the buying and selling rates of 2%.

Exchange tax   No.

Exchange subsidy   No.

Forward exchange market   Exporters and importers are free to take out forward cover with the commercial banks at market-determined rates. Each commercial bank is subject to a prudential limit on its uncovered forward position.

Official cover of forward operations   At its discretion, the BPNG may intervene in the forward exchange market.

Arrangements for Payments and Receipts

Prescription of currency requirements   Contractual commitments to persons residing outside Papua New Guinea and expressed in a foreign currency must be paid in foreign currency. Export proceeds may be received in any foreign currency.

Payment arrangements   No.

Administration of control   Foreign exchange control is administered by the BPNG under the Central Banking Act. Overall policy is determined by the government with the advice of the BPNG. The BPNG has delegated considerable powers to the commercial banks operating in Papua New Guinea, which have been appointed authorized dealers in foreign exchange.

International security restrictions

In accordance with UN sanctions   Certain restrictions are imposed on the making of payments and transfers for current international transactions in respect of the Federal Republic of Yugoslavia (Serbia/Montenegro).

Payment arrears   No.

Controls on trade in gold (coins and/or bullion)

Controls on external trade   The exportation of gold is restricted to licensed gold exporters. For the large mines, the licenses are contained in their respective mining agreements. For exports of alluvial gold, specific export licenses are required from the BPNG.

Controls on exports and imports of banknotes

On exports

  Domestic currency   Travelers wishing to take or send out domestic currency in excess of K 200 in notes and K 5 in coins must obtain approval from the BPNG. Domestic coins issued for numismatic purposes may be taken out freely.

Foreign currency   Overseas visitors are free to take out any currency they brought in and declared on arrival.

Resident Accounts

Foreign exchange accounts permitted   Yes.

Held domestically   Resident business entities are required to obtain BPNG approval, except for term deposits placed for a minimum of 90 days.

Held abroad   These accounts may be permitted, but approval is required.

Accounts in domestic currency convertible into foreign currency   Yes.

Nonresident Accounts

Foreign exchange accounts permitted   Yes.

Domestic currency accounts   Yes.

Convertible into foreign currency   These accounts may be converted, but approval is required.

Blocked accounts   n.a.

Imports and Import Payments

Foreign exchange budget   No.

Financing requirements for imports   No.

Documentation requirements for release of foreign exchange for imports   Authorized dealers may, without referring to the BPNG, approve applications for import transactions that are not subject to quotas or licensing requirements. Authorized dealers may make payments up to K 5,000 upon presentation of commercial invoices. Payments in excess of K 5,000 require a set of shipping documents and a copy of the customs forms, as well as commercial invoices.

Letters of credit   Yes.

Import licenses and other nontariff measures

Negative list   Imports of a limited number of goods are restricted for reasons of health and security, while others are prohibited to protect domestic markets, including sugar, poultry, and pork. The importation of most fresh fruits and vegetables is banned (except for apples, onions, and potatoes for processing). In the event of shortages on the domestic market, special import licenses are issued and imports are subject to a 50% tariff.

Licenses with quotas   Yes.

Import taxes and/or tariffs   The import tariff regime consists of the following rates: (1) zero for essential items (including food staples such as rice and meat not produced domestically); (2) 8% or 11% for basic goods (including some consumer goods and raw materials); (3) 40% for intermediate goods; (4) 55% for luxury goods; (5) 15% or 100% for selected goods that have domestic substitutes, such as tinned mackerel and citrus fruits; and (6) 85% for sugar.

State import monopoly   No.

Exports and Export Proceeds

Repatriation requirements   On June 30, 1999, the retention period of export proceeds was shortened to three months from six months.

Surrender requirements	Export proceeds must be sold to an authorized dealer.
Financing requirements	No.
Documentation requirements	No.
Export licenses	When exporters are not in a position to comply with the conditions of the general authority, they must apply to the BPNG for specific authorization.
Without quotas	Licenses are required for exports of logs, pearls, fishery and marine products, woodchips, sandalwood, rattan, coffee, cocoa, and copra. Log export licenses are issued subject to minimum export price guidelines.
Export taxes	Although exports of unprocessed products are subject to export levies, these have been temporarily waived, except for those on fish (10%) and logs (15% to 70%). Export levies also apply to forestry products.
Other export taxes	Yes.

Payments for Invisible Transactions and Current Transfers

Controls on these transfers	There are restrictions on these payments, but approval is readily granted for most, provided that supporting documentation is submitted. Authorized foreign exchange dealers may approve payments and transfers up to the equivalent of K 500,000 a year for all adult individuals and corporations. Payments and transfers in excess of this amount, except trade-related and debt-service payments, must be referred to the BPNG. For payments or transfers exceeding the equivalent of K 50,000 a year, a certificate of tax payment is required.
Investment-related payments	There are no controls on payment for interest.
Quantitative limits	Payments for the servicing of foreign debt may be approved without a fixed limit by authorized dealers.

Proceeds from Invisible Transactions and Current Transfers

Repatriation requirements	Yes.
Surrender requirements	Residents are not permitted to retain foreign exchange earnings from any source without the approval of the BPNG.
Restrictions on use of funds	Approval is required for the disposal of foreign currency proceeds, other than by sale to an authorized dealer in Papua New Guinea, or for its retention.

Capital Transactions

Controls on capital and money market instruments	There are no controls on inward portfolio investment. Authorized dealers may approve outward investments by resident individuals and corporations up to the equivalent of K 500,000 a year; investment in excess of this limit requires the approval of the BPNG. Income from the investment must be returned to Papua New Guinea as received. Prior clearance from the tax authorities is required for these transactions if the amount exceeds K 50,000 in any calendar year.
On capital market securities	
Shares or other securities of a participating nature	
Purchase abroad by residents	Yes.
Bonds or other debt securities	
Purchase abroad by residents	Yes.

On money market instruments

   Purchase abroad by residents   Yes.

On collective investment securities

   Purchase abroad by residents   Yes.

Controls on derivatives and other instruments

Purchase abroad by residents   Yes.

Controls on credit operations

Commercial credits

   By residents to nonresidents   Yes.

   To residents from nonresidents   Permission is required for these credits; however, authorized foreign exchange dealers may approve offshore foreign currency borrowing by residents other than businesses involved in the forestry sector or mineral resources exploration, without limitation provided that the term is for not less than one year and that interest rates and fees do not exceed the levels specified by the BPNG. Repayment of principal is subject to a six-month moratorium, commencing on the date of disbursements. A maximum debt-to-equity ratio of 5:1 applies to net outstanding borrowing. In the case of a business involved in mineral resource exploration activities, inward investment is considered non–interest bearing equity or loan funds (including preference shares) until the business is successful, at which point any excess above the minimum equity-to-debt ratio specified for that operation can be converted into an interest-bearing loan.

Financial credits

   By residents to nonresidents   Yes.

   To residents from nonresidents   Yes.

Guarantees, sureties, and financial backup facilities

   By residents to nonresidents   Yes.

   To residents from nonresidents   Yes.

Controls on direct investment

Outward direct investment   Yes.

Controls on liquidation of direct investment   Proceeds may be transferred, provided that tax clearance certificates are produced.

Controls on real estate transactions

Purchase abroad by residents   Yes.

Controls on personal capital movements

Transfer of gambling and prize earnings   Yes.

Provisions specific to commercial banks and other credit institutions

Borrowing abroad   Yes.

Maintenance of accounts abroad   Yes.

Lending to nonresidents (financial or commercial credits)   Yes.

Lending locally in foreign exchange   Subject to presentation of commercial invoices for bona fide transactions.

Open foreign exchange position limits   Yes.

Provisions specific to institutional investors   No.

Other controls imposed by securities laws   No.

Changes During 1999

Exports and export proceeds   *June 30*. The retention period for export proceeds was shortened to three months.

PARAGUAY

(Position as of December 31, 1999)

Status Under IMF Articles of Agreement

Article VIII   Date of acceptance: August 23, 1994.

Exchange Arrangement

Currency   The currency of Paraguay is the Paraguayan guaraní.

Exchange rate structure   Unitary.

Classification

Managed floating with no pre-   The authorities are managing their exchange rate policy in order to keep the value of the
announced path for the exchange rate   guaraní roughly unchanged in real effective terms.

Exchange tax   No.

Exchange subsidy   No.

Forward exchange market   Commercial banks are permitted to enter into forward transactions with respect to trade
                                         transactions and on terms that may be negotiated freely with customers.

Arrangements for Payments and Receipts

Prescription of currency   No.
requirements

Payment arrangements

Regional arrangements   Payments between Paraguay and the other LAIA countries are made through accounts
                                         maintained with the Central Bank of Paraguay (CBP) and other central banks participating
                                         in the multilateral clearing arrangements of the LAIA. Clearing takes place every four
                                         months.

Clearing agreements   Yes.

Administration of control   The CBP has the authority to determine foreign exchange policy in consultation with other
                                         agencies of the government. In practice, decisions are taken by the Economic Cabinet on
                                         the advice of the CBP, which is responsible for implementing its decisions. The CBP
                                         supervises, through the Superintendency of Banks, foreign exchange transactions carried
                                         out by banks and exchange houses. The CBP regulates open foreign exchange positions.

International security restrictions No.

Payment arrears   No.

Controls on trade in gold (coins
and/or bullion)

Controls on external trade   The exportation and importation of gold by nonbank residents and industrial users in any
                                         form other than jewelry require the prior authorization of the CBP. Payments for gold im-
                                         ports by industrial users must be made through commercial banks.

Controls on exports and imports of   No.
banknotes

Resident Accounts

Foreign exchange accounts permitted Yes.

692

Held domestically	Yes.
Held abroad	Yes.
Accounts in domestic currency convertible into foreign currency	Yes.

Nonresident Accounts

Foreign exchange accounts permitted	Yes.
Domestic currency accounts	Yes.
Convertible into foreign currency	Yes.
Blocked accounts	No.

Imports and Import Payments

Foreign exchange budget	No.
Financing requirements for imports	No.
Documentation requirements for release of foreign exchange for imports	
Preshipment inspection	All products must be inspected.

Import licenses and other nontariff measures

Negative list

Imports of certain products that may be harmful to public health, national security, or animal or plant health are prohibited. However, these restrictions may be waived to ensure adequate domestic supplies.

Import taxes and/or tariffs

Paraguay, as a member of MERCOSUR, applies its common external tariff, which is composed of 11 rates ranging up to 20%. Paraguay was allowed to exempt 399 items from the CET—these exemptions are to be phased out by 2006 by gradually raising tariff rates to 14% on most capital goods, and to 20% for telecommunications. Typical rates on goods exempt from the CET are zero for raw materials and intermediate goods; 5% for capital goods; 6% for items for tourism; 10% for consumer goods; 15% for vehicles whose c.i.f. value exceeds $10,000; and 20% for vehicles whose c.i.f. value exceeds $20,000. Similarly, on intra-MERCOSUR trade, Paraguay was allowed 427 exceptions to free trade with tariff rates ranging from 6% to 30% to be phased out by 2001. The CBP levies a commission of 0.125% on all import payments made under the LAIA Reciprocal Payments Agreement.

State import monopoly   No.

Exports and Export Proceeds

Repatriation requirements	No.
Financing requirements	No.
Documentation requirements	No.

Export licenses

Without quotas

Exports of logs and unprocessed forest products, raw hides, and wild animals are prohibited. Certain other exports require prior authorization from the appropriate agency. No other exports are restricted, except with regard to technical standards imposed by the National Institute of Technology and Standardization, the Ministry of Industry and Commerce, the Ministry of Public Health, or the Ministry of Agriculture and Livestock, depending on the product exported.

With quotas	Exports of wood and wood products of certain trees are subject to quotas because of risk of depletion.
Export taxes	The CBP levies a commission of 0.125% on all exports made under the LAIA Reciprocal Payments Agreement.

Payments for Invisible Transactions and Current Transfers

Controls on these transfers	
Investment-related payments	There are controls on the transfer of profits.
Prior approval	Only financial enterprises require authorization of the CBP to transfer earnings. The government may grant exemptions from taxes, customs, and import surcharges on proposed investments that are duly registered and approved.

Proceeds from Invisible Transactions and Current Transfers

Repatriation requirements	No.
Surrender requirements	There are no surrender requirements for proceeds from invisibles, except for royalties and remuneration from the binational entities administering the ITAIPU and YACYRETA dams, which are transferred in full to the CBP for the account of the Ministry of Finance.
Restrictions on use of funds	No.

Capital Transactions

Controls on capital and money market instruments	No.
Controls on derivatives and other instruments	
Purchase locally by nonresidents	Nonresidents may purchase foreign exchange forward, up to one year, exclusively for operations relating to trade.
Sale or issue locally by nonresidents	The Superintendency of Banks must be informed of amounts exceeding $10,000 in compliance with money laundering regulations.
Controls on credit operations	No.
Controls on direct investment	No.
Controls on liquidation of direct investment	No.
Controls on real estate transactions	No.
Controls on personal capital movements	No.
Provisions specific to commercial banks and other credit institutions	
Borrowing abroad	Permitted up to a specified proportion of paid-up capital.
Maintenance of accounts abroad	Subject to diversification of depository banks and not to exceed 20% of the local bank's net worth. This limit can be extended up to 70% of the bank's net worth, under special conditions.
Lending to nonresidents (financial or commercial credits)	Permitted up to 5% of the bank's net worth and up to 20%, subject to approval of a guarantee by the Superintendency of Banks.
Lending locally in foreign exchange	Yes.

Purchase of locally issued securities denominated in foreign exchange	Yes.
Differential treatment of deposit accounts in foreign exchange	Yes.
Reserve requirements	Reserves should be constituted in foreign currency. The required ratios vary according to the maturity of deposits.
Investment regulations	
Abroad by banks	The limits are according to those specified in the banking legislation.
Open foreign exchange position limits	Commercial banks may maintain a daily foreign exchange overbought position not exceeding 30% of their effective capital, excluding government bonds denominated in dollars, credit balances in foreign currency of more than one-year maturity for agriculture and livestock; industrial and small- and medium-size businesses; and home and professional service equipment purchases. The daily foreign exchange overbought position may not exceed 100% in cases where the banks do not include within its effective capital the above excluded items. The daily oversold position may not exceed 75% of effective capital. In formulating this position, all foreign exchange components should be included.
Provisions specific to institutional investors	No.
Other controls imposed by securities laws	No.

Changes During 1999

No significant changes occurred in the exchange and trade system.

PERU

Status Under IMF Articles of Agreement

Article VIII	Date of acceptance: February 15, 1961.

Exchange Arrangement

Currency	The currency of Peru is the Peruvian nuevo sol.
Exchange rate structure	Unitary.
Classification	
Independently floating	The exchange rate of the nuevo sol is determined freely by supply and demand. Cross rates with nondollar currencies are determined against the dollar.
Exchange tax	No.
Exchange subsidy	No.
Forward exchange market	Yes.

Arrangements for Payments and Receipts

Prescription of currency requirements	No.
Payment arrangements	
Regional arrangements	Payments between Peru and Argentina, Bolivia, Brazil, Chile, Colombia, the Dominican Republic, Ecuador, Malaysia, Mexico, Paraguay, Uruguay, and Venezuela may be made through accounts maintained with each other by the Central Reserve Bank of Peru (CRBP) and the other central banks concerned within the framework of the multilateral clearing system of the LAIA.
Clearing agreements	Yes.
Administration of control	By law, there are no restrictions on any exchange transactions, including holding, using, purchasing, or selling foreign exchange.
International security restrictions	No.
Payment arrears	No.
Controls on trade in gold (coins and/or bullion)	No.
Controls on exports and imports of banknotes	No.

Resident Accounts

Foreign exchange accounts permitted	Yes.
Held domestically	Yes.
Held abroad	Yes.
Accounts in domestic currency convertible into foreign currency	Yes.

Nonresident Accounts

Foreign exchange accounts permitted	Yes.
Domestic currency accounts	Yes.
Convertible into foreign currency	Yes.
Blocked accounts	No.

Imports and Import Payments

Foreign exchange budget	No.
Financing requirements for imports	No.
Documentation requirements for release of foreign exchange for imports	No.
Import licenses and other nontariff measures	
Negative list	Imports may be prohibited for social, health, or security reasons.
Import taxes and/or tariffs	Tariff rates average 13.4%. A 12% rate is applied to about 84% of import items, and the remaining products are subject to a 20% rate. Imports subject to trade agreements are not subject to these tariffs. Temporary surcharges of 5% and 10% are applied to some agricultural and agro-industrial goods, and some meats and its derivatives, respectively. Raw materials and intermediate goods imported under the Temporary Admission Regime are exempt from import duties.
State import monopoly	No.

Exports and Export Proceeds

Repatriation requirements	No.
Financing requirements	No.
Documentation requirements	No.
Export licenses	No.
Export taxes	No.

Payments for Invisible Transactions and Current Transfers

Controls on these transfers	No.

Proceeds from Invisible Transactions and Current Transfers

Repatriation requirements	No.
Restrictions on use of funds	No.

Capital Transactions

Controls on capital and money market instruments	No.

Controls on derivatives and other instruments	No.
Controls on credit operations	No.
Controls on direct investment	No.
Controls on liquidation of direct investment	No.
Controls on real estate transactions	No.
Controls on personal capital movements	No.
Provisions specific to commercial banks and other credit institutions	
Lending to nonresidents (financial or commercial credits)	Credits granted by resident financial institutions to financial institutions and to individuals or enterprises (residents or nonresidents) are subject to prudential limits.
Differential treatment of deposit accounts in foreign exchange	
Reserve requirements	As a measure of monetary control, there is a difference between the treatment of deposit accounts in domestic currency and deposit accounts in foreign currency, but there is no discrimination between residents and nonresidents. The deposit accounts in foreign currency are subject to a marginal reserve requirement of 20%. However, the CRBP remunerated the reserve requirement with the three-month Libor rate minus 1.375% until October 1, 1999, when the rate of remuneration was increased to the three-month Libor rate minus 0.125%.
Liquid asset requirements	As a measure of prudential regulations, a liquid asset requirement as a percentage of short-term liabilities (20% in foreign currency and 8% in domestic currency) is used.
Open foreign exchange position limits	
On resident assets and liabilities	There is a prudential limit of 100% of the net worth over the long foreign exchange position and a limit of 2.5% over the short foreign exchange position of the financial institution.
Provisions specific to institutional investors	The securities market in Peru is open to foreign investors. No legal restrictions exist on the purchase or sale of domestic securities by nonresidents, or on the purchase or sale of foreign securities by residents. Revenues may be repatriated without restrictions.
Limits (max.) on securities issued by nonresidents and on portfolio invested abroad	The law allows pension funds to invest up to 10% of their portfolio in foreign securities.
Limits (max.) on portfolio invested abroad	The law allows pension funds to invest up to 10% of their portfolio in foreign securities.
Other controls imposed by securities laws	No.

Changes During 1999

Imports and import payments	*August 25.* The temporary surcharge imposed on meat items and their derivatives (56 items) was increased to 10% from 5%.
Capital transactions	
Provisions specific to commercial banks and other credit institutions	*October 1.* The CRBP remuneration for reserve requirement in foreign exchange was increased to the three-month LIBOR rate minus 0.125% from LIBOR minus 1.375%.

PHILIPPINES

(Position as of April 30, 2000)

Status Under IMF Articles of Agreement

Article VIII   Date of acceptance: September 8, 1995.

Exchange Arrangement

Currency   The currency of the Philippines is the Philippine peso.

Other legal tender   Various denominations of gold coins are also legal tender.

Exchange rate structure   Unitary.

Classification

Independently floating   Exchange rates are determined on the basis of demand and supply in the foreign exchange market. However, the Bangko Sentral ng Pilipinas (BSP) acts to limit sharp fluctuations in the exchange rate and intervenes when necessary to maintain orderly conditions in the exchange market. Commercial banks trade in foreign exchange through the Philippine Dealing System (PDS), an electronic screen-based network. The PDS allows trading between 8:30 a.m. and 5:30 p.m. daily among authorized agent banks and the BSP. The system links participants through an electronic screen-based network of sharing information and undertaking transactions. The exchange rate of the peso vis-à-vis the dollar at the beginning of the trading day represents the weighted average of all transactions in the PDS during the preceding day. The amount of foreign exchange that may be sold (over-the-counter) without documentation and prior approval is $10,000. Foreign exchange subsidiaries are exempted from this ruling, provided that they sell dollars only to authorized agent banks and bank-affiliated foreign exchange corporations.

Exchange tax   No.

Exchange subsidy   No.

Forward exchange market   All forward transactions to purchase foreign exchange from nonresidents, including renewals thereof, require prior clearance by the BSP. All forward contracts to sell foreign exchange to nonresidents (including offshore banking units) with no full delivery of principal, including cancellations, rollovers, and renewals thereof, require prior clearance by the BSP. Only banks with expanded derivatives license may enter into transactions covered by nondeliverable forward contracts.

Official cover of forward operations Yes.

Arrangements for Payments and Receipts

Prescription of currency requirements   There are no prescription of currency requirements for outgoing payments, but all foreign exchange proceeds from exports and invisibles must be obtained in the following acceptable currencies: Australian dollars, Bahrain dinars, Belgian francs, Brunei dollars, Canadian dollars, euros, Hong Kong dollars, Indonesian rupiahs, Japanese yen, Kuwaiti dinars, Malaysian ringgit, pounds sterling, Saudi Arabian riyals, Singapore dollars, Swiss francs, Thai baht, U.A.E. dirhams, U.S. dollars, and other such currencies that may be declared acceptable by the BSP. Payments may be made in pesos for exports to ASEAN countries, provided that the BSP is not asked to intervene in the clearing of any balances from this payment scheme. Authorized agent banks may accept notes denominated in the prescribed currencies for conversion into pesos.

Payment arrangements

Bilateral payment arrangements   The BSP entered into a payments agreement with Bank Negara Malaysia. Payments are stipulated in dollars.

Operative   Yes.

PHILIPPINES

Regional arrangements	The Philippines is a member of ASEAN.
Administration of control	Foreign exchange regulations are administered by the BSP on the basis of policy decisions adopted by the Monetary Board.
International security restrictions	No.
Payment arrears	No.

Controls on trade in gold (coins and/or bullion)

Controls on domestic ownership and/or trade

Small-scale miners are required to sell all of their production to the BSP. All forms or types of gold may be bought and sold without specific approval of the BSP. Producers selling gold to the BSP are paid in Philippine pesos on the basis of the latest London fixing price and the prevailing Philippine peso-dollar exchange rate. The gold so acquired is deemed to be part of the official international reserves. The BSP may sell gold grains, pellets, bars, and sheets to local jewelry manufacturers and other industrial users upon application or to banks only for resale to jewelry manufacturers and industrial users, at the BSP's gold-selling price plus a service fee to cover costs, including the costs of conversion and packaging.

Controls on external trade

Gold produced by small-scale miners is required to be sold to the BSP; all other forms of gold may be exported. There are no restrictions on the importation of any form of gold except gold coins, gold coin blanks, and coins without any indication of actual fineness of gold content, which require prior approval of the BSP.

Controls on exports and imports of banknotes

On exports

Domestic currency

Resident and nonresident travelers must obtain prior authorization from the BSP to take out more than ₱10,000 in domestic banknotes and coins or checks, money orders, and other bills of exchange drawn in pesos.

Foreign currency

Departing nonresidents, individual tourists, and emigrants (balikbayans) are allowed to reconvert at airports or other ports of exit unspent pesos up to a maximum of $200 or an equivalent amount in other foreign currency, calculated at the prevailing exchange rates, without proof of sales of foreign exchange to authorized agent banks.

On imports

Domestic currency

Travelers may bring in freely up to ₱10,000 in domestic banknotes and coins and checks, money orders, and other bills of exchange drawn in pesos. The importation exceeding that amount requires prior authorization from the BSP.

Foreign currency

Travelers may bring in freely any amount of foreign currency.

Resident Accounts

Foreign exchange accounts permitted	Yes.
Held domestically	Yes.
Held abroad	Yes.
Accounts in domestic currency convertible into foreign currency	No.

Nonresident Accounts

Foreign exchange accounts permitted	Nonresident accounts may be credited only with the proceeds from inward remittances of foreign exchange or convertible foreign currencies and with peso income earned by non-residents from the Philippines.

Domestic currency accounts	Nonresident peso deposit accounts may be freely withdrawn.
Convertible into foreign currency	Conversion of domestic currency accounts is allowed only up to the equivalent amount of foreign exchange remitted to the Philippines as well as to the equivalent amount of peso income earned by nonresidents, provided the investment was made in a peso time deposit with a maturity of at least 90 days and was registered with the BSP. In order for the funds to be converted into foreign currency for repatriation abroad, investments in bank deposits must be in pesos, must have a maturity of at least 90 days, and must be registered with the BSP. Deposits arising from other investments, such as stocks and government securities, are not subject to the 90-day holding period. The BSP registration document, which is issued directly by the BSP for such investments, will be canceled if the investments are terminated before the end of the 90-day period.
Blocked accounts	No.

Imports and Import Payments

Foreign exchange budget	No.
Financing requirements for imports	No.
Documentation requirements for release of foreign exchange for imports	Commercial banks may sell foreign exchange for payments of imports under LCs, documents against acceptance (DAs), documents against payments (DPs), open account arrangements (OAs), and direct remittances. Registration of DA and OA imports with the BSP for monitoring purposes is needed only if payments are to be made from the banking system; prior approval of the BSP, regardless of maturity, is not required. Payments made subsequent to the original maturity date may be allowed without BSP approval, provided that the importers report the extension of the maturity together with the specific date to which it has been extended. The cumulative length of the maturity periods, including all extensions, may not exceed one year from the date of the draft acceptance of the DA and the bill of lading (BL) date for OAs. Payments of DA and OA obligations whose maturities have exceeded 360 days from the date of the draft acceptance, in the case of DAs, or the date of the BL, in the case of OAs, are subject to approval by the BSP.
Preshipment inspection	Under the Comprehensive Imports Supervision Scheme (CISS), preshipment inspection was required for imports valued at more than $500 from all countries. Imports declared in the shipping documents as off-quality, used, secondhand, scraps, offgrade, or a similar term indicating that the article was not new are subject to CISS inspection even if the value of the imports is less than $500. Effective April 1, 2000, preshipment inspection is no longer required for imports.
Letters of credit	LCs must be opened on or before the date of shipment with a validity period of up to one year. Only one LC may be opened for each import transaction; amendments to such an arrangement need not be referred to the BSP for prior approval except when the amendment extends the total validity of the LC beyond one year.
Other	Senior bank officers responsible for the sale of foreign exchange certify that, in cases other than LCs, DPs, DAs, or OAs, the original documents have been presented and that the bank has taken measures to ensure that the applicant/importer has not purchased foreign exchange from the banking system in excess of the amount of the importation as indicated in the invoice.
Import licenses and other nontariff measures	Generally, all merchandise imports are allowed without a license.
Positive list	Yes.
Negative list	The importation of certain products is regulated or restricted for reasons of public health and safety, national security, international commitments, and development and rationalization of local industries.
Open general licenses	Commodity imports are classified into three categories: freely importable, regulated, and prohibited. To import regulated products, a clearance or permit is required from the appropriate government agency (including the BSP).
Licenses with quotas	Quantitative restrictions are imposed on the imports of rice.

Import taxes and/or tariffs	The import tariff structure consists of four rates: 3%, 10%, 20%, and 30%. Rates on imported capital goods are 3% and 10%, with the former applying to goods without domestic substitutes. Deviations from the standard rates include (1) up to double the applicable standard rate for imports of final goods in industries that have "pioneer" status at the Board of Investment (BOI), and imports of agricultural products for which quantitative restrictions are being removed under the WTO agreement; and (2) duty exemptions for certain imported capital goods registered with the BOI prior to January 1, 1995, or subject to provisions of the Export Development Act. Some 300 products are duty exempt, as are imports of machinery, equipment, and accompanying spare parts used in export manu-facturing. Newly registered firms may only obtain duty reductions on eligible imports up to 3%. Tariff rates in the textile and apparel sectors are 3% for inputs and 30% for final products. Effective January 15, 1999, import tariffs were increased by 3–5 percentage points for seven items (yams, threads, fabrics, garments, pocket lighters, polyamide, and kraft liner), and reduced by 3–22% for three items (iron and steel slabs and scraps; caprolactam and battery separators; and crystal tissues), while tariffs on steel wire rods were unified. Effective April 16, 1999, BOI certification is required at the time the LC is opened to qualify for the preferential rate of 3% for imports of wire rod.
State import monopoly	No.

Exports and Export Proceeds

Repatriation requirements	No.
Financing requirements	Payments for exports may be made in acceptable currencies in the following forms without prior BSP approval: LCs, DPs, DAs, OAs, intercompany open account offsets, consignments, and export advances.
Documentation requirements	All exports must be covered by an export declaration issued by the Department of Trade and Industry duly prepared by the exporter.
Export licenses	Exports of buri seeds and seedlings; abaca and ramie seeds, seedlings, suckers and root stocks, and other planting materials; mangrove; milkfish fry; mother milkfish; pawn-sprawner and fry; selected shells; selected wildlife species; matured coconuts and coconut seedlings; selected raw materials for cottage industries; and stalactites and stalagmites are prohibited.
Without quotas	Yes.
Export taxes	No.

Payments for Invisible Transactions and Current Transfers

Controls on these transfers	The amount of foreign exchange an authorized agent bank may sell to residents for any nontrade purpose, without need of appropriate documentation, is $10,000. Consequently, for sales of foreign exchange exceeding $10,000, the authorized agent's bank requires a written notarized application and supporting documents from the purchaser.
Trade-related payments	
Indicative limits/bona fide test	Yes.
Investment-related payments	The BSP regulates foreign currency loans to ensure that interest and principal owed to creditors can be serviced in an orderly manner and with due regard to the economy's overall debt servicing capacity. Pursuant to the Philippines Constitution, all public and private sector publicly guaranteed obligations from foreign creditors, including offshore banking units and foreign currency deposit units, are referred to the BSP for prior approval. Other private sector loans from these creditors and other financing schemes/arrangements require prior approval and/or registration by the BSP if they are to be serviced using foreign exchange purchased from the banking system. Foreign currency borrowings from foreign currency deposit units (FCDUs) with a maturity exceeding one year are governed by the same guidelines. In the case of short-term FCDU loans, including those obtained by the

private sector, no prior BSP approval is required, provided the borrower/project qualifies for foreign financing.

Prior approval	Service payments relating to foreign loans effected by purchases of foreign exchange through authorized agent banks are limited to those transactions whose original capital transfer has previously been registered with the BSP or are specifically authorized by the BSP to purchase foreign exchange from the banking system. Unregistered loans may be serviced with foreign exchange sourced from outside the banking system.
Quantitative limits	The ceiling is set yearly and is approved by the Monetary Board of the BSP.
Indicative limits/bona fide test	Yes.
Payments for travel	
Quantitative limits	Yes.
Indicative limits/bona fide test	Yes.
Personal payments	
Quantitative limits	Yes.
Indicative limits/bona fide test	Yes.
Foreign workers' wages	
Quantitative limits	Yes.
Indicative limits/bona fide test	Yes.
Credit card use abroad	
Quantitative limits	Yes.
Indicative limits/bona fide test	Yes.
Other payments	
Prior approval	Yes.
Quantitative limits	Yes.
Indicative limits/bona fide test	Yes.

Proceeds from Invisible Transactions and Current Transfers

Repatriation requirements	No.
Restrictions on use of funds	No.

Capital Transactions

Controls on capital and money market instruments

On capital market securities

Shares or other securities of a participating nature

Purchase locally by nonresidents	As a general rule, registration with the BSP or designated custodian bank is not mandatory. Registration is necessary only if the source of the foreign exchange needed for capital repatriation and remittance of dividends, profits, and earnings that accrue thereon is purchased from the banking system.
Sale or issue locally by nonresidents	Sale or issue of securities in the Philippines is allowed only after the proper license to do business in the country is secured by the nonresident from the appropriate government

agency. Prior approval of the BSP is required for all issuances of peso-denominated instruments in the international capital markets that involve (1) inward remittance of foreign exchange to the Philippines and sale thereof for pesos to the local banking system; or (2) if a resident enterprise, or any of its offshore offices, branches, subsidiaries, and affiliates, participates in such transactions as an issuer, guarantor, or beneficiary, and where proceeds are lent to or invested in resident companies.

Purchase abroad by residents	Residents may invest abroad without prior approval and subsequent registration of their investments with the BSP only if (1) the investments are funded by withdrawals from FCDUs; (2) the funds to be invested are not among those required to be sold to authorized agent banks (AABs) for pesos; or (3) the sources of funds are from the banking system but in amounts less than $6 million for an investor a year. For amounts above $6 million (an investor a year), prior approval and registration with the BSP is required. Outward investments of domestic banks, however, are required to be registered with the BSP regardless of the amount.
Sale or issue abroad by residents	Registration with the BSP or a designated custodian bank may be made at the option of the investor. In addition, proceeds of sales of international allocation of initial public offerings (IPOs) and shares of domestic companies listed in foreign stock exchanges must also be reported to the BSP within five days from receipt and remitted to the country. The servicing or transfer of funds pertaining to registered investments using foreign exchange from the banking system in this category is allowed without BSP approval.

Bonds or other debt securities

Purchase locally by nonresidents	Registration with the BSP is necessary only if the foreign exchange needed for capital repatriation and remittance of dividends, profits, and earnings that accrue thereon is purchased from the banking system.
Sale or issue locally by nonresidents	These transactions are allowed only after the proper license to do business in the country is secured from the appropriate government agency.
Purchase abroad by residents	For amounts above $6 million, for which the source is the banking system, prior approval and registration by the BSP is required.
Sale or issue abroad by residents	These transactions are subject to prior approval by the BSP if principal and interest amortization are to be serviced using foreign exchange purchased from the banking system or guaranteed by public sector entities or local banks.

On money market instruments

Sale or issue locally by nonresidents	Yes.
Purchase abroad by residents	Yes.

On collective investment securities

Sale or issue locally by nonresidents	Yes.
Purchase abroad by residents	Yes.

Controls on derivatives and other instruments	Prior BSP approval is required. Only banks and nonbank financial intermediaries performing quasi-banking functions and their affiliates/subsidiaries duly authorized by the BSP are allowed to deal in derivative transactions.
Purchase locally by nonresidents	All forward contracts to sell foreign exchange to nonresidents (including offshore banking units) with no full delivery of principal, including cancellations or rollovers/renewals thereof, are to be submitted for prior clearance to the BSP.
Sale or issue locally by nonresidents	Yes.
Purchase abroad by residents	Yes.
Sale or issue abroad by residents	Yes.

Controls on credit operations	
Commercial credits	Loans of resident private sector borrowers from FCDUs and offshore sources and nonresident loans serviced by foreign exchange purchased outside the banking system no longer require prior BSP approval, except if said loans are guaranteed by the public sector or by

local banks.

To residents from nonresidents

Prior BSP approval and registration are required for short-term trade-related foreign loans by nonbank residents, which are guaranteed by the public sector or by local banks. For those not covered by such guarantees, prior authority to incur the obligation is not required. They are still, however, subject to the registration requirement for debt servicing using foreign exchange from the banking system.

Financial credits

Loans of nonresidents from expanded foreign currency deposit units (EFCDUs), irrespective of maturity, no longer require BSP approval, provided that (1) the loan is serviced using foreign exchange purchased from outside the banking system; and (2) all applicable banking rules and regulations are complied with, including Single Borrower's Limit, which is defined to include lendings and guarantees issued to companies, their subsidiaries, affiliates, and major stockholders all over the world.

By residents to nonresidents

Credits require prior BSP approval. The usual controls on outward remittances and registration requirements apply. Loans of nonresidents from EFCDUs, irrespective of maturity, no longer require BSP approval, provided that (1) the loan is serviced using foreign exchange purchased from outside the banking system; and (2) all applicable banking rules and regulations are complied with, including Single Borrower's Limit, which is defined to include lendings and guarantees issued to companies, their subsidiaries, affiliates, and major stockholders all over the world.

To residents from nonresidents

As a general rule, all foreign loans contracted by nonbank residents with guarantees from the public sector or from local commercial banks require prior BSP approval or registration. Those not covered by such guarantees likewise generally require prior BSP approval and registration to make them eligible for subsequent debt servicing using foreign exchange from the banking system. Loans of resident private sector borrowers from FCDUs/offshore sources and nonresident loans serviced by foreign exchange purchased outside the banking system no longer require prior BSP approval.

Guarantees, sureties, and financial backup facilities

By residents to nonresidents

Guarantees for the account of the public sector, as well as those issued by government-owned and -controlled corporations in favor of nonresidents, require prior BSP approval. Specific guarantees for the account of the private sector covering foreign obligations other than foreign loans do not require prior approval but must be reported to the BSP for registration purposes to be eligible for debt servicing using foreign exchange purchase from the banking system.

To residents from nonresidents

Guarantees issued by foreign banks and financial institutions to secure obligations of residents involved in foreign lending operations require prior BSP approval. Those issued to secure authorized peso loans or FCDU loans, as well as foreign obligations (which do not involve foreign lending) of local firms, do not require prior approval but must be reported to the BSP for registration purposes to be eligible for debt servicing using foreign exchange to be purchased from the banking system in the event of a default by the principal debtor.

Controls on direct investment

Outward direct investment

An applicant's income tax return is required to be submitted to support an application to purchase foreign exchange from the banking system not to exceed $6 million an investor a year for outward investment without prior BSP approval.

Controls on liquidation of direct investment

As a general rule, BSP-registered foreign investments enjoy full and immediate repatriation of capital and remittance of profits, dividends, and other earnings.

Controls on real estate transactions

Purchase abroad by residents

Yes.

Purchase locally by nonresidents

Ownership of land by nonresidents, as well as the exploration, development, and utilization of natural resources, is limited to 40% equity and is subject to the provisions of the Philippines Constitution.

Sale locally by nonresidents

This is allowed in the case of sales of real estate by nonresidents, provided that the transactions that pertain to BSP-registered investments comply with the legal provisions as cited.

Controls on personal capital movements

Gifts, endowments, inheritances, and legacies

By residents to nonresidents   No private land may be transferred or conveyed except to individuals, corporations, or associations qualified to acquire or hold land of the public domain.

Transfer of gambling and prize earnings   Yes.

Provisions specific to commercial banks and other credit institutions

Borrowing abroad   Commercial banks authorized to operate under the expanded foreign currency deposit system may borrow from other FCDUs, nonresidents, and offshore banking units, subject to existing rules on foreign borrowings.

Lending to nonresidents (financial or commercial credits)   Banks may grant commercial credit to nonresidents under any of the following modes of payment without prior BSP approval: (1) LCs; (2) DPs or cash against payment; (3) DAs; (4) OAs; (5) intercompany open account offsets; (6) consignments; and (7) export advances. Commercial banks, which are authorized to operate under the expanded foreign currency deposit system, may grant foreign currency loans to nonresidents, irrespective of maturity, without prior approval of the BSP, provided that (1) the loan is serviced using foreign exchange purchased from outside the banking system; and (2) all applicable banking rules and regulations are complied with, including all limits of lending to a single borrower, which are defined to include lendings and guarantees issued to companies, their subsidiaries, affiliates, and major stockholders all over the world.

Lending locally in foreign exchange   The following foreign currency loans may be granted by FCDUs of commercial banks without prior BSP approval: (1) private sector loans, if they are to be serviced using foreign exchange to be obtained outside the banking system; (2) short-term loans to financial institutions for normal interbank transactions; (3) short-term loans to commodity and service exporters, and producers/manufacturers, provided that the loan proceeds are to be used to finance the import costs of goods and services necessary in the production of goods. In the case of exporters, FCDU loans may also be used to finance the import cost of goods and services in local currency.

Purchase of locally issued securities denominated in foreign exchange   An EFCDU of commercial banks may invest in foreign currency–denominated securities.

Differential treatment of deposit accounts in foreign exchange

Reserve requirements   Effective July 1, 1999, the reserve requirements applied to local currency was reduced to 9% from 10%. The reserve requirement applies only to peso deposits and peso substitute liabilities and not to foreign deposit accounts.

Liquid asset requirements   Banks' liquidity reserve requirements (held in treasury securities) were reduced to 6% on February 1, 1999; to 5% on March 1, 1999; to 4% on April 16, 1999; and to 3% on July 2, 1999. On December 16, 1999, banks' liquidity reserve requirements held against interbank loans were reduced to zero.

Open foreign exchange position limits   Depository banks operating FCDUs or EFCDUs need to maintain full cover for their foreign currency liabilities at all times. For FCDUs, at least 70% of the said cover must be maintained in the same currency of the liability and up to 30% may be denominated in other acceptable foreign currencies. The limit set on a bank's long (overbought) foreign exchange positions may not exceed 5% of their impaired capital or $10 million, whichever is less; no limit is set on short (oversold) foreign exchange positions. Any excess beyond the overbought limit must be settled daily. The BSP sanctions the violation of open position limits. No differential treatment is ascribed to resident and nonresident deposit accounts with respect to liquid asset requirement, as all depository banks under the foreign currency deposit system are required to maintain at all times a 100% asset cover for their foreign currency liabilities, of which 30% must be liquid.

On resident assets and liabilities   Yes.

On nonresident assets and liabilities Yes.

Provisions specific to institutional investors

Limits (max.) on portfolio invested abroad

Except as may be authorized by the Monetary Board, the total equity investments in and/or loans to any single enterprise abroad by any investment house with quasi-banking functions may not at any time exceed 15% of their net worth. Outward investments by residents in amounts exceeding $6 million require prior approval and registration by the BSP. For amounts not exceeding $6 million, the funds to be invested may be purchased from authorized agent banks.

Other controls imposed by securities laws

As a general rule, no securities may be sold or offered for sale to the public within the country unless such securities have been registered and permitted to be sold by the Securities Exchange Commission (SEC). A foreign corporation whose securities are listed and traded in a local stock exchange must designate a transfer agent and registrar in the Philippines. As a general rule, a broker, dealer, or salesman must register with the SEC to do business in the country.

Changes During 1999

Imports and import payments

January 15. Import tariffs were increased by 3–5 percentage points for seven items (yams, threads, fabrics, garments, pocket lighters, polyamide, and kraft liner), and reduced by 3–22% for three items (iron and steel slabs and scraps; caprolactam and battery separators; and crystal tissues), while tariffs on steel wire rods were unified.

April 16. BOI certification is required at the time the LC is opened to qualify for the preferential rate of 3% for imports of wire rod.

Capital transactions

Provisions specific to commercial banks and other credit institutions

February 1. Banks' liquidity reserve requirements were reduced to 6%.

March 1. Banks' liquidity reserve requirements were reduced to 5%.

April 16. Banks' liquidity reserve requirements were reduced to 4%.

July 1. The reserve requirement applied to local currency was reduced to 9% from 10%.

July 2. Banks' liquidity reserve requirements were reduced to 3%.

December 16. Banks' liquidity reserve requirements held against interbank loans were reduced to zero.

Changes During 2000

Imports and import payments

April 1. The preshipment inspection requirement was abolished.

POLAND

(Position as of April 30, 2000)

Status Under IMF Articles of Agreement

Article VIII   Date of acceptance: June 1, 1995.

Exchange Arrangement

Currency   The currency of Poland is the Polish zloty.

Exchange rate structure   Unitary.

Classification

Independently floating   The central exchange rate of the zloty was pegged to a basket of five currencies. Effective January 1, 1999, the currency basket was changed to 55% euro and 45% dollar. The central rate was adjusted under a crawling peg policy at a preannounced rate. Effective March 24, 1999, the monthly devaluation rate of the crawling band was reduced to 0.3% from 0.5%. Until March 23, 1999, the exchange rate of the zloty fluctuated around the central rate at ±12.5%. Effective March 24, 1999, the width of the band was increased to ±15% around the central parity. Effective April 12, 2000, the zloty was allowed to float and trade freely against all currencies. Thus, the exchange arrangement was reclassified to the category independently floating from the category crawling band.

Exchange tax   No.

Exchange subsidy   No.

Forward exchange market   A liquid swap market exists.

Arrangements for Payments and Receipts

Prescription of currency requirements   Yes.

Payment arrangements

Bilateral payment arrangements

Inoperative   There are agreements with Iraq, the Syrian Arab Republic, Tunisia, and Turkey. Outstanding balances are being settled in accordance with the terms of the agreements.

Regional arrangements   Poland is a member of the CEFTA.

Clearing agreements   There are inoperative agreements with members of the former CMEA.

Administration of control   The authority to make basic changes in the Foreign Exchange Law rests with parliament. Regulations are promulgated by the MOF, in cooperation with the president of the National Bank of Poland (NBP). Individual permits are granted by the president of the NBP. The procedures for issuing such permits are established by the president of the NBP in cooperation with the MOF. Decisions concerning individual foreign exchange permits are subject to appeal to the Supreme Administrative Court. Foreign exchange control is exercised by the MOF, the NBP, foreign exchange banks, border guards, custom authorization authorities, and post offices. Effective January 12, 1999, a new foreign exchange law took effect making the zloty an externally convertible currency and allowing offshore zloty accounts. The new law retains some controls on short-term capital transactions, and permits the NBP to take emergency measures should serious risks arise to the stability and integrity of the financial system.

International security restrictions

In accordance with Executive Board Decision No. 144-(52/51)   In compliance with UN Security Council resolutions, Poland imposed and maintained a ban on trade with Iraq and on exports of certain products to Libya. The Polish government bans, in line with relevant UN Security Council resolutions, exports of arms and military equipment to the following countries: Angola (for UNITA forces), Haiti, Iraq, Liberia, Libya, Rwanda, Somalia, and the Federal Republic of Yugoslavia (Serbia/Montenegro).

In accordance with UN sanctions	Yes.
Payment arrears	No.
Controls on trade in gold (coins and/or bullion)	Polish and foreign nationals may take abroad gold coins (money coined after 1850) that bear value in foreign exchange. They may also bring into Poland coins made from precious metals that are legal tender in Poland.
Controls on domestic ownership and/or trade	Resident individuals may hold gold in any form; trading in gold, other than in jewelry form, is subject to permission from the NBP.
Controls on external trade	Polish and foreign nationals may take abroad gold coins that bear value in foreign exchange. They may also bring into Poland coins made from precious metals that are legal tender in Poland.

Controls on exports and imports of banknotes

On exports

Domestic currency	Residents and nonresidents may export up to €6,000. Documentary proof of origin is necessary for amounts exceeding this limit. There are no limitations on nonresident exports of foreign currencies, foreign securities, and traveler's checks. Residents must repatriate foreign exchange within two months of returning to Poland.
Foreign currency	Under the general foreign exchange permit, Polish nationals may take abroad up to €6,000 or its equivalent in foreign currencies, checks, and traveler's checks. Documentary proof of origin is necessary for amounts exceeding this limit. Residents must repatriate foreign exchange within two months of returning to Poland. For official and business travel, allowances are based on separate regulations on business travel and on collective wage agreements. Nonresidents are free to take out of Poland up to €2,000 or its equivalent; higher amounts are allowed, subject to permission.

On imports

Domestic currency	Residents and nonresidents may import up to €6,000. Documentary proof of origin is necessary for amounts exceeding this limit. There are no limitations on nonresident exports of foreign currencies, foreign securities, and traveler's checks. Residents must repatriate foreign exchange within two months of returning to Poland.
Foreign currency	Nonresidents entering Poland are permitted to have up to €2,000 or its equivalent in convertible currencies; higher amounts require permission. Residents must repatriate foreign exchange within two months after returning to Poland.

Resident Accounts

Foreign exchange accounts permitted	Yes.
Held domestically	Yes.
Held abroad	Residents (individuals and enterprises) carrying out economic activity abroad may hold foreign exchange accounts abroad to cover the costs of such activity and during their stay abroad. The NBP must be notified about accounts opened abroad, and quarterly balances in these accounts must be reported to the NBP.
Approval required	Yes.
Accounts in domestic currency convertible into foreign currency	No.

Nonresident Accounts

Foreign exchange accounts permitted   Yes.

Domestic currency accounts   These accounts may or may not pay interest, depending on an agreement with the bank, and they may be credited with funds from any title, but conversion into foreign currency and/or transfer abroad within three months from the date of deposit, in the case of term deposits for amounts exceeding Zl 500,000, is prohibited, except for funds freely transferable abroad.

Convertible into foreign currency   These accounts may be convertible into foreign currency, but approval is required.

Blocked accounts   No.

Imports and Import Payments

Foreign exchange budget   No.

Financing requirements for imports   No.

Documentation requirements for re-lease of foreign exchange for imports   No.

Import licenses and other nontariff measures   Licenses are not required for imports from the convertible currency area, with the exception of imports of radioactive materials and military equipment; alcoholic beverages other than beer; tobacco products; crude oil and oils obtained from bituminous minerals; gasoline and light oils; natural gas and other gaseous hydrocarbons; coal; and goods for industrial assembly of motor vehicles.

Negative list   The importation of passenger cars and other passenger vehicles older than 10 years; trucks, vans, other utility cars, and passenger vehicles older than three years for transportation of more than 10 persons; cars with two-cycle engines; and combine harvesters is prohibited.

Licenses with quotas   The importation of petroleum oils and oils obtained from bituminous minerals is subject to quantitative quotas.

Import taxes and/or tariffs   All commercial imports, regardless of country of origin or provenance, are subject to an ad valorem import tariff. Import tariffs are based on the Harmonized System and the Combined Nomenclature of the EU, with six basic rates: zero on equipment for the disabled, mineral resources, textiles, and cattle hides; up to 3% on other raw materials; 6% to 9% on basic parts of semifinished and finished goods; 12% to 25% on industrial goods; 25% to 30% on agriculture and textile products; and 30% on luxury goods. Imports from developing countries are granted preferential treatment under the GSP. Also, imports from 45 developing countries, tropical products, and many goods that are of interest to developing countries enter Poland duty-free. For the remaining goods imported from non-European developing countries whose per capita GDP is lower than Poland's, duties are reduced by 20% to 30% of the MFN rate. Duties and taxes on imports for export production are refunded. Imports of capital goods for new joint ventures are exempt from customs duties.

State import monopoly   No.

Exports and Export Proceeds

Repatriation requirements   Proceeds should be repatriated immediately.

Financing requirements   No.

Documentation requirements   No.

Export licenses   Licenses are required for exports carried out within the framework of international agreements that stipulate bilateral settlements and for temporary exports of capital goods and transport equipment for leasing motor vehicles.

Without quotas	Licenses are required for exports of radioactive materials and military equipment. Export licenses are required for goods subject to export quotas. Exports of specific species of live poultry are prohibited.
With quotas	Exports of waste and scrap of copper, nickel, aluminum, lead, zinc, and tin are subject to quota restrictions.
Export taxes	No.

Payments for Invisible Transactions and Current Transfers

Controls on these transfers	When payments exceed €20,000, all current operations must be done through domestic banks. Residents and nonresidents must document the payment or transfer to the bank if they exceed €20,000.
Credit card use abroad	Credit card use abroad is permitted, but the transaction must be in compliance with regulations.

Proceeds from Invisible Transactions and Current Transfers

Repatriation requirements	Proceeds must be repatriated immediately. Natural persons receiving proceeds while they are abroad must repatriate the proceeds within two months after returning to Poland.
Restrictions on use of funds	No.

Capital Transactions

Controls on capital and money market instruments	
On capital market securities	
Shares or other securities of a participating nature	
Purchase locally by nonresidents	Purchase of Polish securities by nonresidents is free, except for shares of which the freedom to purchase may be limited by Poland's restrictions of foreign direct investment. Purchases of securities by nonresidents with maturity of less than one year require a permit.
Sale or issue locally by nonresidents	A Securities and Exchange Commission (SEC) permit is required for publicly traded securities.
Purchase abroad by residents	A foreign exchange permit is required for residents to make portfolio investments in securities issued by nonresidents not domiciled or not having their seat in OECD countries or in countries with which the Republic of Poland has not concluded agreements on the promotion and mutual protection of investment. This regulation does not apply when residents purchase securities gratuitously. Residents need a foreign exchange permit to purchase securities with a maturity of less than one year.
Sale or issue abroad by residents	Residents are permitted to issue securities only in OECD countries or in the countries with which the Republic of Poland has concluded agreements on the promotion and mutual protection of investments. Residents need a foreign exchange permit to sell or issue securities with a maturity of less than one year.
Bonds or other debt securities	The same regulations apply as for shares or other securities of a participating nature.
On money market instruments	
Purchase locally by nonresidents	NBP approval is required, except for transactions carried out by the treasury, authorized banks, and other authorized financial institutions.
Sale or issue locally by nonresidents	NBP approval and SEC notification are required.

Purchase abroad by residents	NBP approval is required, except for transactions carried out by authorized banks and other authorized financial institutions.
Sale or issue abroad by residents	A permit is required for maturities of less than one year.

On collective investment securities

Purchase locally by nonresidents	Yes.
Sale or issue locally by nonresidents	Yes.
Purchase abroad by residents	The same regulations apply as for shares or other securities of a participating nature.
Sale or issue abroad by residents	The same regulations apply as for shares or other securities of a participating nature.

Controls on derivatives and other instruments

Purchase locally by nonresidents	As from January 12, 1999, financial derivative instruments listed on the Warsaw Stock Exchange, the Polish Financial Stock S.A., and CeTO S.A. may be traded freely. Operations carried out by authorized banks and other authorized financial institutions may be made freely.
Sale or issue locally by nonresidents	Yes.
Purchase abroad by residents	Authorized institutions may effect these transactions freely.
Sale or issue abroad by residents	Yes.

Controls on credit operations

Commercial credits	The NBP must be notified within 20 days.
By residents to nonresidents	Yes.
To residents from nonresidents	Yes.
Financial credits	
By residents to nonresidents	Financial credits with maturities of less than one year require a permit.
To residents from nonresidents	Financial credit operations with nonresidents resulting in a zloty debt with a maturity of less than one year are prohibited if the value of the transaction exceeds the equivalent of €50,000.
Guarantees, sureties, and financial backup facilities	
By residents to nonresidents	An NBP foreign exchange permit is required for guarantee transactions related to claims that are the result of restricted foreign exchange transactions.
To residents from nonresidents	Yes.

Controls on direct investment

Outward direct investment	An NBP foreign exchange permit is required for direct investments exceeding the equivalent of €1 million, with the exception of purchasing shares and interests of companies based in OECD countries and in the countries with which Poland has ratified agreements on the promotion and mutual protection of investments.
Inward direct investment	There are no controls in the foreign exchange law, but there are sectoral restrictions.

Controls on liquidation of direct investment

The transfer of profits from joint ventures and from investments in shares of Polish companies is not restricted, and invested capital may be repatriated once outstanding obligations to creditors are discharged.

Controls on real estate transactions

Purchase abroad by residents	An NBP foreign exchange permit is required for the purchase abroad by residents (natural persons) of real estate located abroad if the price on the day of such purchase is in excess of the equivalent of €50,000, and for the transfer abroad of the foreign currency required for the purchase of such real estate.

Purchase locally by nonresidents	Nonresidents may acquire real estate or other immovable property in Poland only with permission from the Ministry of the Interior, except in the form of an inheritance. Under the Law on Acquisition of Real Estate by Foreigners, foreigners may also acquire real estate without permit if (1) it is a separate apartment; (2) they have lived in Poland for at least five years after getting a permanent residence visa; (3) they are married to a Polish citizen for at least two years (the purchased real estate must form a part of matrimonial community property); or (4) real estate is purchased by nonresident legal persons for statutory purposes, and the area of real estate does not exceed 4,000 square meters in urban areas. The Council of Ministers may issue a regulation defining other cases where a permit is not required, providing that the area of acquired real estate does not exceed 4,000 square meters in urban and 10,000 square meters in rural areas. The Council of Ministers may also extend the area to be acquired without permit to 12,000 square meters in urban and 30,000 square meters in rural areas.
Sale locally by nonresidents	Yes.

Controls on personal capital movements

Loans	There are no controls on family loans.
By residents to nonresidents	Yes.
To residents from nonresidents	Yes.
Gifts, endowments, inheritances, and legacies	
By residents to nonresidents	NBP approval is needed for gifts above €10,000.
To residents from nonresidents	Yes.
Settlement of debts abroad by immigrants	Yes.
Transfer of gambling and prize earnings	Yes.

Provisions specific to commercial banks and other credit institutions

Borrowing abroad	There are controls on short-term borrowing.
Lending to nonresidents (financial or commercial credits)	Banks are permitted to purchase securities abroad within the limits specified in the regulation by the president of the NBP on the types of securities issued abroad to be purchased by authorized banks.
Differential treatment of deposit accounts in foreign exchange	Banks are not allowed to hold accounts for nonresidents in the form of time deposits in zloty with a maturity of less than three months for amounts exceeding Zl 500,000.
Reserve requirements	The reserve requirement on foreign currency accounts differs from that on zloty accounts.
Differential treatment of deposit accounts held by nonresidents	Effective January 12, 1999, a foreign exchange permit is required for deposit transactions made by nonresidents where the transaction involves deposits exceeding Zl 500,000 maturing in less than three months, and for foreign currency deposit transactions made by residents, except for those related to direct or portfolio investments that require no foreign exchange permits, or for those made from bank accounts maintained by individuals when residing abroad.
Open foreign exchange position limits	A bank's open (net) foreign currency position (long or short) in relation to a single foreign currency may not exceed 15% of the bank's capital. The president of the NBP, on the bank's motion, may consent to a foreign currency paid in consideration for equity to be included in computation of the bank's foreign currency position.
Provisions specific to institutional investors	Insurance companies are not affected by the foreign exchange operations in the country, and an MOF permit is required to commence insurance business. An MOF permit is required for investments by nonresidents in insurance companies through shares allowing for 25%, 33%, 50%, 60%, and 75% of votes, respectively, at general shareholders' meetings. Prudential regulations establishing limits for investment of insurance funds in the country and abroad are provided by the act on insurance operating activity.

Nonresidents are allowed to invest in participating units issued by trust funds. There are no foreign exchange restrictions on the transfer abroad by nonresidents of foreign currency purchase against Polish currency associated with remission of participating units in trust funds.

Other controls imposed by securities laws

No.

Changes During 1999

Exchange arrangement

January 1. The currency composite was changed to a basket composed of 55% euro and 45% dollar.

March 24. The monthly devaluation rate of the crawling band was reduced to 0.3%. The width of the band was increased to ±15% around the central parity.

Arrangements for payments and receipts

January 12. A new foreign exchange law took effect.

Capital transactions

January 12. A new foreign exchange law took effect that differentiates between banks and nonbank entities, noting that banks may conduct some short-term capital transactions, which would require a special foreign exchange permit for nonbanks.

Controls on derivatives and other instruments

January 12. Financial derivative instruments listed on the Warsaw Stock Exchange may be traded freely.

Provisions specific to commercial banks and other credit institutions

January 12. A foreign exchange permit is required for deposit transactions made by non-residents where the transaction involves deposits exceeding Zl 500,000 maturing in less than three months, and for foreign currency deposit transactions made by residents, except for those related to direct or portfolio investments that require no foreign exchange permits, or for those made from bank accounts maintained by individuals when residing abroad.

Changes During 2000

Exchange arrangement

April 12. The zloty was allowed to float and trade freely against all currencies. The exchange arrangement was reclassified to the category independently floating from the category crawling band.

PORTUGAL

(Position as of March 31, 2000)

Status Under IMF Articles of Agreement

Article VIII	Date of acceptance: September 12, 1988.

Exchange Arrangement

Currency	Effective January 1, 1999, the currency of Portugal is the euro. In cash transactions, however, the legal tender remains the Portuguese escudo until 2002, when euro banknotes and coins will be issued.
Exchange rate structure	Unitary.

Classification

Exchange arrangement with no separate legal tender	Portugal participates in a currency union (EMU) comprising 11 members of the EU: Austria, Belgium, Finland, France, Germany, Ireland, Italy, Luxembourg, the Netherlands, Portugal, and Spain. Internal conversion rates in respect to the national currencies of EMU participants were fixed to the euro on January 1, 1999, whereas the external exchange rate of the euro is market determined. The conversion rate between the euro and the Portuguese escudo was set at Esc 200.482 per €1. The ECB has the right to intervene to smooth out fluctuations in external exchange rates.
Exchange tax	No.
Exchange subsidy	No.
Forward exchange market	Yes.

Arrangements for Payments and Receipts

Prescription of currency requirements	No.
Payment arrangements	No.
Administration of control	There are no exchange controls. Foreign trade policy is implemented by the Ministry of Economy, which is responsible for administering trade controls and for issuing import and export licenses, declarations, and certificates.
International security restrictions	
In accordance with Executive Board Decision No. 144-(52/51)	Yes.
In accordance with UN sanctions	In compliance with UN Security Council resolutions and EU regulations, certain restrictions have been imposed on the making of payments and transfers for current international transactions with respect to Iraq, the Taliban (the Islamic State of Afghanistan), the Federal Republic of Yugoslavia (Serbia/Montenegro), and the UNITA movement in Angola.
Payment arrears	No.
Controls on trade in gold (coins and/or bullion)	A customs declaration is required for amounts exceeding Esc 2.5 million.
Controls on exports and imports of banknotes	The exportation or importation by residents or nonresidents of banknotes or coins and traveler's checks exceeding the equivalent of Esc 2.5 million must be declared to customs.

Resident Accounts

Foreign exchange accounts permitted	Yes.

Held domestically	Yes.
Held abroad	Yes.
Accounts in domestic currency convertible into foreign currency	Yes.

Nonresident Accounts

Foreign exchange accounts permitted	Yes.
Domestic currency accounts	Yes.
Convertible into foreign currency	Yes.
Blocked accounts	No.

Imports and Import Payments

Foreign exchange budget	No.
Financing requirements for imports	No.
Documentation requirements for release of foreign exchange for imports	No.
Import licenses and other nontariff measures	
Negative list	Imports of certain products are subject to an import license and are allowed under specific conditions, or are prohibited for reasons of health, public order, or the prevention of commercial fraud. For agricultural products covered by the CAP, an import certificate may be required. A few industrial products, such as steel products and some textiles and clothing, are subject to EU import restrictions when they originate in certain third countries. A more extensive restricted list applying to China includes some textiles and a small number of finished products.
Open general licenses	Products of dual use may require a certificate.
Licenses with quotas	Imports subject to quantitative restrictions require an import license. Generally, licenses are valid for six months for customs clearance purposes.
Other nontariff measures	For products under EU surveillance, the appropriate import documents, when required, are issued for statistical purposes and are granted automatically in four or five days.
Import taxes and/or tariffs	Yes.
State import monopoly	No.

Exports and Export Proceeds

Repatriation requirements	No.
Financing requirements	No.
Documentation requirements	No.
Export licenses	
Without quotas	For agricultural products covered by the CAP, an export certificate may be required. Products of dual use may require a certificate.
Export taxes	No.

Payments for Invisible Transactions and Current Transfers

Controls on these transfers	No.

Proceeds from Invisible Transactions and Current Transfers

Repatriation requirements	No.
Restrictions on use of funds	No.

Capital Transactions

Controls on capital and money market instruments — No.

On capital market securities

Shares or other securities of a participating nature

Sale or issue locally by nonresidents — Until March 1, 2000, when they were lifted, controls were applied on the introduction of foreign securities issued by residents of a non-EU member country that were not quoted on a recognized market of the issuer's country or of the country in which they were issued.

Bonds or other debt securities

Sale or issue locally by nonresidents — Until March 1, 2000, when they were lifted, controls were applied on the introduction of foreign securities issued by residents of a non-EU member country that were not quoted on a recognized market of the issuer's country or of the country in which they were issued.

Controls on derivatives and other instruments — No.

Controls on credit operations — No.

Controls on direct investment

Inward direct investment — Investments are permitted in all sectors except those that, under general law, are closed to private enterprise corporations. Foreign investments should be registered within 30 days after the operation has been made. Projects of special interest to the Portuguese economy are covered by a separate and contractual regime.

Controls on liquidation of direct investment — No.

Controls on real estate transactions — No.

Controls on personal capital movements — No.

Provisions specific to commercial banks and other credit institutions — No.

Open foreign exchange position limits — The prudential minimum own-funds requirements are applied on a nondiscriminatory basis.

Provisions specific to institutional investors

Limits (max.) on securities issued by nonresidents and on portfolio invested abroad — On April 30, 1999, a maximum limit of 10% on nonresident stocks quoted in stock markets of EU member countries was allowed.

Limits (max.) on portfolio invested abroad — Yes.

Limits (min.) on portfolio invested locally	On April 30, 1999, a minimum limit of 50% investment in Portuguese public debt securities with a maturity of over one year was allowed.
Currency-matching regulations on assets/liabilities composition	There is a requirement of 80% of currency matching of assets owned by insurance companies.
Other controls imposed by securities laws	The MOF issues regulations on the eligible assets of insurance companies and pension funds and of securities investment funds.

Changes During 1999

Exchange arrangement	*January 1.* The currency of Portugal became the euro. The exchange rate of the escudo was fixed irrevocably at Esc 200.482 per €1.
Capital transactions	
Provisions specific to institutional investors	*April 30.* A minimum limit of 50% investment in Portuguese public debt securities with maturity of over one year was allowed.
	April 30. A maximum limit of 10% on nonresident stocks quoted in stock markets of EU member countries was allowed.

Changes During 2000

Capital transactions	
Controls on capital and money market instruments	*March 1.* Controls were lifted on the introduction of foreign securities issued by residents of a non-EU member country that were not quoted on a recognized market of the issuer's country or of the country in which they were issued.

QATAR

(Position as of December 31, 1999)

Status Under IMF Articles of Agreement

Article VIII   Date of acceptance: June 4, 1973.

Exchange Arrangement

Currency   The currency of Qatar is the Qatar riyal.

Exchange rate structure   Unitary.

Classification

Conventional pegged arrangement   The official exchange rate for the Qatar riyal is pegged to the SDR at QR 4.7619 per SDR 1, within margins of ±7.25% around this rate. The Qatar Central Bank (QCB) sets daily rates for the dollar, the intervention currency. Exchange rates of commercial banks for transactions in dollars are based on the QCB's buying and selling rates. A spread of QR 0.0087 is applied to exchange transactions with the public. The buying and selling rates of commercial banks for other currencies are based on the QCB's rates for the dollar and on market rates for the currency concerned against the dollar.

Exchange tax   No.

Exchange subsidy   No.

Forward exchange market   In the commercial banking sector, importers may purchase foreign exchange in the forward market.

Arrangements for Payments and Receipts

Prescription of currency requirements   All settlements with Iraq and Israel are prohibited, as are all financial transactions with the Federal Republic of Yugoslavia (Serbia/Montenegro). No other prescription of currency requirements are in force.

Payment arrangements   No.

Administration of control   The QCB is the exchange control authority, but there is no exchange control legislation. Import licenses are issued by the Ministry of Finance, Economy, and Commerce.

International security restrictions   Financial transactions with the Federal Republic of Yugoslavia (Serbia/Montenegro) are prohibited.

In accordance with Executive Board Decision No. 144-(52/51)   Yes.

In accordance with UN sanctions   Yes.

Payment arrears   No.

Controls on trade in gold (coins and/or bullion)

Controls on external trade   For trading purposes, the buying and selling of gold and precious metals require import licenses and are subject to customs duty. Transactions involving Iraq and Israel are prohibited.

Controls on exports and imports of banknotes   No.

Resident Accounts

Foreign exchange accounts permitted	No distinction is made between accounts held by residents and those held by nonresidents.
Held domestically	Yes.
Held abroad	Yes.
Accounts in domestic currency convertible into foreign currency	Yes.

Nonresident Accounts

Foreign exchange accounts permitted	Yes.
Domestic currency accounts	Yes.
Convertible into foreign currency	These accounts may be converted, but approval is required.
Blocked accounts	No.

Imports and Import Payments

Foreign exchange budget	No.
Financing requirements for imports	No.
Documentation requirements for release of foreign exchange for imports	No.
Import licenses and other nontariff measures	Imports of alcoholic beverages, firearms, ammunition, and certain drugs are subject to licensing for reasons of health or public policy.
Negative list	All imports from Iraq and Israel are prohibited, as are imports of pork and its derivatives.
Import taxes and/or tariffs	Imports are generally subject to a customs tariff of 4%, which is the minimum rate applied by members of the GCC. The customs tariff on steel is 20%; on tobacco, 50%; and on alcohol, 100%. Imports from GCC member countries are exempt from tariffs.
State import monopoly	No.

Exports and Export Proceeds

Repatriation requirements	No.
Financing requirements	No.
Documentation requirements	No.
Export licenses	No.
Export taxes	No.

Payments for Invisible Transactions and Current Transfers

Controls on these transfers	No.

Proceeds from Invisible Transactions and Current Transfers

Repatriation requirements	No.

Restrictions on use of funds   No.

Capital Transactions

Controls on capital and money market instruments	No.
Controls on derivatives and other instruments	No.
Controls on credit operations	No.
Controls on direct investment	
Inward direct investment	Noncitizens may engage in simple crafts as well as in commerce, industry, agriculture, and services jointly with Qatar partners, who must hold at least 51% of the capital. Noncitizens may also establish companies specializing in contracting business with Qatar partners, subject to the above conditions, if it is determined that there is a need to establish such companies, or if there is a need for the experience and technology they provide.
Controls on liquidation of direct investment	No.
Controls on real estate transactions	No.
Controls on personal capital movements	
Transfer of assets	
Transfer abroad by emigrants	Yes.
Transfer into the country by immigrants	Yes.
Provisions specific to commercial banks and other credit institutions	No.
Provisions specific to institutional investors	No.
Other controls imposed by securities laws	No.

Changes During 1999

Exchange arrangement   *March 31.* The exchange rate arrangement was reclassified to conventional pegged arrangement from pegged exchange rate within horizontal bands.

ROMANIA

(Position as of January 31, 2000)

Status Under IMF Articles of Agreement

Article VIII	Date of acceptance: March 25, 1998.

Exchange Arrangement

Currency	The currency of Romania is the Romanian leu.
Other legal tender	The transferable ruble continues to be used as a unit of account for outstanding CMEA balances.
Exchange rate structure	Unitary.
Classification	
Managed floating with no pre-announced path for the exchange rate	The exchange rate of the leu is determined in the interbank foreign exchange market. The National Bank of Romania (NBR) intervenes in the exchange market to adjust the exchange rate of the leu and to build up foreign exchange reserves. Dealing in the foreign exchange market is subject to NBR authorization. All commercial banks are authorized to participate in the interbank foreign exchange market. Juridical persons other than authorized commercial banks may purchase or sell foreign exchange through authorized banks. Natural persons may purchase or sell foreign currency either through authorized banks or through foreign exchange offices. The NBR quotes rates for 15 currencies based on the rates for these currencies against the dollar in the countries concerned, and the rates for 11 currencies of the euro zone based on the rates of these currencies against the euro. Foreign exchange offices conduct transactions with banknotes of the above currencies and accept traveler's checks and cards denominated in these currencies.
Exchange tax	No.
Exchange subsidy	No.
Forward exchange market	The forward market is underdeveloped.
Official cover of forward operations	n.r.

Arrangements for Payments and Receipts

Prescription of currency requirements	Payments to and from countries with which Romania has bilateral payment arrangements are made only in convertible currencies and in accordance with the procedures set forth in those arrangements.
Payment arrangements	
Bilateral payment arrangements	
Operative	There are arrangements with China, the Democratic People's Republic of Korea, Pakistan, and some previous CMEA members, aimed at liquidating the balance of the CMEA accounts.
Inoperative	There are arrangements with Albania, Algeria, Costa Rica, Egypt, Greece, India, and the Islamic Republic of Iran. On October 10, 1999, a Memorandum of Understanding was signed with the Islamic Republic of Iran in order to liquidate the clearing account.
Regional arrangements	Romania is a member of the CEFTA and has free trade agreements with the EFTA countries, Turkey, and Moldova. Romania is an associated country to the EU.
Clearing agreements	There are clearing arrangements with Bangladesh and a few countries of the former CMEA, but they are only used to settle previous balances.

Administration of control	The NBR issues rules and regulations related to the control of foreign exchange transactions, and authorizes certain capital transfers.
International security restrictions	No.
Payment arrears	
Private	Yes.
Controls on trade in gold (coins and/or bullion)	
Controls on domestic ownership and/or trade	The NBR has sole authority to purchase or to sell gold in any manner. It may grant permission to certain juridical persons for such purposes.
Controls on external trade	There are no actual authorizations for conducting external trade.
Controls on exports and imports of banknotes	Amounts for the export and import of currency exceeding those detailed below have to be declared at customs and deposited against a receipt. On a further trip to Romania within three years, those amounts may be used; after three years, these are automatically passed to the state budget.
On exports	
Domestic currency	Natural persons may take out lei 500,000 a person a trip.
Foreign currency	Natural persons may take out foreign exchange up to the equivalent of $10,000 a person a trip.
On imports	
Domestic currency	Natural persons may bring into Romania up to lei 500,000 a person a trip.
Foreign currency	Natural persons may bring into Romania up to the equivalent of $10,000 a person a trip.

Resident Accounts

Foreign exchange accounts permitted	These accounts may be held by (1) juridical persons who are registered in Romania (i.e., public institutions, embassies, consulates, other Romanian representatives abroad); (2) autonomous state agencies, commercial companies, associations, clubs, leagues, and any other profit or nonprofit juridical persons authorized to carry on activities within the Romanian territory; (3) foreign branches, subsidiaries, representatives, and agencies; (4) Romanian citizens; (5) natural persons with foreign citizenship; and (6) stateless persons living in Romania.
Held domestically	Foreign exchange operations among residents are forbidden, except those authorized by the NBR.
Held abroad	
Approval required	Resident persons need NBR approval for holding accounts abroad, except the following categories: (1) banks for their activity conducted under the authorization of the NBR; (2) representation, agencies, offices of the Romanian juridical persons, which are not registered as juridical persons abroad, for current expenses necessary to carry out their activities abroad; (3) embassies, consulates, or other representations of Romania abroad; (4) residents legally owning real estate abroad for expenses related to the maintenance and administration of their property; (5) resident natural persons while staying abroad; these accounts may be maintained after their return to Romania; and (6) residents for the amounts which, because of legal obstacles, cannot be repatriated to Romania.
Accounts in domestic currency convertible into foreign currency	Full convertibility is permitted for current account transactions. Convertibility for capital account transactions is limited and requires prior approval of the NBR.

Nonresident Accounts

Foreign exchange accounts permitted	Yes.

Domestic currency accounts	The accounts in domestic currency are account type A, B, and deposit accounts: (1) accounts of type A are for depositing proceeds from current transactions, sales and purchases of foreign currency against leu, where the underlying transaction is of a current nature, transfers from B accounts, and interest earned on A and B accounts; (2) accounts of type B are for capital transactions, i.e., sales and purchases of foreign exchange against leu, where the underlying transaction is of a capital nature, proceeds from capital transactions, and transfers to/from A accounts; and (3) deposit accounts with the prior authorization of the NBR.
Convertible into foreign currency	Full convertibility is permitted for current account transactions stipulated by regulations (profits, dividends, interest, and other income sources resulting from legal transactions). Full convertibility is also permitted for most capital transactions of nonresidents in Romania (direct and real estate investments as well as liquidation of those and capital investments), which are freely allowed by law. Convertibility is also assured for all other capital transactions that are subject to authorization of the NBR. The conversion in foreign currencies is carried out provided that nonresidents submit to commercial banks the justifying documents including the authorization of the NBR in the case of deposit accounts. For the balances of accounts of type A, convertibility is permitted, within 180 days starting from the date of encashment. For the balances of accounts of type B and deposit accounts, convertibility is always permitted.
Approval required	Yes.
Blocked accounts	No.

Imports and Import Payments

Foreign exchange budget	No.
Financing requirements for imports	No.
Documentation requirements for release of foreign exchange for imports	Documentation is required in the case of all import payments.
Other	Yes.
Import licenses and other nontariff measures	Imports, in general, are not subject to licensing. The government may restrict imports for reasons of public health, national defense, and state security, in accordance with the provisions of the WTO.
Negative list	Yes.
Other nontariff measures	There is a custom's fee of 0.5% for imports outside the EU, CEFTA, EFTA, and Turkey.
Import taxes and/or tariffs	Tariff rates range between 3% and 144%, averaging about 19% for all goods on a trade-weighted basis. The 6% import surcharge was reduced to 4% on January 1, 1999, and further to 2% on January 1, 2000. It is applied to about 63% of imports.
State import monopoly	No.

Exports and Export Proceeds

Repatriation requirements	Resident juridical persons must maintain foreign exchange export proceeds in accounts opened at domestic commercial banks or foreign commercial banks authorized to operate in Romania but are free to use the balances in these accounts. Repatriation must be effected: (1) within 90 days from the goods crossing the border; and (2) within 15 days from the due date that appears in the contract.
Financing requirements	No.
Documentation requirements	No.
Export licenses	There are licenses for statistical purposes on certain new materials and low-processed goods.

Export taxes	There is a commission of 0.5% for exports outside the EU, EFTA, CEFTA, and Turkey.

Payments for Invisible Transactions and Current Transfers

Controls on these transfers	Payments and transfers must be documented.

Proceeds from Invisible Transactions and Current Transfers

Repatriation requirements	Repatriation must be effected within: (1) 90 days from completing the work or rendering the services; (2) 5 days from the due date that appears in the contract; and (3) 15 days from completing the work or rendering the services in the case of advance payments.
Restrictions on use of funds	No.

Capital Transactions

Controls on capital and money market instruments	
On capital market securities	
Shares or other securities of a participating nature	
Sale or issue locally by nonresidents	Sale by nonresidents is free, whereas issue requires NBR authorization and National Commission for Securities (NCS) approval.
Purchase abroad by residents	These transactions require NBR authorization.
Sale or issue abroad by residents	These transactions require NBR authorization.
Bonds or other debt securities	
Sale or issue locally by nonresidents	Yes.
Purchase abroad by residents	These transactions require NBR authorization.
Sale or issue abroad by residents	These transactions require NBR authorization.
On money market instruments	
Purchase locally by nonresidents	These transactions require NBR authorization.
Sale or issue locally by nonresidents	These transactions require NBR authorization.
Purchase abroad by residents	These transactions require NBR authorization, except for banks.
Sale or issue abroad by residents	These transactions require NBR authorization, except sale of money market securities by banks.
On collective investment securities	
Sale or issue locally by nonresidents	Sale by nonresidents is free, whereas issue requires NBR authorization and NCS approval.
Purchase abroad by residents	These transactions require NBR authorization.
Sale or issue abroad by residents	These transactions require NBR authorization.
Controls on derivatives and other instruments	
Sale or issue locally by nonresidents	Sale by nonresidents is free, whereas issue requires NBR authorization and NCS approval.
Purchase abroad by residents	These transactions require NBR authorization.
Sale or issue abroad by residents	These transactions require NBR authorization.

Controls on credit operations	Effective September 10, 1999, all credit operations extended by nonresidents to residents with a maturity exceeding one year were liberalized.
Commercial credits	
By residents to nonresidents	Yes.
To residents from nonresidents	Yes.
Financial credits	
By residents to nonresidents	These transactions require authorization, except for commercial banks.
To residents from nonresidents	Yes.
Guarantees, sureties, and financial backup facilities	
By residents to nonresidents	Those related to commercial credits of less than one year maturity or if extended by a commercial bank are free.
To residents from nonresidents	These transactions are free only if not related to financial credits.
Controls on direct investment	
Outward direct investment	These transactions require NBR authorization.
Inward direct investment	Investments of more than 5% in banks require NBR authorization.
Controls on liquidation of direct investment	No.
Controls on real estate transactions	
Purchase abroad by residents	These transactions require NBR authorization.
Controls on personal capital movements	
Loans	These transactions require NBR authorization.
By residents to nonresidents	Yes.
To residents from nonresidents	Yes.
Gifts, endowments, inheritances, and legacies	
By residents to nonresidents	These transactions require NBR authorization.
Transfer of assets	
Transfer abroad by emigrants	Yes.
Transfer of gambling and prize earnings	These transactions require NBR authorization only for residents.
Provisions specific to commercial banks and other credit institutions	
Lending to nonresidents (financial or commercial credits)	Requires NBR authorization for maturities longer than one year.
Differential treatment of deposit accounts in foreign exchange	
Reserve requirements	Interest rates paid on reserves are different for each currency.
Liquid asset requirements	n.r.
Interest rate controls	n.r.
Credit controls	n.r.
Differential treatment of deposit accounts held by nonresidents	n.r.

Investment regulations

Abroad by banks	Yes.
In banks by nonresidents	The authorization of the NBR is required for investments by residents or nonresidents of more than 5% in a bank's equity.

Open foreign exchange position limits n.r.

Provisions specific to institutional investors n.r.

Other controls imposed by securities laws n.r.

Changes During 1999

Arrangements for payments and receipts *October 10*. A Memorandum of Understanding was signed with the Islamic Republic of Iran to liquidate the clearing account.

Imports and import payments *January 1*. The rate of the import surcharge was reduced to 4% from 6%.

Capital transactions

Controls on credit operations *September 10*. All credit operations extended by nonresidents to residents with a maturity exceeding one year were liberalized.

Changes During 2000

Imports and import payments *January 1*. The import surcharge was reduced to 2%.

RUSSIAN FEDERATION

(Position as of December 31, 1999)

Status Under IMF Articles of Agreement

Article VIII   Date of acceptance: June 1, 1996.

Exchange Arrangement

Currency   The currency of Russia is the Russian ruble.

Exchange rate structure   Multiple.

Classification

Independently floating   The Central Bank of Russia (CBR) announces an official exchange rate each day. The official exchange rate is based on interbank market exchange rates and is used for accounting and taxation purposes, and for operations with the MOF. The dollar is the intervention currency of the CBR. The CBR participates in the Moscow Interbank Currency Exchange (MICEX) and interbank markets as a net buyer and seller of the dollar to smooth out short-term fluctuations in the exchange rate; it also trades in foreign exchange through direct dealing on the interbank market outside the organized exchanges.

Until the middle of 1999, a two-session regime for the trading of the dollar on interbank foreign currency exchanges was in effect; sessions took place in the morning and the afternoon. Trading in the morning sessions was subject to two principal limitations. First, authorized banks were only permitted to purchase foreign exchange for payments by resident legal entities in respect of imports, dividends, and certain financial credits. Second, exchange transactions could only take place at rates within a band of ±15% of the average weighted rate of the special session from the previous morning. Offers to purchase foreign exchange at rates that were outside these limits were not entered into the trading system. In addition, exporters were required to surrender 75% of export earnings in the morning session. While the rates at which exchange transactions took place within the special morning sessions could not deviate by more than 15% of the weighted average rate from the previous day's morning session, the rates at which exchange transactions took place outside of the sessions could deviate beyond these limits. In these circumstances, a spread of more than 2% could emerge between the rates within and outside of the special sessions. Access to the trading session in the afternoon was unrestricted. Also, interbank trading was permitted outside the sessions throughout the day. Effective June 29, 1999, the trading sessions of the interbank foreign currency exchanges were unified into a single trading session (UTS). Export proceeds in foreign currency exchanges have to be sold in the UTS or directly to the CBR. On September 30, 1999, on the basis of the obligation taken up by the authorities, the exchange rate system of the Russian Federation has been reclassified to the category independently floating from the category managed floating, no preannounced path.

Exchange tax   There is a 1% tax on purchases of foreign currencies and foreign payment instruments.

Exchange subsidy   No.

Forward exchange market   Forward contracts are sold by authorized banks. The futures markets on the MICEX have been temporarily shut down. Until January 1, 1999, a voluntary standstill was in effect on the servicing of forward currency contracts.

Arrangements for Payments and Receipts

Prescription of currency requirements   Yes.

Payment arrangements

Bilateral payment arrangements

   Operative

   Inoperative

Clearing agreements

Administration of control

International security restrictions

In accordance with Executive Board
Decision No. 144-(52/51)

In accordance with UN sanctions

Payment arrears

Official

**Controls on trade in gold (coins
and/or bullion)**

Controls on domestic ownership and/or
trade

Controls on external trade

**Controls on exports and imports of
banknotes**

On exports

   Domestic currency

   Foreign currency

	There are 24 arrangements.
	Agreements are maintained with the Islamic State of Afghanistan, Bulgaria, China, Cuba, the Czech Republic, Egypt, Hungary, India, Mongolia, Poland, the Slovak Republic, Slovenia, and the Syrian Arab Republic.
	Yes.
	The CBR is responsible for administering exchange control regulations, supervising and monitoring transactions of authorized banks, and regulating banks' open foreign exchange positions.
	Certain restrictions apply against the Federal Republic of Yugoslavia (Serbia/Montenegro).
	Yes.
	Yes.
	Domestic trade in gold is permitted. Monetary gold intended to be part of the country's foreign exchange reserves is purchased by the CBR and the government at world prices quoted on the London market and converted at the market exchange rate.
	Transactions in precious metals (gold and silver bullion) require authorization, and transactions must be effected through authorized banks possessing a special license issued by the CBR.
	Residents and nonresidents are allowed to take out a maximum of Rub 500,000 in banknotes.
	There are no limits on the amount of foreign banknotes a nonresident person may take out of the country, provided that a certificate from an authorized bank on the origin of the funds is presented to customs. Effective June 9, 1999, resident natural persons may take out of the Russian Federation foreign exchange not exceeding $10,000. Amounts exceeding this limit may be taken out only with the authorization of the CBR.

Resident Accounts

Foreign exchange accounts permitted

Held domestically

Held abroad

	Yes.
	Balances on these accounts may be used for effecting current foreign exchange transactions. The use of foreign exchange proceeds for capital transactions, with the exception of certain specific individual transactions, requires a CBR license.
	Resident natural persons may maintain bank accounts abroad only during their stay outside Russia for the purpose of education, employment, medical treatment, or visiting. Upon return to Russia, bank accounts abroad must be closed, and balances must be credited to accounts held in authorized banks operating in the territory of Russia. Resident juridical persons, including branches of Russian banks, may not maintain accounts abroad without special permission from the CBR. Resident banks may open correspondent accounts abroad in accordance with the procedures set out in the CBR's foreign exchange licenses.

Accounts in domestic currency convertible into foreign currency	Yes.

Nonresident Accounts

Foreign exchange accounts permitted Yes.

Domestic currency accounts

Nonresidents may maintain five types of ruble accounts: (1) "T" accounts, which may be credited with proceeds from current international transactions (including proceeds from sales of goods and services to residents of Russia and interest earnings on the account itself), and debited for the servicing of export-import operations by their representative offices in Russia; (2) correspondent ruble accounts for nonresident banks under the same regime applicable to T accounts; (3) "I" accounts, which may be used for investment activities (including privatization operations); (4) nonresident accounts for natural persons; and (5) "S" accounts for transactions involving government securities. The transfer abroad of balances in T accounts and correspondent ruble accounts accumulated after June 1, 1996, is not restricted. The use of balances accumulated up to May 31, 1996, is limited to domestic transactions. I accounts may be used for a wide range of investment activities, including profit and dividend transfers. Balances maintained in I accounts may be transferred abroad without restriction after payment of applicable taxes. Nonresident natural and juridical persons may purchase foreign exchange only with ruble balances held in I accounts. After March 31, 1999, before the balances from any of the five types of accounts may be repatriated, they have to be transferred to transit accounts in authorized banks. No interest is paid on these balances.

Convertible into foreign currency

Effective April 5, 1999, purchases of foreign exchange with ruble balances in correspondent accounts of foreign banks were prohibited. This prohibition was lifted on June 30, 1999. Repatriation and conversion of funds in the government securities market are subject to a one-year waiting period.

Approval required Yes.

Blocked accounts No.

Imports and Import Payments

Foreign exchange budget No.

Financing requirements for imports

Advance payment requirements

The CBR requires that all advance payments of Latvian food and consumer goods exports to Russia be for a maximum of 180 days. On March 29, 1999, a 100% deposit requirement for advance import payments was introduced. This requirement was reduced on April 14, 1999, by the amount of an LC by an authorized bank, the guarantee of a nonresident bank, a contract to cover the risk of nonrepatriation in the case of a default of the nonresident payer, a promissory note issued by a nonresident secured by a nonresident bank, or a special permit from the CBR.

Documentation requirements for release of foreign exchange for imports n.a.

Import licenses and other nontariff measures

Effective January 1, 1999, a ban on private imports of ethyl alcohol was imposed. Licenses are required for imports of various alcoholic products, as well as dual-purpose items, military equipment, medicine, industrial waste, and ozone-destructive substances.

Negative list Yes.

Import taxes and/or tariffs

Most customs duties range from 5% to 15%, but some tariff rates can be up to 30%. The following imports are exempt from duties: medicine, medical supplies and equipment, children's articles, and plant equipment. Imports from CIS countries are exempt from duties. On imports of commodities from developing countries (except those subject to excise duties) the customs duty rate is 75% of the basic rate.

State import monopoly	No.

Exports and Export Proceeds

Repatriation requirements	The repatriation ratio is 100%.
Surrender requirements	This surrender requirement was raised to 75% from 50% effective January 1, 1999. At the same time, the period within which surrender must be effected was shortened to 7 days from 14 days.
Financing requirements	CBR permission is required for foreign exchange transactions associated with deferred payments for exports of goods from Russia for a period exceeding 90 days and for deferrals granted to residents to make advance payments against deliveries of imported goods exceeding 180 days. All payment of Latvian energy, metals, and raw material imports from Russia are to be settled within 180 days.
Documentation requirements	n.a.
Export licenses	Export licensing is limited to a small group of products (e.g., military equipment and arms, precious metals and stones, rare animals and plant species, and dual-purpose items). Export licenses are issued by the Ministry of Trade in accordance with application procedures established by the government.
With quotas	Yes.
Export taxes	By February 28, 1999, export taxes were reintroduced, initially for a period of six months (owing to the need to notify Russia's customs union partners), on a number of commodities, including some varieties of seeds, skins and leather, timber, nonferrous metal products and scrap, coal, crude oil, and petroleum products. In general, the taxes were set at a rate of 5%. During 1999, these taxes were renewed, generally increased, and broadened in scope to include some additional forest products, metals and metal products, fuel products, and chemicals and fertilizers. At the end of 1999, export taxes applied to about 170 items, and rates changed to 30% from 5%, with specific duties on a number of commodities, including a rate of €15 per 1000 kilograms for crude oil and crude petroleum products from bituminous materials.

Payments for Invisible Transactions and Current Transfers

Controls on these transfers	On December 30, 1999, a special procedure was introduced whereby execution of payments by residents exceeding the equivalent of $10,000 in foreign currency for services related to intellectual activity required that a confirmation issued by the Foreign Exchange Control Agency (VEK) be submitted to the bank.

Proceeds from Invisible Transactions and Current Transfers

Repatriation requirements	Yes.
Surrender requirements	Proceeds from invisibles, except those from banking services, are subject to the surrender requirement.
Restrictions on use of funds	No.

Capital Transactions

Controls on capital and money market instruments	In the middle of 1998, the authorities suspended repayments and converted all treasury bills maturing before end-1999 into longer-term paper.

On capital market securities

*Shares or other securities of a
participating nature*

    Purchase locally by nonresidents

Nonresidents may purchase from residents securities denominated in foreign exchange with foreign exchange, provided that the residents obtain a license from the CBR for these transactions, as well as for securities denominated in rubles with rubles.

No prior authorization is required to purchase securities denominated in rubles with rubles. Securities denominated in rubles or in foreign exchange may be purchased with funds from type T ruble accounts. Securities denominated in foreign exchange or in rubles with a maturity of more than one year may be purchased with funds from type I accounts as well as from ruble correspondent accounts of nonresident banks.

The parties must notify the Federal Securities Market Commission (FKRTsB) of transactions involving the purchase by nonresidents of securities issued by residents.

    Sale or issue locally by nonresidents

Nonresidents may sell to residents securities denominated in foreign exchange for foreign exchange, provided the residents have a CBR license allowing such transactions, as well as securities denominated in rubles for rubles. The sale by nonresidents of securities denominated in rubles for rubles does not require prior authorization. The parties to such transactions must notify the FKRTsB of concluded transactions for the purchase by residents of securities issued by nonresidents.

Securities issued by nonresidents are permitted to circulate or be initially placed in the securities market after registration of their prospectus with the FKRTsB. These securities should be denominated in rubles.

Foreign exchange proceeds from the sale of securities are credited to foreign exchange accounts opened by nonresidents in authorized banks, from which they may be freely transferred abroad. Ruble proceeds from the sale of securities and from securities issues may be credited to type T ruble accounts of nonresidents opened in authorized banks, or to ruble correspondent accounts of nonresident banks.

    Purchase abroad by residents

Prior CBR approval is required.

    Sale or issue abroad by residents

CBR approval is required. Proceeds from the sale are credited to current foreign exchange accounts of residents. Exports of securities by residents require prior authorization from the MOF and the State Customs Committee.

Bonds or other debt securities

Russia's domestic debt includes primarily the following types of liabilities: government short-term, zero-coupon bonds (GKOs) and federal bonds (OFZs); government nonmarket bonds (OGNZs); government savings bonds; and domestic foreign exchange securities.

    Purchase locally by nonresidents

Nonresidents may effect operations with Russian issuers of securities included in a list compiled by the CBR by using S accounts in authorized banks. Currently, this list includes GKOs and OFZs, two issues of OGNZs, and Russian issuers' shares and corporate bonds put on a listing of trade organizers, in compliance with the CBR's requirements. As regards OGNZs, investors purchase them from the MOF in compliance with a respective agreement between the MOF and a particular investor. OGNZs are not traded in the secondary market.

On money market instruments

    Purchase locally by nonresidents

For nongovernment instruments, the same regulations apply as for capital markets.

The purchase by nonresidents of GKOs and OFZs is carried out from type S accounts. Nonresidents are no longer permitted to invest new funds in the government securities market.

    Sale or issue locally by nonresidents

The same regulations apply as for securities of a participating nature.

    Purchase abroad by residents

The same regulations apply as for securities of a participating nature.

    Sale or issue abroad by residents

The same regulations apply as for securities of a participating nature.

On collective investment securities

Transactions with nonresidents in foreign exchange may be carried out only if residents have authorization from the CBR to conclude such transactions. The parties should notify the FKRTsB of concluded transactions.

Purchase locally by nonresidents	The FKRTsB should be notified of purchases by nonresidents of collective investment securities issued by residents.
Sale or issue locally by nonresidents	Collective investment securities issued by nonresidents require a registration prospectus for the securities with the FKRTsB. These securities must be denominated in rubles.
	Foreign exchange proceeds from the sale of these securities must be credited to foreign exchange accounts and may be transferred abroad freely.
Purchase abroad by residents	Residents need prior authorization from the CBR to transfer foreign exchange in order to purchase these securities abroad. Funds for these purchases may be transferred from current foreign exchange accounts.
	Residents need prior authorization from the CBR to purchase securities denominated in foreign exchange in Russia.
Sale or issue abroad by residents	The sale abroad by residents of collective investment securities for foreign exchange and the transfer of proceeds from the sale require prior authorization from the CBR. Proceeds from the sale are credited to current foreign exchange accounts.
	Collective investment securities issued by a resident may circulate abroad, provided FKRTsB approval is granted. Residents may issue collective investment securities abroad with prior authorization from the CBR. The export by residents of collective investment securities requires prior authorization from the CBR and the State Customs Committee.

Controls on derivatives and other instruments

Purchase locally by nonresidents	Purchases in foreign exchange are permitted, provided residents have prior authorization from the CBR. The purchase of derivatives with rubles may be carried out freely from type T ruble accounts.
Sale or issue locally by nonresidents	Proceeds from sales of foreign exchange are allowed, provided the residents have prior authorization from the CBR. Foreign exchange proceeds may be transferred abroad freely.
	Ruble proceeds from sales may be used only within the territory of Russia or may be credited to ruble correspondent accounts of nonresident banks.
Purchase abroad by residents	Purchases are permitted, provided prior authorization from the CBR to transfer foreign exchange is granted. The transfer of funds to purchase derivatives abroad must be carried out from foreign exchange accounts.
Sale or issue abroad by residents	Sales are permitted with prior authorization from the CBR. The transfer of proceeds from the sales requires prior authorization from the CBR. Proceeds must be credited to current foreign exchange accounts.

Controls on credit operations

Commercial credits

By residents to nonresidents	Credits in the form of prepayment imported commodities, services, and intellectual property with delivery of more than 90 days may be granted only after government authorization.
	Credits with a maturity of less than 90 days may be extended only after authorization.

Financial credits

By residents to nonresidents	Credits for more than 180 days may be extended only after prior authorization from the CBR.
	Credits with an original maturity of less than 180 days may be extended only after prior authorization from the CBR.
To residents from nonresidents	Residents may borrow with a maturity of more than 180 days only after prior authorization from the CBR or after registration by its territorial branches.
	Credits with an original maturity of less than 180 days may be extended only after prior authorization from the CBR or after registration by its territorial branches.

Guarantees, sureties, and financial backup facilities	
By residents to nonresidents	The performance of obligations under bank guarantees, as well as under surety agreements in which the party extending the surety is a resident but not an authorized bank, may be carried out only after prior authorization from the CBR.

Controls on direct investment

Outward direct investment	Investments must be authorized by the CBR. Capital outflow to Latvia for direct and portfolio investments is not allowed without guarantees of the government of Latvia on the return of the investment and its earnings, and guarantees against the discrimination of entities with Russian capital.
Inward direct investment	Investment effected through joint ventures or through outright ownership is not restricted, except in banking, where it is limited to 12% of the aggregate authorized capital; in the exploration of natural resources, where a special license is required; or in landownership, where it is prohibited. Enterprises with foreign capital shares must register with the Ministry of Economy. Investments exceeding Rub 100 million require a permit from the Council of Ministers. Foreign direct investments are accorded the same rules and privileges with regard to property ownership and economic activities as those accorded to residents. Foreign direct investments may be nationalized or expropriated only in exceptional cases in accordance with legislation, and, in such cases, the investor is entitled to compensation. There are provisions protecting foreign investment, including a "grandfather" clause that protects foreign investment for a three-year period from regulatory acts that would adversely affect their activities and a provision that any restrictions on activities of foreign investors can be introduced only by Russian law or by presidential decree.
	Direct investment by crediting the account of the resident with foreign exchange requires prior authorization from the CBR.
	Direct investments from funds converted into rubles must be registered by the territorial branch of the CBR.

Controls on liquidation of direct investment	Liquidation requires prior authorization from the CBR. The transfer abroad of proceeds is carried out by selling ruble funds credited to type I ruble accounts for foreign exchange, which may be freely exported.
Controls on real estate transactions	Prior authorization from the CBR is required for all real estate transactions.

Controls on personal capital movements

Loans

By residents to nonresidents	Credits may be granted only after prior authorization from the CBR.
To residents from nonresidents	Residents may lend to nonresidents only after prior authorization from the CBR.
Provisions specific to commercial banks and other credit institutions	Effective February 12, 1999, sanctions were introduced on banks violating reporting requirements on foreign exchange transactions. The regulation prohibits access of violating banks to the foreign currency market for transactions on their own account and that of their clients.
Borrowing abroad	Borrowing by authorized banks possessing a general foreign exchange license does not require prior authorization from the CBR.
Maintenance of accounts abroad	Authorized banks may open correspondent accounts in banks abroad pursuant to the terms specified in the banking license issued by the CBR (restrictions may be imposed on the number of banks that may open correspondent accounts). The opening of other types of accounts in banks abroad requires prior authorization from the CBR.
Lending to nonresidents (financial or commercial credits)	Only authorized banks may lend to nonresidents.
Lending locally in foreign exchange	Only authorized banks are allowed to lend to residents in foreign exchange.
Purchase of locally issued securities denominated in foreign exchange	Authorized banks may purchase locally issued securities denominated in foreign exchange without prior authorization from the CBR. Other banks may purchase locally issued securities denominated in foreign exchange only after prior authorization from the CBR.

Differential treatment of deposit accounts in foreign exchange	
Reserve requirements	After March 31, 1999, banks are subject to a 100% reserve requirement on the funds held in the transit accounts of nonresidents.
Investment regulations	The CBR does not consider requests of credit institutions to open branches in Latvia, of Latvian banks and affiliates to start operations in Russia, or of residents of Latvia to participate in existing credit institutions, and it does not allow Russian credit institutions to participate in statutory capital of subsidiaries in Latvia.
Abroad by banks	Direct investments require prior authorization of the CBR.
In banks by nonresidents	Direct investments require prior authorization of the CBR.
Open foreign exchange position limits	Effective January 1, 1999, the open foreign currency position of commercial banks is limited to 20% of capital for all currencies and 10% of capital for any individual currency. These limits are applicable on a stock and transaction date basis. A neutral or long position is required in rubles on a flow basis at value date or the actual date of the delivery of funds to the accounts of the contracting party to the deal.
Provisions specific to institutional investors	Investment by institutional investors in securities denominated in foreign exchange requires prior authorization from the CBR.
Limits (max.) on portfolio invested abroad	Resident insurance companies may invest up to 20% abroad.
Limits (min.) on portfolio invested locally	Resident insurance companies must invest at least 80% locally.
Other controls imposed by securities laws	The federal law governing the securities market prohibits the application of preference to one potential owner over another in the purchase of securities to nonresidents.

Changes During 1999

Status under IMF Articles of Agreement	*January 1.* The voluntary standstill on the servicing of forward currency contracts was lifted.
Exchange arrangement	*June 29.* The trading sessions of the interbank foreign currency exchanges were unified into a single trading session.
	September 30. The exchange rate of Russia has been reclassified to the category independently floating from the category managed floating, no preannounced path.
Arrangements for payments and receipts	*June 9.* Resident natural persons were allowed to take out of Russia foreign exchange not exceeding $10,000.
Nonresident accounts	*March 31.* Before the balances from the five types of nonresident accounts can be repatriated, they must be transferred to transit accounts in authorized banks.
	April 5. Purchases of foreign exchange with ruble balances in correspondent accounts of foreign banks were prohibited.
	June 30. The prohibition to purchase foreign exchange with ruble balances in correspondent accounts of foreign banks was lifted.
Imports and import payments	*January 1.* A ban on private imports of ethyl alcohol was imposed. Licenses are required for the import of a number of items.
	March 29. A 100% deposit requirement for advance import payments was introduced.
	April 14. The deposit requirement for advance import payments was reduced by the amount of an LC by an authorized bank, a guarantee of a nonresident bank, a contract to cover the risk of nonrepatriation in the case of a default of the nonresident payer, a promissory note issued by a nonresident secured by a nonresident bank, or a special permit from the CBR.
Exports and export proceeds	*January 1.* A temporary six-month export tax was introduced on a number of commodities.

January 1. The export surrender requirement was raised to 75%, and the period within which the surrender must be effected was shortened to 7 days from 14 days.

February 28. Export taxes were reintroduced on a number of commodities.

Proceeds from invisible transactions and current transfers

December 30. A special procedure was introduced whereby execution of payments by residents exceeding the equivalent of $10,000 in foreign currency for services related to intellectual activity required a confirmation issued by the VEK to be submitted to the bank.

Capital transactions

Provisions specific to commercial banks and other credit institutions

January 1. The open foreign currency position of commercial banks was limited to 20% of the capital for all currencies and to 10% of capital for any individual currency.

February 12. Sanctions were introduced on banks violating reporting requirements on foreign exchange transactions. The regulation prohibits access of violating banks to the foreign currency market for transactions on their own account and that of their clients.

March 31. Banks were subject to a 100% reserve requirement on the funds in transit accounts.

RWANDA

(Position as of December 31, 1999)

Status Under IMF Articles of Agreement

Article VIII	Date of acceptance: December 10, 1998.

Exchange Arrangement

Currency	The currency of Rwanda is the Rwanda franc.
Exchange rate structure	Unitary.
Classification	
Independently floating	The exchange rate of the Rwanda franc is determined freely in the exchange market in which commercial banks and foreign exchange bureaus operate. Banks may apply a variable commission to these operations. Until January 1, 1999, when it was eliminated, outward and inward transfers were subject to a commission of 4%. The National Bank of Rwanda (NBR) does not announce official exchange rates, but it calculates and publishes daily the average market exchange rate for reference purposes.
Exchange tax	No.
Exchange subsidy	No.
Forward exchange market	Effective May 7, 1999, a forward exchange market was created. However, this market is not yet operational.

Arrangements for Payments and Receipts

Prescription of currency requirements	No.
Payment arrangements	
Regional arrangements	The NBR maintains agreements with the central banks of the CEPGL. Under these arrangements, settlements are made through reciprocal accounts in convertible currency. Payments to and from other member countries of the COMESA are made through the COMESA's clearinghouse, which is currently being restructured.
Clearing agreements	Yes.
Barter agreements and open accounts	An arrangement exists with Uganda, but it is not operational.
Administration of control	Foreign exchange control is vested in the NBR, which has delegated authority to authorized banks and foreign exchange bureaus to carry out some of the controls.
International security restrictions	No.
Payment arrears	
Official	Yes.
Private	Yes.
Controls on trade in gold (coins and/or bullion)	
Controls on domestic ownership and/or trade	Trade is restricted to dealers who are approved by the relevant ministry.
Controls on external trade	Imports and exports of gold require a declaration.

Controls on exports and imports of banknotes

On exports

Domestic currency   A declaration is required for exports of banknotes exceeding the equivalent of $100.

Foreign currency   Only foreign exchange purchased from an authorized dealer may be exported freely. Foreign exchange declared to customs on entry in the country may be reexported upon the presentation of the declaration documents.

On imports

Domestic currency   Declaration is required for the import of banknotes exceeding the equivalent of $100.

Resident Accounts

Foreign exchange accounts permitted   Effective September 3, 1999, foreign currency withdrawals exceeding $2,500 a transaction or $5,000 a year, including transfers to nonresidents, require supporting documentation. The same requirement applies to transfers by residents from their domestic currency accounts to their own foreign currency accounts.

Held domestically   Yes.

Held abroad   These accounts may be opened, but approval is required.

Accounts in domestic currency convertible into foreign currency   No.

Nonresident Accounts

Foreign exchange accounts permitted   Effective September 3, 1999, supporting documentation is required for deposits of foreign currency by residents and nonresidents and deposits from nonresidents' or residents' domestic and/or foreign currency accounts.

Domestic currency accounts   Yes.

Convertible into foreign currency   No.

Blocked accounts   No.

Imports and Import Payments

Foreign exchange budget   No.

Financing requirements for imports   No.

Documentation requirements for release of foreign exchange for imports   Imports are generally paid for after delivery. However, authorized banks can make advance payment upon presentation of supporting documentation showing that such payment is needed. They may also sell up to $50,000 in foreign exchange to importers who request this for imports of goods and services, with supporting documents to be presented later; such transactions must be settled by check or bank transfer. Imports through banks must be accompanied by a pro forma invoice stating the f.o.b. value of the merchandise.

Preshipment inspection   Imports with an f.o.b. value of $5,000 or more ($3,000 for fresh foodstuffs and pharmaceuticals) and any partial deliveries of these goods must be inspected by an international agency with regard to the quality, quantity, price, and customs tariff of the goods before being shipped to Rwanda, unless otherwise provided by the NBR. On December 24, 1999, petroleum products became subject to inspection.

Import licenses used as exchange licenses   Yes.

Import licenses and other nontariff measures

Negative list

All imports of narcotics are prohibited. Certain categories of imports, such as explosives and weapons, require prior approval from the relevant authorities, regardless of origin and value. For reasons of health, the importation of human or veterinary medicines, disinfectants, insecticides, rodent poisons, fungicides, herbicides, and other toxic or potentially toxic chemicals is subject to approval of the relevant pro forma invoices by the Ministry of Health.

Open general licenses

Yes.

Import taxes and/or tariffs

In addition to customs duty, a file processing charge, equal to 0.9% of the f.o.b. value of imported general merchandise (the minimum charge being RF 60,000) and 0.7% of the f.o.b. value for petroleum products, is levied when imports are declared, to cover costs incurred by the inspection agency. Effective January 1, 1999, maximum import tariffs were reduced to 25% from 40%, and the intermediate rates to 15% and 5% from 20% and 10%, respectively. Most capital goods remain subject to a zero tariff.

State import monopoly

No.

Exports and Export Proceeds

Repatriation requirements

Proceeds must be repatriated within seven days from the date of payment and may be held in their entirety on foreign exchange accounts maintained by the exporter at authorized banks.

Financing requirements

No.

Documentation requirements

All exports, except trade samples and personal and household effects of travelers, are subject to prior declaration to the authorized banks.

Export licenses

Without quotas

Yes.

Export taxes

The tax levied on coffee exports was eliminated on January 1, 1999.

Payments for Invisible Transactions and Current Transfers

Controls on these transfers

Investment-related payments

Prior approval

Payments are permitted on loans and for interest payments under contracts to be submitted to the NBR with proof that the funds were initially received locally either in cash or in kind. Approval by an authorized bank is required for payments of profits and dividends and is subject to proof being supplied that taxes for the current fiscal year have been provisioned and to a decision by the board of directors of the company concerned.

Payments for travel

Quantitative limits

Official travel requires a travel authorization by the government or by an authorized agency. Daily allowances are granted for such travel. Businessmen may purchase up to $10,000 in payment instruments for each trip, but the number of business trips is not restricted. A maximum allowance of $4,000 a trip is granted for tourism.

Personal payments

There are no controls on the payment of pensions.

Quantitative limits

For medical costs, unless waived by the NBR, residents may purchase up to $20,000 with supporting documents; prior authorization by the NBR is required for transfers of $20,000 or more. Unless waived by the NBR, purchases of foreign exchange for educational expenses are authorized within a limit of $25,000 a year a student on presentation of supporting documents. Authorized banks may freely approve requests for foreign exchange to cover expenses for a resident's family members living abroad for up to

$1,000 a resident a year and to sell freely up to $10,000 a person to resident nationals taking up residence abroad.

Indicative limits/bona fide test	Yes.
Foreign workers' wages	Salaries and wages earned by foreign nationals employed in Rwanda under contract, net of taxes and employee's share of social security contributions, may be transferred abroad. The net earned income of self-employed foreign nationals, whether engaged in a profession or established as independent traders, may also be transferred abroad after payment of taxes. The employee is liable for income tax and social security contributions.
Prior approval	Yes.
Quantitative limits	Prior authorization from the NBR is required for amounts exceeding $20,000 a year.
Other payments	Transfers of airline receipts are allowed, provided authorized banks ensure that landing and handling taxes have been paid and the amounts of transfer represent only the net amounts of all local expenditures.

Proceeds from Invisible Transactions and Current Transfers

Repatriation requirements	Yes.
Surrender requirements	Proceeds may be sold in the domestic foreign exchange market or may be held in foreign exchange accounts with banks located in the country.
Restrictions on use of funds	No.

Capital Transactions

Controls on capital and money market instruments	Presently, only the money market is operational.
On capital market securities	These transactions are governed by the pertinent business law provisions.
Shares or other securities of a participating nature	
Sale or issue locally by nonresidents	Yes.
Purchase abroad by residents	Prior authorization of the NBR is required.
Bonds or other debt securities	
Sale or issue locally by nonresidents	Yes.
Purchase abroad by residents	Yes.
On money market instruments	
Purchase locally by nonresidents	Nonresidents may participate in the secondary market.
Purchase abroad by residents	Prior authorization of the NBR is required.
On collective investment securities	
Purchase abroad by residents	Prior authorization of the NBR is required.
Sale or issue abroad by residents	Sale proceeds must be repatriated.
Controls on derivatives and other instruments	No.
Controls on credit operations	All credit transactions, including those related to guarantees, sureties, and financial backup facilities, are subject to NBR approval.
Controls on direct investment	
Outward direct investment	Investments are subject to NBR approval.

Controls on liquidation of direct investment	Repatriation of investments by nonresidents is governed by the investment code and must be registered by authorized banks.
Controls on real estate transactions	
Purchase abroad by residents	Prior NBR approval is required.
Controls on personal capital movements	
Loans	
By residents to nonresidents	Prior NBR approval is required.
To residents from nonresidents	Proof of entry of the funds into Rwanda is required at the time of payment.
Gifts, endowments, inheritances, and legacies	
By residents to nonresidents	NBR approval is required.
Settlement of debts abroad by immigrants	NBR approval is required.
Transfer of assets	
Transfer abroad by emigrants	NBR approval is required.
Provisions specific to commercial banks and other credit institutions	
Borrowing abroad	Borrowing is allowed under certain conditions.
Lending to nonresidents (financial or commercial credits)	Lending is allowed under certain conditions.
Open foreign exchange position limits	Effective May 5, 1999, a limit of 20% of a bank's capital and reserves is applied.
Provisions specific to institutional investors	No.
Other controls imposed by securities laws	No.

Changes During 1999

Exchange arrangement	*January 1.* The commission on outward and inward transfers was eliminated.
	May 7. A forward exchange market was created, but it is not yet operational.
Resident accounts	*September 3.* Foreign currency withdrawals exceeding $2,500 a transaction or $5,000 a year, including transfers to nonresidents, required supporting documentation. The same requirement applied to transfers by residents from their domestic currency accounts to their own foreign currency accounts.
Nonresident accounts	*September 3.* Supporting documentation was required for deposits of foreign currency by residents and nonresidents and deposits from nonresidents' or residents' domestic and/or foreign currency accounts.
Imports and import payments	*January 1.* Maximum import tariffs were reduced to 25%, and the intermediate rates to 15% and 5%.
	December 24. Petroleum products became subject to preimport inspection.
Exports and export proceeds	*January 1.* The tax on coffee exports was eliminated.
Capital transactions	
Provisions specific to commercial banks and other credit institutions	*May 5.* The open foreign exchange position was set at 20% of a bank's capital and reserves.

ST. KITTS AND NEVIS

(Position as of December 31, 1999)

Status Under IMF Articles of Agreement

Article VIII   Date of acceptance: December 3, 1984.

Exchange Arrangement

Currency   The currency of St. Kitts and Nevis is the Eastern Caribbean dollar, issued by the ECCB.

Exchange rate structure   Unitary.

Classification

Exchange arrangement with no sepa-   The Eastern Caribbean dollar is pegged to the U.S. dollar, the intervention currency, at
rate legal tender   EC$2.70 per US$1. The ECCB also quotes daily rates for the Canadian dollar and the
                                 pound sterling.

Exchange tax   No.

Exchange subsidy   No.

Forward exchange market   No.

Arrangements for Payments and Receipts

Prescription of currency   Settlements with residents of ECCB countries must be effected in Eastern Caribbean
requirements   dollars.

Payment arrangements

Regional arrangements   St. Kitts and Nevis is a member of the CARICOM.

Administration of control   Exchange control is administered by the MOF and applies to all countries.

International security restrictions   n.a.

Payment arrears   No.

Controls on trade in gold (coins   No.
and/or bullion)

Controls on exports and imports of   No.
banknotes

Resident Accounts

Foreign exchange accounts permitted   U.S. dollar accounts may be operated freely, but permission of the MOF is required to
                                 operate other foreign currency accounts.

Held domestically   These accounts may be credited only with foreign currency earned or received from abroad
                                 and may be freely debited. A minimum balance of US$1,000 must be maintained at all
                                 times to operate a U.S. dollar account. Permission is normally confined to major exporters.

Accounts in domestic currency   n.a.
convertible into foreign currency

Nonresident Accounts

Foreign exchange accounts permitted

The same regulations apply as for residents. Permission to operate foreign currency accounts is normally confined to foreign nationals not ordinarily residing in St. Kitts and Nevis.

Domestic currency accounts

n.a.

Blocked accounts

n.a.

Imports and Import Payments

Foreign exchange budget

No.

Financing requirements for imports

Advance payment requirements

Advance import payments exceeding EC$250,000 require prior approval from the MOF.

Documentation requirements for release of foreign exchange for imports

Payments for authorized imports payable in foreign currency are permitted on presentation of documentary evidence of purchase to a bank.

Import licenses and other nontariff measures

Individual licenses are required for imports that compete with local products unless they come from another member country of the CARICOM.

Open general licenses

Most goods are imported under OGLs.

Import taxes and/or tariffs

St. Kitts and Nevis applies the CET of CARICOM, which ranges up to 30%.

State import monopoly

n.a.

Exports and Export Proceeds

Repatriation requirements

Yes.

Surrender requirements

Export proceeds must be deposited into an ECCB currency account or an approved U.S. dollar account.

Financing requirements

n.a.

Documentation requirements

n.a.

Export licenses

Specific licenses are required for the exportation of certain goods to any destination. However, the regulations governing export licenses are not formally adhered to.

Export taxes

Export duties are levied on a few products.

Payments for Invisible Transactions and Current Transfers

Controls on these transfers

Prior approval of the MOF is required for all transactions exceeding EC$250,000.

Investment-related payments

Profits and dividends may be remitted in full, subject to confirmation of registration by the Commissioner of Inland Revenue for income tax purposes. Information is not available on the payment of amortization of loans or depreciation of direct investments.

Proceeds from Invisible Transactions and Current Transfers

Repatriation requirements

Yes.

Surrender requirements

Proceeds must be sold to a bank or deposited into an approved U.S. dollar account if the proceeds are in U.S. dollars.

Restrictions on use of funds

n.a.

Capital Transactions

Controls on capital and money market instruments	Individuals are permitted to purchase up to EC$250,000 without exchange control approval. All outward capital transfers exceeding that amount require exchange control approval.
On capital market securities	
Shares or other securities of a participating nature	
Purchase locally by nonresidents	For purchases of equity shares, an Alien's Land Holding license is required.
Sale or issue locally by nonresidents	Foreign exchange approval from the MOF is required for amounts exceeding EC$250,000.
Purchase abroad by residents	The same regulations apply as for the sale or issue by nonresidents of capital market securities.
On money market instruments	
Sale or issue locally by nonresidents	The same regulations apply as for the sale or issue by nonresidents of capital market securities.
Purchase abroad by residents	The same regulations apply as for the sale or issue by nonresidents of capital market securities.
On collective investment securities	
Purchase locally by nonresidents	The same regulations apply as for the sale or issue by nonresidents of capital market securities.
Sale or issue locally by nonresidents	The same regulations apply as for the sale or issue by nonresidents of capital market securities.
Sale or issue abroad by residents	The seller of the instruments has to be licensed under the Banking Act, and transfers abroad in excess of EC$250,000 require approval from the MOF.
Controls on derivatives and other instruments	Presently, there is no market in derivatives and other instruments.
Controls on credit operations	
Financial credits	
By residents to nonresidents	MOF approval and payment of a 2.5% Alien's Loans Levy is required for these transactions.
To residents from nonresidents	Foreign exchange approval from the MOF is required for amounts exceeding EC$250,000.
Guarantees, sureties, and financial backup facilities	Foreign exchange approval from the MOF is required for amounts exceeding EC$250,000.
Controls on direct investment	
Outward direct investment	Foreign exchange approval from the MOF is required for amounts exceeding EC$250,000.
Inward direct investment	Investments in equity require an Alien's Land Holding license.
Controls on liquidation of direct investment	The remittance of proceeds of the liquidation of direct investments is permitted, subject to the discharge of any liabilities related to the investment. Transfer of proceeds exceeding EC$250,000 requires MOF approval.
Controls on real estate transactions	
Purchase abroad by residents	Purchasing real estate abroad for private purposes is not normally permitted.
Controls on personal capital movements	
Transfer of gambling and prize earnings	Yes.

Provisions specific to commercial banks and other credit institutions

Lending to nonresidents (financial or commercial credits)

MOF approval and payment of a 2.5% Alien's Loans Levy are required.

Lending locally in foreign exchange

MOF approval is required, which is granted only in the case of projects generating foreign exchange to service the loan. The purchase of locally issued securities denominated in foreign currencies requires MOF approval.

Provisions specific to institutional investors

n.r.

Other controls imposed by securities laws

No.

Changes During 1999

No significant changes occurred in the exchange and trade system.

ST. LUCIA

(Position as of January 31, 2000)

Status Under IMF Articles of Agreement

Article VIII	Date of acceptance: May 30, 1980.

Exchange Arrangement

Currency	The currency of St. Lucia is the Eastern Caribbean dollar issued by the ECCB.
Exchange rate structure	Unitary.
Classification	
Exchange arrangement with no separate legal tender	The Eastern Caribbean dollar is pegged to the U.S. dollar, the intervention currency, at EC$2.70 per US$1. The ECCB also quotes daily rates for the Canadian dollar and the pound sterling.
Exchange tax	No.
Exchange subsidy	No.
Forward exchange market	No.

Arrangements for Payments and Receipts

Prescription of currency requirements	Settlements must be made either in Eastern Caribbean dollars or in U.S. dollars.
Payment arrangements	
Regional arrangements	St. Lucia is a member of the CARICOM.
Administration of control	The MOF is responsible for policy decisions related to exchange control, and its Banking Section is responsible for its administration. Commercial banks have been delegated the authority to approve payments and transfers below US$250,000; in the case of imports with proper customs documentation, they may approve transactions for any amount.
International security restrictions	No.
Payment arrears	No.
Controls on trade in gold (coins and/or bullion)	No.
Controls on exports and imports of banknotes	No.

Resident Accounts

Foreign exchange accounts permitted	Yes.
Held domestically	Yes.
Held abroad	Yes.
Accounts in domestic currency convertible into foreign currency	No.

Nonresident Accounts

Foreign exchange accounts permitted   Yes.

Domestic currency accounts   Yes.

Convertible into foreign currency   Approval is required for transactions exceeding EC$250,000.

Blocked accounts   No.

Imports and Import Payments

Foreign exchange budget   No.

Financing requirements for imports

Advance payment requirements   For advance payments exceeding EC$250,000, prior approval from the MOF is required.

Documentation requirements for release of foreign exchange for imports   Payments in foreign currency for authorized imports are permitted upon application to a local bank and submission of certified customs entry.

Import licenses and other nontariff measures

Negative list   Certain agricultural and manufactured products require individual licenses. There are three levels of licenses: (1) goods originating outside the region; (2) goods from the region (both OECS and CARICOM); and (3) goods imported from non-OECS countries.

Import taxes and/or tariffs   Manufactured goods originating in the region are exempt from the payment of import duties. All imported goods are subject to a consumption tax and a service charge of 4%, except for fertilizers, for which the rate is 0.2%. Live animals, eggs, fish, meat, milk, fertilizers, and most agricultural and manufacturing machinery are exempt from import duties. On January 1, 2000, the fourth phase of the CARICOM CET came into effect.

State import monopoly   The importation of rice, flour, and sugar in bulk form is a state monopoly.

Exports and Export Proceeds

Repatriation requirements   No.

Financing requirements   n.a.

Documentation requirements   n.a.

Export licenses   Export licensing is required for certain primary products.

Without quotas   Yes.

Export taxes   A special fee of US$0.02 per barrel is applied to reexports of petroleum.

Payments for Invisible Transactions and Current Transfers

Controls on these transfers   Approval is required for all transactions exceeding EC$250,000.

Investment-related payments

Quantitative limits   With the approval of the MOF, profits may be remitted in full, subject to confirmation by the Comptroller of Inland Revenue and the National Insurance Scheme that liabilities have been discharged. However, in cases where profits are deemed to be high, the MOF reserves the right to phase remittances over a reasonable period.

Proceeds from Invisible Transactions and Current Transfers

Repatriation requirements	There is no repatriation requirement on proceeds of up to EC$250,000.
Restrictions on use of funds	No.

Capital Transactions

Controls on capital and money market instruments	Outward transfers exceeding EC$250,000 require exchange control approval.
On capital market securities	
Shares or other securities of a participating nature	
Purchase locally by nonresidents	n.r.
Sale or issue locally by nonresidents	Yes.
Purchase abroad by residents	Yes.
Sale or issue abroad by residents	Yes.
Bonds or other debt securities	
Purchase locally by nonresidents	n.r.
Sale or issue locally by nonresidents	Yes.
Purchase abroad by residents	Yes.
Sale or issue abroad by residents	Yes.
On money market instruments	
Purchase locally by nonresidents	n.r.
Purchase abroad by residents	Yes.
On collective investment securities	
Purchase abroad by residents	Yes.
Controls on derivatives and other instruments	
Purchase locally by nonresidents	These transactions require approval from the MOF.
Controls on credit operations	There are controls on all categories of credit operations.
Commercial credits	
By residents to nonresidents	These credits require approval of the MOF. Applications for nonresident loans are submitted by the authorized dealer (or other financial intermediary) to the MOF on behalf of the applicant.
To residents from nonresidents	Yes.
Financial credits	
By residents to nonresidents	Approval of the MOF is required, except for loans to nonresident St. Lucians. Applications are submitted by authorized dealers on behalf of the applicant.
To residents from nonresidents	Yes.
Guarantees, sureties, and financial backup facilities	
By residents to nonresidents	Yes.
To residents from nonresidents	Yes.

Controls on direct investment

Outward direct investment | Yes.

Controls on liquidation of direct investment | n.a.

Controls on real estate transactions

Purchase abroad by residents | Yes.

Purchase locally by nonresidents | Approval is not required for nonresident St. Lucians.

Sale locally by nonresidents | Amounts exceeding EC$250,000 require approval for repatriation of estate proceeds.

Controls on personal capital movements

Loans

   By residents to nonresidents | Yes.

Gifts, endowments, inheritances, and legacies

   To residents from nonresidents | Yes.

Transfer of assets

   Transfer into the country by immigrants | n.r.

Transfer of gambling and prize earnings | Yes.

Provisions specific to commercial banks and other credit institutions

Borrowing abroad | Yes.

Lending to nonresidents (financial or commercial credits) | Yes.

Lending locally in foreign exchange | Lending is restricted to Eastern Caribbean dollars or U.S. dollars.

Purchase of locally issued securities denominated in foreign exchange | Purchase is restricted to securities denominated in Eastern Caribbean dollars or U.S. dollars.

Provisions specific to institutional investors

Limits (max.) on portfolio invested abroad | Institutional investors may invest up to 10% of their statutory deposits in government securities of the Commonwealth of Caribbean Nations.

Limits (min.) on portfolio invested locally | Yes.

Currency-matching regulations on assets/liabilities composition | For every U.S. dollar liability, there must be an equivalent U.S. dollar asset.

Other controls imposed by securities laws | Funds raised from issuing securities must be invested locally.

Changes During 1999

No significant changes occurred in the exchange and trade system.

Changes During 2000

Imports and import payments | *January 1.* The fourth phase of the CARICOM CET came into effect.

ST. VINCENT AND THE GRENADINES

(Position as of January 31, 2000)

Status Under IMF Articles of Agreement

Article VIII   Date of acceptance: August 24, 1981.

Exchange Arrangement

Currency
The currency of St. Vincent and the Grenadines is the Eastern Caribbean dollar, which is issued by the ECCB.

Exchange rate structure
Unitary.

Classification

Exchange arrangement with no separate legal tender
The Eastern Caribbean dollar is pegged to the U.S. dollar, the intervention currency, at EC$2.70 per US$1.

Exchange tax
No.

Exchange subsidy
n.a.

Forward exchange market
No.

Arrangements for Payments and Receipts

Prescription of currency requirements
Settlements with residents of member countries of the CARICOM can be made in any currency. Settlements with residents of other countries may be made in any foreign currency or through an external account in Eastern Caribbean dollars.

Payment arrangements

Regional arrangements
St. Vincent and the Grenadines is a member of the CARICOM.

Administration of control
Exchange control is administered by the MOF and applies to all countries outside the ECCB area. The MOF delegates to authorized dealers the authority to approve some import payments and certain other payments.

International security restrictions
n.a.

Payment arrears
No.

Controls on trade in gold (coins and/or bullion)

Controls on domestic ownership and/or trade
Residents are permitted to acquire and hold gold coins for numismatic purposes only.

Controls on external trade
Imports of gold are permitted under license by the MOF for industrial purposes only.

Controls on exports and imports of banknotes
n.a.

Resident Accounts

Foreign exchange accounts permitted   n.a.

Accounts in domestic currency convertible into foreign currency   n.a.

Nonresident Accounts

Foreign exchange accounts permitted

These accounts may be opened by nonresidents with the authorization of the MOF and credited only with funds in the form of remittances from overseas. Except with the prior permission of the MOF, remittances in Eastern Caribbean currency, foreign currency notes and coins, and payments by residents may not be credited to a foreign currency account. These accounts may be debited for payments abroad without prior authorization from the MOF. The operating banks must submit quarterly statements of the accounts to the MOF.

Domestic currency accounts

External accounts may be opened for nonresidents with the authorization of the MOF. They are maintained in Eastern Caribbean dollars and may be credited with inward remittances in foreign currency and with transfers from other external accounts. Credits and debits to these accounts are subject to the same regulations as for foreign exchange accounts.

Convertible into foreign currency

n.a.

Blocked accounts

n.a.

Imports and Import Payments

Foreign exchange budget

No.

Financing requirements for imports

Advance payment requirements

Advance payments for imports over EC$250,000 require prior approval from the MOF.

Documentation requirements for release of foreign exchange for imports

Payments for authorized imports are permitted upon application and submission of documentary evidence and, where required, of the license.

Import licenses and other nontariff measures

Most goods may be freely imported. Imports of some goods that compete with typical exports of other member countries of the CARICOM and the OECS are subject to licenses.

Negative list

Imports of goods that compete with locally made products are prohibited in some cases.

Import taxes and/or tariffs

The import tariff rates range from zero to 20%. In addition, imports are subject to a consumption tax, ranging from 5% to 50% and levied on the tariff-inclusive value of imports. Goods imported from the member countries of the CARICOM are exempt from import tariffs and are subject only to the consumption tax. A customs service charge of 2.5% is imposed on the c.i.f. value of all imported goods, with certain exceptions. On January 1, 2000, the fourth phase of the CARICOM CET came into effect.

State import monopoly

n.a.

Exports and Export Proceeds

Repatriation requirements

Yes.

Surrender requirements

All export proceeds must be surrendered within six months of receipt.

Financing requirements

n.a.

Documentation requirements

n.a.

Export licenses

Specific licenses are required for the exportation to any destination of some agricultural goods included in the CARICOM marketing protocol and in the CARICOM Oils and Fats Agreement. The licenses are issued by the Ministry of Trade, which, in some cases, has delegated its authority to the St. Vincent Central Marketing Corporation. Exports of goats, sheep, and lobsters are subject to licensing to prevent depletion of stocks.

Export taxes

Until January 1, 1999, when it was removed, a 2% export duty was levied on bananas.

Payments for Invisible Transactions and Current Transfers

Controls on these transfers   Payments for invisibles related to authorized imports are not restricted. Other payments exceeding EC$250,000 must be approved by the MOF. Approval is granted routinely.

Investment-related payments   Information is not available on the payment of amortization of loans or depreciation of direct investments.

Payments for travel

Quantitative limits   The limits are the equivalent of EC$2,500 a year for travel outside the ECCB area, and EC$6,000 a year for business travel.

Indicative limits/bona fide test   These allocations may be increased with the authorization of the MOF.

Personal payments   Information is not available on the transfer of pensions, family maintenance, and alimony.

Proceeds from Invisible Transactions and Current Transfers

Repatriation requirements   Yes.

Surrender requirements   Yes.

Restrictions on use of funds   n.a.

Capital Transactions

Controls on capital and money market instruments   All outward capital transfers over EC$250,000 require prior approval from the MOF.

On capital market securities

Shares or other securities of a participating nature

Purchase abroad by residents   Residents are normally not permitted to purchase foreign currency securities abroad for private purposes.

Bonds or other debt securities

Purchase abroad by residents   Yes.

Sale or issue abroad by residents   Yes.

On money market instruments

Purchase abroad by residents   Yes.

On collective investment securities

Purchase abroad by residents   Yes.

Controls on derivatives and other instruments

Purchase abroad by residents   Yes.

Controls on credit operations

Commercial credits

By residents to nonresidents   MOF approval is required.

Financial credits

By residents to nonresidents   MOF approval is required.

Controls on direct investment

Outward direct investment   Yes.

Controls on liquidation of direct investment	The remittance of proceeds is permitted, subject to the discharge of any liabilities related to the investment.
Controls on real estate transactions	
Purchase abroad by residents	Yes.
Purchase locally by nonresidents	Yes.
Controls on personal capital movements	n.a.
Provisions specific to commercial banks and other credit institutions	
Borrowing abroad	Any borrowing abroad by authorized dealers to finance their domestic operations requires the approval of the MOF.
Provisions specific to institutional investors	n.a.
Other controls imposed by securities laws	n.a.

Changes During 1999

Exports and export proceeds	*January 1.* The 2% export duty levied on bananas was removed.

Changes During 2000

Imports and import payments	*January 1.* The fourth phase of the CARICOM CET came into effect.

SAMOA
(Position as of December 31, 1999)

Status Under IMF Articles of Agreement

Article VIII	Date of acceptance: October 6, 1994.

Exchange Arrangement

Currency	The currency of Samoa is the Samoa tala.
Exchange rate structure	Unitary.
Classification	
Conventional pegged arrangement	The exchange rate is determined on the basis of a fixed relationship with a weighted basket of currencies of Samoa's main trading partners. The Central Bank of Samoa (CBS) has the authority to make discretionary exchange rate adjustments against the currency basket within a margin of up to 2%.
Exchange tax	The exchange levy of 1% charged on gross sales of foreign exchange was eliminated on January 1, 1999.
Exchange subsidy	No.
Forward exchange market	Commercial banks are permitted to make forward exchange contracts.

Arrangements for Payments and Receipts

Prescription of currency requirements	No.
Payment arrangements	No.
Administration of control	Overall responsibility for the administration of exchange control rests with the CBS, which delegates part of its powers to authorized banks. In principle, all payments to nonresidents require the CBS's approval. However, the ANZ Bank (Samoa) Ltd., the National Bank of Samoa, and the Pacific Commercial Bank—the only authorized banks—are empowered to approve certain payments without limits and others up to specified amounts.
International security restrictions	No.
Payment arrears	No.
Controls on trade in gold (coins and/or bullion)	No.
Controls on exports and imports of banknotes	
On exports	
Domestic currency	Residents are allowed to export SAT 2,000 as part of their travel allowance.
Foreign currency	Samoan residents are allowed to export the equivalent of SAT 5,000 in foreign currency. Nonresidents may export the amount of foreign currency they brought into the country.

Resident Accounts

Foreign exchange accounts permitted	Residents who earn foreign exchange in the normal course of their business may open, with the approval of the CBS, external or foreign currency accounts with one of the three commercial banks.

Held domestically	These accounts are permitted, but approval is required.
Held abroad	These accounts are permitted, but approval is required.
Accounts in domestic currency convertible into foreign currency	Yes.

Nonresident Accounts

Foreign exchange accounts permitted	Nonresidents who earn foreign exchange may open a foreign currency deposit account if there is a need to settle overseas commitments. However, approval is required to open these accounts.
Domestic currency accounts	These accounts are permitted, but approval is required.
Convertible into foreign currency	Yes.
Blocked accounts	No.

Imports and Import Payments

Foreign exchange budget	No.
Financing requirements for imports	
Advance payment requirements	The limit for advance payments is SAT 10,000.
Documentation requirements for release of foreign exchange for imports	No limits are imposed on imports under an open account. However, payment requires CBS approval.
Import licenses and other nontariff measures	
Negative list	The importation of a few products is prohibited for reasons of security or health. The importation of used cars requires prior approval of the CBS.
Import taxes and/or tariffs	Import duties are applied on an ad valorem basis on c.i.f. values. The maximum import tariff is 20%. Rates on machinery and agricultural imports are generally levied at 10% or lower, while those on motor vehicles at 20%. As of May 28, 1999, there are only four general rates of duty—zero, 5%, 10%, and 20%.
	In addition, an import excise tax is applied to imports of alcohol, soft drinks, tobacco, petroleum, and passenger cars. Enterprises producing for export may receive full or partial exemption from duties and excise taxes on inputs and capital equipment.
Taxes collected through the exchange system	There is a value-added goods and service tax.
State import monopoly	No.

Exports and Export Proceeds

Repatriation requirements	Yes.
Surrender requirements	Export proceeds must be surrendered to the authorized banks within three months of the date of shipment, except for export proceeds from goods shipped to American Samoa, which must be surrendered to the authorized bank within four weeks of the date of shipment.
Financing requirements	Yes.
Documentation requirements	Certificates validated by an authorized bank are required for exports in excess of SAT 250.

Export licenses

Without quotas   All exports require export licenses issued by the Customs Department. Exports may be prohibited by the Director of Agriculture on grounds of low quality, or by order of the head of state to alleviate domestic shortages.

Export taxes   No.

Payments for Invisible Transactions and Current Transfers

Controls on these transfers   Payments for certain invisibles may be approved by the authorized banks up to specified limits. Payments in excess of these limits, as well as payments for all other invisibles, require the prior approval of the CBS, which is granted when applications are supported by documentary proof that capital transactions are not involved. The CBS's approval process governing the remittance of invisible payments is concerned only with whether a transaction is bona fide.

Trade-related payments

  Prior approval   Yes.

  Quantitative limits   Yes.

  Indicative limits/bona fide test   Yes.

Investment-related payments   A 15% withholding tax is levied on remittances of interest payments on overseas loans, and of dividends at the source. Information is not available for the payment of amortization of loans or depreciation of direct investments.

  Prior approval   Yes.

  Quantitative limits   Yes.

  Indicative limits/bona fide test   Yes.

Payments for travel

  Prior approval   Yes.

  Quantitative limits   Residents and expatriates traveling overseas for private purposes are entitled to a foreign currency allowance equivalent to SAT 400 a person a day, subject to a limit of SAT 5,000 a person a trip; children under 15 years of age are entitled to 50% of the adult allowances. A daily allowance of SAT 600 a person is allotted for business travel, with a limit of SAT 6,000 a trip.

  Indicative limits/bona fide test   Yes.

Personal payments

  Prior approval   Yes.

  Quantitative limits   Authorized banks may approve transfers of gifts to relatives and dependents, either for special family occasions or for maintenance, up to SAT 500 a person a year. Requests for larger amounts may be approved by the CBS on a case-by-case basis.

  Indicative limits/bona fide test   Although no limit is set on remittances to cover expenses for medical treatment abroad, documentary evidence must be provided to support requests for such remittances. There is no specific limit for costs to study abroad, but the amount requested must be supported by documentary evidence confirming that the beneficiary is enrolled at an educational institution abroad and costs are in line with the prevailing costs in the country of study.

Foreign workers' wages

  Prior approval   Expatriate workers with local contracts of one year and longer are considered residents and need CBS approval if they wish to repatriate funds in excess of 80% of their net earnings on a fortnightly or monthly basis. Earnings not repatriated during the contract may be repatriated at the end of the contract.

  Quantitative limits   Yes.

Indicative limits/bona fide test	Yes.
Credit card use abroad	
Prior approval	Yes.
Quantitative limits	Yes.
Indicative limits/bona fide test	Yes.
Other payments	
Prior approval	Yes.
Quantitative limits	Yes.
Indicative limits/bona fide test	As regards subscriptions and membership fees, no specific limit exists, but amounts requested must be supported by documentary evidence.

Proceeds from Invisible Transactions and Current Transfers

Repatriation requirements	Yes.
Surrender requirements	All proceeds must be surrendered to the authorized banks. Resident travelers must, on their return, sell to the banks all unused foreign exchange brought in.
Restrictions on use of funds	No.

Capital Transactions

Controls on capital and money market instruments	All capital transactions (inward and outward) require approval of the CBS. Local money markets are beginning to develop following the introduction of open market operations by the CBS. No capital market has yet developed in Samoa.
On capital market securities	
Shares or other securities of a participating nature	
Purchase abroad by residents	Yes.
Bonds or other debt securities	
Purchase locally by nonresidents	Yes.
Sale or issue locally by nonresidents	Yes.
Purchase abroad by residents	Yes.
Sale or issue abroad by residents	Yes.
On money market instruments	
Purchase abroad by residents	Yes.
Sale or issue abroad by residents	Yes.
On collective investment securities	
Purchase abroad by residents	Yes.
Controls on derivatives and other instruments	No.
Controls on credit operations	All credits operations require CBS approval.
Controls on direct investment	
Outward direct investment	Investments require CBS approval.

Controls on liquidation of direct investment	Repatriation of investments requires CBS approval.
Controls on real estate transactions	
Purchase abroad by residents	Purchases require CBS approval.
Purchase locally by nonresidents	Yes.
Sale locally by nonresidents	Yes.
Controls on personal capital movements	
Loans	
By residents to nonresidents	Yes.
To residents from nonresidents	Yes.
Gifts, endowments, inheritances, and legacies	
By residents to nonresidents	Yes.
To residents from nonresidents	Yes.
Settlement of debts abroad by immigrants	Yes.
Transfer of gambling and prize earnings	There are no restrictions for nonresidents, but residents require approval from the CBS.
Provisions specific to commercial banks and other credit institutions	
Borrowing abroad	Borrowing requires CBS approval.
Maintenance of accounts abroad	Yes.
Lending to nonresidents (financial or commercial credits)	Yes.
Lending locally in foreign exchange	Yes.
Purchase of locally issued securities denominated in foreign exchange	Yes.
Provisions specific to institutional investors	No.
Other controls imposed by securities laws	All outward capital transfers by residents require the specific approval of the CBS.

Changes During 1999

Exchange arrangement	*January 1.* The exchange levy of 1% charged on gross sales of foreign exchange was eliminated.
Imports and import payments	*May 28.* Four general rates of duty remained—zero, 5%, 10%, and 20%.

SAN MARINO
(Position as of December 31, 1999)

Status Under IMF Articles of Agreement

Article VIII   Date of acceptance: September 23, 1992.

Article XIV

Exchange Arrangement

Currency

Effective January 1, 1999, San Marino adopted the euro.

Other legal tender

The monetary agreement between San Marino and Italy, renewed on December 21, 1991, provides for San Marino to issue annually agreed amounts of San Marino lira coins equivalent in form to Italian coinage; these coins are legal tender in both countries. The San Marino gold scudo is also issued, but is legal tender only in San Marino. It is not generally used in transactions because its numismatic value exceeds its defined legal value (Lit 60,000 per 1 scudo).

Negotiations with Italy, on behalf of the EU, regarding conditions under which San Marino may issue euro banknotes and/or coins were begun in late 1999.

Exchange rate structure

Unitary.

Classification

Exchange arrangement with no separate legal tender

Foreign exchange transactions are conducted through commercial banks without restrictions at rates quoted in international markets.

Exchange tax

No.

Exchange subsidy

No.

Forward exchange market

Forward transactions may be conducted through commercial banks without restriction at rates quoted in international markets.

Arrangements for Payments and Receipts

Prescription of currency requirements

Settlements with foreign countries on foreign accounts are made in convertible currencies or in euro.

Payment arrangements

No.

Administration of control

The Central Bank of San Marino (CBSM) may grant foreign exchange dealer status to Sammarinese financial institutions. The Finance and Exchange Agreement with Italy, finalized on July 30, 1999, allows Sammarinese banks to maintain accounts with financial institutions abroad. Previously, Sammarinese banks were allowed to operate on foreign markets only through financial institutions in Italy.

Residents of San Marino are allowed to conduct foreign exchange transactions freely, with settlement effected through authorized Italian intermediaries (the Bank of Italy, the Italian Foreign Exchange Office, authorized banks, and the Postal Administration).

International security restrictions

No.

Payment arrears

No.

Controls on trade in gold (coins and/or bullion)

Laws establish that the CBSM is the sole agency entitled to carry out transactions in gold. The CBSM may authorize other banks or domestic companies to buy gold for production purposes, after ensuring the necessary controls. Currently, there is no gold trade in San Marino.

Controls on external trade

Yes.

Controls on exports and imports of banknotes	To combat money laundering, anyone intending to bring into San Marino cash or bearer securities in excess of Lit 30,000,000 is required to carry out the transaction through financial institutions.
On exports	
Domestic currency	Yes.
Foreign currency	Yes.
On imports	
Domestic currency	Yes.
Foreign currency	Yes.

Resident Accounts

Foreign exchange accounts permitted	Residents are free to maintain any type of deposit accounts, with the exception of membered accounts.
Held domestically	Yes.
Held abroad	Yes.
Accounts in domestic currency convertible into foreign currency	Yes.

Nonresident Accounts

Foreign exchange accounts permitted	Nonresidents are free to maintain any type of deposit accounts, with the exception of membered accounts.
Domestic currency accounts	Yes.
Convertible into foreign currency	Yes.
Blocked accounts	No.

Imports and Import Payments

Foreign exchange budget	No.
Financing requirements for imports	No.
Documentation requirements for release of foreign exchange for imports	No.
Import licenses and other nontariff measures	No license, other than the general business license, is required to engage in trade transactions. Imports from the EU are not subject to restrictions, whereas imports from third countries are subject to control under the relevant EU regulations.
Import taxes and/or tariffs	Customs duties on imports from outside the EU are collected by EU customs authorities on behalf of San Marino. A sales tax is levied on all imports at the time of entry. The structure of this tax corresponds closely to the Italian VAT, but the average effective rate is about 4% lower. Sales taxes levied on imports are rebated when the goods are reexported.
State import monopoly	The importation of electricity, gas, and water is reserved for the public sector.

Exports and Export Proceeds

Repatriation requirements	No.

Financing requirements	No.
Documentation requirements	No.
Export licenses	Exports to the EU are not subject to restrictions, while exports to third countries are governed by relevant EU regulations.
Without quotas	Customs clearance formalities concerning the export of arms, works of art, precursor, and dual-use products must be carried out at the customs offices identified by the EC-San Marino Cooperation Committee.
Export taxes	No.

Payments for Invisible Transactions and Current Transfers

Controls on these transfers	No.

Proceeds from Invisible Transactions and Current Transfers

Repatriation requirements	No.
Restrictions on use of funds	No.

Capital Transactions

Controls on capital and money market instruments	Inward and outward capital transfers, with few exceptions, are not restricted.
On capital market securities	
Shares or other securities of a participating nature	
Sale or issue locally by nonresidents	Sales are subject to authorization, while issues are not allowed to nonresidents.
Bonds or other debt securities	
Sale or issue locally by nonresidents	The same regulations apply as for the sale and issue of shares or other securities of a participating nature.
On money market instruments	The same regulations apply as for the sale and issue of shares or other securities of a participating nature.
On collective investment securities	The same regulations apply as for the sale and issue of shares or other securities of a participating nature.
Controls on derivatives and other instruments	
Sale or issue locally by nonresidents	The same regulations apply as for the sale and issue of shares or other securities of a participating nature.
Controls on credit operations	The granting of financial credits of a considerable amount to a person or a company is subject to the Bank Law provisions as well as those of the Office of Banking Supervision.
Commercial credits	
By residents to nonresidents	Yes.
Financial credits	
By residents to nonresidents	Yes.
Controls on direct investment	
Inward direct investment	Investments require government approval, which is based on conformity with long-term developmental and environmental policy considerations. Foreign investors are accorded

equal treatment with national firms.

Controls on liquidation of direct investment	No.
Controls on real estate transactions	Purchases by domestic companies and nonresidents require approval from the Council of Twelve. Approval is granted on a case-by-case basis.
Purchase locally by nonresidents	Yes.
Controls on personal capital movements	
Loans	
By residents to nonresidents	Except for occasional transactions, this activity is not allowed.
Gifts, endowments, inheritances, and legacies	
By residents to nonresidents	Yes.
Provisions specific to commercial banks and other credit institutions	
Lending to nonresidents (financial or commercial credits)	The granting of financial credits of a considerable amount to a person or a company is subject to the Bank Law provisions as well as those of the Office of Banking Supervision.
Lending locally in foreign exchange	The granting of financial credits of a considerable amount to a person or a company is subject to the Bank Law provisions as well as those of the Office of Banking Supervision.
Investment regulations	
Abroad by banks	Yes.
In banks by nonresidents	Buying of securities of a participating nature exceeding 5% of the Sammarinese bank's capital must be declared to the Office of Banking Supervision.
Provisions specific to institutional investors	
Currency-matching regulations on assets/liabilities composition	Yes.
Other controls imposed by securities laws	No.

Changes During 1999

Exchange arrangement	*January 1.* San Marino adopted the euro as its currency.
Arrangements for payments and receipts	*July 30.* The Finance and Exchange Agreement with Italy was finalized.

SÃO TOMÉ AND PRÍNCIPE

(Position as of December 31, 1999)

Status Under IMF Articles of Agreement

Article XIV	Yes.

Exchange Arrangement

Currency	The currency of São Tomé and Príncipe is the São Tomé and Príncipe dobra.
Exchange rate structure	Unitary.
Classification	
Independently floating	The official exchange rate is computed on a daily basis as a weighted average of the exchange rates of the exchange bureaus, the commercial banks, and the parallel market. The intervention currency is the dollar. Rates for certain other currencies are determined on the basis of exchange rates of the dollar for the currencies concerned.
Exchange tax	The taxation system differs for import payments, transactions in foreign checks, and collection of export proceeds. On import-related exchange transactions, the arrangements are as follows: when an LC is opened, a quarterly rate equivalent to 0.5% (minimum $25 and maximum $500) of the import value is charged and is payable with an additional commission of 0.5% to the Central Bank of São Tomé and Príncipe (CB). A stamp of duty of 0.25% is also payable, as well as a postage levy of $2. On foreign checks for collection, commercial banks charge a commission of $2 a transaction. For the collection of export proceeds, a commission of 0.125% (a minimum of $25 and a maximum of $300) is charged when the LC is opened and an additional fee of 0.125% when the funds are received. A postage levy of $7.50 is also charged.
Exchange subsidy	No.
Forward exchange market	No.

Arrangements for Payments and Receipts

Prescription of currency requirements	No.
Payment arrangements	No.
Administration of control	Import and export licenses are freely granted by the Directorate of External Commerce for statistical purposes.
International security restrictions	No.
Payment arrears	
Official	Yes.
Controls on trade in gold (coins and/or bullion)	
Controls on external trade	The export and import of gold require CB authorization.
Controls on exports and imports of banknotes	
On exports	
Foreign currency	The CB establishes the maximum amount that may be exported.

Resident Accounts

Foreign exchange accounts permitted

Until February 27, 1999, domestic accounts in foreign currency, other than those of credit institutions, could have been freely opened only by export enterprises that were also producers, but the utilization of such accounts for making transfers abroad needed authorization on a case-by-case basis from the CB. Individuals were not allowed to hold foreign currency deposits. On February 28, 1999, all restrictions were lifted.

Held domestically

Yes.

Held abroad

Yes.

Accounts in domestic currency convertible into foreign currency

n.a.

Nonresident Accounts

Foreign exchange accounts permitted

These accounts may be freely opened and credited or debited, including for transfers abroad, as long as they are demand accounts or have a term of up to one year.

Domestic currency accounts

n.a.

Blocked accounts

n.a.

Imports and Import Payments

Foreign exchange budget

No.

Financing requirements for imports

Yes.

Advance payment requirements

Prepayment for imports is permitted only through the opening of LCs or through advance transfer when agreed upon by the CB.

Advance import deposits

When importers open LCs, commercial banks require them to lodge a non-interest-bearing deposit in domestic currency of up to 100% of the value of the LCs, depending on the creditworthiness of the operator.

Documentation requirements for release of foreign exchange for imports

Letters of credit

Yes.

Import licenses and other nontariff measures

Import licenses are automatically granted by the Directorate of External Commerce. All individuals and productive entities are permitted to engage in import activity.

Import taxes and/or tariffs

The tax depends on the type of transaction. The following categories are used: import payments, transactions in foreign checks, and collection of export proceeds.

Taxes collected through the exchange system

Yes.

State import monopoly

Fuels and lubricants are imported by the public fuel enterprise.

Exports and Export Proceeds

Repatriation requirements

All export proceeds must be repatriated and collected through the commercial banks.

Financing requirements

n.a.

Documentation requirements

n.a.

Export licenses

All exports require an export license specifying the quantity and c.i.f. or f.o.b. value of the export.

Export taxes

Taxes collected through the exchange system

A commission of 0.125% is charged on the collection of export proceeds, with a minimum of $25 and a maximum of $300 when the LC is opened, and an additional commission of 0.125% when funds are received. A postage levy of $7.50 is also charged.

Other export taxes

Yes.

Payments for Invisible Transactions and Current Transfers

Controls on these transfers

As of February 28, 1999, all restrictions on these payments were lifted, including the preferential allocation for imports. Commercial banks charge a postage levy of $2 for clients (and $4 for others) on all transactions.

Proceeds from Invisible Transactions and Current Transfers

Repatriation requirements

Yes.

Restrictions on use of funds

Yes.

Capital Transactions

Controls on capital and money market instruments

n.a.

Controls on derivatives and other instruments

n.a.

Controls on credit operations

n.a.

Controls on direct investment

Inward direct investment

Investments, excluding those related to the extraction of hydrocarbons and other mining industries, are permitted on the same basis as domestic investments.

Controls on liquidation of direct investment

No.

Controls on real estate transactions

n.a.

Controls on personal capital movements

n.a.

Provisions specific to commercial banks and other credit institutions

n.a.

Provisions specific to institutional investors

n.a.

Other controls imposed by securities laws

n.a.

Changes During 1999

Resident accounts

February 28. All restrictions on these accounts were eliminated.

Payments for invisible transactions and current transfers

February 28. All restrictions on these payments and transfers were eliminated.

SAUDI ARABIA

(Position as of December 31, 1999)

Status Under IMF Articles of Agreement

Article VIII   Date of acceptance: March 22, 1961.

Exchange Arrangement

Currency
The currency of Saudia Arabia is the Saudi Arabian riyal.

Exchange rate structure
Unitary.

Classification

Conventional pegged arrangement
The exchange rate of the Saudi Arabian riyal is pegged to the SDR at SRls 4.28255 per SDR 1. The intervention currency is the dollar, to which a close relationship is maintained. The Saudi Arabian riyal rate against the dollar is determined by the Saudi Arabian Monetary Agency (SAMA). The SAMA's middle rate, which has been stable since June 1986 at SRls 3.745 per $1, serves—together with the SAMA's selling and buying rates—as the basis for exchange quotations in the market, the banks being permitted to charge up to 0.125% above and below the SAMA's buying and selling rates.

Exchange tax
No.

Exchange subsidy
No.

Forward exchange market
The commercial banking sector has an active forward market to cover exchange risks for up to 12 months.

Arrangements for Payments and Receipts

Prescription of currency requirements
Transactions with, and the use of the currency of, Israel are prohibited.

Payment arrangements
No.

Administration of control
Foreign exchange controls are administered by the SAMA.

International security restrictions

In accordance with Executive Board Decision No. 144-(52/51)
There are restrictions on transactions with Iraq.

In accordance with UN sanctions
In compliance with UN Security Council resolutions, certain restrictions have been imposed on the making of payments and transfers for current international transactions with respect to the former Federal Republic of Yugoslavia (Serbia/Montenegro).

Payment arrears
No.

Controls on trade in gold (coins and/or bullion)

Controls on external trade
Residents may import and export gold in any form, except manufactured gold and jewelry, which are subject to a 12% customs duty. Gold of 14 karats or less may not be imported.

Controls on exports and imports of banknotes
No.

Resident Accounts

Foreign exchange accounts permitted
Yes.

Held domestically
Yes.

Held abroad	Yes.
Accounts in domestic currency convertible into foreign currency	Yes.

Nonresident Accounts

Foreign exchange accounts permitted	These accounts may be opened, but approval is required.
Domestic currency accounts	Yes.
Convertible into foreign currency	These accounts may be opened, but approval is required.
Blocked accounts	No.

Imports and Import Payments

Foreign exchange budget	No.
Financing requirements for imports	No.
Documentation requirements for release of foreign exchange for imports	No.
Import licenses and other nontariff measures	Trade with Israel is prohibited.
Negative list	Limited import restrictions on a few commodities are maintained for religious, health, and security reasons.
Open general licenses	Yes.
Import taxes and/or tariffs	Most imports are subject to customs duties at rates ranging from zero to 12%. For a few goods, the rate is 20% and for tobacco products, 50%. Imports from members of the GCC are exempt from duties, provided that at least 40% of value added is effected in GCC countries and that at least 51% of the capital of the producing firm is owned by citizens of GCC member countries.
State import monopoly	No.

Exports and Export Proceeds

Repatriation requirements	No.
Financing requirements	No.
Documentation requirements	No.
Export licenses	Reexport of certain imported items benefiting from government subsidies is prohibited.
Export taxes	No.

Payments for Invisible Transactions and Current Transfers

Controls on these transfers	No.

Proceeds from Invisible Transactions and Current Transfers

Repatriation requirements	No.
Surrender requirements	No.

Restrictions on use of funds	No.

Capital Transactions

Controls on capital and money market instruments

On capital market securities

Shares or other securities of a participating nature

Purchase locally by nonresidents	Portfolio investment in shares of listed Saudi Arabian joint-stock companies is restricted to Saudi Arabian nationals, Saudi Arabian corporations and institutions, and citizens of the GCC. Indirect portfolio investment in shares issued by Saudi Arabian joint-stock companies is allowed via a special purpose vehicle (country fund), authorized by the SAMA and established and managed by the Saudi American Bank. There are no controls on portfolio investment in government securities.
Sale or issue locally by nonresidents	Nonresidents must seek permission of the Minister of Commerce to sell or issue securities within the Kingdom. There are no controls on the repatriation of the proceeds from the sale of securities issued by nonresidents. Residents may purchase or sell nonresident securities via brokerage services offered by domestic banks.
Sale or issue abroad by residents	For the sale of collective investment securities where the underlying assets are shares of Saudi joint-stock companies, the same regulations apply as for shares or other securities of a participating nature.

Bonds or other debt securities

Sale or issue locally by nonresidents	The same regulations apply as for shares or other securities of a participating nature.

On money market instruments

Sale or issue locally by nonresidents	The same regulations apply as for shares or other securities of a participating nature.

On collective investment securities

Purchase locally by nonresidents	The same regulations apply as for shares or other securities of a participating nature.
Sale or issue locally by nonresidents	The same regulations apply as for shares or other securities of a participating nature.
Sale or issue abroad by residents	In the case of collective investments securities, where the underlying assets are shares of Saudi joint-stock companies, the same regulations apply as for shares or other securities of a participating nature.

Controls on derivatives and other instruments

Sale or issue locally by nonresidents	The same regulations apply as for shares or other securities of a participating nature.

Controls on credit operations

Commercial credits

By residents to nonresidents	Saudi Arabian banks must seek permission from the SAMA.
To residents from nonresidents	The SAMA's permission is required for Saudi Arabian riyal–denominated loans made through Saudi Arabian banks.

Financial credits	The SAMA's permission is required.
By residents to nonresidents	Yes.
To residents from nonresidents	Yes.

Guarantees, sureties, and financial backup facilities

By residents to nonresidents	The SAMA's permission is required.

To residents from nonresidents	Financial institutions that give guarantees to government projects must appear on the SAMA-approved list.
Controls on direct investment	
Inward direct investment	Approved foreign investments in Saudi Arabia enjoy the same privileges as domestic capital. Foreign capital invested in industrial or agricultural projects with at least 25% Saudi Arabian participation is exempt from income and corporate tax for 10 years after production has begun.
Controls on liquidation of direct investment	No.
Controls on real estate transactions	
Purchase locally by nonresidents	Purchase of real estate is restricted to Saudi Arabian citizens, Saudi Arabian corporations, Saudi Arabian institutions, and citizens of the GCC.
Sale locally by nonresidents	Sales of real estate by the citizens of the GCC are free.
Controls on personal capital movements	
Transfer of gambling and prize earnings	Prize earnings are transferable; gambling is prohibited.
Provisions specific to commercial banks and other credit institutions	
Lending to nonresidents (financial or commercial credits)	Saudi banks require the SAMA's permission to lend to nonresidents, except for interbank transactions and commercial credits.
Differential treatment of deposit accounts held by nonresidents	
Reserve requirements	For interbank deposits originating from foreign banks, only domestic currency deposits are subject to the SAMA's reserve requirement.
Investment regulations	
Abroad by banks	The SAMA's approval is required by Saudi Arabian banks before acquiring shares in a company established outside the Kingdom.
In banks by nonresidents	Prior permission of the authorities is required.
Open foreign exchange position limits	Open positions are monitored via prudential reports.
Provisions specific to institutional investors	No.
Other controls imposed by securities laws	No.

Changes During 1999

No significant changes occurred in the exchange and trade system.

SENEGAL

(Position as of January 31, 2000)

Status Under IMF Articles of Agreement

Article VIII   Date of acceptance: June 6, 1996.

Exchange Arrangement

Currency

The currency of Senegal is the CFA franc.

Exchange rate structure

Unitary.

Classification

Exchange arrangement with no separate legal tender

The CFA franc is pegged to the euro at the rate of CFAF 100 per €0.8385. Exchange rates for other currencies are derived from the rate for the currency concerned in the Paris exchange market and the fixed rate between the euro and the CFA franc.

Exchange tax

Authorized banks charge an exchange commission of 2% on purchases and sales of French francs and a commission of 0.1215% to 1%, depending on the amount, on purchases and sales of foreign currencies not directly related to transactions abroad. Other foreign currencies are exchanged at rates and with commissions set freely by the parties involved. In addition, a commission of 0.25% (all of which must be surrendered to the Treasury) is levied by banks on transfers to all countries outside the WAEMU.

Exchange subsidy

No.

Forward exchange market

Forward cover against exchange rate risk is available to residents only for imports of a specified category of goods. All forward cover against exchange rate risk must be authorized by the Ministry of Economy, Finance, and Planning (MEFP). Forward cover may be provided only in the currency of settlement stipulated in the commercial contract. Maturities must correspond to the due date of foreign exchange settlement stipulated in the commercial contract and must not exceed one month. For some specified products, the maturity of forward cover may be extended one time for up to three months. Effective February 1, 1999, residents were authorized to contract forward exchange cover to settle payments related to imports and exports of goods and services.

Arrangements for Payments and Receipts

Prescription of currency requirements

Because Senegal is linked to the French Treasury through an Operations Account, settlements with France, Monaco, and other Operations Account countries (WAEMU and CAEMC members and the Comoros) are made in French francs or the currency of any other Operations Account country.

Payment arrangements

Regional arrangements

An Operations Account is maintained with the French Treasury that links Operations Account countries. All purchases or sales of foreign currencies or euros against CFA francs are ultimately settled through a debit or credit to the Operations Account.

Clearing agreements

All payments related to current transactions between WAMA member countries are eligible for the pertinent clearing arrangements. However, this excludes payments related to subregional trade of finished products not originating in West Africa and transactions between member countries.

Administration of control

Exchange control is administered by the MEFP, which has delegated a part of the approval authority for exchange control to the BCEAO and to authorized banks. The Directorate of Money and Credit examines each request. Customs officers monitor outflows of foreign exchange and confirm imports and exports of goods effected through authorized banks, the Postal Administration, or the BCEAO. The BCEAO and the MEFP exercise exchange controls ex post. Effective February 1, 1999, the amount of transfers authorized without supporting documentation was increased to CFAF 300,000 from CFAF 100,000.

International security restrictions

In accordance with Executive Board
Decision No. 144-(52/51)   Yes.

In accordance with UN sanctions   Yes.

Payment arrears   No.

**Controls on trade in gold (coins
and/or bullion)**

Controls on domestic ownership and/or   There are no restrictions on precious metal brokers.
trade

Controls on external trade   Imports and exports of gold (ingots and coins originating in or bound to non-WAEMU
                                           countries) require prior authorization from the MEFP. Exempt from this requirement are
                                           (1) imports and exports by the Treasury or the BCEAO; (2) imports and exports of manu-
                                           factured articles containing a minor quantity of gold (such as gold-filled or gold-plated
                                           articles); (3) imports and exports by travelers of gold articles up to a combined weight of
                                           500 grams; and (4) imports and exports of gold products covered by Decree 94-668.

**Controls on exports and imports of
banknotes**

On exports

  Domestic currency   CFA franc banknotes may be exported freely by travelers within the WAEMU. However,
                                           the suspension of BCEAO repurchases of exported banknotes continues.

  Foreign currency   The reexportation of foreign banknotes for amounts exceeding the equivalent of
                                           CFAF 500,000 is allowed.

On imports

  Domestic currency   Banknotes and coins issued by the BCEAO may be imported freely by residents or
                                           nonresidents.

  Foreign currency   Nonresidents and residents may bring in any amount of foreign banknotes and coins
                                           (except gold coins) of countries outside the Operations Account area. Residents bringing
                                           in foreign banknotes and foreign currency traveler's checks exceeding the equivalent of
                                           CFAF 50,000 must sell them to an authorized intermediary bank within eight days.

Resident Accounts

Foreign exchange accounts permitted   The opening of these accounts with authorized intermediaries in Senegal is permitted, but
                                           is subject to prior approval by the MEFP with the consent of the BCEAO.

Held domestically   Yes.

Held abroad   Individuals traveling may hold bank accounts abroad to receive foreign currency legiti-
                                           mately exported or earned during their stay abroad. However, residents are required to
                                           repatriate assets held in these accounts within 30 days of their return. MEFP approval is
                                           required to open any other type of account.

**Accounts in domestic currency   No.
convertible into foreign currency**

Nonresident Accounts

Foreign exchange accounts permitted   Nonresidents may hold these accounts with authorized financial institutions. Effective
                                           February 1, 1999, the authorization to open these accounts is subject to prior approval
                                           of the MEFP with the consent of the BCEAO.

Domestic currency accounts   These accounts may not be credited with BCEAO banknotes, French franc notes, or
                                           banknotes issued by central banks that maintain an Operations Account with the French

Treasury. They may not be overdrawn without prior authorization of the MEFP. Funds may be transferred freely between nonresident accounts.

Convertible into foreign currency Nonresident-owned French franc accounts may be debited freely for the purchase by non-residents of foreign currencies on the official exchange market.

Blocked accounts No.

Imports and Import Payments

Foreign exchange budget No.

Financing requirements for imports

Advance payment requirements Advance payments for imports require authorization, and importers may not acquire foreign exchange until the contractual date of the payments.

Documentation requirements for release of foreign exchange for imports Exchange authorization, invoices, and import-export cards are required.

Domiciliation requirements On February 1, 1999, the amount of import transactions originating in countries outside the CFA franc zone required to be domiciled with authorized banks was increased to CFAF 5 million from CFAF 3 million.

Preshipment inspection An inspection is required for the quantity, quality, and price of goods exceeding CFAF 3 million f.o.b.

Import licenses and other nontariff measures Quantitative restrictions may be applied on products for public health and security reasons.

Negative list Narcotics and firearms are prohibited.

Import taxes and/or tariffs On January 1, 2000, the WAEMU introduced a CET with four rates (zero, 5%, 10%, and 20%). Thus, the maximum tariff rate was decreased to 20% from 25%.

State import monopoly No.

Exports and Export Proceeds

Repatriation requirements Proceeds from exports, including those to members of WAEMU and Operations Account countries, must normally be collected within 120 days of the arrival of the goods at their destination and repatriated through BCEAO not later than one month after the due date. Effective February 1, 1999, proceeds of exports between WAEMU countries are no longer required to be repatriated.

Surrender requirements Residents are required to surrender to an authorized bank all proceeds received from non-residents within a month after the due date.

Financing requirements No.

Documentation requirements A customs declaration is required.

Domiciliation All exports having a value in excess of CFAF 3 million must be domiciled. On February 1, 1999, this amount was increased to CFAF 5 million. Effective from that same date, exports between WAEMU countries are no longer subject to domiciliation.

Export licenses Licenses are required for gold exports.

Without quotas Yes.

Export taxes No.

Payments for Invisible Transactions and Current Transfers

Controls on these transfers Payments for invisible transactions to France, Monaco, and Operations Account countries may be made freely. Effective February 1, 1999, (1) payments and incomes of foreign ships in the WAEMU zone and WAEMU ships abroad are included under current operations; (2) indicative ceilings on foreign currency allocations were eliminated; and (3) the amount of foreign currency to be surrendered by residents after travel was increased to CFAF 300,000 from CFAF 50,000.

Trade-related payments

   Indicative limits/bona fide test — Yes.

Investment-related payments

   Prior approval — Yes.

   Indicative limits/bona fide test — Yes.

Payments for travel

   Prior approval — Resident travelers must present a travel document, such as a passport or a national identity card, to authorized banks before an exchange permit will be issued.

   Quantitative limits — Residents traveling for tourism or business purposes to countries in the franc zone that are not members of the WAEMU are allowed to take out banknotes other than CFA franc notes up to the equivalent of CFAF 2 million; amounts in excess of this limit may be taken out in other means of payment. The allowances for travel to countries outside the franc zone are (1) for tourist travel, the equivalent of CFAF 1 million without limit on the number of trips or differentiation by the age of the traveler; (2) for business travel, CFAF 200,000 a day for up to one month, corresponding to a maximum of CFAF 6 million (business travel allowances may be combined with tourism allowances). Allowances in excess of these limits are subject to the authorization of the MEFP.

   Indicative limits/bona fide test — Yes.

Personal payments

   Indicative limits/bona fide test — Yes.

Foreign workers' wages

   Indicative limits/bona fide test — Total net wages may be transferred upon presentation of pay slips, provided the transfer is made within three months following the pay period.

Credit card use abroad

   Prior approval — Yes.

   Quantitative limits — Credit cards issued by resident financial intermediaries and specifically authorized by the MEFP may be used up to the ceilings for tourist and business travel.

   Indicative limits/bona fide test — Yes.

Other payments

   Prior approval — Yes.

   Indicative limits/bona fide test — Yes.

Proceeds from Invisible Transactions and Current Transfers

Repatriation requirements — Yes.

Surrender requirements — Proceeds from invisible transactions with France, Monaco, and the Operations Account countries may be retained. All amounts due from residents of other countries for services and all income earned in those countries from foreign assets must be collected and surrendered, if received in foreign currency, within one month of the due date or the date of receipt.

Restrictions on use of funds — No.

Capital Transactions

Controls on capital and money market instruments	Capital movements between Senegal and France, Monaco, and the Operations Account countries are free of exchange control. Capital transfers to all other countries require the approval of the MEFP, but capital receipts from such countries are permitted freely. All investments abroad by residents of Senegal require prior authorization from the MEFP; up to 75% of such investments may be financed with borrowing from abroad. Effective February 1, 1999, there are no controls on foreign investment in WAEMU states or on foreign borrowing by residents. These operations are required to be reported for statistical purposes only.
	The prior authorization of the RCPSFM is required for the following operations: issuing, marketing of securities and real assets of foreign entities, canvassing, and publicity or advertising for investment abroad.
On capital market securities	
Shares or other securities of a participating nature	
Purchase locally by nonresidents	These purchases are subject to declaration for statistical purposes.
Sale or issue locally by nonresidents	The issue or marketing of securities by nonresident individuals or corporations is subject to a declaration for statistical purposes to the MEFP.
Purchase abroad by residents	These operations require the approval of the MEFP.
Sale or issue abroad by residents	Residents may sell freely securities of a resident company. If such operation leads to the placing of a resident institution under foreign control, investors are required to make a prior declaration to the MEFP. Any sale of securities for disinvestment purposes is also subject to prior declaration to the MEFP. Foreign currency proceeds from the sale of securities must be surrendered to an authorized bank.
Bonds or other debt securities	
Sale or issue locally by nonresidents	Yes.
Purchase abroad by residents	Yes.
Sale or issue abroad by residents	Yes.
On money market instruments	
Sale or issue locally by nonresidents	Residents may sell freely these instruments to nonresidents for disinvestment purposes. All other sales must be declared to the MEFP. Transfers of proceeds from these operations require an exchange permit, which must be submitted to the MEFP for clearance.
Purchase abroad by residents	Prior MEFP authorization is required.
Sale or issue abroad by residents	Yes.
On collective investment securities	
Sale or issue locally by nonresidents	A declaration to the MEFP is required for statistical purposes.
Purchase abroad by residents	Prior MEFP authorization is required.
Sale or issue abroad by residents	Prior MEFP authorization is required.
Controls on derivatives and other instruments	These instruments, which are virtually unknown in Senegal, are governed by the regulations applicable to securities and investments.
Purchase locally by nonresidents	Prior MEFP authorization is required.
Sale or issue locally by nonresidents	Yes.
Purchase abroad by residents	Yes.
Sale or issue abroad by residents	Yes.

Controls on credit operations

Commercial credits

By residents to nonresidents

Commercial credits may be granted freely in connection with merchandise exports if the due date of the payment is within 120 days of the shipment of the merchandise. Commercial credits in connection with the provision of services may be granted freely by residents; no limit is set for the payment due date.

To residents from nonresidents

Nonresidents may grant freely commercial credits to resident institutions. Repayments of commercial credits are generally authorized, subject to the submission of supporting documents.

Financial credits

By residents to nonresidents

These credits require the prior authorization of the MEFP. Transfer abroad of the funds necessary to service these facilities requires an exchange authorization, subject to the approval of the MEFP, and the submission of supporting documents.

To residents from nonresidents

There are no controls on the granting of these loans. The funds required for servicing these facilities must be transferred abroad by an authorized intermediary bank.

Guarantees, sureties, and financial backup facilities

By residents to nonresidents

The granting of guarantees and sureties is subject to prior approval by the MEFP. Transfer abroad of the funds required to service these facilities requires issuance of an exchange permit bearing the signature of the MEFP to accompany the supporting documents.

To residents from nonresidents

The granting of these facilities is subject to declaration to the MEFP for statistical purposes and settlement must be made through an authorized bank. If, however, these transactions take place between a direct investment company resident in Senegal and its parent company located abroad, they are considered to be direct investments and therefore require a prior declaration to the MEFP.

Controls on direct investment

Outward direct investment

Direct investments constitute investments implying control of a company or enterprise. Mere participation is not considered direct investment unless it exceeds 20% of the capital of a company whose shares are quoted on a stock exchange. Until February 1, 1999, all investments, including those made through foreign companies that are directly or indirectly controlled by persons in Senegal and those made by overseas branches or subsidiaries of companies in Senegal, required prior authorization from the MEFP. Effective February 1, 1999, authorization is no longer required for investment abroad consisting of the acquisition by residents of securities for which the issue or marketing by nonresidents has been authorized in advance by the RCPSFM. A maximum of 75% of such investments may be financed by foreign loans.

Inward direct investment

Foreign direct investments in Senegal, including those made by companies in Senegal that are directly or indirectly under foreign control and those made by branches or subsidiaries of foreign companies in Senegal, must be reported to the MEFP for statistical purposes.

Controls on liquidation of direct investment

The liquidation of direct and other investments, whether Senegalese investments abroad or foreign investments in Senegal, must be reported to the MEFP and the BCEAO within 20 days of each operation.

Controls on real estate transactions

Purchase abroad by residents

These purchases require the prior authorization of the MEFP.

Purchase locally by nonresidents

Purchases for purposes other than direct investment in a business, branch, or company are allowed. They require a declaration to the MEFP for statistical purposes.

Sale locally by nonresidents

Sales must be declared to the MEFP. Operations may be settled only after the approval of the MEFP. Following settlement, the liquidation or sale must be reported to the MEFP and to the BCEAO within 20 days of each operation.

Controls on personal capital movements

Loans

   By residents to nonresidents   These transactions are subject to authorization.

   To residents from nonresidents   These transactions are subject to declaration for statistical purposes and submission of a report to the MEFP when granted and when repaid.

Gifts, endowments, inheritances, and legacies

   By residents to nonresidents   Inheritances and legacies are generally authorized.

Settlement of debts abroad by immigrants   Immigrants with resident status must obtain the prior authorization of the MEFP to settle debts contracted abroad while they were nonresidents.

Transfer of assets

   Transfer abroad by emigrants   Subject to prior authorization upon presentation of supporting documents.

Transfer of gambling and prize earnings   Yes.

Provisions specific to commercial banks and other credit institutions

Borrowing abroad   Subject to declaration to the MEFP for statistical purposes and submission of the report to the MEFP when granted and when repaid. Repayment must be reported to the MEFP.

Maintenance of accounts abroad   Banks and other financial institutions may open accounts with their correspondent banks to settle operations for their own account or for their customers. However, banks may not keep amounts exceeding their current requirements in these accounts.

Lending to nonresidents (financial or commercial credits)   Prior MEFP authorization is required.

Purchase of locally issued securities denominated in foreign exchange   Yes.

Differential treatment of deposit accounts in foreign exchange

   Credit controls   Effective February 1, 1999, loans and other assistance granted to nonresidents are subject to the prior authorization of the MEFP, after the consent of the BCEAO has been obtained.

Investment regulations   The same regulations apply as for direct investment.

Provisions specific to institutional investors   No.

Other controls imposed by securities laws   No.

Changes During 1999

Exchange arrangement   *January 1.* The CFA franc was pegged to the euro.

                                  February 1. Residents were authorized to contract forward exchange cover to settle payments related to imports and exports of goods and services.

Arrangements for payments and receipts   *February 1.* The amount of transfers authorized without supporting documentation was increased to CFAF 300,000 from CFAF 100,000.

Nonresident accounts   *February 1.* The authorization to open nonresident accounts is issued by the BCEAO.

Imports and import payments	*February 1.* The amount of import transactions originating in countries outside the CFA franc zone required to be domiciled with authorized banks was increased to CFAF 5 million from CFAF 3 million.
Exports and export proceeds	*February 1.* Exports between WAEMU countries are no longer subject to domiciliation and repatriation requirements.
Payments for invisible transactions and current transfers	*February 1.* Payments and incomes of foreign ships in the WAEMU zone and WAEMU ships abroad are included under current operations. Indicative ceilings on foreign currency allocations were eliminated. The amount of foreign currency to be surrendered by residents after travel was increased to CFAF 300,000 from CFAF 50,000.
Capital transactions	*February 1.* The controls on foreign investment in WAEMU states or on foreign borrowing by residents were eliminated.
Controls on direct investment	*February 1.* Authorization is no longer required for investment abroad consisting of the acquisition by residents of securities for which the issue or marketing by nonresidents has been authorized in advance by the RCPSFM.
Provisions specific to commercial banks and other credit institutions	*February 1.* Loans and other assistance granted to nonresidents are subject to the prior authorization of the MEFP, after the consent of the BCEAO has been obtained.

Changes During 2000

Imports and import payments	*January 1.* The WAEMU introduced a CET with four rates (zero, 5%, 10%, and 20%) for all member countries except Guinea-Bissau. Thus, the maximum import duty was decreased to 20% from 25%.

SEYCHELLES

(Position as of December 31, 1999)

Status Under IMF Articles of Agreement

Article VIII	Date of acceptance: January 3, 1978.

Exchange Arrangement

Currency

The currency of Seychelles is the Seychelles rupee.

Other legal tender

Various commemorative gold coins issued on several occasions since 1976 are also legal tender.

Exchange rate structure

Unitary

The Exchange Control Bill, passed on April 14, 1999, outlawed the parallel market in foreign currency.

Classification

Conventional pegged arrangement

The Seychelles rupee is pegged to a weighted basket of currencies of Seychelles' main trading and tourism partners. The weights are as follows: the euro (31.2%), the Japanese yen (3.7%), the pound sterling (16.8%), the Singapore dollar (10.3%), the South African rand (11.5%), and the U.S. dollar (26.5%). Exchange rates for various currencies are quoted on the basis of their New York closing rates for the U.S. dollar on the previous day, using the U.S. dollar rate for the Seychelles rupee as derived from the fixed parity to the currency basket. The Central Bank of Seychelles (CBS) circulates these rates daily to the commercial banks. The CBS charges a commission of 0.125% on purchases and 0.875% on sales of pounds sterling, and U.S. dollars, and 0.500% on purchases and 1.000% on sales of French francs, respectively.

The commercial banks are authorized to deal in pounds sterling and other currencies at rates based on the exchange rates circulated daily by the CBS for the respective currencies. Other authorized dealers include casinos, guest houses, hotels, restaurants, self-catering establishments, tour operators, travel agents, shipping agents, and ship chandlers. These dealers are restricted to buying only in the course of their licensed activity. They must sell all their foreign currency proceeds to the five commercial banks. All other transactions in foreign exchange are prohibited.

Exchange tax

No.

Exchange subsidy

No.

Forward exchange market

No.

Arrangements for Payments and Receipts

Prescription of currency requirements

No.

Payment arrangements

Regional arrangements

Seychelles is a participant in the COMESA and the Cross-Border Initiative.

Administration of control

The exchange control authorities are the CBS and the MOF. The MOF partially controls foreign trade and domestic marketing through a mechanism of import and price controls.

International security restrictions

No.

Payment arrears

Private

Yes.

Controls on trade in gold (coins and/or bullion)

Controls on domestic ownership and/or trade

Residents may purchase, hold, and sell gold freely in any form, except for dealings in gold bullion, which are restricted to authorized dealers.

Controls on exports and imports of banknotes

On exports

  Domestic currency

Travelers may take out up to SR 100 of domestic currency.

  Foreign currency

Travelers may take out any amount of foreign currency.

On imports

  Foreign currency

Overseas visitors may bring in any amount of currency for travel expenses.

Resident Accounts

Foreign exchange accounts permitted

These accounts are permitted, but approval is required.

Held domestically

Yes.

Held abroad

Yes.

Accounts in domestic currency convertible into foreign currency

n.a.

Nonresident Accounts

Foreign exchange accounts permitted

Yes.

Domestic currency accounts

No.

Blocked accounts

Yes.

Imports and Import Payments

Foreign exchange budget

No.

Financing requirements for imports

No.

Documentation requirements for release of foreign exchange for imports

No.

Import licenses and other nontariff measures

Importers other than individuals are required to obtain import licenses from the Seychelles Licensing Authority, in accordance with objective criteria. In addition, for each shipment of commodities, an importer must apply to the Trade and Commerce Division of the MOF for a permit, the granting of which is discretionary. Permits are normally not granted for cars older than three years and some nonessential commodities.

An import quota system applicable to most imports is in effect. The quota allocation system is based on 75% of importers' 1995 imports. Imports related to the tourist industry are granted a higher percentage of their 1995 imports, and new importers are allocated SR 50,000.

Import taxes and/or tariffs

Imports are subject to taxes of up to 200%, with most goods subject to rates ranging between 5% and 30%.

State import monopoly

The Seychelles Marketing Board has the monopoly on imports of rice, sugar, meat, vegetables, margarine, tomato sauce, animal feed, oil, coffee and tea, fruits, flour, and chili sauce.

Exports and Export Proceeds

Repatriation requirements	Yes.
Surrender requirements	All export proceeds must be converted through domestic commercial banks, who are the only authorized sellers of foreign exchange. Surrender requirements are 20% to the pipeline; 30% to finance essential government imports; and the remaining 50% to be used at the discretion of banks.
Financing requirements	No.
Documentation requirements	No.
Export licenses	No.
Export taxes	No.

Payments for Invisible Transactions and Current Transfers

Controls on these transfers	No.

Proceeds from Invisible Transactions and Current Transfers

Repatriation requirements	Yes.
Surrender requirements	Residents must surrender the proceeds to a commercial bank within 21 days of the transaction.
Restrictions on use of funds	Receipts, with the exception of dividend remittances and transfers of management fees, may be disposed of freely.

Capital Transactions

Controls on capital and money market instruments	
On capital market securities	
Shares or other securities of a participating nature	
Purchase locally by nonresidents	Yes.
Sale or issue locally by nonresidents	Yes.
Controls on derivatives and other instruments	No.
Controls on credit operations	No.
Controls on direct investment	
Inward direct investment	Foreign investment is permitted freely, provided that such investment does not involve ownership of land.
Controls on liquidation of direct investment	No.
Controls on real estate transactions	
Purchase locally by nonresidents	Yes.
Sale locally by nonresidents	Yes.

Controls on personal capital movements	No.
Provisions specific to commercial banks and other credit institutions	
Differential treatment of deposit accounts in foreign exchange	
Liquid asset requirements	The liquidity reserve ratio for commercial banks is set at 70% of their deposit liabilities, while the cash reserve ratio is 2.5%.
Investment regulations	
Abroad by banks	Yes.
In banks by nonresidents	Yes.
Provisions specific to institutional investors	No.
Other controls imposed by securities laws	No.

Changes During 1999

Exchange arrangement	*January 1.* The basket of currencies to which the rupee is pegged was changed to reflect the introduction of the euro.
	April 14. The Exchange Control Bill was passed, outlawing the parallel market in foreign currency.

SIERRA LEONE

(Position as of December 31, 1999)

Status Under IMF Articles of Agreement

Article VIII   Date of acceptance: December 14, 1995.

Exchange Arrangement

Currency   The currency of Sierra Leone is the Sierra Leonean leone.

Exchange rate structure Dual.

Classification

Independently floating   Exchange rates are freely determined in the interbank market. Commercial banks and licensed foreign exchange bureaus may buy and sell foreign exchange with customers and trade among themselves or with the Bank of Sierra Leone (BSL), the central bank, freely. The BSL determines the exchange rate to be used in official transactions, including for customs valuation purposes, which is based on the weighted average mid-rate of purchases and sales made by commercial banks and foreign exchange bureaus during the last five business days and the weekly auction. The official buying and selling rates are set within ±1% of the official mid-rate. Foreign exchange bureaus are limited to spot transactions and are not allowed to sell traveler's checks.

Exchange tax   No.

Exchange subsidy   No.

Forward exchange market No.

Arrangements for Payments and Receipts

Prescription of currency requirements Payments for imports may be made in leones to the credit of an external account in the currency of the exporting country, in pounds sterling, or in U.S. dollars. Receipts from exports to countries other than China may be obtained in leones from an external account in the currency of the importing country or in any specified convertible currency.

Payment arrangements

Bilateral payment arrangements

Inoperative   Yes.

Administration of control The MOF formulates exchange control policy in consultation with the BSL, but the day-to-day administration of exchange control is carried out by the BSL with the assistance of the commercial banks.

International security restrictions No.

Payment arrears

Official   Yes.

Private   Yes.

Controls on trade in gold (coins and/or bullion)

Controls on domestic ownership and/or trade Residents may freely purchase, hold, and sell gold coins in Sierra Leone for numismatic purposes. Also, residents and nonresidents may freely purchase, hold, or sell certain Sierra Leonean commemorative gold coins. Residents are not allowed to hold gold in the form of bars or dust without a valid miner's or dealer's license.

| Controls on external trade | Exports of gold require a license. Imports of gold in any form other than jewelry constituting the personal effects of a traveler require an individual import license. |

Controls on exports and imports of banknotes

On exports

Domestic currency — On leaving Sierra Leone, travelers may take out up to Le 50,000.

Foreign currency — Nonresident travelers may take out any amount of foreign currency notes they declared on arrival. Employees on official business may take out up to the amount of the per diem allowance provided for that purpose. Resident travelers may take out up to $5,000 without restriction. Residents should declare on departure foreign exchange in excess of $5,000 with supporting documents.

On imports

Domestic currency — The importation of domestic banknotes is limited to Le 50,000 for each traveler.

Foreign currency — Commercial banks (authorized dealers) are allowed to import foreign currency to meet their operational requirements.

Resident Accounts

Foreign exchange accounts permitted — Residents are permitted to maintain foreign currency accounts denominated in any convertible currency. These accounts, for which minimum balances vary from bank to bank, earn interest at a rate determined by the commercial banks. They may be credited with funds transferred from abroad, and balances on these accounts may be converted into leones to meet the account holder's local expenditures. Transfers abroad of balances in foreign currency accounts are permitted for current international transactions without prior approval from the BSL, subject to fulfilling the regulation governing the transactions.

Held domestically — Yes.

Held abroad — No.

Accounts in domestic currency convertible into foreign currency — n.r.

Nonresident Accounts

Foreign exchange accounts permitted — The same regulations apply as for resident accounts. All documented inward remittances may also be externalized without reference to the BSL.

Domestic currency accounts — Accounts in leones held on behalf of diplomatic missions, UN agencies, and their accredited staff are designated as external accounts. Leone deposits into external accounts are vetted by the BSL, and balances standing to the credit of the account may be externalized without reference to the BSL.

Convertible into foreign currency — These accounts may be converted into foreign currency, but approval is required.

Blocked accounts — Yes.

Imports and Import Payments

Foreign exchange budget — No.

Financing requirements for imports — n.r.

Documentation requirements for release of foreign exchange for imports — All applications for purchases of foreign exchange to pay for imported goods must be submitted to a commercial bank in Sierra Leone, supported by the following documents: completed exchange control form, original pro forma invoice, final invoice, original bill of lading/airway bill, tax clearance certificate, and preshipment inspection certificate.

Preshipment inspection	All goods imported into Sierra Leone, except petroleum and goods specifically exempted by the MOF, are subject to preshipment inspection and price verification by an international company appointed by the government.
Letters of credit	Goods to be financed with importers' own foreign exchange resources are permitted without LCs established with a local commercial bank.

Import licenses and other nontariff measures

Negative list	All goods, except military goods, may be imported freely without a license.
Import taxes and/or tariffs	A sales tax of 20% of the landed value is levied on all imports except for capital goods and their spare parts, petroleum products, and baby food. All imports by unincorporated businesses are subject to a 2% tax as advance payment of income taxes.
State import monopoly	n.a.

Exports and Export Proceeds

Repatriation requirements	Exporters must repatriate export proceeds within 90 days of the date of export (approval of the BSL is required for an extension beyond 90 days). Proceeds from exports of diamonds that were prefinanced from external sources are not subject to the repatriation requirement.
Financing requirements	n.r.
Documentation requirements	All exporters of commercial goods are required to complete export forms that must be endorsed by the exporter's commercial bank.
Preshipment inspection	All exports, except for those exempted by the MOF, are subject to preshipment inspection and price verification, which is undertaken by an inspection company appointed by the government. Exporters who are subject to inspection must pay an export inspection fee of 1% before clearing their goods through customs.
Export licenses	Licenses are required only for exports of gold and diamonds; these export licenses, valid for one year or six months, are issued by the Department of Mines. Exports of the following articles are prohibited: those containing more than 25% silver; those manufactured or produced more than 75 years before the date of exportation; those mounted or set with diamonds, precious stones, or pearls (excluding personal jewelry or ornaments up to a value not exceeding the equivalent of $1,000); postage stamps of philatelic interest; and works of art.
Without quotas	Yes.
Export taxes	Licensed exporters of diamonds are subject to an administrative fee of 1% and an income tax of 1.5% based on the value in U.S. dollars of diamonds exported. Licensed exporters of gold must pay a 2.5% royalty.

Payments for Invisible Transactions and Current Transfers

Controls on these transfers	Authority to provide foreign exchange for legitimate expenses is delegated to the commercial banks. A tax clearance certificate is required for payments and transfers for certain types of current international transactions.
Payments for travel	
Quantitative limits	The limit is $5,000.
Indicative limits/bona fide test	Applications for travel allowances in excess of the limit must be supported by travel documents, e.g., a ticket or passport.
Personal payments	Information is not available on the payment of pensions.

Foreign workers' wages

Prior approval

Commercial banks may make remittances in favor of nonresident employees of international institutions, agencies, or foreign nongovernmental organizations only up to the remuneration package and in favor of other nonresidents when requests for such payment are supported by a valid work permit, a remuneration package agreement, and a tax clearance certificate.

Proceeds from Invisible Transactions and Current Transfers

Repatriation requirements   No.

Restrictions on use of funds   No.

Capital Transactions

Controls on capital and money market instruments

On capital market securities

Shares or other securities of a participating nature

   Purchase locally by nonresidents

BSL approval is required before a security registered in or outside Sierra Leone may be transferred to or purchased by a nonresident.

   Sale or issue locally by nonresidents

These transactions are not permitted.

   Purchase abroad by residents

Permission of the BSL is required both to purchase securities abroad and to transfer funds abroad to effect the purchase.

All funds accruing on such investment as well as the capital upon termination of the investment must be repatriated to Sierra Leone.

   Sale or issue abroad by residents

Capital in respect of securities registered in Sierra Leone may not be transferred abroad without permission; for permission to be given, the company is usually required to obtain bank certification of the funds brought into Sierra Leone.

On money market instruments

Sale or issue locally by nonresidents   These transactions are not permitted.

Purchase abroad by residents   Purchases funded with domestic resources are not permitted.

Sale or issue abroad by residents   These transactions require BSL approval.

On collective investment securities   These instruments are not yet available in Sierra Leone.

Purchase abroad by residents   Purchases with funds brought from abroad are allowed. BSL certification is required.

Sale or issue abroad by residents   Yes.

Controls on derivatives and other instruments   These instruments are not yet available in Sierra Leone.

Controls on credit operations

Financial credits

By residents to nonresidents

Generally, permission of the BSL is required for the granting of any loan, whether by way of advance or bank overdraft, in Sierra Leone to nonresident entities. Permission of the BSL is also required for nonresident entities to borrow outside Sierra Leone. In addition to the above documentation, the proposed arrangement for repayment should be provided.

To residents from nonresidents   Prior approval of the BSL is required.

Guarantees, sureties, and financial backup facilities	
By residents to nonresidents	Prior approval of the BSL should be obtained for the giving or renewal of any guarantee or similar undertaking, and the resident's exposure must be 100% covered by the nonresident.
To residents from nonresidents	Prior approval of the BSL is required for these transactions and for the transfer of funds to service the facilities.
Controls on direct investment	
Outward direct investment	Investments abroad are not allowed.
Inward direct investment	Yes.
Controls on liquidation of direct investment	No.
Controls on real estate transactions	
Purchase abroad by residents	Permission from the BSL is required.
Controls on personal capital movements	n.r.
Provisions specific to commercial banks and other credit institutions	Commercial banks should not hold more than 25% of their deposit liabilities in foreign currency.
Maintenance of accounts abroad	Yes.
Lending to nonresidents (financial or commercial credits)	Banks are not engaged in foreign lending, and there are no regulations in this respect.
Lending locally in foreign exchange	Banks are not engaged in this lending.
Provisions specific to institutional investors	n.r.
Other controls imposed by securities laws	n.a.

Changes During 1999

No significant changes occurred in the exchange and trade system.

SINGAPORE

(Position as of December 31, 1999)

Status Under IMF Articles of Agreement

Article VIII   Date of acceptance: November 9, 1968.

Exchange Arrangement

Currency   The currency of Singapore is the Singapore dollar.

Other legal tender   Singapore and Brunei currency notes and coins are freely interchangeable at par without charge in Singapore and Brunei Darussalam.

Exchange rate structure   Unitary.

Classification

Managed floating with no pre-   The authorities use the exchange rate as an intermediate target, allowing the Singapore
announced path for the exchange rate   dollar to fluctuate within an undisclosed target band.

Exchange tax   No.

Exchange subsidy   No.

Forward exchange market   Foreign currency futures are traded at the Singapore Exchange (SGX). Banks may hedge their exchange risk through a forward foreign exchange transaction.

Arrangements for Payments and Receipts

**Prescription of currency   No.
requirements**

Payment arrangements

Regional arrangements   Singapore is a member of ASEAN.

Administration of control   Singapore has no exchange controls, although the Monetary Authority of Singapore (MAS) retains responsibility for exchange control matters. The Trade Development Board under the Ministry of Trade and Industry administers import and export licensing requirements for a very small number of products.

International security restrictions

In accordance with UN sanctions   Financial assets owned by residents of Iraq and Libya are blocked. Singapore observes the import and export prohibitions covered by the UN Security Council resolutions.

Payment arrears   No.

**Controls on trade in gold (coins   No.
and/or bullion)**

**Controls on exports and imports of   No.
banknotes**

Resident Accounts

Foreign exchange accounts permitted   Yes.

Held domestically   Yes.

Held abroad   Yes.

Accounts in domestic currency convertible into foreign currency	Yes.

Nonresident Accounts

Foreign exchange accounts permitted	Yes.
Domestic currency accounts	Yes.
Convertible into foreign currency	Yes.
Blocked accounts	Those covered by the UN Security Council resolutions.

Imports and Import Payments

Foreign exchange budget	n.a.
Financing requirements for imports	No.
Documentation requirements for release of foreign exchange for imports	No.
Import licenses and other nontariff measures	Licenses are required for imports of rice. A few imports are controlled for health, safety, or security reasons.
Import taxes and/or tariffs	Very few imports are dutiable. Singapore is a party to the CEPT scheme for the AFTA. Customs duties are levied on imports of liquor, tobacco, petroleum, and automobiles.
State import monopoly	No.

Exports and Export Proceeds

Repatriation requirements	No.
Financing requirements	No.
Documentation requirements	No.
Export licenses	
Without quotas	Export licenses are required for substances that deplete the stratospheric ozone layer, timber, and rubber.
With quotas	Certain exports (e.g., textiles and clothing) are subject to quantitative restrictions and other nontariff barriers in importing countries.
Export taxes	n.a.

Payments for Invisible Transactions and Current Transfers

Controls on these transfers	No.

Proceeds from Invisible Transactions and Current Transfers

Repatriation requirements	No.
Restrictions on use of funds	No.

Capital Transactions

Controls on capital and money market instruments

On capital market securities

Shares or other securities of a participating nature

Sale or issue locally by nonresidents

As of November 26, 1999, financial institutions may, without prior consultation with the MAS, arrange equity listings for nonresidents. (Previously, only nonresident companies with at least 20% of their revenues, profits, or expenses attributable to Singapore could list in Singapore dollars.) The arranging institution must ensure that, if the Singapore dollar proceeds of the initial public offering are not to be used for economic purposes in Singapore, the Singapore dollar proceeds must be converted into foreign currency before drawing down by the issuer.

Bonds or other debt securities

Sale or issue locally by nonresidents

Financial institutions may, without prior consultation with the MAS, arrange Singapore dollar bond issues for nonresidents if the Singapore dollar proceeds from the issuance are used for preapproved economic purposes in Singapore. Financial institutions must consult the MAS when the proceeds are to be used outside Singapore or for purposes not explicitly allowed. The proceeds from all such bond issues must be converted or swapped into foreign currency for use outside Singapore. Effective November 26, 1999, all rated and nonrated sovereigns and foreign corporations are allowed to issue Singapore dollar bonds. (Previously, only foreign entities of good standing were allowed to issue these bonds.) In the case of unrated corporations, the investor base is restricted to sophisticated investors.

Controls on derivatives and other instruments

Unless explicitly allowed by the MAS notice on the noninternationalization of the Singapore dollar, banks must consult the MAS before transacting with nonresidents in Singapore dollar financial derivatives. As of November 26, 1999, there are no controls on Singapore dollar over-the-counter interest rate derivatives. Also from the same date, the MAS allows banks to enter into a repo transaction for any amount in Singapore government securities and Singapore dollar–denominated bonds, on the condition that there is full delivery of collateral. Previously, Singapore dollar repo transactions with foreign entities that exceeded S$20 million had to be approved by the MAS.

Purchase locally by nonresidents

Yes.

Sale or issue locally by nonresidents

Yes.

Controls on credit operations

No.

Controls on direct investment

No.

Controls on liquidation of direct investment

No.

Controls on real estate transactions

Purchase abroad by residents

Yes.

Purchase locally by nonresidents

Foreign investment in residential and other properties (including vacant land) that have been zoned or approved for industrial or commercial use requires government approval. Foreigners may, however, freely purchase residential units in buildings of six or more stories and in approved condominium developments. Foreigners who make an economic contribution to Singapore are given favorable consideration to purchase other residential properties for their own use and, in the case of foreign companies, to accommodate their senior personnel.

Controls on personal capital movements

No.

Provisions specific to commercial banks and other credit institutions

Lending to nonresidents (financial or commercial credits)

Banks and other financial institutions must consult the MAS before extending to nonresidents Singapore dollar credit facilities exceeding S$5 million, where the credit facilities would be used for purposes other than those expressly permitted in the relevant MAS notice.

Banks and other financial institutions need not consult the MAS if nonbank nonresidents use the proceeds from Singapore dollar credit facilities for preapproved economic activities in Singapore or for hedging the Singapore dollar exchange rate and interest rate risks arising from these economic activities.

Lending locally in foreign exchange

Banks' lendings to a single borrower or groups of borrowers, regardless of residency, are subject to a limit of 25% of capital.

Purchase of locally issued securities denominated in foreign exchange

Banks' investments, regardless of currency, are subject to a limit of 40% of capital.

Differential treatment of deposit accounts in foreign exchange

Reserve requirements

Foreign currency deposits accepted under the Asian currency units of banks are not subject to reserve requirements.

Liquid asset requirements

Foreign currency deposits accepted under the Asian currency units of banks are not subject to the liquid asset requirement.

Investment regulations

Abroad by banks

Banks are required to seek prior approval from the MAS to acquire 20% or more of the shares in any company.

In banks by nonresidents

Total foreign shareholding in a local bank was subject to a 40% limit. This limit was abolished on May 17, 1999.

Open foreign exchange position limits

No limits are set by the MAS, but it reviews the internal control systems of banks to ensure that adequate limits and controls are established for treasury activities.

Provisions specific to institutional investors

Insurers may only include 30% of their foreign currency–denominated and overseas assets as part of their admitted assets that goes into the calculation of the solvency of the fund. Of this, 10% must be foreign currency deposits with an approved financial institution, foreign currency fixed-income securities graded AA and above, and equities listed on any stock exchange. Insurers may include an additional 10% of foreign currency–denominated fixed-income assets that are fully hedged to the Singapore dollar as admitted assets. Insurers are allowed to invest assets in relation to the currency of their liabilities.

Limits (max.) on securities issued by nonresidents and on portfolio invested abroad

Yes.

Limits (max.) on portfolio invested abroad

Yes.

Currency-matching regulations on assets/liabilities composition

Yes.

Other controls imposed by securities laws

No.

Changes During 1999

Capital transactions

Controls on capital and money market instruments

November 26. Financial institutions could arrange equity listings for nonresidents without consulting the MAS.

November 26. All rated and nonrated sovereigns and foreign corporations were allowed to issue Singapore dollar bonds.

Controls on derivatives and other instruments

November 26. Banks were allowed to enter into a repo transaction in Singapore government securities and Singapore dollar–denominated bonds listed on the SGX in any amount.

November 26. Controls on Singapore dollar over-the-counter interest rate derivatives were eliminated.

Provisions specific to commercial banks and other credit institutions

May 17. The 40% limit on foreign investment holdings in local banks was abolished.

SLOVAK REPUBLIC

(Position as of January 31, 2000)

Status Under IMF Articles of Agreement

Article VIII   Date of acceptance: October 1, 1995.

Exchange Arrangement

Currency	The currency of the Slovak Republic is the Slovak koruna.
Exchange rate structure	Unitary.
Classification	
Managed floating with no pre-announced path for the exchange rate	The exchange rate of the koruna is determined in the foreign exchange market. The National Bank of Slovakia (NBS) no longer guarantees the koruna's exchange rate but would intervene primarily to smooth large fluctuations in the exchange rate and also if the exchange rate moved to an unacceptable level.
Exchange tax	No.
Exchange subsidy	No.
Forward exchange market	No.

Arrangements for Payments and Receipts

Prescription of currency requirements	No.
Payment arrangements	No.
Administration of control	The foreign exchange authorities are the MOF and the NBS. The MOF exercises jurisdiction in matters relating to other ministries and central bodies of the state administration, budgetary and subsidized state organizations, special-purpose state funds, juridical persons established by separate law who are connected through financial ties to the state budget, and local communities and their budgetary and subsidized organizations. The MOF maintains foreign exchange records and documents pertaining to interstate negotiations on property claims, and implements the results of these negotiations within the country. The NBS exercises jurisdiction pursuant to residents other than those specified above and to nonresidents.
International security restrictions	No.
Payment arrears	No.
Controls on trade in gold (coins and/or bullion)	
Controls on domestic ownership and/or trade	Trade in gold is conducted exclusively by banks to the extent stipulated in their license.
Controls on exports and imports of banknotes	There are reporting obligations on exports and imports of banknotes and coins in Slovak and foreign currencies together exceeding Sk 150,000; and on post or other deliveries containing banknotes and coins together exceeding Sk 20,000.
On exports	
Domestic currency	Yes.
Foreign currency	Yes.
On imports	
Domestic currency	Yes.

Foreign currency   Yes.

Resident Accounts

Foreign exchange accounts permitted   Natural persons are eligible to open foreign exchange accounts during their stay abroad; otherwise, approval from the NBS is required.

Held domestically   No.

Held abroad   A resident may open an account abroad in foreign or Slovak currency, or enter into a contract for the safe custody or deposit of funds in foreign or Slovak currency in an account maintained abroad, only after obtaining a foreign exchange permit from the NBS or the MOF. However, a foreign exchange permit is not required (1) when the resident has a banking or foreign exchange license; (2) in connection with a private individual's stay abroad; (3) to cover the documented operating costs of the resident's local representation or agency abroad; (4) for the purpose of depositing the resident's foreign exchange funds if foreign legislation forbids the transfer of such funds to the country; or (5) for the payment of fees, taxes, and other documented expenses related to the administration and maintenance of real estate owned by the resident abroad.

Accounts in domestic currency convertible into foreign currency   This applies to current international transactions and for permitted capital account transactions.

Nonresident Accounts

Foreign exchange accounts permitted   Yes.

Domestic currency accounts   Yes.

Convertible into foreign currency   This applies only to receipts relating to current transactions.

Blocked accounts   No.

Imports and Import Payments

Foreign exchange budget   No.

Financing requirements for imports   No.

Documentation requirements for release of foreign exchange for imports   No.

Import licenses and other nontariff measures   A system of variable levies accompanies import licensing.

Licenses with quotas   Effective January 1, 1999, a nonautomatic licensing system is applicable to the following goods: (1) brown coal; (2) oil and natural gas imported from Russia; and (3) beer and soft drinks from the Czech Republic. This system also applies to the following products: effective February 1, 1999, shoes from China; effective May 1, 1999, sugar from the Czech Republic; from December 1, 1999, sugar from Poland; and, from May through December 1999, pork and live fatted pigs from the Czech Republic.

Import taxes and/or tariffs   All imports, except those from the Czech Republic, with whom there is a customs union, and from countries with whom the Slovak Republic has preferential agreements, are subject to an ad valorem tariff. Imports from developing countries are granted preferential treatment under the GSP; thus, 48 least-developed countries and 102 developing countries are granted 50% and 100% reductions, respectively, from duties applicable to selected commodities. Imported goods are taxed with a VAT, and there are excise duties on mineral oils, spirits, wine, beer, and tobacco. Since June 1, 1999, imports are also subject to a temporary import surcharge of 7%, which was reduced to 5% on January 1, 2000.

State import monopoly   No.

Exports and Export Proceeds

Repatriation requirements	Residents are required to transfer or import all funds acquired abroad in koruny or foreign exchange into the country without delay, net of fees, taxes, and other expenses incurred abroad in connection with the acquisition of such funds, but not later than 30 days from the date of acquisition, or the date of learning of such acquisition, or from the date of becoming a resident in the country. This duty does not apply to (1) foreign or Slovak currency used by a resident natural person during his/her stay abroad; and (2) reinvestment of earnings from direct investment and from employees' securities, although this is not applicable to cases when such investment requires a foreign exchange permit.
Financing requirements	No.
Documentation requirements	No.
Export licenses	
Without quotas	Export licenses are required for narcotics, poisons, firearms and ammunition, and all dual-use goods and technologies.
With quotas	Export licenses are required for (1) a restricted number of agricultural goods; (2) some strategic industrial goods, such as oil products, fuels, or electricity; (3) hardly renewable raw materials, such as raw wood, or metal waste; and (4) imported goods for preventing speculative import-export activities.
Export taxes	No.

Payments for Invisible Transactions and Current Transfers

Controls on these transfers	
Payments for travel	
Quantitative limits	Official travel by employees of budgetary and subsidized organizations is subject to allowances, depending on the country of destination.

Proceeds from Invisible Transactions and Current Transfers

Repatriation requirements	Residents must repatriate all proceeds in koruny or foreign exchange without delay, net of fees, taxes, and other expenses incurred abroad in connection with the acquisition of such funds, but no later than 30 days from the date of acquisition, or the date of learning of such acquisition, or from the date of becoming a resident in the country.
Restrictions on use of funds	No.

Capital Transactions

Controls on capital and money market instruments	
On capital market securities	
Shares or other securities of a participating nature	
Sale or issue locally by nonresidents	These transactions require a permit from the NBS and the MOF, except (1) when foreign securities are accepted for trading on the main market of the foreign stock exchange, and (2) in the case of foreign exchange transactions in which the government or the NBS participates.
Purchase abroad by residents	These transactions require a foreign exchange permit from the NBS or the MOF except for (1) foreign securities accepted for trading on the main market of the foreign stock

exchange; (2) purchases of employees' securities; and (3) foreign exchange transactions in which the government or the NBS participates.

Sale or issue abroad by residents	These transactions require a foreign exchange permit from the NBS.

Bonds or other debt securities

Purchase locally by nonresidents	These transactions require a foreign exchange permit, except (1) when the government or the NBS participates in the transactions and (2) when a resident accepts a financial credit from a nonresident with a maturity of one year or more.
Sale or issue locally by nonresidents	Effective January 1, 2000, these transactions require a foreign exchange permit from the NBS except when (1) foreign securities are tradable on the main market of the foreign stock exchange; (2) bonds are issued by OECD member countries; or (3) the government or the NBS participates in foreign exchange transactions.
Purchase abroad by residents	These transactions require a foreign exchange permit from the NBS, except when (1) the government or the NBS participates in the foreign exchange transaction; (2) a resident grants a financial credit with maturity of one year or more to an OECD country resident; and (3) the bonds are issued by foreign countries.
Sale or issue abroad by residents	Effective January 1, 2000, a foreign exchange permit from the NBS is required except for bonds or other debt securities with a maturity of more than one year. Issuance of local bonds with a maturity of less than one year is subject to a permit from the MOF, except for government bonds.

On money market instruments

Sale or issue locally by nonresidents	The same regulations apply as for bonds or other debt securities.
Purchase abroad by residents	The same regulations apply as for bonds or other debt securities.
Sale or issue abroad by residents	The same regulations apply as for bonds or other debt securities. In addition, issuance of securities is subject to a permit from the MOF.

On collective investment securities

Sale or issue locally by nonresidents	Nonresidents may perform this activity through the mediation of their branch in the Slovak Republic. A foreign exchange permit is required.
Purchase abroad by residents	The same regulations apply as for bonds or other debt securities.
Sale or issue abroad by residents	The same regulations apply as for bonds or other debt securities.

Controls on derivatives and other instruments

Purchase locally by nonresidents	Yes.
Sale or issue locally by nonresidents	A foreign exchange permit from the NBS and the MOF is required.
Purchase abroad by residents	A resident who is an authorized foreign exchange dealer and is not a bank or a securities trader may enter into contracts for dealing in financial derivatives solely on the basis of a foreign exchange permit. A foreign exchange permit is not required when the contract or business is effected with an authorized foreign exchange dealer within the range allowed by the banking or foreign exchange license.
Sale or issue abroad by residents	The same regulations apply as for purchases abroad by residents.

Controls on credit operations

Commercial credits

By residents to nonresidents	Effective January 1, 2000, a foreign exchange permit from the NBS or MOF is required, except for credits granted by residents of the Slovak Republic to residents of OECD countries.
To residents from nonresidents	Effective January 1, 2000, a foreign exchange permit from the NBS or MOF is required except when (1) the maturity is one year or more, and/or (2) the credit is granted by a resident of an OECD country to a resident of the Slovak Republic.

Financial credits	A foreign exchange permit from the MOF or NBS is required.

By residents to nonresidents	Financial credits with a maturity of one year or more granted by Slovak residents to residents of OECD countries are liberalized.
To residents from nonresidents	Financial credits with a maturity of one year or more are liberalized.
Guarantees, sureties, and financial backup facilities	These transactions require a foreign exchange permit.
By residents to nonresidents	Guarantees with a maturity of one year or more are liberalized.

Controls on direct investment

Outward direct investment	A foreign exchange permit from the NBS and an agreement from the MOF are required, except when the investment is made in an OECD country.

Controls on liquidation of direct investment   No.

Controls on real estate transactions

Purchase abroad by residents	A foreign exchange permit is required, except for OECD countries.
Purchase locally by nonresidents	Nonresidents, with the exception of Slovak citizens, may acquire real estate in the country solely in the following cases: (1) by inheritance; (2) for the purpose of establishing diplomatic representation of a foreign country under conditions of mutuality; (3) when the real estate acquired is co-owned by a married couple, and when one of the partners is a nonresident, or when a nonresident acquires real estate from a spouse, sibling, parent, or grandparent; (4) when there is an exchange of domestic real estate owned by a nonresident for other domestic fixed assets, the price of which, pursuant to separate regulations, does not exceed the price of the original real estate as determined in accordance with separate regulations; (5) when the nonresident has preemptive purchase rights based on share ownership of the real estate; (6) when the real estate was built by the nonresident on his or her own land; (7) when expressly permitted under separate legislation; and, effective January 1, 2000, (8) when branches of foreign banks, commercial insurance companies, security traders, and trustees use the real estate in the course of their core business activity.

Controls on personal capital movements   No.

Provisions specific to commercial banks and other credit institutions	Banks must conduct their activities in accordance with their banking license. In the case of controlled operations not covered in their banking license, the same approval as for other residents is required.
Borrowing abroad	Borrowing is allowed within the extent of the banking foreign exchange license.
Maintenance of accounts abroad	Maintenance of accounts abroad is allowed within the extent of the banking foreign exchange license.
Lending to nonresidents (financial or commercial credits)	Such lending requires a foreign exchange permit when the maturity is less than one year.
Lending locally in foreign exchange	Lending is allowed within the extent of the banking license.
Purchase of locally issued securities denominated in foreign exchange	A foreign exchange permit is required.

Investment regulations

Abroad by banks	A foreign exchange permit from the NBS is required when the banking license does not include dealing in foreign securities. Banking regulations issued on September 16, 1999, amended these previous regulations. There are limits for investing in foreign companies abroad on the basis of the capital of banks.
In banks by nonresidents	The same regulations apply for residents and nonresidents. Five zones—5%, 10%, 20%, 33%, and 50%—for investment are defined, for which the investors are required to seek prior NBS permission.
Open foreign exchange position limits	The nonsecured open foreign exchange position for the Czech koruna, the dollar, the euro, the pound sterling, and the Swiss franc must not exceed 10% of the bank's capital. The nonsecured foreign exchange position for other currencies must not exceed 5% of the bank's capital. The total nonsecured foreign exchange position of banks must not exceed

25%. For the calculation of capital, the same calculation is used as for capital adequacy. Foreign banks' branches are not obliged to reporting; they must, however, keep the prudential banking regulations.

On resident assets and liabilities	Yes.
On nonresident assets and liabilities	Yes.

Provisions specific to institutional investors

Limits (max.) on securities issued by nonresidents and on portfolio invested abroad

Effective December 7, 1999, a new Act on Collective Investment came into effect, limiting securities issued by the same emitter to 10% of the whole equity.

Limits (max.) on portfolio invested abroad

The same regulations apply as for nonresidents.

Other controls imposed by securities laws

A new Act on Securities Amendment and an Act on Bonds Amendment were issued on June 6, 1999, and December 7, 1999, respectively.

Changes During 1999

Imports and import payments

January 1. A nonautomatic licensing system was made applicable to the following goods: (1) brown coal; (2) oil and natural gas imported from Russia; and (3) beer and soft drinks from the Czech Republic. This system is also applied to shoes from China, sugar from the Czech Republic and Poland, and pork and live fatted pigs from the Czech Republic, effective from various dates throughout the year.

June 1. A temporary import surcharge of 7% was introduced.

Capital transactions

Provisions specific to commercial banks and other credit institutions

September 16. The new Banking Act came into effect.

Provisions specific to institutional investors

December 7. The Act on Collective Investment came into effect, limiting securities issued by the same emitter to 10% of the whole equity.

Other controls imposed by securities laws

June 6. A new Act on Securities Amendment was issued.

December 7. An Act on Bonds Amendment was issued.

Changes During 2000

Imports and import payments

January 1. The import surcharge was reduced to 5%.

Capital transactions

Controls on capital and money market instruments

January 1. A foreign exchange permit is no longer required to trade locally foreign securities with a maturity of more than one year that are issued by residents of OECD countries when the government or the NBS participates in the foreign exchange transaction.

Controls on credit operations

January 1. A foreign exchange permit is no longer required for residents to grant credits to residents of OECD countries when the maturity of the loan is one year or more.

Controls on real estate transactions

January 1. Branches of foreign financial institutions were allowed to acquire real estate to operate their business.

SLOVENIA

(Position as of December 31, 1999)

Status Under IMF Articles of Agreement

Article VIII	Date of acceptance: September 1, 1995.

Exchange Arrangement

Currency	The currency of Slovenia is the Slovenian tolar.
Exchange rate structure	Unitary.
Classification	
Managed floating with no pre-announced path for the exchange rate	The external value of the tolar is determined in the interbank exchange market, where the Bank of Slovenia (BOS) may participate. The BOS also may buy and sell foreign exchange in transactions with the government and commercial banks. Natural persons may conduct foreign exchange transactions with banks or foreign exchange offices at freely negotiated rates. Licensed banks may conduct foreign exchange transactions among themselves. Juridical persons may conduct foreign exchange transactions with banks and, up until September 1, 1999, when this possibility was eliminated, between themselves. The BOS publishes daily a moving two-month average exchange rate for customs valuation and accounting purposes, as well as for government transactions.
Exchange tax	No.
Exchange subsidy	No.
Forward exchange market	Yes.

Arrangements for Payments and Receipts

Prescription of currency requirements	No.
Payment arrangements	
Bilateral payment arrangements	
Inoperative	Slovenia maintains payment agreements with the former Yugoslav Republic of Macedonia and Bosnia and Herzegovina. The agreements allow juridical persons to conduct transactions through nonresidents' accounts. Also, there is an agreement with Italy related to trade between the two border regions.
Regional arrangements	Slovenia is a member of the CEFTA.
Administration of control	By virtue of the new Foreign Exchange Law, which entered into force on April 23, 1999, exchange control is exercised by (1) the BOS on the foreign exchange operations of banks and foreign exchange offices; (2) the Foreign Exchange Inspectorate within the MOF on foreign exchange and foreign trade operations of natural and juridical persons other than banks; and (3) the customs authorities, who verify that the necessary conditions are met for the cross-border transfers of goods, as well as banknotes, securities, and gold.
International security restrictions	
In accordance with Executive Board Decision No. 144-(52/51)	Yes.
In accordance with UN sanctions	Slovenia maintains certain restrictions with regard to the Federal Republic of Yugoslavia (Serbia/Montenegro).
Payment arrears	No.

Controls on trade in gold (coins and/or bullion)	n.r.

Controls on exports and imports of banknotes

On exports

Domestic currency — Until September 1, 1999, resident and nonresident natural persons were allowed to take abroad up to SIT 300,000 a person. After September 1, 1999, this limit was raised to SIT 500,000 a person. For any amounts exceeding this, prior approval of the BOS is required.

Foreign currency — Until September 1, 1999, residents were allowed to take abroad up to the equivalent of DM 3,000. On September 1, 1999, this limit was set to the equivalent of SIT 500,000; for any amount in excess of this, prior approval of the BOS is required. For nonresidents, the export of foreign currency is free.

On imports

Domestic currency — Resident and nonresident natural persons may bring into the country up to SIT 500,000 (before September 1, 1999, SIT 300,000) a person. For any amounts exceeding this, prior approval of the BOS is required.

Foreign currency — In accordance with regulations on money-laundering prevention, there are reporting requirements for cash and securities exceeding the equivalent of SIT 2.8 million (before September 1, 1999, SIT 2.2 million) for residents and nonresidents.

Resident Accounts

Foreign exchange accounts permitted — Yes.

Held domestically — Effective April 30, 1999, judicial persons were allowed to maintain foreign exchange accounts while, effective September 1, 1999, all residents may open and operate foreign exchange accounts without restriction after proving their identity.

Held abroad — Effective September 1, 1999, the following residents are allowed to maintain foreign exchange accounts without the approval of the BOS: (1) banks; (2) temporary residents of Slovenia; (3) members of diplomatic missions and consular representatives; (4) residents performing services in international transportation of goods and passengers; and (5) natural persons with a permanent residence in Slovenia and a valid resident visa or work permit issued abroad (with a validity of more than six months).

Approval required — Yes.

Accounts in domestic currency convertible into foreign currency — Yes.

Nonresident Accounts

Foreign exchange accounts permitted — Effective September 1, 1999, withdrawals in cash from these accounts are limited to the equivalent of SIT 500,000 a month (previously SIT 250,000), except for diplomatic, consular, and other international institutions as well as nonresidents employed by these institutions and their family members. Amounts exceeding this limit are subject to BOS approval.

Domestic currency accounts — Effective September 1, 1999, withdrawals in cash from these accounts are limited to SIT 500,000 a month (previously SIT 250,000), except for diplomatic, consular, and other international institutions, as well as nonresidents employed by these institutions, including family members. Withdrawals exceeding this amount are subject to the prior approval of the BOS.

Convertible into foreign currency — Yes.

Blocked accounts	These accounts are blocked for the implementation of UN resolutions and for reasons of national security in relation to the assets pertaining to entities from the former Federal Republic of Yugoslavia (Serbia/Montenegro).

Imports and Import Payments

Foreign exchange budget	No.
Financing requirements for imports	No.
Documentation requirements for release of foreign exchange for imports	Commercial banks may require documents verifying the purpose of the transaction before effecting payment.
Import licenses and other nontariff measures	Licensing requirements in the form of permits, for the purpose of controlling items that effect security and public health, have been retained for specific groups of goods (seeds and planting materials of agricultural and forest plants, materials for breeding animals, pharmaceutical products, military equipment, waste, toxic and explosive substances, and precious metals), as well as original sculptures, statues, and antiques, in accordance with international conventions and codes.
Licenses with quotas	Slovenia maintains a system of import quotas applicable only to certain textile products and clothing. There are annual import quotas, which are allocated to relevant associations of the Chamber of Commerce of Slovenia. Quotas are not applied to imports from countries with which Slovenia has free trade agreements.
Import taxes and/or tariffs	In accordance with the WTO schedule, the bound tariff rate for industrial and agricultural products is 27% except for some agricultural products, for which the bound tariff rate is either 45% or a tariff rate plus a specific duty. However, the conventional rate of duty currently applied is, on average for all sectors, 8.76%; for industry, the rate is 7.68%, and for agriculture, it is 12.6%.
State import monopoly	No.

Exports and Export Proceeds

Repatriation requirements	Exporters are free to agree on payment terms with foreign importers. However, effective September 1, 1999, if the collection of export proceeds is delayed by more than one year, the transactions must be reported to the BOS as credit transactions.
Surrender requirements	Exporters had two business days to sell their proceeds to importers at a freely negotiated exchange rate or to use the proceeds for payments abroad. After that time, they had to sell their proceeds to an authorized bank. Effective September 1, 1999, the surrender requirement was abolished.
Financing requirements	No.
Documentation requirements	No.
Export licenses	Except for certain items that are subject to licensing for security or health reasons, exports are not restricted, in accordance with the international conventions and codes.
Without quotas	Yes.
Export taxes	No.

Payments for Invisible Transactions and Current Transfers

Controls on these transfers	No.

Proceeds from Invisible Transactions and Current Transfers

Repatriation requirements	No.
Restrictions on use of funds	No.

Capital Transactions

Controls on capital and money market instruments

On capital market securities — Foreign securities may be offered in Slovenia only through an authorized participant in the securities market.

Shares or other securities of a participating nature

Purchase locally by nonresidents — Except for the purchase of shares representing (1) nonresidents' participation in voting power, (2) more than 10% of the capital of domestic companies, or (3) those purchased in the primary market, purchases in the country by nonresidents of secondary market–traded securities and derivatives must be conducted through the custody accounts established with licensed domestic banks and held either in tolars or in foreign currency. Effective September 1, 1999, commercial banks are obliged to pay a premium in relation to the balances held in the custody accounts. The premium is set quarterly by the BOS and is not charged on balances held with respect to purchases of shares committed for one year (before September 1, 1999, four years) or more.

Sale or issue locally by nonresidents — Effective September 1, 1999, regulations apply on the purchase abroad of capital market securities by residents.

Purchase abroad by residents — Effective September 1, 1999, residents, other than banks, investment funds, and insurance companies may purchase abroad only shares traded on all stock exchanges of the members of the International Federation of Stock Exchanges (FIBV).

Sale or issue abroad by residents — Effective July 9, 1999, residents offering shares abroad are obliged to acquire the prior approval of the MOF and of the Agency for the Securities Market (ASM).

Bonds or other debt securities

Purchase locally by nonresidents — Purchases of bonds in private placements are treated as credit transactions; for other categories, the same regulations apply as for shares or other securities of a participating nature.

Sale or issue locally by nonresidents — Effective July 9, 1999, the issue of tolar-denominated bonds and other debt securities with a minimum maturity of three years requires the permission of the MOF. Nonresidents may sell bonds and other debt securities through an authorized dealer in the securities market only.

Purchase abroad by residents — Effective September 1, 1999, banks, investment funds, and insurance companies are allowed to purchase freely securities abroad. Other residents may purchase securities issued by OECD member states, international finance institutions, securities with a minimum of AA rating, or securities traded on stock exchanges of the FIBV.

Sale or issue abroad by residents — These transactions are treated as credit operations and have to be reported to the BOS.

On money market instruments

Purchase locally by nonresidents — Effective September 1, 1999, the BOS sets the conditions for these transactions.

Sale or issue locally by nonresidents — The same regulations apply as for capital market securities.

Purchase abroad by residents — The same regulations apply as for capital market securities.

Sale or issue abroad by residents — The BOS sets the conditions for these transactions.

On collective investment securities

Purchase locally by nonresidents — The same regulations apply as for capital market securities.

Sale or issue locally by nonresidents	The MOF sets the conditions for these transactions.
Purchase abroad by residents	The same regulations apply as for capital market securities.
Sale or issue abroad by residents	The same regulations apply as for capital market securities.

Controls on derivatives and other instruments   The same regulations apply as for capital market securities.

Controls on credit operations

Financial credits   Effective February 1, 1999, the deposit requirement for financial loans was eliminated. Effective September 1, 1999, all controls on financial credits were eliminated.

Controls on direct investment

Outward direct investment   Before July 23, 1999, domestic juridical persons had to obtain the permission of the MOF. The permission was granted, provided that (1) the domestic company had been operating with a profit and the funds used did not exceed the amount of the profit, and (2) the taxes and customs had been paid. Domestic natural persons had to inform the MOF of any investments abroad. Effective July 23, 1999, outward direct investments were allowed freely. Residents, however, are obliged to report within 30 days the outward direct investment to the MOF.

Inward direct investment   Effective April 23, 1999, foreign direct investments are not allowed in the production and trade of military equipment, and the provision of mandatory pension and health insurance financed by the budget. If not restricted by a special law, foreign direct investment in other fields is allowed freely. Effective February 1, 1999, foreign banks were allowed to open branches in Slovenia.

Controls on liquidation of direct investment   The transfer of proceeds is free of any controls after all tax obligations in Slovenia have been met.

Controls on real estate transactions

Purchase locally by nonresidents   Nonresidents may acquire the right to own real estate pursuant to the provisions of a law or an international agreement, under condition of reciprocity. Foreign states, however, may acquire the right to own real estate used for diplomatic and consular purposes.

Controls on personal capital movements

Loans   As of February 1, 1999, individuals were allowed to contract loans with nonresidents.

Provisions specific to commercial banks and other credit institutions

Borrowing abroad   Effective February 1, 1999, banks were allowed to increase their net foreign indebtedness.

Maintenance of accounts abroad   Effective September 1, 1999, controls on the accounts of banks abroad were eliminated.

Lending locally in foreign exchange   Effective September 1, 1999, domestic authorized banks were allowed to freely extend credits to other authorized banks as well as credits in foreign currency to other residents. The funds so obtained may be used for payments of imports of goods and services and for settlement of existing obligations from previously extended credits pursuant to this regulation. The Slovenian Export Corporation may extend such credit to authorized banks, provided the funds are used to refinance an export credit.

Differential treatment of deposit accounts in foreign exchange

    Reserve requirements   Banks are obliged to hold minimum reserves with the BOS. The required reserve ratios are applied only on tolar deposits.

    Liquid asset requirements   Banks are required to hold reserves in foreign exchange in the form of liquid assets abroad and investments in foreign currency bills issued by the BOS (at least 60% of the requirement), to ensure overall liquidity of payments abroad and to fulfill their obligations to holders of deposits in foreign exchange, both domestic and foreign persons. Correspondingly, the volume of household and legal entities, as well as of nonresident deposits in foreign exchange, are taken into account for the calculation of the prescribed amount.

Differential treatment of deposit
accounts held by nonresidents

   Reserve requirements — Effective February 1, 1999, the interest-free deposit requirement in relation to deposits of foreign banks was eliminated.

Investment regulations

   Abroad by banks — MOF approval is required.

   In banks by nonresidents — BOS approval is required.

Open foreign exchange position limits — Banks are required to limit their daily foreign exchange exposure to 20% of their capital and their monthly average foreign exchange exposure to 10% of their capital.

   On resident assets and liabilities — Yes.

   On nonresident assets and liabilities — Yes.

Provisions specific to institutional investors — The Law on Insurance Companies and the Law on Investment Funds and Management Companies establish that (1) insurance stock companies may not be owned solely by nonresidents; (2) nonresidents may become stockholders of insurance companies only with the approval of the MOF; (3) if the majority of their shares are owned by nonresidents, insurance companies may not provide reinsurance; (4) mutual insurance funds may be owned solely by residents; (5) more than 20% of shares of management companies may be owned by nonresidents only with the approval of the ASM; (6) more than 10% of shares of authorized management companies (i.e., those authorized to manage investment companies that collect vouchers in the privatization process) may be owned by nonresidents only with the approval of the ASM and the Ministry for Economic Affairs and Development; and (7) investment stock companies' investments in foreign securities (closed investment fund) may not exceed 10% of total investments.

The Law on Pension Insurance establishes that the capital fund of the Pension Insurance Stock Company is owned by the Republic of Slovenia. Voluntary pension funds for extra pension rights are subject to rules for insurance stock companies.

Limits (max.) on securities issued by nonresidents and on portfolio invested abroad — Yes.

Limits (max.) on portfolio invested abroad — Yes.

Limits (min.) on portfolio invested locally — Yes.

Other controls imposed by securities laws — According to the new Law on Securities Markets, which entered into force on July 28, 1999, there are no limitations on foreign ownership of stock brokering companies. Acquisitions of shares and the establishment of subsidiaries and branches by nonresident investment firms are subject to nondiscriminatory prudential rules.

Changes During 1999

Exchange arrangement — *September 1.* Except for banks, juridical persons, except banks, are not allowed to conduct foreign exchange transactions among themselves.

Arrangements for payments and receipts — *April 23.* A new foreign exchange law came into effect.

September 1. The limit for the export of cash in foreign currency was set as the equivalent of SIT 500,000 for resident natural persons.

September 1. The limit for the import of foreign currency above which reporting is required was increased to SIT 2.8 million.

September 1. The limit for the import and export of cash in domestic currency was increased to SIT 500,000 from SIT 300,000.

Resident accounts	*April 30.* Resident juridical persons were allowed to maintain foreign exchange accounts with authorized domestic banks.
	September 1. Slovenia residents were allowed to maintain freely foreign exchange accounts, after proof of identity. Also, several categories of residents were allowed to open foreign exchange accounts abroad.
Nonresident accounts	*September 1.* The limit for cash withdrawals from nonresident foreign exchange and tolar-denominated accounts was increased to SIT 500,000 a month.
Exports and export proceeds	*September 1.* Export proceeds collected later than one year must be reported to the BOS as credit transactions.
	September 1. The export surrender requirement was abolished.

Capital transactions

Controls on capital and money market instruments	*April 23.* The new foreign exchange law introduced changes in the rules on issuing and selling securities.
	July 9. Residents offering shares abroad were obliged to acquire the prior approval of the MOF and the ASM.
	July 9. The issue of bonds by nonresidents requires the permission of the MOF.
	September 1. Conditions on the purchase of money market investments by nonresidents are set by the BOS.
	September 1. Commercial banks must pay a premium on the balances of custody accounts of nonresidents held for one year or more.
	September 1. Residents, other than banks, investment funds, and insurance companies, may purchase abroad only shares traded on the stock exchanges of the FIBV.
	September 1. Banks, investment funds, and insurance companies were allowed to purchase securities abroad freely. Other residents may purchase securities issued by OECD member states, international finance institutions, securities with a minimum of an AA rating, or securities traded on stock exchanges of the FIBV.
Controls on credit operations	*February 1.* The deposit requirement for financial loans was eliminated.
	September 1. All controls on financial credits were eliminated.
Controls on direct investment	*February 1.* Foreign banks were allowed to open branches in Slovenia.
	April 23. Inward direct investments were not permitted in the field of military equipment and in the field of mandatory pension and health insurance financed by the budget. In other sectors, foreign investments may be made freely, unless restricted by a special law.
	July 23. Outward direct investments were permitted, but must be reported within 30 days to the MOF.
Controls on personal capital movements	*February 1.* Individuals were allowed to contract loans with nonresidents.
Provisions specific to commercial banks and other credit institutions	*January 1.* The method for calculating liquid asset requirements for banks was changed.
	February 1. Banks were allowed to raise short-term loans abroad, and the interest-free deposit requirement for pure financial loans with maturities of up to seven years was lifted.
	February 1. The interest-free deposit requirement for foreign bank deposits was eliminated.
	February 1. Banks were allowed to increase their net foreign debt.
	September 1. Funds obtained through foreign exchange loans contracted with authorized domestic banks must be used only for import payments and for the settlement of foreign obligations.
	September 1. Controls on the accounts of banks held abroad were eliminated.
	September 1. Domestic authorized banks were allowed to extend credits in foreign exchange to other authorized banks and to residents.

Other controls imposed by securities laws

July 28. A new Law on Securities Markets came into effect, lifting the limitations on foreign ownership of stock brokering companies.

SOLOMON ISLANDS

(Position as of December 31, 1999)

Status Under IMF Articles of Agreement

Article VIII   Date of acceptance: July 24, 1979.

Exchange Arrangement

Currency   The currency of the Solomon Islands is the Solomon Islands dollar.

Exchange rate structure   Unitary.

Classification

Conventional pegged arrangement   The exchange rate for the Solomon Islands dollar is pegged to a trade-weighted basket of the currencies of the Solomon Islands' four major trading partners. The Central Bank of the Solomon Islands (CBSI) provides the commercial banks with daily limits on the buying and selling rates for the U.S. dollar in transactions with the CBSI and the public. The commercial banks in the Solomon Islands are free to determine their exchange rates for all other foreign currencies.

Exchange tax   A tax of SI$3 is levied on sales of foreign exchange exceeding SI$3,000.

Exchange subsidy   No.

Forward exchange market   Commercial banks may enter into forward contracts with residents of the Solomon Islands in any currency.

Arrangements for Payments and Receipts

Prescription of currency requirements   Contractual commitments in a foreign currency to nonresidents may be met only by payments in the currency specified in the contract. Export proceeds may be received in any foreign currency or in Solomon Islands dollars from an account of an overseas bank with a bank in the Solomon Islands.

Payment arrangements   No.

Administration of control   Exchange control is administered by the CBSI through the Foreign Exchange Control Regulations. The CBSI delegates extensive powers to commercial banks, which have been appointed authorized dealers in foreign exchange and may approve certain transactions up to the equivalent of SI$25,000.

International security restrictions

In accordance with Executive Board Decision No. 144-(52/51)   Certain restrictions have been imposed on the making of payments and transfers for current international transactions in respect of the Federal Republic of Yugoslavia (Serbia/Montenegro).

Payment arrears   No.

Controls on trade in gold (coins and/or bullion)

Controls on domestic ownership and/or trade   Only Solomon Islands nationals may be granted a license to pan for alluvial gold. The CBSI is authorized to buy, sell, and hold gold but has not yet undertaken any such transactions. Commercial mining companies require a license from the Ministry of Natural Resources (MONR) to mine gold.

Controls on external trade   Commercial banks and all other residents are required to obtain a permit issued by the MONR to mine, buy, or export gold.

Controls on exports and imports of banknotes

On exports

Domestic currency — Travelers may not take out amounts in excess of SI$250 without the approval of the CBSI, which is not normally given.

On imports

Foreign currency — Nonresidents visiting the Solomon Islands may bring in any amount of currency for travel expenditures.

Resident Accounts

Foreign exchange accounts permitted — Resident companies may obtain CBSI approval to hold these accounts in cases where there is a genuine need. As of March 1, 1999, exporters were allowed to hold 20% of their export proceeds in foreign currency accounts. The account may be opened only in one currency chosen by the exporter.

Held domestically — These accounts are permitted, but approval is required.

Held abroad — These accounts are permitted, but approval is required.

Accounts in domestic currency convertible into foreign currency — Yes.

Nonresident Accounts

Foreign exchange accounts permitted — Foreign exchange accounts may be held, but proof of bona fide need is required.

Domestic currency accounts — These accounts may be held only at authorized foreign exchange dealers.

Convertible into foreign currency — Balances may be transferred abroad with the approval of the CBSI or authorized dealers. CBSI approval is required for these accounts to be credited from Solomon Islands sources.

Blocked accounts — No mechanism exists for these accounts.

Imports and Import Payments

Foreign exchange budget — No.

Financing requirements for imports — No.

Documentation requirements for release of foreign exchange for imports — Authorized dealers are permitted to approve most transactions up to SI$25,000 without reference to the CBSI.

Import licenses and other nontariff measures — No.

Import taxes and/or tariffs — The rate of import levy is 8%. There is no duty on imports from Melanesian countries.

Taxes collected through the exchange system — A tax of SI$3 is levied on sales of foreign exchange exceeding SI$3,000.

State import monopoly — No.

Exports and Export Proceeds

Repatriation requirements — Proceeds must be received within three months of the date of exportation.

Surrender requirements — Export proceeds must be sold promptly to an authorized dealer, except that exporters are allowed to retain 20% of their export earnings as of March 1, 1999.

Financing requirements	No.

Documentation requirements

Preshipment inspection	Goods exported are inspected by customs officers.
Export licenses	Residents may export goods other than round logs without exchange control formalities, but they must comply with the terms of a general authorization issued by the CBSI. Exports of round logs require specific authority from the CBSI upon presentation of a market price certificate issued by the Ministry of Forestry, Conservation, and Environment.
Without quotas	If exporters cannot meet the conditions of a general authorization (repatriation, surrender, or market level price requirements), they must apply to the CBSI for a specific authorization. Authorization is not needed for goods valued under SI$250 in any one consignment or for certain exempt categories of goods, including most personal effects of passengers.
Export taxes	Exports of logs are subject to an export duty of 35% if valued up to SI$250 per cubic meter and 38% if of greater value.

Payments for Invisible Transactions and Current Transfers

Controls on these transfers

Investment-related payments

Prior approval	Approval is readily granted for the repayment of loans contracted overseas and for payments of services and remittances of dividends, profits, and other earnings accruing to nonresidents from companies in the Solomon Islands, provided it can be shown they are properly due.
Quantitative limits	Limits on the amortization of loans or depreciation of direct investments are based on a previously approved repayment schedule.
Indicative limits/bona fide test	Yes.

Payments for travel

Prior approval	Approval is normally given for the purchase of foreign currency for travel. Applications for travel funds must be submitted to an authorized dealer, and presentation of passports and airline tickets is required.

Personal payments

Prior approval	Approval is readily granted. In the case of medical costs, the application must be supported by an invoice from the medical practitioner, or from an educational institution for studies abroad.
Indicative limits/bona fide test	Yes.

Foreign workers' wages

Prior approval	Approval is readily granted for the remittance of funds of temporary residents.
Indicative limits/bona fide test	Yes.

Credit card use abroad

Prior approval	Yes.

Other payments

Prior approval	Approval is readily granted.
Indicative limits/bona fide test	Yes.

Proceeds from Invisible Transactions and Current Transfers

Repatriation requirements	Yes.

Surrender requirements	Approval is required for the disposal of proceeds other than by sale to an authorized dealer.
Restrictions on use of funds	No.

Capital Transactions

Controls on capital and money market instruments	CBSI approval is required for all capital and money market transactions.
Controls on derivatives and other instruments	There are controls on all transactions in derivatives and other instruments.
Controls on credit operations	Only the acceptance of guarantees, securities, and financial backup facilities from nonresidents is not controlled.
Controls on direct investment	
Outward direct investment	Investment by resident individuals or by companies and other organizations operating in the Solomon Islands is subject to certain limitations and when it is likely to be of benefit to the Solomon Islands.
Inward direct investment	Approval by the Foreign Investment Board (FIB) is required for initial or increased foreign investment.
Controls on liquidation of direct investment	Approval is readily given for the transfer of proceeds. Sales of investments by nonresidents to either a resident or a nonresident require FIB approval.
Controls on real estate transactions	
Purchase abroad by residents	Yes.
Controls on personal capital movements	Only the transfer of assets into the country by immigrants is not controlled.
Provisions specific to commercial banks and other credit institutions	
Borrowing abroad	Yes.
Lending to nonresidents (financial or commercial credits)	Yes.
Lending locally in foreign exchange	Yes.
Purchase of locally issued securities denominated in foreign exchange	Yes.
Differential treatment of deposit accounts in foreign exchange	
Liquid asset requirements	Effective April 15, 1999, the liquid asset requirement was lowered to 7.5% from 40%.
Differential treatment of deposit accounts held by nonresidents	
Reserve requirements	Yes.
Liquid asset requirements	Yes.
Investment regulations	
Abroad by banks	Yes.
Open foreign exchange position limits	Limits are set for each commercial bank at SI$2.5 million.
Provisions specific to institutional investors	Insurance companies must obtain permission from the Commissioner of Insurance to remit reinsurance premiums abroad.
Other controls imposed by securities laws	No.

Changes During 1999

Exports and export proceeds

March 1. Exporters were allowed to retain 20% of export proceeds in a foreign currency account at a domestic financial institution.

Capital transactions

Provisions specific to commercial banks and other credit institutions

April 15. The liquid asset requirement was lowered to 7.5% from 40%.

SOMALIA

(Position as of December 31, 1998)

Status Under IMF Articles of Agreement

Article XIV	Yes.

Exchange Arrangement

Currency	The currency of Somalia is the Somali shilling.
Exchange rate structure	
Dual	There are two exchange markets: (1) the official market, comprising the Central Bank of Somalia (CBS) and the two commercial banks operating as authorized dealers. The rate in this market applies to imports of goods and services and debt-service payments of the government; and (2) a free market, in which the exchange rate is freely negotiated between resident holders of foreign exchange accounts, i.e., export/import accounts and external accounts.
Classification	
Independently floating	The exchange rate of the Somali shilling is determined in the free market by supply and demand.
Exchange tax	No.
Exchange subsidy	No.
Forward exchange market	No.

Arrangements for Payments and Receipts

Prescription of currency requirements	Settlements with other countries must be made in Somali shillings or in specified currencies (dollars, Djibouti francs, euros, Kuwaiti dinars, pounds sterling, Saudi Arabian riyals, Swiss francs, and U.A.E. dirhams); however, residents are not permitted to make settlements with Israel or South Africa.
Payment arrangements	n.a.
Administration of control	Exchange licensing is the responsibility of the CBS.
International security restrictions	n.a.
Payment arrears	Yes.
Controls on trade in gold (coins and/or bullion)	
Controls on domestic ownership and/or trade	Residents may hold and acquire, for numismatic purposes only, gold coins that are not legal tender in any country. With this exception, residents other than the monetary authorities and authorized industrial users are not allowed to hold or acquire gold in any form other than jewelry.
Controls on external trade	Imports and exports of gold in any form other than jewelry require the permission of the CBS; permission is not normally granted except for imports and exports by or on behalf of the monetary authorities and industrial users. Gold imported by jewelers must be melted down within one month to a fineness of not more than 22 karats. Imports of gold that originate in member countries of the EU are exempt from customs duty; imports from elsewhere are subject to a 10% duty.

811

Controls on exports and imports of banknotes

On imports

Domestic currency   Nonresidents may bring in with them up to So. Sh. 1,000. Nonresident Somalis and foreign national travelers without diplomatic status are required, upon their arrival in Somalia, to convert at least $100 or its equivalent to Somali shillings at the airport branch of the Commercial and Savings Bank, which acts on behalf of the CBS.

Resident Accounts

Foreign exchange accounts permitted   These accounts may be credited with foreign exchange transferred from abroad and may be debited for any external payment. Residents may transfer funds to other external accounts. Funds in these accounts may be used for invisible payments as well as for merchandise import payments. All transactions between residents and nonresidents taking place through external accounts are effected at the official exchange rate.

Exporters of goods and services may deposit 40% of their foreign exchange proceeds from exports into export/import accounts. Funds in these accounts may be sold to importers holding export/import accounts and may be used only for merchandise import payments.

Held domestically   Yes.

Held abroad   No.

Accounts in domestic currency convertible into foreign currency   n.a.

Nonresident Accounts

Foreign exchange accounts permitted   Nonresident accounts in foreign currency and external accounts in dollars may be opened with the CBS by foreign embassies, international institutions, and nonresidents.

Domestic currency accounts   n.a.

Blocked accounts   n.a.

Imports and Import Payments

Foreign exchange budget   No.

Financing requirements for imports   All payments for private imports must be effected through LCs. Private importers may establish LCs for imports at a commercial bank on the basis of foreign exchange made available for that purpose through a foreign currency account with the commercial bank; in such a case, the foreign exchange involved is kept in a suspense account until the time of settlement of the LCs.

Advance payment requirements   Yes.

Advance import deposits   A non-interest-bearing cash advance deposit of 100% is required to open LCs for private sector imports; the deposit is retained until the LCs are settled.

Documentation requirements for release of foreign exchange for imports

Letters of credit   Yes.

Import licenses and other nontariff measures   Imports of alcohol, tobacco and tobacco products, crude oil and petroleum products, medical and pharmaceutical products, explosives, precious metals, jewelry, and minerals are subject to prior approval. All other items, except those prohibited for reasons of public safety and social policy, may be imported freely. Imports of goods originating in or shipped from Israel and South Africa are prohibited.

Negative list	Yes.
Import taxes and/or tariffs	n.a.
State import monopoly	No.

Exports and Export Proceeds

Repatriation requirements	All proceeds must be repatriated.
Surrender requirements	Exporters of bananas and livestock may retain 40% of their foreign exchange receipts in export/import accounts and must surrender the remainder to the CBS or to authorized dealers. Exporters of nontraditional goods may retain 70% of their export earnings.
Financing requirements	n.a.
Documentation requirements	For exports other than those made under LC arrangements, an advance payment deposit of 100% of the value of exports is required.
Export licenses	Exports and reexports to Israel are prohibited. Bananas are exported only by SOMALFRUIT. The exportation of various types of ivory, hides and skins, and minerals is subject to prior approval.
Without quotas	Yes.
Export taxes	A tax of 25% is levied on exports of livestock on the basis of minimum export prices used for purposes of duty collection.

Payments for Invisible Transactions and Current Transfers

Controls on these transfers	Payments to Israel are prohibited. To prevent unauthorized capital transfers, payments for current invisibles through external accounts, as well as through the commercial banks selling foreign exchange on their own account, are subject to licensing.
Trade-related payments	
Prior approval	Yes.
Investment-related payments	Information is not available on the payment of amortization of loans and depreciation of direct investments.
Prior approval	Yes.
Payments for travel	The CBS provides foreign exchange only for official travel expenses. Foreign exchange for private travel expenses may be purchased only from holders of external accounts, with the approval of the CBS.
Prior approval	Yes.
Quantitative limits	There is a limit of $200 a person a trip for business and tourist travel.
Indicative limits/bona fide test	The CBS may approve applications for larger amounts in exceptional cases.
Personal payments	
Prior approval	Yes.
Quantitative limits	The limit is $3,000 a year for medical costs. The limit is $1,000 a year for studies abroad.
Indicative limits/bona fide test	The CBS may approve applications for larger amounts in exceptional cases for medical costs and studies abroad.
Foreign workers' wages	Transfers of salaries, wages, gratuities, and allowances paid in Somalia to foreign personnel by enterprises registered under the Foreign Investment Law are allowed up to 50%.
Other payments	
Prior approval	Yes.

Quantitative limits	Information is not available on the payment of subscription and membership fees.

Proceeds from Invisible Transactions and Current Transfers

Repatriation requirements	Proceeds from invisibles must be repatriated and declared.
Surrender requirements	Exporters of services may retain up to 40% of their foreign exchange receipts in external accounts; they must surrender the remainder to the CBS or to authorized dealers within five business days of their receipts.
Restrictions on use of funds	n.a.

Capital Transactions

Controls on capital and money market instruments	Capital transactions are subject to licensing unless they are authorized by the Foreign Investment Law.
On capital market securities	
Shares or other securities of a participating nature	
Purchase abroad by residents	Yes.
Sale or issue abroad by residents	Yes.
On money market instruments	
Purchase abroad by residents	Yes.
Sale or issue abroad by residents	Yes.
On collective investment securities	
Purchase abroad by residents	Yes.
Sale or issue abroad by residents	Yes.
Controls on derivatives and other instruments	n.a.
Controls on credit operations	There are controls on all credit operations.
Controls on direct investment	
Outward direct investment	Yes.
Inward direct investment	Investments must obtain approval from the Foreign Investment Board, which reviews proposals on a case-by-case basis, within a 60-day period.
Controls on liquidation of direct investment	Foreign investment (original investment plus any profit reinvested) may be freely repatriated five years from the date of the registration of the original investment. Repatriation may be effected in convertible currency or, at the investor's option, in the form of physical assets. The Foreign Investment Board may reduce the above-mentioned five-year period. Capital gains resulting from the sale of shares or liquidation of assets are freely transferrable after taxes are paid.
Controls on real estate transactions	
Purchase abroad by residents	Yes.
Controls on personal capital movements	n.a.
Provisions specific to commercial banks and other credit institutions	n.a.

Provisions specific to institutional investors	n.a.
Other controls imposed by securities laws	n.a.

Changes During 1998–99

The IMF has not received from the authorities the information required for a description of the exchange and trade system since 1998.

SOUTH AFRICA

(Position as of February 29, 2000)

Status Under IMF Articles of Agreement

Article VIII   Date of acceptance: September 15, 1973.

Exchange Arrangement

Currency   The currency of South Africa is the South African rand.

Other legal tender   Certain gold coins, including Krugerrands, are legal tender.

Exchange rate structure   Unitary.

Classification

Independently floating   The exchange rate of the rand is determined in the foreign exchange market. The authorities of South Africa do not maintain margins with respect to exchange transactions, but may execute transactions in the exchange market, which are typically dollar/rand transactions.

Exchange tax   No.

Exchange subsidy   No.

Forward exchange market   Subject to certain limitations, authorized dealers are permitted to conduct forward exchange operations, including cover for transactions by nonresidents. They are also permitted to provide forward exchange cover in any foreign currency to residents for any firm and ascertained foreign exchange commitments and accruals due to, or by nonresidents arising from, authorized trade and nontrade transactions. Forward exchange contracts may cover the entire period of the outstanding commitments or accruals. Subject to certain limitations, forward exchange cover may also be provided to nonresidents. Gold mining companies and houses may sell forward anticipated receipts of their future gold sales.

Official cover of forward operations   The South African Reserve Bank (SARB) no longer provides long-term forward cover. The SARB may, however, favorably entertain requests to buy dollars outright forward. The SARB participates only in the short-term (maturities not exceeding 12 months) forward market at its own initiative and on prices quoted in the market by authorized dealers.

Arrangements for Payments and Receipts

Prescription of currency requirements   All countries outside the CMA constitute the nonresident area. The rand is legal tender in Lesotho and Namibia but not in Swaziland. Settlements by or to residents of the CMA with the nonresident area may be made in rand to and from a nonresident account and in any foreign currency (except the currencies of Lesotho, Namibia, and Swaziland). Lilangeni banknotes issued by Swaziland, loti banknotes issued by Lesotho, and Namibia dollar banknotes issued by Namibia are freely convertible into rand at par, but they are not legal tender in South Africa.

Payment arrangements

Regional arrangements   South Africa is part of the CMA. Payments within the CMA are unrestricted.

Administration of control   Exchange licensing is the responsibility of the Treasury, which has delegated this authority to the SARB; in turn, the SARB has permitted dealers to deal with most transactions without prior reference to the SARB.

International security restrictions

In accordance with UN sanctions   South Africa maintains restrictions on current payments and transfers to Iraq.

Payment arrears   No.

Controls on trade in gold (coins and/or bullion)

Controls on domestic ownership and/or trade

Residents of South Africa may purchase, hold, and sell gold coins in South Africa for numismatic purposes and investment, but only monetary authorities, authorized dealers, registered gold producers, and authorized industrial and professional users are allowed to purchase, hold, or sell gold in any form other than jewelry. Gold producers may elect to sell their total output to approved counterparties, provided the SARB has given the necessary exemption from the relevant exchange control regulations. This includes sales to foreign counterparties. The current exchange control regulations pertaining to the repatriation of export proceeds remain applicable to gold exports. The mint strikes gold coins and the Krugerrand, which are legal tender, without a face value, and these are made available in limited numbers to the local market.

Controls on external trade

All exports of gold must be approved in advance by the SARB. Authorized dealers have been permitted by the SARB to approve exports of jewelry constituting the personal effects of a traveler up to a value of R 50,000 (subject to a written declaration that the jewelry will be brought back to South Africa on the traveler's return); and for exports of gold jewelry by manufacturing jewelers, subject to a written declaration that the articles are in fully manufactured form and that the gold content of each does not exceed 85% of the selling price to the ultimate consignee. Furthermore, after approval by the SARB, residents are allowed to export currency coins, including certain gold coins, for sale to numismatists.

Controls on exports and imports of banknotes

On exports

Domestic currency

Banknotes up to R 5,000 may be exported, but this amount is not regarded as part of the basic travel allowance. The limitation does not apply to migrant workers returning to neighboring countries, who are permitted to take with them reasonable amounts in banknotes. There are no limitations on the exportation of domestic currency to Lesotho, Namibia, and Swaziland. Foreign visitors leaving South Africa may take with them up to R 5,000 in SARB banknotes.

South African banknotes repatriated from Angola, Botswana, Democratic Republic of Congo, Malawi, Mozambique, Seychelles, Tanzania, Zambia, and Zimbabwe may be remitted upon providing documentary evidence that they were not exported from South Africa in contravention of the exchange control regulations. The consignment of banknotes must be accompanied by the confirmation of the repatriating bank that the banknotes were acquired from bona fide travelers from South Africa in amounts not exceeding R 5,000 per capita.

Foreign currency

Residents and contract workers leaving South Africa for destinations outside the CMA may take out their allowance in foreign banknotes. Foreign visitors leaving South Africa may take with them any amount of foreign banknotes brought into the country or obtained through the disposal of instruments of exchange brought into and converted in South Africa.

On imports

Domestic currency

The limit on banknotes that may be imported from countries outside the CMA is R 5,000. There are no limitations on the importation of domestic currency from Lesotho, Namibia, and Swaziland.

Resident Accounts

Foreign exchange accounts permitted

Yes.

Held domestically

Natural persons may hold foreign currency deposits with authorized dealers. The requirement to complete forms A and E in respect of sales and purchases of foreign exchange is R 50,000. The R 750,000 that natural persons may invest abroad may also be held in a domestic currency account.

Held abroad	Approval is granted based on the merit of the application, and in most circumstances only if it can be demonstrated that the management of trade receipts and payments can be facilitated. South African natural persons may invest abroad up to an amount of R 750,000 and may retain abroad foreign-earned income. No prior approval is required to open foreign bank accounts for these purposes.
Accounts in domestic currency convertible into foreign currency	No.

Nonresident Accounts

Foreign exchange accounts permitted	Authorized dealers are required to open separate nonresident accounts on behalf of nonresident clients in order to distinguish between normal clearing accounts and foreign exchange trading accounts. The aim of this requirement is to isolate these transactions for monitoring purposes and does not affect the transferability of funds. Foreign currency accounts may be opened for nonresidents and the transferability of the funds is not restricted. The requirement to complete forms A and E for both sales and purchases of foreign exchange is R 50,000.
Domestic currency accounts	These accounts may be credited with all authorized payments by residents, with the proceeds of sales of foreign currency to authorized dealers, and with payments from other nonresident accounts. They may be debited for payments to CMA residents for any purpose (other than loans); for payments to nonresidents for any purpose, by transfer to a local nonresident account or for remittance to any country outside the CMA; for the cost of purchases of any foreign currency; and for payments to account holders residing in South Africa for short periods.
Convertible into foreign currency	Yes.
Blocked accounts	These accounts are opened for emigrants from the CMA and are subject to exchange control restrictions. Cash or proceeds from any other South African asset held at the time of departure and subsequently sold must be credited to this type of account. These funds may not be transferred abroad or to another emigrant blocked account in South Africa but must be retained on deposit with an authorized dealer and used within certain limits for the holder's living expenses while visiting South Africa, for other specified payments to residents, or for investment in any locally quoted securities (such securities may not, however, be exported and sold abroad).

Imports and Import Payments

Foreign exchange budget	No.
Financing requirements for imports	
Advance payment requirements	Payments are allowed before the date of shipment or dispatch, except for capital goods imports. Authorized dealers may permit, without the SARB's approval, advance payment of up to 33.3% of the ex-factory cost of capital goods if suppliers require it or if it is normal in the trade concerned.
Documentation requirements for release of foreign exchange for imports	Importers are automatically granted foreign exchange to pay for current imports upon presenting to their bank the necessary transport and consignment documents (proof of importation) and an import permit when required.
Import licenses and other nontariff measures	
Positive list	Imports that do not require a permit include all goods from Botswana, Lesotho, Malawi, Namibia, Swaziland, and Zimbabwe that are grown, produced, or manufactured in these countries, with the exception of a limited range of agricultural products from Malawi and Zimbabwe.
Negative list	The negative list includes all used goods, including waste and scrap; fish, crustaceans, and mollusks; dairy products; dried fruit; black tea; certain vegetables and agricultural products;

wines; mineral fuels; radioactive chemicals; new pneumatic tires; gold; certain minerals; firearms; gambling machines; ozone-depleting substances; and footwear and footwear components. All importers requiring import permits for trade or manufacturing purposes must be registered with the Sub-directorate of Import and Export Control. The permits are valid for imports from any country.

Licenses with quotas

Import quotas apply to certain agricultural and a number of manufactured products, including clothing and textiles imported from Zimbabwe supported with a Quota and Origin Certificate issued by the Ministry of Industry and Commerce of Zimbabwe.

Import taxes and/or tariffs

Tariff rates range up to 69%. Effective January 4, 1999, a 14% VAT on imports from Botswana, Lesotho, Namibia, and Swaziland was introduced.

State import monopoly

No.

Exports and Export Proceeds

Repatriation requirements

Unless otherwise permitted, all export proceeds must be remitted to South Africa within 30 days of accrual. Exporters may retain export proceeds for 180 days after accrual in customer foreign currency accounts with authorized dealers.

Surrender requirements

Unless otherwise permitted, all export proceeds must be offered for sale within six months of the date of shipment or 30 days of the date of accrual, whichever is sooner. Except for exports made on a cash-on-delivery basis or those for which the full proceeds are received in advance, exporters are permitted to cover forward their export proceeds.

Financing requirements

Authorized dealers may permit exporters to grant credit for up to 12 months, provided the credit is necessary in that particular trade or needed to protect an existing export market or capture a new one.

Documentation requirements

All exports over R 50,000 must be supported by a declaration, irrespective of the country of destination of the goods.

Export licenses

Without quotas

Certain agricultural and manufactured goods exported outside the SACU require export permits. In addition to an export permit, military equipment, firearms, and ammunition require an export license issued by the Department of Defense.

Export taxes

No.

Payments for Invisible Transactions and Current Transfers

Controls on these transfers

Most limits have been removed. Documentary evidence must be produced at the time of applying for foreign currency.

Trade-related payments

Indicative limits/bona fide test

Authorized dealers may permit the transfer of commissions against documentary evidence confirming the amount involved, provided the rate of commission is normal in the particular trade.

Investment-related payments

Prior approval

Prior approval is required for the payment of amortization of loans or depreciation of direct investments.

Payments for travel

Quantitative limits

South African residents traveling abroad for either business or holiday had been allowed R 100,000 for each person 12 years and older, and R 30,000 for each child under 12 years, for a calendar year, without any daily limit, irrespective of the country of destination. Effective February 23, 1999, these limits were increased to R 120,000 and R 35,000, respectively, and further, on February 23, 2000, to R 130,000 and R 40,000, respectively. Corporations qualify for a global travel allowance of R 2,000,000 for a calendar year.

Indicative limits/bona fide test	Exchange allowances in excess of the above limits may be provided with the approval of the SARB.

Personal payments

Quantitative limits

Approval was required for living expenses for students of amounts exceeding R 100,000 a year, or R 200,000 if the student is accompanied by a spouse. On February 23, 1999, these limits were raised to R 120,000 and R 240,000, respectively. On February 23, 2000, the limits were further increased to R 130,000 and R 260,000, respectively. Until February 23, 1999, the student holiday allowance was R 30,000 a year, which was then raised to R 35,000, or R 70,000 if accompanied by a spouse, and further, on February 23, 2000, to R 40,000, or R 80,000 if accompanied by a spouse. Also, prior approval is required for amounts exceeding R 6,000 (previously R 4,000) a month for a receiving family. There are no limits set for alimony payments, but a court order is required. Authorized dealers may effect maintenance transfers at a rate not exceeding R 6,000 for a receiving family unit a month, provided the proposed beneficiaries are either the father, mother, brother, or sister of the applicant and are in necessitous circumstances.

Credit card use abroad

Prior approval

Approval is not required in respect of travel expenditures.

Quantitative limits

Expenditure may not exceed 100% of the corresponding allowance.

Other payments

Prior approval

Authorized dealers may permit technical service fees, legal fees, and court costs incurred outside the CMA against the production of documentary evidence confirming the amount involved. Authorized dealers may grant approval for royalty payments, provided the Department of Trade and Industry has approved the relevant royalty agreement. Authorized dealers may also permit the remittance of profits and dividends, provided it does not involve excessive use of local credit facilities. Income earned from securities held by nonresidents is freely transferable to their country of residence.

Proceeds from Invisible Transactions and Current Transfers

Repatriation requirements

South African residents (private individuals) earning income abroad from any source other than merchandise exports may retain those funds abroad. Corporate entities are required to remit earnings within 30 days of accrual. Entities may retain the proceeds of services rendered for 180 days after accrual in customer foreign currency accounts with authorized dealers.

Restrictions on use of funds

No.

Capital Transactions

Controls on capital and money market instruments

On capital market securities

Shares or other securities of a participating nature

Sale or issue locally by nonresidents

Only the issue of securities by nonresidents requires prior exchange control approval, which is not normally granted.

Purchase abroad by residents

Such purchases by resident individuals are allowed within the R 750,000 foreign investment limit. Resident institutions may acquire investments as part of their approved portfolio investments abroad.

Sale or issue abroad by residents

Approval is required. Servicing should be undertaken from foreign sources if the funds are employed abroad, or from domestic sources if the funds were transferred to South Africa.

Bonds or other debt securities

The same regulations apply as for shares or other securities of a participating nature.

On money market instruments	The same regulations apply as for shares or other securities of a participating nature.
On collective investment securities	
Purchase abroad by residents	Such purchases by resident individuals are allowed within the R 750,000 foreign investment limit.

Controls on derivatives and other instruments

Purchase locally by nonresidents	Nonresidents may freely purchase derivative instruments, options, and futures on the local formal market (SAFEX), but over-the-counter transactions require prior approval.
Sale or issue locally by nonresidents	Yes.
Purchase abroad by residents	Yes.
Sale or issue abroad by residents	Yes.

Controls on credit operations

Commercial credits

By residents to nonresidents

Export credits may be granted for up to six months. Banks may in certain circumstances allow a further extension of six months. Longer-term credit requires exchange control approval. In respect of services, payment has to be received under the terms of the contract between the parties within a reasonable period after rendering the service.

Financial credits

By residents to nonresidents

Financial credits, such as loans, may not be extended without prior approval. However, nonresident wholly owned subsidiaries may borrow locally up to 100% of the total shareholders' investment (i.e., the paid-up equity capital; preference shares; undistributed profits; shareholders' loans from abroad; and, in certain instances, the hard core of shareholders' trade credit). The ability to borrow locally, which is generally granted, increases with the size of local participation by a set formula.

To residents from nonresidents

Prior approval, which is generally granted, is required to ensure that the repayment and servicing of loans do not disrupt the balance of payments and that the level of interest rates paid is reasonable in terms of prevailing international rates. Firms are allowed to borrow abroad using their South African balance sheet as collateral in cases where the investment required exceeds the R 50 million limit (R 250 million in respect of SADC). Ten percent of the borrowing from abroad may be used for outward direct investments.

Guarantees, sureties, and financial backup facilities

By residents to nonresidents

Guarantees or sureties for financial loans require approval but not for trade transactions. Performance bonds may be issued.

Controls on direct investment

Outward direct investment

Exchange control approval is required. Requests by companies are considered in light of national interest, such as the benefit to South Africa's international reserves by, for example, generating exports of goods and services. Companies may be allowed to transfer up to R 50 million to finance approved investments abroad; and up to R 250 million in SADC countries other than Namibia, Swaziland, and Lesotho, where funds already flow freely. Ten percent of the borrowing from abroad may be used to finance outward direct investments.

Individuals over 18 years of age may invest up to R 750,000 overseas or in a foreign currency account in South Africa, provided they obtain a tax clearance certificate from the South African Revenue Service. There are no limits on the type of investment and no requirement to advise the authorities of how the funds are used. Income earned abroad and capital introduced into the Republic on or after July 1, 1997 by private individual residents in South Africa may be retransferred abroad, provided the authorized dealer concerned is satisfied that the income and/or capital had previously been converted to rand, by viewing documentary evidence confirming the amounts involved.

Controls on liquidation of direct investment	No.
Controls on real estate transactions	
Purchase abroad by residents	Such purchases by resident individuals are allowed within the R 750,000 foreign investment limit. Other purchases require prior exchange control approval.
Controls on personal capital movements	
Loans	
By residents to nonresidents	Authorized dealers may allow the transfer of loans within a limit of R 20,000 an applicant during a calendar year. Larger loans by residents to nonresidents are generally not permitted.
To residents from nonresidents	Prior approval, which is generally granted, is required to ensure that the repayment and servicing of the loan do not disrupt the balance of payments and that the level of interest paid is reasonable in terms of prevailing international rates.
Gifts, endowments, inheritances, and legacies	
By residents to nonresidents	Authorized dealers may allow the transfer of monetary gifts, including loans referred to above, within a limit of R 20,000 an applicant during a calendar year. Cash bequests and the cash proceeds of legacies and distributions from estates may be remitted abroad.
Settlement of debts abroad by immigrants	Authorized dealers may provide immigrants with exchange to repay loans received in their previous country of domicile for the specific purpose of financing their relocation to South Africa, provided documentary evidence of the debt is available and the immigrant is not in possession of foreign currency to repay the debt.
Transfer of assets	
Transfer abroad by emigrants	Emigrants are limited to a onetime total of R 400,000 a family or R 200,000 an individual, but this must include any previous investments overseas. All other assets remain blocked in South Africa. The emigrant is subsequently able to repatriate the annual income from those blocked assets, but is prohibited from exiting the assets, either by sale to South African residents or by asset swaps with either a foreign or South African counterpart. Authorized dealers may also authorize the export of any household and personal effects, motor vehicles, caravans, trailers, motorcycles, stamps, and coins (excluding coins that are legal tender in the Republic) for a family unit or single person emigrating, within the overall insured value of R 1 million.
Provisions specific to commercial banks and other credit institutions	
Borrowing abroad	All borrowing abroad by residents requires exchange control approval. Banks may contract short-term working capital loans and short-term trade finance, but all medium-term and long-term commitments require exchange control approval.
Maintenance of accounts abroad	Banks may open nostro accounts at their discretion.
Lending to nonresidents (financial or commercial credits)	Banks may lend up to R 20,000, provided that the total credit made available to an individual from any source does not exceed this amount. Exchange control approval is required for facilities exceeding this amount. Foreign investors are allowed to borrow domestically an amount of rand equal to the value of the foreign exchange they brought into South Africa.
Lending locally in foreign exchange	Yes.
Purchase of locally issued securities denominated in foreign exchange	There are no securities denominated in foreign exchange in South Africa.
Differential treatment of deposit accounts in foreign exchange	
Reserve requirements	Reserve requirements on all deposit accounts held by residents or nonresidents and denominated in either rand or foreign exchange are 2.5% of total deposit liabilities, reduced with specific items.

Liquid asset requirements	The requirement is 5% of adjusted total liabilities.
Investment regulations	Investment in immovable property and shares and loans or advances to certain subsidiaries are limited to 100% of capital plus reserves.
Abroad by banks	Prior approval of the Registrar of Banks and Exchange Control is required.
In banks by nonresidents	No approval is required if the investment is less than 15% of the bank's issued capital.
Open foreign exchange position limits	The limit is 15% of net qualifying capital plus reserves.

Provisions specific to institutional investors

Limits (max.) on securities issued by nonresidents and on portfolio invested abroad	Yes.
Limits (max.) on portfolio invested abroad	On outward portfolio investment, the exchange control authority may authorize up to 15% of total assets for each qualifying institution (i.e., insurance companies, pension funds, and fund managers) to be invested abroad by way of an asset swap. Subject to the overall limit of 15% of total assets, long-term insurers and pension funds were eligible to apply for authorization to avail themselves of foreign currency transfers of up to 10% (before February 23, 2000, 5%) of the net inflow of funds for the calendar year 1999, inclusive of SADC countries.
Other controls imposed by securities laws	No.

Changes During 1999

Imports and import payments

January 4. A 14% VAT on imports from Botswana, Lesotho, Namibia, and Swaziland was introduced.

Payments for invisible transactions and current transfers

February 23. The limit on allowances for living expenses of students abroad was increased to R 120,000 a year, and if the student is accompanied by a spouse to R 240,000 a year. The student holiday allowance was increased to R 35,000, and if the student is accompanied by a spouse, to R 70,000. The limit on travel allowances was set at R 120,000 an adult, and R 35,000 a child under 12 a calendar year.

Capital transactions

Provisions specific to institutional investors

February 23. On outward portfolio investment, the exchange control authority may authorize up to 15% of total South African assets for each qualifying institution to be invested abroad by way of an asset swap. Subject to the overall limit of 15% of total South African assets, long-term insurers, pension funds, and unit trusts through unit trust management companies were eligible to apply for authorization to avail themselves of foreign currency transfers of up to 5% of the net inflow of funds for the calendar year 1998, and an additional 10% in securities listed on stock exchanges in SADC countries.

Changes During 2000

Payments for invisible transactions and current transfers

February 23. The limit on allowances for living expenses of students abroad were increased to R 130,000 a year (R 260,000 if accompanied by the spouse). The student holiday allowance was raised to R 40,000 (R 80,000 if accompanied by the spouse).

February 23. The limits for travel were increased to R 130,000 for an adult and R 40,000 for a child under 12.

Capital transactions

Provisions specific to institutional investors

February 23. The limit on outward portfolio investment was changed to 15% and based on all assets, from solely South African assets. Unit trust management companies no longer qualify for this treatment. Foreign currency transfers are allowed up to 10% of the net inflow of funds (previously 5%), inclusive of SADC countries.

SPAIN

(Position as of December 31, 1999)

Status Under IMF Articles of Agreement

Article VIII   Date of acceptance: July 15, 1986.

Exchange Arrangement

Currency

As of January 1, 1999, the currency of Spain is the euro. In cash transactions, however, the legal tender remains the Spanish peseta until 2002, when euro banknotes and coins will be issued.

Exchange rate structure

Unitary.

Classification

Exchange arrangement with no separate legal tender

Spain participates in a currency union (EMU) comprising 11 members of the EU: Austria, Belgium, Finland, France, Germany, Ireland, Italy, Luxembourg, the Netherlands, Portugal, and Spain. Internal conversion rates in respect to the national currencies of EMU participants were fixed to the euro on January 1, 1999, whereas the external exchange rate of the euro is market determined. The conversion rate between the euro and the Spanish peseta was set at Ptas 166.386 per €1. The ECB has the right to intervene to smooth out fluctuations in external exchange rates.

Exchange tax   No.

Exchange subsidy   No.

Forward exchange market

Options and futures in pesetas are traded in major financial markets.

Arrangements for Payments and Receipts

Prescription of currency requirements

No.

Payment arrangements   No.

Administration of control

The Peninsular Territories of the Spanish State, the Canary Islands, the Balearic Islands, Ceuta, and Melilla constitute a single exchange control territory.

The Directorate-General of Foreign Investment and Commercial Policy has the power to authorize, verify, control, and monitor foreign investments and economic transactions, collections, payments, and transfers with the rest of the world. The Directorate-General of the Treasury and Financial Policy has authority to conduct the investigations and inspections required to prepare or change the policy applied in matters concerning exchange control as well as to initiate, address, and rule on penalties applied with regard to exchange control. In addition, the Bank of Spain (BOS) has authority in a number of areas, such as the following: (1) granting authorization to banks, savings and loans, and other financial institutions, when required, to transact business on the foreign exchange market, and registering institutions open to the public to engage in foreign exchange activities; (2) receiving information on collections, payments, and transfers abroad in which registered institutions are involved, and issuing instructions pertaining to the content, procedures, and frequency for such reporting; and (3) receiving information on financial and commercial credits and loans, accounts abroad held by residents in Spain, and netting operations.

International security restrictions

In accordance with UN sanctions

Spain maintains certain restrictions on the making of payments and transfers for current international transactions in respect to Iraq, the Taliban (the Islamic State of Afghanistan), the UNITA movement in Angola, and the Federal Republic of Yugoslavia (Serbia/Montenegro).

Payment arrears	No.
Controls on trade in gold (coins and/or bullion)	No.
Controls on exports and imports of banknotes	Imports and exports of banknotes in excess of the equivalent of Ptas 1 million must be declared.
On exports	
Domestic currency	Yes.
Foreign currency	Yes.
On imports	
Domestic currency	Yes.
Foreign currency	Yes.

Resident Accounts

Foreign exchange accounts permitted	Yes.
Held domestically	Yes.
Held abroad	Collections and payments between residents and nonresidents through credits or debits to these accounts may be freely made. However, account holders are required to report the opening of such accounts and to provide information pertaining to credit and debit activities occurring in the accounts.
Accounts in domestic currency convertible into foreign currency	Yes.

Nonresident Accounts

Foreign exchange accounts permitted	Yes.
Domestic currency accounts	Yes.
Convertible into foreign currency	Yes.
Blocked accounts	No.

Imports and Import Payments

Foreign exchange budget	No.
Financing requirements for imports	No.
Documentation requirements for release of foreign exchange for imports	No.
Import licenses and other nontariff measures	
Open general licenses	Yes.
Import taxes and/or tariffs	No.
State import monopoly	No.

Exports and Export Proceeds

Repatriation requirements	No.
Financing requirements	No.
Documentation requirements	No.
Export licenses	
Without quotas	Exports of certain defense materials require prior authorization from the Directorate-General of Foreign Trade.
Export taxes	No.

Payments for Invisible Transactions and Current Transfers

Controls on these transfers	According to the Royal Decree on Economic Foreign Transactions, all payments, receipts, and transfers between residents and nonresidents must be declared to the deposit institutions.

Proceeds from Invisible Transactions and Current Transfers

Repatriation requirements	No.
Restrictions on use of funds	No.

Capital Transactions

Controls on capital and money market instruments	
On capital market securities	Residents may purchase securities issued by nonresidents or by residents in a foreign market.
Controls on derivatives and other instruments	No.
Controls on credit operations	
Commercial credits	
By residents to nonresidents	Residents (individuals or legal entities other than registered institutions) are required to file reports to the BOS of loans with a maturity of more than one year granted to nonresidents.
To residents from nonresidents	Residents other than registered institutions are required to file reports to the BOS for credits with a maturity of more than one year.
Financial credits	
By residents to nonresidents	Residents are required to file a declaration with the BOS.
To residents from nonresidents	Residents are required to file a declaration with the BOS.
Controls on direct investment	
Outward direct investment	Prior to April 23, 1999, when outward direct investments were fully liberalized, prior administrative verification was required in the following cases: (1) when the investment amounted to at least Ptas 250 million; (2) when the activity of the entity receiving the investment was the direct or indirect holding of share capital of other entities, irrespective of the amount of the investment; and (3) when the investment was made in a tax haven country.

Inward direct investment	Prior to April 23, 1999, when inward direct investments were fully liberalized, foreign direct investments in Spain were defined in accordance with guidelines established by the OECD that took into account whether effective control over the company had been obtained. Effective control was deemed to exist if the share of the investment was at least 10% of the company's capital. Prior verification was required only when foreign participation exceeded 50% and at least one of the following conditions applied: (1) foreign participation exceeded Ptas 500 million; and (2) foreign investors were residents of tax haven countries. Special authorization was required for non-EU foreign investment in television, radio, air transport, gambling, and defense-related industries. Special authorization was also required for a foreign government's participation in Spanish companies (other than governments of EU countries), unless otherwise regulated by international treaties.
Controls on liquidation of direct investment	No.
Controls on real estate transactions	
Purchase abroad by residents	Prior to April 23, 1999, when outward direct investments were fully liberalized, purchases exceeding Ptas 250 million required prior verification.
Purchase locally by nonresidents	Prior to April 23, 1999, when inward direct investments were fully liberalized, prior verification was required for amounts exceeding Ptas 500 million or if investors were residents of tax haven countries.
Controls on personal capital movements	
Loans	Although residents are free to clear credits and debits with nonresidents and to receive or grant loans, credits, and financing or postpone payments from or to the same, they must report such transactions to the BOS.
Gifts, endowments, inheritances, and legacies	
By residents to nonresidents	Specifically, the free acquisition inter vivos of investments in Spain by nonresidents was subject to the same requirements and formalities as if they were an onerous acquisition, without taking into account the condition of the seller of the investment. Consequently, authorization or prior verification had to be sought in such cases in which Spanish legislation so required for onerous acquisitions in any of the forms of foreign investment. As a result of the liberalization of outward direct investment on April 23, 1999, these requirements were abolished.
To residents from nonresidents	A declaration was required providing the data that the administration of the BOS required for purposes of statistical and fiscal monitoring of these transactions. As a result of the liberalization of outward direct investment on April 23, 1999, this requirement was abolished.
Provisions specific to commercial banks and other credit institutions	
Borrowing abroad	Financial credits obtained should be reported to the BOS.
Maintenance of accounts abroad	Yes.
Lending to nonresidents (financial or commercial credits)	Residents must report loans granted to nonresidents to the BOS.
Lending locally in foreign exchange	This type of operation is subject to the rules and regulations governing interest rates and commissions, rules of procedure, customer information, and publications applicable to credit institutions.
Differential treatment of deposit accounts in foreign exchange	
Reserve requirements	Yes.

Investment regulations

In banks by nonresidents

Community investors, even though they may be authorized credit institutions in other EU countries, must obtain prior administrative notice.

Noncommunity institutions may be denied the authorization if community credit institutions do not enjoy reciprocity in the country of origin of the investor.

Provisions specific to institutional investors

Yes.

Currency-matching regulations on assets/liabilities composition

Regulations differ according to the type of institutional investor.

Other controls imposed by securities laws

A new law on securities markets is in effect, harmonizing Spanish rules with the relevant EU directives.

Changes During 1999

Exchange arrangement

January 1. The currency of Spain became the euro. The conversion rate between the euro and the Spanish peseta was set irrevocably at Ptas 166.386 per €1.

Capital transactions

Controls on direct investment

April 23. Direct inward and outward investments were fully liberalized.

SRI LANKA

(Position as of January 31, 2000)

Status Under IMF Articles of Agreement

Article VIII	Date of acceptance: March 15, 1994.

Exchange Arrangement

Currency	The currency of Sri Lanka is the Sri Lanka rupee.
Exchange rate structure	Unitary.
Classification	
Crawling band	The Central Bank of Sri Lanka (CBSL) announces the daily spot buying and selling rates of the dollar against the Sri Lanka rupee for transactions with commercial banks within margins of 2%, and buys and sells the dollar on a spot basis at those rates.
Exchange tax	No.
Exchange subsidy	No.
Forward exchange market	Forward sales are permitted up to a period of 360 days. The commercial banks provide a forward exchange market in which rates for current transactions are freely determined.

Arrangements for Payments and Receipts

Prescription of currency requirements	Payments to and receipts from the member countries of the ACU with respect to current transactions and settlements are effected in dollars. For settlements with all other countries, payments for imports may be made in any foreign currency or in Sri Lanka rupees provided that the supplier maintains a nonresident rupee account in Sri Lanka. Other payments may be made either in the currency of the country to which the payment is due or by crediting Sri Lanka rupees to a nonresident rupee account with the prior approval of the CBSL.
Payment arrangements	
Regional arrangements	Sri Lanka is a member of the ACU.
Clearing agreements	Yes.
Administration of control	Exchange control is administered by the CBSL's Department of Exchange Control. All remittances of foreign exchange in Sri Lanka must be made through authorized commercial banks in accordance with procedures prescribed by the Controller of Exchange (COE). Remittances may also be made through post offices under permits issued by the COE. The Board of Investments (BOI) handles all applications relating to foreign investments in Sri Lanka.
International security restrictions	
In accordance with UN sanctions	Yes.
Payment arrears	No.
Controls on trade in gold (coins and/or bullion)	
Controls on external trade	The importation of gold for domestic, industrial, or commercial purpose is permitted without restrictions. Effective June 30, 1999, all residents are permitted to trade in gems and gold. Imports of other previous metals have been further liberalized.

829

Controls on exports and imports of banknotes

On exports

Domestic currency   Sri Lanka nationals may each take out of Sri Lanka up to SL Rs 1,000.

Foreign currency   Unspent rupee balances from foreign exchange sold by foreign passport holders may be reconverted into foreign currency notes only at exit points, against original encashment documents issued by the authorized dealers or money changers, and can be taken out. Individuals may take out foreign currency for travel purposes and are required to declare to customs if the amount exceeds $10,000 or its equivalent.

On imports

Domestic currency   Sri Lanka nationals may each bring into Sri Lanka up to SL Rs 1,000.

Foreign currency   Travelers must declare, at entry, foreign exchange holdings exceeding $10,000 or its equivalent. In the case of nonconvertible currencies, a declaration has to be made, irrespective of the amount. Prescribed currencies are not permitted to be imported.

Resident Accounts

Foreign exchange accounts permitted   Yes.

Held domestically   Residents may open and operate resident foreign currency accounts with a minimum balance equivalent to $500 in designated currencies, provided the funds do not relate to any transactions. Effective June 30, 1999, the requirement to close these accounts when balances fall below $500 was relaxed.

Held abroad   These accounts may be opened, but approval is required.

Accounts in domestic currency convertible into foreign currency   Yes.

Nonresident Accounts

Foreign exchange accounts permitted   Sri Lankans employed abroad and nonnationals of Sri Lanka origin who are employed and reside abroad may maintain nonresident foreign currency (NRFC) accounts in designated foreign currencies. Credits to these accounts are limited to remittances from employment earnings abroad, foreign exchange earnings brought into the country by such individuals, approved investment incomes, and interest payments on the accounts. Balances on NRFC accounts may be invested in enterprises approved by the BOI, with some exemptions. Dividends and profits earned and sale proceeds of such investments received in foreign currency may be credited to the NRFC accounts without the prior approval of the COE. Resident foreigners may maintain foreign currency accounts with domestic commercial banks in any of 13 designated currencies without prior exchange control approval. These accounts must be operated by the domestic unit of the bank and not by its Foreign Currency Banking Unit (FCBU). The accounts may be current, savings, or deposit accounts, but withdrawal of funds by check is not permitted. Credits to these accounts are limited to inward remittances and to amounts in Sri Lanka rupees authorized by the COE for remittance abroad. Debits to these accounts are limited to outward remittances and to payments after converting into Sri Lanka rupees.

Domestic currency accounts   These accounts may be held by (1) nonnationals residing outside Sri Lanka; (2) firms and companies registered outside Sri Lanka; (3) Sri Lanka nationals residing outside Sri Lanka; (4) emigrants; and (5) foreign banks. The opening of these accounts for categories (1) through (3), credits from inward remittances, and debits for local disbursements or outward remittances may be effected freely; however, local credits to these require prior approval. Accounts in category (4) are designated as nonresident blocked accounts only when instructions to that effect are received from the COE. Debits to such accounts for local disbursements may be freely effected without prior approval; effective June 30, 1999, interest on blocked funds is permitted for outward remittances net of taxes. However, local credits to them and debits for outward remittances in respect to capital funds over a ceiling of SL Rs 1 million a family (SL Rs 750,000 a person) require prior approval. In category (5), foreign banks may open and operate nonresident accounts with local commercial banks without prior approval of the COE.

Convertible into foreign currency	These accounts may be converted, but prior approval is required.
Blocked accounts	These accounts are used to hold funds, usually of nonresidents, repatriates, and emigrants, that have not been accepted for transfer abroad. Authorized dealers may debit these accounts for local disbursements and credit them on account of pensions and income tax refunds. Balances of nonresident foreign citizens and foreign companies in approved blocked accounts outstanding on March 25, 1991, excluding Sri Lanka citizens who have emigrated or acquired foreign citizenship and Indian and Pakistani expatriates, may be remitted abroad. Sri Lankans who have emigrated and acquired foreign citizenship, and Sri Lanka citizens who have acquired permanent resident status abroad and whose accounts have been blocked for more than five years as of June 30, 1992, are also permitted to remit their account balances abroad. Except in the specified cases, remittances of up to SL Rs 1 million are also allowed from these accounts without prior approval.

Imports and Import Payments

Foreign exchange budget	No.
Financing requirements for imports	
Minimum financing requirements	Authorized dealers may approve applications to remit foreign exchange or to credit nonresident accounts against applications for the opening of an LC, documents against payment (DP), or documents on acceptance (DA) terms, and against proof of a valid import license, where applicable. These requirements do not apply if the value of a consignment does not exceed $3,000 (c.i.f.) with respect to raw materials and spare parts for the use of a particular industry or for personal use.
Advance payment requirements	Advance payments for personal imports are limited to $7,500.
Documentation requirements for release of foreign exchange for imports	Imports could be made on DP and DA terms and LCs.
Preshipment inspection	Inspection is required for certain consumer goods.
Letters of credit	Yes.
Import licenses and other nontariff measures	About 285 items are maintained under license—mostly for public health, public moral, environmental, and national security reasons. Imports of wheat, meslin, and wheat and meslin flour are maintained under license in terms of a past contract entered into by the government with a private flour milling company. Certain machinery imports relating to foreign investment require the approval of the BOI.
Import taxes and/or tariffs	The tariff structure consists of two band rates: 10% and 25%, although the rate for agricultural products remains at 35%. A few categories of products (e.g., tobacco, liquor, crude oil, and some categories of motor vehicles) remain outside this tariff structure. A stamp duty of 2% is levied on LCs for certain imports. A national security levy of 5.5% and a goods and services tax of 12.5% are levied on imports.
State import monopoly	Imports of certain items, including wheat, guns and explosives, and certain chemicals and petroleum products, are restricted to government or state corporations.

Exports and Export Proceeds

Repatriation requirements	Exporters are free either to repatriate export proceeds and have such proceeds credited to any rupee account or an Exporters' Foreign Currency Account (EFCA) with the Domestic Banking Unit (DBU) or FCBU of a bank in Sri Lanka or to retain export proceeds abroad in any commercial bank, provided monies in such accounts are not used for acquisition of property or other capital assets outside Sri Lanka. Special arrangements apply to exports

made under trade and payment agreements and to exports made to a member country of the ACU.

Financing requirements	No.
Documentation requirements	No.
Export licenses	
Without quotas	Licenses are required for exports of coral shanks and shells, timber, ivory and ivory products, and passenger vehicles registered in Sri Lanka prior to 1945.
With quotas	Export quotas are maintained on textiles and apparel used to implement bilateral quotas under the MFA. The Textile Quota Board allocates quotas among exporters based primarily on their past export performance.
Export taxes	No.

Payments for Invisible Transactions and Current Transfers

Controls on these transfers	These are indicative limits/bona fide tests in the case of all these transactions.
Trade-related payments	Remittances of premiums for general insurance are permitted, subject to the country's insurance regulations. Remittances of premiums for reinsurance are permitted.
Indicative limits/bona fide test	For commission, reasonable amounts are allowed for export orders secured through agents abroad, provided that export proceeds have been repatriated to Sri Lanka.
Investment-related payments	Profit remittances of nonresident partners and remittances of dividends to nonresident shareholders of companies whose financial assets are in rupees may be effected through commercial banks without prior approval if they relate to the year of application and do not include undistributed profits of the previous years or reserves of the company. However, relevant documentation is required to remit interim profits or dividends, or final profits or dividends.
Indicative limits/bona fide test	Yes.
Payments for travel	
Indicative limits/bona fide test	Yes.
Personal payments	
Indicative limits/bona fide test	Yes.
Foreign workers' wages	Foreign technical employees of approved enterprises may remit their entire savings after meeting expenses and paying taxes and levies.
Indicative limits/bona fide test	Yes.
Credit card use abroad	Credit card use is allowed only for travel-related purposes.
Indicative limits/bona fide test	Yes.
Other payments	
Indicative limits/bona fide test	Yes.

Proceeds from Invisible Transactions and Current Transfers

Repatriation requirements	No.
Restrictions on use of funds	Funds retained abroad with COE permission and export proceeds permitted to be retained abroad should not be used for the acquisition of property or other capital assets outside Sri Lanka.

Capital Transactions

Controls on capital and money market instruments

Except for the local purchase by nonresidents of shares or other securities of a participating nature, all capital market securities and money market instruments are controlled.

On capital market securities

Shares or other securities of a participating nature

Purchase locally by nonresidents

Investments in shares by nonresidents of up to 100% of the equity capital of existing listed and unlisted public companies are permitted, subject to certain exclusions and limitations, without prior approval, in terms of a general permission granted through a Share Investment External Rupee Account maintained at a commercial bank.

Purchase abroad by residents

Investments abroad by residents are not generally permitted unless there is evidence that they will promote the country's exports and generate reasonable profits.

Controls on derivatives and other instruments

All transactions in derivatives and other instruments are controlled.

Controls on credit operations

Effective June 30, 1999, banks were granted general permission to provide rupee credits to nonresident-controlled companies incorporated locally, except for companies approved under Section 17 of the BOI Act. All other credit operations are controlled.

Controls on direct investment

Outward direct investment

Investments abroad by residents are not generally permitted unless there is evidence that they will promote the country's exports and generate reasonable profits.

Inward direct investment

Approval for foreign investment is granted on the basis of the type of activity. Nonresidents are allowed to invest in local companies up to 100% of the issued capital of such companies, except in certain excluded and restricted activities. Effective January 1, 2000, investments in the banking sector are permitted up to 60% of the equity capital (previously 49%); in insurance businesses, up to 90% (previously 49%); and in the financial services sector, up to 49%, except for certain services. In the case of stock brokering, this limit could be up to 100% if permission is granted by the Securities and Exchange Commission. Foreign investments in unit trusts were permitted, provided the trust deed contains the restriction to invest up to 20% in government securities. Excluded areas of investment include the following: money lending, pawn brokering, retail trading with capital less than $1 million, personal services providers other than for exporters and tourism and coastal fishing. The restricted sectors are the production of goods for export under international quota restrictions; growing and primary processing of cocoa, coconuts, rice, rubber, spices, sugar, and tea; primary processing of nonrenewable natural resources; timber processing industries using local timber; deep sea fishing; water supply; construction of residential buildings; telecommunications; mass communication; mass transportation; professional services; freight; travel; shipping agencies; and education. In these sectors, investments are permitted up to 40% of the equity capital of such companies. In the areas of air transportation, coastal shipping, production of energy and power, large-scale mining of gems, and lotteries, foreign investment is permitted up to a percentage approved by the government of Sri Lanka or the relevant authorities.

Controls on liquidation of direct investment

Proceeds from the sale or liquidation of approved investments, along with the capital appreciation, may be remitted in full. Expatriates leaving Sri Lanka for residence in the country of their permanent domicile are permitted to transfer in full assets representing their retirement funds and savings. Persons who have had small businesses in Sri Lanka are allowed to transfer the capital they originally brought into the country, plus a reasonable amount of savings, subject to certain limits.

Authorized dealers may grant foreign exchange allocations to emigrants upon presentation of appropriate documentation.

Controls on real estate transactions

All real estate transactions are controlled.

Controls on personal capital movements

All personal capital movements are controlled.

Transfer of assets	Remittances of life insurance premiums in foreign currency are not permitted.
Transfer abroad by emigrants	At the time of departure, emigrants may be granted foreign exchange to cover passage to the country of migration by normal direct route. Foreign exchange equivalent up to $2,000 a person may also be purchased at the time of departure. Personal effects of reasonable amounts plus jewelry up to SL Rs 150,000 for each married female, SL Rs 60,000 for unmarried females, SL Rs 30,000 for female emigrants under 12 years of age, and SL Rs 37,500 for male emigrants may be exported. Emigrants have also been permitted to effect capital transfers of up to SL Rs 750,000 an individual, up to a maximum limit of SL Rs 1 million a family unit.
Provisions specific to commercial banks and other credit institutions	There are controls on all transactions by commercial banks and other credit institutions; however, there is no information on open foreign exchange position limits. Effective June 30, 1999, reporting requirements with respect to fund transfers through electronic fund transfer cards were introduced.
Lending locally in foreign exchange	Commercial banks may grant foreign currency loans from their domestic currency banking units to exporters who are in a position to pay their loans in foreign exchange earnings. Development banks are also permitted to extend foreign currency loans to exporters based on their foreign credit lines.
Provisions specific to institutional investors	Yes.
Other controls imposed by securities laws	Yes.

Changes During 1999

Arrangements for payments and receipts	*June 30.* Trade in gems, gold, and other precious metals was liberalized.
Resident accounts	*June 30.* The requirement that resident foreign currency accounts be closed when the balance falls below $500 was relaxed.
Nonresident accounts	*June 30.* Interest payments were allowed on funds in blocked accounts and such interest is remittable after any due taxes have been deducted.
Capital transactions	
Controls on credit operations	*June 30.* Banks were granted general permission to provide rupee credits to nonresident-controlled companies incorporated locally, except for companies approved under Section 17 of the BOI Act.
Provisions specific to commercial banks and other credit institutions	*June 30.* Reporting requirements with respect to fund transfers through electronic fund transfer cards were introduced.

Changes During 2000

Capital transactions	
Controls on direct investment	*January 1.* The limits for foreign equity participation in banking and insurance activities were raised to 60% and 90%, respectively, from 49%. In the case of stock brokering, this limit could be up to 100% if permission is granted by the Securities and Exchange Commission. Foreign investments in unit trusts were permitted, provided the trust deed contains the restriction to invest up to 20% in government securities.

SUDAN

(Position as of December 31, 1999)

Status Under IMF Articles of Agreement

Article XIV	Yes.

Exchange Arrangement

Currency	The currency of Sudan is the Sudanese dinar.
Other legal tender	Until January 1, 1999, when it ceased to be legal tender, the Sudanese pound (LSd) also circulated and had a fixed relationship to the Sudanese dinar (SD) of LSd 10 per SD 1.
Exchange rate structure	Unitary.
Classification	
Independently floating	The official exchange rate is determined in the foreign exchange market, and bank and nonbank authorized dealers are free to determine exchange rates and transact freely within the unified regulatory framework. The Bank of Sudan (BOS) is an active participant in the foreign exchange market and transacts at these freely determined rates. The official exchange rate is calculated as the median rate of all foreign exchange transactions that took place during the previous day.
Exchange tax	No.
Exchange subsidy	No.
Forward exchange market	No.

Arrangements for Payments and Receipts

Prescription of currency requirements	Payments to all countries and all monetary areas (the "convertible area") may be made in foreign currency from any free currency account or special foreign currency account, while receipts from the convertible area may be accepted in any convertible currency.
Payment arrangements	
Bilateral payment arrangements	
Inoperative	There is an agreement with Egypt, which has been suspended since 1992.
Administration of control	No.
International security restrictions	No.
Payment arrears	No.
Controls on trade in gold (coins and/or bullion)	No.
Controls on exports and imports of banknotes	No.

Resident Accounts

Foreign exchange accounts permitted	Yes.
Held domestically	All residents, except the government, public institutions, and public sector enterprises, are allowed to keep foreign exchange in free accounts. These accounts may be credited with any means of payment without restrictions, other than a customs declaration for cash deposits. Withdrawals from these accounts may be used to make transfers abroad, to make transfers to other free accounts, to purchase domestic currency, to make payments

in foreign exchange to domestic institutions authorized to sell goods and services for foreign exchange, and for any other purpose.

Held abroad	Yes.
Accounts in domestic currency convertible into foreign currency	Yes.

Nonresident Accounts

Foreign exchange accounts permitted	Diplomatic, foreign, international, and regional missions and organizations; foreign charities and aid organizations; foreign companies, foreign contractors, and the foreign personnel of these organizations are allowed to open special foreign accounts with authorized banks. These accounts may be credited with transfers from abroad. Special foreign currency accounts may be debited for transfers abroad to finance foreign travel, to purchase local currency in order to finance local payments, to make foreign currency payments to local institutions authorized to sell goods and services for foreign currency, and to finance imports. Withdrawals may be made for the purpose of travel by the account holder or his or her family, and local payments in Sudanese dinars.
Approval required	Approval is required to open these accounts, except in the case of airline companies. Accounts of airline companies may be credited with payments by their passengers, consignors, and agents, who are allowed to buy travel tickets in foreign currency.
Domestic currency accounts	These accounts may be opened by the same individuals and organizations as those allowed to open foreign exchange accounts. Balances may be converted, subject to approval on the basis of documentary evidence.
Convertible into foreign currency	Yes.
Blocked accounts	No.

Imports and Import Payments

Foreign exchange budget	No.
Financing requirements for imports	
Advance import deposits	Authorized banks are free to obtain a deposit of any amount in foreign currency from the importer at least one month before the importer receives the shipping documents. Imports financed at the commercial market rate, including those financed with LCs, may be subject to an advance deposit of up to the full c.i.f. value.
Documentation requirements for release of foreign exchange for imports	Imports must be accompanied by a pro forma invoice, a valid commercial registration certificate, a valid tax clearance certificate, and the written consent of the authorized bodies for certain categories of imports.
Letters of credit	Yes.
Import licenses and other nontariff measures	Licenses are required only for imports through bilateral and preferential trade arrangements.
Negative list	Certain imports, such as wine, drugs, gambling instruments, and weapons, are prohibited for reasons of religion, health, and national security.
Other nontariff measures	Imports from Israel are prohibited.
Import taxes and/or tariffs	The import duty rates range from 6% to 80%.
Taxes collected through the exchange system	Yes.
State import monopoly	No.

Exports and Export Proceeds

Repatriation requirements	All export proceeds must be repatriated within 60 days of the date of the bill of lading.
Surrender requirements	Since June 28, 1999, the surrender requirements to the BOS for cotton exports and gum arabic were eliminated. Other surrender requirements were abolished and replaced with a requirement to sell within 20 days to commercial banks export receipts not required to make current payments. If banks do not sell to customers within 7 days the foreign exchange they obtained from exporters, they must surrender it to the BOS.
Financing requirements	n.a.
Documentation requirements	
Letters of credit	Yes.
Export licenses	Licenses are required for exports under bilateral protocol arrangements and under barter trade.
Without quotas	All exports to Israel are prohibited.
Export taxes	Export taxes are levied on several goods.

Payments for Invisible Transactions and Current Transfers

Controls on these transfers	
Trade-related payments	Insurance for imports must normally be taken out with local companies.
Investment-related payments	
Prior approval	Amortization payments on loans to residents are subject to certification from the BOS regarding the original amount of the foreign loans.

Proceeds from Invisible Transactions and Current Transfers

Repatriation requirements	No.
Restrictions on use of funds	No.

Capital Transactions

Controls on capital and money market instruments	No.
Controls on derivatives and other instruments	No.
Controls on credit operations	No.
Controls on direct investment	No.
Controls on liquidation of direct investment	No.
Controls on real estate transactions	No.
Controls on personal capital movements	No.

Provisions specific to commercial banks and other credit institutions

Differential treatment of deposit accounts in foreign exchange

    Reserve requirements   There is a 10% reserve requirement on foreign currency deposits. The reserve requirement on domestic currency deposits is 20%.

Open foreign exchange position limits

    On nonresident assets and liabilities   Yes.

Provisions specific to institutional investors   No.

Other controls imposed by securities laws   No.

Changes During 1999

Exchange arrangement   *January 1.* The Sudanese pound ceased to be legal tender.

Exports and export proceeds   *June 28.* The surrender requirement for cotton exports and gum arabic was eliminated.

SURINAME

(Position as of December 31, 1999)

Status Under IMF Articles of Agreement

Article VIII   Date of acceptance: June 29, 1978.

Exchange Arrangement

Currency   The currency of Suriname is the Suriname guilder.

Other legal tender   Three gold coins are legal tender.

Exchange rate structure

Multiple   Effective January 1, 1999, a multiple exchange rate regime was created, as commercial banks and foreign exchange bureaus were allowed to set their own exchange rates for foreign exchange acquired from sources other than the Central Bank of Suriname (CBS) with-in a 3% band around the official exchange rate. Other exchange rates in effect are an exchange rate that is applied to imports of fuel, which is more depreciated than the official exchange rate; and a customs rate, which is used to evaluate import taxes. A parallel market exchange rate is also in effect, which at end-December 1999 stood at a premium of about 25% over the official exchange rate.

Classification

Managed floating with no prean-   Since January 1, 1999, the CBS has been an active participant in the parallel market, as it
nounced path for the exchange rate now sells foreign exchange to commercial banks and cambios at the parallel market rate. Official transactions are restricted to government purchases. Commercial banks must sell to their clients at the interbank market rate the foreign exchange acquired from the CBS.

                                    Commercial banks charge commissions of 2% on sales of foreign exchange and 9.25% on transfers.

Exchange tax   No.

Exchange subsidy   n.a.

Forward exchange market   No.

Arrangements for Payments and Receipts

**Prescription of currency   Settlements in Suriname guilders between Suriname and foreign countries are not permit-
requirements**   ted; they must, in general, be made in specified convertible currencies (Australian dollars, Barbados dollars, Canadian dollars, Eastern Caribbean dollars, euros, Guyana dollars, Japanese yen, Norwegian kroner, pounds sterling, Swedish kronor, Swiss francs, Trinidad and Tobago dollars, and U.S. dollars).

Payment arrangements

Bilateral payment arrangements   Yes.

Regional arrangements   Suriname is a member of the CARICOM.

Administration of control   The CBS is empowered to provide foreign exchange for import payments (subject to presentation of an import license that serves as a general authorization for payment); this function has been delegated to commercial banks. The CBS approves import licenses if imports are paid with an LC.

                                    Commercial banks (1) provide foreign exchange for imports. Except for limited amounts of foreign exchange for invisible payments not requiring an exchange license, banks are not permitted to sell foreign exchange unless the remitter submits an exchange license; and (2) may accept, free of license, those inward transfers of foreign exchange that do not result from borrowing abroad.

The Ministry of Trade and Industry (MTI) grants export and import licenses. However, two specified mining companies do not need licenses for their own import requirements. Similar exemptions may be granted to foreign companies for their industrial activities in Suriname, provided that they pay for imports from their own foreign exchange holdings.

The Federal Exchange Commission (FEC) (1) grants licenses for external payments other than imports of goods, (2) approves foreign loans, and (3) appoints authorized banks.

International security restrictions	No.
Payment arrears	
Official	These arrears are owed largely to Brazil.
Controls on trade in gold (coins and/or bullion)	
Controls on domestic ownership and/or trade	Producers of gold may sell only to the authorized gold buyers (the CBS and Grassalco). Locally produced gold must be surrendered to the FEC by sale to the CBS. The authorized gold buyers are permitted, however, to sell nuggets at freely agreed prices for industrial and artistic purposes. Dealings between residents in gold bars and other forms of unworked gold, with the exception of nuggets, are prohibited. As local production does not meet the demand for industrial purposes, the CBS may import some gold. Residents may hold and acquire gold coins in Suriname for numismatic and investment purposes; authorized banks may freely negotiate gold coins among themselves and with other residents. Residents other than the monetary authorities, producers of gold, and authorized industrial and dental users are not allowed to hold or acquire gold in any form other than nuggets, jewelry, or coins, at home or abroad without special permission.
Controls on external trade	Imports and exports of gold in any form other than jewelry require exchange licenses issued by the FEC. Licenses are not normally granted except for imports and exports of coins by authorized banks, and for imports and exports by or on behalf of the monetary authorities, producers of gold, and industrial users. Residents arriving from abroad, however, may bring in gold freely, subject to declaration and provided that they surrender it to the CBS within 20 days. Nonresident travelers may also bring in gold freely, subject to declaration; they may reexport the declared amount freely. Imports of gold coins are duty free, and those of unworked gold are subject to a duty of Sf 1.00 a gram, irrespective of origin. The general tariff for gold ornaments is 60% ad valorem. Imports and exports of all forms of gold are subject to a statistical fee of 0.5%; in addition, imports are subject to a licensing fee of 1.5%.
Controls on exports and imports of banknotes	
On exports	
Domestic currency	Both resident and nonresident travelers may take out up to Sf 100.
Foreign currency	Exports in excess of $10,000 require a written declaration.
On imports	
Domestic currency	Travelers may bring in up to Sf 100.
Foreign currency	Travelers may bring in up to $10,000. Larger amounts must be declared. Nonresidents may take out of the country up to the amount they brought in and declared on entry.

Resident Accounts

Foreign exchange accounts permitted	Nonbank residents are allowed to open foreign currency accounts with domestic and foreign banks and to hold foreign securities, provided that the funds have not been acquired from sales of real estate in Suriname or from exports. Balances in these accounts and holdings of foreign assets may be used freely, except for travel, for which there is a limit of Sf 1,500 a person a year.
Held domestically	Yes.

Held abroad	Yes.
Accounts in domestic currency convertible into foreign currency	n.a.

Nonresident Accounts

Foreign exchange accounts permitted	Nonresidents, whether banks or nonbanks, may open accounts in dollars with domestic banks with the prior permission of the FEC; no overdrafts are permitted. These accounts may not be credited with Suriname guilders.
Domestic currency accounts	Nonresidents other than banks may open accounts in Suriname guilders freely with domestic banks. Certain debits and credits are covered by a general license, and all others are subject to a specific license. These accounts must not be overdrawn, and, except for certain specified purposes, debits must not exceed a total of Sf 3,000 a month. Authorized banks may open nonresident accounts in Suriname guilders in the name of nonresident banks; these accounts also must not be overdrawn. Authorized banks may open nonresident accounts on behalf of nonresidents drawing pensions from the government or under company plans. A special permit is required to transfer pensions abroad. Nonresident accounts in guilders may not be credited with Suriname banknotes mailed from abroad.
Convertible into foreign currency	n.a.
Blocked accounts	n.a.

Imports and Import Payments

Foreign exchange budget	No.
Financing requirements for imports	No.
Documentation requirements for release of foreign exchange for imports	
Import licenses used as exchange licenses	Import licenses serve as a general authorization for payment. In case of payment by LC, the import license must be approved by the CBS.
Import licenses and other nontariff measures	Import licenses are required for all imports and are valid for six months, during which period the goods must be landed and paid for.
Negative list	Imports of the following commodities are prohibited: pigs (excluding those for breeding); chicken, duck, and turkey meat; pork; fish (excluding kwie kwie fish and smoked herring), shrimp, and crab (fresh, cooled, frozen, salted, dried, or precooked); vegetables (excluding potatoes, onions, and garlic); edible roots and tubers; citrus fruits; bananas and plantains; coconuts; green and roasted coffee (excluding decaffeinated); rice and rice products (excluding baby food); sugar (excluding cubes and tablets weighing 5 grams or less a cube or tablet); aromatized or colored sugar or sugar syrup; noodles and macaroni; jam, jelly, and marmalade (excluding those for diabetics); peanut butter; syrups and concentrates for nonalcoholic beverages in packages of less than 5 kilograms (excluding those for diabetics); firewood and other nonprocessed wood; railroad ties; shingles; wooden structures for construction; wooden tiles and panels; wooden tools, handles, and coat hangers; men's and boys' shoes (excluding rubber and plastic boots and sport shoes); and sand, gravel, sidewalk tiles, and road bricks. Imports of some other items, such as explosives and narcotics, are prohibited for reasons of public policy or health.
Open general licenses	Yes.
Licenses with quotas	Commodities subject to quotas include kwie kwie fish, milk powder, potatoes, onions, garlic, fruits and nuts (other than citrus fruits, bananas, plantains, and coconuts), decaffeinated coffee, peanuts, baby food, tomato paste, certain preserved vegetables, matches, furnishings, ready-made clothing, and furniture (excluding that for business establishments, such as offices, theaters, clinics, hotels, restaurants, and libraries).
Other nontariff measures	Yes.

Import taxes and/or tariffs	In addition to customs duties, a license fee of 1.5% is levied on the c.i.f. value of all imports. A statistical fee of 2% is levied on the c.i.f. value of imports of bauxite companies, and 0.5% of the c.i.f. value of other imports.
State import monopoly	n.a.

Exports and Export Proceeds

Repatriation requirements	Certain export companies have received special permission from the FEC to maintain current accounts in foreign currency with their parent companies abroad and to use these for specified payments and receipts (including export proceeds).
Surrender requirements	Bauxite companies are not subject to export surrender requirements but must sell foreign exchange at the official exchange rate to the CBS to pay for their local expenditures. Other exporters, except exporters of rice, are also allowed to retain their export proceeds in dollars and to exchange them at the parallel market rate, and are allowed to buy back up to 85% of the amount surrendered.
Financing requirements	No.
Documentation requirements	To verify prices, the MTI ascertains with the relevant government agency whether the export price as reported by the exporter is in accordance with world market prices.
Letters of credit	Licenses are issued if the exports are covered by LCs opened by buyers abroad.
Export licenses	Exports require licenses issued by the MTI. Export licenses for cattle, pigs, fresh beef and pork, and planting materials are granted only on the advice of the Director of Agriculture, Animal Husbandry, and Fisheries. The export of bamboo wood is prohibited, and that of rice is subject to special regulations.
Export taxes	Exports of processed and semiprocessed wood are subject to a tax of 100% of the f.o.b. value. Exports of bauxite are subject to a statistical fee of 2% of their f.o.b. value, and other exports are subject to a statistical fee of 0.5% of their f.o.b. value.

Payments for Invisible Transactions and Current Transfers

Controls on these transfers	Transactions involving outward remittances of foreign exchange are subject to licensing. Application for a license must be submitted to the FEC at least one month before the intended date for effecting such a transaction.
Investment-related payments	License applications must be supported by an auditor's report and presented to the FEC for verification. Transfers of profits from investments made after July 31, 1953, are permitted. License applications must be supported by an auditor's report and presented to the FEC for verification. Profits must be transferred within three years; otherwise, they are considered to have become part of the firm's working capital and may be transferred only in annual installments of 20%. Transfers in accordance with these decisions have been temporarily suspended. Information is not available on the payment of amortization of loans or depreciation of direct investments.
Quantitative limits	There are quantitative limits for the transfer of profits.
Payments for travel	Travel allowances for residents are subject to licensing and are limited to the equivalent of $1,500 a person a calendar year.
Prior approval	Yes.
Quantitative limits	Yes.
Indicative limits/bona fide test	Yes.
Personal payments	A special permit is required to transfer pensions abroad. Information is not available for payments related to medical costs, studies abroad, and family maintenance.
Prior approval	Yes.

Foreign workers' wages

Prior approval	Yes.
Quantitative limits	The head of a repatriating family may transfer the equivalent of Sf 10,000 plus 10% of his or her total taxable earnings in Suriname accrued during the period of residence. If his or her Surinamese assets exceed the sum thus calculated, the excess may be transferred at a rate of Sf 10,000 a year. Transfers abroad in excess of Sf 10,000 a year may be authorized under exceptional circumstances. Outward transfers for these purposes have been temporarily reduced.
Indicative limits/bona fide test	Yes.

Other payments

Quantitative limits	Authorized banks and the General Post Office have authority to provide foreign exchange up to Sf 150 a month for payment of certain services (bank charges, legal fees, membership dues, copy and patent rights, etc.) as well as for advertising expenses and payments for books.

Proceeds from Invisible Transactions and Current Transfers

Repatriation requirements	Yes.
Surrender requirements	Foreign exchange receipts from invisibles must be surrendered to an authorized bank.
Restrictions on use of funds	Yes.

Capital Transactions

Controls on capital and money market instruments	Subject to certain requirements, residents may purchase or sell in specified countries Surinamese corporate shares that have been designated as negotiable by the FEC.
Controls on derivatives and other instruments	n.a.
Controls on credit operations	
Commercial credits	
To residents from nonresidents	Borrowing by nonbanks requires the prior approval of the FEC.
Financial credits	The foreign transactions of authorized banks are restricted, in principle, to those undertaken for the account of their customers. Banks are required, in principle, to surrender to the CBS any excess of foreign currency purchased.
By residents to nonresidents	Authorized banks may place abroad in short-term dollar assets the amounts corresponding to balances in their nonresident dollar accounts.
Controls on direct investment	
Outward direct investment	Investments are not permitted, but exceptions may be made when it is considered beneficial to Suriname interests. The FEC may, at its discretion, grant licenses for transfers abroad from the estate of a deceased person up to a maximum of Sf 10,000. For estates valued at more than Sf 10,000, further annual transfers are permitted so as to spread them over a period of up to 10 years.
Inward direct investment	Yes.
Controls on liquidation of direct investment	Transfers of the foreign exchange (including loans) imported by a nonresident entrepreneur for the company's use are permitted at any time. Also permitted are transfers of capital proceeds from the sale to residents, or the liquidation of fully or partly foreign-owned companies or other forms of enterprise established by nonresidents with foreign capital after July 31, 1953.

Controls on real estate transactions

Purchase abroad by residents

Residents may not purchase real estate abroad.

Controls on personal capital movements

Transfer of assets

Transfer abroad by emigrants

The FEC may allow emigrants (heads of family) to transfer in foreign exchange the equivalent of Sf 5,000 in a lump sum, and subsequently Sf 5,000 a year.

Provisions specific to commercial banks and other credit institutions

Maintenance of accounts abroad

Authorized banks are permitted to place part of their liquid funds abroad and to use the short-term credit lines extended by their foreign correspondent banks as a source of operating funds. The CBS guarantees the LCs issued by the authorized banks by pledging its balances up to a specified ceiling, while the authorized banks keep their balances abroad at a minimum level. This arrangement applies to the state-controlled Landbouw Bank, De Surinaamsche Bank, and Hakrinbank, but not to the Dutch-owned Algemene Bank Nederland. Authorized banks may place abroad in short-term dollar assets the amounts corresponding to balances in their nonresident dollar accounts.

Open foreign exchange position limits

The foreign transactions of authorized banks are restricted, in principle, to those undertaken for the account of their customers, and banks are required, in principle, to surrender to the CBS any excess of foreign currency purchased.

Provisions specific to institutional investors

n.a.

Other controls imposed by securities laws

No.

Changes During 1999

Exchange arrangement

January 1. A multiple exchange rate structure was introduced, as commercial banks and exchange bureaus were free to set their own exchange rates for foreign exchange acquired from non-CBS sources within a ±3% band around the official rate.

SWAZILAND

(Position as of December 31, 1999)

Status Under IMF Articles of Agreement

Article VIII	Date of acceptance: December 11, 1989.

Exchange Arrangement

Currency	The currency of Swaziland is the Swaziland lilangeni.
Exchange rate structure	Unitary.
Classification	
Conventional pegged arrangement	The lilangeni is pegged to the South African rand at E 1 per R 1. Exchange rates for the U.S. dollar quoted by the Central Bank of Swaziland (CBS) are based on the exchange rate of the South African rand against the U.S. dollar. Rates are also quoted for the Canadian dollar, the euro, the Japanese yen, the pound sterling, and the Swiss franc, based on the London and New York market quotations for these currencies against the U.S. dollar and the euro. The CBS also quotes rates for the currencies of the member states of the PTA, based on their relationship with the SDR as reported by the PTA clearinghouse.
Exchange tax	No.
Exchange subsidy	No.
Forward exchange market	The CBS permits authorized dealers to engage in forward exchange operations. The forward exchange rates are market determined.

Arrangements for Payments and Receipts

Prescription of currency requirements	No.
Payment arrangements	Yes.
Regional arrangements	Swaziland is part of the CMA; no restrictions are applied to payments within the CMA, and, in principle, payments are not controlled. Residents of Swaziland have access to the Johannesburg market, in accordance with the terms and conditions applied in that market.
Administration of control	The CBS, on behalf of the MOF, controls all external currency transactions. In relations with countries outside the CMA, Swaziland applies exchange controls that are generally similar to those of South Africa.
International security restrictions	No.
Payment arrears	No.
Controls on trade in gold (coins and/or bullion)	
Controls on domestic ownership and/or trade	Yes.
Controls on external trade	Yes.
Controls on exports and imports of banknotes	
On exports	
Domestic currency	Exports of up to E 500 are allowed.
Foreign currency	Exports of the applicable travel entitlement are allowed.

On imports

   Domestic currency .   Imports of up to E 500 are allowed.

Resident Accounts

Foreign exchange accounts permitted Yes.

Held domestically   Individuals may hold foreign currency deposits of up to E 100,000 with local authorized dealers.

  Approval required   Approval is granted to export/import-oriented companies.

Held abroad   Individuals may not hold foreign currency deposits abroad, and companies are subject to approval and limited to required working balances.

Accounts in domestic currency convertible into foreign currency Converting these accounts is subject to exchange control approval.

Nonresident Accounts

Foreign exchange accounts permitted These accounts are permitted, but subject to approval.

Domestic currency accounts Yes.

Convertible into foreign currency These accounts may be converted, but are subject to approval.

Blocked accounts Balances in these accounts may be invested in quoted securities within Swaziland and other such investments as may be approved by the CBS.

Imports and Import Payments

Foreign exchange budget No.

Financing requirements for imports

Minimum financing requirements Yes.

Advance payment requirements Advance payments are limited to 33.33% of the ex-factory cost of the goods.

Advance import deposits Yes.

Documentation requirements for release of foreign exchange for imports

Import licenses used as exchange licenses Import licenses entitle the holders to buy the foreign exchange required to make import payments.

Import licenses and other nontariff measures

Open general licenses Swaziland is a member of the SACU, and no import restrictions are imposed on goods originating in any country of the customs union. Imports from South Africa, including goods originating outside the customs union, do not require licenses. Imports from countries outside the customs union require licenses. Ports of entry outside Swaziland may be used, but the Swaziland authorities are responsible for controlling import licenses and payment procedures.

Import taxes and/or tariffs Swaziland applies the customs tariff system of SACU on imports from outside the customs union.

State import monopoly No.

Exports and Export Proceeds

Repatriation requirements	For goods shipped to countries outside the customs area, licensing is administered to ensure that export proceeds are repatriated in the prescribed manner and within the stipulated period.
Surrender requirements	Declaration must be done within 30 days from the date of accrual.
Financing requirements	n.r.
Documentation requirements	Contract notes are required.
Export licenses	
Without quotas	All exports are subject to licensing. For those goods that are shipped to members of the customs area, licenses are used mainly for tax levy purposes.
Export taxes	A sugar export levy applies to export proceeds from the EU market.

Payments for Invisible Transactions and Current Transfers

Controls on these transfers	Payments to nonresidents for current transactions, while subject to control, are not normally restricted. Authority to approve some types of current payments up to established limits is delegated to authorized dealers.
Trade-related payments	
Prior approval	Required for the payment of administrative expenses.
Indicative limits/bona fide test	Yes.
Investment-related payments	Information is not available on the payment of amortization loans or depreciation of direct investments.
Prior approval	Required for interest payments and remittances of profits and dividends.
Indicative limits/bona fide test	Yes.
Payments for travel	
Quantitative limits	For business and holiday travel, permanent residents may purchase in foreign exchange up to E 100,000 an adult a year, and E 30,000 a child under 12 years a year.
Indicative limits/bona fide test	Larger amounts are granted upon application supported by proof of bona fide need.
Personal payments	
Prior approval	Required for the transfers of pensions.
Quantitative limits	Study allowances for students in non-CMA countries are E 160,000 a year for single students, and E 200,000 a year for married students accompanied by their spouse. Travel allowances for students studying in non-CMA countries during vacation periods are E 30,000 a year for single students, and E 60,000 a year for married students accompanied by their spouse.
Indicative limits/bona fide test	Yes.
Foreign workers' wages	
Quantitative limits	The limit varies from one-third up to one-half of the gross monthly income.
Indicative limits/bona fide test	Yes.
Credit card use abroad	
Prior approval	To use credit cards outside the CMA, a resident cardholder must complete a letter of undertaking before departure.
Quantitative limits	Residents may utilize up to 100% of the sanctioned travel facility.
Indicative limits/bona fide test	Yes.

Other payments

Indicative limits/bona fide test	Yes.

Proceeds from Invisible Transactions and Current Transfers

Repatriation requirements	Yes.
Surrender requirements	Yes.
Restrictions on use of funds	Yes.

Capital Transactions

Controls on capital and money market instruments	All inward capital transfers require the prior approval of the CBS and must be properly documented in order to facilitate the subsequent repatriation of interest, dividends, profits, and other income.
On capital market securities	
Shares or other securities of a participating nature	
Purchase locally by nonresidents	Purchases may be processed through normal banking channels either directly in foreign currency or through local currency nonresident accounts with the CMA.
Sale or issue locally by nonresidents	Balances in blocked accounts may be invested in quoted securities and other such investments as may be approved by the CBS.
Purchase abroad by residents	Applications for most outward transfers of capital are considered on their merits.
Sale or issue abroad by residents	Yes.
Bonds or other debt securities	
Purchase locally by nonresidents	Yes.
Sale or issue locally by nonresidents	Yes.
Purchase abroad by residents	These transactions are subject to the prior approval of the CBS.
Sale or issue abroad by residents	These transactions are subject to the prior approval of the CBS.
On money market instruments	All money market transactions are controlled.
On collective investment securities	All transactions in collective investment securities are controlled.
Controls on derivatives and other instruments	All transactions in derivatives and other investments are controlled.
Controls on credit operations	All other credit operations are controlled.
Commercial credits	
To residents from nonresidents	Borrowing in foreign currency is not allowed.
Controls on direct investment	
Outward direct investment	Applications for most outward transfers of capital are considered on their merits.
Inward direct investment	Yes.
Controls on liquidation of direct investment	No.
Controls on real estate transactions	
Purchase abroad by residents	These transactions are subject to the prior approval of the CBS.

Purchase locally by nonresidents	Purchases by nonresidents are subject to approval. Applicants must go through the Land Speculation Board to determine if there is effective local demand.
Sale locally by nonresidents	These transactions are subject to the prior approval of the CBS.
Controls on personal capital movements	All other personal capital movements are controlled.
Settlement of debts abroad by immigrants	Controls apply to funds drawn from blocked accounts.
Transfer of gambling and prize earnings	These transactions require approval.
Provisions specific to commercial banks and other credit institutions	
Borrowing abroad	Residents are not permitted to borrow funds from abroad without prior approval.
Lending to nonresidents (financial or commercial credits)	Yes.
Lending locally in foreign exchange	Yes.
Differential treatment of deposit accounts in foreign exchange	
Reserve requirements	Yes.
Liquid asset requirements	Yes.
Differential treatment of deposit accounts held by nonresidents	
Reserve requirements	Yes.
Liquid asset requirements	Yes.
Credit controls	Yes.
Investment regulations	
In banks by nonresidents	Yes.
Open foreign exchange position limits	
On resident assets and liabilities	Yes.
On nonresident assets and liabilities	Yes.
Provisions specific to institutional investors	
Limits (max.) on securities issued by nonresidents and on portfolio invested abroad	Yes.
Limits (max.) on portfolio invested abroad	Yes.
Limits (min.) on portfolio invested locally	Institutional investors are allowed to invest abroad 15% of their assets in Swaziland by way of asset swaps after obtaining CBS approval.
Other controls imposed by securities laws	No.

Changes During 1999

No significant changes occurred in the exchange and trade system.

SWEDEN

(Position as of January 31, 2000)

Status Under IMF Articles of Agreement

Article VIII	Date of acceptance: February 15, 1961.

Exchange Arrangement

Currency	The currency of Sweden is the Swedish krona.
Exchange rate structure	Unitary.
Classification	
Independently floating	The exchange rate of the Swedish krona is determined on the basis of supply and demand.
Exchange tax	No.
Exchange subsidy	No.
Forward exchange market	Yes.
Official cover of forward operations	The Sveriges Riksbank, the central bank, and certain government agencies participate in the forward exchange rate market.

Arrangements for Payments and Receipts

Prescription of currency requirements	No.
Payment arrangements	No.
Administration of control	No.
International security restrictions	
In accordance with Executive Board Decision No. 144-(52/51)	Yes.
In accordance with UN sanctions	Sweden imposes certain restrictions with regard to payments and transfers in respect of the Federal Republic of Yugoslavia (Serbia/Montenegro). Financial transactions with Iraq are prohibited. Certain restrictions are imposed on Angola. Effective June 1, 1999, restrictions against the Libyan Arab Jamahiriya were lifted and sanctions against the Federal Republic of Yugoslavia (Serbia/Montenegro) were amended, while those applied to areas of the Republic of Bosnia and Herzegovina, under the control of the Bosnian Serb forces, were lifted. Effective December 1, 1999, further amendments were made to sanctions with respect to the Federal Republic of Yugoslavia (Serbia/Montenegro).
Payment arrears	No.
Controls on trade in gold (coins and/or bullion)	No.
Controls on exports and imports of banknotes	No.

Resident Accounts

Foreign exchange accounts permitted	Yes.
Held domestically	Yes.

Held abroad	Residents may open accounts, provided that the amounts are reported to the Swedish National Tax Board for tax control and to the Riksbank for statistical purposes.
Accounts in domestic currency convertible into foreign currency	Yes.

Nonresident Accounts

Foreign exchange accounts permitted	Yes.
Domestic currency accounts	External krona accounts may be held by nonresidents domiciled abroad, including persons who have become nonresidents after emigrating. They may be used for payments and transfers and may be converted into any foreign currency.
Convertible into foreign currency	Yes.
Blocked accounts	These accounts are blocked for the Federal Republic of Yugoslavia (Serbia/Montenegro) and Libya.

Imports and Import Payments

Foreign exchange budget	No.
Financing requirements for imports	No.
Documentation requirements for release of foreign exchange for imports	No.
Import licenses and other nontariff measures	Imports on most iron and steel products from all countries outside the EU, other than Turkey and countries of the EFTA or countries that are parties to the EEA, are subject to import licensing for surveillance purposes. Certain goods from China, such as bicycles, brushes, fireworks, gloves, toys, etc., are also subject to licensing for surveillance purposes. Effective January 1, 2000, imports of shoes from Vietnam are subject to licensing for surveillance purposes.
	Imports from Iraq are prohibited due to UN sanctions. Import restrictions apply to certain categories of food as well as narcotic drugs, weapons, live animals, radioactive materials, and others.
Licenses with quotas	As a result of Sweden's membership in the EU, the importation of textiles and clothing from more than 40 countries is subject to restrictions or licensing for surveillance purposes. Agricultural and fishery products are also subject to import licensing. Some iron and steel products from Kazakhstan, Russia, and Ukraine are also subject to restrictions as are imports of porcelain and shoes from China.
Import taxes and/or tariffs	Alcohol, tobacco, and mineral oils are subject to import taxes and customs duty.
State import monopoly	No.

Exports and Export Proceeds

Repatriation requirements	No.
Financing requirements	No.
Documentation requirements	No.
Export licenses	Exports to Iraq and Angola are prohibited due to UN sanctions, with a few exceptions.
Without quotas	Yes.
Export taxes	No.

Payments for Invisible Transactions and Current Transfers

Controls on these transfers	No.

Proceeds from Invisible Transactions and Current Transfers

Repatriation requirements	No.
Restrictions on use of funds	No.

Capital Transactions

Controls on capital and money market instruments	The control applies only to shares and other securities of a participatory nature that may be affected by laws on inward direct investment in fishing and civil aviation.
On capital market securities	
Shares or other securities of a participating nature	
Purchase locally by nonresidents	Yes.
On money market instruments	
Purchase locally by nonresidents	Yes.
Controls on derivatives and other instruments	No.
Controls on credit operations	No.
Controls on direct investment	
Inward direct investment	Laws on inward investment and establishment apply to investment in fishing, civil aviation, and transport and communications.
Controls on liquidation of direct investment	No.
Controls on real estate transactions	
Purchase locally by nonresidents	A permit may be required.
Controls on personal capital movements	No.
Provisions specific to commercial banks and other credit institutions	
Investment regulations	
Abroad by banks	Yes.
Open foreign exchange position limits	For prudential reasons, there are general guidelines related to credit institutions' and securities firms' net positions in foreign currencies. These guidelines stipulate limits on both positions in a single currency—15% of the capital base—and on the total net position of all currencies—30% of the capital base.
On resident assets and liabilities	Yes.
On nonresident assets and liabilities	Yes.
Provisions specific to institutional investors	
Currency-matching regulations on assets/liabilities composition	The same provisions apply as for open foreign exchange position limits.

Other controls imposed by securities laws

No.

Changes During 1999

Arrangements for payments and receipts

June 1. Sanctions against the Libyan Arab Jamahiriya were lifted. Additionally, sanctions against the Federal Republic of Yugoslavia (Serbia/Montenegro) were amended, while those applied to areas of the Republic of Bosnia and Herzegovina under control of the Bosnian Serb forces were lifted.

December 1. Further amendments were made to sanctions with respect to the Federal Republic of Yugoslavia (Serbia/Montenegro).

Changes During 2000

Imports and import payments

January 1. Imports of shoes from Vietnam were made subject to licensing for surveillance purposes.

SWITZERLAND

(Position as of December 31, 1999)

Status Under IMF Articles of Agreement

Article VIII	Date of acceptance: May 29, 1992.

Exchange Arrangement

Currency	The currency of Switzerland is the Swiss franc.
Exchange rate structure	Unitary.
Classification	
Independently floating	The exchange rate of the Swiss franc is determined by supply and demand. However, the Swiss National Bank (SNB) reserves the right to intervene in the foreign exchange market. All settlements are made at free market rates. The principal intervention currency is the dollar.
Exchange tax	No.
Exchange subsidy	No.
Forward exchange market	No officially fixed premiums and discount rates apply to forward exchange contracts, all of which are negotiated at free market rates.

Arrangements for Payments and Receipts

Prescription of currency requirements	No.
Payment arrangements	No.
Administration of control	No.
International security restrictions	
In accordance with Executive Board Decision No. 144-(52/51)	Certain restrictions have been imposed against Iraq and the Federal Republic of Yugoslavia (Serbia/Montenegro). Restrictions imposed against Libya were terminated on June 30, 1999.
In accordance with UN sanctions	On the basis of UN sanctions, restrictions have been imposed on the making of payments and transfers for current international transactions regarding Iraq and the Federal Republic of Yugoslavia (Serbia/Montenegro). Restrictions imposed against Libya were terminated on June 30, 1999.
Payment arrears	No.
Controls on trade in gold (coins and/or bullion)	
Controls on external trade	Import and export licenses, which are issued freely, are required for commercial imports and exports of certain articles containing gold.
Controls on exports and imports of banknotes	No.

Resident Accounts

Foreign exchange accounts permitted	Yes.
Held domestically	Yes.

Held abroad	Yes.
Accounts in domestic currency convertible into foreign currency	Yes.

Nonresident Accounts

Foreign exchange accounts permitted	Yes.
Domestic currency accounts	Yes.
Convertible into foreign currency	Yes.
Blocked accounts	No.

Imports and Import Payments

Foreign exchange budget	No.
Financing requirements for imports	No.
Documentation requirements for release of foreign exchange for imports	No.
Import licenses and other nontariff measures	
Open general licenses	Licenses are required mostly for agricultural products.
Other nontariff measures	Import controls apply only for defense-sensitive products, and in accordance with UN restrictions.
Import taxes and/or tariffs	In general, customs duties are levied based on the weight of goods instead of their value. On industrial goods, import tariffs are in general very low. On agricultural goods that are produced in Switzerland, they are higher. In the frame of the GATT–Uruguay Round all quantitative restrictions and measures having equivalent effect concerning agricultural products were transformed into tariffs. In order to maintain market access opportunities prevailing in 1986–88, 28 tariff rate quotas were created for specific agricultural goods (e.g., fruits, vegetables, meats, wines, etc.).
State import monopoly	The partial state monopolies for the importation of alcohol of less than 80 proof, butter, and wheat grain were removed on June 30, 1999. The remaining state monopolies apply to imports of alcohol 80 proof and above, salt, and wheat flour within the tariff rate quota.

Exports and Export Proceeds

Repatriation requirements	No.
Financing requirements	No.
Documentation requirements	No.
Export licenses	A system of general and individual licenses applies to controlled exports.
Without quotas	Exports of weapons, dual-use goods for the production of conventional weapons, and weapons of mass destruction are controlled (approval is required). Exports are prohibited in accordance with UN restrictions.
Export taxes	No.

Payments for Invisible Transactions and Current Transfers

Controls on these transfers	No.

Proceeds from Invisible Transactions and Current Transfers

Repatriation requirements	No.
Restrictions on use of funds	No.

Capital Transactions

Controls on capital and money market instruments

On capital market securities — Foreign and domestic bond issues denominated in Swiss francs must be reported to the SNB. The physical importation and exportation of Swiss and foreign securities are unrestricted. In case of major disturbances in the capital markets, the federal government may introduce a permit requirement for certain outward capital transfers (e.g., bond issues).

Controls on derivatives and other instruments — No.

Controls on credit operations — No.

Controls on direct investment — No.

Controls on liquidation of direct investment — No.

Controls on real estate transactions

Purchase locally by nonresidents — Purchases by nonresidents require approval by the canton in which the property is situated. The approval of the canton is subject to supervision and appeal by the federal government.

Controls on personal capital movements — No.

Provisions specific to commercial banks and other credit institutions — No.

Provisions specific to institutional investors — For life and nonlife insurance companies, the overall limit is 30% with limits for equities, bonds, and real estate of 25%, 20%, and 5% of the total portfolio, respectively.

Limits (max.) on securities issued by nonresidents and on portfolio invested abroad — Yes.

Limits (max.) on portfolio invested abroad — Yes.

Other controls imposed by securities laws — No.

Changes During 1999

Arrangements for payments and receipts — *June 30.* Restrictions against Libya were lifted.

Imports and import payments — *June 30.* The state monopoly on imports of alcohol of less than 80 proof, butter, and wheat grain was removed.

SYRIAN ARAB REPUBLIC

(Position as of February 29, 2000)

Status Under IMF Articles of Agreement

Article XIV	Yes.

Exchange Arrangement

Currency

The currency of the Syrian Arab Republic is the Syrian pound.

Exchange rate structure

Multiple

On January 1, 1999, the exchange rate system consisted of four official rates and two unofficial rates. On December 31, 1999, the promotion rate of LS 20.22 per $1, which was used only for payments of allowances to students who started overseas study before January 1, 1991, was eliminated. Currently, the official rates are: (1) the legally designated official rate of LS 11.20/11.25 per $1 applies to the repayment of loans and interests arising from bilateral payments agreements; (2) the budget accounting rate of LS 46.45/46.50 per $1 (also known as the government fee rate) applies to public sector exports of petroleum, all government imports (including essential subsidized commodities and invisibles), and repayment of loans and interest not related to bilateral payments agreements; and (3) the "rate in neighboring countries" of LS 46.00/46.50 per $1 applies to the following transactions: (i) all public and private capital inflows, the 25% of export proceeds surrendered by the private sector, and that part of the 75% of export proceeds retained by private sector exporters that is not used to finance their own imports or sold to other importers; (ii) travel allowances; (iii) tourism and medical expenses; (iv) student allowances; (v) remittances abroad and payments by the public sector approved by the Committee for Foreign Exchange; (vi) all public sector enterprises' foreign exchange transactions; (vii) earnings of staff of UN and diplomatic missions in the Syrian Arab Republic; and (viii) domestic expenses of foreign oil companies.

The unofficial rates are (1) the free market rate, which stood at LS 49.85 per $1 on December 31, 1999, and (2) the "export proceeds" rate, in which a market-determined rate applies to goods that may be imported only with foreign exchange earned through exports. Exporters who do not use all of their export earnings to import goods may sell their retained foreign exchange earnings to importers in this market. In December 1999, the exchange rate in this market stood at LS 56 per $1.

Classification

Conventional pegged arrangement

The official rate is pegged to the dollar at LS 11.20/11.25 per $1, but it applies to a few debt payments relating to bilateral payment arrangements.

Exchange tax

No.

Exchange subsidy

No.

Forward exchange market

No.

Arrangements for Payments and Receipts

Prescription of currency requirements

The Exchange Office (EO) prescribes the currencies that may be obtained for exports. Proceeds from exports to all countries may be obtained in any convertible currency. Prescription of currency requirements are not applied to outgoing payments. All payments to, and receipts from, Israel are prohibited. With few exceptions, non-Syrians visiting the Syrian Arab Republic are required to settle their bills in foreign exchange.

Payment arrangements

Bilateral payment arrangements

Operative

There is an agreement with the Islamic Republic of Iran.

Inoperative	There is an agreement with Russia and Sri Lanka.
Administration of control	The Ministry of Economy and Foreign Trade (MOEFT) determines policy with regard to imports and exports and issues import licenses. The EO issues exchange licenses for invisibles and capital transactions.
International security restrictions	n.a.
Payment arrears	
Official	Yes.
Private	Yes.
Controls on trade in gold (coins and/or bullion)	
Controls on external trade	Imports of gold are subject to import licensing, while export proceeds must be surrendered to the Commercial Bank of Syria (ComBS).
Controls on exports and imports of banknotes	
On exports	
Domestic currency	Syrian banknotes may not be exported. However, travelers to Jordan and Lebanon who are not eligible for a foreign exchange allowance may take with them up to LS 5,000 a trip. Nonresidents leaving the Syrian Arab Republic are not allowed to reconvert Syrian currency into foreign exchange.
Foreign currency	Residents traveling abroad may take with them foreign exchange up to $2,000 a trip to all countries except Jordan and Lebanon.

Resident Accounts

Foreign exchange accounts permitted	Residents are permitted to open foreign exchange accounts. Deposits may be transferred to other resident accounts on condition that their accounts have sources from abroad. Deposits in the form of banknotes may only be withdrawn in that form, unless transferred abroad for medical treatment, education, newspaper subscriptions, and other similar noncommercial purposes. Deposits for a term of 90 days or more accrue a competitive rate of interest.
Held domestically	Yes.
Held abroad	Approval is granted if the resident has activities abroad.
Accounts in domestic currency convertible into foreign currency	No.

Nonresident Accounts

Foreign exchange accounts permitted	After obtaining approval, nonresidents may open accounts in convertible foreign currencies at the ComBS for the deposit of funds from abroad. Balances in such accounts may be sold to local banks, transferred abroad without restriction, or used to pay for authorized imports. Temporary nonresident accounts may be opened in the name of nonresidents temporarily residing in the Syrian Arab Republic. These accounts may not be used, however, for funds received in settlement currencies through payment conventions.
Domestic currency accounts	After obtaining approval, these accounts may be credited with the proceeds in foreign currencies sold to the authorized banks and with other receipts in foreign currencies; they may be debited without prior approval to pay for Syrian exports to the country of the account holder and for expenses in the Syrian Arab Republic.
Blocked accounts	Yes.

Imports and Import Payments

Foreign exchange budget

The foreign exchange requirements of the state trading agencies are met from the annual foreign exchange budget; these agencies automatically receive import licenses upon submission of documentation of their import requirements.

Financing requirements for imports

When foreign exchange is not made available, private imports must be financed with the importers' own resources through external credit arrangements, foreign currency deposits maintained in the Syrian Arab Republic by nonresidents, or foreign exchange purchased from other private or mixed enterprises through the intermediary of the ComBS at the "rate in neighboring countries." Imports of many goods are restricted to specific methods of financing. A number of imports may only be imported using foreign exchange generated through exports.

Advance import deposits

A non-interest-bearing advance deposit is required for public sector imports for an amount equal to 100% of the value of the imports. Private sector imports are not subject to this requirement if they are financed from abroad. If the ComBS requires an LC, an import deposit is required in the amount of 100% of the value of the import plus a 3% fee.

Documentation requirements for release of foreign exchange for imports

Letters of credit

Private importers may choose to import products specified on the permitted list by opening LCs at the ComBS.

Import licenses and other nontariff measures

All imports valued at more than LS 2,000 (LS 1,000 for imports from Lebanon) require licensing. A fee ranging from LS 104 to LS 454 is charged upon the issuance of an import license. Imports from the Syrian free zones are allowed for certain industrial goods and for goods imported directly from the country of origin. Imports of commodities originating in Israel are prohibited.

Positive list

The list of items that the private sector is permitted to import includes certain agricultural goods, industrial goods, and raw materials. Imports of goods not on the permitted list are prohibited, with certain exceptions. Imports must come directly from the country of origin, but the MOEFT has the authority to permit certain goods to be imported from countries other than the country of origin.

Negative list

There is a general list of goods that may not be imported from non-Arab countries. A separate list of prohibited imports from member countries of the Arab Free Trade Area includes only goods prohibited for health, safety, religious, or environmental reasons.

Import taxes and/or tariffs

An import surcharge of 2% is charged on all imports; government imports and imports of certain essential items are exempted. Imports for customs duty purposes are valued at different exchange rates (LS 11.25, LS 23, LS 43, and LS 46.50 per $1), according to the categories of goods, while import tariffs range up to 200%. All previous special levies on imports have been replaced by a unified import surcharge ranging from 6% to 35%.

State import monopoly

Many basic commodities (such as paper, salt, tobacco, wheat, iron and steel, and certain agricultural machinery) are imported only by state trading agencies or, for their own account, by certain private sector importers.

Exports and Export Proceeds

Repatriation requirements

Yes.

Surrender requirements

Until May 7, 1999, exporters were required to repatriate and surrender the proceeds to the ComBS within 60 days of the date of shipment to Lebanon, within four months of the date of export shipment to other Arab countries, and within six months of the date of shipment to any other country. On May 8, 1999, these deadlines were amended and currently exporters are required to repatriate and surrender export proceeds within six months of the date of export shipment to Arab countries and within nine months from the date of shipment to any other country. These periods may be extended to nine months for exports to Arab countries and 12 months for exports to other countries, after the approval of the EO, which is granted upon presentation of a proof of need. Private sector exporters of manufactured goods are required to surrender 25% of their export proceeds to the ComBS at the "rate in the neighboring countries," and to retain the remainder to finance permitted imports. Public sector enterprises may retain 100% of their export proceeds in special foreign currency accounts. In the case of fruits and vegetables, private sector exporters may retain 100% of the proceeds.

Financing requirements	The ComBS may accept prepayments for exports of Syrian products.
Documentation requirements	Exports of a few goods to all countries and all exports to Israel are prohibited.
Letters of credit	Yes.
Guarantees	Yes.
Domiciliation	Yes.
Preshipment inspection	Yes.
Export licenses	Exports of wheat, barley, cotton, cotton yarn, and their derivatives are made by the government organizations dealing in cereals and cotton. Petroleum product exports are handled by the state Petroleum Marketing Office. Exports of certain other commodities are also reserved for government agencies, state trading agencies, or specified companies.
Without quotas	Yes.
Export taxes	Products of agricultural origin are subject to the agricultural production tax of 12.5% ad valorem. The processed products that qualify for tax reimbursement include dried, frozen, and processed fruits and vegetables; ginned cotton, cotton wool, cotton clothing, and cotton seed oil; and olive oil. On January 7, 1999, cotton, cotton seeds, cotton yarn, and textiles also became exempt from the agricultural production tax, provided the goods are exported or processed. On February 1, 2000, additional agricultural products became exempted from the agricultural production tax.

Payments for Invisible Transactions and Current Transfers

Controls on these transfers	Most payments for invisibles must be made at the "rate in the neighboring countries."
Trade-related payments	
Prior approval	Yes.
Investment-related payments	Remittances of profit and dividends must be authorized by the EO upon proof of payment of income tax. Profits from projects approved by the Higher Committee for Investment under the investment law may be repatriated freely. Information is not available on the amortization of loans or depreciation of direct investments.
Prior approval	Yes.
Payments for travel	Residents traveling abroad may take with them foreign exchange up to $2,000 a trip to all countries except Jordan and Lebanon. Of this amount, up to the equivalent of LS 5,000 a trip may be purchased at the official rate for travel to Arab countries (except Jordan and Lebanon), and up to the equivalent of LS 7,500 a trip for travel to non-Arab countries. Travelers to Jordan and Lebanon are not eligible for a foreign exchange allowance, but may take with them up to LS 5,000 a trip in Syrian banknotes. For children 15 years and younger, the allowances are 50% of the above amounts. On departure, residents of Syrian nationality must pay an exit tax of LS 600 a person if traveling to Arab countries and LS 1,500 a person for other destinations. An airport stamp tax of LS 200 is added to this tax.
Quantitative limits	Yes.
Personal payments	
Prior approval	The allowance for medical treatment must be authorized by the Ministry of Health and for studies abroad by the Ministry of Higher Education.
Quantitative limits	The limit for family maintenance and alimony is LS 250 for each transfer and is effected upon presentation of proof of need.

Foreign workers' wages

    Prior approval   Yes.

    Quantitative limits   Up to 60% of the salaries received by foreign technicians and experts employed in the Syrian Arab Republic and 50% of the salaries of personnel of foreign diplomatic and international missions in the Syrian Arab Republic may be transferred. Foreign staff connected with foreign direct investments are allowed to transfer 100% of severance pay.

Credit card use abroad   Yes.

Other payments

    Prior approval   Yes.

Proceeds from Invisible Transactions and Current Transfers

Repatriation requirements   Yes.

Surrender requirements   Proceeds from a few transactions by the public sector relating to bilateral payment agreements must be sold at the old official rate of LS 11.20 per $1, and the remainder plus those from transactions by the private sector must be sold at the "rate of neighboring countries." All Syrian employees working abroad are subject to an annual tax of $50–$700, depending on their profession, and are allowed import tax exemptions on luxury items (valued between $500 and $7,000) if the equivalent funds are surrendered at the budget accounting rate. Syrian government employees who are on leave and working abroad are required to repatriate and convert a minimum of 25% of each year's earnings received in foreign exchange at the "rate of neighboring countries."

Restrictions on use of funds   Yes.

Capital Transactions

Controls on capital and money market instruments   All capital transfers to and from the Syrian Arab Republic take place at the "rate in neighboring countries." Exports of capital require the approval of the EO.

On capital market securities   There is no market in medium- and long-term government bonds in the Syrian Arab Republic. Bonds are issued on an as-needed basis to government-owned banks to supplement their capital base.

    Shares or other securities of a participating nature

      Purchase abroad by residents   Yes.

On money market instruments   The only instruments available in the Syrian Arab Republic are investment bonds issued by the Popular Credit Bank (PCB) as agent of the government. The bonds, which carry an interest rate of 9% a year, have 10-year maturity but have a short-term effective holding period as they are redeemable after three to six months. They may only be purchased by nonbank Syrian residents and by the PCB itself.

    Purchase abroad by residents   Yes.

On collective investment securities   These instruments do not exist in the Syrian Arab Republic.

    Purchase locally by nonresidents   n.r.

    Sale or issue locally by nonresidents   n.r.

    Purchase abroad by residents   Yes.

    Sale or issue abroad by residents   n.r.

Controls on derivatives and other instruments   n.a.

Controls on credit operations   There are controls on all credit operations.

Controls on direct investment

Outward direct investment

Yes.

Inward direct investment

The Syrian Arab Republic provides special facilities for the investment of funds of immigrants and of nationals of Arab states, including a seven-year tax exemption from all taxes in the tourism and agricultural industries. Projects with minimum fixed assets of LS 10 million approved by the government benefit from a number of exemptions from exchange and trade regulations, including exemption from customs duties of imports of required machinery, equipment, and vehicles. Mixed companies with at least 25% public participation are exempted from all taxes for seven years and private companies are exempted for five years; exemption periods may be extended by an additional two years if the company exports at least 50% of its output. Investors are permitted to hold foreign currency accounts to finance convertible currency requirements. These accounts comprise all capital and loans secured in foreign currency and 75% of foreign currency exports. All profits may be transferred freely. The Syrian Arab Republic has investment guarantee agreements with France, Germany, Switzerland, and the United States.

Controls on liquidation of direct investment

Investors are free to repatriate foreign exchange capital after five years from the date of investment. Capital may be repatriated after six months if the project suffers from events beyond the control of the investor.

Controls on real estate transactions

Purchase abroad by residents

Yes.

Purchase locally by nonresidents

Nonresidents and foreign nationals may acquire immovable property only after presenting evidence that they have converted into Syrian pounds the foreign exchange equivalent of the price of property at the authorized local bank.

Sale locally by nonresidents

Proceeds are required to be held in a blocked account and repatriated gradually.

Controls on personal capital movements

n.a.

Provisions specific to commercial banks and other credit institutions

Differential treatment of deposit accounts in foreign exchange

Reserve requirements

Foreign currency deposits are not subject to reserve requirements.

Interest rate controls

Yes.

Credit controls

Yes.

Provisions specific to institutional investors

n.a.

Other controls imposed by securities laws

n.a.

Changes During 1999

Exchange arrangement

January 1. The budget accounting rate was adjusted to LS 46.45/46.50 per $1 from LS 45.45/45.50 per $1.

December 31. The promotion exchange rate was eliminated.

Exports and export proceeds

January 7. The agricultural production tax on cotton, cotton seeds, cotton yarn, and textiles was abolished in certain cases.

May 8. The deadlines for repatriating and surrendering export receipts were raised to six months in the case of exports to Arab countries and to nine months in the case of other countries.

Changes During 2000

Exports and export proceeds

February 1. A number of agricultural products were exempted from the agricultural production tax.

TAJIKISTAN

(Position as of March 31, 2000)

Status Under IMF Articles of Agreement

Article XIV	Yes.

Exchange Arrangement

Currency	The currency of Tajikistan is the Tajik ruble.
Other legal tender	The use of other currencies is allowed.
Exchange rate structure	Unitary.

Classification

Managed floating with no preannounced path for the exchange rate	The official buying and selling rates of the National Bank of Tajikistan (NBT) are based on the rates resulting from multiple-bidding auctions held at the Tajik Interbank Foreign Currency Exchange (TICEX) in Dushanbe. In determining the amount to be auctioned, the NBT considers the availability of international reserves, but the main consideration is to maintain a stable exchange rate. The interbank and retail markets transact at freely determined rates, but these rates are generally based on, and close to, the TICEX rate.
Exchange tax	No.
Exchange subsidy	No.
Forward exchange market	No.

Arrangements for Payments and Receipts

Prescription of currency requirements	Residents of Tajikistan may make and receive payments and transfers in any convertible currency as well as in Tajik rubles. Residents and nonresidents may not use foreign exchange for domestic transactions, except for special cases as defined by the authorities. Commercial transactions with nonresidents must be conducted via correspondent accounts maintained either by authorized commercial banks or by the NBT.

Payment arrangements

Bilateral payment arrangements

Operative	Yes.
Inoperative	There are inoperative agreements with the CIS countries, and negotiations for settlement of balances have been concluded.
Barter agreements and open accounts	Barter trade is allowed only for aluminum and electricity.
Administration of control	The NBT (1) acts as nonexclusive agent for the Republic of Tajikistan in the administration of foreign exchange controls; (2) issues licenses to commercial banks to conduct banking operations and foreign currency operations; (3) is exclusively responsible for the supervision and regulation of financial institutions; (4) manages official foreign exchange reserves; and (5) formulates basic foreign exchange policy. The MOF registers foreign investors for inward direct investment.
International security restrictions	No.

Payment arrears

Official	External arrears to the Kyrgyz Republic and Kazakhstan falling due in the first quarter of 1999 were settled on June 29, 1999. On September 30, 1999, arrears falling due for the second quarter were paid to the Kyrgyz Republic. External arrears to the United States falling due in November were settled on January 21, 2000.

Private	Yes.
Controls on trade in gold (coins and/or bullion)	Trade in gold is regulated by the Committee on Precious Metals and Semiprecious Stones.
Controls on external trade	Joint ventures that extract gold are subject to controls.
Controls on exports and imports of banknotes	
On exports	
Domestic currency	Exports of domestic currency are allowed freely without customs regulations.
Foreign currency	Effective March 30, 2000, foreign exchange may be exported freely up to $2,000. For any amount above this limit, documents proving the legality of the exports must be submitted.
On imports	
Foreign currency	Imports are permitted, provided customs rules are observed.

Resident Accounts

Foreign exchange accounts permitted	All restrictions on foreign exchange cash withdrawals were eliminated on June 4, 1999.
Held domestically	Yes.
Held abroad	These accounts are permitted under the Law on Foreign Currency Control. However, the opening of these accounts requires authorization from the NBT.
Accounts in domestic currency convertible into foreign currency	Yes.

Nonresident Accounts

Foreign exchange accounts permitted	Yes.
Domestic currency accounts	Yes.
Convertible into foreign currency	Yes.
Blocked accounts	No.

Imports and Import Payments

Foreign exchange budget	No.
Financing requirements for imports	No.
Documentation requirements for release of foreign exchange for imports	On June 29, 1999, import documentation requirements in connection with cash withdrawals from commercial banks were eliminated.
Letters of credit	Yes.
Import licenses and other nontariff measures	Effective July 1, 1999, import licensing was introduced on tobacco and tobacco products.
Negative list	The importation of firearms, narcotics, poisons, chemical weapons, and nuclear materials is prohibited.
Licenses with quotas	Effective March 1, 1999, licenses with quotas were introduced on imports of ethyl alcohol and alcohol products.
Import taxes and/or tariffs	As Tajikistan is a member of a customs union, customs duties are the same as in the other member countries of the union. Alumina is exempt from duty. Customs duties are collected on alcohol and cigarette imports in fixed amounts, depending on the quantity of goods imported (liters and units).

State import monopoly	No.

Exports and Export Proceeds

Repatriation requirements	Yes.
Surrender requirements	Foreign exchange proceeds may be either held by exporters in foreign currency accounts with domestic banks or sold in the interbank market.
Financing requirements	Yes.
Documentation requirements	For exports of cotton, a 100% advance payment is required.
Letters of credit	Yes.
Guarantees	Yes.
Export licenses	Effective July 1, 1999, licenses are required for the preparation, processing, and export of tobacco and tobacco products.
With quotas	On March 1, 1999, licenses with quotas were introduced on exports and purchases of ethyl alcohol and alcohol products.
Export taxes	No.

Payments for Invisible Transactions and Current Transfers

Controls on these transfers	
Foreign workers' wages	
Quantitative limits	Yes.

Proceeds from Invisible Transactions and Current Transfers

Repatriation requirements	Yes.
Restrictions on use of funds	No.

Capital Transactions

Controls on capital and money market instruments	
On capital market securities	
Shares or other securities of a participating nature	
Purchase locally by nonresidents	MOF and NBT approval is required for the purchase of 10% of shares, and the purchase of shares among shareholders is restricted.
Sale or issue locally by nonresidents	Yes.
Purchase abroad by residents	NBT approval is required.
Sale or issue abroad by residents	Only juridical persons may issue these instruments; registration with the MOF and approval of the NBT are required.
Bonds or other debt securities	Registration with the MOF is required.
Purchase locally by nonresidents	Yes.
Sale or issue locally by nonresidents	Yes.

Sale or issue abroad by residents	Yes.
On money market instruments	
Purchase locally by nonresidents	Yes.
Sale or issue locally by nonresidents	Sales by nonresidents are permitted.
Purchase abroad by residents	NBT approval is required.
Sale or issue abroad by residents	NBT approval is required.
On collective investment securities	
Purchase locally by nonresidents	Yes.
Sale or issue locally by nonresidents	Yes.
Purchase abroad by residents	NBT approval is required.
Sale or issue abroad by residents	If the security is issued in foreign currency, NBT approval is required.
Controls on derivatives and other instruments	
Purchase abroad by residents	NBT approval is required.
Sale or issue abroad by residents	NBT approval is required.
Controls on credit operations	
Commercial credits	
By residents to nonresidents	There are no controls for loans of up to a 120-day maturity.
To residents from nonresidents	There are no controls for loans of up to a 180-day maturity.
Financial credits	There are no controls for loans of up to a 180-day maturity. For maturities over 180 days, NBT approval is required.
By residents to nonresidents	Yes.
To residents from nonresidents	Yes.
Guarantees, sureties, and financial backup facilities	
By residents to nonresidents	There are no controls for such facilities of up to a 180-day maturity. For those with maturities over 180 days, NBT approval is required.
To residents from nonresidents	Yes.
Controls on direct investment	
Outward direct investment	NBT approval is required.
Controls on liquidation of direct investment	No.
Controls on real estate transactions	
Purchase abroad by residents	NBT approval is required.
Controls on personal capital movements	No.
Provisions specific to commercial banks and other credit institutions	
Borrowing abroad	Only authorized foreign exchange banks may borrow from abroad.
Maintenance of accounts abroad	n.r.
Lending to nonresidents (financial or commercial credits)	Yes.

Lending locally in foreign exchange	Yes.
Purchase of locally issued securities denominated in foreign exchange	There are no such securities in Tajikistan.
Investment regulations	The limit is 20% of capital.
Abroad by banks	Yes.
In banks by nonresidents	Yes.
Open foreign exchange position limits	The aggregate open long and short positions are limited to 30% and 10% of the bank's capital, respectively.
On resident assets and liabilities	Yes.
On nonresident assets and liabilities	Yes.
Provisions specific to institutional investors	No.
Other controls imposed by securities laws	No.

Changes During 1999

Arrangements for payments and receipts	*June 29.* External arrears to the Kyrgyz Republic and Kazakhstan were settled.
	September 30. External arrears falling due in the second quarter were paid to the Kyrgyz Republic.
Resident accounts	*June 4.* All restrictions on foreign exchange cash withdrawals were eliminated.
Imports and import payments	*March 1.* Licenses with quotas were introduced on imports of ethyl alcohol and alcohol products.
	June 29. Import documentation requirements in connection with cash withdrawals from commercial banks were eliminated.
	July 1. Import licensing was introduced on tobacco and tobacco products.
Exports and export proceeds	*March 1.* Licenses with quotas were introduced on exports and purchases of ethyl alcohol and alcohol products.
	July 1. Licenses were required for the preparation, processing, and export of tobacco and tobacco products.

Changes During 2000

Arrangements for payments and receipts	*January 21.* External arrears falling due in November 1999 were paid to the United States.
	March 30. Exports of foreign exchange up to a limit of $2,000 were allowed freely.

TANZANIA

(Position as of December 31, 1999)

Status Under IMF Articles of Agreement

Article VIII	Date of acceptance: July 15, 1996.

Exchange Arrangement

Currency	The currency of Tanzania is the Tanzania shilling.
Exchange rate structure	Unitary.
Classification	
Independently floating	The external value of the Tanzania shilling is determined in the interbank market. The Bank of Tanzania (BOT) intervenes in the interbank market only to smooth movements that are caused by transitory factors.
Exchange tax	No.
Exchange subsidy	No.
Forward exchange market	Authorized dealers may enter into forward contracts for purchases and sales of foreign currencies with their customers in export and import transactions.
Official cover of forward operations	The BOT does not offer forward cover against exchange rate risk.

Arrangements for Payments and Receipts

Prescription of currency requirements	No.
Payment arrangements	
Bilateral payment arrangements	
Inoperative	There is an agreement with Mozambique.
Regional arrangements	Tanzania participates in the COMESA, the SADC, and the EAC.
Clearing agreements	There are agreements with Kenya and Uganda.
Administration of control	The MOF has delegated authority to the customs and the BOT to administer and manage exchange transactions both on the mainland and in Zanzibar. The BOT delegates authority to make payments abroad to all licensed banks.
International security restrictions	n.a.
Payment arrears	Yes.
Controls on trade in gold (coins and/or bullion)	Only authorized persons may buy, borrow, sell, lend, and hold or otherwise deal in gold coins and gold bullion outside Tanzania.
Controls on external trade	Yes.
Controls on exports and imports of banknotes	
On exports	
Domestic currency	Payment in domestic currency to a nonresident requires BOT approval. However, following a currency convertibility agreement reached with Uganda and Kenya, residents may carry and cross any of the three borders with any amount of currency from the three countries.
Foreign currency	Yes.

Resident Accounts

Foreign exchange accounts permitted	There are no limitations as to the amounts.
Held domestically	Yes.
Held abroad	Holding of foreign accounts is allowed for money acquired outside Tanzania; otherwise, operations of offshore foreign currency accounts by individual residents are still subject to restrictions. However, in the case of resident banks and financial institutions, there are no restrictions on the operation of accounts with overseas financial institutions (foreign correspondent banks). Any authorized dealer bank may operate foreign currency accounts abroad in its name on behalf of its customers. Accounts of residents have to be reported to the BOT.
Accounts in domestic currency convertible into foreign currency	These accounts are exceptionally reserved for UN-related organizations.

Nonresident Accounts

Foreign exchange accounts permitted	Yes.
Domestic currency accounts	Nonresident accounts are maintained by foreign nationals temporarily residing in Tanzania; such accounts are to be closed upon leaving the country.
Convertible into foreign currency	No.
Blocked accounts	An authorized bank's approval is required when making any payment or placing any sum to the credit of nonresidents. The bank may direct the sum payable or to be paid or credited to a non–interest bearing blocked account.

Imports and Import Payments

Foreign exchange budget	No.
Financing requirements for imports	
Advance payment requirements	Authorized dealers are permitted to handle cases of advance payments.
Documentation requirements for release of foreign exchange for imports	The release of foreign exchange in excess of $5,000 requires invoices, shipping documents, a single bill of entry form, and a clean report of findings.
Domiciliation requirements	Yes.
Preshipment inspection	A clean report of findings is necessary for import payments subject to preshipment inspection. Imports of goods exceeding $5,000 require a preshipment inspection document.
Letters of credit	Yes.
Import licenses and other nontariff measures	
Negative list	Certain imports to the mainland from any source may be prohibited for reasons of health or security.
Import taxes and/or tariffs	Customs tariffs are levied on the c.i.f. value of imports. Effective July 1, 1999, the four rates are 5%, 10%, 20%, and 25% (previously 30%). Low tariffs are also charged on imports of machinery. Specific duties are levied on alcoholic beverages, tobacco, and petroleum products. Statutory exemptions are granted to the diplomatic corps, as well as to religious, educational, and welfare institutions. Zero rates are applicable to strategic and lead investment sectors.
State import monopoly	No.

Exports and Export Proceeds

Repatriation requirements	Requirements are still in place in the repatriation of export proceeds in foreign currency by exporters and reporting by banking institutions to the BOT of delinquent exporters beyond time allowed.
Financing requirements	n.a.
Documentation requirements	
Letters of credit	Yes.
Domiciliation	Yes.
Export licenses	Licenses from the respective ministries are required for the exportation from the mainland for a few items for health, sanitary, or national heritage reasons.
Without quotas	Yes.
Export taxes	n.a.

Payments for Invisible Transactions and Current Transfers

Controls on these transfers	Presentation of relevant documentary evidence at the time of buying the foreign exchange is required. The BOT examines these documents.
Trade-related payments	The release of foreign exchange for import payments requires invoices, shipping documents, a clean report of findings from an authorized inspection firm, and a single bill of entry form.
Quantitative limits	For trade-related payments exceeding $5,000, proper documentation, such as invoices, shipping documents, and a clean report of findings, is required.
Investment-related payments	The transfer of income from investments by nonresidents is not restricted, provided all tax obligations have been met. Remittances of portfolio and dividends require audited reports and authenticated documents confirming payment of all taxes.
Payments for travel	
Quantitative limits	For travel allowances exceeding $10,000, the traveler has to produce documents certifying that the trip will last more than 40 days.
Personal payments	Proper documentation from the relevant educational or medical institution is required.
Indicative limits/bona fide test	There are bona fide tests for payment of medical costs.
Foreign workers' wages	Foreign workers are obliged to document the transfer with contracts and permits and state the reason of remittance.
Indicative limits/bona fide test	Yes.
Other payments	Applicants for payment of fees related to consultancy, management, and royalty agreements need to furnish contractual documents duly executed by parties thereto, relevant invoice/fees notes, and tax clearances from the Tanzania Revenue Authority certifying that tax obligations have been settled.
Indicative limits/bona fide test	Yes.

Proceeds from Invisible Transactions and Current Transfers

Repatriation requirements	No.
Restrictions on use of funds	No.

Capital Transactions

Controls on capital and money market instruments	Capital transfers to all countries are subject to approval by commercial banks. All transfers of foreign currency funds from residents to nonresidents or to foreign-controlled resident bodies require specific approval from the BOT. Residents may acquire from abroad and sell or issue abroad any security or coupon on which capital, dividends, or interest are payable in foreign currency, provided that the security has been funded exclusively by externally acquired funds. The acquisition must be notified to the BOT for statistical purposes.

On capital market securities

Shares or other securities of a participating nature

Purchase locally by nonresidents	Yes.
Sale or issue locally by nonresidents	Participation of nonresidents in the domestic money and capital markets is restricted.
Purchase abroad by residents	Shares issued abroad may be freely held and transferred by residents provided that such securities were acquired with externally generated funds. These purchases have to be reported to the BOT.
Sale or issue abroad by residents	Yes.

Bonds or other debt securities

Purchase locally by nonresidents	The purchase and redemption must be done in local currency.
Sale or issue locally by nonresidents	Yes.
Purchase abroad by residents	Yes.

On money market instruments

Purchase locally by nonresidents	Yes.
Sale or issue locally by nonresidents	Yes.
Purchase abroad by residents	Yes.
Sale or issue abroad by residents	Yes.

On collective investment securities

Purchase locally by nonresidents	Yes.
Sale or issue locally by nonresidents	Yes.
Purchase abroad by residents	Yes.
Sale or issue abroad by residents	Yes.

Controls on derivatives and other instruments	There are controls on all transactions in derivatives and other instruments.
Controls on credit operations	No BOT approval is required with respect to applications for foreign loans, overdrafts, structured external financing facilities, and deferred payment arrangements exceeding 365 days.

Commercial credits

By residents to nonresidents	Yes.
To residents from nonresidents	BOT approval is required with respect to the receipt of foreign currency by residents and/or receipt of payment in the currency of Tanzania from nonresidents. Any person resident in Tanzania who has a right to receive foreign currency from a nonresident has to comply with directives given by the BOT to ensure the receipt of such foreign currency or such payment.

Financial credits

By residents to nonresidents	Yes.

To residents from nonresidents	Yes.
Guarantees, sureties, and financial backup facilities	There are no restrictions on assurances obtained outside Tanzania, except that the transfer should be externally funded.
By residents to nonresidents	There are restrictions in place for the provision of sureties, guarantees, or financial back-up facilities to nonresident entities, or transfer of funds to service these facilities.

Controls on direct investment

Outward direct investment	Investments require BOT approval, except that banks are permitted to authorize access to foreign currency facilities to residents with respect to outward capital account payments under direct investment as repatriation of capital and income to foreign shareholders.
Inward direct investment	All foreign direct investment must be approved by the Investment Promotion Center; some areas are reserved for investment by the public sector, and certain other areas are reserved exclusively for Tanzania citizens.

Controls on liquidation of direct investment	Repatriation of capital and associated income is done through commercial banks upon presentation of audited accounts indicating declared dividends, profits, or capital to be repatriated, plus authenticated documents from the Tanzania Revenue Authority confirming payment of all relevant taxes.

Controls on real estate transactions	Any person who owns immovable property in Tanzania may assign or transfer such property to beneficiaries abroad provided that the property was acquired through external resources subject to any laws in force in Tanzania.
Purchase abroad by residents	Purchases require BOT approval.
Purchase locally by nonresidents	Yes.
Sale locally by nonresidents	Yes.

Controls on personal capital movements

Loans

By residents to nonresidents	Debt servicing–related remittances by residents require the submission of the relevant contract as approved by a commercial bank together with creditors' demand notes to that effect. Commercial banks have to furnish the BOT with monthly reports on loans serviced.
To residents from nonresidents	BOT approval is required for maturities longer than one year.

Gifts, endowments, inheritances, and legacies

By residents to nonresidents	Yes.
Settlement of debts abroad by immigrants	Yes.

Transfer of assets

Transfer abroad by emigrants	Yes.
Transfer into the country by immigrants	Yes.
Transfer of gambling and prize earnings	Yes.

Provisions specific to commercial banks and other credit institutions

Borrowing abroad	Borrowing is subject to external debt management regulations. Otherwise, banks and financial institutions are allowed to operate credit lines with correspondents.
Lending to nonresidents (financial or commercial credits)	Yes.

Differential treatment of deposit
accounts in foreign exchange

   Reserve requirements   The BOT requires that all statutory reserves be held in local currency and allows banks'
averaging of daily positions and the counting of half their vault cash toward meeting the
requirement.

Open foreign exchange position limits   The limit is 20% of core capital.

Provisions specific to institutional   No.
investors

Other controls imposed by securities   n.a.
laws

Changes During 1999

Imports and import payments   *July 1.* The customs tariff bands were reduced.

THAILAND

(Position as of December 31, 1999)

Status Under IMF Articles of Agreement

Article VIII   Date of acceptance: May 4, 1990.

Exchange Arrangement

Currency   The currency of Thailand is the Thai baht.

Exchange rate structure   Unitary.

Classification

Independently floating   The exchange rate of the baht is determined on the basis of supply and demand in the foreign exchange market. The baht-dollar reference exchange rate is announced daily based on
the average exchange rate of the previous day. The authorities have indicated that exchange
market intervention is limited to smoothing operations.

Exchange tax   No.

Exchange subsidy   No.

Forward exchange market   Financial institutions may engage in spot foreign exchange market transactions with
nonresidents in local currency. Forward transactions need not be related to the underlying
trade and financial transactions. In the case of no underlying trade and investment activities
in Thailand, Thai baht credit facilities, including swap and forward exchange contracts
obtained by a nonresident from all domestic financial institutions combined, are subject to
a maximum outstanding limit of B 50 million. The nonresident's head office, branches,
representative offices, and affiliated companies are counted as one entity.

Arrangements for Payments and Receipts

**Prescription of currency
requirements**   No.

Payment arrangements

Regional arrangements   Thailand is a member of the ASEAN.

Administration of control   The Bank of Thailand (BOT) administers exchange controls on behalf of the MOF, but it
delegates responsibility to authorized banks for approving most transactions. Import and
export licenses are issued by the Ministry of Commerce (MOC).

International security restrictions

In accordance with UN sanctions   Yes.

Payment arrears   No.

**Controls on trade in gold (coins
and/or bullion)**

Controls on domestic ownership and/or
trade   Residents may hold and negotiate domestically gold jewelry, gold coins, and unworked
gold. Purchases or sales of gold on commodity futures exchanges are prohibited.

Controls on external trade   Exporters and importers of gold ornaments exceeding B 500,000 in value must complete
foreign exchange transaction forms at customs when submitting import or export entry
forms. Until August 9, 1999, imports and exports of gold, other than gold jewelry, were
subject to licensing, and exports of gold bullion were prohibited. Effective August 10,
1999, these controls were lifted.

Controls on exports and imports of banknotes

On exports

Domestic currency　　Travelers may take out domestic currency up to B 50,000; those traveling to Vietnam and the countries bordering Thailand are allowed to take out a maximum of B 500,000.

Resident Accounts

Foreign exchange accounts permitted　　Yes.

Held domestically　　Approval is not required if funds originate from abroad and, upon depositing, the depositors must submit the documents showing their obligations to pay in foreign currency to persons residing abroad, resident authorized banks, the Export-Import Bank of Thailand, or the Industrial Finance Corporation of Thailand within three months of the date of deposit, and they may deposit amounts not exceeding their obligations. The total outstanding balances in all accounts should not exceed $5 million for a juridical person and $500,000 for a natural person.

Held abroad　　Approval is required if deposits are made with funds of domestic origin.

Accounts in domestic currency convertible into foreign currency　　No.

Nonresident Accounts

Foreign exchange accounts permitted　　Approval is not required if funds originate from abroad.

Domestic currency accounts　　Yes.

Convertible into foreign currency　　Approval is not required if funds originate from abroad, if they are transferred from other nonresidents' baht accounts, or if baht proceeds are borrowed from authorized banks.

Blocked accounts　　No.

Imports and Import Payments

Foreign exchange budget　　No.

Financing requirements for imports　　No.

Documentation requirements for release of foreign exchange for imports　　Importers are required to complete foreign exchange transaction forms for transactions whose value exceeds B 500,000 when submitting import entry forms to customs, except for certain goods, such as military equipment imported by the Ministry of Defense, donated goods, and samples.

Import licenses and other nontariff measures　　Most commodities may be freely imported, but import licenses are required for certain goods. Milk producers are required to purchase locally produced milk in some quantity when they import skimmed milk into Thailand.

Negative list　　Imports of some goods are prohibited for security or social reasons.

Import taxes and/or tariffs　　Ad valorem and/or specific duties are imposed on imports. In addition, special duties are levied on certain commodities. As of October 3, 1999, surcharges on imports that competed with the output of promoted domestic firms were eliminated.

State import monopoly　　No.

Exports and Export Proceeds

Repatriation requirements　　Export proceeds exceeding B 500,000 must be repatriated immediately after payment is received and within 120 days from the date of export.

Surrender requirements	Foreign exchange proceeds must be surrendered to authorized banks within seven days of receipt. Foreign exchange earners are allowed to deposit their foreign exchange in their foreign currency accounts only if they have obligations to pay out such amounts to nonresidents abroad within three months of the deposit date.
Financing requirements	No.
Documentation requirements	Exporters are required to complete a foreign exchange transaction form for transactions exceeding B 500,000 when submitting the export entry form at customs.
Export licenses	Exports of rice, canned tuna, sugar, certain types of coal and charcoal, and textile products are subject to licensing and quantitative restrictions and, in a few cases, to prior approval, irrespective of destination. All other products may be exported freely.
Without quotas	Yes.
With quotas	Yes.
Export taxes	Exports of wood, wood articles, and hides are subject to higher ad valorem or specific duties.

Payments for Invisible Transactions and Current Transfers

Controls on these transfers	Foreign exchange transaction forms must be completed for transactions of more than $5,000.

Proceeds from Invisible Transactions and Current Transfers

Repatriation requirements	Yes.
Surrender requirements	Proceeds must be surrendered to authorized banks or retained in foreign currency accounts with authorized banks in Thailand within seven days of receipt. Travelers passing through Thailand, foreign embassies, and international organizations are exempted from this requirement.
Restrictions on use of funds	No.

Capital Transactions

Controls on capital and money market instruments	The sale or issue of securities is under the jurisdiction of the Securities Exchange Commission (SEC). Under the securities law, different rules and regulations apply to capital market securities (those with a maturity of more than one year) and short-term money market securities (those debt securities with a maturity of not more than one year). The regulations imposed on capital market securities are generally stricter than those imposed on short-term money market securities. Companies wishing to issue securities to the public need approval from the BOT and the SEC.
On capital market securities	
Shares or other securities of a participating nature	
Purchase locally by nonresidents	Foreign equity participation is limited to 25% of the total amount of shares sold in locally incorporated banks, finance companies, credit finance companies, and asset management companies. The combined shareholdings of an individual and related family members must not exceed 5% of a bank's total amount of shares sold and 10% of that of finance companies and credit foncier companies. Foreign equity participation is limited to 49% for other Thai corporations. Foreign investors are allowed to hold more than 49% of the total shares sold in local financial institutions for up to 10 years, after which the amount of shares will be grandfathered, and the nonresidents will not be allowed to purchase new shares until the ratio of shares held by them is brought down to 49%.

Purchase abroad by residents	Purchases require approval of the BOT.
Sale or issue abroad by residents	Approval is required according to the same rules as in the case of domestic issuance.

Bonds or other debt securities

Sale or issue locally by nonresidents	These transactions require approval of the MOF, BOT, and SEC.
Purchase abroad by residents	Purchases require approval of the BOT.
Sale or issue abroad by residents	The potential issuer must submit an application for approval to the SEC, and permission will be granted if the issuer can prove that the security will be pooled exclusively on primary or secondary markets abroad.

On money market instruments

Sale or issue locally by nonresidents	Yes.
Purchase abroad by residents	These transactions require approval of the BOT.
Sale or issue abroad by residents	These transactions are not allowed. However, finance companies are allowed to issue negotiable certificates of deposit (NCDs) and bills of exchange in foreign currency with more than a one-year maturity for sale to the public abroad or for sale to institutions that are authorized to operate in foreign exchange. The transfer of proceeds associated with these issues or the transfer of funds required to service these instruments may be made freely.

On collective investment securities

Purchase locally by nonresidents	There are no controls on the purchase of securities offered by local fund management companies.
Sale or issue locally by nonresidents	Yes.
Purchase abroad by residents	These transactions require approval of the BOT.
Sale or issue abroad by residents	The launching of funds requires approval from the SEC, both locally and abroad, and only local fund management companies are allowed to issue this instrument. In addition, funds managed by local firms will be deemed to have Thai nationality regardless of the nationality of the majority of the unit holders. The transfer of proceeds and the transfer of funds required to service these instruments may be made freely.

Controls on derivatives and other instruments	
Purchase locally by nonresidents	In the case that there are no underlying trade and investment activities in Thailand, Thai baht credit facilities, including swap and forward exchange contracts obtained by a nonresident from all domestic financial institutions combined, are subject to a maximum outstanding limit of B 50 million. The nonresident's head office, branches, representative offices, and affiliated companies are counted as one entity.
Sale or issue locally by nonresidents	The issuance of warrants or equity-related instruments and bonds by nonresidents in the local market is subject to approval by the SEC. The approval criteria are based on the soundness of the underlying stock. There is no discriminatory practice against nonresidents for participating in the financial market.
Purchase abroad by residents	The purchase of derivative instruments by residents and the transfer of funds require approval by the BOT.
Sale or issue abroad by residents	The sale of derivative instruments by residents and the transfer of funds require BOT approval.
Controls on credit operations	In the case that there are no underlying trade and investment activities in Thailand, Thai baht credit facilities, including swap and forward exchange contracts obtained by a nonresident from all domestic financial institutions combined, are subject to a maximum outstanding limit of B 50 million. The nonresident's head office, branches, representative offices, and affiliated companies are counted as one entity.
Commercial credits	Credits may be contracted in the form of deferred payments, bilateral netting, or open accounts. Most payments are settled within 120 days of the exportation of goods.

Financial credits

  By residents to nonresidents

Only authorized banks are allowed to grant financial credits subject to the rule of net foreign exchange position. Residents may only grant loans to their affiliated companies if they own at least 25% of total shares in the company and up to $10 million a year without approval from the BOT.

  To residents from nonresidents

There is no control on these credits. Repayment of financial credits to nonresidents may be made freely as long as residents have an obligation to pay nonresidents in foreign currency.

Controls on direct investment

Outward direct investment

Investments exceeding $10 million a year require approval from the BOT.

Inward direct investment

Foreign capital may be brought into the country without restriction, but proceeds must be surrendered to authorized banks or deposited in foreign currency accounts with authorized banks in Thailand within seven days of receipt.

Controls on liquidation of direct investment

All proceeds may be repatriated without restriction upon submission of supporting evidence.

Controls on real estate transactions

Purchase abroad by residents

Approval of the BOT is required.

Purchase locally by nonresidents

The purchase of property is not allowed with funds that originate from abroad. The foreign ownership limit for condominiums is 40% of the total value. Ownership of property by foreign entities with majority shareholding in Thai financial institutions is, at present, governed by the Commercial Banking Act or the Act on the Undertaking of Finance Business, Securities Business, and Credit Foncier Business.

Sale locally by nonresidents

Yes.

Controls on personal capital movements

Loans

  By residents to nonresidents

Approval of the BOT is required.

Gifts, endowments, inheritances, and legacies

  By residents to nonresidents

Thai residents are allowed to send up to $100,000 to their relatives abroad, who hold permanent resident permits, without approval from the BOT.

Transfer of assets

  Transfer abroad by emigrants

Thai emigrants are allowed to transfer abroad up to $1 million a year without approval from the BOT.

Transfer of gambling and prize earnings

Gambling is illegal in Thailand.

Provisions specific to commercial banks and other credit institutions

In the case that there are no underlying trade and investment activities in Thailand, Thai baht credit facilities, including swap and forward exchange contracts obtained by a nonresident from all domestic financial institutions combined, are subject to a maximum outstanding limit of B 50 million. The nonresident's head office, branches, representative offices, and affiliated companies are counted as one entity.

Lending to nonresidents (financial or commercial credits)

Government financial institutions, except the Export-Import Bank of Thailand, are not allowed to practice foreign lending activities. Authorized banks in Thailand may lend to nonresidents in foreign currency without restriction.

Lending locally in foreign exchange

Commercial lending to particular industries denominated in foreign currencies may be partially (50%) included as foreign assets in order to recognize the potential risk that banks may not be fully repaid as exchange rate risk is heightened.

Differential treatment of deposit accounts held by nonresidents

  Liquid asset requirements

Commercial banks are required to maintain at least 6% of their nonresident foreign exchange deposits in the form of (1) nonremunerated balance at the BOT (at least 2%);

(2) vault cash (at most 2.5%); and (3) eligible securities (the rest). Finance companies and finance and securities companies are not allowed to accept foreign exchange deposits.

Investment regulations

Abroad by banks

Commercial banks are allowed to buy or hold shares in a limited company (including public companies) in an amount not exceeding 10% of the total shares sold and 20% of their capital fund. Banks may seek approval to hold shares above the 10% limit in the following cases: (1) companies set up for supporting functions; (2) companies that operate as financial arms, such as leasing companies and factoring companies; (3) companies set up to manage foreclosed properties; and (4) companies set up to manage projects that are beneficial to the economy, especially infrastructure projects.

In banks by nonresidents

Foreign investors may invest in Thai commercial banks up to 25% of the total amount of shares sold. Foreign investors may be allowed, on a case-by-case basis, to hold up to 100% of shares sold in commercial banks, finance companies, and credit foncier companies for a period of 10 years, which will be grandfathered. However, after the 10-year period, they will not be allowed to purchase additional shares unless their holding is less than 49% of the total amount of shares sold.

Open foreign exchange position limits

The rule on net foreign exchange exposure limits allows commercial banks to maintain positions in terms of their first-tier capital of no more than 15% oversold or overbought.

On resident assets and liabilities

Yes.

On nonresident assets and liabilities

Yes.

Provisions specific to institutional investors

Limits (max.) on securities issued by nonresidents and on portfolio invested abroad

Approval of the BOT is required.

Limits (max.) on portfolio invested abroad

Mutual funds and provident funds have to invest their total portfolio in the domestic market. The criteria for insurance companies to invest abroad are as follows: (1) the fund may be invested in equity and debenture issued by juridical persons incorporated under the ASEAN Agreement or the United Nation's Economic and Social Commission for Asia and the Pacific Agreement to specifically operate reinsurance business; and (2) the funds may be invested in equity issued by nonresident juridical persons other than specified in (1) with approval from the authorities, and by using the surplus funds. Total investments under (1) and (2) must not exceed 5% of total assets.

Limits (min.) on portfolio invested locally

Portfolio investment of life and nonlife insurance companies is governed by the acts and notifications of the MOC. The criteria are as follows: (1) total investment in debenture and equity should not exceed 30% of the company's assets; (2) investment in unit trust should not exceed 20% of total assets; (3) rediscount of state enterprise bonds should not exceed 20% of total assets; and (4) investment in securities abroad must not exceed 5% of total assets and should have approval from the appropriate authority. The criteria for investment of provident fund are as follows: (1) investment of at least 60% in government bonds, state enterprise bonds, deposits at commercial banks, and debt instruments issued by commercial banks; and (2) investment of not more than 40% in promissory notes of finance companies, stocks, and other debt instruments. In addition, the ceiling on investment in stocks is 25% of the portfolio, and that on any single stock is 5% of the portfolio.

Other controls imposed by securities laws

Under the Securities Act, there are no controls for nonresidents to have equity participation in Thai security companies. However, a 50% limit on a nonresident's equity participation in any company is imposed. Foreign security companies are permitted access to the Thai securities market in the form of representative offices whose roles are limited to providing research material for their parent companies. In addition, they are allowed to enter into joint partnership with Thai security companies and to provide professional consultancy services.

Changes During 1999

Arrangements for payments and receipts

August 10. The prohibition on exporting and importing gold was eliminated.

Imports and import payments

October 3. Surcharges on imports that compete with the output of promoted domestic firms were eliminated.

TOGO

(Position as of January 31, 2000)

Status Under IMF Articles of Agreement

Article VIII
Date of acceptance: June 1, 1996.

Exchange Arrangement

Currency
The currency of Togo is the CFA franc.

Exchange rate structure
Unitary.

Classification

Exchange arrangement with no separate legal tender
The CFA franc is pegged to the euro, the intervention currency, at the fixed rate of CFAF 100 per €0.8385, which is the official buying and selling rate. Exchange rates for other currencies are derived from the rate for the currency concerned in the Paris foreign exchange market and the fixed rate between the euro and the CFA franc.

Exchange tax
There is a bank commission of 0.25% on transfers to all countries outside the WAEMU, which must be surrendered to the Treasury.

Exchange subsidy
No.

Forward exchange market
Effective February 1, 1999, residents were authorized to contract forward exchange cover to settle payments related to imports and exports of goods and services.

Arrangements for Payments and Receipts

Prescription of currency requirements
Because Togo is linked to the French Treasury through an Operations Account, settlements with France, Monaco, and other Operations Account countries (WAEMU and CAEMC members and the Comoros) are made in French francs or the currency of any other Operations Account country. Settlements with countries outside the Operations Account area are free.

Payment arrangements

Regional arrangements
An Operations Account is maintained with the French Treasury that links Operations Account countries. All purchases or sales of foreign currencies or euros against CFA francs are ultimately settled through a debit or credit to the Operations Account.

Clearing agreements
There is a clearing arrangement within the framework of the WAMA between the WAEMU states and Cape Verde, The Gambia, Ghana, Guinea, Liberia, Mauritania, Nigeria, and Sierra Leone.

Administration of control
Exchange control is administered jointly by the MOF and the BCEAO. Since February 1, 1999, most of the authority to supervise foreign exchange transactions has been delegated to authorized banks, which are required to report these operations to the MOF. The only operations that continue to require prior authorization of the MOF or the BCEAO involve residents' investments abroad, domestic accounts in foreign exchange, and residents' accounts abroad. Effective February 1, 1999, the amount of transfers authorized without supporting documentation was raised to CFAF 300,000 from CFAF 100,000.

The advertising or offering for sale of foreign or domestic securities in Togo requires the authorization of the RCPSFM.

International security restrictions
No.

Payment arrears

Official
Yes.

Controls on trade in gold (coins and/or bullion)

Controls on external trade

Imports and exports of gold from or to any other country require prior authorization from the MOF.

Controls on exports and imports of banknotes

On exports

Domestic currency

The export of CFA franc banknotes by travelers is not prohibited. However, the BCEAO repurchase of exported banknotes remains suspended. Furthermore, transfers of BCEAO banknotes between the authorized intermediaries and their correspondents located outside the WAEMU are strictly prohibited.

Foreign currency

The reexportation of foreign banknotes by nonresidents is allowed up to the equivalent of CFAF 500,000; the reexportation of foreign banknotes above these ceilings requires documentation demonstrating either the importation of the foreign banknotes or their purchase against other means of payment registered in the name of the traveler or through the use of nonresident deposits in local banks. Residents traveling outside the WAEMU area are allowed to take out banknotes up to the equivalent of CFAF 2 million a person. Larger amounts may be exported in the form of traveler's checks, bank drafts, or other means of payment.

On imports

Domestic currency

There are no restrictions on the importation by resident and nonresident travelers of banknotes and coins issued by the BCEAO; however, the amounts must be declared at customs.

Foreign currency

Residents and nonresidents may bring in any amount of foreign banknotes and coins (except gold coins) of countries outside the Operations Account area. Nonresidents bringing in foreign banknotes and foreign currency traveler's checks exceeding the equivalent of CFAF 1 million are required to declare all the means of payment they are carrying when entering or exiting Togo.

Resident Accounts

Foreign exchange accounts permitted

Effective February 1, 1999, residents are allowed to open foreign exchange accounts with local banks or with banks abroad after obtaining authorization from the MOF, subsequent to the approval of the BCEAO.

Held domestically

Prior approval is required to open these accounts.

Held abroad

The opening of accounts abroad by residents is subject to prior MOF authorization, subsequent to the approval of the BCEAO.

Accounts in domestic currency convertible into foreign currency

No.

Nonresident Accounts

Foreign exchange accounts permitted

Effective February 1, 1999, authorization is issued by the BCEAO.

Domestic currency accounts

Because the BCEAO has suspended the repurchase of banknotes circulating outside the WAEMU area, nonresident accounts may not be credited or debited with BCEAO banknotes. However, transfers of funds between nonresident accounts are not restricted.

Convertible into foreign currency

Nonresidents may debit freely their accounts in CFA francs for the purpose of purchasing foreign currency on the official foreign exchange market.

Blocked accounts

No.

Imports and Import Payments

Foreign exchange budget	No.
Financing requirements for imports	No.
Documentation requirements for release of foreign exchange for imports	Importers may purchase foreign exchange for import payments after establishing bank payment order accounts and submitting supporting documents, but not earlier than eight days before shipment if a documentary credit is opened, or on the due date of payment if the products have already been imported.
Domiciliation requirements	All imports from countries outside the franc zone exceeding CFAF 500,000 must be domiciled with an authorized bank. Effective February 1, 1999, this limit was raised to CFAF 5 million.
Preshipment inspection	All imports through the port exceeding CFAF 3 million are subject to inspection. Overland imports are subject to prior inspection when their value exceeds CFAF 1.5 million.
Letters of credit	LCs may be opened for all import operations, regardless of origin.
Import licenses and other nontariff measures	Certain imports, e.g., narcotics, are prohibited from all sources.
Positive list	Yes.
Open general licenses	Licenses are issued for imports of pharmaceuticals, explosives, and firearms. Imports of potatoes may be prohibited during the period when local production is adequate to meet local demand (between August and February).
Other nontariff measures	Yes.
Import taxes and/or tariffs	On January 1, 2000, the WAEMU introduced a CET with four rates (zero, 5%, 10%, and 20%) for all member countries except Guinea-Bissau. In addition, a statistical tax of 3% and a VAT of 18% are imposed on all imports. With the exception of the VAT, which is assessed on the basis of the c.i.f. value of imports inclusive of fiscal import duties, all other taxes are levied on c.i.f. values.
State import monopoly	No.

Exports and Export Proceeds

Repatriation requirements	The due date for payment of exports to foreign countries, including the Operations Account area, may not be later than 180 days after the arrival of the goods at their destination. Effective February 1, 1999, proceeds from exports to WAEMU countries no longer need to be repatriated.
Surrender requirements	The proceeds must be surrendered within one month of the due date to the BCEAO through authorized intermediaries; authorized diamond purchasing officers, however, may retain foreign currency proceeds in foreign currency accounts with authorized banks in Togo.
Financing requirements	No.
Documentation requirements	
Letters of credit	Yes.
Domiciliation	All export transactions over CFAF 5 million must be domiciled with an authorized bank. Effective February 1, 1999, exports to WAEMU countries need not be domiciled.
Export licenses	Gold, diamonds, and all other precious metals are subject to MOF authorization. Exports to all countries require licenses in certain cases.
Without quotas	Yes.
Export taxes	
Other export taxes	Phosphate rock is subject to a specific export tax.

Payments for Invisible Transactions and Current Transfers

Controls on these transfers	Payments for invisibles to France, Monaco, and the Operations Account countries are permitted freely; most of those to other countries are also permitted freely, subject to the provision of supporting documents. Effective February 1, 1999, payments and incomes of foreign ships in the WAEMU zone and WAEMU ships abroad are included under current operations.
Investment-related payments	Current transfers abroad of funds required to service loans are unrestricted. These must, however, be carried out through an authorized bank and are to be reported for statistical purposes to the MOF. Payments for depreciation of direct investments require prior authorization from the MOF, since this type of depreciation is not specifically mentioned in the regulations.
Prior approval	Loan repayments abroad are unrestricted. Notification to the MOF is required for statistical purposes.
Indicative limits/bona fide test	The MOF verifies transactions that require its authorization.
Payments for travel	
Quantitative limits	Effective February 1, 1999, limits on foreign exchange allowances were eliminated. The threshold of foreign exchange to be surrendered by residents after travel was raised to CFAF 300,000 from CFAF 50,000.
Indicative limits/bona fide test	Allowances in excess of the equivalent of CFAF 2 million in foreign banknotes must be exported in the form of traveler's checks, bank drafts, or other means of payment.
Personal payments	There is no control on the payment of pensions.
Indicative limits/bona fide test	Yes.
Foreign workers' wages	The transfer of the entire net salary of a foreign national working in Togo is permitted upon presentation of the appropriate pay voucher, residence permit, or work permit, provided that the transfer takes place within three months of the pay period.
Indicative limits/bona fide test	Bona fide tests are conducted by authorized agents.

Proceeds from Invisible Transactions and Current Transfers

Repatriation requirements	Proceeds from invisible transactions with countries that are not WAEMU members must be repatriated.
Surrender requirements	Proceeds from transactions with WAEMU members may be retained. Effective February 1, 1999, all amounts due from residents of other countries in respect of services and all income earned in those countries from foreign assets must be collected and surrendered within one month of the due date or the date of receipt.
Restrictions on use of funds	No.

Capital Transactions

Controls on capital and money market instruments	Transfers of capital abroad by residents for investment purposes are subject to controls. Capital inflows to WAEMU countries are unrestricted, with the exception of direct investment, which is subject to prior declaration, and certain borrowing operations, which require prior authorization of the MOF. If, however, the purchase of the securities has been authorized by the RCPSFM, MOF authorization is not required. A maximum of 75% of investment abroad may be financed by foreign loans.
	In line with the new direction of economic policy aimed at attracting foreign investment, new exchange laws currently being adopted by the WAEMU member states provide for the elimination of all controls on capital inflows.
	In the implementation of the provisions indicated in this document, the term "foreigner" refers to countries that are not members of the franc zone. However, with respect to the

local issue and offer for sale of foreign securities, the term "foreigner" refers to all countries outside the territory of the member state concerned.

With the exception of the issue and sale in the country of foreign securities, operations in securities are not covered explicitly by specific laws. However, by their nature, these operations are still subject to the provisions governing foreign investment and lending.

Effective February 1, 1999, transfers by nonresidents related to the sale of an investment were allowed. The reinvestment abroad by a resident of proceeds from the sale of an investment is subject to the prior approval of the MOF. Foreign investment in WAEMU countries became unrestricted. Such operations are subject to reporting for statistical purposes. The prior authorization of the RCPSFM is required for the issuance and marketing of securities and capital assets of foreign entities, as well as for the advertising of investments abroad. Any investment by residents abroad requires the prior approval of the MOF.

On capital market securities

Shares or other securities of a participating nature

Sale or issue locally by nonresidents

The issue of securities and the sale of corporate or foreign securities in Togo by nonresidents requires prior authorization by the RCPSFM.

Securities issued or offered for sale by a nonresident with prior authorization may be purchased freely by a resident. The same applies to payments for these purchases by residents, subsequent to the presentation of supporting documentation.

There are no controls on the sale of securities resulting from the divestiture of investment in the form of a transfer between a nonresident and a resident, subject to the regulations governing the financial settlement of the operation.

Settlement of securities transactions by transfer abroad or by credit to a nonresident account requires an exchange authorization to be submitted to the MOF for approval, accompanied by supporting documentation.

Purchase abroad by residents

The purchase of securities abroad by residents and the transfer abroad of funds for this purpose are subject to prior authorization by the MOF.

Sale or issue abroad by residents

Residents may sell local corporate securities abroad. If these operations result in foreign control of Togolese establishments, foreign investors are required to make a prior declaration to this effect to the MOF. The sale of securities to liquidate an investment abroad is subject to prior declaration to the MOF. The proceeds in foreign exchange from the sale or liquidation must be surrendered to an authorized intermediary bank.

Residents may also issue securities abroad, except for those constituting a loan. Issuance of the latter to nonresidents must be made through an authorized bank and must be reported to the MOF for statistical purposes.

Because authorization to borrow abroad is no longer required, the transfer abroad of funds to repay loans does not require authorization. Such operations must be reported to the MOF for statistical purposes.

Bonds or other debt securities

The same regulations apply as for shares and other securities of a participating nature.

On money market instruments

Purchase locally by nonresidents

Nonresidents may acquire money market instruments through local banks.

Sale or issue locally by nonresidents

The sale or issue by nonresidents of money market instruments on the local market is subject to prior authorization by the RCPSFM. The transfer of the proceeds from these operations is unrestricted if the issue itself has received prior authorization, and must be effected through an authorized bank and reported to the MOF for statistical purposes.

Purchase abroad by residents

Yes.

Sale or issue abroad by residents

There are no controls on the sale of money market instruments abroad by residents. Sales to liquidate an investment must be declared in advance. The proceeds in foreign exchange of the sale or liquidation must be surrendered to an authorized intermediary bank. The issue by residents of money market instruments abroad is governed by the provisions pertaining to borrowing.

On collective investment securities	The same regulations apply as for money market instruments.
Controls on derivatives and other instruments	These instruments are almost nonexistent in the franc zone. They are covered by the regulatory framework that applies generally to securities and investments. Effective February 1, 1999, transfers relating to option purchases were allowed.
Purchase abroad by residents	Yes.

Controls on credit operations

Commercial credits

By residents to nonresidents

There are no controls on the granting of commercial credits by residents to nonresident entities on the following conditions:

(1) Claims arising from the export of goods must be recovered and the corresponding amounts repatriated through the BCEAO within 30 days of the payment due date stipulated in the commercial contract. In principle, the due date stipulated in the commercial contract must be within 180 days.

(2) Claims arising from the payment of services must also be encashed and surrendered on the exchange market within an overall maximum time frame of two months from the payment due date. There is no administratively established limit for this due date.

To residents from nonresidents

There are no controls on the granting of commercial credits by nonresidents to resident entities. Repayments of commercial credits are generally authorized on the provision of documentation attesting to the authenticity of the commercial transaction or provision of service and the payment due date.

Financial credits

By residents to nonresidents

The granting of financial credits, guarantees, sureties, and backup credit facilities by residents to nonresident entities is comparable to an investment abroad and requires the prior authorization of the MOF. The transfer abroad of the funds needed to service these facilities requires that an exchange authorization be submitted to the MOF, accompanied by supporting documentation.

To residents from nonresidents	Effective February 1, 1999, foreign borrowing by residents is no longer restricted.
Guarantees, sureties, and financial backup facilities	The same regulations apply as for financial credits.
By residents to nonresidents	Yes.
To residents from nonresidents	Yes.

Controls on direct investment

Outward direct investment	Prior MOF authorization is required. A maximum of 75% of such investments may be financed by foreign loans.
Inward direct investment	For statistical purposes, investments must be reported to the MOF before they are made. The MOF may request postponement of the projects within two months of receiving the declaration.
Controls on liquidation of direct investment	The liquidation of investments must be reported to the MOF within 20 days of each operation.

Controls on real estate transactions

Purchase abroad by residents	Yes.
Purchase locally by nonresidents	There are controls on purchases when they do not involve direct investment in an enterprise, a branch, or a company.
Sale locally by nonresidents	Yes.

Controls on personal capital movements

Loans

   By residents to nonresidents   Residents are free to contract loans with nonresidents, provided that the transactions are carried out through authorized banks and are reported to the MOF for statistical purposes.

   To residents from nonresidents   Lenders must obtain prior authorization from the MOF, unless the amount is CFAF 100 million or less and the interest does not exceed the normal market rate. Loans to finance imports and exports also do not require authorization.

Gifts, endowments, inheritances, and legacies

   By residents to nonresidents   Except for inheritances and dowries, which are in general specifically authorized, these settlements require prior authorization by the MOF.

Settlement of debts abroad by immigrants   Immigrants who have acquired resident status must obtain prior authorization from the MOF to settle debts incurred abroad while they were nonresidents.

Transfer of assets

   Transfer abroad by emigrants   Upon proof of their income, emigrants may transfer freely their pensions, rents, or salaries through authorized banks up to CFAF 300,000 without supporting documentation. Amounts above this limit may be transferred upon authorization by the MOF.

Provisions specific to commercial banks and other credit institutions

Borrowing abroad   Authorized agents are free to borrow from abroad.

Maintenance of accounts abroad   Banks and financial institutions are not authorized to keep liquid assets outside the WAEMU zone, except to meet the needs of their current operations.

Lending to nonresidents (financial or commercial credits)   In accordance with the general provisions of the exchange regulations, these operations may be executed freely with respect to commercial credits. Effective February 1, 1999, other loans granted to nonresidents are subject to the prior authorization of the MOF, after the approval of the BCEAO.

Lending locally in foreign exchange   Local lending in foreign exchange or purchases of securities issued locally and denominated in foreign exchange require prior authorization by the MOF.

Purchase of locally issued securities denominated in foreign exchange   Such purchases require prior authorization by the MOF.

Differential treatment of deposit accounts in foreign exchange

   Credit controls   Yes.

Investment regulations   The same regulations apply in general to all residents, investors, and beneficiaries of foreign investments.

   Abroad by banks   Yes.

   In banks by nonresidents   Yes.

Provisions specific to institutional investors   Effective February 1, 1999, controls are imposed by the Insurance Code of the Inter-African Conference on Insurance Markets.

Other controls imposed by securities laws   Yes.

Changes During 1999

Exchange arrangement   *January 1.* The CFA franc peg to the French franc was replaced with a peg to the euro.

        February 1. Residents were authorized to contract forward exchange cover to settle payments related to imports and exports of goods and services.

Arrangements for payments and receipts	*February 1.* Most of the authority for supervising foreign exchange transactions was delegated to authorized banks.
	February 1. The amount of transfers authorized without supporting documentation was raised to CFAF 300,000 from CFAF 100,000.
Resident accounts	*February 1.* Residents are allowed to open foreign exchange accounts with local banks or with banks abroad after obtaining authorization from the MOF with the approval of the BCEAO.
Nonresident accounts	*February 1.* Authorizations to open nonresident accounts are issued by the BCEAO.
Imports and import payments	*February 1.* The limit for the domiciliation requirement was raised to CFAF 5 million.
Exports and export proceeds	*February 1.* Proceeds from exports to WAEMU countries were no longer required to be repatriated.
	February 1. Exports to WAEMU countries need not be domiciled.
Payments for invisible transactions and current transfers	*February 1.* Payments and incomes of foreign ships in the WAEMU zone and WAEMU ships abroad are included under currrent operations.
	February 1. Limits on foreign exchange allowances were eliminated. The threshold of foreign exchange to be surrendered by residents after travel was raised to CFAF 300,000 from CFAF 50,000.
Capital transactions	*February 1.* Transfers related to the sale of foreign securities by residents and to proceeds of disinvestments by nonresidents were allowed. Foreign investment in WAEMU countries became unrestricted. Such operations are subject to reporting for statistical purposes. The prior authorization of the RCPSFM is required for the issuance and marketing of securities and capital assets of foreign entities, as well as for the advertising of investments abroad. Any investment by residents abroad requires the prior approval of the MOF.
Controls on derivatives and other instruments	*February 1.* Transfers relating to option purchases were allowed.
Controls on credit operations	*February 1.* Foreign borrowing by residents became unrestricted.
Provisions specific to commercial banks and other credit institutions	*February 1.* Loans granted to nonresidents are subject to the prior authorization of the MOF with the approval of the BCEAO.
Provisions specific to institutional investors	*February 1.* Restrictions are imposed by the Insurance Code of the Inter-African Conference on Insurance Markets.

Changes During 2000

Imports and import payments	*January 1.* The WAEMU introduced a CET with four rates (zero, 5%, 10%, and 20%) for all member countries except Guinea-Bissau.

TONGA

(Position as of December 31, 1999)

Status Under IMF Articles of Agreement

Article VIII   Date of acceptance: March 22, 1991.

Exchange Arrangement

Currency   The currency of Tonga is the Tongan pa'anga.

Exchange rate structure   Unitary.

Classification

Conventional pegged arrangement   The external value of the pa'anga is determined on the basis of a weighted basket of currencies comprising the U.S. dollar, the Australian dollar, and the New Zealand dollar.

Exchange tax   No.

Exchange subsidy   No.

Forward exchange market   Commercial banks are allowed to provide forward exchange cover, but their gross foreign exchange liabilities must not exceed T$1 million. Provision of forward exchange cover for squash exporters requires the approval of the MOF.

Arrangements for Payments and Receipts

Prescription of currency requirements   No.

Payment arrangements   No.

Administration of control   Foreign exchange transactions are regulated by the MOF.

International security restrictions   No.

Payment arrears   No.

Controls on trade in gold (coins and/or bullion)   No.

Controls on exports and imports of banknotes   No.

Resident Accounts

Foreign exchange accounts permitted   No.

Accounts in domestic currency convertible into foreign currency   No.

Nonresident Accounts

Foreign exchange accounts permitted   No.

Domestic currency accounts   No.

Blocked accounts   No.

Imports and Import Payments

Foreign exchange budget	No.
Financing requirements for imports	No.
Documentation requirements for release of foreign exchange for imports	No.
Import licenses and other nontariff measures	Licenses are required for all imports, but they are issued freely for selected imports, e.g., motor vehicles.
Licenses with quotas	Import quotas apply only to fresh eggs and are intended to protect domestic producers, but the restriction is not enforced. The importation of certain items is restricted for cultural or environmental reasons or to protect the health and safety of residents.
Import taxes and/or tariffs	Import tariffs of up to 35% are levied on an ad valorem basis. Imports of a few items (petroleum, tobacco, and alcoholic beverages) are subject to either specific tariffs or ad valorem rates of up to 300%. The tariff rate on motor vehicles is 45%. Imports by the reigning monarch, by the public sector, and by diplomatic missions; imports under certain technical assistance agreements; and imports of personal effects are exempt from tariffs. Imports are also subject to a 20% port and services tax, except for items under the Industrial Development Incentives Act, which qualify for concessional rates, and imports of government and quasi-government organizations, which are exempt.
State import monopoly	No.

Exports and Export Proceeds

Repatriation requirements	Yes.
Surrender requirements	All export proceeds must be repatriated within 12 months, but this regulation is not enforced.
Financing requirements	No.
Documentation requirements	No.
Export licenses	Licenses are required for all exports weighing more than 10 kilograms. Licenses are granted liberally except for squash.
Without quotas	Yes.
Export taxes	No.

Payments for Invisible Transactions and Current Transfers

Controls on these transfers	Commercial banks are authorized to provide foreign exchange for invisible payments, but there are controls on all these payments, except for the use of credit cards abroad and the transfer of costs of family maintenance or alimony.
Trade-related payments	
Prior approval	Yes.
Quantitative limits	Yes.
Indicative limits/bona fide test	Yes.
Investment-related payments	Shipping and airline agencies may remit income earned from activities in Tonga upon producing income statements relating to local business activities that have been submitted to their respective head offices. There are no controls on the payment of amortization of loans or depreciation of direct investments.
Prior approval	Yes.

Quantitative limits	Yes.
Indicative limits/bona fide test	Yes.
Payments for travel	
Prior approval	Yes.
Quantitative limits	Yes.
Indicative limits/bona fide test	Yes.
Personal payments	There are no controls on transfer of costs of family maintenance or alimony.
Prior approval	Yes.
Quantitative limits	Yes.
Indicative limits/bona fide test	Yes.
Foreign workers' wages	
Prior approval	Yes.
Quantitative limits	Yes.
Indicative limits/bona fide test	Yes.
Other payments	
Prior approval	No prior approval is required for payment of consulting and legal fees.
Quantitative limits	Yes.
Indicative limits/bona fide test	Yes.

Proceeds from Invisible Transactions and Current Transfers

Repatriation requirements	No.
Restrictions on use of funds	No.

Capital Transactions

Controls on capital and money market instruments	
On capital market securities	
Shares or other securities of a participating nature	
Purchase abroad by residents	The acquisition of foreign financial assets is, in principle, prohibited, but in practice the control is not strictly enforced because the repatriation requirement is not enforced.
Bonds or other debt securities	
Purchase abroad by residents	Yes.
Controls on derivatives and other instruments	No.
Controls on credit operations	No.
Controls on direct investment	
Inward direct investment	Licenses are required for direct foreign investment. High-technology projects are readily approved. Intermediate projects are accepted if there is a local partner, and simple projects that can be undertaken by locals are likely to be rejected. Investment in certain sectors, including wholesale and retail, transportation and some tourism-related activities, and all resource-based activities, such as fishing, are prohibited. However, joint ventures may be

allowed if the project is deemed beneficial to the country. No time period has been specified for the approval process, which can be quite lengthy, but once licensed, foreign projects in manufacturing and tourism are fully eligible for incentives.

Controls on liquidation of direct investment	No.
Controls on real estate transactions	No.
Controls on personal capital movements	No.
Provisions specific to commercial banks and other credit institutions	
Borrowing abroad	Yes.
Maintenance of accounts abroad	Yes.
Provisions specific to institutional investors	No.
Other controls imposed by securities laws	No.

Changes During 1999

No significant changes occurred in the exchange and trade system.

TRINIDAD AND TOBAGO

(Position as of January 31, 2000)

Status Under IMF Articles of Agreement

Article VIII	Date of acceptance: December 13, 1993.

Exchange Arrangement

Currency	The currency of Trinidad and Tobago is the Trinidad and Tobago dollar.
Exchange rate structure	Unitary.
Classification	
Conventional pegged arrangement	The Central Bank of Trinidad and Tobago (CBTT) allows the exchange rate to move within a narrow range and maintains an informal ceiling on the exchange rate of TT$6.30 per US$1.
Exchange tax	No.
Exchange subsidy	No.
Forward exchange market	Banks are allowed to conduct foreign exchange transactions, both spot and forward, with the public without limitation.

Arrangements for Payments and Receipts

Prescription of currency requirements	Settlements may be made in Canadian dollars, euros, Japanese yen, Myanmar kyats, Norwegian kroner, Swedish kronor, Swiss francs, pounds sterling, and U.S. dollars.
Payment arrangements	
Regional arrangements	Trinidad and Tobago is a member of CARICOM.
Clearing agreements	Trinidad and Tobago is the agent for the inoperative Carribean Multilateral Clearing Facility.
Administration of control	Authority to administer exchange control is vested in the CBTT acting under the authority of the MOF.
International security restrictions	No.
Payment arrears	No.
Controls on trade in gold (coins and/or bullion)	
Controls on domestic ownership and/or trade	Residents are permitted to purchase, hold, or sell gold coins for numismatic purposes. Unless specifically permitted by the MOF, one party to transactions in gold between residents must be an authorized bank.
Controls on external trade	Exports of gold are controlled by the Ministry of Trade and Industry and are subject to specific export licenses, which are normally issued only to monetary authorities.
Controls on exports and imports of banknotes	
On exports	
Domestic currency	For amounts exceeding TT$20,000, a customs declaration is required.
Foreign currency	For amounts exceeding US$5,000, a customs declaration is required.
On imports	
Domestic currency	Residents and nonresidents may bring in up to TT$20,000 freely, but for larger amounts, a customs declaration is required.

Foreign currency	Resident and nonresident travelers may bring in notes up to the equivalent of US$5,000 freely, but for larger amounts, a customs declaration is required.

Resident Accounts

Foreign exchange accounts permitted	Yes.
Held domestically	Yes.
Held abroad	Yes.
Accounts in domestic currency convertible into foreign currency	Yes.

Nonresident Accounts

Foreign exchange accounts permitted	Yes.
Domestic currency accounts	Yes.
Convertible into foreign currency	Yes.
Blocked accounts	No.

Imports and Import Payments

Foreign exchange budget	No.
Financing requirements for imports	No.
Documentation requirements for release of foreign exchange for imports	No.
Import licenses and other nontariff measures	Duty-free licenses are granted to local concessionary manufacturers for imports of certain inputs for manufacturing.
Negative list	Imports of firearms, ammunition, and narcotics are tightly controlled.
Open general licenses	All goods, unless exempted for reasons of health and security, may be imported under OGL arrangements.
Other nontariff measures	All imports of food and drugs must satisfy prescribed standards. Imports of meat, live animals, plants, and mining materials are subject to specific regulations.
Import taxes and/or tariffs	The customs duty rates on most goods range from 5% to 20%. The rate on agricultural produce is 40%. The duty rates on new motor vehicles range from 25% to 45%. All goods originating from CARICOM countries are exempt from duties, as are imports of some foodstuffs, fertilizers, and raw materials. Local enterprises producing import substitutes or export goods may be granted exemptions from customs duties by the Ministry of Trade and Industry and the Tourism Industrial Development Company, Ltd. On January 1, 2000, the fourth phase of the CARICOM CET came into effect.
State import monopoly	Imports of animal feed, flour, rice, petroleum, and edible oil are traded principally by state companies.

Exports and Export Proceeds

Repatriation requirements	In practice, the foreign-owned petroleum company operating in Trinidad and Tobago repatriates all foreign exchange after providing for the equivalent of its local currency needs.
Financing requirements	No.
Documentation requirements	No.

Export licenses	Individual licenses are required for some foodstuffs, firearms and explosives, animals, gold, petroleum and petroleum products, and certain products not produced locally. Export licenses for all other commodities are granted under OGL. General licenses may also be issued at the discretion of the Ministry of Trade and Industry.
Without quotas	Yes.
With quotas	Yes.
Export taxes	No.

Payments for Invisible Transactions and Current Transfers

Controls on these transfers	No.

Proceeds from Invisible Transactions and Current Transfers

Repatriation requirements	No.
Restrictions on use of funds	No.

Capital Transactions

Controls on capital and money market instruments	Cross-border trading of shares of companies listed on the respective stock exchanges is permitted among the residents of Barbados, Jamaica, and Trinidad and Tobago; residents and companies of the other two countries are designated as residents of Trinidad and Tobago for exchange control purposes in cross-border trading.
On capital market securities	
Shares or other securities of a participating nature	The holding of shares in local companies is subject to compliance with the provisions of the Financial Institutions Act.
Controls on derivatives and other instruments	No.
Controls on credit operations	No.
Controls on direct investment	
Inward direct investment	Holding shares in local companies is subject to compliance with the provisions of the Foreign Investment Act.
Controls on liquidation of direct investment	No.
Controls on real estate transactions	
Purchase locally by nonresidents	Holding interest in real estate is subject to compliance with the provisions of the Foreign Investment Act.
Controls on personal capital movements	No.
Provisions specific to commercial banks and other credit institutions	
Differential treatment of deposit accounts in foreign exchange	
Reserve requirements	The reserve requirement applied to domestic currency deposits is 21%. A supplemental reserve requirement of 5% applies, which can be held in treasury securities. A reserve requirement of 9% applies to nonbank institutions.
Liquid asset requirements	A liquid asset ratio of 25% on foreign currency deposits is required.

Open foreign exchange position limits	A liquid asset ratio of 25% on foreign currency deposits is required.
Provisions specific to institutional investors	
Limits (max.) on portfolio invested abroad	Yes.
Limits (min.) on portfolio invested locally	Insurance companies are required to hold at least 80% of their investment assets locally.
Other controls imposed by securities laws	The Insurance Act imposes other controls.

Changes During 1999

Exchange arrangement	*March 31.* The exchange rate arrangement was reclassified to the category conventional pegged arrangement from the category independently floating.

Changes During 2000

Imports and import payments	*January 1.* The fourth phase of the CARICOM CET came into effect.

TUNISIA

(Position as of February 29, 2000)

Status Under IMF Articles of Agreement

Article VIII   Date of acceptance: January 6, 1993.

Exchange Arrangement

Currency   The currency of Tunisia is the Tunisian dinar.

Exchange rate structure   Unitary.

Classification

Crawling peg   The exchange rate of the Tunisian dinar is determined in the interbank market in which commercial banks, including offshore banks acting on behalf of their resident customers, conduct transactions at freely negotiated rates, but there is no limit on the spread between the buying and selling rates. The Central Bank of Tunisia (CBT) intervenes in the market and publishes an indicative interbank exchange rate for foreign currencies and banknotes by the following day, at the latest. Resident banks trade freely in foreign currencies in the spot market among themselves, with their foreign correspondents, and with nonresident banks in Tunisia.

Exchange tax   No.

Exchange subsidy   No.

Forward exchange market   Importers and exporters are authorized to obtain forward exchange cover on the interbank market as of the date the contract is signed or the date on which the foreign commercial paper is domiciled, depending on the arrangements for the product concerned. Forward rates are freely negotiated by the transactor of the authorized counterpart bank. Forward cover may be established for up to 12 months for imports and up to 9 months for exports. Persons who provide services are eligible for exchange cover for up to 12 months, to be provided within 30 days of the date on which the claim originated. Resident borrowers of foreign exchange may purchase 3-month, 6-month, and 12-month foreign currency options in dollars and euros.

Official cover of forward operations   The reinsurance company manages this exchange cover mechanism for banks and financial institutions in respect of their borrowings abroad.

Arrangements for Payments and Receipts

Prescription of currency requirements   Settlements between Tunisia and other countries may be made in any convertible currency (traded in the interbank market) or in convertible Tunisian dinars through foreign accounts. Payments to Israel are prohibited.

Settlements between Tunisia and Algeria, Libya, Mauritania, and Morocco may be effected through convertible accounts in the national currencies concerned at the respective central banks.

Payment arrangements   No.

Administration of control   Exchange control is administered by the CBT and the Ministry of Trade (MOT). The CBT delegates authority over payments for imports and most invisibles to the authorized banks, whereas the MOT administers foreign trade control, which issues import and export authorization for products not covered by the liberalization of foreign trade.

International security restrictions

In accordance with UN sanctions   Yes.

Payment arrears   No.

Controls on trade in gold (coins and/or bullion)

Controls on domestic ownership and/or trade | Yes.

Controls on external trade | The CBT has a monopoly over the importation and exportation of monetary gold. Imports and exports of gold in other forms require joint approval from the CBT and the MOT.

Controls on exports and imports of banknotes

On exports

Domestic currency | Exports of banknotes and coins are prohibited.

Foreign currency | Nonresident travelers wishing to reexport the foreign exchange equivalent of amounts exceeding D 1,000 must declare to customs the foreign currencies they are importing upon their entry into Tunisia. There is no ceiling on the reconversion of Tunisian banknotes by nonresident travelers. Foreign exchange from dinar reconversion may be reexported upon presentation of a foreign exchange voucher or receipt if the amount to be reexported is less than D 1,000 or if the foreign exchange used in the purchase of the dinars was received abroad in the form of a check, draft, money order, or any other evidence of a claim or by debiting a foreign account in foreign currency or convertible dinars. The foreign exchange import declaration approved by customs is also required if the amount of foreign exchange from dinar reconversion exceeds the equivalent of D 1,000 derived from the surrender of foreign currencies physically imported from abroad.

On imports

Domestic currency | Imports of banknotes and coins are prohibited.

Resident Accounts

Foreign exchange accounts permitted | Yes.

Held domestically | (1) Professional accounts in foreign currency may be opened by (i) any resident natural person, (ii) any Tunisian juridical person, and (iii) any foreign juridical person in Tunisia with the foreign currency assets in connection with their activities. These accounts may be credited with (i) a maximum of 50% of foreign exchange proceeds from the account holder's exports and foreign currency loans contracted in conformity with the regulations in force; (ii) interest accrued on the balances of these accounts; and (iii) transfers from the account holder's other professional accounts in the same currency or any other currency. The accounts may be debited for (i) payment of any current operation pertaining to the activity for which they were opened, and (ii) any other transaction with general or specific authorization. Balances may be placed on the foreign exchange market.

(2) Special accounts in foreign currency may be opened by (i) natural persons of Tunisian nationality changing their normal residence to Tunisia from abroad; (ii) resident natural persons of Tunisian nationality or Tunisian juridical persons for their nontransferable assets legitimately acquired abroad; (iii) natural persons of foreign nationality residing in Tunisia; (iv) foreign juridical persons with branches in Tunisia; and (v) Tunisian diplomats and civil servants stationed abroad. Funds legitimately acquired abroad, not from the exportation of goods or services from Tunisia, may be credited to these accounts. They may be debited for (i) foreign exchange sold on the interbank market; (ii) foreign exchange remitted to the account holder, his or her spouse, parents, and offspring to undertake foreign travel; (iii) amounts credited to another special account in foreign currency or convertible dinars; and (iv) any payments abroad, including those for the acquisition of movable or real estate property located abroad or ownership rights abroad, for foreign claims, and for payments for imports subject to applicable foreign trade formalities.

Approval required | A declaration of holdings is required for special accounts only.

Held abroad | Residents may open accounts abroad, but prior approval is required. Resident banks may freely open correspondent current accounts abroad.

Accounts in domestic currency convertible into foreign currency

Professional accounts in convertible dinars may be opened by resident natural or juridical persons with resources in foreign exchange, subject to CBT authorization. These accounts may be credited and debited under the terms laid down by the CBT in the authorization to open such accounts.

Special accounts in convertible dinars may be opened by the same natural and juridical persons that may open special foreign exchange accounts. These special accounts may be credited with the dinar proceeds from sales on the interbank market of funds legitimately acquired abroad, but not from the exportation of goods or services from Tunisia. They may be debited for (1) payments of any kind in Tunisia; (2) the acquisition of foreign currencies either for remittance to the account holder, his or her spouse, parents, and offspring, or for making payments abroad, particularly for the acquisition of movable or real estate property located abroad, or ownership rights abroad, for foreign claims and for payments for imports subject to applicable foreign trade formalities; and (3) amounts credited to another special account in foreign currency or convertible dinars. A declaration of holdings is required.

Special export earnings accounts in convertible dinars may be opened by Tunisian or foreign natural persons residing in Tunisia who earn profits from the exportation of goods or services and/or who are shareholders or partners in a resident company earning profits from the exportation of goods or services. These accounts may be freely credited with (1) 5% of the export earnings realized by the account holder or received from companies in which he or she is a shareholder (this amount was increased to 10% on February 18, 2000), (2) proceeds from sales on the interbank market of foreign exchange representing income or revenue from assets acquired abroad by debiting the account, and (3) interest on balances in the account.

They may be freely debited for (1) payments of any kind in Tunisia; (2) purchases on the interbank market of foreign exchange to be used for foreign travel by the account holder, his or her spouse, parents, or offspring; and (3) payments in connection with a current operation or to acquire rights and interests abroad not involving real property.

Nonresident Accounts

Foreign exchange accounts permitted

Foreign accounts in convertible currencies may be opened freely by all nonresidents regardless of nationality. These accounts may be credited with (1) receipts in convertible foreign currencies (banknotes must be declared at customs); (2) foreign exchange remitted to the account holder by a nonresident; (3) authorized payments by residents in favor of the account holder; (4) interest payable by the authorized intermediaries on foreign exchange deposits in the accounts whenever they can use the funds thus deposited at remunerative rates; (5) transfers from other foreign accounts; and (6) the amount of cashed checks, traveler's checks, or drafts expressed in convertible currencies and made out by a nonresident to the order of the account holder. All other crediting requires prior authorization from the CBT, either directly or by delegation.

These accounts may be debited freely for (1) payments of any kind in Tunisia; (2) transfers abroad or delivery of foreign currency to the account holder, to any other nonresident beneficiary, or to residents with the status of permanent representatives or salaried employees of the account holder; and (3) transfers to other foreign accounts.

Domestic currency accounts

Domestic nonresident accounts may be opened freely by authorized intermediaries in the name of foreigners residing temporarily in Tunisia. These accounts may be credited without authorization from the CBT with the following: (1) transfers of funds carried out in convertible currencies from a foreign country; (2) revenue of any kind accruing in Tunisia to the holder of the account (in particular the nontransferable part of remuneration for services rendered by that person in Tunisia); (3) liquid assets from estates opened in Tunisia; (4) proceeds from the repayment of loans previously granted in dinars with funds from the account holder's internal nonresident account; and (5) transfers from another internal nonresident account opened in the name of the account holder. These accounts may be debited for (1) support of the account holder and his or her family in Tunisia; (2) payment of costs of managing property in Tunisia, (3) lending to residents; and (4) transfers to another internal nonresident account opened in the name of the account holder.

Special dinar accounts may be freely opened by foreign enterprises holding contracts in Tunisia approved by the CBT. Such enterprises are authorized to open for each contract a single special account in dinars, in which they may deposit the portion of the contract price payable in dinars to cover their local expenses. Such accounts may also be credited with funds from a foreign account in convertible foreign currency, the dinar equivalent of any transfer in convertible foreign currency from abroad, and interest accruing on funds deposited in the account. The account may be freely debited for the enterprise's contract-related expenses in Tunisia. Any transfer operations from such accounts must be authorized by the CBT. Interest is paid at rates comparable to those applied to resident accounts in dinars.

Capital accounts may be opened freely in the name of a nonresident natural person of foreign nationality or by a nonresident juridical person. Subject to certain conditions, capital accounts may be credited, without the prior approval of the CBT, with the proceeds of sales on the stock exchange, or the contractual or advance redemption of transferable Tunisian securities; with the sales proceeds of real estate through an attorney at the Supreme Court, or of rights to real estate situated in Tunisia; and with funds from another capital account. Irrespective of the account holder's country of residence, capital accounts may be freely debited for the living expenses in Tunisia of the account holder and his or her family up to D 100 a person a week, provided that total withdrawals from one or more capital accounts in a calendar year do not exceed D 2,000. In addition, a capital account holder traveling in Tunisia between November 1 and March 31 may withdraw from the account an amount equal to the foreign exchange imported for the trip and surrendered to the CBT, an authorized intermediary, or a subagency, provided that total withdrawals for the living expenses of the account holder and his or her family do not exceed D 2,000 a year. Such accounts may also be debited, subject to certain conditions, for expenses connected with the management of Tunisian securities; for the maintenance, repair, and insurance of real estate and all taxes; and for transfer to the credit of another capital account. Balances on capital accounts are freely transferable between nonresidents of foreign nationality, with the exception of juridical persons governed by public law. Subject to certain conditions, they may also be debited to assist the account holder's parents and offspring residing in Tunisia, at a maximum rate of D 50 a person a month. These accounts do not pay interest and may not be overdrawn. Natural and juridical persons of French or Italian nationality holding capital accounts may transfer all funds in their accounts regardless of the date of deposit.

Suspense accounts may be opened by all nonresidents regardless of nationality and may be used for crediting all proceeds accruing to nonresidents and awaiting utilization. These proceeds may, upon general or specific approval, be used in Tunisia for specific purposes, transferred abroad, or transferred to other nonresident accounts. Subject to certain conditions, suspense accounts may be debited, without the prior authorization of the CBT, for purchases of Tunisian securities, subscriptions to issues of short-term debentures or bonds, portfolio management expenses in respect of certain securities, payments to the Tunisian government or public institutions, or payment of the expenses of managing securities deposited in a suspense file opened in the name of the account holder. They may also be debited for settlement of living expenses incurred in Tunisia by the account holder and his or her family up to D 100 a person a week, provided that the total withdrawals in any calendar year from one or more accounts do not exceed D 2,000 a family. In addition, a suspense account holder traveling in Tunisia between November 1 and March 31 of the next year may withdraw from the account an amount equal to the foreign exchange imported for the trip and surrendered to the CBT, an authorized intermediary, or a subagency, provided that total withdrawals for the living expenses of the account holder and his or her family do not exceed D 2,000 a year. Up to D 50 a person a month may be debited to assist the offspring or parents of the resident account holder. Natural and juridical persons of French or Italian nationality holding suspense accounts may transfer all funds in their accounts regardless of the date of deposit. These accounts do not pay interest.

Convertible into foreign currency

Foreign accounts in convertible dinars may be opened freely by all nonresidents regardless of nationality. These accounts may be credited freely with (1) the dinar proceeds from sales of foreign currency on the interbank market (banknotes must be declared at customs); (2) proceeds from authorized payments by residents in favor of the account holder; (3) proceeds from the conversion of the amount of cashed checks, traveler's checks, or drafts expressed in foreign currency and made out by a nonresident to the order of the account holder; (4) transfers from other foreign accounts; and (5) interest on balances in these accounts. No other amount may be credited to these accounts without authorization from the CBT, granted either directly or by delegation.

These accounts may be freely debited for (1) payments of any kind in Tunisia, and (2) purchases on the interbank market of foreign currency either for transfers abroad or for delivery to the account holder, to any other nonresident beneficiary, or to residents with the status of representatives or salaried employees of the account holder.

Blocked accounts	No.

Imports and Import Payments

Foreign exchange budget	No.
Financing requirements for imports	No.
Documentation requirements for release of foreign exchange for imports	Importers must receive a customs code.
Domiciliation requirements	Yes.
Import licenses and other nontariff measures	On March 16, 1999, Morocco and Tunisia signed a free trade agreement, providing for the immediate liberalization of 2,000 products, and for the complete phasing out of tariff barriers between the two countries by December 2007. All imports are free except those that have an impact on law and order, hygiene, health, morals, protection of fauna and flora, and cultural heritage, and are effected by an import certificate domiciled with an authorized intermediary. Goods not liberalized need an import authorization granted through the MOT. Imports of raw materials, semifinished products, spare parts, and equipment that are paid from sources outside Tunisia and do not involve the payment or delivery of foreign currency may be effected without foreign trade formalities by enterprises for their own use up to a value of D 100,000. Furthermore, companies exclusively engaged in exporting goods or services and companies established in a free trade zone may import freely, without foreign trade formalities, any goods required for their production process, subject only to customs declaration. All imports from Israel are prohibited. Some items, a list of which is drawn up by the MOT, are subject to technical import controls.
Negative list	Goods not covered by the liberalization of foreign trade and those that have an impact on law and order, hygiene, health, morals, protection of flora and fauna, and cultural heritage are included in a list issued by decree. Cars of certain categories remain temporarily subject to import licenses.
Import taxes and/or tariffs	In addition to customs duties, imports are subject to the value-added tax and, in some cases, to the consumption tax. Certain imports destined for domestic investment projects are eligible for full or partial exemption from import duties.
State import monopoly	No.

Exports and Export Proceeds

Repatriation requirements	Proceeds must be repatriated within 10 days of the payment due date. If no credit is extended, payment is due within 30 days of the date of shipment. Nonresident companies exclusively engaged in exporting goods or services and covered by the Investment Incentives Code, as well as nonresident international trading companies and nonresident enterprises constituted in a free trade zone, are not required to repatriate or surrender their export proceeds.
Surrender requirements	Resident exporters may credit up to 50% of their foreign exchange export proceeds and their foreign currency loans contracted in accordance with existing exchange regulations to their professional accounts.
Financing requirements	No.

Documentation requirements

Domiciliation	Exports of goods covered by the liberalization of foreign trade must be domiciled within eight days of the date of shipment.
Preshipment inspection	Some products listed by the MOT are subject to export controls.
Export licenses	On March 16, 1999, Morocco and Tunisia signed a free trade agreement, providing for the immediate liberalization of 2,000 products, and for the complete phasing out of tariff barriers between the two countries by December 2007. Most exports are free, and certain goods may be exported with an authorization issued by the MOT.
Without quotas	Yes.
Export taxes	No.

Payments for Invisible Transactions and Current Transfers

Controls on these transfers

Investment-related payments	Transfers for reimbursement of principal on loans in foreign exchange arranged freely by resident financial institutions and resident enterprises may be freely executed.
Payments for travel	
Quantitative limits	Effective October 25, 1999, the annual limits for tourist travel were increased to D 1,000 from D 500 an adult and to D 500 from D 250 a child under the age of 10. The business allowance for exporters is 10% of export proceeds for the current year, with an annual limit of D 80,000. The annual limit for business travel by importers ranges from D 5,000 to D 30,000, depending on turnover, and the annual limit for business travel by other professions ranges from D 2,000 to D 20,000, depending on turnover declared to the tax authorities. The allowance for promoters of new projects is up to D 5,000 and is granted only once for the duration of the project.
Indicative limits/bona fide test	Yes.
Personal payments	There are no restrictions on the transfer of pensions.
Prior approval	Alimony payments to the ex-spouse and children in a definitive judgment are freely transferable.
Quantitative limits	The annual allowance for expenses related to stays abroad for reasons of health is D 750. Persons accompanying patients may transfer up to D 250 a trip in the case of medical or paramedical staff and D 500 in all other cases. The annual settlement and the monthly living expense allowances for students studying abroad are D 1,500 and D 700, respectively. Education allowances are freely transferable up to a ceiling of D 6,000 a year.
Indicative limits/bona fide test	The limit of D 750 for expenses related to stays abroad for reasons of health may be exceeded if the patient's condition requires several trips abroad during the same year.
Foreign workers' wages	
Quantitative limits	Contractually employed foreign nationals may transfer up to 50% of their earnings. For foreign experts employed by the public sector, limits on transfers are specified in their contracts; otherwise, the restrictions for contractually employed foreign nationals will apply.
Indicative limits/bona fide test	Yes.
Credit card use abroad	Only operators holding business travel allowances are authorized to use credit cards abroad.
Prior approval	Yes.
Quantitative limits	Holders of business travel allowances may use their credit cards abroad only to the extent of their transfer entitlements for these allowances.
Indicative limits/bona fide test	Yes.
Other payments	There are controls on the payment of consulting fees.

Proceeds from Invisible Transactions and Current Transfers

Repatriation requirements

Residents are required to repatriate all remuneration for services rendered to nonresidents and all proceeds from invisible transactions received from abroad.

Surrender requirements

The facilities associated with professional accounts in foreign exchange apply to proceeds from services to nonresidents.

Restrictions on use of funds

Foreign exchange deposited in professional accounts must be used in accordance with the rules governing the operation of accounts of this type.

Capital Transactions

Controls on capital and money market instruments

There are controls on all transactions in capital and money market instruments.

On capital market securities

Shares or other securities of a participating nature

Purchase locally by nonresidents

Stocks may be freely acquired with foreign exchange transferred from abroad by foreign nonresidents in companies established in Tunisia. However, for stocks with voting rights and for acquisitions that result in foreign ownership exceeding 50% of capital shares listed in the stock exchange and for unlisted shares, the approval of the High Investment Commission (HIC) is required. Authorization is not required from the HIC for acquisitions of Tunisian securities entailing voting rights or shares in companies established in Tunisia (1) between associates or shareholders in the same company who are foreign nationals; (2) transacted by nonresident natural or juridical persons established in Tunisia, for securities and corporate shares that have already been acquired, within the limit of 50% or more; and (3) provided as a guarantee for management activities of foreign directors in companies established in Tunisia.

Sale or issue locally by nonresidents

Nonresidents may freely transfer net real proceeds from the sale of shares of companies established in Tunisia that were purchased with foreign exchange transferred from abroad for an investment made in accordance with the legislation in force.

Purchase abroad by residents

The accumulation of assets abroad by residents is subject to authorization. However, resident exporters may transfer D 40,000 to D 200,000 annually to finance equity participation in companies located abroad. The holders of special accounts in foreign currency or convertible dinars or special export earnings accounts may purchase securities abroad by debiting these accounts.

Sale or issue abroad by residents   Yes.

Bonds or other debt securities

Purchase locally by nonresidents

Subscription by nonresident foreign nationals of debt securities issued by state or resident companies is subject to approval.

Sale or issue locally by nonresidents   Yes.

Purchase abroad by residents   Yes.

Sale or issue abroad by residents   Yes.

On money market instruments

Purchase locally by nonresidents   Yes.

Sale or issue locally by nonresidents   Yes.

Purchase abroad by residents   Yes.

Sale or issue abroad by residents   Yes.

On collective investment securities

Purchase locally by nonresidents
Nonresidents may freely acquire shares of Tunisian mutual funds with foreign exchange transferred from abroad. However, the approval of the HIC is required if the acquisition raises the foreign ownership to more than 50% of the mutual fund's capital.

Sale or issue locally by nonresidents
Nonresidents may freely transfer net real proceeds from sales of Tunisian mutual fund shares acquired with foreign exchange transferred from abroad.

Purchase abroad by residents
Yes.

Sale or issue abroad by residents
Yes.

Controls on derivatives and other instruments
There are controls on all transactions in derivatives and other instruments. Resident banks may engage among themselves and with their correspondent banks in foreign exchange swaps maturing in up to 12 months.

Controls on credit operations
There are controls on all credit transactions.

Commercial credits

By residents to nonresidents
These credits require approval from the CBT, except for credits in foreign currency granted on the money market to refinance import or export operations of nonresident industrial enterprises established in Tunisia and short-term credits in dinars to finance the local operating expenses of nonresident enterprises established in Tunisia.

To residents from nonresidents
Resident financial institutions and other resident enterprises may freely contract foreign currency loans from nonresidents up to an annual limit of D 10 million and D 3 million, respectively.

Financial credits
Resident financial institutions and other resident enterprises may freely contract foreign currency financial loans from nonresidents up to an annual limit of D 10 million and D 3 million, respectively; all other loans require approval from the CBT.

By residents to nonresidents
Yes.

To residents from nonresidents
Yes.

Guarantees, sureties, and financial backup facilities

By residents to nonresidents
Resident banks may freely grant bid bonds, performance bonds, advance payment bonds, contract holdback bonds, or any other bonds to resident exporters of goods or services to guarantee their obligations to nonresidents. They may also freely grant guarantees for the payment by resident importers of their purchases from nonresident suppliers. The issue and establishment of repayment guarantees for foreign currency loans freely contracted by residents are not subject to approval.

To residents from nonresidents
At the request, and with the counterguarantee, of a nonresident bank, resident banks may freely grant the usual bank guarantees required of nonresident service providers by resident transactors in connection with business contracts, work contracts, service contracts, etc.

Controls on direct investment

Outward direct investment
To transfer capital abroad, residents must obtain approval from the CBT; however, to support their export activities, exporters may freely transfer amounts ranging from D 40,000 to D 200,000 a calendar year to cover the installation, maintenance, and operating costs of branches and subsidiaries or to finance equity participation, and D 20,000 to D 100,000 to cover installation, maintenance, and operating costs of liaison or representative offices.

Inward direct investment
Foreigners may invest freely in most economic sectors. However, the participation of foreigners in certain service industries not exclusively engaged in export activities requires the approval of the HIC if such participation exceeds 50% of the capital stock.

Controls on liquidation of direct investment
All foreign direct investments carried out legitimately in Tunisia with foreign exchange transferred from abroad are guaranteed the right to repatriate the net proceeds from the sale or liquidation of the invested capital, even if the net proceeds exceed the initial value of foreign exchange invested.

Controls on real estate transactions

Purchase abroad by residents

Purchases require prior approval from the CBT.

Purchase locally by nonresidents

Purchases require prior approval from the CBT.

Sale locally by nonresidents

Authorization is required for sales other than those made to a resident and involving real estate that is the subject of a land title. These sales are recorded in the Land Registry solely upon presentation of documentation showing that the price was deposited by the buyer to a suspense or capital account maintained in the name of the vendor in the books of a licensed intermediary.

Controls on personal capital movements

Loans

By residents to nonresidents

Yes.

To residents from nonresidents

Yes.

Gifts, endowments, inheritances, and legacies

By residents to nonresidents

Authorization is not required to take possession of an inheritance established in Tunisia for the benefit of a nonresident. The transfer of proceeds from gifts, endowments, and inheritances not previously guaranteed is subject to approval.

To residents from nonresidents

Authorization is not required for gifts from nonresidents to residents, and for taking possession of an inheritance established abroad for a resident. Proceeds from gifts and inheritances must be declared and repatriated.

Settlement of debts abroad by immigrants

Yes.

Transfer of assets

Transfer abroad by emigrants

Yes.

Transfer into the country by immigrants

Nonresident Tunisian nationals returning definitively to the country must declare and repatriate their assets or proceeds and revenue from their holdings abroad.

Transfer of gambling and prize earnings

Yes.

Provisions specific to commercial banks and other credit institutions

Borrowing abroad

Resident financial institutions may freely contract foreign currency loans from nonresidents up to a limit of D 10 million.

Maintenance of accounts abroad

Resident banks may freely open "correspondent" accounts with foreign banks of their choice.

Lending to nonresidents (financial or commercial credits)

The approval of the CBT is required for loans granted by resident banks to nonresidents. However, resident banks may freely grant loans on the foreign exchange money market to nonresident industrial enterprises established in Tunisia for operating expenses and to finance imports and exports. In addition, effective May 24, 1999, resident banks may extend dinar loans to offshore companies to finance local (dinar-denominated) operational expenses. Such loans cannot be used to purchase foreign exchange, and must be located in a special account.

Lending locally in foreign exchange

Resident banks may freely extend credit to finance import and export operations. They may also lend their foreign currency surpluses to other resident banks and to their correspondent banks, in exchange for loans in another currency with the same maturity.

Purchase of locally issued securities denominated in foreign exchange

Yes.

Differential treatment of deposit accounts in foreign exchange	
Reserve requirements	Tunisia has no reserve ratio on foreign currency deposit accounts.
Interest rate controls	Interest rates on foreign currency deposits are freely negotiated between the bank and account holder, except that remuneration of the foreign currency accounts of residents may in no case be more than a half point below the rates of muneration published by the CBT for foreign currency amounts above or equal to D 10,000.
Differential treatment of deposit accounts held by nonresidents	
Reserve requirements	The dinar deposits of nonresidents are included in the calculation of the reserve requirements base.
Interest rate controls	Interest rates on dinar and convertible dinar deposits of nonresidents are freely negotiated, except in the case of demand accounts, on which there is a cap of 2%. As for foreign currency accounts, their remuneration is freely negotiated with banks. Dinar balances in suspense accounts and capital accounts do not earn interest.
Investment regulations	
Abroad by banks	Yes.
In banks by nonresidents	Approval is required for any acquisition of capital stakes in a bank that may result in the transfer of a significant proportion of a bank's assets potentially changing its financial structure or the focus of its activities.
Open foreign exchange position limits	Net open positions of banks operating in the foreign exchange market resulting from both spot and forward transactions are limited to 10% of banks' net equity capital in each currency, with a global limit of 20% for position in all currencies.
On resident assets and liabilities	Yes.
Provisions specific to institutional investors	
Limits (max.) on securities issued by nonresidents and on portfolio invested abroad	Yes.
Limits (max.) on portfolio invested abroad	Yes.
Other controls imposed by securities laws	Any acquisition on the stock exchange of a twentieth, tenth, fifth, third, half, or two-thirds of the capital of a company that is involved in public deposit taking must be declared to that company, to the Financial Board, and to the Securities Exchange.

Changes During 1999

Resident accounts	*February 12.* The maximum portion of export proceeds that may be freely credited to professional foreign currency accounts was increased to 50% from 40%, and authorization was granted to credit these accounts with 50% of any foreign currency loans legitimately contracted by the account holder.
Imports and import payments	*March 16.* Morocco and Tunisia signed a free trade agreement, providing for the immediate liberalization of 2,000 products, and for the complete phasing out of tariff barriers between the two countries by December 2007.
Payments for invisible transactions and current transfers	*October 25.* The annual allowance for tourist travel was increased to D 1,000 from D 5,000 for adults and to D 500 from D 250 for children under the age of 10.
Capital transactions	
Provisions specific to commercial banks and other credit institutions	*May 24.* Resident banks may extend dinar loans to offshore companies to finance local (dinar-denominated) operational expenses. Such loans cannot be used to purchase foreign exchange, and must be located in a special account.

Changes During 2000

Resident accounts   *February 18.* The percentage of profits that may be credited to special export earnings accounts in convertible currencies was increased to 10% from 5%.

TURKEY

(Position as of June 30, 2000)

Status Under IMF Articles of Agreement

Article VIII   Date of acceptance: March 22, 1990.

Exchange Arrangement

Currency   The currency of Turkey is the Turkish lira.

Exchange rate structure   Unitary.

Classification

Crawling peg   In December 1999, the Central Bank of Turkey (CBT) modified its exchange arrangement by moving to a preannouncement of the exchange rate path of the lira against the current basket comprising the dollar and the euro (in amounts equivalent to $1 and €0.77).

Exchange tax   A 0.1% banking and insurance transaction tax is applied to sales of foreign exchange against the Turkish lira.

Exchange subsidy   No.

Forward exchange market   Banks may deal with forward transactions within the framework of the open position limits set according to the communiqué on total net foreign exchange positions/capital base ratio, and there is no limit on forward transactions of precious metal brokerage institutions.

Official cover of forward operations Banks may enter into swap transactions with the CBT with terms of quarterly periods up to 12 months, provided that the CBT is ready to engage in such transactions.

Arrangements for Payments and Receipts

Prescription of currency requirements   Certain commercial transactions with Poland are made through special accounts denominated in dollars.

Payment arrangements

Clearing agreements   There is an agreement with Poland.

Barter agreements and open accounts There is a banking agreement with Poland.

Administration of control   The Undersecretariat of the Treasury and the CBT administer the exchange controls; the Undersecretariat of the Treasury authorizes banks to engage in foreign exchange operations, and regulates and supervises banks' open foreign exchange position limits together with the CBT.

International security restrictions

In accordance with Executive Board Decision No. 144-(52/51)   Turkey maintains certain restrictions on the making of payments and transfers for current international transactions to the government of Iraq and the Federal Republic of Yugoslavia (Serbia/Montenegro).

In accordance with UN sanctions   Yes.

Payment arrears   No.

Controls on trade in gold (coins and/or bullion)

Controls on domestic ownership and/or trade   Domestic purchases and sales in Turkey of unprocessed gold imported by the CBT and by precious metals intermediary institutions can only be conducted at the Istanbul Gold Exchange. The purchase and sale of precious metals, stones, and articles are free within the country.

Controls on external trade   Exports and imports of precious metals, stones, and articles are free. Unprocessed gold may be imported by the CBT and by precious metals intermediary institutions that are members

909

of the Precious Metals Exchange (PME) without being subject to the provisions of the Foreign Trade Regime, but the gold must be surrendered to the Istanbul Gold Exchange (IGE) within three days.

Banks may open gold deposit accounts in the name of natural and juridical entities residing in Turkey and abroad. The account holders may freely use balances on their accounts. Within the framework of the banking regulations, banks may extend gold credits to juridical and natural persons involved in the jewelry business, upon the physical delivery of the gold purchased by their institutions, and against the gold held in the gold deposit accounts. The buying and selling prices of gold are freely determined by banks. The precious metal intermediary institutions, who are members of the PME, may obtain gold from abroad for their own account and/or for the account of their customers who are involved in the jewelry business. However, the raw-gold credit should be transferred to the IGE within three days, and the buying and selling operations should take place in the IGE.

Travelers may bring into and take out of the country ornamental articles made from precious metals and stones of which the value does not exceed the equivalent of $15,000. The taking out of ornamental articles exceeding this value is dependent on their declaration upon arrival or proof that they have been purchased in Turkey.

Controls on exports and imports of banknotes	
On exports	
Domestic currency	Travelers may freely take abroad up to the equivalent of $5,000.
Foreign currency	Travelers may freely take up to the equivalent of $5,000 out of the country. To take out more than this amount, nonresidents must declare banknotes upon arrival, and residents must present a document confirming that the foreign banknotes were purchased for invisible transactions.

Resident Accounts

Foreign exchange accounts permitted	Yes.
Held domestically	Yes.
Held abroad	Yes.
Accounts in domestic currency convertible into foreign currency	No.

Nonresident Accounts

Foreign exchange accounts permitted	Yes.
Domestic currency accounts	Yes.
Convertible into foreign currency	No.
Blocked accounts	No.

Imports and Import Payments

Foreign exchange budget	No.
Financing requirements for imports	No.
Documentation requirements for release of foreign exchange for imports	No.
Import licenses and other nontariff measures	
Negative list	The importation of goods prohibited by law, such as narcotics, weapons, foreign coins

made of metals other than gold, and ammunition, is allowed only with a special permit. Old, used, reconditioned, defective, substandard, soiled, or poor-quality goods may be imported only with special permission from the Undersecretariat of the Treasury, but certain used goods that are not older than five years may be imported freely.

Licenses with quotas	Quotas are implemented as a requirement for the harmonization of the import policy of Turkey with that of the EU.
Import taxes and/or tariffs	No.
State import monopoly	No.

Exports and Export Proceeds

Repatriation requirements	Foreign exchange receipts must be repatriated within 180 days of the date of shipment. Exporters are allowed to use those proceeds for payments on imports and invisible transactions.
Surrender requirements	Receipts must be surrendered within 180 days of the date of repatriation. If exchange receipts are surrendered within 90 days, exporters are entitled to retain 30% of proceeds, which they may deposit in foreign exchange accounts with commercial banks, keep abroad, or dispose of freely. Exporters may retain export proceeds abroad up to the equivalent of $50,000. Banks, special financial institutions, and post and telegraphic offices are required to sell to the foreign currency notes market and to the CBT the predetermined ratio of all foreign exchange they obtain from exports, invisible transactions, and gold accounts within a period agreed to by the CBT. Since April 1, 1999, this ratio has been set at zero.
Financing requirements	No.
Documentation requirements	
Letters of credit	Yes.
Guarantees	Yes.
Preshipment inspection	Yes.
Export licenses	
Without quotas	Exports are generally free, but for the exportation of a few goods, permission from authorized institutions is required in advance. Exportation of certain goods requires registration for purposes of information on the importing country, price, quantity, and the method of payment, etc.
With quotas	A few products are subject to quotas.
Export taxes	
Taxes collected through the exchange system	Export taxes on nuts and unprocessed leather are collected through the exchange system.

Payments for Invisible Transactions and Current Transfers

Controls on these transfers	
Credit card use abroad	
Quantitative limits	Credit cards are allowed to be used on a revolving basis up to the equivalent of $10,000 for travel and expenses abroad; balances exceeding the equivalent of $10,000 must be settled within 30 days.
Indicative limits/bona fide test	Yes.

Proceeds from Invisible Transactions and Current Transfers

Repatriation requirements	No.

Restrictions on use of funds	No.

Capital Transactions

Controls on capital and money market instruments	Sales or issue of these instruments by nonresidents is subject to the permission of the Capital Market Board (CMB).
On capital market securities	
Shares or other securities of a participating nature	
Sale or issue locally by nonresidents	Sales by nonresidents (including investments, partnerships, and mutual funds abroad) of all kinds of securities and other capital instruments through the banks and intermediary institutions authorized according to the legislation on capital transactions may be made freely. The transfer of the income from such securities and instruments, as well as the proceeds from their sale, may be effected freely through banks and special finance institutions.
Purchase abroad by residents	Purchases and sales by residents of the securities traded in foreign financial markets are free, provided that the transactions are carried out by banks, special finance institutions, and intermediary institutions authorized according to the legislation on capital transactions, and that the transfer of their purchase value abroad is made through banks and special financial institutions.
Bonds or other debt securities	
Sale or issue locally by nonresidents	Sale or issue of these instruments by nonresidents is subject to the permission of the CMB.
On money market instruments	
Sale or issue locally by nonresidents	Yes.
On collective investment securities	
Sale or issue locally by nonresidents	Yes.
Controls on derivatives and other instruments	No.
Controls on credit operations	
Commercial credits	
To residents from nonresidents	Residents may freely obtain credits from abroad provided that they channel such credits through the banks or special finance institutions. Effective December 4, 1999, the maturity of prefinancing credits was extended to 18 months from one year.
Financial credits	
To residents from nonresidents	Credits with a maturity of over one year must be registered at the debt log maintained by the Undersecretariat of the Treasury.
Controls on direct investment	
Outward direct investment	Residents may freely export capital in cash up to $5 million or its equivalent in other foreign currencies through banks or special financial institutions and capital in kind within the framework of the provisions of the customs legislation, for the purpose of investment, incorporating companies for commercial purposes, participating in an enterprise, or opening branches abroad. The permission to export capital in cash and/or in kind exceeding $5 million is given by the ministry to which the Undersecretariat of the Treasury is attached.
Inward direct investment	Permission from the Undersecretariat of the Treasury within the framework of the Encouragement of Foreign Capital Law is required. In establishing partnership or joint companies in the Turkish private sector, foreign investors must bring at least $50,000 of capital.
Controls on liquidation of direct investment	Proceeds may be transferred abroad, but must be reported to the CBT.

Controls on real estate transactions

Purchase locally by nonresidents

Nonresidents may acquire real estate in Turkey for tourism, petroleum, and banking activities if approved by the Council of Ministers. The acquisition of real estate in villages of Turkey by nonresidents is prohibited. If nonresidents acquire real estate via inheritance in villages of Turkey, it must be liquidated. For nonresidents to acquire real estate exceeding 30 hectares in independent rural areas not belonging to a village, a decision of the Council of Ministers is required. Nonresidents may not acquire real estate in forbidden military and security areas.

Controls on personal capital movements

Loans

By residents to nonresidents

The control applies only to commodity credits of more than two years for the export of nondurable goods, and of more than five years for the export of other goods. Approvals for credits are granted by the Undersecretariat of Foreign Trade.

To residents from nonresidents

Controls are applied only to prefinancing credits with a maturity of more than 18 months.

Provisions specific to commercial banks and other credit institutions

Borrowing abroad

Before January 1, 1999, when the tax was reduced to zero, credits obtained by banks from abroad were subject to a 4% tax, which was earmarked for the Resource Utilization Support Fund.

Lending to nonresidents (financial or commercial credits)

Resident banks may extend credits to nonresidents in foreign exchange up to the total amount of the foreign exchange credits they have obtained and their foreign exchange deposit accounts, and also in Turkish liras, provided that the amount of the credits is within the limits determined in the Banking Law for banks or in the communiqué regarding Special Financial Institutions.

Lending locally in foreign exchange

Resident banks may not extend credits to residents in foreign exchange except to exporters, investors, financial leasing firms, Turkish entrepreneurs working abroad, residents who are conducting business related to international tenders held in Turkey, and residents who are conducting business related to defense industry projects that have been approved by the Undersecretariat of the Defense Industry.

Differential treatment of deposit accounts in foreign exchange

Reserve requirements

On December 10, 1999, the reserve requirement ratio for deposits in local currency was reduced to 6% from the previous 8%, while that for deposits in foreign currency, except domestic interbank deposits, remained at 11%. Two percent of the Turkish lira deposits must be placed with the CBT, calculated as a weekly average. Special financial houses are obliged to hold the same reserves for the domestic and foreign currency collected in current and participation accounts.

Liquid asset requirements

Domestic deposits and other domestic liabilities of banks are subject to a 6% liquidity re-serve, of which a minimum of 4% has to be held in government bonds, 2% must be met with deposits at the CBT, and a maximum of 2% cash in the vault. Foreign exchange deposits and other foreign exchange liabilities of banks are subject to a 3% liquidity re-serve, of which a minimum of 1% must be held in government bonds and a maximum of 2% cash in the vault. For domestic and foreign exchange liabilities other than deposits, 8% and 11% liquidity respectively has to be held in the form of free deposits at the CBT.

Investment regulations

Abroad by banks

According to a new act, promulgated on June 23, 1999, the Banking Regulation and Supervision Agency (BRSA) was established. Thus, the opening of branches or representative offices abroad by banks founded in Turkey is now subject to the permission of the BRSA. Likewise, the opening of a company abroad by banks or banks' participation in a previously established company abroad requires the permission of the BRSA. Banks that fail to meet the standard ratios according to the Banks Act may not acquire new shares in partnerships. However, until the BRSA begins its operations, the responsibility for granting permits is governed by the previous law.

In banks by nonresidents	Effective June 23, 1999, any acquisition of shares whereby the capital shares held by one person exceed 10% (previously 5%), 20%, 33%, or 50% of the capital of the bank, and any transfer of shares whereby the capital shares held by one person fall below these limits, are subject to prior permission of the BRSA. Transactions that result in reducing the number of shareholders to less than five or in shares being assigned without permission may not be registered. These rules are valid for the acquisition of voting rights and pledging of shares. The assignment of preferential shares requires BRSA approval, irrespective of the above limits.
Open foreign exchange position limits	All foreign exchange–indexed assets and liabilities have to be taken into account fully as foreign assets and foreign liabilities. On January 1, 1999, the ratio of total net foreign exchange position to capital base was reduced to 30% from 50%. This was further reduced to 25% on August 31, 1999, and to 20% on September 30, 1999. On December 21, 1999, regulations were approved requiring banks to calculate foreign exchange exposure limits on a consolidated basis. This requirement became effective on June 30, 2000.

Provisions specific to institutional investors

Limits (max.) on portfolio invested abroad	Only for investment trusts that invest the maximum of 25% of their capital and reserve funds on securities in their portfolios.
Other controls imposed by securities laws	No.

Changes During 1999

Exports and export proceeds	*April 1.* The ratio of surrender requirement for special financial institutions and post and telegraphic offices was set at zero.
Capital transactions	
Controls on credit operations	*December 4.* The maturity for prefinancing credits obtained by residents from abroad was extended to 18 months from one year.
Provisions specific to commercial banks and other credit institutions	*January 1.* The ratio of total net foreign exchange position to capital base was reduced to 30% from 50%, and all foreign exchange–indexed assets and liabilities were included in the calculation.
	January 1. For domestic deposits and other domestic liabilities, up to 2% and for foreign exchange deposits and other foreign liabilities, up to 1% of cash accounts of banks is taken into account in the calculation of liquidity requirements.
	January 1. The rate of tax on credits obtained by banks from abroad was reduced to zero from 4%.
	June 23. The BRSA was established, and the acquisition of shares allowed by one person was increased to 10% from 5%.
	August 31. The ratio of total net foreign exchange position to capital base was reduced to 25% from 30%.
	September 30. The ratio of total net foreign exchange position to capital base was reduced to 20% from 25%.
	December 10. Reserve requirements on domestic currency deposits were reduced to 6% from 8%. A 2% liquidity reserve must be kept in deposits at the CBT.

Changes During 2000

Capital transactions	
Provisions specific to commercial banks and other credit institutions	*June 30.* Banks were required to calculate foreign exchange exposure limits on a consolidated basis.

TURKMENISTAN

(Position as of January 31, 2000)

Status Under IMF Articles of Agreement

Article XIV	Yes.

Exchange Arrangement

Currency

The currency of Turkmenistan is the Turkmen manat.

Exchange rate structure

Dual.

Classification

Conventional pegged arrangement

The official (cash and noncash) exchange rate is determined at a weekly central bank auction in which authorized commercial banks participate. The official rate has remained unchanged since April 1998 at manat 5,200 per $1. Access to the foreign exchange auction is limited to authorized banks, and bids are screened by the Central Bank of Turkmenistan (CBT) and the Foreign Currency Committee (FCC). Banks participate in the auctions on behalf of their customers and for transactions approved by the CBT and the FCC. Bids are submitted at the rate established in the previous auction; if demand exceeds the foreign exchange supplied by the CBT, the excess demand is shifted to the next session.

The commercial banks' cash foreign exchange window was closed in December 1998, except with respect to a short positive list of transactions: (1) medical treatment abroad; (2) educational support for students abroad; and (3) official travel by public officers. The CBT charges banks a commission of 1% for converting noncash foreign exchange into cash foreign exchange. There is no buy/sell spread on the official rate.

Exchange tax

A 50% exchange tax on cash receipts from gas exports is levied. Effective October 1, 1999, a 20% tax on purchases of foreign exchange by enterprises and individuals was introduced. This tax was eliminated on January 31, 2000.

Exchange subsidy

No.

Forward exchange market

No.

Arrangements for Payments and Receipts

Prescription of currency requirements

Settlements with Russia and a few other countries of the FSU are made through a system of correspondent accounts. Settlements with countries with which Turkmenistan has bilateral payment arrangements are effected in accordance with the procedures set forth in these agreements. Barter transactions, other than gas exports, must take place through the State Commodity Exchange. All other transactions are made in convertible currencies.

Payment arrangements

Bilateral payment arrangements

  Operative

Yes.

  Inoperative

The bilateral agreements with Malaysia and the Islamic Republic of Iran are inoperative.

Clearing agreements

Trilateral agreements are maintained with Armenia and the Islamic Republic of Iran, and with Ukraine and the Islamic Republic of Iran.

Barter agreements and open accounts

There are barter trade agreements, primarily for gas and oil exports to Iran and Ukraine, respectively, and there is an agreement with Kazakhstan for the export of electricity.

Administration of control

The CBT, along with the Ministry of Economy and Finance (MEF), the Foreign Exchange Committee, and the Tax Authority, is empowered to issue exchange control regulations depending on the type of operation involved. The use of official foreign exchange reserves is controlled to a large extent by the President of Turkmenistan.

International security restrictions	No.
Payment arrears	
Official	Yes.
Controls on trade in gold (coins and/or bullion)	
Controls on domestic ownership and/or trade	Yes.
Controls on external trade	A license is required to engage in international trade in gold.
Controls on exports and imports of banknotes	Local and foreign banknotes may be freely exported and imported, provided funds are declared on arrival and departure.

Resident Accounts

Foreign exchange accounts permitted	Juridical and natural persons may hold foreign exchange accounts with local commercial banks.
Held domestically	These accounts may be opened if the holder possesses a certificate of registration issued by the Ministry of Foreign Economic Relations (MFER); the authorized bank determines the amount and currency of denomination of interest payable on these accounts. All external payments made from balances of these accounts must be approved by the CBT; however, cash withdrawals from the accounts in foreign currency may be made without the approval of the CBT.
Held abroad	With the permission of the CBT, Turkmen citizens residing overseas may open foreign exchange accounts abroad for the duration of their residence abroad.
Accounts in domestic currency convertible into foreign currency	n.a.

Nonresident Accounts

Foreign exchange accounts permitted	Juridical and natural persons are eligible.
Domestic currency accounts	n.a.
Blocked accounts	n.a.

Imports and Import Payments

Foreign exchange budget	No.
Financing requirements for imports	n.a.
Documentation requirements for release of foreign exchange for imports	n.a.
Import licenses and other nontariff measures	
Negative list	Imports of goods on a small negative list (arms, narcotics, antiques) are prohibited. Approval of the president or the Cabinet of Ministers (CM) is required to import these goods.
Import taxes and/or tariffs	Excise taxes are levied on alcoholic beverages, cigarettes, jewelry, and cars. Goods in transit are exempt.
State import monopoly	No.

Exports and Export Proceeds

Repatriation requirements	Yes.
Surrender requirements	The private sector and joint-venture enterprises are exempt from surrender requirements, as are public enterprises in the cotton sector. Surrender requirements for other enterprises are 50%, all of which is to be surrendered to the CBT. The gas sector, however, has a surrender requirement of 25% in effect (in addition to the 50% tax).
Financing requirements	n.a.
Documentation requirements	n.a.
Export licenses	All exports, except gas, have to be channeled through the Stock Commodity Exchange.
With quotas	Quantitative and price restrictions are imposed on exports of cotton and other raw materials to protect domestic supplies.
Export taxes	
Taxes collected through the exchange system	There is a 50% foreign exchange tax on gas. Also, 0.01% of the value of licensed products paid for convertible currencies is collected as a fee. The fee on exports to the Baltic countries, Russia, and other countries of the FSU is 0.1% of the ruble value of the licensed product. The customs department also charges an administration fee of 0.2%.

Payments for Invisible Transactions and Current Transfers

Controls on these transfers	All payments require prior approval of the exchange control authorities.
Trade-related payments	
Prior approval	Yes.
Investment-related payments	Information is not available on the payment of amortization of loans or depreciation of direct investments.
Prior approval	Yes.
Quantitative limits	After the payment of taxes, profits may be reinvested in Turkmenistan, held in bank accounts in national or other currencies, or transferred abroad.
Payments for travel	
Prior approval	Residents must possess valid passports to purchase foreign exchange for travel abroad.
Quantitative limits	The limit is $1,000 a transaction, without a limit on the number of transactions.
Personal payments	
Prior approval	Yes.
Foreign workers' wages	
Prior approval	Yes.
Credit card use abroad	
Prior approval	Yes.
Other payments	
Prior approval	Yes.

Proceeds from Invisible Transactions and Current Transfers

Repatriation requirements	Yes.

Surrender requirements	Proceeds must be sold to commercial banks, except for the retained portion allowed in the case of enterprises. Effective January 4, 1999, banks have been required to resell all foreign exchange received from customers to the CBT at the auction rate.
Restrictions on use of funds	n.a.

Capital Transactions

Controls on capital and money market instruments	Both inward and outward capital transfers are subject to CBT approval.
On capital market securities	
Shares or other securities of a participating nature	
Purchase locally by nonresidents	The nonresidents' share in the equity of a resident company is limited to 49%. Nonresidents may purchase only registered shares.
Sale or issue locally by nonresidents	These transactions are subject to quota and licensing by the CM.
Purchase abroad by residents	These transactions are subject to quota and licensing by the CM.
Sale or issue abroad by residents	These transactions are subject to quota and licensing by the CM.
On money market instruments	These transactions are subject to quota and licensing by the CM.
On collective investment securities	n.r.
Controls on derivatives and other instruments	There are no transactions in derivatives in Turkmenistan.
Controls on credit operations	A CBT license or its approval is required for residents. Nonresidents need only CBT approval.
Controls on direct investment	
Outward direct investment	Yes.
Inward direct investment	Investments by juridical persons are permitted, in principle, in all sectors. Investors are required to obtain an authorization from the MFER; if the amount exceeds $500,000, the approval of the CM is required. Foreign participation in joint-stock companies is limited to 49%.
Controls on liquidation of direct investment	Foreign investors have the right to recover investments within six months of liquidation.
Controls on real estate transactions	
Purchase abroad by residents	Yes.
Controls on personal capital movements	
Transfer of gambling and prize earnings	Yes.
Provisions specific to commercial banks and other credit institutions	A CBT license is required. Provided the license is granted, no controls apply to individual transactions.
Borrowing abroad	Yes.
Maintenance of accounts abroad	Yes.
Lending to nonresidents (financial or commercial credits)	Yes.
Lending locally in foreign exchange	Yes.
Purchase of locally issued securities denominated in foreign exchange	Yes.

Provisions specific to institutional investors	A CBT and/or an MEF license is required, depending on the type of institutional investors.
Other controls imposed by securities laws	Institutional investors are required to meet minimum capital requirements. Responsibility rests with the CM, the CBT, and/or the MEF, depending on the type of investors.

Changes During 1999

Exchange arrangement	*October 1.* A 20% tax on purchases of foreign exchange by enterprises and individuals was introduced.
Proceeds from invisible transactions and current transfers	*January 4.* Banks were required to resell all foreign exchange received from customers to the CBT at the auction rate.

Changes During 2000

Exchange arrangement	*January 31.* The 20% tax on purchases of foreign exchange was eliminated.

UGANDA

Status Under IMF Articles of Agreement

Article VIII   Date of acceptance: April 5, 1994.

Exchange Arrangement

Currency   The currency of Uganda is the Uganda shilling.

Exchange rate structure   Unitary.

Classification

Independently floating   The external value of the Uganda shilling is determined in the interbank foreign exchange market. Certain transactions may be effected in foreign exchange bureaus that are licensed to buy and sell foreign exchange at freely negotiated rates.

Exchange tax   No.

Exchange subsidy   No.

Forward exchange market   Authorized banks may deal with customers in the forward exchange market.

Arrangements for Payments and Receipts

Prescription of currency requirements   Authorized payments, including those for imports to nonresidents, may be made in Uganda shillings to the credit of an external account in Uganda or in any other currency that is appropriate to the country of residence of the payee.

Payment arrangements

Bilateral payment arrangements

   Inoperative   Uganda maintains clearing arrangements with Burundi, the Democratic Republic of Congo, and Rwanda. Trade and payment agreements exist with Algeria, Cuba, Egypt, the Democratic People's Republic of Korea, and Libya.

Regional arrangements   Following the East African Cooperation Agreement, the Uganda, Kenya, and Tanzania shillings are now freely convertible in the three countries. Excess holdings of Kenya and/or Tanzania shillings are repatriated to the respective central banks for immediate credit in dollars.

Clearing agreements   The Bank of Uganda (BOU) settles accounts in dollars with COMESA member countries through the COMESA clearinghouse. Residents of member countries may use national currencies in day-to-day payments during a transaction period of two calendar months; the monetary authorities settle net balances at the end of this period in convertible currencies.

Administration of control   The BOU has delegated a broad range of responsibilities to authorized banks and exchange bureaus. Import and export control regulations are administered by the Ministry of Tourism, Trade, and Industry (MTTI).

International security restrictions

In accordance with UN sanctions   No transactions are allowed with a country facing UN sanctions.

Payment arrears

Official   Yes.

Private   Yes.

Controls on trade in gold (coins and/or bullion)

Controls on domestic ownership and/or trade	Residents may hold and acquire gold coins for numismatic purposes. Only monetary authorities and licensed dealers are allowed to hold or acquire gold in any form other than jewelry.
Controls on external trade	Dealing in gold in any form other than jewelry constituting the personal effects of a traveler requires licenses issued by the Ministry of Energy and Mineral Development. On the basis of these licenses, the MTTI issues export and import permits.
Controls on exports and imports of banknotes	No.

Resident Accounts

Foreign exchange accounts permitted	Yes.
Held domestically	Yes.
Held abroad	Yes.
Accounts in domestic currency convertible into foreign currency	Yes.

Nonresident Accounts

Foreign exchange accounts permitted	Yes.
Domestic currency accounts	Yes.
Convertible into foreign currency	Yes.
Blocked accounts	No blocked accounts exist; however, an account could be blocked if it is required by the law.

Imports and Import Payments

Foreign exchange budget	No.
Financing requirements for imports	No.
Documentation requirements for release of foreign exchange for imports	No.
Import licenses and other nontariff measures	
Negative list	The importation of pornographic materials is prohibited. Imports of firearms and ammunition require special permission. The ban on tobacco products was lifted on April 1, 1999.
Import taxes and/or tariffs	Customs duties are applied at one of three rates of up to 15%. For countries outside COMESA, the rates are zero, 7%, and 15%; for COMESA members zero, 4%, and 6%. Duties for intermediate goods and raw materials range up to 7%, while the rate for machinery is zero. On April 1, 1999, ad valorem excise duties on imports of tobacco products were introduced.
State import monopoly	No.

Exports and Export Proceeds

Repatriation requirements	No.
Financing requirements	No.
Documentation requirements	No.
Export licenses	No.
Export taxes	No.

Payments for Invisible Transactions and Current Transfers

Controls on these transfers	No.

Proceeds from Invisible Transactions and Current Transfers

Repatriation requirements	No.
Restrictions on use of funds	No.

Capital Transactions

Controls on capital and money market instruments	No.
Controls on derivatives and other instruments	No.
Controls on credit operations	No.
Controls on direct investment	No.
Controls on liquidation of direct investment	No.
Controls on real estate transactions	
Purchase locally by nonresidents	Resident foreign nationals may purchase land, whereas nonresident foreign nationals may only be granted a lease not exceeding 99 years.
Controls on personal capital movements	No.
Provisions specific to commercial banks and other credit institutions	
Differential treatment of deposit accounts in foreign exchange	
Reserve requirements	Banks must hold 20% of foreign deposits in reserve on their own account. Banks must also maintain (unremunerated) cash reserves on deposit with the central bank, amounting to 8% of time deposits and 9% of demand deposits. These requirements are in addition to liquidity requirements, which are based on total deposits, regardless of currency denomination.
Open foreign exchange position limits	Commercial banks are allowed to have an open position equivalent to 20% of core capital.
On resident assets and liabilities	Yes.
On nonresident assets and liabilities	Yes.

Provisions specific to institutional investors   No.

Other controls imposed by securities laws   No.

Changes During 1999

Imports and import payments   *April 1.* The ban on the imports of tobacco products was lifted, and ad valorem excise duties on imports of tobacco products were introduced.

UKRAINE

(Position as of February 29, 2000)

Status Under IMF Articles of Agreement

Article VIII   Date of acceptance: September 24, 1996.

Exchange Arrangement

Currency   The currency of Ukraine is the Ukrainian hryvnia.

Exchange rate structure   Unitary.

Classification

Managed floating with no pre-   The interbank foreign exchange market was reopened on March 19, 1999. The proceeds
announced path for the exchange rate from the surrender of foreign exchange may be sold either in the official currency exchange
                                    (birzha) or the interbank market. The official exchange rate is determined daily as the aver-
                                    age weighted exchange rate used by commercial banks in the interbank market.

                                    On August 6, 1999, the authorities effectively abandoned the exchange rate band, which, on
                                    February 9, 1999, had been widened to Hrv 3.4–4.6 from Hrv 2.5–3.5 per $1. However, no
                                    formal announcement has yet been made regarding the elimination of the exchange rate
                                    band. The National Bank of Ukraine (NBU) continues to influence the exchange rate
                                    through interventions in the interbank market. The exchange rate arrangement was reclassi-
                                    fied to the category managed floating with no preannounced path for the exchange rate
                                    from the category pegged exchange rate within horizontal bands.

                                    On February 21, 2000, the NBU began to set the exchange rate of the hryvnia as the
                                    weighted average exchange rate of transactions by authorized banks in the interbank
                                    exchange market.

Exchange tax   A tax of 1% is levied on cash transactions at foreign exchange bureaus.

Exchange subsidy   No.

Forward exchange market   No.

Arrangements for Payments and Receipts

Prescription of currency   Payments to and receipts from all countries are settled in foreign currencies. Nonbarter
requirements   trade with the Baltics, Russia, and other countries of the FSU is now settled mainly in con-
                                    vertible currencies, especially the dollar. Settlement may also be in national currencies.

Payment arrangements

Bilateral payment arrangements

  Inoperative   There are arrangements with the Baltics, Russia, and other countries of the FSU.

Regional arrangements   Yes.

Barter agreements and open accounts   Barter continues to be a major form of trade for Ukrainian companies in their transactions
                                    with the Baltics, Russia, and the other countries of the FSU. The use of barter in foreign
                                    trade transactions is prohibited for a group of goods determined by the Ukrainian Cabinet
                                    of Ministers.

Administration of control   The NBU, the State Tax Administration, the State Customs Service, and the Ministry of
                                    Foreign Economic Relations and Trade (merged with the MOF) administer exchange
                                    controls.

International security restrictions

In accordance with UN sanctions   Restrictions on payments and on the provision of financial services to Iraq, the Taliban
                                    (the Islamic State of Afghanistan), and the UNITA movement in Angola are maintained.

Payment arrears	n.a.

Controls on trade in gold (coins and/or bullion)

Controls on domestic ownership and/or trade	Residents are required to obtain a license from the MOF to deal in precious stones and metals. The NBU licenses commercial bank transactions in precious metals for monetary use.
Controls on external trade	Permission for residents to export precious metals and precious stones is granted by the Ministry of Economy in consultation with the MOF. Individual licenses to export precious metals for monetary use are issued by the NBU.

Controls on exports and imports of banknotes

On exports

Domestic currency	Residents may export up to the equivalent of 10 times the nontaxed minimum wage (HRV 17), while the limit for nonresidents is five times the nontaxed minimum wage. Juridical persons require a license from the NBU.
Foreign currency	Resident natural persons may export the amount declared to the customs service at the time of entry and/or $1,000 in cash or traveler's checks without documentation, and up to the equivalent of $4,000 in cash or traveler's checks with permission from an authorized bank. Nonresident natural persons may export the amount declared to the customs service at the time of entry and/or $1,000 in cash without permission, and $1,000 in cash and $5,000 in traveler's checks with permission. The exportation of currency by residents and nonresidents in excess of the established norms requires a permit from the NBU.

On imports

Domestic currency	Resident and nonresident natural persons are permitted to import domestic currency up to the amounts declared in a customs declaration upon exit from Ukraine. Juridical persons must obtain a permit from the NBU to import domestic currency.
Foreign currency	Resident and nonresident natural persons are permitted to import up to the equivalent of $50,000 in cash; for amounts in excess of this limit, permission from the NBU is required. Residents and nonresidents require a permit issued by the NBU to import foreign currency in amounts in excess of these limits.

Resident Accounts

Foreign exchange accounts permitted	Yes.
Held domestically	Certain conditions apply to these accounts.
Held abroad	A license from the NBU is required, except when the account is opened during a temporary stay abroad.
Accounts in domestic currency convertible into foreign currency	These accounts are convertible in cases where an obligation to a nonresident exists.

Nonresident Accounts

Foreign exchange accounts permitted	Resident juridical persons of Armenia, Belarus, Kazakhstan, Lithuania, Moldova, Russia, and Uzbekistan must have a license from their respective central banks in order to open accounts with authorized Ukrainian banks. Natural persons of Belarus, Kazakhstan, and Russia do not require such a license in order to open accounts during a temporary stay in Ukraine.
Domestic currency accounts	"P" accounts may be opened for the permanent representative office of a foreign company, firm, or international organization established without the status of a legal entity, through which a nonresident conducts all or part of his or her entrepreneurial activities in Ukraine. P accounts may be credited with the proceeds from current international transactions from any economic activity in Ukraine.

"N" accounts may be opened by a representative office of a nonresident legal entity, an institution, or a person who represents its interests in Ukraine and does not engage in entrepreneurial activities in the territory of Ukraine. The holders of N accounts are regarded as nonresidents for exchange control purposes, although they are treated as residents for tax purposes. N accounts may be credited with funds by selling foreign exchange to the servicing bank in order to effect settlement associated solely with the maintenance of the representative office, or with funds received by embassies and consulates for providing consular services. All N account holders may purchase foreign exchange on the interbank currency market to transfer funds abroad, including interest accrued on the balance in the account.

Convertible into foreign currency	P account holders may (1) convert and transfer to a nonresident legal person (which it represents) the proceeds from transactions effected in Ukraine for the sale of goods and work services, interest accrued on deposit accounts and balances in such a type P account, and the balance in an account when ceasing activities in Ukraine; and (2) credit to their own account in foreign currency resources designated for labor compensation of nonresident employees and for business trip and representative office expenses abroad. N account holders other than foreign diplomatic, consular, commercial, and other official missions and their offices may not purchase foreign exchange on the interbank market to transfer funds abroad from their N account. Nonresident natural persons may convert and transfer abroad funds from settlement accounts in hryvnias. Approval to convert these accounts into foreign currency is required.
Blocked accounts	No.

Imports and Import Payments

Foreign exchange budget	No.
Financing requirements for imports	
Advance payment requirements	The restriction on advance import payments was eliminated on July 1, 1999.
Documentation requirements for release of foreign exchange for imports	In order to purchase foreign exchange on the interbank market in group 1 of the foreign exchange nomenclature of the NBU and transfer it abroad to pay for imports, residents must provide the bank with copies of the pertinent import contracts. In addition, a resident needs to obtain a certificate from the State Tax Administration (STA) confirming information on the resident's bank account and registration as a legal entity. A certificate from the STA is also required to transfer any foreign exchange to accounts of nonresidents registered in offshore zones.
Domiciliation requirements	Yes.
Preshipment inspection	Inspection is not mandatory but may be performed by the Ukrainian Chamber of Commerce and Industry at the request of nonresidents.
Letters of credit	Yes.
Import licenses and other nontariff measures	
Negative list	Yes.
Other nontariff measures	Nontariff measures are limited to those for national safety and environmental reasons.
Import taxes and/or tariffs	There are three customs duty rates with a trade-weighted average rate of about 5% (including energy imports). The first category (preferred duty rate) applies to goods from countries with which Ukraine has a free trade agreement, imports from developing countries, and imports from countries that have a preferential agreement with Ukraine. The second category (concessional duty rate) applies to imports from countries that have entered into MFN agreements with Ukraine. The third category applies to imports from other sources. A uniform, nondiscriminatory 2% import surcharge was in effect between July 1, 1999, and December 31, 1999.
	A VAT of 20% is levied on most imports.
State import monopoly	No.

Exports and Export Proceeds

Repatriation requirements

Exporters must repatriate all foreign exchange proceeds through domestic commercial banks within 90 days of shipment.

Surrender requirements

There is a 50% surrender requirement and proceeds are required to be channeled through the interbank foreign exchange market.

Financing requirements

n.a.

Documentation requirements

Preshipment inspection

Inspection is not mandatory but may be performed by the Ukrainian Chamber of Commerce and Industry at the request of residents.

Export licenses

With quotas

Goods subject to voluntary export restraints or other international agreements and those falling under the "special export regime"—coal, precious metal scrap, and alcoholic spirits—are also subject to export quotas and licenses. The licenses required for these goods are, however, freely provided, except in the case of precious metal scrap. For grain exports, it is required that sales for the export market be undertaken through the agricultural commodity exchange. Export contract preregistration is limited to goods subject to voluntary export restraints or antidumping actions. Registration of exports is automatic and for statistical purposes only.

Export taxes

Taxes are applied to exports of livestock, skins, and hides. Effective September 30, 1999, this tax was extended to exports of sunflower seeds.

Payments for Invisible Transactions and Current Transfers

Controls on these transfers

A nonresident requires a certificate from the STA stating that there are no outstanding tax liabilities associated with the underlying transaction.

Investment-related payments

Information is not available on the payment of amortization of loans or depreciation of direct investments. Proceeds, including interest, from investment in treasury bills held by nonresidents that were not rescheduled were blocked in 1998. On August 31, 1999, this restriction was lifted.

Payments for travel

Quantitative limits

The foreign currency limit for tourists is $10,000, including $5,000 in cash and $5,000 in traveler's checks a trip; for business travel, the limit is $10,000 (cash and/or traveler's checks). In addition, credit cards for international payment systems issued by Ukrainian banks may be used abroad.

Indicative limits/bona fide test

Yes.

Personal payments

Pension payments are made in accordance with agreements concluded between the Pension Fund of Ukraine and the corresponding organizations of other countries. Transfers of personal funds of natural persons (alimony, pensions, and funds for family maintenance) are performed in accordance with existing regulations.

Quantitative limits

Transfers in excess of the standard amounts require an NBU license.

Indicative limits/bona fide test

Yes.

Credit card use abroad

Residents may use abroad credit cards issued by Ukrainian banks.

Other payments

Prior approval

Yes.

Quantitative limits

The limit is $20 for membership dues.

Indicative limits/bona fide test

Yes.

Proceeds from Invisible Transactions and Current Transfers

Repatriation requirements	Proceeds, except those of a few organizations with international operations, such as the national airlines, are subject to repatriation requirements.
Restrictions on use of funds	Yes.

Capital Transactions

Controls on capital and money market instruments	
On capital market securities	
Shares or other securities of a participating nature	
Purchase locally by nonresidents	Yes.
Sale or issue locally by nonresidents	Yes.
Purchase abroad by residents	Yes.
Sale or issue abroad by residents	Yes.
Bonds or other debt securities	
Sale or issue locally by nonresidents	Repayment of investments in treasury bills that were not rescheduled was blocked until August 31, 1999.
Purchase abroad by residents	An NBU license is required.
Sale or issue abroad by residents	Yes.
On money market instruments	
Purchase locally by nonresidents	Yes.
Sale or issue locally by nonresidents	Yes.
Purchase abroad by residents	Yes.
Sale or issue abroad by residents	Yes.
On collective investment securities	An NBU license is required.
Purchase locally by nonresidents	Yes.
Sale or issue locally by nonresidents	Yes.
Purchase abroad by residents	Yes.
Sale or issue abroad by residents	Yes.
Controls on derivatives and other instruments	There are controls on all transactions in derivatives and other instruments.
Controls on credit operations	
Commercial credits	
By residents to nonresidents	An NBU license is required if the repayment deadline exceeds 90 days.
Financial credits	All financial credits must be registered with the NBU.
Guarantees, sureties, and financial backup facilities	
By residents to nonresidents	Commercial banks require a license from the NBU.
To residents from nonresidents	Yes.

Controls on direct investment

Outward direct investment	Investments require an individual NBU license.
Inward direct investment	Foreign investments in most types of businesses are permitted, although licenses are required in some cases. Investments in insurance and businesses engaged in intermediation activities require a license from the MOF, and investments in the banking sector require a license from the NBU. Foreign investment in Ukraine must be made in convertible currency or in kind. The Russian ruble is not regarded as a convertible currency for this purpose.

Controls on liquidation of direct investment

The transfer of proceeds, after payment of taxes due, is guaranteed.

Controls on real estate transactions

Purchase abroad by residents	An NBU license is required.
Purchase locally by nonresidents	Yes.
Sale locally by nonresidents	Yes.

Controls on personal capital movements

Loans

By residents to nonresidents	An NBU license is required.
To residents from nonresidents	Natural persons are not allowed to receive loans in foreign currency.

Gifts, endowments, inheritances, and legacies

By residents to nonresidents	There are no controls with regard to natural persons.
To residents from nonresidents	There are no controls with regard to legal persons.

Transfer of assets

Transfer abroad by emigrants	Transfers by nonresident natural persons are not restricted after settlement of tax liabilities.
Transfer into the country by immigrants	Transfers by nonresident natural persons are unrestricted.

Provisions specific to commercial banks and other credit institutions

Borrowing abroad	Borrowing exceeding one year requires registration with the NBU.
Maintenance of accounts abroad	Yes.
Lending to nonresidents (financial or commercial credits)	An NBU license is required.
Lending locally in foreign exchange	This type of lending may be done only for financing a limited range of "critical imports." The provision of foreign exchange to service private sector loans contracted by residents may not be made at an interest rate higher than 20%. Effective March 16, 1999, the restrictions on granting credits in foreign exchange locally were eliminated.
Purchase of locally issued securities denominated in foreign exchange	Yes.

Investment regulations

Abroad by banks	An NBU license is required.
In banks by nonresidents	Yes.
Open foreign exchange position limits	Open foreign exchange positions are set according to standards established by the NBU.
On resident assets and liabilities	Yes.
On nonresident assets and liabilities	Yes.

Provisions specific to institutional investors	No.
Other controls imposed by securities laws	n.a.

Changes During 1999

Exchange arrangement

February 9. The exchange rate band was widened.

March 19. The interbank foreign exchange market was reopened.

August 6. The band was effectively abandoned to give way to a policy of managed floating. The exchange arrangement was reclassified to the category managed floating with no prearranged path for the exchange rate from the category pegged exchange rate within horizontal bands.

Imports and import payments

July 1. A uniform, nondiscriminatory import surcharge of 2% was introduced.

July 1. The restriction on advance import payments was eliminated.

Exports and export proceeds

September 30. An export duty on sunflower seeds was introduced.

Payments for invisible transactions and current transfers

August 31. The restriction on transferring proceeds from treasury bonds held by nonresidents was eliminated.

Capital transactions

Provisions specific to commercial banks and other credit institutions

March 16. The restrictions on granting credits in foreign exchange locally were eliminated.

Changes During 2000

Exchange arrangement

February 21. The NBU began to set the exchange rate of the hryvnia as the weighted average exchange rate of transactions by authorized banks in the interbank exchange market.

Imports and import payments

January 1. The uniform, nondiscriminatory 2% import surcharge was eliminated.

UNITED ARAB EMIRATES

(Position as of December 31, 1999)

Status Under IMF Articles of Agreement

Article VIII	Date of acceptance: February 13, 1974.

Exchange Arrangement

Currency	The currency of the United Arab Emirates is the U.A.E. dirham.
Exchange rate structure	Unitary.
Classification	
Conventional pegged arrangement	The exchange rate of the U.A.E. dirham is pegged to the SDR at Dh 4.76190 per SDR 1 within margins of ±7.25%. The U.A.E. dirham has maintained a stable relationship with the dollar, the intervention currency, since November 1997 at Dh 3.6730 per $1 (buying rate) and Dh 3.6725 per $1 (selling rate).
Exchange tax	No.
Exchange subsidy	No.
Forward exchange market	The United Arab Emirates Central Bank (UAECB) maintains a swap facility, which the commercial banks may use to purchase dirhams spot and sell dirhams forward for periods of one week, one month, and three months. For each bank, maximum limits of $20 million outstanding for one-month and three-month swaps and $10 million outstanding for one-week swaps are in effect. There is also a limit of $3 million a day on purchases by each bank for one-month and three-month swaps. This facility is designed to provide temporary dirham liquidity to commercial banks. Swap facilities are not available to banks having a short position in dirhams, except for the covering of forward transactions for commercial purposes.
Official cover of forward operations	Yes.

Arrangements for Payments and Receipts

Prescription of currency requirements	There are no prescription requirements, but settlements with Israel are prohibited.
Payment arrangements	No.
Administration of control	No.
International security restrictions	No.
Payment arrears	No.
Controls on trade in gold (coins and/or bullion)	No.
Controls on exports and imports of banknotes	No.

Resident Accounts

Foreign exchange accounts permitted	Yes.
Held domestically	Yes.
Held abroad	Yes.

Accounts in domestic currency convertible into foreign currency	Yes.

Nonresident Accounts

Foreign exchange accounts permitted	These accounts may be opened by banks and by trade, financial, and industrial companies incorporated outside the United Arab Emirates that have no local branches; by branches of local institutions in foreign countries; and by embassies and diplomatic agencies. Additionally, these accounts may be opened by U.A.E. citizens working abroad and by foreigners working in the United Arab Emirates who have no residency.
Domestic currency accounts	Yes.
Convertible into foreign currency	Yes.
Blocked accounts	No.

Imports and Import Payments

Foreign exchange budget	No.
Financing requirements for imports	No.
Documentation requirements for release of foreign exchange for imports	No.
Import licenses and other nontariff measures	Only licensed parties may enter the import trade. Importers may import only the commodities specified in their licenses.
Negative list	Imports of a few commodities are prohibited for health, security, or moral reasons.
Other nontariff measures	Imports from Israel are prohibited, as are imports of products manufactured by foreign companies blacklisted by the Arab League.
Import taxes and/or tariffs	Most imports are subject to a customs duty of 4% of the c.i.f. value. Imports of alcohol and tobacco are subject to higher rates. Imports originating from members of the GCC are exempt from duties.
State import monopoly	No.

Exports and Export Proceeds

Repatriation requirements	No.
Financing requirements	No.
Documentation requirements	No.
Export licenses	No.
Export taxes	No.

Payments for Invisible Transactions and Current Transfers

Controls on these transfers	No.

Proceeds from Invisible Transactions and Current Transfers

Repatriation requirements	No.

| **Restrictions on use of funds** | No. |

Capital Transactions

Controls on capital and money market instruments

On capital market securities

Shares or other securities of a participating nature

| Purchase locally by nonresidents | At least 51% of the shares of U.A.E. corporations must be held by U.A.E. nationals or organizations. |

| Sale or issue locally by nonresidents | Yes. |

Bonds or other debt securities

| Sale or issue locally by nonresidents | Yes. |

On collective investment securities

| *Purchase locally by nonresidents* | Yes. |

| *Sale or issue locally by nonresidents* | Yes. |

| **Controls on derivatives and other instruments** | No. |

| **Controls on credit operations** | No. |

Controls on direct investment

| Inward direct investment | At least 51% of the equity of companies, other than branches of foreign companies, must be held by nationals of the United Arab Emirates. Nationals of the other member countries of the GCC are permitted to hold (1) up to 75% of the equity of companies in the industrial, agricultural, fisheries, and construction sectors; and (2) up to 100% of the equity of companies in the hotel industry. Furthermore, nationals of the other member countries of the GCC are permitted to engage in wholesale and retail trade activities, except in the form of companies, in which case they are subject to the Company Law. |

| **Controls on liquidation of direct investment** | No. |

Controls on real estate transactions

| Purchase locally by nonresidents | Yes. |

| **Controls on personal capital movements** | No. |

| **Provisions specific to commercial banks and other credit institutions** | Commercial banks operating in the United Arab Emirates are prohibited from engaging in nonbanking operations. |

| Lending to nonresidents (financial or commercial credits) | Banks operating in the United Arab Emirates are required to maintain special deposits with the UAECB equal to 30% of their placements with, or loans to, nonresident banks in dirhams with a remaining life of one year or less. The profits of certain banks are subject to a fee levied by local authorities at an annual rate of 20%. |

Investment regulations

| *Abroad by banks* | Banks are not allowed to lend more than 7% of their capital base to one foreign institution. They are also not allowed to invest more than 25% of their own funds in shares or bonds issued by commercial companies. Loans to foreign governments with a first-class credit rating and placement in such countries' financial institutions are exempt from such limits. |

| *In banks by nonresidents* | Nonresidents cannot acquire more than 20% of the share capital of any national bank. |

Provisions specific to institutional investors	No.
Other controls imposed by securities laws	No.

Changes During 1999

Exchange arrangement
March 31. The exchange rate arrangement was reclassified to the conventional pegged arrangement category from the pegged exchange rates within horizontal bands category.

UNITED KINGDOM

(Position as of December 31, 1999)

Status Under IMF Articles of Agreement

Article VIII	Date of acceptance: February 15, 1961.

Exchange Arrangement

Currency	The currency of the United Kingdom is the pound sterling.
Other legal tender	Gold sovereigns and britannias are legal tender, but do not circulate.
Exchange rate structure	Unitary.
Classification	
Independently floating	The exchange rate of the pound sterling is determined on the basis of supply and demand. However, the authorities may intervene at their discretion to moderate undue fluctuations in the exchange rate.
Exchange tax	No.
Exchange subsidy	No.
Forward exchange market	Banks are allowed to engage in forward exchange transactions in any currency, and they may deal among themselves and with residents and nonresidents in foreign notes and coins at free market exchange rates.

Arrangements for Payments and Receipts

Prescription of currency requirements	No.
Payment arrangements	No.
Administration of control	No.
International security restrictions	
In accordance with Executive Board Decision No. 144-(52/51)	Yes.
In accordance with UN sanctions	The United Kingdom suspended financial sanctions against Libya on April 6, 1999. Restrictions against Iraq continue to be enforced. In the case of the Federal Republic of Yugoslavia (Serbia/Montenegro), funds are frozen. In addition, funds of the government of the former Yugoslav Republic of Macedonia and the Federal Republic of Yugoslavia (Serbia/Montenegro) are frozen on the basis of an EU regulation, and new investments in the Federal Republic of Yugoslavia (Serbia/Montenegro) are banned.
Payment arrears	No.
Controls on trade in gold (coins and/or bullion)	
Controls on domestic ownership and/or trade	Gold bullion and gold coins are not subject to controls. Gold coins have also been issued in Jersey and the Isle of Man and are legal tender there. Except under license granted by the Treasury, it is an offense to melt down or break up any metal coin that is for the time being current in the United Kingdom or that, having been current there, has at any time after May 16, 1969, ceased to be so. There is a gold market in London in which gold bars are freely traded.
Controls on external trade	The exportation of gold in manufactured form more than 50 years old and valued at £8,000 or more for each item, or matching set of items, also requires a license from the Department of National Heritage.

Controls on exports and imports of banknotes	No.

Resident Accounts

Foreign exchange accounts permitted	Yes.
Held domestically	Yes.
Held abroad	Yes.
Accounts in domestic currency convertible into foreign currency	Yes.

Nonresident Accounts

Foreign exchange accounts permitted	Yes.
Domestic currency accounts	Yes.
Convertible into foreign currency	Yes.
Blocked accounts	Yes.

Imports and Import Payments

Foreign exchange budget	No.
Financing requirements for imports	No.
Documentation requirements for release of foreign exchange for imports	No.
Import licenses and other nontariff measures	Imports of cereals and cereal products, beef and veal, mutton and lamb, poultry meat, and dairy products other than butter and cheese are subject to minimum import prices enforced through autonomously imposed variable import levies. Imports of many other agricultural, horticultural, and livestock products are subject to EU regulations.
Negative list	Yes.
Open general licenses	Most imports are admitted to the United Kingdom under an OGL.
Licenses with quotas	The remaining restrictions concern textiles and clothing under the MFA and are maintained under various EU bilateral agreements with third countries that are not members of the MFA; certain steel products from Russia and Ukraine that are subject to the EU bilateral agreements; autonomous EU-wide restrictions on imports of certain steel products from Kazakhstan; EU-wide tariff quotas on certain products produced in the Czech Republic and the Slovak Republic; and EU-wide quotas on three categories of goods originating in China. A double-checking system is in operation with Bulgaria, the Czech Republic, Romania, and the Slovak Republic on certain steel products. On April 1, 1999, this system was extended to certain steel products from Poland. Imports of cars from Japan are also subject to restraint under a separate agreement (the Elements of Consensus) between the EU and the Japanese government. A few articles may be imported under OGLs (i.e., without limit as to quantity or value).
Import taxes and/or tariffs	Yes.
State import monopoly	No.

Exports and Export Proceeds

Repatriation requirements	No.

Financing requirements	No.
Documentation requirements	No.
Export licenses	Exports of certain products are controlled for reasons of national security, animal welfare, national heritage, and in accordance with international agreements.
Without quotas	Yes.
Export taxes	No.

Payments for Invisible Transactions and Current Transfers

Controls on these transfers	No.

Proceeds from Invisible Transactions and Current Transfers

Repatriation requirements	No.
Restrictions on use of funds	No.

Capital Transactions

Controls on capital and money market instruments	No.
Controls on derivatives and other instruments	No.
Controls on credit operations	No.
Controls on direct investment	
Inward direct investment	The Secretary of State for Trade and Industry may prohibit a proposed transfer of control of an important U.K. manufacturing undertaking to a nonresident where the transfer is considered contrary to the interests of the United Kingdom or a substantial part of it. If it is considered that the national interest cannot appropriately be protected in any other way, property in such a proposal or completed transfer may be compulsorily acquired against compensation. Both prohibition and vesting orders are subject to parliamentary approval. These powers have not been used to date.
Controls on liquidation of direct investment	No.
Controls on real estate transactions	No.
Controls on personal capital movements	No.
Provisions specific to commercial banks and other credit institutions	
Open foreign exchange position limits	Net spot liabilities in foreign currencies (i.e., the net amount of foreign currency resources funding sterling assets) form part of a bank's eligible liabilities that are subject to a 0.15% non-interest-bearing deposit requirement with the Bank of England and may also be subject to calls for special deposits to be placed with the bank. Amounts between £100 million and £400 million are eligible for interest payment. This rule applies to banks as well as to building societies. There is currently no special deposit call.
Provisions specific to institutional investors	No.
Other controls imposed by securities laws	No.

Changes During 1999

Arrangements for payments and receipts

April 6. Sanctions against Libya were suspended.

Imports and import payments

April 1. The double-checking system for certain steel products was extended to include imports from Poland.

UNITED STATES

(Position as of December 31, 1999)

Status Under IMF Articles of Agreement

Article VIII Date of acceptance: December 10, 1946.

Exchange Arrangement

Currency	The currency of the United States is the dollar.
Exchange rate structure	Unitary.
Classification	
Independently floating	The exchange rate of the dollar is determined freely in the foreign exchange market.
Exchange tax	No.
Exchange subsidy	No.
Forward exchange market	Yes.

Arrangements for Payments and Receipts

Prescription of currency requirements	No.
Payment arrangements	
Regional arrangements	The United States is a member of NAFTA.
Administration of control	No.

International security restrictions

The Department of the Treasury (Treasury) administers economic sanction programs involving direct or indirect financial or commercial transactions with Cuba, the Islamic Republic of Iran, Iraq, the Democratic People's Republic of Korea, Libya, Sudan, the Federal Republic of Yugoslavia (Serbia/Montenegro), the Taliban (the Islamic State of Afghanistan, as of July 7, 1999), the UNITA movement in Angola and its senior officials, foreign terrorist organizations, and significant narcotics traffickers centered in Colombia, as specified under the following: (1) the Cuban Assets Control Regulations, (2) the Iranian Assets Control Regulations and the Iranian Transactions Regulations, (3) the Iraqi Sanctions Regulations, (4) the Foreign Assets Control Regulations, (5) the Libyan Sanctions Regulations, (6) the Sudanese Sanctions Regulations, (7) the Federal Republic of Yugoslavia (Serbia/Montenegro) Kosovo Sanctions Regulations, (8) the UNITA (Angola) Sanctions Regulations, (9) the Terrorism Sanctions Regulations, (10) the Foreign Terrorist Organizations Sanctions Regulations, (11) Executive Order No. 13129, and (12) the Narcotics Trafficking Sanctions Regulations, respectively.

The Treasury also has administrative responsibility for the blocked accounts of the above countries and groups of persons. Although most transactions with respect to the Republic of Montenegro are authorized, funds blocked prior to May 10, 1996, and December 27, 1995, remain blocked until released in accordance with applicable law and without prejudice to the claims of the successor states to the former Federal Republic of Yugoslavia. The Treasury also prohibits new investment in Myanmar, under the Burmese Sanctions Regulations; restricts certain offshore transactions involving strategic merchandise to certain countries, under the Transaction Control Regulations; prohibits donative transfers, or those that pose a risk of furthering terrorist acts in the United States by the government of Syria, under the Terrorism List Governments Sanctions Regulations; and, effective February 23, 1999, prohibits imports into the United States from certain entities that proliferate nuclear, biological, or chemical weapons, under the Weapons of Mass Destruction Trade Control Regulations.

In accordance with Executive Board Decision No. 144-(52/51)	Certain restrictions are imposed on the making of payments and transfers for current international transactions. Property and property interest of the government of Sudan have been blocked, and certain transactions with respect to the UNITA movement have been prohibited.
In accordance with UN sanctions	The Treasury administers economic sanction programs on the basis of UN decisions involving direct or indirect financial or commercial transactions with Iraq and with UNITA and its senior officials.
Payment arrears	No.
Controls on trade in gold (coins and/or bullion)	
Controls on external trade	No controls are imposed except for the countries and groups of persons to which international security restrictions apply.
Controls on exports and imports of banknotes	Individuals leaving or entering the United States with more than $10,000 in domestic or foreign currency, traveler's checks, money orders, or negotiable bearer securities must declare these to customs at the point of exit or entry.

Resident Accounts

Foreign exchange accounts permitted	Yes.
Held domestically	Yes.
Held abroad	Yes.
Accounts in domestic currency convertible into foreign currency	Yes.

Nonresident Accounts

Foreign exchange accounts permitted	Yes.
Domestic currency accounts	Yes.
Convertible into foreign currency	Yes.
Blocked accounts	Accounts blocked are those of Cuba, the Islamic Republic of Iran, Iraq, the Democratic People's Republic of Korea, Libya, Sudan, the Federal Republic of Yugoslavia (Serbia/ Montenegro), UNITA and its senior officials, Middle East terrorists, foreign terrorist organizations, certain foreign terrorist governments, and significant narcotics traffickers centered in Colombia; residual accounts are blocked under sanctions against the Federal Republic of Yugoslavia (Serbia/Montenegro) and the Bosnian Serbs.

Imports and Import Payments

Foreign exchange budget	No.
Financing requirements for imports	No.
Documentation requirements for release of foreign exchange for imports	No.
Import licenses and other nontariff measures	
Negative list	The importation of goods and services that originate in Cuba, the Islamic Republic of Iran, Iraq, the Democratic People's Republic of Korea, Libya, Sudan, and the Federal Republic of Yugoslavia (Serbia/Montenegro) or that were produced or provided by certain entities that proliferate nuclear, biological, or chemical weapons is prohibited unless specifically

authorized by the Treasury. The importation of certain goods from Angola is also prohibited unless specifically authorized by the Treasury.

Licenses with quotas	Bilateral import quota agreements on textiles and clothing exist with numerous countries. These are to be phased out over 10 years beginning in 1995 under the ATC, negotiated in the Uruguay Round of Multilateral Trade Negotiations.

The ATC provided for the gradual and complete integration of apparel and textile products into the WTO regime over a 10-year transition period, and the gradual phasing out of quantitative restrictions on textile and apparel exports to the United States. "Integrated products" have been removed from the scope of the ATC's special safeguard mechanism, and any applicable quotas have been eliminated. Integration is taking place in four stages: in 1995, 16% of the volume of textile and apparel trade was integrated; at the beginning of year 4 and year 7, an additional 17% and 18%, respectively, will be integrated; and after year 10, all remaining products will be integrated. With regard to the phasing out of quotas, the vast majority of quotas affecting imports to the United States will be subject to automatic "growth-on-growth" liberalization during each year of the transition period.

Import taxes and/or tariffs	Import tariffs are generally low, with higher-than-average rates for imports of beverages and tobacco, textiles and clothing, and leather and footwear. As a result of the Uruguay Round, all tariff lines are bound.
State import monopoly	No.

Exports and Export Proceeds

Repatriation requirements	No.
Financing requirements	No.
Documentation requirements	No.
Export licenses	The Department of Commerce (DOC) controls the export and reexport of dual-use commodities, technology, and software for reasons of national security, foreign policy, nonproliferation, and short supply. Except for shipment to U.S. territories and possessions, which are treated as part of the United States, most exports outside the United States are subject to the Export Administration Regulations. Several agencies of the U.S. government maintain export controls on items other than dual-use articles and services: the Treasury, which controls certain financial transactions, or the Department of Agriculture, which controls the export of livestock, dairy, and poultry items.
Without quotas	Ammunition may be exported only under license issued by the Office of Defense Trade Controls in the Department of State. The DOC administers controls directly on exports of crime control and detection equipment, as well as on instruments and related technical data, to all countries except other members of NATO, Australia, Japan, and New Zealand. The DOC administers controls directly on exports of other goods from the United States and on reexports of goods of U.S. origin from any area.
Export taxes	n.a.

Payments for Invisible Transactions and Current Transfers

Controls on these transfers	No.

Proceeds from Invisible Transactions and Current Transfers

Repatriation requirements	No.
Restrictions on use of funds	No.

Capital Transactions

Controls on capital and money market instruments

On capital market securities

Shares or other securities of a participating nature

    Purchase locally by nonresidents

Laws on inward direct investment apply to purchases in the United States by nonresidents. The control applies only to the purchases by nonresidents of securities that may be restricted by laws on inward direct investment and on establishment in the nuclear energy, maritime, communications, and air transport industries.

    Sale or issue locally by nonresidents

Foreign mutual funds are restricted. This restriction applies only to (1) nonresident issuers that are defined as investment companies under the Investment Company Act and (2) the use of small business registration forms and a small-issues exemption by nonresident issuers.

On money market instruments

Sale or issue locally by nonresidents

Foreign mutual funds are restricted. The control applies only to nonresident issuers that are defined as investment companies under the Investment Company Act.

On collective investment securities

Sale or issue locally by nonresidents

The same regulations apply as for shares and other securities of a participating nature.

Controls on derivatives and other instruments

No.

Controls on credit operations

Financial credits

By residents to nonresidents

The Johnson Act prohibits, with certain exceptions, persons within the United States from dealing in financial obligations or extending loans to foreign governments that have defaulted on payments of their obligations to the U.S. government. The Act does not apply to those foreign governments that are members of both the IMF and the World Bank.

Controls on direct investment

Outward direct investment

There are controls on certain transactions with or involving Cuba, the Islamic Republic of Iran, Iraq, the Democratic People's Republic of Korea, Libya, Myanmar, Sudan, the Federal Republic of Yugoslavia (Serbia/Montenegro), the UNITA movement and its senior officials, foreign terrorists who disrupt the Middle East peace process, foreign terrorist organizations, certain foreign terrorist governments, and significant narcotics traffickers centered in Colombia.

Foreign acquisitions of control that threaten to impair national security may be suspended or prohibited. Investments involving ownership interest in banks are subject to federal and state banking laws and regulations.

Inward direct investment

Laws on inward direct investment apply to purchases in the United States by nonresidents. This control applies only to investments that may be restricted by laws on inward direct investment and establishment in the nuclear energy, maritime, communications, and air transport industries. Foreign acquisitions of control that threaten to impair national security may be suspended or prohibited. Investments involving ownership interest in banks are subject to federal and state banking laws and regulations. However, as noted above, there are controls on certain transactions with or involving Cuba, Iraq, the Democratic People's Republic of Korea, Libya, foreign terrorists who disrupt the Middle East peace process, Terrorism List governments, foreign terrorist organizations, Sudan, Syria, significant narcotics traffickers centered in Colombia, and certain foreign terrorist governments. The Omnibus Trade Act contains a provision, the Exon-Florio Amendment, authorizing the president to suspend or prohibit foreign acquisitions, mergers, and takeovers in the United States if he determines that the foreign investor might take action that would threaten to impair national security and if existing laws, other than the International Emergency

Economic Powers Act and the Exon-Florio Amendment itself, are not, in the president's judgment, adequate or appropriate to protect national security.

Controls on liquidation of direct investment	No.
Controls on real estate transactions	
Purchase locally by nonresidents	Ownership of agricultural land by foreign nationals or by corporations, in which foreign owners have an interest of at least 10% or substantial control, must be reported to the Department of Agriculture. Certain states in the United States impose various controls on foreign nationals' purchases of land within their borders.
Controls on personal capital movements	No.
Provisions specific to commercial banks and other credit institutions	
Investment regulations	Banks are subject to prudential oversight in these areas.
Open foreign exchange position limits	The foreign currency positions of banks, whether overall or with respect to individual currencies, are not subject to quantitative limitations, but banks are subject to prudential oversight.
Provisions specific to institutional investors	No.
Other controls imposed by securities laws	No.

Changes During 1999

Arrangements for payments and receipts	*February 23.* A sanctions program restricting imports from certain entities that proliferate nuclear, biological, or chemical weapons was put into place.
	July 7. A sanctions program blocking property and property interests of the Taliban (the Islamic State of Afghanistan) and its agents and controlled entities and prohibiting certain other transactions with the Taliban or within the territory of Afghanistan controlled by the Taliban came into effect.

URUGUAY

(Position as of December 31, 1999)

Status Under IMF Articles of Agreement

Article VIII	Date of acceptance: May 2, 1980.

Exchange Arrangement

Currency	The currency of Uruguay is the Uruguayan peso.
Exchange rate structure	Unitary.
Classification	
Crawling band	The exchange rate for the Uruguayan peso is determined in the exchange market, where the Central Bank of Uruguay (CBU) intervenes to ensure that the rate remains within a band. The exchange rate band is depreciated daily at a predetermined monthly rate, and the CBU announces its intervention buying and selling rates daily.
	The rate of depreciation against the dollar is 0.6% per month and the total width of the band is 3%.
Exchange tax	Purchases of foreign exchange by public sector institutions are subject to a tax of 2%, with the exception of those by the CBU and official banks, which are exempt from the tax.
Exchange subsidy	No.
Forward exchange market	No.

Arrangements for Payments and Receipts

Prescription of currency requirements	All settlements of balances under the multilateral clearing system are made in dollars.
Payment arrangements	
Bilateral payment arrangements	
Operative	There is an arrangement with the Islamic Republic of Iran in effect through July 31, 2000.
Inoperative	A bilateral payment arrangement with Cuba is inoperative.
Regional arrangements	Payments between Uruguay and the other LAIA countries may be made through accounts maintained with each other by the central banks within the framework of the multilateral clearing system of the LAIA.
Clearing agreements	Yes.
Administration of control	Operations are carried out through authorized banks, finance houses, exchange houses, and the Bank of the Republic. Exchange houses must be authorized by the CBU.
International security restrictions	No.
Payment arrears	No.
Controls on trade in gold (coins and/or bullion)	
Controls on domestic ownership and/or trade	Residents and nonresidents may freely purchase, hold, and sell financial gold with a fineness of not less than 0.9.
Controls on external trade	Residents may freely import and export gold with a fineness of not less than 0.9. Gold for industrial purposes is subject to the general policy that governs the exportation, importation, and trading of goods.

Controls on exports and imports of banknotes	No.

Resident Accounts

Foreign exchange accounts permitted	Yes.
Held domestically	Yes.
Held abroad	Yes.
Accounts in domestic currency convertible into foreign currency	Yes.

Nonresident Accounts

Foreign exchange accounts permitted	Yes.
Domestic currency accounts	Yes.
Convertible into foreign currency	Yes.
Blocked accounts	No.

Imports and Import Payments

Foreign exchange budget	No.
Financing requirements for imports	No.
Documentation requirements for release of foreign exchange for imports	No.
Import licenses and other nontariff measures	
Negative list	Imports of used cars are prohibited.
Open general licenses	All imports are subject to registration that is generally valid for 180 days; goods must be cleared through customs during that period.
Import taxes and/or tariffs	Under MERCOSUR, a CET exists among Argentina, Brazil, Paraguay, and Uruguay. There are 11 tax rates. Initially, the maximum rate was 20%. However, a surcharge, imposed in 1997, and whose removal is planned in 2001, raised this maximum to 23%. Uruguay was granted exemption to the surcharge for capital and certain intermediate goods. Regionally produced capital and telecommunications goods are subject to tariffs of 14% and 16%, respectively. Parties to MERCOSUR are permitted to exempt up to 300 goods from the CET until 2001, at which time they are to converge to the CET. In addition, for Uruguay, tariffs on capital goods, telecommunications, buses, and trucks will not converge until 2006.
	Import duties among MERCOSUR countries were generally eliminated, with certain exceptions. In Uruguay's case, exemptions on pharmaceuticals, plastics, automobile parts, textiles, and dairy products remained in place through 1999. Duties on wheat, tires, paper, glass, sugar, textiles, and apparel are computed on the basis of "minimum export prices," which provide a basis for a sliding surcharge on these goods, depending on the difference between the minimum prices and declared c.i.f. import prices.
State import monopoly	No.

Exports and Export Proceeds

Repatriation requirements	No.
Financing requirements	No.
Documentation requirements	No.
Export licenses	
Without quotas	Occasionally, and for special reasons (e.g., stock position, protection, or sanitary considerations), certain exports are prohibited or are subject to special requirements.
Export taxes	Exports of dry, salted, and pickled hides are subject to a 5% tax.

Payments for Invisible Transactions and Current Transfers

Controls on these transfers	No.

Proceeds from Invisible Transactions and Current Transfers

Repatriation requirements	No.
Restrictions on use of funds	No.

Capital Transactions

Controls on capital and money market instruments	The Capital Market Securities and Negotiable Obligations Law provides a framework in which financial markets are largely self-regulating but supervised by the CBU. Mutual and private pension funds as well as insurance companies are regulated separately. Although private pension funds must hold an implicit legal minimum ratio of 55% in the form of government securities, the transitory maintenance of time deposits with the CBU is permitted without limitations. In the public sector, the type of operations permitted depends on the type of institution. Government agencies are covered by their own bylaws, and the central government and departmental governments are covered by their own procedures, which are more restrictive.
On collective investment securities	The Mutual Funds Law defines instruments and contains several requirements regarding conflict of interest and safekeeping.
Controls on derivatives and other instruments	n.r.
Controls on credit operations	No.
Controls on direct investment	
Inward direct investment	The Law for the Promotion and Protection of Investment requires identical treatment of domestic and foreign investors and free transfer of capital. It provides for certain exemptions from wealth and value-added taxes and for the reduction of social security taxes to a 3% rate. It establishes national priorities and provides corresponding incentives. It exempts from tariffs imported inputs whose domestic production has been reduced or discontinued.
Controls on liquidation of direct investment	No.
Controls on real estate transactions	No.
Controls on personal capital movements	n.a.

Provisions specific to commercial banks and other credit institutions

Differential treatment of deposit accounts in foreign exchange

Reserve requirements

There is a minimum mandatory reserve requirement (10%) for local currency and another for foreign currency, except for 30- to 180-day deposits, on which the local currency reserve requirement is 4% and the foreign currency reserve requirement is 10%. These reserve requirements are for currency holdings and notes, and demand deposits at the CBU in their respective currencies. Nonresident deposits placed with nonresidents are exempt from the foreign currency reserve requirement. Also, when establishing such reserves, the deposit at the CBU should be in an amount of not less than 50% of the minimum mandatory reserve requirement. There is a minimum interest-bearing mandatory reserve requirement of 10% in local currency on total deposits and other obligations covered by the non-interest-bearing reserve requirement regime. This reserve requirement may be established by a deposit at the CBU. There was also an 11.5% mandatory holding in dollar-denominated treasury notes on foreign currency deposits and liabilities under the reserve requirement regime, excluding those of nonresidents applying to placements with nonresidents. Effective December 1, 1999, this requirement was replaced with an interest-bearing reserve requirement of 11.5% in foreign currency on total deposits and other obligations covered by the non-interest-bearing requirement regime, and it may be established by holding dollar-denominated cetificates of deposit issued by the CBU.

Open foreign exchange position limits

A ceiling on the asset position of foreign or local currency of 150% of the book value equity less administrative fixed assets (i.e., fixed assets, investments, and deferred charges) was established. There is also a ceiling on the asset or liability position of foreign currency–denominated "operations to be settled" (i.e., future contracts and sales of securities subject to repurchase agreements) of 20% of the book value equity less administrative fixed assets.

Provisions specific to institutional investors

Limits (max.) on portfolio invested abroad

Insurance companies must hold a maximum of 5% of total assets, except for life insurance contracts, where companies can hold 20% of required provisions. Private pension funds are permitted to invest only in domestic issuer securities, including those issued abroad. These funds must deal in domestic formal markets according to CBU regulations.

Limits (min.) on portfolio invested locally

Private pension funds must hold a minimum ratio of total assets of 55% in the form of government securities. In the public sector, the type of operations permitted depends on the type of institution. Government agencies are covered by their own bylaws, and the central government and departmental governments are covered by their own procedures, which are more restrictive.

Currency-matching regulations on assets/liabilities composition

Insurance companies must match assets with liabilities.

Other controls imposed by securities laws

No.

Changes During 1999

Capital transactions

Provisions specific to commercial banks and other credit institutions

December 1. A minimum interest-bearing mandatory reserve requirement of 11.5% in foreign currency on total deposits and other obligations covered by the non-interest-bearing requirement replaced the mandatory holding in dollar-denominated treasury notes requirement.

UZBEKISTAN

(Position as of June 30, 2000)

Status Under IMF Articles of Agreement

Article XIV	Yes.

Exchange Arrangement

Currency	The currency of Uzbekistan is the Uzbek sum.
Exchange rate structure	
Unitary	There were three exchange rates: (1) the official exchange rate, (2) the exchange rate prevailing on the Uzbek Republican Currency Exchange, and (3) the over-the-counter exchange rate. Effective May 1, 2000, the multiple exchange rate system was unified. Purchases and sales of foreign exchange are effected at the exchange rate established on the basis of supply and demand conditions on the domestic foreign exchange market.
Classification	
Managed floating with no pre-announced path for the exchange rate	The official rate is fixed by the Central Bank of Uzbekistan (CBU) on a weekly basis, taking into account current rates in the exchange and over-the-counter currency markets. Exchange rates for currencies that are not traded are determined from cross rates in the international market.
Exchange tax	Effective January 15, 1999, Uzbekistan introduced a 5% tax on purchases of foreign exchange. The following purchases of foreign exchange are exempt from this tax: those effected from budgetary resources, those used for repayment of principal and interest on credits in foreign currency guaranteed by the government, and those authorized by banks for subsequent sale on the domestic foreign exchange market.
Exchange subsidy	No.
Forward exchange market	No.

Arrangements for Payments and Receipts

Prescription of currency requirements	Settlements with countries with which Uzbekistan maintains bilateral payment agreements are effected in accordance with the terms of the agreements. Transactions with other countries are settled in convertible currencies.
Payment arrangements	
Bilateral payment arrangements	
Operative	Uzbekistan maintains agreements with Russia and Ukraine.
Inoperative	Agreements with Belarus, Indonesia, the Islamic Republic of Iran, Kazakhstan, Latvia, Malaysia, and Moldova are inoperative.
Regional arrangements	Yes.
Clearing agreements	These are effected on the basis of intergovernmental agreements.
Administration of control	Transactions in foreign currency are administered by the CBU and authorized banks. The primary responsibilities of the Ministry of Foreign Economic Relations (MFER) are to regulate foreign economic activities and to represent Uzbekistan in foreign economic interests; to attract foreign investments and provide for their effective use; to develop foreign economic relations; and to certify imports and exports. The MFER implements external trade policy through the issuance of licenses and quotas. The Ministry of Justice registers enterprises with foreign investments.
International security restrictions	No.

Payment arrears

Private   Yes.

Controls on trade in gold (coins and/or bullion)

Controls on domestic ownership and/or   Yes.
trade

Controls on external trade   Gold is imported and exported on the basis of licenses issued by the MFER.

Controls on exports and imports of banknotes

On exports

   Domestic currency   n.r.

   Foreign currency   Foreign exchange not exceeding the equivalent of $1,500 may be exported without restriction. The export of amounts in excess of this requires confirmation that the foreign exchange was held in an account at an authorized bank that has a general license to operate in foreign exchange.

On imports

   Domestic currency   n.r.

   Foreign currency   Individuals may import up to $10,000 in banknotes without restriction. Imports of foreign banknotes above that amount are subject to a customs charge of 1% of the amount in excess of $10,000.

Resident Accounts

Foreign exchange accounts permitted   Following the simplification of procedures for the opening of foreign exchange accounts for small- and medium-size businesses on March 4, 2000, all enterprises, regardless of ownership, were allowed to open accounts in domestic and foreign currencies at various banks, beginning June 1, 2000.

Individuals are permitted to open bearer foreign exchange accounts.

Held domestically   Yes.

Held abroad   The CBU may approve the opening of accounts abroad by individuals and legal entities that are residents of the Republic of Uzbekistan. CBU approval is not required for accounts opened by resident individuals during temporary stays abroad.

Accounts in domestic currency convertible into foreign currency   Importers must present a preregistered contract before they may purchase foreign exchange.

Nonresident Accounts

Foreign exchange accounts permitted   The opening, with prior CBU approval, of bearer foreign exchange accounts is allowed.

Domestic currency accounts   Yes.

Convertible into foreign currency   Yes.

Approval required   Importers must present a preregistered contract before they may purchase foreign exchange.

Blocked accounts   De facto local currency accounts of importers may be blocked (with the consent of the latter) by banks while awaiting conversion.

Imports and Import Payments

Foreign exchange budget	No.
Financing requirements for imports	No.
Documentation requirements for release of foreign exchange for imports	
Preshipment inspection	Preshipment inspection is performed at the importers' request as an alternative to ex ante registration of import contracts.
Letters of credit	Yes.
Import licenses used as exchange licenses	All imports are subject to prior contract registration except imports from the importers' own source of foreign exchange.
Other	Yes.
Import licenses and other nontariff measures	Imports of medicines require import licenses from the Ministry of Health; imports of weapons, precious metals, uranium, and other radioactive substances require import licenses from the MFER; imports of foreign movies and videos require import licenses from the Ministry of Cultural Affairs.
Negative list	The importation of publications, manuscripts, video and audio equipment, and photographs aimed at undermining state and social order are prohibited.
Licenses with quotas	Yes.
Other nontariff measures	Tenders are held for imports of major food items (e.g., sugar and wheat).
Import taxes and/or tariffs	The average tariff rate is 29%; the rate on most consumer goods is 30%. The minimum import duty is 3%. In addition, excise taxes ranging from 20% to 35% apply to 20 groups of imported consumer goods. A 20% charge is applied to imports of goods bought in duty-free shops in excess of $1,000. Goods shipped in by shuttle traders are subject to a charge of 50% of the value in excess of $1,000. The rate for goods sent to individuals is 50% without application of limits established for duty-free imports.
Taxes collected through the exchange system	There is a 5% tax on the purchase of foreign exchange to effect imports, except in the case of the acquisition of foreign exchange using budget resources.
State import monopoly	No.

Exports and Export Proceeds

Repatriation requirements	Yes.
Surrender requirements	Effective January 1, 1999, proceeds in foreign currencies from nontraditional exports of goods and services are subject to a 50% surrender requirement to authorized banks at the over-the-counter bid rate.
	Proceeds in foreign currencies from centralized exports, including gold, are subject to a 100% surrender requirement to the CBU at the over-the-counter foreign exchange market purchase rate.
Financing requirements	Goods may be exported provided that a prepayment has been made, an LC has been opened, or a foreign bank guarantee has been obtained.
Documentation requirements	
Letters of credit	Yes.
Guarantees	Yes.
Export licenses	Exports of weapons, precious metals, uranium, and other radioactive substances require licenses from the MFER; exports of research data require licenses from the State Committee on Science and Technology; and exports of works of art require licenses from the Ministry of Cultural Affairs.

| With quotas | Exportation of crude oil, gas condensate, lint and cotton fiber, and ferrous metals is subject to export licensing in the amount of established quotas. Exports of sugar, alcohol, vegetable oil, wheat and flour products, meat and poultry, tea, raw hides and skins, dried milk, and antiques are prohibited. |

Export taxes

| Other export taxes | Enterprises producing and exporting goods to CIS countries in freely convertible currencies are exempt from VAT and excises. Excise taxes apply to exports of certain types of goods. An excise tax is applicable to alcoholic and nonalcoholic beverages, construction materials, and cigarettes exported by trading companies. |

Payments for Invisible Transactions and Current Transfers

Controls on these transfers

Trade-related payments

   Indicative limits/bona fide test   Yes.

Investment-related payments

   Indicative limits/bona fide test   Yes.

Payments for travel

   Indicative limits/bona fide test   Yes.

Personal payments

   Indicative limits/bona fide test   Yes.

Foreign workers' wages   n.r.

Credit card use abroad

   Indicative limits/bona fide test   Yes.

Other payments

   Indicative limits/bona fide test   Yes.

Proceeds from Invisible Transactions and Current Transfers

Repatriation requirements	Yes.
Surrender requirements	Surrender requirements also apply to proceeds from exports of services.
Restrictions on use of funds	No.

Capital Transactions

Controls on capital and money market instruments

On capital market securities

  Shares or other securities of a participating nature

    Purchase locally by nonresidents   Yes.

    Sale or issue locally by nonresidents   Yes.

    Purchase abroad by residents   Yes.

    Sale or issue abroad by residents   Yes.

Bonds or other debt securities	n.r.
On money market instruments	n.r.
On collective investment securities	
Purchase locally by nonresidents	Yes.
Sale or issue locally by nonresidents	Yes.
Purchase abroad by residents	Yes.
Sale or issue abroad by residents	Yes.
Controls on derivatives and other instruments	n.r.
Controls on credit operations	All credit operations are subject to controls.
Controls on direct investment	
Outward direct investment	Enterprises established abroad with the participation of Uzbek investors must be registered with the MFER.
Inward direct investment	Enterprises may establish joint ventures as foreign direct investment upon registration with the Ministry of Justice. Foreign equity capital participation is allowed up to 100%. A foreign participation of at least 30% is required for access to fiscal incentives.
Controls on liquidation of direct investment	Yes.
Controls on real estate transactions	
Purchase locally by nonresidents	Yes.
Sale locally by nonresidents	Yes.
Controls on personal capital movements	
Loans	n.r.
Gifts, endowments, inheritances, and legacies	n.r.
Settlement of debts abroad by immigrants	n.r.
Transfer of assets	
Transfer abroad by emigrants	Yes.
Transfer into the country by immigrants	Yes.
Provisions specific to commercial banks and other credit institutions	
Borrowing abroad	Yes.
Maintenance of accounts abroad	Yes.
Lending to nonresidents (financial or commercial credits)	Yes.
Lending locally in foreign exchange	Banks are allowed to make loans in foreign currencies, subject to the limit on the foreign currency open position.
Differential treatment of deposit accounts in foreign exchange	
Reserve requirements	Yes.
Liquid asset requirements	Yes.

Differential treatment of deposit accounts held by nonresidents	n.r.
Investment regulations	
Abroad by banks	Yes.
In banks by nonresidents	Yes.
Open foreign exchange position limits	
On resident assets and liabilities	Yes.
On nonresident assets and liabilities	Yes.
Provisions specific to institutional investors	n.r.
Other controls imposed by securities laws	No.

Changes During 1999

Exchange arrangement — *January 15.* A 5% tax on purchases of foreign exchange was imposed.

Exports and export proceeds — *January 1.* A surrender requirement of 50% on proceeds from decentralized exports to authorized banks was established for all enterprises, regardless of form of ownership.

Changes During 2000

Exchange arrangement — *May 1.* The multiple exchange rate system was unified.

Resident accounts — *March 4.* The procedures for opening foreign exchange accounts were simplified for small- and medium-size businesses.

June 1. All enterprises, regardless of ownership, were allowed to open accounts in domestic and foreign currencies at various banks.

VANUATU

(Position as of January 31, 2000)

Status Under IMF Articles of Agreement

Article VIII	Date of acceptance: December 11, 1982.

Exchange Arrangement

Currency	The currency of Vanuatu is the Vanuatu vatu.
Exchange rate structure	Unitary.
Classification	
Conventional pegged arrangement	The external value of the vatu is determined on the basis of an undisclosed transactions-weighted (trade and tourism receipts) basket of currencies of Vanuatu's major trading partners. The Reserve Bank of Vanuatu (RBV) buys from and sells to commercial banks U.S. dollars only. However, it also deals in Australian dollars, New Zealand dollars, euros, pounds sterling, and Japanese yen with other customers. The RBV quotes rates daily for the vatu against the above currencies. Buying and selling rates of the vatu against the currencies in the basket are quoted once a day within margins ranging between 0.25% and 0.30% around the middle rate.
Exchange tax	n.r.
Exchange subsidy	n.r.
Forward exchange market	Commercial banks provide forward exchange rate cover facilities.

Arrangements for Payments and Receipts

Prescription of currency requirements	n.r.
Payment arrangements	n.r.
Administration of control	n.r.
International security restrictions	No.
Payment arrears	No.
Controls on trade in gold (coins and/or bullion)	n.r.
Controls on exports and imports of banknotes	n.r.

Resident Accounts

Foreign exchange accounts permitted	Yes.
Held domestically	Yes.
Held abroad	Yes.
Accounts in domestic currency convertible into foreign currency	Yes.

Nonresident Accounts

Foreign exchange accounts permitted	Yes.
Domestic currency accounts	Yes.
Convertible into foreign currency	The decision to approve the convertibility of domestic currency accounts into foreign currency is left to commercial banks.
Blocked accounts	n.r.

Imports and Import Payments

Foreign exchange budget	No.
Financing requirements for imports	No.
Documentation requirements for release of foreign exchange for imports	No.
Import licenses and other nontariff measures	The importation of frozen chicken pieces, T-shirts bearing a Vanuatu motif, firearms and ammunition, animals and plants, and transistor and telephone equipment is restricted through import-licensing arrangements. A similar restriction is applied to the importation of rice, sugar, flour, canned fish, and tobacco products.
Positive list	Yes.
Import taxes and/or tariffs	Import duties have a structure of eight rates ranging from zero to 30%. Most basic items are now duty free, and the rate of protected goods is 30%.
	Effective January 1, 2000, duties on certain imported commodities under the protected goods category were reduced to 50% from 55%. Additionally, the VT 385 duty per liter of fuel was reduced to VT 350.
State import monopoly	No.

Exports and Export Proceeds

Repatriation requirements	n.r.
Financing requirements	n.r.
Documentation requirements	n.r.
Export licenses	The exportation of logs and flitches has been banned for environmental reasons. Under special circumstances, small parcels of logs may be exported if they cannot be processed by any company in Vanuatu. Any proposal to export logs requires approval of the Council of Ministers. Export permits issued by the Environmental Unit and Forestry Department are also required for sandalwood and rare or endangered species.
Without quotas	For conservation purposes, exports of certain products, such as trochus, green snails, bêches-de-mer, mother-of-pearl, aquarium fish, and crustaceans, as well as coconut crops, are subject to authorization. Exports of copra and cocoa are channeled through the Vanuatu Commodities Marketing Board (VCMB). Effective April 4, 1999, exports of kava may be undertaken by individuals subject to authorization from the Quarantine Office. Artifacts having a special value, either as a result of ceremonial use or because they are more than 10 years old, are subject to authorization from the Cultural Center.
Export taxes	There are taxes on exports of logs, unworked shells, and wood in the rough, whether or not stripped of bark or sapwood, or roughly squared.

Payments for Invisible Transactions and Current Transfers

Controls on these transfers	n.r.

Proceeds from Invisible Transactions and Current Transfers

Repatriation requirements	n.r.
Surrender requirements	n.r.
Restrictions on use of funds	n.r.

Capital Transactions

Controls on capital and money market instruments	n.r.
Controls on derivatives and other instruments	n.r.
Controls on credit operations	n.r.
Controls on direct investment	n.r.
Controls on liquidation of direct investment	n.r.
Controls on real estate transactions	n.r.
Controls on personal capital movements	n.r.
Provisions specific to commercial banks and other credit institutions	n.r.
Provisions specific to institutional investors	n.r.
Other controls imposed by securities laws	n.r.

Changes During 1999

Exports and export proceeds	*April 1.* The restrictions on kava exports were eliminated.

Changes During 2000

Imports and import payments	*January 1.* Duties on certain imported commodities were reduced to 50% from 55%. The VT 385 duty per liter of fuel was reduced to VT 350.

(Position as of December 31, 1999)

Status Under IMF Articles of Agreement

Article VIII	Date of acceptance: July 1, 1976.

Exchange Arrangement

Currency	The currency of República Bolivariana de Venezuela is the Venezuelan bolívar.
Other legal tender	Venezuelan gold coins are legal tender, but they do not circulate.
Exchange rate structure	Unitary.
Classification	
Crawling band	The exchange rate is determined by supply and demand, but the Central Bank of República Bolivariana de Venezuela (CBV) intervenes in the market. The CBV determines the reference exchange rate daily. The level and monthly adjustments of the central rate are Bs 508.50 per $1 and Bs 7 per $1, respectively. The exchange rate band is ±7.5% around the central rate.
Exchange tax	No.
Exchange subsidy	No.
Forward exchange market	Futures on the bolívar-dollar exchange rate were established in 1997. However, the Venezuelan Chamber of Options and Futures Compensations suspended its operations on November 13, 1998, because of low liquidity of the settled contracts and financial losses.

Arrangements for Payments and Receipts

Prescription of currency requirements	No.
Payment arrangements	
Regional arrangements	Payments between República Bolivariana de Venezuela and the other LAIA countries, Jamaica, and Malaysia may be settled through the accounts maintained with each other at the CBV.
Clearing agreements	Yes.
Administration of control	No.
International security restrictions	No.
Payment arrears	
Official	Arrears are maintained on interest payments related to external public debt that is under litigation.
Private	Yes.
Controls on trade in gold (coins and/or bullion)	
Controls on external trade	The exportation of nonmonetary gold (other than jewelry for personal use) and gold coins is subject to prior authorization from the CBV.
Controls on exports and imports of banknotes	Imports and exports of banknotes are subject to prior authorization from the CBV.
On exports	
Domestic currency	Yes.

Foreign currency	Yes.
On imports	
Domestic currency	Yes.
Foreign currency	Yes.

Resident Accounts

Foreign exchange accounts permitted	Yes.
Held domestically	Yes.
Held abroad	Yes.
Accounts in domestic currency convertible into foreign currency	No.

Nonresident Accounts

Foreign exchange accounts permitted	Yes.
Domestic currency accounts	Yes.
Convertible into foreign currency	No.
Blocked accounts	These apply only in cases of inheritance, preventive judicial measures, and narcotics traffic activities.

Imports and Import Payments

Foreign exchange budget	No.
Financing requirements for imports	No.
Documentation requirements for release of foreign exchange for imports	No.
Import licenses and other nontariff measures	Some imports are subject to licensing for environmental, health, or security reasons. There are minimum prices for certain imports.
Positive list	Imports of military arms must be authorized by the Defense Ministry. Imports of nonmilitary weapons must be authorized by the Ministry of Domestic Affairs and Justice.
Negative list	Importation of used motor vehicles is prohibited, except for hearses, prison vans, and ambulances.
Licenses with quotas	A small number of agricultural products are subject to tariff quotas.
Import taxes and/or tariffs	There are four basic ad valorem tariff rates on manufactured goods (5%, 10%, 15%, and 20%), except for motor vehicles, which are subject to a special regime under the Andean Community. The MEIV (Tariffs on Imported Components for Vehicles) on motor vehicles is 35% for passenger cars; 15% for cargo and commercial vehicles, except for vehicles under 4,500 kg, such as pickup trucks, for which the rate is 35%; and 3% for vehicle components. The industrial free zone of Paraguana and the free port of Margarita Island enjoy a special customs regime that includes exemptions from customs tariffs. Duty-free access is granted to imports from Argentina, Bolivia, Brazil, Chile, Colombia, Costa Rica, Ecuador, El Salvador, Guatemala, Honduras, Mexico, Paraguay, Peru, Uruguay, and CARICOM countries under trade agreements. There is a temporary surcharge of 15% over import duties on about 800 products and a customs handling fee of 2%.
State import monopoly	No.

Exports and Export Proceeds

Repatriation requirements	No.
Surrender requirements	The state petroleum company is required to surrender its export proceeds to the CBV.
Financing requirements	No.
Documentation requirements	No.
Export licenses	No.
Export taxes	There is an export tax on hydrocarbons.

Payments for Invisible Transactions and Current Transfers

Controls on these transfers	No.

Proceeds from Invisible Transactions and Current Transfers

Repatriation requirements	No.
Restrictions on use of funds	No.

Capital Transactions

Controls on capital and money market instruments	
On capital market securities	
Shares or other securities of a participating nature	
Purchase locally by nonresidents	Foreign investors are allowed to purchase corporate stocks in the Caracas Stock Exchange but must inform the Superintendency of Foreign Investment (SIEX) of such purchases at the end of each calendar year.
Sale or issue locally by nonresidents	Authorization from the CBV is required.
Sale or issue abroad by residents	Authorization from the CBV is required.
Bonds or other debt securities	
Sale or issue locally by nonresidents	Authorization from the CBV is required.
Sale or issue abroad by residents	Authorization from the CBV is required.
On collective investment securities	
Sale or issue locally by nonresidents	Authorization by the CBV is required.
Controls on derivatives and other instruments	There are some regulations for market participants.
Controls on credit operations	No.
Controls on direct investment	
Inward direct investment	Mass media, communications, newspapers in Spanish, and security services are reserved for national ownership. New investments do not require prior authorization from the SIEX but must be registered with the SIEX after the fact, and approval is automatically granted if the new investment is consistent with national legislation. Foreign enterprises may establish subsidiaries in República Bolivariana de Venezuela without prior authorization as long as they are consistent with the commercial code. The SIEX must, however, be notified within

60 working days about newly established subsidiaries. Investment in the petroleum and iron sectors is subject to specific regulations.

Controls on liquidation of direct investment

Owners of direct investment have the right to reexport the proceeds of liquidation while SIEX checks the performance of the commitments of foreign investors in accordance with national legislation.

Controls on real estate transactions

No.

Controls on personal capital movements

Transfer of assets

Banks must report to the Superintendancy of Banks on a monthly basis any transfer above $10,000, or its equivalent, to or from another country.

Provisions specific to commercial banks and other credit institutions

Purchase of locally issued securities denominated in foreign exchange

There are limits regulated by the CBV in relation to foreign exchange position limits.

Differential treatment of deposit accounts in foreign exchange

Reserve requirements

Reserve requirements of 17% apply to deposits, obligations, and debit operations.

Differential treatment of deposit accounts held by nonresidents

Reserve requirements

Reserve requirements of 17% apply to deposits, obligations, and debit operations.

Investment regulations

Commercial banks are not allowed to invest in stocks in excess of 20% of paid-in capital.

Abroad by banks

Yes.

In banks by nonresidents

Yes.

Open foreign exchange position limits

On resident assets and liabilities

Yes.

On nonresident assets and liabilities

Yes.

Provisions specific to institutional investors

No.

Other controls imposed by securities laws

No.

Changes During 1999

No significant changes occurred in the exchange and trade system.

VIETNAM

(Position as of December 31, 1999)

Status Under IMF Articles of Agreement

Article XIV	Yes.

Exchange Arrangement

Currency
The currency of Vietnam is the Vietnamese dong.

Exchange rate structure
Unitary.

Classification

Pegged exchange rate within horizontal bands
Until February 24, 1999, trading in the interbank market had to take place at exchange rates within ranges stipulated daily by the State Bank of Vietnam (SBV). Only the SBV; state-owned banks, such as the Bank of Investment and Development; joint-stock banks; joint-venture banks; and branches of foreign banks could participate in the interbank market.

Effective February 25, 1999, the SBV quotes as interbank market rate the daily average exchange rate in the interbank market during the previous business day. Participating banks may not quote rates representing more than a 0.1% depreciation of the previous business day's official rate.

Exchange tax
No.

Exchange subsidy
No.

Forward exchange market
The SBV permits commercial banks and some economic entities to enter into forward and swap transactions with maturities of one to six months. The rate is set daily by the commercial banks within ranges, i.e., the percentage depreciation of the previous day's average spot exchange rates in the interbank market. The SBV does not enter into forward or swap transactions with commercial banks. Economic entities are allowed to enter into forward and swap transactions with commercial banks.

Arrangements for Payments and Receipts

Prescription of currency requirements
No.

Payment arrangements

Bilateral payment arrangements

Operative
Vietnam maintains bilateral payment arrangements with Belarus, China, Lao PDR, and Russia.

Administration of control
Exchange control is administered by the SBV.

International security restrictions
n.a.

Payment arrears

Official
Yes.

Controls on trade in gold (coins and/or bullion)

Controls on external trade
Yes.

Controls on exports and imports of banknotes	
On exports	
Domestic currency	A bank permit is required for amounts exceeding VND 5 million upon leaving Vietnam.
Foreign currency	A bank permit is required for amounts exceeding $3,000.
On imports	
Domestic currency	Amounts in excess of VND 5 million must be declared upon entering Vietnam.
Foreign currency	Amounts in excess of $3,000 must be declared to customs.

Resident Accounts

Foreign exchange accounts permitted	Yes.
Held domestically	Residents who are organizations with foreign currency sources originating from current transactions, capital transactions, or other stated sources are entitled to open and maintain foreign currency accounts at authorized banks for receiving and making payments, remittances, and transfers in foreign exchange as specified by the SBV.
	Resident private individuals who have foreign currencies transferred from abroad via banks or who bring foreign currencies into Vietnam and have a border-gate customs certification, together with other legal sources of foreign currencies, are entitled to open and maintain foreign currency accounts at licensed banks. These accounts may be used for receiving overseas remittances for export of goods and services or assistance funds allowed by law; cash from overseas (certified by border-gate customs offices); transfers in foreign currencies in cash or account transfers for salaries, bonuses, or allowances; and other sources of foreign currencies permitted by the SBV. The accounts may be used for making payments to overseas organizations or individuals for goods or services to organizations and to individuals in Vietnam who are allowed to invoice in foreign currency for certain goods provided and services rendered; remitting foreign currency abroad for certain personal purposes; selling foreign currency to credit institutions that are allowed to conduct foreign exchange activities; withdrawing foreign currency in cash for savings and other stated purposes; investing in foreign currency–denominated securities; and other stated purposes as specified by the SBV.
	Depositors are entitled to earn interest in foreign currencies and withdraw principal and interest in foreign currencies.
Held abroad	Resident enterprises operating in specified sectors that contract with foreign organizations may open and use foreign currency accounts overseas subject to the submission of various documents to and approval of the SBV in order to open foreign currency accounts abroad to facilitate the conducting of current overseas transactions; to deposit security for international bid contracts; to conduct clearing transactions; or to meet the requirements of treaties, agreements, or commitments signed with foreign countries, foreign-invested enterprises operating in accordance with the Foreign Investment Law of Vietnam, and certain credit institutions. Other organizations not engaged in the above-mentioned activities, but that wish to open and use an overseas foreign currency account, must obtain the approval of the Prime Minister or the SBV.
Accounts in domestic currency convertible into foreign currency	Yes.

Nonresident Accounts

Foreign exchange accounts permitted	Nonresident organizations operating in Vietnam and nonresident organizations or nonresident individuals operating overseas and (1) having foreign currencies transferred through a bank into the country upon entering Vietnam and holding the appropriate border-gate certification, or (2) carrying other legal sources of foreign currencies in Vietnam are entitled to open and maintain foreign currency accounts at licensed banks.

In addition, holders of nonresident foreign currency accounts are permitted to make withdrawals in either foreign currency or Vietnamese dong.

Approval required	Yes.
Domestic currency accounts	Nonresidents who have domestic currency converted from foreign currency and other legal income may open these accounts.
Convertible into foreign currency	Yes.
Blocked accounts	Yes.

Imports and Import Payments

Foreign exchange budget	The budget is indicative only and, therefore, not binding.
Financing requirements for imports	Priorities are assigned to certain types of imports. Highest priority is given to critical imports, such as petroleum products and fertilizer. Lowest priority is given to imports of goods that compete with domestically produced goods and imports of other consumer goods.
Documentation requirements for release of foreign exchange for imports	No.
Import licenses and other nontariff measures	Importation may only be carried out in accordance with the registered business activity of the enterprise. Only a few foreign trade enterprises are allowed to import a broad range of goods. A number of imports require a license issued by the Ministry of Trade (MOT). In addition, the importation of certain products is controlled by other ministries for broadly defined health, safety, and moral reasons.
Negative list	Prohibited imports are weapons, ammunition, explosives, and other military equipment; nonmedical drugs and toxic chemicals; "reactionary and/or pornographic" cultural products; fireworks and children's toys that detrimentally influence personality, education, social order, and safety; cigarettes (excluding limited quantities imported during personal travel); most used consumer goods; most used vehicles, including bicycles and motorcycles, and used parts; and passenger vehicles.
Licenses with quotas	All import quotas are formally approved by the government. The Ministry of Planning and Investment (MOPI), in coordination with the MOT, may also impose ad hoc temporary quantity controls. Imports of steel, cement, fertilizer, petroleum products, and sugar are subject to quantitative controls. In addition, the imports of certain ceramic and granite floor tiles, glass products, newspaper and other printing paper, some types of construction steel, vegetable oils, sugar, motorcycles, and cars with less than 16 seats require an import license from the MOT.
Other nontariff measures	A broad range of additional nontariff measures exists.
Import taxes and/or tariffs	Effective January 31, 1999, import tariffs range up to 50%, and the number of tariff rates was reduced to 15. Most imports of machinery, equipment, and medicine are exempt from tariffs. Certain imports of foreign enterprises, incorporated under the Law on Foreign Investment, are also exempt from tariffs. Tariff rates of 50% to 60% are applied to imports of garments and footwear, soft drinks, cosmetics, and automobiles.
State import monopoly	No.

Exports and Export Proceeds

Repatriation requirements	All receipts must be repatriated, but no deadline is specified.
Surrender requirements	All resident enterprises are required to sell 50% of foreign currency to banks, except foreign-owned enterprises without government guarantee for foreign exchange balances, and 100% if they are nonprofit organizations.
Financing requirements	No.

Documentation requirements	n.a.
Export licenses	Prohibited exports are weapons, ammunition, explosives, and other military equipment; antiques; nonmedical drugs and toxic chemicals; timber and timber products from natural forests; wild and/or rare native animals; and certain plants.
Without quotas	State-owned firms with an annual export turnover of more than $5 million may obtain permanent direct foreign trading rights, whereas those with an annual export turnover in the range of $2 million to $5 million may obtain temporary direct foreign trading rights.
With quotas	Exports of rice and of textiles and garments in quota-regulated markets are subject to quotas.
Export taxes	
Other export taxes	Yes.

Payments for Invisible Transactions and Current Transfers

Controls on these transfers	All transactions require individual authorization from the MOF. Payments for invisibles related to authorized imports are not restricted.
Investment-related payments	
Prior approval	Profit and dividend remittances are subject to a tax of 5% to 10%.
Indicative limits/bona fide test	Information is not available on indicative limits for interest payments.
Payments for travel	
Prior approval	For foreign currency provided from a bank's account, SBV permission is not required. For foreign currency provided from other sources, SBV permission is required.
Quantitative limits	Yes.
Indicative limits/bona fide test	Yes.
Personal payments	
Prior approval	For foreign currency provided from a bank's account, SBV permission is not required. For foreign currency provided from other sources, SBV permission is required.
Foreign workers' wages	
Prior approval	Yes.
Credit card use abroad	
Prior approval	Yes.
Other payments	
Prior approval	Yes.

Proceeds from Invisible Transactions and Current Transfers

Repatriation requirements	All proceeds must be repatriated, but no deadline is specified.
Surrender requirements	All resident enterprises are required to sell 50% of foreign currency to banks, except foreign-owned enterprises without government guarantee for foreign exchange balances, and 100% if they are nonprofit organizations.
Restrictions on use of funds	Restrictions are the same as with other foreign exchange holdings.

Capital Transactions

Controls on capital and money market instruments	There are controls on all transactions in capital and money market instruments and in collective investment securities.
Controls on derivatives and other instruments	
Sale or issue locally by nonresidents	SBV approval is required.
Purchase abroad by residents	SBV approval is required.
Controls on credit operations	Enterprises are subject to external borrowing ceilings.
Commercial credits	
By residents to nonresidents	Yes.
To residents from nonresidents	For short-term credit, borrowing enterprises must observe the required conditions of the SBV. For medium- and long-term credit, enterprises, based on conditions required by the SBV, must sign contracts and then register the borrowings and repayment schedules with the SBV before disbursement. State-owned enterprises' borrowing contracts must be approved by the SBV. Under this requirement, state-owned enterprises must report the borrowing and repayment schedules to the SBV.
Financial credits	
By residents to nonresidents	n.r.
To residents from nonresidents	Yes.
Controls on direct investment	
Outward direct investment	The authorized agency's approval is required and the capital must be registered with the SBV.
Inward direct investment	The authority to grant foreign investment licenses is entrusted to the MOPI for projects over $1 million; for projects under $1 million, to the provincial authorities concerned. The forms of foreign investment are regulated by the relevant investment laws.
Controls on liquidation of direct investment	n.a.
Controls on real estate transactions	
Purchase locally by nonresidents	Land may not be owned by foreign investors but must be leased from the state.
Controls on personal capital movements	There are controls on all personal capital movements.
Provisions specific to commercial banks and other credit institutions	
Borrowing abroad	SBV approval is required.
Maintenance of accounts abroad	SBV approval is required.
Lending to nonresidents (financial or commercial credits)	Yes.
Lending locally in foreign exchange	Permission is given only for imports and other permitted purposes.
Differential treatment of deposit accounts in foreign exchange	
Reserve requirements	Through end-February 1999, reserve requirements on foreign currency were set at 10% and held in foreign currency. Normally, the obligation was met by holding dollars. However, banks were allowed to hold the reserves in euros or yen instead of dollars if more than 50% of the obligation arose from deposits held in these other currencies. Effective March 1, 1999, the SBV expanded the coverage of the reserve requirements to all deposit-taking institutions. The reserve requirements on deposits in foreign and local currency were unified at the level of 7% (5% for rural joint-stock banks and credit cooperatives).

Interest rate controls	The maximum foreign exchange lending rate is 7.5% a year. For enterprises, the maximum foreign exchange deposit rates are 0.5% a year on demand deposits and 3% a year on fixed deposits of less than one year.
Open foreign exchange position limits	The SBV has gradually increased maximum limits on open positions in individual foreign currency to 15% from 10%. Open position limits for local currency are also 15%. The aggregate open position limits remain unchanged at 30%. Forward and swap positions are included in the calculation of open position limits. These regulations apply to all banks.
Provisions specific to institutional investors	n.a.
Other controls imposed by securities laws	n.a.

Changes During 1999

Exchange arrangement	*February 25.* The SBV quotes as the official rate the daily average exchange rate of the previous day of the interbank market. Based on this rate, commercial banks set their own rate within a band of ±0.1%.
Imports and import payments	*January 31.* The maximum import tariff rate was reduced to 50%, and the number of tariff rates was reduced to 15.
Capital transactions	
Provisions specific to commercial banks and other credit institutions	*March 1.* The coverage of the reserve requirements was expanded to all deposit-taking institutions and was unified at 7%.

REPUBLIC OF YEMEN

(Position as of December 31, 1999)

Status Under IMF Articles of Agreement

Article VIII	Date of acceptance: December 10, 1996.

Exchange Arrangement

Currency	The currency of the Republic of Yemen is the Yemeni rial.
Exchange rate structure	Unitary.
Classification	
Independently floating	The exchange rate of the Yemeni rial is determined by supply and demand.
Exchange tax	No.
Exchange subsidy	No.
Forward exchange market	No.

Arrangements for Payments and Receipts

Prescription of currency requirements	No.
Payment arrangements	No.
Administration of control	Exchange control authority is vested with the Central Bank of Yemen (CBY).
International security restrictions	No.
Payment arrears	
Official	Yes.
Private	Yes.
Controls on trade in gold (coins and/or bullion)	No.
Controls on exports and imports of banknotes	
On exports	
Domestic currency	Exports of rial banknotes are prohibited.
On imports	
Domestic currency	Imports of rial banknotes are prohibited.

Resident Accounts

Foreign exchange accounts permitted	Yes.
Held domestically	Yes.
Held abroad	Yes.
Accounts in domestic currency convertible into foreign currency	Yes.

Nonresident Accounts

Foreign exchange accounts permitted	Yes.
Domestic currency accounts	Yes.
Convertible into foreign currency	Yes.
Blocked accounts	Yes.

Imports and Import Payments

Foreign exchange budget	No.
Financing requirements for imports	No.
Documentation requirements for release of foreign exchange for imports	
Letters of credit	Yes.
Import licenses used as exchange licenses	All importers holding an import license for wheat or flour may obtain the necessary foreign exchange from the CBY. This system was eliminated on January 30, 1999.
Import licenses and other nontariff measures	
Negative list	Some imports are banned for security and religious reasons, and three categories of goods are banned for economic reasons. Imports from Israel are prohibited, as well as certain types of used machinery.
Open general licenses	Yes.
Import taxes and/or tariffs	Currently, there are four tariff rates: 5%, 10%, 15%, and 25%.
State import monopoly	Imports of petroleum products are reserved for the Yemen Petroleum Company.

Exports and Export Proceeds

Repatriation requirements	No.
Financing requirements	No.
Documentation requirements	No.
Export licenses	Exports are registered for statistical purposes. Exports to Israel are prohibited.
Export taxes	No.

Payments for Invisible Transactions and Current Transfers

Controls on these transfers	No.
Investment-related payments	Information is not available on the payment of amortization of loans or depreciation of direct investments.

Proceeds from Invisible Transactions and Current Transfers

Repatriation requirements	No.
Restrictions on use of funds	No.

Capital Transactions

Controls on capital and money market instruments	No.
Controls on derivatives and other instruments	No.
Controls on credit operations	
Commercial credits	
To residents from nonresidents	Yes.
Financial credits	
To residents from nonresidents	Short-term foreign loans by the public sector are prohibited. Approval by the Council of Ministers is required for contracting medium- and long-term foreign loans by the public sector.
Guarantees, sureties, and financial backup facilities	
To residents from nonresidents	Yes.
Controls on direct investment	No.
Controls on liquidation of direct investment	Liquidation of direct investments is free for approved and registered projects.
Controls on real estate transactions	No.
Controls on personal capital movements	No.
Provisions specific to commercial banks and other credit institutions	
Differential treatment of deposit accounts in foreign exchange	Foreign exchange deposits held at the CBY are nonremunerated.
Open foreign exchange position limits	Commercial and specialized banks are required to observe prudential regulations regarding currency exposure and to report their positions.
On resident assets and liabilities	Yes.
On nonresident assets and liabilities	Yes.
Provisions specific to institutional investors	No.
Other controls imposed by securities laws	No.

Changes During 1999

Imports and import payments	*January 30.* The importation of wheat and flour was liberalized.

ZAMBIA

(Position as of December 31, 1999)

Status Under IMF Articles of Agreement

Article XIV	Yes.

Exchange Arrangement

Currency	The currency of Zambia is the Zambian kwacha.
Exchange rate structure	Unitary.
Classification	
Independently floating	The official rate is market determined, and the spread between the Bank of Zambia's (BOZ) buying and selling rates is currently fixed at 1.6%, but can be adjusted within a range of 1–2%. On the basis of the bids and offers received, as well as other budgetary considerations (such as government and BOZ requirements, donor assistance funds, and export earnings), the BOZ determines the amount of foreign exchange to be sold to or purchased from the market through the dealing window. The exchange rates prevailing in the interbank market follow closely those established at the BOZ's dealing window.
Exchange tax	No.
Exchange subsidy	No.
Forward exchange market	No.

Arrangements for Payments and Receipts

Prescription of currency requirements	No.
Payment arrangements	
Regional arrangements	Zambia is a member of COMESA and SADC.
Administration of control	All exchange controls have been abolished. The Ministry of Commerce, Trade, and Industry is responsible for trade arrangements.
International security restrictions	No.
Payment arrears	
Official	Yes.
Private	Yes.
Controls on trade in gold (coins and/or bullion)	
Controls on external trade	Imports and exports of gold in any form other than jewelry require approval from the Ministry of Mines.
Controls on exports and imports of banknotes	Amounts exceeding $5,000 must be declared for statistical purposes.

Resident Accounts

Foreign exchange accounts permitted	Yes.
Held domestically	Yes.

Held abroad	Yes.
Accounts in domestic currency convertible into foreign currency	Yes.

Nonresident Accounts

Foreign exchange accounts permitted	Yes.
Domestic currency accounts	Yes.
Convertible into foreign currency	Yes.
Blocked accounts	Yes.

Imports and Import Payments

Foreign exchange budget	No.
Financing requirements for imports	No.
Documentation requirements for release of foreign exchange for imports	
Letters of credit	Yes.
Import licenses and other nontariff measures	Licenses for statistical purposes are required, but they are granted automatically by commercial banks. Personal and household effects, trade samples, diplomatic shipments, and vehicles brought in temporarily are exempted from this requirement. Effective November 26, 1999, a license for the trade of petroleum products is required. The license is granted by the Energy Regulation Board to all oil marketing companies that undertake to adhere to specific guidelines pertaining to fuel uplift and import, pricing, and storage.
Negative list	There are restrictions on imports of firearms, ammunition, and ivory.
Import taxes and/or tariffs	MFN tariff rates range from zero to 25%. In addition, there is a 5% Import Declaration Fee. A number of products are subject to specific rates. Imports from COMESA countries are subject to a tariff equivalent to 60% of the MFN tariff. Some imports are exempt under the Investment Act.
State import monopoly	No.

Exports and Export Proceeds

Repatriation requirements	No.
Financing requirements	No.
Documentation requirements	All exports must be declared on the prescribed export declaration form for statistical purposes.
Export licenses	Yes.
Without quotas	Export declarations are required for most goods (mainly for statistical purposes), although they are administered routinely by commercial banks under authority delegated by the Ministry of Commerce, Trade, and Industry. There are restrictions on exports of firearms, ammunition, and ivory.
With quotas	White maize and fertilizers may be subject to a quota if domestic supply is short.
Export taxes	No.

Payments for Invisible Transactions and Current Transfers

Controls on these transfers	All payments for invisibles, except external debt-service payments, may be effected through banks and foreign exchange bureaus without the prior approval of the BOZ, subject to the requirement that no taxes are due.

Proceeds from Invisible Transactions and Current Transfers

Repatriation requirements	No.
Restrictions on use of funds	No.

Capital Transactions

Controls on capital and money market instruments	Outward transfers are free of controls. No controls apply to the sale of assets among nonresidents and between residents and nonresidents.
Controls on derivatives and other instruments	No.
Controls on credit operations	
Commercial credits	All borrowing must be registered with the BOZ for statistical purposes.
Controls on direct investment	No.
Controls on liquidation of direct investment	No.
Controls on real estate transactions	No.
Controls on personal capital movements	No.
Provisions specific to commercial banks and other credit institutions	
Borrowing abroad	Information on borrowing abroad is submitted to the BOZ for statistical purposes.
Open foreign exchange position limits	
On resident assets and liabilities	Yes.
On nonresident assets and liabilities	Yes.
Provisions specific to institutional investors	No.
Other controls imposed by securities laws	No.

Changes During 1999

Imports and import payments	*November 26.* The trade of petroleum products was tied to a license.

ZIMBABWE

(Position as of January 31, 2000)

Status Under IMF Articles of Agreement

Article VIII   Date of acceptance: February 5, 1995.

Exchange Arrangement

Currency	The currency of Zimbabwe is the Zimbabwe dollar.
Exchange rate structure	Unitary.
Classification	
Conventional pegged arrangement	On March 31, 1999, the exchange rate was pegged, de facto, at Z$38 per US$1, as the result of an agreement between the monetary authorities and the main commercial banks. Technically, however, the monetary authorities have not announced a formal pegging of the rate. Thus, the exchange rate system of Zimbabwe has been reclassified to the category conventional pegged arrangement from the category independently floating.
Exchange tax	No.
Exchange subsidy	No.
Forward exchange market	No.

Arrangements for Payments and Receipts

Prescription of currency requirements	All payments by nonresidents to residents must be effected in any of 17 currencies freely convertible through authorized dealers, with the exception of payments otherwise specified or effected through nonresident accounts.
Payment arrangements	
Bilateral payment arrangements	
Operative	There is an arrangement with Malaysia.
Administration of control	Exchange control is administered by the Reserve Bank of Zimbabwe (RBZ) under powers delegated to it by the MOF. Authorized dealers have been empowered to approve certain foreign exchange transactions.
International security restrictions	No.
Payment arrears	
Official	Yes.
Controls on trade in gold (coins and/or bullion)	
Controls on domestic ownership and/or trade	No person, either as principal or agent, may deal in or possess gold unless that person is (1) the holder of a license or permit; (2) the holder or distributor of a registered mining location from which gold is being produced; or (3) the employee or agent of any of the persons mentioned in (1) and (2) above and authorized by an employer or principal to deal in or possess gold that is already in the lawful possession of such employer or principal. A mining commissioner may issue to any person a permit authorizing the acquisition, possession, or disposal of any gold, provided the quantity does not exceed one troy ounce. In all other cases, permission can be issued only by the Secretary for Mines.
	Three types of licenses may be issued under the terms of the Gold Trade Act: a gold dealing license, a gold recovery works license, and a gold assaying license. Each holder or distributor of a registered mining location is required to lodge to the holder of a gold dealing license, not later than the tenth day of every month, all gold won by him from his

mining location, except any gold for which the Minister or mining commissioner has given him special authority to deal in otherwise. Any person intending to smelt gold or any article containing gold must first obtain a license issued by a district commissioner under the terms of the Secondhand Goods Act that authorizes the possession of smelting equipment.

Controls on external trade

The exportation of gold in unmanufactured form is controlled and licensed by the Ministry of Mines; these controls do not apply to the RBZ. No export licenses for gold are issued. The importation of gold is controlled by the Gold Trade Act, which requires those intending to import gold into Zimbabwe to meet certain requirements.

Controls on exports and imports of banknotes

On exports

Domestic currency

Travelers may take out, as part of their travel allowance, up to Z$2,000.

Foreign currency

As part of their travel allowance, travelers may annually take out up to the equivalent of US$500 a day for business travel and up to US$5,000 for holiday travel. Nonresident travelers may take out the traveler's checks they brought in, less the amount they sold to authorized dealers. Upon departure, nonresident travelers may reconvert unspent Zimbabwean currency into foreign currencies on presentation of exchange certificates.

On imports

Domestic currency

A traveler may bring in up to Z$2,000.

Foreign currency

Foreign currency and traveler's checks may be imported without restriction but must be sold or exchanged in Zimbabwe only through authorized dealers or foreign exchange bureaus.

Resident Accounts

Foreign exchange accounts permitted

Resident individuals may open foreign currency accounts in one of the denominated currencies in local branches of authorized dealers. Funds in these accounts are traded at market-determined exchange rates. Funds withdrawn from these accounts and converted into local currency, however, may not be redeposited in the account, except in the case of the amount of the initial investment and income or capital gains from investments in listed companies on the stock exchange or money market accounts.

Held domestically

Yes.

Held abroad

These accounts may be opened, but approval is required.

Accounts in domestic currency convertible into foreign currency

A resident may only convert funds in a domestic account into foreign currency when purchasing traveler's checks for holiday travel payments.

Nonresident Accounts

Foreign exchange accounts permitted

These accounts may be credited with foreign currencies, with payments from other nonresident accounts, or with payments by residents that would be eligible for transfer outside Zimbabwe. Nonresident accounts may be debited for payments to residents, for payments to other nonresident accounts, or for payments abroad. Nonresident individuals may open foreign currency accounts in one of the denominated currencies in local branches of authorized dealers. Funds in these accounts are traded at market-determined exchange rates. Funds withdrawn from these accounts and converted into local currency, however, may not be redeposited in the account, except in the case of the initial investment, and income or capital gains from investments in the stock exchange.

Approval required

Yes.

Domestic currency accounts

Yes.

| Convertible into foreign currency | Nonresidents may only convert domestic currency accounts into foreign currency when emigrating and taking out their surplus earnings. |

Convertible into foreign currency — Nonresidents may only convert domestic currency accounts into foreign currency when emigrating and taking out their surplus earnings.

Approval required — Yes.

Blocked accounts — Only former residents residing outside Zimbabwe may maintain emigrants' accounts in Zimbabwe. Cash assets held in Zimbabwe in the names of emigrants must be blocked in these accounts, and all payments to and from these accounts are subject to various exchange restrictions.

Imports and Import Payments

Foreign exchange budget — No.

Financing requirements for imports

Advance payment requirements — Authorized dealers were allowed to approve advance payments for imports up to US$50,000. Effective January 2, 2000, authorized dealers are no longer permitted to effect advance payments for imports without prior RBZ approval.

Documentation requirements for release of foreign exchange for imports — Authorized dealers may approve applications to effect payments for authorized imports, provided the necessary documentation is submitted. Payments for imports into Zimbabwe may not be made in domestic currency through a local nonresident account.

Domiciliation requirements — Yes.

Import licenses and other nontariff measures — There are no import-licensing requirements. Imports of certain goods (mostly agricultural and processed food products) require a special permit issued by the Ministry of Lands and Agriculture.

Negative list — The negative list for imports includes, in addition to items restricted for health or security reasons, nonmonetary gold, pearls, precious and semiprecious stones, and some jewelry items.

Open general licenses — Yes.

Licenses with quotas — No quotas are in force, but seasonal restrictions are applied to certain agricultural products.

Import taxes and/or tariffs — The customs duty regime consists mainly of ad valorem duties, which range up to a maximum of 100% for luxuries with a surtax of 10% on finished goods, and specific duties on a number of products. Generally, imports are subject to an additional tax (between 12.5% and 20%) equivalent to the sales taxes imposed on goods sold domestically. Government imports and capital goods for statutory bodies are exempt from customs duties. On August 13, 1999, the import surcharge was decreased to 10% from 15%.

State import monopoly — Maize may be imported only by the Grain Marketing Board or by others with the permission of the Board. Petroleum is imported by the National Oil Company.

Exports and Export Proceeds

Repatriation requirements — Yes.

Surrender requirements — Until August 1999, exporters were required to sell export proceeds in the market within a specified period. Effective August 9, 1999, exporters are allowed to retain 100% of their export proceeds in foreign currency accounts for 60 days; following that period, the foreign exchange must be sold in the market.

Financing requirements — Goods may not be exported without permission unless the customs authorities are satisfied that payment has been made in an approved manner or will be made within three months of the date of shipment (or a longer period if permitted by the RBZ).

Payments for exports must be received in foreign currency transferred into Zimbabwe through the banking system, except when there are special arrangements.

Documentation requirements

Letters of credit	Yes.
Domiciliation	Yes.

Export licenses

Without quotas — Export licenses are required for the following: (1) any ore, concentrate, or other manufactured product of chrome, copper, lithium, nickel, tin, or tungsten; (2) petroleum products; (3) jute and hessian bags; (4) road or rail tankers for carrying liquids or semiliquids; (5) bitumen, asphalt, and tar; (6) wild animals and wild animal products; (7) certain wood products; (8) ammonium nitrate; and (9) armaments. Export-licensing requirements are imposed for reasons of health and social welfare, as well as to ensure an adequate domestic supply of essential products. Export permits are required from the Ministry of Lands and Agriculture for some basic agricultural commodities, including maize, oilseeds, cheese, milk, seeds, potatoes, citrus fruits, apples, bananas, and tomatoes.

Export taxes — No.

Payments for Invisible Transactions and Current Transfers

Controls on these transfers — Foreign exchange to pay for invisibles related to imports and, within certain limits, for other purposes is provided by commercial banks under delegated authority. Applications for foreign exchange exceeding the limits established for commercial banks are approved by the RBZ, which deals with each case on its merits.

Trade-related payments

Prior approval — Required for payment of commissions.

Quantitative limits — The limits for freight and insurance are 30% of f.o.b. value of goods transported, but for goods that are of exceptional mass in relation to value, up to 80% of the f.o.b. value may be approved. For commission, the following limits apply: (1) conforming commission—up to 2.5% of c.i.f. value; (2) buying commission—up to 5% of f.o.b. value; (3) foreign travel agents—up to 10% of sales; and (4) selling commission—up to 7.5% of f.o.b. value.

Indicative limits/bona fide test — Yes.

Investment-related payments — All investment-related transfers are subject to prior RBZ approval.

Prior approval — Required for payment of profits and dividends. Specific applications are submitted to authorized dealers for approval without reference to the RBZ.

Quantitative limits — A corporation may be authorized to remit by way of dividends to foreign shareholders, including dividends due to former residents of Zimbabwe, up to 100% of the corporation's net after-tax profits, provided that an application for the remittance of a dividend is submitted to an authorized dealer within 12 months from the end of the financial year in respect of which the dividend is payable.

Indicative limits/bona fide test — Yes.

Payments for travel

Prior approval — Yes.

Quantitative limits — The basic foreign exchange allowance for travel is US$5,000 a year a person regardless of age. The basic foreign exchange allowance for business travel is up to US$500 a day.

Indicative limits/bona fide test — Yes.

Personal payments — Remittance of pensions of former residents is guaranteed under the constitution.

Prior approval — With RBZ approval, foreign exchange is provided for education abroad beyond the secondary school level for certain diploma and degree courses.

Quantitative limits	For medical treatment, the limit is US$20,000 a trip for the patient and one companion. A travel allowance up to US$250 a person a day may be allowed. For studies abroad, the limit is US$50,000 a year, and the annual limit is US$2,000 for alimony and child support payments.
Indicative limits/bona fide test	Applications for additional amounts must be submitted to the RBZ for approval.
Foreign workers' wages	Expatriate workers may remit their monthly salaries, subject to RBZ approval.
Prior approval	Yes.
Quantitative limits	Amounts of up to a third of gross salary may be remitted.
Indicative limits/bona fide test	Yes.
Credit card use abroad	
Prior approval	Yes.
Quantitative limits	Credit cards may be used abroad for holiday and business travel only, up to the limits set for those transactions.
Indicative limits/bona fide test	Yes.
Other payments	
Prior approval	Yes.
Quantitative limits	The annual limit for subscriptions for a company is US$20,000.
Indicative limits/bona fide test	Yes.

Proceeds from Invisible Transactions and Current Transfers

Repatriation requirements	Yes.
Surrender requirements	Receipts from invisibles must be sold to authorized banks within a reasonable period of time.
Restrictions on use of funds	Only surplus funds are required to be repatriated through the banking system.

Capital Transactions

Controls on capital and money market instruments	Inward transfers of capital through normal banking channels are not restricted. Outward transfers of capital are controlled.
On capital market securities	
Shares or other securities of a participating nature	
Purchase locally by nonresidents	Foreign investors are permitted to participate in the Zimbabwe Stock Exchange (ZSE) using currency received in Zimbabwe through normal banking channels. The initial investment plus any capital gains and dividend income may be remitted without restriction. Foreign investors may also subscribe for up to 35% of primary issues of bonds and stocks. Nonresidents are not permitted to purchase bonds and stocks from the secondary market.
Sale or issue locally by nonresidents	Nonresident investors are allowed to sell their bonds and stocks in the secondary market.
Purchase abroad by residents	Yes.
Sale or issue abroad by residents	Yes.
Bonds or other debt securities	
Purchase locally by nonresidents	Yes.
Sale or issue locally by nonresidents	Yes.

Purchase abroad by residents	Yes.
Sale or issue abroad by residents	Yes.
On money market instruments	
Purchase locally by nonresidents	Former residents holding blocked assets and new emigrants are allowed to invest their funds in government external bonds with a maturity of 12 years and an annual interest rate of 4%.
Sale or issue locally by nonresidents	Yes.
Purchase abroad by residents	Yes.
Sale or issue abroad by residents	Yes.
On collective investment securities	
Purchase locally by nonresidents	Yes.
Sale or issue locally by nonresidents	Yes.
Purchase abroad by residents	Yes.
Sale or issue abroad by residents	Yes.
Controls on derivatives and other instruments	No derivative transactions with foreign currency implications are permitted.
Controls on credit operations	
Commercial credits	
By residents to nonresidents	Yes.
To residents from nonresidents	The limit on foreign borrowing without prior approval of the External Loans Coordinating Committee is US$5 million. Gold producers undertaking new expansion projects are permitted access to offshore financing in the form of gold loans.
Financial credits	
By residents to nonresidents	Residents are not permitted to provide credit to nonresidents without RBZ approval.
To residents from nonresidents	Yes.
Guarantees, sureties, and financial backup facilities	
By residents to nonresidents	Yes.
To residents from nonresidents	Yes.
Controls on direct investment	
Outward direct investment	These investments require RBZ or MOF approval on a case-by-case basis.
Inward direct investment	Direct foreign investment in various sectors is subject to the prior approval of the Zimbabwe Investment Center, normally with the following conditions: (1) up to 100% foreign ownership is allowed in the following priority sectors: manufacturing, mining, quarry and mineral exploration, and development of hotels for tourism; (2) up to 70% foreign shareholding is permitted in specialized services such as management consultancy and construction, etc.; and (3) a maximum of 35% foreign ownership (reserved sector list) is allowed in selected sectors where foreign investors wishing to participate may only do so in joint-venture partnership with Zimbabwean firms or individuals. The reserved sector list is as follows: (a) primary production of food and cash crops; (b) primary horticulture; (c) game, wildlife ranching, and livestock; (d) forestry; (e) fishing and fish farming; (f) poultry farming; (g) employment agencies; (h) estate agencies; (i) valet services; (j) armaments manufacture, marketing, and distribution; (k) public water provision for domestic and industrial purposes; (l) rail operations; (m) grain mill products; (n) bakery products; (o) sugar products; (p) tobacco packaging and grading; and (q) tobacco products.
Controls on liquidation of direct investment	Effective April 1, 1999, all foreign investments, irrespective of their source, that have been undertaken through normal banking channels since May 1993, may be repatriated. In all

cases, specific applications must be submitted to the RBZ in respect of repatriation of capital. Repatriation at accelerated rates that depend on discounted sale prices of net equity is allowed for investments effected before 1979.

Controls on real estate transactions

Purchase abroad by residents

Yes.

Purchase locally by nonresidents

Yes.

Controls on personal capital movements

Loans

By residents to nonresidents

Yes.

To residents from nonresidents

Yes.

Gifts, endowments, inheritances, and legacies

By residents to nonresidents

Yes.

To residents from nonresidents

Yes.

Settlement of debts abroad by immigrants

Yes.

Transfer of assets

Transfer abroad by emigrants

Applications for emigrant status must be submitted to the RBZ; the settling-in allowance that emigrants may remit abroad is limited to US$1,000 a person or US$2,000 a family. In exceptional cases, the exchange control authorities will consider applications exceeding this maximum. All those applying for emigrant status are required to liquidate their assets within six months and to invest the total proceeds, less any settling-in allowance granted, in 4%, 12-year Zimbabwe government external bonds. If emigrants are unable to comply with the six-month limit, the matter may be referred to the RBZ.

Transfer of gambling and prize earnings

Lottery prizes due to nonresidents may be transferred, except the first prize.

Provisions specific to commercial banks and other credit institutions

Borrowing abroad

Borrowing abroad is subject to exchange control rules and regulations and the External Loans Coordinating Committee.

Maintenance of accounts abroad

Maintaining accounts abroad is subject to exchange control rules and regulations.

Lending to nonresidents (financial or commercial credits)

Lending to nonresidents is subject to exchange control rules and regulations. However, it is usually not permitted.

Lending locally in foreign exchange

These transactions are subject to exchange control rules and regulations.

Purchase of locally issued securities denominated in foreign exchange

Yes.

Differential treatment of deposit accounts in foreign exchange

There are rules that allow for differential treatment of local exporters and companies operating in the export promotion zone.

Reserve requirements

Yes.

Liquid asset requirements

Yes.

Interest rate controls

Yes.

Credit controls

Controls apply to mortgage rates of building societies.

Investment regulations

Abroad by banks

Investment abroad by local banks in offshore entities is subject to exchange control approval.

In banks by nonresidents	Acquiring equity by nonresidents in local banks listed on the ZSE is subject to the ZSE's rules and regulations. For banks not listed in the ZSE, these are subject to exchange control approval.
Open foreign exchange position limits	Authorized dealers are subject to overnight net foreign currency exposure limits. The net open position limits of foreign exchange dealers is US$2 million or 10% of their capital base, and their capital requirements are 5% (core/Tier I) and 10% (total capital).
On resident assets and liabilities	Yes.
On nonresident assets and liabilities	Yes.
Provisions specific to institutional investors	Local institutional investors are not permitted to invest in securities registered offshore.
Limits (max.) on securities issued by nonresidents and on portfolio invested abroad	Yes.
Limits (max.) on portfolio invested abroad	Yes.
Limits (min.) on portfolio invested locally	Purchase of shares by foreign investors is limited to 40% of the total equity of the company, with a limit of 10% for one investor. These limits are in addition to any existing foreign shareholdings in the companies.
Currency-matching regulations on assets/liabilities composition	Yes.
Other controls imposed by securities laws	No.

Changes During 1999

Exchange arrangement	*March 31.* The exchange rate arrangement of Zimbabwe has been reclassified to the category conventional pegged arrangement from the category independently floating.
Imports and import payments	*August 13.* The import surcharge was decreased to 10% from 15%.
Exports and export proceeds	*August 9.* Exporters were allowed to retain their export proceeds in foreign currency accounts for 60 days.
Capital transactions	
Controls on liquidation of direct investment	*April 1.* The policy allowing the creation of 12-year and 20-year 4% government bonds out of blocked profits accruing on pre-1993 investment was abolished.

Changes During 2000

Imports and import payments	*January 2.* Authorized dealers are no longer permitted to effect advance payments for imports without prior RBZ approval.

APPENDICES

	Total number of countries with this feature	Afghanistan, Islamic State of	Albania	Algeria	Angola	Antigua and Barbuda	Argentina	Armenia	Aruba	Australia	Austria	Azerbaijan	Bahamas, The	Bahrain	Bangladesh	Barbados	Belarus	Belgium	Belize	Benin	Bhutan	Bolivia	Bosnia and Herzegovina
Status under IMF Articles of Agreement																							
Article VIII	152			•		•	•	•	•	•	•		•	•	•	•			•	•	•	•	
Article XIV	33	•	•		•							•					•						•
Exchange rate arrangements																							
Exchange arrangement with no separate legal tender	38					◊					⊕								⊕	▲			
Currency board arrangement	8						•																•
Conventional pegged arrangement	45														▼								
Pegged exchange rate within horizontal bands	6																						
Crawling peg	5																					•	
Crawling band	6																						
Managed floating with no pre-announced path for the exchange rate	27			•								•					•						
Independently floating	50	•	•		•				•	•													
Exchange rate structure																							
Dual exchange rates	13	•											•										
Multiple exchange rates	5																•						
Arrangements for payments and receipts																							
Bilateral payments arrangements	61	•	•		•							•			•	—	•			•		•	
Multiple exchange rates	60	—	•		•	•	•					—				•							—
Controls on payments for invisible transactions and current transfers	100	•		•	•	•				•		•	•		•	•	•		•	•	•	•	
Proceeds from exports and/or invisible transactions																							
Repatriation requirements	105	•	•	•	•	—			•			•	•		•	•	•		•	•		•	•
Surrender requirements	75	•		•	•				•				•		•	•	•		•	•		•	•
Capital transactions																							
Controls on:																							
Capital market securities	125	—	•	•	•		•		•	•		•	•		•	•	•		•	•		•	
Money market instruments	110	—	•	•	•		•		•	•		•	•		•	•	•		•	•		•	
Collective investment securities	103	—	•	•	•		•		•			•	•		•	•	•	•	•	•		•	
Derivatives and other instruments	83	—	•	•	•		•		•	•		■	•		•	—	•		•	•		•	
Commercial credits	108	—	•	•	•				•	•		•	•		•	•	•		•	•		•	•
Financial credits	113	—	•	•	•				•	•		•	•		•	•	•		•	•		•	•
Guarantees, sureties, and financial backup facilities	93	—	•	•	•				•			•			•	•	—		•	•		•	
Direct investment	147	•	•	•	•		•		•	•	•	•	•	•	•	•	•	•	•	•		•	
Liquidation of direct investment	54	•			•				•						•				•	•		•	
Real estate transactions	136	—	•	•	•	•	•	•	•	•		•	•		•	•	•		•	•		•	•
Personal capital movements	90	—	•	—	•				•			•	•			—		—	▲	•		•	•
Provisions specific to:																							
Commercial banks and other credit institutions	158	—	•	•	•	•	•		•	•	•	•	•	•	•	•		•	•	•		•	•
Institutional investors	83	—	■		—	—	•		•			•	•		•	•	—		•	•		•	

For key and footnotes, see page 988

Frameworks for Current and Capital Transactions in Member Countries[1]
first country page)[2]

Botswana	Brazil	Brunei Darussalam	Bulgaria	Burkina Faso	Burundi	Cambodia	Cameroon	Canada	Cape Verde	Central African Republic	Chad	Chile	China, People's Rep. of	Hong Kong SAR	Colombia	Comoros	Congo, Dem. Rep. of the	Congo, Republic of	Costa Rica	Côte d'Ivoire	Croatia	Cyprus	Czech Republic	Denmark	Djibouti	Dominica	Dominican Republic	Ecuador	Egypt	El Salvador	Equatorial Guinea	Eritrea	Estonia	Ethiopia
•	•	•	•	•			•	•		•	•	•	•	•		•		•	•	•	•	•	•	•	•	•	•	•		•	•		•	
				•	•				•				•			•													•		•		•	
			▲		▲		▲	▲									▲		▲							◇		◆			▲			
		•	•										•												•								•	
▼																																		
																	•																	
					•	•											•		•						•									•
	•						•			•		•		•		•											•							
(•)	•			(•)	•				•							•			•							(•)	(•)							
•	•		•	•	•		•				•					•			•						•	•					•			
	•	•	•	•	•		—	•	•		•				•	•		•	•	•		•	•	•		•	•				•	•	—
	•	•	•	•	•	•		•	•		•	•	•		•	•		•		•				•	•				•			•	
	•	•	•	•	•		•	•		•	•	•	•	•	•	•	•	•	•	•	•	•	•	•		•	•				•	•	
	•		•	•	•	•		•	•		•		•		•	•		•		•		•				•	•	•			•	•	
•	•		•	•	•	—	•		•		•	•	•		•	•		•	•	•				•	•		•		•		•	•	
•	•		•	•	•	—	•		•		•	•	•		•	—	•	•		•	•	•	•		•	•	•				•	•	
	•		•		•	—	•		•		•	•	•		•	—		•		•		•	•		•	•		•			•	—	
	•		•	•	■	—	■		—	•		•	•		•	—		•		•	•	•			—		•	•			•	—	
	•		•	•	•	•	•		•	•		•	•		•	•		•		•	•	•			•	•	•				•	•	
	•	•	•	•	•	•		•	•		•	•	•		•	•		•		•	•	•		•	•	•	•				•	•	
	•		•	•	•	•	•		•	•		•	•		•	•		•		•		•			•	•					•	•	—
	•	•	•	•	•	•	•		•	•		•	•	•	•	•	•	•	•	•	•	•	•		•	•		•			•	•	•
	•		•	•	•		•		•		•	•		•	•	—	•	•		•	•				•		•				•		
	•	•	•	•	•		•	—	•		•	•	•		•	—	•	—	•		•	•	•	•		•		•			•	•	•
	•	•	•	•	•	•	•		•		•	•	•		•	—		—	—	•	•	•	•	•		•	◇	•			•	•	•
•	•	•	•	•	•		•		•	•		•	—	•		•		•	•	•	•	•	•	•	•		•	•		•	•	•	•	•
•	•				•			•			—	—	—	•			•	—		—	—	•	•	•	•	•	•				•	•	—	•	•

	Fiji	Finland	France	Gabon	Gambia, The	Georgia	Germany	Ghana	Greece	Grenada	Guatemala	Guinea	Guinea-Bissau	Guyana	Haiti	Honduras	Hungary	Iceland	India	Indonesia	Iran, Islamic Rep. of	Iraq	Ireland	Israel	Italy
Status under IMF Articles of Agreement																									
Article VIII	•	•	•	•	•	•	•	•	•	•	•	•	•	•	•	•	•	•	•	•			•	•	•
Article XIV																					•	•			
Exchange rate arrangements																									
Exchange arrangement with no separate legal tender		⊕	⊕	▲		⊕				◊			▲										⊕		⊕
Currency board arrangement																									
Conventional pegged arrangement	▼																								
Pegged exchange rate within horizontal bands																									
Crawling peg																									
Crawling band																•	•							•	
Managed floating with no pre-announced path for the exchange rate												•													
Independently floating				•	•			•				•		•	•	•			•	•					
Exchange rate structure																									
Dual exchange rates																					•				
Multiple exchange rates																									
Arrangements for payments and receipts																									
Bilateral payments arrangements	—							•			•	•	•	•		•							—		
Multiple exchange rates	—				•						•	•	•	•		•							—		
Controls on payments for invisible transactions and current transfers	•			•			•		•	•	•	•	•						•		•	•			
Proceeds from exports and/or invisible transactions																									
Repatriation requirements	•			•				•		•	•	•				•	•		•		•	•			
Surrender requirements	•			•				•		•	•		•			•			•		•	•			
Capital transactions																									
Controls on:																									
Capital market securities	•	•		•				•	•	•		•	•	—		•	•	•	•	—	•			•	
Money market instruments	•		•	•				•		•		•	—			•	•	•	•	•	•			•	
Collective investment securities	•		•	•				•		•		•	—			•	•		•	•	•			•	•
Derivatives and other instruments	•		•	•	•			•		•		•	—			•	•		•	—	•			•	
Commercial credits	•		•	•				•		•		•	•	•	—	•			•	•	•				
Financial credits	•		•	•	•			•		•		•	•			•			•	•	•				
Guarantees, sureties, and financial backup facilities	•		•	•						—	•	•	•		•	•			•	•	•			•	
Direct investment	•	•	•	•				•	•			•	•		•	•			•	•	•	•		•	•
Liquidation of direct investment	•		•	•							•		—						•		•	•			
Real estate transactions	•	•		•	•			•		•		•	•	—		•	•	•	•	—	•			•	•
Personal capital movements	•			—	—			•		◊		•	•	—		•			•		•			•	
Provisions specific to:																									
Commercial banks and other credit institutions	•	•		—	•	•		•				•	•	•	•	•	•	•	•	•	•			•	•
Institutional investors	•	•	•	—		—	•					•	—			•	•	•	•	•	—			•	•

For key and footnotes, see page 988

Frameworks for Current and Capital Transactions in Member Countries[1]
first country page)[2]

	Jamaica	Japan	Jordan	Kazakhstan	Kenya	Kiribati	Korea, Republic of	Kuwait	Kyrgyz Republic	Lao People's Dem. Rep.	Latvia	Lebanon	Lesotho	Liberia	Libyan Arab Jamahiriya	Lithuania	Luxembourg	Macedonia, fmr. Yugoslav Rep.	Madagascar	Malawi	Malaysia	Maldives	Mali	Malta	Marshall Islands	Mauritania	Mauritius	Mexico	Micronesia, Fed. States of	Moldova	Mongolia	Morocco	Mozambique	Myanmar	Namibia
	•	•	•	•	•	•	•	•	•		•	•	•			•	•	•	•	•	•		•	•	•	•	•	•	•	•	•	•			•
										•		•	•							•													•	•	
						◆											⊕								◆				◆						
																•																			
								▼			▼															▼								▼	
	•				•					•	•										•					•									
		•		•			•							•					•						•				•	•	•		•		
										•	•			•					•		•			•		•		•		•		•	•	•	
		•	•			•						•	•						•		•			•		•				•	•	•	•	•	
			•											•					•		•			•		•				•			•		•
	■			•	•	—	•	•	•		•	•		•				•	•	•	•	•	—	•	•	•	—	•	•	•	•	—		
	•		•	•	—	•	•	•			•	•		•				•	■	•	•		—	•	•	—	•	—	•	•	•	—		
	•		•			—	•				•	•		•			■	■	•	•		—	•	—	•	•	—	•	•	•	•		
	■		•		•	—	•	•	■		•	—		—			■	■	•	•		—	•	—	•	—	•	—	•	•	•	—	•	
		•		—			—				•	•		•			•	■	•	•			—	•		•	•	—	■	•	•	•	•	
		•		—			—				•	•	•	•			•	•	•	•			—	•		•	•	—	■	•	•	•	•	•
			•			—						•		•			•	—	•	•			•				—	■	•	•	•	•	
	•	•	•	•	•	•					•	•		•			•	—	•	•			—	—			•	•		•	•	•	•	
	•			—		•					•			•			•	•	—	—			•	•	—	—	•	•		•	•	•	•	•
	■		•	—	•	•					—	—		•			•	—	•	—			—	—			■	•	•	•	•	—	•
	•	•	•	—	•		•	•		•	—	•		■			•	■	•	—	—	•	■	•	•	—		•	•	•	•	•
	•	•	•	—		•		•	—	•	—				—	•	■	—	—	•	■	•	•	—	•	—	•	—	•	•	•	—	•

	Nepal	Netherlands	Netherlands Antilles	New Zealand	Nicaragua	Niger	Nigeria	Norway	Oman	Pakistan	Palau	Panama	Papua New Guinea	Paraguay	Peru	Philippines	Poland	Portugal	Qatar	Romania	Russian Federation	Rwanda	St. Kitts and Nevis	St. Lucia	St. Vincent and the Grenadines
Status under IMF Articles of Agreement																									
Article VIII	•	•	•	•	•	•		•	•	•	•	•	•	•	•	•	•	•	•	•	•	•	•	•	•
Article XIV							•																		
Exchange rate arrangements																									
Exchange arrangement with no separate legal tender		⊕				▲					◆	◆						⊕					◊	◊	◊
Currency board arrangement																									
Conventional pegged arrangement																									
Pegged exchange rate within horizontal bands																									
Crawling peg					•																				
Crawling band																									
Managed floating with no pre-announced path for the exchange rate							•	•						•						•					
Independently floating				•									•		•	•	•				•				
Exchange rate structure																									
Dual exchange rates																									
Multiple exchange rates																					•				
Arrangements for payments and receipts																									
Bilateral payments arrangements															•	•				•	•				
Multiple exchange rates					•	•	•						•							•	•	•			
Controls on payments for invisible transactions and current transfers	•	•				•	•		•	•			•		•	•				•	•	•	•	•	•
Proceeds from exports and/or invisible transactions																									
Repatriation requirements	•					•	•			•			•					•		•	•	•	•		•
Surrender requirements						•							•								•		•		•
Capital transactions																									
Controls on:																									
Capital market securities	•	•				•	•	•	•	•			•		•	•				•	•	•	•	•	•
Money market instruments	•	•				•	•			•			•		•	•				•	•	•	•	•	•
Collective investment securities	—	•				•				•			•		•	•				•	•	•	•	•	•
Derivatives and other instruments	—	•				•				•			•	•	•	•				•	•	•		•	•
Commercial credits	•	•				•	•			•			•		•	•				•	•	•	•	•	•
Financial credits	•	•				•				•			•		•	•				•	•	•	•	•	•
Guarantees, sureties, and financial backup facilities	•	•				•				•			•		•	•				•	•	•	•	•	—
Direct investment	•	•	•	•		•		•	•	•	•		•		•	•	•			•	•	•	•	•	•
Liquidation of direct investment	•					•	•													•	•			—	
Real estate transactions	•	•	•			•			•	•			•		•	•				•	•	•	•	•	•
Personal capital movements	•	•				•	•			•			•		•	•			•	•	•	•	•	•	—
Provisions specific to:																									
Commercial banks and other credit institutions	•	•	•		•	•	•	•			•	•	•		•	•	•	•			•	•		•	•
Institutional investors	■	•		•			•		—	•						•	•	•	•	■	•		■	•	—

Frameworks for Current and Capital Transactions in Member Countries[1]
first country page)[2]

	Samoa	San Marino	São Tomé and Príncipe	Saudi Arabia	Senegal	Seychelles	Sierra Leone	Singapore	Slovak Republic	Slovenia	Solomon Islands	Somalia	South Africa	Spain	Sri Lanka	Sudan	Suriname	Swaziland	Sweden	Switzerland	Syrian Arab Republic	Tajikistan	Tanzania	Thailand	Togo	Tonga	Trinidad and Tobago	Tunisia	Turkey	Turkmenistan	Uganda	Ukraine	United Arab Emirates	United Kingdom	United States
	•	•		•	•	•	•	•	•	•	•		•	•	•		•	•	•	•			•	•	•	•	•	•	•		•	•	•	•	•
			•									•				•					•	•								•					
		◆			▲									⊕																					
	▼					▼					▼															▼									
																												•	•						
													•																						
								•	•	•									•													•			
			•				•		•	•					•			•	•				•	•							•	•		•	•
							•		•																•						•	•			
																	•			•															
			•						•	—							•	•					•	•					•	•	•			
			•				•		•								•		•	•			•	•					•	•	—			
	•			•			•		•		•		•		•		•		•		•		•	•			•	•	•			•			
			•		•	•	•		•		•		•		•		•		•		•		•	•			•	•	•			•			
	•		•		•				•	•	•		•				•	•			•		•	•			•	•	•			•			
	•	•	—	•	•	•	•	•	•	•	•	•	•		•		—	•	•		•	•	•	•	•		•	•	•		•	•			•
	•	•	—	•	•		•		•	•	•	•	•		•		—	•	•		•	•	•	•	•		•	•	•		•	•			•
	•	•	—	•	•		■		•	•	•	•	•		•		—	•	•		•	•	•	•	•		•	•	■		•	•			•
	•	•	—	•	•		■	•	•		•	•	•	—	•		—	•	•		•	•	•	•			•	•	—		•				
	•	•	—	•			•		•		•	•	•	•	•		•	•			•	•	•	•			•	•	•		•				
	•	•	—	•			•		•		•	•	•	•	•		•	•			•	•	•	•			•	•	•		•				
	•		—	•	•		•		•								•	•			•	•	•	•			•	•	•		•	•			
	•	•	—	•	•		•		•	•	•	•	•				•	•	•	•	•	•	•	•	•	•	•	•	•		•	•	•	•	•
	•			•					•	•							•				•	•	•												
	•	•	—	•	•		•	•	•	•							•	•	•	•	•	•	•	•		•	•	•	•	•	•	•		•	•
	•	•	—		•		■	•	•		•	—	•		⊕		•	—	•	•	•		—	•	•		•	•	•	•	•				
	•	•	—	•	•	•	•	•	•	•	•		•	•	•		—	•	•	•		•	•	•	•		•	•	•		•	•			
		•	—				■	•	•	•	•		—		•	•		—	•	•	•	—		•	•			•	•	•	•				

	Uruguay	Uzbekistan	Vanuatu	Venezuela, Rep. Bolivariana of	Vietnam	Yemen, Republic of	Zambia	Zimbabwe
Status under IMF Articles of Agreement								
Article VIII	•		•	•		•		•
Article XIV		•			•		•	
Exchange rate arrangements								
Exchange arrangement with no separate legal tender								
Currency board arrangement								
Conventional pegged arrangement			▼					✛
Pegged exchange rate within horizontal bands					✱			
Crawling peg								
Crawling band	•			•				
Managed floating with no pre-announced path for the exchange rate		•						
Independently floating						•	•	
Exchange rate structure								
Dual exchange rates								
Multiple exchange rates								
Arrangements for payments and receipts								
Bilateral payments arrangements	•	•	■		•			•
Multiple exchange rates		•		•	•	•	•	•
Controls on payments for invisible transactions and current transfers		•	■		•			•
Proceeds from exports and/or invisible transactions								
Repatriation requirements		•	■		•			•
Surrender requirements		•	■		•			
Capital transactions								
Controls on:								
Capital market securities		•	■	•	•			•
Money market instruments		■	■		•			•
Collective investment securities		•	■	•	•			•
Derivatives and other instruments	■	■	■		•			•
Commercial credits		•	■		•	•		•
Financial credits		•	■		•	•		•
Guarantees, sureties, and financial backup facilities		•	■		—	•		•
Direct investment		•	■	•	•			•
Liquidation of direct investment		•	■		—			•
Real estate transactions		•	■		•			•
Personal capital movements	—	•	■		•			•
Provisions specific to:								
Commercial banks and other credit institutions	•	•	■	•	•	•	•	•
Institutional investors	•	■	■		—			•

- Indicates that the specified practice is a feature of the exchange system.
- — Indicates that data were not available at time of publication.
- ■ Indicates that the specific practice is not regulated.
- ◆ Indicates that member uses the currency of another member as legal tender.
- ◊ Indicates that member participates in the ECCU.
- ▲ Indicates that the arrangement is pegged to the French franc.
- ⊕ Indicates that member participates in the euro area.
- ✛ Indicates that flexibility is limited to a single currency.
- ▼ Indicates that the composite is a basket of other currencies.
- ✛ Indicates that the country participates in the ERM II of the EMS.
- ✱ Indicates other band arrangements.

[1] The listing includes Hong Kong SAR, Aruba, and the Netherlands Antilles.

[2] Usually December 31, 1999.

Status Under IMF Articles of Agreement

Article VIII

Article XIV

Exchange Arrangement

Currency

Other legal tender

Exchange rate structure

Unitary

Dual

Multiple

Classification

Exchange arrangement with no separate legal tender

Currency board arrangement

Conventional pegged arrangement

Pegged exchange rate within horizontal bands

Crawling peg

Crawling band

Managed floating with no pre-announced path for the exchange rate

Independently floating

Exchange tax

Exchange subsidy

Forward exchange market

Official cover of forward operations

Arrangements for Payments and Receipts

Prescription of currency requirements

Payment arrangements

Bilateral payment arrangements

Operative

Inoperative

Regional arrangements

Clearing agreements

Barter agreements and open accounts

Administration of control

International security restrictions

In accordance with Executive Board
Decision No. 144-(52/51)

In accordance with UN sanctions

Payment arrears

Official

Private

**Controls on trade in gold (coins
and/or bullion)**

Controls on domestic ownership and/or
trade

Controls on external trade

**Controls on exports and imports of
banknotes**

On exports

  Domestic currency

  Foreign currency

On imports

  Domestic currency

  Foreign currency

Resident Accounts

Foreign exchange accounts permitted

Held domestically

  Approval required

Held abroad

  Approval required

**Accounts in domestic currency
convertible into foreign currency**

Nonresident Accounts

Foreign exchange accounts permitted

Approval required

Domestic currency accounts

Convertible into foreign currency

Approval required

Blocked accounts

Imports and Import Payments

Foreign exchange budget

Financing requirements for imports

Minimum financing requirements

Advance payment requirements

Advance import deposits

**Documentation requirements for re-
lease of foreign exchange for imports**

Domiciliation requirements

Preshipment inspection

Letters of credit

Import licenses used as exchange
licenses

Other

**Import licenses and other nontariff
measures**

Positive list

Negative list

Open general licenses

Licenses with quotas

Other nontariff measures

Import taxes and/or tariffs

Taxes collected through the exchange
system

State import monopoly

Exports and Export Proceeds

Repatriation requirements

Surrender requirements

Financing requirements

Documentation requirements

Letters of credit

Guarantees

Domiciliation

Preshipment inspection

Other

Export licenses

Without quotas

With quotas

Export taxes

Taxes collected through the exchange
system

Other export taxes

Payments for Invisible Transactions and Current Transfers

Controls on these transfers

Trade-related payments

   Prior approval

   Quantitative limits

   Indicative limits/bona fide test

Investment-related payments

   Prior approval

   Quantitative limits

   Indicative limits/bona fide test

Payments for travel

   Prior approval

   Quantitative limits

   Indicative limits/bona fide test

Personal payments

   Prior approval

   Quantitative limits

   Indicative limits/bona fide test

Foreign workers' wages

   Prior approval

   Quantitative limits

   Indicative limits/bona fide test

Credit card use abroad

   Prior approval

   Quantitative limits

   Indicative limits/bona fide test

Other payments

   Prior approval

   Quantitative limits

   Indicative limits/bona fide test

Proceeds from Invisible Transactions and Current Transfers

Repatriation requirements

Surrender requirements

Restrictions on use of funds

Capital Transactions

Controls on capital and money market instruments

On capital market securities

Shares or other securities of a participating nature

Purchase locally by nonresidents

Sale or issue locally by nonresidents

Purchase abroad by residents

Sale or issue abroad by residents

Bonds or other debt securities

Purchase locally by nonresidents

Sale or issue locally by nonresidents

Purchase abroad by residents

Sale or issue abroad by residents

On money market instruments

Purchase locally by nonresidents

Sale or issue locally by nonresidents

Purchase abroad by residents

Sale or issue abroad by residents

On collective investment securities

Purchase locally by nonresidents

Sale or issue locally by nonresidents

Purchase abroad by residents

Sale or issue abroad by residents

Controls on derivatives and other instruments

Purchase locally by nonresidents

Sale or issue locally by nonresidents

Purchase abroad by residents

Sale or issue abroad by residents

Controls on credit operations

Commercial credits

By residents to nonresidents

To residents from nonresidents

Financial credits

By residents to nonresidents

To residents from nonresidents

Guarantees, sureties, and financial backup facilities

By residents to nonresidents

To residents from nonresidents

Controls on direct investment

Outward direct investment

Inward direct investment

Controls on liquidation of direct investment

Controls on real estate transactions

Purchase abroad by residents

Purchase locally by nonresidents

Sale locally by nonresidents

Controls on personal capital movements

Loans

By residents to nonresidents

To residents from nonresidents

Gifts, endowments, inheritances, and legacies

By residents to nonresidents

To residents from nonresidents

Settlement of debts abroad by immigrants

Transfer of assets

Transfer abroad by emigrants

Transfer into the country by immigrants

Transfer of gambling and prize earnings

Provisions specific to commercial banks and other credit institutions

Borrowing abroad

Maintenance of accounts abroad

Lending to nonresidents (financial or commercial credits)

Lending locally in foreign exchange

Purchase of locally issued securities denominated in foreign exchange

Differential treatment of deposit accounts in foreign exchange

Reserve requirements

Liquid asset requirements

Interest rate controls

Credit controls

Differential treatment of deposit accounts held by nonresidents

Reserve requirements

Liquid asset requirements

Interest rate controls

Credit controls

Investment regulations

Abroad by banks

In banks by nonresidents

Open foreign exchange position limits

On resident assets and liabilities

On nonresident assets and liabilities

Provisions specific to institutional investors

Limits (max.) on securities issued by nonresidents and on portfolio invested abroad

Limits (max.) on portfolio invested abroad

Limits (min.) on portfolio invested locally

Currency-matching regulations on assets/liabilities composition

Other controls imposed by securities laws

Changes During 1999

Status under IMF Articles of Agreement

Exchange arrangement

Arrangements for payments and receipts

Resident accounts

Nonresident accounts

Imports and import payments

Exports and export proceeds

Payments for invisible transactions and current transfers

Proceeds from invisible transactions and current transfers

Capital transactions

Controls on capital and money market instruments

Controls on derivatives and other instruments

Controls on credit operations

Controls on direct investment

Controls on liquidation of direct investment

Controls on real estate transactions

Controls on personal capital movements

Provisions specific to commercial banks and other credit institutions

Provisions specific to institutional investors

Other controls imposed by securities laws

Changes During 2000

Status under IMF Articles of Agreement

Exchange arrangement

Arrangements for payments and receipts

Resident accounts

Nonresident accounts

Imports and import payments

Exports and export proceeds

Payments for invisible transactions and current transfers

Proceeds from invisible transactions and current transfers

Capital transactions

Controls on capital and money market instruments

Controls on derivatives and other instruments

Controls on credit operations

Controls on direct investment

Controls on liquidation of direct investment

Controls on real estate transactions

Controls on personal capital movements

Provisions specific to commercial banks and other credit institutions

Provisions specific to institutional investors

Other controls imposed by securities laws